Male Order

AttaGirl Press Bestsellers

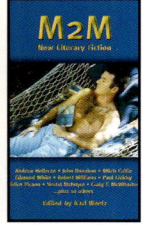

Edited by Lambda Literary Award-winner Karl Woelz. Stories by legendary authors Andrew Holleran, Edmund White, Felice Picano, plus rising stars Paul Lisicky, Mitch Cullin, Tom House, Robin Lippincott, Greg Herren, Dan Jaffe and 11 others.

$16.95

The long-awaited debut novel of noted book critic and essayist David McConnell.

"He is tough and satanic, like Hervé Guibert... His style is completely original and unforgettable." *Edmund White*

$22.00/Hardbound

Lambda Literary Award Finalist 2002
Reflective, expressionistic poems written during the holidays, chronicling this award-winning author's life.

$17.95/Hardbound

Lambda Literary Award Winner 2001
"These are some of the funniest pieces about queer sex and politics that I have ever read." *Patrick Califia*

$14.95

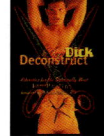

Order by phone:
Phone: 415/255-0404
Toll Free: 800/462-6654

Or order online:
www.attagirlpress.com

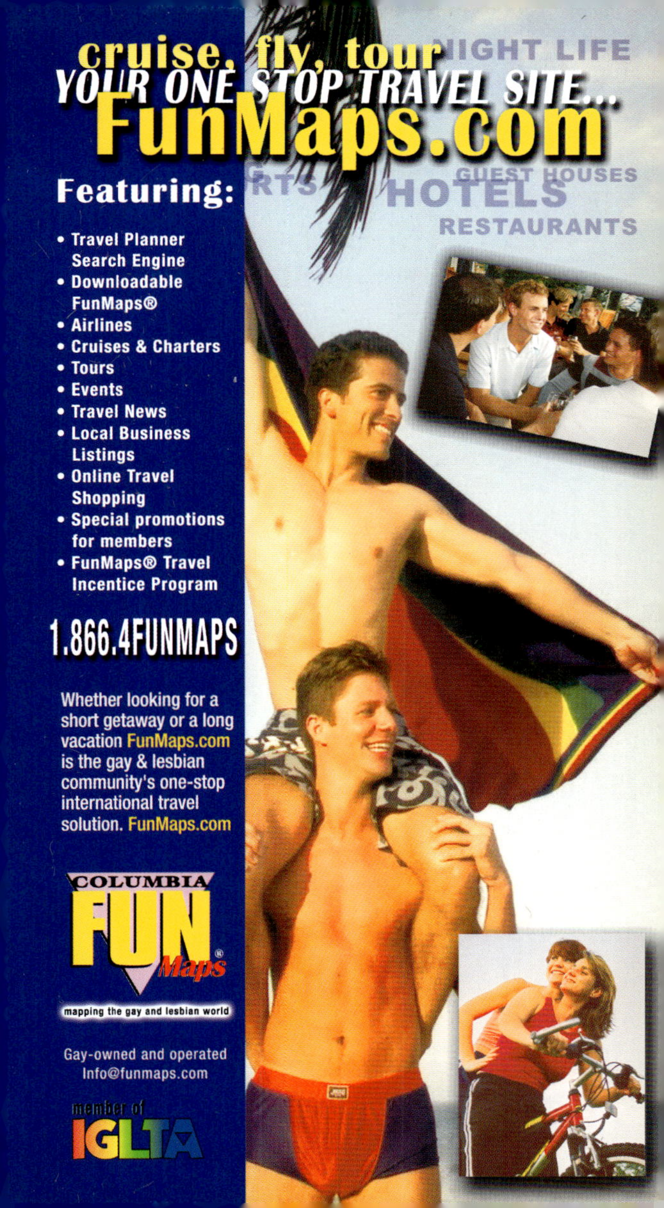

cruise, fly, tour
YOUR ONE STOP TRAVEL SITE...
FunMaps.com

NIGHT LIFE
GUEST HOUSES
HOTELS
RESTAURANTS

Featuring:

- Travel Planner Search Engine
- Downloadable FunMaps®
- Airlines
- Cruises & Charters
- Tours
- Events
- Travel News
- Local Business Listings
- Online Travel Shopping
- Special promotions for members
- FunMaps® Travel Incentice Program

1.866.4FUNMAPS

Whether looking for a short getaway or a long vacation FunMaps.com is the gay & lesbian community's one-stop international travel solution. FunMaps.com

COLUMBIA FUN Maps®

mapping the gay and lesbian world

Gay-owned and operated
Info@funmaps.com

member of
IGLTA

MEET MEN

 LOCAL VOICE PERSONALS
For <u>Your</u> Local System call: **(800) 289.1489**

For amazing Voice & Video dating, visit us online at **MEGAMATES.COM**

18+ ©2004 PC LLC

ANYWHERE

BROWSE ALL ADS
FREE
use code 3087
REPLY TO ADS FREE

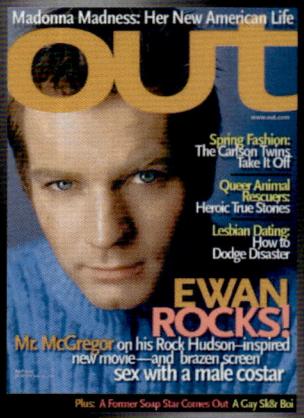

MANSHOTS

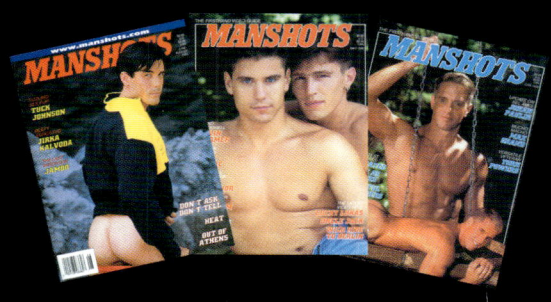

This year over 1,000 new gay videos will be released. How do you find the best videos for you?

Manshots provides readers with all they need to choose the right video. Each issue is jam-packed with revealing reviews, fantastic photos, intimate interviews, and insider industry news.

Subscribe to MANSHOTS today!

WWW.MANSHOTS.COM
Subscribe online or call (212) 557-1565

MORE THAN JUST A MAGAZINE

XODUS USA
ACTIVE WEAR

WWW.XODUS-USA.COM

Magnets.Cards.Posters.Calendars.shirts.Tattoos

Anywhere you are traveling... **We** are ready to **play.**

n2mansex.com™

Image courtesy of Raging Stallion Studios

Sharing our playground with you!

CAMP REHOBOTH
CREATING COMMUNITY

FOR MORE INFORMATION ABOUT REHOBOTH BEACH
VISIT WWW.CAMPREHOBOTH.COM OR CALL 302-227-5620

No straight men were harmed in the making of these films.

sean cody.com

Straight, Muscular and Raw Men.

the Damron Men's Travel Guide

Publisher	**Damron Company**
President & Editor-in-Chief	**Gina M. Gatta**
Managing Editor	**Ian Philips**
Deputy Editor	**Erika O'Connor**
Assistant Editor	**Chane Binderup**
Director of Art & Advertising	**Kathleen Pratt**
Cover Photo	**Jack Slomovits**
Cover Design	**Rick Avila**

Board of Directors
Mikal Shively, Gina M. Gatta, Edward Gatta, Jr., Louise Mock

In Memory of Bob Damron and Dan Delbex

How to Contact Us
Mail: PO Box 422458, San Francisco, CA 94142-2458
Email: info@damron.com
Web: www.damron.com
Fax: 415/703-9049
Phone: 415/255-0404 & 800/462-6654 [9am-5pm (PST) Mon-Fri]

Damron Company reserves the right to make its own independent judgement as to the acceptability of advertising copy and illustrations in advertisements. Advertiser and advertising agency assume liability for all content (including text, representation, photographs and illustrations) of advertisements printed and also assume responsibility for any claims arising therefrom against the publisher. Offers to sell products that appear in the *Damron Men's Travel Guide* are subject to all laws and regulations and are void where so prohibited.

Copyright ©2003 Damron Company Inc.

All rights reserved. Reproduction of the *Damron Men's Travel Guide* in whole or in part without written permission from the Damron Company is prohibited.

National Resources

LGBT INFO LINES
Gay/Lesbian National Hotline — [888] 843-4564

AIDS/HIV
CDC National HIV/AIDS/STDs Hotlines — [800] 342-2437
TTY: [800] 243-7889
en español: [800] 344-7432

Sexual Health Information Line (Canada) — [613] 563-2437

LEGAL RIGHTS
Lambda Legal Defense Fund (New York City, NY) — [212] 809-8585

National Gay/Lesbian Task Force (Washington, DC) — [202] 393-5177
TTY: [202] 393-2284

YOUTH SERVICES
Hetrick-Martin Institute (New York City, NY) — [212] 674-2400

LYRIC (Lavender Youth Recreation/Information Center) hotline (San Francisco, CA) — *CA only:* [800] 246-7743 / [415] 863-3636

CHEMICAL DEPENDENCY
Alternatives — [800] 342-5429
Pride Institute — [800] 547-7433

GAY TRAVEL
International Gay/Lesbian Travel Association (IGLTA) — [800] 448-8550

National Association of Lesbian/Gay Community Centers (Garden Grove, CA) — [714] 534-0862

T.A.G. (Travel Alternatives Group) — [415] 437-3800

Damron Website & Database — www.damron.com

Using this Guide

Call first! Not because we haven't (in fact, we call several times a year!), but because every element of a listing, from hours to area codes, may have changed since we've hung up the phone.

Info Lines & Services This is the category for the gay center. At our website, www.damron.com, we extensively list hotlines, social or support groups as well as services like the state tourism board or the personal guide with a limo.

Accommodations Most accommodations (especially B&Bs) require advance reservations. It's a good idea to request a brochure ahead of time, and to be clear about deposit and cancellation policies when making reservations.

Bars & Nightclubs Many codes apply only a few nights a week, especially when we've noted "theme nights". You should call the bar to verify what is scheduled for which nights. Bars coded **BW** (beer/wine) might not serve both.

Restaurants All restaurants listed are gay-friendly; those with mostly gay/lesbian clientele are coded **MW**.

Cafes are casual hangouts serving coffee and pastries, but not full menus.

Entertainment & Recreation Something touristy, maybe a little kitschy, definitely unusual or commonly overlooked, that even your friends who've lived there all their lives won't mind doing.

Publications If you want to know what's new, get one when you get to town. They're usually free and distributed in many of the locations we list. Your best bet, however, is to go right to the local LGBT or alternative bookstore to get the latest issue and/or lowdown.

Gyms are workout facilities, not bathhouses. They're mostly straight, unless coded **MW** or **MO**.

Men's Clubs include sex clubs, bathhouses, playspaces, and sex-oriented groups.

Men's Services are mostly telephone dating services.

Cruisy Areas In many cities, you're more likely to meet vice cops than partners at public grounds. Try the local bar or bathhouse instead if you're bent on picking up. To avoid entrapment, read the notice about "Cruisy Areas," page 4.

Unconfirmed means we've called, several times, but no one answered. The phone still works but everything else may be different. Definitely call first.

Events Calendar Lists those "can't-miss" events for the upcoming year — from circuit parties to bear jamborees to street fairs and festivals.

Tour Operators A brief description of what kinds of tours the tour operator offers.

As Damron has done since 1964, we reward the best letters (those packed with new info of openings and closings we haven't already found) with a **FREE COPY** of next year's edition.

Table of Contents

United States of America

Alabama	24
Alaska	26
Arizona	28
Arkansas	39
California	41
Colorado	163
Connecticut	172
Delaware	177
District of Columbia	180
Florida	186
Georgia	248
Hawaii	260
Idaho	278
Illinois	280
Indiana	295
Iowa	304
Kansas	308
Kentucky	312
Louisiana	316
Maine	341
Maryland	347
Massachusetts	350
Michigan	377
Minnesota	387
Mississippi	392
Missouri	394
Montana	402
Nebraska	404
Nevada	406
New Hampshire	411
New Jersey	413
New Mexico	418
New York	424
North Carolina	458
North Dakota	467
Ohio	468
Oklahoma	484
Oregon	489

Table of Contents

Pennsylvania	495
Rhode Island	511
South Carolina	513
South Dakota	516
Tennessee	517
Texas	522
Utah	539
Vermont	542
Virginia	546
Washington	550
West Virginia	559
Wisconsin	561
Wyoming	568
International	
Canada	570
Caribbean	605
Mexico	616
Costa Rica	632
Austria • Vienna	638
Czech Republic • Prague	640
England • London	642
France • Paris	649
Germany • Berlin	657
Italy • Rome	663
The Netherlands • Amsterdam	665
Spain • Madrid, Barcelona & Sitges	671
National Advertisers	**326**
Tours & Events	
2004 Tours & Tour Operators	681
Events Calendar	688
Film Festivals	697
Leather, Fetish & Bear Events	701
Conferences & Retreats	705
Spiritual Gatherings	706
Circuit Parties	707
Male Order	717

Who We Are

In 1964, a businessman published a book of all the gay bars he knew from his constant travels across the United States. This book could fit comfortably in the palm of your hand. Despite its small size, it was an impressive accomplishment. Each one of the listings he had visited himself. Every last copy of that book he sold himself. The name of this pioneering businessman—**Bob Damron**.

Almost forty years later, his little book, the **Damron Men's Travel Guide** (originally **Bob Damron's Address Book**), is still a bestseller. And it has remained the model for the countless gay travel guides to follow in its wake. Today, Damron's list of ever-expanding titles includes: the **Damron Women's Traveller** for lesbians, the **Damron City Guide**, a full-color map guide, and **Damron Accommodations** with thousands of expanded B&B listings and color photos.

How We Maintain the Accuracy of Our Listings

Our editors contact every single listing in our database annually, usually by phone, fax, or email. They also receive updated information directly from business owners and you, our readers. If you send in new, verifiably correct information, Damron will send you a free copy of the next edition as our way of saying a very sincere "thank you" for your help.

PLEASE READ THIS NOTICE ABOUT "CRUISY AREAS"

Certain locations are categorized as "Cruisy Areas." These areas include but are not limited to parks, rest stops, and beaches. Information regarding these areas is furnished to Damron by various sources and, due to time and other constraints, Damron is unable to investigate these areas. Areas marked as "AYOR" (At Your Own Risk) may involve risk and the reader should proceed with caution. However, the absence of an AYOR rating does not guarantee the safety or security of any area. Therefore, Damron makes no warranty or representation as to the safety, security, or status of those areas marked as cruisy areas. Damron urges readers to avoid sexual activity within Cruisy Areas.

BEWARE – MOST POLICE DEPARTMENTS IN THE USA HAVE COPIES OF THE MEN'S TRAVEL GUIDE.

Vacation rentals...

VillasandCondos.Com LLC

Specializing in gay owned
and gay friendly villas and condos.

Mexico - Hawaii - Palm Springs

Affordable luxury for every budget

Why settle for less?

Call us toll free 1.877.421.6367
Phone: 360.277.9228
www.VillasandCondos.com

IGLTA

SUPER SLIPPERY
Longer lasting, never sticky and latex safe.

ORDER TODAY ON ErosUSA.com

A PJUR GUARRANTEE

Pjur Eros Original, Pjur Basic and Pjur Power are longer lasting, making them cheaper drop-per-drop than other brands. Our products never become sticky and they're 100% latex safe.

BE SURE IT'S PJUR

Look for the Pjur mark and feel confident that you are getting genuine Pjur products.

Personal Pleasure Products

do you cruise?

All-gay cruise & resort vacations.

For a new 2004 brochure detailing all our vacations, see your travel agent, visit our website, or call us at
800-6-ATLANTIS

Atlantis
THE WAY WE PLAY

www.atlantisevents.com

CST#2033720-40

RSVP

The first and the leading gay vacations. RSVP takes the whole ship and resort and creates a gay & lesbian paradise. We offer the best land tours available, and all a great value.

2003 Club RSVP Ixtapa
At Club Med® Village in Cancún November 8-15

2004 RSVP Cruises

Caribbean
Holland America Oosterdam
7-day cruise
Feb. 22-29, 2004

Mexican Riviera
Holland America Oosterdam
7-day cruise
April 25 - May 2, 2004

Budapest - Prague
Amadeus Symphony
7-day riverboat + 2 day tour
Sept, 2004

2003 - 2004 Tours

African Safari
Highlights of Ireland
Machu Picchu Peru

(multiple departures for tours)

800-328-RSVP(7787)

Ship registry: Oosterdam, Netherlands.
CST #2020963-50
Information subject to change.

American Airlines®

RSVPVACATIONS.COM

PINKPAGES &
www.lesgaypinkpages.com

One great community... Two great resources!

Advertise in the original lifestyle magazine and business directory for the gay & lesbian community.

PINK PAGES

FOR ADVERTISING INFORMATION, CALL 773.769.6328.

chicago – denver – seattle – new york

not even our subway lines are straight

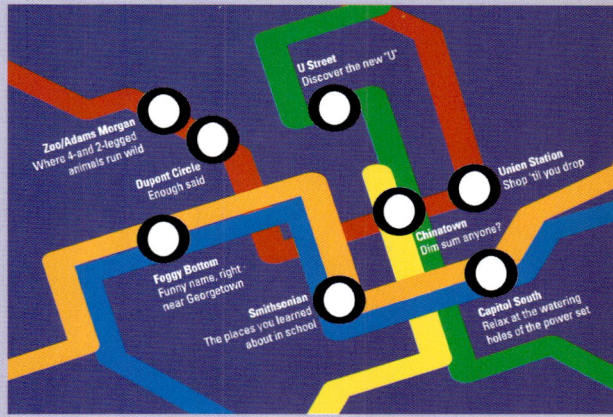

Zoo/Adams Morgan — Where 4-and 2-legged animals run wild
Dupont Circle — Enough said
U Street — Discover the new "U"
Foggy Bottom — Funny name, right? near Georgetown
Smithsonian — The places you learned about in school
Chinatown — Dim sum anyone?
Union Station — Shop 'til you drop
Capital South — Relax at the watering holes of the power set

washington, dc

for more info on all the best places to visit in washington, dc, call 800.422.8644 ext. 361 and request the glbt travelers guide. or go straight to our website at www.prideindc.org.

celebrate freedom to be. join us for

May
Black Lesbian & Gay Pride Day

June
Capital Pride Festival, Parade

October
Reel Affirmations Film Festival

WASHINGTON DC
THE AMERICAN EXPERIENCE

Washington, DC Convention and Tourism Corporation

Gay life matters...

NEWS • ENTERTAINMENT • POLITICS
RIGHTS • FAMILY • WORK

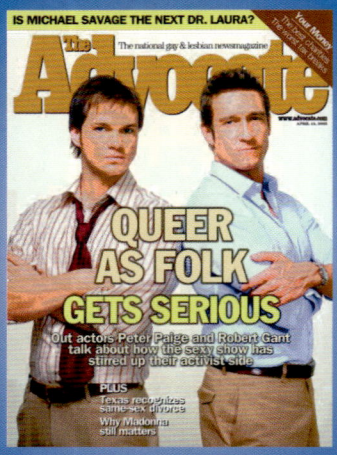

Keep up-to-date

on our place in today's world.

Subscribe to *The Advocate*,

the national gay and lesbian newsmagazine

at

or call (800) 827-0561

noodle
a gay asian magazine

www.noodlemagazine.com

take a vacation from the politically correct world, and find out why instinct is america's number one gay men's magazine

sexy.

funny.

smart.

contemporary.

instinct magazine
fashion. dating. relationships. fitness. health. media. auto. home.

to subscribe: call 888.454.6784 or fax 818.205.9093
to advertise: call 818.205.9033
www.instinctmag.com

sex•body•self•mind•love•art•uncharted

XODUS
MAGAZINE

an Evolutionary
Next generation
Gay magazine

www.xodusmag.com

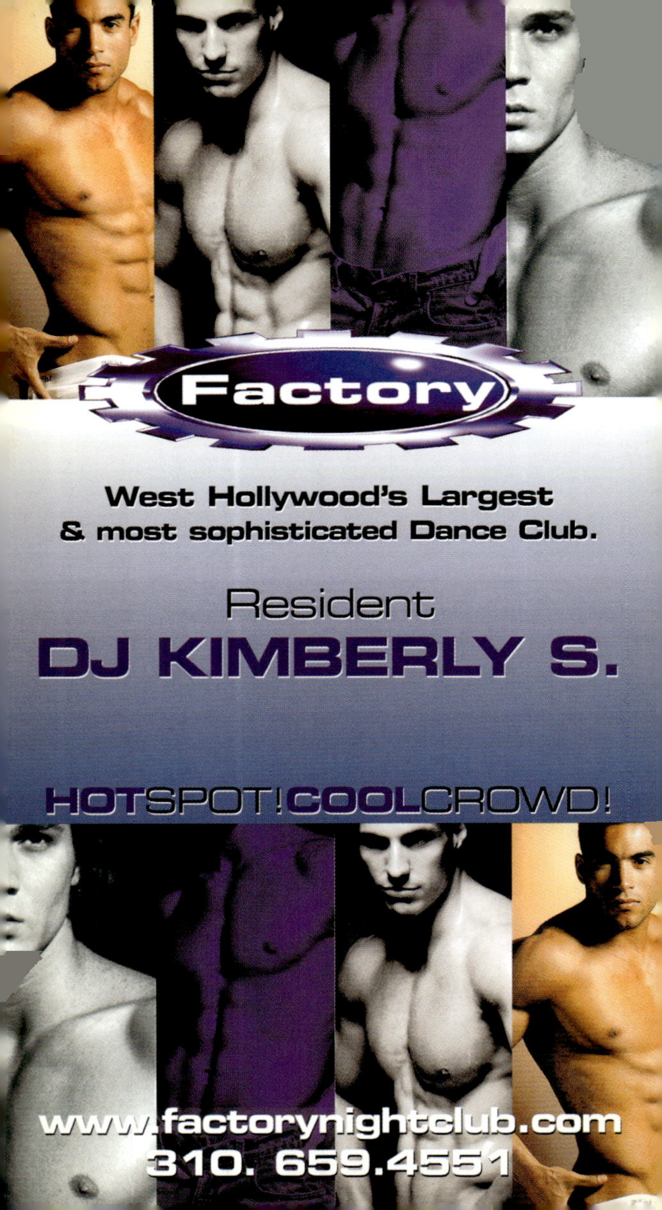

Factory

West Hollywood's Largest & most sophisticated Dance Club.

Resident
DJ KIMBERLY S.

HOTSPOT! COOLCROWD!

www.factorynightclub.com
310. 659.4551

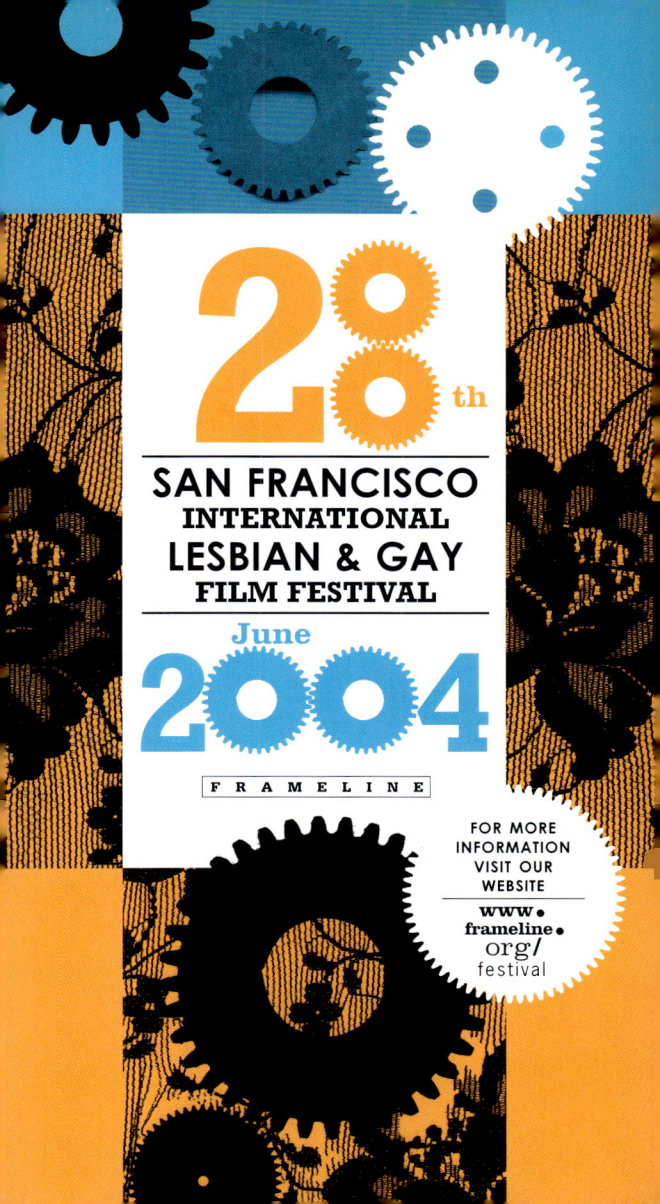

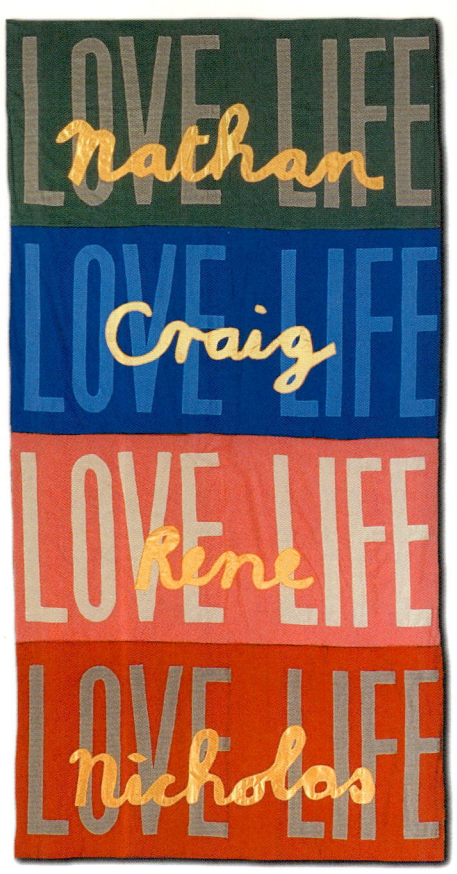

gay travel news

Where to go?
What to see?
Where to stay?
How to get there?

www.gaytravelnews.com

Gaytravelnews is <u>different</u>! Only qualified TAG-Approved™ inns, hotels and resorts are accepted on the site, based on their progressive corporate policies and practices, not on ad purchase. Visit today! Operated by Community Marketing, Inc. www.mark8ing.com

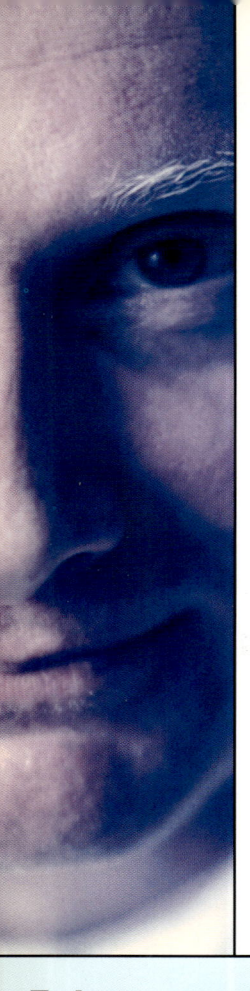

DREAM TRIPS ARE TRAVEL FOR THE SOUL

Destination Foundation grants dream trips to people in the San Francisco Bay Area living with life-threatening illnesses. Dream trips are much more than a "vacation" they are alternative medicine to heal the spirit, mind and body - a welcome respite from the everyday challenges of a life-threatening illness.

To learn more and to make a donation:

Destination Foundation, Inc.
584 Castro Street #114
San Francisco, CA 94114
(415) 477-9097
www.destinationfoundation.org

JACK**SLOMOVITS**
photographs
212 691 4345
www.jackny.com
www.gayvow.com

design: www.blowsquish.com

Alabama • *USA*

USA

ALABAMA

Statewide

■ PUBLICATIONS

➤ **Southern Voice** 404/876-1819
weekly lgbt newspaper for AL, FL (panhandle), GA, LA, MS, TN w/ resource listings

➤ **TLW Magazine** 727/522-8888
Southeast's largest entertainment magazine for gay men

Anniston

■ CRUISY AREAS

Cheaha Park Cheaha Scenic Dr *midday & early evenings, head towards the walking trail*

Auburn

■ ACCOMMODATIONS

Black Bear Camp [MO,SW,N,NS,WC,GO] 10565 US Hwy 280 W, Waverly **334/887-5152** *hot tub, kitchen*

Birmingham

■ ACCOMMODATIONS

The Tutwiler Wyndham [GF,WC] 2021 Park Pl N (at 21st St N) **205/322-2100** *also restaurant & lounge*

■ BARS

Kings Knight [M,D,DS,V,WC] 2627 7th Ave S (btwn 26th & 27th) **205/326-3637** *4pm-3am, till 4am wknds, cruise/ show bar, 2 patios*

Misconceptions Tavern [MW,V,WC] 3719 3rd Ave S (btwn 37th & 38th) **205/592-3800** *noon-3am, patio*

■ NIGHTCLUBS

22nd Street Jazz Cafe [GF,D,MR,F,E] 710 22nd St S (at 7th Ave S) **205/252-0407** *5pm-close, clsd Sun-Tue*

The Club Latroy [MW,D,MR,DS,19+,WC,$] 316 20th St S (btwn 3rd & 4th Aves S) **205/322-8338** *11pm-close Fri-Sat, also restaurant*

The Quest Club [M,D,DS,PC,WC] 416 24th St S (at 5th Ave S) **205/251-4313** *24hrs, 18+ Wed-Sun, patio*

■ RESTAURANTS

Anthony's [WC,GO] 2131 7th Ave S (at 20th) **205/324-1215** *lunch & dinner, Sun brunch, clsd Mon, cont'l/ Italian, full bar*

Bottega Cafe & Restaurant [WC] 2240 Highland Ave (btwn 22nd & 23rd) **205/939-1000** *lunch & dinner, clsd Sun, full bar*

Highlands Bar & Grill [WC] 2011 11th Ave S (at 20th St) **205/939-1400** *6pm-10pm, bar from 4pm, clsd Sun-Mon*

John's [WC] 112 21st St N (btwn 1st & 2nd Ave N) **205/322-6014** *11am-10pm, clsd Sun, full bar*

PT's Sports Grill [WC] 350 Hollywood Blvd (at Hwy 280 S) **205/879-8519** *11am-close*

Silvertron Cafe 3813 Clairmont Ave S (at 39th St S) **205/591-3707** *11am-10pm, till 9pm Sun, also full bar, more gay Mon*

■ ENTERTAINMENT & RECREATION

Magic City Diamonds 2117 University Blvd (at 22nd, at Baptist church) **205/591-4382, 205/595-4414** *7pm-9pm Th only, alternative square dance club*

Terrific New Theater 2821 2nd Ave S (in Dr Pepper Design Complex) **205/328-0868**

■ MEN'S SERVICES

➤ **Megaphone Birmingham** **800/289-1489** *Call for the local # nearest you! Meet Hot Men in your area! FREE to Browse & Respond to voice ads. Use code 3087. Also try MEGAMATES.COM*

Mobile • Alabama

EROTICA

Alabama Adult Books 801 3rd Ave N (at 8th) **205/322-7323** *24hrs*

Birmingham Adult Books [★] 7610 1st Ave N (at Oporto-Madrid Blvd) **205/836-1580** *24hrs, booths*

The Downtown Bookstore 2731 8th Ave N (at 28th St) **205/328-5525** *video arcade, booths*

Pleasure Books 7606 1st Ave N (at 77th St) **205/836-7379** *video arcade, booths*

Top Hat Cinema 9221 Todd Dr **205/833-8221** *theater, booths*

CRUISY AREAS

Cahaba River Rd Park [AYOR] at Jefferson/ Shelby county line (on Hwy 280 E, exit before Cahaba River bridge & turn left)

Rushton Park [AYOR] Highland Park area *hustlers*

Decatur

ACCOMMODATIONS

Days Inn [GF,SW,WC] 810 6th Ave NE (Hwy 31 N at Church) **256/355-3520, 800/DAYS-INN** *also Mexican restaurant*

RESTAURANTS

The Waffle House 710 6th Ave NE (btwn Layfayette & Walnut) **256/355-2871** *24hrs, popular afterhours*

Geneva

ACCOMMODATIONS

Spring Creek Campground [M,SW,N,GO] 163 Campground Rd (at Hwy 52 & Country Rd 4) **334/684-3891** *cabins, tent & RV sites, some theme wknds w/ DJ*

Huntsville

BARS

Club Ozz [MW,NH,D,E,WC] 1204 Posey (at Larkin) **256/534-5970** *7pm-2am, DJ Th-Sun, shows Th-Sun, patio*

NIGHTCLUBS

Upscale [MW,D,F,DS,19+,WC] 2021 Golf Rd **256/881-8820** *8pm-close Fri-Sat, 'Alabama's largest alternative entertainment complex'*

Lafayette

ACCOMMODATIONS

Blue Willow Inn [M,SW,GO] 302 Lafayette St S **334/864-9008** *seasonal (June-Aug)*

Mobile

see also Pensacola, Florida

INFO LINES & SERVICES

Pink Triangle AA Group at Cornerstone MCC **251/479-9994 (AA#), 251/476-4621 (church)** *7pm Th & Sat*

BARS

Bienville Cruise Pub [M,NH] 22 S Conception (at Conti) **251/432-8077** *24hrs*

Gabriel's Downtown [MW,K,V,PC] 55 S Joachim St (at Government) **251/432-4900** *4:30pm-close, from 7pm Sat, from 3pm Sun*

NIGHTCLUBS

B-Bob's Downtown [M,D,B,P,DS,PC,WC] 213 Conti St (at Joachim) **251/433-2262** *5pm-close, from 3pm Sun, 2 level multi-venue club, home den of Gulf Coast Bears, also gift shop*

On The Roxx [MW,D] 20 S Conception (at Conti) **251/432-9056** *10am-close*

Troopers [MW,D,DS,PC,WC] 215 Conti St (near Joachim) **251/433-7436** *9pm-close Wed-Sat, shows Th (open since 1965!)*

CAFES

Big E's Delicatessen [WC] 263 St Francis St (at N Jackson St) **251/694-0585** *lunch Mon-Fri, private parties & catering services*

Alabama • *USA*

■ MEN'S SERVICES

➤ **Megaphone Mobile**
800/289-1489 *Call for the local # nearest you! Meet Hot Men in your area! FREE to Browse & Respond to voice ads. Use code 3087. Also try MEGAMATES.COM*

Montgomery

■ ACCOMMODATIONS

Lattice Inn [GF,SW,GO] 1414 S Hull St **334/832-9931** *full brkfst, hot tub*

Tuscaloosa

■ BARS

Michael's [MW,D,DS] 2201 6th St (at 22nd Ave) **205/758-9223** *5pm-close Tue-Wed & Fri-Sat*

■ CRUISY AREAS

River Road Park [AYOR] along Black Warrior River *also check out the nature trails on the other side of the park*

ALASKA

Anchorage

■ INFO LINES & SERVICES

AA Gay/ Lesbian 2110 E Northern Lights #103 (at Community Center) **907/344-2474, 907/344-2474** *7pm Mon & Fri*

Gay/ Lesbian Helpline
907/258-4777, 888/901-9876 *6pm-11pm*

Identity, Inc 2110 E Northern Lights Blvd #103 **907/929-4528** *community center, newsletter*

■ ACCOMMODATIONS

Alaska Bear Company B&B [GS] 535 E 6th Ave (at Fairbanks) **907/277-2327**

Alaska's Jewel Lake [GS,GO] 8125 Jewel Lake Rd (at Rasberry) **907/245-7321** *B&B, full brkfst, some shared baths*

Gallery B&B [GS,WC,GO] 1229 'G' St (at 12th) **907/274-2567**

Susitna Sunsets [GF,NS,GO] 9901 Conifer St **907/346-1067** *B&B, private-entry garden suite*

■ BARS

Mad Myrna's [MW,NH,D,F,K,DS] 530 E 5th Ave (at Fairbanks) **907/276-9762** *3pm-3am*

Raven [MW,NH,WC] 708 E 4th Ave **907/276-9672** *1pm-3am*

■ RESTAURANTS

At Last a Deli 701 W 36th Ave #16 (at Arctic Blvd) **907/563-3354** *6:30am-6pm, till 4pm Sat, clsd Sun*

China Lights 12110 Business Blvd, Eagle River **907/694-8080** *11:30am-10pm, till 10:30pm wknds*

Garcia's 1901 Business Blvd (next to Safeway), Eagle River **907/694-8600** *lunch & dinner, till midnight Fri-Sat, Mexican*

Kodiak Kafe 225 E 5th Ave (btwn Cordova & Barrow) **907/258-5233** *brkfst & lunch*

O'Brady's Burgers & Brew 6901 E Tudor Rd (in Chugach Square) **907/338-1080** *11am-midnight, noon-10pm Sun*

Simon & Seafort's 420 'L' St (btwn 4th & 5th) **907/274-3502** *lunch weekdays, dinner nightly, seafood & prime rib, full bar*

■ BOOKSTORES

Cyrano's Bookstore & Cafe [F,E,BW,WC] 413 'D' St (btwn 4th & 5th) **907/274-2599** *noon-midnight, clsd Mon-Wed in winter, also playhouse & resident theater company*

■ PUBLICATIONS

Anchorage Press **907/561-7737** *alternative paper*

■ MEN'S SERVICES

The Confidential Connection®! **907/563-6338** *The hottest local guys! 18+ Record & Listen FREE! Use access code 499*

■ EROTICA

Le Shop 305 W Dimond Blvd **907/522-1987**

Swingers Books & Gifts 710 W Northern Lights Blvd (at Arctic) **907/561-5039**

Sitka • Alaska

Fairbanks

■ INFO LINES & SERVICES
Gay/ Lesbian Info Line
907/458-8288 24hrs

■ ACCOMMODATIONS
Ah, Rose Marie Downtown B&B [GS,GO] 302 Cowles St (at 3rd Ave) **907/456-2040** full brkfst

Billie's Backpackers Hostel [GF,F] 2895 Mack Rd **907/457-2034** B&B, hostel & campsites

Crabtree Guest House [M] 724 College Rd **907/458-8288** kitchens, shared baths

Fairbanks Hotel [GF,GO] 517 3rd Ave (btwn Cushman & Lacey) **907/456-6411, 888/329-4685** recently restored to art deco style

■ BARS
Alaskan Experience [GF,D,S] 3175 College Rd (at Alaskaland) **907/456-5960** 10pm-3am Fri-Sat (seasonal), gay after 11pm Fri-Sat only

■ EROTICA
Fantasyland Video 1765 Richardson Hwy **907/488-0879** 24hrs

Homer

■ ACCOMMODATIONS
Island Watch B&B [GF,NS,WC] 4241 Claudia St (at W Hill Rd) **907/235-2265** full brkfst, kitchens

The Shorebird Guest House [★GS,NS,WC,GO] 4774 Kachemak Dr **907/235-2107, 888/934-2378** cottage rental, beach access

Skyline B&B [GS,GO] 63540 Skyline Dr **907/235-3823** full brkfst, hot tub

■ ENTERTAINMENT & RECREATION
Alaska Fantastic Fishing Charters **800/478-7777** deluxe cabin cruiser for big-game fishing (halibut)

Juneau

■ INFO LINES & SERVICES
SEAGLA (Southeast Alaska Gay & Lesbian Alliance) 907/586-4297 also publishes newsletter

■ ACCOMMODATIONS
A Pearson's Pond Luxury Suites & Adventure Spa [GF,NS] 4541 Sawa Circle **907/789-3772, 888/658-6328** B&B resort & spa

Alaska Suites Juneau [GF,NS] 2141-2145 Crowhill Rd, Douglas **907/789-3772, 888/658-6328** 1-bdrm condos, waterview balconies

■ RESTAURANTS
Inn at the Waterfront 455 S Franklin St **907/586-2050** 5pm-9pm, full bar

Ketchikan

■ ACCOMMODATIONS
Anchor Inn by the Sea [GF,NS] 4672 S Tongass Hwy **907/247-7117, 800/928-3308**

■ ENTERTAINMENT & RECREATION
Southeast Sea Kayak [GF] 1430 Millar St **907/225-1258, 800/287-1607**

Palmer

■ ACCOMMODATIONS
Alaska Garden Gate B&B [GS,GO] 1351 S Middle Mesa Rd **907/746-2333** B&B inn, full brkfst, hot tub

Sitka

■ ACCOMMODATIONS
A Crescent Harbor Hideaway [GF] 709 Lincoln St **907/747-4900** restored historic waterfront home, wildlife & marine tours

■ CAFES
Backdoor Cafe 104 Barracks (behind Old Harbor Books on Lincoln St) **907/747-8856** 7am-5pm, 9am-3pm Sun

Mojo Café 256 Katlian St **907/747-0667** 6:30am-3pm, clsd wknds

Arizona • USA

ARIZONA

Apache Junction

■EROTICA

The Airport Video (Adult Resort) [MW,SW,AYOR] 10145 E Apache Tr (exit Crismon Rd off I-60 E, 30 min from Phoenix) **480/380-9843** *24hrs, sauna*

Bisbee

■BARS

St Elmo's [GF,E] 36 Brewery Gulch Ave **520/432-5578** *10am-1am, live bands Fri-Sat*

Bullhead City

includes Laughlin, Nevada

■BARS

The Lariat Saloon [MW,NH,MR,WC] 1161 Hancock Rd (at 95) **928/758-8479** *10am-1am*

■CRUISY AREAS

Karen's Adult Video Hwy 95 (near Mohave Jct, S of town)

Cottonwood

■RETAIL SHOPS

Seasons Party Shoppe [GO] 11 N Main St #C (on Rte 89-A, N of 260) **928/649-1747** *pride items, party supplies, costumes*

Flagstaff

■ACCOMMODATIONS

Hotel Monte Vista [GF] 100 N San Francisco St **928/779-6971, 800/545-3068** *historic 1927 lodging, full bar*

■BARS

Charlie's [GF,F,E,WC] 23 N Leroux (at Aspen) **928/779-1919** *11am-1am*

Monte Vista Lounge [GF,E] 100 N San Francisco St (at Aspen) **928/774-2403** *noon-1am, from 11am Fri-Sun*

■RESTAURANTS

Café Olé [BW,WC] 119 S San Francisco (at Butler) **928/774-8272** *lunch & dinner, clsd Sun*

Monsoon's 1551 S Milton **928/774-2266** *lunch & dinner, Asian*

Pasto [BW,WC] 19 E Aspen (at San Francisco) **928/779-1937** *dinner only, Italian*

■BOOKSTORES

Aradia Books 116 W Cottage (at Beaver) **928/779-3817** *10:30am-5:30pm, clsd Sun, lesbian/ feminist, some gay men's titles*

■EROTICA

Image 620 E Rte 66, Ste 100 **928/226-8335** *videos & adult gifts*

■CRUISY AREAS

Thorpe Park [AYOR]

Fort Mohave

■EROTICA

Karen's Adult Bookstore & Ladies Lingerie 4350 Hwy 95 #1 **928/763-5600**

Golden Valley

■EROTICA

Pleasure Palace Adult Bookstore 3583 US Hwy 68 #7 **928/565-5600**

Jerome

■ACCOMMODATIONS

The Cottage Inn Jerome [GS,GO] **928/634-0701** *full brkfst*

■RESTAURANTS

Red Rooster Cafe [E,GO] 363 Main St **928/634-7087** *10:30am-4pm, clsd Tue, live music wknds*

Kingman

■ACCOMMODATIONS

Kings Inn Best Western [GF,F,SW,WC] 2930 E Andy Devine **520/753-6101, 800/750-6101** *also bakery*

■CAFES

The Fountain Cafe 310 E Beale St **928/718-2333** *7am-5pm*

Phoenix • Arizona

Lake Powell

■ ACCOMMODATIONS

Dreamkatchers of Lake Powell B&B
[GS] 435/675-5828, 888/479-9419
8-person spa on deck

Mesa

■ EROTICA

Castle Megastore 8315 E Apache Tr
480/986-6114 *24hrs*

Mohave Valley

■ EROTICA

Eros Adult Emporium 10185 Harbor Ave 928/768-6300

Phoenix

see also Scottsdale & Tempe

■ INFO LINES & SERVICES

1 N 10 602/234-2752 (also TDD)
community center & switchboard, youth services

AA Lambda Club 2622 N 16th St
602/264-1341 *noon, 6pm & 8pm, 10pm*

■ ACCOMMODATIONS

➤ **Arizona Royal Villa Resort**
[MO,SW,N,NS,GO] 1110 E Turney Ave #8
602/266-6883, 888/266-6884
hot tub

➤ **Arizona Sunburst Inn**
[MO,SW,N,GO] 6245 N 12th Pl (at Rose Ln) 602/274-1474, 800/974-1474
hot tub

➤ **Casa de Mis Padres** [MO,SW,N,GO]
5965 E Orange Blossom Ln
480/675-0247, 800/996-4108
luxury multi-room suites, 5 minutes to Old Town Scottsdale

Larry's B&B [MW,SW,N,NS,WC,GO]
502 W Claremont Ave (btwn Maryland & Bethany Home) 602/249-2974
full brkfst, hot tub

Maricopa Manor B&B Inn
[GS,SW,WC,GO] 15 W Pasadena Ave
602/274-6302, 800/292-6403
hot tub

ARIZONA SUNBURST INN

"A Man's Bed & Breakfast Place"

Heated Pool • Hot Tub • Color TV
Tropical Garden Setting
Clothing Optional
The Inn Place to stay in Phoenix
The Valley of the Sun

6245 N. 12th Place   Phoenix, AZ 85014

1-800-974-1474

Fax: 1-602-264-3503
E-mail: Sunbrstinn@aol.com
Web: www.azsunburst.com

ARIZONA ROYAL VILLA

Phoenix's Largest Male Complex

from $69.95 sgl / $79.95 dbl

- very central
- private baths
- pool & hot tub
- clothing optional
- day passes $10
- gated complex

1110 E. Turney Ave., Phoenix, AZ 85014
(602) 266-6883 · (888) 266-6884
www.royalvilla.com

PHOENIX ◆ SCOTTSDALE

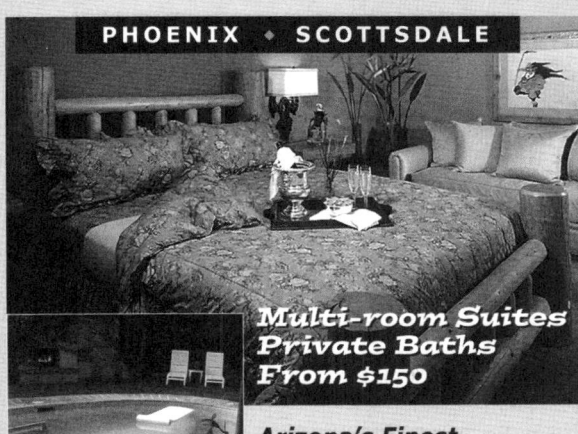

**Multi-room Suites
Private Baths
From $150**

**Arizona's Finest
Bed & Breakfast
Near Old Town Scottsdale**

◆Heated Pool ◆Expanded Continental Breakfast ◆In-Suite Color Cable TVs and VCRs ◆Ralph Lauren Linens and Robes ◆One-half acre of Lush Gardens ◆Business and Leisure Travel ◆Fax, Private Phones, Computer Ports ◆Galleries and World-Class Shopping Nearby ◆Major Credit Cards ◆Extended Stay Discounts ◆Gay Owned and Operated

Casa de Mis Padres

5965 E. Orange Blossom Lane
Phoenix, AZ 85018
480-675-0247
800-996-4108

WWW.CASADMP.COM

Arizona • USA

➤ **Yum Yum Tree Guest House**
[GS,SW,GO] 90 W Virginia Ave #1 (at 3rd Ave) **602/265-2590**, **877/986-8733**

■BARS

Amsterdam [MW,E] 718 N Central Ave (btwn Roosevelt & Fillmore) **602/258-6122** *4pm-1am, upscale*

Apollo's [M,NH,K] 5749 N 7th St (S of Bethany Home) **602/277-9373** *10am-1am, diverse crowd*

Buddy's [MW,NH,E,S] 1560 E Osborn Rd (at N 16th St) **602/266-0477** *1pm-1am, from 10am wknds, male strippers Th*

The Bunkhouse Saloon [M] 4428 N 7th Ave (at Indian School) **602/200-9154** *noon-1am, patio*

Cash Inn Country [W,D,CW,WC] 2140 E McDowell Rd (at 22nd St) **602/244-9943** *4pm-1am, clsd Mon*

Charlie's [M,D,CW,WC] 727 W Camelback Rd (at 7th Ave) **602/265-0224** *2pm-1am, till 3am Fri-Sat, Sun bbq*

Cruisin' Central [M,WC] 1011 N Central Ave (at Roosevelt) **602/253-3376** *6am-1am, from 10am Sun, hustlers*

Harley's 155/ Harley's II [M,NH,D,B,L,V] 155 W Camelback Rd (btwn 3rd & Central Aves) **602/274-8505** *noon-1am*

Incognito Lounge [MW,D,S,WC] 2424 E Thomas Rd (at 24th St) **602/955-9805** *8pm-1am, till 3am Fri-Sat, clsd Mon-Wed*

Johnny Mc's/ Up Yours [M,NH] 138 W Camelback Rd (btwn 3rd & Central Aves) **602/266-0875** *10am-1am, 2 bars*

Marlys' [MW,NH] 15615 N Cave Creek Rd (btwn Greenway Pkwy & Greenway Rd) **602/867-2463** *3pm-1am*

Nasty's Sports Bar [MW,NH,K] 3108 E McDowell Rd (at 32nd St) **602/267-8707** *noon-1am*

Nu Towne Saloon [★M,NH,WC] 5002 E Van Buren (at 48th St) **602/267-9959** *10am-1am, popular Sun & Tue, patio, cruisy*

Phoenix • Arizona

Oz [MW,NH] 1805 W Bethany Home Rd
602/242-5114 *1am-1pm*

Paco Paco's [M,D,MR-L,TG,DS] 3045 N 16th St (at Thomas) **602/263-8424** *7pm-1am, clsd Mon-Tue*

Padlock [M,L] 998 E Indian School Rd (at 10th St) **602/266-5640** *3pm-1am*

Pookie's Cafe [MW,E,V,WC] 4540 N 7th St (at Camelback) **602/277-2121** *11am-midnight, Sun brunch*

Pumphouse II [M,NH] 4132 E McDowell Rd (at 41st) **602/275-3509** *noon-1am*

Roscoe's on 7th [MW,F] 4531 N 7th St (at Minnezona) **602/285-0833** *3pm-1am, from 11am Sun, sports bar*

Triangles [MW,NH,D] 5008 W Northern Ave **623/937-0940** *11am-1am, from 10am wknds*

The Waterhole [MW,NH,F,K] 8830 N 43rd Ave (at Dunlap) **623/937-3139** *11am-1am*

Winks [★M,C,DS] 5707 N 7th St (btwn Bethany Home & Missouri) **602/265-9002** *10am-1am*

■ NIGHTCLUBS

Boom [★M,D,S,YC,WC] 1724 E McDowell (at 16th St) **602/254-0231** *4pm-1am, till 3am Fri, till 6am Sat, clsd Sun-Wed, dancers Fri, circuit crowd Sat*

Club Pulse [M,D,YC] 3702 N 7th St (at Weldon) **602/212-9888** *5pm-1am*

■ RESTAURANTS

Alexi's [WC] 3550 N Central (at Osborn) **602/279-0982** *lunch & dinner, dinner only Sat, clsd Sun, int'l, full bar, patio*

Hamburger Mary's [GO] 5111 N 7th St (N of Camelback) **602/240-6969** *11am-1am, from 10am wknds, till 3am Fri-Sat, Sun brunch*

Katz's Deli 5144 N Central (at Camelback) **602/277-8814** *6:30am-2:30pm, from 8am Sun, kosher*

Los Dos Molinos 8646 S Central Ave **602/243-9113** *lunch & dinner, clsd Sun-Mon, homecooking*

Persian Garden Cafe 1335 W Thomas Rd (at N 15th Ave) **602/263-1915** *11am-9pm, till 10pm Fri-Sat, clsd Sun*

Arizona • *USA*

Pookie's Cafe [MW,E,V,WC] 4540 N 7th St (at Camelback) **602/277-2121** *11am-midnight, Sun brunch, also full bar*

Vincent Guerithault on Camelback [WC] 3930 E Camelback Rd #204 (at 40th St) **602/224-0225** *Southwestern*

■ BOOKSTORES

The Bookstore 4230 N 7th Ave **602/279-3910** *9am-8:30pm, till 6pm Sat, till 5pm Sun, independent*

■ RETAIL SHOPS

Energy Tanning [WC] 4700 N Central #114 (at Camelback) **602/285-1861** *locations valley-wide*

Movies on Central [WC] 4700 N Central #121 (at Highland) **602/274-0994** *11am-10pm, till 9pm Sun, lgbt video rentals & sales*

Root Seller Gallery 1605 N 7th Ave (at McDowell Rd) **602/712-9338** *10am-6pm, lgbt books & gifts*

➤ **Unique on Central** [WC] 4700 N Central Ave #105 (at Highland) **602/279-9691, 800/269-4840 (mail order)** *10am-9pm, till 8pm Sun, cards & gifts*

■ PUBLICATIONS

Echo Magazine 602/266-0550 *bi-weekly lgbt newsmagazine*

HeatStroke News 602/264-3646 *bi-weekly lgbt newspaper*

Ionaz 602/308-4662 *entertainment guide*

X-Factor 602/266-0550 *adult video reviews, classified ads, bar & club listings*

■ MEN'S CLUBS

➤ **Chute** [MO,B,L] 1440 E Indian School Rd **602/234-1654** *24hrs*

➤ **Flex Complex** [SW,PC] 1517 S Black Canyon Hwy (btwn 19th Ave & I-17) **602/271-9011** *24hrs*

Renovated
Steamroom
and Wet Area
New
Big Screen
Satellite TV
New
Videos in
select rooms
New
rates and
specials
New
membership
specials...

...*same
great place*
to meet friendly
Bears and
Leathermen
in PHOENIX,
Arizona.

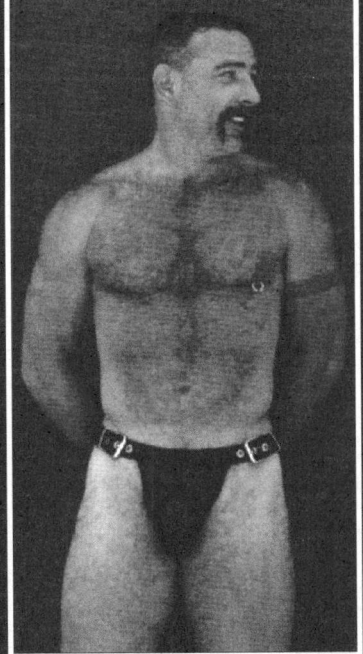

1440 E. Indian School Rd., PHOENIX, AZ
85014   602-234-1654
24 hour Private Men's Health Club Est 1994

Image and leatherwear: leathermasters.com

Arizona • USA

■Men's Services

The Confidential Connection®!
602/252-3333 *The hottest local guys! 18+ Record & Listen FREE! Use access code 499*

➤ **Megaphone Phoenix**
800/289-1489 *Call for the local # nearest you! Meet Hot Men in your area! FREE to Browse & Respond to voice ads. Use code 3087. Also try MEGAMATES.COM*

■Erotica

Adult Shoppe 111 S 24th St (at Jefferson) **602/306-1130** *24hrs; also 5021 W Indian School Rd (at 51st Ave), 623/245-3008 & 2345 W Holly St, 602/253-7126*

Castle Megastore 300 E Camelback (at Central) **602/266-3348** *24hrs; also 5501 E Washington, 602/231-9837; 8802 N Black Canyon Fwy, 602/995-1641; 8315 E Apache Tr, 480/986-6114*

International Bookstore 3640 E Thomas Rd (at 36th St) **602/955-2000**

Pleasure World [V] 4029 E Washington (at 40th St) **602/275-0015** *also 1838 NW Grand Ave, 602/252-6446 & 6327 N 59th Ave, 623/939-3411*

Tuff Stuff 1716 E McDowell Rd (at 17th St) **602/254-9651** *10am-6pm, till 4pm Sat, clsd Sun-Mon, leather shop*

■Cruisy Areas

Dreamy Draw Park [AYOR] Squaw Peak Pkwy (off Northern) *go E along the driveway to the back—popular w/ 9-5ers*

La Pradera Park [AYOR] 39th Ave (at Glendale), Glendale

Papago Park [AYOR] Galvin Pkwy (btwn McDowell Rd & Van Buren St)

Thunderbird Park [AYOR] I-17 N to Bell Rd (then W to 59th Ave), Glendale *popular w/ 9-5ers*

Washington Park [AYOR] 21st Ave (N of Bethany Home) *nights*

Prescott

■Info Lines & Services

Prescott Pride Center [WC] 111 Josephine St **928/445-8800** *1:30pm-5:30pm Tue, Th & Sat, call for calendar of events*

■Accommodations

Briar Wreath Inn B&B [GS,GO] 232 S Arizona Ave (at Gurley) **928/778-6048** *full brkfst, hot tub*

■Cruisy Areas

Granite Creek Park [AYOR]

Heritage Park [AYOR] Willow Creek Rd (3 miles S of Hwy 89)

Scottsdale

■Accommodations

Fountain Hills Inn B&B [M,SW,GO] 10621 N Eagle Ln, Fountain Hills **480/816-5000, 866/837-7800** (outside AZ only)

ScottsDale Resorts Accommodations [GF,SW,NS] 7025 E Greenway Pkwy #250 **480/515-2300, 888/868-4378** *rental homes, villas & condos*

Southwest Inn at Eagle Mountain [GF,NS] 9800 N Summer Hill Blvd, Fountain Hills **480/816-3000, 800/992-8083** *on 18-hole golf course*

■Bars

BS West [MW,D,V,WC] 7125 E 5th Ave (in pedestrian mall) **480/945-9028** *1pm-1am*

■Restaurants

AZ-88 7553 E Scottsdale Mall **480/994-5576** *11am-1am, food till midnight, from 5pm wknds, upscale, bar popular w/ gay men Fri-Sat evenings*

Malee's 7131 E Main **480/947-6042** *lunch & dinner, Thai, full bar*

■Erotica

Zorba's Adult Book Shop 2924 N Scottsdale Rd (N of Thomas) **480/941-9891** *arcade*

Tucson • Arizona

Sedona

■ ACCOMMODATIONS

A-Lodge at Sedona—A Luxury B&B Inn [GS,NS] 125 Kallof Pl **928/204-1942, 800/619-4467** *Mission-style B&B inn w/ Red Rock views*

Apple Orchard Inn [GF,SW,NS,WC] 656 Jordan Rd **928/282-5328, 800/663-6968** *full brkfst*

Casita Blanca [MW,WC] **928/567-2938** *straw-bale cottage*

Iris Garden Inn [GF,NS,WC] 390 Jordan Rd **928/282-2552, 800/321-8988** *motel, jacuzzi*

Opening Doors [GS] 325 Navahopi Rd (at Jordan Rd) **928/282-2125** *spiritual retreat*

Southwest Inn at Sedona [GF,NS] 3250 W Hwy 89-A **928/282-3344, 800/483-7422**

Two Angels Guesthouse [MW,NS,GO] **928/204-2083** *lesbian-owned/ run*

■ RESTAURANTS

Judi's 40 Soldier Pass Rd **928/282-4449** *11:30am-9pm, full bar*

Piñon Bistro [WC,GO] 1075 Hwy 260 (Rte 89A), Cottonwood **928/649-0234** *dinner Th-Sun, clsd Mon-Wed*

Tempe

■ RESTAURANTS

Restaurant Mexico 120 E University Dr **480/967-3280** *11am-9pm, till 10pm Fri-Sat, clsd Sun*

■ BOOKSTORES

Changing Hands 6428 S McClintock Dr **480/730-0205** *new & used, lgbt section*

■ EROTICA

Modern World 1812 E Apache (at McClintock Dr) **480/967-9052**

Tucson

■ INFO LINES & SERVICES

AA Gay/ Lesbian 3269 N Mountain Ave (at MCC) **520/624-4183** *8pm Th*

Wingspan, Southern Arizona's LGBT Community Center 300 E 6th St (at 5th Ave) **520/624-1779, 520/624-0348** *10am-7pm Mon-Fri, till 5pm Sat, resources, youth support, library, film festival & more*

■ ACCOMMODATIONS

Adobe Desert Vacation Rentals [GS,NS] **520/578-3998**

Adobe Rose Inn B&B [GF,SW] 940 N Olsen Ave **520/318-4644, 800/328-4122** *full brkfst, hot tub*

Armory Park Guesthouse [GF] 219 S 5th Ave **520/206-9252** *renovated 1896 residence (owner's) w/ 2 detached guest units*

Casa Alegre B&B Inn [GF,SW,NS] 316 E Speedway Blvd **520/628-1800, 800/628-5654** *full brkfst, hot tub*

Catalina Park Inn [GS,NS,GO] 309 E 1st St **520/792-4541, 800/792-4885**

Clarion Hotel Randolph Park [GF,SW,WC] 102 N Alvernon Wy **520/795-0330, 800/252-7466** *full brkfst, jacuzzi*

Desert Trails B&B [GF,SW] 12851 E Speedway Blvd **520/885-7295, 877/758-3284** *adobe hacienda on 3 acres bordering Saguaro Nat'l Park*

Elysian Grove Market B&B [GS,NS] 400 W Simpson **520/628-1522** *full brkfst, renovated historic adobe, kitchen in suite*

Gateway Villas B&B [GS,SW,NS,GO] 228 N 4th Ave (at 9th St) **520/740-0767, 888/239-8125** *jacuzzi, some kitchens*

Hacienda del Sol Guest Ranch Resort [GF,F,SW,WC] 5601 N Hacienda del Sol Rd **520/299-1501, 800/728-6514**

Hotel Congress [GF,F] 311 E Congress **520/622-8848, 800/722-8848** *also Cup Cafe & full bar*

Natural B&B [GS,NS,GO] **520/881-4582** *non-toxic/ allergenic, full brkfst, massage available*

Royal Elizabeth B&B Inn [GS,SW,NS,GO] 204 S Scott Ave (at Broadway) **520/670-9022, 877/670-9022** *historic 1878 downtown mansion, full brkfst, hot tub*

Arizona • USA

➤ **Tortuga Roja Men's B&B** [MO,SW,N,NS,WC,GO] 2800 E River Rd **520/577-6822, 800/467-6822** *hot tub*

The Tree House [GS,NS,GO] 53-A Spring Canyon (at Tombstone Canyon Rd), Bisbee **520/432-1307** *secluded 1-bdrm guest house, full brkfst, hot tub*

■ BARS

Congress Tap Room [GF,NH,D,A,E] 311 E Congress (at Hotel Congress) **520/622-8848** *10am-1am, dance club from 9pm, theme nights*

IBT's (It's About Time) [MW,D,S,WC] 616 N 4th Ave (at University) **520/882-3053** *11am-1am*

Venture-N [M,L] 1239 N 6th Ave (at Stone) **520/882-8224** *10am-1am,*

Woody's [M,V,WC] 3710 N Oracle (at Prince) **520/292-6702** *noon-1am, from 11am wknds*

The Yard Dog Saloon [GS,TG,WC] 2449 N Stone (N of Grant) **520/624-3858** *6am-1am, from 10am Sun*

■ CAFES

The Cottage Bakery Cafe 800 N Kolb **520/722-1129** *7am-9pm, till 11pm Fri-Sat, 8am-8pm Sun*

Rainbow Planet Coffee House [MW] 606 N 4th Ave (at University) **520/620-1770** *7am-11pm, 8am-midnight Fri-Sat*

■ RESTAURANTS

Blue Willow 2616 N Campbell (at Grant) **520/327-7577** *brkfst served all day*

Cafe Terra Cotta [WC] 3500 E Sunrise **520/577-8100** *full bar*

The Grill on Congress 100 E Congress (at Scott) **520/623-7621** *24hrs, full bar*

November Bar & Grill 4001 N Romero Rd (at Roger) **520/407-9622** *lunch & dinner, dinner only Fri, also full bar*

■ BOOKSTORES

Antigone Books [WC] 411 N 4th Ave (at 7th St) **520/792-3715** *10am-6pm, till 9pm Fri-Sat, noon-5pm Sun, lgbt*

TORTUGA ROJA
Men's Bed & Breakfast

2800 East River Road
Tucson, Arizona 85718

520.577.6822
800.467.6822

www.tortugaroja.com
redtrtl@tortugaroja.com

Eureka Springs • Arkansas

■RETAIL SHOPS

Desert Pride [WC,GO] 300 E 6th St #1A (at 5th Ave) **520/388-9829** *noon-7pm, till 6pm wknds, pride gifts*

■PUBLICATIONS

The Observer 520/622-7176

■MEN'S SERVICES

➤ **Megaphone Tucson** **800/289-1489** *Call for the local # nearest you! Meet Hot Men in your area! FREE to Browse & Respond to voice ads. Use code 3087. Also try MEGAMATES.COM*

■EROTICA

The Bookstore Southwest 5754 E Speedway Blvd **520/790-1550**

Caesar's Adult Shop 2540 N Oracle Rd (btwn Glen & Grant) **520/622-9479**

Continental Adult Shop 2655 N Campbell (at Grant), Tuscon **520/327-8402** *private rooms, arcade*

Hydra 145 E Congress (at 6th) **520/791-3711** *vinyl, leather, toys, shoes*

■CRUISY AREAS

Fort Lowell Park [AYOR]

Gollob Park [AYOR] off Prudence (S of the Hilton Hotel)

Greasewood Park [AYOR] W Speedway *beware of cacti*

Redington Pass *upper Tanque Verde Falls, clothing-optional, gay area is beyond straight area*

Tanque Verde Falls [AYOR] E on Tanque Verde Rd (to Upper Tanque Verde Falls parking area)

ARKANSAS

Batesville

■CRUISY AREAS

Riverside Park [AYOR]

Crossett

■CAFES

Pig Trail Cafe [★] Rte 16 (E of Elkins) **479/643-3307** *6am-9pm*

Eureka Springs

■ACCOMMODATIONS

11 Singleton House B&B [GF,NS] 11 Singleton **479/253-9111**, **800/833-3394** *1890s Victorian, full brkfst, jacuzzi*

1905 Basin Park Hotel [GS] 12 Spring St **479/253-7837**, **800/643-4972** *1905 historic hotel*

Arbour Glen Victorian Inn B&B [GF] 7 Lema **479/253-9010**, **800/515-4536** *historic Victorian home w/ guest house, full brkfst, jacuzzis, fireplaces*

Comfort Inn of Eureka Springs [GF,SW,WC] Hwy 62 E (at Jct 23 S) **479/253-5241**, **800/828-0109** *3-story Victorian hotel*

Eureka Springs Cottages [GS] historic downtown **479/253-7409**, **800/799-7409** *B&B inn in heart of downtown, full gourmet brkfst, hot tub*

Heart of the Hills Inn [GS,GO] 5 Summit **479/253-7468**, **800/253-7468** *historic inn near downtown, full brkfst*

Home Suite Home [GF,GO] **888/933-4050** *suites or cottage, jacuzzi*

Morningstar Retreat on the Kings River [GF,NS] Hwy 221 S & Kings River **479/253-5995**, **800/298-5995** *cottages, jacuzzi*

Palace Hotel & Bath House [GF] 135 Spring St **479/253-7474** *historic bath house open to all*

Pond Mountain Lodge & Resort [GS,SW,NS,WC,GO] **479/253-5877**, **800/583-8043** *full brkfst*

Wildflower Cottages [GS] 22 Hale **479/253-9173**, **866/847-9776** *private cottages, hot tub*

The Woods Resort [MW,NS,GO] 50 Wall St (off Hwy 62) **479/253-8281** *cottages, jacuzzis, kitchens, treehouse hot tub*

■BARS

Center Street Restaurant & Bar [★GF,D,E] 10 Center St **479/253-8102** *5pm-10pm Th-Sun, Mexican/ South American*

Arkansas • USA

Chelsea's Corner Cafe [GF] 10 Mountain St (at Center St) **479/253-6723** *11am-2am, till 10pm Sun, patio*

■ RESTAURANTS

Autumn Breeze Hwy 23 S **479/253-7734** *5pm-9pm, clsd Sun, cont'l*

Cottage Inn Hwy 62 W **479/253-5282** *seasonal, 5pm-9pm, clsd Sun-Mon, Mediterranean, full bar*

Ermilio's 26 White **479/253-8806** *5pm-9pm, Italian, full bar*

Gaskins Cabin Restaurant [GS] 2883 Hwy 23 N (Hwy 187) **479/253-5466** *5pm-9pm Th-Sat*

Jim & Brent's Bistro [BYOB] 173 S Main **479/253-7457** *5pm-10pm, clsd Wed-Th*

Sonny's Pizzeria 119 N Main St (at Mountain) **479/253-2329** *3pm-9pm, from 11am Wed, till 10pm Fri-Sat, clsd Tue*

Fayetteville

■ INFO LINES & SERVICES

AA Gay/ Lesbian 568 W Sycamore **479/443-6366** (AA#) *7pm Th, 10am Sat*

■ BARS

Sycamore Pub [MW,NH,D,V,PC,GO] 716 W Sycamore #2 (at Gregg Ave) **479/571-1300** *8pm-2am, clsd Mon-Tue, DJ Fri-Sat*

■ NIGHTCLUBS

Ron's Place [★MW,D,DS,PC,GO] 523 W Poplar **479/442-3052** *9pm-2am Th-Sun*

■ CAFES

The Common Grounds 412 W Dickson (at West) **479/442-3515** *7am-2am, from 9am wknds*

■ BOOKSTORES

Hastings Bookstore 3009 N College Ave (Fiesta Square Shopping Center) **479/521-0244** *9am-11pm*

Passages 2332 N College Ave **479/442-5845** *new age bookstore*

■ EROTICA

Curry's Video Concepts 612 N College Ave **479/521-0009**

■ CRUISY AREAS

Flat Rock Beach [AYOR] 10 miles W of town *nude beach*

Lake Fayetteville [AYOR] take second left after the mall on your right *check the woods*

Fort Smith

■ BARS

Kinkead's [★GS,D,DS,18+] 1004 1/2 Garrison Ave (at Towson) **479/783-9988** *3pm-1am, till midnight Sat, clsd Sun*

■ NIGHTCLUBS

Burnzee's on the Hill [★MW,D,DS,PC] 1217 South W (at Towson & 'U') **479/494-7300** *9pm-5am, from 4pm Sun, clsd Mon-Tue*

Hot Springs

■ NIGHTCLUBS

Our House Lounge & Restaurant [★MW,D,WC] 660 E Grand Ave **501/624-6868** *7pm-3am, till 2am Sat, clsd Sun, [DS] monthly*

■ CRUISY AREAS

Degray Lake [AYOR] Lakeside area *afternoon in the woods*

Desota Park [AYOR] just out of town (off Central Ave) *check out road across from the park*

Jonesboro

■ CRUISY AREAS

Craighead Forest Park [AYOR] *seasonal*

Little Rock

■ BARS

Backstreet [MW,D,DS,PC,WC] 1021 Jessie Rd #Q (btwn Cantrell & Riverfront) **501/664-2744** *9pm-5am*

The Factory [M,NH,D,F,E,K,WC,GO] 412 S Louisiana St (btwn 4th & Center) **501/372-3070** *5pm-2am, 8pm-1am Sat, clsd Sun-Mon*

Angeles Nat'l Forest • California

■NIGHTCLUBS

The Aquarium
[MW,NH,D,MR,TG,E,K,DS,PC,WC,GO] 824 W Capitol (at Izard) **501/375-8580** *Fri 5pm-2am, from 9pm Sat, clsd Sun-Th*

Discovery: The Experience
[★GS,D,TG,DS,PC,WC] 1021 Jessie Rd (btwn Cantrell & Riverfront) **501/664-4784** *9pm-5am Sat only*

■RESTAURANTS

Vino's Pizza [BW] 923 W 7th St (at Chester) **501/375-8466** *11am-midnight, till 10pm Tue-Wed*

■ENTERTAINMENT & RECREATION

The Weekend Theatre [BW,GO] 1001 W 7th St (at Chester) **501/374-3761** *plays & musicals on wknds*

■RETAIL SHOPS

A Twisted Gift Shop 1007 W 7th St (at Chester) **501/376-7723** *11am-10pm, clsd Tue, gift shop; also 7201 Asher Ave, 501/568-4262*

Wild Card 400 N Bowman (at Maralynn) **501/223-9071** *10am-8pm, noon-5pm Sun, novelties & gifts*

■MEN'S SERVICES

▶ **Megaphone Little Rock**
800/289-1489 *Call for the local # nearest you! Meet Hot Men in your area! FREE to Browse & Respond to voice ads. Use code 3087. Also try MEGAMATES.COM*

CALIFORNIA

Amador City

■ACCOMMODATIONS

Imperial Hotel [GF,GO] 14202 Hwy 49 (at Water St) **209/267-9172, 800/242-5594** *B&B, brick Victorian hotel from Gold Rush era, full brkfst*

Anaheim

■NIGHTCLUBS

Bravo [MW,D] 1490 S Anaheim Blvd **714/533-2291** *gay Sat only*

■MEN'S SERVICES

The Confidential Connection®!
714/539-5500 *The hottest local guys! 18+ Record & Listen FREE! Use access code 499*

The Gay Connection 900/505-6339
Talk and/ or meet with other men from the area, at only 99¢ per minute.

▶ **Megaphone Anaheim**
714/905-0050 *Voice Personals! Meet Hot Men in your area! FREE to Browse & Respond to voice ads. Use code 3087. Also try MEGAMATES.COM*

Voice MALE 714/636-9500 *The city's hottest & wildest all-male voice club. Chat one on one! Use access code 5111*

■CRUISY AREAS

Yorba Regional Park [AYOR] La Palma Ave (exit Wilson, turn right) *days*

Angeles Nat'l Forest

■CRUISY AREAS

Beach in the Upper Big Tujunga Canyon (UBTC) [AYOR] Hwy 2, exit Angeles Crest Hwy, head N, turn left to UBTC Rd, turn right (btwn marker 4.5 & 4.8) *little nude beach along creek*

Cajon Pass [AYOR] Rte 66 (W of I-15) *many warnings, including that the San Andreas fault will be directly under your feet!*

Mill Creek Summit [AYOR] *just SE of the road at the summit btwn Pasadena & Palmdale*

California • USA

Arcata

■RESTAURANTS

Wildflower Bakery & Cafe 1604 'G' St
707/822-0360 *8am-8pm, 9am-1pm Sun, vegetarian*

■BOOKSTORES

Northtown Books 957 'H' St
707/822-2834 *10am-7pm, till 9pm Fri, till 6pm Sat, noon-5pm Sun, lgbt section*

■CRUISY AREAS

Azalea State Reserve [AYOR] along Mad River (on N Bank Rd) *6 miles N of Arcata*

Arnold

■ACCOMMODATIONS

Dorrington Inn at Big Trees [GS,GO] 3450 Hwy 4, Dorrington
209/795-2164, 888/874-2164 *cottages & suites, 3 hours from San Francisco, 18 miles from Bear Valley*

Atascadero

■EROTICA

Diamond Adult World 5915 El Camino Real (at Traffic Wy)
805/462-0404

Auburn

■CAFES

Wolf Mountain Coffee [TG,WC,GO] 13428 Lincoln Wy (at Foresthill Rd/I-80) **530/888-8195** *5:30am-9pm, 7am-6pm Sun, relaxing woodsy atmosphere, internet access*

Bakersfield

■ACCOMMODATIONS

Rio Bravo Resort, Hotel & Spa [GS,SW,WC] 11200 Lake Ming Rd
661/872-5000, 888/517-5500 *outdoor activities*

■NIGHTCLUBS

Club Paradise [M,NH,D,K] 902 19th St (btwn 'O' & 'Q' Sts) **661/327-5247** *5pm-2am*

■EROTICA

Cinema 19 1224 19th St (btwn 'L' & 'M', across from The Mint)
661/323-7711

Deja Vu 1524 Golden State Hwy (at Chester Ave) **661/322-7300**

Wildcat Books 2620 Chester Ave (at 21st) **661/324-4243**

■CRUISY AREAS

Beach Park [AYOR] 21st & Oak Sts

Kern River Canyon [AYOR] 5 miles to Forest Service land *nude beach*

Benicia

see Vallejo

Berkeley

see East Bay

Big Bear Lake

■ACCOMMODATIONS

Alpine Retreats [GS,NS,GO] 433 Edgemoor (at Big Bear Blvd)
818/535-9272 *indoor spas, fireplaces, private entrances*

Eagles' Nest B&B [GF] 41675 Big Bear Blvd **909/866-6465, 888/866-6465** *5 cottages, full brkfst*

The Greenbriar [GS,GO] 943 Greenbriar (at Sycamore & Kuffel Canyon), Sky Forest **909/336-4433,**
866/205-4433 *B&B in Lake Arrowhead area, full brkfst*

Grey Squirrel Resort [GF,SW,WC,GO] **909/866-4335, 800/381-5569** *19 private rental homes*

Hillcrest Lodge [GS,WC] 40241 Big Bear Blvd **909/866-6040,**
800/843-4449 *motel, smokefree rms available, cabins, jacuzzi suites*

Knickerbocker Mansion Country Inn [GS,NS,WC,GO] 869 Knickerbocker Rd **909/878-9190, 877/423-1180** *log mansion on lake, full brkfst*

Majestic Moose Lodge [GF,SW] 39328 Big Bear Blvd (at Cienga)
909/866-2435, 877/585-5855 *cabins, jacuzzis*

Clear Lake • California

Rainbow View Lodge [GS,NS] 2726 View Dr (at Hilltop), Running Springs **888/868-1810**

Big Sur

■ACCOMMODATIONS

Lucia Lodge [GF] Hwy 1 **831/667-2391, 866/424-4787** *ocean view cabins (newly remodeled), restaurant, Rockslide Lounge, store*

Bodega Bay

■ACCOMMODATIONS

Marina View Guest Suite on Bodega Dunes [MW,GO] 2015 Sandpiper Ct (at Whaleship & Bay Flat Rd) **707/478-4492** *guest house, hot tub, views of bay & dunes*

Buena Park

■BARS

Ozz Supper Club [MW,D,F,E,C,P] 6231 Manchester Blvd **714/522-1542** *9pm-2am, from 6pm Fri-Sat, from 3pm Sun, clsd Mon & Wed, call for events*

Burney

■ACCOMMODATIONS

Burney Mountain Guest Ranch [GF,SW,WC,GO] 22800 Hat Creek, Powerhouse #2 (at Hwy 299), Cassek **530/335-4087** *cabins, full brkfst, close to some of best fly-fishing in state, hot tub*

Cambria

■ACCOMMODATIONS

The J Patrick House B&B [GF,NS] 2990 Burton Dr (1/2 mile off Hwy 1) **805/927-3812, 800/341-5258** *authentic log cabin, fireplaces*

Carmel

see also Monterey

■ACCOMMODATIONS

Happy Landing Inn [GF,NS,WC] Monte Verde (btwn 5th & 6th) **831/624-7917** *Hansel & Gretel 1925 inn, full brkfst*

■CRUISY AREAS

Garrapata State Beach [AYOR] 10 miles S of crossroads (on right side of Hwy 1) *nude sunbathing*

Ocean Ave Beach [AYOR]

Chico

■INFO LINES & SERVICES

Stonewall Alliance Center 341 Broadway #416 **530/893-3336** *1pm-5pm, till 7pm Tue-Fri, recorded info, meetings*

■ACCOMMODATIONS

Inn at Shallow Creek Farm [GF,NS] 4712 Road DD, Orland **530/865-4093, 800/865-4093**

■CRUISY AREAS

Bidwell Park [AYOR] *near cedar grove area at '5 mile' recreation area, & at swimming hole 'M' in Upper Bidwell Park*

Chula Vista

■MEN'S SERVICES

➤ **Megaphone Chula Vista** **619/734-1110** *Voice Personals! Meet Hot Men in your area! FREE to Browse & Respond to voice ads. Use code 3087. Also try MEGAMATES.COM*

■EROTICA

F St Bookstore [WC] 1141 3rd Ave (at Naples) **619/585-3314** *24hrs*

Clear Lake

■ACCOMMODATIONS

Blue Fish Cove Resort [GF,SW] 10573 E Hwy 20, Clearlake Oaks **707/998-1769** *lakeside resort cottages, boat facilities & rentals*

Edgewater Resort [SW,GO] 6420 Soda Bay Rd (at Hohape Rd), Kelseyville **707/279-0208, 800/396-6224** *'gay-owned, straight-friendly,' also camping, theme wknds*

Sea Breeze Resort [GS,SW,NS,WC,GO] 9595 Harbor Dr, Glenhaven **707/998-3327** *cottages*

California • USA

RESTAURANTS

The Brentwood 6278 E Hwy 20, Lucerne **707/274-2301** *dinner only (brkfst, lunch & dinner wknds), clsd Tue-Wed*

Kathy's Inn [WC] 14677 Lake Shore Dr, Clearlake **707/994-9933** *lunch Wed-Fri, open from 4pm wknds, clsd Mon-Tue, full bar*

Cloverdale

see also Healdsburg

ACCOMMODATIONS

Vintage Towers B&B [GF,NS] 302 N Main St (at 3rd) **707/894-4535, 888/886-9377** *Queen Anne mansion, full brkfst*

Concord

INFO LINES & SERVICES

AA Gay/ Lesbian 2118 Willow Pass Rd **925/939-4155** (AA#) *7:30pm Tue*

Rainbow Community Center 2118 Willow Pass Rd #500 (at Diablo) **925/692-0090** *10am-5pm, clsd Sun*

MEN'S SERVICES

➤ **Megaphone Concord** **800/289-1489** *Call for the local # nearest you! Meet Hot Men in your area! FREE to Browse & Respond to voice ads. Use code 3087. Also try MEGAMATES.COM*

EROTICA

Lingerie Etc 2294 Monument Blvd (at Buskirk) **925/676-2962**

Costa Mesa

BARS

Tin Lizzie Saloon [M,NH,WC] 752 St Clair (at Bristol) **714/966-2029** *11am-2am*

NIGHTCLUBS

Lion's Den [MW,D,K,DS,YC] 719 W 19th St (at Pomona) **949/645-3830** *9pm-2am, clsd Mon-Tue, straight Sat, Latino Fri*

CRUISY AREAS

Wilson Park [AYOR] Hwy 55 S (exit Wilson, turn right) *days*

Crescent City

CRUISY AREAS

Foot of 'A' St [AYOR] at Front St *days*

Cupertino

BARS

Dar's Hideaway [MW,NH,E] 10095 Saich Wy (at Stevens Creek Blvd) **408/255-7474** *5pm-2am, DJ every other Sat*

CRUISY AREAS

Stevens Creek Canyon Park [AYOR] Foothill Blvd *at first road turn left below the dam, go down, then go up to the top parking area on the right*

Danville

BARS

Bleu [★MW,D,E,GO] 519 San Ramon Valley Blvd **925/831-0963** *5pm-2am, clsd Mon, theme nights, College Night Wed, DJ Fri-Sat, comedy Sun, [DS] 1st Sun, also lounge*

Davis

see also Sacramento

INFO LINES & SERVICES

LGBT Resource Center [WC] University House Annex **530/752-2452** *10am-5pm, clsd wknds, info, referrals, mtgs, library*

CAFES

Cafe Roma [★YC] 231 'E' St (btwn 2nd & 3rd) **530/756-1615** *6am-10pm, 6:30am-9pm wknds*

MEN'S SERVICES

➤ **Megaphone Davis 800/289-1489** *Call for the local # nearest you! Meet Hot Men in your area! FREE to Browse & Respond to voice ads. Use code 3087. Also try MEGAMATES.COM*

East Bay • California

East Bay

includes Berkeley & Oakland, see also Concord, Danville, Fremont, Lafayette, Hayward, Pleasant Hill, San Lorenzo, Walnut Creek

■ INFO LINES & SERVICES

La Peña [MR] 3105 Shattuck Ave, Berkeley **510/849-2568** *10am-5pm Tue-Fri, box office open 1pm-6pm Wed-Sat, multicultural center, hosts meetings, dances, performance art, events, also cafe 5:30pm-9:30pm Wed-Sun*

Pacific Center 2712 Telegraph Ave (at Derby), Berkeley **510/548-8283** *10am-10pm, noon-3pm & 7pm-10pm Sat, 6pm-9pm Sun*

■ ACCOMMODATIONS

Bates House B&B [GS,NS,GO] 399 Bellevue Ave (at Van Buren), Oakland **510/893-3881**

Elmwood House [GS,NS,GO] **510/540-5123**

Washington Inn [GF,NS,WC] 495 10th St (at Broadway), Oakland **510/452-1776** *historic boutique hotel*

■ BARS

Bench & Bar [★M,D,MR-L,DS,P,S,YC,WC] 2111 Franklin St **510/444-2266** *3pm-2am, Latin Fri, strippers*

Cabel's Reef [MW,D,MR,K,DS] 2272 Telegraph Ave (at Grand), Oakland **510/451-3777** *2pm-2am*

White Horse [MW,D,WC] 6551 Telegraph Ave (at 66th), Oakland **510/652-3820** *1pm-2am, from 3pm Mon-Tue, popular wknds*

■ CAFES

Cafe Sorrento 2510 Channing (at Telegraph), Berkeley **510/548-8220** *11am-9pm, Italian*

Cafe Strada [★WC] 2300 College Ave (at Bancroft), Berkeley **510/843-5282** *6:30am-midnight, students, great patio & white mochas*

Mimosa Cafe [BW] 462 Santa Clara (at Grand), Oakland **510/465-2948** *11am-9pm, from 9am wknds, till 2pm Sun, clsd Mon*

■ RESTAURANTS

Bette's To Go 1807 4th St (at Hearst), Berkeley **510/548-9494** *6:30am-5pm, from 8am wknds, sandwiches*

Chez Panisse [BW,R] 1517 Shattuck Ave (at Cedar), Berkeley **510/548-5525** *clsd Sun, upscale nouvelle Californian, also cafe*

La Mediterranée [BW] 2936 College Ave (at Ashby), Berkeley **510/540-7773** *10am-10pm, till 11pm wknds*

Mama's Royale [★W,BW,WC] 4012 Broadway (at 40th), Oakland **510/547-7600** *7am-3pm, from 8am wknds, come early for excellent wknd brunch*

Oakland Taqueria 120 11th St (at Oak St), Oakland **510/893-4060** *11am-midnight, from 6pm wknd*

■ ENTERTAINMENT & RECREATION

Oakland East Bay Gay Men's Chorus **800/706-2389**

■ BOOKSTORES

Boadecia's Books [WC,GO] 398 Colusa Ave (1/2 mile from Solano), North Berkeley **510/559-9184** *11am-6pm Sun-Mon, noon-8pm Tue-Fri, 11am-8pm Sat, lgbt*

Cody's [WC] 2454 Telegraph Ave (at Haste), Berkeley **510/845-7852** *10am-10pm, frequent readings & lectures, lgbt section*

Easy Going 1385 Shattuck (at Rose), Berkeley **510/843-3533**, **510/843-6725** *10am-7pm, till 6pm Sat, noon-6pm Sun, travel books & accessories*

Shambhala Booksellers [WC] 2482 Telegraph Ave (at Dwight), Berkeley **510/848-8443** *11am-7pm, clsd Mon, spiritual*

■ RETAIL SHOPS

Ancient Ways 4075 Telegraph Ave (at 41st), Oakland **510/653-3244** *11am-7pm, extensive occult supplies, classes, readings, runs several events annually*

California • USA

■ PUBLICATIONS

San Francisco Bay Times [★]
415/626-0260 *bi-weekly, a 'must read' for Bay Area resources*

■ MEN'S CLUBS

➤ **Steamworks** [★,PC] 2107 4th St (at Addison), Berkeley **510/845-8992** *24hrs, call for recorded info*

■ MEN'S SERVICES

The Confidential Connection®!
510/814-6699 *The hottest local guys! 18+ Record & Listen FREE! Use access code 499*

Voice MALE 510/749-9966 *The city's hottest & wildest all-male voice club. Chat one on one! Use access code 5111*

■ EROTICA

Good Vibrations 2504 San Pablo (at Dwight Wy), Berkeley **510/841-8987** *clean, well-lighted sex toy store, also mail order, workshops & events*

Hollywood Adult Books 5686 Telegraph Ave (at 57th), Oakland **510/654-1169**

L'Amour Shoppe 1905 San Pablo Ave, Oakland **510/465-4216**

El Cajon

■ MEN'S SERVICES

➤ **Megaphone El Cajon**
619/387-0383 *Voice Personals! Meet Hot Men in your area! FREE to Browse & Respond to voice ads. Use code 3087. Also try MEGAMATES.COM*

■ EROTICA

F St Bookstore [WC] 158 E Main (at Magnolia) **619/447-0381** *24hrs*

Escondido

■ MEN'S SERVICES

➤ **Megaphone Escondido**
760/708-0800 *Voice Personals! Meet Hot Men in your area! FREE to Browse & Respond to voice ads. Use code 3087. Also try MEGAMATES.COM*

■ EROTICA

F St Bookstore [WC] 237 E Grand Ave (at Juniper) **760/480-6031**

Romantix Video Specialties [WC] 2322 S Escondido Blvd **760/745-6697**

Eureka

■ ACCOMMODATIONS

Abigail's Elegant Victorian Mansion Historic B&B Inn [GF,NS] 1406 'C' St **707/444-3144** *full brkfst, sauna*

Carter House Victorians [GF,NS,WC] 301 'L' St **707/444-8062, 800/404-1390** *enclave of 4 unique inns, full brkfst, restaurant, wine shop*

■ BARS

Lost Coast Brewery Pub [GF,F,BW,WC] 617 4th St (btwn 'G' & 'H') **707/445-4480** *11am-midnight, kitchen open till midnight*

The Shanty [MW,NH] 213 3rd St (at 'C') **707/442-2053** *noon-2am, from 10am Sat*

■ NIGHTCLUBS

Club Triangle (Club West)
[GF,D,A,F,E,18+,YC,WC] 535 5th St (at 'G' St) **707/444-2582** *9pm-2am, gay Sun only*

■ RESTAURANTS

Folie Deuce [BW,R,WC] 1551 'G' St, Arcata **707/822-1042** *dinner only, clsd Sun-Mon, bistro*

■ BOOKSTORES

Booklegger [WC] 402 2nd St (at 'E' St) **707/445-1344** *10am-5:30pm, 11am-4pm Sun, mostly used, lgbt section*

■ EROTICA

Good Relations [WC] 308 2nd St **707/441-9570** *bisexual-owned/ run*

■ CRUISY AREAS

The Rockpile [AYOR] on 'T' St

Fairfield

see Vacaville

Fresno • California

Ferndale

■ACCOMMODATIONS
Collingwood Inn B&B [GF,NS,WC,GO] 831 Main St (at Hwy 101) **707/786-9219, 800/469-1632** *full brkfst*

The Gingerbread Mansion Inn [★GF,NS] 400 Berding St **707/786-4000, 800/952-4136** *grand Victorian lady, full brkfst*

Fontana

■EROTICA
Romantix 14589 Valley Blvd (at Cherry) **909/350-4717** *24hrs*

Fort Bragg

■ACCOMMODATIONS
Annie's Jug Handle Beach B&B [GS,GO] 32980 Gibney Ln **707/964-1415, 800/964-9957** *on Hwy 1 across from Pacific Ocean, full brkfst*

Aslan House [GF] 24600 N Hwy 1 **707/964-1952** *beach house, hot tub, partial ocean view*

The Cleone Gardens Inn [GF,NS] 24600 N Hwy 1 **707/964-2788, 800/400-2189 (CA only)** *country garden retreat on 9-1/2 acres, cottages, hot tub*

■RESTAURANTS
Purple Rose Mill Creek Dr **707/964-6507** *5pm-9pm, clsd Mon-Tue, Mexican*

■ENTERTAINMENT & RECREATION
Skunk Train California Western foot of Laurel St **707/964-6371, 800/777-5865**

■BOOKSTORES
Windsong Books & Records 324 N Main (at Redwood Ave) **707/964-2050** *10am-5:30pm, till 4pm Sun, mostly used*

Fremont

■INFO LINES & SERVICES
The Edge [WC] 39160 State St **510/790-2887** *call for hours, drop-in center, community bulletin board, support groups & services*

■MEN'S SERVICES
➤ **Megaphone Fremont** **800/289-1489** *Call for the local # nearest you! Meet Hot Men in your area! FREE to Browse & Respond to voice ads. Use code 3087. Also try MEGAMATES.COM*

■EROTICA
L'Amour Shoppe 40555 Grimmer Blvd (at Fremont) **510/659-8161**

■CRUISY AREAS
Central Park (aka Lake Elizabeth) [AYOR] Pasoe Padre & Stevenson *trails right of lake & parking lot*

Fresno

■INFO LINES & SERVICES
Serenity Fellowship AA 900 N Fulton #D (btwn Olive & Belmont) **559/221-6907** *8pm Th*

■BARS
The Den [M,CW,B,L,MR,V,OC,BW] 4538 E Belmont Ave (at Maple) **559/255-3213** *4pm-2am, uniform club, beer busts & other events*

North Tower Circle [★MW,D] 2777 N Maroa **559/229-4188** *8pm-2am, from 5pm Th-Sun, patio*

Red Lantern [M,NH,CW,WC] 4618 E Belmont Ave (at Maple) **559/251-5898** *2pm-2am*

■NIGHTCLUBS
Bam Bam's Cafe [GF,D,S,V,18+,YC,PC,GO] 2915 N Maroa Ave (btwn Shields & Clinton) **559/226-2267, 559/270-9730** *9pm-close Fri-Sat only, alcohol-free, 16+*

Deja Vu/ Starz Lounge [M,D,DS,V,GO] 708 N Blackstone (btwn Olive & Belmont, on Bremer) **559/445-0878** *9pm-2am, Latin music & drag show Th*

California • *USA*

■ MEN'S SERVICES
The Confidential Connection®!
559/271-9999 *The hottest local guys! 18+ Record & Listen FREE! Use access code 499*

➤ **Megaphone Fresno**
800/289-1489 *Call for the local # nearest you! Meet Hot Men in your area! FREE to Browse & Respond to voice ads. Use code 3087. Also try MEGAMATES.COM*

■ EROTICA
Only For You 2123 N Maroa Ave **559/225-3225** *lgbt*

Wildcat Book Store 1535 Fresno St (at 'G' St) **559/237-4525** *video arcade*

■ CRUISY AREAS
LA-SF Time Out [AYOR] US 99 (at Kingsburg, S of Fresno) *go to cheap motel next to rest area; rest stop activity discouraged*

Garberville

■ ACCOMMODATIONS
Giant Redwoods RV & Camp [GF] **707/943-3198** *campsites, RV, located off the Avenue of the Giants on the Eel River*

Garden Grove

■ INFO LINES & SERVICES
The Center Orange County 12832 Garden Grove Blvd #A (btwn Harbor & Fairview) **714/534-0862** *9am-9pm, 10am-2pm Sat, clsd Sun*

■ BARS
Frat House [★MW,D,MR,DS,S,YC,WC] 8112 Garden Grove Blvd (at Beach Blvd) **714/373-3728** *3pm-2am, strippers*

■ MEN'S SERVICES
➤ **Megaphone Garden Grove**
714/467-9991 *Voice Personals! Meet Hot Men in your area! FREE to Browse & Respond to voice ads. Use code 3087. Also try MEGAMATES.COM*

■ EROTICA
A-Z Bookstore 8192 Garden Grove Blvd (at Beach) **714/534-9349** *24hrs wknds*

Party House 8743 Garden Grove Blvd (at Magnolia) **714/534-9996**

Romantix 12686 Garden Grove Blvd (at Harbor) **714/638-8595**

Romantix 8745 Garden Grove Blvd (btwn Beach & Magnolia) **714/534-9823**

Video Rental & Preview Center 8745 Garden Grove Blvd **714/534-9922**

Grass Valley
see also Nevada City

Gualala

■ ACCOMMODATIONS
Breakers Inn [GS] 39300 S Hwy 1 **707/884-3200, 800/BREAKER** *oceanfront*

North Coast Country Inn [GF,NS] 34591 S Hwy 1 **707/884-4537, 800/959-4537** *hot tub*

Half Moon Bay

■ ACCOMMODATIONS
Mill Rose Inn [GF,NS] 615 Mill St **650/726-8750, 800/900-7673** *classic European elegance by the sea, full brkfst, hot tub*

■ RESTAURANTS
Moss Beach Distillery 140 Beach Wy (at Ocean) **650/728-5595** *lunch & dinner, Sun brunch*

Pasta Moon [WC] 315 Main St (at Mill) **650/726-5125** *lunch & dinner, full bar*

San Benito House [WC] 356 Main St **650/726-3425** *deli daily, dinner Th-Sun, Mediterranean, bar*

Hayward

■ INFO LINES & SERVICES
Lighthouse Community Center 1217 'A' St (near 2nd St) **510/881-8167** *noon-5pm Sat (call for other hours), variety of support groups & social events*

■ BARS
Rainbow Room [MW,D,E] 21859 Mission Blvd (at Sunset) **510/582-8078** *noon-2am, from 10am wknds*

# Kernville • California

Turf Club [MW,D,DS] 22519 Main St (at 'A') 510/881-9877 *noon-2am, from 10am wknds, patio*

■ NIGHTCLUBS
ClubUniverse Main [GS,D,S,WC] 22554 Main St (btwn 'A' & 'B') 510/733-2334 *11am-2am, 10am-2am wknds, hip-hop Sat, strippers Sun*

■ MEN'S SERVICES
➤ **Megaphone Hayward** 800/289-1489 *Call for the local # nearest you! Meet Hot Men in your area! FREE to Browse & Respond to voice ads. Use code 3087. Also try MEGAMATES.COM*

■ EROTICA
L'Amour Shoppe 22553 Main St (btwn 'A' & 'B') 510/886-7777

■ CRUISY AREAS
Municipal Parking Lot [AYOR] btwn Main & Mission, 'A' & 'B' Sts *evenings*

Healdsburg

see also Russian River

■ ACCOMMODATIONS
Camellia Inn [GF] 211 North St 707/433-8182, 800/727-8182 *Italianate Victorian*

Madrona Manor [GF,F,SW,NS,WC] 707/433-4231, 800/258-4003 *full brkfst, elegant Victorian country inn, also restaurant*

Tzabaco Lodge [GF,SW,GO] 615 Bailhache (at Redwood Hwy) 707/433-4443 *private rental home, waterfall*

■ RESTAURANTS
Chateau Souverain 400 Souverain Rd, Geyserville 707/433-8281 *lunch daily, dinner Fri-Sun only, brunch Sun, fine dining*

Hemet

■ NIGHTCLUBS
Club Don't You Know [MW,D,TG,F,K,WC,GO] 133 N Harvard St (at Florida) 909/658-5939 *3pm-1am, till 2am Fri-Sat*

Hermosa Beach

■ EROTICA
Tender Box 809 Pacific Coast Hwy (at 7th) 310/318-2882

USJ Video & Books 544 Pacific Coast Hwy (at 6th) 310/374-9207

Huntington Beach

■ MEN'S SERVICES
➤ **Megaphone Huntington Beach** 714/590-0400 *Voice Personals! Meet Hot Men in your area! FREE to Browse & Respond to voice ads. Use code 3087. Also try MEGAMATES.COM*

■ EROTICA
Paradise Specialties 7344 Center (at Gothard) 714/898-0400

Idyllwild

■ ACCOMMODATIONS
The Rainbow Inn [GS,NS,GO] 909/659-0111 *full brkfst, patio, also conference center*

Imperial Beach

■ EROTICA
Romantix 1177 Palm Ave (at Florida) 619/575-5081 *24hrs*

Jamestown

■ ACCOMMODATIONS
The Homestead at Table Mountain B&B [GF,NS,GO] 17307 Table Mountain Rd (at Chicken Ranch Rd) 209/984-3712 *B&B, full brkfst*

Joshua Tree Nat'l Park

■ ACCOMMODATIONS
Joshua Desert Retreats [GS,NS,SW,GO] Witt Rd (at Amboy Hwy), Twentynine Palms 310/558-5544

Kernville

■ ACCOMMODATIONS
River View Lodge [GS,NS,GO] 2 Sirretta 760/376-6019, 877/885-6333 *resort on Kern River, jacuzzi*

California • USA

Klamath

■ACCOMMODATIONS

Rhodes' End B&B [GF,NS] 115 Trobitz Rd **707/482-1654** *full brkfst, hot tub*

Laguna Beach

■INFO LINES & SERVICES

AA Gay/ Lesbian 714/556-4555 (AA#)

■ACCOMMODATIONS

By The Sea Inn [GF,SW,WC] 475 N Coast Hwy **949/497-6645, 800/297-0007** *hot tub*

California Riviera 800 1027 N Coast Hwy #A **949/376-0305, 800/621-0500** *8am-5pm, beach cities hotel reservation service*

Casa Laguna B&B Inn [GF,SW,NS,GO] 2510 S Coast Hwy **949/494-2996, 800/233-0449** *inn & cottages overlooking the Pacific*

The Coast Inn [MW,SW,NS,GO] 1401 S Coast Hwy **949/494-7588, 800/653-2697** (reservations only) *oceanside accommodations w/ 2 bars & restaurant*

Holiday Inn Laguna Beach [GF,F,SW,WC] 696 S Coast Hwy **949/661-5000, 800/533-9748**

Laguna Brisas Spa Hotel [GS,SW,WC] 1600 S Coast Hwy (at Bluebird) **949/497-7272, 888/296-6834** *resort hotel, in-room whirlpool spas*

Laguna Cliffs Marriott Resort & Spa [GF,SW,WC] 25135 Park Lantern, Dana Point **949/661-5000, 800/533-9748**

Laguna Magical Cottages [GS] 217 & 223 Nyes Pl **949/494-4554** *2 rental cottages on Laguna Beach*

■BARS

Main St [MW,E,P] 1460 S Coast Hwy **949/494-0056** *2pm-2am, from 5pm wknds*

Woody's at the Beach [M,F] 1305 S Coast Hwy (at Cress) **949/376-8809** *4pm-2am, also restaurant, 6pm-10pm, monthly T-dances in summer, patio*

■NIGHTCLUBS

Boom Boom Room [★M,D,DS,S,V] 1401 S Coast Hwy (at The Coast Inn) **949/494-7588** *11:30am-2am, from 11am wknds, strippers*

■CAFES

The Koffee Klatch 1440 S Coast Hwy (btwn Mountain & Pacific Coast Hwy) **949/376-6867** *7am-11pm, till midnight Fri-Sat*

Zinc Cafe [BW,WC] 350 Ocean Ave (at Broadway) **949/494-6302** *7am-4:30pm, till 5pm wknds, patio, also market*

■RESTAURANTS

Cafe Zoolu [WC] 860 Glenneyre **949/494-6825** *dinner, clsd Mon*

The Cottage 308 N Coast Hwy (at Aster) **949/494-3023** *lunch & dinner*

Dizz's As Is 2794 S Coast Hwy **949/494-5250** *open 5:30pm, seating at 6pm, clsd Mon, full bar, patio*

Drew's Caribbean Cafe [BW,GO] 31732 Pacific Coast Hwy (at 3rd), South Laguna Beach **949/499-6311** *5pm-9pm, till 10pm Fri-Sat, clsd Mon-Tue*

Madison Square & Garden Cafe 320 N Coast Hwy **949/494-0137** *8am-3pm, from 7am wknds, clsd Tue*

Mark's Restaurant 858 S Coast Hwy (at Thalia) **949/494-6711** *dinner only, full bar*

■ENTERTAINMENT & RECREATION

West St Beach

■RETAIL SHOPS

GayMartUSA 168 Mountain Rd **949/497-9108**

Jewelry by Poncé 1417 S Coast Hwy **949/497-4154, 800/969-RING** *11am-7pm Wed-Sun, by appt Mon-Tue, lgbt commitment rings & other jewelry*

■PUBLICATIONS

Orange County/ Long Beach Blade **949/494-4898**

Lake Tahoe • California

MEN'S SERVICES
➤ **Megaphone Laguna Beach** 800/289-1489 *Call for the local # nearest you! Meet Hot Men in your area! FREE to Browse & Respond to voice ads. Use code 3087. Also try MEGAMATES.COM*

EROTICA
Video Horizons 31678 Coast Hwy (at 3rd Ave) 949/499-4519

CRUISY AREAS
Heisler Park [AYOR] N side of park *also take path to the ocean, then climb over the rocks to the right*

Lake Tahoe
see also Lake Tahoe, Nevada

ACCOMMODATIONS
➤ **Black Bear Inn** [GS,NS,GO] 530/544-4411, 800/431-4411 *full brkfst, hot tub, fireplaces*

Grinnin' Bear Cabin [GS,NS] 530/582-8703, 800/289-1522

Ridgewood Inn [GF] 1341 Emerald Bay Rd 530/541-8589 *small country inn, hot tub*

Silver Shadows Lodge [GF,SW] 1251 Emerald Bay Rd, South Lake Tahoe 530/541-3575 *motel*

NIGHTCLUBS
Faces [MW,D] 270 Kingsbury Grade, Stateline, NV 775/588-2333 *5pm-2am, till 4am Fri-Sat*

CAFES
Syd's Bagelry 550 North Lake Blvd, Tahoe City 530/583-2666 *6:30am-5pm*

RESTAURANTS
Driftwood Cafe [WC] 4119 Laurel Ave (at Poplar) 530/544-6545 *7am-2pm, homecooking*

Passaretti's 1181 Emerald Bay Rd/ Hwy 50 530/541-3433 *11am-9pm, Italian*

CRUISY AREAS
El Dorado Beach [AYOR] btwn Rufus Allen Blvd & Lakeview, South Lake Tahoe

See photos of every room, plus rates and amenities at:
www.tahoeblackbear.com *or call* 800.431.4411

California • USA

Private Beach [AYOR] off Pine St (near Park), South Lake Tahoe *private beach behind resorts*

Lancaster

■ NIGHTCLUBS

Back Door [MW,D,K,DS] 1255 W Ave 'I' (at 13th St W) **661/945-2566** *4pm-2am*

■ CRUISY AREAS

Appolo Park [AYOR] Ave 'G' & 50 W

Long Beach

■ INFO LINES & SERVICES

AA Gay/ Lesbian (Atlantic Alano Club) 441 E 1st St (at Linden) **562/432-7476**

The Gay & Lesbian Community Center of Greater Long Beach 2017 E 4th St (at Cherry) **562/434-4455** *9am-10pm, till 6pm Sat, 5pm-9pm Sun, also newsletter*

■ ACCOMMODATIONS

Beachrunners' Inn [MW,GO] 231 Kennebec Ave (at Juniperro & Broadway) **562/856-0202, 866/221-0001** *B&B, near beach, hot tub*

Queen Mary [GF,WC] 1126 Queens Hwy **562/435-3511, 800/437-2934** *historic ocean liner*

■ BARS

The Brit [M,NH] 1744 E Broadway (at Cherry) **562/432-9742** *10am-2am*

The Broadway [MW,NH,K,WC] 1100 E Broadway (at Cerritos) **562/432-3646** *10am-2am*

Club Broadway [W,NH,V,WC] 3348 E Broadway (at Redondo) **562/438-7700** *11am-2am*

The Crest [M,L] 5935 Cherry Ave (at South) **562/423-6650** *2pm-2am*

The Falcon [M,NH,WC] 1435 E Broadway (at Falcon) **562/432-4146** *7am-2am*

Long Beach • California

Fire Island [M,D,CW,K,S,WC] 3325 E Anaheim St (at Redondo) **562/597-0014** *6pm-2am, from 7pm Sat, go-go boys, cocktail patio*

Mineshaft [★M,WC] 1720 E Broadway (btwn Gaviota & Hermosa) **562/436-2433** *10am-2am*

Pistons [M,B,L] 2020 E Artesia (at Cherry) **562/422-1928** *6pm-2am, till 4am Fri-Sat, from 3pm Sun, patio*

Que Será [GS,D,A,E] 1923 E 7th St (at Cherry) **562/599-6170** *7pm-2am, from 5pm Fri, from 1pm Sun*

Ripples [★M,D,MR,F,E,K,S,V,YC] 5101 E Ocean (at Granada) **562/433-0357** *noon-2am, patio, T-dance Sun, Latin night 2nd Sat, Asian night 3rd Sat*

Silver Fox [M,K,V,WC] 411 Redondo (at 4th) **562/439-6343** *4pm-2am, from noon wknds, popular happy hour*

Sweetwater Saloon [M,NH,WC] 1201 E Broadway (at Orange) **562/432-7044** *10am-2am, popular days, cruisy*

The Underground [M,NH,L,K,V] 17817 Lakewood Blvd (S of 91), Bellflower **562/633-6394** *5pm-2am, Latin Wed, fetish nights Fri-Sat*

■CAFES

Cafe Haven 1708 E Broadway (at Gaviota) **562/437-3785** *6am-midnight, till 1am Tue, till 3am Fri-Sat*

■RESTAURANTS

Egg Heaven 4358 E 4th St **562/433-9277** *7am-2pm, till 3pm wknds*

➤ **Hamburger Mary's** [MW] 740 E Broadway (at Alamitos) **562/983-7001** *11am-2am, from 7am wknds, full menu & Sun champagne brunch*

House of Madame JoJo [★MW,BW,WC] 2941 E Broadway (btwn Temple & Redondo) **562/439-3672** *5:30pm-10pm, Mediterranean*

Omelette Inn 108 W 3rd St (at Pine) **562/437-5625** *7am-2:30pm*

Original Park Pantry [MW,WC] 2104 E Broadway (at Junipero) **562/434-0451** *lunch & dinner, int'l*

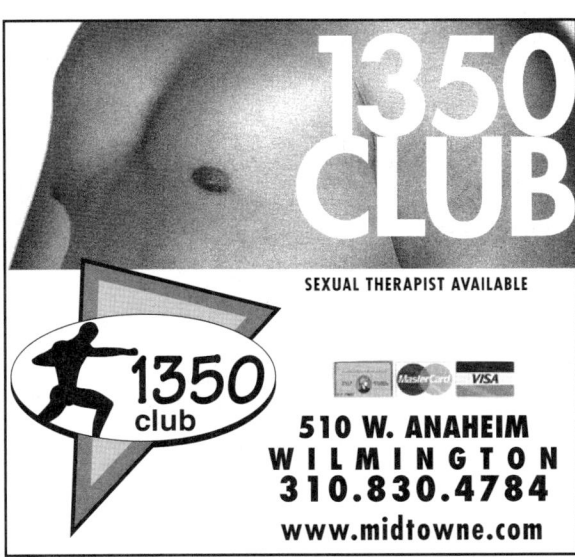

California • *USA*

Porch Cafe [MW,GO] 2708 E 4th St (at Ohio Ave) **562/433-0118** *7am-2pm, till 3pm wknds, garden patio*

■ RETAIL SHOPS

Hot Stuff 2121 E Broadway (at Junipero) **562/433-0692** *11am-7pm, 10am-6pm wknds, cards, gifts & adult novelties, serving community since 1980*

Toto's Revenge [GO] 2947 E Broadway (at Orizaba) **562/434-2777, 877/688-8686** *10am-9pm, unique cards & gifts, dog-friendly, mail-order*

■ MEN'S CLUBS

➤ **1350 Club** [PC] 510 W Anaheim St (at Neptune), Wilmington **310/830-4784** *24hrs*

■ MEN'S SERVICES

➤ **Megaphone Long Beach** **562/485-4008** *Voice Personals! Meet Hot Men in your area! FREE to Browse & Respond to voice ads. Use code 3087. Also try MEGAMATES.COM*

■ EROTICA

The Crypt on Broadway 1712 E Broadway (btwn Cherry & Falcon) **562/983-6560** *leather, toys*

The Rubber Tree 5018 E 2nd St (at Granada) **562/434-0027** *gifts for lovers, women-owned*

■ CRUISY AREAS

Please Note: All cruisy areas for Long Beach have been removed by request of various lgbt community organizations.

LOS ANGELES

■

Los Angeles is divided into 7 geographical areas:
LA—Overview
LA—West Hollywood
LA—Hollywood
LA—West LA & Santa Monica
LA—Silverlake
LA—Midtown
LA—Valley

LA—Overview

■ INFO LINES & SERVICES

Alcoholics Together Center 1773 Griffith Park Blvd (at Hyperion) **323/663-8882, 323/936-4343 (AA#)** *12-step groups*

LA Gay & Lesbian Center's Village 1125 N McCadden Pl (at Santa Monica) **323/860-7302** *cyber-center, cafe, theaters, library, call for events & hours*

Los Angeles Gay & Lesbian Center 1625 N Schracer Blvd **323/993-7400** *9am-9pm, till 1pm Sat, clsd Sun, wide variety of services*

Midway Car Rental **888/682-0166**

■ ENTERTAINMENT & RECREATION

The Celebration Theatre 7051-B Santa Monica Blvd (at La Brea) **323/957-1884** *lgbt theater*

Gay Men's Chorus **323/467-9741**

The Getty Center 1200 Getty Center Dr, Brentwood **310/440-7300** *clsd Mon, LA's world-class museum; of course, it's still in LA so you'll need to make reservations for parking (!)*

Highways 1651 18th St, Santa Monica **310/315-1459 (reservation line), 310/453-1755 (admin line)** *'full-service performance center'*

IMRU Gay Radio KPFK LA 90.7 FM **818/985-2711** *7pm Mon*

Outfest **213/480-7088** *lgbt media arts foundation that sponsors the annual lgbt film festival each July (see Film Festival Calendar in back Events section)*

Purple Circuit Hotline **818/953-5072** *lgbt theater listings*

■ RETAIL SHOPS

The Art of Raymond Helgeson 11350 Alethea Dr, Sunland **818/352-0557**

■ PUBLICATIONS

Adelante Magazine **323/256-6639** *bilingual lgbt magazine*

Community Yellow Pages 8235 Santa Monica Blvd Penthouse Ste, West Hollywood **323/848-3033, 800/745-5669** *annual survival guide to lgbt southern CA & Bay Area*

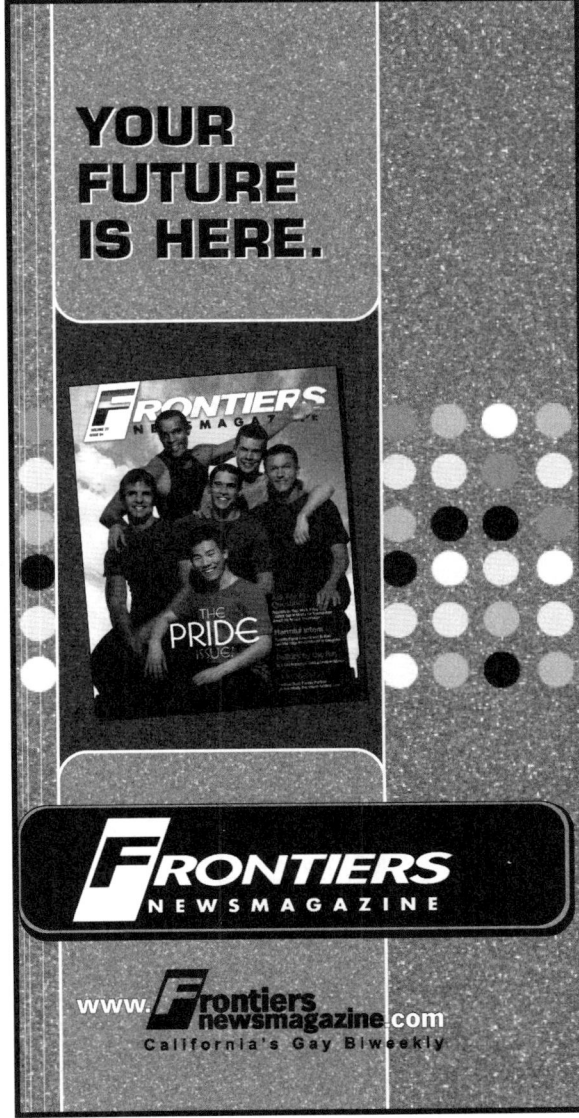

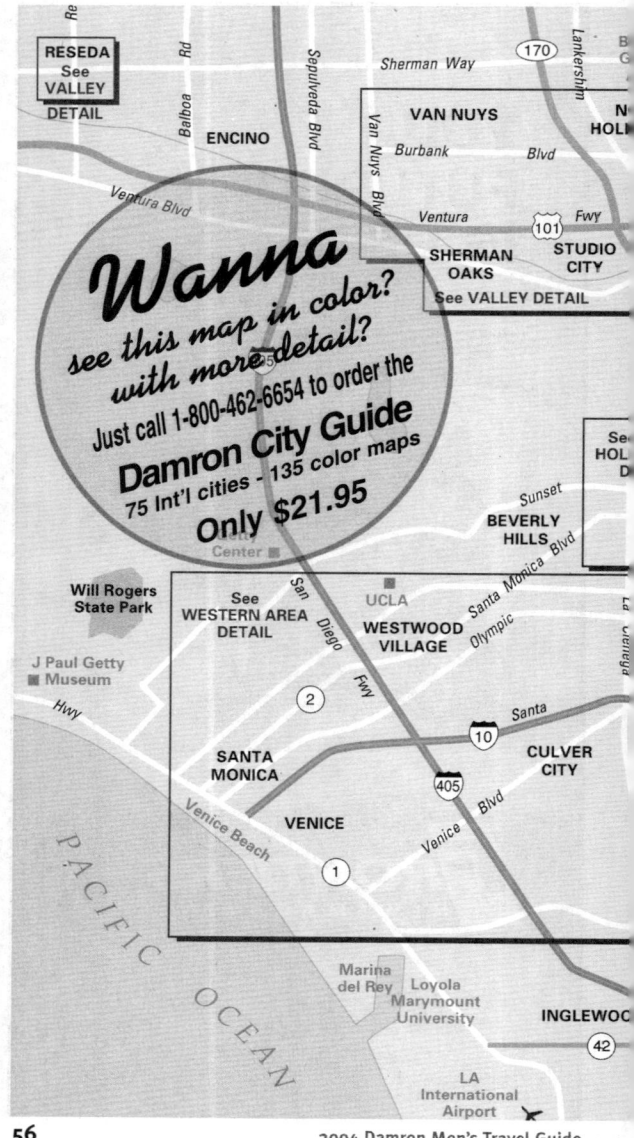

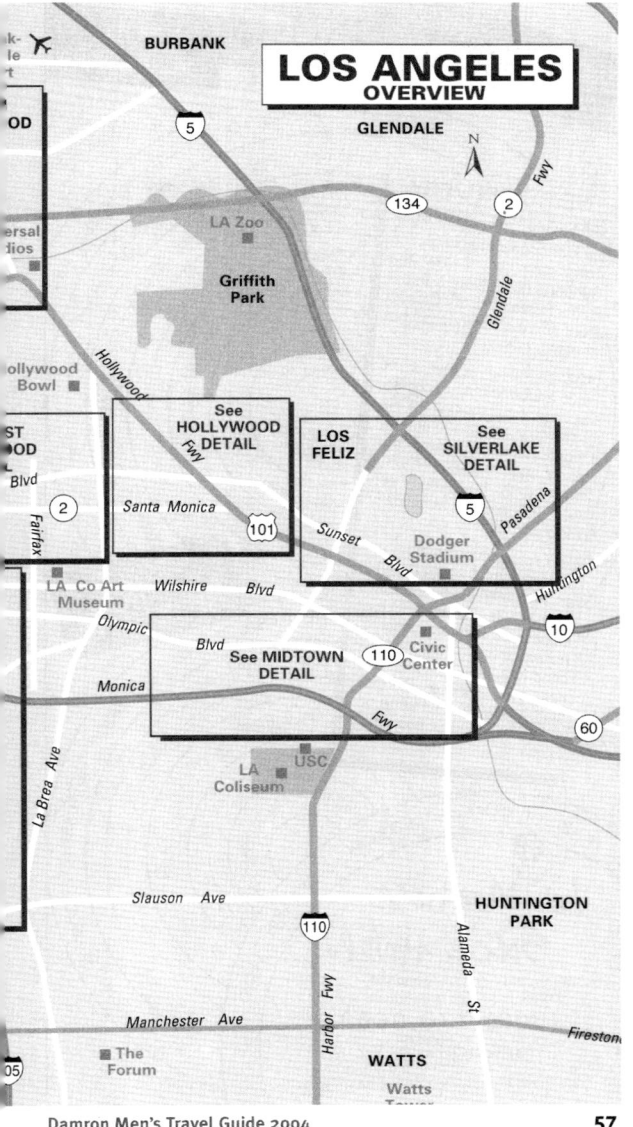

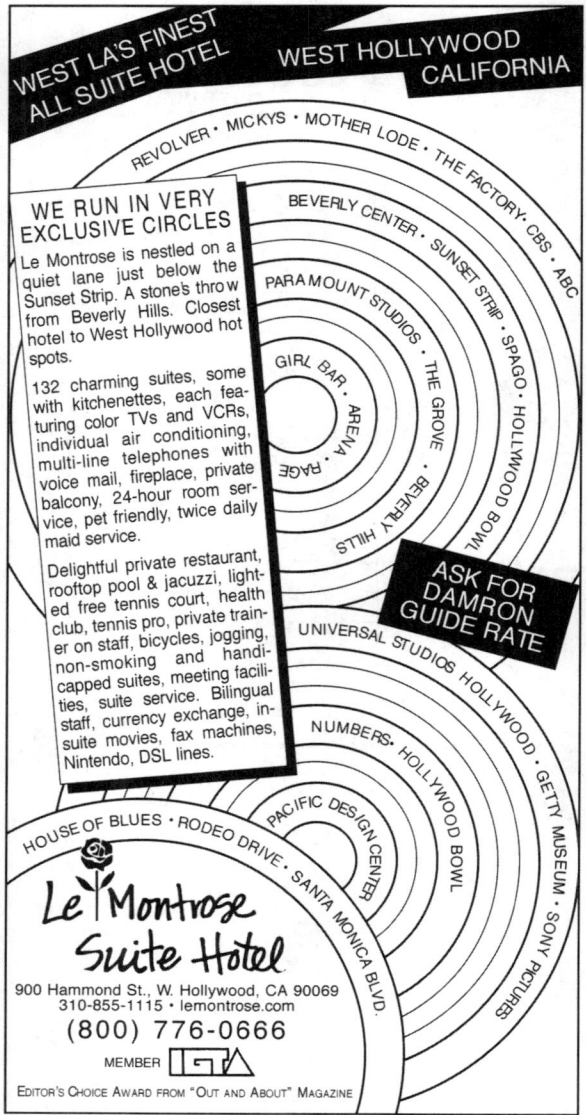

RE-DISCOVER WEST HOLLYWOOD!

WHEN WAS THE LAST TIME YOU VISITED?

A lot has changed – come and see what is truly **ONLY IN WEST HOLLYWOOD!**

The Legendary Sunset Strip: Still the home of LA's music scene.

The Avenues of Art and Design: 30 Art Galleries, The *Pacific Design Center*, and the *Museum of Contemporary Art*.

Santa Monica Blvd: See What a 34 million dollar face lift can do. Visit your favorites *Factory, Micky's, Rage* and *Revolver* and check out all the new hot spots *Fubar, Felt* and *Here*.

For more information on our city call *1-800-368-6020* or visit our web site at *www.visitwesthollywood.com* for hotel packages and special events.

8687 Melrose Ave. Suite M38
West Hollywood, CA 90069

WEST HOLLYWOOD

GOOD **Will** & AMAZING **Grace**

LE PARC.

733 N. West Knoll Dr.
West Hollywood, CA 90069

Res: (800) 5-SUITES
Local: (310) 855-8888

IGLTA

SUMMIT
HOTELS & RESORTS

web: **leparcsuites.com**
e.mail: **leparcres@aol.com**

Le Parc
SUITE HOTEL

California • USA

Divas Magazine 323/255-1021
bilingual lgbt magazine

Fab! 323/655-5716 *hip gay newspaper w/ club listings*

➤ **Frontiers** 323/848-2222 *huge lgbt newsmagazine w/ listings for everything*

Gay-LA 323/660-4520 *monthly guide to LA*

➤ **Gloss Magazine** 415/552-2051 *CA arts/ entertainment magazine, bi-weekly*

IN Los Angeles 323/848-2200 *gay news & entertainment magazine for LA*

➤ **Odyssey Magazine** 323/874-8788 *all the dish on LA's club scene*

■ MEN'S SERVICES

The Confidential Connection®! 310/854-6666, 323/734-7822 *The hottest local guys! 18+ Record & Listen FREE! Use access code 499*

The Gay Connection 900/505-6338 *Talk and/or meet with other men from the area, at only 99¢ per minute.*

LA—West Hollywood

■ INFO LINES & SERVICES

➤ **West Hollywood Convention & Visitors Bureau** 800/368-6020

■ ACCOMMODATIONS

Élan Hotel Modern [GS,WC,GO] 8435 Beverly Blvd (at Croft) 323/658-6663, 888/611-0398

The Grafton on Sunset [GS,SW,WC] 8462 W Sunset Blvd (at La Cienega) 323/654-4600, 800/821-3660 *sundeck, panoramic views, located in heart of Sunset Strip*

8585 Santa Monica Boulevard
Ramada Property of the Year Award
www.thegayhotel.com

California • USA

The Grove Guesthouse [MW,SW,GO]
1325 N Orange Grove Ave (at Sunset)
323/876-8887, 888/524-7683
1-bdrm villa, hot tub

Holloway Motel [GS] 8465 Santa
Monica Blvd (at La Cienega)
323/654-2454, 888/654-6400
centrally located

Hyatt West Hollywood [GS,SW,NS,WC]
8401 Sunset Blvd (at Kings Rd)
323/656-1234, 800/233-1234
on the Sunset Strip

Just Right Reservations
978/934-9931 *Inns & B&Bs, also Palm Springs, Provincetowm & Boston, MA*

▶ **Le Montrose Suite Hotel**
[★GF,SW,NS,WC] 900 Hammond St (at Sunset) 310/855-1115,
800/776-0666 *rooftop patio, gym, restaurant*

▶ **Le Parc Suite Hotel** [★GF,F,SW,WC]
733 N West Knoll Dr (at Melrose)
310/855-8888, 800/578-4837
tennis courts, also restaurant

▶ **Ramada Plaza Hotel—West Hollywood** [GF,F,SW,WC] 8585 Santa
Monica Blvd (at La Cienega)
310/652-6400, 800/845-8585 *art deco, 15% off w/ mention of Damron*

▶ **San Vicente Inn-Resort**
[MO,SW,N,GO] 845 N San Vicente Blvd
(at Santa Monica) 310/854-6915
hot tub

Southern Comforts [M,SW,NS,GO]
310/305-2984, 800/889-7359
garden patio, koi pond

Sunset Marquis Hotel & Villas
[GS,SW,WC] 1200 Alta Loma Rd (1/2 blk S of Sunset Blvd) 310/657-1333,
800/858-9758 *full brkfst, sauna, hot tub*

Valadon Hotel [GF,SW,WC] 8822
Cynthia St (at Larrabee) 310/854-1114,
800/835-7997
all-suite hotel, hot tub

■ **BARS**

Comedy Store [GF] 8433 Sunset Blvd
(at La Cienega) 323/650-6268 *8pm-2am, stand-up club*

Fubar [★M,E] 7994 Santa Monica Blvd
(at Crescent Hts) 323/654-0396 *4pm-2am, theme nights, DJ Fri-Sat, beer bust Sun*

Gold Coast [★M,NH,WC] 8228 Santa
Monica Blvd (at La Jolla)
323/656-4879 *11am-2am, from 10am wknds*

▶ **Here Lounge** [MW,P] 696 N
Robertson Blvd (at Santa Monica)
310/360-8455 *4pm-2am, swanky & stylish, DJ nightly, also juice bar*

Improvisation [GF] 8162 Melrose Ave
(at Crescent Heights) 323/651-2583
stand-up comedy

Micky's [★M,D,F,V,YC,GO] 8857 Santa
Monica Blvd (at San Vicente)
310/657-1176 *noon-2am, after-hours wknds*

Mother Lode [★M,NH,K,WC] 8944
Santa Monica Blvd (at Robertson)
310/659-9700 *2pm-2am, beer bust Sun*

The Normandie Room [GS,NH,WC]
8737 Santa Monica Blvd (at Hancock)
310/659-6204 *5pm-2am, great cosmopolitans*

Numbers [★M,F,WC] 8741 Santa
Monica Blvd (at Hancock, 2nd flr)
310/652-7700 *5pm-2am*

Revolver [★M,A,K,V] 8851 Santa
Monica Blvd (at San Vicente)
310/659-8851 *4pm-2am*

Spike [★MW,D,WC] 7746 Santa Monica
Blvd (at Spaulding) 323/656-9343
from 5pm, after-hours Th-Sun, clsd Mon-Tue, cruise bar, patio

Tempest [★GS,D,E] 7323 Santa Monica
Blvd (E of Fuller Ave) 323/850-5115
8:30pm-close, theme nights, patio

Tiki Bar at Tahiti [M] 7910 W 3rd St
(W of Fairfax) 323/651-1213 *6pm-close, more gay Wed, also restaurant*

Trunks [M,NH,V,YC] 8809 Santa Monica
Blvd (at Larrabee) 310/652-1015
1pm-2am

Viper Room [GF,D,S,$] 8852 Sunset
Blvd (btwn San Vicente & Larrabee)
310/358-1880 *9pm-2am*

LA—West Hollywood • California

■ NIGHTCLUBS

7969 [GS,D,TG,DS,S] 7969 Santa Monica Blvd (at Fairfax) **323/654-0280** *9pm-2am, drag Mon & Fri*

The Factory [★M,D,S,V,YC] 652 N La Peer Dr (at Santa Monica) **310/659-4551** *9pm-2am Wed-Sun*

La Plaza [M,D,MR-L,S] 739 N La Brea Ave (at Melrose) **323/939-0703** *8pm-2am, clsd Tue, shows nightly at 10:15pm & midnight*

Rage [★M,D,F,S,V,YC,WC] 8911 Santa Monica Blvd (at San Vicente) **310/652-7055** *11am-2am, lunch & dinner daily*

Thrust [M,D,$] 7070 Hollywood Blvd (at LaBrea, at The Ruby) **866/398-2169** *after-hours, from 3am Sat night only*

Ultra Suede [GS,D,A,E] 661 N Robertson Blvd (at Santa Monica) **310/659-4551** *9pm-2am Wed-Sun*

■ CAFES

Eat-Well [★] 8252 Santa Monica Blvd (at La Jolla) **323/656-1383** *7am-3pm & 5:30pm-10pm, 8am-3pm wknds*

Mani's Bakery [WC] 519 S Fairfax Ave (at Maryland Dr) **323/938-8800** *6:30am-midnight, coffee & dessert bar*

Who's On Third Cafe 8369 W 3rd St (at Orlando) **323/651-2928** *7:30am-3pm, from 8am wknds*

■ RESTAURANTS

The Abbey [★MW,WC] 692 N Robertson (at Santa Monica) **310/289-8410** *8am-2am, full bar, patio*

African Restaurant Row Fairfax btwn Olympic & Pico *many Ethiopian, Nigerian & other African restaurants to choose from on this block*

Alto Palato 755 N La Cienega Blvd (at Waring) **310/657-9271** *5pm-10:30pm, pasta, full bar*

Baja Bud's [WC] 8575 Santa Monica Blvd (at La Cienega) **310/659-1911** *10am-10pm, till 11pm Fri-Sat, healthy Mexican, patio*

Benvenuto Cafe [WC] 8512 Santa Monica Blvd (at La Cienega) **310/659-8635** *lunch Tue-Fri, dinner nightly, Italian, patio*

Bossa Nova [BW,WC] 685 N Robertson Blvd (at Santa Monica) **310/657-5070** *11am-11pm, Brazilian, patio*

Cafe La Boheme [WC] 8400 Santa Monica Blvd (btwn Benecia Ave & Fox Hills Dr) **323/848-2360** *5:30pm-1am Fri-Sat, till midnight Sun-Th, eclectic Californian, full bar, patio*

Canter's Deli [WC] 419 N Fairfax (btwn Melrose & Beverly) **323/651-2030** *24hrs, hip after-hours, Jewish/ American*

Il Pastaio 400 N Cannon Dr (at Brighton Wy), Beverly Hills **310/205-5444** *homemade pasta*

Il Piccolino Trattoria [WC] 350 N Robertson Blvd (btwn Melrose & Beverly) **310/659-2220** *lunch & dinner, clsd Sun, patio*

Kachina Grill [WC] 8948 Santa Monica Blvd (at N Robertson) **310/657-4832** *11am-11pm, till 1am wknds, Mexican*

Koo Koo Roo [BW,WC] 8520 Santa Monica Blvd (at La Cienega Blvd) **310/657-3300** *11am-11pm, lots of healthy chicken dishes*

L'Orangerie 903 N La Cienega Blvd (btwn Melrose & Santa Monica) **310/652-9770** *dinner only, clsd Mon, haute French, patio*

Louise's Trattoria [BW] 7505 Melrose Ave (at Gardner) **323/651-3880** *11am-11pm, till midnight Fri-Sat, Italian, great foccacia bread*

Lucques [WC] 8474 Melrose Ave (at La Cienega) **323/655-6277** *lunch & dinner, French, full bar, patio*

Marco's Trattoria [WC] 8136 Santa Monica (at Crescent Hts) **323/650-2771** *11am-10pm*

Marix Tex Mex [MW,WC] 1108 N Flores (btwn La Cienega & Fairfax) **323/656-8800** *11:30am-11pm, great margaritas*

Mark's Restaurant [★] 861 N La Cienega Blvd (at Santa Monica) **310/652-5252** *6pm-10pm, till 11:30pm Fri-Sat, Sun brunch, full bar*

North [★] 8029 W Sunset (at Laurel Canyon, enter rear) **323/654-1313** *7pm-2am, '70s ski lodge decor, full bar*

Damron Men's Travel Guide 2004

Circus of Books
THE LOCAL BOOKSTORE WITH INTERNATIONAL APPEAL

8230 Santa Monica Blvd
West Hollywood
323/656-6533
6am - 2am
(7 Days a Week)

4001 Sunset Blvd
Silverlake
323/666-1304
6am - 2am
(7 Days a Week)

COMPLETE NEWSSTAND
BOOKS FOR ALL INTERESTS
ADULT VHS, DVD RENTAL & SALES
TOYS • LUBES • CONDOMS • HARDCORE MAGS
JEWELRY & GIFT ITEMS

www.circusofbooks.com
Email: circuswh@pacbell.net

coral sands MOTEL

1730 N Western Ave.
Hollywood, CA 90027

INFO: (323) 467-5141
FAX: (323) 467-4683
www.coralsands-la.com

For Reservation Only:
(800) 367-7263   (800) 421-3650
California   U.S. Continental

A legend in the gay community

LA—West Hollywood • California

Real Food Daily [★BW,WC] 414 N La-
Cienega (btwn Beverly & Melrose)
310/289-9910 *11:30am-11pm,
organic vegetarian*

Sante Libre 345 N La Brea (btwn
Melrose & Beverly) **323/857-0412**
10am-10pm, pastas, salads & wraps

Sapori Cucina [WC] 8945 Santa
Monica Blvd (at Robertson)
310/275-9518 *Italian*

Skewers [BW] 8939 Santa Monica Blvd
(at Robertson) **310/271-0555** *11am-
10pm, Middle Eastern, lowfat grill*

Tango Grill [MW,BW,WC] 8807 Santa
Monica Blvd (at San Vicente)
310/659-3663 *11:30am-11:30pm,
Argentinian*

Tommy Tang's [★BW] 7313 Melrose
Ave (at Poinsettia) **323/937-5733**
*noon-10pm, till 11pm wknds,
drag night Tue*

Trocadero [WC] 8280 Sunset Blvd (at
Sweetzer) **323/656-7161** *6pm-2am,
patio, full bar*

Yukon Mining Co [★BW,WC] 7328
Santa Monica Blvd (at Fuller)
323/851-8833 *24hrs, brunch wknds*

■ BOOKSTORES

A Different Light [★] 8853 Santa
Monica Blvd (btwn San Vicente &
Larrabee) **310/854-6601**
10am-10pm, lgbt

Book Soup 8818 W Sunset Blvd (at
Larrabee) **310/659-3110** *9am-
midnight, lgbt section*

■ RETAIL SHOPS

Don't Panic 802 N San Vicente Blvd (at
Santa Monica Blvd) *campy T-shirts,
lgbt gifts*

Dorothy's Surrender 7985 Santa
Monica Blvd #111 (at Laurel)
323/650-4111 *10am-11:30pm,
gifts, magazines*

Perfect Beat 8941 Santa Monica Blvd
310/273-3337 *11am-midnight, till
2am Fri-Sun, club music*

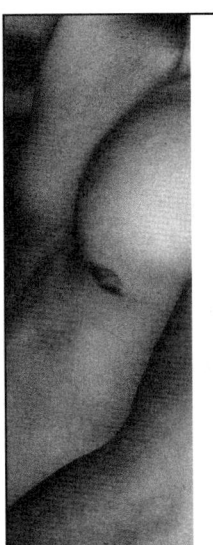

**MELROSE SPA
7269 MELROSE AVE.
HOLLYWOOD
323.937.2122**

SEXUAL THERAPIST AVAILABLE

www.midtowne.com

RAMADA INN-HOLLYWOOD

An Unforgettable Experience

- Charming, boutique-style hotel
- Complimentary deluxe continental breakfast
- 130 elegantly furnished rooms featuring hair dryer, private bath & lighted vanity, phone with voice mail and data port, in-room coffee maker and satellite TV with pay-per-view movies and HBO
- Heated pool, sauna & fitness center
- New restaurant, bar, lounge, meeting and boardroom
- Private meeting room available
- 5000 sq.ft. of versatile meeting and function space

Minutes to West Hollywood, Los Feliz, Silver Lake, Universal Studios Hollywood, The Greek and Pantages Theaters, LA Convention Center, exciting nightlife, world class restaurants and shopping on Melrose Avenue, Rodeo Drive and the Sunset Strip.

ASK ABOUT OUR SPECIAL PACKAGES

The Lion King
Universal Studios
City Pass

Central Reservations
1-800-800-9733
Ask for Property #2954
Ask for Special Promo Code LP12

1160 North Vermont, Hollywood, CA 90029
323-315-1800 / 800-800-9733 / fax 323-660-8069
www.gayhollywoodhotel.com
email:gayinfo@ramadahollywood.com

LA—Hollywood • California

Raving Rainbow.com 8515 Santa Monica Blvd **310/358-1935** *11am-7:30pm, clsd Sun, circuit party supplies, pride gear*

Syren 7225 Beverly Blvd **323/936-6693, 800/667-9736** *clsd Sun-Mon, leather & latex*

■ GYMS & HEALTH CLUBS

Easton's Gym [GF] 8053 Beverly Blvd (at Crescent Hts) **323/651-3636**

■ MEN'S CLUBS

➤ **Melrose Spa** [★PC] 7269 Melrose Ave (at Poinsettia) **323/937-2122** *24hrs*

Slammer 3688 Beverly Blvd (2 blks E of Vermont) **213/388-8040** *8pm-4am, from 2pm wknds*

■ MEN'S SERVICES

➤ **Megaphone West Hollywood** **323/450-1144** *Voice Personals! Meet Hot Men in your area! FREE to Browse & Respond to voice ads. Use code 3087. Also try MEGAMATES.COM*

■ EROTICA

➤ **Circus of Books** 8230 Santa Monica Blvd (at La Jolla) **323/656-6533**

➤ **Drake's** 8932 Santa Monica Blvd (at San Vicente) **310/289-8932** *also 7566 Melrose Ave, 323/651-5600*

Grand Opening! 8442 Santa Monica Blvd **323/848-6970, 877/731-2626** *11am-8pm, noon-5pm Sun, sex toy store especially for women, everyone welcome*

Hardart Phallic Replicating Service 4213 Cromwell Ave 90027-1355 **323/667-1501** *send legal-size SASE for brochure*

Hustler Hollywood 8920 Sunset Blvd (at San Vicente) **310/860-9009** *chic erotic department store, also cafe*

Pleasure Chest 7733 Santa Monica Blvd (at Genesee) **323/650-1022**

Tomkat Theatre 7734 Santa Monica Blvd (at Genesee) **323/650-9551** *24hrs wknds, cruisy*

LA—Hollywood

■ ACCOMMODATIONS

➤ **Coral Sands Hotel** [M,SW] 1730 N Western Ave (at Hollywood Blvd) **323/467-5141, 800/367-7263** *hot tub, sauna, weights, cruisy*

Holiday Inn Hollywood [GF,F,SW,WC] 2005 N Highland (at Franklin) **323/876-8600** *exercise room, jacuzzi*

Hollywood Celebrity Hotel [GF] 1775 Orchid Ave (btwn Hollywood & Franklin) **323/850-6464, 800/222-7017** *1930s art deco hotel*

Hollywood Metropolitan Hotel [GF,NS,WC] 5825 Sunset Blvd (btwn Bronson & Van Ness) **323/962-5800, 800/962-5800** *also restaurant*

➤ **Ramada Inn & Hollywood— Universal Studios** [GF,SW,WC] 1160 N Vermont Ave (at Santa Monica) **323/660-1788, 800/800-9733**

■ BARS

Faultline [★M,D,B,L,V] 4216 Melrose Ave (at Normandie) **323/660-0889** *4pm-2am, 2pm-4am Fri-Sat, clsd Mon, patio*

Spit [★M,D,A,L,V] 4216 Melrose Ave (at Faultine) **323/969-2530** *9pm-3am 3rd Sat, cruisy*

Spotlight [M,NH,WC] 1601 N Cahuenga (at Hollywood) **323/467-2425** *6am-2am*

Stone [M,NH,MR-A,K,S,V] 5221 Hollywood Blvd (near Harvard) **323/466-6061** *7pm-2am, gay Fri only*

Study [★M,NH,MR-AF] 1723 N Western (at Hollywood) **323/464-9551** *2pm-2am*

■ NIGHTCLUBS

Beige at 360° Restaurant & Lounge [★MW,D,F] 6290 Sunset Blvd (at Vine) **323/871-2995** *Tue only*

The Circus/ Arena [★M,D,MR-L,S,V] 6655 Santa Monica Blvd (at Seward) **323/462-1291** *9pm-2am Tue & Fri-Sat, more gay Tue & Fri*

Tempo [M,D,MR-L,S] 5520 Santa Monica Blvd (at Western) **323/466-1094** *9pm-2pm, till 3am Th-Sat, from 2pm Sun*

California • USA

■ RESTAURANTS

360° Restaurant & Lounge [★D,WC,GO] 6290 Sunset Blvd (at Vine) **323/871-2995** *dinner, great views, jazz wknds*

Hollywood Canteen 1006 N Seward St (at Santa Monica) **323/465-0961** *11:30am-midnight, till 1am Fri-Sat, dinner only Sat, clsd Sun, classic*

La Poubelle [WC] 5907 Franklin Ave (at Bronson) **323/465-0807** *5:30pm-2am, French/Italian*

Lucy's Cafe El Adobe [S] 5536 Melrose Ave (near Gower St) **323/462-9421** *lunch & dinner, clsd Sun, Mexican, patio*

Musso & Frank Grill 6667 Hollywood Blvd (near Las Palmas) **323/467-7788** *11am-11pm, clsd Sun-Mon, the grand-dame diner/ steak house of Hollywood: great pancakes, potpie & martinis!*

Off Vine [BW] 6263 Leland Wy (at Vine) **323/962-1900** *lunch & dinner, Sun brunch*

Prado [WC] 244 N Larchmont Blvd (at Beverly) **323/467-3871** *lunch & dinner, dinner only Sun, Caribbean*

Quality [WC] 8030 W 3rd St (at Laurel) **323/658-5959** *8am-3pm, homestyle brkfst*

Rosco's House of Chicken & Waffles 1514 N Gower (at Sunset) **323/466-7453** *8:30am-midnight*

■ RETAIL SHOPS

Archaic Idiot/ Mondo Video-A-Go-Go 4328 Melrose (at Vermont) **323/953-8896** *noon-10pm, vintage clothes, cult & lgbt videos*

Videoactive [WC] 2522 Hyperion Ave (at Griffith Park Blvd) **323/669-8544** *10am-11pm, till midnight wknds, lgbt & adult videos*

■ GYMS & HEALTH CLUBS

Gold's Gym [GF] 1016 N Cole Ave (near Santa Monica & Vine) **323/462-7012**

LA—West LA & Santa Monica • California

■ MEN'S CLUBS

➤ **Flex Complex** [SW] 4424 Melrose Ave (btwn Normandie & Vermont) 323/663-7786 *24hrs, patio, steam*

Hollywood Spa [★PC] 1650 N Ivar (near Hollywood & Vine) 323/463-5169 *24hrs*

The Zone [PC] 1037 N Sycamore Ave (at Santa Monica) 323/464-8881

■ EROTICA

Highland Books 6775 Santa Monica Blvd (at Highland) 323/463-0295 *24hrs*

Mr S Leather & Fetter USA 4232 Melrose Ave (at New Hampshire) 323/663-7765

Romantix 6315-1/2 Hollywood Blvd (at Vine) 323/464-9435

■ CRUISY AREAS

Hollywood Bowl Overlook [AYOR] Mulholland Dr (W from Hollywood Fwy) *top of observation deck*

LA—West LA & Santa Monica

■ ACCOMMODATIONS

The Georgian Hotel [GF,F,WC] 1415 Ocean Ave (btwn Santa Monica & Broadway), Santa Monica 310/395-9945, 800/538-8147

The Inn at Venice Beach [GF,WC] 327 Washington Blvd (at Via Dolce), Marina Del Rey 310/821-2557, 800/828-0688

The Linnington [MW,GO] 2052 Linnington Ave (at S Beverly Glen Blvd) 310/441-9107 *B&B, jacuzzi*

W Hotel Los Angeles [GF,F,SW] 930 Hilgard Ave (at Le Conte) 310/208-8765, 800/421-2317 *suites, gym, day spa*

■ BARS

Annex [M,NH,D,MR-AF,K,WC] 835 S La Brea (at Arbor Vitae), Inglewood 310/671-7323 *4pm-2am*

The Dolphin [MW,NH,K,WC] 1995 Artesia Blvd (at Aviation Blvd), Redondo Beach 310/318-3339 *4pm-2am, from 2pm wknds, patio*

El Capitan [MW,NH,K,BW] 13825 S Hawthorne Blvd (at 138th), Hawthorne 310/675-3436 *4pm-2am, from noon Fri-Sun*

Friendship [MW,NH,K,WC] 112 W Channel Rd (at Pacific Coast Hwy), Santa Monica 310/454-6024 *noon-2am, patio, beach access, upstairs lounge*

Roosterfish [★M,NH] 1302 Abbot Kinney Blvd (at Cadiz), Venice 310/392-2123 *11am-2am, patio*

■ NIGHTCLUBS

Insomnia [GS,D,$] 3414 W Washington Blvd (4th Ave) 310/833-3300 *midnight-dawn Sat, patio*

Red Dragon [★M,D,MR-A,18+,$] 5515 Wilshire Blvd (at El Rey Theatre) *2nd Sat*

■ CAFES

Anastasia's Asylum 1028 Wilshire Blvd (at 11th St), Santa Monica 310/394-7113 *8am-1am, plenty veggie, live music evenings*

■ RESTAURANTS

12 Washington 12 Washington Blvd (at Pacific), Venice 310/822-5566 *dinner from 6pm, cont'l*

Baja Cantina 311 Washington Blvd (at Sanborn), Venice 310/821-2252 *lunch & dinner Mon-Fri, also brunch wknds*

Border Grill 1445 Fourth St (at Broadway), Santa Monica 310/451-1655 *lunch & dinner*

Cantalini's Salerno Beach Restaurant [BW,E] 193 Culver Blvd (at Vista del Mar), Playa del Rey 310/821-0018 *lunch 11:30am-3pm Tue-Fri, dinner 4pm-10pm Tue-Sun, clsd Mon, Italian, homemade pastas, live music Sun nights*

Drago [WC] 2628 Wilshire Blvd (btwn 26th & Princeton), Santa Monica 310/828-1585 *lunch Mon-Fri, dinner nightly, Sicilian Italian*

Golden Bull 170 W Channel Rd (at Pacific Coast Hwy), Santa Monica 310/230-0402 *dinner only, Sun brunch (summers), American, full bar*

California • USA

Joe's 1023 Abbot Kinney Blvd, Venice **310/399-5811** *lunch Tue-Fri, dinner nightly, wknd brunch, clsd Mon, French/ Californian*

The Local Yolk 3414 Highlands Ave (at Rosecranz), Manhattan Beach **310/546-4407** *6:30am-2:30pm*

Real Food Daily [BW,WC] 514 Santa Monica Blvd (btwn 5th & 6th), Santa Monica **310/451-7544** *11:30am-10pm, organic vegetarian*

Wolfgang Puck Cafe 1323 Montana Ave (at 14th St), Santa Monica **310/393-0290** *colorful entrees à la Puck (fast-food versions)*

■ RETAIL SHOPS

David Aden Gallery 361 Vernon, Venice Beach **310/396-2949** *9am-5pm, fine-art photography, large selection of male imagery*

■ MEN'S CLUBS

Roman Holiday 12814 Venice Blvd (at Beethoven), Mar Vista **310/391-0200** *24hrs*

■ MEN'S SERVICES

➤ **Megaphone Santa Monica** **310/883-2299** *Voice Personals! Meet Hot Men in your area! FREE to Browse & Respond to voice ads. Use code 3087. Also try MEGAMATES.COM*

■ CRUISY AREAS

Palisades Park [AYOR] Ocean Ave (btwn Montana & Adelaide) *after 2am*

Will Rogers State Park [AYOR] Hwy 1 (N of Santa Monica), Malibu

Zuma Beach [AYOR] Westward Beach Rd (N of Kaman), Malibu

LA—Silverlake

■ ACCOMMODATIONS

Sanborn GuestHouse [GS,NS,GO] 1005 1/2 Sanborn Ave (near Sunset) **323/666-3947, 800/663-7262** *private unit w/ kitchen*

■ BARS

AKBar [★GS,NH,D,WC] 4356 W Sunset Blvd (at Fountain) **323/665-6810** *7pm-2am, from 6pm Fri, hip, DJ Tue*

Cuffs [★M,L,WC] 1941 Hyperion Ave (near Fountain) **323/660-2649** *4pm-2am, cruise bar*

Gauntlet II [★M,L,WC] 4219 Santa Monica Blvd (at Hoover) **323/669-9472** *4pm-2am, from 2pm Sat, uniform bar*

Little Joy [GS,NH,MR-L] 1477 W Sunset Blvd (at Portia) **213/250-3417** *4pm-2am, from 1pm wknds*

The Other Side [M,NH,E,P,OC] 2538 Hyperion Ave (at Griffith Park) **323/661-4233** *noon-2am*

Silverlake Lounge [M,NH,MR-L,E] 2906 Sunset Blvd (at Silver Lake Blvd) **323/663-9636** *3pm-2am*

Woody's Hyperion [★M,NH,D,MR,WC] 2810 Hyperion Ave (at Rowena) **323/660-1503** *4pm-2am, Latin Sat*

■ NIGHTCLUBS

Dragstrip 66 [★GS,D,A,DS,$] 2500 Riverside Dr (at Fletcher, in Rudolpho's) **323/969-2596** *9pm-4am 2nd Sat, trashy pansexual rock 'n' roll club*

Rudolpho's [MW,D,E] 2500 Riverside Dr (at Fletcher) **323/669-1226** *8pm-2am, more gay Sat, theme nights, salsa music & dance lessons, patio*

■ CAFES

The Coffee Table 2930 Rowena Ave **323/644-8111** *7am-11pm, till midnight wknds, patio, fab mosaic magic*

■ RESTAURANTS

Casita Del Campo [★] 1920 Hyperion Ave **323/662-4255** *11am-10pm, till 11:30pm Fri-Sat, Mexican, patio*

Cha Cha Cha [MW,WC] 656 N Virgil (at Melrose) **323/664-7723** *8am-10pm, till 11pm Fri-Sat, Caribbean*

The Cobalt Cantina [★MW,WC] 4326 Sunset Blvd (at Fountain) **323/953-9991** *lunch & dinner, Cal-Mex, full bar, patio*

The Crest Restaurant 3725 Sunset Blvd (at Lucille) **323/660-3645** *8am-10pm, diner/ Greek*

Da Giannino [BW] 2630 Hyperion Ave (at Griffith Park Blvd) **323/664-7979** *dinner only, clsd Mon, patio*

LA—Midtown • California

El Conquistador [BW] 3701 W Sunset Blvd (at Lucille) **323/666-5136** *lunch Wed-Sun, dinner nightly, Mexican, patio*

The Flying Leap Cafe 2538 Hyperion Ave (below The Other Side bar)

Lunch to Latenite Kitchen [GO] 4348 Fountain Ave (at Sunset Blvd) **323/664-3663** *noon-1am, 10am-3am Fri-Sat, from veggie entrees to chicken & dumplings*

Vida 1930 Hillhurst Ave (at Franklin, in Los Feliz) **323/660-4446** *6pm-11pm, clsd Mon, hip w/ Asian accent*

Zen Restaurant [E,K] 2609 Hyperion Ave (at Griffith Park Blvd) **323/665-2929, 323/665-2930** *open late, Japanese, full bar*

■ENTERTAINMENT & RECREATION

Plush Life Cabaret 1920 Hyperion Ave (at Casita Del Campo) **323/969-2596** *Sat*

■RETAIL SHOPS

Rough Trade 3915 Sunset Blvd **323/660-7956** *noon-10pm, clsd Mon, toys, leather, gifts*

■GYMS & HEALTH CLUBS

Body Builders [GF] 2516 Hyperion Ave (at Tracy) **323/668-0802**

■EROTICA

➤ **Circus of Books** 4001 Sunset Blvd (at Sanborn) **323/666-1304**

LA—Midtown

■BARS

The Redhead Bar (Redz) [W,NH,MR-L] 2218 E 1st St (btwn Soto & Chicago, Boyle Hts) **323/263-2995** *2pm-midnight, till 2am wknds*

Score [MW,NH,D,MR-L,S] 107 W 4th St (at Main) **213/625-7382** *2pm-2am, from 11:30am wknds, beer bust Fri & Sun*

MIDTOWNE SPA
615 SOUTH KOHLER
LOS ANGELES
213.680.1838
www.midtowne.com

Private men's spa
Safe + Discreet
Always open
Also in...
Denver
Milwaukee
Texas

California • USA

◾NIGHTCLUBS

Jewel's Catch One Disco
[★MW,D,A,MR-AF,K,WC] 4067 W Pico Blvd (at Crenshaw) **323/734-8849** *5pm-2am, clsd Mon-Tue, dancers Wed*

◾RESTAURANTS

Cassell's 3266 W 6th St (at Vermont) **213/480-8668** *10:30am-4pm, clsd Sun, great burgers*

Du-Par's 6333 W 3rd St (at the Farmer's Market) **323/933-8446** *6am-10pm, plush diner schmoozing*

◾MEN'S CLUBS

➤ **Midtowne Spa—Los Angeles** [SW,PC] 615 S Kohler (at Central) **213/680-1838** *24hrs*

LA—Valley

includes San Fernando & San Gabriel Valleys

◾BARS

Apache Territory [★M,D,K,WC] 11608 Ventura Blvd (at Laurel Canyon), Studio City **818/506-0404** *3pm-2am*

The Bullet [M,L,WC] 10522 Burbank Blvd (at Cahuenga), North Hollywood **818/762-8890** *noon-2am, patio*

Gold 9 [M,NH,K,WC] 13625 Moorpark St (at Woodman), Sherman Oaks **818/986-0285** *1pm-2am*

The Lodge [★M,D,MR-L,MR-AF,S,WC] 4923 Lankershim Blvd (at Vineland), North Hollywood **818/769-7722** *2pm-2am, till 3am wknds, theme nights*

Moonshadow [★MW,NH,D,K,S,WC] 10437 Burbank Blvd (at Cahuenga), North Hollywood **818/508-7008** *1pm-2am*

Rawhide [★M,D,CW,WC] 10937 Burbank Blvd (near Vineland), North Hollywood **818/760-9798** *7pm-midnight Tue-Wed, 8pm-2am wknds, from 2pm Sun, clsd Mon & Th, Latin music wknds*

Silver Rail [MW,NH] 11518 Burbank Blvd (btwn Colfax & Lankershim) **818/980-8310** *4pm-2am, from noon wknds*

◾NIGHTCLUBS

Bananas Bar & Nightclub [★MW,NH,D,MR,K,S,WC,GO] 7026 Reseda Blvd (at Sherman Way), Reseda **818/996-2976** *4pm-2am, clsd wknds, patio, Latin Wed*

La Victoria [GS,D,MR-L,F,S] 19655 Sherman Wy (at Corbin Ave), Reseda **818/998-8464** *9pm-2am, more gay Wed-Th*

Oil Can Harry's [M,D,CW,S] 11502 Ventura Blvd (at Tujunga & Colfax), Studio City **818/760-9749** *8pm-2am, from 7:30pm Tue & Th, clsd Sun, dance lessons Tue & Th*

Queen Mary [★GF,D,K,DS] 12449 Ventura Blvd (at Whitsett), Studio City **818/506-5619** *7pm-2am, clsd Mon-Tue, shows wknds*

◾CAFES

Coffee Junction [E] 19221 Ventura Blvd (E of Tampa), Tarzana **818/342-3405** *7am-7pm, till 11pm Fri-Sat, 8am-11pm Sun*

Stonewall Gourmet Coffee Company [★WC] 12135 Victory Blvd, North Hollywood **818/506-4736** *7am-midnight, till 1am Fri-Sat, from 8am Sun*

◾RESTAURANTS

Du-Par's 12036 Ventura Blvd (at Laurel Canyon), Studio City **818/766-4437** *6am-1am, till 3am Fri-Sat, plush diner schmoozing*

Du-Par's 75 W Thousand Oaks Blvd, Thousand Oaks **805/373-8785** *6am-10:30pm, till 11:30pm wknds, plush diner schmoozing*

◾GYMS & HEALTH CLUBS

Gold's Gym 6233 N Laurel Canyon Blvd (at Oxnard), North Hollywood **818/506-4600**

◾MEN'S CLUBS

The North Hollywood Spa [V] 5636 Vineland (at Burbank) **818/760-6969** *24hrs, no membership req'd*

Roman Holiday [SW] 14435 Victory Blvd (at Van Nuys), Van Nuys **818/780-1320** *24hrs*

Marin County • California

■ MEN'S SERVICES

➤ **Megaphone San Fernando Valley**
818/465-0500 *Voice Personals! Meet Hot Men in your area! FREE to Browse & Respond to voice ads. Use code 3087. Also try MEGAMATES.COM*

■ EROTICA

Le Sex Shoppe 12323 Ventura Blvd (at Laurel Canyon), Studio City **818/760-9352** *24hrs*

Le Sex Shoppe 21625 Sherman Wy (at Nelson), Canoga Park **818/992-9801**

Le Sex Shoppe 4539 Van Nuys Blvd (at Ventura), Sherman Oaks **818/501-9609** *24hrs*

Le Sex Shoppe 4877 Lankershim Blvd (at Houston), North Hollywood **818/760-9529** *24hrs*

Video & Stuff 11612 Ventura Blvd (at Colfax), Studio City **818/761-3162**

Manhattan Beach

see also LA—West LA & Santa Monica

■ ACCOMMODATIONS

➤ **Sea View Inn at the Beach**
[GF,SW] 3400 Highland Ave
310/545-1504 *non-smoking rms available, courtyard*

Marin County

includes Corte Madera, Mill Valley, San Rafael, Sausalito, Tiburon

■ INFO LINES & SERVICES

Spectrum Center for LGBT Concerns [WC] 1000 Sir Francis Drake Blvd #10, San Anselmo **415/457-1115** *11am-5pm, 3pm-6:30pm Th, clsd wknds, referrals, social/ support groups*

■ ACCOMMODATIONS

Acqua Hotel [GF,NS,WC] 555 Redwood Hwy, Mill Valley **415/380-0400, 888/662-9555**

RELAX.

Sea View Inn at the beach

3400 Highland Avenue
Manhattan Beach, CA 90266
310.545.1504 310.545.4052 fax
www.seaview-inn.com

(OR NOT)

Swim in our Pool.

Run on the Beach.

Surf.

Ride our free Bikes.

Walk to the Pier.

Shop.

Play Volleyball.

Rollerblade.

California • USA

Beach House, Bolinas CA [GS,NS,GO] **415/927-2644 x2** *cottage*

Marin Suites Hotel [GF] 45 Tamal Vista Blvd (at Lucky Dr), Corte Madera **415/924-3608, 800/362-3372** *all-suite hotel w/ full kitchens*

Panama Hotel [GF,NS,F] 4 Bayview St, San Rafael **415/457-3993, 800/899-3993** *cottages, some shared baths*

Tiburon Lodge & Conference Center [GF,SW] 1651 Tiburon Blvd, Tiburon **415/435-3133, 800/762-7770**

Waters Edge [GS,NS,WC] 25 Main St, Tiburon **415/789-5999, 877/789-5999**

■ RESTAURANTS

Guaymas 5 Main St (at ferry dock), Tiburon **415/435-6300** *gourmet Mexican, great views of the Bay*

■ ENTERTAINMENT & RECREATION

Black Sand Beach take last exit before Golden Gate Bridge, go right on Outlook Rd, look for dirt parking lot, Golden Gate Nat'l Rec Area *popular nude beach, look for trail*

■ RETAIL SHOPS

Cowgirl Creamery 80 4th St, Pt Reyes Station **415/663-9335** *10am-6pm Wed-Sun, handmade cheeses, picnic lunches to go*

Marina del Rey

■ ACCOMMODATIONS

The Inn at Venice Beach [GF,WC] 327 Washington Blvd, Venice **310/821-2557, 800/828-0688** *European-style inn*

Marysville

■ CRUISY AREAS

Riverfront Park [AYOR]

Mendocino

■ ACCOMMODATIONS

Agate Cove Inn [GF,NS] 11201 N Lansing **707/937-0551, 800/527-3111** *full brkfst, fireplaces*

Blair House & Cottage [GF,NS] 45110 Little Lake St (at Ford St) **707/937-1800, 800/699-9269**

Brewery Gulch Inn [GS] 9401 Coast Hwy 1 N **707/937-4752, 800/578-4454** *oceanview B&B made of salvaged redwood, full gourmet brkfst, jacuzzi*

Glendeven Inn [GF,NS,WC] 8205 N Hwy 1, Little River **707/937-0083, 800/822-4536** *full brkfst, farmhouse on the coast, also private rental home*

Hill House Inn [GS] 10701 Palette Dr **707/937-0554, 800/422-0554** *also restaurant*

Inn at Schoolhouse Creek [GS,NS] 7051 N Hwy 1, Little River **707/937-5525, 800/731-5525** *B&B w/ cottages & suites, full brkfst, hot tub, fireplaces*

MacCallum House Inn [GS,NS,WC] 45020 Albion St (at Lansing) **707/937-0289, 800/609-0492** *also restaurant, full bar*

McElroy's Inn [GF,NS] 998 Main St **707/937-1734, 888/262-3576 (CA only)** *in the village*

Mendocino Coastal Reservations [GF] **800/262-7801, 707/937-5033**

Mendocino Hotel & Garden Suites [GF,NS] 45080 Main St **707/937-0511, 800/548-0513** *garden cottages*

Orr Hot Springs [GF,SW,N] 13201 Orr Springs Rd, Ukiah **707/462-6277** *mineral hot springs, swimming, hostel-style cabins, private cottages & campsites, clothing-optional, guests must bring all own food*

The Philo Pottery Inn [GS,GO] 8550 Hwy 128, Philo **707/895-3069** *historic country inn, lesbian-owned/ run*

Seagull Inn [GF,NS,WC] 44594 Albion St **707/937-5204, 888/937-5204**

Stanford Inn by the Sea—A Country Inn [GF,SW,NS,WC] Coast Hwy 1 & Comptche-Ukiah Rd **707/937-5615, 800/331-8884** *full brkfst, fireplaces*

■ RESTAURANTS

Cafe Beaujolais [R,WC] 961 Ukiah **707/937-5614** *from 5:45pm*

Napa Valley • California

Menlo Park
see Palo Alto

Merced
■CRUISY AREAS
Applegate Park [AYOR] off 'M' St

Mill Valley
see Marin County

■BOOKSTORES
The Depot Bookshop & Cafe 87 Throckmorton **415/383-2665** *7am-7pm, independent*

Modesto
see also Stockton

■NIGHTCLUBS
The Mustang Club [MW,D,E,K] 413 N 7th St (at 'B' St) **209/522-0393** *4pm-2am, from 6:30pm wknds, Wed ladies night, men's night Th, karaoke Sun, open 35+ years!*

■CAFES
Espresso Caffe 3025 McHenry Ave (at Rumble) **209/571-3337** *7:30am-7pm, clsd wknds*

■EROTICA
L'Amour Shoppe 1507-B 9th St **209/521-7987**

Liberty Adult Book Store 1030 Kansas Ave **209/524-7603**

Montebello
■BARS
Chico Bar [M,D,MR-L,S] 2915 W Beverly Blvd (at Garfield) **323/721-3403** *9pm-2am, clsd Mon-Tue in winter, strippers Wed*

■CRUISY AREAS
Legg Lake [AYOR] N end

Monterey
■ACCOMMODATIONS
Gosby House Inn [GF,NS,WC] 643 Lighthouse Ave (at 18th), Pacific Grove **831/375-1287, 800/527-8828** *full brkfst*

Monterey Fireside Lodge [GF] 1131 10th St **831/373-4172, 800/722-2624** *hot tub, fireplaces, smokefree rms available*

■BARS
Lighthouse Bar & Grill [MW,F] 281 Lighthouse Ave (at Dickman), New Monterey **831/373-4488** *3:30pm-2am, Sun brunch from noon*

■NIGHTCLUBS
Norma Jean [MW,D,MR-L,S] 10639 Merritt, Castroville **831/633-2090** *8pm Fri only, also Franco's restaurant next door, 11am-9pm Fri-Sun*

■RESTAURANTS
Fisherman's Grotto 39 Fisherman's Wharf #1 **831/375-4604** *11am-9pm*

Tarpy's Roadhouse 2999 Hwy 68 (at Canyon Dr) **831/647-1444**

Mountain View
■NIGHTCLUBS
King of Clubs Nightclub [MW,NH,D,CW,MR,TG,K,S] 893 Leong Dr (at Moffett Blvd) **650/968-6366** *6pm-close, Latin & dance music Fri-Sat, Club Fever Sun, CW Tue, karaoke Mon & Th*

■MEN'S SERVICES
➤ **Megaphone Mountain View 800/289-1489** *Call for the local # nearest you! Meet Hot Men in your area! FREE to Browse & Respond to voice ads. Use code 3087. Also try MEGAMATES.COM*

Napa Valley
■ACCOMMODATIONS
Beazley House B&B Inn [GF,NS,WC] 1910 First St, Napa **707/257-1649, 800/559-1649** *full brkfst*

The Chablis Inn [GS,SW,NS,WC,GO] 3360 Solano Ave (Redwood Rd at Hwy 29), Napa **707/257-1944, 800/443-3490** *motel, hot tub, kids/ pets ok*

Chateau de Vie [GS,GO] 3250 Hwy 128, Calistoga **707/942-6446, 877/558-2513** *full brkfst, hot tub*

California • USA

Halo Vineyard [M,R,SW,NS,GO] 3750 Silverado Trail, Calistoga **707/963-8195** *country house on 10 acres surrounded by vineyards*

The Ink House B&B [GF,NS] 1575 St Helena Hwy, St Helena **707/963-3890** *Italianate Victorian, full brkfst*

La Belle Epoque B&B Inn [GF,NS] 1386 Calistoga Ave, Napa **707/257-2161, 800/238-8070** *in historic Old Town, full brkfst*

Meadowlark Country House [GF,SW,N,NS,GO] 601 Petrified Forest Rd, Calistoga **707/942-5651, 800/942-5651** *B&B, full brkfst, hot tub*

The Mount View Hotel [SW] 1457 Lincoln Ave, Calistoga **707/942-6877, 800/816-6877** *jacuzzi, spa, cottages*

Oliver House B&B [GF,GO] 2970 Silverado Trail N (at Deer Park), St Helena **707/963-4089, 800/682-7888** *B&B, European-style chalet in heart of the wine country*

Stone Oaks Vineyard [GS,SW] Silverado Trail, Napa **916/452-8434** *rental home, jacuzzi*

White Sulphur Springs Resort & Spa [GF,SW] 3100 White Sulphur Springs Rd, St Helena **707/963-8588, 800/593-8873** (in CA & NV only) *Napa Valley retreat*

■RESTAURANTS

Brannan's [GF,GO] 1374 Lincoln Ave (at Washington), Calistoga **707/942-2233** *lunch & dinner, brunch wknds, new American/ wine country cuisine, full bar*

Flat Iron Grill [GF,GO] 1440 Lincoln Ave (at Washington), Calistoga **707/942-1220** *lunch & dinner, New York-style restaurant, traditional American classics*

Travigne 1050 Charter Oak Ave (Hwy 29), St Helena **707/963-4444** *11:30am-10pm, Italian, also wine bar*

■MEN'S SERVICES

➤ **Megaphone Napa Valley** **800/289-1489** *Call for the local # nearest you! Meet Hot Men in your area! FREE to Browse & Respond to voice ads. Use code 3087. Also try MEGAMATES.COM*

Nevada City

■ACCOMMODATIONS

The Flume's End [GS] 317 S Pine St **530/265-9665**

■CAFES

Java John's [GO] 306 Broad St **530/265-3653** *6:30am-5pm*

■RESTAURANTS

Friar Tucks [★WC] 111 N Pine St (at Commercial) **530/265-9093** *dinner from 5pm, American/ fondue, full bar*

Nice

■ACCOMMODATIONS

Gingerbread Cottages B&B [GS,SW,NS] 4057 E Hwy 20 **707/274-0200** *lakefront w/ private beach, fireplaces, antiques & art, hot tub*

Oakland

see East Bay

Oceanside

■BARS

Greystokes [MW] 1903 S Coast Hwy (btwn Kelly & Vista Wy) **760/757-2955** *2pm-2am, from 11am wknds, also restaurant, patio*

Ted's Capri Lounge [M,NH,WC] 207 N Tremont (at Mission) **760/722-7284** *2pm-2am, from noon wknds*

■MEN'S SERVICES

➤ **Megaphone Oceanside** **760/405-4005** *Voice Personals! Meet Hot Men in your area! FREE to Browse & Respond to voice ads. Use code 3087. Also try MEGAMATES.COM*

■EROTICA

Romantix 316 Pier View Wy (off S Coast Hwy) **760/757-7832** *24hrs*

■CRUISY AREAS

Buddy Todd Park [AYOR] on Mesa Dr (btwn Mission Rd & El Camino Real)

Orange County

see Anaheim, Costa Mesa, Garden Grove, Huntington Beach, Laguna Beach, Newport Beach

Palm Springs • California

Oxnard

MEN'S SERVICES
➤ **Megaphone Oxnard**
805/200-0299 *Voice Personals! Meet Hot Men in your area! FREE to Browse & Respond to voice ads. Use code 3087. Also try MEGAMATES.COM*

CRUISY AREAS
Oxnard Shores Beach [AYOR] 5th St (past Harbor Blvd) *head to sand dunes*

Pacific Grove

RESTAURANTS
Pasta Mia Trattoria/ The Pizza Grotto 481 Lighthouse Ave
831/375-7709, 831/375-9268
dinner from 4:30pm, Italian, cocktails, beer/ wine

Palm Springs

INFO LINES & SERVICES
AA Gay/ Lesbian 760/324-4880 (AA#)

Desert Pride Center 1733 N Palm Canyon Dr, Ste D (north of Vista Chino)
760/327-2313 *1pm-9pm, 9am-5pm wknds, programs & services, AA meetings*

ACCOMMODATIONS
2022 Casa Diego Baristo [MW,SW,GO]
2022 E Baristo Rd (at Sunrise)
760/320-1124, 52-322/223-4676 (Mexico #) *vacation rental, spa*

➤ **The 550** [★MO,B,V,SW,N,GO]
550 Warm Sands Dr (at Ramon)
760/320-7144, 800/669-0550
hot tub, kitchens

All Worlds Resort [★MO,SW,N,GO]
526 Warm Sands Dr (at Ramon)
760/323-7505, 800/798-8781
4 pools & 4 spas & large steam room

the 550

**A PRIVATE MEN'S RESORT
CLOTHING IS NEVER REQUIRED!**

Our rooms & suites offer color TV's
with the hottest in all male channels.
A heated pool and hot tub offered
with outdoor fog mist amidst a view
of the majestic mountain vistas.
Access to dry and steam sauna,
full library of adult videos
and provocative nature walk.
Each morning your day starts with
a full continental breakfast plus
evening mixers. More importantly,
a relaxing and sensual place for
men who like real men.

550 Warm Sands Drive, Palm Springs, CA 92264 Adjacent to the All Worlds Resort
1-800-798-8781 Fax 1-760-323-1055 1-760-323-7505

Damron Men's Travel Guide 2004

Palm Spring's Hottest New Resorts!
Come for the Sun... Stay for the Men!

Ambiente Inn
AND THE BLACK PALM
AN INN WITH A FETISH EDGE

TWO RESORTS!
One Clothing OPTIONAL...
the other STRICLTY NUDE!

INTERNATIONALLY
Themed ONE BEDROOM
Suites+Kitchens+TV+DVD

Look us up online: www.ccgay.com
Reservations: (760) 770-1697... call Today!

Casa DeAgua

- A Luxurious Guesthouse for Gentlemen
- Fabulously Restored 1936 Spanish Hacienda
- Complimentary Rolls-Royce Transportation

866/416-2350   760/416-2350
www.CasaDeAgua.com

1146 E. El Alameda   Palm Springs, CA 92262

Chestnutz

An Exceptional Resort For Men in Palm Springs

Put a Little Fun in Your Life!

800.621.6973 • 760.325.5269 • www.chestnutz.com
641 San Lorenzo Road • Palm Springs, CA 92264

The largest Clothing Optional Resort in the Palm Springs Area.

Take a walk on the wild side!
800-472-0836
760-324-1350

Lively Atmosphere
Passes Available
NEW! The Dungeon
Pool & Jacuzzi
Nude Beach
Steamroom
Sauna
Waterfalls

CCBC RESORT HOTEL

www.ccbcresort.com
68369 Sunair Rd.
Cathedral City, CA. 92234

choose paradise

14 Intimate Rooms
Outdoor Showers
Jaccuzzi
Adult Channels
Clothing Optional

The Desert Paradise Resort Hotel

1-800-342-7635 - Palm Springs, CA.
www.desertparadise.com

EL MIRASOL
VILLAS RESORT

PALM SPRINGS
www.elmirasol.com
800.327.2985

the hacienda
at warm sands

Sweet Dreams. Style. Comfort. Luxury.

One of the "Top 10 North American Gay Guesthouses"

800/359.2007   760/327.8111
www.thehacienda.com
586 Warm Sands Drive • Palm Springs, CA 92264

Out & About's "5 Palms Award"

- 4 POOLS
- 2 JACUZZIS
- STEAM ROOM
- OUTDOOR FIREPLACE
- FULLY EQUIPPED GYM
- OUTDOOR COOLING MIST
- CLOTHING ALWAYS OPTIONAL

No shirt, No shoes GOOD service
NO PANTS! Even BETTER service.

BROCHURES & RESERVATIONS:
800 962-0186
www.innexile.com
760 327-6413
545 WARM SANDS DR.
PALM SPRINGS, CA 92264

INN Exile
A MAN'S RESORT

In the heart of Warm Sands

INNdulge
PALM SPRINGS
"to pamper, pleasure or gratify oneself"

Complimentary Continental breakfast
Gym on site • VCRs, video library
Pool & Jacuzzi open 24 hours
Complimentary guest internet station
Summer & seasonal specials

CLOTHING FOREVER OPTIONAL!

For Adventurous
Gay Men

"A solid, consistent top choice, with 24 tastefully renovated rooms, a spectacular view and very attractive pool."
Out & About

★★★★

800.833.5675 • 760.327.1408
Fax 760.327.7273
In the heart of Warm Sands
601 Grenfall Road • Palm Springs, CA 92264
www.inndulge.com • info@inndulge.com

IGLTA

California • USA

All-Gay-Hotels.com 800/422-5416 *go online or call, hotel reservations at over 80 hotels & resorts, open daily*

➤ **Ambiente Inn** [MO,GO] 37112 Palo Verde Dr (at Palm Canyon Dr), Cathedral City 760/770-1697

The Atrium [★MO,SW,N,GO] 981 Camino Parocela (at Warm Sands) 760/322-2404, 800/669-1069 *steam & spa, porn channels*

Avalon [MO,SW,N,GO] 568 Warm Sands (at Ramon) 760/322-2404, 800/669-1069 *spa & steam, porn channels*

Bacchanal [★MO,SW,NS,GO] 589 S Grenfall Rd (at Parocela) 760/323-0760, 800/806-9059 *full brkfst, kitchens, 9-man hot tub*

Ballantines Hotel [GF,SW] 1420 N Indian Canyon Dr 760/320-1178, 800/485-2808 *'50s chic*

BauHouse in the Desert [GS,SW,WC] 2470 S Yosemite Dr (at Camino Real & Hwy 111) 760/325-7050 *rental home*

Caliente Tropics Resort [GS,F,SW,NS,GO] 411 E Palm Canyon Dr 760/327-1391, 866/468-9595

➤ **Camp Palm Springs** [★MO,SW,N,GO] 1466 N Palm Canyon Dr (at Monte Vista) 760/322-2267, 800/793-0063 *kitchens, sauna*

Canyon Boys Club [★MO,SW,N,GO] 960 N Palm Canyon Dr (btwn Tachevah & El Alameda) 760/322-4367, 800/295-2582 *kitchens, hot tub & patios*

➤ **Casa de Agua Guesthouse** [MO,SW,N,NS,GO] 1146 E El Alameda 760/416-2350, 866/416-2350

➤ **CCBC Resort Hotel** [★MO,SW,N,WC,GO] 68-369 Sunair Rd (btwn Melrose & Palo Verde), Cathedral City 760/324-1350, 800/472-0836 *free shuttle around town*

The ♥ Of Warm Sands.

Clothing Optional
Continental Breakfast
Heated Swimming
Pool & Jacuzzi
Studio & Full Apartments
Observation Deck
In-room Adult Movies

Warm Sands Villas

PALM SPRINGS

866.357.5695
www.warmsandsvillas.com
555 Warm Sands Drive

Palm Springs • California

Chaps Inn [MO,SW,GO] 312 E Camino Monte Vista **760/327-8222, 800/445-8916 (also TTY)** *catering to leather & bears mostly, hot tub*

▶ **Chestnutz** [MO,SW,N,NS,GO] 641 San Lorenzo Rd (at Random) **760/325-5269, 800/621-6973** *full brkfst, hot tub*

▶ **The Citadel** [MO,SW,N,NS,WC,GO] 1491 Via Soledad (at Sonora & S Palm Canyon) **760/325-2686, 877/644-4111** *full brkfst, jacuzzi, Out & About rated 4 Palms (see ad in front color section)*

Cobalt [MO,SW,N,NS,GO] 526 S Camino Real (at Ramon Rd) **760/416-0168, 888/289-9555** *suites, jacuzzi*

Columns Resort [★MO,SW,N,WC,GO] 537 Grenfall Rd (at Ramon) **760/325-0655, 800/798-0655** *studios, hot tub*

The Desert Bear [MO,SW,N,GO] 530 Mel Ave **760/325-6767, 877/464-7695** *hot tub*

Desert Oasis 800 **800/615-7805** *7:30am-6:30pm, 8:30am-4:30pm Sat, clsd Sun, hotel reservation service*

Desert Palms Inn [M,SW,GO] 67-580 E Palm Canyon Dr (at Gene Autry Tr), Cathedral City **760/324-3000, 800/801-8696** *also bar & restaurant*

▶ **Desert Paradise Resort Hotel** [★MO,SW,N,NS,GO] 615 Warm Sands Dr (at Parocela) **760/320-5650, 800/342-7635** *jacuzzi, firepit, outdoor shower*

The East Canyon Hotel & Spa [★MO,SW,GO] 288 E Camino Monte Vista **760/320-1928, 877/324-6835** *boutique hotel, day spa, 5 Palm award winner by Out & About*

▶ **El Mirasol Villas** [★MO,SW,N,NS,GO] 525 Warm Sands Dr (at Ramon) **760/327-5913, 800/327-2985** *newly renovated bungalows in a garden setting, steam room & jacuzzi*

Escape 2 Palm Springs Condo Rentals [GF,SW,NS,GO] **760/323-4848** *weekly rental*

TERRAZZO men's resort

**** Out & About 4 Palms and Editor's Choice

- 40' Pool
- 10 Man Spa
- Luxury Rooms
- Breakfast & Lunch
- Free Snacks
- On-Site Gym
- Concierge

it's all about You!

866.837.7996
terrazzo-ps.com
1600 E Palm Canyon Dr - Palm Springs 92264

---

www.triangle-inn.com
JOIN US FOR SOME SUN AND FUN!

TRIANGLE INN PALM SPRINGS
A DESERT RESORT FOR MEN

**** Out & About's "Four Palms Award" 2001

800-732-7555 • 760-322-7993

Palm Springs • California

➤ **The Hacienda at Warm Sands**
[★MO,V,SW,N,NS,WC,GO] 586 Warm Sands Dr (at Parocela) 760/327-8111, 800/359-2007 *2 pools & hot tub*

Harlow Club Hotel [MO,SW]
175 E El Alameda (at Palm Canyon) 760/323-3977, 888/547-7881 *hot tub, gym*

Indianola Tiki Guest House
[MO,SW,GO] 354 E Stevens Rd (at Indian Canyon) 760/323-3203, 877/337-0393 *hip '50s 'Polynesian Pop' style, full kitchens*

➤ **Inn Exile** [★MO,F,SW,N,GO]
545 Warm Sands Dr (at Ramon) 760/327-6413, 800/962-0186 *hot tub, gym*

➤ **INNdulge Palm Springs**
[★MO,SW,N,GO] 601 Grenfell Rd (at Parocela) 760/327-1408, 800/833-5675 *hot tub*

Just Right Reservations
978/934-9931 *inns & B&Bs, also W Hollywood, Santa Monica, Malibu, Provincetown, MA & Boston, MA*

➤ **La Posada** [★MO,SW,N,WC,GO]
120 W Vereda Sur (at N Palm Canyon) 760/323-1402, 888/411-4949 *resort, jacuzzi, private garden, mtn views*

La Posada East [★MO,SW,N,WC,GO]
280 East Mel Ave 760/323-1402, 888/411-4949 *all-suite inn, sauna, hot tub, mtn views*

Las Palmas Hotel [M,SW,NS,GO]
1404 N Palm Canyon Dr 760/327-6883, 866/552-7272 *resort*

Lions Head at Villa Escondida
[MO,SW,N,WC,GO] 280 E Mel Ave (at Indian Canyon) 760/323-2868, 888/888-2062 *B&B, jacuzzi*

m4maccommodations.com [MO] 1146 E El Alameda (at Avenida Cabelleros) 866/416-2350 *luxurious gay guest house & condo vacation rentals w/ 5-star amenities*

Mirage [MO,SW,N,GO] 555 Grenfall Rd (at Ramon) 760/322-2404, 800/669-1069 *private resort, kitchens, waterfall, spa & steam, porn channels*

California • USA

Mojave [GF,SW,WC] 73721 Shadow Mountain Dr, Palm Desert **760/346-6121, 800/391-1104** *hot tub, spa services*

Mountain View Villa [GS,SW,NS] **305/294-1525 (FL#)** *vacation rental at Mesquite Country Club*

Ruby Montana's Coral Sands Inn [GS,SW,WC,GO] 210 W Stevens Rd (at N Palm Canyon) **760/325-4900, 866/820-8302** *resort*

Santiago Resort [MO,SW,N,NS] 650 San Lorenzo Rd (at Mesquite) **760/322-1300, 800/710-7729** *hot tub, sauna & shower garden, brkfst & lunch included*

➤ **Terrazzo Resort** [MO,SW,NS,WC,GO] 1600 E Palm Canyon Dr (btwn Calle Marcus & Sunrise) **760/778-5883, 866/837-7996** *resort, full brkfst*

Tortuga del Sol [MO,SW,N,GO] 715 San Lorenzo **760/416-3111, 888/541-3777** *resort*

➤ **Triangle Inn Palm Springs** [★MO,SW,N,GO] 555 San Lorenzo Rd (at Random Rd) **760/322-7993, 800/732-7555** *hot tub*

Villa Mykonos [MW,SW] 67-590 Jones Rd (at Cree), Cathedral City **760/321-2898, 800/471-4753**

The Villa Palm Springs [★MW,F,SW,GO] 67-670 Carey Rd (at Cree), Cathedral City **760/328-7211, 877/778-4552** *2 restaurants & bars*

Villa Royale [★GF,SW] 1620 Indian Trail **760/327-2314, 800/245-2314** *jacuzzi, also Europa Restaurant*

The Village Inn [GS,SW] 855 N Indian Canyon Dr **760/320-8622, 866/320-8622** *hotel, hot tub*

➤ **Vista Grande Villa** [★MO,SW,N,GO] 574 Warm Sands Dr (at Ramon) **760/322-2404, 800/669-1069** *private resort*

➤ **Warm Sands Villas** [MO,SW,N,NS,GO] 555 Warm Sands Dr (at Ramon) **760/323-3005, 800/357-5695** *hot tub, jacuzzi*

■ BARS

Badlands [M,NH] 200 S Indian Canyon Dr (at Arenas) **760/778-4326** *9am-2am*

The Barracks [M,L] 67-625 E Palm Canyon (at Canyon Plaza), Cathedral City **760/321-9688** *2pm-2am, cruisy, also LeatherSmiths leather store*

Dates [MW] 67-670 Carey Rd (at The Villa resort), Cathedral City **760/328-7211** *11am-midnight, poolside bar, patio, also cafe w/ lunch & dinner*

Desert Palms' Poolside Bar [★M,F] 67-580 E Palm Canyon Dr (at the Desert Palms Inn), Cathedral City **760/324-3000, 800/801-8696** *10am-close*

Ground Zero [MW,D,K] 36-737 Cathedral Canyon Dr (at Commercial), Cathedral City **760/321-0031** *2pm-2am, CW Tue & Sat, patio*

Hunter's Video Bar [★M,D,V] 302 E Arenas Rd (at Calle Encilia) **760/323-0700** *10am-2am*

Sidewinders [M,CW,L] 67-555 E Palm Canyon Dr (at E Eagle Canyon Way), Cathedral City **760/328-9919** *1pm-2am, from 11am wknds*

Spike's Wonder Bar & Grill [★] 241 Tahquitz Canyon Wy **760/322-5280**

Streetbar [★M,NH,E,K,WC] 224 E Arenas Rd (at Indian) **760/320-1266** *10am-2am*

Tool Shed [M,NH,L] 600 E Sunny Dunes Rd (at Palm Canyon) **760/320-3299** *7am-2am, till 4am Fri-Sat, call for events, also leather shop*

Toucan's Tiki Lounge [MW,D,E,K,DS,S] 2100 N Palm Canyon Dr **760/416-7584** *2pm-2am, karaoke Th, go-go dancers*

Twisters [M,D] 67-555 E Palm Canyon #A104, Cathedral City **760/770-3711** *2pm-2am, DJ Fri-Sun, T-dance Sun*

■ NIGHTCLUBS

Heaven [MW,D,K,C,V] 611 S Palm Canyon Dr **760/416-0950** *6pm-2am Mon, from 8pm Th, till 4am Fri-Sat, clsd Sun & Tue-Wed*

■ RESTAURANTS

Atlas [D] 210 S Palm Canyon Dr **760/325-8839** *lunch & dinner, cosmopolitan fusion*

Palm Springs • California

Billy Reed's 1800 N Palm Canyon Rd (at Vista Chino) **760/325-1946** *bakery, full bar*

Blame It on Midnight [E] 777 E Tahquitz Canyon Wy **760/323-1200** *5pm-10pm, till 11pm wknds, clsd Mon in summer, also full bar, patio*

Boomerang's Bistro [BW] 394 N Palm Canyon Dr **760/416-3348** *lunch & dinner, brunch wknds, urban, patio*

El Gallito Mexican Restaurant [BW] 68820 Grove St (at Palm Canyon), Cathedral City **760/328-7794**

Las Casuelas 368 N Palm Canyon Dr (btwn Amado & Alejo) **760/325-3213** *10am-11pm, Mexican*

The Left Bank 150 E Vista Chino (at Indian Canyon) **760/320-6116** *lunch & dinner, French, full bar*

Maria's Italian Cuisine [BW] 67-778 Hwy 111 (at Perez), Cathedral City **760/328-4378** *4:30pm-8:30pm, clsd Mon*

Rainbow Cactus Cafe [P] 212 S Indian Canyon (at Arenas) **760/325-3868** *lunch & dinner, Sun brunch only, Californian, full bar*

Red Tomato [BW,WC] 68-784 E Palm Canyon (btwn Date Palm & Cathedral Canyon), Cathedral City **760/328-7518** *4pm-10pm, Italian*

Shame on the Moon [WC] 69-950 Frank Sinatra Dr (at Hwy 111), Rancho Mirage **760/324-5515** *5pm-10:30pm, cont'l, full bar, patio*

Simba's [E] 190 N Sunrise **760/778-7630** *lunch & dinner, ribs, clsd summers*

Tomboyz Cafe [BW] 214 E Arenas Rd (at Indian) **760/322-9915** *8am-10pm*

The Wilde Goose [E,C] 67-938 Hwy 111 (at Perez), Cathedral City **760/328-5775** *5pm-close, cont'l/ wild game, full bar*

■ENTERTAINMENT & RECREATION

Ruddy's 1930s General Store Museum 221 S Palm Canyon Dr **760/327-2156** *10am-4pm Th-Sun, 'the most you can spend is 95¢'*

■RETAIL SHOPS

Blink 319 E Arenas Rd (at Indian Canyon) **760/323-1667** *noon-10pm, books, queer gifts & clothing*

Bravo for Men 328 N Palm Canyon Dr (at Amado) **760/322-3077** *10am-6pm*

GayMartUSA 305 E Arenas Rd (at Indian Canyon) **760/416-6436** *10am-midnight*

Tuff Stuff 169 E Alego **760/864-8539** *custom leather, some bear & pride items, also small boutiques in Tool Shed & Sidewinders bars*

■PUBLICATIONS

The Bottom Line **760/323-0552** *the desert's lgbt bar guide & classifieds*

Desert Daily Guide **760/320-3237** *lgbt weekly*

■GYMS & HEALTH CLUBS

Basic Gym [GF] 1584 S Palm Canyon Dr (at E Olancha) **760/320-1009** *6am-7pm, 8am-5pm Sat, clsd Sun, day passes $10*

Gold's Gym [GF] 40-70 Airport Center Dr (at Ramon) **760/322-4653**

World Gym Palm Springs [M,MR,WC,GO] 1751 N Sunrise Way (at Vista Chino) **760/327-7100** *5am-10pm, from 6am wknds, day passes available, steam & sauna, club-quality sound system*

■MEN'S SERVICES

The Confidential Connection®! **760/322-9200** *The hottest local guys! 18+ Record & Listen FREE! Use access code 499*

▶ **Megaphone Palm Springs** **800/289-1489** *Call for the local # nearest you! Meet Hot Men in your area! FREE to Browse & Respond to voice ads. Use code 3087. Also try MEGAMATES.COM*

■EROTICA

Hidden Joy Book Shop 68-424 Commercial (at Cathedral Canyon), Cathedral City **760/328-1694** *24hrs*

World Wide Book Store 68-300 Ramon Rd (at Cathedral Canyon), Cathedral City **760/321-1313**

California • USA

Palo Alto

■ACCOMMODATIONS
Creekside Inn [GS,SW,NS,WC] 3400 El Camino Real (at Page Mill Rd) **650/493-2411, 800/492-7335** *restaurant*

Hotel Avante [GS,SW] 860 El Camino Real, Mountain View **650/940-1000, 800/538-1600** *jacuzzi*

■BOOKSTORES
Books Inc 157 Stanford Shopping Center **650/321-0600** *9:30am-9pm, 10am-8pm Sat, 11am-6pm Sun, general, lgbt section*

■MEN'S SERVICES
➤ **Megaphone Palo Alto** **800/289-1489** *Call for the local # nearest you! Meet Hot Men in your area! FREE to Browse & Respond to voice ads. Use code 3087. Also try MEGAMATES.COM*

Pasadena

■BARS
Boulevard/ Club S Karaoke [M,NH,K,P] 3199 E Foothill Blvd (at Sierra Madre Villa) **626/356-9304** *6pm-2am, from 3pm Fri-Sun, piano bar Sun*

Encounters [MW,NH,D,YC] 203 N Sierra Madre Blvd (at Foothill) **626/792-3735** *4pm-2am, 3pm-2am wknds*

■RESTAURANTS
Twin Palms 101 W Green St (at De Lacey Ave) **626/577-2567** *lunch & dinner, huge menu, unusual combos*

■MEN'S SERVICES
➤ **Megaphone Pasadena** **800/289-1489** *Call for the local # nearest you! Meet Hot Men in your area! FREE to Browse & Respond to voice ads. Use code 3087. Also try MEGAMATES.COM*

■EROTICA
Romantix 45 E Colorado (at Raymond) **626/683-9468** *24hrs*

Pescadero

■ACCOMMODATIONS
Costanoa [GS] 2001 Rossi Rd **650/879-1100, 800/738-7477** *also tent bungalows & cabins, 1 hour S of San Francisco*

Estancia del Mar [GF,NS] **650/879-1500** *cottage rentals w/ ocean views*

Petaluma

■ACCOMMODATIONS
Old Palms of Petaluma B&B [GF,WC] 2 Liberty St (at 6th St) **707/658-2554** *full brkfst*

■RESTAURANTS
Twisted Vines [★] 16 Kentucky St (in Lanmart Bldg) **707/766-8162** *lunch & dinner, clsd Sun, also wine store*

■BOOKSTORES
Copperfield's Books 140 Kentucky St (btwn Western & Washington, downtown) **707/762-0563** *9am-9pm, till 6pm Sun, new & used books, also great little cafe*

Pismo Beach

■ACCOMMODATIONS
The Palomar Inn [GS] 1601 Shell Beach Rd, Shell Beach **805/773-4204, 888/384-4004**

Placerville

■ACCOMMODATIONS
Rancho Cicada Retreat [M,SW,N,GO] **209/245-4841** *riverside retreat, campsites, tents & cabins*

Shafsky House B&B [GF,NS,GO] 2942 Coloma St (at Spring St/ Hwy 49) **530/642-2776** *full brkfst*

Pleasant Hill

■EROTICA
Lingerie Etc 2298 Monument Blvd (at Buskirk) **925/676-2962**

Riverton • California

Pomona

■BARS

Alibi East [M,D] 225 S San Antonio Ave (at 2nd) **909/623-9422** *10am-2am, till 4am Fri-Sat, also Back Alley Bar [M], from 9pm Fri-Sat*

The Hookup [MW,F,K,V,WC,GO] 1047 E 2nd St (at Pico) **909/620-2844** *noon-2am, from 10am wknds, karaoke Wed, levi/ leather beer bust Sun*

■NIGHTCLUBS

Robbie's [MW,D,MR-L,S] 390 E 2nd St (at College Plaza) **909/620-4371** *6pm-2am, clsd Mon-Th, call for events*

■EROTICA

Mustang Books & Videos 961 N Central (at Foothill Blvd), Upland **909/981-0227** *24hrs*

Red Bluff

■CRUISY AREAS

Dog Island Park [AYOR] *days*

Park along the river [AYOR] *early evenings*

Redding

■BARS

Rainbow Lounge & Grille [MW,NH,D,F,K,WC,GO] 2151 Market St (at Gold St, off Pine St) **530/247-1691** *6pm-2am, from 4pm Sun, food served Fri-Sat, karaoke Wed*

■NIGHTCLUBS

Club 501 [MW,D,F,YC] 1244 California St (at Center & Division, enter rear) **530/243-7869** *6pm-2am, from noon Sun*

■CAFES

Judy's Espresso [GF,WC] 1100 Hartnell Ave (at Churncreek) **530/221-8081** *6:30am-6pm, snow cones & coffee drinks*

■CRUISY AREAS

Clear Creek Rd [AYOR] 13 miles W of Hwy 273 (4 miles W of old 99) *nude beach, summers*

Lake Redding Park [AYOR] *near boat ramp*

Redondo Beach

see also Los Angeles—West LA & Santa Monica

■ACCOMMODATIONS

Palos Verdes Inn [GF,F,SW,WC] 1700 S Pacific Coast Hwy **310/316-4211** *jacuzzi*

Redwood City

■ENTERTAINMENT & RECREATION

Redwood Roller Rink [MW,MR,18+] 1303 Main St (at Beech St) **650/369-5558** *gay skate night Wed 8pm-10:30pm, PJ night 1st Wed, underwear night last Wed of month*

■EROTICA

Secrets 13 739 El Camino Real (at Brewster) **650/364-6913** *24hrs*

Riverside

see also San Bernardino

■NIGHTCLUBS

Menagerie [M,D,K,DS,WC] 3581 University Ave (at Orange) **909/788-8000** *4pm-2am*

VIP Nightclub & Restaurant [MW,D,F,K,DS] 3673 Merrill Ave (at Magnolia) **909/784-2370** *3pm-2am*

■MEN'S SERVICES

➤ **Megaphone Riverside** **800/289-1489** *Call for the local # nearest you! Meet Hot Men in your area! FREE to Browse & Respond to voice ads. Use code 3087. Also try MEGAMATES.COM*

■EROTICA

Romantix 3945 Market St (at 9th) **909/788-5194** *24hrs*

Riverton

■CRUISY AREAS

Bull Creek Rd [AYOR] off Hwy 50 *trail along river*

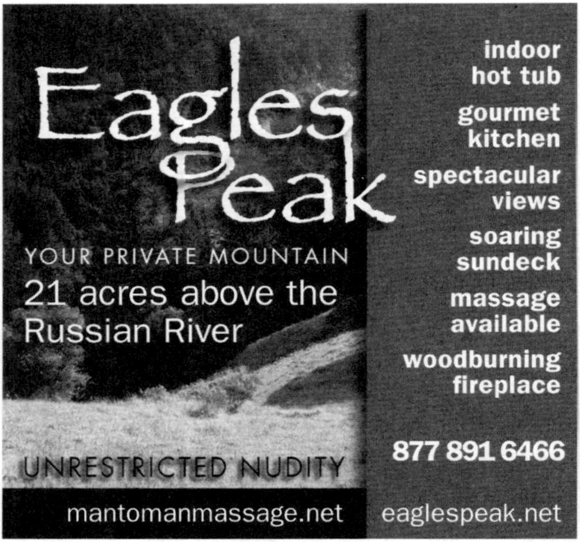
Eagles Peak
YOUR PRIVATE MOUNTAIN
21 acres above the Russian River
UNRESTRICTED NUDITY
mantomanmassage.net
indoor hot tub
gourmet kitchen
spectacular views
soaring sundeck
massage available
woodburning fireplace
877 891 6466
eaglespeak.net

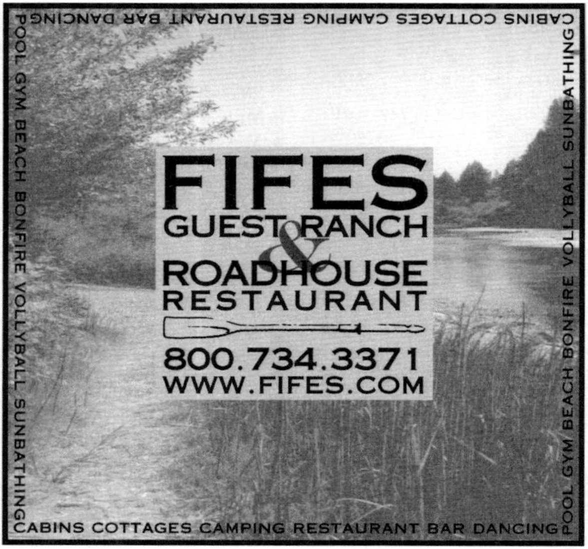
CABINS COTTAGES CAMPING RESTAURANT BAR DANCING
POOL GYM BEACH BONFIRE VOLLYBALL SUNBATHING
FIFES
GUEST RANCH
&
ROADHOUSE
RESTAURANT
800.734.3371
WWW.FIFES.COM
CABINS COTTAGES CAMPING RESTAURANT BAR DANCING
POOL GYM BEACH BONFIRE VOLLYBALL SUNBATHING

Russian River • California

Russian River
includes Cazadero, Forestville, Guerneville & Monte Rio

INFO LINES & SERVICES
Sonoma Tourism 800/576-6662

ACCOMMODATIONS
Applewood [GF,F,SW,NS,WC,GO] 13555 Hwy 116 (at Mays Canyon), Guerneville **707/869-9093, 800/555-8509** *full brkfst*

Camellia House on the Russian River [GS] **707/566-6714** *rental home on the river*

➤ **Eagle's Peak** [MO,GO] 11644 Our Peak Rd (at McPeak Rd), Forestville **707/887-9218, 877/891-6466** *vacation house w/ deck & spa on 26 acres*

Fern Falls [MW,NS,GO] **707/632-6108**

➤ **Fifes Guest Ranch & Roadhouse Restaurant** [GS,F,SW,NS,WC,GO] 16467 River Rd (at Brookside Ln), Guerneville **707/869-0656, 800/734-3371** *cabins & campsites, 2 bars [M,D], cruisy*

Grandma's House [MW,GO] 20280 River Blvd, Monte Rio **707/865-1865**

➤ **Highlands Resort** [MW,SW,N] 14000 Woodland Dr, Guerneville **707/869-0333** *country retreat on 4 wooded acres, hot tub*

Huckleberry Springs Country Inn & Spa [GS,V,SW,NS] 8105 Old Beedle, Monte Rio **707/865-2683, 800/822-2683** *private cottages, spa, massage therapy*

Powder River Ranch [GS,GO] 7390 Covey Rd (at River Rd), Forestville **707/696-8040** *studio cottage, jacuzzi*

Retreat Resort & Spa [GS,SW,NS,GO] 14711 Armstrong Woods Rd, Guerneville **707/869-2706, 866/737-3529**

THE WILLOWS

A Guesthouse on the Russian River
12 Private Bedrooms
Camping and Self-contained R.V.'s
• 5-Acre secluded riverside park • Sundeck overlooking private beach
• Complimentary continental breakfast • Free use of canoes, hot tub & sauna • Friendly relaxed atmosphere • Community kitchen, BBQ, fireplace • Near the ocean & seal watching • In the wine country • All major credit cards accepted

P.O. Box 465, 15905 River Road Guerneville, CA 95446
(707) 869-2824 • (800) 953-2828

HIGHLANDS RESORT

Cabins with fireplaces
Rooms, Camping and
Day use.
Swimming Pool and
Hot Tub.
Nude Sunbathing

Located a short walk
from town on 3 acres
of redwood trees and
beautiful gardens..

Open all year!

HIGHLANDS RESORT

P.O. Box 346/14000 Woodland Dr.
Guerneville, CA 95446
www.HighlandsResort.com
(707) **869-0333** Fax (707) 869-0370

California • USA

Rio Villa Beach Resort [GF,GO] 20292 Hwy 116 (at Bohemian Hwy), Monte Rio **707/865-1143** *cabins on the river*

River Village Resort & Spa [GS,SW,WC] 14880 River Rd, Guerneville **707/869-8139**, **800/529-3376** *cottages, hot tub*

Russian River Getaways [MW,GO] 14075 Mill St (at 4th St), Guerneville **707/869-4560, 800/433-6673** *vacation rental service*

Russian River Guesthouse [GS,NS] **707/869-9636, 877/247-4837** *2-bdrm rental hideaway, kids ok, weekly rental, bi-owned/ run*

Russian River Reservations [GO] **707/887-9219, 800/767-1759** *reservation service for rental homes*

➤ **Russian River Resort/ Triple 'R' Resort** [MW,E,V,SW,N,WC,GO] 16390 4th St (at Mill), Guerneville **707/869-0691, 800/417-3767** *hot tub, bar, restaurant*

Russian River View Retreat [GF,NS] **707/869-3040** *vacation home w/ deck, hot tub*

Schoolhouse Canyon Park [GF,SW] 12600 River Rd (at Oddfellows Park Rd), Guerneville **707/869-2311** *open May-Sept, private beach, camping & RV*

Tim & Tony's Treehouse [GS,NS,N,NS,GO] **707/887-9531, 888/887-9531** *studio cottage, hot tub, sauna*

Village Inn & Restaurant [GS,NS,WC,GO] 20822 River Blvd, Monte Rio **707/865-2304, 800/303-2303** *historic inn w/ restaurant & full bar*

➤ **The Willows** [MW,NS] 15905 River Rd (at Hwy 116), Guerneville **707/869-2824, 800/953-2828** *country lodge, camping*

Xen Resort & Spa [GS,SW] 16484 4th St (at Mill St), Guerneville **707/869-0600, 888/773-4897**

■ BARS

Mc T's Bullpen [GS,NH,WC] 16246 1st St (at Church), Guerneville **707/869-3377** *8am-2am, sports bar, patio*

The Pink Elephant [GF,NH,E] 9895 Main St, Monte Rio **707/865-0500** *11am-2am*

Rainbow Cattle Co [GS,NH] 16220 Main St (at Armstrong Woods Rd), Guerneville **707/869-0206** *6am-2am*

The Russian River Eagle [MW,NH,A,B,L,WC] 16225 Main St (at Armstrong Woods Rd), Guerneville **707/869-3400** *1pm-2am*

■ NIGHTCLUBS

Club Fab [★M,D,DS] 16135 River Rd (at Armstrong Woods Rd), Guerneville **707/869-5708** *9pm-2am, till 4am Sat, 4pm-close Sun, clsd Mon-Wed*

■ CAFES

Coffee Bazaar 14045 Armstrong Woods Rd (at River Rd), Guerneville **707/869-9706** *6am-8pm, soups, salads & pastries*

■ RESTAURANTS

Cape Fear Cafe 25191 Main St, Duncans Mills **707/865-9246** *9am-9pm*

Chez Marie [GO] 6675 Front St (Hwy 116), Forestville **707/887-7503** *dinner from 6pm, clsd Mon-Tue*

Flavors Unlimited 16450 Main St/ River Rd, Guerneville **707/869-0425** *hours vary, custom-blended ice cream*

Pasta Boys [MW,WC] 16390 4th St (at Triple 'R' Resort), Guerneville **707/869-0691** *full bar, patio*

River Inn Restaurant [WC] 16141 Main St, Guerneville **707/869-0481** *seasonal hours, local favorite*

■ ENTERTAINMENT & RECREATION

The Nude Beach on Russian River at Wohler Bridge, Guerneville

■ BOOKSTORES

River Reader [WC] 16355 Main St (at Mill), Guerneville **707/869-2240** *10am-6pm, extended summer hours*

■ RETAIL SHOPS

Guerneville 5&10 [GO] 16252 Main St, Guerneville **707/869-3404** *10am-6pm, old-fashioned five & dime*

Touch of Greene [GO] 16377 B Main St, Guerneville **707/869-3180** *10am-6pm, till 5pm Sun, bath & body shop, massage*

Sacramento • California

Up the River 16212 Main St (at Armstrong Woods Rd), Guerneville **707/869-3167** *cards, gifts, T-shirts & more*

Sacramento

■INFO LINES & SERVICES

Gay AA 601 Alhambra Blvd (at Clunie Clubhouse in McKinley Park) **916/454-1100** *11am Sun*

Lambda Community Center 1927 'L' St **916/442-0185** *noon-9pm, clsd Sun, youth groups, discussion groups, referrals, library*

Northall Gay AA 2631 Riverside Blvd, unit 'B' **916/454-1100** *8pm nightly, men's meeting 8pm Tue*

■ACCOMMODATIONS

Capitol Park B&tB [GF,GO] 1300 'T' St (at 13th) **916/414-1300, 877/753-9982** *full brkfst*

Inn at Parkside [GS,GO,WC] 2116 6th St (at 'U' St) **916/658-1818, 800/995-7275** *B&tB inn, full brkfst, jacuzzi*

Verona Village River Resort [MW] 6985 Garden Hwy, Nicolaus **530/656-1321** *RV space, restaurant, full bar, store, marina*

■BARS

The Bolt [M,NH,L] 2560 Boxwood St (at El Camino) **916/649-8420** *5pm-2am, volleyball in summer*

The Depot [★M,NH,TG,V,WC] 2001 'K' St **916/441-6823** *4pm-2am, till 4am Fri-Sat, from 2pm wknds*

Lil' Galley Two [M,NH,A,CW,MR,TG,F,K,DS,YC,WC,GO] 1011 Del Paso Blvd (at Globe) **916/922-9994** *10am-2am, karaoke Fri-Sat, smoking patio*

The Mercantile Saloon [M,NH,WC] 1928 'L' St (at 20th St) **916/447-0792** *10am-2am*

The Townhouse [M,NH,D,K,WC] 1517 21st St (at 'P' St) **916/441-5122** *3pm-2am, also restaurant, karaoke wknds*

■NIGHTCLUBS

Club 21 [W,D,MR,F,C,V,GO] 1119 21st St (at L St) **916/443-1537** *9pm-2am Wed-Sun, Bojangles men's night Wed [18+], cabaret Th, also Isabella's Mexican/ Italian restaurant*

Faces [★MW,D,CW,TG,K,DS,V,WC] 2000 'K' St (at 20th St) **916/448-7798** *4pm-2am*

■RESTAURANTS

Ernesto's 1901 16th St (at 'S' St) **916/441-5850** *10am-10pm, till 11pm Fri-Sat, Mexican, full bar*

Hamburger Mary's 1630 'J' St (at 17th) **916/441-4340** *11am-10pm, till 11pm Fri-Sat, full bar*

Jack's Urban Eats 20th & Capitol **916/444-0307** *lunch Mon-Fri, dinner nightly; also at 2535 Fair Oaks Blvd, 916/481-5225*

Rick's Dessert Diner 2322 'K' St (at 24th) **916/444-0969** *10am-midnight*

Thai Palace 3262 'J' St (33rd St) **916/447-5353** *lunch & dinner*

■ENTERTAINMENT & RECREATION

Lavender Library, Archives & Cultural Exchange of Sacramento 1414 21st St **916/492-0558** *clsd Mon-Wed, call for hours*

■BOOKSTORES

The Open Book [WC] 910 21st St (btwn 'I' & 'J' Sts) **916/498-1004** *10am-11pm, till midnight Fri-Sat, lgbt, also coffeehouse*

■PUBLICATIONS

➤ **Gloss Magazine** **415/552-2051** *CA arts/ entertainment magazine, bi-weekly*

MGW (Mom Guess What) **916/441-6397** *lgbt newspaper*

Outword News Magazine **916/329-9280** *lgbt newspaper*

■MEN'S SERVICES

The Confidential Connection®! **916/489-9800** *The hottest local guys! 18+ Record & Listen FREE! Use access code 499*

California • USA

The Gay Connection 900/505-6338
Talk and/or meet with other men from the area, at only 99¢ per minute.

➤ **Megaphone Sacramento**
916/340-1414 *Voice Personals! Meet Hot Men in your area! FREE to Browse & Respond to voice ads. Use code 3087. Also try MEGAMATES.COM*

■ EROTICA

'G' Spot [★GO] 2009 'K' St (at 20th) 916/441-3200

Goldie's I 201 N 12th St (at North 'B' St) 916/447-5860 *24hrs; also* 2138 Del Paso Blvd, 916/922-0103

Goldie's Outlet 1800 Del Paso Blvd (at Oxford Blvd) 916/920-8659

Kiss-N-Tell 4201 Sunrise Blvd (at Fair Oaks) 916/966-5477

L'Amour Shoppe 2531 Broadway (at 26th) 916/736-3467

■ CRUISY AREAS

American River Access [AYOR] off La Rivera Dr, near Howe Ave & Watt Ave

Beach & levee on American River [AYOR] at end of N 10th St, off Richards Blvd

Paradise Beach [AYOR] on American River

Salinas

■ EROTICA

L'Amour Shoppe 325 E Alisal St 831/758-9600

San Bernardino

see also Riverside

■ INFO LINES & SERVICES

AA Gay/ Lesbian 909/825-4700

Gay/ Lesbian Community Center Hotline 2286 N LeRoy 909/882-4488 *7:30pm-9pm*

■ NIGHTCLUBS

The Lark [MW,D,E,K,WC] 917 Inland Center Dr 909/884-8770 *noon-2am, DJ Fri-Sat, huge patio*

■ MEN'S SERVICES

➤ **Megaphone San Bernardino**
909/663-0300 *Voice Personals! Meet Hot Men in your area! FREE to Browse & Respond to voice ads. Use code 3087. Also try MEGAMATES.COM*

■ EROTICA

Bearfacts Book Store 1434 E Baseline 909/885-9176 *24hrs*

■ CRUISY AREAS

Perris Hill Park [AYOR] Highland Ave (turn right just after courts) *days*

San Clemente

■ CRUISY AREAS

Calafia State Beach [AYOR] to the left, off the fwy (from Hwy 5 S)

San Onofre Beach State Park [AYOR] at N end of Camp Pendleton

San Diego

■ INFO LINES & SERVICES

AA Gay/ Lesbian 1730 Monroe Ave #B 619/298-8008 *Live & Let Live Alano*

Lesbian/ Gay Men's Community Center 3909 Centre St (at University) 619/692-2077 *9am-10pm, till 7pm Sat, clsd Sun*

➤ **Turn Key Real Estate**
619/299-DEAN

■ ACCOMMODATIONS

All-Gay-Hotels.com 800/422-5416 *go online or call, hotel reservations at over 200 hotels & resorts, open daily*

Balboa Park Inn [GF] 3402 Park Blvd (at Upas) 619/298-0823, 800/938-8181

Beach Area B&B/ Elsbree House [GF,NS] 5054 Narragansett Ave (at Sunset Cliffs Blvd) 619/226-4133, 800/607-4133 *near beach*

The Beach Place [MW,N,GO] 2158 Sunset Cliffs Blvd (at Muir) 619/225-0746 *apts, hot tub, near beach*

RESIDENTIAL AND INVESTMENT SALES

PURCHASE AND REFINANCE LOANS

Personal Attention
it's what you deserve

Listing Broker
Buyers Broker
Loan Broker

1031 Tax Free Exchanges
Relocation Specialist
Free Pre-Qualification

Dean M. Burrows
MBA, Broker, CRS

619-299-DEAN (3326)
www.deanburrows.com

Meeting the needs of men of all ages.
Heated Pool & Spa.
Centrally located. Downtown, parks, theaters, buses, trolleys, zoo, beaches, airport, train depot, Mexico, fishing, Sea World and tours.
Friendly and personable but still private.
(From single rooms to harbor view suites)

GRAPE STREET HOTEL

505 W. Grape Street & 1970 State Street
San Diego, CA 92101
619-234-6787 • 800-692-5101 • FAX 619-231-3501
www.grapestreethotel.com • men@grapestreethotel.com

HARBOR HOUSE RESORT
642 W. HAWTHORN • SAN DIEGO, CA 92101

Phone: 1-888-338-9966 • Fax: 1-888-338-9977
Email: HarborHouseUSA@aol.com
Web: www.HarborHouseResort.com
www.MobyDicksBar.com

San Diego • California

The Bristol Hotel [GS,WC] 1055 First St **619/232-6141, 800/662-4477** *restaurant, great collection of pop art*

Casa Granada [GS,NS,GO] 1720 Granada Ave (at Date St) **619/501-5911, 866/524-2312** *near beach*

Dmitri's Guesthouse [MW,SW,N,NS,WC] 931 21st St (at Broadway) **619/238-5547** *overlooks downtown, hot tub*

➤ **Grape Street Hotel** [MO,SW,WC,GO] 505 W Grape St **619/234-6787, 800/692-5101** *downtown guest house, hot tub*

➤ **Harbor House Resort** [MW,GO] 642 W Hawthorn (btwn Columbia & State) **619/338-9966, 888/338-9966** *outdoor jacuzzis, also Moby Dick's bar*

➤ **Hillcrest Inn Hotel** [MW,WC] 3754 5th Ave (btwn Robinson & Pennsylvania) **619/293-7078, 800/258-2280**

Inn Suites Hotel [GF,F,SW,WC] 2223 El Cajon Blvd (btwn Louisiana & Mississippi) **619/296-2101** *also restaurant*

Keating House [GF,NS,GO] 2331 2nd Ave (at Juniper) **619/239-8585, 800/995-8644** *Victorian B&B, full brkfst*

Mike's Place [M,GO] 1252 Lincoln Ave (at Washington St) **619/235-4127** *private guest cottage*

Park Manor Suites [GF] 525 Spruce St (btwn 5th & 6th) **619/291-0999, 800/874-2649** *1926 hotel*

Villa Serena B&B [GF,NS,SW] 2164 Rosecrans St (btwn Udall & Voltaire) **619/224-1451, 866/559-2728** *hot tub, residential neighborhood*

California • USA

■BARS

➤ **Bourbon Street** [★M,E] 4612 Park Blvd (at Adams) **619/291-4043** *2pm-2am, from 11am wknds*

The Brass Rail [MW,D,WC] 3796 5th Ave (at Robinson) **619/298-2233** *noon-2am*

The Caliph [M,E,K,P,OC] 3100 5th Ave (at Redwood) **619/298-9495** *11am-2am, piano bar*

Chee Chee Club [M,NH] 929 Broadway (at 9th Ave) **619/234-4404** *6am-2am, hustlers*

Cheers [M,NH,F] 1839 Adams Ave (at Park) **619/298-3269** *11am-2am*

Flick's [★M,V,YC] 1017 University Ave (at 10th Ave) **619/297-2056** *2pm-2am*

The Hole [M,D,L,S] 2820 Lytton St (at Rosecrans) **619/226-9019** *4pm-2am, from noon Fri-Sun, Wet Underwear Mon*

Kickers [★M,D,K,WC] 308 University Ave (at 3rd Ave) **619/491-0400** *7pm-2am, Latin Mon, karaoke Wed, CW Th-Sat, T-dance Sun*

The Loft [M,NH,WC] 3610 5th Ave (at Brookes) **619/296-6407** *11am-2am*

Martini's Bar & Grill [MW,NH,F,P,GO] 3940 4th Ave (btwn Washington & University) **619/293-0232** *11:30am-11pm, 11am-midnight Fri-Sat, Sun brunch from 10am*

Moby Dick's Patio Bar & Deli [MW,F,S] 642 W Hawthorn (at Harbor House Resort) **619/338-9942** *10am-midnight, deli open noon-10pm, strippers Fri-Sun*

➤ **No 1 Fifth Ave** (no sign) [M,V] 3845 5th Ave (at University) **619/299-1911** *noon-2am, patio*

California • USA

Numbers [★M,D,K,S,V,WC] 3811 Park Blvd (at University) **619/294-9005** *1pm-2am, go-go boys Tue-Sat, karaoke Sun, patio*

Patti's Front Office [W,NH,K,GO] 6156 Fairmont Ave (at Mission Gorge Rd) **619/280-1400** *1pm-midnight, till 2am Fri-Sat, more gay after 6pm, karaoke Fri-Sat*

Pecs [M,L,WC] 2046 University Ave (at Alabama) **619/296-0889** *noon-2am, patio, cruisy*

Redwing Bar & Grill [M] 4012 30th St (at Lincoln) **619/281-8700** *10am-1am, till 2am Fri-Sat, lounge, patio*

San Diego Eagle [M,NH,L,WC] 3040 North Park Wy (at 30th) **619/295-8072** *4pm-2am, from 2pm wknds*

Shooterz/ Club Odyssey [M,NH,D] 3815 30th St (at University) **619/574-0744** *3pm-2am, till 4am Th-Sat, sports & cruise bar*

SRO Lounge [M,NH,OC] 1807 5th Ave (at Elm) **619/232-1886** *10am-2am*

Top of the Park [★M] 3167 5th Ave (at Park Manor Suites) **619/296-0057** *5pm-midnight, popular Fri happy hour*

Wolf's [M,L,BW] 3404 30th St (at Upas) **619/291-3730** *8pm-2am, leather shop in back*

■ **NIGHTCLUBS**

Axiom [M,D,S] 655 4th Ave **619/231-6700** *gay Fri only, go-go boys & girls*

Bacchus House [M,D,MR,TG,E,DS,S,V,YC,WC,GO] 3054 University Ave (at 30th St) **619/299-2032** *4pm-2am, strippers*

Club Montage [★M,D,E,V,WC,$] 2028 Hancock St (at Washington Ave) **619/294-9590** *9pm-4am Th-Sat, rooftop patio*

San Diego • California

Rich's [★M,D,V,YC] 1051 University Ave (at Vermont) 619/295-2195, 619/497-4588 (club line) *open Wed-Sun*

■ CAFES

The Big Kitchen [WC] 3003 Grape St (at 30th) 619/234-5789 *8am-2pm, 7:30am-3pm wknds*

David's Coffeehouse [MW,E] 3766 5th Ave (at Robinson) 619/296-4173 *7am-midnight, till 1am wknds, coffeehouse for positive people & friends, patio*

Espresso Roma UCSD Price Center #76 (at Voight), La Jolla 858/450-2141 *7am-8pm, 8am-6pm Sat, clsd Sun*

Extraordinary Desserts 2929 5th Ave 619/294-7001 *8:30am-11pm, till midnight Fri, 11am-midnight Sat, 11am-11pm Sun, the name says it all*

■ RESTAURANTS

The Abbey Café [MW,GO] 127 E University Ave (in Hillcrest) 619/692-0311 *10am-11pm, from 3pm Mon, also coffee & tea house, specialty desserts, full bar*

Adams Avenue Grill [BW,WC,GO] 2201 Adams Ave (at Mississippi) 619/298-8440 *lunch, dinner, brunch wknds, bistro*

Bayou Bar & Grill [WC] 329 Market St (btwn 3rd & 4th) 619/696-8747 *lunch & dinner, Sun brunch, Creole/Cajun*

Cafe Eleven [WC] 1440 University Ave (at Normal) 619/260-8023 *dinner, clsd Mon, French*

Cafe W [GF] 3680 6th Ave (at Pennsylvania Ave) 619/291-0200 *6pm-10pm, till 11pm Fri-Sat, clsd Tue, urban chic, patio*

California Cuisine [WC] 1027 University Ave (at 10th Ave) 619/543-0790 *11am-10pm, from 5pm wknds, clsd Mon, some veggie, also bar*

City Deli 535 University Ave (at 6th Ave) 619/295-2747 *7am-midnight, till 2am wknds, NY deli, full bar*

The Cottage 7702 Fay (at Klein), La Jolla 858/454-8409 *7:30am-3pm, fresh-baked items*

Crest Cafe [WC] 425 Robinson (btwn 4th & 5th) 619/295-2510 *7am-midnight*

➤ **Hamburger Mary's** [WC] 308 University Ave (at 3rd) 619/491-0400 *9am-11pm, full bar, patio*

Hash House A Go Go 3628 5th Ave 619/298-4646 *7:30am-9pm, till 10pm Fri-Sat, great brkfst*

Liaison [WC] 2202 4th Ave (at Ivy) 619/234-5540 *dinner only, clsd Mon, French country, prix fixe dinner*

Lips 2770 5th Ave (at Olive) 619/295-7900 *Sun brunch, clsd Mon, 'the ultimate in drag dining', Bitchy Bingo Wed, celeb impersonation Th, DJ wknds*

The Mission [MW] 3795 Mission Blvd (at San Jose), Mission Beach 858/488-9060 *brkfst & lunch; also 2801 University Ave in North Park, 619/220-8992*

Mixx [MW,GO] 3671 5th Ave 619/299-6499 *dinner only, 'cuisine w/ no ethnic boundaries'*

■ ENTERTAINMENT & RECREATION

Diversionary Theatre 4545 Park Blvd #101 (at Madison) 619/220-0097 (box office #), 619/220-6830 *lgbt theater*

Torrey Pines Beach State Park ('Blacks Beach') *popular nude beach*

Damron Men's Travel Guide 2004

Your complete guide to Southern California news, entertainment & happenings!

More Copies, More Often, To More Locations Throughout All Of Southern California Than Any Other Gay & Lesbian Publication, Period!

Michael G. Portantino • Publisher

San Diego/SoCal Edition
619.299.6397
1730 Monroe Ave. Ste A San Diego, CA 92116

1.800.438.8786

www.gaylesbiantimes.com

open 24 hours
CLUB SAN DIEGO

3955 4th avenue • San Diego CA

VIP suites and jr suites • 52 private rooms
26 TV rooms • 300 lockers • 2 video lounges
steam room • sauna Jacuzzi • smoking lounge
snack room • 12 hour time limits
One night memberships

(619)•295•0850

California • USA

■BOOKSTORES

Groundworks Books [WC] UCSD Student Center 0323 (at Gilman Dr), La Jolla **858/452-9625** *10am-8pm, till 5pm Fri-Sat, clsd Sun, alternative, lgbt section*

➤ **Obelisk the Bookstore** [WC] 1029 University Ave (at 10th) **619/297-4171** *10am-10pm, till 11pm Fri-Sat, from 11am Sun, lgbt*

■RETAIL SHOPS

Auntie Helen's [WC] 4028 30th St (at Lincoln) **619/584-8438** *10am-5pm, clsd Sun-Mon, thrift shop benefits PWAs*

Flesh Skin Grafix 1155 Palm Ave, Imperial Beach **619/424-8983** *tattoos & piercing*

Mastodon 4638 Mission Blvd (at Emerald), Pacific Beach **858/272-1188** *body piercing*

Rainbow Road 141 University Ave (at 3rd) **619/296-8222** *10am-10pm, gay gifts*

■PUBLICATIONS

➤ **Gay/ Lesbian Times** 1730 Monroe Ave, Ste A **619/299-6397, 800/438-8786** *lgbt newsmagazine*

➤ **Gloss Magazine** **415/552-2051** *CA arts/ entertainment magazine, bi-weekly*

San Diego Buzz 3316 4th Ave **619/291-6690** *bi-weekly, news, entertainment & listings*

Update **619/299-0500**

■GYMS & HEALTH CLUBS

Frog's Athletic Club 901 Hotel Circle S (at Washington), Mission Valley **619/291-3500** *$10-15 day passes*

■MEN'S CLUBS

➤ **Club San Diego** [PC] 3955 4th Ave (btwn Washington & University) **619/295-0850** *24hrs*

➤ **Mustang Spa** [SW,PC] 2200 University Ave (at Mississippi) **619/297-1661** *24hrs*

Obelisk Bookstore
A SOURCE LIKE NO OTHER
www.obeliskbooks.com

1029 University Avenue   San Diego, CA 92103   619.297.4171

MUSTANG SPA

San Diego's Hottest Private Mens Club

- Huge Heated Indoor Pool
- 20-Man Jacuzzi
- Euro-Steam Room
- Dry Sauna
- Solarium
- 2 Video Lounges
- TV Rooms w/3 Channels
- Private Rooms
- Lockers
- Digital Stereo
- and Much, Much More...

Open 24 Hours

Visa & MasterCard Accepted

2200 University Ave, San Diego, CA
(619) 297-1661

San Francisco • California

➤ **Vulcan Steam & Sauna** [PC]
805 W Cedar St (at Pacific Hwy)
619/238-1980 *24hrs*

■MEN'S SERVICES
➤ **Megaphone San Diego**
858/707-7770 *Voice Personals! Meet Hot Men in your area! FREE to Browse & Respond to voice ads. Use code 3087. Also try MEGAMATES.COM*

■EROTICA
Adult Emporium [GO] 3576 Main St
619/239-1878 *24hrs*

The Crypt 3847 Park Blvd (at University) **619/692-9499** *24hrs; also* 4094 30th St, **619/284-4724**

F St Bookstore 2004 University Ave (at Florida) **619/298-2644** *24hrs*

F St Bookstore 751 4th Ave (at 'F' St) **619/236-0841** *24hrs*

F St Bookstore 7865 Balboa Ave (at Mercury), Kearny Mesa **858/292-8083** *24hrs*

F St Bookstore 7998 Miramar Rd (at Dowdy) **858/549-8014** *24hrs*

F St Bookstore 4650 Border Village (at San Ysidro Blvd), San Ysidro
619/690-2070

Gemini Adult Books [WC]
5265 University Ave (at 52nd)
619/287-1402

Midnight Books 1407 University Ave (at Richmond) **619/299-7186** *24hrs*

Midnight Books 3606 Midway Dr (at Kemper) **619/222-9973** *24hrs*

Pleasureland 836 5th Ave (btwn 'E' & 'F' Sts) **619/237-9056** *24hrs*

Ringold Alley [GO] 3408 30th St (at Upas St) **619/295-7464** *leather, fetish & accessories*

Romantix Midnight Videos 4792 El Cajon Blvd (at 48th) **619/582-1997** *24hrs*

Sensual Delights [WC] 1220 University Ave (at Vermont) **619/291-7400** *safer sex gifts*

■CRUISY AREAS
Please Note: All cruisy areas for San Diego have been removed because the SDPD aggressively polices these areas.

SAN FRANCISCO

San Francisco is divided into 7 geographical areas:
SF—Overview
SF—Castro & Noe Valley
SF—South of Market
SF—Polk Street Area
SF—Downtown & North Beach
SF—Mission District
SF—Haight, Fillmore, Hayes Valley

SF—Overview

■INFO LINES & SERVICES
AA Gay/ Lesbian **415/674-1821**

GLBT Hotline of San Francisco
415/355-0999 *5pm-9pm Mon-Fri, peer-counseling, info*

LYRIC (Lavender Youth Recreation/ Information Center) 127 Collingwood (between 18th & 19th) **415/703-6150, 800/246-7743** (CA only) *support & social groups, also crisis counseling for lgbt youth under 24 at* **415/863-3636** *(hotline #)*

The San Francisco LGBT Community Center 1800 Market St (at Octavia) **415/865-5555** *cyber center, mtg rooms, cafe, classes & more*

■ACCOMMODATIONS
Dockside Boat & Bed [GF,NS]
57 Clay St, Oakland **510/444-5858, 800/436-2574** *private yachts, charters available*

■ENTERTAINMENT & RECREATION
Beach Blanket Babylon [★GF] 678 Green St (at Powell, in Club Fugazi) **415/421-4222** *the USA's longest running musical revue & wigs that must be seen to be believed; also restaurant & full bar*

Black Sand Beach first exit past Golden Gate Bridge (Alexander) (go left under Fwy, right on Outlook Rd, look for dirt parking lot), Golden Gate Nat'l Rec Area *popular nude beach, look for trail*

Castro Theatre 429 Castro (at Market) **415/621-6120** *art house cinema, many lgbt & cult classics, live organ evenings*

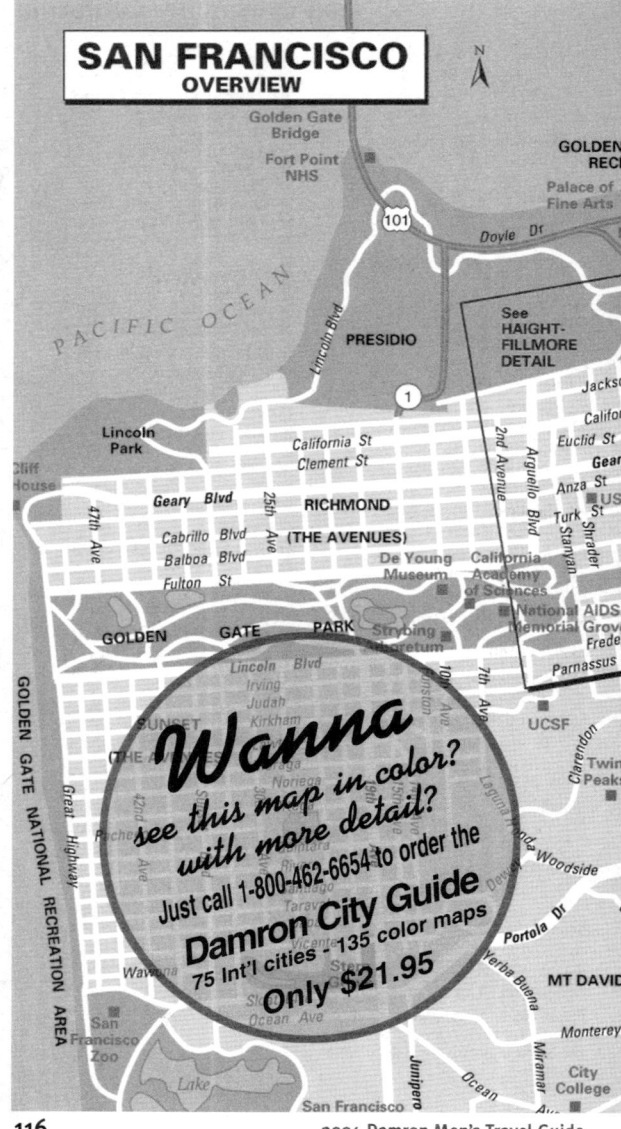

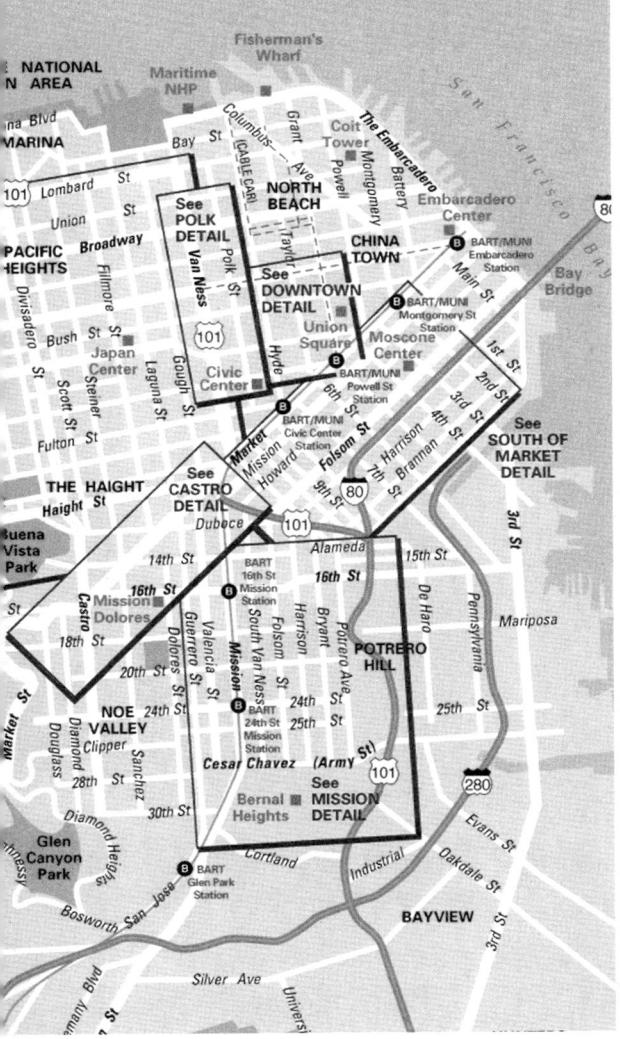

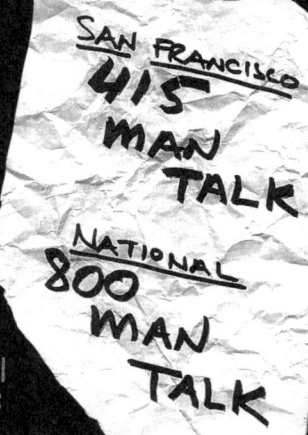

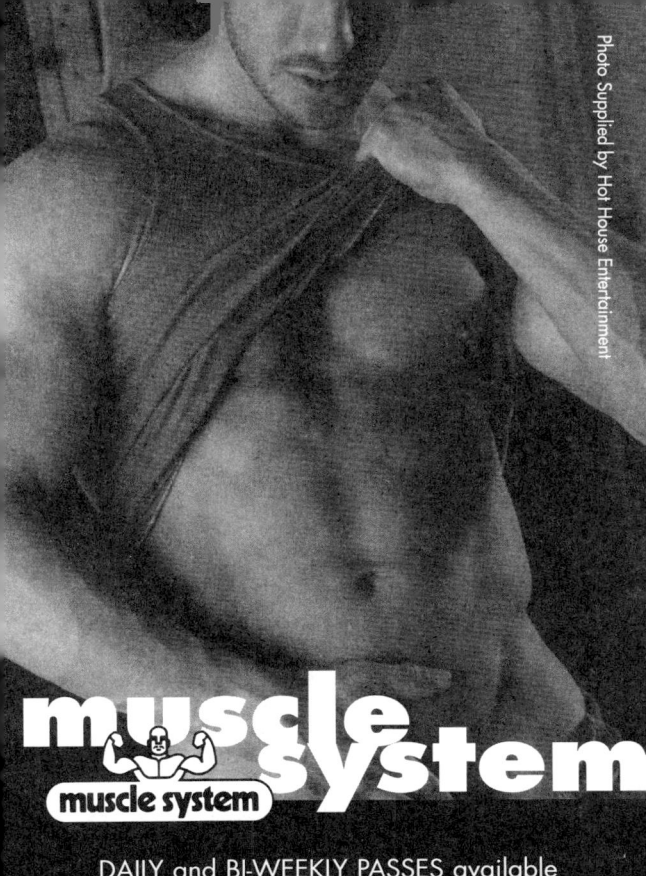

muscle system

DAILY and BI-WEEKLY PASSES available

FREE WEIGHTS & MACHINES • CARDIO
TANNING • SAUNA

Convenient San Francisco Location:
2275 Market St.
(415) 863-4700

▲ Member of the PRIDE Group of Affiliate Gyms ▲

California • USA

Cruisin' the Castro 415/550-8110
5-star walking lesbian/gay history tour of the Castro (Goldrush-present), lunch included

➤ **Frameline** 415/703-8650 *lgbt media arts foundation that sponsors the annual SF Int'l Lesbian/Gay Film Festival each June (see Film Festival Calendar in back Events section)*

The Marsh 1062 Valencia (at 22nd St) 415/641-0235 *queer-positive theater*

Monday Night Gay Comedy [★MW,$] 1800 Market St (at LGBT Community Center) 415/541-5610 *7:30pm every other Mon, call for info*

➤ **National AIDS Memorial Grove** [WC] Golden Gate Park (on corner of Middle Drive East & Bowling Green Dr) 415/750-8340, 888/294-7683 *guided tours available 9:30am-12:30pm every Th*

The New Conservatory Theatre Center 25 Van Ness Ave, Lower Lobby (at Market) 415/861-8972 *gay theater in historic Masonic Bldg*

Out 4 Travel [MW,GO] 510/548-8671 *Bay Area information, custom & ready-made itineraries, guided tours available*

SF GayTours.com 415/648-7758, 877/734-2986 *SF Queer History tour, commitment ceremonies*

Theatre Rhinoceros 2926 16th St (at S Van Ness) 415/861-5079 *lgbt theater*

Victorian Home Walks [GO] 415/252-9485 *custom-tailored walking tours w/ San Francisco resident*

■PUBLICATIONS

BAR (Bay Area Reporter) 415/861-5019 *the weekly lgbt newspaper*

➤ **Gloss Magazine** 415/552-2051 *CA arts/entertainment magazine, bi-weekly*

➤ **Odyssey Magazine** 415/621-6514 *all the dish on SF's club scene*

QSF Magazine 800/999-9718 **(subscriptions)** *glossy w/ extensive arts, clubs & restaurant listings for the City*

San Francisco Bay Times [★] 415/626-0260 *bi-weekly, a 'must read' for Bay Area resources*

San Francisco Spectrum 415/255-9760 *lgbt news, entertainment, personals & events, monthly*

■MEN'S CLUBS

➤ **Steamworks** [★PC] 2107 4th St (at Addison), Berkeley 510/845-8992 *24hrs, call for recorded info, live DJ wknds*

➤ **Watergarden** [★PC] 1010 The Alameda, San Jose 408/275-1215 *24hrs, great outdoor patio & jacuzzi, Latin TV*

■MEN'S SERVICES

➤ **The Connector** 415/626-8255, 800/626-8255 *900-50-50-500 from SF/LA/Sac/SD, 900-388-5847 (DV8-LTHR) Nationwide, MC/VISA/AE/DISC*

➤ **Megaphone San Francisco** 415/430-1199 *Voice Personals! Meet Hot Men in your area! FREE to Browse & Respond to voice ads. Use code 3087. Also try MEGAMATES.COM*

SF—Castro & Noe Valley

■ACCOMMODATIONS

18th Inn Castro [MW,GO] 415/252-7192 *Victorian guest house in the Castro*

24 Henry & Village House [M,NS,GO] 24 Henry St & 4080 18th St (btwn Sanchez & Noe) 415/864-5686, 800/900-5686 *B&B, some shared baths, 1-bdrm apt also available*

Albion House Inn [GF,NS] 135 Gough St (at Fell) 415/621-0896, 800/625-2466 or 800/400-8295 *full brkfst*

Beck's Motor Lodge [GF] 2222 Market St (at Sanchez) 415/621-8212 *in the heart of the Castro (ie, cruisy)*

THE PARKER
GUEST HOUSE

SAN FRANCISCO'S
PREMIER GAY GUEST HOUSE

- 21 rooms in the heart of the Gay Castro area
- Beautiful public rooms, gardens and steam spa
- Complete business traveler amenities & on-site parking
- Rates from $119— includes breakfast and wine social

"EDITOR'S CHOICE"
Out & About
1998-2003

520 Church Street, San Francisco, CA 94114
TOLL FREE 1-888-520-7275
www.parkerguesthouse.com   IGLTA

Tan Line Optional.

Photo by: Cliff Baker

Open:
Mon-Sat 8am-10pm
Sun 10am-6pm

TWO CONVENIENT LOCATIONS
3985 17th Street (at Castro)
  (415) 626-8222
2286 Union Street
  (415) 292-4490

Sun·Days TANNING CENTERS

Odyssey
THE PARTYZINE

San Francisco...
Los Angeles...
Hawaii...

FOR THE LATEST ISSUE...
SEND $3.00 ($5.00 CANADA)

Odyssey Magazine
7985 Santa Monica Blvd. #447
West Hollywood CA. 90046

LA: 323.874.8788
SF: 415.621.6514
E: ODYSSEYZ@PACBELL.NET

WWW.ODYSSEYMAGAZINE.NET

PHOTO: LATINJOCKS.COM   DESIGN: SIT & CLICK 323.270.5608

memorial day weekend SAN FRANCISCO

gus presents
COLOSSUS

may 23-25, 2004

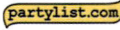

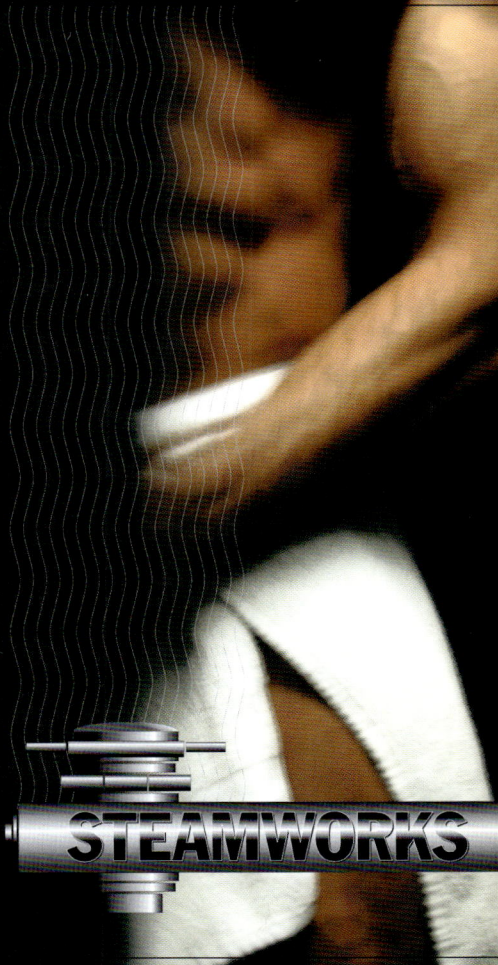

The San Francisco Bay Area's Unique Collection of Boutique Hotels & Escapes

Central Reservations for all Joie de Vivre Hotels
800.738.7477

These hotels are all distinctive Joie de Vivre properties.

www.jdvhospitality.com
Access Code: JV

Acqua Hotel

Mill Valley • 888.662.9555

Nob Hill Lambourne

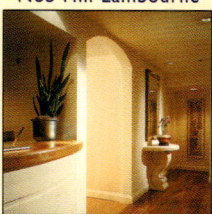

Nob Hill • 800.274.8466

escape, explore, experience

Commodore Hotel

Union Square • 800.338.6848

Hotel Del Sol

Marina District • 877.433.5765

Hotel Bijou

Union Square • 800.771.1022

Maxwell Hotel

Union Square • 888.734.6299

Savoy Hotel

Union Square • 800.227.4223

Phoenix Hotel

Civic Center • 800.248.9466

Archbishop's Mansion

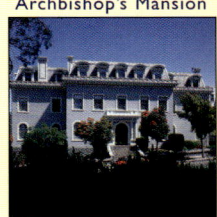

Alamo Square • 800.543.5820

Photos: Cesar Rubio, Nathanael Bennett, Russell Abrahams, Chris Opel

Reach California twice monthly.

Left Coast Nightlife, Reviews, Food & Interviews
SAN FRANCISCO • LOS ANGELES • PALM SPRINGS • SAN DIEGO

*The Hyatt Regency
San Francisco
The only Four Diamond Luxury
hotel on the upscale revitalized
waterfront, invites you to experience
San Francisco.*

*Located on the beautiful Embarcadero
waterfront, this is the perfect getaway
with 805 guestrooms. Just minutes
away from the city's best attractions,
world-class shopping and fabulous
entertainment.*

*Five metro stops away from the Castro.
Cost: $1.00. Take the Metro!*

*So join us this weekend…
the best of the Bay Area is just a
phone call away.*

Special ~ Make your reservation early!
Call 1-800 233-1234
and request the *"Pride Corporate Rate"*.
Our liberal cancellation policy is 24 hours
before your arrival. Please note that
weekend nights are Friday, Saturday and
Sunday. However, rate may be available
over other days too! This rate is based on
availability and higher rates may apply.

*The Nob Hill Hotel San Francisco
835 Hyde Street
San Francisco, CA 94109*
Toll Free at (1877) 662-4455 or (415) 203-2730
Web-www.nobhillhotel.com   Email-nobhill@nobhillhotel.com

1906 Victorian Boutique Hotel
Complimentary:
Continental Breakfast, Morning
Paper, Safety Deposit Boxes
Guest Computer Service with DSL,
Evening Wine & Sherry Tasting,
and Daily 24-Hour Fitness Club passes.

Rates starting from:

$89-$245

nightly

In room Microwave/Refrigerator/Coffee Makers
CD Clock Radio/Hair Dryer/Iron & Ironing Board
Reserved parking/Italian Restaurant w/Room service
Two line guest room phone w/ modem hook up and
Voice mail/Wake up calls, & Business Center w/DSL
Elegant Suites w/Jacuzzi Tubs & English Style Garden

Mention **Damron** *and receive our special* **$65.00** *Rate!!!*

California • USA

➤ **Belvedere House** [★MW,NS,GO] 598 Belvedere St (at 17th St) **415/731-6654, 877/226-3273** *wall-to-wall books, art & style, just up the hill from the heart of the Castro*

Casa Buena Vista [GF,NS] near Market & Castro **916/974-7409, 916/813-3119 (cell)** *rental apts*

Castillo Inn 48 Henry St **415/864-5111, 800/865-5112**

Castro Suites [M,NS,GO] 927 14th St (at Noe) **415/437-1783** *furnished apts*

Castro Victorian Vacation Rental [GS,GO] **415/621-3580** *furnished apts in the Castro*

Church Street B&B [GS,NS] 325 Church St (at 15th) **415/621-7600, 800/222-2160** *restored 1905 Edwardian*

Clipper House/ Noe Valley Victorian [NS] 164 Clipper St **415/821-4872** *self-contained garden flat in private home, weekly or monthly rental only*

Dolores Park Inn [GF,NS] 3641 17th St (btwn Church & Dolores) **415/621-0482** *Italianate Victorian mansion*

➤ **Edwardian San Francisco** [GF,NS] 1668 Market St (btwn Franklin & Gough) **415/864-1271, 888/864-8070** *some shared baths, hot tub, jacuzzi*

Friends [MW,GO] **415/826-5972** *B&B in private home*

Inn on Castro [MW,NS,GO] 321 Castro St (btwn 16th & 17th) **415/861-0321** *full brkfst*

Just Off Castro [M,GO] 4408 18th St **415/621-2915** *Victorian, some shared baths*

Le Grenier [MW] 347 Noe St (at 16th St) **415/864-4748** *suite*

Noe's Nest B&B [GF,NS] 3973 23rd St (at Noe) **415/821-0751** *kitchens, fireplace*

➤ **The Parker Guest House** [★M,NS,GO] 520 Church St (at 17th) **415/621-3222, 888/520-7275** *guest house complex w/ gardens, steam spa*

SF Noe Valley Tourist Apt [GS,NS,GO] 225 28th St (at Church) **415/695-9782, 415/312-0138 (cell)**

The Summit [MO,N,NS,GO] 433 Burnett Ave (at Gardenside Dr) **415/821-0612** *guest house, jacuzzi*

Terrace Place [M,GO] **415/241-0425** *guest suite*

Tom's Place [M,L,GO] 4510 18th St (at Douglass) **415/861-0516** *slinged play area*

Travelodge Central [GF] 1707 Market St (at Valencia) **415/621-6775, 800/578-7878**

➤ **The Willows Inn** [MW,NS,GO] 710 14th St (at Church) **415/431-4770** *'amenities, comfort, great location'*

■ BARS

The Bar on Castro [★M,NH,WC] 456 Castro St **415/626-7220** *3pm-2am, from noon wknds*

The Cafe [★MW,D,YC] 2367 Market St **415/861-3846** *2pm-2am, deck overlooking Castro & Market*

Cafe du Nord [GF,A,F,E] 2170 Market St (at Sanchez) **415/861-5016** *6pm-2am, live music, theme nights*

Daddy's [★M,NH,L] 440 Castro St **415/621-8732** *9am-2am, from 8am wknds, very cruisy, Red Hanky Beer Bust Tue*

The Detour [★M,NH] 2348 Market St (at Castro) *2pm-2am, hip cruise bar*

The Edge [★M,NH,L] 4149 18th St **415/863-4027** *noon-2am, classic cruise bar*

Harvey's [★MW,NH,E,WC] 500 Castro St **415/431-4278** *11am-2am, from 9am wknds, also restaurant*

Martuni's [★GS,NH,P] 4 Valencia St (at Market) **415/241-0205** *4pm-2am, lounge, great martinis*

Men's Room [M,NH] 3988 18th St **415/861-1310** *noon-2am*

The Metro [M,K] 3600 16th St (at Noe) **415/703-9751, 415/703-9750 (restaurant)** *11am-2am, overlooks Market St, also Chinese restaurant*

Did you know there is a NATIONAL memorial dedicated to all lives touched by AIDS, and it is right here in San Francisco's Golden Gate Park? For more information visit our website at www.AIDSmemorial.org, or call 415-750-8340.

A place for remembrance and renewal

THE NATIONAL AIDS MEMORIAL GROVE ENSURES THAT THE GLOBAL TRAGEDY OF AIDS WILL NEVER BE FORGOTTEN.

The Willows Inn

Comfort

In-room amenities

Great Castro Location

A room for every budget

Come see why our guests keep coming back

800-431-0277
www.WillowsSF.com
Innkeeper@willowsSF.com

Edwardian San Francisco Hotel

A small boutique hotel that possesses character with a distinctly European flavor

Recipient of the *New York Times' Budget Choice*.

☆ Centrally located six blocks east of Castro Street
☆ On San Francisco's main corridor of public transportation
☆ City tours available ☆ Hotel recently renovated
☆ Charming rooms ☆ Jacuzzi available in selected rooms
☆ Visa, Mastercard & American Express welcome

We are pleased to offer accommodations at reasonable rates featuring rooms with direct dial phone, cable TV, coffee and fresh flowers.

**1668 MARKET STREET • SAN FRANCISCO, CA 94102
TEL (415) 864-1271 • 1-888-864-8070 • FAX (415) 861-8116
www.edwardiansfhotel.com**

BELVEDERE HOUSE
Bed and Breakfast
A place to be and let be.

toll free 1.877.B and B SF
phone 1.415.731.6654
fax 1.415.681.0719
email
Info@GayBedAndBreakfast.net

---

598 Belvedere Street
(at 17th Street, right above the Castro)

10% DISCOUNT
for reservations four weeks in advance.*

Rooms from $85.00/night.
Stay one week, get ONE NIGHT FREE.*

Your very popular gay stay in the City.
Walk to the bars, restaurants, shops and all the fun.
Great views on Golden Gate Park, Golden Gate Bridge, Pacific Ocean.*

Full breakfast until noon.
Laundry service available.

California • USA

➤ **Midnight Sun** [★M,V] 4067 18th St **415/861-4186** *2pm-2am, from noon wknds*

The Mint [MW,K,V] 1942 Market St (at Buchanan) **415/626-4726** *11am-2am, popular karaoke bar nights, restaurant*

The Mix [M,NH] 4086 18th St **415/431-8616** *noon-2am, from 9am wknds, heated patio, wknd bbq*

Moby Dick's [M,NH,V] 4049 18th St

Pendulum [★M,MR-AF] 4146 18th St **415/863-4441** *6am-2am*

Pilsner Inn [★M,NH,YC] 225 Church St (at Market) **415/621-7058** *10am-2am, great patio*

SF Badlands [★M,NH,D,WC] 4121 18th St (at Castro) **415/626-9320** *2pm-2am, wknd beer busts*

The Transfer [M,NH] 198 Church St (at Market) **415/861-7499** *11am-2am, from 6am wknds*

Twin Peaks [M,OC,WC] 401 Castro St **415/864-9470** *noon-2am*

Whiskey Lounge/ Red Grill [★MW] 4063 18th St **415/255-2RED** *5pm-close, cozy bar upstairs, restaurant downstairs*

■ CAFES

Cafe Flore [★MW,BW] 2298 Market St **415/621-8579** *7am-11pm, great patio to see & be seen, come early for a seat*

Jumpin' Java 139 Noe St (at 14th St) **415/431-5282** *6am-10pm, from 7am wknds*

Just Desserts [MW] 248 Church St **415/626-5774** *7am-10pm, from 8am wknds, delicious cakes, quiet patio*

Orbit Room Cafe 1900 Market St (at Laguna) **415/252-9525** *8am-1am, till 2am Fri-Sat, till midnight Sun, great view of Market St, also bar*

Samovar 498 Sanchez (at 18th St) **415/626-4700** *early morning to late eve, tea lounge*

Starbucks [B] 4094 18th St **415/626-6263** *5:30am-10pm, till 11pm wknds, always a bear jamboree*

SF—Castro & Noe Valley • California

Sweet Inspiration 2239 Market St **415/621-8664** *popular wknd nights, fabulous desserts*

■ RESTAURANTS

2223 Market [★WC] 2223 Market St **415/431-0692** *dinner, brunch wknds, full bar*

Anchor Oyster Bar [MW,BW] 579 Castro St (at 19th) **415/431-3990**

Bagdad Cafe [MW] 2295 Market St **415/621-4434** *24hrs, American*

Blue [★BW] 2337 Market St (btwn Castro & Noe) **415/863-2583** *11:30am-11pm, wknd brunch, home-cooking served w/ style*

Cafe Cuvee [GO] 2073 Market St (at 14th St) **415/621-7488** *dinner Tue-Sat, brunch wknds, clsd Mon*

Caffe Luna Piena [★MW] 558 Castro St (btwn 18th & 19th) **415/621-2566** *lunch & dinner, clsd Mon, patio*

China Court [BW] 599 Castro **415/626-5358** *lunch Mon-Fri, dinner nightly*

Chloe's [★] 1399 Church St (at 26th St) **415/648-4116** *8am-3pm, come early for wknd brunch*

Chow [★] 215 Church St **415/552-2469** *11am-11pm, till midnight Th-Sat, eclectic & affordable*

Cove Cafe [MW,WC] 434 Castro St **415/626-0462** *7am-10pm*

Eric's Chinese Restaurant [★] 1500 Church St (at 27th St) **415/282-0919** *11am-9pm*

Home [★] 2100 Market St (at Church) **415/503-0333** *American*

Hot 'N Hunky [MW] 4039 18th St **415/621-6365** *11am-midnight, burgers*

It's Tops 1801 Market St (at Octavia) **415/431-6395** *8am-3pm, 8pm-3am, vintage diner*

La Tasca [GO] 1760 Market St (near Gough) **415/863-3516** *open till 1am, wknd brunch, tapas menus*

Lalo's 2247 Market St **415/621-5256** *Mexican, full bar, popular Sun afternoon w/ $2 Sundays & go-go boys*

M&L Market (May's) 691 14th St (at Market) **415/431-7044** *11:30am-4pm, clsd Sun, great huge sandwiches*

Ma Tante Sumi [MW] 4243 18th St (at Diamond) **415/552-6663** *5:30pm-10pm, cont'l/ Japanese*

Mecca [★DS,WC] 2029 Market St (at Dolores) **415/621-7000** *dinner from 5:30pm, American, swanky bar, DJ nightly, drag show Sun, valet parking*

Orphan Andy's [GO] 3991 17th St **415/864-9795** *24hrs, diner*

Pasta Pomodoro [★MW] 2304 Market St **415/558-8123** *open till midnight, inexpensive Italian; also 24th & Noe location*

Patio Cafe [MW] 531 Castro St **415/621-4640** *enclosed patio, popular brunch*

Red Grill 4063 18th St **415/255-2733** *steak & seafood, also Whiskey Lounge upstairs*

The Sausage Factory [MW,BW] 517 Castro St **415/626-1250** *noon-1am, pizza & pasta*

Sparky's 242 Church St (at Market) **415/626-8666** *24hrs, diner, popular after-hours*

Tin-Pan Asian Bistro [★] 2251 Market St **415/565-0733** *11am-11pm, wknd brunch, sake cocktails*

Tita's Hale'aine [★WC] 3870 17th St (btwn Sanchez & Noe) **415/626-2477** *dinner Tue-Sun, lunch wknds, traditional Hawaiian, plenty veggie*

Welcome Home [★MW,BW] 464 Castro St **415/626-3600** *8am-11pm, home-style*

Zuni Cafe [★] 1658 Market St (at Franklin) **415/552-2522** *clsd Mon, upscale cont'l/ Mediterranean, full bar*

■ ENTERTAINMENT & RECREATION

Castro Country Club [MW] 4058 18th St **415/552-6102** *noon-11pm, from 10am wknds, alcohol & drug-free club*

Pink Triangle Park nr Market & Castro *'in remembrance of lgbt victims of the Nazi regime'*

California • USA

■ BOOKSTORES

A Different Light [★] 489 Castro St **415/431-0891** *10am-10pm, lgbt bookstore & queer info clearinghouse, cruisy late nights & wknds*

Aardvark Books 227 Church St **415/552-6733** *10:30am-10:30pm, mostly used, good lgbt section*

Books, Inc [WC] 2275 Market St **415/864-6777** *10am-11pm, lgbt section*

Get Lost 1825 Market St (at Guerrero) **415/437-0529** *10am-7pm, till 6pm Sat, 11am-5pm Sun, stylish travel book store, lgbt section*

■ RETAIL SHOPS

A Taste of Leather 2370 Market (near Castro) **415/552-4500** *noon-8pm, 10am-10pm wknds*

Best in Show 300 Sanchez St (at 16th St) **415/863-7387** *pet supplies*

Cold Steel America 2377 Market St (at 17th St) **415/621-7233** *piercing & tattoo studio; also 1783 Haight St, 933-7233*

Does Your Father Know? 548 Castro St **415/241-9865** *9:30am-10pm, till 11pm Fri-Sat, 9am-9pm Sun, lgbt gifts & videos*

Does Your Mother Know? 4079 18th St **415/864-3160** *9:30am-10pm, cards & T-shirts*

Don't Panic 541 Castro St **415/553-8989** *10am-10pm, 11am-9pm Sun, T-shirts, gifts & more*

Gotham Body Piercing 3991 17th St **415/701-1970** *noon-8pm, 11am-6pm Sun*

Image Leather 2199 Market St (at Sanchez) **415/621-7551** *9am-10pm, 11am-7pm Sun, custom leather clothing, accessories & toys*

Just for Fun [WC] 3982 24th St (at Noe) **415/285-4068** *9am-8pm, till 7pm Sat, 10am-6pm Sun, gift shop*

California • USA

National Product 1845 Market St (at Guerrero) **415/255-1920** *clsd Mon-Tue, 'art & unusual gifts,' great cards*

Nomad 1745 Market (at Valencia) **415/563-7771** *noon-7pm, clsd Wed, piercing (walk-in), jewelry*

Rolo 2351 Market St **415/431-4545** *11am-8pm, till 7pm Sun, designer labels; also 450 Castro location, 415/626-7171*

Under One Roof [WC] 549 Castro **415/252-9430** *11am-7pm, 100% donated to AIDS relief*

GYMS & HEALTH CLUBS

Gold's Gym Castro [★MW] 2301 Market St **415/626-4488** *day passes available*

➤ **Muscle System** [★MO] 2275 Market St **415/863-4700** *day passes available*

MEN'S CLUBS

➤ **Eros** 2051 Market St (btwn Church & Dolores) **415/864-3767** *safer sex club, theme nights, massage available*

EROTICA

Auto-Erotica 4077-A 18th St, 2nd flr **415/861-5787**

➤ **Castro Gulch** 2353 Market St (at Castro) **415/934-8524** *11am-midnight, toys, videos, men's sexy clothing, fetish items*

➤ **Jaguar** 4057 18th St **415/863-4777**

Le Salon 4126 18th St **415/552-4213**

The MMO (Mercury Mail Order) 4084 18th St **415/621-1188** *leather, toys & more*

Romantasy Exquisite Corsetry **415/585-0760** *call for appt, corsets & fetish clothing*

CRUISY AREAS

Collingwood Park [AYOR] (btwn 18th & 19th Sts) *Castro merry-go-round, after bars close*

Enjoy the best!
Clean, comfortable.
Friendly, diverse crowd.
Steamroom, sauna & showers.
Professional massage.

EROS
2051 Market St.
415 864-3767
www.erossf.com

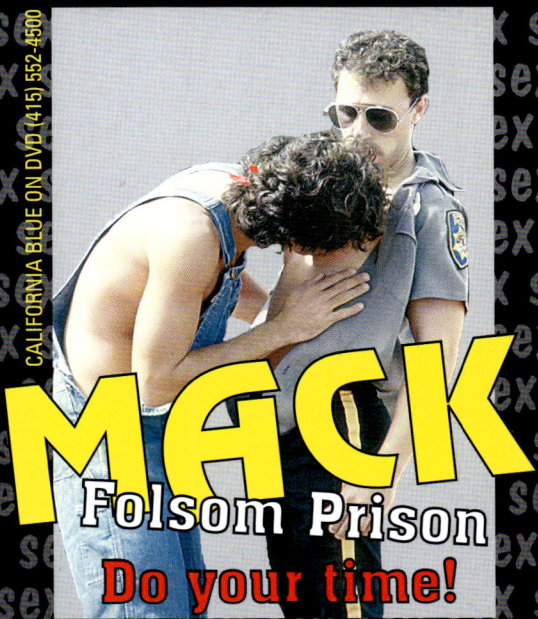

San Francisco

Howard Johnson
EXPRESS INN

385 9th St.
(415) 431-5131
(800) 446-4656

- FREE Continental Breakfast
- FREE HBO
- FREE Microwave/Refrigerator
- Jacuzzi Rooms available

Centrally located in San Francisco
(South of Market)
Walking distance from bars and clubs
Easy transportation

Newly Renovated!

SF—South of Market • California

SF—South of Market

■ACCOMMODATIONS

Argent Hotel [GF] 50 3rd St
415/974-6400, 800/974-7477
sauna

➤ **Howard Johnson Express Inn**
[GS,WC] 385 9th St (at Harrison)
415/431-5131, 800/446-4656
motel

The Mosser Hotel [GS,NS]
54 4th St (btwn Market & Mission)
415/986-4400, 800/227-3804
1913 landmark, also restaurant & full bar

Ramada Market St [GF,WC]
1231 Market St (btwn 8th & 9th)
415/626-8000, 800/227-4747

➤ **Renoir Hotel** [GS,NS,WC]
45 McAllister St (at Market St)
415/626-5200, 800/576-3388
boutique-style

■BARS

The Eagle Tavern [★M,L,E] 398 12th St
(at Harrison) 415/626-0880 *noon-2am, great beer bust Sun, patio*

Hole in the Wall Saloon [★M,NH,L]
289 8th St (at Folsom) 415/431-4695
noon-2am, 'a nasty little biker bar'

Loading Dock [M,L]
1525 Mission (btwn 11th & S Van Ness)
415/864-1525 *8pm-2am Th-Sun, uniform bar w/ strict dress code*

Lone Star Saloon [★M,B,L]
1354 Harrison St (btwn 9th & 10th)
415/863-9999 *noon-2am, from 9am wknds, patio, bear bar, beer bust wknds*

My Place [M,NH,L] 1225 Folsom St
(btwn 8th & 9th) 415/863-2329
noon-2am, very cruisy

Powerhouse [M,NH,L] 1347 Folsom St
(at Dore Alley) 415/552-8689 *4pm-2am, theme nights, popular wknds w/ DJ, patio, cruisy*

Standard Rooms $89-$149   Suites $175-$250

- *Gay-friendly boutique hotel in historic landmark building*
- *Near cable cars, Union Square, theaters and shopping*
- *Walking distance to Folsom St., SOMA bars/clubs, Castro 15 min.*
- *135 renovated rooms, café, 2 bars, Brazilian restaurant*
- *Best view of Gay Pride Parade from Market Street rooms and suites (last Sunday June)*
- *Ideal for Folsom St. Fair leather event (last weekend Sept.), Castro Street Fair (1st weekend Oct.) and Halloween in the Castro (Oct. 31)*

Renoir Hotel
San Francisco

45 McAllister At Market St., San Francisco, CA 94102
www.renoirhotel.com • 800-576-3388 • Fax 415-626-0916   **IGLTA**

California • USA

■ NIGHTCLUBS

1015 Folsom [★GS,D,$] 1015 Folsom St (at 6th) **415/431-1200** *10pm-4:30am, call for events*

Asia SF [★GS,D,MR-A,S,$] 201 9th St (at Howard) **415/255-2742** *10:30pm-close Wed-Sat, theme nights, go-go boys, also Cal-Asian restaurant w/ en-drag service 5pm-10pm*

Endup [M,D,MR] 401 6th St (at Harrison) **415/357-0827** *clsd Tue, theme nights, popular Sun mornings*

Fag Fridays [★M,D,YC,$] 401 6th St (at The Endup) **415/263-4850** *10pm-5:30am Fri*

First Sunday [GS,D] 1190 Folsom St (at The Cat Club) *8pm-2am 1st Sun only, lounge-y, 'the only lgbt club you could bring your grandmother to'*

Futura [★M,D,MR-L,S,$] **415/665-6715** *call for times & location, hot (¡muy caliente!) dancers*

Mass [M,D,$] 1015 Folsom St (at 6th St) **415/431-1200 (1015 Folsom #)** *6pm-midnight 1st Sun*

Mezzanine [GS,D,MR,TG,E,WC,$] 444 Jessie (at Mint) **415/820-9669** *10pm-7am, clsd Mon-Wed, 'fusion of clubbing & art,' theme nights*

The Stud [★MW,D,YC] 399 9th St (at Harrison) **415/252-7883** (info line), **415/863-6623** *5pm-2am, theme nights, outrageous Trannyshack Tue*

Sugar [★M,D,A,YC] 399 9th St (at The Stud) **415/252-7883** (Stud #) *9pm-5am Sat, great music & wall-to-wall alternababes*

Trannyshack [★M,D,TG,GO] 399 9th St (at The Stud) **415/863-6623** *10pm-3am Tue, weekly party for trannies & their friends & admirers*

■ CAFES

Brain Wash [★E,BW] 1122 Folsom St (at 7th St) **415/861-3663, 415/431-9274** *7am-11pm, laundromat & cafe*

XXX DVD & VIDEO
NO DEPOSIT RENTALS
SEX TOYS
FALCON GEAR
LEATHER
PRIDE ITEMS
PREVIEW BOOTHS
EROTIC MAGAZINES

CRUISE ZONE AHEAD
SF'S HOTTEST ARCADE EXPERIENCE!

THE GULCH
947 Folsom 415.495.6402
2352 Market 415.934.8524
ALSO VISIT
960 Folsom 415.543.2124
1020 Geary 415.776.5940

www.sincityvideo.com

SF—South of Market • California

Pick Me Up 298 9th St (at Folsom) **415/864-7425** *6:30am-7pm, from 8am Sat, 10am-5pm Sun*

■ RESTAURANTS

Ananda Fuara 1298 Market St (at 9th) **415/621-1994** *8am-8pm, till 3pm Wed, clsd Sun, vegetarian*

Bacar Restaurant & Wine Salon [E,WC] 448 Brannan St (btwn 3rd & 4th) **415/904-4100**

Boulevard [★] 1 Mission St (at Steuart) **415/543-6084** *lunch Mon-Fri & dinner daily, one of SF's finest*

Butter 354 11th St (at Folsom) **415/863-5964** *6pm-2am, clsd Sun-Mon, 'white trash bistro', full bar*

Fringale [WC] 570 4th St (btwn Bryant & Brannan) **415/543-0573** *lunch & dinner, clsd Sun, French bistro*

Hawthorne Lane 22 Hawthorne St (btwn 2nd & 3rd, off Howard) **415/777-9779** *dinner nightly, lunch Mon-Fri*

Le Charm 315 5th St (at Folsom) **415/546-6128** *lunch & dinner, dinner only wknds*

Lulu [★WC] 816 Folsom St (at 4th St) **415/495-5775** *lunch & dinner, upscale Mediterranean, full bar*

Manora's Thai Cuisine 1600 Folsom (at 12th) **415/861-6224** *lunch & dinner*

Mary's 12th & Folsom [WC] 1582 Folsom St (at 12th St) **415/626-1985** *11:30am-10:30pm, 9am-midnight wknds, full bar*

The Slanted Door [★R] 100 Brannan **415/861-8032** *Vietnamese*

Tu Lan 8 6th St (at Market) **415/626-0927** *lunch & dinner, Vietnamese, dicey neighborhood but delicious (& cheap) food*

Woodward's Garden [WC] 1700 Mission St (at Duboce) **415/621-7122** *dinner seating at 6pm & 8pm, clsd Sun-Mon*

California • USA

■RETAIL SHOPS

A Taste of Leather 1339 Folsom (btwn 9th & 10th) **415/252-9166, 800/367-0786** *noon-8pm, till midnight Fri-Sat*

Dandelion [GO] 55 Potrero Ave (at Alameda St) **415/436-9500, 888/548-1968** *10am-6pm, clsd Sun-Mon, gifts, books, erotica & more*

Leather Etc 1201 Folsom St (at 8th St) **415/864-7558** *10:30am-7pm, 11am-6pm Sat, noon-5pm Sun*

Mr S Leather 310 7th St (at Folsom) **415/863-7764** *11am-7pm, noon-6pm Sun, erotic goods, custom leather & latex*

Stompers 323 10th St (at Folsom) **415/255-6422** *11am-7pm, till 6pm Sun, boots, cigars & gloves*

Stormy Leather 1158 Howard St (btwn 7th & 8th) **415/626-1672** *noon-7pm, leather, latex, toys & magazines*

■GYMS & HEALTH CLUBS

Gold's Gym San Francisco [★] 9th & Brannan **415/552-4653** *day passes available*

■MEN'S CLUBS

➤ **Blow Buddies** [★MO,LV,PC,GO] 933 Harrison (btwn 5th & 6th) **415/777-4323** *open late Th-Sun*

➤ **Mack Folsom Prison** [L,PC] 1285 Folsom (at 9th) **415/252-1221** (info line), **415/844-3959** *open nightly, 24hrs wknds, fetish parties*

Power Exchange Mainstation [18+,$] 74 Otis St (btwn S Van Ness & Gough) **415/487-9944** *9pm-4am, till 6am wknds, 4 flrs*

■EROTICA

➤ **City Entertainment** 960 Folsom St (at 5th) **415/543-2124** *24hrs wknds*

➤ **Folsom Gulch** 947 Folsom (btwn 5th & 6th) **415/495-6402** *24hrs wknds*

Golden Gate Video #4 99 6th St (at Mission) **415/495-5573**

■CRUISY AREAS

Folsom St [AYOR] btwn 5th & 6th *late*

SF—Polk Street Area

■ACCOMMODATIONS

➤ **Essex Hotel** [GF,NS] 684 Ellis St **415/474-4664, 800/443-7739** (in CA)

Hostelling International—San Francisco City Center [GF,NS,GO] 685 Ellis St (at Larkin) **415/474-5721, 800/909-4776** *hostel*

The Monarch Hotel [GF] 1015 Geary St (at Polk) **415/673-5232, 800/777-3210** *completely renovated*

Nob Hill Motor Inn [GF] 1630 Pacific Ave (at Van Ness Ave) **415/775-8160, 800/343-6900** *hotel*

The Phoenix Hotel [★GF,SW] 601 Eddy St (at Larkin) **415/776-1380, 800/248-9466** *1950s style motor lodge*

■BARS

The Cinch [M,NH,WC] 1723 Polk St (at Clay) **415/776-4162** *6am-2am, patio, lots of pool tables & no attitude*

Club Rendez-Vous [M,S] 1312 Polk St (at Bush) **415/309-2582** *9am-2am*

Edinburgh Castle [GF,NH,E] 950 Geary St (at Polk) **415/885-4074** *5pm-2am, mostly straight but rockin' Scottish pub w/ single malts, beer, darts & authentic fish & chips*

Gangway [M,NH] 841 Larkin St (btwn Geary & O'Farrell) **415/776-6828** *6am-2am*

Jezebel's Joint [GS,D,A,TG,S] 510 Larkin (at Turk) **415/345-9832** *4pm-2am, from 9pm Sat, theme nights*

Kimo's [M,NH,DS] 1351 Polk St (at Pine) **415/885-4535** *8am-2am, live bands upstairs [GS,A,YC]*

Lush Lounge [★GS,NH,E,WC] 1092 Post (at Polk) **415/771-2022** *4pm-2am, from 3pm Fri-Sun, martini bar & piano lounge*

Reflections [M,NH] 1160 Polk St (near Sutter) **415/771-6262** *6am-2am*

■NIGHTCLUBS

Divas [M,NH,D,TG,S] 1081 Post St (at Larkin) **415/928-6006, 415/474-DIVA** *6am-2am, TS/TVs & their admirers*

the *Essex*
❖ HOTEL ❖

With a European charm and tradition, the Essex is only one block from Polk Street. Close to shopping, bars, restaurants, theatres, and the City's gay life!

415-474-4664

single from $69 and up

1-800-453-7739 USA

1-800-443-7739 CA

684 Ellis Street · San Francisco, CA · 94109

California • USA

N' Touch [M,NH,D,MR-A,S] 1548 Polk St (at Sacramento) **415/441-8413** *3pm-2am, also Club NRG Th, go-go boys Th-Sat*

Tango Tango [GS,K] 1550 California, 2nd flr (at Polk) **415/775-0442** *4pm-2am*

■CAFES

Quetzal [★E,V,BW] 1234 Polk St (at Sutter) **415/673-4181** *6am-11pm, internet access, roasts own coffee*

■RESTAURANTS

Antica Trattoria 2400 Polk St (at Union) **415/928-5797** *dinner Tue-Sun, Italian*

California Culinary Academy [★] 625 Polk St (at Turk) **415/771-3500** *lunch & dinner, cooking school where future top chefs serve up what they've learned*

El Super Burrito 1200 Polk St (at Sutter) **415/771-9700** *9am-11pm*

Grubstake II [MW,BW] 1525 Pine St (at Polk) **415/673-8268** *5pm-4am, from 10am wknds, diner*

Tai Chi [★] 2031 Polk St (at Pacific) **415/441-6758** *lunch Mon-Fri, dinner nightly, Chinese*

■BOOKSTORES

A Clean Well Lighted Place For Books 601 Van Ness Ave (at Turk) **415/441-6670** *10am-11pm, till 9pm Sun, general, lgbt section*

■EROTICA

➤ **Frenchy's** 1020 Geary St (at Polk) **415/776-5940** *24hrs, videos, magazines, toys*

Good Vibrations [W] 1620 Polk St (btwn Sacramento & Clay) **415/345-0400** *11am-7pm, till 8pm Fri-Sat, clean, well-lighted sex toy store, also mail order*

➤ **The Locker Room Bookstore** 1038 Polk St (at Post) **415/775-9076**

The Magazine 920 Larkin St (at Geary) **415/441-7737**

■CRUISY AREAS

Polk St [AYOR] btwn Geary & California Sts *hustlers*

SF—Downtown & North Beach

■ACCOMMODATIONS

Allison Hotel [GF] 417 Stockton St (at Sutter) **415/986-8737, 800/628-6456** *some shared baths*

Amsterdam Hotel [GF] 749 Taylor St (at Sutter) **415/673-3277, 800/637-3444** *European-style*

Andrews Hotel [GF] 624 Post St (at Taylor) **415/563-6877, 800/926-3739** *Victorian hotel, also Italian restaurant*

Canterbury Hotel [GF,WC] 750 Sutter St (at Taylor) **415/474-6464, 800/227-4788** *also Murray's Glasshouse restaurant & bar*

Carlton Hotel [GF] 1075 Sutter (at Larkin) **415/673-0242, 800/922-7586** *also restaurant*

Cartwright Hotel on Union Square [GF] 524 Sutter St (at Powell) **415/421-2865, 800/919-9779** *B&B-inn on Union Square*

The Commodore Hotel [GF] 825 Sutter St (at Jones) **415/923-6800, 800/338-6848** *also popular Red Room lounge*

Dakota Hotel [GF] 606 Post St (at Taylor) **415/931-7475** *near Union Square*

Galleria Park Hotel [GF,WC] 191 Sutter St (at Kearny) **415/781-3060, 800/792-9639** *live jazz Wed-Sun*

Grand Hyatt San Francisco [GF] 345 Stockton St (at Sutter) **415/398-1234, 800/233-1234** *restaurant & lounge, gym*

Halcyon Hotel [GS,GO] 649 Jones St (at Post) **415/929-8033, 800/627-2396**

Harbor Court Hotel [GF,WC] 165 Steuart St (btwn Howard & Mission) **415/882-1300, 800/346-0555** *in the heart of the Financial District, gym*

Hostelling International—San Francisco Downtown [GS,WC] 312 Mason St (at Geary) **415/788-5604, 800/909-4776** *hostel, shared baths, open kitchen, internet access*

SF—Downtown & North Beach

Hotel Bijou [GS,NS,WC] 111 Mason St (at Eddy) **415/771-1200, 800/771-1022**

Hotel Cosmo [GF] 761 Post St (at Jones) **415/673-6040, 800/252-7466**

Hotel Diva [GF] 440 Geary (at Mason) **415/885-0200, 800/553-1900** *also Italian restaurant*

Hotel Griffon [GF,WC] 155 Steuart St (at Mission) **415/495-2100, 800/321-2201** *gym, also restaurant, bistro/ cont'l*

Hotel Monaco [GF] 501 Geary St (at Taylor) **415/292-0100, 800/214-4220** *pets ok, also full bar*

Hotel Nikko San Francisco [GS,SW,NS,WC] 222 Mason St **415/394-1111, 800/645-5687**

Hotel Palomar [GS] 12 4th St (at Market) **415/348-1111, 877/294-9711** *boutique hotel*

Hotel Triton [GF,WC] 342 Grant Ave (at Bush) **415/394-0500, 800/433-6611** *designer theme rms*

Hotel Vintage Court [GF,NS,WC] 650 Bush St (at Powell) **415/392-4666, 800/654-1100** *also world-famous 5-star Masa's restaurant, French*

➤ **Hyatt Regency San Francisco** [GF] 5 Embarcadero Center (at California) **415/788-1234, 800/233-1234** *luxury waterfront hotel*

Juliana Hotel [GF,WC] 590 Bush St (at Stockton) **415/392-2540, 800/328-3880** *featured on 'Lifestyles of the Rich & Famous'*

King George Hotel [GF,F,WC] 334 Mason St (at Geary) **415/781-5050, 800/288-6005** *also The Bread & Honey Tearoom*

Maxwell Hotel [GF] 386 Geary St (at Mason) **415/986-2000, 888/734-6299** *1908 art deco masterpiece, full brkfst*

Monticello Inn [GF,F] 127 Ellis St (at Powell) **415/392-8800, 800/669-7777**

➤ **Nob Hill Hotel** [GS,NS,WC] 835 Hyde St (btwn Bush & Sutter) **415/885-2987, 877/662-4455** *European-style hotel, jacuzzi*

Nob Hill Lambourne [GF] 725 Pine St (at Powell) **415/433-2287, 800/274-8466**

Prescott Hotel [GF] 545 Post St (btwn Taylor & Mason) **415/563-0303, 800/283-7322** *small luxury hotel*

Ramada Union Square [GF,WC] 345 Taylor St (at Ellis) **415/673-2332, 800/228-2828** *restaurant & full bar*

Savoy Hotel [GF] 580 Geary St (at Jones) **415/441-2700, 800/227-4223** *also popular restaurant & bar*

Serrano Hotel [GF,WC] 405 Taylor St (at O'Farrell) **415/885-2500, 877/294-9709**

Sir Francis Drake Hotel [GF] 450 Powell St (at Sutter) **415/392-7755, 800/227-5480** *also restaurant & Starlight Room*

The Touchstone Hotel [GF,WC] 480 Geary St (btwn Mason & Taylor) **415/771-1600, 800/524-1888**

Tuscan Inn [GF,WC] 425 North Point St (at Mason) **415/561-1100, 888/206-7718**

Villa Florence Hotel [GF] 225 Powell St (at Geary) **415/397-7700, 800/553-4411** *also restaurant*

The York Hotel [GS,NS,WC] 940 Sutter St (at Leavenworth) **415/885-6800, 800/808-9675** *boutique hotel, also cabaret*

■ BARS

Aunt Charlie's Lounge [M,NH,DS] 133 Turk St (at Taylor) **415/441-2922** *noon-midnight, 10am-2am wknds, drag shows wknds*

Ginger's Trois [M,NH,P] 246 Kearny St (at Sutter) **415/989-0282** *10am-10pm, from 2pm Sat, clsd Sun*

Hob Nob [M,NH] 700 Geary St (at Leavenworth) **415/771-9866** *6am-2am*

Plush Room [★GS,C,WC] 940 Sutter St (at York Hotel) **415/885-6800, 800/808-9675** *cabaret w/ world-class performers*

Damron Men's Travel Guide 2004

California • USA

■NIGHTCLUBS

➤ **Fresh at Ruby Skye—Pour Homme** [M,D] 420 Mason (at Geary) **415/693-0777** *6pm-midnight Sun, T-dance, check listings for dates*

■CAFES

Caffe Trieste [★] 601 Vallejo St **415/392-6739** *get a taste of the real North Beach (past & present) & a great cappuccino*

■RESTAURANTS

Cafe Claude [E,BW] 7 Claude (near Bush & Kearny) **415/392-3505** *11:30am-close, clsd Sun, live jazz wknds, as close to Paris as you can get in SF*

Dottie's True Blue Cafe [GO] 522 Jones St (at Geary) **415/885-2767** *7:30am-3pm, clsd Tue-Wed, great brkfst*

Mario's Bohemian Cigar Store Cafe [BW] 566 Columbus Ave (at Union) **415/362-0536** *great foccacia sandwiches*

Masa's [★WC] 650 Bush St (at Hotel Vintage Court) **415/989-7154** *dinner Tue-Sat, world-famous 5-star French restaurant*

Max's on the Square [★] 398 Geary St (at Mason) **415/646-8600** *lunch & dinner, seafood, full bar*

Millennium 246 McAllister St (at Hyde, at the Abigail Hotel) **415/487-9800** *dinner only, Euro-Mediterranean, upscale vegetarian*

Moose's [★] 1652 Stockton (btwn Filbert & Union) **415/989-7800** *upscale bistro menu*

Original Joe's 144 Taylor (btwn Turk & Eddy) **415/775-4877** *lunch & dinner, Italian, since 1937, also art deco cocktail lounge*

■BOOKSTORES

City Lights Bookstore 261 Columbus Ave, North Beach (at Pacific) **415/362-8193** *10am-midnight, historic beatnik bookstore, many progressive titles, lgbt section, whole flr dedicated to poetry*

Nob Hill Adult Theatre
"Famous From The Day We Opened"

www.nobhilltheatre.com

Erotic Dancers!

San Francisco's premier LIVE NUDE MALE entertainment venue, celebrating 35 years! Over 25 shows daily from 12 noon 'til past midnight.

Online Theatre!

www.nobhilltheatre.com

Online members get a FULL VIEW of our theatre. High quality 8-cam Internet streams of the pre-show, stage, locker-room, showers, and our WILD Underground Sex Studio. *PLUS* hot pics and chat!

Adult Arcade!

75 channel adult video arcade with hot action and horny guys.

$10 OFF Before Noon
$5 All Night Parking @ Bush & Stockton

729 Bush St. @ Powell
More Info: 415.781.9468

California • USA

RETAIL SHOPS
Billy Blue 54 Geary (at Grant) **415/781-2111, 800/772-BLUE** *10am-6pm, clsd Sun*

EROTICA
Circle J Video 369 Ellis St (at Jones) **415/474-6995**

➤ **Club 220** [GO] 220 Jones St (at Turk) **415/673-3384** *male dancers, Asian night Sun*

➤ **Nob Hill Theater** [MO] 729 Bush St (at Powell) **415/989-8552** *8am-2:30am, male dancers, over 25 shows daily, 8 live hot internet video feeds*

SF—Mission District

ACCOMMODATIONS
Andora Inn [MW,F,NS,GO] 2438 Mission (btwn 20th & 21st) **415/282-0337, 800/967-9219** *near Castro*

➤ **The Inn San Francisco** [GF,NS] 943 S Van Ness Ave (btwn 20th & 21st) **415/641-0188, 800/359-0913** *Victorian mansion, hot tub*

BARS
El Rio [GS,NH,MR-L,E] 3158-A Mission St (at Cesar Chavez) **415/282-3325** *3pm-2am, till midnight Mon, patio*

Lexington Club [★W,NH,GO] 3464 19th St (at Lexington) **415/863-2052** *3pm-2am*

Phone Booth [MW,NH] 1398 S Van Ness Ave (at 25th) **415/648-4683** *noon-2am*

Sadie's Flying Elephant [GS,NH] 491 Potrero (at Mariposa) **415/551-7988** *4pm-2am, K'vetsh queer open mike 9pm 1st Sun*

Wild Side West [GS,WC] 424 Cortland, Bernal Heights (at Bennington) **415/647-3099** *1pm-2am, patio, magic garden*

NIGHTCLUBS
26 Mix [GS,D,YC] 3024 Mission St (btwn 26th & Cesar Chavez) **415/826-7378** *5pm-2am, intimate dance club*

The Inn San Francisco

Distinct San Franciscan hospitality.

Gracious 1872 Victorian Mansion.

Historic residential neighborhood.

Antiques, fresh flowers, beverages.

Spa tubs, hot tubs, fireplaces.

Sundeck, lovely English Garden.

Full Buffet Breakfast.

943 SOUTH VAN NESS AVENUE, SAN FRANCISCO, CA 94110
(415)641-0188 • (800)359-0913 • FAX: (415)641-1701
E-MAIL: innkeeper@innsf.com
www.innsf.com

SF—Mission District • California

Club Papi SF [M,D,MR-L] 550 Barneveld (at Space 550, 2 blks off Bayview) **415/675-9763** *monthly party, call for dates*

Esta Noche [M,D,MR-L,TG,S] 3079 16th St (at Mission) **415/861-5757** *1pm-2am, salsa & disco in a classic Tijuana dive*

Sundance Saloon [★M,D,CW,GO] 550 Barneveld (at Space 550, 2 blks off Bayshore Blvd) **415/820-1403** *6pm-11pm Sun, lessons at 6pm, DJ from 7:30pm*

■ CAFES

Cafe Commons [WC] 3161 Mission St (btwn Cesar Chavez & Valencia) **415/282-2928** *6am-5pm, from 8am wknds, sandwiches, patio*

Farleys 1315 18th St (at Texas St, Potrero Hill) **415/648-1545** *7am-10pm, from 8am wknds*

■ RESTAURANTS

42 Degrees 499 Illinois St, China Basin (near 16th St & 3rd) **415/777-5558** *Wed-Sat only, jazz supper club, full bar*

Charanga [★BW,WC] 2351 Mission St (at 20th St) **415/282-1813** *lunch & dinner, clsd Sun-Mon, tapas*

Delfina 3621 18th St (at Dolores) **415/552-4055** *5:30pm-10pm, excellent Tuscan cuisine*

El Farolito [★] 2777 Mission St (at 24th) **415/824-7877** *delicious, cheap burritos & more*

Firecracker [★] 1007 1/2 Valencia St (at 21st) **415/642-3470** *Chinese*

Herbivore [BW] 983 Valencia (near 21st St) **415/826-5657** *11am-10pm, till 11pm wknds, vegan*

Just For You [★MW] 1453 18th St, Potrero Hill (btwn Missouri & Connecticut) **415/647-3033** *7am-2pm, 8am-3pm wknds, Southern brkfst*

Klein's Delicatessen [W,BW] 501 Connecticut St (at 20th St, Potrero Hill) **415/821-9149** *7am-7pm, 8am-5pm Sun, sandwiches & salads, patio*

Pancho Villa [BW,WC] 3071 16th St (btwn Mission & Valencia) **415/864-8840** *10am-midnight; also El Toro at 18th St & Valencia*

Pauline's Pizza Pie [★MW,BW] 260 Valencia St (btwn 14th & Duboce) **415/552-2050** *5pm-10pm, clsd Sun-Mon, gourmet pizza*

Picaro [BW,WC] 3120 16th St (at Valencia) **415/431-4089** *dinner only, Spanish tapas bar*

Slow Club [WC] 2501 Mariposa (at Hampshire) **415/241-9390** *lunch Mon-Fri, dinner Mon-Sat, wknd brunch, full bar*

Ti-Couz [BW,WC] 3108 16th St (at Valencia) **415/252-7373** *11am-11pm, from 10am wknds, dinner & dessert crepes*

Yamo Thai Kitchen 3406 18th St (at Mission) **415/553-8911** *11am-9:30pm, clsd Sun*

■ ENTERTAINMENT & RECREATION

Brendita's Latin Tour **415/921-0625** *walking tours of the Mission District*

Metronome Ballroom [GS,$] 1830 17th St (at De Haro) **415/252-9000** *dance lessons, salsa to swing, dance parties wknds, call for events*

■ BOOKSTORES

Dog Eared Books [WC] 900 Valencia St (at 20th) **415/282-1901** *10am-10pm, till 8pm Sun, new & used, good lgbt section*

Modern Times Bookstore [WC] 888 Valencia St **415/282-9246** *10am-9pm, 11am-6pm Sun, progressive, lgbt section, readings*

■ RETAIL SHOPS

Black & Blue Tattoo [W] 381 Guerrero **415/626-0770**

Body Manipulations 3234 16th St (btwn Guerrero & Dolores) **415/621-0408** *noon-7pm, piercing (walk-in basis), jewelry*

■ EROTICA

Good Vibrations [W] 1210 Valencia St (at 23rd) **415/282-6454**, **415/974-8980** *noon-7pm, 11am-8pm Th-Sat, clean, well-lighted sex toy store, also mail order*

▶ **Mission St News** 2086 Mission St (at 17th) **415/626-0309** *24hrs*

California • USA

SF—Haight, Fillmore, Hayes Valley

■ ACCOMMODATIONS

Alamo Square Inn [GF,NS] 719 Scott St (at Fulton) **415/922-2055, 800/345-9888** *Victorian mansions, full brkfst*

The Archbishop's Mansion [GF,NS,GO] 1000 Fulton St (at Steiner) **415/563-7872, 800/543-5820** *one of SF's grandest homes*

Baby Bear's House [GS,NS,GO] 1424 Page St (btwn Central & Masonic) **415/255-9777** *1892 Victorian near the Castro*

The Chateau Tivoli [GF,NS] 1057 Steiner St (at Golden Gate) **415/776-5462, 800/228-1647** *historic SF B&B*

Francisco Bay Inn [GF] 1501 Lombard St (at Franklin) **415/474-3030, 800/410-7007** *motel*

Hayes Valley Inn [GS] 417 Gough St (at Hayes) **415/431-9131, 800/930-7999** *European-style pension*

Hostelling International—Fisherman's Wharf [GS,F,WC] Fort Mason, Bldg 240 (at Franklin) **415/771-7277, 800/909-4776** *hostel, shared baths*

Hotel Del Sol [★GS,NS,SW] 3100 Webster St (at Greenwich) **415/921-5520, 877/433-5765**

Hotel Majestic [GF,WC] 1500 Sutter St (at Gough) **415/441-1100, 800/869-8966** *one of SF's earliest grand hotels, also restaurant, full bar*

Inn 1890 [GS,NS,GO] 1890 Page St (near Stanyan) **415/386-0486, 888/INN-1890** *Victorian near Golden Gate Park*

Inn at the Opera [GF,NS,WC] 333 Fulton St (at Franklin) **415/863-8400, 800/325-2708**

Jackson Court [GF,NS] 2198 Jackson St (at Buchanan) **415/929-7670**

Metro Hotel [GF,F] 319 Divisadero St (at Haight) **415/861-5364**

The Queen Anne Hotel [★GF,WC,GO] 1590 Sutter St (at Octavia) **415/441-2828, 800/227-3970** *1890 landmark*

Radisson Miyako Hotel [GF,WC] 1625 Post St (at Laguna) **415/922-3200, 800/533-4567** *in Japantown*

Shannon-Kavanaugh Guest House [GF,WC,GO] 722 Steiner St (at Hayes) **415/563-2727** *1-bdrm garden apt*

Southern Comforts [GF,NS,WC,GO] **310/305-2984, 800/889-7359** *1800s Victorian mansion*

Stanyan Park Hotel [GF,WC] 750 Stanyan St (at Waller) **415/751-1000** *historic Victorian*

■ BARS

An Bodhran [GF,NH,E] 668 Haight St (btwn Pierce & Scott) **415/431-4724** *4pm-2am; from 6pm Sat, traditional Irish pub w/ live bands Wed & Sun*

Hayes & Vine [GS] 377 Hayes St (at Gough) **415/626-5301** *5pm-midnight, till 1am wknds, 3pm-9pm Sun, wine bar*

The Lion Pub [GS] 2062 Divisadero St (at Sacramento) **415/567-6565** *3pm-2am*

Marlena's [M,NH,P,DS,WC] 488 Hayes St (at Octavia) **415/864-6672** *noon-2am, from 10am wknds, drag shows wknds*

Noc Noc [GF,BW] 557 Haight St (at Fillmore) **415/861-5811** *5pm-2am*

Traxx [M,NH] 1437 Haight St (at Masonic) **415/864-4213** *noon-2am*

■ NIGHTCLUBS

The Top [GF,D,A] 424 Haight St (at Webster) **415/864-7386** *7pm-2am, theme nights, call for events*

■ CAFES

Fillmore Grind 711 Fillmore (at Hayes) **415/775-5680** *6:30am-7pm*

■ RESTAURANTS

Alamo Square Seafood 803 Fillmore (at Grove) **415/440-2828** *dinner only*

Blue Muse [WC] 409 Gough St (at Fell) **415/626-7505** *9:30am-10pm, Sun brunch, cont'l, full bar*

San Jose • California

Cafe Delle Stelle [★BW] 395 Hayes (at Gough) **415/252-1110** *lunch & dinner, Italian*

Cha Cha Cha 1801 Haight St (at Shrader) **415/386-7670** *open till 11pm, Cuban/ Cajun, excellent sangria, worth the wait!*

Eliza's [★] 2877 California (at Broderick) **415/621-4819** *lunch & dinner, excellent Chinese food & stylish decor*

Ella's 500 Presidio Ave (at California) **415/441-5669** *brkfst & lunch wkdays, popular wknd brunch*

Garibaldi's [WC,GO] 347 Presidio (at Sacramento) **415/563-8841** *lunch & dinner, Mediterranean, full bar*

Greens Fort Mason, Bldg 'A' (near Van Ness & Bay) **415/771-6222** *lunch Tue-Sun, dinner nightly, Sun brunch, gourmet vegetarian*

Jardinière [★] 300 Grove St (at Franklin) **415/861-5555** *5pm-midnight, till 10:30pm Sun-Mon, oh-so-chic Californian-French cuisine, full bar*

Joubert's [★BW,R,GO] 4115 Judah St (at 46th Ave) **415/753-5448** *dinner Wed-Sun, lunch wknds, South African vegetarian*

Kan Zaman [BW] 1793 Haight (at Shrader) **415/751-9656** *5pm-midnight, noon-2am wknds, Mediterranean, hookahs & tobacco available*

Suppenküche [GO] 601 Hayes (at Laguna) **415/252-9289** *dinner, Sun brunch, German cuisine served at communal tables*

Thep-Phanom [★BW] 400 Waller St (at Fillmore) **415/431-2526** *5:30pm-10pm, excellent Thai food, worth the wait!*

■ENTERTAINMENT & RECREATION

Kabuki Springs & Spa 1750 Geary Blvd (at Fillmore) **415/922-6000** *traditional Japanese bath w/ extensive menu of spa sevices*

■RETAIL SHOPS

La Riga 1391 Haight St (at Masonic) **415/552-1525** *11am-7pm, leather*

Mainline Gifts 1928 Fillmore St (at Bush) **415/563-4438** *hours vary*

Psychic Eye 301 Fell St (at Gough) **415/863-9997** *10am-10pm, 11am-7pm Sun, New Age & occult books & supplies, also readings & classes*

Spundae Records 678 Haight **415/575-1580**

■CRUISY AREAS

Land's End [AYOR] NW tip of SF *inquire locally*

San Jose

■INFO LINES & SERVICES

AA Gay/ Lesbian **408/374-8511** *24hr helpline*

Billy DeFrank Lesbian/ Gay Community Center [WC] 938 The Alameda **408/293-2429, 408/293-3040** *noon-10pm, till 6pm Sat, clsd Sun*

■ACCOMMODATIONS

Hensley House B&B [MW,GO] 456 N 3rd St **408/298-3537, 800/498-3537** *located in a historic landmark, full brkfst, hot tub*

Hotel De Anza [GF,F,WC,NS] 233 W Santa Clara St **408/286-1000, 800/843-3700** *art deco gem*

■BARS

Mac's Club [M,NH,D] 39 Post (btwn 1st & Market) **408/288-8221** *noon-2am*

Renegades [MW,NH] 393 Stockton (at Julian) **408/275-9902** *noon-2am, patio*

■NIGHTCLUBS

Muevelo [M,D,MR-L,$] 175 N San Pedro (at Club Wild) **408/535-8677** *9pm-2am 1st Sat*

■RESTAURANTS

Eulipia Restaurant & Bar 374 S 1st St (at San Carlos) **408/280-6161** *dinner only, clsd Mon*

■ENTERTAINMENT & RECREATION

Tech Museum of Innovation 201 S Market St (at Park Ave) **408/294-8324** *10am-5pm, clsd Mon, open daily in summer, a must-see for digital junkies*

California • USA

■ PUBLICATIONS

Out Now Newsmagazine 1020 The Alameda **408/293-1598** *lgbt newspaper*

■ MEN'S CLUBS

➤ **Watergarden** [★PC] 1010 The Alameda **408/275-1215** *24hrs, great outdoor patio & jacuzzi, Latin Th*

■ MEN'S SERVICES

➤ **Megaphone San Jose 408/514-1111** *Voice Personals! Meet Hot Men in your area! FREE to Browse & Respond to voice ads. Use code 3087. Also try MEGAMATES.COM*

■ EROTICA

Leather Masters 969 Park Ave **408/293-7660** *fetish clothes, toys, etc*

Pleasures from the Heart 1427 The Alameda (at Hamilton & Winchester) **408/292-4040** *also 1575-C S Winchester Blvd, Campbell, 408/871-1826*

San Luis Obispo

■ INFO LINES & SERVICES

Wayne McCaughan Community Pride Center 11573 Los Osos Valley Rd, Ste 'B' **805/541-4252** *2pm-6pm, clsd wknds*

■ ACCOMMODATIONS

Casa De Amigas B&B [MW,NS,GO] 1202 8th St, Los Osos **805/528-1964**

The Madonna Inn [GF] 1000 Madonna Rd **805/543-3000, 800/543-9666** *theme rooms (our fave is the Caveman Room)*

The Palomar Inn [GS] 1601 Shell Beach Rd, Shell Beach **805/773-4204, 888/384-4004**

➤ **Temptation Ranch at Hidden Springs** [MO,N,NS,GO] Hidden Springs Ranch Rd, Santa Margarita **888/213-7733** *cabins & house on private lake, hot tub*

San Luis Obispo • California

■ CAFES

Linnaea's Cafe 1110 Garden (at Marsh)
805/541-5888 *7am-midnight, till 7pm Sun*

Outspoken, A Beverage Bistro [GO]
1422 Monterey (at California)
805/545-7664 *6:30am-5:30pm, 8am-2pm wknds*

■ RESTAURANTS

Big Sky Cafe 1121 Broad (at Marsh)
805/545-5401 *7am-10pm, 8am-9pm Sun*

■ ENTERTAINMENT & RECREATION

Pirates Cove Beach left turn off Avila

■ BOOKSTORES

Coalesce Bookstore & Garden Wedding Chapel 845 Main St, Morro Bay **805/772-2880** *10am-5:30pm, 11am-4pm Sun, lgbt section*

Volumes of Pleasure [WC,GO]
1016 Los Osos Valley Rd, Los Osos
805/528-5565 *10am-6pm, noon-5pm Sun, general, lgbt section*

■ RETAIL SHOPS

Boxworks [GF,GO] 778 Higuera St (in Network Downtown SLO)
805/545-9940 *10am-5:30pm, unique cards & gifts, mention Damron & receive a 10% discount!*

■ PUBLICATIONS

GALA News & Reviews
805/541-4252 *news & events for Central California coast*

■ CRUISY AREAS

Diamond Cove [AYOR] W of Pirates Cove & down a cliff

Morro Rock [AYOR] along Embarcadero, Morro Bay *late*

Pismo Dunes [AYOR] Grand Ave to beach

California • USA

San Mateo

■CRUISY AREAS
Coyote Point [AYOR] off US 101 (btwn San Mateo & Burlingame) *beach & parking lot*

San Rafael
see Marin County

Santa Barbara

■INFO LINES & SERVICES
Pacific Pride Foundation 126 E Haley St #A-11 **805/963-3636** *9am-5pm Mon-Fri, social/ educational & support services, youth groups, HIV/AIDS services*

■ACCOMMODATIONS
Blue Dolphin Inn [GS,NS,WC,GO] 420 W Montecito St **805/965-2333, 877/722-3657** *1900s Victorian*

Fess Parker's DoubleTree Resort [GF] 633 E Cabrillo Blvd (at Garden) **800/879-2929**

Glenborough Inn [GS,NS] 1327 Bath St (at Sola) **805/966-0589, 888/966-0589** *4 different homes w/ 4 different personalities, full brkfst, fireplaces*

Inn of the Spanish Garden [GF,SW,NS,WC] 915 Garden St (at Carrillo) **805/564-4700, 866/564-4700**

Old Yacht Club Inn [GF] 431 Corona Del Mar Dr **805/962-1277, 800/676-1676 & 800/549-1676 (CA only)** *only B&B on beach*

■BARS
Hades Bar & Nightclub [MW,D,K,S] 235 W Montecito St **805/962-2754** *4pm-2am, clsd Mon*

■CAFES
Hot Spot Espresso Bar & Reservation Service 36 State St **805/564-1637** *24hrs*

■RESTAURANTS
Sojourner Cafe [BW,WC] 134 E Canon Perdido (at Santa Barbara) **805/965-7922** *11am-11pm, till 10pm Sun*

Zelo [★D,E] 630 State (at Ortega) **805/966-5792** *lunch & dinner, clsd Mon, full bar, also nightclub from 10pm nightly*

■BOOKSTORES
Chaucer's Books 3321 State St (at Las Positas Rd) **805/682-6787** *9am-9pm, till 10pm Fri-Sat, till 6pm Sun, general, lgbt section*

■RETAIL SHOPS
Boxworks [GO] 1221 State St, #11 (at Victoria, in Victoria Court Shops) **805/568-1115** *10am-5:30pm, unique cards & gifts, mention Damron & receive a 10% discount!*

■EROTICA
For Adults Only 223 Anacapa **805/963-9922** *23hrs*

The Riviera Adult Superstore 4135 State St **805/967-8282** *pride items*

■CRUISY AREAS
Cabrillo Beach [AYOR] E of wharf

East Beach [AYOR]

Padero Ln Beach [AYOR]

Santa Clara

■NIGHTCLUBS
Tinker's Damn (TD's) [M,D] 46 N Saratoga (at Stevens Creek) **408/243-4595** *3pm-2am, 1pm-2am wknds*

■EROTICA
Borderline 36 N Saratoga Ave (at Stevens Creek) **408/241-2177** *toys, videos*

L'Amour Shoppe 2329 El Camino Real **408/296-7076** *24hrs*

Santa Cruz

■INFO LINES & SERVICES
AA Gay/ Lesbian **831/475-5782** (AA#)

The Diversity Center 177 Walnut Ave **831/425-5422** *1pm-3pm, 2pm-5pm Sun, call for events*

Santa Rosa • California

ACCOMMODATIONS

Chateau Victorian B&B Inn [GS,NS] 118 First St **831/458-9458**

Compassion Flower Inn [GS,WC,GO] 216 Laurel St **831/466-0420** *medical marijuana-friendly*

Quan Yin House [GS,GO] Redwood St (at Bay Ave) **831/423-5671, 510/459-3208**

NIGHTCLUBS

Blue Lagoon [GS,D,A,TG,V,WC] 923 Pacific Ave **831/423-7117** *4pm-2am*

Dakota [MW,D,WC] 1209 Pacific Ave (at Soquel) **831/454-9030** *4pm-2am, from 2pm wknds, salsa Mon, women's night Wed, men's night Th*

RESTAURANTS

Costa Brava Taco Stand 505 Seabright **831/423-8190** *8am-11pm, till 10pm Sun-Mon*

Crêpe Place [WC] 1134 Soquel Ave (at Seabright) **831/429-6994** *11am-midnight, 10am-1am Fri-Sat, full bar, garden patio*

Saturn Cafe [GO] 145 Laurel (at Pacific) **831/429-8505** *11:30am-3:30am, till 4:30am Fri-Sat*

BOOKSTORES

Book Loft 1207 Soquel Ave (at Seabright) **831/429-1812** *10am-10pm, noon-6pm Mon, till 6pm Sun, mostly used*

Bookshop Santa Cruz [WC] 1520 Pacific Garden Mall **831/423-0900** *9am-10pm, general, lgbt section*

PUBLICATIONS

Manifesto 831/761-3176 *monthly*

GYMS & HEALTH CLUBS

Heartwood Spa Hot Tub & Sauna Garden [GF] 3150-A Mission Dr (off Soquel, behind hospital) **831/462-2192** *noon-11pm, women-only Sun night*

Kiva Retreat House Spa 702 Water St (at Ocean) **831/429-1142** *noon-11pm, till midnight Fri-Sat, women only 9am-1:30pm Sun*

MEN'S SERVICES

➤ **Megaphone Santa Cruz** **800/289-1489** *Call for the local # nearest you! Meet Hot Men in your area! FREE to Browse & Respond to voice ads. Use code 3087. Also try MEGAMATES.COM*

CRUISY AREAS

Laguna Creek Beach [AYOR] 7 miles N of town

Santa Maria

INFO LINES & SERVICES

Pacific Pride Gay/ Lesbian Resource Center 819 W Church St (at Depot) **805/349-9947** *9am-5pm Mon-Fri*

CAFES

Cafe Monet [WC] 1555 S Broadway (at Battles) **805/928-1912** *6:30am-5:30pm, clsd Sun*

EROTICA

Book Adventure [AYOR] 306 S Blosser Rd (btwn Cook & Cypress) **805/928-7094**

Diamond Adult World 938 W Main St (at Western) **805/922-2828**

Santa Rosa

INFO LINES & SERVICES

Santa Rosa AA 707/544-1300 (AA#)

NIGHTCLUBS

Club Cosmo [MW,D,V] 720 Adams (at Michele's) **707/577-8270** *seasonal June-Dec, call for info*

CAFES

Aroma Roasters [MW,WC,GO] 95 5th St (Railroad Square) **707/576-7765** *6am-11pm, till midnight Fri-Sat, 7:30am-11pm Sun*

RESTAURANTS

Syrah 205 5th St (at Davis) **707/568-4002** *lunch & dinner, clsd Sun-Mon, creative California/ French*

California • USA

■ BOOKSTORES
North Light Books [GO] 550 E Cotati Rd, Cotati **707/792-4300** *9am-9pm, till 7pm Fri, 10am-8pm Sun, strong lgbt emphasis, also coffeehouse*

Sawyer's News 733 4th St (btwn 'D' & 'E') **707/542-1311** *7am-9pm, till 10pm Fri-Sat, till 7pm Sun*

■ PUBLICATIONS
We the People 707/581-1809

■ MEN'S SERVICES
➤ **Megaphone Santa Rosa** **800/289-1489** *Call for the local # nearest you! Meet Hot Men in your area! FREE to Browse & Respond to voice ads. Use code 3087. Also try MEGAMATES.COM*

■ EROTICA
Santa Rosa Adult Books 3301 Santa Rosa Ave (at Todd) **707/542-8248**

Sausalito
see Marin County

Sebastopol

■ CAFES
Coffee Catz [E,WC] 6761 Sebastopol Ave (at Hwy 116) **707/829-6600** *7am-8pm, till 10pm Fri-Sat*

■ EROTICA
The Sensuality Shoppe 2371-A Gravenstein Hwy S **707/829-3999** *open daily, toys, books, videos, woman-owned/ run*

Sequoia Nat'l Park

■ ACCOMMODATIONS
Organic Gardens B&B [GF,NS,GO] 44095 Dinely Dr, Three Rivers **559/289-4608** *5 miles from entrance to Sequoia Nat'l Park*

Sonoma

■ ACCOMMODATIONS
A Wine Country Teahouse [MW,GO] 9556 Frederica Ave, Kenwood **707/833-6998**

Cedars of Sonoma [GS] 10203 Barnett Valley Rd (at Burnside), Sebastopol **707/829-1000** *cabin on 20 acres*

Gaige House Inn [GF,SW] 13540 Arnold Dr, Glen Ellen **707/935-0237, 800/935-0237** *in the Wine Country*

Jackaroo Cottage [GS,GO] 14045 Arnold Dr (at Hill Rd), Glen Ellen **707/758-7135** *hot tub*

Springville

■ ACCOMMODATIONS
Great Energy [MW,SW,NS] **559/539-2382** *retreat in foothills of Sierra Nevada mtns*

Stockton
see also Modesto

■ NIGHTCLUBS
Paradise [MW,D,E,V,YC] 10100 N Lower Sacramento Rd (near Grider) **209/477-4724** *6pm-2am, from 3pm Sun*

■ EROTICA
Jaybird Books 332 N California (at Miner) **209/941-8607**

Sunnyvale

■ ACCOMMODATIONS
Wild Palms Hotel [GF,SW,WC] 910 E Fremont Ave (at Wolfe Ave) **408/738-0500, 800/538-1600** *hot tub*

■ MEN'S SERVICES
➤ **Megaphone Sunnyvale** **800/289-1489** *Call for the local # nearest you! Meet Hot Men in your area! FREE to Browse & Respond to voice ads. Use code 3087. Also try MEGAMATES.COM*

Sutter Creek

■ ACCOMMODATIONS
Foxes Inn of Sutter Creek [GF,GO] 77 Main St (at Keys St) **209/267-5882, 800/987-3344** *full brkfst*

Tiburon
see Marin County

Ventura • California

Torrance

■INFO LINES & SERVICES
South Bay Center 2235 Sepulveda Blvd (btwn Crenshaw & Arlington) **310/328-6550** *support/ education*

Ukiah

■BARS
Perkins St Grill [GF,D] 228 E Perkins St **707/462-0327** *lunch & dinner, clsd Mon, Californian*

■CRUISY AREAS
Jensen's Truck Stop [AYOR] Lovers Ln *nights*

Lake Mendocino [AYOR] at the overlook *days only*

Upland

■NIGHTCLUBS
Oasis [M,D,DS,WC] 1386 E Foothill Blvd #H (at Grove) **909/920-9590** *7pm-2am Wed-Sat, from 8pm Sun, drag Th & Sun [18+]*

■EROTICA
Mustang Books 961 N Central (at Foothill) **909/981-0227** *24hrs*

The Toy Box 1999 W Arrow Rte (at Central) **909/920-1135** *24hrs*

Vacaville

■INFO LINES & SERVICES
Solano County Pride 707/427-2356

■MEN'S SERVICES
➤ **Megaphone Vacaville**
800/289-1489 *Call for the local # nearest you! Meet Hot Men in your area! FREE to Browse & Respond to voice ads. Use code 3087. Also try MEGAMATES.COM*

Vallejo

■NIGHTCLUBS
Nobody's Place [MW,D,WC] 437 Virginia St (at Sonoma Blvd) **707/645-7298** *noon-2am, patio*

■MEN'S SERVICES
➤ **Megaphone Vallejo**
800/289-1489 *Call for the local # nearest you! Meet Hot Men in your area! FREE to Browse & Respond to voice ads. Use code 3087. Also try MEGAMATES.COM*

Van Nuys

■MEN'S SERVICES
➤ **Megaphone Van Nuys**
800/289-1489 *Call for the local # nearest you! Meet Hot Men in your area! FREE to Browse & Respond to voice ads. Use code 3087. Also try MEGAMATES.COM*

■EROTICA
Diamond Adult World 6406 Van Nuys Blvd (at Victory) **818/997-3665** *24hrs*

Ventura

■INFO LINES & SERVICES
AA Gay/ Lesbian 805/389-1444 (AA#)

Rainbow Alliance Gay/ Lesbian Center 2021 Sperry Ave, Ste 3 **805/339-6340** *8:30am-6pm, clsd wknds*

■ACCOMMODATIONS
La Mer B&B [GS,GO] 411 Poli St (at Oak St) **805/643-3600** *European-style B&B, full brkfst*

■BARS
Paddy McDermott's [MW,D,E,K,DS,P] 2 W Main St (at Ventura) **805/652-1071** *2pm-2am*

■EROTICA
Three Star Books 359 E Main St **805/653-9068** *24hrs*

■CRUISY AREAS
Bates Beach [AYOR] Rincon Point (btwn Ventura & Santa Barbara) *N beyond the sea wall*

Surfers Point [AYOR] N of the Ventura Pier (btwn fairgrounds & Ocean) *go N along beach to Hobo's Jungle*

California • USA

Victorville

BARS
West Side 15 [MW] 16868 Stoddard Wells Rd (off I-15) 760/243-9600 *3pm-2am, from 2pm Sun*

EROTICA
Oasis Adult Dept Store 14949 Palmdale Rd 760/241-0788

CRUISY AREAS
Grady Trammel Park [AYOR] 3/4 mile N of West Side 15 bar (on Stoddard Wells Rd)

Visalia

CRUISY AREAS
Mooney Grove Park [AYOR] *days*

Walnut Creek

INFO LINES & SERVICES
AA Gay/ Lesbian 193 Mayhew Wy (at Buskirk) 925/939-4155 *8:30pm Fri & 5:30pm Sat*

NIGHTCLUBS
Club 1220 [MW,D,WC] 1220 Pine St (at Civic Dr) 925/938-4550 *4pm-2am*

MEN'S SERVICES
➤ **Megaphone Walnut Creek** 800/289-1489 *Call for the local # nearest you! Meet Hot Men in your area! FREE to Browse & Respond to voice ads. Use code 3087. Also try MEGAMATES.COM*

White Hall

CRUISY AREAS
Digger Indian [AYOR] off Hwy 50, in El Dorado Forest area (btwn White Hall & Kyburz) *summers*

Whittier

INFO LINES & SERVICES
Together in Pride AA 11931 Washington Blvd (at the church) 562/696-6213 (church #) *7:30pm Th*

Willits

RESTAURANTS
Purple Thistle 50 S Main St 707/459-4750 *4:30pm-8pm, till 9pm wknds, Japanese, also Sun brunch 9am-3pm (different menu)*

BOOKSTORES
Leaves of Grass 630 S Main St 707/459-3744 *10am-5:30pm, noon-4pm Sun, alternative*

CRUISY AREAS
Eel River [AYOR] 15 miles N of town *warm summer days*

Yosemite Nat'l Park

ACCOMMODATIONS
The Ahwahnee Hotel [GF,F,SW] Yosemite Valley Floor 559/252-4848 *incredibly dramatic & expensive grand fortress*

Highland House B&B [GF] 3125 Wild Dove Ln (at Jerseydale Rd), Mariposa 209/966-3737, 888/477-5089

The Homestead [GF,NS] 41110 Rd 600, Ahwahnee 559/683-0495, 800/483-0495 (US#) *cottages*

The Lakehouse B&B at Bass Lake [GF,NS] 39131 Lake Drive (at Hill), Bass Lake 559/683-8220 *full brkfst, hot tub*

Narrow Gauge Inn [GF,SW] 48571 Hwy 41, Fish Camp 559/683-7720 *country inn, 4 miles from Yosemite, hot tub*

The Yosemite Bug Lodge & Hostel [GF,F,SW,NS,WC] 6979 Hwy 140, Midpines 209/966-6666 *hostel w/ dorms, cabins, private rms & tents*

Yosemite View Lodge [GF,SW] 11136 Hwy 140, El Portal 209/379-2681, 888/742-4371

Yosemite's Apple Blossom Inn B&B [GF,WC] 44606 Silver Spur Tr 559/642-2001, 888/687-4281 *hot tub*

CRUISY AREAS
Rest Stop [AYOR] at turn to Glacier Point on road to valley

Boulder • Colorado

COLORADO

Statewide

■PUBLICATIONS

DiverseCity Magazine
303/300-3699 *lgbt magazine for various cities around Colorado, monthly magazine*

➤ **Out Front Colorado**
303/778-7900 *statewide lgbt newspaper*

Alamosa

■ACCOMMODATIONS

Cottonwood Inn [GF,NS] 123 San Juan Ave **719/589-3882, 800/955-2623** *full brkfst*

Aspen

■INFO LINES & SERVICES

Aspen Gay/ Lesbian Community Hotline 970/925-9249 *recorded local info & events*

■ACCOMMODATIONS

Aspen Mountain Lodge [GF,SW,NS] 311 W Main St **970/925-7650, 800/362-7736** *full brkst, hot tub*

Hotel Aspen [GF,SW,NS] 110 W Main St **970/925-3441, 800/527-7369** *hot tub*

Hotel Lenado [GF] 200 S Aspen St **970/925-6246, 800/321-3457** *full brkfst, hot tub, bar*

Sardy House [GF,SW] 128 E Main St **970/925-2525, 800/321-3457** *hot tub*

■BARS

Double Diamond [GF,S] 450 S Galena **970/920-6905** *seasonal, 9pm-2am*

■NIGHTCLUBS

Club Chelsea [GF,WC] 415 Hyman Ave (at Galena) **970/477-2280** *8pm-2am*

■RESTAURANTS

Jimmy's 205 S Mill St (at Hopkins) **970/925-6020** *5:30pm-11:30pm, also bar*

Syzygy [E,WC] 520 E Hyman **970/925-3700** *seasonal, 6pm-10pm, bar till 2am*

■BOOKSTORES

Explore Booksellers & Bistro [F,WC] 221 E Main (at Aspen) **970/925-5336** *10am-9pm, also gourmet vegetarian restaurant*

Boulder

■ACCOMMODATIONS

The Briar Rose B&B [GF,NS] 2151 Arapahoe Ave (at 22nd St) **303/442-3007**

The Historic Earl House Inn [GF] 2429 Broadway (at Maxwell St) **303/938-1400** *full brkfst*

■BARS

The Foundry [GF,D,S,WC] 1109 Walnut **303/447-1803** *11am-1:30am, also cafe from 6am*

■CAFES

Walnut Cafe [★WC] 3073 Walnut (at 30th) **303/447-2315** *7am-4pm, patio*

■BOOKSTORES

Left Hand Books 1200 Pearl St, lower level (E of Broadway) **303/443-8252** *noon-9pm, till 8pm Sat, till 4pm Sun*

Word Is Out [WC] 1731 15th St (btwn Canyon & Arapahoe) **303/449-1415** *10am-7pm, noon-5pm Sun, lgbt sections*

■RETAIL SHOPS

Enchanted Ink [GO] 1200 Pearl St #35 **303/440-6611** *tattoos, piercing, henna, lesbian-owned/ run*

■EROTICA

The News Stand 1720 15th St (at Grove) **303/442-9515**

■CRUISY AREAS

Dream Canyon [SW,N] Lost Angel Rd (off Sugarloaf Mtn Rd) *inquire locally for detailed directions*

Colorado • USA

Breckenridge

■ACCOMMODATIONS

The Bunkhouse Lodge [MO,N,GO]
13203 Hwy 9 **970/453-6475** *full brkfst, hot tub, also Bunkhouse Bar* [CW,BYOB]

Colorado Springs
(includes Manitou Springs)

■INFO LINES & SERVICES

Pikes Peak Gay/ Lesbian Community Center Helpline 719/471-4429
1pm-5pm Tue-Sat, call for events

■ACCOMMODATIONS

Arthur's Retreat at Chalice House [GS] 1120 N Wahsatch Ave (at Uintah) **719/475-7505, 888/475-7505** *full brkfst, hot tub*

Authentic B&B Inns of the Pikes Peak Region 888/892-2237

Blue Skies Inn B&B [GS,NS] 402 Manitou Ave (at Mayfair), Manitou Springs **719/685-3899, 800/398-7949** *Gothic Revival, full brkfst*

Columbine Inn [GS] 10755 Ute Pass Ave, Green Mountain Falls **888/684-9576** *also restaurant*

Old Town Guest House B&B [GF,WC] 115 S 26th St **719/632-9194, 888/375-4210** *full brkfst, hot tub*

Pikes Peak Paradise [GF,NS] Woodland Park **719/687-6656, 800/728-8282** *full brkfst, hot tub, mansion w/ view of Pikes Peak*

Quality Inn—Garden of the Gods [GF,SW] 555 W Garden of the Gods **719/593-9119, 800/828-4347**

■NIGHTCLUBS

Hide & Seek Complex
[★MW,D,CW,S,YC,WC] 512 W Colorado (at Walnut) **719/634-9303** *10:30am-2am, till 5am Fri-Sat, 5 bars, 4 dance flrs, restaurant*

■RESTAURANTS

Dale Street Cafe 115 E Dale (at Nevada) **719/578-9898** *11am-9pm, till 9:30pm Fri-Sat, clsd Sun*

■MEN'S SERVICES

➤ **Megaphone Colorado Springs**
800/289-1489 *Call for the local # nearest you! Meet Hot Men in your area! FREE to Browse & Respond to voice ads. Use code 3087. Also try MEGAMATES.COM*

■EROTICA

First Amendment Adult Bookstore
220 E Fillmore (at Nevada)
719/630-7676

Romantix 1613 La Shelle Wy (off 'B' St)
719/538-9675

XXX-Treme Mature Fantasy Store
620 Peterson Rd **719/638-0200**

■CRUISY AREAS

Iron Horse Park [AYOR] Fort Carson

Palmer Park [AYOR] *many undercover cops*

Crawford

■RESTAURANTS

Mad Dog Ranch Fountain Cafe
131 Hwy 92 **970/921-7632** *seasonal, bkfst, lunch & dinner*

Crested Butte

■ACCOMMODATIONS

Inn at Rockhouse Ranch [GF] 13931 County Rd 730, Gunnison
970/641-0601, 800/641-0601
full brkfst, in Ohio Valley Creek

Denver

■INFO LINES & SERVICES

AA Gay/ Lesbian 303/322-4440

Lesbian/ Gay/ Bisexual Community Services Center of Colorado [WC]
1050 Broadway, 2nd flr
303/733-7743, 303/837-1598 (TDD) *10am-6pm Mon-Fri, extensive resources & support groups*

■ACCOMMODATIONS

Bobby's Place [MO,NS,GO]
303/831-8266, 800/513-7827

Capitol Hill Mansion B&B [GF] 1207 Pennsylvania (at 12th) **303/839-5221, 800/839-9329** *full brkfst, jacuzzi*

Colorado • USA

Elyria's Western Guest House [M,NS,GO] 1655 E 47th Ave (near I-70 & Brighton) 303/291-0915 *historic neighborhood*

The Gregory Inn, LoDo [GF,GO] 2500 Arapahoe St (at 25th St) **303/295-6570, 800/925-6570** *jacuzzis*

Hotel Monaco [GF,NS] 1717 Champa St (at 17th) 303/296-1717, 800/397-5380 *gym, spa, also Italian restaurant*

The Oxford Hotel [GF,F] 1600 17th St 303/628-5400, 800/228-5838 *also restaurant & Cruise Room art deco lounge*

Radisson Hotel Denver Stapleton Plaza [GF,SW,WC] 3333 Quebec St (at 35th) 303/321-3500, 800/333-3333 *also restaurant*

Ramada Inn Denver Downtown [GS,SW,WC] 1150 E Colfax Ave (at Downing) 303/831-7700, 800/292-6232 *hotel, hot tub, full brkfst, in the heart of Capitol Hill*

Royal Host Motel [GF,WC] 930 E Colfax Ave (at Ogden) 303/831-7200 *next to Charlie's*

■BARS

60 South [GS,D,E,K,DS,WC] 60 S Broadway (at Bayaud) 303/777-0193 *2pm-2am*

The Atrium Bar & Grill [GS,D,F] 554 S Broadway 303/744-1923 *7am-2am*

BJ's Carousel [★GS,NH,TG,F,K,S,WC,GO] 1380 S Broadway (at Arkansas) 303/777-9880 *noon-2am, from 10am wknds, also restaurant, karaoke Wed, male strippers Tue & Th*

Brick's [M,NH,WC] 1600 E 17th Ave (at Franklin) 303/377-5400 *11am-2am, lunch Mon-Fri, brunch wknds*

The Brig [M,NH,DS,S] 117 Broadway (btwn 1st & 2nd Aves) 303/777-9378 *noon-2am, male dancers Mon, Fri-Sat*

Broadways [M,NH,D] 1027 Broadway (at 11th Ave) 303/623-0700 *2pm-2am, from noon wknds, dancing/DJ wknds*

C's [W,D] 7900 E Colfax Ave (at Trenton) 303/322-4436 *5pm-midnight, till 2am Fri-Sat*

Cafe Cero [GS,NH,F,R] 1446 S Broadway (btwn Arkansas & Florida) 303/282-1446 *4pm-1:30am Tue-Sat, also restaurant, Italian, food served 5pm-10:30pm*

Charlie's [★M,D,CW,WC] 900 E Colfax Ave (at Emerson) 303/839-8890 *11am-2am, 2 clubs, also restaurant*

The Compound [M,NH,D,A] 145 Broadway (at 2nd Ave) 303/722-7977 *7am-2am*

The Den [MW,NH,WC] 5110 W Colfax Ave (at Sheridan) 303/623-7998 *11am-2am, from 10am wknds, also restaurant, dinner Tue-Sat, brunch Sun*

Denver Detour [★W,E,WC] 551 E Colfax Ave (at Pearl, use back entrance) 303/861-1497 *11am-2am, lunch & dinner served*

The Denver Wrangler [M,B,WC] 1700 Logan Ave (at 17th Ave) 303/837-1075 *11am-2am, levi/ bear*

Down Under Denver [MW,NH,F,GO] 266 S Downing, unit 'B' (at Alameda, enter on alley) 303/777-4377 *3pm-2am, from 11am Sun*

El Chapultepec [★GF,E,$] 1962 Market St (at 20th) 303/295-9126 *7am-2am, live jazz & blues*

Fox Hole [MW] 2936 Fox St (at 20th St) 303/298-7391 *8pm-2am, from 6pm Fri, from 3pm wknds, clsd Mon-Wed, clsd winters*

JR's Bar [★M,NH,V,YC,GO] 777 E 17th Ave 303/831-0459 *3pm-2am*

The Longhorn [M,NH,S,WC] 3014 E Colfax Ave (at St Paul) 303/393-2900 *7am-2am, strippers Wed, Fri-Sat*

The Old Tequila Rose [M,NH,MR-L] 5190 Brighton Blvd 303/295-2819 *noon-2am*

R&R Denver [GS,NH] 4958 E Colfax Ave (at Elm) 303/320-9337 *1pm-2am, from 11am wknds*

Safari Bar [MW,D,DS] 500 Denargo St (at 31st) 303/298-7959 *noon-2am, mostly men wknds*

The Triangle [M,L] 2036 Broadway (at 20th Ave) 303/293-9009 *3pm-2am, from noon Sun*

Colorado • USA

■NIGHTCLUBS

Oxygen at La Rumba [MW,D,E] 99 W 9th Ave (at Broadway) 303/572-8006 *8pm-2am Fri only*

The Wave Nightclub [MW,D,S,WC] 2101 Champa St (at 21st) 303/299-9283 *9pm-close Wed, Fri-Sat*

■CAFES

Bump & Grind Cafe 439 E 17th Ave (at Pennsylvania) 303/861-4841 *7am-3:30pm, wknd brunch 10am-2pm, clsd Mon*

Diedrich Coffee [★] 1201 E 9th (at Downing) 303/837-1275 *6am-11pm, from 7am wknds*

Java Creek [WC] 287 Columbine St (at 3rd Ave) 303/377-8902 *8am-6pm, 9am-4pm Sun*

■RESTAURANTS

The Avenue Grill 630 E 17th Ave (at Washington) 303/861-2820 *11:30am-11pm, till 11:30pm wknds*

Benny's 301 E 7th Ave (at Grant St) 303/894-0788 *8am-11pm, 9am-10pm wknds, Mexican*

Dazzle [E] 930 Lincoln St (at 9th) 303/839-5100 *dinner from 4pm, from 5pm wknds, also lounge*

Joseph's Southern Food, Carry Out & Drive In [GS,GO] 2868 Fairfax St (at I-70 & Colorado Blvd) 303/333-5332 *7am-9pm, clsd Mon, traditional southern, also bakery, ice cream parlor, candy*

Las Margaritas [★WC] 1066 Old S Gaylord St 303/777-0194 *11am-10pm, bar till 2am, Mexican*

Painted Bench 400 E 20th Ave (at Logan) 303/863-7473 *lunch & dinner, dinner only Sat, clsd Sun, full bar*

Paris on the Platte 1553 Platte (at 15th) 303/455-2451 *8am-1am, till 3am wknds, popular after-hours*

Racine's 850 Bannock St (btwn 8th & 9th) 303/595-0418 *brkfst, lunch, dinner & Sun brunch, full bar*

Wazee Supper Club 1600 15th St (at Wazee) 303/623-9518 *11am-2am, noon-midnight Sun, full bar*

Zaidy's Deli 121 Adams (at First) 303/333-5336 *6:30am-5pm, till 8pm Wed-Fri, from 7:30am wknds*

■ENTERTAINMENT & RECREATION

Colorado OUT Spoken PBS KBDI, channel 12 303/861-0829 *11pm Sun, lgbt news & entertainment TV program*

■BOOKSTORES

Isis Books & Gifts [WC] 5701 E Colfax Ave (at Ivanhoe) 303/321-0867 *10am-7pm, till 6pm Fri-Sat, noon-5pm Sun, New Age, metaphysical*

Relatively Wilde [WC,GO] 42 S Broadway (at Ellsworth) 303/777-0766, 866/779-4533 *10am-6pm, noon-5pm Sun, lgbt*

Tattered Cover Book Store [WC] 2955 E 1st Ave (at Milwaukee) 303/322-7727, 800/833-9327 *9am-11pm, 10am-6pm Sun, local independent; also 1628 16th St, 4 flrs*

■RETAIL SHOPS

Arco Iris Design 82 S Broadway 303/765-5116 *pride jewelry & design*

Bound By Design 1336 E Colfax (at Humboldt) 303/830-7272, 303/832-TAT2 *piercing & tattoos*

Heaven Sent Me [WC] 116 S Broadway (btwn Alameda & Virginia) 303/733-9000 *also pride items, clothing, gifts*

■PUBLICATIONS

H Ink 303/534-4042 *bi-monthly party guide*

➤ **Out Front Colorado** 303/778-7900 *statewide bi-weekly lgbt newspaper, since 1976*

Pride Magazine 773/769-6328 *also publish Denver Pink Pages*

■GYMS & HEALTH CLUBS

Broadway Bodyworks [MW,WC] 160 S Broadway (at Maple) 303/722-4342 *$10 day passes*

■MEN'S CLUBS

Community Country Club [PC] 2151 Lawrence St 303/297-2601

Denver Swim Club [★V,YC,SW,PC] 6923 E Colfax Ave (at Olive) 303/321-9399

Denver • Colorado

➤ **Midtowne Spa—Denver** [PC] 2935 Zuni St (at 29th) **303/458-8902** *24hrs*

MEN'S SERVICES

The Confidential Connection®! **303/831-8800** *The hottest local guys! 18+ Record & Listen FREE! Use access code 499*

➤ **Megaphone Denver** **800/289-1489** *Call for the local # nearest you! Meet Hot Men in your area! FREE to Browse & Respond to voice ads. Use code 3087. Also try MEGAMATES.COM*

Voice MALE 303/831-8330 *The city's hottest & wildest all-male voice club. Chat one on one! Use access code 5111*

EROTICA

Adult Book & Video 4810 Pontiac St **303/288-9529** *24hrs*

Circus Cinema 5580 N Federal Blvd **303/455-3144** *24hrs*

The Crypt 131 Broadway (btwn 1st & 2nd) **303/733-3112** *leather & more*

Crypt Adult Entertainment 139 Broadway (btwn 1st & 2nd) **303/778-6584** *all-male theaters & arcades*

Dove Theater 3480 W Colfax **303/893-0037** *24hr wknds*

Galaxy Theater 633 E Colfax Ave (at Washington) **303/831-8319** *24hrs*

Las Vegas Adult Palace 550 W Mississippi Ave (at Santa Fe) **303/698-9119** *24hrs*

Pandora's Lingerie 4380 E Alameda, Glendale **303/778-8828**

Pleasure Entertainment Center 127 S Broadway (at Bayaud) **303/722-5852** *open 23hrs; also 3250 W Alameda, 303/ 934-2373 & 3490 W Colfax, 303/ 825-6505*

CRUISY AREAS

Cheesman Park [AYOR] near Pavilion

Colorado • USA

Durango

■ ACCOMMODATIONS

Leland House B&B [★GF,WC]
721 E 2nd Ave **970/385-1920**,
800/664-1920 *rms & suites, full brkfst*

Rochester Hotel [★GF,NS,WC]
721 E 2nd Ave **970/385-1920**,
800/664-1920 *Western-style house, full brkfst*

■ CRUISY AREAS
Narrow Gauge Train Station [AYOR]

Fort Collins

■ INFO LINES & SERVICES
The Lambda Community Center
149 W Oak, Ste 8 **970/221-3247**

■ ACCOMMODATIONS
Never Summer Nordic [GS]
970/482-9411 *camping in yurts (portable Mongolian round houses) in Rockies, sleep 5-9, mtn-biking & skiing*

■ BARS
Choice City Shots [MW,NH,D,S,WC,GO]
124 LaPorte Ave (at College)
970/221-4333 *3pm-2am, from 4pm Th-Sat, DJ Fri-Sat*

■ NIGHTCLUBS
Club Static [★GS,D,A,V,WC] 1437 E
Mulberry St (at Link Ln) **970/493-0251**
6pm-2am, more gay Fri

Grand Junction

■ BARS
Quincy's [GF,NH,WC] 609 Main St (btwn
7th & Main) **970/242-9633** *7am-2am, gay after 8pm, theater crowd*

■ RESTAURANTS
Leon's Taqueria 505 30th Rd
970/242-1388 *lunch & dinner*

■ EROTICA
24 Road Video Exchange 639 24 Rd
(at Mesa Mall) **970/243-4112**

Winter Park • Colorado

■ CRUISY AREAS
Hawthorne & Lincoln Parks [AYOR]
Walker Wildlife Area [AYOR] Hwy 6, 50 W of Mesa Mall (near the CO river) *in the woods*

Greeley

■ CRUISY AREAS
Island Grove Park [AYOR]

Hotchkiss

■ ACCOMMODATIONS
Leroux Creek Inn & Vineyards
1220 3100 Rd **970/872-4746**

■ RESTAURANTS
Zach's Bar-B-Q 721 East Bridge St **970/872-3199**

Lakewood

■ EROTICA
Romantix 1569 N Wadsworth Blvd (at Colfax) **303/232-2332**

Mancos

■ ACCOMMODATIONS
Old Mancos Inn [GS,GO] 200 W Grand Ave **970/533-9019** *some shared baths*

Pueblo

■ BARS
Pirate's Cove [MW,NH,WC] 105 Central Plaza (off 1st & Union) **719/542-9624** *2pm-2am, clsd Mon*

■ CRUISY AREAS
Mineral Palace Park [AYOR] 17th St (13th St, exit off I-25)

Springfield

■ CAFES
Crossroads Travel Plaza 2780 Hwy 287 (at Hwy 160) **719/523-6977** *24hrs, truck stop diner*

Steamboat Springs

■ ACCOMMODATIONS
Elk River Estates [GF,GO] **970/879-7556** *full brkfst, suburban town house*

Vail

■ ACCOMMODATIONS
Antlers at Vail [GF,SW] 680 W Lionshead Pl **970/476-2471, 800/843-8245** *apts, hot tub*

■ RESTAURANTS
Larkspur Restaurant & Market [WC] 458 Vail Valley Dr (in the Golden Peak Lodge) **970/479-8050** *lunch & dinner, fine dining, also bar, patio, ski-in/out*

Sweet Basil [WC] 193 E Gore Creek Dr **970/476-0125** *lunch & dinner, bar*

Winter Park

■ ACCOMMODATIONS
The Bear Paw Inn [GS] 871 Bear Paw Dr **970/887-1351** *massive log lodge on top of mtn w/ spectacular views of Rocky Mtn Nat'l Park*

Silverado II [GF,SW] 490 Kings Crossing Rd **970/726-5753, 800/551-9943** *condo ski resort*

Connecticut • *USA*

CONNECTICUT

Avon

■RESTAURANTS
Fat Cat Café 124 Simsbury Rd **860/674-1310** *lunch & dinner, clsd Mon, American*

Bethel

■RESTAURANTS
Bethel Pizza House 206 Greenwood Ave **203/748-1427** *11am-11pm*

Emerald City Cafe [E,R] 269 Greenwood Ave **203/778-4100** *lunch, dinner & Sun brunch, clsd Mon, cont'l*

Bridgeport

■RESTAURANTS
Bloodroot Restaurant 85 Ferris St **203/576-9168** *lunch Tue & Th-Sat, dinner Tue-Sat, brunch only Sun, clsd Mon, vegetarian*

■BOOKSTORES
Bloodroot [WC] 85 Ferris St **203/576-9168** *clsd Mon, call for hours, also vegetarian restaurant*

■MEN'S SERVICES
The Confidential Connection®! 203/394-6222 *The hottest local guys! 18+ Record & Listen FREE! Use access code 499*

▶ **Megaphone Bridgeport 800/289-1489** *Call for the local # nearest you! Meet Hot Men in your area! FREE to Browse & Respond to voice ads. Use code 3087. Also try MEGAMATES.COM*

■EROTICA
Boston Book & Video 2053 Boston Ave **203/335-9705**

■CRUISY AREAS
Main St [AYOR] *near downtown hustlers*

Bristol

■CRUISY AREAS
The Rockwell Park [AYOR] Rte 72

Danbury

■BARS
Triangles Cafe [★MW,D,S] 66 Sugar Hollow Rd, Rte 7 **203/798-6996** *5pm-1am, till 2am Fri-Sat, patio*

■RESTAURANTS
Goulash Place [BW] 42 Highland Ave **203/744-1971** *lunch & dinner, clsd Mon, Hungarian*

■CRUISY AREAS
The Oldtown [AYOR] Dikes Pt Park, E side of Lake Candlewood

Enfield

■EROTICA
Bookends 44 Enfield St/ Rte 5 **860/745-3988**

Groton

■ACCOMMODATIONS
Flagship Inn & Suites [GF,WC,GO] 470 Gold Star Hwy (Rte 184, off I-95) **860/445-7458, 888/800-0770** *gym passes, in-room movies*

Hammonasset

■CRUISY AREAS
Hammonasset State Beach [AYOR]

Hartford

■INFO LINES & SERVICES
Project 100/ The Community Center [WC] 1841 Broad St (at New Britain) **860/724-5542** *8:30am-8pm*

■ACCOMMODATIONS
Butternut Farm [GS] 1654 Main St, Glastonbury **860/633-7197** *full brkfst*

Holiday Inn East Hartford [GF,SW,WC] 363 Roberts St, East Hartford **860/528-9611** *also restaurant*

The Mansion Inn [GF] 139 Hartford Rd (at Main St), Manchester **860/646-0453** *B&B, full brkfst, in-room fireplaces*

metroline

30 Years Strong

When traveling in southern New England, ask for the number one rated news resource and area guide for the gay community since 1974.

1.888.233.8334 / www.metroline-online.com

MetroStore

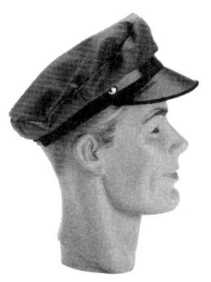 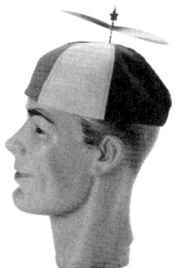

for all things gay and fabulous

When in Hartford, stop by MetroStore for a selection of magazines, videos, gift items, jewelery, dance music, cards, novelties and much, much more...
"100% gay owned and operated." 495 Farmington Avenue • 860.231.8845

Connecticut • USA

■ BARS

Chez Est [★MW,D,E,DS]
458 Wethersfield Ave (at Main St)
860/525-3243 *3pm-1am, till 2am Fri-Sat*

The Polo Club [MW,D,E,K,DS,S] 678 Maple Ave (btwn Preston & Mapleton) **860/278-3333** *8pm-1am, till 2am Fri-Sat, karaoke Mon, male strippers Tue*

■ NIGHTCLUBS

Webster Theatre [GS,D,E] 31 Webster St (at Whitmore) **860/246-8001** *9pm-2am, goth/ fetish party 1st Sat*

■ RESTAURANTS

Arugula [R] 953 Farmington Ave, West Hartford **860/561-4888** *lunch & dinner, clsd Sun-Mon, Mediterranean*

Peppercorn's 357 Main St
860/547-1714 *lunch & dinner, contemporary Italian*

Pond House Cafe [BYOB] 155 Asylum Ave **860/231-8823** *11am-2:30pm & 5pm-9pm, Sun brunch, clsd Mon, patio*

Trumbull Kitchen 150 Trumbull St (at Pearl St) **860/493-7417** *lunch & dinner Mon-Fri, dinner only wknds, global cuisine/ tapas*

■ RETAIL SHOPS

➤ **MetroStore** 493 Farmington Ave (at Sisson Ave) **860/231-8845** *8:30am-8pm, till 5:30pm Tue, Wed & Sat, clsd Sun, magazines, travel guides, leather, video rentals & more*

■ PUBLICATIONS

➤ **Metroline** **860/233-8334** *regional newspaper & entertainment guide, covers CT, RI & MA*

■ MEN'S SERVICES

The Confidential Connection®!
860/293-3969 *The hottest local guys! 18+ Record & Listen FREE! Use access code 499*

➤ **Megaphone Hartford**
800/289-1489 *Call for the local # nearest you! Meet Hot Men in your area! FREE to Browse & Respond to voice ads. Use code 3087. Also try MEGAMATES.COM*

■ EROTICA

Aircraft Book & News 349 Main St (at Pratt), East Hartford **860/569-2324**

Amazing Express 1870 Berlin Tpke/ Rte 15, Wethersfield **860/257-8663**

Erotic Video [AYOR] 35 W Service Rd (at Hwy 91 N) **860/549-1896** *24hr wknds, hustlers*

Very Intimate Pleasures 100 Brainard Ave (exit 27, off I-91) **860/246-1875**

■ CRUISY AREAS

Bushnell Park [AYOR] S of Asylum Ave (downtown exit off I-84)

The Dikes [AYOR] E to W Service Rd of I-91 N *Riverside Park*

Manchester

■ CAFES

Cafe on Main 1071 Main St
860/647-7444 *7am-2pm, clsd Tue*

■ EROTICA

Amazing Superstore 249 Broad St (at Middle Tpke) **860/646-1629**

Meriden

■ EROTICA

The D/ S Toy Chest [W] 975 Broad St (at rear) **203/639-0622** *huge fetish boutique!*

■ CRUISY AREAS

Hubbard Park [AYOR]

Mystic

■ ACCOMMODATIONS

Mermaid Inn of Mystic [MW,GO]
2 Broadway **860/536-6223,**
877/692-2632

New Britain

■ CRUISY AREAS

Walnut Hill Park Veteran's Monument [AYOR]

Norfolk • Connecticut

New Haven

INFO LINES & SERVICES
New Haven Gay/ Lesbian Community Center 50 Fitch St 203/387-2252 *6pm-9pm Mon, Wed-Fri*

ACCOMMODATIONS
The Inn at Oyster Point [GS,GO] 104 Howard Ave (at 6th St) 203/773-3334, 866/978-3778 *full brkfst, jacuzzi*

Three Chimneys Inn at Yale University [GF,NS,WC] 1201 Chapel St (at Park) 203/789-1201, 800/443-1554 (outside CT only) *B&B inn, full brkfst*

BARS
168 York St Cafe [MW,GO] 168 York St 203/789-1915 *3pm-1am, till 2am Fri-Sat, patio*

The Bar [GS,D,WC] 254 Crown St 203/495-8924 *4pm-1am, more gay Tue*

Partners [MW,NH,D] 365 Crown St (at Park St) 203/776-1014 *5pm-1am, till 2am Fri-Sat, The Krypt every other Sat [MO,L]*

NIGHTCLUBS
Gotham Citi Cafe [GS,D,DS] 130 Crown St (at Church) 203/498-2484 *clsd Sun-Tue, more gay Sat, drag shows*

CAFES
Chapel Sweet Shoppe 1042 Chapel St 203/624-2411 *10am-8pm, noon-6pm Sun, full ice cream fountain, seasonal outside cafe*

RESTAURANTS
168 York St Cafe [MW,GO] 168 York St 203/789-1915 *3pm-1am, till 2am Fri-Sat, seasonal Sun brunch, full bar, patio*

Beach Head Cafe 3 Cosey Beach Ave 203/469-5450 *dinner only, seafood, Italian*

EROTICA
Fairmont Theatre 33 Main St 203/467-3832

Nu Haven Book & Video 754 Chapel St (at State) 203/562-5867

Very Intimate Pleasures 170 Boston Post Rd, Orange 203/799-7040

CRUISY AREAS
East Rock State Park [AYOR] lower parking lot *days*

Long Wharf Dr [AYOR] parking lot *hustlers*

New London

BARS
Frank's Place [MW,D,E,WC] 9 Tilley St 860/443-8883 *6pm-1am, till 2am Fri-Sat, patio*

Heroes [MW,NH,D] 33 Golden St 860/442-4376 *4pm-1am, till 2am wknds, 3pm-1am Sun*

BOOKSTORES
Greene's Books & Beans [WC] 140 Bank St (at Golden) 860/443-3312 *9am-5pm, till 4pm Sat, 11am-4pm Sun, also cafe*

EROTICA
Video Expo 591 Rte 12 #8, Groton 860/448-0787

CRUISY AREAS
Ocean Park Beach [AYOR] near boardwalk

New Milford

CRUISY AREAS
Lynn Deming Park [AYOR]

Norfolk

ACCOMMODATIONS
Manor House B&B [GF,NS] 69 Maple Ave 860/542-5690 *1898 Victorian Tudor estate, full brkfst, fireplaces, whirlpool*

Connecticut • USA

North Stonington Village

■ACCOMMODATIONS
Antiques & Accommodations [GF]
800/554-7829 *B&B*

Norwalk

■INFO LINES & SERVICES
Triangle Community Center 16 River St **203/853-0600** *7:30pm-9:30pm Mon-Fri*

■CRUISY AREAS
Cranbury Park [AYOR] on Grumman Ave

Merritt Pkwy Commuter Lot [AYOR] Rte 15, exit 38 (Rte 123, New Canaan Ave) *main lot, turn right*

Norwich

■BOOKSTORES
Magazines & More 77 Salem Tpke #105 **860/886-6247** *10am-6pm, till 8pm Th-Fri, till 5pm Sat, clsd Sun, lgbt*

Preston

■ACCOMMODATIONS
The Mandrake Inn [GS,WC] 124 Rte 2A (at Rtes 2 & 12) **860/892-1485**

Ridgefield

■RESTAURANTS
Gail's Station House 378 Main St **203/438-9775** *brkfst & lunch, dinner Fri-Sun, great cheddar corn pancakes*

■CRUISY AREAS
Riverside on Rte 7 [AYOR] opposite Ridgefield Motor Inn

South Windsor

■ACCOMMODATIONS
The Watson House [GS,WC,GO] 1876 Main St (at Sullivan Ave) **860/282-8888**

Stamford

■CRUISY AREAS
Cove Island Beach [AYOR]
Scalzi Park [AYOR]

Wallingford

■NIGHTCLUBS
Club Out [MW,D,DS] 8 N Turnpike Rd *9pm Fri only*

Washington Depot

■RESTAURANTS
GW Tavern 20 Bee Brook Rd (Rte 47) **860/868-6633** *11:30am-10pm, till 2am wknds*

Waterbury

■EROTICA
Video Books of Waterbury 90 S Main St **203/573-1066**

■CRUISY AREAS
Lakewood Park/ Twin Lakes Annex [AYOR] Farmwood Rd *days*

Westport

■BARS
Cedar Brook Cafe [MW,D,S,WC] 919 Post Rd E **203/221-7429** *8pm-1am Mon, till 2am Fri-Sat, 6pm-11pm Sun*

■ENTERTAINMENT & RECREATION
Sherwood Island State Park Beach left to gay area

Willimantic

■EROTICA
Dan's Adult World 1110 Main St **860/456-3780**

Rehoboth Beach • Delaware

DELAWARE

Statewide

■ INFO LINES & SERVICES
Gay & Lesbian AA 302/856-6452

New Castle

■ EROTICA
Discount Adult Books 174 S DuPont Hwy (near 13/40 split) 302/328-4812

Rehoboth Beach

■ INFO LINES & SERVICES
Camp Rehoboth 39 Baltimore Ave 302/227-5620 *10am-5pm Mon-Fri, community center, also magazine*

■ ACCOMMODATIONS
An Inn by the Bay [GS,NS,GO] 205 Savannah Rd, Lewes 302/644-8878, 866/833-2565 *hot tub*

At Melissa's B&B [GF] 36 Delaware Ave (btwn 1st & 2nd) 302/227-7504, 800/396-8090

Cabana Gardens B&B [MW,SW,NS,GO] 20 Lake Ave (at 3rd St) 302/227-5429 *rooftop deck*

Chesapeake Landing B&B [GF,SW,NS,GO] 101 Chesapeake St (at King Charles) 302/227-2973 *full brkfst, lakefront, near Poodle Beach*

Delaware Inn B&B [GF,SW,GO] 55 Delaware Ave 302/227-6031, 800/246-5244 *near beach*

The Hidden Treasure B&B [MO,GO] 302/945-9456 *full brkfst, hot tub, 8 miles out of town*

Lord Hamilton Seaside B&B Inn [MW,GO] 20 Brooklyn Ave (at 1st) 302/227-6960, 877/227-6960 *near beach & boardwalk*

The Ram's Head [MO,SW,N,GO] 302/226-9171 *hot tub, gym*

Rehoboth Guest House [MW,GO] 40 Maryland Ave (at King Charles) 302/227-4117, 800/564-0493 *seasonal, Victorian beach house*

The Royal Rose Inn [GS,GO] 41 Baltimore Ave 302/226-2535 *sundeck*

SILVER LAKE
The guest house on the lake...by Poodle Beach

One of the "Top 10 North American Gay Guesthouses." Out & About
"The best of the bunch." Fodor's Gay Guide

133 Silver Lake Drive • Rehoboth Beach, DE 19971
www.silverlakeguesthouse.com • 800/842-2115

Delaware • USA

Shore Inn at Rehoboth [M,SW,N,GO]
703 Rehoboth Ave (near Church)
302/227-8487, 800/597-8899
hot tub

➤ **Silver Lake Guest House**
[MW,NS,GO] 133 Silver Lake Dr
302/226-2115, 800/842-2115
near Poodle Beach

Summer Place Hotel [GS] 30 Olive Ave
(at 1st) **302/226-0766,
800/815-3925** *also apts, near beach*

The Sussex House [GS,NS,GO]
601 Bayard Ave (at New Castle Ave)
302/227-7860, 877/787-7392
rental house, 2 blks to beach

■ BARS

The Blue Moon [★MW] 35 Baltimore
Ave (btwn 1st & 2nd) **302/227-6515**
*4pm-2am, clsd Jan, popular happy hour,
also restaurant, dinner, Sun brunch*

Dogfish Head Brewings & Eats
[GF,F,E] 320 Rehoboth Ave
302/226-2739 *micro-brewery, wood-grilled food*

Double L Bar [M,L] 622 Rehoboth Ave
302/227-0818 *3pm-2am, clsd Sun*

■ NIGHTCLUBS

The Beach House Restaurant & Bar
[W,D,E,WC] 316 Rehoboth Ave
302/227-4227

■ CAFES

Java Beach 167 Rehoboth Ave
302/226-3377 *7am-6pm, open later
in summer, patio*

Lori's Café 39 Baltimore Ave (at 1st)
302/226-3066 *seasonal, call for hours*

■ RESTAURANTS

Back Porch Cafe [WC] 59 Rehoboth
Ave **302/227-3674** *lunch & dinner,
Sun brunch, seasonal*

Celsius [WC] 50-C Wilmington Ave
302/227-5767 *dinner nightly, Sun
brunch, French-Mediterranean*

Cloud Nine [★D,K,WC] 234 Rehoboth
Ave (at 2nd) **302/226-1999** *4pm-
2am, fusion bistro, karaoke Th in
summer*

Wilmington • Delaware

The Cultured Pearl 19-A Wilmington Ave (off 1st St) **302/227-8493** *5pm-10pm Th-Sun, pan-Asian, cocktail lounge*

Dos Locos [★] 10 N 1st St (btwn Baltimore & Rehoboth) **302/227-3353** *seasonal, Mexican, full bar*

Iguana Grill 52 Baltimore Ave **302/227-0948** *11am-10pm, till 2am Th-Sat (summers), Southwestern, full bar, patio*

La La Land 22 Wilmington Ave **302/227-3887** *6pm-1am (seasonal), seafood, full bar, patio*

Purple Parrot Grill [K,WC] 247 Rehoboth Ave **302/226-1139** *dinner, karaoke Fri-Sat*

Sydney's Side Street Restaurant & Blues Place [E] 25 Christian St (at 2nd St) **302/227-1339** *4pm-1am (seasonal), full bar, patio*

Tijuana Taxi [WC] 207 Rehoboth Ave (at 2nd St) **302/227-1986** *5pm-10pm, from noon wknds*

Yum-Yum Pan Asian Bistro [★] 37 Wilmington Ave **302/226-0400** *name says it all, patio, T-dance Sun*

■ ENTERTAINMENT & RECREATION

Carpenter's Beach below S end of Boardwalk at foot of Queen St

Poodle Beach S of boardwalk *popular gay beach*

■ BOOKSTORES

Lambda Rising [WC] 39 Baltimore Ave (btwn 1st & 2nd) **302/227-6969** *10am-midnight, 11am-8pm Sun-Th & till 10pm Fri-Sat (winters), lgbt*

■ PUBLICATIONS

➤ **EXP Gayzette** **302/227-5787, 877/397-6244** *bi-weekly gay magazine for Mid-Atlantic*

Letters from Camp Rehoboth **302/227-5620** *newsmagazine w/ events & entertainment listings*

Visions Today **302/656-1809, 800/944-0100** *quarterly, covers Rehoboth, Philadelphia, New Hope, Wilmington & surrounding area*

■ GYMS & HEALTH CLUBS

Body Shop 401 N Boardwalk (at Virginia) **302/226-0920** *$10 day pass*

The Firm Fitness Center 6 Camelot Shopping Ctr/ Rte 1 **302/227-8363**

■ CRUISY AREAS

Cape Henlopen State Park Beach [AYOR] *go N past the 2nd lookout tower in the dunes*

Wilmington

■ BARS

814 Club [MW,D,TG] 814 Shipley St (btwn 8th & 9th) **302/657-5730** *5pm-1am, also restaurant*

■ NIGHTCLUBS

Baxter's [MW,D,CW,F,K] 2006 Pennsylvania Ave **302/654-9858** *4pm-1am*

Everybody's [MW,D,MR-AF,AYOR] 11 E 4th St (upstairs) *opens 10pm Wed-Sat, unconfirmed*

Excalibur [M,D,CW,E,K,S,V,YC,GO] 839 N Orange St (at 8th St) **302/777-2225** *5pm-2am, clsd Sun, 2 flrs*

■ RESTAURANTS

Mrs Robino's [WC] 520 N Union (at Pennsylvania) **302/652-9223** *lunch & dinner, family-style Italian, bar*

■ PUBLICATIONS

➤ **EXP Gayzette** **302/227-5787, 877/397-6244** *bi-weekly gay magazine for Mid-Atlantic*

Visions Today **302/656-1809, 800/944-0100** *quarterly, covers Rehoboth, Philadelphia, New Hope, Wilmington & surrounding area*

■ MEN'S SERVICES

The Confidential Connection®! **302/478-4330** *The hottest local guys! 18+ Record & Listen FREE! Use access code 499*

■ CRUISY AREAS

8th St [AYOR] btwn Shipley & Tetnell

Brandywine Park [MR-AF,AYOR] *footbridge & woods*

District of Columbia • USA

DISTRICT OF COLUMBIA

Washington

■ INFO LINES & SERVICES

Gay/ Lesbian Hotline (at Whitman-Walker Clinic) 202/833-3234 *7pm-11pm*

Triangle Club 2030 'P' St NW 202/659-8641 *various 12-Step groups, call for times*

Washington, DC Convention & Tourism 1212 New York Ave NW #600 800/422-8644

■ ACCOMMODATIONS

1836 California [GS] 1836 California St NW (btwn 18th & 19th) 202/462-6502 *historic (ca 1900) house, sundeck*

➤ **The Bed & Breakfast at the William Lewis House** [★M,GO] 1309 'R' St NW (at 13th) 202/462-7574, 800/465-7574 *turn-of-the-century, hot tub, full brkfst wknds*

Bull Moose B&B on Capitol Hill [GS,NS,GO] 101 5th St NE (at 'A' St) 202/547-1050, 800/261-2768 *Victorian row house*

The Carlyle Suites Hotel [GS,F,WC] 1731 New Hampshire Ave NW (btwn 'R' & 'S' Sts) 202/234-3200, 866/468-3532 *art deco, also bar, popular gay Sun brunch*

Center City Hotel [GF] 1201 13th St NW 202/682-5300, 888/250-5396 *near Dupont Circle, internet access*

DC GuestHouse [GS,GO] 1337 10th St NW 202/332-2502 *full brkfst*

The Embassy Inn [GF] 1627 16th St NW 202/234-7800, 800/423-9111 *small hotel w/ B&B atmosphere*

Embassy Suites Alexandria [GS,SW] 1900 Diagonal Rd, Alexandria, VA 703/684-5900, 800/362-2779 *full brkfst*

Embassy Suites—Chevy Chase Pavilion [GF,SW,WC] 4300 Military Rd NW 202/362-9300, 800/362-2779

EMBASSY SUITES HOTEL®

WASHINGTON, DC DOWNTOWN

1250 22ND STREET NW, WASHINGTON, DC 20037
202-857-3388
www.embassysuitesDCmetro.com/downtown

Ideally located between Dupont Circle and Georgetown, we offer spacious two-room suites and a complimentary full, cooked-to-order breakfast every morning. In the evening, unwind at our manager's reception featuring complimentary alcoholic and non-alcoholic beverages from 5:30–7:30 nightly. We are within walking distance of the Dupont Circle and Foggy Bottom metro stations, as well as a wide variety of nightlife, restaurants, museums and attractions. Our friendly and professional staff awaits you. Please ask for the special "DAM" rate code!

You are *always* welcome at the Bed and Breakfast at the

WILLIAM LEWIS HOUSE

Washington's Finest

(202) 462-7574
(800) 465-7574

Warm, Cozy, Convenient
Close to 17th St.
Close to Dupont Circle
Close to Gay Attractions
Minutes from the Mall
Close to Metro
Great Restaurants Nearby
Perfect for Business
Great for Sightseeing
Friendly, Affordable, First Class
Accommodations

Visa, Mastercard, American Express and Discover Accepted
Smoking Permitted in the Garden
Reservations Recommended
Off Street Parking Available
E-mail: Info@WLewisHous.com
Web: Http:// www.WLewisHous.com
Fax (202)462-1608

Gay Owned and Operated

District of Columbia • USA

Embassy Suites Tysons Corner [GF,SW,WC] 8517 Leesburg Pike, Vienna, VA **703/883-0707, 800/362-2779** full brkfst

➤ **Embassy Suites Washington, DC** [GF,SW] 1250 22nd St NW **202/857-3388, 800/362-2779** full brkfst

FourSeventeen [GS,GO] 417 'A' Street SE (at 5th St) **202/543-1481** B&B in private home

Hotel Helix [GF,WC] 1430 Rhode Island Ave NW **202/462-9001, 866/508-0658**

Hotel Madera [GF,WC] 1310 New Hampshire Ave NW **202/296-7600, 800/368-5691** boutique hotel, Firefly bistro adjacent

Hotel Monaco [GF,WC] 700 'F' St NW **202/628-7177, 800/202-5411** boutique hotel

Hotel Rouge [GF,WC] 1315 16th St NW (at Rhode Island) **202/232-8000, 800/368-5689** ultra hip, high-tech luxury hotel, also restaurant & bar

Kalorama Guest House at Kalorama Park [GS] 1854 Mintwood Pl NW (at Columbia Rd) **202/667-6369** Victorian town house

Kalorama Guest House at Woodley Park [GS,NS] 2700 Cathedral Ave NW (off Connecticut Ave) **202/328-0860**

One Washington Circle Hotel [GF,SW,WC] One Washington Cir NW **202/872-1680, 800/424-9671** suites w/ kitchens, also restaurant & piano bar

Radisson Barcelo Hotel Washington [GF,F,SW] 2121 'P' St NW (at 21st St) **202/293-3100, 800/333-3333**

The River Inn [GF,WC] 924 25th St NW (at 'K' St) **202/337-7600, 800/424-2741** also Dish restaurant

Savoy Suites Hotel [GF,WC] 2505 Wisconsin Ave NW (at Calvert, in Georgetown) **202/337-9700, 800/944-5377** also Italian restaurant

Swann House Historic B&B [GS,SW] 1808 New Hampshire Ave NW (at Swann St) **202/265-4414** Victorian mansion in Dupont Circle, swimming, roof deck

Topaz Hotel [GF,WC] 1733 'N' St NW **202/393-3000, 800/424-2950** boutique hotel, also restaurant & bar

Washington Plaza [GF] 10 Thomas Cir NW (at 14th & Massachusetts) **202/842-1300, 800/424-1140** full-service hotel, also restaurant

■BARS

1409 Playbill Cafe [MW,F] 1409 14th St NW **202/265-3055** 4pm-2am, till 3am Fri-Sat, also theater

Apex [MW,D,K,V,YC,WC,$] 1415 22nd St NW (btwn 'P' & 'Q' Sts) **202/296-0505** 9pm-2am, till 3am Fri-Sat, clsd Sun-Mon & Wed

Back Door Pub [M,D,MR-AF,F,S,WC] 1104 8th St SE, 2nd flr (at 'L' St) **202/546-5979** 5pm-2am, till 3am Fri-Sat

Carlyle Cafe [GS,F,WC] 1731 New Hampshire (at 18th & 'R' Sts, in the Carlyle Suites) **202/234-3200** 5pm-midnight, till 2am Fri-Sat, art deco bar, dinner served, internet access

Club Chaos [MW,D,MR,TG,F,DS,WC] 1603 17th St NW (at 'Q' St) **202/232-4141** 5pm-1am, till 2am Wed-Th, till 3am Fri-Sat, 11am-3pm Sun, clsd Mon, Sun brunch

DC Eagle [★M,L,WC] 639 New York Ave NW (btwn 6th & 7th) **202/347-6025** 4pm-2am, till 3am Fri-Sat

DIK Bar [M,D,K,OC] 1635 17th St NW **202/328-0100** 4pm-2am, till 3am wknds

Ellington's on 8th [MW,F,E] 424-A 8th St SE **202/546-8308** dinner, Sun brunch, clsd Mon-Tue, live jazz

The Fireplace [M,NH,MR,V,WC] 2161 'P' St NW (at 22nd St) **202/293-1293** 1pm-2am, wknds till 3am

Green Lantern/ Tool Shed [M,NH,K,V] 1335 Green Court NW (in alley) **202/347-4533** 4pm-2am, from 1pm wknds, The Tool Shed [L] upstairs

JR's Bar [★M,N,F,V,YC] 1519 17th St NW (at Church) **202/328-0090** noon-2am, till 3am Fri-Sat, cruisy, hot cocktail hour

Larry's Lounge [MW,NH,WC] 1840 18th St NW (at 'T' St) **202/483-1483** 4pm-1am, till 3am Fri-Sat

182 2004 Damron Men's Travel Guide

Washington • District of Columbia

Marx Cafe [GS,D,F,BW] 3203 Mt Pleasant St NW **202/518-7600** *4pm-2am, till 3am wknds, brunch wknds*

Mr Henry's Capitol Hill [★GF,MR,E] 601 Pennsylvania Ave SE (at 6th St) **202/546-8412** *11:30am-midnight, till 1am wknds, live jazz, also restaurant*

Mr P's/ The Loft [M,MR,S,V] 2147 'P' St NW (at 22nd) **202/293-1064** *2pm-2am, from noon Sun, patio, very cruisy, The Loft upstairs [M,L,V]*

Nob Hill [MW,NH,D,MR-AF,S] 1101 Kenyon NW (at 11th St) **202/797-1101** *8pm-close, clsd Mon-Tue, dancers, also Ebony II upstairs*

Omega [★M,MR,K,S,V] 2122 'P' St NW (enter rear) **202/223-4917** *4pm-2am, 8pm-3am Sat*

Remington's [★M,D,DS,V] 639 Pennsylvania Ave SE (btwn 6th & 7th) **202/543-3113** *4pm-2am, till 3am Fri-Sat, 2 flrs, T-dance Sun*

Sheridan's [MW,D,CW,DS,P,GO] 713 8th St SE **202/546-6955** *10pm-close Sat, T-dance Sun from 5pm*

Titan [MW,D,F,V] 1337 14th St NW (at Hamburger Mary's) **202/232-7010** *5pm-midnight, till 2am Fri-Sat*

■ NIGHTCLUBS

Atlas/ Lizard Lounge [M,D] 1223 Connecticut Ave NW (at 18th & N, at MCCXXIII) **202/331-4422** *8pm Sun only, call for info*

Bachelors Mill [★M,D,MR-AF,S,WC] 1104 8th St SE (downstairs at Back Door Pub) **202/544-1931** *5pm-close, 2 flrs*

Chief Ike's Mambo Room [GF,D,E,WC] 1725 Columbia Rd NW (at Ontario) **202/332-2211** *4pm-close, till 3am Fri, 6pm-3am Sat, clsd Sun, live music Wed-Th, also restaurant, American*

Cobalt [M,D,E,DS] 17th & 'R' Sts NW **202/462-6569** *4pm-2am, from 3pm wknds, till 3am Fri-Sat*

The Deep End [★M,D,MR-AF] 1214 18th St NW (at Andula) **202/462-9057** *9:30pm-2:30am Wed only*

The Edge [MW,D,MR,F,S,V,18+,WC,$] 56 'L' St SE (at Half St) **202/488-1200** *from 10pm Mon, Wed & Sat only, Mon Afrodiziac [M,S]*

La Cage Aux Follies [★M,S,V] 18 'O' St SE (at S Capitol) **202/554-3615** *9pm-2am, till 3am Fri-Sat, nude dancers*

Velvet [★M,D,F,DS,V,YC,$] corner of S Capitol & 'K' St SE (at Nation) **202/554-1500** *10pm-6am Sat*

Wet [M,S] 52 'L' St SE (at Half St) **202/488-1200** *8pm-2am, till 3am Fri-Sat, clsd Sun, go-go boys*

Ziegfeld's [MW,D,A,MR,E,DS,S,WC] 1345 Half St SE (at 'O' St) **202/554-5141** *9pm-3am, till 2am Th & Sun, clsd Mon-Wed, also Secrets w/ male dancers*

■ CAFES

Cafe Luna [★MW] 1633 'P' St NW (at 17th) **202/387-4005** *8am-11pm, from 10am wknds, till 1:30am Fri-Sat*

Cyber STOP Café [★] 1513 17th St NW (btwn 'P' & 'O' Sts NW) **202/234-2470** *7am-midnight, from 8am wknds, internet access, great people-watching*

Jolt n' Bolt [★] 1918 18th St NW (at Florida) **202/232-0077** *8am-10pm, till midnight Fri-Sat, patio*

Soho Tea & Coffee [WC] 2150 'P' St NW **202/463-7646** *6am-5am, till 2am Mon, till 4am Th, 8:30am-1am Sun, cybercafe & more, patio*

Xando/ Cosi [★] 1647 20th St **202/332-6364** *till midnight, till 2am Fri-Sat, full bar from 4pm, make your own s'mores*

■ RESTAURANTS

17th Street Bar & Grill [★] 1516 Rhode Island Ave NW (at 17th) **202/872-1126** *brkfst, lunch & dinner, popular Sun brunch, patio*

Annie's Paramount Steak House [★] 1609 17th St NW (at Corcoran) **202/232-0395** *11am-11pm, 24hrs Fri-Sat, full bar*

Banana Cafe & Piano Bar [E,P,GO] 500 8th St SE (at 'E' St) **202/543-5906** *lunch & dinner, Puerto Rican/ Cuban, some veggie, famous margaritas*

Cafe Berlin [WC] 322 Massachusetts Ave NE (btwn 3rd & 4th) **202/543-7656** *lunch & dinner, dinner only Sun, German, patio*

District of Columbia • USA

Cafe Japoné [★MR-A,K] 2032 'P' St NW (at 21st) **202/223-1573** *6pm-2am, Japanese, full bar, live jazz*

Chartwell Grill [WC] 1914 Connecticut Ave (in The Churchill Hotel) **202/797-2000** *brkfst, lunch, dinner,*

Dupont Italian Kitchen & Bar 1637 17th St NW (at 'R' St) **202/328-3222, 202/328-0100** *11am-midnight*

Food For Thought [NS] 1811 14th St NW (at the Black Cat) **202/797-1095** *8pm-1am, 7pm-1am Fri-Sat, mostly vegan/veggie, indie/punk music shows*

Gabriel [R,WC] 2121 'P' St NW (at 21st) **202/956-6690** *6:30pm-10:30pm, 4pm-midnight Tue, from 7pm wknds, Sun brunch, Mediterranean/Latin, full bar*

Guapo's [WC] 4515 Wisconsin Ave NW (at Albemarle) **202/686-3588** *dinner, lunch only on Sun, Mexican, full bar*

The Islander 1201 'U' St (at 12th) **202/234-4955** *lunch & dinner, Caribbean, full bar*

Jaleo [WC] 480 7th St NW (at 'E' St) **202/628-7949** *lunch & dinner, tapas*

La Frontera Cantina 1633 17th St NW (btwn 'R' & 'Q') **202/232-0437** *11am-11pm, till 1am Fri-Sat, Tex-Mex*

Lauriol Plaza 1835 18th St NW (at 'S') **202/387-0035** *Latin American*

Mercury Grill [GO] 1602 17th St NW **202/667-5937** *lunch Mon-Fri, dinner nightly, full bar, patio*

Occidental Grill 1475 Pennsylvania Ave NW (btwn 14th & 15th) **202/783-1475** *political player hangout*

Pepper's [★WC] 1527 17th St NW (btwn 'P' & 'Q') **202/328-8193** *11:30am-2am, Sun brunch, int'l, full bar*

Rocklands 2418 Wisconsin Ave NW (at Calvert) **202/333-2558** *lunch & dinner, bbq & take-out*

Sala Thai 2016 'P' St NW (at 21st) **202/872-1144** *lunch & dinner*

Skewers [★] 1633 'P' St NW (at 17th) **202/387-7400** *11:30am-11pm, Middle Eastern, full bar*

Soul Vegetarian 2606 Georgia Ave NW **202/328-7685** *11am-9pm, till 3pm Sun (brunch), all-vegan menu*

Trio 1537 17th St NW (at 'Q' St NW) **202/232-6305** *7:30am-midnight, American, full bar, sidewalk cafe*

Two Quail [★GO] 320 Massachusetts Ave NE **202/543-8030** *lunch Mon-Fri, dinner nightly, brunch Sun, full bar*

■ ENTERTAINMENT & RECREATION

Anecdotal History Tours [GF] **301/294-9514** *guided tours*

Gay Men's Chorus of Washington **202/338-7464**

Hillwood Museum & Gardens [R] 4155 Linnean Ave NW (at Tilden St NW) **202/686-5807, 877/445-5966** *9am-5pm Tue-Sat*

Phillips Collection 1600 21st St NW (at 'Q' St) **202/387-0961** *clsd Mon, America's oldest museum of modern art, near Dupont Circle*

■ BOOKSTORES

ADC Map & Travel Center 1636 'I' St NW (at 17th St) **202/628-2608, 800/544-2659** *9am-6:30pm, till 5:30pm Fri, 11am-5pm Sat, clsd Sun, extensive maps & travel guides*

Kramer Books & Afterwords [WC] 1517 Connecticut Ave NW (at 'Q') **202/387-1400** *7:30am-1am, 24hrs wknds, also cafe*

Lambda Rising [WC] 1625 Connecticut Ave NW (btwn 'Q' & 'S' Sts) **202/462-6969** *10am-10pm Sun-Th, till midnight Fri-Sat, lgbt*

■ RETAIL SHOPS

Leather Rack 1723 Connecticut Ave NW (btwn 'R' & 'S' Sts) **202/797-7401**

▶ **Pleasure Place** 1710 Connecticut Ave NW (btwn Florida Ave & R St) **202/483-3297** *10am-10pm, till midnight Wed-Sat, noon-7pm Sun, erotica, clubwear, leather, adult toys, DVDs, clothing & more*

▶ **Pleasure Place** [WC] 1063 Wisconsin Ave NW, Georgetown (btwn 'M' & 'K' Sts) **800/386-2386** *10am-10pm, till midnight Wed-Sat, noon-7pm Sun, erotica, clubwear, leather, adult toys, DVDs, clothing & more*

Washington • District of Columbia

Universal Gear 1601 17th St NW (at 'Q') **202/319-0136** *11am-10pm Sun-Th, till midnight Fri-Sat, casual, club, athletic & designer clothing*

■ PUBLICATIONS

➤ **EXP Gayzette** **302/227-5787, 877/397-6244** *bi-weekly gay magazine for Mid-Atlantic*

MW (Metro Arts & Entertainment) **202/638-6830** *extensive club listings*

Washington Blade **202/797-7000** *huge lgbt newspaper w/ extensive resource listings*

■ GYMS & HEALTH CLUBS

Results—The Gym [GF] 1612 'U' St NW (at 17th St) **202/518-0001** *also cafe*

Washington Sports Club 1835 Connecticut Ave NW (at Columbia & Florida) **202/332-0100** *day-passes $10-25*

■ MEN'S CLUBS

Crew Club 1321 14th St NW (at Rhode Island) **202/319-1333** *24hrs*

GHC (The Gloryhole) 24 'O' St SE (at S Capitol & Half, downstairs) **202/863-2770** *24hrs*

■ MEN'S SERVICES

➤ **Megaphone Washington DC** **800/289-1489** *Call for the local # nearest you! Meet Hot Men in your area! FREE to Browse & Respond to voice ads. Use code 3087. Also try MEGAMATES.COM*

■ EROTICA

B&K Newsstand Video Arcade 1004 'F' St (at 10th) **202/628-8306**

➤ **Pleasure Place** 1710 Connecticut Ave NW (btwn Florida Ave & R St) **202/483-3297** *10am-10pm, till midnight Wed-Sat, noon-7pm Sun, erotica, clubwear, leather, adult toys, DVDs, clothing & more*

➤ **Pleasure Place** [WC] 1063 Wisconsin Ave NW, Georgetown (btwn 'M' & 'K' Sts) **800/386-2386** *10am-10pm, till midnight Wed-Sat, noon-7pm Sun, erotica, clubwear, leather, adult toys, DVDs, clothing & more*

■ CRUISY AREAS

25th St NW [AYOR] btwn 'N' & 'M' Sts

The Pleasure Place

Washington's Premier Erotic Boutique

Serving the community since 1979

Leathergear, clubwear, thongs, lubricants, condoms, DVDs, videos, toys galore & more...!

- For Mail Orders: 1-800-386-2386
- Visit our online catalogue at: www.pleasureplace.com
- Email: pleasure@pleasureplace.com

• Open Daily •

Georgetown:
1063 Wisconsin Ave, NW
(202) 333-8570

Dupont Circle:
1710 Connecticut Ave, NW
(202) 483-3297

Photo by Martin Schulman

Florida • USA

FLORIDA

Statewide

■PUBLICATIONS

HOTSPOTS! Magazine
954/928-1862 *Florida's weekly bar guide w/ hot shots*

➤ **Southern Voice** 404/876-1819 *weekly lgbt newspaper for AL, FL (panhandle), GA, LA, MS, TN w/ resources*

➤ **TLW Magazine** 727/522-8888 *Southeast's largest entertainment magazine for gay men*

Amelia Island

■ACCOMMODATIONS

The Amelia Island Williams House B&B [GF,WC] 103 S 9th St 904/277-2328, 800/414-9258 *jacuzzi, fireplace*

Ash Street Inn [GS,SW,GO] 102 S 7th St (at Ash St) 904/277-6660, 800/277-6660 *B&B, full brkfst, jacuzzi*

■RESTAURANTS

Beech Street Grill 801 Beech St (at 8th St), Fernandina Beach 904/277-3662 *dinner only*

Bretts 1 Front St 904/261-2660 *lunch Mon-Sat, dinner nightly*

■CRUISY AREAS

Burney Park [AYOR]

Peters Point [AYOR]

Auburndale

■BARS

Alternative Bar [GS,NH,CW,BW,GO] 404 Eaker St (at Hwy 92) 863/965-9018 *noon-2am*

Boca Raton

■CRUISY AREAS

Spanish River Park [AYOR]

Bradenton

■RESTAURANTS

Greasy Spoon 5604 15th St E/ Old 301 941/739-9810 *6am-3pm, diner*

■EROTICA

C&U Bookmart [AYOR] 4949 14th St W 941/755-9076 *24hrs*

■CRUISY AREAS

Anthony Rossi Park (aka Waterfront Park)

Coquina Beach [AYOR]

ManGroves [AYOR] Manatee Ave (off Palma Sola Bay) *on right, after crossing the first bridge, towards Anna Maria Island*

Cape Canaveral

■CRUISY AREAS

Jetty Park & Beach [AYOR] *days*

Merritt Island National Refuge [AYOR] on the road to Playalinda Beach (off Rte 402 E)

Cape Coral

see Fort Myers

Clearwater

see also Dunedin, New Port Richey, Port Richey & St Petersburg

■BARS

Pro Shop Pub [★M,NH] 840 Cleveland St (at Prospect) 727/447-4259 *11:30am-2am, from 1pm Sun*

■EROTICA

X-Factor 12880 US 19 N 727/524-3604

Cocoa

■BARS

Drama Club [MW,K,DS,GO] 9 Stone St (off Brevard) 321/639-8228 *5pm-2am*

Cocoa Beach

■RESTAURANTS

Flaminias [BW] 3210 S Atlantic Ave 321/783-9908 *dinner only, Italian*

MICHAEL'S

Casual Fine Dining & Deck Bar

Dinner 5-10pm Wed-Sun
Happy Hour 3-6pm Closed Monday.
116 Madison Ave. Daytona Beach
(just minutes from beach)
386-323-0607

Florida • USA

Lobster Shanty [WC] 2200 S Orlando Ave **321/783-1350** *lunch & dinner, full bar*

Mango Tree [WC] 118 N Atlantic Ave **321/799-0513** *opens 6pm, clsd Mon, fine dining & single malt Scotch bar*

Daytona Beach

■ INFO LINES & SERVICES

Lambda Center 320 Harvey Ave (at Hollywood) **386/255-0280** *support groups, youth services & 12-step mtgs*

■ ACCOMMODATIONS

Acapulco Hotel & Resort [GF,F,WC] 2505 S Atlantic Blvd (at Int'l Speedway Blvd) **386/761-2210, 800/245-3580** *jacuzzi*

Best Western Mayan Inn Beachfront [GF,SW,WC] 103 S Ocean Ave **386/252-2378, 800/443-5323** *ocean views, lounge*

The Villa B&B [GF,SW,N,NS,GO] 801 N Peninsula Dr **386/248-2020** *historic Spanish mansion, spa*

■ BARS

The Zone Bar & Grill [M,NH,B,F,BW,GO] 322 Seabreeze Blvd (at Oleander), Daytona Beach **386/257-6464, 386/428-3763** *4pm-midnight, till 2am Fri-Sat*

■ NIGHTCLUBS

The Other Place Nite Club [MW,D,DS,TG] 642 S Atlantic Ave, Ormond Beach **386/677-1006** *7pm-2am*

Rumors Bar & Niteclub [MW,D,TG,E,S,V,WC,GO] 1376 N Nova Rd **386/252-3776** *noon-2am*

■ RESTAURANTS

Anna's Trattoria [BW] 304 Seabreeze Blvd **386/239-9624** *dinner only, clsd Mon, Italian*

Frappes North [R] 123 W Granada Blvd **386/615-4888** *lunch & dinner, clsd Sun, patio*

➤ **Michael's** [M,WC,GO] 116 Madison Ave (at N Beach St) **386/323-0607** *dinner only, clsd Mon, video bar, patio*

Sapporo 501 Seabreeze Ave **386/257-4477** *lunch Mon-Fri, dinner 7 days, Japanese, full bar*

Sweetwater's [WC] 3633 Halifax Dr, Port Orange **386/761-6724**

■ PUBLICATIONS

➤ **TLW Magazine** **727/522-8888** *Southeast's largest entertainment magazine for gay men*

■ MEN'S SERVICES

➤ **Megaphone Daytona Beach** **800/289-1489** *Call for the local # nearest you! Meet Hot Men in your area! FREE to Browse & Respond to voice ads. Use code 3087. Also try MEGAMATES.COM*

■ CRUISY AREAS

Boardwalk & Beach [AYOR] *around bandshell*

N Wild Olive Ave [AYOR] *from Ora St to Earl St (in front of sightseeing tower & bandshell) nights, also the W side at Adventure Lands fenceline*

Reed Canal Park [AYOR] *head N on Nova Rd (right on Reed Canal Rd)*

Delray Beach

■ ACCOMMODATIONS

Crane's BeachHouse [GF,SW] 82 Gleason St (at Atlantic Ave) **561/278-1700, 866/372-7263** *hotel*

■ BARS

Lulu's Place [MW,P] 640 E Atlantic Ave Bay 6 (at E Federal Hwy) **561/278-4004** *4pm-2am*

Dunedin

see also St Petersburg

■ BARS

1470 West [MW,D,K,DS,WC] 325 Main St (at Douglass) **727/736-5483** *4pm-2am, karaoke Wed, patio*

Englewood Beach

■ ACCOMMODATIONS

Florida Beach Rental [GF,GO] 2045 Arkansas Ave **513/705-9608**

Fort Lauderdale • Florida

Fort Lauderdale

■ INFO LINES & SERVICES

Gay/ Lesbian Community Center [WC] 1717 N Andrews Ave (at 17th St) **954/463-9005** *10am-10pm, noon-6pm wknds, outreach, also Stonewall Library*

➤ **Greater Fort Lauderdale Convention & Visitors Bureau** 1850 Eller Dr, Ste 303 **800/227-8669 (code 187)** *call for free 'Rolling Out the Rainbow Carpet' guide*

Lambda South Inn [WC] 1231 E Las Olas Blvd **954/761-9072** *mtg-space for lgbt in recovery*

www.GayFloridaRealty.com *Log on & see current MLS listings in your destination Florida city. Search for a gay or lesbian realtor or mortgage broker.*

■ ACCOMMODATIONS

Alhambra Beach Motel [GF,SW,GO] 3021 Alhambra St **954/525-7601** *motel, close to gay beach*

Bahama Hotel [GF,SW,WC] 401 N Fort Lauderdale Beach Blvd (at Bayshore) **954/467-7315, 800/622-9995** *full gym, also The Deck restaurant & bar*

➤ **Banyan Marina Resort** [GF,SW] 111 Isle of Venice **954/524-4430, 800/524-4431 (reservations, US only)** *waterfront apts*

The Blue Dolphin [★MO,V,SW,WC,GO] 725 N Birch Rd (at Vistamar) **954/565-8437, 800/893-2583** *rooms & apts, near beach*

➤ **Brigantine for Men** [MO,SW,N,GO] 2831 Vistamar St (at Bayshore) **954/565-6911, 877/565-6911** *newly redecorated rooms, near ocean*

➤ **The Cabanas** [M,SW,NS,GO] 2209 NE 26th St **954/564-7764, 866/564-7764**

California Dream Inn [GF,GO] 300-315 Walnut St, Hollywood **954/923-2100** *located directly on ocean*

Caribbean Quarters Inn [GS,GO] 3012 Granada St (at Fort Lauderdale Beach Blvd) **954/523-3226, 888/414-3226** *B&B inn, jacuzzi, courtyard gardens*

➤ **Cheston House** [MO,SW,N,GO] 520 N Birch Rd (at Viramar) **954/566-7950, 866/566-7950**

Comfort Suites Airport & Cruise Port [GS,SW] 1800 S Federal Hwy (at 17th St) **954/767-8700, 800/760-0000**

➤ **Coral Reef Guesthouse** [MO,SW,N,GO] 2609 NE 13th Ct (off Sunrise Blvd) **954/568-0292, 888/365-6948** *12-man jacuzzi, very secluded*

➤ **Deauville Inn** [GS,SW,GO,WC] 2916 N Ocean Blvd (Oakland Park Blvd & A1A) **954/568-5000** *in the heart of Fort Lauderdale Beach*

Doubletree Fort Lauderdale Oceanfront Hotel [GF,SW] 440 Seabreeze Blvd **954/524-8733**

Doubletree Guest Suites Fort Lauderdale Galleria [GF,SW] 2670 E Sunrise Blvd **954/565-3800** *bar & grille, patio w/ tiki bar, jacuzzi, health club*

Edun House [MO,SW,N,NS,GO] 2733 Middle River Dr (near Oakland Park Blvd) **954/565-7775, 800/479-1767** *patio*

Eighteenth Street Inn [GS,SW,GO] 712 SE 18th St **954/467-7841, 888/828-4466**

➤ **Elysium Resort** [M,SW,NS,GO] 552 N Birch Rd (at Terramar) **954/564-9601, 800/533-4744** *sundeck, near beach*

➤ **Embassy Suites Hotel** [GF,SW,WC] 1100 SE 17th St **954/527-2700, 800/362-2779** *full brkfst, hot tub*

➤ **The Flamingo-Inn Amongst the Flowers** [MO,SW,NS,GO] 2727 Terramar St (near Birch) **954/561-4658, 800/283-4786** *totally renovated Dec 2001, hot tub*

Fort Lauderdale Manhattan Tower Apartment Hotel [GS,SW,GO] 701 Bayshore Dr (at A1A) **954/564-1117** *hotel, near beach, pets ok*

➤ **Gigi's Resort by the Beach** [GF,SW,GO] 3005 Alhambra St (at Birch) **954/463-4827, 800/910-2357** *on the beach, hot tub*

Damron Men's Travel Guide 2004   **189**

Florida • USA

➤ **The Grand Resort**
[MO,SW,NS,WC,GO] 539 N Birch Rd (at Windamar) **954/630-3000, 800/818-1211** *sundeck, spa, ocean views*

Holiday Inn Fort Lauderdale [GF] 999 Fort Lauderdale Beach Blvd **954/563-5961**

➤ **Inn Leather Guesthouse**
[MO,L,SW,GO] 610 SE 19th St (at SW 1st Ave) **954/467-1444, 877/532-7729** *sling in each room, dungeon, hot tub*

➤ **Lambton Court** [MO,SW,GO] 840 NE 17th Terrace **954/462-3977, 866/222-7905** *apt-motel*

➤ **Liberty Apartment & Garden Suites** [MW,SW,WC,GO] 1501 SW 2nd Ave (at Sheridan), Dania Beach **954/927-0090, 877/927-0090** *furnished apts, weekly rates*

➤ **The Mangrove Villas**
[M,SW,N,WC,GO] 1100 N Victoria Park Rd (at 11th St) **954/527-5250, 800/238-3538** *self-contained houses*

Manor Inn [MO,SW,N,NS,GO] 2408 NE 6th Ave (at NE 24th St), Wilton Manors **954/566-8223** *B&B, hot tub*

The New Zealand House B&B [M,SW,N,WC,GO] 908 NE 15th Ave (at Sunrise) **954/523-7829, 888/234-5494** *Key West-style guest house*

➤ **Orton Terrace** [MO,SW,N,GO] 606 Orton Ave (at Terramar) **954/566-5068, 800/323-1142**

➤ **Palm Plaza Resort** [MO,SW,GO] 2801 Rio Mar St (at Birch) **954/260-6568** *tropical gardens, near beach*

➤ **Pineapple Point Guest House** [MO,SW,N,WC,GO] 315 NE 16th Terr (at NE 3rd Ct) **954/527-0094, 888/844-7295** *luxury guest house, spa*

Richard's Inn [MO,SW,N,GO] 1025 NE 18th Ave (at Sunrise) **954/563-1111, 800/516-1111**

➤ **The Royal Palms Resort** [★M,SW,GO] 2901 Terramar St (at Birch) **954/564-6444, 800/237-7256** *rated one of the very best gay accommodations in the USA by Out & About*

➤ **Saint Sebastian Guest House** [MO,SW,GO] 2835 Terramar St (at Orton) **954/568-6161, 800/425-8105** *Bahamian-style*

➤ **The Schubert Resort** [★MO,SW,WC,GO] 855 NE 20th Ave **954/763-7434, 866/763-7435** *full brkfst, hot tub, 2 full bars*

Sea Grape House Inn [M,SW,N,GO] 1109 NE 16th Pl (at Dixie Hwy) **954/525-6586, 800/447-3074** (code: 44) *2 clothing-optional pools, 7-man spa*

➤ **Sheraton Yankee Trader** [GF,SW] 321 N Fort Lauderdale Beach Blvd (A1A) **954/467-1111, 800/958-5551** *beachfront hotel*

Sun n' Splash [MO,SW,N,GO] 1135 N Victoria Park Rd (at 13th) **954/467-2669, 888/842-9352**

➤ **Villa Venice Resort** [MO,SW,GO] 2900 Terramar St (at Orton) **954/564-7855, 877/284-5522** *2 blks to beach*

➤ **Windamar Beach Resort** [M,SW,N,GO] 543 Breakers Ave (near Bayshore) **954/561-0039, 800/205-5464** *just steps from the ocean*

➤ **The Worthington Guest House** [MO,SW,NS,GO] 543 N Birch Rd (at Terramar) **954/563-6819, 800/445-7036** *resort, hot tub*

■ BARS

Anywayz [MW,E,K] 1753 N Andrews Sq **954/766-2552** *2pm-2am, till 3am Fri-Sat, from noon Sun*

➤ **Bill's Filling Station** [★M,NH,F,WC] 1243 NE 11th Ave (at 13th St) **954/525-9403** *11am-2am, till 3am wknds, from noon Sun, patio*

Boardwalk [★M,NH,S] 1721 N Andrews Ave **954/463-6969** *noon-2am, till 3am Fri-Sat, strippers from 5pm*

The Bushes [★M,NH,WC] 3038 N Federal Hwy (at Oakland Park Blvd) **954/561-1724** *9am-2am, till 3am wknds*

Cathode Ray Club [★M,D,E,S,V] 1307 E Las Olas Blvd (at 13th Ave) **954/462-8611** *2pm-2am, till 3am Fri-Sat, 3 bars & restaurant*

GREATER FORT LAUDERDALE

Rolling out the rainbow carpet.

Relax in the attitude-free ambience of Greater Fort Lauderdale. Feel free in the gay-friendly hotels, countless bars and restaurants and enjoy unrivaled nightlife. For your free Rainbow Map and Guide, call 800-22-SUNNY, code 958.

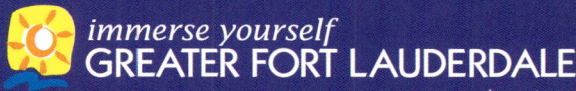

immerse yourself
GREATER FORT LAUDERDALE
www.sunny.org/rainbow

Mangrove Villas Guest House

Fort Lauderdale, Florida

It's more than home.

Spacious Individual Villas
Extended-stay
Apartment Units

- **Heated pool** *(clothing optional)*
- **Kitchens**
- **Internet & email access**
- **Housekeeping service**
- **Gated off-street parking**

800.238.3538
or
954.527.5250

**1100 NORTH VICTORIA PARK ROAD,
FORT LAUDERDALE, FLORIDA 33304**

info@mangrovevillas.com
www.mangrovevillas.com

Orton Terrace
THE AFFORDABLE INN PLACE FOR OUT MEN

Steps to Beach

Guest Rooms

1 & 2 Bedroom Apartments
All with refrigerators, microwaves,
27" TV's, stereos, VCR's, and videos

DSL Computer Access

Heated Pool

Barbeque Grill

Continental Breakfast
for late risers from 8-noon

**606 Orton Avenue
Ft. Lauderdale, FL 33304**

954-566-5068 fx 954-564-8646

800-323-1142
www.ortonterrace.com

luxury charm magic

for those whose standards of excellence
in luxury accommodations are higher than most

steps from Fort Lauderdale's sun-kissed beaches...

under towering royal palms, amid the lush and exotic
tranquil gardens of The Royal Palms, celebrate the
pristine luxury of distinctive, 5-star accommodations,
where life is a rare blend of effortless endeavors.

they call it magic... we call it home

5-Star Rating 1991-2004 Out & About
★ ★ ★ ★ ★

2901 Terramar St., Fort Lauderdale Beach
ph: **954.564.6444**
    800.237.7256
e: info@royalpalms.com

www.royalpalms.com

BANYAN MARINA RESORT
Apartments on the canals of the Venice of the Americas

Enter through flowers into a scene amenable at first glance: heated swimming pool, tranquil yacht marina and the great Banyan tree. Minutes away from the beach and fashionable Las Olas Blvd's shops, restaurants and nightclubs.
German ownership, gay friendly, and highly recommended by Fodor's and Frommer's Travel Guide.

waterfront accommodations
fully equipped kitchens
luxuriously furnished
data ports

www.banyanmarina.com
111 Isle of Venice, Fort Lauderdale. Ph: (954) 524-4430
Fx: (954) 764-4870 E: info@banyanmarina.com

The Cabanas
OUT&ABOUT

866.564.7764
www.TheCabanasGuesthouse.com
Something for everyone
Receive a gift for mentioning The Mens Guide

designed by Victor Mauro

Cheston House
A Men's Resort

WHERE ELEGANCE MEETS AFFORDABILITY...

Ft. Lauderdale Beach's newest gay resort...

520 N. Birch Road, Ft. Lauderdale Beach, FL 33304
954.566.7950 • 866.566.7950
www.ChestonHouse.com

- Welcoming All [And Their Pets]
- Heated Pool
- Rooms & Suites
- 2 Blocks to Beach
- Gay Owned/Operated

come SLEEP with US

866.595.1522 • 954.568.5000 • WWW.THEDEAUVILLEINN.COM
2916 N OCEAN BLVD • FT. LAUDERDALE, FL

DEAUVILLE

Elysium Resort
FORT LAUDERDALE

Paradise Awaits...
OVERSIZED HOT TUB • 180 YARDS TO BEACH
CLOTHING OPTIONAL POOLS

954.564.9601 • 800.533.4744
WWW.ELYSIUMRESORT.NET

PHOTO: RAYMOND VINO ©2003 • DESIGN: BLUE DOOR PRODUCTIONS, INC. (954) 713.8126

Great Location! It's that simple...

Located on 17th Street Causeway, within walking distance of dining, night life and the Intracoastal Waterway.

EMBASSY SUITES Hotel®
1100 SE 17th St. Causeway
Fort Lauderdale, FL 33316
Ph.:954-527-2700
Fax: 954-760-7202

www.embassysuitesftl.com
e-mail: reservations@embassysuitesftl.com
© 2002 Hilton Hospitality Inc.
*Subject to state and local laws.

- Spacious 2 Rm. Suites
- Complimentary Breakfast Daily
- Manager's Reception Nightly*
- Free Shuttle to Ft. Lauderdale Airport & Port Everglades
- Tropical Outdoor Pool
- 2 Miles from Beach
- High Speed Internet
- HHonors Points & Miles®

THE FLAMINGO
Inn Amongst The Flowers
FORT LAUDERDALE BEACH

Design: Blue Door Productions, Inc. (954) 713.8126

An Adventure In
INDULGENCE
LUXURY • SOPHISTICATION • ELEGANCE

954.561.4658 • 800.283.4786

★★★★★

WWW.THEFLAMINGORESORT.COM

The Closest to the Gay Beach!

- Uniquely Decorated Rooms
- Sun Deck
- Tropical Setting
- Private Baths

Gigi's
RESORT BY THE BEACH

800-910-2357
954-463-4827
email: gigisresort@aol.com

3005 Alhambra St., Ft. Lauderdale • www.gigisresort.com

MORNING...
NOON...
NIGHT...

800.818.1211
954.630.3000

🇺🇸 **MILITARY & STUDENT RATES**

FT. LAUDERDALE'S LARGEST MEN'S RESORT

The Grand Resort

T-1 INTERNET
CLOTHING OPTIONAL AREAS
HEATED POOL
10-MAN JACUZZI
LUXURIOUS BUSINESS SUITES

GRANDRESORT.NET

954.467.1444 — 877.532.7729 — www.InnLeather.com

INN LEATHER
GUESTHOUSE

610 South East 19th Street — Fort Lauderdale — Florida 33316

Lambton Court

Daily, Weekly and Extended Stay

- minutes to Fort Lauderdale Beach
- walk to the Galleria Mall, Fine Restaurants and Trendy Shops
- centrally located to all Fort Lauderdale's celebrated Nightlife
- facilities include heated pool, off street parking, laundry

1.866.222.7905

www.**LambtonCourt**.com

840 NE 17th Terrace, Fort Lauderdale, FL 33304 | 954.462.3977 | lambtoncourt@aol.com

---

LIBERTY SUITES

Affordable Daily, Weekly & Monthly Stays

Beautiful Apartments ★ Best Rates In Town
Terrific Location ★ Pets Always Welcome

Your Home Away From Home For Vacation & Relocation

Toll free (877) 927-0090 ★ Local (954) 927-0090
1501 SW Second Avenue, Ft. Lauderdale (Dania Beach) FL 33004

Near Gay Dania & Nude Haulover Beaches
www.LibertySuites.com

Come play with us!

palm plaza resort .com

Photo by: SylvesterQ
Graphics: Georgios Atzemouglou

Clothing optional pool - Steps to Gay beach - Low Rates
9542606568

---

rekindle...

PINEAPPLE POINT

5 Palm Rating — OUT&ABOUT

888-844-7295 • 954-527-0094
315 NE 16th Terrace • Ft. Lauderdale, FL 33301
PINEAPPLEPOINT.COM

PHOTO & DESIGN ©2002 BLUE DOOR PRODUCTIONS 954.713.8126

www.saintsebastianguesthouse.com

1.800.425.8105

the other fabulous gay guesthouse on Fort Lauderdale Beach!

saint sebastian
guest house

2835 Terramar St. Fort Lauderdale, FL 33304

STEPS AWAY FROM:

St. Sebastian "most friendly" Beach,

Chic Las Olas &

Trend Setting Wilton Manors

Dataports • Weight Room • 24 Hour Deli
Business Center • 2 Pools

www.sheratontrader.com

Sheraton Yankee Trader
Fort Lauderdale Beach   (800) 958-5551

Villa Venice
on Fort Lauderdale Beach

stay with us once...
you'll stay again

Clothing optional heated pool...
Guest laundry & internet...
Poolside tropical breakfast...
Just steps to our famous beach...

877.284.5522
954.564.7855

www.VillaVenice.com

Windamar Beach RESORT

*Owned and Operated by
the Townhouse of New York*

One block from the beach • Clothing Optional
Happy Hour • Continental Breakfast
High Speed Internet • Pet Friendly
Daily, Weekly, Monthly

543 Breakers Avenue
Ft. Lauderdale, FL 33304
954.561.0039
866.554.6816

www.windamarbeachresort.com

KEY WEST AND SOUTH BEACH COME TO FORT LAUDERDALE

SCHUBERT RESORT
Fort Lauderdale, Florida

- 30 oversized suites
- café & full service liquor bars
- heated pool
- 10 person jacuzzi
- sun decks
- clothing optional area
- individually controlled air in each suite
- internet and e-mail access
- conference room available
- minutes from sizzling nightlife and beaches

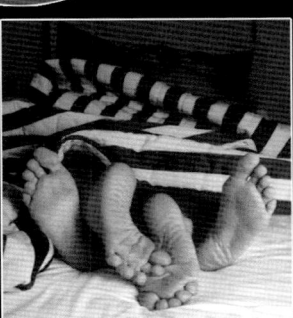

"You're going to enjoy your stay at the Schubert" — tony dee

WWW.SCHUBERTRESORT.COM
855 NORTHEAST TWENTIETH AVENUE
FORT LAUDERDALE, FLORIDA 33304
PHONE: 954-763-7434
TOLL FREE: 1-866-763-7435
FAX: 954-763-4132

Florida • USA

The Corner Pub [GS,NH,GO] 1915 N Andrews Ave **954/564-7335** *noon-close*

Cubby Hole [M,NH,L,F,WC] 823 N Federal Hwy (at 8th St) **954/728-9001** *11am-2am, till 3am Fri-Sat, from noon Sun, internet access*

Fort Lauderdale Eagle [★M,L,WC] 1951 Powerline Rd/ NW 9th Ave (at NW 19th St) **954/462-7224** *noon-2am, till 3am wknds, 'Florida's largest leather club', also HardWear Leather shop*

Georgie's Alibi [★MW,F,V,WC] 2266 Wilton Dr (at NE 6th Ave) **954/565-2526** *11am-2am, till 3am Sat, sports bar*

Hideaway [M,V] 2022 NE 18th St (at Federal Hwy) **954/566-8622** *2pm-2am, till 3am wknds, cruise bar*

Jackhammer [M,D,L,WC] 1725 N Andrews Square (at 17th Ct) **954/522-5855** *theme nights, cruisy*

Johnny's [M,NH,F,S,WC] 1116 W Broward Blvd (at 11th Ave) **954/522-5931** *10am-2am, till 3am Fri-Sat, from noon Sun, male dancers nightly*

Junkyard [M,D,GO] 3073 NE 6th Ave (just S of Oakland Park Blvd) **954/816-7195** *11am-2am, till 3am Fri-Sat, patio*

Kicks Sports Bar [MW,NH] 2008 Wilton Dr (at NE 20th St), Wilton Manors **954/564-8480** *4pm-2am, from noon wknds*

Mona's [M,NH] 502 E Sunrise Blvd (at 6th Ave) **954/525-6662** *noon-2am, till 3am wknds*

Ramrod [★M,D,B,L] 1508 NE 4th Ave (at 16th St) **954/763-8219** *3pm-2am, till 3am wknds, bbq Sun, cruise bar, patio, also Dungeon Bear Leather store*

Royal Tea Dance [M,D] 219 S Atlantic Blvd (at Atlantis Nightclub, enter rear) **954/779-2544** *4pm-8pm Sun only*

■ NIGHTCLUBS

Boom [★M,D,E,K,DS,GO] 2234 Wilton Dr **954/630-3556** *4pm-2am, 3pm-3am wknds, Club Evolution Fri-Sat, T-dance Sun*

Coliseum [M,D,E,S,18+] 2520 S Miami Rd (at US1 & State Rd 84) **954/832-0100** *9pm-6am Fri-Sat only, 18+ Fri*

Copa [M,D,MR,F,E,S,YC] 2800 S Federal Hwy (N of airport) **954/463-1507** *10pm-6am, oldest gay bar in FL*

End Up [M,D] 19 N Federal Hwy, Dania Beach **954/922-6960** *4pm-4am, from 11pm wknds*

The Sea Monster [MW,D,TG,WC,GO] 2 S New River Dr W (under the Andrews Drawbridge, across from Las Olas shopping center) **954/463-4641** *9pm-3am, 4pm-2am Sun, clsd Mon-Th, Latin night Fri, more men Sun for T-dance*

The Voodoo Lounge [M,D,DS] 111 SW 2nd Ave (at Moffat St) **954/522-0733** *gay Sun only for drag show*

■ RESTAURANTS

Bar Amici Restaurant [★E] 1301 E Las Olas Blvd **954/467-3266** *lunch & dinner, Sun brunch w/ live jazz, Italian, full bar*

Bite Me! [GO] 827 E Oakland Park Blvd **954/565-3225** *11am-4pm, clsd Sun, sandwiches, wraps & salads*

Chardee's [MW,D,E,K,P,WC] 2209 Wilton Dr (at NE 6th Ave) **954/563-1800** *dinner from 6pm, also bar, open 4:30pm-2am, karaoke Sun*

Costello's [E] 2345 Wilton Dr, Wilton Manors **954/563-7752** *dinner nightly, also Gin Mill martini bar next door*

The Deck [E,WC] 401 N Atlantic Blvd (at the Bahama Hotel) **954/463-7436** *also bar*

Grandma's French Cafe 3354 N Ocean Blvd (N of Oakland Park Blvd) **954/564-3671** *lunch & dinner, clsd Mon, also ice cream parlor*

Hamburger Mary's [★] 2449 Wilton Dr, Wilton Manors **954/567-1320** *full bar*

Hi-Life Cafe 3000 N Federal Hwy #12 (at Oakland Park Blvd, in the Plaza 3000) **954/563-1395** *dinner Tue-Sun, bistro*

Lester's Diner [★] 250 State Rd 84 **954/525-5641** *24hrs, more gay late nights*

Mustards Bar & Grill [WC,GO] 2256 Wilton Dr (btwn 4th & 6th) **954/565-5116** *4pm-10pm, till 11pm wknds, Mediterranean/ California cuisine*

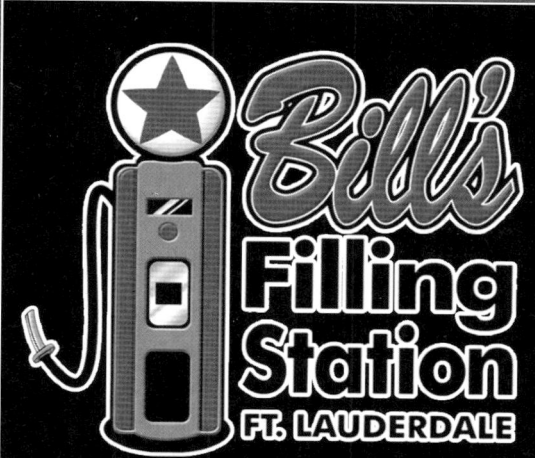

Florida • USA

Simply Delish Cafe [R] 2287 Wilton Dr, Wilton Manors **954/565-8646** *7am-3pm daily, 5pm-9pm Tue-Sun*

Sukothai [★] 1930 E Sunrise Blvd **954/764-0148** *lunch Mon-Fri, dinner nightly, Thai*

Tropics Cabaret & Restaurant [MW,P,WC] 2000 Wilton Dr (at 20th) **954/537-6000** *dinner, also piano bar 4pm-2am, till 3am Sat*

Victoria Park [★BW,R] 900 NE 20th Ave (at Sunrise Blvd) **954/764-6868** *dinner Wed-Sat, brkfst & lunch wknds, clsd Mon-Tue*

■ ENTERTAINMENT & RECREATION

Gold Coast Roller Rink 2604 S Federal Hwy **954/523-6783** *8pm-midnight Tue, gay skate*

John U Lloyd State Park—Dania Beach [AYOR] Dania *popular gay beach, first parking lot over the bridge, off Dania Beach Blvd, walk right*

Pontoon Pride Rides 719 NW 19th St, 201 **954/648-1507** *Fort Lauderdale's only gay pontoon charter!*

■ BOOKSTORES

Pride Factory & CyberCafe 845 N Federal Hwy (at Sunrise) **954/463-6600** *10am-10pm, till 11pm Fri-Sat, 11am-8pm Sun, books, gifts, cybercafe*

■ RETAIL SHOPS

Audace 813 E Las Olas Blvd (at 8th St) **954/522-7503** *10am-11pm, from 11am Sun, men's underwear & sportswear*

Catalog Xtreme 850 NE 13th St **954/524-5050** *10am-10pm, till 9pm Sat, 11am-7pm Sun*

Clothes Encounters 1952 E Sunrise Blvd (at US 1) **954/522-2228** *10am-7pm, clsd Sun, clubwear, gifts & more*

Hard Wear Leather 1949 Powerline Rd/ NW 9th Ave (at NW 19th St) **954/523-4444** *noon-9pm, 3pm-3am Fri-Sat, clsd Sun, alterations, leather wear & gear, adult toys*

Hard Wear Leather 1743 N Andrews Sq **954/523-4444** *alterations, leather wear & gear, adult toys*

We R R You? 1735 N Andrews Ave Extn **954/779-1122, 877/937-7817** *noon-midnight, till 2am Fri-Sat, DVDs, videos, leather, pride items, etc*

■ PUBLICATIONS

The 411 **954/567-1981** *weekly entertainment guide*

Express Gay News **954/568-1880**

■ GYMS & HEALTH CLUBS

Better Bodies [GO] 2270 Wilton Dr, Wilton Manors **954/561-7977**

Firm Fitness 928 N Federal Hwy (at Sunrise) **954/767-6277**

■ MEN'S CLUBS

➤ **Club Fort Lauderdale** [★SW,PC] 110 NW 5th Ave (at Broward) **954/525-3344** *24hrs*

Clubhouse II [V,PC] 2650 E Oakland Park Blvd **954/566-6750** *24hrs, gym*

■ MEN'S SERVICES

➤ **Megaphone Fort Lauderdale** **800/289-1489** *Call for the local # nearest you! Meet Hot Men in your area! FREE to Browse & Respond to voice ads. Use code 3087. Also try MEGAMATES.COM*

■ EROTICA

Fetish Factory 855 E Oakland Park Blvd **954/563-5777**

Midnight News [MO] 2652 E Oakland Park Blvd (at Federal Hwy) **954/564-5015** *cruisy location*

Secrets 4509 N Pine Island Rd (btwn Oakland Park & Commercial), Sunrise **954/748-5855**

Tropixxx Video 1514 NE 4th Ave (at 16th St), Wilton Manors **954/522-5988**

■ CRUISY AREAS

Beach at Sebastian St [AYOR]

Dania Pier [AYOR] Dania Beach (S of John U Lloyd State Park) *nights*

Deerfield Beach [AYOR]

Fort Lauderdale Beach [★AYOR] opposite 18th St NE (btwn Oakland Park & Sunrise Blvds) *dune area cruisy all night & gay beach during the day*

North Lauderdale Beach [AYOR]

Pompano Beach [AYOR] 16th St & A1A (N of Atlantic)

Setting A New Standard

Always Open
Guest Memberships
Steam Room
Sauna
Whirlpool
Private Dressing Rooms
Outdoor Pool & Patio
Gym
18+ only

THE **CLUB**
FT. LAUDERDALE

A PRIVATE MEN'S CLUB
110 NW 5th Ave. • Ft. Lauderdale, FL • (954)525-3344
www.the-clubs.com

Florida • USA

Fort Myers

■INFO LINES & SERVICES
Mark Griffin, Realtor
800/726-1498

■BARS
Office Pub [M,NH] 3704 Cleveland Ave (at Grove) **239/936-3212** *noon-2am, bear night 1st Sun, leather Fri*

Tubby's [M,K,S,GO] 4350 Fowler St (at Colonial) **239/274-5001** *2pm-2am*

■NIGHTCLUBS
The Bottom Line (TBL) [MW,D,V,S,WC] 3090 Evans Ave (at Hanson) **239/337-7292** *2pm-2am*

■RESTAURANTS
Oasis [BW,WC] 2260 Martin Luther King Blvd (at Hendry St) **239/334-1566** *brkfst & lunch only*

■ENTERTAINMENT & RECREATION
Lovers Key State Recreation Area [N] 8700 Estero Blvd (5 miles S of Fort Myers Beach) *nudist area, more gay in back area*

Sam's I-75 to exit 25, then E on Palm Beach Blvd; go N on State Rd 31 past the civic center (Ruden Rd turn left) *nudist area, more gay in back area*

■MEN'S SERVICES
➤ **Megaphone Fort Myers** 800/289-1489 *Call for the local # nearest you! Meet Hot Men in your area! FREE to Browse & Respond to voice ads. Use code 3087. Also try MEGAMATES.COM*

■CRUISY AREAS
Bunche Beach [AYOR] John Morris Pkwy *S end of beach*

Jaycee's Park [AYOR] at the end of Beach Blvd, Cape Coral *also Treeline Road, just past rest area at same exit off I-75*

Fort Walton Beach

■ACCOMMODATIONS
Spring Creek Campground [M,SW,N,GO] 163 Campground Rd (at Hwy 52 & Country Rd 4), Geneva, AL **334/684-3891** *cabins, tent & RV sites, some theme wknds w/ DJ*

■NIGHTCLUBS
Club Insashaible [GF,D,TG,E,K,C,DS,S,GO] 217 Hwy 98 E **850/664-2966** *5pm-midnight, 7pm-4am Th-Sat, 3pm-1am Sun, clsd Mon*

Gainesville

■INFO LINES & SERVICES
Gay/ Lesbian/ Bisexual Community Switchboard 352/332-0700 *3pm-7pm Mon, Wed & Fri, noon-4pm Sat*

www.GayFloridaRealty.com *Log on & see current MLS listings in your destination Florida city. Search for a gay or lesbian realtor or mortgage broker.*

■BARS
Spikes [★MW,NH] 4130 NW 6th St **352/376-3772** *5pm-2am*

The University Club [MW,D,K,S,YC,WC] 18 E University Ave (enter rear) **352/378-6814** *5pm-2am, till 11pm Sun, 3 levels, patio*

■BOOKSTORES
Wild Iris Books [WC] 802 W University Ave (at 8th St) **352/375-7477** *10am-6pm, 11am-5pm Sun, feminist/ lgbt*

■CRUISY AREAS
Bivens Arm Nature Park [AYOR] *days*

Bolen's Bluff Dock [AYOR] US 441 S (past Praynes Prairie, on the right) *days*

Hollywood

see also Miami

■ACCOMMODATIONS
Ocean Mist Motel [GF] 1500 N Ocean Dr **954/922-1744, 954/610-6880** *deck*

■BARS
Dinopete's [GS,D,F,E,K] 4221 N State Rd 7 (at Sterling) **954/966-4441** *4pm-close, clsd Sun, restaurant, karaoke Th*

Trixie's Show Bar [M,DS,S] 600 S Dixie Hwy (S of Hollywood Blvd) **954/923-9322** *8pm-2am, strippers*

■NIGHTCLUBS
Manhattan Lounge [GS,D,F] 219 N 21st Ave (near Hollywood Blvd) **954/922-1144** *11am-4am*

Florida • USA

■ EROTICA

Hollywood Book & Video
1235 S State Rd 7 (at Washington)
954/981-2164

■ CRUISY AREAS
Young Circle [AYOR]

Inverness

■ ACCOMMODATIONS

Camp David [MO,N] 2000 S Bishop's Point Rd 352/344-3445 *camping/ RV retreat*

Islamorada

■ ACCOMMODATIONS

Casa Morada [GF,SW] 136 Madeira Rd 305/664-0044, 888/881-3030 *luxury all-suite hotel w/ private island*

Lookout Lodge Resort [GF] 87770 Overseas Hwy, mile marker 88 (at Plantation Blvd) 305/852-9915, 800/870-1772 *waterfront resort*

■ EROTICA

The Romance Store 82185 Overseas Hwy (Mile Marker 82) 305/664-8228, 800/326-8905 *10am-6pm, clsd Sun*

Jacksonville

■ BARS

616 [MW,NH,K] 616 Park St (at I-95) 904/358-6969 *4pm-2am, patio*

Boot Rack Saloon [M,CW,BW,WC] 4751 Lenox Ave (at Cassat Ave) 904/384-7090 *3pm-2am, cruise bar, patio, also toy store*

The Metro [★MW,D,K,DS,P,S,V,18+,WC] 2929 Plum St 904/388-8719, 904/388-7192 *4pm-2am, from 6pm Sat, till midnight Mon, 7 bars, male strippers, also The Loft [NS]*

The Norm [W,D,E,WC] 2952 Roosevelt Blvd (at College) 904/384-9929 *4pm-2am*

Park Place Lounge [MW,NH,D,WC] 931 King St (at Post) 904/389-6616 *noon-2am*

Third Dimension [M,D,A,MR,K,S,WC] 711 Edison Ave (btwn Riverside & Park) 904/353-6316 *3pm-2am, from 6pm Sat, from 5pm Sun, 5 bars*

■ CAFES

Fuel Coffee House [F,E] 1037 Park St (at Post) 904/425-3835 *9am-3am, till 10pm Sun, till midnight Mon-Tue*

■ RESTAURANTS

Dir-T-SuzE's Bar & Grill [K,GO] 910 King St (at College St) 904/387-2899 *dinner, full bar*

European Street Cafe [★BW,WC,GO] 2753 Park St (at King) 904/384-9999 *10am-10pm*

■ RETAIL SHOPS

Daddy's Closet 2929 Plum St (inside The Metro) 904/777-3692 *9pm-2am Th-Sat, leather wear, gifts & club supplies*

Rainbows & Stars 1046 Park St (in historic 5-Points) 904/356-7702 *noon-8pm, clsd Sun, pride giftstore*

■ PUBLICATIONS

➤ **TLW Magazine** 727/522-8888 *Southeast's largest entertainment magazine for gay men*

■ MEN'S CLUBS

Club Jacksonville [SW,PC] 1939 Hendricks Ave 904/398-7451 *24hrs*

■ MEN'S SERVICES

➤ **Megaphone Jacksonville** 800/289-1489 *Call for the local # nearest you! Meet Hot Men in your area! FREE to Browse & Respond to voice ads. Use code 3087. Also try MEGAMATES.COM*

Jacksonville Beach

■ BARS

Bo's Coral Reef [MW,D,S] 201 5th Ave N (at 2nd St) 904/246-9874 *2pm-2am*

■ CRUISY AREAS

5th Ave Beach [AYOR] *S to boardwalk*

Neptune Beach [AYOR] at 13th *dunes, just S*

Key Biscayne

■ CRUISY AREAS

Bear Cut Park [AYOR] in Crandon Beach Park

214   2004 Damron Men's Travel Guide

tlw
MAGAZINE

WHATEVER YOU'RE LOOKING FOR
WE'VE GOT IT!

www.tlwmagazine.com
INFO@tlwmagazine.com

P.O. Box 21512
St. Petersburg, FL 33742
727-522-8888

design: graphic art / model: chuck / photo: pictureman

Key West • Florida

Key West

INFO LINES & SERVICES

➤ **Floridakeys.com** *comprehensive vacation planning site*

Gay/ Lesbian AA 305/296-8654

Gay/Lesbian Community Center 1075 Duval St, Unit C-14 **305/292-3223** *many mtgs & groups, call for info*

➤ **Key West Business Guild** 305/294-4603, 800/535-7797

KISS (Keep It Simple, Sweetie) 1215 Petronia St (at MCC) **305/294-8912** *variety of AA meetings*

www.GayFloridaRealty.com *Log on & see current MLS listings in your destination Florida city. Search for a gay or lesbian realtor or mortgage broker.*

ACCOMMODATIONS

Alexander Palms Court [GF,SW,GO] 715 South St (at Vernon) **305/296-6413, 800/858-1943** *hot tub*

➤ **Alexander's Guest House** [MW,SW,N,WC,GO] 1118 Fleming St (at Frances) **305/294-9919, 800/654-9919** *sundeck, hot tub, private patios*

Ambrosia House Tropical Lodging [GF,SW] 615 & 618-622 Fleming St (at Simonton) **305/296-9838, 800/535-9838** *captain's house*

Andrews Inn [GF,SW,NS] Zero Whalton Ln (at Duval) **305/294-7730, 888/263-7393**

The Artist House [GS,SW,NS] 534 Eaton St (at Duval) **305/296-3977, 800/582-7882** *full brkfst (seasonal), jacuzzi, patio*

➤ **Atlantic Shores Resort** [★MW,F,SW,N,WC] 510 South St (at Duval) **305/296-2401, 800/547-0717** *resort w/ pool, pier, bars, restaurant & T-dance Wed & Sun*

Author's Key West [GF,SW] 725 White St (entrance on Petronia) **305/294-7381, 800/898-6909**

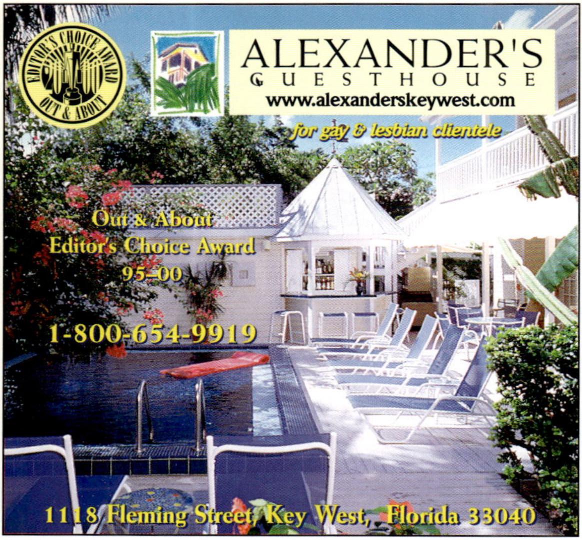

key west's oceanfront alternative

the complete waterfront resort

- open to the public
- party deck, bar & grill
- world famous tea dance
- comfortable guestrooms
- cinema shores
- diner shores
- central to area attractions

ATLANTIC SHORES RESORT · KEY WEST

510 SOUTH ST., KEY WEST, FL • 305.296.2491
VISIT US ONLINE AT **GLResorts.com**
OR CALL TOLL FREE 866.900.3892

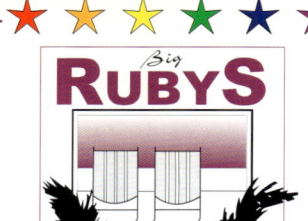

Big RubyS

France ✦ Costa Rica ✦ U.S.A.

L'Orangerie
Aigues-Mortes ✦ France

Magnificently appointed 15th century residence in the historic town of Aigues-Mortes in the south of France.

tél. ++ 33 (0) 4 66 73 90 48

france@bigrubys.com

La Plantacion
Manuel Antonio ✦ Costa Rica

Luxurious bungalows set in extensive tropical gardens , overlooking the pacific ocean

tél. (++506) 777 1332

costarica@bigrubys.com

Big Rubys
Key West ✦ Florida

Elegant 19th century guesthouse set in he heart of key west.
Full breakfast included.

tél. (++1) 305 296 2323

keywest@bigrubys.com

www.bigrubys.com
award winning guesthouse

Our 24 Man Hot-tub

Key West's Most Sought After All-Male Accommodations

Choose either:
**The Oasis Guesthouse or Coral Tree Inn
822/823 Fleming Street, Key West
800-362-7477**

www.keywest-allmale.com

www.islandhousekeywest.com
1 800-890-6284
305-294-6284
IHKeyWest@aol.com

IsLAnd HouSe

"The best gay men's resort in the world..."
BOYZ Magazine

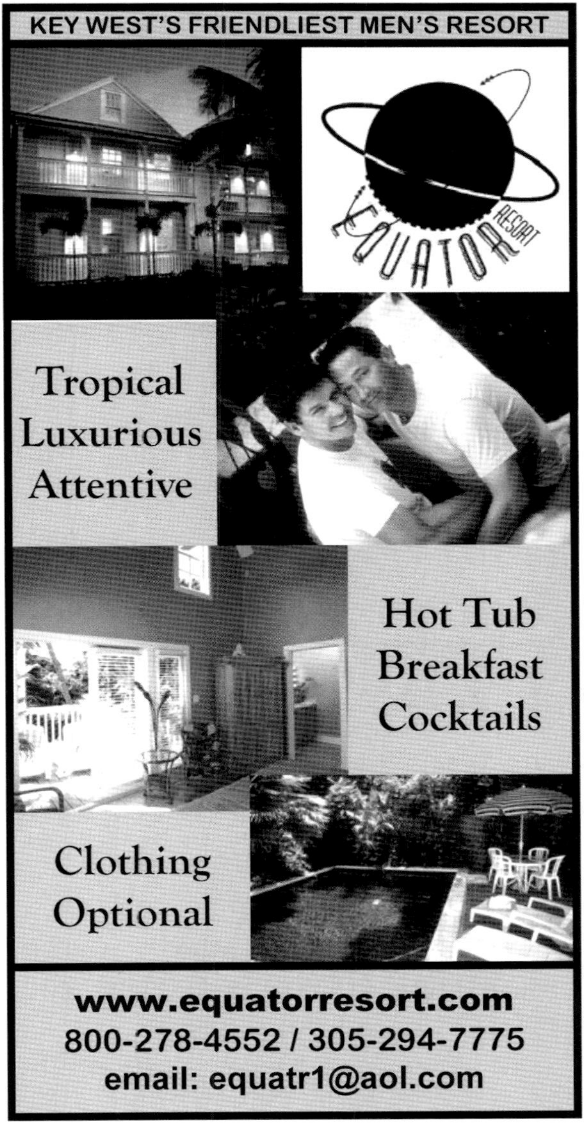
KEY WEST'S FRIENDLIEST MEN'S RESORT
EQUATOR RESORT
Tropical
Luxurious
Attentive
Hot Tub
Breakfast
Cocktails
Clothing
Optional
www.equatorresort.com
800-278-4552 / 305-294-7775
email: equatr1@aol.com

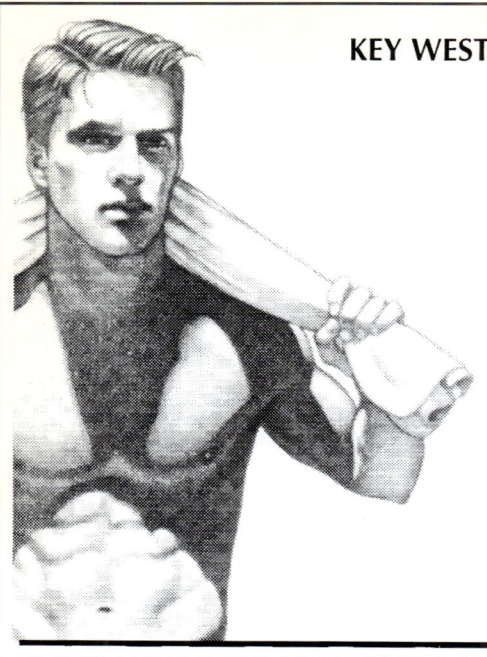

KEY WEST

LIGHTHOUSE COURT

Experience a fantasy vacation at Key West's largest all-male, clothing optional private compound.
- Courtyard Café • Poolside Video Bar
- Health Club • Heated Pool & Spa.

All 45 rooms/cabanas/cottages/suites offer air conditioning, phones, TV's, Bahama fans, mini-bars. Some with kitchens. Central location next to Key West Lighthouse and across from Hemingway House.

902 Whitehead, Key West, FL 33040
(305) 294-9588
www.lighthousecourt.com

Key West • Florida

Avalon B&B [GF,SW] 1317 Duval St (at United) **305/294-8233, 800/848-1317** *restored Victorian, near beach*

Bananas Foster B&B [GF,GO] 537 Caroline St (at Simonton St) **305/294-9061, 800/653-4888** *hot tub, spa*

Beach Bungalow & Beach Guest Suite [GS] **305/294-1525** *vacation rental, 3-day minimum stay*

➤ **Big Ruby's Guesthouse** [M,SW,N,WC,GO] 409 Appelrouth Ln (at Duval & Whitehead) **305/296-2323, 800/477-7829** *full brkfst, evening wine, non-smoking available*

Blue Parrot Inn [GF,SW,N,WC,GO] 916 Elizabeth St (at Olivia) **305/296-0033, 800/231-2473**

Chelsea House [MW,SW,N,WC,GO] 707 Truman Ave (at Elizabeth) **305/296-2211, 800/845-8859**

Coconut Grove Guesthouse for Men [MO,SW,N] 815 Fleming St (at William St) **305/296-5107, 800/262-6055** *2 historic homes*

Colours Destinations Int'l [MW,GO] **954/825-0321, 877/932-6652** *hotel reservation service*

➤ **Coral Tree Inn/ Oasis Guest House** [M,SW,N,WC,GO] 822 & 823 Fleming St (at Margaret) **305/296-2131, 800/362-7477** *sundeck*

The Courtyard of Key West [GF] 910 Simonton St (at Truman) **305/296-1148, 800/296-1148** *apt suites*

Cuban Club Suites [GF] 1102-1108 Duval St (at Virginia) **305/296-0465, 800/432-4849** *award-winning historic hotel*

Curry House [MO,SW,N,GO] 806 Fleming St (at William) **305/294-6777, 800/633-7439** *full brkfst, hot tub, sundeck*

Cypress House [GF,SW] 601 Caroline (at Simonton) **305/294-6969, 800/525-2488** *sundeck*

Deja Vu Resort [GF,SW,N] 611 Truman Ave (at Simonton) **305/292-9339** *hot tub*

Duval House [GF,SW,NS,GO] 815 Duval St (at Petronia) **305/292-9491, 800/223-8825** *Victorians w/ gardens, sundeck*

Eaton Lodge [GF,SW] 511 Eaton St (at Duval) **305/292-2170, 800/294-2170** *hot tub*

➤ **Equator Guest House** [MO,SW,N,NS,WC,GO] 818 Fleming St (at William) **305/294-7775, 800/278-4552** *hot tub*

➤ **Fleur de Key Guesthouse** [★M,SW,N,NS,WC,GO] 412 Frances St (at Eaton) **305/296-4719, 800/932-9119** *luxury guest house, hot tub*

Heartbreak Hotel [MW,GO] 716 Duval St (near Petronia) **305/296-5558** *kitchens*

Heron House [GF,SW,WC] 512 Simonton St (at Fleming) **305/294-9227, 800/294-1644** *evening wine*

➤ **Island House** [MO,F,SW,N,NS,WC,GO] 1129 Fleming St (at White) **305/294-6284, 800/890-6284** *some shared baths, hot tub, sauna, steam, gym, very cruisy*

Key Lodge Motel [GF,SW] 1004 Duval St (at Truman) **305/296-9915, 800/845-8384**

Key West Harbor Inn B&B [MW,SW,NS,WC] 219 Elizabeth St (at Greene) **305/296-2978, 800/608-6569** *hot tub*

Knowles House B&B [GS,SW,N,NS,GO] 1004 Eaton St (at Grinnell) **305/296-8132, 800/352-4414** *restored 1880s Conch house*

La Casa de Luces [GF,WC] 422 Amelia St (at Whitehead) **305/296-3993, 800/432-4849** *early 1900s Conch house & condos, jacuzzi*

La Te Da [★MW,S,SW,N,21+,WC,GO] 1125 Duval St (at Catherine) **305/296-6706, 877/528-3320** *full brkfst, tropical setting, also restaurant & 3 bars*

Lightbourn Inn [GF,SW,NS,WC,GO] 907 Truman Ave (at Packer) **305/296-5152, 800/352-6011**

Florida • USA

➤ **Lighthouse Court** [MO,SW,N] 902 Whitehead St (at Olivia) **305/294-9588** *poolside cafe, spa*

Marquesa Hotel [GF,SW,WC] 600 Fleming St (at Simonton) **305/292-1919, 800/869-4631** *also Cafe Marquesa 6pm-11pm, full bar*

The Mermaid & the Alligator [GS,SW,NS,GO] 729 Truman Ave (at Windsor Ln) **305/294-1894, 800/773-1894** *full brkfst*

Nassau House [GF,SW,NS,WC,GO] 1016 Fleming St (at Grinnell) **305/296-8513, 800/296-8513** *sundeck, hot tub*

The New Orleans House Guesthouse [M,GO] 724 Duval St, upstairs (at Angela) **305/293-9800, 888/293-9893**

Pier House Resort & Caribbean Spa [GF,SW,NS,WC] 1 Duval St (at Front) **305/296-4600, 800/327-8340** *private beach, hot tub, restaurants, bars, spa*

Pilot House Guest House [GS,SW,N,NS,WC] 414 Simonton St (at Eaton) **305/293-6600, 800/648-3780** *Victorian mansion, hot tub*

Sea Isle Resort [★M,SW,N,WC,GO] 915 Windsor Ln (at Olivia) **305/294-5188, 800/995-4786** *hot tub, gym, sundeck*

Seascape Tropical Inn [GF,SW,NS] 420 Olivia St (at Duval) **305/296-7776, 800/765-6438** *also cottages, hot tub, sundeck*

Sheraton Suites Key West [GF,SW,WC] 2001 S Roosevelt Blvd **305/292-9800, 800/452-3224** *hot tub, also restaurant*

Simonton Court Historic Inn & Cottages [GF,SW] 320 Simonton St (at Caroline) **305/294-6386, 800/944-2687** *built in 1880s*

Travelers Palm [GF,SW] 915 Center St **305/294-9560, 800/294-9560** *3 locations in Old Town Key West*

Tropical Inn [GF,SW] 812 Duval St (at Petronia) **305/294-9977, 888/611-6510** *hot tub, sundeck*

Watson House [GS,SW,GO] 525 Simonton St (btwn Fleming & Southard) **305/294-6712, 800/621-9405** *spa*

■ **BARS**

The 801 Bourbon Bar [★MW,NH,D,C,DS,P,S] 801 Duval St (at Petronia) **305/294-4737** *11am-4am, Sun bingo, also One Saloon [M,L]*

Bourbon Street Pub [★M,S,V,SW,WC] 724 Duval St (at Angela) **305/296-1992** *11am-4am, popular daytime bar, start your 'Duval Crawl' here*

Donnie's Club International [M,NH,WC] 900 Simonton St (at Olivia) **305/294-2655** *noon-4am*

Kwest Men [★M,S] 705 Duval St **305/292-8500** *3pm-4am, strippers*

La Te Da [★MW,C,P,WC,GO] 1125 Duval St (at Catherine) **305/296-6706** *3 bars & restaurant*

■ **NIGHTCLUBS**

Aqua [MW,D,DS,V] 711 Duval St **305/294-0555** *2pm-2am, till 4am Th-Sat, also Tiki Bar, Th-Sat from 10pm, garden w/ waterfall*

➤ **Tea by the Sea** [★MW,F,SW,N,WC] 510 South St (at Atlantic Shores Resort) **305/296-2491, 877/778-7711** *6pm-10pm Wed & 7pm-11pm Sun, T-dance at this complete resort w/ pool, bars, restaurant, rooms*

Wax [★GF,D,YC] 422 Appelrouth Ln (at Whitehead) **305/296-6667** *9pm-4am, patio*

■ **CAFES**

Croissants de France [MW,BW] 816 Duval St (at Petronia) **305/294-2624** *7:30am-6pm, restaurant open till 3pm, French pastries, patio*

■ **RESTAURANTS**

Alice's [★] at La Te Da accommodations **305/296-6706 x39** *brkfst & lunch Tue-Sun, dinner nightly, fusion, award-winning chef*

Antonia's [★] 615 Duval St (at Southard) **305/294-6565** *6pm-11pm, Italian, full bar*

Bo's Fish Wagon [★] 801 Caroline (at Williams) **305/294-9272** *lunch, dinner in-season only, 'seafood & eat it'*

Key West • Florida

Camille's 1202 Simonton (at Catherine) **305/296-4811** *8am-3pm, 6pm-10pm, no dinner Sun-Mon, bistro, hearty brkfst*

Kelly's Caribbean Bar Grill & Brewery 301 Whitehead St (at Caroline) **305/293-8484** *lunch & dinner, owned by actress Kelly McGillis*

La Trattoria Venezia [MW] 524 Duval St (at Fleming) **305/296-1075** *5:30pm-10:30pm, Italian, full bar*

Lobos [BW] 611 1/2 Duval St **305/296-5303** *11am-6pm, noon-4pm Sun*

Louie's Backyard [★] 700 Waddell Ave (at Vernon) **305/294-1061** *lunch & dinner, fine dining, bar from 11:30am-2am, deck*

Mangia Mangia [BW] 900 Southard St (at Margaret St) **305/294-2469** *dinner only, fresh pasta, patio*

Mangoes [WC] 700 Duval St (at Angela) **305/292-4606** *11:30am-11pm, 'Floribbean' cuisine, full bar*

New York Pizza Cafe [GF] 1075 Duval St (Duval Square) **305/292-1991** *open till midnight, very reasonable prices*

Pisces 1007 Simonton St (at Truman) **305/294-7100** *6pm-11pm, tropical French, full bar*

Rooftop Cafe 310 Front St (at Duval) **305/294-2042** *lunch & dinner, best Key Lime pie, full bar*

Seven Fish [★] 632 Olivia St (at Elizabeth) **305/296-2777** *6pm-10pm, clsd Tue*

Square One [WC] 1075 Duval St (at Truman) **305/296-4300** *6pm-10pm, American, full bar*

■ Entertainment & Recreation

Bahia Honda State Park & Beach 35 miles N of Key West *Viking Beach is best*

BluQ Sailing [M,GO] 201 William St (at Caroline) **305/923-7245** *all-gay sails, daily sailing, snorkeling, kayaking & sunset cruises, day trips include all gear & meals*

Fort Zachary Taylor Beach *more gay to the right*

Moped Hospital 601 Truman **305/296-3344** *forget the car—mopeds are a must for touring the island*

Sebago Gay Cruises [MW,BW,$] 200 William St (at historic Key West Seaport) **305/292-4768** *9pm-11pm Tue [MO], 9pm-11pm Sat [MW], full cash bar*

■ Bookstores

Blue Heron Books 826 Duval (btwn Petronia & Olivia) **305/296-3508** *10am-9pm, till 6pm Sun, lgbt section*

Flaming Maggie's 830 Fleming St (at Margaret) **305/294-3931** *lgbt bookstore & coffeehouse*

Key West Island Books 513 Fleming St (at Duval) **305/294-2904** *10am-9pm, new & used rare books, lgbt section*

■ Retail Shops

Fast Buck Freddie's [WC] 500 Duval St (at Fleming) **305/294-2007** *10am-6pm, till 8pm Fri-Sat, from 11am Sun, clothing, gifts*

Fausto's Food Palace 522 Fleming St (at Duval) **305/296-5663** *8am-8pm, till 7pm Sun, cruisy grocery store*

In Touch 715 Duval St (at Angela) **305/292-7293** *9:30am-11pm, gay gifts*

Xposure 505 Southard (at Duval) **305/293-8199** *clubwear, swimwear, accessories, etc*

■ Publications

Celebrate! **305/295-8292**

Southern Exposure **305/294-6303**

■ Gyms & Health Clubs

Bodies on South 2740 N Roosevelt Blvd **305/292-2930**

Club Body Tech [MW] 1075 Duval St (at Virginia) **305/292-9683** *full gym, steam room, massage therapy available*

Florida • USA

■EROTICA

Leather Master 418-A Appelrouth Ln (btwn Duval & Whitehead) **305/292-5051, 800/565-9447** *11am-11pm, noon-8pm Sun, custom leather, toys & more; also 504 Petronia location, 305/ 292-9911*

Leatherotica [GO] 405-B Petronia St **305/294-3000, 800/655-1505** *10am-midnight, 11am-9pm Sun*

Truman Books & Video 922 Truman Ave **305/295-0120** *arcade*

■CRUISY AREAS

'Dick Dock' [AYOR] pier at end of Reynolds St *late*

Fleming St [AYOR]

Kissimmee

■ACCOMMODATIONS

Ramada Plaza Gateway [GF,F,WC] 7470 Hwy 192 W **407/396-4400, 800/327-9170 ext 688** *1 mile from Walt Disney World*

Lake Worth

■BARS

The Mad Hatter Bar & Grill [MW,NH,F] 1532 N Dixie Hwy (16th Ave) **561/547-8860** *11am-2am, from noon Sun*

Lakeland

■ACCOMMODATIONS

Sunset Motel [GF,SW,WC,GO] 2301 New Tampa Hwy **863/683-6464** *motels, apts & private home on 3 acres*

■BARS

Pulse [M,D,S,WC] 1030 E Main St **863/683-6021** *4pm-2am, till midnight Sun*

■CRUISY AREAS

Saddle Creek Park [AYOR] Hwy 92

Largo

■EROTICA

Buddies of Largo 13801 66th St **727/539-7979**

Leesburg

■NIGHTCLUBS

Attitudes [MW,D,K,DS,S] 1850 E Main St/ Hwy 441 **352/728-1968** *6pm-2am, clsd Mon-Tue*

Madeira Beach

see also St Petersburg

Madison

■ACCOMMODATIONS

The Mystic Lake Manor [MO,SW,N,WC,GO] **850/973-8435** *full brkfst, hot tub*

Marathon

■EROTICA

➤ **The Lion's Den Adult Bookstore** 2315 Overseas Hwy (MM 48.2 on US-1) **305/289-3399**

Melbourne

■INFO LINES & SERVICES

www.GayFloridaRealty.com *Log on & see current MLS listings in your destination Florida city. Search for a gay or lesbian realtor or mortgage broker.*

■ACCOMMODATIONS

Crane Creek Inn B&B [GS,SW,NS] 907 E Melbourne Ave **321/768-6416** *full brkfst, hot tub, on the waterfront*

■BARS

Cold Keg [★MW,D,S,WC] 4060 W New Haven Ave (1/2 mile E of I-95) **321/724-1510** *2pm-2am*

■ENTERTAINMENT & RECREATION

Canova Beach [AYOR] *cruisy nights*

■CRUISY AREAS

Melbourne Harbor Marina [AYOR]

Paradise Beach [AYOR]

Miami—Greater Miami • Florida

MIAMI

Miami is divided into
3 geographical areas:
Miami—Overview
Miami—Greater Miami
Miami—Miami Beach/ South Beach

Miami—Overview

■INFO LINES & SERVICES
Switchboard of Miami
305/358-4357 *24hrs, gay-friendly info & referrals for Dade County*

■PUBLICATIONS
Contax Guide 305/757-6333 *club listings & more*

TWN (The Weekly News)
305/757-6333 *lgbt newspaper for South Florida*

Miami—Greater Miami

■INFO LINES & SERVICES
Lambda Dade AA [WC] 317 NE 24th St (off Biscayne) **305/573-9608**

■ACCOMMODATIONS
Miami River Inn [GF,SW,WC]
118 SW S River Dr **305/325-0045, 800/468-3589** *B&B located in Miami's Little Havana district, jacuzzi*

Rick's Place [MO,GO] 547 NE 94th St (at NE 5th) **305/751-3040, 305/756-9899**

■BARS
Cactus Bar & Grill [M,MR,F,S,V]
2041 Biscayne Blvd (at 20th Terr)
305/438-0662 *4pm-2am, Latin night Wed & Sat, Wall-to-Wall Men Fri*

Sugar's [M,NH,D,V,WC] 17060 W Dixie Hwy (at 172nd), North Miami Beach **305/940-9887** *3pm-6am*

Damron Men's Travel Guide 2004

Florida • USA

Uranus Bar [M,NH,D,V] 55 NE 24th St (at N Miami Ave) 305/573-1010 4pm-5am, video cruise bar, leather night Fri, DJ/dancing Sat & Sun T-dance

■NIGHTCLUBS

Club Boi [M,D,MR-AF] 726 NW 79th St (1 blk west of I-95) 305/836-8995 Fri-Sat midnight-close

Club Ozone [M,D,DS] 6620 Red Rd/ SW 57th Ave 305/667-2888, 305/667-4684 9pm-5am, Latin Tue, patio

➤ **Cupid's Cabaret** [★MO,D,MR,S,PC,GO] 1060 NE 79th St (1/2 mile E of Biscayne Blvd) 305/756-2694 5pm-5am, nude dancers

Steel [★MW,D] 5922 S Dixie Hwy (at US Hwy 1) 305/663-4567 9pm-5am, from 4pm Sun, clsd Mon-Tue, goth Wed & Sat [A,18+], Tease Fri [W,D], garden terrace

■CAFES

Gourmet Station [GO] 7601 Biscayne Blvd (at NE 71st St) 305/756-9899 also catering

■RESTAURANTS

The Bal Harbour Bistro [WC,GO] 9700 Collins Ave (in the Bal Harbour Shops), Bal Harbour 305/861-4544 10am-10pm, full bar, patio

Magnum Lounge & Restaurant [★GS,E,P] 709 NE 79th St 305/757-3368 6pm-midnight, bar open 5pm-2am, cont'l

■BOOKSTORES

Lambda Passages Bookstore 7545 Biscayne Blvd (at 76th) 305/754-6900 11am-9pm, noon-6pm Sun, lgbt/ feminist

■RETAIL SHOPS

Frivole Couture 14700 NW 7th Ave 305/769-5828

■MEN'S CLUBS

Club Body Center Miami [★MO,SW,PC] 2991 Coral Wy 305/448-2214 24hrs, poolside cook-outs, over 30 years popular!

■EROTICA

Biscayne Books & Video 117 Biscayne Blvd 305/891-3475 24hrs

Cloverleaf Book & Video 14907 NW 7th Ave 305/681-2001 24hrs

Happy Books 9514 S Dixie Hwy 305/670-9203 24hrs

Perrine Books & Video 18093 S Dixie Hwy 305/233-3913

■CRUISY AREAS

Alice Wainwright Park [AYOR]

Bear Cut Beach [AYOR]

Biscayne Boulevard [AYOR] cruisy hitchhikers

Matheson Hammock Beach [AYOR] on Old Cutler Rd (S of Kendall Dr)

Miami—Miami Beach/ South Beach

■ACCOMMODATIONS

The AAA Shelborne Beach Resort— South Beach [GF,F,SW,WC] 1801 Collins Ave (at 18th) 305/531-1271, 800/327-8757 full brkfst, tropical gardens

Abbey Hotel [GS] 300 21st St (at Collins) 305/531-0031, 888/612-2239 chic restored art deco, full brkfst, gym

Aqua Hotel & Lounge [GS,SW] 1530 Collins Ave 305/538-4361

The Bayliss [MW] 504 14th St 305/538-5620 tropical art deco hotel

The Beachcomber [GF] 1340 Collins Ave (at 13th St) 305/531-3755, 888/305-4683 intimate art deco hotel

The Blue Moon Hotel [GF] 944 Collins Ave 305/673-2262, 800/724-1623 Mediterranean-style hotel, also bar

The Bohemia [MO,N,NS,GO] 825 Michigan Ave (at 8th St) 305/534-1322, 888/883-4565 apts, studios, hot tub

Brigham Gardens [GS] 1411 Collins Ave (at 14th) 305/531-1331 art deco guest house

The Cardozo Hotel [GF,F,WC] 1300 Ocean Dr 305/535-6500, 800/782-6500 Gloria Estefan's plush hotel

Castle Palms [MO,SW,N,GO] 305/672-2080, 888/327-9118 gym, sauna, hot tub

Miami Beach/ South Beach • Florida

The Century [GF,F] 140 Ocean Dr
305/674-8855, 888/982-3688
restored art deco, Joia restaurant, celebrity hangout

Chesterfield Hotel [GS] 855 Collins Ave **305/531-5831, 800/244-6023**

The Colony Hotel [GF,F,WC] 736 Ocean Dr (at 7th St) **305/673-0088, 800/226-5669** *newly renovated*

Delano Hotel [GF,F,SW,WC] 1685 Collins Ave **305/672-2000, 800/555-5001** *hip hotel, great bar scene (see & be seen)*

Delores Guesthouse [GS] 1420 Collins Ave **305/673-0800** *1 blk from beach*

Destinations International–Mantell [MW,SW,GO] 255 W 24th St **305/532-9341, 877/932-6652** *hotel reservation service for several art deco hotels & apts*

The European Guesthouse [MW,GO] 721 Michigan Ave (btwn 7th & 8th) **305/673-6665** *B&B, full brkfst, hot tub*

Florida Hotel Network [★] **800/293-2419** *reservations & rentals*

Florida Sunbreak **305/532-1516, 800/786-2732** *vacation rental condos, suite hotels & homes*

Fountainbleu Hilton Resort & Spa [GF,F,SW,WC] 4441 Collins Ave **305/538-2000, 800/548-8886**

Golden Tulip Casablanca Hotel [GS,SW] 6345 Collins Ave (at 63rd St) **305/868-0010, 800/813-6676** *studios*

The Hotel [GF,F,SW] 801 Collins Ave **305/531-2222, 877/843-4683** *interior design by Todd Oldham*

Hotel Astor [★GF,F,SW,WC] 956 Washington Ave (at 10th St) **305/531-8081, 800/270-4981** *also Metro restaurant*

Hotel Impala [GS,F,WC] 1228 Collins Ave **305/673-2021, 800/646-7252** *luxury hotel near beach*

ISLAND HOUSE
SOUTH BEACH'S LARGEST GAY GUESTHOUSE

**Rooms, Studios, Suites
Complimentary Breakfast
Weekend Happy Hour
One Block to Beach
Walk to Nightlife
Ocean Drive & Lincoln Road
V.I.P Club Guestlist**

800-382-2422   305-864-2422
1428 Collins Avenue Miami Beach, FL 33139
IHSOBE@Bellsouth.net
Fax: 305-865-2220
IslandHouseSouthBeach.com   IGLTA

South Beach

"Without Question the Best of South Beach's Gay Guesthouses." **FODOR'S**

Walk everywhere!

Miami Beach's ONLY Bed & Breakfast

THE JEFFERSON HOUSE
BED & BREAKFAST

- Deluxe, gourmet breakfast included
- Blocks from beach, clubs, dining, and shopping
- High-speed guest Internet computer
- Cable TV/VCR's CD Players & AC

1018 Jefferson Avenue, Miami Beach, FL 33139
Phone (305) 534-5247 Fax (305) 534-5953

Toll Free: 877-599-5247
www.thejeffersonhouse.com
email: stay@thejeffersonhouse.com

THE ROYAL PALMS

- LUXURIOUS ROOMS WITH 320 COUNT FRETTE EGYPTIAN LINENS
- BOSE SOUND SYSTEM
- PRIVATE 2 LINE PHONE
- VOICE EMAIL
- COMPUTER ACCESS
- CLOTHING-OPTIONAL TROPICAL HEATED POOL
- 10 MAN SPA
- PRIVATE COMPOUND WITH LUSH, EXOTIC FLORA
- COMPLIMENTARY CONTINENTAL BREAKFAST
- COMPLIMENTARY WINE, BEER, BEV'S & SNACKS
- STEPS TO BEACH

800~237~PALM
www.royalpalms.com

ph 954-564-6444 fx 954-564-6443
email info@royalpalms.com
2901 Terramar Street
Fort Lauderdale Beach, FL 33304
Gay Owned & Operated

IGLTA

Just 35 miles from Miami!

Miami Beach/ South Beach • Florida

Hotel Leon [GF,F,WC] 841 Collins Ave (at 8th St) **305/673-3767** *stylish decor, popular w/ photo industry*

Hotel Nash [GF,F,SW,WC] 1120 Collins Ave **305/674-7800** *sleek & modern new boutique hotel, also restaurant & spa, near gay beach*

Hotel Ocean [★GS,F,WC] 1230-38 Ocean Dr **305/672-2579, 800/783-1725** *great location, jacuzzi*

Hotel Shelley [GS,WC] 844 Collins Ave **305/531-3341, 800/414-0612** *1930s art deco hotel*

➤ **The Indian Creek Hotel** [GF,F,SW,WC,GO] 2727 Indian Creek Dr **305/531-2727, 800/491-2772** *simple & away from the action*

➤ **Island House Miami Beach** [MO,GO] 715 82nd St **305/864-2422, 800/382-2422** *patio*

➤ **Island House South Beach** [MO,GO] 1428 Collins Ave **305/864-2422, 800/382-2422** *SoBe's largest men's guest house, full brkfst*

➤ **Jefferson House B&B** [M,F,SW,NS,GO] 1018 Jefferson St **305/534-5247, 877/599-5247** *private tropical garden, full brkfst, near beach*

The Kent [GS,F,WC] 1131 Collins Ave (at 11th St) **305/531-6771, 800/688-7678** *on the beach, garden bar*

Lily Guesthouse [MW,WC] 835 Collins Ave **305/535-9900, 888/742-6600** *studios, suites*

The Loft Hotel [GS] 952 Collins Ave **305/534-2244** *affordable boutique hotel*

Marlin Hotel [GS,WC] 1200 Collins Ave **305/531-8800, 800/688-7678** *fabulous studios w/ full kitchens, stereo & WebTV*

Miami Habitat [GS] 2999 NE 191 St #404, Aventura **305/935-4641, 800/385-4644** *furnished apts & hotel rooms in Art Deco District, also charter boats*

The Nassau Suite Hotel [GS] 1414 Collins Ave **305/532-0043, 866/859-4177** *renovated art deco, near beach*

The National Hotel [GS,F,SW,WC] 1677 Collins Ave **305/532-2311, 800/327-8370** *on beach*

Ocean Surf Hotel [GF,WC] 7436 Ocean Terrace (near 75th St & Collins Ave) **305/866-1648, 800/555-0411** *restored art deco in quiet North Beach*

The Park Central [GF,F,SW] 640 Ocean Dr **305/538-1611, 800/727-5236** *ocean views*

The Pelican [★GS,F] 826 Ocean Dr (btwn 8th & 9th Sts) **305/673-3373, 800/773-5422** *designer theme rooms*

Penguin Hotel [MW,F,WC] 1418 Ocean Dr **305/534-9334, 800/235-3296** *renovated art deco*

The Raleigh, Miami Beach [GF,SW,WC] 1775 Collins Ave (at Ocean Front) **305/534-6300, 800/848-1775** *outdoor gym*

The Savoy Hotel [GS,SW,WC] 425 Ocean Dr (at 5th St) **305/532-0200, 800/237-2869** *art-deco-meets-eclectic boutique hote*

South Seas [GF,F,SW] 1751 Collins Ave **305/538-1411, 800/345-2678** *clean & basic, beach access, brkfst included*

The Tides [GS,F,SW] 1220 Ocean Dr **305/604-5070, 800/688-7678** *showcase Island Outpost hotel, gym*

The Tropics Hotel & Hostel [GS,SW] 1550 Collins Ave (btwn 15th & 16th Sts) **305/531-0361** *near beach & attractions*

Villa Paradiso Guesthouse [GF] 1415 Collins Ave **305/532-0616** *studios*

The Wave Hotel [GF,F] 350 Ocean Dr **305/673-0401, 800/501-0401** *tropical style*

The Winterhaven [GS,F] 1400 Ocean Dr **305/531-5571, 800/395-2322** *ocean views*

Florida • USA

■BARS

Laundry Bar [MW,NH,E,DS] 721 N Lincoln Ln **305/531-7700** *7am-5am, more men Th, more women Sat, drag show Mon, also laundromat*

Lime Bar [GF,NH,D,TG,E,WC] 1771 West Ave (at Alton Rd & 18th St) **305/534-9993, 786/306-2995** *5pm-5am, clsd Mon-Tue, martini bar, gay Sat only*

Loading Zone [M,L] 1426-A Alton Rd (at 14th Ct) **305/531-5623** *10pm-5am, heavy cruising, leather shop*

■NIGHTCLUBS

Billboardlive [M,D] 15th & Ocean Dr (at ocean steps) **305/538-2251** *Sun only, T-dance, call for exact dates*

Blue [GS,D,DS] 222 Espanola Way (at Collins) **305/534-1009** *10pm-5am, drag show Sun*

Crobar [★GF,D,WC] 1445 Washington Ave (at the Cameo Theater) **305/531-5027** *10pm-5am, gay Sun for Anthem*

Pump [★M,D,WC] 841 Washington Ave (btwn 8th & 9th) **305/538-7867** *4am-close Fri-Sat, world-famous DJs & hot circuit crowd*

Rize at Maze Nightclub [MO,D,TG,DS,WC,GO] 1771 West Ave (at Alton Rd) **305/534-9975, 786/306-2995** *10pm-5am Sat only, occasional theme/ circuit parties*

Score [★MW,D,DS,V] 727 Lincoln Rd (at Meridian) **305/535-1111** *4 bars, lounge opens 3pm, dance club 10pm-5am*

Twist [★M,D,DS,S,V,WC] 1057 Washington Ave (at 11th) **305/538-9478** *1pm-5am*

■CAFES

News Cafe [★] 800 Ocean Dr **305/538-6397** *24hrs, healthy sandwiches*

■RESTAURANTS

11th Street Diner 11th & Washington **305/534-6373** *24hrs, full bar*

A Fish Called Avalon [WC] 700 Ocean Dr **305/532-1727** *6pm-11pm, full bar*

Balans 1022 Lincoln Rd (btwn Michigan & Lennox) **305/534-9191** *8am-midnight, till 1am Fri-Sat, int'l*

Big Pink 157 Collins (at 2nd St) **305/532-4700** *9am-1am, till 2am Fri-Sat, 'real food for real people'*

El Rancho Grande 1626 Pennsylvania Ave (S of Lincoln) **305/673-0480** *11:30am-10pm, Mexican*

The Front Porch 1418 Ocean Dr **305/531-8300** *8am-10:30pm, healthy homecooking, full bar*

Joe's Stone Crab 11 Washington Ave **305/673-0365** *lunch & dinner, seasonal*

Larios on the Beach 820 Ocean Dr **305/532-9577** *11:30am-11:30pm, till 2am Fri-Sat, Cuban*

Madame's Cabaret & Lounge [GF,NH,MR,TG,E,C,DS,WC] 239 Sunny Isles Blvd (at 163rd St & Collins Ave), Sunny Isles Beach **305/945-2040** *6pm-midnight, till 1am Fri-Sat, clsd Tue-Wed, Southern comfort food, full bar*

Nemo 100 Collins Ave (at 1st St) **305/532-4550** *chic decor, Pacific Rim & South American cuisine*

Nexxt Cafe [★] 700 Lincoln Rd (at Euclid Ave) **305/532-6643** *9am-11pm*

Ortanique on the Mile [★] 278 Miracle Mile **305/446-7710** *Caribbean, full bar*

Pacific Time 915 Lincoln Rd (btwn Jefferson & Michigan) **305/534-5979** *lunch Mon-Fri, dinner nightly, pan-Pacific*

Spiga 1228 Collins Ave (at 12th St) **305/534-0079** *homemade pastas*

Sushi Rock Cafe [★] 1351 Collins Ave (at 14th) **305/532-2133** *full bar*

Tiramisu 721 Lincoln Rd **305/532-4538** *lunch & dinner, Italian*

Yuca 501 Lincoln Rd (at Drexel Ave) **305/532-9822** *New Cuban cuisine, great afternoon tapas & cocktails*

Narnaja • Florida

ENTERTAINMENT & RECREATION

Beach Scooter Rentals 1461 Collins Ave **305/532-0977**

Fritz's Skate & Bike 730 Lincoln Rd (at Euclid & Meridian) **305/532-1954** *rentals, in pedestrian mall*

The Gay Beach 12th St & Ocean *where the boys are*

Lincoln Rd Lincoln Rd (btwn West & Collins Aves) *pedestrian mall that embodies the rebirth of South Beach*

BOOKSTORES

The 9th Chakra 530 Lincoln Rd (btwn Drexel & Pennsylvania) **305/538-0671** *clsd Mon, New Age books, supplies, gifts*

RETAIL SHOPS

Whittall & Shon 900 Washington Ave (at 9th) **305/538-2606** *11am-9pm, till 11pm Fri-Sat, funky clothes & clubwear*

PUBLICATIONS

Wire 1800 Sunset Harbor Dr, Ste 2103 **305/588-0000**

GYMS & HEALTH CLUBS

David Barton Gym [GF] 1685 Collins Ave (in the Delano Hotel) **305/674-5757**

Idol's Gym 719 Lincoln Ln (behind Lincoln Rd) **305/532-0089** *24hrs, $10 day pass*

Ironworks Gym [★] 1676 Alton Rd **305/531-4743** *5:30am-midnight, $15 day pass*

MEN'S SERVICES

Jet Set Escorts **305/538-1770** *we accept all major credit cards*

➤ **Megaphone Miami** **800/289-1489** *Call for the local # nearest you! Meet Hot Men in your area! FREE to Browse & Respond to voice ads. Use code 3087. Also try MEGAMATES.COM*

EROTICA

Pleasure Emporium 1019 5th St **305/673-3311** *24hrs*

Romantix Adult Emporium 8831 SW 40th St **305/226-8332**

Romantix Emporium 19800 S Dixie Hwy **305/255-2190**

CRUISY AREAS

23rd St Beach [AYOR]

Flamingo Park [AYOR] 12th St (btwn Meridian & Alton) *late nights, after bars close*

Haulover Beach Park [AYOR] North Miami Beach *popular nude beach, N of station #27*

North Shore State Park [AYOR] Collins Ave (btwn 79th & 89th Sts)

Mt Dora

ACCOMMODATIONS

The Dora Way B&B [GF] 1123 Dora Wy (at Old Rte 441) **352/735-5994** *B&B furnished w/ antiques & 1950s collectibles, hot tub*

Naples

INFO LINES & SERVICES

Lesbian/ Gay AA 2740 Bayshore Dr (at New Attitudes Club) **239/262-6535** *8pm Th*

ACCOMMODATIONS

Naples Park House [GF,NS] 655 106th Ave N (at 7th Ave) **212/581-7737** *rental home near beach, patio*

BARS

The Galley [MW,NH,K,S,GO] 509 3rd St S **239/262-2808** *3pm-2am, till midnight Sun*

CAFES

Cafe Flamingo 536 9th St N **239/262-8181** *7:30am-2pm, Sun brunch*

CRUISY AREAS

The Beach [AYOR] 16th-18th Ave S

Lowdermilk Park [AYOR] Gulf Shore Blvd N

Vanderbilt Beach [AYOR] Hwy 846 (off I-75)

Narnaja

EROTICA

Dixie Adult Super Store 27338 S Dixie Hwy **305/247-5127**

Florida • USA

Ocala

BARS
The Connection [MW,NH,D,S,WC] 3331 S Pine Ave/ US 441 **352/620–2511** *2pm-2am*

BOOKSTORES
Barnes & Noble 3500 SW College Rd (at Hwy 200) **352/854–3999** *9am-10pm, lgbt section*

EROTICA
Secrets of Ocala 815 N Magnolia Ave **352/622–3858**

Ocoee

ENTERTAINMENT & RECREATION
Think It's Not When It Is **407/877–6564** *theater company promoting positive lgbt images*

Orlando

INFO LINES & SERVICES
Gay, Lesbian & Bisexual Community Center of Central Florida 946 N Mills Ave **407/228–8272** *noon-9pm, till 5pm Sat, clsd Fri & Sun, full-service community center, helpline*

ACCOMMODATIONS
B&B Orlando [GS,SW,NS,GO] 2603 Coventry Ln **407/291–2127**

EO Inn & Spa [GS,F,NS] 227 N Eola Dr (at Robinson) **407/481–8485, 888/481–8488** *rooftop terrace, hot tub, cafe on-site*

➤ **Parliament House Motor Inn** [★MW,D,MR,F,S,YC,SW,WC,GO] 410 N Orange Blossom Tr **407/425–7571** *also 5 bars (open at 8pm)*

➤ **Rick's B&B** [M,N,SW,GO] **407/396–7751, 407/414–7751 (cell)** *full brkfst, patio, near Walt Disney World*

The Veranda B&B [GF,SW,NS,WC] 115 N Summerlin Ave **407/849–0321, 800/420–6822** *hot tub*

Rick's Bed and Breakfast

Concierge Accommodations at a B&B Rate

PO Box 22318
Orlando, FL 32830
(407) 396-7751 • (407) 414-7751
Email: RICKsBnB@aol.com
Web: www.ricksbedandbreakfast.com

Florida • USA

The Winter Park Sweet Lodge [GS,GO] 271 S Orlando Ave (at Fairbanks Ave), Winter Park **407/644-6099** *motel*

■ BARS

The Cactus Club [M,P] 1300 N Mills Ave **407/894-3041** *3pm-2am, patio*

Copper Rocket [GF,BW,WC] 106 Lake Ave (at 17-92), Maitland **407/645-0069** *11:30am-2am, 4pm-midnight Sun, also restaurant*

Full Moon Saloon [M,L] 500 N Orange Blossom Tr **407/648-8725** *noon-2am, popular Sun afternoon, patio*

Hank's [M,NH,BW,WC] 5026 Edgewater Dr **407/291-2399** *noon-2am, patio*

Lava Lounge [M,NH,MR,TG,V,WC] 1235 N Orange Ave, Ste 101 **407/895-9790** *5pm-2am, from 7pm Sat, clsd Sun-Mon, upscale lounge, patio (w/ DJ Sat)*

The Peacock Room [GF,NH,E] 1321 N Mills Ave (at Montana) **407/228-0048** *4pm-2am, trendy, lounge*

Stable [M,CW,L] 410 N Orange Blossom Tr (at Parliament House) **407/425-7571** *6pm-2am*

Studz [M,NH,K] 4453 Edgewater Dr **407/523-8810** *4pm-2am, from noon wknds, karaoke Mon, boxer-shorts night Wed*

Will's Pub [GF,NH,F,BW,WC] 1820-50 N Mills Ave **407/898-5070** *2pm-2am; also Loch Haven Motor Inn, 407/896-3611*

Wylde's [M,NH] 3535 S Orange Blossom Tr **407/835-1889** *4pm-2am*

■ NIGHTCLUBS

The Club [★GS,D,DS,S,V,18+$] 578 N Orange Ave **407/872-0066** *10pm-3am, more gay Sat*

Club Quest [MW,D,MR,DS,18+] 745 Bennett Rd **407/228-8226** *10pm-3am Fri-Sat only*

Heaven [M,D,GO] 360 State Ln (behind Bank of America) **407/872-7188** *1am-8am Sat only*

▶ **Parliament House Motor Inn** [★MW,D,MR,F,S,SW,WC,GO] 410 N Orange Blossom Tr **407/425-7571** *10:30am-3am, 5 bars*

Southern Nights [★MW,D,MR,DS,S,18+,WC] 375 S Bumby Ave **407/898-0424** *4pm-3am, from 8pm Sat, from 9pm Sun, Latin Mon, more men Fri for Where the Boyz Are go-go dancers, patio*

■ CAFES

The Coffee House of Thornton Park 412 E Washington St (at Summerlin) **407/426-8989** *8am-4:30pm, till 6pm wknds*

White Wolf Cafe & Antique Shop [E,BW,WC] 1829 N Orange Ave (at Princeton) **407/895-5590** *11am-10pm, till 11pm Fri-Sat, clsd Sun*

■ RESTAURANTS

Brian's 1409 N Orange Ave (at Virginia) **407/896-9912** *6am-4pm, popular Sun*

Dexter's of Thornton Park 808 E Washington St **407/648-2777** *lunch & dinner, American, also cafe & wine bar, trendy*

Dexter's of Winter Park 558 W New England (at N Pennsylvania Ave), Winter Park **407/629-1150** *lunch & dinner, American, also cafe & wine bar, trendy*

Harvey's Bistro 390 N Orange Ave (in Bank of America bldg) **407/246-6560** *popular cocktail hour*

Hemingway's at the Hyatt [★] 1 Grand Cypress Blvd, Lake Buena Vista **407/239-1234** *dinner, cont'l*

Hue 629 E Central Blvd (at N Summerlin Ave) **407/849-1800** *lunch & dinner, wknd brunch, new American, full bar*

La Fontanella [BW,WC] 900 E Washington **407/425-0033** *lunch & dinner, clsd Mon, seafood/ Italian, patio*

The Rainbow Cafe [MW] at Parliament House **407/425-7571 x711** *7am-11pm, till 4am Fri-Sat, till 3am Sun*

Taqueria Quetzalcoatl [BW] 480 N Orlando Ave #120 (at Gay Rd), Winter Park **407/691-0208** *11am-9pm, till 10pm Fri-Sat, from 8am Sun*

Setting A New Standard

Always Open
Guest Memberships
Steam Room
Sauna
Whirlpool
Private Dressing Rooms
Outdoor Pool & Patio
Gym
18+ only

THE CLUB ORLANDO
ATHLETIC VENTURES

A PRIVATE MEN'S CLUB
450 E. Compton St. • Orlando, Florida • (407) 425-5005
www.the-clubs.com

HS-03455

Florida • USA

■ENTERTAINMENT & RECREATION

The Enzian Theater [BW] 1300 S Orlando Ave (at Magnolia), Maitland **407/629-0054** *art house cinema & cafe*

Family Values WPRK 91.5 FM **407/646-2915** *noon Fri, lgbt radio*

Universal Studios Florida 1000 Universal Studios Pl **407/363-8000, 800/232-7827**

Walt Disney World Resort **407/824-4321** *don't even pretend you came to Orlando for any other reason*

■BOOKSTORES

Mojo 930 N Mills Ave (at E Marks St) **407/896-0204** *noon-8pm, 1pm-6pm Sun, lgbt bookstore*

Urban Think Bookstore 625 E Central Blvd **407/650-8004** *10am-9pm, 11am-6pm Sun-Mon, lgbt section*

■RETAIL SHOPS

Annex 498-B N Orange Blossom Tr **407/835-8998** *1pm-9pm, till midnight Fri-Sat, new & gently worn clothing for men*

Harmony Designs [WC,GO] 496 N Orange Blossom Tr **407/481-9850** *6pm-1am, pride store*

Rainbow City [WC] 936 N Mills Ave **407/898-6096** *10am-9pm, till 6pm Sun*

Realm Clothing & Accessories 934 N Mills Ave **407/895-2475** *1pm-9pm, clsd Sun, club clothing, swimwear*

Urban Body 12 N Summerlin **407/481-7979** *11am-7:30pm, noon-5pm Sun, men's clothing*

■PUBLICATIONS

➤ **TLW Magazine** **727/522-8888** *Southeast's largest entertainment magazine for gay men*

Watermark **407/481-2243** *bi-weekly lgbt newspaper*

■MEN'S CLUBS

➤ **Club Orlando** [PC] 450 E Compton St **407/425-5005** *24hrs*

■MEN'S SERVICES

➤ **Megaphone Orlando** **800/289-1489** *Call for the local # nearest you! Meet Hot Men in your area! FREE to Browse & Respond to voice ads. Use code 3087. Also try MEGAMATES.COM*

■EROTICA

Fairvilla Video 1740 N Orange Blossom Tr **407/425-5352**

Midnight News at Parliament House **407/425-7571**

Video Express 98 N Orange Blossom Trail **407/839-8835**

■CRUISY AREAS

Lake Fairview Beach [AYOR] Lee Rd (at US 441)

Palm Beach

■ACCOMMODATIONS

Heart of Palm Beach [GF,SW] 160 Royal Palm Wy **561/655-5600, 800/523-5377** *European-style hotel, also restaurant, full bar*

■RESTAURANTS

Ta-Boo [D,P,WC] 221 Worth Ave **561/835-3500** *11:30am-10:30pm*

Panama City

■ACCOMMODATIONS

Casa de Playa [MW,SW,NS,GO] 20304 Front Beach Rd, Panama City Beach **850/236-8436** *guest house, steps from Gulf of Mexico, jacuzzi, patios*

Spring Creek Campground [M,SW,N,GO] 163 Campground Rd (at Hwy 52 & Country Rd 4), Geneva, AL **334/684-3891** *cabins, tent & RV sites, some theme wknds w/ DJ*

Wisteria Inn [GS,SW,NS] 20404 Front Beach Rd, Panama City Beach **850/234-0557** *hot tub*

■BARS

La Royale Lounge & Liquor Store [MW,NH,WC] 100 Harrison (at Beach Dr) **850/763-1755** *3pm-3am, courtyard*

Splash Bar [M,NH,S,V,18+,GO] 6520 Thomas Dr, Panama City Beach **850/236-3450** *6pm-2am, till 4am Fri-Sat, male dancers Th-Sat*

Sarasota • Florida

■ **NIGHTCLUBS**

Fiesta Room [MW,D,DS,WC]
110 Harrison Ave (at Beach Dr)
850/763-1755 8pm-3am

■ **CRUISY AREAS**

Phillip's Inlet County Beach [AYOR]
1/2 mile W of Ramsgate Harbor

Pensacola

■ **INFO LINES & SERVICES**

AA Gay/ Lesbian 415 N Alcaniz (at Larova) **850/433-8528** 7:30pm Mon & Fri

■ **BARS**

Round-Up [★M,NH,WC] 706 E Gregory St (near 9th Ave) **850/433-8482**
2pm-3am, patio

■ **NIGHTCLUBS**

Emerald City [★MW,D,S,18+,WC] 406 E Wright St (at Alcaniz) **850/433-9491**
5pm-3am, patio

■ **RETAIL SHOPS**

Gulf Coast Pride [WC] 801-C N 9th Ave (at Jackson) **850/433-1443**
11am-7pm, clsd Sun, gifts, toys, magazines

■ **PUBLICATIONS**

➤ **TLW Magazine** 727/522-8888
Southeast's largest entertainment magazine for gay men

■ **CRUISY AREAS**

The Bluffs [AYOR] Scenic Dr

Gulf Islands Nat'l Seashore Park [AYOR] btwn Pensacola & Navarre beaches

Johnson Beach [AYOR] Perdido Key E of town

Navarre Beach [AYOR] Rte 399 W *park on dead-end street, then walk E*

Port Charlotte

■ **BARS**

Charlotte's Web [M,NH,GO]
1193 Enterprise Dr, unit 6-B (at US 41) **941/627-4777** 7pm-2am, 6pm-midnight Sun

■ **RETAIL SHOPS**

The Realm 2721 Tamiami Tr
941/766-1933 11am-8pm, clsd Sun, fetishwear

Port Richey

■ **BARS**

Waterside Landing [MW,D,K,S,WC]
7737 Grand Blvd (2 blks off US 19)
727/841-7900 6pm-2am

Port St Lucie

■ **NIGHTCLUBS**

VIP's [GS,D,L,E,S,18+,GO] 8283 S Federal Hwy (at Fiesta Square) **772/340-7777**
5pm-2am, 1pm-midnight Sun

Sarasota

■ **INFO LINES & SERVICES**

Friends Group (Gay AA)
1844 17th St, Bldg C (enter off Osprey)
941/951-6810 8pm Mon

Gay Info Line **941/923-4636** 24hrs, recorded info

www.GayFloridaRealty.com *Log on & see current MLS listings in your destination Florida city. Search for a gay or lesbian realtor or mortgage broker.*

■ **ACCOMMODATIONS**

The Cypress [GF,NS] 621 Gulfstream Ave S **941/955-4683** *B&B inn overlooking Sarasota Bay, full brkfst*

Siesta Holidays [GF,SW,NS] 1017 Seaside Dr & 1011 Crescent St, Siesta Key **941/312-9882, 800/720-6885**
2 locations, near Crescent Beach

Vera's Place [MO,SW,N,GO] 3913 Chapel Dr **941/351-3171, 941/359-8881**

■ **BARS**

Club Tri-Angles [M,D,E,DS,V,WC]
1330 Martin Luther King Jr Wy
941/953-5945 1pm-2am, patio

■ **EROTICA**

Tamiami Books 7338 S Tamiami Tr
941/923-7626 24hrs

■ **CRUISY AREAS**

North Lido Beach [AYOR]

Florida • USA

Satellite Beach

■EROTICA

Space Age Books & Temptations
63 Ocean Blvd 321/773-7660

South Beach

see Miami Beach/ South Beach

St Augustine

■ACCOMMODATIONS

The Saragossa Inn B&B [GS,GO]
34 Saragossa St (at Sevilla)
904/808-7384 *full brkfst*

St Petersburg

see also Tampa

■INFO LINES & SERVICES

Gay Information Line (The Line)
727/586-4297 *volunteers 7pm-11pm, touchtone service 24hrs*

www.GayFloridaRealty.com *Log on & see current MLS listings in your destination Florida city. Search for a gay or lesbian realtor or mortgage broker.*

■ACCOMMODATIONS

Berwin Oak Guesthouse [MO,NS,GO]
5103 28th Ave S (at 51st St S), Gulfport
727/321-4272 *comprised of 2 apts, courtyard w/ bar, deck & hot tub*

Inn at the Bay B&B & Tea Room
[GF,WC] 126 4th Ave NE (at 1st St)
727/822-1700, 888/873-2122
full brkfst, jacuzzi

El Morocco Resort Motel [GF,SW,GO]
16333 Gulf Blvd (at Madiera Beach Causeway) 727/391-1675 *across from Gulf of Mexico, beach access*

Pier Hotel [GS,NS,GO] 253 2nd Ave N
(at 2nd St) 727/822-7500,
800/735-6607 *in museum district, live music nightly at cocktail hour*

➤ **Suncoast Resort** [★MW,SW,WC,GO]
3000 34th St S/ Hwy 19 S (at 32nd Ave S) 727/867-1111 *6 bars & 2 restaurants, tennis, even a gay shopping mall (see ad page 213)*

■BARS

The Back Room Bar @ Surf & Sand Bar [M,NH,K,WC] 14601 Gulf Blvd, Madiera Beach 727/391-2680 *noon-2am, from 1pm Sun, beach access, patio*

Grand Central Station [M,NH,S,WC]
2612 Central Ave (at 26th)
727/327-8204 *2pm-2am, male dancers Th-Sun, patio*

Haymarket Pub [M,NH,WC] 8308 4th
St N (at 83rd) 727/577-9621 *4pm-2am, upscale*

Oar House [M,NH,F,K] 4807 22nd Ave S
727/327-1691 *10am-2am, 1pm-2am Sun, free buffet every afternoon*

Sharp A's [★MW,D,K,WC]
4918 Gulfport Blvd S (at 49th), Gulfport
727/327-4897 *2pm-2am*

Sports Page Bar [W,D,E,K,WC]
13344 66th St N (at Ulmerton Rd),
Largo 727/538-2430 *4pm-2am, from 1pm Sun*

➤ **Suncoast Resort**
[★MW,D,D,S,S,SW,WC,GO] 3000 34th St
S/ Hwy 19 S (at 32nd Ave S)
727/867-1111 *6 bars & 2 restaurants*

VIP Lounge & Mexican Food Grill
[GF,WC] 10625 Gulf Blvd
727/360-5062 *9am-2am, food served 11am-11pm*

■NIGHTCLUBS

Georgie's Alibi
[MW,NH,D,F,DS,S,V,WC,GO] 3100 3rd Ave
N (at 31st St N) 727/321-2112 *11am-2am, 3 bars, patio*

■CAFES

Beaux Arts [MW] 2635 Central Ave
727/328-0702 *noon-5pm, 8pm Sat open mic*

■RESTAURANTS

Alex's Restaurant 104 Patricia Ave,
Dunedin 727/736-6163 *7am-2pm, 8am-3pm wknds, homestyle*

➤ **Suncoast Resort** [★MW,WC,GO]
3000 34th St S/ Hwy 19 S (at 32nd Ave
S) 727/867-1111 *Flamingo restaurant w/ indoor & patio dining*

Tampa • Florida

■RETAIL SHOPS

The MC Film Festival Video & Music Store 3000 34th St S #2 (in Suncoast Resort) 727/866-0904 *nonerotic lgbt videos, CDs & pride gifts, also business center*

Tampa Bay Leather Company 3000 34th St S (in Suncoast Resort) 727/865-3010 *noon-midnight, till 2am Fri, leather, fetish*

■PUBLICATIONS

The Gazette 813/689-7566 *the Suncoast's monthly gay/ lesbian newsmagazine*

➤ **TLW Magazine** 727/522-8888 *Southeast's largest entertainment magazine for gay men*

■EROTICA

4th St Books & Video 1427 4th St S (at Newton) 727/821-8824 *24hrs*

Pig Boy Leather [GO] 2429 Central Ave 727/327-7450 *noon-7pm, till 10pm Fri-Sat, clsd Sun-Mon, leather, fetish*

■CRUISY AREAS

Pass-a-Grille Beach [AYOR] *below 8th St*

Tallahassee

■INFO LINES & SERVICES

The Family Tree 1406 Hays St, Ste 4 850/222-8555 *lgbt community center, call for hours*

■ACCOMMODATIONS

Twelve Oaks B&B [MO,SW,N,GO] 984 Boston Hwy/ County Rd 149 (at US Hwy 19), Monticello 850/997-1272 *full brkfst, hot tub*

■BARS

Brothers [MW,D,MR,S,V,18+,WC] 926 W Tharpe St (near Old Bainbridge) 850/386-2399 *4pm-2am*

■RESTAURANTS

The Village Inn [★] 2690 N Monroe St (at Sharer Rd) 850/385-2903 *6am-3am, 24hrs wknds*

■PUBLICATIONS

➤ **TLW Magazine** 727/522-8888 *Southeast's largest entertainment magazine for gay men*

■MEN'S SERVICES

➤ **Megaphone Tallahassee** 800/289-1489 *Call for the local # nearest you! Meet Hot Men in your area! FREE to Browse & Respond to voice ads. Use code 3087. Also try MEGAMATES.COM*

■CRUISY AREAS

Lost Lake [AYOR] Spring Hill Rd

Tampa

see also St Petersburg

■INFO LINES & SERVICES

Gay Information Line (The Line) 727/586-4297 *volunteers 7pm-11pm, touchtone service 24hrs*

Gay/ Lesbian Community Center of Tampa [WC] 3708 W Swann Ave 813/875-8116 *call for hours*

■ACCOMMODATIONS

Gram's Place B&B GuestHouses/ Hostel & Music [GS,P,BYOB,N] 3109 N Ola Ave 813/221-0596 *hot tub*

Ruskin House B&B [MW] 120 Dickman Dr SW, Ruskin 813/645-3842 *1910 Victorian home, 30 minutes S of Tampa & 30 minutes N of Sarasota*

Sawmill Camping Resort [★GS,E,SW,N,NS,GO] 21710 US Hwy 98, Dade City 352/583-0664 *RV hookups, cabins, tent spots*

■BARS

2606 [★M,L,S,WC,GO] 2606 Armenia Ave (at St Conrad) 813/875-6993 *8pm-3am, from 6pm Sun, strippers wknds, also leather shop from 9pm*

Baxter's [M,NH,S,WC] 1519 S Dale Mabry (at W Neptune) 813/258-8830 *noon-3am*

City Side [MW,NH,K] 3703 Henderson Blvd (at Dale Mabry) 813/254-6466 *noon-3am, patio*

Joey's [M,NH,GO] 9002 N Florida Ave (at Busch) 813/935-9771 *3pm-3am, till midnight Mon-Tue*

Keith's Bar [M,NH,S,GO] 14905 N Nebraska (at Bearss) 813/971-3576 *1pm-3am, strippers Fri*

Florida • USA

Ki Ki Ki III [M,BW] 1908 W Kennedy Blvd (at Melville) **813/254-8183** *11am-3am, from 1pm Sun*

Metropolis [MW,NH,S,WC] 3447 W Kennedy Blvd (at Himes) **813/871-2410** *noon-3am, from 1pm Sun, strippers Fri-Sat*

■NIGHTCLUBS

Babylon [M,NH,D,F,S] 105 W Martin Luther King Blvd (at Tampa St) **813/237-8883** *3pm-3am, male dancers*

The Chambers [MW,D,F,DS,18+] 1701 N Franklin St **813/223-1300** *5pm-3am, from 8:30 Sun, clsd Mon-Tue, 2 flrs, fetish night Sun, also restaurant, also Pig Boy Leather*

Valentine's [MW,D,K,DS] 7522 N Armenia Ave (btwn Waters & Sligh) **813/936-1999** *3pm-3am*

■CAFES

Sacred Grounds [MW,E] 4819 E Busch Blvd **813/983-0837** *6:30pm-1am, till 2am Fri-Sat, till midnight Sun, clsd Mon*

■RESTAURANTS

Ho Ho Chinese [WC,GO] 533 S Howard **813/254-9557** *11:30am-10pm, full bar*

Taqueria Quetzalcoatl [BW] 402 S Howard Ave (at Azeele St) **813/259-9982** *11am-11pm, from noon Sun, Mexican*

Tropics Cabaret & Restaurant [MW,E,P] 2801 S MacDill **813/837-1836** *5:30pm-close, bar open from 4pm*

■ENTERTAINMENT & RECREATION

United Skates of America 5121 N Armenia **813/876-5826** *lgbt skate 9pm-11:30pm Tue, seasonal*

■BOOKSTORES

Tomes & Treasures 406-408 S Howard Ave (at Swann) **813/251-9368** *11am-midnight, from 10am wknds, lgbt, also coffeehouse till midnight, till 10pm Sat, gallery*

■RETAIL SHOPS

The Leather Rooster [GO] 3441-B W Kennedy Blvd (at Himes) **813/877-6005** *pride items, new & used leather*

■PUBLICATIONS

The Gazette **813/689-7566** *Florida's gay/lesbian newsmagazine*

➤ **TLW Magazine** **727/522-8888** *Southeast's largest entertainment magazine for gay men*

Watermark **407/481-2243** *bi-weekly lgbt newspaper*

■GYMS & HEALTH CLUBS

Metro Flex Fitness 2511 Swann Ave (at Armenia) **813/876-3539**

■MEN'S CLUBS

Club Tampa [★PC] 215 N 11th St **813/223-5181** *24hrs*

■MEN'S SERVICES

The Confidential Connection®! **813/626-6080** *The hottest local guys! 18+ Record & Listen FREE! Use access code 499*

➤ **Megaphone Tampa** **800/289-1489** *Call for the local # nearest you! Meet Hot Men in your area! FREE to Browse & Respond to voice ads. Use code 3087. Also try MEGAMATES.COM*

■EROTICA

Buddies Video 4322 W Crest Ave (at Hillsborough) **813/876-8083** *24hrs*

Playhouse Theatre 4421 N Hubert (at Alva) **813/873-9235** *24hrs*

Tres Equis 6222 B Adamo Dr **813/740-8664** *24hrs*

■CRUISY AREAS

Ben T Davis Beach [AYOR] E side of Campbell Causeway

Lettuce Lake Park [AYOR] Fletcher Ave & I-75

Picnic Island [AYOR] across from the military base (on E side) *gay beach*

Titusville

■CRUISY AREAS

Playalinda Beach [AYOR]

West Palm Beach • Florida

Venice

■ CRUISY AREAS

Casperson Beach [AYOR] *at W end of Venice Ave at promenade*

Venus

■ ACCOMMODATIONS

Camp Mars [M,SW,N,GO] 326 Goff Rd **863/699-6277** *campground w/ cabins, tents, RV hookups, 2 hours from Fort Lauderdale & Miami*

West Palm Beach

■ INFO LINES & SERVICES

Compass Community Center [WC] 7600 S Dixie Hwy **561/533-9699** *10am-8:30pm, noon-8pm Sat, clsd Sun*

■ ACCOMMODATIONS

Hibiscus House B&B [GS,SW,NS,GO] 501 30th St **561/863-5633, 800/203-4927** *full brkfst, jacuzzi*

Tropical Gardens B&B [MW,SW,NS,GO] 419 32nd St (Old Northwood Historic District) **561/848-4064, 800/736-4064**

■ BARS

5101 Bar [M,NH,K,WC] 5101 S Dixie Hwy **561/585-2379** *7am-3am, till 4am Fri-Sat, noon-3am Sun*

HG Rooster's [★M,NH,WC] 823 Belvedere Rd (btwn Parker & Lake) **561/832-9119** *3pm-3am, till 4am Fri-Sat*

Kozlow's [★M,NH,WC] 6205 Georgia Ave (at Colonial) **561/533-5355** *noon-2am, till 4am wknds, patio, DJ wknds*

Leather & Spurs WPB [M,NH,CW,L,BW] 5812 S Dixie Hwy **561/547-1020** *7pm-3am, from 9pm Th-Sat, till 4am Fri-Sat, from 8pm Sun*

■ NIGHTCLUBS

➤ **Cupids** [M,D,S] 4430 Forest Hill Blvd **561/642-5299** *5pm-5am, strip club*

Cupids — A CLUB LIKE NO OTHER

NUDE MEN 7 DAYS A WEEK
7pm - 5am / Full Liquor Bar

4430 FOREST HILL BLVD., WEST PALM BEACH, FL
561.642.5299 / WWW.CUPIDSCABARET.COM

Florida • USA

Kashmir [M,D,S] 1651 S Congress Ave
561/649-5557 10pm-5am Wed-Sun

Respectable Street [GF,D,A,E]
518 Clematis St **561/832-9999** 9pm-3am, till 4am Fri-Sat, clsd Sun-Tue, retro & new wave nights

■RESTAURANTS

Rhythm Cafe [BW] 3800-A S Dixie Hwy
561/833-3406 6pm-10pm, clsd Sun-Mon

■BOOKSTORES

Changing Times Bookstore
911 Village Blvd #806 (at Palm Beach Lakes) **561/640-0496** 10am-7pm, till 9pm Fri, noon-5pm Sun, lgbt section

■RETAIL SHOPS

Eurotique 3109 45th St #300
561/684-2302 11am-7pm, noon-6pm Sat, clsd Sun, PVC, leather, books, videos

Studio 205 600 Lake Ave (at North 'L' St), Lake Worth **561/533-5272** 9am-9pm, 8am-4pm Sun, gay pride items, books & home accessories

■CRUISY AREAS

Bert Winters Park [AYOR] Ellison Wilson Rd (in Juno Beach)

Boynton Beach [AYOR] on A1A

Delray Beach [AYOR] A1A

MacArthur Park Beach [AYOR]

Seawall [AYOR] summers

Wilton Manors

see Fort Lauderdale

Winter Park

■BARS

Lighthouse Lounge [GS,NH,D,K] 7124 Aloma Ave (at Forsythe) **407/678-9070** 4pm-2am

■CRUISY AREAS

Cady Way [AYOR] street bordering Ward Memorial Park

GEORGIA

Statewide

■PUBLICATIONS

➤ **Southern Voice** 404/876-1819
weekly lgbt newspaper for AL, FL (panhandle), GA, LA, MS, TN w/ resource listings

➤ **TLW Magazine** 727/522-8888
Southeast's largest entertainment magazine for gay men

Athens

■BARS

Georgia Bar [GF,NH,WC] 159 W Clayton (at Lumpkin) **706/546-9884** 3pm-2am, clsd Sun, more gay weeknights

The Globe [GF] 199 N Lumpkin (at Clayton) **706/353-4721** 4pm-2am, till 1am Mon-Tue, clsd Sun, 55 single-malt scotches

■NIGHTCLUBS

Boneshakers [MW,D,S,18+,WC] 433 E Hancock Ave **706/543-1555** 8pm-3am, from 9:30pm Fri, till 4am Sat, clsd Sun

Forty Watt Club [GF,E,WC]
285 W Washington St (at Pulaski)
706/549-7871 9pm-2am, clsd Sun, live music venue

■CAFES

Espresso Royale Cafe [WC] 297 E Broad St (at Jackson) **706/613-7449** 7am-midnight, from 8am wknds, best coffee in Athens

■RESTAURANTS

The Bluebird 493 E Clayton
706/549-3663 8am-3pm, popular brunch wknds

The Grit [WC] 199 Prince Ave
706/543-6592 11am-10pm (clsd 3pm-5pm Sat-Sun), great wknd brunch

■BOOKSTORES

Barnett's Newsstand 147 College Ave (at Clayton) **706/353-0530** 7:30am-10pm, 8am-11pm Fri-Sat, 8am-10pm Sun

■CRUISY AREAS

Bishop Park [AYOR] Sunset Dr days

College Square [AYOR] Clayton & College

Atlanta • Georgia

Atlanta

■ INFO LINES & SERVICES

Atlanta Gay/ Lesbian Center 170 11th St (off Juniper) **404/523-7500** *5:30pm-9pm Mon-Fri, social services, clinic, library*

Galano Club 585 Dutch Valley Rd (at Monroe) **404/881-9188** *lgbt recovery club, call for mtgs times*

Gay Helpline 404/525-4357 *24hrs, live 6pm-11pm, info & counseling*

■ ACCOMMODATIONS

Abbett Inn [GS,NS,GO] 1746 Virginia Ave **404/767-3708** *1880s Victorian*

Ansley Inn B&B [GS,NS,GO] 253 15th St **404/872-9000, 800/446-5416** *full brkfst, near gay nightlife in Midtown*

The Cottage Off Peachtree [GS,GO] 137 Ridgeland Wy NE **404/237-3914** *B&B, some shared baths, hot tub*

The Georgian Terrace Hotel [GF,SW,WC] 659 Peachtree St **404/897-1991, 800/555-8000**

Guests Atlanta [GS,NS,GO] 811 Piedmont Ave NE **404/872-5846, 800/724-4381** *urban guest house*

Hello Atlanta [MW,NS,GO] 1865 Windemere Dr **404/892-8111** *hot tub*

Lynwood Place B&B [MO,SW,N,GO] 767 Lynwood St SE (at Boulevard) **404/622-5622** *hot tub*

Midtown Guest House [GS,GO] 971 Piedmont Ave (at 10th St) **404/931-8791** *in the heart of midtown*

Sheraton Atlanta Hotel [GF,F,SW,WC] 165 Courtland St (at International Blvd) **404/659-6500, 800/325-3535** *3 restaurants, full bar, gym*

■ BARS

Atlanta Eagle [★M,D,B,L,GO] 306 Ponce de Leon Ave NE (at Argonne) **404/873-2453** *8pm-3am, from 6pm Sun, also American Bear Saloon inside from 5pm, also leather store*

Blake's (on the Park) [MW,NH,P,S,V] 227 10th St (at Piedmont) **404/892-5786, 888/441-8984** *3pm-2am, Sun brunch*

Buddies [M,NH] 2345 Cheshire Bridge Rd (at La Vista) **404/634-5895** *1:30pm-4am, till 3am Sat, till midnight Sun*

▶ **Bulldogs** [★M,NH,D,L,MR,V] 893 Peachtree St NE (btwn 7th & 8th) **404/872-3025** *2pm-4am, till 3am Sat, cruise bar*

Burkhart's Pub [MW,NH,F,K,S,WC] 1492-F Piedmont Ave (at Monroe, in Ansley Mall) **404/872-4403** *4pm-4am, 2pm-3am wknds, patio*

Colours [M,D,MR-AF,DS] 1492-B Piedmont Ave (in Ansley Mall) **678/702-0872** *10pm-4am Wed-Fri, till 3am Sat*

Eddie's Attic [GS,E] 515-B N McDonough St (at Trinity Place), Decatur **404/377-4976** *4pm-close, rooftop deck, restaurant*

Felix's on the Square [M,F] 1310-G Piedmont Ave (Ansley Square) **404/249-7899** *2pm-close, noon-midnight Sun, also restaurant*

Fountainhead Lounge [GS,D,MR] 485-A Flat Shoals Ave **404/522-7841** *9pm-3am*

Halo [GS,F] 817 W Peachtree (at 6th) **404/962-7333**

Haze [GS] 40 7th St (at Cypress) **404/249-8900** *8pm-close, more gay Wed*

Hoedowns [★M,D,CW,E,WC] 931 Monroe Dr #B (at Midtown Promenade) **404/876-0001** *3pm-3am, clsd Sun-Mon*

Le Buzz [MW,NH,D,F,K,S,WC] 585 Franklin Rd A-10 (at S Marietta Pkwy, in Longhorn Plaza), Marietta **770/424-1337** *5pm-3am, from 7pm Sat, clsd Sun, DJ Fri-Sat, patio*

Mary's [MW,NH,V] 1287 Glenwood Ave (at Flat Shoals) **404/624-4411** *5pm-2am, till 3am Fri-Sat, 5pm-midnight Sun, friendly cocktail bar*

The Metro [★M,D,MR,S,V] 1080 Peachtree St (at 11th) **404/874-9869** *4pm-4am, till 3am Sat, clsd Sun, go-go boys nightly, Latin Tue*

Georgia • USA

Midtown Saloon & Grill [★M,NH,F] 738 Ponce de Leon Ave NE (at Ponce de Leon Plaza) **404/874-1655** 2pm-4am, food served 6pm-midnight Mon-Fri, patio

Miss Q's [M,NH] 560-B Amsterdam (in Midtown Outlets) **404/875-6255** 4pm-close, 3pm-midnight Sun, big-screen TV

Model T [M,NH,K,DS,OC,WC] 699 Ponce de Leon Ave NE (at Barnett) **404/872-2209** 9am-3am, noon-midnight Sun, cruisy

New Order Lounge [M,NH,E,OC,WC] 1544 Piedmont Ave NE (at Monroe, in Ansley Square Center) **404/874-8247** 2pm-2am, till 3am wknds

Opus I [M,NH,WC] 1086 Alco St NE (at Cheshire Bridge) **404/634-6478** 9am-4am, from 12:30pm Sun

Oscar's [M,V] 1510-C Piedmont Ave (in Ansley Mall) **404/874-7748** 3pm-4am, till 3am Sat, from 3pm Sun

The Palace [M,D,MR-AF] 91 Broad St (at Martin Luther King) **404/522-3000** 5pm-close, 3 levels

The Phoenix [M,NH] 567 Ponce de Leon (at Monroe) **404/892-7871** 9am-4am, from 12:30pm Sun, hustlers

Red Chair [★MW,F,V] 550-C Amsterdam Ave (at Monroe) **404/870-0532** 5:30pm-11pm, also restaurant, Sun brunch

Rico's View on Ponce [M,NH,K,S,V] 736 Ponce de Leon, NE (at Ponce de Leon Pl) **404/873-3220** 11am-4am, till 3am Sat, 12:30pm-midnight Sun, rooftop patio

Swinging Richard's [M,S,$] 1400 Northside Dr NW (btwn I-75 & Northside Dr) **404/352-0532** 6:30pm-4am, clsd Sun-Mon, gay strip club, nude dancers

Tripps [M,NH] 1931 Piedmont Circle (at Cheshire Bridge) **404/724-0067** 9am-4am, till 3am Sat, clsd Sun, free buffet at 3pm

Atlanta • Georgia

Woofs on Piedmont [M,NH,F,GO]
2425 Piedmont (at Lindbergh)
404/869-9422

■ NIGHTCLUBS

The Armory [★MW,D,MR,S,V,YC,WC] 836 Juniper St NE (at 7th) **404/881-9280** *4pm-4am, clsd Sun, 4 bars*

➤ **Backstreet** [★GS,D,MR,C,S,V,YC,PC,$] 845 Peachtree St NE (btwn 5th & 6th, enter rear) **404/873-1986** *24hrs, 3 flrs, gift shop, home of Charlie Brown's XXX-Rated Cabaret Th-Sat*

Blu [★M,D,$] 960 Spring St (at 10th) **404/877-1221** *from 11pm Sat only*

The Chamber [GF,D,S] 2115 Faulkner Rd (at Cheshire Bridge) **404/248-1612** *10pm-4am Th-Fri, till 3am Sat, fetish crowd, 18+ Th, theme nights*

Chaparral [MW,D] 2715 Buford Hwy **404/634-3737** *10pm-4am, gay Fri & Sun only*

Da Boxx [D,MR,S] 521 Tift St (at Murphy) **404/681-2699** *from 10pm Tue, Fri-Sat*

The Heretic [★M,D,L,F,S,WC] 2069 Cheshire Bridge Rd (at Piedmont) **404/325-3061** *9am-4am, 12:30pm-midnight Sun, 3 bars, patio, call for theme nights, also Heretic Leathers toy shop*

Masquerade [GF,D,F,E,18+,$] 695 North Ave NE (at Ponce de Leon), **404/577-8178**, **404/577-2002** *10pm-4am Th-Fri, till 3am Sat, 7pm-midnight Sun*

MJQ Concourse [★GF,D,A,S,YC] 736 Ponce de Leon Ave (at Ponce de Leon Pl) **404/870-0575** *10pm-3am*

Traxx [GS,D,MR-AF,E,18+] 339 Marietta St NW (at Simpson) **404/681-4422** *10pm-3am, more gay Mon, Th & wknds*

■ CAFES

Caribou Coffee 1551 Piedmont Ave (at Monroe) **404/733-5539** *6am-11pm, 7am-midnight wknds*

Georgia • USA

Intermezzo 1845 Peachtree Rd NE **404/355-0411** *11am-3am, till 4am Fri-Sat, classy, full bar, great desserts*

■ RESTAURANTS

Agnes & Muriel's [★BW] 1514 Monroe Dr (near Piedmont) **404/885-1000** *11am-11pm, till midnight Fri-Sat, from 10am wknds, patio*

Apres Diem 931 Monroe Dr #C-103 **404/872-3333** *lunch & dinner, French bistro, live jazz Wed, full bar*

The Big Red Tomato Bistro 980 Piedmont Rd NE (at 10th St) **404/870-9881** *lunch, dinner & Sun brunch, Italian, full bar, patio*

Bridgetown Grill [★WC] 689 Peachtree (across from Fox Theater) **404/873-5361** *11am-11pm, funky Caribbean*

The Colonnade 1879 Cheshire Bridge Rd NE **404/874-5642** *lunch Wed-Sun, dinner nightly, traditional Southern*

Cowtippers [TG,WC] 1600 Piedmont Ave NE (at Monroe) **404/874-3469** *11:30am-11pm, steak house*

Dunk N' Dine [★MW,TG] 2277 Cheshire Bridge Rd (at Lenox) **404/636-0197** *24hrs, downscale diner, queens abound*

Einstein's [★WC] 1077 Juniper (at 12th) **404/876-7925** *11am-midnight, till 1am Fri-Sat, wknd brunch, full bar, patio*

The Flying Biscuit Cafe [★BW,WC] 1655 McLendon Ave (at Clifton) **404/687-8888** *7am-10pm, healthy brkfst all day*

Majestic Diner [★AYOR] 1031 Ponce de Leon (at Clayton Terr) **404/875-0276** *24hrs, diner right from the '50s, cantankerous waitresses included*

Murphy's [★WC] 997 Virginia Ave NE (at N Highland Ave) **404/872-0904** *11am-10pm, till midnight Fri, from 8am wknds*

R Thomas [BW,WC] 1812 Peachtree Rd NE (btwn 26th & 27th) **404/872-2942** *24hrs, healthy Californian/ juice bar, popular late night*

Ria's Bluebird Cafe [★BW,TG,WC] 421 Memorial Dr **404/521-3737** *8am-3pm, gourmet brunch in quaint old diner*

Atlanta • Georgia

Swan Coach House 3130 Slaton Dr NW, Buckhead **404/261-0636** *lunch only Mon-Sat, clsd Sun*

Veni Vidi Vici 41 14th St **404/875-8424** *lunch Mon-Fri, dinner 5pm-11pm nightly, upscale Italian*

Watershed 406 W Ponce de Leon, Decatur **404/378-4900** *11am-10pm, Sun brunch, wine bar, gift shop, owned by Emily Saliers of the Indigo Girls*

■ ENTERTAINMENT & RECREATION

Alternative Talk WRFG 89.3FM **404/523-8989** (station #), **404/523-3471** (office #) *5pm-5:30pm Fri, radio program for Atlanta's African-American lgbt community*

Funny That Way Theater Company **404/893-3399, 404/627-6672** *lgbt theater, seasonal musicals, call for schedule*

Lambda Radio WRFG 89.3 FM **404/523-8989** *6pm Tue, lgbt radio program*

Little 5 Points, Moreland & Euclid Ave S of Ponce de Leon Ave *hip & funky area w/ too many restaurants & shops to list*

Martin Luther King, Jr Center for Non-Violent Social Change 449 Auburn Ave NE **404/524-1956** *includes King's birth home, the church where he preached in the 60s & his gravesite*

Piedmont Park [AYOR] SE part of the park (off Monroe & 10th St) *hilltop sunbathing, cruisy parking lot*

Theatre OUTlanta **404/371-0212** *lgbt theater group, call for performance location*

■ BOOKSTORES

▶ **Brushstrokes** 1510-J Piedmont Ave NE (near Monroe) **404/876-6567** *10am-10pm, till 11pm Fri-Sat, lgbt variety store*

**THREE STORES IN ONE MALL
OVER 4200 SQ. FT**

a variety store
**Sun-Thurs: 10-10
Fri & Sat: 10-11**

a place for music & movies
**Sun-Thurs: 10-10
Fri & Sat: 10-11**

a gift for everyone
**Mon & Tues 11-7
Wed - Sat 10-10
Sun: 12-8**

For you, your loved ones,
your co-workers, your home,
& your pets

**www.brushstrokesatlanta.com
info@brushstrokesatlanta.com**

**THREE STORES IN ONE MALL
OVER 4200 SQ. FT**

BRUSHSTROKES
404.876.6567

SENSORY⚡OVERLOAD ™
404.876.6567

CAPULETS
404.876.9003

**Ansley Square
1510 Piedmont Ave.
Atlanta 30324**

Georgia • USA

➤ **Outwrite Bookstore & Coffeehouse** [F,WC] 991 Piedmont Ave NE (at 10th) **404/607-0082** *9am-11pm, lgbt, music, videos, gifts, cafe*

■ RETAIL SHOPS

➤ **The Boy Next Door** 1447 Piedmont Ave NE (btwn 14th & Monroe) **404/873-2664** *10am-8pm, noon-6pm Sun, clothing*

➤ **Capulets** 1510 Piedmont Ave, #D (at Monroe) **404/876-9003** *candles, incense, gifts*

The Junkman's Daughter 464 Moreland Ave (at Euclid) **404/577-3188** *11am-7pm, hip stuff*

Metropolitan Deluxe [WC] 1034 N Highland NE (at Virginia) **404/892-9337** *10am-10pm, till 11pm Fri-Sat, till 7pm Sun, flowers & gifts*

Piercing Experience 1654 McLendon Ave NE (at Clifton) **404/378-9100** *noon-9pm, till 5pm Sun, clsd Mon*

■ PUBLICATIONS

David Atlanta 404/876-4076

Out & Active 404/873-6004 *free gay/ lesbian resource & entertainment guide*

➤ **Southern Voice** 404/876-1819 *weekly lgbt newspaper for AL, FL (panhandle), GA, LA, MS, TN w/ resource listings*

■ GYMS & HEALTH CLUBS

Extreme Bodyworks [MW] 2201 Faulkner Dr NE (at Cheshire Bridge) **404/321-6507** *cruisy*

The Fitness Factory [★GF] 500 N Amsterdam (in Amsterdam Outlets) **404/815-7900** *full gym*

■ MEN'S CLUBS

➤ **Flex** [SW] 76 4th St (at Spring St) **404/815-0456** *24hrs*

Fort Troff [L,V,PC,GO] 701 Edgehill (at 10th & Howell Mill) **404/873-5520** *dungeon party Sat, dress code*

FIND WHAT YOU'RE LOOKING FOR IN ATLANTA

FLEX

ATLANTA, GA
404-815-0456
76 4TH STREET NW
30308

WWW.FLEXBATHS.COM

ATLANTA • CLEVELAND • LOS ANGELES
NEW ORLEANS • PHOENIX • COLUMBUS

Augusta • Georgia

The Sanctuary [PC] 1417 Dutch Valley Pl 404/874-4838 *dungeon, men's night Wed-Th & Sat, pansexual Fri, 3pm-8pm Sun, clsd Mon, women's night last Sat*

MEN'S SERVICES

➤ **Megaphone Atlanta** 800/289-1489 *Call for the local # nearest you! Meet Hot Men in your area! FREE to Browse & Respond to voice ads. Use code 3087. Also try MEGAMATES.COM*

EROTICA

4skins 2 593 Westminster Dr NE (at Monroe) 404/685-1700 *custom leather, also location inside Atlanta Eagle*

Heaven 2628 Piedmont (at Sidney Marcus Blvd) 404/262-9113

Inserection 505 Peachtree St NE 404/888-0878 *call for other locations*

The Poster Hut/ Scream Boutique 2175 Cheshire Bridge Rd 404/633-7491 *clothing, toys*

Southern Nights Videos 2205 Cheshire Br Rd (at Lenox Rd) 404/728-0701 *24hrs*

Starship 2275 Cheshire Bridge Rd 404/320-9101 *leather & more, 7 locations in Atlanta*

CRUISY AREAS

Dutch Valley Rd [AYOR] off Monroe Dr

Piedmont Park [AYOR] near Botanical Garden

Tara Theatre [AYOR] Cheshire Bridge Rd *parking lot*

Wildwood Park [AYOR] 1050 Barclay Circle, Marietta *on trails off gravel path*

Augusta
see also Aiken, South Carolina

ACCOMMODATIONS

➤ **Parliament Resort** [MO,L,V,BYOB,SW,N,PC,GO] 1250 Gordon Hwy 706/722-1155 *24hrs, motel complex w/ hot tub, maze & dungeon*

Parliament Resort
Augusta, GA
1250 Gordon Hwy.
Augusta, GA 30901
Ph: (706) 722-1155
www.p-house.com

Georgia's Hottest Gay Men's Resort !

Gay Owned & Operated

65 Rooms

Must Be 18 or Older

Cafe'
Pool
Hot Tub
Pride Shop
Steam Room
Video Lounge

Georgia • USA

■NIGHTCLUBS

Club Argos/ The Tower of Argos
[M,D,B,L,E,K,C,DS,WC] 1923 Walton Way (at Baker) **706/481-8829** *9pm-3am, clsd Sun, 2 stories, levi/ leather wknds, 4th Fri gothic*

The Coliseum [MW,D,S] 1632 Walton Wy **706/733-2603** *8pm-3am, clsd Sun*

Gravity [M,D] 825 E Buena Vista Ave, N Augusta, SC *5pm-5am*

Blue Ridge

■RESTAURANTS

Great Eats Deli [YC,BYOB,WC] 611 E Main St (at Carter St) **706/632-3094** *11am-4pm, soups, sandwiches, desserts*

Carrollton

■CRUISY AREAS
Lake Carroll Rec Area [AYOR]

Columbus

■EROTICA
Foxes Cinema 3009 Victory Dr **706/689-2211**

■CRUISY AREAS
Callaway Gardens & Showers [AYOR] at Robin Lake Beach

South Lumpkin Road Park [AYOR]

Dahlonega

■ACCOMMODATIONS
Mountain Laurel Creek [GS,NS,GO] 202 Talmer Grizzle Rd (at Hwy 19 & McDonald Rd) **706/867-8134** *B&B, full brkfst, jacuzzi, garden, creek*

■RESTAURANTS
Renee's Cafe 135 N Chestatee (at Hawkins) **706/864-6829** *dinner only, clsd Sun-Mon, gourmet*

Smith House 84 S Chestatee St **706/864-3566** *lunch & dinner, clsd Mon, family-style Southern*

Dalton

■RESTAURANTS
Dalton Depot 110 Depot St **706/226-3160** *11am-10pm, clsd Sun, bar*

Decatur
see Atlanta

Dewy Rose

■ACCOMMODATIONS
The River's Edge [M,F,E,SW,N,NS,WC] 2311 Pulliam Mill Rd **706/213-8081** *cabins, camping, RV*

Gainesville

■RETAIL SHOPS
The British Nook [GO] 475-D Dawsonville Hwy (at Shallowford Rd) **770/536-1026** *10am-6pm, till 5pm Sat, clsd Sun, giftshop specializing in foods & giftware from UK & Ireland*

Lake Lanier

■ENTERTAINMENT & RECREATION
Mile Marker 21 ('Cocktail Cove') *a rainbow rendezvous for the pleasure-boating crowd—look for the pink triangle*

Macon

■ACCOMMODATIONS
Lumberjack's Camping Resort [M,SW,GO] 50 Hwy 230 (at Hwy 41), Unadilla **478/783-2267** *on 150 acres, jacuzzi*

■NIGHTCLUBS
Club Synergy [★MW,D,K,S,WC] 425 Cherry St (at MLK, Jr Blvd) **478/755-9383** *8pm-2am, till 3am Fri & 4am Sat, clsd Sun-Tue, 4 bars*

■CRUISY AREAS
Central City Park [AYOR]

Marietta
see Atlanta

Mountain City

■ACCOMMODATIONS
The York House [GF,NS,WC] 416 York House Rd **706/746-2068, 800/231-9675** *1896 historic country inn, located btwn Clayton & Dillard, full brkfst*

Valdosta • Georgia

Savannah

■ INFO LINES & SERVICES
First City Network 307 E Harris St
912/236-CITY *infoline, newsletter*

■ ACCOMMODATIONS
912 Barnard Victorian B&B
[MW,NS,GO] 912 Barnard St
912/234-9121 *full brkfst, shared baths, fireplaces, garden*

Catherine Ward House Inn [GS,GO]
118 E Waldburg St (at Abercorn)
912/234-8564, 800/327-4270
Victorian Italianate B&B, full brkfst, jacuzzi

Fox House Inn [GS,NS,GO]
536 E Harris St (btwn Price & E Broad)
912/644-7444 *full brkfst*

Green Palm Inn [GS,NS,GO]
548 E President St (at Houston)
912/447-8901, 888/606-9510 *full brkfst*

Paradise Inn [GF,SW,NS,GO] 512 Tattnall St (at Gaston) **912/443-0200, 888/846-5093** *newly renovated 1866 town house*

Park Avenue Manor [MW,NS]
107-109 W Park Ave **912/233-0352**
1889 Victorian B&B, full brkfst

Under the Rainbow Inn [MW,GO]
104-106 West 38th St **912/790-1005**

■ BARS
Blaine's Backdoor Bar [MW,NH]
13 E Perry St (enter rear)
912/233-6765 *11am-3am, clsd Sun*

Chuck's Bar [GS,NH,YC] 305 W River St
912/232-1005 *6pm-3am, clsd Sun*

Faces II [M,NH] 17 Lincoln St (at Bryan)
912/233-3520 *noon-3am*

Teasers [MW,WC] 416 W Liberty St (at Martin Luther King) **912/238-4788**
4pm-3am, till 2am Sun, also restaurant

■ NIGHTCLUBS
Club One [MW,D,F,S,V] 1 Jefferson St (at Bay) **912/232-0200** *5pm-3am, till 2am Sun, 'home of the Lady Chablis'*

■ CAFES
B Matthews Bakery [GO] 325 E Bay St (at Habersham St) **912/233-1319**
6am-7pm, from 8am wknds

■ RESTAURANTS
Barbary Coast Burritos [WC,GO]
103 W Congress St (at Whitaker St)
912/447-1099 *opens 11am*

Clary's Cafe 404 Abercorn (at Jones)
912/233-0402 *7am-4pm, country cookin'*

Good Eats 606 Abercorn
912/447-5444 *lunch Tue-Sat, dinner Tue-Sun, Sun brunch*

■ ENTERTAINMENT & RECREATION
Savannah Walks, Inc [GF]
912/238-9255 *walking tours of downtown Savannah*

■ BOOKSTORES
Hannah Banana Books [WC] 4515 Habersham St (at 61st) **912/353-7447**
9:30am-7pm, clsd Sun, lgbt section

Moon Dance 306 W St Julian St
912/236-9003 *10am-6pm, till 8pm Fri-Sat, 11am-5pm Sun, lgbt books, metaphysical supplies, gifts*

■ RETAIL SHOPS
Urban Cargo [MW,GO] 146 Whitaker St (at Oglethorpe) **912/341-0061** *10am-6pm, noon-5pm Sun, pride items*

■ MEN'S SERVICES
▶ **Megaphone Savannah**
800/289-1489 *Call for the local # nearest you! Meet Hot Men in your area! FREE to Browse & Respond to voice ads. Use code 3087. Also try MEGAMATES.COM*

■ EROTICA
Home Run Video & News [GO]
4 E Liberty St (at Bull St)
912/236-5192 *large lgbt section*

■ CRUISY AREAS
Monterey Square [AYOR] Bull St

Valdosta

■ NIGHTCLUBS
Mixxers [MW,D,MR,TG,E,K,DS,18+,WC,GO]
118 N Patterson St (at Toombs St)
229/242-2355 *8pm-close Th-Sat*

■ CRUISY AREAS
Langdale Park [AYOR] N Valdosta Rd *days*

Hawaii • *USA*

HAWAII

Please note that cities are grouped by islands:
Hawaii (Big Island)
Kauai
Maui
Molokai
Oahu (includes Honolulu)

STATEWIDE

■ACCOMMODATIONS

Bed & Breakfast Honolulu (Statewide) [GF] 3242 Kaohinani Dr (at Pelekane), Oahu **808/595-7533, 800/288-4666** *414 locations statewide, clientele & ownership vary*

Pacific Ocean Holidays Oahu **808/923-2400, 800/735-6600** *Hawaii vacation packages*

HAWAII (BIG ISLAND)

Captain Cook

■ACCOMMODATIONS

Affordable Hawaii at Pomaika'i (Lucky) Farm B&B [GS,NS] 83-5465 Mamalahoa Hwy **808/328-2112, 800/325-6427** *working, century-old Kona farm, full brkfst*

Aloha Guesthouse [GS,N,NS,WC,GO] 84-4780 Mamalahoa Hwy **808/328-8955, 800/897-3188** *full brkfst, hot tub*

Areca Palms Estate B&B [GF,NS] **808/323-2276** *full brkfst, jacuzzi*

Diver Dan's B&B Hawaii [M,GO] 81633 Papio Dr (in Papa Bay) **808/328-8073, 800/573-3299** *view of Kona coastline, diving & snorkeling*

Horizon Guest House [GS,SW,NS,WC,GO] **808/328-2540, 888/328-8301** *full brkfst*

Kealakekua Bay B&B [GS,NS] **808/328-8150, 800/328-8150** *villa & 2-bdrm guest house*

Hilo

■ACCOMMODATIONS

Aloha Hawaii Healing Retreat [W,F,SW] 400 Hualani #325 (at Monono) **808/965-1244, 888/967-8622** *all-inclusive holistic healing retreat*

Oceanfront B&B [GF,WC] 1923 Kalanianaole St (3 miles from intersection of Hwys 11 & 19) **808/934-9004, 800/363-9524** *2 units w/ ocean views*

Our Place Papaikou's B&B [GS,GO] 27-228 Mamalahoa Hwy, Papaikou, Hilo **808/964-5250** *3-rm tropical healing retreat, 4 miles N of Hilo*

■CAFES

Kope-Kope 1261 Kilauea Ave #220 (in Hilo Shopping Center) **808/933-1221** *espresso bar*

■RESTAURANTS

Cafe Pesto 308 Kamehameha Ave **808/969-6640** *pizzas, salads, pastas*

■ENTERTAINMENT & RECREATION

Richardson's Beach at end of Kalanianaole Ave (Keaukaha)

■BOOKSTORES

Borders 301 Maka'ala St (at Kanoelehua Hwy) **808/933-1410** *lgbt section*

■CRUISY AREAS

Reeds 'Gay' Bay Tearooms [AYOR] Banyan Dr *1st beach S of the hotels*

Honaunau-Kona

■ACCOMMODATIONS

Dragonfly Ranch Healing Arts Retreat [GS,NS] 1 1/2 miles down City of Refuge Rd **808/328-2159, 800/487-2159** *near ancient sanctuary w/ friendly dolphins*

Kailua-Kona

■ACCOMMODATIONS

1st Class B&B Kona Hawaii [GF,NS] 77-6504 Kilohana St **808/329-8778, 888/769-1110** *full brkfst, ocean views*

E walea by the Sea B&B [GS,SW,NS,GO] 25 Puako Beach Dr **808/882-1331** *on Kohala coast*

Big Island • Hawaii

➤ **Hale Kipa 'O Pele** [★MW,GO]
808/329-8676, 800/528-2456
hot tub, plantation-style B&B

Hawaiian Oasis B&B [GF,SW,WC] 74-4958 Kiwi St **808/327-1701** *hot tub*

KonaLani Coffee Plantation Inn [M,GO] 76-5917H Mamalahoa Hwy, Holualoa **808/324-0793** *full brkfst*

Leilani—The Kona Coast [GF,GO] 77-6461 Leilani St (at Lako) **808/327-1704** *vacation rental*

Pu'ukala Lodge B&B [MW,NS,GO] **808/325-1729, 888/325-1729**

Royal Kona Resort [GF,SW,F,E,WC] 75-5852 Ali'i Dr **808/329-3111, 800/222-5642** *private beach*

■ BARS

Mask Bar & Grill [★MW,NH,D,E,K] 75-5660 Kopiko St (at Cathedral Plaza) **808/329-8558** *9am-2am, only gay & lesbian bar on the island*

■ RESTAURANTS

Cassandra's Greek Taverna 75-5719 Alii Dr **808/334-1066** *11:30am-10pm, from 4:30pm wknds*

Edward's at Kanaloa [GO] 78-261 Manukai St (at Kamehameha III) **808/322-1003** *8am-2pm & 5pm-9pm, Mediterranean, bar from 8am-9pm*

Huggo's [E,K] 75-5828 Kahakai Rd (on Kailua Bay) **808/329-1493** *lunch & dinner, from 5:30pm wknds, seafood & steak, patio*

■ ENTERTAINMENT & RECREATION

Eco-Adventures [GO] 75-5660 Palani Rd (in King Kamehameha's Kona Beach Hotel) **808/329-0076, 800/949-3483** *complete Hawaiian vacations—any island, any adventure*

■ CRUISY AREAS

Kahaluu Beach Park [AYOR]

Nude Beach (Honokohau Beach) [AYOR] *5 miles S of airport*

Plantation-style home on a gated tropical estate

Expansive covered decks, ceilings fans & jacuzzi

Interior atrium with lava rock falls & koi pond

Only 5 miles to the beach and all activities

Two suites with private baths

Large bungalow with kitchen

USA/Canada (800)-LAVAGLO
International (808) 329-8676
PO Box 5252
Kailua-Kona, Hawaii 96745
www.gaystayhawaii.com

HALE KIPA 'O PELE
A distinctive Bed & Breakfast on the Big Island of Hawai'i

Hawaii • USA

Queen's Bath Beach [AYOR] off Hwy 19, N of Kailua-Kona *left on Honokohau Harbor Rd, right before marina, park at dead end & walk over rocks & down path to beach (not a nude beach—tickets given for nudity)*

Ninole

■ACCOMMODATIONS

Pu'u Puanani Hawaiian Vacation Home [GS,NS,WC,GO] 32-949 Mamalahoa Hwy **808/963-6789, 808/640-4703** *2 units in 1 guest house on 11 acres, hot tub, ocean views*

Pahoa

■ACCOMMODATIONS

Absolute Paradise B&B [MO,SW,N,NS,GO] **808/965-1828, 888/285-1540** *B&B, full brkfst, outdoor hot tub, some shared baths*

➤ **Big Island Cabanas** [M,SW,N,NS,WC,GO] **808/965-7056** *cabanas in compound*

Kalani Oceanside Retreat [GS,F,SW,N,NS,WC,GO] **808/965-7828, 800/800-6886** *coastal retreat & spa, full brkfst, hot tub*

Pamalu—Hawaiian Country House [GS,SW,NS,GO] **808/965-0830** *country retreat on 5 secluded acres*

Paradise Cliffs [GS,NS,GO] **808/965-8640** *B&B, ocean views*

Rainbow Dreams Cottage [GS,NS,GO] 13-6412 Kalapana Beach Rd **415/824-7062** *oceanfront cottage*

Rainbow's Inn & Adventures [GS,SW,NS,WC,GO] **808/965-9011** *B&B hideaway*

■ENTERTAINMENT & RECREATION

Kehena Beach off Hwy 137 (trailhead at 19-mile marker phone booth) *lava rock trail to clothing-optional beach*

Rainbow Adventures [GO] **808/965-9011** *custom-made excursions*

Big Island Cabanas
... on the island of Hawaii

King Beds
Outdoor Showers
Pool and Hot Tub
Clothing Optional

Grand Opening Specials!
www.BigIslandCabanas.com
GRGnDVD@BigIslandCabanas.com
808.965.7056

Kauai • Hawaii

■CRUISY AREAS

Steam Vents [AYOR] 3 miles S of Pahoa on Keaau-Pahoa Rd *early evenings*

Volcano Village

■ACCOMMODATIONS

The Chalet Kilauea Collection [GF,NS] 998 Wright Rd **808/967-7786, 800/937-7786** *full brkfst, hot tub*

Hale Ohia Cottages [GS,GO] **808/967-7986, 800/455-3803** *hot tub*

KAUAI

■INFO LINES & SERVICES
Lambda Aloha 808/823-6248

Anahola

■ACCOMMODATIONS

Aliomanu Palms—A Kauai Beachfront B&B [GS,GO] 4880 Aliomanu Rd (at Kuhio Hwy), Anahola **808/822-1021** *B&B, on the beach*

Mahina Kai Ocean Villa [★GS,SW,N,NS,GO] 4933 Aliomanu Rd **808/822-9451, 800/337-1134** *B&B villa, hot tub, near gay beach*

Hanalei

■NIGHTCLUBS

Tahiti Nui [GF,F,E,K,WC] 5-5134 Kuhio Hwy (near Hanalei Center) **808/826-6277** *11am-2am, luaus Wed*

Kapaa

■ACCOMMODATIONS

Aloha Dude Vacation Rentals [GS,NS,GO] **808/822-3833** *guest house & apt*

➤ **Aloha Kauai B&B** [MW,SW,NS,WC,GO] 156 Lihau St **808/822-6966, 800/262-4652** *full brkfst*

Anuenue Plantation B&B [M,NS,GO] **808/823-8335, 888/371-7716** *plantation house & cottage w/ 360° ocean & mtn views, full brkfst*

Aloha Kauai BED & BREAKFAST

156 Lihau Street
Kapaa, Kauai,
Hawaii 96746
Mainland Reservations
1-800-262-4652
While in Hawaii
(808) 822-6966

- **Complete Breakfast • Swimming Pool**
- **In-Room TV • In-Room Ceiling Fans**
- **Close to Beaches, Scenic Attractions, Hiking Trails, Restaurants & Shopping**

After a dip in the pool our expansive living room with South Pacific decor is the perfect place to relax at day's end with refreshments served daily from 5 o'clock. Let us show you a little Hawaiian hospitality with the personal service you deserve.

Hawaii • USA

Kauai Coconut Beach Resort
[GF,SW,WC] 484 Kuhio Hwy
808/822-3455, 800/222-5642
oceanfront resort, tennis, nightly luau

Kauai Kualapa Cottage [GF] 1471
Kualapa Pl 808/822-1626 *private
cottage overlooking hidden valley, 10
minutes to beaches*

Kauai Waterfall B&B [MW,SW,NS,GO]
5783 Haaheo St 808/823-9533,
800/996-9533 *hot tub, overlooking
Wailua River State Park Waterfall*

Mohala Ke Ola B&B Retreat
[GF,SW,NS,GO] 5663 Ohelo Rd (at
Kuamoo Rd/ Hwy 580) 808/823-6398,
888/465-2824 *jacuzzi, lomilomi
massage*

Royal Drive Cottages [GS,NS,WC,GO]
147 Royal Dr 808/822-2321 *private
garden cottages, kitchenettes*

■RESTAURANTS

A Pacific Cafe [R] 4-831 Kuhio Hwy
#200 808/822-0013 *dinner only*

Bull Shed 796 Kuhio Hwy
808/822-3791 *5:30pm-10pm, steak &
seafood, full bar*

Eggbert's [GO] 4-484 Kuhio Hwy (in
Coconut Plantation Marketplace)
808/822-3787 *7am-3pm & 5pm-
9pm, popular for brkfst*

Me Ma's Thai 4361 Kuhio Hwy (in
shopping center) 808/823-0899
lunch Mon-Fri, dinner nightly

■ENTERTAINMENT &
RECREATION

Men's Bonfire 808/823-6248
Fri night, call for location

■CRUISY AREAS

Donkey Beach [AYOR] off Hwy 56, N of
Kapaa (btwn 11 & 12-mile markers)
*walk along cane field, down through
ironwood trees & then to the right on the
dirt road to the beach*

Kilauea

■ACCOMMODATIONS

Kalihiwai Jungle Home [GS,N,NS,GO]
808/828-1626 *clifftop rental home,
near beaches*

Kauai Vacation Hideaway
[MW,NS,WC] 4180 N Waiakalua St
808/828-0228, 888/858-6562 *overlooks Pacific, private path to secluded
beach, jacuzzi, 4-day minimum*

■CAFES

Mango Mama's Fruitstand Cafe
4640 Hookui Rd (at Kuhio Hwy)
808/828-1020 *7am-6pm, natural
foods, fruit smoothies & more*

■CRUISY AREAS

Secret Beach [AYOR] *inquire locally*

Lihue

■ENTERTAINMENT &
RECREATION

Lydgate State Park Beach off Hwy 56
btwn Lihue & Kapaa (S of Wailua River)
*gay beach btwn the condos & the golf
course*

■BOOKSTORES

Borders Bookstore & Cafe 4303
Nawiliwili Rd 808/246-0862 *9am-
10pm, till 11pm Fri-Sat, till 8pm Sun,
large lgbt section*

Poipu Beach

■ACCOMMODATIONS

Poipu Plantation Resort [GS,GO] 1792
Pe'e Rd, Poipu Beach 808/742-6757,
800/634-0263 *rooms & cottages, hot
tub*

Puunene

■RESTAURANTS

Roy's Bar & Grill 2360 Kiahuna
Plantation Dr 808/742-5000 *5:30pm-
9:30pm*

Wailua

■RESTAURANTS

Caffe Coco [E] 4-369 Kuhio Hwy
808/822-7990 *lunch Tue-Fri, dinner
nightly, clsd Mon*

Maui • Hawaii

MAUI

■ INFO LINES & SERVICES
Out In Maui Community Info line
808/244-4566 *recorded events info*

■ PUBLICATIONS
Out In Maui 808/244-4566 *(24hr info)* *monthly lgbt newspaper, free at locations throughout HI*

Haiku

■ ACCOMMODATIONS
Hale Huelo B&B [GS,GO] Door of Faith Church Rd, Huelo (at Hana Hwy) 808/572-8669 *ocean views*

Halfway to Hana House [GF,NS] 101 W Waipio Rd 808/572-1176 *studio w/ ocean view*

Huelo Point Flower Farm [GS,SW,GO] 808/572-1850 *vacation rentals, oceanfront estate*

Maui Vacation Retreat [GF,SW,N,GO] 655 Haumana Rd (at Hana Hwy) 866/675-6700

Hana

■ ACCOMMODATIONS
Hale Ohia [GS] 49625 Hana Hwy (at mile marker 27) 808/248-7045 *rental home, hot tub*

➤ **Hana Accommodations** [GS,GO] 808/248-7868, 800/228-4262 *studios & tropical cottages*

Hana Alii Holidays 808/248-7742, 800/548-0478 *reservations service*

Heavenly Flora [GF,SW,NS,GO] 70 Maia Rd 808/248-8680 *private rental home*

Na Pualani 'Ohana [GS,WC,GO] 808/248-8935, 800/628-7092 *2 full units, ocean & mtn views, lanai*

Huelo

■ ACCOMMODATIONS
Cliff's Edge [GF] 808/572-4530, 800/532-MAUI *seasonal*

Huelo Point Lookout [GF,SW] 808/573-0914

Discover the "Other" Maui

Hana Accommodations and Plantation Houses

Waterfalls, secluded beaches, natural sunbathing, Hiking in Bamboo jungles, ocean trails and Hot Tub all just *steps* away from our tropical cottages in beautiful Hana.

Celebrating 17 years of Award Winning Hospitality
800 228-4262
www.HANA-MAUI.com
check out our California site
www.TemptationRanch.com
888 213-7733

Hawaii • USA

Kaanapali

■ACCOMMODATIONS

The Royal Lahaina Resort
[GF,F,SW,WC] 2780 Kekaa Dr
808/661-3611, 800/222-5642
full-service resort

Kahului

■INFO LINES & SERVICES

AA Gay/ Lesbian 101 W Kam Ave (at Kahului Union Church) **808/874-3589** *6:30pm Wed*

Kihei

■INFO LINES & SERVICES

AA Gay/ Lesbian Kalama Park South Pavilion **808/874-3589** *7:30am Sun*

■ACCOMMODATIONS

Andrea's Maui Condos
[GS,SW,NS,WC,GO] **800/289-1522, 530/582-8703** *1 & 2-bdrm beachfront condos*

➤ **Anfora's Dreams** [GS,SW,GO]
323/467-2991, 800/788-5046
rental condo near ocean, hot tub

Eva Villa [GF,WC] 815 Kumulani Dr
808/874-6407, 800/884-1845
near Wailea beaches

Jack & Tom's Maui Condos/ Maui Suncoast Realty [GS,GO]
808/874-1048, 800/800-8608 *fully equipped condos & apts, non-smoking rooms available*

Ko'a Kai Rentals [GS,SW,NS,GO]
1993 S Kihei Rd #401 **808/879-6058, 800/399-6058 x33** *inexpensive rentals*

Koa Lagoon [GF,SW,WC] 800 S Kihei Rd
808/879-3002, 800/367-8030
oceanfront suites

Anfora's Dreams
MAUI CONDOS

Affordable, completely furnished deluxe units from singles to large homes with your total comfort in mind...
• Pool • Jacuzzi • Beach Access •
Starting from $79.00 a day

The Best Deal On Maui!
(800) 788-5046 or **(323) 467-2991**

PO Box 74030, Los Angeles, CA 90004
mauicondo@earthlink.net
www.home.earthlink.net/~mauicondo

Maui • Hawaii

Maui Oceanfront Inn [GS]
2980 S Kihei Rd 808/879-7744,
800/263-3387 *hotel*

Two Mermaids on the Sunny Side of Maui B&B [GS,NS,SW] 2840 Umalu Pl
808/874-8687, 800/598-9550
jacuzzi, near beach

Wailana Inn [GS,N,NS,GO] 14 Wailana Pl 808/874-3131, 800/399-3885
studios, rooftop hot tub, near beach

■Nightclubs
Odyssey Nights at Hapa's Brew Haus [MW,D,K] 41 E Lipoa St (in Lipoa Center) 808/879-9001 *8pm-2am Tue only*

■Cafes
Stella Blues 1215 S Kihei Rd
808/874-3779 *8am-9pm, deli*

■Erotica
The Love Shack 1794 S Kihei Rd (across from Tony Roma's)
808/875-0303

■Cruisy Areas
Kalama Park [AYOR]

Lahaina

■Accommodations
➤ **Maui Kaanapali Villas** [GS,SW]
45 Kai Ala Dr 808/667-7791,
800/922-7866 *private condos on the beach*

■Restaurants
Lahaina Coolers 180 Dickenson St
808/661-7082 *8am-2am, int'l, patio*

■Retail Shops
Skin Deep Tattoo 626 Front St (across from the Banyan Tree) 808/661-8531
tattooing, adult toys, T-shirts

■Cruisy Areas
Front St [AYOR] along Beach Walk

Makawao

■Accommodations
Hale Ho'okipa Inn B&B [GF,WC]
32 Pakani Pl 808/572-6698,
877/572-6698 *gracious old Hawaiian plantation home*

■Restaurants
Cassanova Restaurant & Deli
1188 Makawao Ave 808/572-0220
lunch & dinner, Italian, full bar till 2am, live music Wed-Sat

Makena

■Entertainment & Recreation
Little Beach at Makena [MW] *Pilani Hwy south to Wailea, right at Wailea Ike Dr, left on Wailea Alanui Dr to public beach, then take trail up hill at end of beach*

Pukalani

■Accommodations
Heavenly Gate Vacation Rental
[GS,NS,GO] 276 Hiwalani Loop (at Iolani St) 808/276-2917, 808/276-5783
bungalow home, tropical gardens

Wailea

■Accommodations
The Palms at Wailea [SW,NS]
3200 Wailea Alanui Drive Unit #2203
808/572-4530 *condo, near beach*

■Cafes
Maui Rainbow Factory [GO] near Little Beach at Makena (1 mile S of Maui Prince Hotel) *shave ice, fresh fruit smoothies*

Wailuku

■Erotica
Paradise Spice 1010 Lower Main #B
808/249-2449 *toys, magazines, DVDs*

Hawaii • USA

MOLOKAI

Kamalo

■ACCOMMODATIONS
Wavecrest Oceanfront Condo [GS,SW,GO] Wavecrest C-314 (at Hwy 450) 707/953-3106 (CA#)

Kaunakakai

■ACCOMMODATIONS
Molokai Beachfront Escapes [GF,SW,GO] 808/248-7868, 800/228-4262 *beachfront units*

KAUI

Waimea

■ACCOMMODATIONS
➤ **Waimea Plantation Cottages** [GS,SW] 808/338-1625, 800/922-7866 *seaside condos*

OAHU

■PUBLICATIONS
Odyssey Magazine Hawaii 808/955-5959 *everything you need to know about gay Hawaii*

Pocket Guide to Hawaii PO Box 88245 96830-8245 808/923-2400 *distributed free in the islands or $5 by mail order*

Aiea

■EROTICA
C 'n' N Liquor Aiea Shopping Center 808/487-2944

Suzie's 98-115 Kamehameha Hwy, 2nd flr (in Aiea Shopping Center) 808/487-6969 *24hrs*

Video Warehouse 98-019 Kamehameha Hwy (at Hekaha St) 808/487-1750 *24hrs, booths*

THE PERFECT START TO YOUR HAWAIIAN HOLIDAY.
FRESH FLOWER LEI GREETING ON ARRIVAL.
• WEDDING ITINERARIES AVAILABLE •
• FRESH LEIS SHIPPED - WORLD WIDE •

CALL - TOLL FREE
1-888-534-7644 OR FAX: (808) 732-7134
http://www.leisofhawaii.com

HAWAII'S FIVE BEST ALTERNATIVES.

Choose from three intimate Waikiki locations, near dining, shopping, alternative bars and activities, or venture to Maui or Kauai for a quiet vacation getaway.

Aston Waikiki Circle Hotel
Overlooking famous Waikiki Beach, rooms offer panoramic ocean views. Colorful & bright details enhance the fun of Waikiki.

Maui Kaanapali Villas
Fronting the best stretch of beach in West Maui, this condo resort offers you privacy and comfort on 11 acres of landscaped grounds.

Waikiki Joy Hotel
Waikiki's premier boutique hotel. In-room Jacuzzi, stereo system, 1 free hour karaoke, free continental breakfast. IGLTA member.

Waimea Plantation Cottages
Private seaside cottages on Kauai, surrounded by a 27-acre coconut grove – reminiscent of the way Hawaii used to be.

Ask for the "Property Special"
CALL YOUR TRAVEL SPECIALIST OR 800-922-7866

ASTONHOTELS.COM
AOL Keyword: ASTON HAWAII

ASTON ResortQuest HAWAII
A Vacation Well Spent.™

Aston Coconut Plaza Hotel
Waikiki's answer to a bed & breakfast. Gazebo front and Mexican tile add to country charm. Complimentary breakfast daily.

© Aston Hotels & Resorts® Hawaii 2003

Hawaii • USA

Honolulu

INFO LINES & SERVICES

Gay/ Lesbian AA 277 Ohua (at Waikiki Health Center) **808/946-1438** *8pm daily*

The Gay/ Lesbian Community Center 2424 S Beretania (btwn Isenberg & University) **808/951-7000** *10am-6pm, noon-4pm Sun*

➤ **Leis of Hawaii** 888/534-7644 *personalized Hawaiian greeting service, complete w/ fresh flower leis*

ACCOMMODATIONS

Aloha Hale [GF,SW,GO] 2427 Kuhio Ave (at Uluniu) **808/735-1287, 888/632-3218** *condos, sauna, jacuzzi*

➤ **Ashton Coconut Plaza Hotel** [GF,SW,WC] 450 Lewers St, Waikiki (at Ala Wai) **808/923-8828, 800/922-7866** *near beach*

➤ **Aston Waikiki Circle Hotel** [GS] 2464 Kalakaua Ave (at Uluniu St) **808/923-1571, 800/922-7866** *overlooking Waikiki Beach*

Breakers Hotel [GF,SW] 250 Beachwalk **808/923-3181, 800/426-0494** *also bar & grill*

➤ **The Cabana at Waikiki** [★M,GO] 2551 Cartwright Rd (off Kapahulu Ave) **808/926-5555, 877/902-2121** *1-bdrm suites w/ kitchens & lanais, 8-man spa, 1 blk to gay Queen's Surf beach*

Kolohe's B No B [MO,GO] 441 Kanekapolei St #102A (at Ala Wai Blvd) **808/923-2408** *in private home, DSL internet access*

➤ **Nui Kai** [MW,R,SW,NS,WC,GO] 718/783-2331 *oceanfront condo at base of Diamond Head w/ huge lanai & ocean & Diamond Head views, 5-minute walk to Queen's Surf Beach*

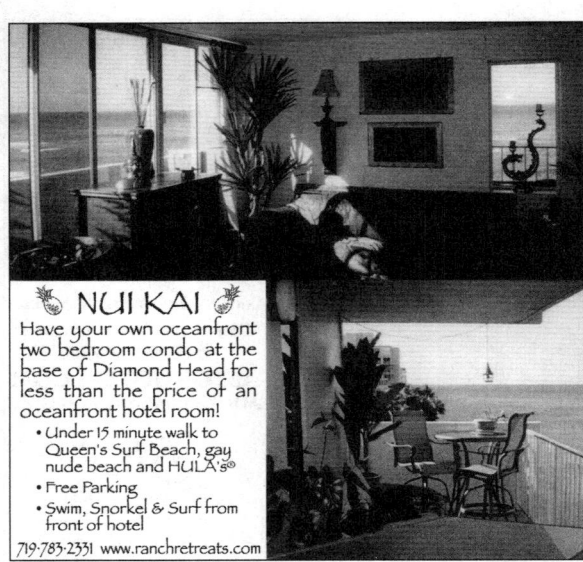

PARADISE FOR RENT: WAIKIKI

THE ONLY GAY OWNED & OPERATED "OCEAN VIEW" UNITS IN WAIKIKI
2 MINUTE WALK TO QUEEN'S SURF GAY BEACH
KING-SIZE BEDS
NEW BATHROOMS
MARBLE FLOORS
POOL
HULA'S BAR ON 2ND FLOOR

Queen's Surf Vacation Rentals at the Waikiki Grand Hotel
134 Kapahulu Avenue

Call toll-free:
(888)336-4368
In Hawaii: (808)923-1814
www.gaywaikiki.com
reservations@queenssurf.com

Oahu • Hawaii

➤ **Queen's Surf Vacation Rentals**
[GS,SW,NS,GO] 134 Kapahulu (at Lemon Rd, in Waikiki Grand Hotel)
808/923-1814, 888/336-4368 *ocean views*

Waikiki GLBT Vacation Rentals
[GF,NS,WC] 2092 Kuhio Ave #1903
808/922-1659, 800/543-5663 *reservation service, ask for Walt Flood*

➤ **Waikiki Grand Hotel** [GS]
134 Kapahulu Ave **800/922-7866**

➤ **Waikiki Joy Hotel** [GS,F,K,SW]
320 Lewers St **808/923-2300, 800/922-7866** *boutique hotel*

Waikiki Parkside Hotel [GF,SW,NS,WC]
1850 Ala Moana Blvd (at Kalia & Ena)
808/955-1567, 800/237-9666

■ BARS

➤ **Angles** [MW,NH,D,S,V] 2256 Kuhio Ave, 2nd flr, Waikiki (at Seaside)
808/926-9766, 808/923-1130 (infoline) *10am-2am, DJ Wed-Sun, free internet access, male dancers Th & Sun*

➤ **Hula's Bar & Lei Stand**
[★MW,D,TG,F,S,V,YC] 134 Kapahulu Ave (2nd flr of Waikiki Grand Hotel)
808/923-0669 *10am-2am, near gay beach, go-go boys Th & Sun*

In Between [GS,NH,K] 2155 Lau'ula St, Waikiki (off Lewers, across from Planet Hollywood) **808/926-7060** *2pm-2am*

Michelangelo's [M,NH,F] 444 Hobron Ln #P-8 (in Eaton Square Shopping Center, Waikiki) **808/951-0008** *10am-2am, from 6am wknds, sports bar, cruisy*

■ NIGHTCLUBS

Fusion Waikiki [★M,D,A,TG,K,S,V]
2260 Kuhio Ave, upstairs (at Seaside)
808/924-2422 *9pm-4am, from 8pm Fri-Sat, from 10pm Sun, go-go boys Wed*

Venus Nightclub [GS,D,MR-A,DS,S,YC]
1349 Kapiolani Blvd (below China House restaurant, at Piikoi)
808/951-8671, 808/955-2640 *8pm-4am, drag shows Th & Sat, male dancers Fri-Sat*

THIS PUBLIC SERVICE MESSAGE IS BROUGHT TO YOU BY:

CALL YOUR TRAVEL AGENT TODAY! AND WHEN YOU STOP BY: MENTION THIS AD FOR A COOL GIFT!

Angles Waikiki • 2256 Kuhio Ave., Honolulu, HI 96815 • www.angleswaikiki.com • (808) 926-9766

Oahu • Hawaii

■ CAFES

Caffe Giovannini [GO] 1888 Kalakaua Ave, Waikiki (across from the Wave) **808/979-2299** *9am-11pm, patio*

Mocha Java Cafe 1200 Ala Moana Blvd (in Ward Center) **808/591-9023** *8am-9pm, till 5pm Sun*

■ RESTAURANTS

Café Che Pasta [MW,D,E] 1001 Bishop St (enter off Alakea St) **808/524-0004, 808/531-4140** (info line) *11am-8pm, from 5pm Sat, clsd Sun, full bar*

Cafe Sistina [WC] 1314 S King St **808/596-0061** *lunch Mon-Fri, dinner nightly, northern Italian, full bar*

Eggs n' Things 1911-B Kalakaua Ave **808/949-0820** *11pm-2pm, diner, popular after-hours*

Indigo 1121 Nu'uanu Ave **808/521-2900** *lunch Tue-Fri, dinner Tue-Sat, Eurasian, live jazz Tue*

Keo's In Waikiki [★R] 2028 Kuhio Ave **808/951-9355** *7:30am-10:30pm*

La Cucaracha 102 Nahua Rd (at Kuhio Ave) **808/922-2288** *1pm-midnight, Mexican, full bar*

Lewers St Steak & Seafood [WC] 412 Lewers St (at the Marc Suites) **808/926-1881** *dinner only, full bar*

Singha Thai [E] 1910 Ala Moana Blvd **808/941-2898** *4pm-11pm*

■ ENTERTAINMENT & RECREATION

Dive Shack 1778 Ala Moana Blvd, lower lobby, Ste 4 **808/949-3483, 888/922-3483** *various diving trips, free hotel pick-up*

Honolulu Gay/ Lesbian Cultural Foundation 1877 Kalakaua Ave **808/941-0424 x18** *annual film festival Memorial Day wknd, art exhibits, concerts, plays, call for events*

See over 2,500 works of art by Douglas Simonson, master of the male nude, online at **www.douglassimonson.com.** In Hawaii, private showings at the artist's studio are by appointment (call 737-6275 for studio location). For free brochure write to: Douglas Simonson, 758 Kapahulu Ave. Box 328-D, Honolulu HI 96816.

THE ART OF DOUGLAS SIMONSON

© 2003 by Douglas Simonson

Hawaii • USA

LikeHike 808/455-8193 *gay hiking tours every other Sun*

Queens Surf Beach Kapiolani Park *popular gay beach*

Rainbow Sailing Charters [MW,GO] 808/396-5995 *whale-watching, snorkeling, sunset cocktail cruises & commitment ceremonies*

■ RETAIL SHOPS

The Art of Raymond Helgeson 311 Ohua Ave #203-C 808/922-3082

➤ **Douglas Simonson—Artists Studio** 758 Kapahulu Ave, Box 328 96816 808/737-6275 *call for appt & location*

Eighty Percent Straight 2139 Kuhio Ave, Waikiki 808/923-9996 *10am-10pm, till 11pm Fri-Sat, lgbt clothing, books, videos, cards, toys*

■ PUBLICATIONS

DaKine Magazine 808/923-7378 *lgbt newsmagazine for Oahu, club & nightlife listings, monthly*

Odyssey Magazine Hawaii 808/955-5959 *everything you need to know about gay Hawaii*

Pocket Guide to Hawaii 808/923-2400 *distributed free in the islands or $5 by mail order*

■ MEN'S CLUBS

➤ **Max's Gym** [★V,18+,PC] 444 Hobron Ln, 4th flr (at Ala Moana Blvd, in Eaton Square) 808/951-8232 *24hrs, also Cafe Max*

P-10A [S,V,18+,PC,$] 444 Hobron Ln, #P-10A (next to Michelangelo's) 808/942-8536 *6pm-6am, 24hrs wknds, low rates, drug- & alcohol-free, nude dancers Fri-Sat*

Shop us online at www.adultdhv.com

MAGAZINES · GAY PRIDE PRODUCTS · BOOKS · CD ROMS · GREETING CARDS
ADULT NOVELTIES · CALENDARS · DVD's with no regional coding & MORE!

The Most Incredible Selection of Adult Videos!

870 Kapahulu Ave. Honolulu, HI
Ph. (808) 735-6066
Just one mile from Waikiki!

Diamond Head Video
Open 9am-Midnight 365 days a year

Hawaii • USA

■ MEN'S SERVICES

The Confidential Connection®!
808/596-7222 *The hottest local guys! 18+ Record & Listen FREE! Use access code 499*

▶ **Megaphone Honolulu**
800/289-1489 *Call for the local # nearest you! Meet Hot Men in your area! FREE to Browse & Respond to voice ads. Use code 3087. Also try MEGAMATES.COM*

■ EROTICA

▶ **Diamond Head Video**
870 Kapahulu Ave (near Genki Sushi)
808/735-6066

Esquire Bookstore [AYOR] 39 N Hotel St (at top of stairs) *24hrs*

Risque II Theatre/ Bookstore [AYOR] 32 N Hotel St, in Chinatown (upstairs)
808/531-7318 *24hrs*

Suzie's 2162 Kalakaua Ave (at Lewers)
808/922-4071 *24hrs*

Velvet Video 2155 Lau'ula St, Waikiki, 2nd flr (above In Between)
808/924-0868 *booths*

■ CRUISY AREAS

Ala Moana Beach Park [AYOR]
near Waikiki Yacht Club

Kailua

■ ACCOMMODATIONS

Hale Pueo [GS,NS,GO] 1142 Koohoo Pl (off of A'alapapa in Lanikai neighborhood) 808/262-2820, 888/712-5698

■ EROTICA

▶ **Diamond Head Video** Aikahi Park Shopping Ctr (near Kaneohe Marine Base) 808/254-6066

Wahiawa

■ EROTICA

Entertainment Today 177 S Kamehameha Hwy (near AF base)

Windward Coast

■ ACCOMMODATIONS

Ali'i Bluffs Windward B&B
[GS,SW,NS,GO] 46-251 Ikiiki St, Kane'ohe
808/235-1124, 800/235-1151

IDAHO

Statewide

■ PUBLICATIONS

Diversity Newsmagazine
208/336-3870 #2 *statewide lgbt newspaper, monthly*

Boise

■ INFO LINES & SERVICES

AA Gay/ Lesbian 23rd & Woodlawn (at First Congregational Church)
208/344-6611 *8pm Sun & Tue*

The Community Center 919-A N 27th St (at Jordan) 208/336-3870 *volunteer staff, 24hr info line*

■ ACCOMMODATIONS

Bed & Buns [MO,N,GO] 10325 Victory Rd (at Five Mile Rd) 208/362-1802
B&B, hot tub, pets ok

■ BARS

The Lucky Dog [MW,NH] 1108 Front St (at 11th) 208/333-0074 *5pm-close, 3pm-2am wknds, patio*

■ NIGHTCLUBS

The Balcony Club [★GS,D,WC,GO]
180 N 8th St #224 (at Idaho)
208/336-1313 *2pm-2am, theme parties*

Emerald City Club [MW,D,S] 415 S 9th (at Myrtle) 208/342-5446 *10am-2am*

■ CAFES

Flying M Coffeehouse [E] 500 W Idaho (at 5th St) 208/345-4320
6:30am-10pm, till 11pm Fri-Sat, 7:30am-6pm Sun

■ RESTAURANTS

The Klatsch [E,BW] 409 S 8th (across from 8th St Marketplace)
208/345-0452 *brkfst, lunch & dinner, till 3pm Sun-Mon, organic*

■ ENTERTAINMENT & RECREATION

Flicks & Rick's Cafe American
[F,E,BW,WC] 646 Fulton St
208/342-4288 *opens 4pm, from noon wknds, 4 movie theaters, patio*

Twin Falls • Idaho

■ RETAIL SHOPS
The Edge 1101 W Idaho St (at 11th) **208/344-5383** *6:30am-10pm, 9am-7pm Sun, gifts, also cafe*

■ MEN'S SERVICES
➤ **Megaphone Boise 800/289-1489** *Call for the local # nearest you! Meet Hot Men in your area! FREE to Browse & Respond to voice ads. Use code 3087. Also try MEGAMATES.COM*

■ EROTICA
Pleasure Boutique 424 N Orchard **208/433-1161** *toys, videos*

■ CRUISY AREAS
Ann Morrison Park [AYOR] *near baseball fields*

Coeur d'Alene
see also Spokane, Washington

■ ACCOMMODATIONS
The Clark House on Hayden Lake [★GF,NS,GO] 5250 E Hayden Lake Rd, Hayden Lake **208/772-3470, 800/765-4593** *mansion on 12-acre estate, full brkfst, hot tub*

■ BARS
Mik-N-Mak's [MW,NH,D,K,S] 406 N 4th (at Wallace) **208/667-4858** *2pm-2am, from noon wknds*

Idaho Falls

■ CRUISY AREAS
Park South of Broadway [AYOR] *S of water tower on Capitol parking lot S of bathrooms & gazebo*

Lava Hot Springs
see also Pocatello

■ ACCOMMODATIONS
Lava Hot Springs Inn [GF,SW,NS,WC] **208/776-5830** *full brkfst*

■ BOOKSTORES
Aura Soma Lava 97 N 2nd St E (at Portneuf River Rd) **208/776-5800, 800/757-1233** *open wknds, open wkdays during summer, 10am-5pm, metaphysical & lgbt books*

■ CRUISY AREAS
Hot Pools [AYOR]

Moscow

■ BOOKSTORES
Bookpeople 521 S Main (btwn 5th & 6th) **208/882-7957** *9am-8pm*

Pocatello

■ NIGHTCLUBS
Charleys [MW,D,E,WC] 331 E Center **208/232-9606** *5pm-2am, from 7pm Sun*

■ CAFES
Main St Coffee & News 234 N Main (btwn Lander & Clark) **208/234-9834** *7am-8pm, till 4pm Sat, 9am-4pm Sun*

■ EROTICA
Pegasus Book Store 246 W Center **208/232-6493**
The Silver Fox 143 S 2nd St (at Center) **208/234-2477**

■ CRUISY AREAS
Ross Park [AYOR] *upper level*

Powell

■ CRUISY AREAS
Jerry Johnson Hot Springs [AYOR] US 12 *days*

Sand Point

■ CRUISY AREAS
Cedar St Bridge [AYOR]

Stanley

■ ACCOMMODATIONS
Las Tejanas B&B [GF,NS] Hwy 75, Lower Stanley **208 /774-3301** *May-Sept, natural hot tub, full brkfst*

Twin Falls

■ CRUISY AREAS
City Park [AYOR] Shoshone & 4th Ave E
Rock Creek Park [AYOR] *on Addison Ave W days*

Illinois • USA

ILLINOIS

Statewide

PUBLICATIONS
Prairie Flame 217/753-2887
lgbt newspaper for downstate IL

Alton

see also St Louis, Missouri

NIGHTCLUBS
Bubby & Sissy's [MW,D,DS,WC]
602 Belle (at 6th) **618/465-4773**
3pm-2am, till 3am Fri-Sat, drag Sun

CRUISY AREAS
Rock Springs Park [AYOR] College Ave (at Rock Springs Dr)

Atkinson

EROTICA
➤ **The Lion's Den Adult Bookstore**
313 S State St (Exit 27, off I-80)
309/936-7066 *24hrs*

Aurora

see also Chicago

EROTICA
Denmark Book Store 1300 US Hwy 30
(2 miles S of Rte 34) **630/898-9838**
24hrs

Bloomington

BARS
Bistro [MW,D,WC] 316 N Main St (at Jefferson) **309/829-2278** *8pm-1am, till 2am Fri-Sat*

EROTICA
Risque's 1506 N Main (at Division)
309/827-9279 *24hrs*

CRUISY AREAS
Forest Park [AYOR]

Blue Island

NIGHTCLUBS
The Edge [MW,NH,TG,C,DS,S,WC] 13126 S Western (at Grove) **708/597-8379**
8pm-2am, till 3am Fri-Sat, from 4pm Sun

Buckley

EROTICA
➤ **The Lion's Den Adult Bookstore**
362 E 800 North Rd (exit 272, off I-57)
217/394-2601 *24hrs*

Calumet City

see also Chicago & Hammond, Indiana

BARS
Dick's R U Crazee [M,NH] 48 154th Pl (at Forsythe) **708/862-4605** *7pm-2am, from 9pm Mon, till 3am Wed, Fri & Sat*

John L's Place [MW,NH,TG,WC] 335 154th Pl **708/862-2386** *7pm-close*

NIGHTCLUBS
Pour House [GS,D] 103 155th Pl (at Forsythe) **708/891-3980** *8pm-2am, till 3am Wed, Fri-Sat, clsd Tue*

CRUISY AREAS
Shabonna Woods & Sandridge Forest Preserves [AYOR]

Carbondale

INFO LINES & SERVICES
AA Lesbian/ Gay 618/549-4633

ACCOMMODATIONS
Rainbow Ranch Gay Campsite
[M,SW,GO] 90 Old Cape Rd, Jonesboro
618/833-7926 *wooded creekside campsite*

NIGHTCLUBS
The Upside Downtown
[GF,NH,D,E,S,V,GO] 213 E Main St
618/549-4270 *10pm-2am, clsd Mon-Tue*

CRUISY AREAS
Crab Orchard Lake [AYOR] Cambria Neck Ln *exit off Rte 13 onto Cambria Rd, drive 1 mile N, on right side of Cambria Rd is side rd called Cambria Neck Ln, turn right onto it*

Chicago—Overview • Illinois

Centreville
see also St Louis, Missouri

■NIGHTCLUBS

Boxers 'n' Briefs [M,D,F,DS,S,WC] 55 Four Corners Ln (next to PT's Show Club) **618/332-6141** *6pm-2am, 7pm-6am Fri-Sat, clsd Mon, nude dancers, drag every other Th*

Champaign/Urbana

■ACCOMMODATIONS

The Little House on the Prairie [GS,SW,GO] RR 2, Patterson Rd (by Country Club Rd), Sullivan **217/728-4727** *Queen Anne Victorian, full brkfst, hot tub*

■BARS

Ruby's [MW,NH,D,A,B,L,DS,WC] 207 W Clark (btwn State & Randolph St), Champaign **217/359-8644** *5pm-close, goth Mon*

■NIGHTCLUBS

Chester Street [MW,D,DS,WC,GO] 63 Chester St (at Water St), Champaign **217/356-5607** *5pm-1am*

■CAFES

Espresso Royale 602 E Daniel (at 6th St), Champaign **217/328-1112** *7am-11pm*

■RESTAURANTS

Fiesta Cafe [GO] 216 S 1st St (at White, near U of IL campus), Champaign **217/352-5902** *11am-1am, Mexican*

■EROTICA

I-Block Arcade & Theatre 213 S Neil St (btwn White & Clark), Champaign **217/351-8897** *video booths, basement theater*

Illini Video Arcade 33 E Springfield Ave (S Neil exit, off I-74), Champaign **217/359-8529** *24hrs*

Urbana News 602 Cunningham (next to Five Points Tavern), Urbana **217/384-0188** *24hrs*

■CRUISY AREAS

Crystal Lake Park [AYOR] at Park & University Sts

CHICAGO

Chicago is divided into 5 geographical areas:
Chicago—Overview
Chicago—North Side
Chicago—Boystown/ Lakeview
Chicago—Near North
Chicago—South Side

Chicago—Overview

■INFO LINES & SERVICES

AA Gay/ Lesbian Boystown Al-Anon Club [WC] 909 W Belmont Ave, 2nd flr (btwn Clark & Sheffield) **773/529-0321** *5pm-11pm, from 8:30am wknds*

Horizons Community Services 961 W Montana (at Fullerton & Sheffield) **773/472-6469** *9am-10pm, till 5pm Fri, 11am-3pm Sat, clsd Sun*

■ENTERTAINMENT & RECREATION

Bailiwick Arts Center 1229 W Belmont **773/883-1090** *many lgbt-themed productions, popular Pride Series*

Cafe Pride Lakeview Presbyterian, 716 W Addison (at Broadway) **773/784-2635** *lgbt coffeehouse, for youth only, 8pm-midnight Fri*

Chicago Neighborhood Tours [GF] 78 E Washington St (at the Chicago Cultural Center) **312/742-1190** *the best way to make the Windy City your kind of town*

The Hancock Observatory 875 N Michigan Ave (in John Hancock Center) **888/875-8439** *renovated 94th-flr observatory w/ outside Skywalk*

Leather Archives & Museum 6418 N Greenview **773/761-9200** *by appt*

Sears Tower Skydeck 233 S Wacker Dr (enter at Jackson Blvd) **312/875-9696** *see the City from one of the world's tallest bldgs*

COMING TO THE WINDY CITY?

Lambda Publications

... we've got the community covered

The voice of the gay, lesbian, bi & trans community, serving the Chicago & suburban communities since 1985

Windy City Times
Nightspots bar guide
BLACKlines
En La Vida
OUT! Resource Guide

and now ...

Windy
City
Radio
FM 105.9

THE VOICE OF THE GLBT COMMUNITY

www.wctimes.com
outlines@suba.com, WCTeditor@aol
(773) 871-7610
Fax (773) 871-7609
1115 West Belmont, Suite 2-D,
Chicago, IL 60657

www.wctimes.com

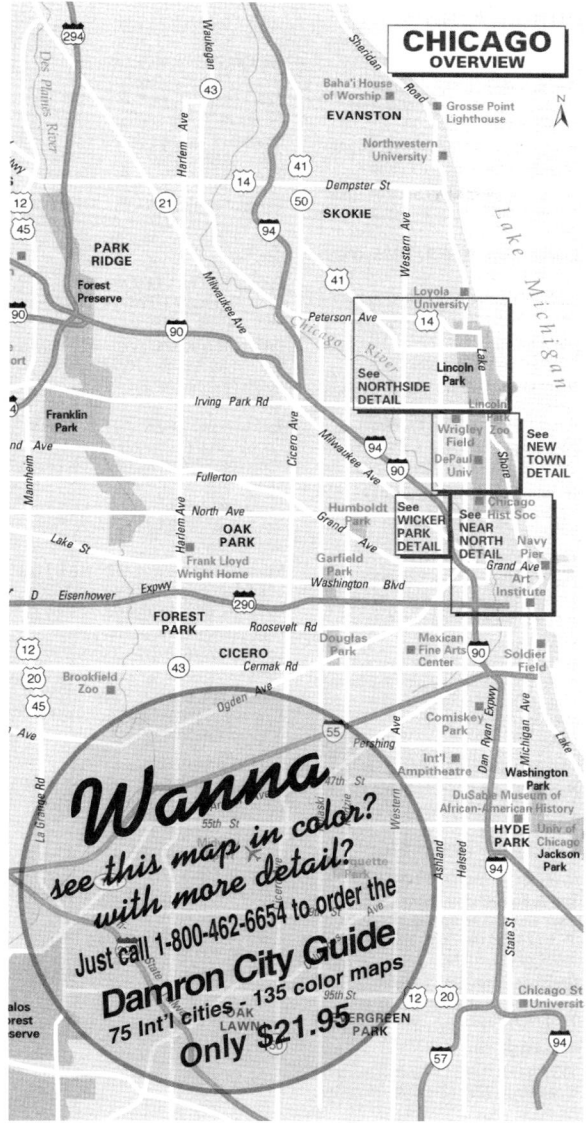

Illinois • USA

■ PUBLICATIONS

The Alternative Phone Book 773/472-6319 *directory of local businesses*

BLACKlines 773/871-7610 *monthly news & features for Black lgbts*

boi magazine 773/975-0264 *slick glossy w/ bar listings, articles, photos & circuit dish*

Chicago Free Press 773/325-0005 *lgbt newspaper*

En La Vida 773/871-7610 *monthly news & features for Latino/a lgbts*

Gay Chicago 773/327-7271 *weekly, extensive resource listings*

Nightspots 773/871-7610 *news, views, art & recreation focusing on African-American lgbt community*

Pink Pages 773/769-6328 *lgbt business directory & lifestyle magazine*

➤ **Windy City Times** 773/871-7610 *weekly lgbt newspaper & weekly calendar guide*

■ MEN'S SERVICES

The Gay Connection 900/847-6338 *Talk and/or meet with other men from the area, only 99¢ per minute.*

➤ **Megaphone Chicago** 800/289-1489 *Call for the local # nearest you! Meet Hot Men in your area! FREE to Browse & Respond to voice ads. Use code 3087. Also try MEGAMATES.COM*

■ CRUISY AREAS

Humboldt Park [AYOR] North Ave & Sacramento *near pavilion & bushes*

Chicago—North Side

■ ACCOMMODATIONS

The Ardmore House [M,GO] 1248 W Ardmore Ave (at Magnolia) 773/728-5414 *Victorian B&B, full brkfst wknds, hot tub*

Greenview Inn B&B [GS,GO] 7318 N Greenview Ave (at Chase) 773/743-1043

■ BARS

1137 [M,NH,L] 1137 W Granville (E of Broadway) 773/973-0006 *9am-2am*

Big Chicks [MW,NH,D,V,WC] 5024 N Sheridan (btwn Foster & Argyle) 773/728-5511 *4pm-2am, from 3pm wknds, patio, Sun bbq*

Charmer's Lounge [M,NH] 1502 W Jarvis (at Greenview) 773/465-2811 *6pm-2am, from 4pm wknds, till 3am Sat*

Chicago Eagle [MW,L,WC] 5015 N Clark St (at Argyle) 773/728-0050 *8pm-4am, till 5am Sat, dress code Tue, Fri & Sat*

Clark's on Clark [★M,NH] 5001 N Clark St (at Argyle) 773/728-2373 *4pm-4am, till 5am Sat*

Different Strokes [M,NH,MR,S] 4923 N Clark St (at Argyle) 773/989-1958 *noon-2am, till 3am Sat, dancers 5pm wknds*

Jackhammer [★M,NH,D,L,S,V] 6406 N Clark St (at Devon) 773/743-5772 *4pm-4am, till 5am Fri, from 2pm wknds, patio*

Legacy 21 [M,NH] 3042 W Irving Park Rd (at Kedzie) 773/588-9405 *7pm-4am, till 5am Sat,*

Madrigal's [MW,MR-L,K,S] 5316 N Clark St (at Balmoral) 773/334-3033 *5pm-2am, till 3am Sat, strippers Tue-Sun*

Scot's [MW,NH] 1829 W Montrose (at Damen) 773/528-3253 *3pm-2am, from 11am wknds*

Touché [★M,L] 6412 N Clark St (at Devon) 773/465-7400 *5pm-4am, from 3pm wknds*

■ NIGHTCLUBS

@tmosphere [MW,D,GO] 5355 N Clark (at W Balmoral Ave) 773/784-1100 *3pm-2am, till 3am Sat*

■ RESTAURANTS

Chicago Diner [BW] 3411 N Halsted St 773/935-6696 *11am-10pm, from 10am wknds, hip & vegetarian*

Fireside 5739 N Ravenswood (at Rosehill) 773/878-5942 *11am-4am, from 10am Sun, Cajun & pizza, patio, full bar*

The Room [MW] 5900 N Broadway 773/989-7666 *dinner nightly, Sun brunch*

Chicago—Boystown • Illinois

Tendino's [WC] 5335 N Sheridan (at Broadway) 773/275-8100 *11am-11pm, till midnight wknds, pizza, full bar*

Tomboy [★BYOB,WC,GO] 5402 N Clark (at Balmoral) 773/907-0636 *5pm-10pm, till 11pm wknds, clsd Tue*

■ Entertainment & Recreation

Hollywood Beach [★] at Hollywood & Sheridan Sts *'the' gay beach*

■ Bookstores

KOPI: A Traveler's Cafe [E] 5317 N Clark St (at Summerdale) 773/989-5674 *8am-11pm, till midnight Fri, from 9am Sat, from 10am Sun*

■ Retail Shops

Bad Boys Chicago [GO] 1500 W Balmoral 773/334-9993 *men's clothing, accessories*

Eagle Leathers 5005 N Clark St 773/728-7228

Gay Mart 3457 N Halsted St (at Cornelius) 773/929-4272 *11am-7pm, till 6pm Sun*

Specialty Video Films [GO] 5307 N Clark St (at Foster) 773/878-3434 *10am-10pm, till 11pm Fri-Sat, foreign, cult, art house, lgbt & erotic videos*

■ Gyms & Health Clubs

Cheetah Gym 5248 N Clark St (at Foster) 773/728-7777

■ Men's Clubs

Man's Country [PC,S] 5017 N Clark St (at Argyle) 773/878-2069 *24hrs, nude strippers Fri-Sat*

Man's World [PC] 4862 N Clark St (at Lawrence) 773/728-0400 *24hrs Fri-Sat*

■ Erotica

Admiral Theater 3940 W Lawrence 773/478-8111

■ Cruisy Areas

Hollywood Beach [AYOR] along lake (at 5700 N)

Lincoln Park [AYOR] E of Lake Shore Dr (btwn Foster & Montrose)

Chicago—Boystown/ Lakeview

■ Accommodations

Best Western Hawthorne Terrace [GF,WC] 3434 N Broadway (at Hawthorne Pl) 773/244-3434, 888/675-2378 *located in the heart of Chicago's gay community*

City Suites Hotel [GF] 933 W Belmont Ave (btwn Clark & Sheffield) 773/404-3400, 800/248-9108 *European style*

Majestic Hotel [GF] 528 W Brompton Ave (at Addison) 773/404-3499, 800/727-5108 *romantic 19th-century atmosphere*

➤ **Villa Toscana B&B** [MW,NS,WC,GO] 3447 N Halsted St 773/404-2643, 800/404-2643 *1890s coach house*

The Willows [GS] 555 W Surf St (at Broadway) 773/528-8400, 800/787-3108 *19th-century French flair*

■ Bars

Annex 3 [MW,NH,WC] 3160 N Clark St (at Belmont) 773/327-5969 *noon-2am, till 3am Sat*

Beat Kitchen [GF,F,E] 2100 W Belmont (btwn Hoyne & Damen) 773/281-4444 *11:30am-2am*

Berlin [★MW,D,TG,S,V,WC] 954 W Belmont (at Sheffield) 773/348-4975 *5pm-4am, from 8pm-5am Sat, from 8pm Mon, go-go boys Tue*

Blues [★GF,E] 2519 N Halsted 773/528-1012, 773/549-9436 *8pm-2am, till 3am Sat, classic Chicago blues spot*

Bobby Love's [MW,NH,K,WC] 3729 N Halsted St (at Waveland) 773/525-1200 *3pm-2am, from noon wknds, till 3am Fri-Sat*

Buck's Saloon [M,NH] 3439 N Halsted St (btwn Cornelia & Newport) 773/525-1125 *10am-2am, from 11am Sun, patio*

Buddies [★MW,CW,F] 3301 N Clark St (at Aldine) 773/477-4066 *3pm-2am, from 9am wknds, till 3am Fri-Sat, restaurant from 3pm, 9am wknds*

Damron Men's Travel Guide 2004

Illinois • USA

Cell Block [M,D,B,L,WC] 3702 N Halsted (at Waveland) 773/665-8064 *4pm-2am, from 2pm wknds, also Holding Cell, from 10pm Th-Sat w/ strict leather/ latex/ uniform code, also Leather Cell store*

Charlie's Chicago [M,D,CW] 3726 N Broadway (btwn Waveland & Grace) 773/871-8887 *3pm-4am, till 5am Sat*

The Closet [★MW,NH,V] 3325 N Broadway St (at Buckingham) 773/477-8533 *2pm-4am, till 5am Sat, from noon wknds*

Cocktail [MW,NH,D,S,V,WC] 3359 Halsted St (at Roscoe) 773/477-1420 *4pm-2am, from 2pm wknds, till 3am Sat, go-go dancers Tue & Th-Fri*

Gentry on Halsted [GS,E,P] 3320 N Halsted (at Aldine) 773/348-1053 *4pm-2am, till 3am Sat, piano bar*

Little Jim's [★M,NH] 3501 N Halsted St (at Cornelia) 773/871-6116 *noon-4am, till 5am Sat*

Lucky Horseshoe [M,NH,S] 3169 N Halsted St (at Briar) 773/404-3169, 800/443-3169 *3pm-2am, from noon wknds, dancers nightly, patio*

Manhandler [★M,NH,V] 1948 N Halsted St (at Armitage) 773/871-3339 *noon-4am, till 5am Sat, patio*

The North End [M,NH,WC] 3733 N Halsted St (at Grace) 773/477-7999 *3pm-2am, till 3am Sat, from 1pm wknds, sports bar*

Roscoe's [★MW,NH,D,S,V] 3354-56 N Halsted St (at W Roscoe) 773/281-3355 *2pm-2am, noon-3am Sat, 6 bars, patio cafe in summer*

Sidetrack [★M,NH,V,WC] 3349 N Halsted St (at Roscoe) 773/477-9189 *3pm-2am, from 2pm wknds, rooftop open in summer*

Spin [GS,D,S,V] 800 W Belmont (enter on Halsted) 773/327-7711 *4pm-2am, from 2pm wknds, 3 bars, '80s Th*

Villa Toscana

A Bed and Breakfast with European Charm in the Heart of Gay Chicago

Just steps from the gay nightlife, theaters, bars, restaurants, and Wrigley Field

Newly Redecorated
Air Conditioned
Private Phones
Cable TV
Continental Breakfast

3447 N. Halsted Street
Chicago, IL 60657
1-800-404-2643

www.villa-toscana.com (online reservations)

Chicago—Boystown • Illinois

■ NIGHTCLUBS

Circuit/ Rehab [M,D,MR,K,S] 3641 N Halsted St (at Addison) **773/325-2233** *9pm-4am, till 5am Sat, clsd Mon-Tue, also Club Rehab from 4pm, Latin Wed-Th, Latin T-dance Sun*

Felt [MW,F] 3341 N Halsted **773/404-8100** *5pm-2am, small lounge, specialty martinis*

Manhole [★M,D,L,V] 3458 N Halsted St (at Cornelia) **773/975-9244** *9pm-4am, till 5am Sat*

Smart Bar [★GF,D,A,E] 3730 N Clark St (downstairs at the Metro) **773/549-4140** *10pm-4am, till 5am Sat*

■ CAFES

Pick Me Up Cafe & All Nite Express Lounge 3408 N Clark **773/248-6613** *3pm-3am, 24hrs Fri-Sat, brkfst all day*

■ RESTAURANTS

Angelina Ristorante [WC] 3561 N Broadway (at Addison) **773/935-5933** *5:30pm-11pm, Sun brunch, Italian, full bar*

Ann Sather's [★] 929 W Belmont Ave (at Sheffield) **773/348-2378** *7am-9pm, Swedish diner & Boystown fixture*

Buddies Restaurant & Bar [★MW,WC] 3301 N Clark St (at Aldine) **773/477-4066** *3pm-11pm, from 9am wknds, full bar*

Cornelia's [WC] 750 W Cornelia Ave (at Halsted) **773/248-8333** *clsd Mon, dinner nightly, upscale Italian, full bar*

Kit Kat Lounge & Supper Club [GO] 3700 N Halsted (at W Waveland Ave) **773/525-1111** *5:30pm-1am Tue-Sun, brunch Sun (seasonal), great martini menu*

Kitsch'n On Roscoe 2005 W Roscoe (at Damen) **773/248-7372** *9am-10pm, till 3pm Sun, brunch wknds, full bar*

TOYS FOR BIG BAD BOYS
3505 North Halsted/Chicago, IL 60657
773.868.0914

www.cupidssextoys.com

BERKELEY   CHICAGO   SAN JUAN   AND NOW IN TORONTO

STEAMWORKS

24/7 MEN'S GYM/SAUNA   3246 N HALSTED
773.929.6080   WWW.STEAMWORKSONLINE.COM

RAM BOOKSTORE

CHICAGO'S BIGGEST AND BEST BACKROOM!

3511 N Halsted
525-9528

Illinois • USA

The Pepper Lounge [MW] 3441 N Sheffield (btwn Newport & Clark) **773/665-7377** *6pm-1:30am, till midnight Sun, clsd Mon, supper club, Italian*

The Raw Bar & Grill [E,WC] 3720 N Clark St (at Waveland) **773/348-7291** *5pm-2am, seafood*

Technicolor [WC] 3210 N Lincoln Ave (at Belmont & Ashland) **773/665-2111** *dinner, clsd Mon, kitschy decor, eclectic fusion menu*

Voltaire [MW,C] 3441 N Halsted **773/281-9320** *3pm-2am, till 3am Sat, from 11am Sun, full bar*

■ BOOKSTORES

Unabridged Books [★] 3251 N Broadway St (at Aldine) **773/883-9119** *10am-10pm, till 8pm wknds, large lgbt section*

■ RETAIL SHOPS

Bad Boys Chicago [GO] 3352 N Halsted St **773/549-7701** *men's clothing, accessories*

Flashy Trash 3525 N Halsted **773/327-6900** *contemporary & vintage clothing*

Specialty Video Films [GO] 3221 N Broadway St (at Belmont) **773/248-3434** *10am-10pm, till 11pm Fri-Sat, foreign, cult, art house, lgbt & erotic videos*

Uncle Fun 1338 W Belmont (at Racine) **773/477-8223** *heaven for kitsch lovers*

Universal Gear 3153 N Broadway (at Belmont) **773/296-1090** *11am-10pm, till 11pm Fri-Sat, casual, club, athletic & designer clothing*

■ GYMS & HEALTH CLUBS

Chicago Sweat Shop [GF] 3215 N Broadway (at Belmont) **773/871-2789**

■ MEN'S CLUBS

➤ **The Steamworks Gym & Sauna** [★PC] 3246 N Halsted St (N of Belmont) **773/929-6080** *24hrs*

■ EROTICA

Adult Fantasy 2928 N Broadway (at Oakdale) **773/525-9705** *24hrs*

Batteries Not Included 3420 N Halsted (at Roscoe) **773/935-9900** *50% of all profits donated to charity*

➤ **Cupid's Leather Sport** 3505 N Halsted (at Cornelia) **773/868-0914** *11am-midnight*

Male Hide Leathers 2816 N Lincoln Ave (at Diversey) **773/929-0069** *noon-8pm, till 5pm Sun, clsd Mon*

The Pleasure Chest 3155 N Broadway (at Belmont Ave) **773/525-7152**

➤ **The Ram Bookstore** 3511 N Halsted St (at Cornelia) **773/525-9528** *24hrs*

Chicago—Near North

■ ACCOMMODATIONS

Allegro [GF,F,E,WC] 171 W Randolph (at LaSalle) **312/236-0123, 800/643-1500**

Best Western Inn of Chicago [GF,F,WC] 162 E Ohio St (at Michigan Ave) **312/787-3100, 800/557-2378**

Comfort Inn & Suites Downtown [GF] 15 E Ohio St **312/894-0900, 888/775-4111**

Days Inn Gold Coast [GF,WC] 1816 N Clark St (at Lincoln) **312/664-3040, 800/329-7466**

Flemish House of Chicago [GS,GO] 68 E Cedar St (btwn Rush & Lake Shore Dr) **312/664-9981** *B&B, studios & apts in greystone row house*

Gold Coast Guesthouse [GF,NS] 113 W Elm St (btwn Clark & LaSalle) **312/337-0361** *long-term rates available*

The Hotel Burnham [GF] One W Washington St (at Dearborn) **312/782-1111, 877/294-9712**

Hotel Monaco [GF] 225 N Wabash (at S Water & Wacker Pl) **312/960-8500, 866/610-0081** *upscale, gym*

Hyatt Regency Chicago [GF] 151 E Wacker Dr (at Michigan Ave) **312/565-1234, 800/233-1234** *restaurant, cafe & bar*

Millennium Knickerbocker Hotel [GF,F,WC] 163 E Walton Pl (Michigan Ave) **312/751-8100, 800/621-8140** *gym, restaurant & martini bar*

Chicago—Near North • Illinois

Old Town Chicago B&B Inn [GS] 312/440-9268 *jacuzzi, roof deck, gym*

■ BARS

Artful Dodger [GF,D] 1734 W Wabansia (at Hermitage, in Wicker Park) 773/227-6859 *5pm-2am, 8pm-3am Sat*

Club Foot [GF,NH,D,A] 1824 W Augusta (in Wicker Park) 773/489-0379 *8pm-2am, till 3am Sat, kitschy*

Davenport's [GS,C,P] 1383 N Milwaukee (in Wicker Park) 773/278-1830 *6pm-midnight, till 3am Sat, clsd Tue*

Gentry on State [★M,E,P,V] 440 N State (at Illinois) 312/664-1033 *4pm-2am, till 3am Sat*

Second Story Bar [M,NH] 157 E Ohio St (at Michigan Ave) 312/923-9536 *noon-2am, till 3am Sat*

■ NIGHTCLUBS

Baton Show Lounge [MW,DS,WC] 436 N Clark St (btwn Illinois & Hubbard) 312/644-5269 *showtimes at 8:30pm, 10:30pm, 12:30am, clsd Mon-Tue, reservations advised*

Boom Boom Room at Red Dog [★GF,D,S,$] 1958 W North Ave (enter in alley behind Border Line Tap, in Wicker Park) 773/278-1009 *10:30pm-4am Mon*

The Crobar [★GF,D] 1543 N Kingsbury (at Sheffield) 312/337-5001 *10pm-4am, clsd Mon-Th, more gay Sun*

The Rails [M,D,MR-AF,MR-L,S,$] 1675 N Elston Ave (at North Ave, at Prop House in Wicker Park) 708/802-1705, 312/486-2086 *11pm-4am Fri only*

Second City [GF,E] 1616 N Wells St (at North) 312/337-3992, 877/778-4707 *legendary comedy club, call for reservations*

■ CAFES

Earwax Records 1564 N Milwaukee Ave (in Wicker Park) 773/772-4019 *11am-midnight, till 1am Fri-Sat, from 10am wknds*

■ RESTAURANTS

The Berghoff 17 W Adams St (at State) 312/427-3170 *11am-9pm, till 10pm Sat, clsd Sun, German, great mashed potatoes*

Blackbird 619 W Randolph (at Des Plaines) 312/715-0708 *lunch Mon-Fri, dinner nightly, clsd Sun*

Fireplace Inn 1448 N Wells St (at North Ave) 312/664-5264 *dinner nightly, lunch wknds, bbq, full bar*

Iggy's [21+] 700 N Milwaukee, River North (at Chicago) 312/829-4449 *dinner nightly, till 4am Th-Sat, till 2am Sun, int'l, full bar, patio*

Kiki's Bistro 900 N Franklin St (at Locust) 312/335-5454 *French, full bar*

Manny's 1141 S Jefferson St (at Roosevelt) 312/939-2855 *5am-4pm, clsd Sun, killer corned beef*

Shaw's Crab House [WC] 21 E Hubbard (at State St) 312/527-2722 *lunch & dinner, full bar*

■ BOOKSTORES

After-Words New & Used Books [WO] 23 E Illinois 312/464-1110 *9am-9pm, till 11pm Fri-Sat, noon-7pm Sun, internet access*

Barbara's Bookstore [★WC] 1350 N Wells St (at Schiller, in Old Town) 312/642-5044 *9am-10pm, 10am-9pm Sun, lgbt section; also 700 E Grand Ave at Navy Pier, 312/222-0890; also Oak Park, 708/848-9140*

Quimby's Queer Store [★WC] 1854 W North Ave (at Wolcott, in Wicker Park) 773/342-0910 *noon-10pm, till 6pm Sun, alternative literature & comics*

■ EROTICA

Adonis 6 E Walton (at State St) 312/440-1913 *24hrs*

Bijou Theatre 1349 N Wells St (at North Ave) 312/943-5397 *24hrs*

Erotic Warehouse [WC] 1246 W Randolph (at Elizabeth) 312/226-5222 *24hrs*

Mimi's Adult Bookstore 3203 N Cicero (at Belmont) 773/283-0980 *24hrs*

■ CRUISY AREAS

Grant Park [AYOR] btwn Michigan Ave & the lake

Illinois • USA

Chicago—South Side

■ INFO LINES & SERVICES
Church of the Open Door Community Center 5954 S Albany Ave **773/778-3030** *variety of resources & programs, focusing on African-American lgbt/sgl as well as wider African-American communities*

■ BARS
Club Escape [MW,D,MR-AF,F] 1530 E 75th St (at Stoney Island) **773/667-6454** *4pm-2am, till 3am Sat*

Inn Exile [M,D,V,WC] 5758 W 65th St (at Menard, near Midway Airport) **773/582-3510** *8pm-2am, till 3am Sat*

Jeffery Pub [★MW,D,MR-AF,E,WC] 7041 S Jeffery (at 71st) **773/363-8555** *6pm-4am, from 11am Fri-Sun*

■ NIGHTCLUBS
Escapades [M,D,V] 6301 S Harlem **773/229-0886** *10pm-4am, till 5am Sat*

■ BOOKSTORES
57th St Books 1301 E 57th St, Hyde Park (at Kimbark St) **773/684-1300** *10am-10pm, till 8pm Sun, lgbt section, readings*

■ EROTICA
Slightly Sinful 12300 S Cicero (at 123rd) **708/388-6902**

De Kalb

■ EROTICA
Paperback Grotto 157 E Lincoln Hwy (at 2nd) **815/758-8061**

Decatur

■ BARS
The Firehouse Bar [MW,D,E,K,S,V,GO] 550 N Morgan (at Eldorado St) **217/428-7411** *6pm-2am*

The Flashback Lounge [MW,NH,D,K] 2239 E Wood St (at 22nd) **217/422-3530** *9am-2am, karaoke Fri*

■ CRUISY AREAS
Fairview Park [AYOR] in the back

Du Quoin

■ ACCOMMODATIONS
The Pit [MW,18+,SW,N,WC,GO] 7403 Persimmon Rd **618/542-9470** *primitive camping*

Elgin
see also Chicago

Elk Grove Village
see also Chicago

■ NIGHTCLUBS
Hunters [★M,D,V] 1932 E Higgins (at Busse) **847/439-8840** *4pm-4am, patio*

Forest Park
see also Chicago

■ NIGHTCLUBS
Hideaway [M,D,K,DS,V] 7301 W Roosevelt Rd (at Marengo) **708/771-4459** *3pm-2am, till 3am Fri-Sat, male dancers*

Nut Bush [M,D,K,DS,V] 7201 Franklin (at Harlem) **708/366-5117** *3pm-2am Mon, till 3am Fri-Sat, from 1pm wknds, bingo Th*

Franklin Park

■ NIGHTCLUBS
Temptations [★MW,D,TG,E,DS,WC] 10235 W Grand Ave (at Mannheim) **847/455-0008** *6pm-4am, till 5am Fri-Sat*

Galesburg

■ ACCOMMODATIONS
The Fahnestock House [GS,GO] 591 N Prairie St (at Losey) **309/344-0270** *full brkfst, Queen Anne Victorian*

■ EROTICA
Romantix 595 N Henderson St (at Losey) **309/342-7019**

Paris • Illinois

Granite City
see also St Louis, Missouri

■NIGHTCLUBS
Inside Out [★MW,E,DS,V] 3145 W Chain of Rocks Rd **618/797-0700** *8pm-2am, till 3am Sat, from 2pm Sun, clsd Mon-Tue (open Tue in summers for volleyball)*

■CRUISY AREAS
Lewis & Clark Park [AYOR] Rte 3, 2 miles N of I-270 *closes at dusk*

Hoffman Estates

■CRUISY AREAS
Beverly Lake Forest Preserve [AYOR] Rte 72 (btwn 25 & 59)

Ina

■CRUISY AREAS
Rend Lake [AYOR] off I-57 (S of Mt Vernon, N of Carbondale) *near boat ramp*

Joliet

■NIGHTCLUBS
Maneuvers & Co [MW,D,TG,DS] 118 E Jefferson (at Chicago) **815/727-7069** *8pm-2am, till 3am Fri-Sat, patio, frequent events*

■CRUISY AREAS
Hammill Woods [AYOR] Rte 59 (2 miles N of Hwy 52)

Kankakee

■CRUISY AREAS
Kankakee River State Park [AYOR] Rte 102 *across from main entrance, Dan Uze Area*

LaGrange

■CRUISY AREAS
Airie Crown Forest Preserve [AYOR] *summers*

Leroy

■CRUISY AREAS
Moraine View State Park [AYOR] *around Dawson Lake & Timber Point*

Long Grove

■RETAIL SHOPS
The Long Grove Popcorn Shoppe [GO] 318 Old McHenry Rd **847/821-9101** *10am-5pm, from 11am Sun, try the 'Pride Pop,' also gourmet coffee & doggie treats*

Marion

■EROTICA
➤ **The Lion's Den Adult Bookstore** exit 45, off I-57 **618/995-1586** *24hrs*

Marseilles

■CRUISY AREAS
Illinois State Park [AYOR] *summers*

Marshall

■EROTICA
Hyway News [AYOR] 1801 N Illinois 1 (at I-70) **217/826-8936** *24hrs, cruisy*

Montrose

■EROTICA
➤ **The Lion's Den Adult Bookstore** 401 Frontage Rd (Exit 105, off I-70) **217/924-4524** *24hrs*

Morris

■EROTICA
Forty-Seven Video 50 Gore Rd (N of exit 112, off I-80) **815/942-8309** *24hrs*

Ottawa

■EROTICA
Brown Bag Video 3042 N Rte 71 (at I-80) **815/434-0820** *24hrs*

■CRUISY AREAS
Matthiessen State Park [AYOR] 5 miles S of I-80 (at Rte 178/ Utica exit) *river area*

Paris

■CRUISY AREAS
Twin Lakes Park [AYOR] Hwy 1, N of town (W side of park)

Illinois • USA

Peoria

■ NIGHTCLUBS
Red Fox Den [MW,D,E,DS]
800 N Knoxville Ave (at Glendale)
309/674-8013 *9pm-4am*

■ PUBLICATIONS
Prairie Flame 217/753-2887
lgbt newspaper for downstate IL

■ EROTICA
Brown Bag Video 801 SW Adams (at Oak) **309/676-3003**

The Green Door 2610 W Farmington Rd (near Sterling Ave) **309/674-4337**

Mary's Adult Bookstore
7814 N Sommer **309/692-7477**

Swingers World 335 SW Adams (at Harrison) **309/676-9275** *24hrs*

Prospect Heights

see also Chicago

■ CRUISY AREAS
Camp Pine/ Cook County Forest Preserve [AYOR] Euclid Ave (1/4 mile E of River Rd)

Quincy

■ NIGHTCLUBS
Irene's Cabaret
[★MW,D,B,L,MR,TG,F,E,K,DS,WC,GO] 124 N 5th St (at Washington Park, enter rear)
217/222-6292 *9pm-2:30am, from 7pm Fri-Sat, till 3:30am Sat, clsd Sun-Mon, 21+*

■ EROTICA
Chelsea Bookstore 5000 Gardner Expwy (2 miles S of Quincy)
217/224-7000

■ CRUISY AREAS
Parker Heights Park [AYOR] *parking lot by archery range*

Rock Island

see also Davenport, Iowa

■ BARS
Augie's [MW,NH] 313 20th St (at 3rd)
309/788-7389 *3pm-3am*

■ NIGHTCLUBS
JR's [MW,D,K,S,WC] 325 20th St (at 4th Ave) **309/786-9411** *3pm-3am, also restaurant*

■ RETAIL SHOPS
Rainbow Gifts [GF,MR,TG,GO] 311 17th St **309/786-0873** *noon-7pm, till 6pm wknds, from 10am Sat, pride items*

■ EROTICA
Centennial Video Center 309 20th St
309/794-1682 *arcade, booths*

Rockford

■ BARS
Oh Zone [MW,D,E,K,S] 1014 Charles St (at E State) **815/964-9663** *5pm-2am, noon-midnight Sun*

■ NIGHTCLUBS
The Office Niteclub [★MW,D,E,DS,S,V]
513 E State St (btwn 2nd & 3rd)
815/965-0344 *5pm-2am, noon-midnight Sun*

■ RESTAURANTS
Lucernes [WC] 845 N Church St (at Whitman) **815/968-2665** *5pm-11pm, clsd Mon (also Sun summers)*

Maria's 828 Cunningham St (at Corbin)
815/968-6781 *5pm-9pm, clsd Sun-Mon*

Schiller Park

■ CRUISY AREAS
Schiller Park Woods [AYOR] E of River Rd

Bloomington • Indiana

Springfield

ACCOMMODATIONS

The Henry Mischler House [GF,NS,GO] 802 E Edwards St (btwn 8th & 9th Sts) **217/525-2660** *full brkfst*

BARS

Jimmez & Co [MW,D,K,DS,YC,WC] 2143 N 11th St **217/525-6717** *6pm-1am*

The Station House [MW,NH,D,WC] 304-306 E Washington (btwn 3rd & 4th Sts) **217/525-0438** *10am-1am, till 3am Fri-Sat, from noon Sun*

CAFES

Lil' Jimmy's Diner [GO] 1629 1/2 Peoria Rd (at North Grand Ave) **217/753-1055** *6am-10pm, till 2pm Sun, brkfst, lunch & dinner*

ENTERTAINMENT & RECREATION

Triangle Camping Club [MW] **217/753-2887** *seasonal camping in central IL, call for info*

BOOKSTORES

Sundance 1428 E Sangamon Ave (at Peoria Rd) **217/788-5243** *10am-6pm, clsd Sun, new age books & gifts, lgbt titles*

PUBLICATIONS

Prairie Flame 217/753-2887 *lgbt newspaper for downstate IL*

CRUISY AREAS

Douglas Park [AYOR] MacArthur & Jefferson

Riverside Park [AYOR]

Washington Park [AYOR] *by the bells*

Waukegan

see also Chicago

CRUISY AREAS

Illinois Beach State Park [AYOR] *trails & by bird sanctuary*

Wood River

see also Alton

CRUISY AREAS

Belk Park [AYOR]

INDIANA

Anderson

CRUISY AREAS

Meridian Plaza [AYOR] Jackson & Main Sts *late*

Bloomington

BARS

The Other Bar [MW,NH,WC] 414 S Walnut (btwn 2nd & 4th) **812/332-0033** *5pm-3am, 4pm-midnight Sun, patio*

Uncle Elizabeth's [MW,NH] 502 N Morton (at 9th) **812/331-0060** *4pm-3am, 5pm-midnight Sun, patio*

NIGHTCLUBS

Bullwinkle's [MW,D,K,S] 201 S College St (at 4th St) **812/334-3232** *8pm-3am, clsd Sun*

RESTAURANTS

Village Deli [MW] 409 E Kirkwood **812/336-2303** *7am-10pm, till 4pm wknds*

RETAIL SHOPS

Athena Gallery [WC] 108 E Kirkwood Ave (at Walnut) **812/339-0734** *10:30am-6pm, till 9pm Fri, noon-5pm Sun, clothing, drums, incense, gifts, etc*

Fourth Street Emporium [GO] 212 W 4th St **812/334-3567** *10am-6pm, noon-5pm Sun, clsd Mon, antiques mall*

EROTICA

College Ave Bookstore 1013 N College Ave (at 14th) **812/332-5160** *24hrs*

CRUISY AREAS

Cascades Park [AYOR] *beware of cops late evenings!*

Morgan-Monroe State Forest [AYOR] Rte 37 (btwn Bloomington & Martinsville)

Indiana • USA

Brazil

■CRUISY AREAS
Forest Park [AYOR] near baseball field

Clarksville

■EROTICA
Theatair X 4505 Hwy 31 (1/2 mile N of I-65) 812/282-6976 24hrs

Columbus

■CRUISY AREAS
Mill Race Park [AYOR]

Nobblitt Park [AYOR] 17th St (1 1/2 blks W of Washington) walk to train bridge

Crown Point

■CRUISY AREAS
Lake Country Fairgrounds [AYOR] W side of lake & parking lot

Elkhart

see also South Bend

■INFO LINES & SERVICES
Info Helpline 800/808-4357 24hrs

Evansville

■BARS
Scottie's [MW,NH,D,F,E,K,DS] 2207 S Kentucky Ave (1/2 mile N of I-164) 812/421-1092 4pm-3am, till 12:30am Sun, karaoke Tue, bear/ leather night 1st Fri, patio, also gift shop upstairs

■NIGHTCLUBS
Someplace Else [MW,D,K,DS] 930 Main St (at Sycamore) 812/424-3202 4pm-3am, 2pm-midnight Sun, also gift shop

■BOOKSTORES
AA Michael Books [WC] 1541 S Green River Rd (at Covert) 812/479-8979 10am-6pm, till 8pm Fri, 10am-5pm Sat, noon-5pm Sun

■EROTICA
Bookmart of Evansville 519 N Main (by Lucky Lady) 812/423-2011 24hrs

Fulton Ave Bookmart 201 S Fulton Ave 812/421-0222

■CRUISY AREAS
The Levee [AYOR]

Mesker Park [AYOR] police patrols are heavy

Sunset Park [AYOR] police patrols are heavy

Fort Wayne

■INFO LINES & SERVICES
Gay/ Lesbian AA at Up the Stairs Community Center 260/424-1199 (Helpline #) 7:30pm Tue & Sat, call for complete schedule

Up the Stairs Community Center 514 E Washington Blvd 260/422-2450 7pm-10pm, till midnight Fri-Sat, youth group, library, space for various groups including lesbian/ gay helpline, also newsletter

■ACCOMMODATIONS
The Doctor's Inn [MO,GO]
1205 Fairfield Ave 260/420-5545

■BARS
Hide-n-Seeks Pub & Eatery
[M,NH,D,F] 1008 N Wells St 260/423-2202 5pm-3am, till 12:30am Sun

Up the Street [W,D,DS,WC] 2322 S Calhoun (at Creighton) 260/456-7166 6pm-3am, 5pm-1am Sun, clsd Mon

■NIGHTCLUBS
After Dark [MW,D,DS,S,WC]
1601 S Harrison St 260/456-6235 noon-3am, 6pm-1am Sun

■RETAIL SHOPS
Boudoir Noir 512 W Superior St 260/420-0557 11am-10pm, till 1pm Fri-Sat, gifts, toys, leather

Indianapolis • Indiana

■CRUISY AREAS

Foster Park [AYOR] near picnic shelters be alert—major crackdown on cruising in Fort Wayne

Pearl St [AYOR] from Harrison to Ewing be alert—major crackdown on cruising in Fort Wayne

Sweeney Park [AYOR] be alert—major crackdown on cruising in Fort Wayne

Fountain City

■CRUISY AREAS

Portland Arch [AYOR] trails

Gary

■EROTICA

Romantix Michigan Street Theatre #2 8801 Melton Rd/ US 20 (at Ripley Rd) 219/938-2194 24hrs

Trucker's World [AYOR] 25th Ave & Burr St (off I-80/ 94)

■CRUISY AREAS

Marquette Park [AYOR] W section at Holman & State

Miller Beach [AYOR] Lake St

Hammond

■ACCOMMODATIONS

Sibley Court Yard Inn [MO,PC] 629 Sibley St (at Calumet) 219/933-9604

■RESTAURANTS

Phil Smidt & Son 1205 N Calumet Ave (at Indianapolis Blvd) 219/659-0025 lunch & dinner, clsd Mon, seafood, bar

■CRUISY AREAS

State St & Sibley Blvd [AYOR] btwn Hohman & State Line Ave

Indiana Dunes

■ACCOMMODATIONS

The Gray Goose Inn B&B [GS] 350 Indian Boundary Rd (at I-95), Chesterton 219/926-5781, 800/521-5127 full brkfst

Indianapolis

■INFO LINES & SERVICES

AA Gay/ Lesbian 317/632-7864 call for mtg times & locations

■ACCOMMODATIONS

Kurt's B&B Inn [MO,SW,N,GO] 3212 Lupine Dr (near 34th St & High School Rd) 317/291-5728

Renaissance Tower Historic Inn [GF] 230 E 9th St (btwn Delaware & Alabama) 317/261-1652, 800/676-7786 studio suites, full kitchens

Yellow Rose Inn [GS,NS] 1441 N Delaware St 317/636-7673 Victorian B&B, rooftop hot tub

■BARS

501 Eagle [★M,D,L] 501 N College 317/632-2100 5:30pm-3am, from 7:30pm Sat, clsd Sun

Downtown Olly's [M,NH] 822 N Illinois St (at St Clair) 317/636-5597 11am-midnight, from 3pm Sat, sports bar

Illusions [GS,D,K,DS] 1446 E Washington (at Arsenal) 317/266-0535 7am-3am, noon-midnight Sun

The Metro [MW,F,K,P,WC] 707 Massachusetts Ave (at College) 317/639-6022 4pm-3am, noon-12:30am Sun, piano bar Mon, karaoke Th, patio, also restaurant, Sun brunch, Metropolis giftshop upstairs

Varsity Lounge [M,NH,F] 1517 N Pennsylvania St (S of 16th) 317/635-9998 10am-3am, noon-midnight Sun

■NIGHTCLUBS

Club Cabaret [★MW,D,C,DS,WC] 151 W 14th St (at Capitol) 317/951-8569 8pm-3am Th-Sat only

Greg's [★M,D,CW,V,WC] 231 E 16th St (at Alabama) 317/638-8138 4pm-3am, 6pm-12:30am Sun, CW Wed, Fri & Sun, patio

➤ **Talbott Street** [GS,D,DS,GO] 2145 N Talbott St (at 22nd St) 317/931-1343 9pm-4am, 6pm-2am Sun, clsd Mon-Th, VIP lounge

Indiana • USA

The Ten [★MW,D,S,WC] 1218 N Pennsylvania St (at 12th, enter rear) **317/638-5802** *6pm-3am, clsd Sun*

The Unicorn Club [★M,S,PC] 122 W 13th St (at Illinois) **317/262-9195** *8pm-3am, till 2:30am Sun, male dancers*

■ CAFES

Cath's Coffee & Tea House [E] 5401 N College (at 54th) **317/251-2677** *6:30am-7pm, 8am-3pm Sun*

■ RESTAURANTS

Aesop's Tables [BW,WC] 600 N Massachusetts Ave (at East) **317/631-0055** *11am-9pm, till 10pm Fri-Sat, authentic Mediterranean*

English Ivy's 944 N Alabama (at 10th) **317/822-5070** *till 3am Mon-Sat, 11am-12:30am Sun, eclectic, also full bar*

Peter's [R] 8505 Keystone Crossing Blvd **317/465-1155, 800/479-0909** *dinner only, clsd Sun, upscale dining, full bar, large wine selection*

Ruthellen's [P, 21+,GO] 825 N Pennsylvania St (btwn E St Claire & E 9th St) **317/631-7884** *lunch Tue-Fri, dinner Tue-Sun, Sun brunch, clsd Mon, eclectic menu, full bar, piano Wed, Fri-Sat*

■ ENTERTAINMENT & RECREATION

Indianapolis Men's Chorus PO Box 2919 46206-2919 **317/931-9464**

Key Cinemas 4044 S Keystone Ave (at S Carson Ave) **317/784-7454** *alternative cinema*

■ BOOKSTORES

Borders 5612 Castleton Corner Ln (at 86th St) **317/849-8660** *9am-10pm, 10am-8pm Sun, some lgbt titles*

Out Word Bound 625 N East St (at Massachusetts Ave) **317/951-9100** *11:30am-9pm, till 10pm Fri-Sat, from 10am Sat, noon-6pm Sun, lgbt books & gifts, special events*

INDY'S PREMIER DANCE CLUB & SHOW BAR
2145 N. TALBOTT STREET, INDIANAPOLIS
phone: 317-931-1343 fax: 317-931-1344
www.talbottstreet.com

The area's leading LGBT publication, established over 10 years ago... and still growing!

OUTlines
Indiana's Gay & Lesbian Newspaper

NEWS TO READ, THINGS TO DO, PLACES TO GO, PEOPLE TO MEET!

For subscription info or advertising rates... call, write or e-mail us!

(317) 923-8550
133 W. Market Street, Suite 105
Indianapolis, IN 46204-2801
editor@indygaynews.com

the WORKs

A Social Club for Gay Gentlemen

- Single Day or Annual Memberships • Suites
- Video Rooms • Lockers
- Tanning • Gifts & Novelties
- Nautlus™ & Universal™ Machines • Steam • Sauna
- Air Conditioning • In/Out Privileges • Outdoor Patio • Free Parking • Giant Screen Movie Room
- Phones • Security Boxes • Close to Indy's Nighlife • We NEVER Close!!!

web: www.TheWorks4men.com
email: TheWorks@TheWorks4men.com

Discreet & Comfortable. Courteous & Efficient Staff.
100% Gay Owned and Operated.

(317) 547-9210

4120 N. Keystone Ave.
Indianapolis, IN 46205-2843
We gladly accept VISA, MasterCard & American Express

Setting A New Standard

Always Open
Guest Memberships
Steam Room
Sauna
Whirlpool
Private Dressing Rooms
Outdoor Pool & Patio
Gym
18+ only

THE CLUB INDIANAPOLIS

A PRIVATE MEN'S CLUB
620 N. Capitol Avenue • Indianapolis, IN • (317)635-5796
www.the-clubs.com

Indiana • USA

■RETAIL SHOPS
Metropolis 707 Massachusetts Ave (upstairs at The Metro) **317/639-6022** *hours vary*

■PUBLICATIONS
➤ **OUTlines—The Indiana Gay/Lesbian Newspaper** **317/923-8550** *lgbt newsmagazine w/ extensive resources*

The Word **317/725-8840** *lgbt newspaper*

■MEN'S CLUBS
➤ **Club Indianapolis** [SW,PC] 620 N Capitol Ave (at North & Walnut) **317/635-5796** *24hrs*

➤ **The Works** [PC,GO] 4120 N Keystone Ave (at 38th) **317/547-9210** *24hrs*

■MEN'S SERVICES
The Confidential Connection®! **317/791-1234** *The hottest local guys! 18+ Record & Listen FREE! Use access code 499*

➤ **Megaphone Indianapolis** **800/289-1489** *Call for the local # nearest you! Meet Hot Men in your area! FREE to Browse & Respond to voice ads. Use code 3087. Also try MEGAMATES.COM*

Voice MALE **317/782-0700** *The city's hottest & wildest all-male voice club. Chat one on one! Use access code 5111*

■EROTICA
Indy News 20 E Maryland (at Meridian) **317/632-7680** *6am-7pm, till 6pm wknds*

Southern Nights Videos 3760 Commercial Dr **317/329-5505** *videos, DVDs, toys, etc*

Southside News 8063 Madison Ave **317/887-1020** *6am-8pm, till 7pm Sun*

Jeffersonville

■EROTICA
Adult Bookstore 4505 Hwy 31 E **812/283-5019** *24hrs*

Kokomo

■BARS
Club Millennium [MW,D,F,K,DS,S] 1400 W Markland Ave (at Park) **765/452-1611** *8pm-2am, clsd Sun-Tue, karaoke Wed-Th*

■CRUISY AREAS
Foster Park [AYOR] near tennis courts

Highland Park [AYOR] near 'Old Ben'

Lafayette

■BARS
The Sportsman [MW,NH,D] 644 Main St (at Columbia) **765/742-6321** *1pm-4am, from 4pm Sat, clsd Sun, DJ Fri-Sat*

■EROTICA
Fantasy East 2311 Concord Rd (at Teal) **765/474-2417**

■CRUISY AREAS
Happy Hollow Park [AYOR] W Lafayette

Lake Station

■NIGHTCLUBS
Encompass Nightclub & Lounge [★MW,D,F,E,C,DS,P,S,V,WC] 2415 Rush St (at I-80/94 & Ripley St) **219/962-4640** *7pm-3am, till 1am Sun, cabaret Fri-Sat, male strippers Mon & Fri*

Leroy

■CRUISY AREAS
Stoney Run Park [AYOR]

Logansport

■CRUISY AREAS
Spencer Park [AYOR] near tennis courts & trails along Eel River

Madison

■ACCOMMODATIONS
Lanham House B&B Inn [GS,NS,GO] 703 W Main (at Mill) **812/273-3198**

South Bend • Indiana

■CRUISY AREAS

Clifty St Park [AYOR] btwn poplar & oak groves

Third St [AYOR] btwn Broadway fountain & Mulberry

Vaughn Dr [AYOR] along river

Merrillville
see also Gary & Hammond

■CRUISY AREAS

Deep River Park [AYOR] County Line Rd, Old 30

Michigan City

■NIGHTCLUBS

Helen's [M,D,TG,F,DS,S,WC] 4960 W US 20 (at 520) **219/874-1100** *5pm-2am, till 3am Th-Sat, 2pm-12:30am Sun, male strippers last Fri, patio (in-season), also restaurant (reservations recommended)*

Mishawaka
see also South Bend

■CRUISY AREAS

Battel Park [AYOR] by rock walk going to river

Central Park [AYOR] 100 Center & Univ Park Malls

Country Marketplace [AYOR] 100 Center & Univ Park Malls

Merrifield Park [AYOR]

Muncie

■BARS

Mark III Tap Room [MW,NH,D,MR,TG,F,K,DS,GO] 107 E Main St (at Walnut) **765/284-3840** *2pm-2am, till 3am Wed & Fri-Sat*

■CAFES

The MT Cup 1606 W University Ave (at N Dill St) **765/287-1995** *7am-midnight, from 7:30am wknds, sandwiches & baked goods*

■CRUISY AREAS

McCulloch Park [AYOR] on Broadway (past the Muncie Mall)

Peru

■CRUISY AREAS

Mississinewa Lake Rec Area [AYOR] btwn points 4 & 5 on 'Lost Sister Trail'

Richmond

■BARS

Coachman [MW,D,K,DS,WC] 911 E Main St (at N 9th St) **765/966-2835** *7pm-3am, DJ Fri-Sat, karaoke Th*

■CRUISY AREAS

Glen Miller Park [AYOR] US Hwy 40 (roughly 2 miles E of Richmond)

Springwood Park [AYOR] Waterfall Rd (off US 27/ Chester Blvd)

South Bend

■ACCOMMODATIONS

Council Oak Inn [MO,N,GO] near airport **574/273-6416, 574/315-7098** *B&B in private home, full brkfst, private decks*

■BARS

Jeannie's Tavern [GF,TG,GO] 621 S Bendix (at Ford St) **574/288-2962** *10am-3am*

Vickies Inc [MW,NH,TG,F,K,GO] 112 W Monroe (at S Michigan Ave) **574/232-4090** *2pm-3am, from 3pm Mon, from noon Fri-Sat, clsd Sun, football party every Sat in season, karaoke Sat*

■NIGHTCLUBS

Seahorse II Cabaret [MW,D,DS,WC] 1902 Western Ave (at Brookfield) **574/237-9139** *8pm-3am, 7pm-midnight Sun, clsd Tue*

Starzbar [★M,D,S,WC] 1505 S Kendall St (at Indiana) **574/288-7827** *9pm-3am, from 8pm Fri-Sat, clsd Sun, underwear night Th, amateur night Wed*

Truman's Nightclub & Lounge/ Little T's [★MW,D,F,K,DS] 100 N Center St, Mishawaka **574/259-2282, 574/259-7507** *8pm-3am, clsd Mon, Little T's sports bar [K], open Fri-Sat 6pm-2am, till 12:30am Sun, also gift shop, pride items, clothing*

Indiana • *USA*

■Erotica
Pleasureland Museum
114 W Mishawaka Ave (at Main)
574/259-6776 *24hrs*

Romantix 2715 S Main St (at Ewing)
574/291-1899

■Cruisy Areas
East Race Area [AYOR]
Potawatami Park [AYOR]
Rum Village Park [AYOR] W Ewing Ave
Safetyville [AYOR] old Storyland zoo

Terre Haute

■Nightclubs
Zimmer's Nightclub & Restaurant
[MW,D,TG,F,DS,S] 1500 Locust St (at 15th St) **812/232-3036** *5pm-3am, 7pm-12:30am Sun, clsd Mon, also restaurant, amateur shows Wed & Sun, professional shows Fri-Sat*

■Cruisy Areas
City Park [AYOR] S 1st Ave
Deming Park [AYOR]

Valparaiso

■Cruisy Areas
Court House [AYOR]

Vincennes

■Cruisy Areas
The Circle [AYOR] Patrick Henry Dr
George Rodgers Clark Memorial Park [AYOR]
Greg Park [AYOR]

Young America

■Cruisy Areas
Lion's Park [AYOR] 2-1/4 miles W of Indiana State Rd 18

Iowa

Statewide

■Publications
Accessline 319/232-6805 *lgbt newspaper*

Lavender Magazine 612/871-2237 (MN#), 877/515-9969 *lgbt newsmagazine for MN, WI, IA, ND, SD*

Ames

■Info Lines & Services
LGBT Alliance 515/294-2104
7pm Wed, also LGBT Student Services 515/294-5433

■Restaurants
Lucallen's 400 Main St (at Kellogg)
515/232-8484 *11am-9pm, till 10pm Fri-Sat, Italian, full bar*

■Erotica
Romantix 117 Kellogg (at Lincoln Wy)
515/232-7717 *24hrs*

Boone

■Cruisy Areas
McHose Park [AYOR]
Roadside Park [AYOR] 1 mile W on US-30

Burlington

■Accommodations
Arrowhead Motel, Inc [GS,WC]
2520 Mt Pleasant St **319/752-6353**

■Bars
Steve's Place [GF,NH,F,WC]
852 Washington (at Central Ave)
319/752-9109 *10am-2am, also restaurant*

■Erotica
Venus News 219 S Main
319/753-5455

■Cruisy Areas
Hunt Woods [AYOR] 1 mile S of town *days*
Rest Area [AYOR] Hwy 61 S (along the Skunk River)

Des Moines • Iowa

Cedar Falls
see also Waterloo

■ BOOKSTORES

Gateways 109 E 2nd St (at Main)
319/277-3973 *noon-5:30pm Fri, 9:30am-4pm Sat, clsd Sun-Th, gay section*

Cedar Rapids

■ INFO LINES & SERVICES

Gay/ Lesbian Resource Center
305 2nd St SE #324 **319/366-2055**
7pm-9pm Mon & Th, 24hr recorded info, referrals

■ NIGHTCLUBS

Club Basix [MW,D,L,TG,K,DS,GO]
3916 1st Ave NE (btwn 39th & 40th)
319/363-3194 *5pm-2am, from 3pm wknds, karaoke Th*

■ RESTAURANTS

The Happy Chef 1906 Blairs Ferry Rd NE **319/395-7793** *24hrs, all-American, salad bar*

■ ENTERTAINMENT & RECREATION

CSPS Arts Center 1103 3rd St SE
319/364-1580 *many lgbt events*

■ EROTICA

Adult Shop 630 66th Ave SW
319/362-4939 *24hrs*

■ CRUISY AREAS

Ellis Park [AYOR]

Shaver Park [AYOR] 'J' Ave & Wenig Rd NE *days*

Council Bluffs
see also Omaha, Nebraska

■ EROTICA

Romantix 3216 1st Ave (at Broadway)
712/328-2673 *24hrs*

Romantix 50662 189th St
712/366-1764 *24hrs*

Davenport
see also Rock Island, Illinois

■ ACCOMMODATIONS

Traveler Motel [GS] 433 14th St (near I-74 & US 61), Bettendorf
563/355-0285 *XXX motel*

■ BARS

811 Lockdown [M,GO] 811 W 2nd St (at Warren) **563/322-3292** *11:30am-11:30pm, till 2am Fri-Sat, also restaurant*

Mary's on 2nd [MW,NH,D,E,V,WC] 832 W 2nd St **563/884-8014** *4pm-2am, from noon Sun (2pm summer), patio*

■ NIGHTCLUBS

Club Fusion [MW,D,DS,S,GO] 813 W 2nd St (at Warren) **563/326-3452** *4pm-2am, patio, deck*

Liquid [M,D,19+,DS,S,WC,GO]
822 W 2nd St (at Centennial Bridge)
563/324-9675 *4pm-2am, male & female strippers, huge patio bar, volleyball, theme parties*

■ EROTICA

TR Video 3727 Hickory Grove Rd (at Fairmont & Hickory Grove)
563/386-7914

■ CRUISY AREAS

Credit Island Park [AYOR] W River Dr (W end) *daytime*

Davenport Levee [AYOR] under the Centennial Bridge *dusk*

Le Clair Park [AYOR] on riverfront from Main to Ripley *late*

Des Moines

■ INFO LINES & SERVICES

LGBT Community Center of Central Iowa **515/277-7884** *24hrs recorded info, mtgs, newsletter*

■ ACCOMMODATIONS

The Cottage B&B [GF,GO] 1094 28th St (at Cottage Grove) **515/277-7559**

The Hotel Savery [GF,SW,FWC]
401 Locust St (at 4th) **515/244-2151, 800/798-2151** *luxury hotel & spa*

Kingman House [MW,WC]
2920 Kingman Blvd **515/279-7312, 515/996-2829** *full brkfst*

Iowa • USA

Quality Inn & Suites Des Moines
[GF,SW] 4995 N Merle Hay Rd
515/278-2381 *hot tub*

Racoon River Retreat [M,WC,GO]
515/279-7312, 515/996-2829
log house & bunk house & campsites, seasonal, full brkfst, hot tub

■ BARS

The Blazing Saddle [★M,D,L,DS,S,WC]
416 E 5th St (btwn Grand & Locust)
515/246-1299 *2pm-2am, from noon wknds*

Dally's Pub & Emporium
[MW,D,F,E,K,DS,WC] 430 E Locust (1 blk S of Grand, btwn E 4th & 5th)
515/243-9760 *2pm-2am*

Faces [MW,D,K,DS,WC] 416 E Walnut (at 4th St) 515/280-5463 *9am-2am, DJ wknds, karaoke Sun-Mon*

■ NIGHTCLUBS

The Frathouse [MW,DS] 508 Clifton (at 7th) 515/284-1074 *9pm-2am Wed, Fri-Sat*

The Garden [MW,D,S,K,V,YC,WC]
112 SE 4th St 515/243-3965 *8pm-2am, clsd Mon-Tue, patio*

■ CAFES

Chat Noir Cafe [WC] 644 18th St (at Woodland) 515/244-1353 *lunch & dinner, clsd Sun-Mon*

Java Joe's [E] 214 4th St (at Court Ave)
515/288-5282 *7:30am-11:30pm, till 1am Fri-Sat, 9am-11pm Sun, gallery next door*

Zanzibar's Coffee Adventure
2723 Ingersoll (at 28th St)
515/244-7694 *6:30am-9pm, till 11pm Fri-Sat, till 6pm Sun*

■ RESTAURANTS

ArtHouse [GO] 2811 Ingersoll Ave (W of 28th St) 515/243-6601 *brkfst & lunch Mon-Sat, clsd Sun, also gallery, art openings & art bar 2nd Fri of month*

Chicago Dog, Deli & Pizza [GO]
1733 Grand Ave 515/243-3085
10am-9pm, clsd Sun

Paradise Pizza 2025 Grand, West Des Moines 515/222-9959 *11am-9pm, till 10pm Fri-Sat*

■ ENTERTAINMENT & RECREATION

First Friday Breakfast Club, Inc
[MO,R] 1501 Woodland (at Woodland)
515/288-2500, 515/284-0880
7am-8:15am 1st Fri, cont'l brkfst, guest speakers, call for info & reservation, reservations required for guests

■ BOOKSTORES

Borders 4100 University #115 (at 42nd), West Des Moines 515/223-1620
9am-11pm, till 9pm Sun, lgbt section, also cafe

■ PUBLICATIONS

LGBT Newsletter 515/277-7884
monthly newsletter of the LGBT Community Center of Central Iowa

■ MEN'S SERVICES

➤ **Megaphone Des Moines**
800/289-1489 *Call for the local # nearest you! Meet Hot Men in your area! FREE to Browse & Respond to voice ads. Use code 3087. Also try MEGAMATES.COM*

■ EROTICA

Gallery Book Store 1000 Cherry (at 10th) 515/244-2916 *24hrs*

Romantix 1401 E Army Post Rd (at SE 14th St) 515/256-1102 *24hrs*

Romantix 2020 E Euclid (at Delaware)
515/266-7992 *24hrs*

■ CRUISY AREAS

Gay Loop [AYOR] 8th St (btwn Crocker & Center)

West River Dr [AYOR] N of downtown, by the river (off 2nd Ave N)

Dubuque

■ BARS

One Flight Up [MW,D,F,DS] 44-48 Main St 563/582-8357 *5pm-2am*

■ EROTICA

Gentleman's Bookstore 30 Main St, upstairs (at Hwy 151) 563/556-9313

■ CRUISY AREAS

2nd St [AYOR] Ice Harbor area

Julien Dubuque Monument Park
[AYOR]

Waterloo • Iowa

Fort Dodge

■EROTICA

Romantix Mini Cinema 15 N 5th St (on the square) **515/955-9756**

Grinnell

■INFO LINES & SERVICES

Stonewall Resource Center Grinnell College 641/269-3327 4:30pm-11pm Mon-Th, library, also quarterly newsletter

Iowa City

■INFO LINES & SERVICES

AA Gay/ Lesbian 319/338-9111 (AA#)

■BARS

Deadwood [★GF,NH] 6 S Dubuque St **319/351-9417** 10am-2am, mostly straight, fun college crowd

Studio 13 [MW,D,DS,S,19+,GO] 13 S Linn St (in the alley btwn Linn & Dubuque Sts) **319/338-7145** 5pm-2am

■BOOKSTORES

Prairie Lights Bookstore [WC] 15 S Dubuque St (at Washington) **319/337-2681** 9am-10pm, till 6pm Sun, also cafe

■RETAIL SHOPS

New Pioneer Co-op & Bakehouse [GF] 22 S Van Buren **319/338-9441, 319/358-5513** 7am-10pm, health food store & deli; also Coralville location at 1101 2nd St (at 12th Ave)

Vortex 211 E Washington **319/337-3434** 10am-7pm, till 8pm Fri-Sat, noon-5pm Sun, unique gifts

■EROTICA

Just A Bit Different 116 E 9th St (near 1st Ave), Coralville **319/338-7978**

Romantix 315 Kirkwood Ave (at Gilbert) **319/351-9444** 24hrs

■CRUISY AREAS

Natural Preserves [AYOR] Cou Falls Rd (10 miles N on Hwy 965, near Swisher) local sunbathing spot known as the 'hill'

Lansing

■ACCOMMODATIONS

Suzanne's B&B [GF,NS] 120 N 3rd St (30 miles S of La Crosse, WI) **319/538-3040** clsd Jan, full brkfst, shared bath, sauna, fireplace

Marshalltown

■EROTICA

Adult Odyssey 907 Iowa Ave E **641/752-6550** videos, toys, leather

Newton

■ACCOMMODATIONS

La Corsette Maison Inn [GF] 629 1st Ave E **641/792-6833** upscale B&B w/ 4-star restaurant

■EROTICA

➤ **The Lion's Den Adult Bookstore** 7717 Hwy F 48 W (Exit 159, off I-80) **641/792-9301** 24hrs

Ottumwa

■EROTICA

Cinema X 317 E Main St (downtown exit, off Rte 34) **641/683-1481** clsd Mon

■CRUISY AREAS

Greater Ottumwa Park [AYOR]

Sioux City

■BARS

3 Cheers [MW,NH,D,S,WC] 414 20th St **712/255-8005** Wed-Sat

Jones Street Station [MW,D,DS] 412 Jones St **712/258-6922** 5pm-2am, clsd Mon

■EROTICA

Romantix 511 Pearl St **712/277-8566** 24hrs

Waterloo

■INFO LINES & SERVICES

Access 319/232-6805 weekly info & support

Iowa • USA

■NIGHTCLUBS
Club Metro [MW,D,S] 510 Mulberry St (btwn E 4th & E Park Ave, alley entrance) **319/232-2239** *7pm-2am, clsd Mon, underwear night Th*

■EROTICA
Adult Cinema 16 315 E 4th St **319/234-7459**

Romantix 1507 Laporte Rd (at Lock) **319/249-9340** *24hrs*

■CRUISY AREAS
Cedar Bend Park [AYOR] along river

KANSAS

Statewide

■PUBLICATIONS
➤ **The Liberty Press** 316/652-7737, 785/842-7714 (in Lawrence) *statewide lgbt newspaper*

Midwest Times 816/348-7600 *lgbt newspaper covering Missouri & Kansas*

Abilene

■RETAIL SHOPS
Triangle Artworks [GO] 1605 NW 3rd St (at Van Burren) **785/263-7849** *clsd Sun-Mon, gallery & gifts, ask about gay discount*

Blue Rapids

■CRUISY AREAS
Roadside Park [AYOR] 1 mile E on US-77

Dodge City

■ACCOMMODATIONS
Boot Hill B&B [GF] 603 W Spruce St (at 5th St) **620/225-7600** *full brkfst, across from Boot Hill Museum*

■CRUISY AREAS
Rest Stop [AYOR] 7 miles E on US 56 *late*

Emporia

■BOOKSTORES
Town Crier 716 Commercial St **620/343-9649** *9am-8pm, till 6pm Sat, 10am-2pm Sun, some lgbt magazines*

Ford

■RETAIL SHOPS
Gary's Stop [GF,F] 807 Main St **620/369-2216** *truck stop, diesel, food & drinks, pleather!*

Great Bend

■CRUISY AREAS
Fort Zarah Rest Area [AYOR] on Santa Fe Trail (on Hwy 56) *2 miles E of Great Bend*

Hutchinson

■CRUISY AREAS
Carey Park [AYOR] Main St (at the very south end)

Junction City

■NIGHTCLUBS
Xcalibur Club [GS,D,K,DS,GO] 384 Grant Ave **785/762-2050** *6pm-2am, from 2pm Fri-Sun, clsd Mon, more gay Wed, bears 4th wknd*

■EROTICA
After Dark Video 785/762-4747 *24hrs*

Kansas City
see also Kansas City, Missouri

■PUBLICATIONS
Midwest Times 816/348-7600 *lgbt newspaper covering Missouri & Kansas*

■MEN'S SERVICES
➤ **Megaphone Kansas City** **800/289-1489** *Call for the local # nearest you! Meet Hot Men in your area! FREE to Browse & Respond to voice ads. Use code 3087. Also try MEGAMATES.COM*

■CRUISY AREAS
Pierson Park [AYOR] Wyandotte County (off Nieman Rd) *Mon-Fri*

Kensington

■CRUISY AREAS
Rest Stop [AYOR] on Hwy 36

Liberty Press

Proudly Serving Lesbian and Gay Kansans Since 1994.

WE RING YOUR BELL

Readers Views News Features Op/Ed Reviews Comics Horoscopes Resource Directory Travel Tell Trinity Books Controversy Movies

DON'T MISS ANOTHER ISSUE!

Call, write or visit our website for your FREE sample copy

WWW.LIBERTYPRESS.NET

(316) 652-PRESS
editor@libertypress.net
PO Box 16315
Wichita, KS 67216

Kansas • USA

Lawrence

■Bars
Teller's Restaurant & Bar [GF,WC]
746 Massachusetts St (at 8th)
785/843-4111 *11am-2am, more gay Tue pm, also Italian restaurant*

■Nightclubs
Granada [GS,D,MR,WC]
1020 Massachusetts (at 11th)
785/842-1390 *7pm-2am, clsd Sun, retro Fri*

Jazzhaus [GF,E] 926-1/2 Massachusetts St **785/749-3320, 785/749-1387** *4pm-2am*

Last Call [GF,D] 729 New Hampshire St (at 7th) **785/838-4623** *8pm-2am, till 3am Fri, till 4am Sat, clsd Sun-Tue, more gay Wed*

■Cafes
Henry's 11 E 8th St (btwn Massachusetts St & New Hampshire St) **785/331-3511** *7am-2am, also full bar upstairs*

Java Break [GO] 17 E 7th St (btwn Mass & New Hampshire Sts) **785/749-5282** *24hrs, sandwiches, desserts*

■Bookstores
The Dusty Bookshelf [GO]
708 Massachusetts St **785/749-4643** *10am-8pm, till 10pm Fri-Sat, noon-6pm Sun, lgbt section*

■Retail Shops
Naughty But Nice 1741 Massachusetts St (btwn 17th & 18th) **785/832-1000** *10am-1am, till 3am Fri-Sat, noon-10pm Sun, pride items, erotica*

■Cruisy Areas
Memorial Drive [AYOR] E of Jayhawk Blvd

Riverfront Park [AYOR] at the intersection of US 24-40-59

Wells Overlook County Park [AYOR] 1.4 miles S of Lawrence on US 59

Liberal

■Bookstores
Second Street Bookstore 11 W 2nd St **620/624-8105** *9:30am-8pm, from 11am Sun, gay magazine section*

Luray

■Cruisy Areas
Rest Stop [AYOR] at intersection of Hwys 18 & 281

Manhattan

■Bookstores
The Dusty Bookshelf [GO]
700 N Manhattan **785/539-2839** *10am-8pm, till 6pm Sat, 1pm-5pm Sun*

■Cruisy Areas
Turtle Creek Park [AYOR]

Neodesha

■Cruisy Areas
Rest Area [AYOR] US 75 (2 miles N of town) *beware cops*

Olathe

■Cruisy Areas
Cedar Lake [AYOR] off K-7 Hwy

Salina

■Cruisy Areas
Thomas Park [AYOR] 1/2 mile S of I-70 (at 9th St exit)

Topeka

■Info Lines & Services
AA Gay/ Lesbian 785/234-6131 *8pm Fri, call Marcus for location*

■Bars
Club Cosmos [MW,NH,D,K]
1421 SW Lane St (at 15th)
785/290-2582 *6pm-2am*

■Bookstores
Barnes & Noble 6130 SW 17th St #101 **785/273-9600** *9am-11pm, till 9pm Sun, lgbt section*

Wichita • Kansas

■ RETAIL SHOPS

The Enchanted Willow Alchemy Shoppe [GO] 418 SW 6th Ave 785/235-3776 *hours vary, pride items, pagan supplies*

■ EROTICA

Adult Entertainment Center 903 N Kansas Ave 785/235-6010

Sinsations 4720 SW Topeka Blvd (S from I-470) 785/862-5002 *video arcade*

■ CRUISY AREAS

Gage Park [AYOR] *beware of cops!*

Shunga Park [AYOR] 29th St & Fairlawn Rd

Wichita

■ INFO LINES & SERVICES

Land of Awes Info Line 316/269-0913 *touchtone info*

One Day at a Time Gay AA 2821 S Hydraulic 316/522-7411 *8pm Mon-Fri, 7pm Sat, 12:30pm Sun*

■ ACCOMMODATIONS

Hawthorn Suites [GF,WC] 2405 N Ridge Rd 316/729-5700 *brkfst buffet*

■ BARS

J's Lounge [MW,E,K,C,WC] 513 E Central (at Emporia) 316/262-1363 *4pm-2am, karaoke Mon, cabaret, patio*

Kirby's Beer Store [GF,F,S] 3227 E 17th (at Holyoke) 316/685-7013 *2pm-2am*

The Link [MO,D,L,WC,GO] 1507 E Pawnee (at K-15) 316/265-5465 *2pm-2am, leather night 3rd Sat*

Ralph's [GS,NH,K] 3210 E Osie (at George Washington) 316/682-4461 *3pm-2am, karaoke Th & Sat*

Side Street Saloon [M,D,WC] 1106 S Pattie (near Lincoln & Hydraulic) 316/267-0324 *2pm-2am, patio*

Trade Bar & Cafe [MW,F,K,V] 2959 S Hillside 316/683-3080 *11am-2am, from noon wknds, clsd Mon-Tue, karaoke Sun, smokefree section, patio, also The Roosterfish (coffee shop & bookstore)*

■ NIGHTCLUBS

Club M [M,D,F,S,18+] 458 N Waco (at Central) 316/262-8130 *9pm-2am Fri, 10pm-3am Sat, 8pm-2am Sun, 18+ Fri & Sun, male dancers Fri-Sat, also restaurant*

Fantasy Complex [MW,D,CW,DS,S,WC] 3201 S Hillside (at 31st) 316/682-5494 *3pm-2am, clsd Mon, also South Forty (CW bar)*

■ CAFES

Riverside Perk 1144 Bitting Ave (at 11th) 316/264-6464 *7am-10pm, till midnight Fri-Sat, from 10am Sun, internet access, also Lava Lounge juice bar next door*

■ RESTAURANTS

Moe's Sub Shop 2815 S Hydraulic (at Wassall) 316/524-5511 *11am-8pm, clsd Sun*

Old Mill Tasty Shop 604 E Douglas (at St Francis) 316/264-6500 *11am-3pm, 8am-5pm Sat, clsd Sun, old-fashioned soda fountain, lunch menu*

Tanya's Soup Kitchen 725 E Douglas (behind Black Canyon Grill) 316/267-5349 *lunch Mon-Sat, dinner Wed-Sat*

The Upper Crust 7038 E Lincoln 316/683-8088 *lunch only, clsd wknds, homestyle*

■ ENTERTAINMENT & RECREATION

Cabaret Oldtown Theatre 412 1/2 E Douglas (at Topeka) 316/265-4400 *edgy, kitschy productions*

Mosley Street Melodrama [F,$] 234 N Mosley St (btwn 1st & 2nd St) 316/263-0222 *melodrama, homestyle buffet & full bar!*

■ RETAIL SHOPS

Holier Than Thou Body Piercing 1111 E Douglas Ave (at Washington) 316/266-4100 *11am-8pm, clsd Sun*

Mother's 3100 E 31st St S (at Hillside) 316/686-8116 *hours vary, lgbt gifts*

Kansas • USA

MEN'S SERVICES
The Confidential Connection®! 316/267-3366 *The hottest local guys! 18+ Record & Listen FREE! Use access code 499*

▶ **Megaphone Wichita** 800/289-1489 *Call for the local # nearest you! Meet Hot Men in your area! FREE to Browse & Respond to voice ads. Use code 3087. Also try MEGAMATES.COM*

EROTICA
Circle Cinema/ Video 2570 S Seneca St (at Crawford St) 316/264-2245 *24hrs*

Fetish Lingerie 2150 S Broadway (btwn E Clark St & E Kinkaid St) 316/264-7800 *leather, toys, clubwear, all sizes available*

Priscilla's 6143 W Kellogg (at Dugan) 316/942-1244

Xcitement Video 220 E 21st St (at Broadway) 316/832-1816

Xcitement Video 1515 S Oliver (at Harry) 316/688-5343 *24hrs*

Xcitement Video 1306 E Harry (at Pattie) 316/269-9036 *24hrs*

CRUISY AREAS
Chisholm Trail Park [AYOR] Oliver & 29th St *days*

Sedgwick County Park [AYOR] Zoo Blvd (W of I-235)

KENTUCKY

Statewide

PUBLICATIONS
▶ **The Letter** 502/636-0935 (news), 502/772-7570 (advertising) *statewide lgbt newspaper*

▶ **TLW Magazine** 727/522-8888 *Southeast's largest entertainment magazine for gay men*

Ashland

CRUISY AREAS
Central Park [AYOR] *beware of cops on bikes!*

Bowling Green

CRUISY AREAS
City Water Tower [AYOR] park beneath it (on Hospital Hill)

Campbellsville

CRUISY AREAS
Green River Dam [AYOR] Hwy 55 (below dam)

Covington
see also Cincinnati, Ohio

ACCOMMODATIONS
First Farm Inn [GF] 2510 Stevens Rd, Petersburg 859/586-0199, 800/277-9527 *1800s farmhouse B&B, full brkfst, near Cincinnati*

BARS
Rosie's Tavern [GS,NH,GO] 643 Bakewell St 859/291-9707 *3pm-2:30am*

Woolly's [M,NH,D,K,DS] 828 Monmouth, Newport 859/431-7408 *4pm-2:30am*

Yadda Club [MW,NH,MR,F,E,K,WC] 404 Pike St (at Main St) 859/491-5600 *3pm-1am, noon-2:30am wknds, clsd Mon, T-dance Sun, patio*

CRUISY AREAS
Devou Park [AYOR] Covington exit, off Rte 75

Harned

ACCOMMODATIONS
Kentucky Holler House [MW,NS] 270/547-4507 *B&B on 48 acres*

Hazard

CRUISY AREAS
Carr Creek Dam [AYOR]

Jamestown

CRUISY AREAS
Kendall Recreation Area [AYOR] below Wolf Creek Dam (10 miles S on Hwy 127) *also pull-off areas & overlook above dam*

Louisville • Kentucky

Lexington

■ INFO LINES & SERVICES
Gay/ Lesbian AA 859/245-7471 (private home), 859/276-2917 (AA#) *8pm Mon & Wed, 7:30pm Fri, call for location*

Pride Center of the Bluegrass 389 Waller Ave #100 859/253-3233 *10am-3pm Mon-Sat*

■ ACCOMMODATIONS
The Bear & Boar B&B Resort [MO,GO] Wood Creek Lake, London 606/862-6557 *also camping*

■ BARS
The Bar Complex [★MW,D,S,WC] 224 E Main St 859/255-1551 *4pm-1am, till 3:30am Sat, clsd Sun*

Crossings [M,NH,D,L,S,WC] 117 N Limestone St 859/233-7266 *4pm-1am, clsd Sun*

■ NIGHTCLUBS
Club 141 [★MW,D,A,S,WC] 141 W Vine St (at Limestone) 859/233-4262 *8:30pm-1am, till 3am wknds, clsd Sun-Mon*

■ RESTAURANTS
Alfalfa [E] 557 S Limestone 859/253-0014 *lunch & dinner, healthy multi-ethnic, folk music nightly*

Natasha's Cafe & Boutique 112 Esplanade 888/901-8412 *eclectic, Turkish coffee, internet access*

■ BOOKSTORES
Joseph-Beth [WC] 161 Lexington Green Circle 859/273-2911, 800/248-6849 *9am-10pm, till 11pm Fri-Sat, 11am-9pm Sun, also cafe*

Sqecial Media 371 S Limestone St 859/255-4316 *also pride items*

■ PUBLICATIONS
GLSO (Gay/ Lesbian) News 859/253-3233 *local news & calendar*

▶ **The Letter** 502/636-0935 (news), 502/772-7570 (advertising) *statewide lgbt newspaper*

■ MEN'S SERVICES
The Confidential Connection®! 859/254-3800 *The hottest local guys! 18+ Record & Listen FREE! Use access code 499*

■ EROTICA
2004 Video 2004 Family Circle Dr (at New Circle Dr) 859/255-1002 *24hrs*

The New Bookstore 940 Winchester Rd 859/252-2093

■ CRUISY AREAS
Jacobsen Park [AYOR] Richmond Rd (3 miles W of Lexington) *take 3 rights inside park to sunbathing area*

Woodland Park [AYOR] E High St

Louisville

■ INFO LINES & SERVICES
LGBT Hotline 502/454-7613 *counseling 6pm-10pm, 24hr hotline, AA referrals*

■ ACCOMMODATIONS
Bernheim Mansion B&B [GS,SW,GO] 1416 S 3rd St (at Hill) 502/638-1387, 800/303-0053 *Victorian mansion, full brkfst, hot tub*

Columbine Inn [GF,NS] 1707 S 3rd St (near Leet St) 502/635-5000, 800/635-5010 *1896 Greek Revivial mansion, full brkfst*

Inn at the Park [GF,NS] 1332 S 4th St (at Park Ave) 502/637-6930, 800/700-7275 *restored mansion, full brkfst*

Mansion at River Walk [GF] 704 E Main St (at State St), New Albany, IN 812/941-8100, 812/944-7313 *Italianate B&B, full brkfst*

■ BARS
Magnolia Bar [GF,NH,YC] 1398 S 2nd St (at Magnolia) 502/637-9052 *5pm-4am*

Teddy Bears Bar & Grill [M,NH,WC] 1148 Garvin Pl (at St Catherine) 502/589-2619 *11am-4am, from 1pm Sun*

Tink's Pub [W,NH] 2235 S Preston St 502/634-8180 *4pm-close, from 11am Sat, from 1pm Sun*

Tryangles [M,K,S,WC] 209 S Preston St (at Market) 502/583-6395 *4pm-4am, from 1pm Sun, Levi's bar*

Kentucky • USA

NIGHTCLUBS

The Connection Complex
[★MW,D,C,P,V,WC] 120 S Floyd St (at Market) **502/585-5752** *5pm-4am, 5 bars*

CAFES

Sumshee's Family Room [E]
202 S Preston **502/589-2018** *7am-close, also gallery*

RESTAURANTS

Cafe Mimosa 1216 Bardstown Rd **502/458-2233** *lunch & dinner, Vietnamese, Chinese & sushi*

El Mundo [★] 2345 Frankfort Ave **502/899-9930** *clsd Sun*

Lynn's Paradise Cafe [MW,GO] 984 Barret Ave (at Baxter) **502/583-3447** *7am-10pm, till 2pm Mon, also bar*

Queenie's Pizza & Such [GO] 2622 S 4th St **502/636-3708** *11am-10pm, till 11pm Fri-Sat, 4pm-8pm Sun, clsd Mon*

Rudyard Kipling [E] 422 W Oak St **502/636-1311** *lunch Mon-Fri, dinner from 5:30pm Mon-Sat*

ENTERTAINMENT & RECREATION

Community Chorus **502/327-4099**

BOOKSTORES

Carmichael's 1295 Bardstown Rd (at Longest Ave) **502/456-6950** *8am-10pm, till 11pm Fri-Sat, from 10am Sun, large lgbt section*

Hawley Cooke Booksellers 3024 Bardstown Rd (in Gardiner Lane Shopping Center) **502/456-6660, 800/844-7323** *9am-9pm, 10am-6pm Sun; also 4600 Shelbyville Rd, Shelbyville Plaza, 502/893-0133*

PUBLICATIONS

➤ **The Letter** **502/636-0935** (news), **502/772-7570** (advertising) *statewide lgbt newspaper*

MEN'S SERVICES

The Confidential Connection®!
502/584-8080 *The hottest local guys! 18+ Record & Listen FREE! Use access code 499*

➤ **Megaphone Louisville**
800/289-1489 *Call for the local # nearest you! Meet Hot Men in your area! FREE to Browse & Respond to voice ads. Use code 3087. Also try MEGAMATES.COM*

EROTICA

Arcade Adult Bookstore 2822 7th St (at Arcade) **502/637-8388**

Blue Movies 244 W Jefferson St (at 3rd) **502/585-4627** *24hrs*

The Erotic Touch 3423 Taylor Blvd (at Longfield Ave) **502/363-9448**

➤ **The Lion's Den Adult Bookstore** 2517 7th St (at Central) **502/636-9002**

➤ **The Lion's Den Adult Bookstore** 626 W Broadway (at 7th) **502/681-5111**

Louisville Manor 4600 Dixie Hwy/ US 61 **502/449-1443** *24hrs*

Showboat Adult Bookstore 3524 S 7th St (at Berry Blvd) **502/361-0007** *hustlers*

The Toy Store 1857 Berry Blvd (at 7th) **502/366-7563**

Madisonville

CRUISY AREAS

Grapevine Lake [AYOR]

Madisonville City Park [AYOR]
Park Ave (off Pennyrile Pkwy) *go W thru 3 traffic lights, go left & drive 1 mile*

Morehead

CRUISY AREAS

Cave Run State Park [AYOR]

Daniel Boone Campground [AYOR]

Newport

BARS

The Crazy Fox Saloon [GS,NH]
901 Washington Ave **859/261-2143** *3pm-2:30am*

CRUISY AREAS

James Taylor Park [AYOR] *on Newport Levee*

Vol. 9, No. 2 — February 1998

the LETTER

Kentucky's Gay, Lesbian, Bisexual and Transgender Newspaper

Now in Eight States!

The Most Widely Respected GLBT Newspaper in Mid-America

Featuring

- ✔ Full Local & National News Coverage
- ✔ Entertainment & Lively Personals
- ✔ Health & Religion News
- ✔ Complete State Service Directory
- ✔ Much more!

PO Box 3882
Louisville, KY 40201

News/Administration:	502/636-0935
Advertising:	502/772-7570
Entertainment:	812/284-3448
Fax:	502/635-6469
Email:	WillNich@aol.com
Web:	www.theletter.net

Kentucky • USA

Owensboro

■CRUISY AREAS
English Park [AYOR] 1st St

Paducah

■NIGHTCLUBS
Chip's Place [GS,NH,D,S,WC]
2118 Bridge St (at Wayne Sullivan Dr)
270/575-1995 *6pm-3am Wed-Sat*

■EROTICA
Tammy's Books 243 Brown (at Irvin Cobb Dr) 270/442-5584

Radcliff

■EROTICA
Adult Video [AYOR] 1744 Dixie

■CRUISY AREAS
Radcliff City Park [AYOR]

Somerset

■INFO LINES & SERVICES
Lesbigay Info 606/678-5814 *call Linda for info*

■CRUISY AREAS
Alpine Rest Area [AYOR] S Hwy 27 Daniel Boone Nat'l Forest

Waitsboro Recreation Area [AYOR] S Hwy 27

Upton

■EROTICA
➤ The Lion's Den Adult Bookstore
270/369-8171

Versailles

■ACCOMMODATIONS
Rose Hill Inn [GF] 233 Rose Hill
800/307-0460 *1823 Victorian mansion, full brkfst*

LOUISIANA

Statewide

■PUBLICATIONS
➤ Ambush Mag 504/522-8049
lgbt newspaper

➤ Southern Voice 404/876-1819
weekly lgbt newspaper for AL, FL (panhandle), GA, LA, MS, TN w/ resource listings

➤ TLW Magazine 727/522-8888
Southeast's largest entertainment magazine for gay men

Alexandria

■NIGHTCLUBS
Unique Bar & Lounge
[★MW,D,TG,S,WC] 3217 Industrial St
318/448-0555 *9pm-2am, clsd Tue*

Baton Rouge

■INFO LINES & SERVICES
Freedom of Choice/ Gay AA
333 E Chimes St (at the Wesley Foundation) 225/924-0030 (AA#)
8pm Th & 9pm Sat

The Lambda Group 1733 Florida Blvd
225/907-3665, 225/383-0777 (info line #) *lgbt educational/ support groups, drop-in center, hotline*

■ACCOMMODATIONS
Brentwood House [MO,NS,GO]
225/924-4989 *home stay in 100+-yr-old house, hot tub, clothing-optional on deck & in house*

■BARS
George's Place [★MW,NH,K,S,WC] 860 St Louis 225/387-9798 *3pm-2am, from 5pm Sat, clsd Sun, strippers Tue*

Hound Dog [MW,NH,WC] 668 Main St (at 7th) 225/344-0807 *noon-2am, clsd Sun, also giftshop*

■NIGHTCLUBS
Icon [M,D,S,18+,WC] 2183 Highland Rd
225/242-9491 *9pm-2am, clsd Sun-Tue*

Natchitoches • Louisiana

■RESTAURANTS

Drusilla Seafood 3482 Drusilla Ln (at Jefferson Hwy) **225/923-0896** *dinner till 10pm*

Ralph & Kacoo's 6110 Bluebonnet Blvd (off I-10 & Perkins) **225/766-2113** *lunch & dinner, Cajun*

■BOOKSTORES

Hibiscus Bookstore 635 Main St (btwn 6th & 7th) **225/387-4264** *11am-6pm, clsd Sun, lgbt*

Folsom

■ACCOMMODATIONS

Woods Hole Inn [GF,NS] 78253 Woods Hole Ln (at Thompson Rd) **985/796-9077** *suites & cabin*

Gretna

see New Orleans

Harvey

see New Orleans

Lafayette

■INFO LINES & SERVICES

AA Gay/ Lesbian 1119-C Johnson St **337/991-0830 (AA)** *8pm Wed*

■BARS

Backstreet Men's Club [MW,OC] 110 Polk St (at Garfield) **337/269-0430** *5pm-2am, till midnight Sun, cruisy*

Jules' Downtown [MW,D,K,S,WC] 533 Jefferson **337/264-8000** *8pm-2am*

■NIGHTCLUBS

Sound Factory [M,D,S,YC] 209 Jefferson St (at Cypress) **337/269-6011** *6pm-2am, noon-midnight Sun*

■RESTAURANTS

Gabriel's Restaurant [GF,E,K,P,WC,GO] 100 N Main St, St Martinville **337/394-4446** *lunch & dinner Wed-Sat, brkfst & live music Sat, full bar, courtyard*

■CRUISY AREAS

Garrand Park [AYOR]

Lake Charles

■ACCOMMODATIONS

Aunt Ruby's [GS,GO] 504 Pujo St (at Hodges) **337/430-0603** *full brkfst*

■NIGHTCLUBS

Crystal's [MW,D,CW,F,S,WC] 112 W Broad St **337/433-5457** *8pm-2am, from 9pm Fri-Sat, till 4am Fri, clsd Sun*

■CAFES

Creole Coffeehouse 311 Broad St (at Ryan) **337/433-0857** *7am-5pm, clsd Sun*

■RESTAURANTS

Pujo St Café [GO] 901 Ryan St (at Pujo) **337/439-2054** *11am-9:30pm, till 10pm wknds*

Metairie

see New Orleans

Monroe

■BARS

Bangkok Bar [MW,D,18+,MR,TG,DS,S,V,WC,GO] 812 N 3rd St (at Louisville Ave) **318/699-0097** *9pm-2am, clsd Sun-Mon*

The Corner Bar [MW,NH,MR,E,K,18+,GO] 512 N 3rd St (at Pine) **318/329-0046** *6:30pm-2am, clsd Sun*

■CRUISY AREAS

Forsyth Park [AYOR]

Monroe Boat Dock & Picnic Area [AYOR]

Natchitoches

■ACCOMMODATIONS

Chez des Amis B&B [GF,NS,GO] 910 Washington St (at Texas St) **318/352-2647** *full brkfst*

Louisiana • USA

New Orleans

■ INFO LINES & SERVICES

Lesbian/ Gay Community Center of New Orleans 2114 Decatur St
504/945-1103 *2pm-8pm, from noon Th-Fri, 11am-6pm Sat, noon-6pm Sun, call first*

■ ACCOMMODATIONS

1227 Easton House [GS,NS,GO]
1227 N Rendon St (btwn Esplanade & Grand Rte St John) 504/488-5543, 877/311-1023 *full brkfst, some shared baths*

1415 Creole Gardens [GS,WC]
1415 Prytania (at Melpomene)
504/569-8700, 866/773-8700 *hotel*

1850's Creole Cottage [GS]
French Quarter 504/527-5360, 888/523-5235 *apt*

1896 O'Malley House B&B [GS,GO]
120 S Pierce St (at Canal St)
504/488-5896, 866/226-1896
B&B, jacuzzi

214 Chartres [GS] French Quarter
504/527-5360, 888/523-5235
condo, jacuzzi

➤ **A Creole House** [GS,NS] 1013 St Ann (btwn Burgundy & Rampart)
504/524-8076, 888/251-0090
1830s bldg furnished in period style

Aaron Ingram Haus [GS,GO] 1012 Elysian Fields Ave (btwn N Rampart & N Claude) 504/949-3110 *apts, courtyard*

Alexander's on the Point B&B [GS]
531 Seguin St (at Eliza St)
504/362-1030, 888/560-6652

➤ **Alternative Accommodations/ French Quarter Accommodation Service** [GF] 1001 Marigny St
504/949-5815, 800/209-9408
4 guest houses

Andrew Jackson Hotel [GF] 919 Royal St (btwn St Philip & Dumaine)
504/561-5881, 800/654-0224

Antebellum Guest House [GS,N,GO]
1333 Esplanade Ave (at Maris St)
504/943-1900 *B&B, full brkfst, hot tub, private courtyard*

Audubon Garden Cottage [GS,GO]
5033 S Saratoga St (at Soniat St)
504/895-4130, 504/669-1880
private cottage

B&W Courtyards B&B [GS,GO] 2425 Chartres St (btwn Mandeville & Spain)
504/945-9418, 800/585-5731 *hot tub*

Big Easy/ French Quarter Lodging [GS,GO] 233 Cottonwood Dr, Gretna
504/433-2563, 800/368-4876
free reservation service

The Biscuit Palace [GF,WC] 730 Dumaine (btwn Royal & Bourbon)
504/525-9949 *1820s Creole mansion in the French Quarter*

Block-Keller House [GS,NS,WC,GO]
3620 Canal St (at Telemachus)
504/483-3033, 877/588-3033

Bon Maison Guest House [★MW,GO]
835 Bourbon St (btwn Lafittes & Bourbon Pub) 504/561-8498
1833 town house, patio

➤ **Bourgoyne Guest House** [★MW]
839 Bourbon St (at Dumaine St)
504/524-3621, 504/525-3983
1830s Creole mansion, courtyard

Bourbon Orleans Hotel [★GF,F,SW]
717 Orleans (at Bourbon St)
504/523-2222, 800/521-5338

Casa de Marigny Creole Guest Cottages [GS,SW] 818 Frenchmen St (at Dauphine) 504/948-3875 *private cottages*

Creole Inn [GS,NS,GO] 2471 Dauphine St (at Spain) 504/948-3230
B&B in private home, garden

Crescent City Guest House [GS,N,GO]
612 Marigny St (at Chartres)
504/944-8722, 877/203-2140
near French Quarter, hot tub

Doubletree Hotel [GF,F,SW] 300 Canal St (btwn S Peters & Tchoupitoulas)
504/581-1300, 888/874-9074
gym, restaurants & lounge

Elysian Fields Inn [GS,WC,GO]
930 Elysian Fields Ave (N Rampart)
504/948-9420, 866/948-9420
1860s inn, jacuzzi

➤ **Elysian Guest House** [MW,GO]
1008 Elysian Fields Ave (at Rampart St)
504/940-0540 *1880s Victorian 'double,' large hot tub*

Five Continents B&B [GS,GO]
1731 Esplanade Ave (at Claiborne)
504/943-3536, 800/997-4652
full brkfst

Louisiana • USA

Fourteen Twelve Thalia Suite [GS,GO] 1412 Thalia (btwn Prytania & Coliseum) **504/522-0453** *1-bdrm apt in the Lower Garden District*

French Quarter B&B [MW,SW,GO] 1132 Ursulines (btwn N Rampart & St Claude Ave) **504/525-3390, 800/823-6785 (pin 00)** *B&B*

French Quarter Corporate Apts [GS,GO] **504/495-2387** *1-bdrm apts & condos*

➤ **French Quarter Reservation Service** [MW,GO] **504/523-1246, 800/523-9091**

French Quarter Suites [GF,SW,WC] 1119 N Rampart (at Ursulines) **504/524-7725, 800/457-2253** *hotel, kitchens, hot tub*

➤ **The Frenchmen Hotel** [★GS,SW,NS,WC] 417 Frenchmen St (where Esplanade, Decatur & Frenchmen intersect) **504/948-2166, 888/365-2775** *1860s Creole town houses*

Gallier Street Guesthouse [M,SW,N,GO] 822 Gallier St (at Dauphine & Burgundy) **504/949-3100, 877/949-3100** *B&B near French Quarter, full brkfst wknds, hot tub*

Garden District B&B [GF] 2418 Magazine St (at First St) **504/895-4302**

The Gillham Pierce House B&B [GS,SW,GO] 1407 Esplanade Ave (at N Villere) **504/944-2115, 866/226-6392**

Green House Inn [MW,SW,GO] 1212 Magazine St (at Erato) **504/525-1333, 800/966-1303** *gym, hot tub*

HH Whitney House on the Historic Esplanade [GS,NS,GO] 1923 Esplanade Ave (at N Prieur St) **504/948-9448, 877/944-9448** *1865 B&B, hot tub, some shared baths*

➤ **Historic Rentals** [GS,GO] **800/537-5408** *1-bdrm apts in French Quarter*

Hotel de la Monnaie [GF,SW,WC] 405 Esplanade Ave (btwn Decatur & N Peters) **504/947-0009** *all-suite hotel, hot tub, courtyard*

Hotel Monaco—New Orleans [GF] 333 St Charles Ave **504/561-0010** *boutique hotel in former Masonic Temple*

Hotel Royal [GS,NS,WC] 1006 Royal St (at St Philip) **504/524-3900, 800/776-3901** *1830s Creole town house*

House of David [GS,GO] 735 Touro St (at Dauphine) **504/948-3438, 888/948-3440** *hot tub, private courtyard*

Kerlerec House [GS,GO] 922-928 Kerlerec (at Dauphine St) **504/948-6047, 888/948-3440** *1 blk from the French Quarter, gardens*

Kim's 940 Guest House [MW,GO] 940 Elysian Fields Ave **504/258-2224** *guest house in 100-yr-old bldg, kids/pets ok, also dance club [MW]*

La Dauphine, Residence des Artistes [GS,NS,GO] 2316 Dauphine St (btwn Elysian Fields & Marigny) **504/948-2217** *B&B, no unregistered overnight guests, 3-night minimum stay*

La Maison Marigny B&B on Bourbon [GS,NS,GO] 1421 Bourbon St (at Esplanade) **504/948-3638, 800/570-2014** *on the quiet end of Bourbon St*

La Residence [GS,NS] Esplanade & Marais Sts **504/832-4131** *1-bdrm apt,*

Lafitte Guest House [GS,NS,GO] 1003 Bourbon St (at St Philip) **504/581-2678, 800/331-7971** *elegant French manor house*

➤ **Lamothe House Hotel** [GS,SW,GO] 621 Esplanade Ave (btwn Royal & Chartres) **504/947-1161, 800/367-5858** *Victorian guest house*

Lanata House [GS,SW,GO] 1220 Chartres St #5 (at Gov Nicholls) **504/522-0374** *furnished residential units*

Le Papillon Guesthouse [GS,GO] 2011 N Rampart St (at Touro St) **504/948-4993** *restored 1830s guest house*

Lions Inn [MO,SW,NS,GO] 2517 Chartres St (btwn Spain & Franklin) **504/945-2339, 800/485-6846** *1850s home, hot tub, patio*

New Orleans • Louisiana

➤ **Macarty Park Guesthouse**
[GS,SW,GO] 3820 Burgundy St
504/943-4994, 800/521-2790
hot tub, also cottages & condos

Maison Dauphine [M,GO] 2460
Dauphine St (btwn Spain & St Roch)
504/943-0861 *near French Quarter*

Maison de Mandeville Guesthouse
[GF,WC,GO] 708 Mandeville St (at Royal
St) 504/944-9200, 800/977-6963
B&B

Maison Rouge [GS] 1 blk N of French
Quarter (at Ursulines St)
504/527-5360, 888/523-5235

Marigny Manor House [GS,NS,GO]
2125 N Rampart St 504/943-7826,
877/247-7599 *in historic 1850s Greek Revival, hot tub*

Mazant Guest House [GF] 906 Mazant
(at Burgundy) 504/944-2662

Montblanc House [M,GO] 2011
Burgundy St (at Frenchmen)
504/945-4965, 888/475-3557
B&B, hot tub

New Orleans Historic Reservations
[GS,GO] 531 Seguin St (at Eliza St)
504/362-1030, 888/560-6652 *B&B & private condo suites in French Quarter & surrounding areas*

Olde Town Inn [GS] 1001 Marigny St
504/949-5815, 800/209-9408
historic guest house, tropical courtyard, walk-ins welcome

Olde Victorian Inn—French Quarter
[GS,SW,GO] 914 N Rampart St (at
Dumaine St) 504/522-2446,
800/725-2446 *B&B, full brkfst*

Parkview Marigny B&B [GS,NS,GO]
726 Frenchmen St (at Dauphine)
504/945-7875, 877/645-8617
Creole town house

➤ **Pauger Guest Suites** [GS,SW,WC,GO]
1722 Pauger St 504/944-2601 *near French Quarter*

Pecan Tree Inn of New Orleans [GF]
2525 N Rampart St (at Roch St)
504/943-6195, 800/460-3667
courtyards, fireplaces, kitchens

BOURGOYNE GUEST · HOUSE

Old World Charm in the heart of the French Quarter.

**Antiques • Charming courtyard
Private Baths • Kitchens**

839 BOURBON

NEW ORLEANS, LA. 70116
(504) 525-3983 OR 524-3621

Elysian Guest House

1008 Elysian Fields Avenue
New Orleans, LA 70117
Phone/FAX: **504-940-0540/940-0599**
www.elysianguesthouse.com

- 5 blocks to French Quarter/Riverfront
- Very large rooms, baths, mini-kitchens
- Private entrances, hot-tub, nudity
- TV/VCR, phone, parking, smoking
- Leather/Country dance bars in block
- Gay owned & operated

*Through our gates
pass happy guests!
Tom & Terry*

WHEN ARE THE BEST RATES? MON THRU THURS ALL YEAR ROUND!

Maybe you've tried them all...

Going solo
Two in a tango
Ménage a trois

But have you ever gone for a little...

French Quarter Quartet

Experience the French Quarter like a local, by making one of our cozy, historical townhouses your home away from home. You'll find an authentic New Orleans flavor with a friendly, local touch. Visit us on the web and explore all four of our unique properties. You'll love our house blend of offbeat charm and vintage New Orleans decadence. Stay with us and feel like a native.

**Lamothe House · St. Peter Guest House · Frenchmen Hotel · A Creole House
Call for reservations: 800-367-5858 or visit us at WWW.FQQUARTET.COM**

FRENCH QUARTER
ACCOMMODATIONS

Make Your Plans NOW!

French Quarter Reservation Service

N'AWLINS OLDEST & LARGEST GAY RESERVATION SERVICE

1-800-523-9091

504-523-1246 • FAX 504-527-6327
1000 Bourbon St., PMB #263, New Orleans, LA 70116

IGLTA

e-mail: fqrsinc@bellsouth.net
www.neworleansgay.com

Macarty Park Guest House

3820 Burgundy Street
New Orleans, LA 70117
504-943-4994
504-943-4999 FAX
1-800-521-2790
www.macartypark.com
macpar@aol.com

Go for a splash in our refreshing in-ground pool or spacious hot tub 24-hours a day!
Enjoy beautiful cottages and rooms with color cable TV, phone, internet access and private baths!

FRENCH QUARTER

Historic, Charming Apartments

$75 AND UP

Convenient to all Bars, Restaurants, and Entertainment

GAY-OWNED

800-537-5408

www.historicrentals.com

New Orleans • Louisiana

The Pontchartrain Hotel [GF]
2031 St Charles Ave (at Josephine St)
504/524-0581, 800/777-6193
jacuzzi

Radisson Hotel New Orleans [GF,F,SW]
1500 Canal St (at LaSalle St)
504/522-4500

The Rathbone Mansion Esplanade
[GS,GO] 1227 Esplanade Ave (at St Claude) **504/947-2100, 800/947-2101** *hot tub, patio*

Rober House Condos [GS,SW,WC,GO]
822 Ursulines Ave (at Dauphine)
504/529-4663 *non-smoking room available, courtyard*

Royal Barracks Guest House [GF,NS]
717 Barracks St (at Bourbon)
504/529-7269, 888/255-7269
jacuzzi, private patios

Royal St Courtyard [MW,GO] 2438 Royal St (at Spain) **504/943-6818, 888/846-4004** *historic 1884 guest house, full kitchens, hot tub*

Southern Comforts [GS,SW,NS,WC,GO]
310/305-2984, 800/889-7359
French Quarter rentals, hot tub

➤ **St Peter House Hotel** [GS] 1005 St Peter St (at Burgundy) **504/524-9232, 888/604-6226** *antique-furnished early-1800s bldg*

Sully Mansion [GF,NS,GO] 2631 Prytania St (at Fourth) **504/891-0457, 800/364-2414** *1890s mansion in heart of Garden District*

Sun & Moon B&B [GS,NS]
1037 N Rampart St (at Ursulines)
504/529-4652, 800/638-9169
Creole cottage

Sun Oak Museum & Guesthouse
[GS,GO] 2020 Burgundy St
504/945-0322 *Greek Revival Creole cottage*

➤ **Ursuline Guest House** [★GS,GO]
708 Ursulines Ave (btwn Royal & Bourbon) **504/525-8509, 800/654-2351** *hot tub, evening socials*

PAUGER GUEST SUITES

FROM $55

- Rooms, Suites, Apartments
- Walk to French Quarter
- Free Parking
- Refrigerator or Kitchens

Call: Glenn Delatte
(504) 944-2601

Ursuline Guest House

Your Inn in the French Quarter located in a charming historic 19th century guest house with modern comforts.

Gay owned, operated and proudly serving our community since 1964.

Steps away from the exciting clubs and nightlife of Bourbon Street, the world famous shopping and fine dining of Royal Street and many cultural attractions.

Complimentary continental breakfast and wine served daily.

Enjoy the hot tub in our lush tropical courtyard.

Safetydeposit boxes and limited parking available.

**708 Rue Des Ursulines
New Orleans, LA 70116
504-525-8509
800-654-2351
504-525-8408 Fax
ursulineguesthouse.com**

National Advertisers

Key to the Codes

▶ an Advertiser – please mention Damron when patronizing businesses that support us by advertising!

★	very popular
MO	Men Only
GF	Gay-Friendly (mostly straight)
GS	Gay/Straight
MW	gay men and lesbians (Men and Women)
M	mostly gay Men
W	mostly Women (lesbians)
WO	Women Only
NH	NeighborHood bar
D	Dancing (DJ spinning—usually Fri-Sat)
A	Alternative music (modern rock)
CW	Country/Western
B	Bears
L	Leather & fetish
MR	MultiRacial clientele
MR-A	mostly Asian-American
MR-AF	mostly African-American
MR-L	mostly Latino/a-American
TG	TransGender-friendly
F	hot Food served from a kitchen or grill
E	live Entertainment (bands, comedy, spoken word, etc.)
K	Karaoke (usually only on some nights)
C	Cabaret
DS	Drag shows
P	Piano bar
S	Strippers & go-go dancers
V	Videos shown
18+	must be 18 years or older
YC	Young/Collegiate types
OC	Older/more mature Crowd
BW	Beer and/or Wine only
BYOB	Bring Your Own Bottle (of alcohol)
R	Reservations required
SW	Swimming on-site or nearby
N	Nudity permitted in some areas
NS	Non-Smoking building
PC	Private Club
WC	WheelChair accessible (bathrooms too)
GO	Gay-Owned and/or operated (includes lesbian-owned)
$	cover charge ($7 and up)
AYOR	At Your Own Risk
LGBT	Lesbian/Gay/Bisexual/Transgender

new england's largest
gay, lesbian and bisexual newspaper
for over 12 years

www.innewsweekly.com

450 Harrison Avenue Suite 414 > Boston, MA 02118 > 617/426-8246

World's Foremost Gay and Lesbian Hotels

**If you think All gay and lesbian hotels are the same,
You haven't experienced our world...**

WORLD'S FOREMOST GAY & LESBIAN HOTELS

www.foremostgayhotels.com

At last, an uncommon philosophy rules for gay and lesbian accommodations worldwide. One shared vision has been born for the gay and lesbian traveler. Extraordinary accommodations, unique to the destination property, unforgettable in character and consistency of the total experience, yet all focused on welcoming you, the gay and lesbian traveler, with an unforgettable combination of attractive facilities and amenities, pampering and comforting services, and delightful decor which awakens your spirit to a new world of gay and lesbian travel. It is after all what you expect and have been seeking in your travel accommodations – all comparable to the finest mainstream properties. The time has come for the World's Foremost Gay and Lesbian Hotels.

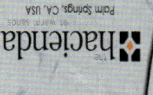
Palm Springs, CA, USA

San Francisco, CA, USA
Bethlehem, NH, USA

Provincetown, MA, USA

Cairns, Australia

Quepos, Costa Rica

Key West, FL, USA

Fort Lauderdale, FL, USA

We're going your way

**All the news for your Life.
And your Style.
In New Orleans,
and across the South.**

Southern Voice is a Window Media Publication

Party from Coast to Coast!

Party from coast to coast on your private luxury railcar with an itinerary of your choosing (for up to six travelers).

AMERICA RAILCAR CHARTERS

www.AmericaRailcarCharters.com

480-390-9123

OUT&ABOUT
ESSENTIAL INFORMATION FOR GAY AND LESBIAN TRAVELERS

sex & travel | summer resorts | nude travel | winter resorts

Guides to over 150 destinations worldwide.

Guides to resort towns, nude travel, solo travel, circuit events and more.

Available online at www.outandabout.com

Go Out Shopping at Home

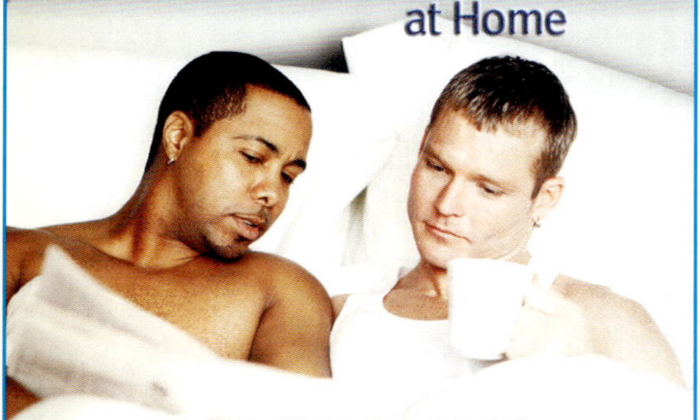

OUR △ TRIBE®

Our Tribe Cardpack brings the finest collection of products and services to your door!

Our gay postcard catalog is mailed quarterly. Email or write today!

Subscribe FREE Online:
www.outtribe.com

✓ **Yes!** I want my FREE issue of *Our Tribe Cardpack*.

Name _____

Address _____

City _____ State _____ Zip _____

e-mail _____

Mail to: *Our Tribe Cardpack*, 70-A Greenwich Ave #380, New York, NY 10011-8300
Our Tribe Cardpack is mailed discreetly in a shrink wrapped package.
You will receive the next quarterly issue. Offer valid in USA only. Ad Sales: 212-462-0036
e-mail: **freeissue@outtribe.com** *Remember to include your snail-mail address.*

SHOP TILL YOU DROP – AT HOME.

Get Your First Issue Free
When You Subscribe Online
Or Call 1-800-642-7535
www.venusmagazine.com

Nightsweats & T-cells ♥

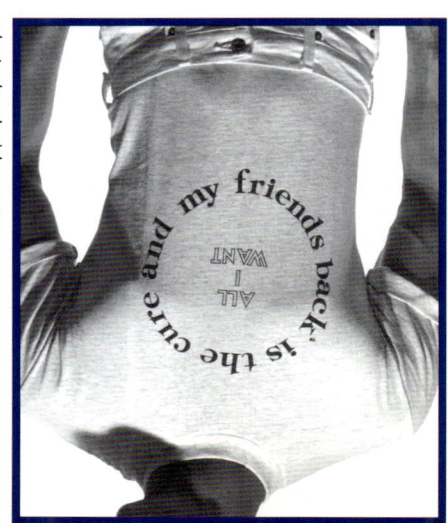

photo by david morgan

20 Years
16 Million Dead
Thousands of Shirts
Hundreds of Paychecks

Custom Screenprinting
&
Graphic Design

800-859-8685

owned & operated
by people living with hiv/aids

New Orleans • Louisiana

■ BARS

Anglès [MW,NH,D,K,DS,WC] 2301 N Causeway Blvd (at 34th), Metairie 504/834-7979 *5pm-close, karaoke Th*

Armstrong Café & Bar [MW,D,F,S] 822 N Rampart St 504/525-3533, 504/525-4898 *6pm-close, also PR1 [S,P]*

Big Daddy's [MW,NH,WC] 2513 Royal (at Franklin) 504/948-6288 *24hrs*

Bourbon Pub & Parade [★MW,D,S,V,18+,YC] 801 Bourbon St (at St Ann), 504/529-2107 *24hrs, T-dance Sun*

Café Lafitte in Exile/ The Balcony Bar [★MW,D,S,V] 901 Bourbon St (at Dumaine) 504/522-8397 *24hrs, Balcony Bar upstairs w/ cyber bar*

Chet's Queen's Pub [MW,NH,P,WC] 706 Franklin Ave (at Royal) 504/948-4200

The Corner Pocket [★M,NH,DS,S] 940 St Louis (at Burgundy) 504/568-9829 *24hrs, male dancers nightly, hustlers*

► **Country Club** [★GS,F,C,S,NW] 634 Louisa St (at Chartres) 504/945-0742 *11am-1am, from 10am Fri-Sun, a gay country club!*

Cowpoke's [M,NH,D,C,W,E,K] 2240 St Claude (at Elysian Fields) 504/947-0505 *4pm-2am, dance lessons 8pm Tue, karaoke Wed, also The Barn theater space*

The Double Play [M,NH,TG] 439 Dauphine (at St Louis) 504/523-4517 *24hrs*

The Four Seasons [★M,NH,E,K,DS,GO] 3229 N Causeway Blvd (at 18th), Metairie 504/832-0659 *3pm-4am, also the Outback Bar, patio*

The Friendly Bar [★M,NH,WC] 2301 Chartres St (at Marigny) 504/943-8929 *11am-3am*

Golden Lantern [M,NH] 1239 Royal St (at Barracks) 504/529-2860 *24hrs*

Good Friends Bar [★M,NH,K,P,WC] 740 Dauphine (at St Ann) 504/566-7191 *24hrs, also Queens Head Pub Th-Sun, piano sing-along*

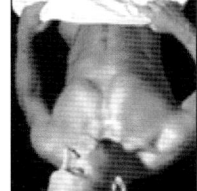

The only happy hour where you can wear a suit or take it off!

Skinny-dipping daily till 1 am

The **Country Club**
New Orleans

www.countryclubneworleans.com

Heated Pool Bar & Clubhouse

In an historic Georgian, plantation-style mansion, just 5 minutes from the French Quarter

(504)945-0742
634 Louisa Street,
New Orleans, LA 70117

Pool is always open!

Year-Round
Mon.–Thurs. 11 am – 1 am
Fri.–Sun. 10 am – 1 am

Everyone is welcome!

Get A Room! Get A Car! Get A Flight!

GayAmerica.COM

Original & ONLY
Official Web Site of
Southern Decadence
since 1995 TN/TM/SM

Official Southern Decadence
SouthernDecadence.COM

AMBUSH MAG.COM

Gulf South Entertainment & Travel Guide
Since 1982 • Texas-Florida
828-A Bourbon St. • New Orleans, LA 70116-3137
504.522.8049 • 504.522.8047
info@ambushmag.com

Original & ONLY
Official Web Site of
Gay Mardi Gras
since 1995 TN/TM/SM

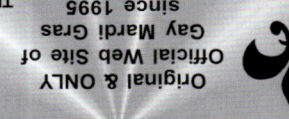

Official Gay Mardi Gras
GayMardiGras.COM

**Discount Hotels • Flights
Rental Cars • Events • Pics**

New Orleans • Louisiana

■ RESTAURANTS

Bluebird Café [★] 3625 Prytania St (btwn Foucher & Antonine) 504/895-7166 *7am-3pm, from 8am wknds, great brkfsts, cash only*

Café Sbisa 1011 Decatur 504/522-5565 *dinner & Sun brunch, French Creole, patio*

Casamento's 4330 Magazine (at Napoleon Ave) 504/895-9761 *lunch & dinner, clsd Mon (also clsd June-Aug), best oyster loaf in city*

Clover Grill [★] 900 Bourbon St (at Dumaine) 504/523-0904 *24hrs, diner fare*

Commander's Palace [R] 1403 Washington Ave (in Garden District) 504/899-8221 *lunch & dinner, upscale Creole, jazz brunch wknds*

Feelings Cafe [P] 2600 Chartres St (at Franklin Ave) 504/945-2222 *dinner nightly, lunch Fri, Sun brunch, Creole, also piano bar Fri-Sat*

Fiorella's Cafe [★] French Market Pl (at Gov Nicholls & Ursulines) 504/528-9566 *7am-midnight, till 2am Th-Sat, clsd Sun, homecooking*

La Peniche 1940 Dauphine St (at Touro St) 504/943-1460 *24hrs, diner*

Lafitte's Restaurant 2031 St Charles Ave (in Pontchartrain Hotel) 504/524-0581 *7am-2:30pm & 5pm-9pm, Creole, the setting for part of Anne Rice's The Witching Hour*

Mama Rosa 616 N Rampart (at Toulouse & St Louis) 504/523-5546 *11am-10pm, till 11pm Fri-Sat, Italian*

Mona Lisa [BW] 1212 Royal St (at Barracks) 504/522-6746 *11am-10:30pm, Italian*

Nola [WC] 534 St Louis St (btwn Chartres & Decatur) 504/522-6652 *lunch (except Sun) & dinner, fusion Creole*

Old Dog New Trick Café [★BW,WC] 517 Frenchmen St 504/943-6368 *11:30am-9pm, till 10pm wknds, vegetarian, wknd brunch, patio*

Olivier's [WC] 204 Decatur St 504/525-7734 *lunch & dinner, Creole*

Red Bike Bakery & Café 746 Tchoupitoulas (off Julia) 504/529-2453 *lunch daily, dinner Tue-Sat, outdoor dining*

■ CAFES

PJ's [★] 634 Frenchmen St 504/949-2292 *7am-11pm, till midnight Fri-Sat*

Rainbows [MW,D] 3536 18th St (btwn Edenborn & N Arnoult), Metairie 504/454-3200 *8pm-close, clsd Mon-Wed*

■ NIGHTCLUBS

735 Bourbon [M,D,E,DS] 735 Bourbon St (at Orleans) 504/527-0703 *24hrs*

Club City Lights [M,N,H,WC] 834 N Rampart (at St Ann) 504/525-0002 *6pm-close*

The Full Moon [M,NH] 424 Destrehan, Harvey 504/341-4396 *9pm-close, clsd Sun-Wed*

OZ [★ M,D,DS,S,V,C,WC] 800 Bourbon St (at St Ann) 504/593-9491 *24hrs*

Le Roundup [M,NH,CW,TG] 819 St Louis (at Dauphine) 504/561-8330 *24hrs*

MRB [★MW,NH] 515 St Philip (at Decatur) 504/524-2558 *24hrs, patio*

Ninth Circle [M,NH,TG] 700 N Rampart (at St Peter) 504/524-7654 *24hrs*

Phoenix [★M,N,H,B,L,F,GO] 941 Elysian Fields Ave (at N Rampart) 504/945-9264 *24hrs, cruise room, bbq Sun, also The Eagle* [D] *9pm-5am Mon (bring your own meat), bear night*

Rawhide 2010 [★M,N,H,A,B,L,V] 740 Burgundy (at St Ann) 504/525-8106 *24hrs, underground sound*

Seventh Circle [M,N,H,S] 820 N Rampart (at St Ann) 504/523-6588 *24hrs, upscale, strippers*

Society Page [M,NH,TG] 542 N Rampart (at Toulouse) 504/593-9941 *3pm-3am, till 5am Fri-Sat*

Voodoo at Congo Square [M,NH] 718 N Rampart (at Orleans) 504/527-0703 *24hrs*

Setting A New Standard

- Always Open
- Guest Memberships
- Steam Room
- Sauna
- Whirlpool
- Private Dressing Rooms
- Outdoor Pool & Patio
- Gym
- 18+ only

THE CLUB
NEW ORLEANS

A PRIVATE MEN'S CLUB

515 Toulouse Street • New Orleans, LA • (504) 581-2402
www.the-clubs.com

New Orleans • Louisiana

Poppy's Grill [WC] 717 St Peter (at Royal & Bourbon) 504/524-3287 *24hrs, diner*

Praline Connection 542 Frenchmen St (at Chartres) 504/943-3934 *10:30am-9pm, soul food; also a location at 901 St Peters St, 504/ 523-3973 w/ a Sun gospel jazz brunch*

Quarter Scene 900 Dumaine St (at Dauphine) 504/522-6533 *lunch & dinner, dinner only Tue, homecooking*

Quartermaster 1100 Bourbon St 504/529-1416 *24hrs, sandwiches & more*

Sammy's Seafood 627 Bourbon St (across from Pat O' Brien's) 504/525-8442 *11am-midnight, Creole/ Cajun*

Secret Garden 538 St Philip St (at Decatur) 504/524-2041 *5:30pm-10pm, Creole, garden dining, romantic*

Vaqueros 4938 Prytania (at Robert) 504/891-6441 *Southwestern/ Mexican, good margaritas*

Vera Cruz [WC] 7537 Maple (at Hilliard) 504/866-1736 *5pm-11pm, from 11am Th-Fri, clsd wknds, Mexican*

■ ENTERTAINMENT & RECREATION

Café du Monde 1039 Decatur St (Old Jackson Square) 504/587-0835, 800/772-2927 *till you've a had a beignet—fried dough, powdered w/ sugar, that melts in your mouth—you haven't been to New Orleans & this is 'the' place to have them 24hrs a day*

Gay Heritage Tour 909 Bourbon St 504/945-6789 *call for details, departs from Alternatives giftshop*

Haunted History Tour 888/644-6787 *guided 2-1/2-hr tours of New Orleans' most famous haunts, including Anne Rice's home*

Mardi Gras World 233 Newton St 504/361-7821, 800/362-8213 *tour this year-round Mardi Gras float workshop, take the free ferry from the base of Canal St*

FIND WHAT YOU'RE LOOKING FOR IN NEW ORLEANS

FLEX

New Orleans, LA
504-598-3539
700 BARONNE STREET
70113

www.FLEXBATHS.COM

ATLANTA • CLEVELAND • LOS ANGELES
NEW ORLEANS • PHOENIX • COLUMBUS

Louisiana • USA

Pat O'Brien's [G:F] 718 St Peter St (btwn Bourbon & Royal)

St Charles Streetcar Canal St (btwn Bourbon & Royal Sts) 504/827-7802 (RTA #) *it's not named Desire, but you should still ride it; Blanche, if you want to see the Garden District*

BOOKSTORES

Bookstar [WC] 414 N Peters (in Jax Brewery Complex) 504/523-6411 *9am-10pm*

Faubourg Marigny Bookstore [WC] 600 Frenchmen St (at Chartres) 504/943-9875 *10am-8pm, till 6pm Sun, natural food store*

Hit Parade [★] 741 Bourbon St 504/524-7700 *noon-midnight, 11am-2am Fri-Sat, lgbt books, designer circuit clothing & more*

Postmark New Orleans [G0] 631 Toulouse St (btwn Chartres & Royal) 504/529-2052, 800/285-4247 *10am-6pm, from noon Sun, gifts*

Queen Fashions 907 Bourbon St 504/524-4335 *wigs, footwear, accessories & more; also 3001 19th St, Metairie, 504/828-9888*

Rab-Dab 508 St Philip St 504/525-3577 *11am-6pm, men's clothing/clubwear & gifts*

Rings of Desire 1128 Decatur St 504/524-6147 *piercing studio*

Second Skin Leather 521 St Philip St (btwn Decatur & Chartres) 504/561-8167 *10am-10pm, till 8pm Sun*

CRUISY AREAS

Belle Promenade [AYOR]

Capitol Lakes [AYOR] *also adjacent area*

Riverwalk [AYOR] *very interesting*

Something Different [G0] 5300 Tchoupitoulas (in Riverside Market) 504/891-9056 *10am-9pm, till 7pm Sat, 11am-6pm Sun, cards, novelties*

PUBLICATIONS

➤ **Ambush Mag** 504/522-8049 *lgbt newspaper*

➤ **Southern Voice** 404/878-1819 *weekly lgbt newspaper for AL, FL (panhandle), GA, LA, MS, TN w/ resource listings*

The Whiz 504/947-0816, 504/782-2056 *weekly gay guide to New Orleans*

MEN'S CLUBS

➤ **The Club New Orleans** [★PC] 515 Toulouse St (at Decatur) 504/581-2402 *24hrs*

➤ **Flex-New Orleans** [V] 700 Baronne St 504/598-3539 *24hrs*

MEN'S SERVICES

➤ **Megaphone New Orleans** 800/289-1489 *Call for the local # nearest you! Meet Hot Men in your area! FREE to Browse & Respond to voice ads. Use code 3087. Also try MEGAMATES.COM*

EROTICA

Airline Bookstore 1404 26th St (off Bainbridge), Kenner 504/468-2931

Bourbon Strip Tease 205 Bourbon St 504/581-6633

Chartres St Conxxxion 107 Chartres St (off Canal St) 504/588-8006 *24hrs*

Gargoyles 1215 Decatur St (at Gov Nicholls) 504/529-4387 *leather/ fetish/ goth store*

Panda Bear [WC] 415 Bourbon St (at St Louis) 504/529-3593 *leather & toys*

Paradise [WC] 41 W 24th St (at Crestview), Kenner 504/461-0000

MAINE

Statewide

■ PUBLICATIONS

► **In Newsweekly** 617/426-8246
New England's largest lgbt newspaper

Aroostook County

■ ACCOMMODATIONS

Magic Pond Wildlife Sanctuary & Guest House [W,NS,GO] Blaine 207/429-8787 *artist-owned cottage*

Augusta

■ ACCOMMODATIONS

Maple Hill Farm B&B Inn [GS,NS,WC,GO] 207/622-2708, 800/622-2708 *historic Victorian farmhouse, full brkfst, swimming pond*

■ NIGHTCLUBS

PJ's (aka Papa Joe's) [★MW,D,F,P] 80 Water St (btwn Laurel & Bridge) 207/623-4041 *7pm-1am Wed-Sat, piano bar, patio*

■ CRUISY AREAS

Waterfront Park [AYOR] E side of the Memorial Bridge (off Western Ave)

Bailey Island

■ ACCOMMODATIONS

See View Cottage [GS,GO] 37 Pebble Ln (at Oceanside Rd) 207/833-6023 *ocean view, pets ok*

Bangor

■ ACCOMMODATIONS

Maine Wilderness Lake Island [MW] 26 5th St 207/990-5839 *weekly rental cabins for summer*

■ NIGHTCLUBS

The Spectrum [MW,D,K,DS,WC] 190 Harlow St (next to Federal Bldg) 207/942-3000 *8pm-1am, till 2am Sat, clsd Sun-Wed, karaoke Th*

Shreveport

■ BARS

Johns Wall St Pub [MW,NH,D,MR,TG,K,DS,18+,GO] 235 Wall St (at Stoner) 318/678-8300

Korner Lounge II [M,NH] 800 Louisiana (near Cotton) 318/222-9796 *5pm-midnight, till 2am Fri-Sat*

■ NIGHTCLUBS

Central Station [★MW,D,CW,TG,S,WC] 1025 Marshall (btwn Fairfield & Creswell) 318/222-2216 *3pm-2am, till 6am wknds*

■ EROTICA

Fun Shop Too 9434 Mansfield Rd 318/688-2482 *clsd Sun*

■ CRUISY AREAS

Bickham-Dickson Park [AYOR] E King's Hwy (at 3132)

Slidell

■ BARS

Billy's [MW,NH,F] 2600 Hwy 190 W 985/847-1921 *7pm-2am, 5pm-midnight Sun, clsd Mon-Wed*

Maine • USA

Bar Harbor

ACCOMMODATIONS
Manor House Inn [GF] 106 West St (near Bridge St) 207/288-3759, 800/437-0086 *open May-Nov, 1880s Victorian mansion, full brkfst, jacuzzi*

RESTAURANTS
Mama DiMatteo's [GO] 34 Kennebec Pl (at Rodick St) 207/288-3666 *5pm-9pm, clsd Sun-Mon, open year-round, upscale casual dining, seafood, steak & pasta, full bar*

CRUISY AREAS
Lakewood [AYOR] Town Hill Rd (1 mile from Hulls Cove) *Follow trail to the 'Ledges'*
Thompson Island [AYOR] Mt Desert Island

Bath

ACCOMMODATIONS
The Galen C Moses House [GS,NS,GO] 1009 Washington St 207/442-8771, 888/442-8771 *full brkfst*
The Inn at Bath [GS,NS,WC,GO] 969 Washington St 207/443-4294, 800/423-0964 *1810 B&B, full brkfst*

Boothbay Harbor

ACCOMMODATIONS
Hodgdon Island Inn [GS,SW,NS,GO] Barter's Island Rd (at Sawyer's Island Rd), Boothbay 207/633-7474 *1810 sea captain's home, full brkfst*
Sur La Mer Inn [GF,NS,GO] 18 Eames Rd, PO Box 663 207/633-7400, 800/791-2026 *luxury oceanfront B&B*

Brunswick

RESTAURANTS
Star Fish Grill 100 Pleasant St/ Rte 1 (at Mill St) 207/725-7828 *dinner only, clsd Mon, fresh seafood & natural meats, full bar*

BOOKSTORES
Gulf of Maine Books 134 Maine St (at Pleasant) 207/729-5083 *9:30am-5:30pm, clsd Sun*

Camden

ACCOMMODATIONS
Norumbega [GF] 63 High St 207/236-4646, 877/363-4646 *inn, circa 1886, restaurant*

Caribou

INFO LINES & SERVICES
Gay/ Lesbian Phoneline 398 S Main St 800/468-2088 (ME only) *7pm-9pm Mon-Fri, social & networking group for northern ME & NW New Brunswick, Canada*

Corea

ACCOMMODATIONS
The Black Duck Inn on Corea Harbor [GS,NS,GO] Crowley Island Rd (Rte 195), Corea Harbor 207/963-2689, 877/963-2689 *full brkfst, restored farmhouse on harbor, also cottages*

RESTAURANTS
Fisherman's Inn 7 Newman St, Winter Harbor 207/963-5585 *seasonal, 4:30pm-9pm*

Deer Isle

RESTAURANTS
Fisherman's Friend School St, Stonington 207/367-2442 *open April-Oct, 11am-8pm*

Farmington

BOOKSTORES
Devaney, Doak & Garrett Booksellers 193 Broadway 207/778-3454 *hours vary, lgbt section*

BOOKSTORES
Pro Libris Bookshop 10 3rd St (at Union) 207/942-3019 *10am-6pm, clsd Sun-Mon, new & used*

CRUISY AREAS
Valley Avenue Park [AYOR] along river bank

Ogunquit • Maine

Freeport

■ ACCOMMODATIONS

The Bagley House [GS,NS,GO]
1290 Royalsborough Rd, Durham
207/865-6566, 800/765-1772
full brkfst

Hallowell

■ RESTAURANTS

Slate's [E] 167 Water St (Franklin)
207/622-9575 *lunch & dinner, till 2pm Sun*

Hancock

■ RESTAURANTS

Le Domaine Restaurant & Inn
207/422-3395 *open June-Oct, 6pm-9pm, clsd Sun-Mon*

Kennebunkport

■ ACCOMMODATIONS

Arundel Meadows Inn [GF,SW,NS]
1024 Portland Rd (at Walker Ln),
Arundel 207/985-3770 *full brkfst, hot tub*

The Colony Hotel [GF,FSW,NS,WC]
140 Ocean Ave (at Kings Hwy)
207/967-3331, 800/552-2363
seasonal, oceanfront property w/ private beach

White Barn Inn [GF,SW,F] 37 Beach St
207/967-2321

■ RESTAURANTS

Bartley's Dockside by the bridge
207/967-5050 *lunch & dinner May-Dec, lunch only Jan-April, full bar*

Kittery

■ EROTICA

Amazing Rte 236 N (1 mile from traffic circle), Eliot 207/439-6285

see also Portsmouth, New Hampshire

Lewiston

■ ACCOMMODATIONS

Ware Street Inn B&B [GF] 52 Ware St (at College St) 207/783-8171, 877/783-8171

■ BARS

The Sportsman's Club
[★MW,NH,D,E,K,DS] 2 Bates St (at Main) 207/784-2251 *8pm-1am, clsd Mon-Tue, oldest gay bar in Maine*

■ EROTICA

Paris Book Store 297 Lisbon St (at Chestnut) 207/783-6677

■ CRUISY AREAS

West Pitch Park [AYOR] at Great Falls Plaza, Auburn

Newcastle

■ ACCOMMODATIONS

The Tipsy Butler B&B [GS,NS]
11 High St 207/563-3394 *on the Damariscotta River*

Ogunquit

■ ACCOMMODATIONS

Abalonia [M,NS,GO] 207/646-4804,
800/311-4345 *B&B, renovated farmhouse*

Admiral's Inn Resort Hotel
[MW,SW,NS,GO] 87 Main St (at Agamenticus) 207/646-7093,
888/263-6318 *hot tub*

Beach Haven Ogunquit [GF,GO]
69 Cottage St 207/646-5639
5 minutes to beach, seasonal

Beauport Inn & Suites on Clay Hill
[GS,WC] 339 Agamenticus/ Clay Hill Rd
207/361-2400, 800/646-1898 *full brkfst*

Beaver Dam Campground [GF,SW]
551 School St, Rte 9, Berwick
207/698-2267 *campground on beautiful 20-acre spring-fed pond*

Belm House Vacation Units [MW,GO]
207/641-2637 *rental units w/ kitchens*

Black Boar Inn [MW,GO] 47 Main St
207/646-2112 *B&B built in 1674, full gourmet brkfst, tea*

Maine • USA

► The Carriage Trade Inn [MW,NS,GO] 254 Shore Rd
207/646-0650, 866/500-0650 B&B, also 1 suit for weekly rental, walking distance to Perkins Cove, beach & clubs, 3-night minimum

Distant Sands B&B [GS,NS,GO]
207/646-8686 18th-c farmhouse, overlooks Ogunquit River, also cottage

The Heritage of Ogunquit [MW,NS,GO] PO Box 1788 03907
207/646-5050 mostly lesbian clientele, gay men welcome, efficiencies & B&B, hot tub

The HideAway 65 Main St
207/646-3787, 617/524-0080 guest house

Leisure Inn [GS,GO] 73 School St
207/646-2737 seasonal

Moon Over Maine B&B [MW,GO] Berwick Rd **207/646-6666, 800/851-6837** hot tub

Ogunquit Beach Inn & Vacation Apartments [M,GO] 67 School St
207/646-1112, 888/976-2463 5 minutes to beach, also house & apt rentals

The Ogunquit House [*MW,GO] 17 Glen Ave **207/646-2967** clsd Jan-Feb, Victorian B&B, also cottages

OgunquitCottages.com [MW,NS,GO] 25 Mill St, N Reading, MA 01864
207/646-3840, 978/664-5813 weekly rentals, seasonal (June-Sept), near bars & beach

Rockmere Lodge B&B [GS,NS,GO] 150 Stearns Rd **207/646-2985** Maine shingle cottage, near beach

Sunrise Rental Properties [M,GO] 35 Kings Ln (at Main St) **207/641-2007** rental cottages & condos

Two Village Square [M,SW,NS,GO] 2 Village Square Ln **207/646-5779, 412/323-9652** (winter #) open May-Oct, Victorian w/ ocean views, hot tub

---

THE CARRIAGE TRADE INN — OGUNQUIT, MAINE

Carriage Trade

AN OGUNQUIT INN

OPEN YEAR-ROUND

6 beautifully appointed rooms with private baths

Suite available with kitchen and fireplace

Walk to Perkins Cove and Ogunquit Sq.

Minutes from Kittery Outlets
and historic Portsmouth

254 Shore Rd. • 207/646-0650 • www.carriagetradeinn.com • 866/500-0650

Portland • Maine

Portland

■ INFO LINES & SERVICES
Gays in Sobriety 32 Thomas St (at United Church of Christ)
207/774-4060 6:30pm Sun

■ ACCOMMODATIONS
Auberge by the Sea B&B [GF,NS] 103 East Grand Ave, Old Orchard Beach 207/934-2355 *private beach path*

▶ **The Inn at St John** [GS,WC,GO] 939 Congress St 207/773-6481, 800/636-9127 *unique historic inn*

The Percy Inn [GF,NS] 15 Pine St (at Longfellow Square) 207/871-7638, 888/417-3729 *B&B at Longfellow Square*

Wild Iris Inn [GF,NS] 273 State St 207/775-0224, 800/600-1557 *in downtown Portland*

■ BARS
Blackstones [M,N,WC] 6 Pine St (off Longfellow Square) 207/775-2885 4pm-1am, from 3pm Sun, *leather/ fetish 3rd Sat*

Somewhere [MW,NH,MR,P,WC] 117 Spring St (at High) 207/871-9169

Una [GS,F] 505 Fore St 207/828-0300 4:30pm-1am, *martini & wine bar*

The Wine Bar [GS] 38 Wharf St 207/773-6667 *5pm-close*

La Pizzeria [BW,GO] 25 Main St (Rte 1) 207/646-1143 *open April-Dec, lunch & dinner*

Poor Richard's Tavern 125 Shore Rd (at Pine Hill) 207/646-4722 *seasonal, 5:30pm-9pm, clsd Sun (Sun brunch off-season), full bar*

Southside Pizza [GO] 185 Main St/ US Rte 1 207/646-8800 11am-1am, *also wraps, smoothies, salads*

■ PUBLICATIONS
▶ **In Newsweekly** 617/426-8246 *New England's largest lgbt newspaper*

■ CRUISY AREAS
Ogunquit Beach [AYOR] 200 yds N of beach entrance

Maine

Yellow Monkey Guest House/ Hotel [GS,WC,GO] 280 Main St 207/646-9056 *seasonal, jacuzzi, gym*

■ BARS
Front Porch Cafe [GS,F,P] Ogunquit Square 207/646-3976, 207/646-6655 *open April-Jan, 9pm-close, also Rooftop Cafe & Martini Lounge from 4pm, from 11:30am wknds*

■ NIGHTCLUBS
The Club [★M,D,F,K,V,GO] 237 Main St 207/646-6655 *open April-Jan, 9pm-1am, 4pm wknds from 11:30am wknds*

Maine Street [★MW,D,F,CD,S,V,GO] 195 Main St/ US Rte 1 207/646-5101 3pm-1am, *T-dance 4pm-8pm Sun (summers)*

■ CAFES
Bread & Roses 24-A Main St 207/646-4227 *7am-7pm, open later wknds*

Fancy That Cafe Village Square (corner of Beach St & Rte 1) 207/646-4118 *April-Oct, 6:30am-11pm*

Sister Mary Catherine's Internet Cafe [GF,GO] 757A Post Rd (Rte 1) (at 9B & Rte 1), Wells 207/646-6611 *8am-4pm, till 6pm Fri-Sat, till 3pm Sun*

■ RESTAURANTS
Arrows [★R] Berrick Rd (18 miles W of Center) 207/361-1100 *open April-Dec, 6pm-9pm, clsd Mon-Tue, eclectic*

The Cape Neddick Inn [R,WC] 1233 Rte 1, York 207/363-2899 *5:30pm-10pm, clsd Mon-Tue*

Clay Hill Farm [P] 207/646-2272 (2 miles W of Rte 1) *dinner, clsd Mon-Tue, seafood, also piano bar*

Five-O [★] 50 Shore Rd 207/646-6365 *5pm-1am, from 11am wknds, full bar*

Grey Gull Inn 475 Webhannet Dr, Wells 207/646-7501 *New England fine dining, also accommodations*

Johnathan's [WC] 92 Bourne Ln 207/646-4777 *5pm-8:30pm, till 10pm wknds, veggie/ seafood, full bar*

Maine • USA

NIGHTCLUBS

The Underground [★BW,D,E,K,DS]
3 Spring St 207/773-3315 4pm-1am,
from 8pm Mon-Tue, DJ Th-Sun

RESTAURANTS

Katahdin 106 High St (at Spring)
207/774-1740 5pm-9:30pm, till
10:30pm Fri-Sat, clsd Sun-Mon,
American menu, bar

Siam Restaurant [BW,WC,GO] 339 Fore
St (at Pearl) 207/773-8389 lunch &
dinner, Thai

Street & Co [★ BW,WC] 33 Wharf St
(btwn Dana & Union) 207/775-0887
5:30pm-9:30pm, till 10pm Fri-Sat,
seafood

UFFA 190 State St (at Congress)
207/775-3380 dinner Wed-Sat,
brunch Fri-Sun, clsd Tue

Walter's Cafe 15 Exchange St
207/871-9258 11am-3pm & 5pm-
9pm (open later Fri-Sat), dinner only
Sun, seafood/pasta

BOOKSTORES

Longfellow Books 1 Monument Wy
207/772-4045 9am-7pm, lgbt section

RETAIL SHOPS

Communiques 3 Moulton St (at
Commercial) 207/773-5181 9am-
5:30pm, till 9pm summers, cards, gifts,
clothing

Condom Sense 424 Fore St (at Union)
207/871-0356 hours vary

Drop Me A Line [GO] 611 Congress St
(at High) 207/773-5547 10am-6pm,
till 5pm Sun, gift shop

PUBLICATIONS

Casco Bay Weekly 207/775-6601,
800/286-6601 weekly alternative
newspaper

MEN'S SERVICES

➤ **Megaphone Portland**
800/289-1489 Call for the local #
nearest you! Meet Hot Men in your area!
FREE to Browse & Respond to voice ads.
Use code 3087. Also try MEGAMATES.COM

Čuropean Charm...

The Victorian Inn at St. John

...in the heart of Portland

- Continental breakfast
- Non-smoking rooms available
- Walking distance to historic Old Port/Arts District
- Free Cable/HBO
- Local Calls
- Airport pick-up
- Parking

(207) 773-6481
(800) 636-9127

939 Congress Street, Portland, Maine 04102
info@innatstjohn.com • www.innatstjohn.com

Baltimore • Maryland

Waterville

■ EROTICA

Treasure Chest [★] 5 Sanger Ave (at Main) 207/873-7411 *clsd Sun*

York Harbor

■ RESTAURANTS

York Harbor Inn Rte 1A 207/363-5119 *lunch Mon-Fri, dinner Th-Sat, Sun brunch, also the Cellar Pub, also lodging*

MARYLAND

Annapolis

■ INFO LINES & SERVICES

AA Gay/ Lesbian 199 Duke of Gloucester St (at St Anne's Parish) 410/268-5441 *8pm Tue*

■ ACCOMMODATIONS

Two-0-One B&B [GS,NS,GO] 201 Prince George St (at Maryland Ave) 410/268-8053 *full brkfst*

William Page Inn [GS,NS,GO] 8 Martin St 410/626-1506, 800/364-4160 *renovated 1908 home, full brkfst, jacuzzi*

Baltimore

■ INFO LINES & SERVICES

AA Gay/ Lesbian 410/663-1922

Gay/ Lesbian Community Center 241 W Chase St (at Read) 410/837-5445 *call for hours*

■ ACCOMMODATIONS

Abacrombie Badger Fine Food & Accommodations [GS,NS] 58 W Biddle St (at Cathedral) 410/244-7227, 888/922-3437 *also restaurant*

Biltmore Suites [GF] 205 W Madison St (at Park) 410/728-6550, 800/868-5064 *Victorian hotel*

Clarion Hotel–Mt Vernon Square [GF,FWC] 612 Cathedral St (at W Monument) 410/727-7101, 800/292-5500 *jacuzzis*

Embassy Suites Hotel Baltimore at BWI [GF,SW] 1300 Concourse Dr, Linthicum 410/850-0747, 800/362-2779 *full brkfst*

■ EROTICA

Video Expo 666 Congress St (at State) 207/774-1377

■ CRUISY AREAS

Cutter Street [AYOR] *at the foot of the street on the Eastern Promenade*

Rockland

■ ACCOMMODATIONS

Captain Lindsey House Inn [GF,NS,WC] 5 Lindsey St 207/596-7950, 523-2145

The Old Granite Inn [GF,WC] 546 Main St 207/594-9036, 800/386-9036 *1880s stone guest house, full brkfst, harbor views*

Rockport

■ RESTAURANTS

Chez Michel Rte 1, Lincolnville Beach 207/789-5600 *dinner, Sun brunch, clsd Mon, full bar*

Lobster Pound Rte 1, Lincolnville Beach 207/789-5550 *11:30am-8pm May-Sept, full bar*

Sebago Lake

■ ACCOMMODATIONS

Bear Mountain Village [GS] 207/583-2541 (summer), 207/782-2275 (winter) *on lake, cottages, campsites*

■ RESTAURANTS

Sydney's Rte 302, Naples 207/693-3333 *open April-Jan, 4pm-9pm, till 9:30pm Sat, full bar*

Tenants Harbor

■ ACCOMMODATIONS

Blueberry Cove Camp [GF] Harts Neck Road 207/372-6333, 617/878-2897 (off-season) *cabins & campsites, near Penobscot Bay*

Eastwind Inn [GF,R] 207/372-6366, 800/241-8439 *clsd Dec-April, full brkfst, rooms & apts, also restaurant*

Maryland • USA

Harbor Inn Pier 5 [G,S,F,WC]
711 Eastern Ave (at President)
410/539-2000 on waterfront, full brkfst, restaurant, cigar bar

Mr Mole B&B [★G,SG] 1601 Bolton St (at McMechen) 410/728-1179, 866/811-2477 suites on Bolton Hill

BARS

The Allegro [M,D,DS,V] 1101 Cathedral St (at Chase) 410/837-3906 6pm-2am, 18+ Th, T-dance Sun

Atlantis [M,S] 615 Fallsway (at Centre St) 410/727-9099 5pm-2am, nude dancers open Sun, clsd Mon

Baltimore Eagle [★M,L,WC]
2022 N Charles St (enter on 21st)
410/823-2453 3pm-2am, leather store, patio

Central Station [★M,W,D,F,K,V] 1001 N Charles St (at Eager) 410/752-7133 4pm-2am, 2 bars, also sidewalk cafe

Club Bunns [MW,D,MR,S]
608 W Lexington St (at Greene St)
410/234-2866 5pm-2am, male strippers Wed

The Drinkery [M,N,H,X] 203 W Read St (at Park) 410/225-3100 11am-2am, from 9:30am wknds

The Gallery Bar & Studio Restaurant [MW,WC] 1735 Maryland Ave (at Lafayette) 410/539-6965 2pm-1:30am, dinner nightly

Hippo [★MW,D,TG,E,K,P,V,WC] 1 W Eager St (at Charles) 410/547-0069, 410/576-0018 4pm-2am, 3 bars

Leon's [M,NH,F,WC] 870 Park Ave (at Chase) 410/539-4993, 410/539-4850 11am-2am, also Tyson's Place restaurant, Sun brunch

The Quest [M,NH] 3607 Fleet St (at Conkling) 410/563-2617 4pm-2am

NIGHTCLUBS

Club 1722 [GS,D,18+,PC]
1722 N Charles St (at Lafayette)
410/727-7431 after-hours Th-Sat, also Sun-Wed, 18+ Th-Fri only, members only Sat, dress code

Orpheus [GF,D,A,18+] 1001 E Pratt St (at Exeter) 410/276-5599 goth Fri & 1st Th, fetish party Sat, disco Sun

CAFES

Donna's Coffee Bar [BW] 2 W Madison (at Charles) 410/385-0180 7:30am-11pm, 9am-midnight wknds

RESTAURANTS

Alonso's [WC] 415 W Cold Spring Lake (at Keswick Rd) 410/235-3433 11am-midnight, till 1am Fri-Sat, Italian, full bar

Café Hon [WC] 1002 W 36th St (at Roland) 410/243-1230 7am-9pm, 9am-10pm wknds

Loco Hombre 413 E Cold Spring Ln (at Roland) 410/889-2233 11am-10pm

Mount Vernon Stable & Saloon 909 N Charles St (btwn Eager & Read) 410/685-7427 lunch & dinner, Sun brunch, some veggie, also bar

Spike & Charlie's Restaurant/ Wine 1225 Cathedral St (at Preston) 410/752-8144 5:30pm-11:30pm, clsd Mon

BOOKSTORES

Lambda Rising [WC] 241 W Chase St (at Read) 410/234-0069 10am-10pm, lgbt

PUBLICATIONS

▶ **EXP Gayzette** 302/227-5787, 877/397-6244 bi-weekly gay magazine for Mid-Atlantic

Gay Life 410/837-7748 lgbt newspaper

MEN'S SERVICES

▶ **Megaphone Baltimore**
800/289-1489 Call for the local # nearest you! Meet Hot Men in your area! FREE to Browse & Respond to voice ads. Use code 3087. Also try MEGAMATES.COM

The Paradox [★MW,D,MR,F,E,V,18+,WC] 1310 Russell St (at 13th) 410/837-9110 11pm-5am, midnight-6am Sat, more gay Sat, 18+ Fri

Paloma's [G,F,D,F,E,K] 15 W Eager St (at Cathedral) 410/783-9004 8pm-2am, till 4am wknds, karaoke Mon, also The Other Place cafe & bar [E]

Maryland • Hyattsville

Cumberland

■ ACCOMMODATIONS

Red Lamp Post B&B [MW,NS,GO] 849 Braddock Rd 301/**777-7476** *full brkfst, dinner available, hot tub*

■ RESTAURANTS

Acropolis 47 E Main St, Frostburg 301/**689-8277** *4pm-10pm, clsd Sun-Mon, full bar*

Au Petite Paris [R,WC] 86 E Main St 301/**689-8946** *6pm-9:30pm, clsd Sun-Mon, also lounge*

Edgewood

■ EROTICA

Bush River Books & Video 3909 Pulaski Hwy (Rte 40), Abingdon 410/**676-9051** *24hrs*

Frederick

■ CRUISY AREAS

C&O Canal [AYOR] Rte 340 S from Frederick (last left before Potomac River bridge); *go 1.5 miles, cross RR tracks*

Gambrill State Park [AYOR] W of Frederick (off I-70) *go to the summit, turn left*

Greenbelt

see also Washington, District of Columbia

Hagerstown

■ CRUISY AREAS

Greenbelt Park [AYOR]

Hyattsville

see also Washington, District of Columbia

Bettsville

see also Washington, District of Columbia

Boonsboro

■ NIGHTCLUBS

Deer Park Lodge [M,D,DS,GO] 21614 National Pike 301/**797-7672** *7pm-2am, till midnight Sun, clsd Mon-Wed*

Cockeysville

■ RESTAURANTS

The York Inn [E,P] 10010 York Rd 410/**666-0006** *3pm-10pm, till 11pm wknds, clsd Mon, full bar*

College Park

see also Washington, District of Columbia

Havre de Grace

■ ACCOMMODATIONS

La Clé D'Or [GS,GO] 226 N Union Ave (at Chesapeake Bay), 410/**939-6562**, 888/**484-4837** *1868 home of the Johns Hopkins family, full brkfst, hot tub*

Hyattsville

see also Washington, District of Columbia

■ EROTICA

Big Top Books 429 E Baltimore 410/**547-2495**

Chained Desires 136 W Read St 410/**528-8441** *leather & more*

Earle Theater 4845 Belair Rd 410/**488-5134**

Greenmount Books, Inc 3222 Greenmount Ave (at 33rd St) 410/**467-0403**

■ CRUISY AREAS

Druid Hill Park [MR-AF,YC,AYOR] W side of town (near Park Cir)

Lake Montebello Park [AYOR] Lake Montebello Terr (at Hartford Rd) *in the woods*

Wyman Dell Park [AYOR] Charles St (btwn 29th & 33rd) *hustlers on the sidewalk, cruising on the Wyman Park Dr side*

Hagerstown

S Potomac St & Summit St [AYOR]

Maryland • USA

Laurel

see also Washington, District of Columbia

■ EROTICA
Route 1 News Agency
106 Washington Blvd (at Main)
410/880-4253

Potomac

see also Washington, District of Columbia

Princess Anne

■ ACCOMMODATIONS
The Alexander House Booklovers B&B [GF] 30535 Linden Ave (at corner of Beckford) 410/651-5195 *literary-themed B&B, full brkfst*

Rock Hall

■ ACCOMMODATIONS
Tallulah's on Main [GS,WC,GO] 5750 Main St (at Sharp St) 410/639-2596 *small suite hotel*

Rockville

see also Washington, District of Columbia

■ CRUISY AREAS
Lake Needwood [AYOR] N of Rte 28 (off Avery Rd)

Salisbury

■ EROTICA
Salisbury News Agency
616 S Salisbury Blvd (near Vine)
410/543-4469

■ CRUISY AREAS
Salisbury City Park [AYOR] near the Wicomico Civic Ctr (off Rte 50) *zoo & baseball diamond area*

Silver Spring

see also Washington, District of Columbia

MASSACHUSETTS

Statewide

■ PUBLICATIONS
▶ **In Newsweekly** 617/426-8246 *New England's largest lgbt newspaper*

Acton

■ RESTAURANTS
Acton Jazz Café [E,NS,$] 452 Great Rd/ Rte 2-A 978/263-6161 *5:30pm-10pm, Sun brunch & lunch seasonal, clsd Mon, full bar*

Amherst

■ ACCOMMODATIONS
Ivy House B&B [GS,GO] 1 Sunset Ct 413/549-7554 *full brkfst*

■ RESTAURANTS
Amber Waves [WC] 63 Main St, Amherst 413/253-9200 *11:30am-9pm, till 10pm Th-Sat, from 12:30pm Sun, Thai*

■ BOOKSTORES
Food For Thought [WC] 106 N Pleasant St (at Main) 413/253-5432 *10am-6pm, till 8pm Wed-Fri, noon-5pm Sun, progressive bookstore*

Attleboro

■ EROTICA
State Line Video 1124 Washington St (off I-95, Broadway exit), South Attleboro 508/761-4900

Barre

■ ACCOMMODATIONS
Jenkins Inn & Restaurant [GF,FNS,GO] 978/355-6444, 800/378-7373 *also restaurant & full bar*

Winterwood [GF,NS] 19 N Main St, Petersham 978/724-8885 *Greek Revival mansion, fireplaces*

■ RESTAURANTS
Barre Mill 90 Main St, South Barre 978/355-2987, 978/355-6417 *dinner Wed-Sat, noon-8pm Sun, clsd Mon-Tue, Italian*

Boston • Massachusetts

Berkshires

ACCOMMODATIONS

The B&B at Howden Farm [MW,NS,GO]
Rannapo Rd, Sheffield
413/229-8481 *full brkfst*

Broken Hill Manor [GF,W,GO]
771 West Rd (at Rte 23), Sheffield
413/528-6159, 877/535-6159

Walker House [GS,NS,WC]
64 Walker St, Lenox 413/637-1271,
800/235-3098 *1804 guest house*

463 Beacon St Guest House [GF,GO]
463 Beacon St 617/536-1302
residential area, near Boston's heart

82 Chandler B&B [GS,NS,GO]
82 Chandler St 617/482-0408,
888/482-0408 *historic town house*

RESTAURANTS

Café Lucia 80 Church St, Lenox
413/637-2640 *dinner only, clsd Sun-Mon*

Church Street Café 65 Church St,
Lenox 413/637-2745 *clsd Sun-Mon*

Gateways [WC] 51 Walker St, Lenox
413/637-2532 *dinner, clsd Sun-Mon*

Windflower Inn [GF,SW,NS]
684 S Egremont Rd, Great Barrington
413/528-2720, 800/992-1993
country inn in the Berkshires, full brkfst

Boston

INFO LINES & SERVICES

GLBT Helpline 617/267-9001
6pm-11pm, 5pm-10pm wknds

ACCOMMODATIONS

CRUISY AREAS

Berkshire Athenaeum [AY,OR] Pittsfield

Burbank Park [AY,OR] on Onota Lake,
Pittsfield

EROTICA

Video Expo 1021 South St/ Rte 20,
Pittsfield 413/496-8055

Two townhouses in the heart of
Boston ◆ Telephones ◆ Color
TV's ◆ Central Air ◆ Outdoor
Decks ◆ Private & Shared Baths
◆ Continental Breakfast &
Parking ◆ Close To
All Major Sights & Nightlife
◆ Reasonable Rates
◆ MC, VISA & AMEX

22 Edgerly Road
Boston, MA 02115
Phone: 617-267-2262
Fax: 617-267-1920
1-800-230-0105
Web: www.oasisgh.com
Email: info@oasisgh.com

BOSTON

On the edge of historic Back Bay and the wonderfully eclectic South End, Boston's most exciting small hotel offers visitors a myriad of fringe benefits.

All rooms newly renovated

BOSTON'S BEST VALUE.

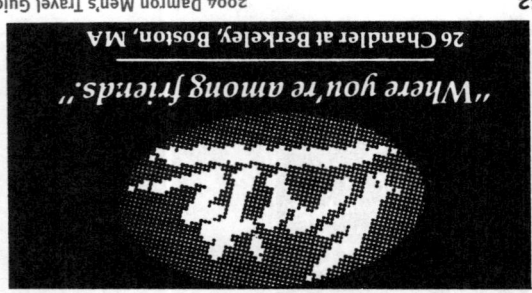

CHANDLER INN
HOTEL

1-800-842-3450

www.chandlerinn-fritz.com

26 Chandler at Berkeley, Boston, MA 02116 (617) 482-3450

"Where you're among friends."

26 Chandler at Berkeley, Boston, MA

BEST OF BOSTON
2001 ★ 2002

Best Singles Scene-Gay. Awarded by **Boston** Magazine

ALL ACCESS!
COME ENJOY THE ALL NEW ALL ACCESS CLUB CAFÉ!

"Without a question, the all-inclusive homo hotspot on Thursdays."

Improper Bostonian

Club Café
RESTAURANT & LOUNGE

209 Columbus Avenue
at Berkeley Street
Boston Massachusetts
617.536.0966
www.clubcafe.com

83CLUBCAFÉ03
CELEBRATING OUR TWENTIETH YEAR!
XX

Massachusetts • USA

't Amsterdammertje [MW,SG,GO] 617/471-8454, 800/484-6401 x1676 *full brkfst, near Boston, Euro-American B&B*

➤ **Chandler Inn** [GF] 26 Chandler St 617/482-3450, 800/842-3450

The Charles Street Inn [GS,WC,GO] 94 Charles St (at Mount Vernon, Beacon Hill) 617/314-8900, 877/772-8900 *B&B, jacuzzi*

Clarendon Square Inn [MW,GO] 198 W Brookline St (btwn Tremont & Columbus) 617/536-2229

Encore B&B [GF,GO] 116 W Newton St (at Tremont) 617/247-3425 *19th-c town house in Boston's South End*

Just Right Reservations [GS,GO] 978/934-9931 *inns & B&Bs for Boston, Provincetown, West Hollywood, Santa Monica, Malibu & Palm Springs*

Nine Zero [GF] 90 Tremont St (at Bosworth) 617/772-5800, 866/646-3937 *luxury hotel, full bkfst, jacuzzi*

Oasis Guest House [★GS,NS,WC,GO] 22 Edgerly Rd 617/267-2262 *in Back Bay*

Rutland Square House B&B [GS,NS,GO] 56 Rutland Square 617/247-0018, 800/786-6567 *Victorian town house*

Taylor House B&B [GS,NS,GO] 50 Burroughs St 617/983-9334, 888/228-2956 *Italianate Victorian*

■ BARS

The Alley [M,NH,D,LWC] 14 Pie Alley (at Court Square) 617/263-1449 *10:30am-2am, from noon Sun, cruisy*

Boston Eagle [M,NH] 520 Tremont St (near Berkeley) 617/542-4494 *3pm-2am, from noon Sun*

Boston Ramrod [★M,D,LWC] 1254 Boylston St (at Ipswich, 1 blk from Fenway Park) 617/266-2986 *noon-2am, Bear night Th*

Chaps/ Vapor Nightclub [M,D,F] 100 Warrenton St (at Stuart) 617/422-0862, 617/695-9500 *(info line) 5pm-2am, clsd Mon, piano bar Mon, Latino night Wed, T-dance Sun from noon*

■ CAFES

Diesel Café [GO] 257 Elm St (in Davis Square), Somerville 617/629-8717 *7am-midnight, till 1am Fri-Sat, from 8am wknds*

Static Café [M,D,S,19+] 13 Lansdowne (at Axis) 617/262-2437 *10pm-2am Mon*

The Middle East [GF,A,F,E,YC] 472 Massachusetts Ave (in Central Square), Cambridge 617/497-0576 *11am-1am, till 2am wknds, live music*

Manray [GS,A,19+,YC] 21 Brookline St (off Mass Ave, in Central Square), Cambridge 617/864-0400 *9pm-2am, clsd Sun-Tue, more gay on campus Th & liquid Sat (disco/ new wave), goth Wed, Fetish Fri*

Lust at Aria [M,D,19+] 246 Tremont St 617/338-7080 *10pm Wed only*

Buzz [★M,D,S,$] 67 Stuart St 617/267-8969 *10pm-2am Sat, go-go boys*

Avalon [★M,D,YC,S] 15 Lansdowne St 617/262-2424 *9pm-2am Th-Sun, more gay Sun*

■ NIGHTCLUBS

Paradise [M,D,S] 180 Massachusetts Ave, Cambridge 617/494-0700 *7pm-1am, till 2am Th-Sat*

Milky Way Lounge & Lanes [GS,F,E,K] 403 Centre St, Jamaica Plain 617/524-3740 *6pm-1am, live music, poetry, only occasional performances Sat-Sun*

Machine [★M,D,V,YC,WC] 1254 Boylston St (below Boston Ramrod) 617/536-1950 *10pm-2am Fri-Sat*

Jacque's [★M,TG,CDS] 79 Broadway (at Stuart) 617/426-8902 *11am-midnight*

➤ **Fritz** [★M,NH] 26 Chandler St (in the Chandler Inn) 617/482-4428 *noon-2am, sports bar, Sat & Sun brunch*

Dedo's [M,NH,F,P] 69 Church St (btwn Stuart & Arlington, in Theater District) 617/338-9999 *5pm-1am*

➤ **Club Café** [★MW,F,P,VWC] 209 Columbus (at Berkeley) 617/536-0966 *11:30am-2am, from 2pm Sat, 3 bars including Moonshine [V], also restaurant Euro-American B&B*

Boston • Massachusetts

ENTERTAINMENT & RECREATION

Boston Gay Men's Chorus 617/424-8900 *diverse array of classical & pop, concerts usually held in Dec, March & June*

Freedom Trail *start at the Visitor Information Center in Boston Common (at Tremont & West Sts), the most famous cow pasture & oldest public park in the US, & follow the red line to some of Boston's most famous sites*

Isabella Stewart Gardner Museum 280 The Fenway 617/566-1401 *Venetian palazzo filled w/ Old Masters to impressionists, lovely courtyard, clsd Mon*

The Mapparium 175 Huntington Ave (in the Christian Science Center) 617/450-3790 *the map's out of date, but where else can you walk through a 30-ft stained-glass globe*

Museum of Afro-American History/ Black Heritage Trail 46 Joy St (at Smith Ct, on Beacon Hill) 617/725-0022 *exhibits in the African Meeting House, the oldest standing African-American church in the US*

Theater Offensive 617/542-4214 *New England's foremost presenter of lgbt theater; Out on the Edge festival in Sept*

BOOKSTORES

Calamus Bookstore [★] 92-B South St 617/338-1931, 888/800-7300 9am-7pm, noon-6pm, lgbt, also cards, music, jewelry, videos, magazines

Trident Booksellers & Café [BW,WC] 338 Newbury St (off Mass Ave) 617/267-8688 *9am-midnight, good magazine browsing*

Unicorn Books 1210 Massachusetts Ave (at Appleton), Arlington Hts 781/646-3680 *10am-9pm, till 5pm wknds, from noon Sun, spiritual*

We Think The World of You [★] 540 Tremont St (btwn Berkeley & Clarendon) 617/574-5000 *10am-7pm, till 6:30pm Sat, 11:30am-5:30pm Sun, lgbt*

Wordsworth 30 Brattle St (at Mt Auburn, in Harvard Square), Cambridge 617/354-5201 *9am-11pm, 10am-10pm Sun, some lgbt titles*

Damron Men's Travel Guide 2004   355

Francesca's [★ MW,WC] 564 Tremont St (at Clarendon) 617/482-9026 *8am-11pm, till midnight wknds, excellent pastries*

Geoffry's Café [BW,GO] 160 Commonwealth Ave 617/266-1122 *9am-10pm, till 11pm wknds, great desserts*

RESTAURANTS

Brandy Pete's 267 Franklin St (at Congress) 617/439-4165 *lunch & dinner Mon-Fri only*

Buddha's Delight 3 Beach St, 2nd flr 617/451-2395 *11am-9:30pm, Chinese, vegetarian*

Casa Romero 30 Gloucester St 617/536-4341 *5pm-10pm, till 11pm wknds, Mexican*

City Girl Caffe [GO] 204 Hampshire St (at Prospect), Cambridge 617/864-2809 *11am-9pm, from 10am wknds, clsd Mon, Italian, great sandwiches*

Club Café [★ MW,E,V,WC] 209 Columbus (at Berkeley) 617/536-0966 *dinner & wknd brunch, also 3 bars*

Flux [★ GO] 1 Appleton St (at Tremont St) 617/695-3589 *5:30pm-midnight, Sun from 4pm, American comfort food*

Icarus 3 Appleton St (off Tremont) 617/426-1790 *dinner only*

Johnny D's [D,E] 17 Holland St (in Davis Square) (at Buckingham) 617/776-2004 *dinner Tue-Sat & wknd brunch, live music nightly*

Laurel 142 Berkeley St (at Columbus) 617/424-6711 *lunch & dinner, Sun brunch*

Rabia's [WC] 73 Salem St (at Cross St) 617/227-6637 *lunch & dinner, fine Italian*

Ristorante Lucia 415 Hanover St 617/367-2353 *great North End pasta*

Trattoria Pulcinella 147 Huron Ave (at Concord), Cambridge 617/491-6336 *fine Italian, cash only*

Massachusetts • USA

RETAIL SHOPS

- ► **City Video** 240 Newbury St (at Fairfield) 617/536-2489 *10am-11pm, lgbt section; also 23 White St, Cambridge (Porter Square Shopping Center), 617/354-7587*

PUBLICATIONS

Bay Windows 617/266-6670 *lgbt newspaper*

► **In Newsweekly** 617/426-8246 *New England's largest lgbt newspaper*

GYMS & HEALTH CLUBS

Metropolitan Fitness [GF] 209 Columbus 617/536-3006

Mike's Gym II [★GO] 560 Harrison Ave (at Waltham St) 617/338-6210, 617/338-6677

MEN'S SERVICES

► **Megaphone Boston** 800/289-1489 *Call for the local # nearest you! Meet Hot Men in your area! FREE to Browse & Respond to voice ads. Use code 3087. Also try MEGAMATES.COM*

EROTICA

Amazing Express 1258 Boylston St (at Ipswich) 617/859-8911 *also 57 Stuart St, 617/338-1252*

Eros Boutique 581-A Tremont St, 2nd flr 617/425-0345 *fetishwear & toys*

Hubba Hubba 534 Massachusetts Ave (at Brookline, in Central Square), Cambridge 617/492-9082 *fetish & drag gear*

Marquis de Sade 92 South St 617/426-2120

CRUISY AREAS

The Esplanade [AYOR] *across foot bridge at end of Dartmouth St. go to the right*

The Fens [AYOR] *near the Ramrod bar*

Brockton

CRUISY AREAS

N end of DW Field Park trails [AYOR]

2004 Damron Men's Travel Guide

Massachusetts • Lawrence

Brookline
see Boston

Cambridge
see Boston

Cape Cod
see also Provincetown listings

■ INFO LINES & SERVICES
Gay/Lesbian AA Cape Cod Hospital (at Whitcomb Pavilion), Hyannis
508/775-7060 *6pm Sun*

■ ACCOMMODATIONS
15 Park Square [M,NS,GO] 15 Park Square (at Main St), Hyannis
508/771-4760 *guest house, shared baths*

The Capeside Cottage B&B [GF,SW,NS] 320 Woods Hole Rd, Woods Hole 508/548-6218, 800/320-2322 *full brkfst*

Gull Cottage [M,WC] 10 Old Church St, Yarmouth Port 508/362-8747 *near beach, shared bths*

Woods Hole Passage [GF] 186 Woods Hole Rd, Falmouth 508/548-9575, 800/790-8976 *full brkfst, near beaches*

■ NIGHTCLUBS
Club 477 [MW,D,MC] 477 Yarmouth Rd, Hyannis 508/775-9835, 800/393-6161 *6pm-1am, Cape Cod's largest gay complex*

■ ENTERTAINMENT & RECREATION
Friday Night Gaymes [M,O,21+,GO] Sagamore 508/888-9278

■ CRUISY AREAS
Boardwalk [AYOR] Jarvis St (off 6-A, exit 1), Sandwich *nights*

Crow's Pasture [AYOR] exit 9 before Suicide Alley (N on 6-A, then right on to Sea St), Dennis *conservation area*

Fresh Pond Conservation Area [AYOR] Rte 134 (at Fresh Pond), Dennis

Kalmus Park Beach [AYOR] end of Ocean St, Hyannis *behind parking lot*

Chelsea
see Boston

Dedham

■ EROTICA
Amazing Express 530 Providence Hwy/ Rte 1 781/320-9377

Greenfield

■ ACCOMMODATIONS
Brandt House [GF] 29 Highland Ave 413/774-3329, 800/235-3329 *full brkfst*

The Charlemont Inn [GF,E,GO] Rte 2, Mohawk Trail, Charlemont 413/339-5796 *restaurant, full bar*

■ BOOKSTORES
World Eye Bookshop 156 Main St 413/772-2186 *9am-7pm, till 8pm Fri, till 6pm Sat, noon-5pm Sun, lgbt section*

Haverhill

■ BARS
Friend's Landing [★,MW,D,F,K,C,WC] 85 Water St 978/374-9400 *6pm-1am, till 2am Fri, clsd Mon, 6 bars, waterfront deck*

Ipswich

■ CRUISY AREAS
Crane's Beach [AYOR] 1/2 mile to the right

Lawrence

■ CRUISY AREAS
The Common [AYOR] near Haverhill St

Ryder Woods Conservation Area [AYOR] Rte 130 to Cotuit Rd (toward Mashpee for 3.5 miles), Sandwich *trails along the lake*

Skaket Beach [AYOR] Dennis *off to the right*

West Side of Sandy Nook Beach [AYOR] Sandwich

Massachusetts • USA

Lincoln

■ ACCOMMODATIONS

Thoreau's Walden B&B [GF] 2 Concord Rd 781/259-1899 *full brkfst, near historic Walden Pond*

Lowell

■ EROTICA

Tower News 101 Gorham St 978/452-8693

Lynn

■ CRUISY AREAS

Moody St [AYOR]

■ BARS

Fran's Place [MW,D,K,S,WC] 776 Washington (at Sagamore) 781/598-5618 *4pm-2am*

The Pub at 47 Central [M,NH,D,L,K,S,GO] 47 Central Ave 781/586-0551 *2pm-2am, DJ wknds*

■ CRUISY AREAS

Lynn Beach [AYOR] Red Rock to Swampscott line

Martha's Vineyard

■ ACCOMMODATIONS

Arbor Inn [GF] 222 Upper Main St, Edgartown 508/627-8137, 888/748-4383 *B&B, some shared baths*

Four Gables [GS,NS] 41 New York Ave, Oak Bluffs 508/696-8384 *inn near beach, sundeck*

MP's [MW,NS,GO] 508/693-0253

The Shiverick Inn [GS,NS,GO] 5 Pease's Pt Wy, Edgartown (at Pent Ln) 508/627-3797, 800/723-4292 *restored 1840 mansion*

Martha's Vineyard (cont.)

■ RESTAURANTS

The Black Dog Tavern [WC] Beach St Extension #21 508/693-9223 *7am-9pm*

Le Grenier 96 Main St, Vineyard Haven 508/693-4906 *5:30pm-close, French*

Louis' Café [GO] 350 State Rd, Vineyard Haven 508/693-3255 *Italian, plenty veggie*

■ BOOKSTORES

Bunch of Grapes 44 Main St, Vineyard Haven 508/693-2291, 800/693-0221 *9am-6pm, some lgbt titles*

Medford

■ EROTICA

Amazing Express 423 Mystic Ave/ Rte 38 781/391-7438

Milton

■ CRUISY AREAS

Blue Hills [AYOR] Wampatuck Rd trails & parking lot

Nantucket

■ ACCOMMODATIONS

The Chestnut House [GF,NS] 3 Chestnut St 508/228-0049 *also cottage*

■ CRUISY AREAS

Dunes W of Surfside [AYOR]

New Bedford

■ BARS

Le Place [★MW,D,K] 20 Kenyon St 508/990-1248 *2pm-2am*

Puzzles [MW,D,F,K,S,WC] 428 N Front St (at Phillips Ave) 508/997-0466 *2:30pm-close, from 4pm Sun-Wed, DJ Fri-Sat, strippers Fri & Mon*

■ ENTERTAINMENT & RECREATION

Horseneck Beach Westport *cruising in the dunes to the right of the main gate*

■ EROTICA

Video Expo 10 Sconticut Square/ Rte 6, Fairhaven 508/991-8191

Northampton • Massachusetts

The Iron Horse [GF,FNS] 20 Center St
413/584-0610 7:30pm-close, live
music, all ages
Pearl Street [GS,D,YC] 10 Pearl St
413/584-7777 7:30pm-1am, live
music

CAFES

Bart's Homemade 235 Main St
413/584-0721 7:30am-11pm, till
midnight Fri-Sat, cafe menu & ice cream
(i)
Haymarket Café [★] 15 Amber Ln
413/586-9969 10am-11pm

RESTAURANTS

Bela [WC,GO] 68 Masonic St
413/586-8011 noon-8:45pm, clsd
Sun-Mon, vegetarian
Cha Cha Cha 134 Main St
413/586-7311 11:30am-10pm, till
11pm Fri-Sat, noon-9pm Sun, Mexican
Green Street Café [BW,GO] 64 Green
St (at Main) 413/586-5650 lunch &
dinner
La Cazuela [BW] 7 Old South St
413/586-0400 5pm-9pm,
Southwestern
Paul & Elizabeth's [BW,WC]
150 Main St (in Thorne's Marketplace)
413/584-4832 lunch & dinner,
seafood

RETAIL SHOPS

Dorset Men's Wear 112 Main St
413/586-6482 club clothes, underwear
Pride & Joy [WC] 20 Crafts Ave
413/585-0683 open 7 days, lgbt books
& gifts

PUBLICATIONS

▶ In Newsweekly 617/426-8246
New England's largest lgbt newspaper
▶ Metroline 860/233-8334 covers
CT, RI & MA

CRUISY AREAS

Northampton Meadows [AYOR] next
to the Connecticut River (dirt roads)
not far from I-91 rest areas
Pulaski Park [AYOR] Main St summer
nights

Newburyport

ACCOMMODATIONS

46 High Road B&B [GS,NS]
46 High Rd, Newbury 978/462-4664
full brkfst

RESTAURANTS

Glenns Restaurant [E,WC] 44 Merrimac
St 978/465-3811 5:30pm-10pm, from
4pm wknds, clsd Mon, bar open till
midnight

CRUISY AREAS

Demarest Lloyd State Park [AYOR]
South Dartmouth, go left out of parking
lot to to end of beach

Newton

see Boston

Northampton

ACCOMMODATIONS

Clarion Hotel & Conference Center
[GF,SW,WC] 1 Atwood Dr
413/586-1211, 800/582-2929
full brkfst, also restaurant & bar
Clark Tavern Inn B&B [GF,SW,NS]
98 Bay Rd, Hadley 413/586-1900
full brkfst
Corner Porches [GS,NS] 82 Baptist
Corner Rd, Ashfield 413/628-4592
full brkfst
The Hotel Northampton [GF,WC]
36 King St 413/584-3100,
800/547-3529 in the heart of down-
town
The McKinley House [MW,GO]
3 McKinley Ave (at Rte 10),
Easthampton 413/527-5116 1900s
Colonial, full brkfst, some shared baths
Old Red Schoolhouse [MW,GO] 67
Park St 413/584-1228 apts & studios

NIGHTCLUBS

Diva's [★,MW,D,S,YC] 492 Pleasant St
(at Conz St) 413/586-8161 8pm-1am,
from 7pm Wed, from 4pm Sun, clsd Mon,
Goth Tue [18+], drag Wed [18+], dancers
Fri [19+], Latin Sun

Massachusetts • USA

Northborough

EROTICA
Amazing Superstore 15 Belmont St/ Rte 9 508/366-3807

Peabody

EROTICA
Amazing Superstore 82 Newbury St/ Rte 1 978/535-7999

Plymouth

ACCOMMODATIONS
Symphony Hollow B&B [GS,GO] 127 Brook St, Plympton 781/585-7823, 888/655-1200 *on 7 acres, full brkfst, gardens, fireplaces*

Provincetown

INFO LINES & SERVICES
➤ **In Town Reservations, Real Estate & Travel** [GO] 4 Standish St 508/487-1883, 800/67P-TOWN (677-8696)

➤ **Provincetown Business Guild** 508/487-2313, 800/637-8696

ACCOMMODATIONS
1807 House [MW,GO] 54 Commercial St (btwn W Vine & Point St) 508/487-2173, 888/522-1807 *50 ft from beach*

➤ **Admiral's Landing Guest House** [M,NS,GO] 158 Bradford St (btwn Conwell & Pearl) 508/487-9665, 800/934-0925 *1840s Greek Revival home & studio efficiencies*

➤ **Aerie House & Beach Club** [MW,GO] 184 Bradford St (at Miller Hill) 508/487-1197, 800/487-1197 *hot tub, sundeck*

---

www.InTownReservations.com

- ▲ Condo & House Rentals
- ▲ B&B & Motel Bookings ▲ Show Tickets
- ▲ Limo Service ▲ Real Estate Sales
- ▲ Local Tours ▲ Full Service Travel Agency
- ▲ Computer Rental Stations

1-800-67P-TOWN ▲ 508-487-1883
4 Standish Street

IN TOWN RESERVATIONS
▲ PROVINCETOWN ▲ PUERTO VALLARTA ▲

PROVINCETOWN 365

A favorite season, your own reasons

Funded in Part by the Provincetown Tourism Board

provincetown BUSINESS GUILD

888.637.8013 for your free Gay Guide to Provincetown

www.ptown.org

The best place to ORGanize your visit!

Massachusetts • USA

➤ **Ampersand Guesthouse** [M,NS,GO] 6 Cottage St **508/487-0959, 800/574-9645** *1880s Greek Revival, sundeck*

Anchor Inn Beach House [★GS,NS,WC] 175 Commercial St **508/487-0432, 800/858-2657** *private beach*

The Archer Inn [M,NS,GO] 26 Bradford St (at Pleasant) **508/487-2529, 800/263-6574** *also cottage, 1930s theme, sundeck*

Bayberry Accommodations [MW,NS,GO] 16 Winthrop St **508/487-4605, 800/422-4605** *newly renovated, award-winning home*

Beachfront Realty 139 Commercial St **508/487-1397** *vacation rentals*

Beaconlight Guest House [★M,NS,GO] 12 Winthrop St **508/487-9603, 800/696-9603** *hot tub, sundecks, parking, award-winning*

Benchmark Inn & Central [MW,SW,NS,WC,GO] 6-8 Dyer St **508/487-7440, 888/487-7440** *hot tub, sauna, harbor views*

➤ **Boatslip Resort** [★M,SW,GO] 161 Commercial St (at Atlantic) **508/487-1669, 800/451-7547** *seasonal, also several bars & popular T-dance*

The Bradford Carver House [MW,NS,GO] 70 Bradford St **508/487-4966, 800/826-9083** *restored mid-19th-c home, centrally located*

Brass Key Guesthouse [★MW,SW,NS,WC,GO] 67 Bradford St (at Carver) **508/487-9005, 800/842-9858** *luxury inn w/ hot tub*

Burch House [GS] 116 Bradford St **508/487-9170** *seasonal, studios, some shared baths*

Cape Inn [GF,SW,WC] **508/487-1711, 800/422-4224** *also restaurant & bar*

ADMIRAL'S LANDING
158 Bradford Street, Provincetown
800.934.0925 508.487.9665
Heated Spa - Fireplaces - Year-Round

WWW.ADMIRALSLANDING.COM

provincetown's premier waterfront resort

your place on the cape

open to the public
sun deck, bar & grill
heated pool
world famous tea dance
waterfront guestrooms
central to area attractions

161 Commercial St., Provincetown, MA 02657 • 508.487.1669
visit our website at GLResorts.com
or call toll free 866.900.3892

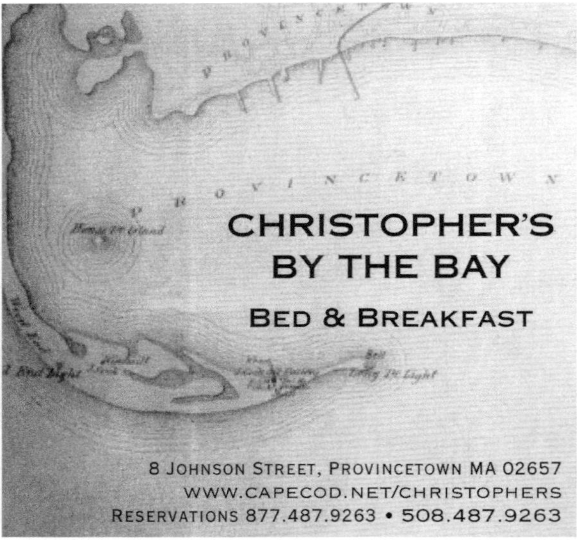

CHRISTOPHER'S BY THE BAY

BED & BREAKFAST

8 JOHNSON STREET, PROVINCETOWN MA 02657
WWW.CAPECOD.NET/CHRISTOPHERS
RESERVATIONS 877.487.9263 • 508.487.9263

· PROVINCETOWN ·
CROWN & ANCHOR
"Your Vacation Party Begins At The Crown"

Walk out your door and be in the center of it all!

A Waterfront Hotel in Provincetown's **Largest** Entertainment Complex.

The Complex Includes
- 19 Hotel Rooms
- 6 Bars • 3 Clubs
- In Ground Heated Pool
- A Full Service Restaurant
- The Largest Show Spaces In P-Town

WWW.ONLYATTHECROWN.COM
508.487.1430
247 COMMERCIAL STREET • P-TOWN, MA 02657

Provincetown • Massachusetts

The Captain & His Ship [GS,GO]
164 Commercial St (btwn Winthrop & Central) 508/487-1850, 800/400-2278 *seasonal, sundeck*

Captain Lysander's Inn [GF]
96 Commercial St (at Mechanic)
508/487-2253 *sundeck w/ harbor view, also apt & cottage*

Captain's House B&B [M,NS,GO]
350-A Commercial St (at Center)
508/487-9353, 800/457-8885 *patio*

Carl's Guest House [MO,N,NS,GO]
68 Bradford St (at Court St)
508/487-1650, 800/348-2275

Carpe Diem Guesthouse [MW,NS,GO]
12 Johnson St 508/487-4242,
800/487-0132 *full German brkfst, hot tub*

The Carriage House Guesthouse
[GS,GO] 7 Central St 508/487-8855,
800/309-0248 *1700s guest house w/ luxurious modern rooms, hot tub*

Chicago House [MW,GO] 6 Winslow St (at Bradford) 508/487-0537,
800/733-7869 *rooms & apts*

➤ **Christopher's by the Bay**
[MW,NS,GO] 8 Johnson St (at Bradford)
508/487-9263, 877/487-9263
full brkfst, some shared baths, patio

The Clarendon House [GS,NS]
118 Bradford St (btwn Ryder & Alden)
508/487-1645, 800/669-8229
also cottage, hot tub, roof deck

Coat of Arms [GS,GO] 7 Johnson St
508/487-0816, 800/224-8230

The Commons Guest House & Bistro
[GS,GO] 386 Commercial St (at Pearl)
508/487-7800, 800/487-0784
deck w/ full bar, also restaurant

➤ **Copper Fox** [GS,GO] 448
Commercial St 508/487-8583
apts & suites

➤ **Crown & Anchor** [MW,SW,NS,GO]
247 Commercial St 508/487-1430
also cabaret & poolside bars

➤ **Crowne Pointe Historic Inn**
[MW,SW,NS,WC,GO] 82 Bradford St
508/487-6767, 877/276-9631
1800s mansion, full brkfst, hot tub, 2 large jacuzzis

Massachusetts • USA

Designer's Dock [GS,GO]
349 Commercial St **508/487-0385, 800/724-9888** *weekly condos in town & on beach, seasonal*

➤ **Dexter's Inn** [MW,NS,GO] 6 Conwell St (at Railroad) **508/487-1911, 888/521-1999** *sundeck*

The Dunes Motel & Apartments [MW] **508/487-1956, 800/475-1833** *seasonal, rooms & apts, decks*

➤ **Elephant Walk Inn** [M,GO] 156 Bradford St (at Conwell) **508/487-2543 or 954/730-0664 (Nov-April), 800/889-9255** *sundeck, parking*

Esther's [GS] 186 Commercial St **508/487-7555, 888/873-5001** *restaurant & piano bar on premises*

➤ **Fairbanks Inn** [★MW,NS,GO] 90 Bradford St **508/487-0386, 800/324-7265** *lesbian-owned/run*

Gabriel's Apartments & Guest Rooms [★MW,N,NS,GO] 104 Bradford St **508/487-3232, 800/969-2643** *full brkfst, hot tub*

The Gallery Inn [M] 3 Johnson St **508/487-3010, 800/676-3010** *seasonal*

Gifford House Inn [MW,GO] 9-11 Carver St **508/487-0688, 800/434-0130** *seasonal, also several bars & 11 Carver restaurant (dinner only, seafood)*

Gracie House [MW,NS] 152 Bradford St (at Conwell) **508/487-4808** *historic, restored Queen Anne*

Grand View Inn [MW,NS,GO] 4 Conant St **508/487-9193, 888/268-9169** *decks*

Harbor Lights of Provincetown [MW,NS,GO] 163 Bradford St (at Law St) **508/487-8246** *1-bdrm apt, parking*

Heritage House [★MW,GO] 7 Center St **508/487-3692** *shared baths*

The Inn at Cook Street [GF,NS,GO] 7 Cook St **508/487-3894, 888/266-5655** *intimate & quiet*

Ireland House [MW,GO] 18 Pearl St (at Arch) **508/487-7132** *1820s B&B*

DEXTER'S INN

circa 1800

A Traditional Cape Cod Guest House

**Private Baths - Sundeck - Parking - TV's - Fridges
Central Location - Airport Pickup - Brochure
OPEN YEAR ROUND
6 Conwell Street, Provincetown, MA 02657
508-487-1911 Toll-free 888-521-1999
email: dextersinn@aol.com
www.ptowndextertsinn.com**

Spacious, elegant, affordable rooms in the heart of Provincetown. Private baths, color tv's, vcr's, phones, refrigerators, optional A/C, sun deck. Parking and continental breakfast.

156 Bradford Street
Provincetown, MA 02657
(508) 487-2543
Reservations: (800) 889-WALK

ELEPHANT WALK INN

email: info@elephantwalkinn.com
website: www.elephantwalkinn.com

THE FAIRBANKS INN

"Exceptional, Exquisite..."
*Five Palms & Editors Choice Award
8 Years Running — Out & About*

"One of the outstanding reasons to visit New England."
—*Yankee Magazine*

"One of the top places to stay in town."
— *Frommer's*

90 Bradford Street, Provincetown
1-800-324-7265   508-487-0386
www.fairbanksinn.com

www.ProvincetownFavorites.com

The Internet Resource to find accommodations. Please visit our website where you will find an extensive range of guest houses and inns with amenities to suit every taste and budget as well as a complete travel Guide to Gay Provincetown.

PROVINCETOWN Favorites!

ADMIRAL'S LANDING
800 934-0925

AERIE HOUSE & BEACH CLUB
800 487-1197

AMPERSAND GUESTHOUSE
800 574-9645

THE COPPER FOX
508-487-8583

DEXTER'S
888 521-1999

PRINCE ALBERT GUEST HOUSE
800 992-0859

REVERE GUESTHOUSE
800 487-2292

SUNSET INN
800 965-1801

THE TUCKER INN
800 477-1867

WATERSHIP INN
800 330-9413

www.ProvincetownFavorites.com

Provincetown • Massachusetts

John Randall House [MW,GO]
140 Bradford St (at Standish)
508/487-3533, 800/573-6700
open year-round

Kensington Gardens [MW,NS,WC,GO]
15 Cottage St **508/487-2620, 888/220-2700**

Labrador Landing [MW,GO]
47 Commercial St **917/597-1500**
luxury cottages on West End

Land's End Inn [GS,NS,GO]
22 Commercial St **508/487-0706, 800/276-7088** *seasonal*

Locust Court [GS] 32 Court St
860/896-1879 *rental home, fireplace, private yard & deck*

Lotus Guest House [MW,GO]
296 Commercial St (at Standish)
508/487-4644, 888/508-4644
seasonal, decks, garden

Moffett House [M,L,GO] 296-A
Commercial St **508/487-6615, 800/990-8865** *levi/ leather-friendly*

The Oxford [MW,NS,GO] 8 Cottage St
508/487-9103, 888/456-9103
newly renovated Revival, parking

➤ **The Prince Albert Guest House**
[M,NS,GO] 166 Commercial St
508/487-0859, 800/992-0859

Provincetown Inn [GS,SW,WC]
1 Commercial St (at Rotary)
508/487-9500, 800/942-5388
waterfront, private beach, poolside bar & grill, theater

Ptown Beach House [GS]
359 Commercial St (btwn Johnson & Center Sts) **941/587-3443** *condo right on waterfront*

➤ **The Ranch Guestlodge** [M,NS,GO]
198 Commercial St **508/487-1542, 800/942-1542** *shared baths, sundeck, also bar*

The Red Inn [GF,NS,WC,GO]
15 Commercial St (at Point)
508/487-7334, 866/473-3466

SNUG COTTAGE

Historic 19th century inn

178 Bradford Street Provincetown
800 432 2334
www.snugcottage.com
email: info@snugcottage.com

GET HOT GET HIP GET COOL GET SERVICED

Provincetown's year-round boutique style guesthouse...
service without the attitude!

GET BOY!!!

Where the boys play and stay while in Ptown

378 Commercial Street, Provincetown, MA 02657
800.575.1850 toll free / 508.487.0383 local
Check out our groovy web page
www.somersethouseinn.com
getserviced@somersethouseinn.com

Surfside Hotel & Suites

Newly Renovated Oceanfront Rooms

Provincetown, MA · 543 Commercial St.
(800) 421-1726 · www.surfsideinn.cc

Stay with us!

Walking distance to P-Town Shops, Restaurants & Marina. Private Beach Visit our New Lighthouse Bar!

Massachusetts • USA

➤ **Revere Guesthouse** [MW,NS,GO] 14 Court St (btwn Commercial & Bradford) **508/487-2292, 800/487-2292** *restored 1820s home, also apt*

Romeo's Holiday [MW,N,GO] 97 Bradford St (btwn Gosnold & Masonic) **508/487-6636, 877/MY-ROMEO** *hot tub*

Roomers [M,GO] 8 Carver St (at Commercial St) **508/487-3532** *seasonal, Greek Revival*

Rose & Crown Guest House [GS,GO] 158 Commercial St **508/487-3332** *also cottage*

Sandpiper Beach House [GS,NS,GO] 165 Commercial St **508/487-1928, 800/354-8628**

Seasons, An Inn for All [MW,NS,GO] 160 Bradford St (at Pearl) **508/487-2283, 800/563-0113** *Victorian B&B, full brkfst*

The Secret Garden Inn [MW] 300-A Commercial St **508/487-9027, 866/786-9646**

Shiremax Inn [MW,GO] 5 Tremont St (btwn Franklin & School) **508/487-1233, 888/744-7362** *seasonal, also apts*

➤ **Snug Cottage** [GS,GO] 178 Bradford St **508/487-1616, 800/432-2334** *boutique B&B*

➤ **Somerset House** [★MW,NS,GO] 378 Commercial St (at Pearl) **508/487-0383, 800/575-1850**

The Stationmaster's Cottage [GS,NS,GO] North Truro **508/487-1329** *cottage w/ ocean view, summers only*

➤ **Sunset Inn** [MW,N,GO] 142 Bradford St (at Center) **508/487-9810, 800/965-1801** *seasonal, some shared baths*

➤ **Surfside Hotel & Suites** [GS,SW] 543 Commercial (at Kendall Ln) **508/487-1726, 800/421-1726** *seasonal, waterfront hotel w/ lots of amenities, private beach*

Fine lodging in the heart of Provincetown.

The Tucker Inn

A Quintessential, Historic B&B

"this place is a real find."
– Fodors Gay Guide to the USA

Heated Spa, Fireplaces, Private Garden

800.477.1867
508.487.0381

12 Center Street
Provincetown

info@theTuckerInn.com
www.TheTuckerInn.com

White Wind Inn
A Provincetown Landmark℠

The Place to see... And be seen

EDITOR'S CHOICE AWARD — OUT & ABOUT

WWW.WHITEWINDINN.COM
174 Commercial Street • 1-888-449-9463

WEST END INN
quiet • intimate • authentic

44 Commercial St., Provincetown, MA 02657
508/487-9555   800/559-1220
www.westendinn.com

Massachusetts • USA

Three Peaks Guest House
[MW,TG,NS,GO] 210 Bradford St (at Howland) **508/487-1717, 800/286-1715** *1870s Victorian, sundeck*

➤ **The Tucker Inn** [MW,NS,GO] 12 Center St **508/487-0381, 800/477-1867** *patio*

Victoria House [MW,WC,GO] 5 Standish St **508/487-4455**

➤ **Watership Inn** [★M,NS,GO] 7 Winthrop St **508/487-0094, 800/330-9413** *sundeck*

➤ **West End Inn** [GF,GO] 44 Commercial St **508/487-9555, 800/559-1220** *seasonal*

➤ **White Wind Inn** [MW,GO] 174 Commercial St (at Winthrop) **508/487-1526, 888/449-9463** *well-appointed*

■BARS

➤ **The Boatslip Beach Resort** [★MW,D,F,YC] 161 Commercial St (at Central) **508/487-1669, 800/451-7547** *seasonal, popular T-dance 3:30pm daily, special events, also restaurant, seafood*

Governor Bradford [GF,F,E,K,DS] 312 Commercial St (at Standish) **508/487-2781** *11am-1am, from noon Sun, 'drag karaoke' in season, also restaurant*

PiedBar [★MW,D,F,E,P,S,WC] 193-A Commercial St (at Court St) **508/487-1527** *seasonal May-Oct, noon-1am, mostly men 6:30pm-9:30pm at After Tea T-Dance*

Porchside Lounge [M,NH,P] 11 Carver St (in the Gifford House accommodations) **508/487-0688** *5pm-1am, lobby lounge from 10pm*

Steve's Alibi [★GS,NH,DS] 291 Commercial St **508/487-2890** *11am-1am, drag shows Wed-Mon in season, local favorite*

➤ **Vault** [M,O,L] 247 Commercial St (downstairs in the Crown & Anchor) **508/487-1430** *9pm-1am*

➤ **Wave Video Bar** [MW,NH,K] 247 Commercial St (in the Crown & Anchor) **508/487-1430** *6pm-1am, from noon in season, karaoke Wed, T-dance Fri-Sat from 6pm*

■NIGHTCLUBS

Atlantic House (The 'A-House') [★M,D] 6 Masonic Pl **508/487-3821** *9pm-1am, weekly theme parties, also The Little Bar [M,NH] & the Macho Room [M,L]*

Club Purgatory [M,D,L] 9-11 Carver St (at Bradford St) **508/487-8442** *9pm-1am, theme nights, popular Sun for Bound*

➤ **Paramount** [★MW,D,E,DS,$] in Crown & Anchor accommodations **508/487-1430** *10pm-1am wknds, seasonal, Power T Sun 6pm-9pm (no cover Sun)*

■CAFES

No Ordinary Joe 148-A Commercial St **508/487-6656** *7:30am-11pm, great coffee w/ a view*

Post Office Cafe Cabaret [MW,E] 303 Commercial St (upstairs) **508/487-3892** *8am-midnight (brkfst till 1pm), call for off-season hours*

■RESTAURANTS

Bayside Betsy's [WC] 177 Commercial St **508/487-0120** *brkfst, lunch & dinner on waterfront, also Mixers Cocktails 11:30am-1am*

Bubala's by the Bay [★] 183-185 Commercial **508/487-0773** *seasonal, 8am-11pm, bar till 1am, patio*

Café Blasé 328 Commercial St **508/487-9465** *brkfst, lunch & dinner, patio, full bar*

Chester [★] 404 Commercial St **508/487-8200** *dinner from 6pm, seasonal*

Ciro & Sal's [R] 4 Kiley Ct (btwn Bangs St & Lovett's Ct) **508/487-6444**

Clem & Ursie's 89 Shank Painter Rd **508/487-2333** *11am-8pm, outdoor dining*

Fanizzi's [★WC] 539 Commercial St **508/487-1964** *seasonal, full bar*

Front Street Restaurant [MW] 230 Commercial St **508/487-9715** *seasonal, bistro 6pm-10:30pm, bar till 1am*

Grand Central [★] 5 Masonic Pl **508/487-7599** *dinner, seasonal, full bar*

Randolph • Massachusetts

L'Uva Restaurant 133 Bradford St
508/487-2010 *classic Mediterranean/ New American, outdoor garden & full bar*

Lobster Pot [WC] 321 Commercial St (harborside) **508/487-0842** *noon-10pm*

Martin House 157 Commercial St **508/487-1327** *6pm-close, clsd Wed, outdoor dining (summers)*

The Mews Restaurant & Cafe [★WC] 429 Commercial St (btwn Lovett's & Kiley) **508/487-1500** *dinner, lunch wknds, also Cafe Mews upstairs*

Napi's Restaurant [WC] 7 Freeman St **508/487-1145, 800/571-6274** *int'l/ seafood*

Sal's Place [★] 99 Commercial St **508/487-1279** *seasonal, seafood/ Italian, deck, on the water*

Spiritus Pizza [★] 190 Commercial St **508/487-2808** *noon-2am, great espresso shakes & late-night hangout for a slice*

Tofu A Go-Go! 336 Commercial St #6 (upstairs) **508/487-6237** *seasonal, lunch & dinner, vegetarian, vegan & macrobiotic*

■ ENTERTAINMENT & RECREATION

Art's Dune Tours [GO] 9 Washington Ave 02657 **508/487-1950, 800/894-1951** *day trips, sunset tours & charters through historic sand dunes & Nat'l Seashore Park*

Ptown Bikes [GO] 42 Bradford **508/487-8735** *rentals*

Spaghetti Strip *nude beach, 1.5 miles S of Race Point Beach*

■ BOOKSTORES

Now, Voyager 357 Commercial St **508/487-0848** *10am-11pm (11am-5pm off-season), lgbt*

Provincetown Bookshop 246 Commercial St **508/487-0964** *10am-11pm (till 5pm off-season)*

■ RETAIL SHOPS

➤ **City Video** 193 Commercial St **508/487-4493** *10am-11pm, lgbt section*

Details in Whalers Wharf **508/487-4474** *10am-11pm (in summer), call for off-season hours, lgbt gifts*

Don't Panic 200 Commercial St **508/487-1280** *seasonal, 10am-10pm, lgbt gifts*

Piercings by the Bearded Lady [GO] 336 Commercial St #4 **508/487-7979** *1pm-7pm, clsd Sun*

■ PUBLICATIONS

➤ **In Newsweekly** 617/426-8246 *New England's largest lgbt newspaper*

Provincetown Banner **508/487-7400** *newspaper*

Provincetown Magazine **508/487-1000** *seasonal, Provincetown's oldest weekly magazine*

■ GYMS & HEALTH CLUBS

Mussel Beach [MW] 35 Bradford St (btwn Montello & Conant) **508/487-0001** *6am-9pm, till 8pm in winter*

Provincetown Gym [MW] 82 Shank Painter Rd (at Winthrop) **508/487-2776**

■ EROTICA

MG Leather Inc [GO] 338 Commercial St (at Standish St) **508/487-4036** *11am-6pm, leather, fetish*

■ CRUISY AREAS

The Boatyard [AYOR] behind Boatslip Beach Club *late*

Herring Cove Beach [AYOR]

Quincy

see also Boston

■ RETAIL SHOPS

Body Xtremes 414 Hancock St, North Quincy **617/471-5836** *body piercing & jewelry; also The Xtreme tattoo parlor across the street (617/ 984-0956)*

Randolph

■ BARS

Randolph Country Club [★MW,D,F,K,C,S,V,SW,WC] 44 Mazzeo Dr **781/961-2414** *2pm-2am, from 10am summer, 2 dance clubs, volleyball*

Massachusetts • *USA*

Reading

■EROTICA
Video Expo 1349 Main St/ Rte 28
781/942-7804

Saugus

■NIGHTCLUBS
Vision [GF,D,S,18+] 168 Broadway (Rte 1 N, Godfried's Plaza) **781/231-5111** *from 10pm, occasional gay after-hours parties*

■RETAIL SHOPS
➤ **City Video** Godfried's Plaza, Rte 1 N **781/231-2993** *10am-11pm, lgbt & large adult video selection*

Somerville
see Boston

Springfield

■INFO LINES & SERVICES
Gay/ Lesbian Info Service
413/731-5403

■BARS
Hob Nob Cafe/ Daddy's [M,NH,L] 234 Chestnut St (E of Main) **413/785-1234** *11am-2am, Daddy's open 9pm-2am Fri-Sat only*

Judge's Chambers [M] 405 Dwight St, 2nd flr **413/743-0566** *6pm-2am*

➤ **Pub/ Quarry** [MW,NH,D,S,WC] 382 Dwight (at Taylor) **413/734-8123** *2pm-2am, from noon wknds, also The Krypt 2nd & 4th Sat [MO,L]*

■NIGHTCLUBS
Xstatic [M,D,DS,S] 240 Chestnut St **413/736-2618** *9pm-2am Wed-Sat, from 6pm Sun*

■EROTICA
Video Expo 486-B Bridge St
413/747-9812

The Pub

MASS OLDEST 32 YEARS

382 Dwight St.
Springfield, MA 01103
413/734-8123
Weekdays 2-2
Sat & Sun Noon - 2 AM

WMASS LARGEST 8,000 Sq. Ft.

Underground
The Quarry Saloon
Leather/Levi bar
Thur - Sat 9 PM - 2 AM

Satan's Lair Dance Bar
Fri & Sat 9 PM - 2 AM

Ann Arbor • Michigan

Stoneham

■ CRUISY AREAS

Sheep's Fold Conservation Area [AYOR] Rte I-93 exit 33 (off Rte 28) *top of the hills*

Waltham

■ BOOKSTORES

Synchronicity Transgender Bookstore 14 Felton St (at Moody) **781/899-2212** *over 100 TG titles*

■ EROTICA

Video Expo 465 Moody St **781/894-5063**

Ware

■ ACCOMMODATIONS

The Wildwood Inn [GS,NS,WC] 121 Church St **413/967-7798, 800/860-8098** *1880s Victorian, full brkfst, some shared baths*

Watertown

see also Boston

■ CRUISY AREAS

Bird Sanctuary [AYOR] near VFW Hall along the Charles River

Weymouth

■ EROTICA

Amazing Express 138 Bridge St, North Weymouth **781/335-0446**

Williamstown

■ ACCOMMODATIONS

River Bend Farm B&B [GF] 643 Simonds Rd **413/458-3121** *historic home, seasonal*

Worcester

■ INFO LINES & SERVICES

AA Gay/ Lesbian 1 Freeland St **508/752-9000** *7pm Sat*

■ BARS

MB Lounge [M,NH,WC] 40 Grafton St (at Franklin) **508/799-4521** *3pm-2am*

■ NIGHTCLUBS

Art Bar [★GF,D,S,WC] 90 Commercial St **508/754-7742** *9pm-2am, clsd Mon, more gay Tue only*

■ RETAIL SHOPS

Glamour Boutique 850 Southbridge St, Auburn **508/721-7800** *noon-8pm, call for Sun hours, large-size dresses, wigs, etc*

■ GYMS & HEALTH CLUBS

Midtown Athletic Club [GF] 22 Front St, 2nd flr (in Midtown Mall) **508/798-9703**

MICHIGAN

Statewide

■ PUBLICATIONS

Between the Lines **248/615-7003, 888/615-7003** *lgbt weekly*

➤ **Cruise Magazine** **248/545-9040** *gay entertainment listings*

Out Post **313/702-0272** *bi-weekly nightlife guide for SE Michigan*

Ann Arbor

■ INFO LINES & SERVICES

Lesbian/ Gay AA **734/482-5700**

■ BARS

\'aut\ Bar [★MW,NH,F,WC] 315 Braun Ct (at Catherine) **734/994-3677** *4pm-2am, from 10am Sun (brunch), 2 flrs, patio, also restaurant, American/ Mexican*

■ NIGHTCLUBS

The Nectarine [GS,D,V,18+,YC] 516 E Liberty **734/994-5436** *9pm-2am, Tue '80s night & Fri gay night*

■ RESTAURANTS

Dominick's [WC] 812 Monroe St (at Tappan Ave) **734/662-5414** *10am-10pm, Italian, full bar*

The Earle [BW,WC] 121 W Washington (at Ashley) **734/994-0211** *6pm-10pm, till midnight Fri-Sat, clsd Sun (summer), cont'l*

Seva 314 E Liberty **734/662-1111** *11am-9pm, from 10am wknds, vegetarian, also cafe & wine bar*

Michigan • USA

■ ENTERTAINMENT & RECREATION

The Ark [GF,S] 316 S Main St (btwn William & Liberty) **734/761-1451** *concert house*

■ BOOKSTORES

Common Language [WC] 215 S 4th Ave (at Liberty) **734/663-0036** *open daily, lgbt*

Crazy Wisdom Books 114 S Main (btwn Huron & Washington) **734/665-2757** *10am-10pm, till 11pm Wed-Sat, 11am-7pm Sun, holistic & metaphysical*

Nicola's Books 2513 Jackson Rd (at Maple, in Westgate) **734/662-4110**

Battle Creek

■ NIGHTCLUBS

Partners [MW,D,K,WC] 910 North Ave (at Morgan) **269/964-7276** *6pm-2am*

■ EROTICA

Eastown Capri 686 W Michigan (at Grand) **269/964-3070**

Bellaire

■ ACCOMMODATIONS

Bellaire B&B [GS,GO] 212 Park St (at Antrim) **231/533-6077, 800/545-0780** *stately 1879 home*

Coldwater

■ EROTICA

➤ **The Lion's Den Adult Bookstore** 570 Jonesville Rd (exit 16, off I-69) **517/278-9577** *24hrs*

Detroit

■ INFO LINES & SERVICES

Affirmations Lesbian/ Gay Community Center 195 W 9-Mile Rd (at Woodward), Ferndale **248/398-7105** *9am-9pm, till 5pm Sat, 1pm-9pm Sun*

■ ACCOMMODATIONS

The Atheneum Suite Hotel [GF,WC] 1000 Brush St (at Lafayette) **313/962-2323, 800/772-2323** *luxury hotel, restaurant & lounge, gym*

Milner Hotel [GF] 1538 Centre St **313/963-3950, 800/521-0592** *downtown*

Shorecrest Motor Inn [GF,WC] 1316 E Jefferson Ave **313/568-3000, 800/992-9616** *downtown, also restaurant*

Woodbridge Star B&B [GS,NS] 3985 Trumbull Ave **313/831-9668**

■ BARS

Adam's Apple [M,NH] 18937 W Warren (at Artesian) **313/240-8482** *3pm-2am*

Club Gold Coast [★M,D,S,WC] 2971 E 7-Mile Rd (at Conant) **313/366-6135** *7pm-2am*

Detroit Eagle [★M,D,L,WC] 1501 Holden (at Trumbull) **313/873-6969** *8pm-2am, from 5pm Fri & Sun, clsd Mon-Tue, patio*

Diamond Jim's Saloon [M,NH,D,CW,B,L,MR,K,GO] 19650 Warren (1 blk E of Evergreen) **313/336-8680** *3pm-2am, clsd Mon, dance lessons*

Gigi's [M,D,TG,K,D,S,GO] 16920 W Warren (at Clayburn, enter rear) **313/584-6525** *noon-2am, from 2pm wknds, dancers Mon & Fri, karaoke Sun, drag shows Sat, talent contest Battle of the Bitches Th*

Hayloft Saloon [M,NH,B,OC,WC] 8070 Greenfield Rd (S of Joy Rd) **313/581-8913** *3pm-2am, levi/ leather bar*

Male Box [M,NH,D,K,GO] 3537 E 7-Mile Rd (btwn Conant & Ryan) **313/892-5420** *2pm-2am, CW Wed, Sun T-dance*

Detroit • Michigan

Menjo's [★M,D,V,YC] 928 W McNichols (at Hamilton) **313/863-3934** *noon-10pm, till 2am Wed-Sun, popular happy hour*

Pronto [★MW,F,V] 608 S Washington (at 6th St), Royal Oak **248/544-7900** *10am-2am Wed-Sat, till midnight Sun-Tue, also cafe*

R&R Saloon [M,D,L,F] 7330 Michigan Ave (at Central) **313/849-2751** *2pm-2am*

Rattlebox [★M,F,K] 8832 Greenfield Rd (at Joy) **313/273-2224** *4pm-2am, after-hours Sat, from 2pm Sun*

Stingers Lounge [MW,NH,F,DS,GO] 19404 Sherwood (at 7-Mile) **313/892-1765** *6pm-5am, from 8pm wknds*

Vibrations [M,MR-AF,F] 12327 Gratiot Ave (btwn Outer Dr & Houston-Whittier) **313/526-8423** *9pm-2am, from 6pm Sun*

The Woodward Bar & Grill [★M,F,K] 6426 Woodward Ave (at Milwaukee, rear entrance) **313/872-0166** *2pm-2am, lounge*

The Works [M,D,V] 1846 Michigan Ave (at Rosa Parks) **313/961-1742** *5:30pm-2am, till 4am Fri, till 6am Sat, clsd Sun*

■ NIGHTCLUBS

Backstreet [★M,D,18+,WC,$] 15606 Joy Rd (at Greenfield) **313/493-7595** *9pm-2am Wed & Sat, 5 levels*

Numbers [M,D,MR,F,V,YC] 17518 Woodward (at McNichols) **313/868-9145, 313/869-9524** *10pm-4am, clsd Mon*

Off Broadway East [M,D,MR,YC] 12215 Harper Ave (at Dickerson) **313/521-0920** *9pm-2am, Wed & Sat popular*

Q [M,D,18+] 141 W 9 Mile (at Woodward), Ferndale **248/582-7227** *9pm-close Wed & Fri-Sun*

The Rainbow Room [MW,D,K,DS] 6640 E 8-Mile Rd (at Mound) **313/891-1020** *7pm-2am Wed-Sun*

Stiletto's [W,D,E] 1641 Middlebelt Rd (at Michigan Ave), Inkster **734/729-8980** *8pm-2am Th-Sun*

Temple [M,D,TG,MR-AF,DS,WC] 2906 Cass Ave (btwn Charlotte & Temple) **313/832-2822** *11am-2am, popular wknds*

Zippers [★MW,D,MR-AF,S,WC] 6221 E Davison (at Mound) **313/892-8120** *9pm-2am Fri-Sun*

■ CAFES

Avalon Bakery [GO] 422 W Willis (at Cass) **313/832-0008** *6am-6pm, clsd Sun-Mon*

■ RESTAURANTS

Cass Cafe 4260 Cass Ave (at Forest) **313/831-1400** *11am-2am, 5pm-midnight Sun, full bar*

Como's [WC] 22812 Woodward (at 9-Mile), Ferndale **248/548-5005** *11am-2am, till 3:30am Th-Sat, Italian, full bar*

La Dolce Vita [MW,WC] 17546 Woodward Ave (at McNichols) **313/865-0331** *lunch & dinner, Sun brunch, clsd Mon, Italian, patio*

Sweet Lorraines [WC] 29101 Greenfield Rd (at 12-Mile), Southfield **248/559-5985** *11am-10pm, till midnight Fri-Sat*

Twingo's [GO] 4710 Cass Ave **313/832-3832** *11am-11pm, till 2am Th-Sat, till 8pm Sun, nouvelle French, full bar, live jazz Fri-Sat*

Vivio's 2460 Market St (btwn Gratiot & Russell) **313/393-1711** *lunch & dinner, clsd Sun, Italian, full bar*

■ BOOKSTORES

Chosen Books [WC] 120 W 4th St (btwn Main St & Woodward), Royal Oak **248/543-5758** *noon-10pm, lgbt*

Just 4 Us 211 W 9-Mile Rd (at Woodward), Ferndale **248/547-5878** *clsd Sun, also espresso bar*

■ RETAIL SHOPS

The Dressing Room 42621 Garfield Rd, Clinton Township **586/280-0412** *1pm-8pm, noon-5pm Sat, clsd Sun, cross-dressing boutique*

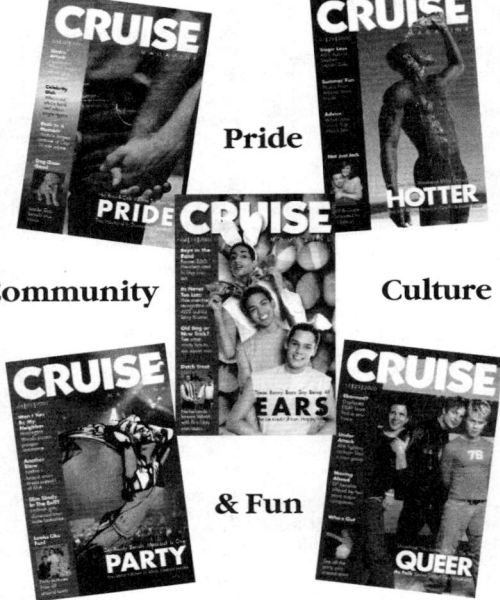

BODY ZONE

Metro Detroit's busiest Gay Health Club with the HOTTEST GUYS. Tourists welcome with temporary membership. Open 24-7. Huge steam room, whrilpool, gym, TV & video lounge, tanning, pool table, lockers, 75 plus rooms, TV rooms w/12 channels, digital stereo, & monthly theme nights.

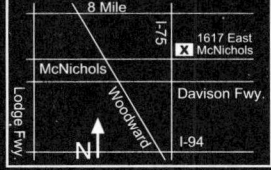

THE HOTTEST PLACE TO BE IN DETROIT!

**1617 E. McNICHOLS @ I-75
DETROIT · 313-366-9663
PRIVATE GAY HEALTH CLUB ·
MEMBERSHIP REQUIRED · 18+ ONLY**

Michigan • USA

■Publications

Between the Lines 248/615-7003, 888/615-7003 *statewide lgbt weekly*

➤ **Cruise Magazine** 248/545-9040 *statewide gay entertainment listings*

Metra 248/543-3500 *covers IN, IL, MI, OH, PA, WI & Ontario, Canada*

■Men's Clubs

➤ **Body Zone** [★V,PC] 1617 E McNichols (at I-75) 313/366-9663 *24hrs, gym & steam, sauna & tanning, $7 day pass*

TNT Health Club [★MO,V,18+,PC,GO,$] 13333 W 8-Mile Rd (at Schaefer, enter rear) 313/341-5322 *24hrs*

■Men's Services

The Confidential Connection®! 313/962-7070 *The hottest local guys! 18+ Record & Listen FREE! Use access code 499.*

The Gay Connection 900/468-6338 *Talk and/or meet with other men from the area, at only 99¢ per minute.*

➤ **Megaphone Detroit** 800/289-1489 *Call for the local # nearest you! Meet Hot Men in your area! FREE to Browse & Respond to voice ads. Use code 3087. Also try MEGAMATES.COM*

Voice MALE 313/237-0500 *The city's hottest & wildest all-male voice club. Chat one on one! Use access code 5111*

■Erotica

24hr Video 17438 Woodward Ave (N of McNichols Rd) 313/869-2955 *11am-4am*

Escape Adult Bookstore 18728 W Warren (8 blks W of Southfield) 313/336-6558

Fifth Wheel Adult Books 9320 Michigan Ave (at Wyoming) 313/846-8613

Noir Leather [WC] 124 W 4th (at Center), Royal Oak 248/541-3979

Uptown Book Store 16541 Woodward Ave (at 6-Mile Rd) 313/869-9477

Flint

■Bars

Club MI [★MW,D,S,MR] 2402 N Franklin St (at Davison) 810/234-9481 *1pm-2am*

Pachyderm Pub [MW,NH,D,MR,TG,F,P,GO] G-1408 E Hemphill Rd (btwn I-475 & Saginaw St), Burton 810/744-4960 *3pm-2am, video bar & restaurant, outdoor courtyard, T-dance Sun & Wed*

State Bar [★MW,D,K,WC] 2510 S Dort Hwy 810/767-7050 *3pm-2am*

■Nightclubs

Club Quorum [M,D,S,MR-AF,BYOB] 3212 N Saginaw St (at McClellan) 810/789-7940 *10:30pm-3am Fri only*

Club Triangle [★MW,D,18+] 2101 S Dort (at Lippincott) 810/767-7550 *7pm-2am, clsd Mon*

■Cafes

The Good Beans Cafe [E,WC,GO] 328 N Grand Traverse (at 1st Ave) 810/237-4663 *7:30am-4pm, till 9pm Th-Fri, open some wknds*

■Retail Shops

Margo's 11394 N Saginaw (10 miles N of Flint), Clio 810/670-6218 *10am-6pm Tue-Sat, leather, apparel & motorcycle parts*

Grand Rapids

■Bars

The Apartment [M,NH,WC] 33 Sheldon NE (at Library) 616/451-0815 *noon-2am, from 2pm Sun*

Diversions [★MW,D,S,V,18+,WC] 10 Fountain St NW (at Division) 616/451-3800 *8pm-2am, also cafe*

■Nightclubs

The Carousel [M,D,S,WC] 76 S Division St (at Oakes) 616/454-4499 *2pm-2am, from 4pm wknds*

■Cafes

Discussions [E,K,GO,WC] 6 Jefferson SE (at Fulton) 616/456-5060 *8:30am-2am, till midnight Sun, from 10am wknds*

Mount Pleasant • Michigan

■ RESTAURANTS

Brandywine 1345 Lake Drive SE (in East town) **616/774-8641** *lunch & dinner*

Gaia Cafe 208 Diamond Ave SE (at Lake) **616/454-6233** *8am-8pm, till 3pm wknds, clsd Mon, vegetarian*

■ MEN'S CLUBS

Diplomat Health Club [PC] 2324 S Division Ave (at Whithey) **616/452-3754** *24hrs*

■ MEN'S SERVICES

➤ **Megaphone Grand Rapids** **800/289-1489** *Call for the local # nearest you! Meet Hot Men in your area! FREE to Browse & Respond to voice ads. Use code 3087. Also try MEGAMATES.COM*

■ EROTICA

Cini-Mini I 1358 Plainfield NE (at Spencer) **616/454-2444** *also Cini-Mini II at 415 Bridge St NW, 616/454-7531*

Houghton

■ EROTICA

Backroom Multi Entertainment [GO] 109 Sheldon Ave (at Bridge) **906/482-0637**

Jackson

■ CRUISY AREAS

Michigan Ave [AYOR] btwn Jackson & Mechanic Sts

Kalamazoo

■ INFO LINES & SERVICES

Kalamazoo Gay/ Lesbian Resource Center 629 Pioneer St **269/349-4234, 888/377-7271** *educational/ support groups, youth group, hotline*

■ BARS

Tradewinds [MW,NH,D] 562 Portage St (at Walnut) **269/383-1814** *4pm-2am, theme nights*

■ NIGHTCLUBS

Brother's Bar [MW,D,K,S,PC] 209 Stockbridge (btwn Portage & Burdick) **269/345-1960** *2pm-2am, patio*

The Zoo [M,D,K,18+] 906 Portage St (at Vine) **269/385-9191, 269/342-4229** *4pm-2am*

■ EROTICA

Triangle World [WC] 551 Portage Rd (at Walnut) **269/373-4005**

Lansing

■ INFO LINES & SERVICES

Lansing Lesbian/ Gay Hotline **517/332-3200** *7pm-10pm, 2pm-5pm Sun, clsd Sat*

■ BARS

Esquire [MW,NH] 1250 Turner (at Clinton) **517/487-5338** *3pm-2am, from noon Wed & Sat*

■ NIGHTCLUBS

Spiral [M,D,V,18+] 1247 Center St (at Clinton) **517/371-3221, 866/477-4725** *8pm-2am, clsd Mon, theme nights*

X-cel [M,D,S,YC] 224 S Washington Square **517/484-2399** *9pm-2am, clsd Mon*

■ BOOKSTORES

Community News Center [WC] 418 Frandor Shopping Center **517/351-7562** *9am-9pm, till 7pm Sun*

Marquette

■ BOOKSTORES

Sweet Violets 413 N 3rd St (btwn Michigan & Arch) **906/228-3307** *10am-6pm, clsd Sun, feminist, some gay men's titles*

■ EROTICA

Backroom Obsessions [GO] 215 S Front St (at Main) **906/458-2116**

■ CRUISY AREAS

Presque Isle Point [AYOR]

Shinas Park—Picnic Rocks [AYOR]

Mount Pleasant

■ CRUISY AREAS

Chipwater Park [AYOR] *summers*

Michigan • USA

Petoskey

■ CRUISY AREAS
Rotary Point [AYOR]
opposite Holiday Inn

Pontiac

■ NIGHTCLUBS
Club Flamingo [MW,D,S,WC]
352 Oakland Ave (at Montcalm)
248/253-0430 4pm-2am, from 2pm Sat

■ CRUISY AREAS
Dog Run [AYOR] Clarkston

Port Huron

■ NIGHTCLUBS
Seekers [MW,D,S] 3301 24th St (btwn Oak & Little) **810/985-9349** 7pm-2am, from 4pm Fri-Sat, from 2pm Sun

■ CRUISY AREAS
Lighthouse Beach [AYOR]
Pine Grove Park [AYOR]

Saugatuck

■ ACCOMMODATIONS
The Bunkhouse B&B [MW,SW,GO]
269/543-4335, 877/226-7481

Campit Campground [MW,SW,GO]
269/543-4335, 877/226-7481
seasonal, campsites & RV hookups, also B&B

The Country Place Inn [GS,SW]
2135 Blue Star Hwy, Fennville
269/857-4535, 877/694-4963
Victorian country estate, full brkfst, hot tub, massage therapy

Douglas House B&B [GS,GO]
41 Spring St, Douglas **269/857-1119, 313/922-4220** *near gay beach*

➤ **The Dunes Resort**
[MW,D,TG,F,E,DS,SW,WC,GO] 333 Blue Star Hwy, Douglas **269/857-1401**
motel & cottages, open year-round

Hunter's Lodge [GS,GO] 2790 Blue Star Hwy (at US 31), Douglas
269/857-5402

A boutique motel with retro charm!

A wonderful choice for discriminating travelers seeking a Lake Michigan cottage atmosphere with the Saugatuck/Douglas amenities and nightlife within easy walking distance.

56 Blue Star Hwy. • Douglas, MI 49406
(269) 857-5211
www.thepinesmotorlodge.com

Michigan • USA

Kirby House [GS,SW,NS,GO] 294 W Center (at Blue Star Hwy) **269/857-2904, 800/521-6473** *full brkfst, Queen Anne manor*

Moore's Creek Inn [GS,NS] 820 Holland St (at Lucy) **269/857-5241** *full brkfst, old-fashioned farmhouse*

➤ **The Pines Motor Lodge** [GS,NS,GO] 56 Blue Star Hwy (at Center St), Douglas **269/857-5211** *quaint '50s-style motel, also retro gift gallery*

The Spruce Cutter's Cottage [GS,GO] 6670 126th Ave (at Blue Star Hwy & M-89), Fennville **269/543-4285, 800/493-5888**

Timber Bluff 2731 Lakeshore Dr, Fennville **269/857-2586** *cottages on Lake Michigan, short drive to Saugatuck*

■ BARS

➤ **Dunes Disco** [MW,D,TG,E,C,DS,GO] 333 Blue Star Hwy (at the Dunes Resort) **269/857-1401** *9am-2am, 6 bars, cabaret, patio*

■ CAFES

Uncommon Grounds 127 Hoffman (at Water) **269/857-3333** *7:30am-9:30pm, open later on wknds, coffee & juice bar*

The Yum Yum Gourmet Cafe [GS,GO] 98 Center St, lower level (at Union St), Douglas **269/857-4567** *ice cream, gelato, sorbet*

■ RESTAURANTS

Blue Frog To Go [MW] in the Dunes Resort **269/857-1401 x143** *11am-7pm, till 9pm Fri-Sat, open May-Oct only, take-out only*

Pumpernickel's 202 Butler St (at Mason) **269/857-1196** *seasonal, 8am-3pm (clsd Wed in winter), sandwiches & fresh breads*

Restaurant Toulouse [WC] 248 Culver St (at Griffith) **269/857-1561** *dinner, country French, full bar*

■ RETAIL SHOPS

Circa Antiques, Arts & Accessories [GO] 98 Center St (at Union St), Douglas **269/857-7676** *antiques, arts, furnishings & accessories from a range of periods*

Glitter and Garden [GO] 98 Center St, lower level (at Union St), Douglas **269/857-4567** *garden & holiday shop, unique items & gifts*

Groovy! Groovy! Retro Gift Gallery [GO] 56 Blue Star Hwy (at Center St), Douglas **269/857-2171** *funky gifts & goods*

Hoopdee Scootee 133 Mason (at Butler) **269/857-4141** *10am-9pm, till 6pm Sun (till 5pm in winter), clothing, gifts*

■ CRUISY AREAS

Oval Beach [AYOR] *walk north*

Park on Water St [AYOR]

Sault Ste-Marie

■ BOOKSTORES

Open Mind Books 223 Ashmun St (at Ridge) **906/635-9008, 877/635-9008** *11am-5pm, clsd Sun-Mon, progressive*

Sawyer

■ EROTICA

➤ **The Lion's Den Adult Bookstore** **269/426-6099**

South Haven

■ ACCOMMODATIONS

Yelton Manor B&B [GS,NS,WC] 140 North Shore Dr (at Dyckman) **269/637-5220** *full brkfst, jacuzzi*

St Clair

■ ACCOMMODATIONS

William Hopkins Manor [GF] 613 N Riverside Ave **810/329-0188** *full brkfst*

Traverse City

■ ACCOMMODATIONS

Neahtawanta Inn [GF,SW,WC] 1308 Neahtawanta Rd **231/223-7315** *sauna*

■ NIGHTCLUBS

Side Traxx Nite Club [MW,D,WC] 520 Franklin **231/935-1666** *8pm-2am*

Hinckley • Minnesota

■BOOKSTORES
The Bookie Joint 120 S Union St (btwn State & Front) **231/946-8862** *10am-6pm, 11am-5pm Sat, clsd Sun, pride gifts, used books*

■CRUISY AREAS
Bryant Park [AYOR]

Westend Beach

Union Pier

■ACCOMMODATIONS
Blue Fish Guest House & Cottage [GS,NS,GO] 16070 Lake Shore Rd (at Union Pier Rd) **269/469-2907** *cottage & guest house available*

Fire Fly Resort [GS,NS,GO] 15657 Lakeshore Rd **269/469-0245** *1 & 2-bdrm units*

Westland

■CRUISY AREAS
Wm P Holliday Park [AYOR] *summers*

Ypsilanti

■EROTICA
Cross Street Video 515 W Cross **734/482-6944**

MINNESOTA

Albert Lea

■ACCOMMODATIONS
Days Inn Albert Lea [GS,SW,WC] 2306 E Main St (at 35W) **507/373-6471**

Bemidji

■CRUISY AREAS
Diamond Point Park [AYOR] *summers*

The Indian Trail [AYOR] *below Lake Blvd (btwn 10th & 12th St)*

Brainerd

■ACCOMMODATIONS
Hallett House B&B [GS,GO] 22418 Hwy 6, Deerwood **218/546-5433, 877/546-5433** *B&B, located on 13 private acres, full brkfst, jacuzzi, fireplaces*

Duluth

see also Superior, Wisconsin

■ACCOMMODATIONS
Stanford Inn B&B [GF,GO] 1415 E Superior St **218/724-3044** *full brkfst*

■BOOKSTORES
At Sara's Table [WC] 1902 E 8th **218/723-8569** *9am-6pm, clsd Tue in winter, also cafe*

■EROTICA
Wabash Books 114 E 1st **218/723-1980**

■CRUISY AREAS
Leif Ericsson Park [AYOR]

Park Point Beach [AYOR] *summers*

Edina

■CAFES
Cafe Nikita 3940 W 50th St (W of France Ave, in the Edina 5-0 Mall) **952/848-1655** *8am-6pm, till 5pm Sat, clsd Sun, brkfst & lunch*

Ely

■ACCOMMODATIONS
Log Cabin Hideaways [GF,NS] 1321 N Hwy 21 **218/365-6045** *remote wilderness cabins, wood-fired sauna & hot tub, no running water/ electricity*

Grand Marais

■ACCOMMODATIONS
Snuggle Inn B&B [GF,NS,GO] 8 Seventh Ave W (at Hwy 61) **218/387-2847, 800/823-3174**

Hastings

■ACCOMMODATIONS
Thorwood & Rosewood Inns [GF,NS,WC] 315 Pine St (at 4th) **651/437-3297, 888/846-7966** *full brkfst*

Hinckley

■ACCOMMODATIONS
Dakota Lodge B&B [GS,NS,WC] **320/384-6052** *full brkfst, hot tub, fireplaces*

Minnesota • USA

Kenyon

ACCOMMODATIONS
Dancing Winds Farmstay Retreat [GS,NS,GO] 6863 County 12 Blvd **507/789-6606** *B&B & working dairy farm, also tentsites, work exchange*

Mankato

CAFES
The Coffee Hag [E,WC] 329 N Riverfront **507/387-5533** *7:30am-11pm, till midnight Fri, 9am-midnight Sat, clsd Mon*

EROTICA
Pure Pleasure 2102 N Riverfront Dr **507/388-6871** *24hrs*

Minneapolis/ St Paul

INFO LINES & SERVICES
AA Intergroup 7204 W 27th St, Ste 113, St Louis Park **952/922-0880**

OutFront Minnesota 310 38th St E #204, Minneapolis **612/822-0127, 800/800-0350** *info line w/ 24 hr pre-recorded visitor info*

ACCOMMODATIONS
Cover Park Manor [GF,NS] 15330 58th St N (at Peller), Stillwater **651/430-9292, 877/430-9292** *full brkfst, in-room jacuzzi & fireplace*

➤ **Hotel Amsterdam** [M,GO] 828 Hennepin Ave (btwn 8th & 9th), Minneapolis **612/288-0459** *shared baths*

Millennium Hotel Minneapolis [GF,F,SW,WC] 1313 Nicollet Mall (btwn W Grant & 13th St), Minneapolis **612/332-6000, 800/522-8856**

hotel**amsterdam**
the inn that's **out**

for information and reservations telephone 612.288.0459

conveniently located above The Saloon bar.

9th & hennepin ▼ downtown minneapolis
www.gaympls.com

Minneapolis/ St Paul • Minnesota

■ BARS

19 Bar [M,NH,BW,WC] 19 W 15th St (at La Salle), Minneapolis 612/871-5553 3pm-1am, from 1pm wknds

Bev's Wine Bar [GF] 250 3rd Ave N (at Washington Ave), Minneapolis 612/337-0102 4:30pm-1am, from 6pm Sat, clsd Sun-Mon, patio

Boom [M,F,V,GO] 401 E Hennepin Ave (at 4th), Minneapolis 612/378-3188 4pm-1am, also Oddfellows

Brass Rail [★M,K,DS,P,S,V,WC] 422 Hennepin Ave (at 4th), Minneapolis 612/333-3016 noon-1am, from 11am Sun, karaoke Wed, dancers Th-Sat

Bryant Lake Bowl [GF,A,F,E,WC] 1810 W Lake St (at corner of Bryant), Minneapolis 612/825-3737 8am-1am, bar, theater & bowling alley

Jetset [MW,NS] 115 N First St, Minneapolis 612/339-3933 5pm-close, clsd Sun-Mon, upscale

Minneapolis Eagle [M,L,F] 515 Washington Ave S (btwn Portland & 5th Ave), Minneapolis 612/338-4214 11am-1am, till 3am Fri-Sat, from noon wknds, patio, dress code enforced from 9pm Fri-Sat

Over the Rainbow [MW,D,F,K,S,GO] 719 N Dale St (at Minnehaha), St Paul 651/487-5070 11am-1am

Times Bar/ Jitters [GF,E,K,C] 201 & 205 E Hennepin Ave (at 2nd St NE), Minneapolis 612/617-8098 11am-1am, also cafe & restaurant

The Town House [★MW,D,E,C,DS,P] 1415 University Ave (at Elbert), St Paul 651/646-7087 3pm-1am, from noon wknds, theme nights, piano lounge from 9pm Th-Sat

Trikkx [M,D,F,S,WC] 490 N Robert St (at 9th St), St Paul 651/224-0703 4pm-1am, till 2am wknds, bear party 4th Fri, also restaurant

■ NIGHTCLUBS

The Bolt [M,D,MR,F,WC,GO] 513 Washington Ave S (at Portland), Minneapolis 612/338-4214 7pm-1am, till 3am Fri-Sat

Gay 90s [★MW,D,MR,E,K,DS,WC] 408 Hennepin Ave (at 4th), Minneapolis 612/333-7755 8am-1am (dinner nightly), 9-bar complex, also Men's Room [MO,L]

Ground Zero/ The Front [★GS,D,S,WC] 15 NE 4th St (at Hennepin), Minneapolis 612/378-5115 9pm-1am, clsd Sun-Tue, more gay Th & Sat for Bondage-A-Go-Go, also The Front from 8pm

Lucy's [MW,D,K,S,GO] 601 N Western Ave (at Thomas Ave), St Paul 651/228-9959 3pm-1am, from noon wknds, go-go boys Fri

Margarita Bella [GS,D,MR-L,F,DS,NS,GO] 1032 3rd Ave NE (at Central), Minneapolis 612/331-7955 9pm-1am, more gay Wed, drag shows Th, also restaurant 11am-9pm

► The Saloon [★M,D,F,K,WC,GO] 830 Hennepin Ave (at 9th), Minneapolis 612/332-0835 9am-1am, after-hours till 4am Th-Sat, from 10am Sun, Latin Tue, also The Tank [L,V] Sun from 9pm

Velvet Rope [MW,D,DS,18+,WC] 2554 Como Ave (at Warehouse Nightclub) 651/645-4618 8:30pm-1am Th only, drag king night last Th of month

■ CAFES

Anodyne at 43rd [E,WC] 4301 Nicollet Ave (at 43rd), Minneapolis 612/824-4300 6:30am-10pm, from 7am Sat, from 8am-9pm Sun, till midnight Fri-Sat

Cafe Barbette [MW,BW] 1600 W Lake St (at Irving), Minneapolis 612/827-5710 7am-1am, French/ American

Cahoots 1562 Selby Ave (at Snelling), St Paul 651/644-6778 7am-9:30pm, 7:30am-11pm wknds

Moose & Sadie's 212 3rd Ave N (at 2nd St), Minneapolis 612/371-0464 7:30am-11pm, till 1:30am Fri-Sat, 9am-10pm Sun, warehouse district cafe

Uncommon Grounds [GS] 2809 Hennepin Ave (at 28th Ave), Minneapolis 612/872-4811 5pm-1am, outdoor seating

The Urban Bean 3255 Bryant Ave S (at 33rd), Minneapolis 612/824-6611 7am-11pm, patio

Minnesota • USA

Vera's Cafe 2901 Lyndale Ave S (at 29th St W), Minneapolis **612/822-3871** *7am-11pm, cozy coffeehouse, light meals*

■ RESTAURANTS

Al's Breakfast [★] 413 14th Ave SE (at 4th), Minneapolis **612/331-9991** *6am-1pm, from 9am Sun, great hash*

Bobino Cafe & Wine Bar 222 E Hennepin Ave, Minneapolis **612/623-3301** *lunch & dinner nightly, classic bistro, also martini bar*

Cafe Brenda 300 1st Ave N, Minneapolis **612/342-9230** *lunch Mon-Fri, dinner Mon-Sat, clsd Sun, vegetarian & seafood*

Campiello 1320 W Lake St (at Hennepin), Minneapolis **612/825-2222** *dinner & Sun brunch*

D'Amico Cucina [E] 100 N 6th St (btwn 1st & 2nd Aves), Minneapolis **612/338-2401** *dinner nightly, a la carte, full bar, live music wknds*

Goodfellows 40 S 7th (at Hennepin), Minneapolis **612/332-4800** *lunch & dinner, clsd Sun, upscale American*

King & I Thai 1346 LaSalle Ave (at W Grant), Minneapolis **612/332-6928** *full bar, free valet parking*

Murray's 26 S 6th St (at Hennepin), Minneapolis **612/339-0909** *lunch Mon-Fri, dinner nightly, steak & potatoes*

Palomino Euro Bistro 825 Hennepin Ave (at 9th St), Minneapolis **612/339-3800** *11am-1am, 5pm-12:30am Sun, Italian/ Mediterranean*

Rudolph's Bar-B-Que [WC] 1933 Lyndale (at Franklin), Minneapolis **612/871-8969** *11am-1am, full bar*

■ ENTERTAINMENT & RECREATION

32nd St Beach E side of Lake Calhoun (33rd & Calhoun Blvd), Minneapolis *gay beach*

Fresh Fruit KFAI 90.3 FM, Minneapolis **612/341-0980** *7pm-8pm Th, gay radio program, also a variety of lgbt programs 9pm-11pm Sun*

Twin Cities Gay Men's Chorus 528 Hennepin Avenue #307, Minneapolis **612/339-7664**

Twin Lake Beach [N] in Wirth Park (33rd & Calhoun Blvd), Minneapolis *hard to find, inquire locally*

■ BOOKSTORES

A Brother's Touch [WC] 2327 Hennepin Ave (at 24th), Minneapolis **612/377-6279** *11am-7pm, till 6pm Sat, noon-5pm Sun, lgbt*

Magus Books, Ltd 1316 SE 4th St (at 13th/ 14th), Minneapolis **612/379-7669, 800/996-2387** *10am-8pm, till 6pm wknds, from noon Sun, spirituality, also mail order*

■ RETAIL SHOPS

Cellar Leather 2315-B Hennepin Ave S (at Dupont Ave & 24th St), Minneapolis **612/377-5897**

Leather by Boots Minnesota [GO] **612/366-0879** *sells at local bars 9pm-close*

The Rainbow Road [WC] 109 W Grant (at LaSalle), Minneapolis **612/872-8448** *10am-10pm, lgbt retail & video*

Sister Fun 1604 W Lake St (at James), Minneapolis **612/672-0263** *noon-7pm, 1pm-5pm Sun, clsd Mon, kitschy stuff*

■ PUBLICATIONS

Lavender Magazine **612/871-2237, 877/515-9969** *lgbt newsmagazine for MN, WI, IA, ND, SD*

■ GYMS & HEALTH CLUBS

The Firm [MW] 245 Aldrich Ave N (at Glenwood), Minneapolis **612/377-7222** *day passes*

■ MEN'S SERVICES

➤ **Megaphone Minneapolis** **800/289-1489** *Call for the local # nearest you! Meet Hot Men in your area! FREE to Browse & Respond to voice ads. Use code 3087. Also try MEGAMATES.COM*

■ EROTICA

Denmark Books 459 W 7th St, St Paul **651/222-2928**

Fantasy Gifts [WC] 709 W Lake (at Lyndale), Minneapolis **612/824-2459**

➤ **Lickety Split** 251 3rd Ave S, Minneapolis **612/333-0599** *24hrs*

Minnesota • USA

Triangle @ SexWorld 241 2nd Ave N, 3rd flr (at Washington), Minneapolis **612/672-0556** *24hrs*

■CRUISY AREAS

'Bare Ass' Beach [AYOR] E bank of the Mississippi (btwn the Franklin Ave & I-94 bridges), Minneapolis *esp summer afternoons*

Crosby Farm [AYOR] Shepard Rd (near Hwy 5, overlooking the Mississippi River), St Paul

Joy Park [AYOR] Silver Lake, North St Paul

Loring Park [AYOR] 15th St (near 35 W & I-94 exchange), Minneapolis

Moorhead

see also Fargo, North Dakota

■INFO LINES & SERVICES

Pride Collective & Community Center 116 12th St S (at Main Ave) **218/287-8034** *3pm-5pm Tue & Sat, referrals, support/ social groups*

■NIGHTCLUBS

The I-Beam [MW,D,F,V,WC] 1021 Center Ave **218/233-7700** *8pm-1am*

■CAFES

Atomic Coffee [GO] 15 4th St S (at Main) **218/299-6161** *7am-11pm, from 9am wknds, till 10pm Sun, also gallery*

Rochester

■INFO LINES & SERVICES

Gay/ Lesbian Community Service 507/281-3265 *5pm-7pm Mon & Wed*

■CRUISY AREAS

Eastwood Park [AYOR] County Rd 14 N (off US 52)

Soldiers Field Park [AYOR]

Rushford

■ACCOMMODATIONS

Windswept Inn [GF,GO] 207 N Mill St **507/864-2545**

Two Harbors

■ACCOMMODATIONS

Grand Superior Lodge [GS,SW,F] 2826 Hwy 61 E (near Gooseberry Falls State Park) **218/834-3796, 800/627-9565** *log cabins on Lake Superior, hot tub*

Wolverton

■RESTAURANTS

District 31 Victoria's [BW,R] 101 First St **218/995-2000** *5:30pm-9:30pm, clsd Sun*

MISSISSIPPI

Statewide

■PUBLICATIONS

➤ **Southern Voice 404/876-1819** *weekly lgbt newspaper for AL, FL (panhandle), GA, LA, MS, TN w/ resource listings*

➤ **TLW Magazine 727/522-8888** *Southeast's largest entertainment magazine for gay men*

Biloxi

■ACCOMMODATIONS

Lofty Oaks Inn [GF,SW] 17288 Hwy 67 **228/392-6722, 800/280-4361** *full brkfst, hot tub*

■BARS

The Golden Turtle [GS,NH,D,F] 1834 Beach Blvd (at Veterans) **228/385-3070** *noon-2am*

Just Us Lounge [MW,NH,S] 906 Division St (at Caillavet) **228/374-1007** *24hrs*

■NIGHTCLUBS

Barcode [MW,D,S,K] 153 Veterans Ave **228/380-0092** *3pm-7am*

■EROTICA

Adult Theatre 222 Iberville Dr **228/435-5625**

Adult Video Arcade 1854 Beach Blvd **228/388-4212** *24hrs*

The Arcade Books 1620 Pass Rd (enter thru dead-end alley) **228/435-2802** *clsd Sun*

Vicksburg • Mississippi

■ CRUISY AREAS

Beach Hwy [AYOR] btwn Biloxi & Gulfport

Gulf Coast Beach [AYOR] *btwn Holiday Inn & Coliseum*

Brookhaven

■ CRUISY AREAS

Bypass btwn I-55 & US Hwy 51 [AYOR] S frontage Rd of US Hwy 84

Holly Springs

■ ACCOMMODATIONS

Somerset Cottage [GS,NS] 135 W Gholson Ave **662/252-4513** *hot tub*

Jackson

■ INFO LINES & SERVICES

Gay/ Lesbian Community Info Line 601/346-4379 *24hrs, switchboard for many organizations, including youth group*

Lambda AA 4872 N State St (at Unitarian Church) **601/346-4379** *7pm Mon & Wed, 6pm Sat*

■ ACCOMMODATIONS

Microtel Inns & Suites [GF,SW,WC] 614 Monroe St **601/352-8282**

■ BARS

Jack's Construction Site (JC's) [MW,NH,BW,BYOB] 425 N Mart Plaza **601/362-3108** *5pm-close*

■ NIGHTCLUBS

Club City Lights [MW,D,MR-AF,S,BW,BYOB] 200 N Mill St **601/353-0059** *10pm-close Fri-Sat*

Jack & Jill's [MW,D,S,BW,BYOB,WC] 3911 Northview Dr (at Meadowbrook) **601/982-5225** *9pm-close Fri-Sat*

■ MEN'S SERVICES

The Confidential Connection®! 601/982-7030 *The hottest local guys! 18+ Record & Listen FREE! Use access code 499*

■ EROTICA

Terry Road Books [AYOR] 1449 Terry Rd **601/353-9156** *24hrs*

■ CRUISY AREAS

Battlefield Park [AYOR] Terry Rd (at Hwy 80) *afternoons*

Smith Park [AYOR]

Natchez

■ BARS

Under the Hill Saloon [GF,NH,E] 33 Silver St **601/446-8023** *10am-close*

Ovett

■ ACCOMMODATIONS

Camp Sister Spirit [W,F,NS,GO] **601/344-1411, 601/645-6479** *120 acres of camping & RV sites, volunteer-run, men welcome, clean & sober space*

Oxford

■ CRUISY AREAS

The Grove [AYOR]

Sardis Lake Beach [AYOR]

Pascagoula

■ CRUISY AREAS

Beach Park [AYOR]

Rest Area [AYOR] east & westbound (off I-10)

Tupelo

■ NIGHTCLUBS

Rumors [GS,D,S,WC] 637 Hwy 145 (10 miles S of Tupelo), Shannon **662/767-9500, 662/213-4891** *8pm-1am Th-Sun*

■ CRUISY AREAS

Chickasaw Village & Old Town Site Scenic Overlooks [AYOR] Natchez Trace Pkwy *closes at sunset*

Confederate Grave Site [AYOR] Hwy 78-Natchez Trace Pkwy interchange (5 miles N)

Vicksburg

■ EROTICA

Hill City News & Novelty 1214 Washington St **601/638-4435**

Missouri • USA

MISSOURI

Statewide

■PUBLICATIONS
Midwest Times 816/348-7600 *lgbt newspaper covering Missouri & Kansas*

Ava

■ACCOMMODATIONS
Cactus Canyon Campground [MO,N,GO] 16 miles E of Ava on Hwy 14 (N 1 mile on County 223) **417/683-9199**

Boonville

■EROTICA
Passions LLC 17701 Old Five Dr **660/882-9426** *24hrs*

Venus [GS,GO] 11654 Old Hwy 40 (at I-70, exit 98) **660/882-2388** *24hrs, DVDs, videos, toys, arcades, 3 theaters (1 all-gay)*

Branson

see also Springfield & Eureka Springs, Arkansas

■CRUISY AREAS
Table Rock Lake Dam [AYOR] Fish Hatchery area

Bridgeton

■EROTICA
Fantasy Video 3419 N Lindbergh Blvd (S of I-70) **314/344-0016** *24hrs*

Cape Girardeau

■ACCOMMODATIONS
Rose Bed Inn [GS,F,GO] 611 S Sprigg St **573/332-7673, 866/767-3233** *B&B, full brkfst, hot tub, gourmet dining by reservation*

■NIGHTCLUBS
Independence Place [MW,D,TG,DS] 5 S Henderson St (at Independence) **573/334-2939** *8:30pm-1:30am, from 7pm Fri-Sat, clsd Sun, live shows Sat*

■CRUISY AREAS
Capaha Park [AYOR]

Columbia

■BARS
Music Cafe [GF,E] 120 S 9th St **573/815-9995** *4pm-1:30am*

SoCo Club [GS,D,A,F,K,DS,WC] 128 E Nifong Blvd #E (at Providence Rd) **573/499-9483** *6:30pm-1:30am, clsd Sun, karaoke Tue, patio*

■CAFES
Ernie's Cafe 1005 E Walnut (at 10th) **573/874-7804** *6:30am-3pm*

RagTag Cinemacafe [F,BW] 23 N 10th St **573/443-4359** *independent & alternative cinema, also theater, music & dance*

■RETAIL SHOPS
Trailside Cafe & Bike Shop [GF,F,GO] 700 1st St (at Pike St), Rocheport **573/698-2702** *8am-7pm, clsd Mon, clsd in winter*

■EROTICA
Eclectics [★] 1122-A Wilkes Blvd **573/443-0873**

Olde Un Theatre/ Midwest Adult Book Store 101 E Walnut St (at 1st) **573/442-6622**

Venus [GS,GO] 1004 Old Hwy 63 N **573/442-4319** *10am-1am, DVDs, videos, toys, 3 theaters (1 all-gay)*

■CRUISY AREAS
Cosmopolitan Park [AYOR] W side of town (off Business Loop 70)

Jefferson City

■ACCOMMODATIONS
Jefferson Inn B&B [GF] 801 W High St **573/635-7196** *full brkfst*

Kansas City

■INFO LINES & SERVICES
Gay/ Lesbian Community Center 207 Westport Rd #212 **816/931-4420** *10am-8pm, clsd Sun, call for events*

Live & Let Live AA 3535 Broadway (at Knickerbocker Pl) **816/531-9668** *noon & 6pm daily, 7pm Sat*

Kansas City • Missouri

ACCOMMODATIONS

➤ **Hydes Guesthouse** [M,NS,GO] 816/561-1010 *in historic Hyde Park*

Ken's Place [MW,N,GO] 13 W 38th St (at Baltimore) **816/753-0533** *some shared baths, near gay bars*

LaFontaine Inn [GF,GO] 4320 Oak St **816/753-4434**

The Porch Swing Inn [GF,GO] 702 East St, Parkville **816/587-6282, 866/587-6282** *B&B, full brkfst, hot tub*

Sleep Inn [GF,SW,WC] 7611 NW 97th Terrace (at Tiffany Springs Rd) **816/891-0111, 800/424-6423** *hotel*

Su Casa B&B [GF,SW,NS] 9004 E 92nd St **816/965-5647, 866/632-2136** *Southwest-style home*

BARS

Balanca's [MW,D,E] 1809 Grand Ave (at 11th) **816/474-6369** *6pm-3am, from 3pm wknds, 2 flrs*

Buddies [M,NH] 3715 Main St (at 37th) **816/561-2600** *6am-3am, clsd Sun*

DB Warehouse Complexx [★M,D,B,L,F,WC] 1915 Main St (at 20th) **816/471-1575** *11am-3am, 5 bars, also leather shop*

The Fox [M,NH,TG,V] 7520 Shawnee Mission Pkwy (at Metcalf), Overland Park, KS **913/384-0369** *2pm-2am*

Missie B's [M,NH,D,TG,K,S] 805 W 39th St (at SW Trafficway) **816/561-0625** *noon-3am, clsd Sun*

Papa Joe's [★MW,NH,DS] 1020 McGee (at E 10th St) **816/842-4123** *8am-1:30am, 11am-midnight Sun*

Push [MW,NH,D,MR,TG,E,K,C,DS] 823 Walnut (at 9th St) **816/472-7855** *7pm-1:30am, clsd Sun-Mon, theme nights, Whip Me Wednesdays [L], karaoke Th*

Sidekicks [MW,D,CW,DS,WC] 3707 Main St (at 37th) **816/931-1430** *2pm-3am, clsd Sun-Mon, drag shows Fri*

Sidestreet Bar [M,NH,GO] 413 E 33rd St (at Gilliam) **816/531-1775** *10am-1:30am, clsd Sun*

Missouri • USA

Soakie's [MW,D,MR-AF,F,DS,WC] 1308 Main St (at 13th) **816/221-6060** *10am-3am*

Time Out [MW,NH,D,TG,K,S,GO] 1321 Grand (at Truman) **816/421-1288** *noon-3am, clsd Sun, Latino night Sat*

Wilde's [M,D,P,V,WC] 3611 Broadway (at 36th/ Valentine) **816/931-0501** *4:30pm-1:30am, clsd Sun*

■ NIGHTCLUBS

The Hurricane [GF,D,E] 4048 Broadway (at Westport Rd) **816/753-0884** *2pm-3am, from 5pm wknds, live bands*

XO [GS,D,K] 3954 Central (btwn Westport & Broadway) **816/753-0112** *9pm-3am, clsd Sun-Tue, gay Th only*

■ CAFES

Broadway Cafe 4106 Broadway Blvd (at Westport) **816/531-2432** *7am-11pm, 8:30am-midnight wknds*

Muddy's [WC] 1719 W 39th St (at Bell) **816/756-1997** *7am-midnight, 8am-6pm Sun*

Planet Cafe [★GO] 3535 Broadway Blvd (at 35th) **816/561-7287** *7am-11pm, till midnight Fri-Sat, from 10am wknds*

■ RESTAURANTS

Classic Cup Cafe [WC] 301 W 47th St (at Central) **816/753-1840** *7am-10pm*

The Corner Restaurant [WC] 4059 Broadway (at Main) **816/931-6630** *brkfst & lunch*

Sharp's 63rd St Grill [BW,WC] 128 W 63rd St **816/333-4355** *7am-10pm, till 11pm Fri-Sat, from 8am Sat, from 9am Sun*

Strouds 1014 E 85th St (btwn Troost & Holmes) **816/333-2132** *4pm-10pm, lunch Fri-Sun, fried chicken*

■ ENTERTAINMENT & RECREATION

Heartland Men's Chorus **816/931-3338**

Unicorn Theatre 3820 Main **816/531-3033** *contemporary American theater*

■ RETAIL SHOPS

In The Life 205 Westport Rd (btwn Main & Broadway) **816/753-4757, 866/753-4757** *10am-7pm, noon-6pm Sun, clsd Tue, lgbt*

■ PUBLICATIONS

➤ **EXP Magazine** **314/367-0397, 877/397-6244** *bi-weekly gay magazine for MO, IL & KS*

KC Exposures **816/753-4500** *weekly gay magazine, calendar, listings*

Midwest Times **816/348-7600** *lgbt newspaper covering Missouri & Kansas*

■ MEN'S CLUBS

➤ **Hydes KC** **816/561-1010** *hours vary, call for location*

■ EROTICA

Erotic City 8401 E Truman Rd (at I-435) **816/252-3370** *24hrs, arcade*

Hollywood at Home 9063 Metcalf (at 91st), Overland Park, KS **913/649-9666**

Ray's Video & Newsstand 3324 Main St (at 34th) **816/753-7692** *24hrs*

■ CRUISY AREAS

Country Club Plaza [AYOR]

Loose Park [AYOR] *oh, really!*

Lake Ozark

■ ACCOMMODATIONS

Paradise House [GS,GO] 299 Flynn Rd (at Hwy 54) **573/365-4397** *B&B in private home, hot tub*

Nelson

■ EROTICA

➤ **The Lion's Den Adult Bookstore** RR1 Hwy J Box 163 (Exit 84, off I-70) **660/859-2741** *24hrs*

Noel

■ ACCOMMODATIONS

Rivertown Park/ Noel Rafting [GF,WC] **417/475-6460, 800/475-6460** *May-Sept, campsites & canoe rental*

St Louis • Missouri

Overland

■ EROTICA

TLC Priscilla's 10210 Page Ave (E of Ashby) 314/423-8422

Poplar Bluff

■ NIGHTCLUBS

Realities Dance Club [MW,D,DS,GO] 67 Hwy S 573/686-0740 *8pm-1:30am Fri-Sat only*

Springfield

■ INFO LINES & SERVICES

AA Gay/ Lesbian 601 E Walnut St (at Christ Episcopal Church Annex) 417/823-7125 (AA #) *6pm Sat*

Gay & Lesbian Community Center of the Ozarks [WC] 518 E Commercial St 417/869-3978 *6pm-10pm Fri-Sun, transgender support group 7pm Sun, youth group 4pm Tue, many other groups, newsletter*

■ BARS

The Edge [MW,D,K,DS,WC,GO] 424 N Boonville 417/831-4700 *4pm-1:30am, clsd Sun*

Martha's Vineyard [MW,NH,D,DS,18+,WC] 217-221 W Olive St 417/864-4572, 417/831-6144 *4pm-1:30am, till midnight Sun, also martini lounge, patio*

RoniSuz [M,GO] 821 W College St (at Grant) 417/864-0036 *4pm-11pm*

■ EROTICA

TLC Priscilla's 1918 S Glenstone (at Sunshine) 417/881-8444

■ CRUISY AREAS

Phelps Grove Park [AYOR]

St Joseph

■ NIGHTCLUBS

Labels Nightclub [GS,D,E,C,DS,V,WC] 107 S 6th St (at Felix) 816/232-2269 *7pm-1:30am, clsd Sun-Tue, 2 flrs*

■ CRUISY AREAS

Small Park [AYOR] *downtown*

St Louis

■ INFO LINES & SERVICES

Gay/ Lesbian Hotline 314/367-0084 *6pm-10pm, clsd Sun*

Steps Alano Club 1935-A Park Ave 314/436-1858 *lgbt 12-step mtgs, call for mtg schedule*

■ ACCOMMODATIONS

2049 Sidney [GS,GO] 2049 Sidney St (at McNair) 314/772-2049, 866/772-2049 *B&B, jacuzzi*

➤ **A St Louis Guesthouse** [M,N,NS,GO] 1032-38 Allen Ave (at Menard) 314/773-1016 *in historic Soulard district, hot tub*

Brewers House B&B [MW,GO] 1829 Lami St (at Lemp) 314/771-1542, 888/767-4665 *1860s home, jacuzzi*

Napoleon's Retreat B&B [GS,NS,GO] 1815 Lafayette Ave (at Mississippi) 314/772-6979, 800/700-9980 *restored 1880s town house, full brkfst*

Park Avenue Mansion—A B&B Guesthouse [GS] 2007 Park Ave (at Mississippi) 314/588-9004, 866/588-9004 *B&B inn, full brkfst, jacuzzi*

Two Boys Inn B&B [MW,GO] 2712 S Compton Ave (at Magnolia) 314/773-6700

■ BARS

Absolutli Goosed Martini Bar, Etc [MW,NH,GO] 3196 S Grand (4 blks S of Tower Grove Park) 314/772-0400 *4pm-close, from 5pm Sat, clsd Mon-Tue, also desserts, appetizers*

Blake's [MW,D,DS] 7101 S Broadway (at Blow St) 314/481-9178 *5pm-1:30am, from 6pm Sat, clsd Sun-Tue*

Clementine's [★M,NH,F,WC] 2001 Menard (at Allen) 314/664-7869 *10am-1:30am, 11am-midnight Sun*

Club Escapades [MW,D,K,S] 113 W Main St, Belleville, IL 618/222-9597 *5pm-2am*

The Drake Bar [MW,E,P,WC] 3500 Papin St (at Theresa, 1 blk NE of Grand & Chouteau) 314/865-1400 *4pm-1:30am, clsd Sun, patio*

Missouri • USA

Freddie's [MW,NH,D,K,V] 4112-14 Manchester Ave **314/371-1333** 2pm-1:30am, clsd Sun, show tunes Tue, karaoke Wed-Th

Grey Fox Pub [MW,NH,TG,F,S] 3503 S Spring (at Potomac) **314/772-2150** 3pm-1:30am, from 11am Sat, clsd Sun, patio

Inside Out [MW,F,DS,V] 3145 W Chain of Rocks Rd, Granite City, IL **618/797-0700** 7pm-2am, till 3am Sat, clsd Mon, outdoor complex

JJ's Clubhouse & Bar [M,NH,B,L,WC] 3858 Market St (at Vandeventer) **314/535-4100** 4pm-3am, clsd Sun

Loading Zone [★MW,V,WC,GO] 16 S Euclid (at Forest Park Pkwy) **314/361-4119** 3pm-1:30am, clsd Sun

Novak's Bar & Grill [W,E,K,S,WC] 4146 Manchester **314/531-3699** 4pm-1:30am, patio

Rainbow's End [MW,NH,F,DS,WC] 4060 Chouteau (at Manchester) **314/652-8790** 9am-close, patio, also leather shop

Soulard Bastille [M,NH,F] 1027 Russell (at Menard) **314/664-4408** 11am-1:30am, from 11am Fri-Sun

Tangerine [GF,D,F,E] 1405 Washington Ave (at 14th) **314/621-7335** 5:30pm-10pm Mon-Th, 5pm-11pm Fri-Sat, hipster lounge & restaurant

V-Bar [MW,E,K,DS,V] 17 S Vandeventer (at Forest Park Pkwy) **314/652-0171** 9pm-1:30am, clsd Sun

■ NIGHTCLUBS

Bubby & Sissy's [MW,D,V,WC] 602 Belle St (at 6th St), Alton, IL **618/465-4773** 3pm-2am, till 3am Fri-Sat, from noon Sun

The Complex/ Angles [★MW,D,F,DS,V,WC] 3515 Chouteau (at Grand) **314/772-2645** 5pm-3am, from 9pm Tue, clsd Mon, multiple bars, patio

Faces Complex [MW,D,F,DS,V,18+] 130 4th St (at Missouri), East St Louis, IL **618/271-7410** 11pm-6am, from 9pm Wed & Sun, clsd Mon-Tue, 3 levels, patio

A St. Louis Guesthouse

Located in Historic Soulard
next door to Clementines

Accommodations with:
- Private Bath
- Phone
- Hot Tub in Courtyard

1032-38 Allen Ave., St. Louis, MO 63104
www.stlouisguesthouse.com
(314) 773-1016

St Louis • Missouri

The Galaxy [GF,A,L,E,$] 1227 Washington Ave **314/231-2404, 314/231-6968** *hours vary, fetish night Mon*

Magnolia's [★M,D,CW,F,K,C,WC] 5 S Vandeventer (at Forest Park Pkwy) **314/652-6500** *6pm-3am, Gateway Fri-Sun [L]*

Velvet Lounge [GS,D] 1301 Washington Ave (at 13th Ave) **314/241-8178, 314/241-2997** *9pm-3am Fri-Sat*

■CAFES

Classical Coffee 313 Belt Ave (at Waterman) **314/361-1317** *7am-3pm, till 4pm Wed, from 8am Sat, 9am-2pm Sun*

Coffee Cartel [★] 2 Maryland Plaza (at Euclid) **314/454-0000** *24hrs*

MokaBe's [★E,WC] 3606 Arsenal (at S Grand) **314/865-2009** *11am-1am*

■RESTAURANTS

Cafe Balaban [★WC] 405 N Euclid Ave (at McPherson) **314/361-8085** *pizza, Sun brunch, full bar*

Chez Leon [GO] 4580 Laclede Ave (at Euclid) **314/361-1589** *5:30pm-10pm, till 11pm Fri-Sat, 5pm-9pm Sun, clsd Mon, French bistro, full bar*

Dressel's 419 N Euclid (at McPherson) **314/361-1060** *lunch & dinner, great Welsh pub food, full bar*

Duff's [WC] 392 N Euclid Ave (at McPherson) **314/361-0522** *lunch & dinner, clsd Mon, fine dining, full bar*

Kirk's Bistro & Bar 512 N Euclid (at Washington) **314/361-1456** *5pm-10pm, till 11pm Fri-Sat, Sun brunch*

Majestic Bar & Restaurant 4900 Laclede (at Euclid) **314/361-2011** *6am-1:30am, diner fare*

On Broadway Bistro [WC] 5300 N Broadway (at Grand) **314/421-0087** *11am-1am, full bar*

Ted Drewes Frozen Custard [★] 6726 Chippewa (at Jameson) **314/481-2652** *11am-11pm, seasonal, a St Louis landmark; also 4224 S Grand Blvd, 314/352-7376*

Missouri • USA

Tomatillo Mexican Grill 9641 Olive Blvd (at Warson) **314/991-4995** *11am-10pm, till midnight wknds*

Tony's [R] 410 Market St (at Broadway) **314/231-7007** *dinner only, clsd Sun, Italian fine dining*

Zinnia 7491 Big Bend Blvd (at Shrewsbury), Webster Groves **314/962-0572** *lunch Tue-Fri & dinner Tue-Sun, bistro*

■ ENTERTAINMENT & RECREATION

Anheuser-Busch Brewery Tours/ Grant's Farm 314/577-2626, 314/843-1700 *all-American kitsch: see the Clydesdales in their air-conditioned stables, or visit the Busch family estate that was once the home of Ulysses S Grant*

Int'l Bowling Museum & Hall of Fame 111 Stadium Plaza (across from Busch Stadium) **314/231-6340** *5,000 yrs of bowling history (!) & 4 free frames*

Lavender Limelight Radio Show KDHX 88.1FM **314/664-3688** *7pm Th, lgbt radio show*

Opera Theatre of Saint Louis [WC] 539 Garden Ave (at Edgar & Big Bend) **314/961-0171**

■ BOOKSTORES

Left Bank Books 399 N Euclid Ave (at McPherson) **314/367-6731** *10am-10pm, 11am-6pm Sun, strong lgbt section*

■ RETAIL SHOPS

➤ **Boxers** 310 N Euclid Ave (at Maryland) **314/454-0209** *11am-6pm, 1pm-5pm Sun, men's underwear*

Daily Planet News 243 N Euclid Ave (at Maryland) **314/367-1333** *7am-8pm*

Heffalump's 387 N Euclid Ave (at McPherson) **314/361-0544** *11am-8pm, till 6pm Mon, till 10pm Fri-Sat, noon-5pm Sun, gifts*

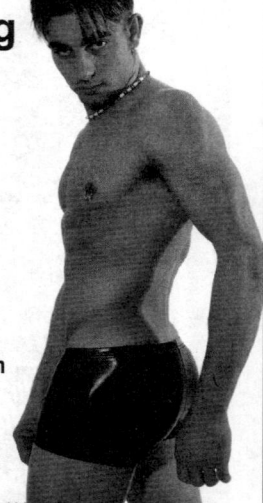

When dressing down is as important as dressing up.

Boxers

In The Central West End

http://www.eBoxersOnline.com
Free Shipping!

**310 N. Euclid
St. Louis, Missouri 63108**
314.454.0209

• 2(x)ist • JM • RIPS • LASC • ManSilk • /baskit/ • N2N • Sauvage • Go Softwear •

Setting A New Standard

Always Open
Guest Memberships
Steam Room
Sauna
Whirlpool
Private Dressing Rooms
Outdoor Pool & Patio
Gym
18+, only

A PRIVATE MEN'S CLUB
2625 Samuel Shepard Dr. • St. Louis, MO • (314)533-3666
www.the-clubs.com

Missouri • USA

■PUBLICATIONS

➤ **EXP Magazine** 314/367-0397, 877/397-6244 *bi-weekly gay magazine for MO, IL & KS*

Vital Voice 314/865-3787
bi-monthly news & feature publication

■MEN'S CLUBS

➤ **Club St Louis** [PC,SW]
2625 Samuel Shepard Dr (at Jefferson) 314/533-3666 *24hrs*

■MEN'S SERVICES

The Confidential Connection®!
314/231-2600 *The hottest local guys! 18+ Record & Listen FREE! Use access code 499*

The Gay Connection 900/346-6338
Talk and/or meet with other men from the area, at only 99¢ per minute.

➤ **Megaphone St Louis**
800/289-1489 *Call for the local # nearest you! Meet Hot Men in your area! FREE to Browse & Respond to voice ads. Use code 3087. Also try MEGAMATES.COM*

■EROTICA

Cheap Trx 3211 S Grand Blvd
314/664-4011 *body piercing, sex supplies*

Friends & Luvers 3550 Gravois (at Grand) 314/771-9405 *10am-10pm, noon-7pm Sun, fetish clothes, toys, videos, dating service*

■CRUISY AREAS

Creve Coeur Park [AYOR] Dorset Rd W (off Hwy 2-70)

Steelville

■ACCOMMODATIONS

Country's Getaway [MW,N] 119 Big Bend Ln (near Hwy 8) 573/775-5534 *campground (open May 15-Oct 31), 100 miles SW of St Louis*

Waynesville

■EROTICA

➤ **The Lion's Den Adult Bookstore**
25965 Hwy 17 (Exit 153, off I-44) 573/774-9957 *24hrs*

MONTANA

Billings

■NIGHTCLUBS

The Loft [MW,D,K] 2910 2nd Ave N (at 29th) 406/259-9074 *4:30pm-2am, karaoke Wed*

■EROTICA

Big Sky Books 1203 1st Ave N
406/259-0051

The Victorian [GS,P] 2019 Minnesota Ave (at 21st) 406/245-4293 *noon-midnight, clsd Sun-Mon, videos, magazines, arcade, fireplace, also HIV testing 5pm-9pm Wed-Sat & monthly Hep B/C testing*

Boulder

■ACCOMMODATIONS

Boulder Hot Springs Hotel & Retreat [GF,F,SW,N,NS,WC]
406/225-4339 *massage, workshops*

Bozeman

■ACCOMMODATIONS

Gallatin Gateway Inn [GF,F,SW,WC]
76405 Gallatin Rd/ Hwy 191
406/763-4672, 800/676-3522 *hot tub, smokefree rooms available, dinner nightly*

Lehrkind Mansion B&B [GS,NS]
719 N Wallace Ave 406/585-6932, 800/992-6932 *Queen Anne Victorian, full brkfst, hot tub*

■CAFES

The Leaf & Bean [E,WC] 35 W Main
406/587-1580 *6:30am-10pm, till 11pm Fri-Sat*

■EROTICA

Ms Kitty's Adult Store 12 N Wilson
406/586-6989

Butte

■ACCOMMODATIONS

Snookums at the Skookum [MW]
3541 Harrison Ave 406/533-0919
also apts w/ kitchens

Missoula • Montana

■ BARS
Snookums at the Skookum [MW]
3541 Harrison Ave **406/533-0919**
7pm-2am, clsd Mon-Tue

■ RESTAURANTS
Matt's Place 2339 Placer (btwn Montana & Rowe) **406/782-8049**
11:30am-7pm, clsd Sun-Mon, classic soda fountain diner

Pekin Noodle Parlor 117 S Main, 2nd flr **406/782-2217** *5pm-11pm, till 3am Fri-Sat, clsd Tue*

Pork Chop John's 8 W Mercury **406/782-0812** *10:30am-7:30pm, clsd Sun*

Uptown Cafe 47 E Broadway **406/723-4735** *lunch & dinner, bistro, full bar*

■ EROTICA
Rocky Adult Book Store
121 W Broadway (at Montana)
406/723-7218

Gardiner

■ BOOKSTORES
Silvertip Bookstore [GO] 501 Scott St **406/848-2225** *7am-8pm, from 8am Sat, from 9am Sun (summers), winter hours vary, internet access & cafe*

Great Falls

■ RESTAURANTS
Black Diamond Bar & Supper Club 64 Castner, Belt **406/277-4118** *5pm-10pm, clsd Mon, steaks & seafood, 20 miles from Great Falls*

■ CRUISY AREAS
Gibson Park [AYOR]

Helena

■ INFO LINES & SERVICES
PRIDE **406/442-9322, 800/610-9322 (in MT)** *info, newsletter, political advocacy & education*

Kalispell

■ INFO LINES & SERVICES
Flathead Valley Alliance
406/758-6707 *referrals*

■ ACCOMMODATIONS
Cottonwood Hill Farm Inn [GF,NS]
2928 Whitefish Stage Rd
406/756-6404, 800/458-0893
renovated farmhouse

Livingston

■ ACCOMMODATIONS
Yellowstone River Inn Cabins [GS,NS]
4950 Hwy 89 S **406/222-2429, 888/669-6993** *cabins*

Missoula

■ INFO LINES & SERVICES
Gay/ Lesbian AA 532 University Ave (at Lifeboat) **406/543-0011** *7pm Mon*

Western Montana Gay/ Lesbian Community Center 615 Oak St **406/543-2224** *lgbt resource center*

■ ACCOMMODATIONS
Brooks St Motor Inn [GF,WC]
3333 Brooks St (at MacDonald)
406/549-5115, 800/538-3260
motel, hot tub

Foxglove Cottage B&B [GS,SW,NS,GO]
2331 Gilbert Ave **406/543-2927**
1800s guest house

Holland Lake Lodge [GF,WC,GO] 1947 Holland Lake Lodge (at Hwy 83), Swan Valley **406/754-2282, 877/925-6343** *resort w/ lakefront cabins, restaurant & bar*

■ BARS
Amvets Club [GS,D,F] 525 Ryman (at Broadway) **406/543-9174** *noon-2am, beer bust Th*

The Oxford [★GF] 337 N Higgins (at Pine) **406/549-0117** *8am-2am, 24hr cafe*

■ CAFES
The Catalyst 111 N Higgins **406/542-1337** *7am-6pm*

The Raven Cafe 130 E Broadway **406/829-8188** *8am-midnight, till 3pm Sun, pool table*

Montana • USA

■RESTAURANTS
Montana Club/ Red Baron Casino [WC] 2620 Brooks **406/543-3200** *6:30am-10pm, till midnight wknds, casino open till 2am*

■BOOKSTORES
Fact & Fiction [WC] 220 N Higgins **406/721-2881** *9am-8pm, 10am-5pm Sat, noon-4pm Sun*

University Center Bookstore Campus Dr (at U of MT) **406/243-4921** *8am-6pm, from 10am Sat, clsd Sun, gender studies section*

■CRUISY AREAS
McCormick Park [AYOR] W side of Orange St Bridge

Ronan

■ACCOMMODATIONS
North Crow Ranch [MW,N,NS,GO] 2360 N Crow Rd **406/676-5169** *hot tub, camping, call in advance*

NEBRASKA

Columbus

■CRUISY AREAS
Pawnee Park [AYOR]

Grand Island

■ACCOMMODATIONS
Midtown Holiday Inn [GF,SW,WC] 2503 S Locust **308/384-1330** *hot tub, non-smoking rooms available, also Images Pink Cadillac Lounge*

Relax Inn [GF,SW,WC] 507 W 2nd St **308/384-1000**

■BARS
Desert Rose Saloon [GF,WC] 3235 S Locust (at 34th) **308/381-8919** *7pm-1:30am, clsd Sun-Tue*

Nathan Detroit's [GF,NH,F,WC] 316 N Pine St **308/384-3655** *11am-1am*

■RESTAURANTS
Tommy's 1325 S Locust **308/381-0440** *24hrs*

■GYMS & HEALTH CLUBS
Health Plex Fitness Center [GF] 2909 W Hwy 30 **308/384-1110**

■EROTICA
Exclusively Yours Shop 214 N Locust **308/381-6984**

K&L Market 2007 E Hwy 30 **308/382-0910**

Sweet Dreams Shop 217 W 3rd St **308/381-6349**

■CRUISY AREAS
Ashley Park [AYOR] Capital & St Paul Rd

Pier Park [AYOR] S Locust St & Bismark

Stolley Park [AYOR]

Kearney

■BARS
Captain's Table [GF,F] 110 S 2nd Ave (at Holiday Inn) **308/237-5971** *noon-11pm, later wknds*

■RETAIL SHOPS
Hastings Store 9 W 39th St **308/234-1130** *10am-11pm, gay gifts & books*

■CRUISY AREAS
Harmon Park [OC,AYOR] 29th St & 5th Ave *near rock garden & stage area*

Lincoln

■INFO LINES & SERVICES
AA Gay/ Lesbian 2748 'S' St, 3rd flr (at 28th, at The Meeting Place) **402/438-5214** *7:30pm Mon*

■BARS
Panic [MW,E,K,WC,GO] 200 S 18th St (at 'N' St) **402/435-8764** *4pm-1am, from 1pm wknds, patio, internet access*

■NIGHTCLUBS
The Q [MW,D,E,K,S] 226 S 9th (btwn 'M' & 'N' Sts) **402/475-2269** *8pm-1am, clsd Mon, 19+ Tue, also The Vault [M], 10pm-1am Fri-Sat only, cruise bar*

■RETAIL SHOPS
Avant Card 1323 'O' St (btwn 13th & 14th) **402/476-1918** *hours vary; also Gateway Mall location (61st & 'O' St), 402/ 476-1918*

Omaha • Nebraska

■ EROTICA

Adult Books & Cinema X 921 'O' St
402/435-9323 *24hrs*

■ CRUISY AREAS

15th St [AYOR] from 'A' St to State Capitol

Antelope, Pioneer & Van Dorn Parks [AYOR]

McCook

■ CRUISY AREAS

Rest Area [AYOR] 2 miles E of McCook, on Hwy 6 & 34

Norfolk

■ CRUISY AREAS

Ta-Ha-Zooka Park [AYOR]

Omaha

■ INFO LINES & SERVICES

AA Gay/ Lesbian 851 N 74th (at Presbyterian Church) **402/556-1880** *8:15pm Fri*

Rainbow Outreach Center 1719 Leavenworth St **402/341-0330** *6pm-9pm, noon-5pm Sat, clsd Sun, movie night Fri, 24hr info*

■ ACCOMMODATIONS

Castle Unicorn [GS,GO] 57034 Deacon Rd (at Hwy 34 & I-29), Pacific Jct, IA **712/527-5930** *medieval style B&B*

The Cornerstone Mansion Inn [GF,NS] 140 N 39th St (at Dodge) **402/558-7600, 888/883-7745** *1894 historic mansion, commitment ceremonies*

■ BARS

Connections [MW,D,K,S,WC,GO] 1901 Leavenworth St (at 19th) **402/933-3033** *4pm-1am*

DC's Saloon [MW,D,CW,S,WC] 610 S 14th St (at Jackson) **402/344-3103** *2pm-1am*

Diamond Bar [M,WC] 712 S 16th St **402/342-9595** *11am-2pm, then 9pm-close*

Gilligan's Pub [MW,NH,F,K,WC] 1407 Harney St (at 14th St) **402/449-9147** *4pm-1am, till 4am Fri-Sat*

The Omaha Mining Company [M,D,S,18+,WC] 1715 Leavenworth St (btwn 17th & 18th) **402/449-8703** *2pm-1am, till 4am Fri-Sat, 18+ from 1:30am-4am, very cruisy*

■ NIGHTCLUBS

Joy [MW,D,DS,S,V,YC,GO] 1516 Jones (at 15th) **402/341-7337** *4pm-1am, clsd Mon-Wed, After Joy till 4am*

The Max [★M,D,DS,V,WC,$] 1417 Jackson (at 15th St) **402/346-4110** *4pm-1am, 5 bars, DJ Wed-Sun, shows Fri & Sun, patio, cover Fri-Sat*

■ CAFES

Stage Right [E] 401 S 16th (at Harney) **402/346-7675** *7am-11pm, from 10am wknds, till 5pm Sun*

■ RESTAURANTS

Dixie Quick's 1915 Leavenworth St **402/346-3549** *dinner Th-Sat, Sun brunch, Southern*

French Cafe 1017 Howard St **402/341-3547** *lunch & dinner, Sun brunch, full bar*

■ ENTERTAINMENT & RECREATION

HGRA (Heartland Gay Rodeo Association) **402/203-4680**

River City Mixed Chorus **402/341-7464**

■ BOOKSTORES

New Realities [WC] 1026 Howard St (in the Old Market) **402/342-1863** *11am-10pm, till 11pm Fri-Sat, till 6pm Sun, progressive*

■ RETAIL SHOPS

Villain's 3629 'Q' St **402/731-0202** *noon-8pm, till 5pm Sun, tattooing, piercing*

■ MEN'S SERVICES

▶ **Megaphone Omaha** **800/289-1489** *Call for the local # nearest you! Meet Hot Men in your area! FREE to Browse & Respond to voice ads. Use code 3087. Also try MEGAMATES.COM*

■ CRUISY AREAS

Glen Cunningham Lake [AYOR] W side

Hanscom Park [AYOR] *west end*

Levi Carter Park [AYOR] in Carter Lake (near the airport)

Nebraska • USA

Scottsbluff

■RESTAURANTS
Pasta Villa [GO] 1455 10th St (at 'O' St), Gering **308/436-5900** *11am-8pm, clsd Sun-Mon*

■CRUISY AREAS
Riverside Zoo Park [AYOR]

NEVADA

Carson City

■MEN'S SERVICES
➤ **Megaphone Carson City** **800/289-1489** *Call for the local # nearest you! Meet Hot Men in your area! FREE to Browse & Respond to voice ads. Use code 3087. Also try MEGAMATES.COM*

■CRUISY AREAS
Mills Park [AYOR] N end

Elko

■CRUISY AREAS
Elko City Park [AYOR]

Lake Tahoe

see also Lake Tahoe, California

■ACCOMMODATIONS
The Mountain Retreat [MW,SW,GO] 275 Tramway Dr (at Boulder Ct), Stateline **530/582-5670** *luxury town house, hot tub, sundeck*

■NIGHTCLUBS
Faces [MW,D] 270 Kingsbury Grade, Stateline **775/588-2333** *5pm-2am, till 4am Fri-Sat*

■CRUISY AREAS
Secret Beach [AYOR] Rte 28 N (off Hwy 50 to Spooner Jct) *approx 6 miles, look for parked cars & follow trails down hill*

Las Vegas

■INFO LINES & SERVICES
The Gay/ Lesbian Community Center of Southern Nevada 953 E Sahara Ave #B-25 **702/733-9800** *11am-7pm, 10am-3pm Sat, clsd Sun*

■ACCOMMODATIONS
➤ **Blue Moon Resort** [MO,SW,WC,GO] 2651 Westwood Dr **702/361-9099, 866/798-9194** *private resort, steam room & jacuzzi grotto*

Las Vegas Rainbow [MO,SW,N,GO] 1800 Chapman Dr (at Oakey/ 15th St) **702/699-8977, 866/DOROTHY** *decadent B&B, full brkfst, also bar, hot tub*

Lucky You B&B [M,SW,N,GO] **702/384-1129** *hot tub, sauna, shared baths*

Oasis Guesthouse [M,SW,GO] 662 Rolling Green Dr (at Twain & Paradise) **702/369-1396** *full brkfst, jacuzzi*

Viva Las Vegas Villas [GS,NS,GO] 1205 Las Vegas Blvd **702/384-0771, 800/574-4450** *campy themed rooms, on-site disco, commitment ceremonies*

■BARS
Backdoor Lounge [MW,NH,D,S,SW,WC] 1415 E Charleston (near Maryland Pkwy) **702/385-2018** *24hrs, patio, Latin nights Fri-Sat, strippers Sun*

Backstreet [★MW,D,CW,WC] 5012 S Arville Rd (at Tropicana) **702/876-1844** *24hrs, DJ Wed-Sun*

Badlands Saloon [M,NH,D,CW,WC,GO] 953 E Sahara #22 (in Commercial Center) **702/792-9262** *24hrs*

The Buffalo [★M,B,L,V,WC] 4640 Paradise Rd (at Naples) **702/733-8355** *24hrs*

Cobalt Las Vegas [M,F,DS,S,V,YC] 900 E Karen Ave #H-102 (in Commercial Center) **702/696-0226** *24hrs, strippers*

Flex [MW,D,E,K] 4371 W Charleston (at Arville) **702/385-3539** *24hrs*

Freezone [MW,NH,D,TG,F,K,DS,S,YC,GO] 610 E Naples **702/794-2300** *24hrs, also restaurant, karaoke Sun*

Goodtimes [M,NH,D,K,WC] 1775 E Tropicana (at Spencer, in Liberace Plaza) **702/736-9494** *24hrs, DJ Mon*

Las Vegas • Nevada

Icon [MW,NH,V,WC] 4633 Paradise Rd (at Naples) 702/791-0100 *3pm-close*

The Las Vegas Eagle [M,L] 3430 E Tropicana (at Pecos) 702/458-8662 *24hrs, DJ Wed, Fri & Sat, also The Annex bar 8pm-4am Wed & Fri*

Las Vegas Lounge [NH,TG,E,S,GO] 900 E Karen Ave (at Maryland Pkwy) 702/737-9350 *24hrs*

Snick's Place [MO,NH] 1402 S 3rd St (at Imperial) 702/385-9298 *24hrs*

The Spotlight Lounge [★M,NH,D,E] 957 E Sahara (at Commerical Center's entrance) 702/696-0202 *24hrs*

■ NIGHTCLUBS

➤ **The Gipsy** [★M,D,S,V,YC] 4605 S Paradise Rd (at Naples) 702/731-1919 *9pm-close, Latin night Mon, go-go boys*

House of Blues [GF,D,F,S,$] 3950 Las Vegas Blvd S (at Hacienda Ave, in Mandalay Bay) 702/632-7600

SRO [MW,D,S] 1700 E Flamingo (btwn Mayland Pkwy & Spencer) 702/796-1136 *gay Tue only for Adam from 11pm, 2 dance flrs, go-go dancers*

■ CAFES

Espresso Roma Cafe [E] 4440 S Maryland Pkwy 702/369-1540 *7am-midnight, from 8am wknds, open mic Sun-Mon*

■ RESTAURANTS

Coyote Cafe [WC] 3799 S Las Vegas Blvd (in MGM Grand) 702/891-7349, 888/757-2572 *8:30am-10:30pm, the original Santa Fe chef*

Hamburger Mary's 4503 Paradise Rd 702/735-4400 *24hrs*

Mama Jo's 3655 S Durango 702/869-8099 *lunch & dinner, Italian*

The Raw Truth 2381 Windmill Ln 702/450-9007 *8am-10pm, noon-6pm Sun, organic vegan, juice bar*

Sushi Boy Desu 4632 S Maryland Pkwy #12 702/736-8234 *11am-10pm*

Las Vegas • Nevada

■ ENTERTAINMENT & RECREATION

Crystal Palace Skating Rink 4680 Boulder Hwy 702/458-7107 *8:30pm-11pm 3rd Mon, lgbt skate*

Cupid's Wedding Chapel [GS] 827 Las Vegas Blvd S (1 blk N of Charleston) **702/598-4444, 800/543-2933** *commitment ceremonies*

The Forum Shops at Caesars 3570 Las Vegas Blvd S (in Caesars Palace) *you saw it in 'Showgirls' & many other movies, now come shop for yourself*

King Tutankhamun's Tomb & Museum 3900 Las Vegas Blvd S (in the Luxor Las Vegas) **702/262-4555** *exact replica of the tomb when Howard Carter opened it in 1922*

La Cage 2901 Las Vegas Blvd (at the Riviera) **702/794-9433** *7pm-9pm, clsd Tue, the biggest drag show in town: Frank Marino & friends impersonate the divas, from Joan Rivers to Tina Turner*

Las Vegas Gay & Lesbian Chorus **702/594-3393**

Liberace Museum 1775 E Tropicana Ave **702/798-5595** *this is one queen's closet you have to look into—especially if you love pianos, clothes & cars covered w/ diamonds*

'O' at the Bellagio 3600 Las Vegas Blvd S **888/488-7111 (reservations only), 702/693-7111 (general info)** *Cirque du Soleil tops themselves w/ this show-stopper in a specially constructed aquatic theater (it costs a pretty penny but a far more fun than losing your shirt in the casino)*

■ BOOKSTORES

Borders [WC] 2323 S Decatur (at Sahara) **702/258-0999** *9am-11pm, till 9pm Sun, lgbt section, cafe*

Get Booked 4640 Paradise #15 (at Naples) **702/737-7780** *10am-midnight, till 2am Fri-Sat, lgbt*

■ RETAIL SHOPS

The Fig Leaf [M] 4367 W Charleston **702/259-5510** *10am-6pm, clsd Sun, unique fashions, erotic wear, clubwear*

HANDS ON
THERAPEUTIC
Massage

Las Vegas' #1 Choice in Massage Therapy!

To make an appointment for a table massage to your home or hotel room, please call **702-458-8777**

www.handsonmassagelv.com
License #M12-00341-1-087429 & License #302-519-3

Nevada • USA

Glamour Boutique 714 E Sahara Ave #250 **702/697-1800, 866/692-1800** *large-size dresses, wigs, etc*

Sin City 1013 Charleston (at Main) **702/387-6969** *24hrs, piercing & tattoo studio*

■ PUBLICATIONS

Las Vegas Night Beat 1140 Almond Tree Ln #304 **702/369-8441**

Out Las Vegas 702/650-0636 *monthly lgbt entertainment newspaper*

Out Las Vegas Bugle 702/369-6260 *lgbt newspaper*

■ GYMS & HEALTH CLUBS

➤ **Hands On Therapeutic Massage** 4354 Annie Oakley Dr (at Brighthill Ave) **702/458-8777** *licensed massage therapists visit home or hotel rm, 'open to all men & women; mention ad for discount*

The Las Vegas Athletic Club [GF] 5090 S Maryland Pkwy **702/798-5822** *5am-10pm, 8am-8pm wknds, day passes $15*

■ MEN'S CLUBS

Apollo Spa & Health Club [MO,SW] 953 E Sahara Ave #A19 (near Paradise & Maryland, at Commercial Center entrance) **702/650-9191** *24hrs*

Hawks Gym [MO,PC,GO,$] 953-35B, Ste 102 (at E Sahara) **702/731-4295** *24hrs wknds*

■ MEN'S SERVICES

➤ **Megaphone Las Vegas** **800/289-1489** *Call for the local # nearest you! Meet Hot Men in your area! FREE to Browse & Respond to voice ads. Use code 3087. Also try MEGAMATES.COM*

■ EROTICA

Adult Super Store 3850 W Tropicana **702/798-0144** *24hrs, cruisy theaters*

Adult World/ Mini Theaters [V] 3781 Meade Ave (at Valley View) **702/579-9735** *24hrs*

Bare Essentials Fantasy Fashions [GO] 4029 W Sahara Ave (near Valley View Blvd) **702/247-4711** *exotic/ intimate apparel, toys*

Desert Adult Books 4350 N Las Vegas Blvd (at Nellis) **702/643-7982** *24hrs*

Fantasy World Arcade/ Theaters 6760 Boulder Hwy (btwn Sunset & Russell) **702/433-6311** *24hrs*

Industrial Road Adult Books 3427 Industrial Rd (at Spring Mtn) **702/734-7667** *24hrs*

Pal Joey's 3084 S Highland #C **702/734-7589** *fetishwear, videos, arcade, also tattoos & piercing*

Price Video 700 E Naples Dr #102 (at Swenson) **702/734-1342**

Rancho Adult Entertainment Center 4820 N Rancho #D (at Lone Mtn) **702/645-6104** *24hrs*

Video West [GO] 5785 W Tropicana (at Jones) **702/248-7055** *also 4637 S Paradise Rd,* 702/735-1469

■ CRUISY AREAS

Boulder Beach at Lake Mead [AYOR] Lake Mead Blvd, Rte 147 (turn left, then right onto 8.0 Rd, road number 89 on the map) *2 miles of rough road, may take 30 minutes*

Jaycee Park [AYOR] Eastern & St Louis (N of Sahara)

Sunset Park [AYOR]

Laughlin

see Bullhead City, Arizona

Reno

■ INFO LINES & SERVICES

A Rainbow Place, Northern Nevada's GLBT Community Center 33 St Lawrence Ave (at Tahoe) **775/789-1780, 800/627-1168 (24hrs)** *noon-9pm, clsd Sun, movie night Wed, library, meetings, resources, also newsletter, also crisis line* 800/627-1168

■ ACCOMMODATIONS

Holiday Inn & Diamonds Casino [GF,SW,WC] 1000 E 6th St (at Wells Ave) **775/786-5151** *restaurant*

■ BARS

1099 Club [★MW,NH,S,V,WC] 1099 S Virginia St (at Vassar) **775/329-1099** *24hrs, patio*

Concord • New Hampshire

The Cadillac Lounge [GF,NH,D,CW,B,L,TG,GO] 144 West St (at 1st) **775/348-7827** *noon-4am*

Carl's Pub [MW,NH,D] 3310 S Virginia St (at Moana) **775/829-8886** *1pm-3am, patio*

Five Star Saloon [M,NH,D,WC] 132 West St (at 1st) **775/329-2878** *24hrs*

The Patio [MW,NH] 600 W 5th St (btwn Washington & Ralston) **775/323-6565** *11am-2am*

The Quest [M,D,TG,DS] 210 W Commercial Row (at West) **775/333-2808** *24hrs, Latin drag shows*

■ NIGHTCLUBS

Visions [★M,D,E,YC] 340 Kietzke Ln (btwn Glendale & Mill) **775/786-5455** *3pm-close, from noon wknds, gift shop Wed-Sun*

■ CAFES

Sassy's Cafe & Deli 195 N Edison (at Mill) **775/856-3501** *7:30am-4pm, clsd wknds*

■ BOOKSTORES

Borders 4995 S Virginia St **775/448-9999** *9am-10pm, lgbt section*

Sundance Books 1155 W 4th St (at Keystone) **775/786-1188** *9am-9pm, 10am-6pm wknds*

■ PUBLICATIONS

The Outlands **775/324-7866** *calendar, resources, features, classifieds, listings*

Reno Informer **877/835-4664** *northern Nevada's lgbt newspaper*

Sierra Voice **775/322-7866** *monthly, bar & resource listings, community events, arts & entertainment*

■ MEN'S CLUBS

Steve's [PC] 1030 W 2nd St (at Keystone) **775/323-8770** *24hrs, spa*

■ MEN'S SERVICES

► **Megaphone Reno** **800/289-1489** *Call for the local # nearest you! Meet Hot Men in your area! FREE to Browse & Respond to voice ads. Use code 3087. Also try MEGAMATES.COM*

■ EROTICA

The Chocolate Walrus 160 E Grove **775/825-2267** *clsd Sun*

Fantasy Faire 1298 S Virginia (at Arroyo) **775/323-6969** *leather & fetish*

'G' Spot [★GO] 138 West St (btwn 1st & 2nd) **775/333-6969**

Suzie's 195 Kietzke Ln (at E 2nd St) **775/786-8557** *24hrs*

■ CRUISY AREAS

Crissie Caughlin Park [AYOR] W end of the park *days*

Idlewild Park [AYOR] W 2nd St (baseball field at the W end of park)

Virginia City

■ CRUISY AREAS

Union St [AYOR] behind Pipers Opera House *nights*

Winnemuca

■ CRUISY AREAS

Button Point [AYOR] I-80, exit 187 (3 miles E of Winnemuca)

NEW HAMPSHIRE

Statewide

■ INFO LINES & SERVICES

Rainbow Resources **603/224-1686** *active social & support groups, info for NH & VT*

■ PUBLICATIONS

Equality Press 26 S Main St, PMB 145, Concord 03301 **603/738-3763** *non-profit lgbt newspaper of the granite state*

► **In Newsweekly** **617/426-8246** *New England's largest lgbt newspaper*

Bristol

■ ACCOMMODATIONS

The Cliff Lodge [GO] 77 Ravine Dr **603/744-8660** *cabins, restaurant*

Concord

■ CRUISY AREAS

Rollings Park [AYOR] S end of town

New Hampshire • *USA*

Dover

■CRUISY AREAS

Dover Point [AYOR] bayside park
go N over the Great Bay bridge

Durham

■ACCOMMODATIONS

Three Chimneys Inn [GF,F,NS,WC]
17 Newmarket Rd (Rte 108, off Rte 4)
603/868-7800, 888/399-9777
1649 house, near Portsmouth

Fitzwilliam

■ACCOMMODATIONS

Hannah Davis House [GS,NS]
603/585-3344 *historic 1820 Federal bldg, full brkfst*

Hampton

■CRUISY AREAS

Hampton Beach [AYOR] *summers*

Keene

■ACCOMMODATIONS

The Post & Beam B&B [GS,NS,GO]
18 Centre St, Sullivan **603/847-3330, 888/376-6262** *1797 Colonial armstead, full brkfst*

■CRUISY AREAS

Chesterfield Gorge [AYOR] 5 miles W of town (off Rte 9)

Littleton

■ACCOMMODATIONS

Comfort Inn & Suites [GF,SW,WC]
703 US Rte 5S (at I-91), St Johnsbury, VT
802/748-1500, 800/424-6423

Manchester

■BARS

313 [★MW,D,F,E,K,DS,P,V,18+,WC] S Maple St **603/628-6813** *6pm-1am, from 4pm Fri-Sat, from noon Sun, 18+ Tue & Th*

The Breezeway [MW,NH,D,GO] 14 Pearl St **603/621-9111** *5pm-1:30am, T-dance Sun*

Club Front Runner [★MW,D,TG,E,DS,PC]
22 Fir St (at Elm St) **603/623-6477**
5pm-1:30am, from 3pm Sun, clsd Mon, DJ Th-Sat

■MEN'S SERVICES

➤ **Megaphone Manchester**
800/289-1489 *Call for the local # nearest you! Meet Hot Men in your area! FREE to Browse & Respond to voice ads. Use code 3087. Also try MEGAMATES.COM*

■CRUISY AREAS

Weston Observatory Park [AYOR]
Reservoir Rd

Nashua

■CRUISY AREAS

Greeley Park [AYOR] off Manchester St (woods on right) *days*

Main St [AYOR] around City Hall

Newfound Lake

■ACCOMMODATIONS

The Inn on Newfound Lake
[GS,SW,GO] 1030 Mayhew Tpke Rte 3-A, Bridgewater **603/744-9111, 800/745-7990** *restaurant, full bar*

Plymouth

■ACCOMMODATIONS

Federal House Inn Historic B&B
[GS,GO] 27 Rte 25 (Rte 3 traffic circle)
603/536-4644, 866/536-4644
full brkfst, hot tub

Portsmouth

■EROTICA

Moonlight Reader 940 Rte 1 Bypass N
603/436-9622

Spaulding Book & Video [GO]
80 Spaulding Tpke **603/430-9760**

■CRUISY AREAS

Hilton Park [AYOR] Dover Rte Rd

Pierce Island [AYOR] dock area

Asbury Park • New Jersey

Surry

■ ACCOMMODATIONS

The Surry House [GS,SW,WC,GO] 50 Village Rd (at Crain Rd) 603/352-2268 *B&B in private home, full brkfst*

White Mtns

■ ACCOMMODATIONS

The Horse & Hound Inn [GF,F,GO] 205 Wells Rd, Franconia 603/823-5501, 800/450-5501 *clsd April & Nov, also restaurant*

The Inn at Bowman [GS,SW,NS,GO] Rte 2, Randolph 603/466-5006 *country inn, hot tub*

Inn at Crystal Lake [GS,NS,GO] Rte 153 Eaton Center (at Rte 16), North Conway 603/447-2120, 800/343-7336

Mulburn Inn at Bethlehem [GS,NS] 2370 Main St/ Rte 302, Bethlehem 603/869-3389, 800/457-9440 *Victorian B&B, hot tub*

The Notchland Inn [GS,F,NS,GO] Rte 302, Hart's Location 603/374-6131, 800/866-6131 *1860s mansion on 100 acres, full brkfst*

Riverbend Inn B&B [GS,NS,GO] 273 Chocorua Hwy (at Rte 113), Chocorua 603/323-7440, 800/628-6944 *full brkfst, located on the Chocorua River*

Wildcat Inn & Tavern [GF,E] Rte 16A, Jackson Village 603/383-4245, 800/228-4245 *full brkfst, 2 restaurants*

Will's Inn [GF,SW,NS] Rte 302, Glen 603/383-6757, 800/233-6780 *New England motor inn, 2-bdrm cottages*

■ RESTAURANTS

Polly's Pancake Parlor Rte 117 (exit 38 off 93 N), Sugar Hill 603/823-5575 *7am-2pm, till 3pm wknds, clsd winters*

■ CRUISY AREAS

Dugway Scenic Rest Stop [AYOR] Still Rd, Conway

Scenic Rest Area [AYOR] on left of Rte 16 N, Chocorua

Schouler Park [AYOR] North Conway

Wilton

■ ACCOMMODATIONS

The Fountain House [GF,NS,GO] 55 Burns Hill Rd (at NH Rte 31) 603/654-5000, 888/222-7330 *B&B inn, full brkfst, jacuzzi*

NEW JERSEY

Statewide

■ PUBLICATIONS

PM Entertainment Magazine 631/587-8669, 631/543-1963 *events, listings, classifieds & more for Long Island, NJ & NYC*

Asbury Park

■ BARS

Anybodys [M,NH,B,L,MR,TG,18+,GO] 108 St James Pl (at Cookman Ave) *4pm-2am, patio, volleyball*

Georgie's [MW,NH,NS,WC] 810 5th Ave (at Main) 732/988-1220 *1pm-2am, from noon wknds*

■ NIGHTCLUBS

Paradise [MW,D,E,P,SW] 101 Asbury Ave (at Ocean Ave) 732/988-6663 *4pm-2am, 2 dance flrs, also piano bar & tiki/ pool bar in summer*

■ RESTAURANTS

Cafe on Mattison 620 Mattison Ave 732/869-9666 *brkfst, lunch & dinner, clsd Mon*

Moonstruck 517 Lake Ave (at Grand) 732/988-0123 *dinner only, clsd Mon, also bar*

The Talking Bird Restaurant [★MW,GO] 224 Cookman Ave (at St James Place) *midnight-4am, Fri-Sat only, popular 'after-closing' spot, near gay bars*

■ CRUISY AREAS

Boardwalk [AYOR] near Convention Hall

New Jersey • USA

Atlantic City

ACCOMMODATIONS

➤ **Ocean House** [MO,V,SW,N,GO] 127 S Ocean Ave **609/345-0198** *intimate atmosphere*

Surfside Resort Hotel [GS,SW,GO] 18 S Mt Vernon Ave (at Pacific) **609/347-0808, 888/277-7873** *upscale straight-friendly hotel, sundeck, hot tub, also bar, restaurant in summer*

BARS

Brass Rail Bar & Grill [★GS,NH,F,K,S,GO] at Club Tru Complex **609/347-0808** *24hrs, go-go boys Sun*

Oak Room [GF,P,GO] at Surfside Resort Hotel **609/347-0808** *9pm-1:30am Fri-Sat only, seasonal, upscale piano lounge*

Reflections [MW,NH,V] 135 S South Carolina Ave (at Pacific) **609/348-1115** *5pm-5am*

NIGHTCLUBS

Club Tru [★GS,D] 9 S Martin Luther King, Jr Blvd (btwn Atlantic & Pacific Aves) **609/344-2222** *10pm-2am, several bars*

Studio Six Video Dance Club [★MW,D,E,V] 18 S Mt Vernon Ave **609/348-3310** *10pm-close, go-go boys*

RESTAURANTS

Dock's Oyster House [WC] 2405 Atlantic Ave **609/345-0092** *dinner*

Mama Mott's [WC] 151 S New York Ave (at Pacific) **609/345-8218** *dinner nightly, Italian & seafood*

White House Sub Shop 2301 Arctic Ave (at Mississippi) **609/345-1564** *10am-10pm, till 11pm Fri-Sat, from 11am Sun*

PUBLICATIONS

➤ **EXP Gayzette** **302/227-5787, 877/397-6244** *bi-weekly gay magazine for Mid-Atlantic*

OCEAN HOUSE
127 South Ocean Avenue
Atlantic City, NJ 08401
609-345-0198

The beachblock, centrally located, clothing optional, intimate atmosphere guest house exclusively for men.
CALL/WRITE FOR BROCHURE

Highlands • New Jersey

■ **MEN'S SERVICES**
➤ **Megaphone Atlantic City**
800/289-1489 *Call for the local # nearest you! Meet Hot Men in your area! FREE to Browse & Respond to voice ads. Use code 3087. Also try MEGAMATES.COM*

■ **EROTICA**
Atlantic City News 101 S Martin Luther King Jr Blvd (at Pacific) **609/344-9444** *24hrs*

Belmar

■ **CRUISY AREAS**
Belmar Beach [AYOR] *btwn 2nd & 3rd*

Boonton

■ **NIGHTCLUBS**
Connexions [MW,D,CW,F,S] 202 Myrtle Ave (off Washington) **973/263-4000** *11:30am-2am, from 4pm wknds, CW Tue*

Camden

see also Philadelphia, Pennsylvania

■ **ENTERTAINMENT & RECREATION**
The Walt Whitman House 328 Mickle Blvd (btwn S 3rd & S 4th Sts) **856/964-5383** *the last home of America's great & controversial poet*

Cape May

■ **ACCOMMODATIONS**
Highland House [GF,NS] 131 N Broadway (at York) **609/898-1198** *B&B, gazebo*

The Virginia Hotel [GF] 25 Jackson St (btwn Beach Dr & Carpenter's Ln) **609/884-5700, 800/732-4236** *also The Ebbitt Room restaurant*

■ **BARS**
The King Edward Room [M] 301 Howard St (at The Chalfonte Hotel) **609/884-8409**

■ **CAFES**
Brad's Beachfront Cafe 314 Beach Dr (at Jackson) **609/898-6050** *7am-10pm in summer*

■ **CRUISY AREAS**
Cape May Promenade [AYOR] Beach Ave (btwn Broadway & 2nd)

Cherry Hill

see also Philadelphia, Pennsylvania

■ **CRUISY AREAS**
Cooper River Park [AYOR] Cuthbert Blvd S (off Rte 70) *turn left at North Park Dr, area behind & E of the Hilton*

Clifton

■ **CRUISY AREAS**
3rd Ward Park [AYOR] *by the boat house*

Rte 3 West [AYOR] *pull-off after IHOP*

Collingswood

see also Philadelphia, Pennsylvania

Egg Harbor City

■ **BARS**
Red Moon Saloon [GS,NH,F,K] 5027 White Horse Pike **609/965-4755** *4pm-3am, more gay Sat, also restaurant*

■ **EROTICA**
United Video Adult World 25 White Horse Park **609/965-1110** *24hrs wknds*

Florence

■ **EROTICA**
Florence Book Store Rte 130 S (4 miles S of Rte 206) **609/499-9853**

Folsom

■ **NIGHTCLUBS**
The Rainbow [MW,D,F,DS,S] 40 E Black Horse Pike (Rte 322) **609/567-4499** *3pm-close, free happy hour buffet 3pm-8pm, also tiki bar, Italian restaurant till 10pm, go-go boys*

Highlands

■ **ACCOMMODATIONS**
Sandy Hook Cottage B&B [GS,NS,GO] 36 Navesink Ave (Rte 36) **732/708-1923** *hot tub*

New Jersey • USA

Hoboken

■NIGHTCLUBS
Maxwell's [★GF,A] 1039 Washington St **201/656-9632** *live music venue*

Howell

■EROTICA
Video Express 6825 Hwy 9 **732/363-9680**

Jersey City

■NIGHTCLUBS
Albert's [M,D] 360 Marin Blvd (at 1st) **201/222-3282** *10pm-3am Fri-Sat only*

Lambertville

see also New Hope, Pennsylvania

■ACCOMMODATIONS
York Street House B&B [GF,NS] 42 York St **609/397-3007, 888/398-3199** *1909 Manor house*

Long Branch

see also Asbury Park

■CRUISY AREAS
Boardwalk [AYOR] W end

Morristown

■INFO LINES & SERVICES
Gay Activist Alliance in Morris County 21 Normandy Hts Rd (at Unitarian Fellowship) **973/285-1595** *info line 7:30pm-10:30pm, also recorded info*

New Brunswick

■INFO LINES & SERVICES
Pride Center of New Jersey 1048 Livingston Ave **732/846-2232** *info line & mtg space for various groups, call for info*

■BARS
The Den [★M,D,CW,MR,S,V,WC] 700 Hamilton St (at Douglas), Somerset **732/545-7329** *8pm-2am, from 9pm Sat, clsd Mon, DJ Fri-Sat, CW Fri*

■RESTAURANTS
The Frog & the Peach [WC] 29 Dennis St (at Hiram Square) **732/846-3216** *lunch Mon-Fri, dinner nightly, full bar*

Stage Left [★MW,WC] 5 Livingston Ave (at George) **732/828-4444** *full bar, expensive*

■CRUISY AREAS
Johnson Park [AYOR] *parking lot & trails (along river) Highlands Park*

Newark

■BARS
Murphy's Tavern [MW,NH,D,MR-AF,F] 59 Edison Pl (btwn Broad & Mulberry) **973/622-9176** *11:30am-2am, DJ Th-Sat*

■MEN'S SERVICES
The Confidential Connection®! **973/243-7000** *The hottest local guys! 18+ Record & Listen FREE! Use access code 499*

The Gay Connection **900/468-6338** *Talk and/or meet with other men from the area, at only 99¢ per minute.*

➤ **Megaphone Newark** **800/289-1489** *Call for the local # nearest you! Meet Hot Men in your area! FREE to Browse & Respond to voice ads. Use code 3087. Also try MEGAMATES.COM*

■CRUISY AREAS
Ferry St [AYOR] *iron-bound area*

Ocean City

■CRUISY AREAS
58th St Pavilion [AYOR] *late*

Corson's Inlett State Park [AYOR] Ocean Dr (near Strathmere Ocean City bridge) *beach & trails*

Orange

■CRUISY AREAS
Big Rock at South Mtn Reservation [AYOR] Crest Dr (to Washington Rock)

Toms River • New Jersey

Plainfield

■ ACCOMMODATIONS

The Pillars of Plainfield B&B
[GS,NS,GO] 922 Central Ave (at 9th St)
**908/753-0922, 888/PILLARS
(745-5277)** *full brkfst, Georgian/Victorian mansion*

Princeton

■ CRUISY AREAS

Herrontown Woods Park [AYOR] off Snowden Ln, btwn mailbox 586 & 603 (no sign, entrance looks like private driveway)

Rahway

■ CAFES

Eat to the Beat Coffeehouse [E] 1465 Irving St (at E Cherry) **732/381-0505** *11am-10pm, till midnight Fri-Sat, clsd Mon*

■ CRUISY AREAS

Milton Lake [AYOR] Lake Ave (off St George Ave) *turn right before cemetery, follow paths to lake*

Rahway River Park [AYOR]

Red Bank

■ BOOKSTORES

Earth Spirit 16 W Front St (at Broad) **732/842-3855** *11am-7pm, till 8pm Fri, noon-5pm Sun, New Age bookstore & center*

River Edge

■ NIGHTCLUBS

Feathers [★M,D,K,S,V,YC,WC] 77 Kinder Kamack Rd (at Grand) **201/342-6410** *9pm-2am, till 3am Sat, theme nights*

■ CRUISY AREAS

Park & Ride [AYOR] off Rte 4 (across the street from Feathers nightclub)

Rosemont

■ RESTAURANTS

The Cafe [BYOB] 88 Kingwood-Stockton Rd **609/397-4097** *8am-3pm, dinner 5pm-9pm Wed-Sun, clsd Mon*

Sandy Hook

■ ENTERTAINMENT & RECREATION

Gunnison Nude Beach Beach G parking lot (near Gunnison Park, S end) *at the beach go right (all the way) to the gay section, cruisy area yr-round*

Sayreville

■ NIGHTCLUBS

Colosseum [MW,D,K,S,18+] 7090 Rte 9 N (at Rte 35 N) **732/316-0670** *9pm-3am, clsd Mon, drag Tue, salsa Sat*

■ RESTAURANTS

Cagney's Pub & Restaurant [D,K] 3276 Washington Rd **732/525-5586** *3pm-2am, also bar*

Seaside Heights

■ CRUISY AREAS

Franklin Ave & Boardwalk [AYOR] *summers only*

Sergeantsville

see New Hope, Pennsylvania

Somerville

■ CAFES

Sanctuary Cafe 41 W Main St (at Division) *internet access, gay coffeehouse 2nd Th*

■ ENTERTAINMENT & RECREATION

Gay Coffeehouse 41 W Main St (at Division, at Sanctuary cafe) **908/685-0779** *2nd Th*

Stockton

■ ACCOMMODATIONS

Woolverton Inn [GF,WC] 6 Woolverton Rd **609/397-0802, 888/264-6648** *full brkfst, jacuzzi*

Toms River

■ CRUISY AREAS

Winding River [AYOR] Rte 37 (near Garden State Pkwy)

New Jersey • USA

Trenton

■BARS
Buddies Pub [MW,NH,D,K] 677 S Broad St (at Madison) **609/989-8566** *5pm-1:30am, from 6pm wknds, DJ wknds*

■CRUISY AREAS
Clinton & State St [AYOR]

West Paterson

■CRUISY AREAS
Homo Beach [AYOR] river btwn Union Blvd & Little Falls

Westville

see also Philadelphia, Pennsylvania

■NIGHTCLUBS
Bounce Night Club [M,D,MR,TG,F,K,DS,S,V,18+,YC,WC] 1102 Rte 130 S (at I-295) **856/845-1010** *9pm-2am, clsd Sun-Tue*

NEW MEXICO

Statewide

■PUBLICATIONS
Out! Magazine **505/243-2540** *lgbt*

Alamogordo

■ACCOMMODATIONS
Best Western Desert Aire Motor Inn [GF,SW,WC] 1021 S White Sands Blvd **505/437-2110**

■CRUISY AREAS
Alameda Park [AYOR] off White Sands Blvd *nights*

Foothills Park [AYOR] 1st St E (past Scenic Dr) *days*

Albuquerque

includes Bernalillo, Corrales, Placitas & Rio Rancho

■INFO LINES & SERVICES
AA Gay/ Lesbian [NS,WC] **505/266-1900 (AA#)**

Common Bond Info Line **505/891-3647** *24hrs, covers lgbt community*

MPower Community Center 120 Morningside NE **505/232-2990** *for gay & bi men 18-29, weekly & monthly events*

Steve Benoit 609 11th St NW **505/245-7653, 800/658-6149** *associate realtor: buyer's agent, seller's agent, relocation specialist*

■ACCOMMODATIONS
Brittania & W E Mauger Estate B&B [GF,NS] 701 Roma Ave NW (at 7th) **505/242-8755, 800/719-9189** *intimate Queen Anne house, full brkfst*

Casa de Alegria B&B [GS,NS,WC,GO] 5 Alegria Ln (at Old Church Rd), Corrales **505/890-0176, 888/320-3456** *full brkfst, hot tub*

Casitas at Old Town [GS,NS,GO] 1604 Old Town Rd NW **505/843-7479** *classic adobe bldg, private patios*

El Peñasco [W,NS,GO] **505/771-8909, 888/576-2726** *private historic adobe guest house, halfway btwn Albuquerque & Santa Fe*

Golden Guesthouses [MW,NS,GO] 2645 Decker NW **505/344-9205, 888/513-GOLD**

Hacienda Antigua B&B [GS,SW,NS] 6708 Tierra Dr NW (close to corner of 2nd & Osuna) **505/345-5399, 800/201-2986** *full brkfst, hot tub*

Nuevo Dia [GF,WC] 11110 San Rafael Ave NE (at Browning) **505/856-7910** *guest house, hot tub*

Wyndham Albuquerque Hotel [GF,SW] 2910 Yale Blvd SE (at Gibson) **505/843-7000, 800/227-1117** *4-star hotel, also Rojo Bar & Grill*

Albuquerque • New Mexico

■BARS

Albuquerque Mining Co (AMC)
[★M,D,S,V,WC,GO] 7209 Central Ave NE (at Louisiana) **505/255-4022** *6pm-2am, till midnight Sun, also Pit Bar*

Albuquerque Social Club [★MW,D,PC]
4021 Central Ave NE (enter rear)
505/255-0887 *3pm-midnight, till 2am Fri-Sat*

Empire [M,D,TG,F,E,V,GO]
4310 Central Ave SE (at Washington)
505/255-1668 *clsd Mon-Tue*

Foxes Lounge [MW,D,DS] 8521 Central Ave NE (btwn Wisconsin & Wyoming)
505/255-3060 *10am-2am, noon-midnight Sun*

The Ranch [M,D,CW,B,L,WC]
8900 Central SE (at Wyoming)
505/275-1616 *noon-2am, till midnight Sun*

■NIGHTCLUBS

Pulse/ Blu [★M,D,E,$] 4100 Central Ave SE (at Montclaire, in Nob Hill)
505/255-3334 *Blu Lounge 5pm-2am, Pulse Th-Sat only*

■RESTAURANTS

Artichoke Café 424 Central Ave
505/243-0200 *lunch Mon-Fri, dinner nightly, bistro*

Chef du Jour [WC] 119 San Pasquale SW (at Central) **505/247-8998** *lunch Th-Sat, dinner Fri-Sat*

Flying Star Cafe [WC] 3416 Central SE (2 blks W of Carlisle) **505/255-6633** *6am-11pm, till midnight wknds*

Frontier 2400 Central SE (at Cornell)
505/266-0550 *24hrs, good brkfst burritos*

Romano's Macaroni Grill
2100 Louisiana NE (at Winrock Mall)
505/881-3400 *lunch & dinner, Italian*

Sadie's Cocinita [★] 6230 4th St NW (near Osuna) **505/345-5339** *11am-10pm, till 9pm Sun, New Mexican*

■ENTERTAINMENT & RECREATION

Hugs & Hot Air Ballooning [GF,GO]
12272 N Hwy 14, Cedar Crest
505/450-8692 *scenic balloon rides*

■BOOKSTORES

Bird Song 1708 Central SE
505/268-7204 *11am-7pm, used, lgbt section*

Page One 11018 Montgomery NE
505/294-2026, 800/521-4122 *9am-10pm, till 8pm Sun*

Sisters & Brothers Bookstore
4011 Silver Ave SE (btwn Morningside & Montclair) **505/266-7317,**
800/687-3480 (orders only) *10am-6pm, noon-5pm Sun, clsd Mon, lgbt*

■RETAIL SHOPS

In Crowd [WC,GO] 3106 Central SE (at Richmond) **505/268-3750** *10am-6pm, noon-4pm Sun, local & folk art*

■PUBLICATIONS

Out! Magazine **505/243-2540** *lgbt newsmagazine*

■GYMS & HEALTH CLUBS

Betty's Bath & Day Spa 1835 Candelaria NW **505/341-3456**
full-service spa, men's night Tue

Pride Gym [MO,18+,PC] 1803 3rd St NW (4 blks S of I-40, exit 158)
505/242-7810 *tanning, clothing-optional sundeck, after-hours parties, day passes available*

■MEN'S SERVICES

▶ **Megaphone Albuquerque**
800/289-1489 *Call for the local # nearest you! Meet Hot Men in your area! FREE to Browse & Respond to voice ads. Use code 3087. Also try MEGAMATES.COM*

■EROTICA

Castle Superstore 5110 Central Ave SE (at San Mateo) **505/262-2266**

Mr Peepers 4300 Edith Blvd NE (at Candelaria) **505/343-8063** *24hrs*

Not Too Naughty 5319 Menual Blvd NE **505/881-2112** *toys, videos, DVDs, magazines, men's sexy clothing, fetish items*

New Mexico • USA

Too Naughty 9134 Central Ave SE **505/293-3507** *toys, videos, DVDs, magazines, men's sexy clothing, fetish items*

Video Maxxx 810 Comanche NE (at I-25) **505/341-4000** *leather, novelties, books, etc*

Viewpoint [★] 6406 Central Ave SE (at San Pedro) **505/268-6373** *24hrs*

Carlsbad

■ CRUISY AREAS

Riverside Park [AYOR] at Blodgett St cul-de-sac *nights*

Chimayo

■ ACCOMMODATIONS

Casa Escondida B&B [GF,NS] **505/351-4805, 800/643-7201** *full brkfst, hot tub*

Cloudcroft

■ ACCOMMODATIONS

Good Life Inn B&B [GF,GO] 164 Karr Canyon Rd (At Hwy 82) **505/682-5433, 866/543-3466** *luxurious suites, full brkfst, hot tub*

Clovis

■ CRUISY AREAS

Main St [AYOR] btwn 2nd & 7th

Farmington

■ ACCOMMODATIONS

Days Inn [GF,WC] 1901 E Broadway **505/325-3700**

■ CRUISY AREAS

Brookside Park [AYOR] Dustin & 20th

Hobbs

■ EROTICA

Oasis Video & Bookstore Hwy 132 & Hwy 83 (10 miles N of town) **505/392-2310**

Stateline Adult Book Store 6100 W Carlsbad Hwy 62 (across from airport) **505/393-3616**

Las Cruces

■ INFO LINES & SERVICES

Southwest Gay Men's Association **505/541-1736, 505/522-1390**

■ CAFES

Tommy's Cake Shop & Cafe [GF] 1609 El Paseo (at Montana) **505/526-6599** *7am-7pm, till 6pm Mon, 8am-4pm Sun, alternative night Th w/ karaoke* [GS,YC]

■ RETAIL SHOPS

Spirit Winds Gifts & Cafe 2260 S Locust St **505/521-0222** *7am-9pm, till 9:30pm Fri-Sat, 9:30am-6pm Sun, live music wknds, patio*

■ PUBLICATIONS

Normal Heart 505/522-1390 *newsletter*

■ CRUISY AREAS

Burn Lake [AYOR] btwn W Amador & Westgate

Madrid

■ ACCOMMODATIONS

Madrid Lodging [GF,NS,WC] 14 Opera House Rd **505/471-3450** *suite, hot tub*

■ BARS

Mineshaft Tavern [GF,E] 2846 State Hwy 14 **505/473-0743** *noon-10pm, till 2am wknds, hosts annual He/ She Bang in Sept, also restaurant from 11am*

■ CAFES

Java Junction 2855 State Hwy 14 **505/438-2772** *8am-7pm, also B&B*

Ruidoso

■ RESTAURANTS

Mountain Annie's [GF,E,BW,WC] 2710 Sudderth (at Mechem) **505/257-7982** *11am-9pm, clsd wknds, patio, gazebos*

■ CRUISY AREAS

Downtown Park [AYOR] off Meechum Dr

Santa Fe • New Mexico

Santa Fe

INFO LINES & SERVICES
AA Gay/ Lesbian 505/982-8932

ACCOMMODATIONS
Alexander's Inn [GS,NS,GO] 529 E Palace Ave (at Delgado) **505/986-1431, 888/321-5123** full brkfst, hot tub

➤ **Arius Compound** [GF] **505/982-8859, 800/735-8453** 4 adobe casitas, hot tub, patio

Casa Torreon [GF,NS,GO] 1613 Calle Torreon **505/982-2826, 505/982-6815** adobe guest house w/ kitchen

El Farolito B&B [GS,GO] 514 Galisteo St (at Paseo de Peralta) **505/988-1631, 888/634-8782** adobe compound w/ casitas

Four Kachinas Inn [GS,NS,WC,GO] 512 Webber St **505/982-2550, 800/397-2564** courtyard, near the Plaza

Hacienda Nicholas [GS,NS,WC,GO] 320 E Marcy St **505/986-1431, 888/321-5123** full brkfst

Inn at Mountaintop [GS,GO] **505/621-7958** private cottages, hot tub, secluded 10 acres, call for directions

➤ **Inn of the Turquoise Bear B&B** [MW,NS,GO] 342 E Buena Vista St **505/983-0798, 800/396-4104** Out & About Editors' Choice Award 1999-03 & Santa Fe Heritage Preservation Award 1999, New Mexico Preservation Award 2000

La Tienda Inn & Duran House [GF,NS,WC] 445-447 W San Francisco St **505/989-8259, 800/889-7611** adobe compound

Leadfeather [MW,NS,GO] 3888 State Rd 14 (at Hwy 42) **505/438-3131** B&B on scenic Turquoise Trail

The Madeleine Inn [GS,NS,GO] 106 Faithway St **505/986-1431, 888/321-5123** Queen Anne Victorian, full brkfst, hot tub

ARIUS COMPOUND

SANTA FE VACATION RENTALS ON HISTORIC CANYON ROAD

Classic Adobe Casitas surrounded by gardens and fruit trees, patios, fountain, outdoor redwood hot tub. Tile floors, corner fireplaces, one or two bedrooms, fully equipped kitchens Ideally located in Santa Fe's historic East Side, walking distance to restaurants, museums, galleries & plaza. Great for outdoor weddings. Rentals by the night or week.

old world charm at affordable rates

800-735-8453 · 505-982-8859
WWW.ARIUSCOMPOUND.COM
po box 1111, santa fe, nm 87504 • info@ariuscompound.com

New Mexico • USA

Marriott Residence Inn [GF,SW,NS,WC]
1698 Galisteo St (at St Michaels)
505/988-7300, 800/331-3131
suites, hot tub

Michael's Casa Quintana
[GS,NS,WC,GO] 114 Quintana St
505/984-1869 *1,100-sq-ft adobe home rental*

Open Sky [GF,NS,WC,GO]
134 Turquoise Trail Ct **505/471-3475**
B&B & guest house , jacuzzi, great views

Our Haven Santa Fe [GS,GO]
828/669-7580 *adobe guest house, private gardens*

Tano Road Casita [GS] 15 Tano Pt Ln
505/989-7802, 505/989-7803
studio guest house

The Triangle Inn—Santa Fe
[MW,WC,GO] 14 Arroyo Cuyamungue
(12 miles N of Santa Fe)
505/455-3375, 877/733-7689
7 adobe casitas, smokefree available, hot tub

Villas de Santa Fe [GS,SW,WC]
400 Griffin St **505/988-3000,
800/869-6790** *villa-style suites, gym, courtyard*

The Water Street Inn [GF,NS,WC]
427 W Water St **505/984-1193,
800/646-6752** *historic adobe inn, jacuzzi*

■ NIGHTCLUBS

The Paramount/ Bar B Lounge
[★GS,D,F,E] 331 Sandoval (at Montezuma) **505/982-8999** *5pm-close, from 7pm Sun, more gay Wed for Trash Disco & Sat for Galaxy Lounge, also pizza restaurant*

Swig [GS,D,F,GO] 135 W Palace Ave, 3rd flr (at Grant) **505/955-0400** *5pm-2am, clsd Sun-Mon, swank lounge, tapas served*

Inn of the Turquoise Bear

gay headquarters for visitors to santa fe, new mexico
an historic bed and breakfast on the Witter Bynner Estate

- Walk to Plaza, museums, galleries, restaurants & gay nightlife
- Close to opera, theater, skiing, hiking, biking, tours of pueblos & archaeological sites
- 11 rooms, private baths & entrances
- Secluded gardens & patios
- TV/VCRs
- Southwest Decor
- Expanded continental breakfasts & sunset refreshments

www.turquoisebear.net
342 E. Buena Vista Street • Santa Fe, NM 87501-4423 • 800.396.4104
505.983.0798 • FAX 505.988.4225 • IGLTA • email: bluebear@newmexico.com

Taos • New Mexico

■ RESTAURANTS

Anasazi Restaurant [WC]
113 Washington Ave (at The Inn of the Anasazi) 505/988-3236 brkfst, lunch, dinner & Sun brunch

Cafe Pasqual's [★BW] 121 Don Gaspar (at Water St) 505/983-9340 brkfst, lunch, dinner & Sun brunch, Southwestern

Cowgirl Hall of Fame 319 S Guadalupe (btwn Aztec & Guadalupe) 505/982-2565 11am-2am, from 8:30am wknds, till midnight Sun, Southwestern

Dave's Not Here [BW] 1115 Hickox St (at Cortez) 505/983-7060 11am-9pm, clsd Sun, New Mexican

Geronimo's 724 Canyon Rd (at Camino del Monte Sol) 505/982-1500 lunch daily, dinner Tue-Sun, eclectic gourmet, full bar from 11am-11pm

Paul's [BW,WC] 72 Marcy St (at Lincoln & Washington) 505/982-8738 lunch Mon-Sat, dinner nightly, modern int'l

Santacafe [WC] 231 Washington Ave 505/984-1788 lunch & dinner, Southwestern/ Asian

Vanessie of Santa Fe [★MW,P] 434 W San Francisco (at Guadalupe) 505/982-9966 5:30pm-10:30pm (bar till 1am), steak house, piano bar

■ ENTERTAINMENT & RECREATION

Ten Thousand Waves [N] 3451 Hyde Park Rd (4 miles out of town) 505/992-5025 Japanese health spa & lodging, sit under the stars & look at the mtns, clothing-optional in all tubs

■ BOOKSTORES

Downtown Subscription 376 Garcia St (at Acequia Madre) 505/983-3085 7am-7pm, newsstand & coffee shop

■ RETAIL SHOPS

The Ark 133 Romero St (at Agua Fria) 505/988-3709 9:30am-7pm, 10am-6pm Sat, 11am-5pm Sun, spiritual

Silver City

■ ACCOMMODATIONS
West Street Inn 505/534-2302

■ CAFES
Piñon Cafe & Bakery [BW,GO] 602 N Bullard St (at 6th St) 505/534-9168 NY-style deli menu for brkfst & lunch, fine Italian/ seafood dinner menu, espresso, patio

■ RESTAURANTS
Diane's Restaurant & Bakery [BW] 510 N Bullard 505/538-8722

Taos

■ ACCOMMODATIONS

Adobe & Stars B&B [GS,NS,WC] 584 State Hwy 150 (at Valdez Rim Rd) 505/776-2776, 800/211-7076 full brkfst, fireplaces, patios

Brooks Street Inn [GF,NS] 505/758-1489, 800/758-1489 full brkfst

Dobson House [GF,NS] 475 Tune Dr 505/776-5738 luxury suites, full brkfst, N of Taos

The Dreamcatcher B&B [GF,NS,WC] 416 La Lomita (Valverde) 505/758-0613, 888/758-0613 full brkfst, hot tub

Orinda B&B [GS,NS] 461 Valverde St (on Valverde Park) 505/758-8581, 800/847-1837 full brkfst

San Geronimo Lodge [★GS,SW,NS,WC] 1101 Witt Rd (at Kit Carson) 505/751-3776, 800/894-4119 full brkfst, hot tub & massage available

Sonterra Condominiums [GS,NS] 206 Siler Rd 505/758-7989, 800/257-6010

New York • USA

NEW YORK

Adirondack Mtns

■ACCOMMODATIONS

Country Road Lodge B&B [GF,NS]
115 Hickory Hill Rd, Warrensburg
518/623-2207 *full brkfst, secluded retreat*

The Doctor's Inn [GF,NS] Trudeau Rd, RR1, Box 375, Saranac Lake
518/891-3464, 888/518-3464
full brkfst, some shared baths

King Hendrick Motel [GF,SW,WC]
1602 State Rte 9, Lake George
518/792-0418, 866/521-6883
cabins available

Rainbow Woods Campgrounds
[MO,SW] 134 Rte 74 (at Rte 9), Schroon Lake **518/532-9728** *also inn, jacuzzi*

■CRUISY AREAS

Cooperas Pond Trail [AYOR] off E side of Rte 86 (at junction of Rtes 86 & 7), Lake Placid

Albany

see Capital District

Angelica

■ACCOMMODATIONS

Jones Pond Campground
[MO,SW,N,GO] 9835 Old State Rd
716/567-8100 *May-Oct 15, theme wknds, campsites & RV*

Beacon

■RESTAURANTS

Quinn's Restaurant 330 Main St
845/831-8065 *5am-2pm, great bread*

■RETAIL SHOPS

Kringle's Christmas House 475 Main St (at Tiorondа Ave) **877/323-7660**
10am-5pm, clsd Tue, gifts

Binghamton

see also Scranton, Pennsylvania

■INFO LINES & SERVICES

AA Gay/ Lesbian 438 Chenango St (at United Methodist Church)
607/722-5983 *7pm Sat*

BARA (Binghamton Area Rainbow Association) PO Box 3308 13902
607/772-3216

■ACCOMMODATIONS

Serenity Farms [GS,SW,GO]
607/656-4659 *B&B, camping, on 100 acres*

■BARS

Squiggy's [MW,NH,D] 34 Chenango St (at Court) **607/722-2299** *5pm-1am, till 3am Fri-Sat, clsd Sun, DJ Fri-Sat*

■NIGHTCLUBS

Prism [M,D,MR,S,GO] 201 State St (at Hawley) **607/772-0710** *3pm-close, from 7pm Fri-Sat, clsd Mon-Tue*

■CAFES

Lost Dog Cafe [★E,BW,WC] 222 Water St **607/771-6063** *11am-10pm, till 11pm Fri-Sat, clsd Sun*

■RESTAURANTS

The Whole in the Wall 43 S Washington St **607/722-5138**
11:30am-9pm, clsd Sun-Mon

■ENTERTAINMENT & RECREATION

Rainbow Dreams **607/723-4091**
lgbt chorus

■MEN'S CLUBS

NEMA **607/656-4388** *private fisting parties, monthly*

■EROTICA

North Street Bookshop 17 Washington Ave (at North), Endicott
607/785-1588

■CRUISY AREAS

Oneida Campground [AYOR]

Capital District • New York

Buffalo

■ BARS

Buddies [MW,D,E,WC] 31 Johnson Park (at S Elmwood) **716/855-1313** *1pm-4am, from noon wknds*

Cathode Ray [M,NH,V,WC] 26 Allen St (at N Pearl) **716/884-3615** *1pm-4am*

Fugazi [GS,V] 503 Franklin St (near Allen St) **716/881-3588** *5pm-2am, from 8pm wknds, clsd Mon, cocktail lounge*

The Underground [M,NH,D,K] 174 Delaware Ave (at Johnson) **716/853-0092**

■ NIGHTCLUBS

Club Marcella [MW,D,DS,WC] 622 Main St **716/847-6850** *9pm-4am, from 4pm Fri, clsd Mon-Tue, 19+ Th*

■ CAFES

Teasel [GO] 100 Elmwood (at Allen St) **716/332-6472** *7am-11pm, 8am-midnight Fri-Sat, 9am-9pm Sun, tearoom*

■ BOOKSTORES

Talking Leaves 3158 Main St (btwn Winspear & Hertel Aves) **716/837-8554** *10am-6pm, till 8pm Wed-Th, clsd Sun; also 951 Elmwood Ave, 716/884-9524*

■ PUBLICATIONS

Erie Gay News **814/456-9833** *covers news & events in the Erie, Cleveland, Pittsburgh, Buffalo & Chautauqua County, NY region*

■ MEN'S CLUBS

Fort Erie Steam Baths (see listing in Fort Erie, ON, Canada)

■ MEN'S SERVICES

➤ **Megaphone Buffalo** **800/289-1489** *Call for the local # nearest you! Meet Hot Men in your area! FREE to Browse & Respond to voice ads. Use code 3087. Also try MEGAMATES.COM*

■ EROTICA

Village Books & News 3104 Delaware Ave (at Sheridan), Kenmore **716/877-5027** *24hrs*

Capital District

includes Albany, Schenectady & Troy

■ INFO LINES & SERVICES

Gay AA at L/G Community Center, Albany **518/462-6138** *7:30pm Sun & Mon*

Lesbian/ Gay Community Center 332 Hudson Ave, Albany **518/462-6138** *7pm-10pm, till 11pm Fri-Sat, 2pm-10pm Sun, also cafe*

■ ACCOMMODATIONS

The Morgan State House [GF,NS] 393 State St, Albany **518/427-6063, 888/427-6063** *1800s town house*

■ BARS

Alibi's [GS,F,GO] 1100 Madison Ave, Albany **518/489-0606** *5:30pm-2am, till 4am Fri-Sat, casual lounge, also Peking restaurant*

Blythewood [M,NH,F,WC] 50 N Jay St (off Union), Schenectady **518/382-9755** *9pm-4am, from 4pm Sun*

Cafe Hollywood [GF,NH,V] 275 Lark St (at Hamilton), Albany **518/472-9043** *3pm-4am*

Clinton Street Pub [MW,NH,D,E,K] 159 Clinton St, Schenectady **518/377-8555** *8am-4am, noon Sun*

Oh Bar [M,NH,MR,V,WC] 304 Lark St (at Madison), Albany **518/463-9004** *2pm-4am*

Players [M,NH,F,K,GO] 77 Central Ave, Albany **518/472-3588** *2pm-4am, Sun brunch*

Rome [★GS,NH,F,GO] 286 Lark St (at Hamilton), Albany **518/436-4096** *6pm-2am, till 4am Th-Sat*

Waterworks Pub [M,NH,D,F,E,K,WC] 76 Central Ave (btwn Lexington & Northern), Albany **518/465-9079** *1pm-4am, garden bar, DJ wknds*

■ NIGHTCLUBS

Club Phoenix [MW,D,TG,K,GO] 348 Central Ave, Albany **518/462-4862** *4pm-4am*

Fuze Box [GS,E,K,GO] 12 Central Ave, Albany **518/432-4472** *8pm-4am, from 2pm Fri, swing dancing Th*

New York • USA

■ Restaurants

Bomber's Burrito Bar [GO]
258 Lark St, Albany 518/463-9636
11am-11pm, till 10pm Sun

Cafe Lulu [BW] 288 Lark St (at Madison), Albany 518/436-5660 *4pm-midnight, till 1am Fri-Sat, Mediterranean*

Debbie's Kitchen 456 Madison Ave (btwn Lark St & Washington Park), Albany 518/463-3829 *10am-9pm, 11am-6pm Sat, clsd Sun*

El Loco Mexican Cafe 465 Madison Ave (btwn Lark & Willett), Albany 518/436-1855 *11:30am-10pm, till 11pm Fri-Sat, clsd Mon, healthy Tex-Mex, full bar*

Shades of Green 187 Lark St, Albany 518/434-1830 *11am-9pm, clsd wknds, vegetarian*

Stephanie's On the Park Restaurant [GO,E] 462 Madison Ave, Albany 518/449-2492 *dinner, Sun brunch, bar till 2am Fri-Sat, clsd Mon, cont'l/ Indonesian*

Yono's [E] 64 Colvin Ave (at Armory Center), Albany 518/436-7747 *5:30-10pm, clsd Sun-Mon, Indonesian/ cont'l, live music*

■ Entertainment & Recreation

Homo Radio WRPI 91.5 FM, Troy 518/276-6248 *noon-2pm Sun*

Two Rivers 518/449-0758 *lgbt outdoor club*

■ Retail Shops

GPA Video/ Deja View 37 Central Ave (at Henry Johnson Blvd), Albany 518/433-1605 *lgbt video sales/ rentals, also adult novelties*

Romeo's Gifts 299 Lark St (at Madison), Albany 518/434-4014 *11am-9pm, noon-5pm Sun*

■ Publications

Community 518/462-6138 x7 *monthly newsjournal*

■ Men's Clubs

River Street Club [MO,V,N,NS,PC,WC,GO] 540 River St (at corner of River & Hoosick St), Troy 518/272-0340 *noon-11pm, till 2am Fri-Sat, full gym, sauna, steam, jacuzzi, tanning*

■ Erotica

Amazing Troy 516 River St (at Hoosic), Troy 518/272-7577

Cinema Art Theatre [M] 289 River St, Troy 518/274-6676

King Street Video 14 King St, Troy 518/272-4714 *24hrs Th-Sat*

■ Cruisy Areas

Empire State Plaza [AYOR] Albany

Lark, State & Willet Sts [AYOR] near Washington Park, Albany

Catskill Mtns

■ Accommodations

Bradstan Country Hotel [GF,C,P] 1561 Rte 17-B/ White Lake 845/583-4114 *also piano bar & cabaret, 6pm-1am Fri-Sat*

Country Suite [GF,NS,WC,GO] Rte 23, Windham 518/734-4079, 888/883-0444 *B&B, Victorian style farmhouse, full brkfst, some shared baths, antique shop*

Full Moon Resort [GS,SW,NS] Valley View Rd (at County Rt 47), Oliverea 845/254-5117, 845/254-5179 *hotel, cabins available, located on 100 acres, commitment ceremonies*

The Nightingale Inn [GS,GO] 2372 State Rte 81, Earlton 518/634-7305 *full brkfst*

Palenville House B&B [GS,NS,GO] 3292 Rte 23A, Palenville 518/678-5649, 877/689-5101 *Victorian guest house, full brkfst, hot tub, some shared baths*

Point Lookout Mountain Inn [GF,NS,WC] The Mohican Trail, Rte 23, East Windham 518/734-3381 *hot tub, near skiing, also restaurant*

River Run B&B [GF,NS] Fleischmanns 845/254-4884 *full brkfst, Queen Anne Victorian*

Village Green [GO] 12 Tinker St 845/679-0313 *B&B*

Fire Island • New York

The Wild Rose Inn [GF,NS,GO] 66 Rock City Rd, Woodstock 845/679-8783 *Victorian B&B*

The Woodstock Inn on the Millstream [GF,WC] 48 Tannery Brook Rd, Woodstock 845/679-8211, 800/697-8211 *swimming hole*

■ RESTAURANTS

Catskill Rose 5355 Rte 212, Mt Tremper 845/688-7100 *5pm-close Th-Sun, full bar, patio*

■ ENTERTAINMENT & RECREATION

Frog Hollow Farm Old Post Rd, Esopus 845/384-6424 *riding school, also summer cottage rental*

Healing Waters Farms [GS,GO] State Rte 206 (1 mile W of Walton, at Lower Third Brook Rd) 607/865-4420 *seasonal, carriage museum, petting zoo, shops*

■ BOOKSTORES

Golden Notebook [WC] 29 Tinker St, Woodstock 845/679-8000 *10:30am-7pm, till 6pm Sun (till 9pm summers), lgbt section*

Cherry Creek

■ ACCOMMODATIONS

The Cherry Creek Inn [GS,GO] 1022 West Rd (at Center Rd) 716/296-5105 *B&B, full bkfst*

Cooperstown

see Sharon Springs

Corning

■ ACCOMMODATIONS

Rufus Tanner House B&B [GS,NS,WC] 60 Sagetown Rd, Pine City 607/732-0213 *full brkfst, jacuzzi*

Cortland

■ BOOKSTORES

Mandolin Winds Bookstore 33 Main St (at Central) 607/758-7460 *10am-7pm, till 4pm Sat, clsd Sun, lgbt section*

Elmira

■ NIGHTCLUBS

ANGLES Ultimate Dance Club [★MW,D,F,S,18+,GO] 511-513 Railroad Ave (btwn Clinton & 3rd) 607/737-7676 *5pm-1am, till 3am Fri-Sat*

■ EROTICA

Deluxe Books 123 Lake St 607/734-9656

Findley Lake

■ ACCOMMODATIONS

The Blue Heron Inn [GF,NS] 10412 Main St (at Shadyside Rd) 716/769-7852 *B&B, full brkfst*

Fire Island

see also Long Island

■ INFO LINES & SERVICES

AA Gay/ Lesbian 631/669-1124

■ ACCOMMODATIONS

A Summer Place Realty [MW,GO] Bayview Walk (at Main Walk), Cherry Grove 631/597-6140 *rentals, private homes & apts, also sales*

Belvedere Hotel [MO,SW,WC] 631/597-6448 *Venetian-style palace, hot tub, jacuzzi, gym*

Black Sheep in Exile B&B [MW,NS,GO] 71 Bay Walk E, The Pines 631/597-6565 *full brkfst, gourmet dinner available*

Bob Howard Real Estate The Pines 631/597-9400, 212/819-9400 *great source for rentals*

Botel [M,F,SW,WC] The Pines 631/597-6500 *also restaurant*

D Katen Fire Island Properties, Ltd [GO] 36 Fire Island Blvd, The Pines 631/597-7000 *weekly, monthly & seasonal rentals*

Dune Point Guesthouse [MW,WC,GO] 631/597-6261 *hot tub*

GroveHotel [M,SW,N,WC,GO] Dock Walk, Cherry Grove 631/597-6600 *non-smoking room available, also 4 bars*

New York • USA

Holly House [MW,NS] Holly Walk near Bayview Walk, Cherry Grove **631/597-6911** *seasonal, shared baths*

Island Properties Real Estate [GO] 37 Fire Island Blvd, The Pines **631/597-6900** *weekly, monthly & seasonal rentals*

Pines Harbor Realty [GO] **631/597-7575, 888/597-7575** *weekly, monthly & seasonal rentals*

Pines Place [GS,SW,GO] **631/597-6162** *guest house, 2 locations, some shared baths*

■BARS

Cherry's [★MW,F,E,DS,P] 158 Bayview Walk, Cherry Grove **631/597-6820** *seasonal, noon-4am, patio, restaurant*

The Island Club & Grille [M,D,E,P] 36 Fire Island Blvd, The Pines **631/597-6001** *seasonal, 6pm-4am, from 4pm wknds, grille open 6pm-11pm, clsd Wed, also piano bar*

■NIGHTCLUBS

GroveHotel (aka the Ice Palace) [MW,D,DS,WC] Cherry Grove **631/597-6600** *hours vary*

The Pavilion [★MW,D,WC] Fire Island Blvd, The Pines **631/597-6131** *seasonal, noon-8am, also restaurant*

■RESTAURANTS

Cherry Grove Pizza Dock Walk (under the GroveHotel), Cherry Grove **631/597-6766** *11am-11pm*

Rachel's at the Grove [MW] Lewis Walk, Cherry Grove **631/597-4174** *brkfst, lunch & dinner, also bar*

Top of the Bay [★MW] Dock Walk at Bay Walk, Cherry Grove **631/597-6699** *seasonal, 7pm-midnight, outdoor dining*

■ENTERTAINMENT & RECREATION

Invasion of the Pines the Pines dock (July 4th wknd) *4th of July, come & enjoy the annual fun as boatloads of drag queens from Cherry Grove arrive to terrorize the posh Pines*

■RETAIL SHOPS

All American Boy Harbor Walk, The Pines **631/597-7758** *noon-5:30pm, 10am-7:30pm wknds, clothing*

■GYMS & HEALTH CLUBS

Pines Gym [★M] Harbor Walk, The Pines **631/597-7867** *where the boys of Fire Island work out*

■CRUISY AREAS

Meat Rack [AYOR] trail btwn Cherry Grove & W end of Pines *where the boys of Fire Island really work out*

Forest Hills

■BARS

Bartini's [M,D,F,S] 1 Station Square *4pm Sun only*

Geneva

■ACCOMMODATIONS

Belhurst Castle [GF,F] State Rte 14 S (near Snell Rd) **315/781-0201** *fireplaces, also restaurant*

Glens Falls

■BARS

Seventy South Street Pub [GS,D] 70 South St **518/798-9809** *noon-4am*

■NIGHTCLUBS

Club Twenty-Two [M,NH,D,TG,F,K,DS,S,18+,WC,GO] 22 South St (at Glen St) **518/792-4510** *4pm-4am*

■CRUISY AREAS

Aviation Mall [AYOR] trails in woods behind the mall

City Park [AYOR] downtown

Highland

see also Poughkeepsie, New Paltz

■ACCOMMODATIONS

Inn at Applewood [GS,NS,GO] 120 North Rd **845/691-2516** *full brkfst, also restaurant [WC]*

■NIGHTCLUBS

Prime Time [M,D,K,S,18+] Rte 9 W **845/691-8550** *9:30pm-4am Th-Sat, theme parties, X-rated bingo*

■RESTAURANTS

The Would Restaurant [GO] 120 North Rd (off Rte 9 W) **845/691-9883** *dinner nightly, full bar, patio*

Long Island—Nassau • New York

Hudson

■ACCOMMODATIONS

Hudson City B&B [GS,GO] 326 Allen St (at Rte 9-G/ 3rd St) **518/822-8044** *18th-c Victorian, full brkfst, hot tub*

St Charles Hotel [GF] 16-18 Park Pl **518/822-9900** *also 2 restaurants*

Van Schaack House [GF,NS,GO] 20 Broad St (at Albany Rd), Kinderhook **518/758-6118** *B&B, full brkfst*

Ithaca

■INFO LINES & SERVICES

AA Gay/ Lesbian First Baptist Church (at Dewitt Park) **607/273-1541** *6pm Sun*

■BARS

Common Ground [★MW,D,MR,E,YC,WC] 1230 Danby Rd/ Rte 96-B (at Comfort) **607/273-1505** *4pm-1:30am, clsd Mon, also restaurant 5pm-8pm Wed-Sat & Sun brunch*

■RESTAURANTS

ABC Cafe [BW] 308 Stewart Ave (at Buffalo) **607/277-4770** *brkfst, lunch & dinner, wknd brunch, clsd Mon, vegetarian*

■ENTERTAINMENT & RECREATION

Out Loud Chorus **800/367-1463**

■BOOKSTORES

Borealis Bookstore [WC] 205 N Aurora St **607/277-5608** *11am-9pm, noon-5pm Sun, independent alternative w/ lgbt section*

■CRUISY AREAS

Reservoir at Upper Six Mile Creek [AYOR] at Van Etten Dam Waterfalls

Stewart Park [AYOR]

Jamestown

■BARS

Rascals [M,D,DS,S] 701 N Main St/ Rte 60 (at 7th) **716/484-3220** *3pm-2am, DJ Fri-Sun*

Sneakers [MW,D,WC] 100 Harrison (at Institute) **716/484-8816** *2pm-2am, clsd Tue*

■ENTERTAINMENT & RECREATION

The Lucy-Desi Museum 212 Pine St **716/484-0800** *for those who love Lucy*

Kingston

■RESTAURANTS

Armadillo Bar & Grill 97 Abeel St **845/339-1550** *lunch & dinner, clsd Mon, Southwestern, full bar, patio*

■EROTICA

Ulster Video & Gifts 584 Ulster Ave **845/331-6023**

Lake George

■ACCOMMODATIONS

Tea Island Motel [GF] 3020 Lake Shore Dr **518/668-2776**

Livingston Manor

■ACCOMMODATIONS

Magical Land of Oz B&B [GS,GO] 753 Shandelee Rd **845/439-3418** *rooms have Oz theme, shared baths, hot tub*

LONG ISLAND

■

Long Island is divided into 2 geographical areas:
Long Island—Nassau County
Long Island—Suffolk County
see also Fire Island

Long Island—Nassau

■INFO LINES & SERVICES

Gay/ Lesbian Switchboard of Long Island (GLSB of LI) **631/665-3700** *seasonal, 7pm-10pm only*

■BARS

Blanche [M,NH,E,S] 47-2 Boundary Ave, South Farmingdale **516/694-6906** *7pm-4am, from 3pm Sun, dancers Fri-Sat*

New York • USA

■NIGHTCLUBS

City [M,D] 508 Walt Whitman Blvd/ Rte 110, Melville **631/425-7575** *10pm-4am, gay Fri only*

Deluxe [MW,D] 2686 Hempstead Tpke (at Big Bamboo), Levittown **516/520-1332** *9pm-4am Wed only*

Sutra [M,D] 106 Adams Ave, Hauppauge **631/231-8080** *Sat only*

■RESTAURANTS

RS Jones 153 Merrick Ave (off Sunrise), Merrick **516/378-7177** *dinner, clsd Mon, Tex-Mex*

■ENTERTAINMENT & RECREATION

Jones Beach Field #6

Pride for Youth Coffeehouse [MW,D] 2050 Bellmore Ave, Bellmore **516/679-9000** *7:30pm-11:30pm Fri, ages 13-20, live music*

■PUBLICATIONS

Outlook Long Island **631/968-7780 x1**

PM Entertainment Magazine **516/845-0759** *events, listings, classifieds & more for Long Island, NJ & NYC*

Long Island—Suffolk

■INFO LINES & SERVICES

Gay/ Lesbian Switchboard of Long Island (GLSB of LI) **631/665-3700** *7pm-10pm only*

LIGALY (Long Island Gay & Lesbian Youth) 34 Park Ave, Bay Shore **631/665-2300** *lgbt youth organization w/ center*

■ACCOMMODATIONS

Centennial House of East Hampton [GS,SW,NS,GO] 13 Woods Ln, East Hampton **631/324-9414** *full brkfst, also cottage*

Comfort Inn [GF,SW,WC] 2695 Rte 112 (exit 64 off LI Expwy), Medford **631/654-3000, 800/626-7779** *(out-of-state reservations only)* also **Gateway Lounge** [F]

The Country Place [GS,NS] 29 Hands Creek Rd, East Hampton **631/324-4125** *near beach*

Cozy Cabins Motel [MW,GO] **631/537-1160** *seasonal, hot tub*

East Hampton Village B&B [GS,NS] 172 Newtown Ln (at McGuirk St), East Hampton **631/324-1858** *lovely turn-of-the-century home*

EconoLodge—MacArthur Airport [GF,NS,WC] 3055 Rte 454, Ronkonkoma **631/588-6800, 800/553-2666** *budget motel*

EconoLodge—Smithtown/ Hauppauge [GF] 755 Rte 347, Smithtown **631/724-9000, 800/553-2666**

Hampton Resorts & Hospitality [GF,SW,WC] 1655 Country Rd 39, Southampton **631/283-6100** *boutique hotels, jacuzzi*

Summit Motor Inn [GF] 501 E Main St (at Brentwood Rd), Bay Shore **631/666-6000, 800/869-6363**

Sunset Beach [GF,F] 35 Shore Rd, Shelter Island **631/749-2001** *seasonal*

■BARS

Club 608 [MW,NH] 608 Sunrise Hwy (at Belmont Ave), West Babylon **631/661-9580** *8pm-4am*

The Long Island Eagle [M,NH,L] 94 N Clinton Ave (at Union Blvd), Bay Shore **631/968-2750** *9pm-4am, from 4pm Sun*

■NIGHTCLUBS

Adam's Wood Lounge [MO,MR,S,18+,WC,$] 194D Fehr Way (at Cleveland), N Bay Shore **631/374-1119, 631/667-5305** *seasonal hours (please call), nude dancers, juice bar only*

Bunkhouse [★M,D,K,S,WC,GO] 192 N Main St/ Montauk Hwy (at Foster Ave), Sayville **631/567-2865** *7pm-4am*

Honey's [MW,D,DS,OC] 667 Montauk Hwy, Bayport **631/472-3243** *7:30pm-4am, from 4pm Sun*

Thunders [★MW,D,E,S,GO] 1017 E Jericho Tpke, Huntington Station **631/423-5241** *9pm-4am, clsd Mon, Wed & Sun, 18+ Th, popular Th-Fri, male dancers Sat, huge outdoor area, 2 flrs*

NYC—Overview • New York

■ RESTAURANTS

Babette's 66 Newtown Ln, East Hampton **631/329-5377** *brkfst, lunch & dinner, healthy*

■ ENTERTAINMENT & RECREATION

Fowler Beach Southampton

■ PUBLICATIONS

PM Entertainment Magazine **516/845-0759** *events, listings, classifieds & more for Long Island, NJ & NYC*

■ MEN'S SERVICES

➤ **Megaphone Long Island** **800/289-1489** *Call for the local # nearest you! Meet Hot Men in your area! FREE to Browse & Respond to voice ads. Use code 3087. Also try MEGAMATES.COM*

■ EROTICA

Heaven Sent Me 1601 Arctic Ave, Bohemia **631/567-6600** *24hrs*

■ CRUISY AREAS

Beach at end of Two Mile Hollow Rd [AYOR] East Hampton *go left*

Fowle Beach [AYOR] Southampton *go right*

Smith Point Park [AYOR] Fire Island Nat'l Seashore (at end of William Floyd Pkwy), Shirley

Millbrook

■ ACCOMMODATIONS

Inn at Rose Hill Farm [GF,SW] 86 Barmore Rd (at Taconic Pkwy & Rte 55), La Grangeville **845/677-5611** *seasonal (clsd Jan), luxurious Old World-style B&B, full brkfst, hot tub*

New Paltz

■ RESTAURANTS

Northern Spy Cafe [WC] Rte 213, High Falls **845/687-7298** *dinner nightly & Sun brunch, clsd Wed, full bar*

Ristorante Locust Tree 215 Hugenot St (behind conference center) **845/255-7888** *dinner, clsd Mon-Tue, Euro-Italian, full bar, patio*

NEW YORK CITY

■

New York City is divided into 8 geographical areas:
NYC—Overview
NYC—Soho, Greenwich & Chelsea
NYC—Midtown
NYC—Uptown
NYC—Brooklyn
NYC—Queens
NYC—Bronx
NYC—Staten Island

NYC—Overview

■ INFO LINES & SERVICES

AA Gay/ Lesbian Intergroup at Lesbian/ Gay Community Center **212/647-1680**

Gay/ Lesbian Switchboard of New York Project **212/989-0999** *4pm-8pm Mon-Fri, noon-5pm Sat*

Lesbian/ Gay Community Services Center [★WC] 208 W 13th **212/620-7310** *many group mtgs & resources, also cafe*

■ ACCOMMODATIONS

Manhattan Getaways [GS] **212/956-2010** *B&B rooms & private apts throughout Manhattan*

■ NIGHTCLUBS

Avalon [M,D] 6th Ave & 20th St (at the old Limelight) **212/807-7780** *from 10pm Sun*

Deep [M,D] 16 W 22nd St (btwn 5th & 6th Aves)

■ ENTERTAINMENT & RECREATION

Before Stonewall: A Lesbian & Gay History Tour 476 13th St (at Big Onion Walking Tours) **212/439-1090**

Townhouse Tours **347/693-1484** *walking tours of New York's gay history*

Damron Men's Travel Guide 2004

New York • *USA*

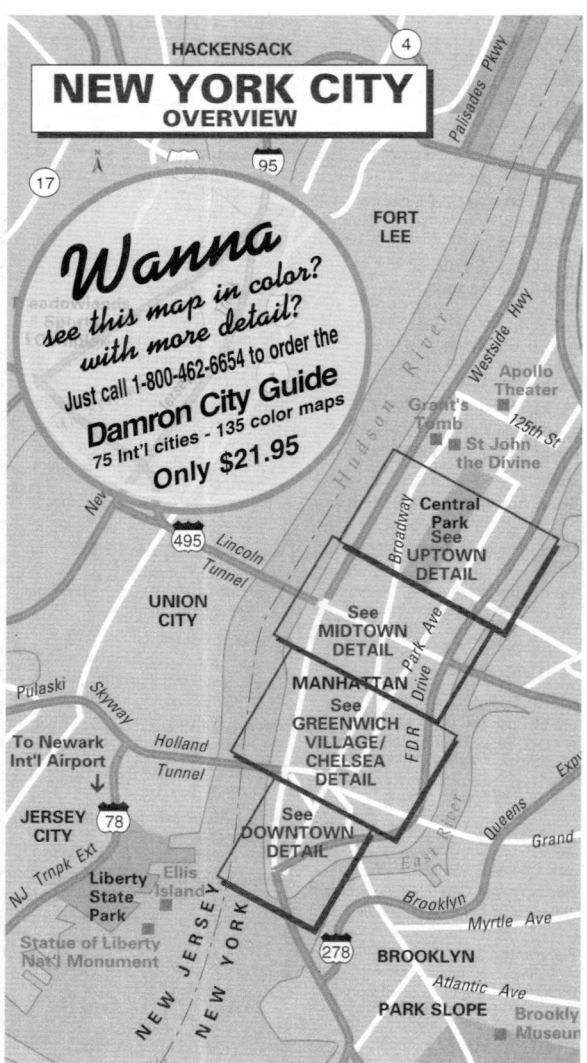

"THE INDISPENSABLE GUIDE TO ALL THINGS GAY"
-DETAILS MAGAZINE

HX MAGAZINE

CONTACT
GARY LACINSKI
ASSOCIATE PUBLISHER
PHONE 212·352·3535
FAX 212·352·3596
E-MAIL glacinski@hx.com

THE LARGEST AND MOST INFLUENTIAL GAY PUBLICATION IN NEW YORK

NEW YORK CITY'S AWARD WINNING WEEKLY NEWSPAPER

read it online: gaycitynews.com

434   2004 Damron Men's Travel Guide

The 11th Original
GLBT EXPO

Blending Business & Entertainment For Over a Decade

Saturday, March 20, 2004 • 10AM – 7PM
Sunday, March 21, 2004 • 12PM – 6PM
Jacob Javits Convention Center
38th Street & 11th Ave. • NYC
Directions : 212.216.2000

See and Be Seen at "The Event" for The GLBT Community.

With over 20,000 attendees and over 1.3 million visits to our website, Top Business Leaders and The Best Entertainment have ranked this event #1 in the nation!

Bring this ad to receive $2 off Regular Admission of $12 1-Day OR $18 2-Day

RDP Group Productions
30 Tower Lane
Avon, CT 06001
Tel: 800.243.9774
Fax: 860.677.6869
info@rdpgroup.com
www.RDPgroup.com

Photos: Raymond Vino ©2002 • Design: www.BlueDoorProductions.com

"This is nothing like the 'green sign' hotel your parents stayed in!"

- In the heart of the historic Financial District
- Close to shopping at Century 21, across from the World Trade Center site
- Walk to South Street Seaport, Statue of Liberty/Ellis Island Ferry and many other historic sites
- Convenient to Greenwich Village, Chelsea, Little Italy, Chinatown, Soho and Tribeca
- NYC's high-tech hotel. T-1 Internet and PC's

Holiday Inn®
Wall Street District

15 Gold Street • New York, NY 10023
tel: 212.232.7700 • fax: 212.425.7800
Reservations: 212.232.7800

NYC—Soho, Greenwich & Chelsea • New York

■ PUBLICATIONS

➤ **Gay City News** 646/452-2500
lgbt newspaper, weekly

➤ **HX Magazine** 212/352-3535
complete weekly guide to gay New York at night

New York Blade News 212/268-2701
weekly lgbt newspaper

Next 212/627-0165 *party paper*

PM Entertainment Magazine
516/845-0759 *events, listings, classifieds & more for Long Island, NJ & NYC*

■ MEN'S SERVICES

➤ **Megaphone New York**
800/289-1489 *Call for the local # nearest you! Meet Hot Men in your area! FREE to Browse & Respond to voice ads. Use code 3087. Also try MEGAMATES.COM*

NYC—Soho, Greenwich & Chelsea

■ ACCOMMODATIONS

Abingdon Guesthouse [GS,NS,WC] 13 8th Ave (at W 12th St) 212/243-5384 *quiet, mature clientele*

Chelsea Inn [GF] 46 W 17th St (btwn 5th & 6th Aves) 212/645-8989, 800/640-6469 *European-style inn*

Chelsea Mews Guest House [MO,NS,GO] 344 W 15th St (btwn 8th & 9th Aves) 212/255-9174 *some shared baths*

➤ **Chelsea Pines Inn** [M,GO]
317 W 14th St (btwn 8th & 9th Aves) 212/929-1023, 888/546-2700 *some shared baths*

The Chelsea Savoy Hotel [GS,WC] 204 W 23rd St (at 7th Ave) 212/929-9353

➤ **Colonial House Inn** [M,N,GO]
318 W 22nd St (btwn 8th & 9th Aves) 212/243-9669, 800/689-3779

N E W   Y O R K

Winner! Out & About Editor's Chice Award
Outstanding Achievement in Gay Travel

"The ultimate in fabulous stays" —*Let's Go NYC*

CHELSEA PINES INN

The Premiere Bed and Breakfast in the Heart of Gay New York

Charming Rooms from $89

Private or semi-private bath
Phone/Cable TV/Refrigerator/Hair dryer/Irons in all rooms
Air conditioning/Central heating/Free Internet access
Continental Breakfast included
Walk to Christopher Street, all bars, clubs, shops
Advance Reservations Suggested
All Major Credit Cards Accepted

317 West 14th Street, New York City 10014
Tel: 212.929.1023 Fax: 212.620.5646
E.Mail: cpiny@aol.com
Visit our website: www.chelseapinesinn.com

New York • USA

The Gramercy Park Hotel [GF]
2 Lexington Ave (at E 21st St)
212/475-4320, 800/221-4083 *aging hotel across from Gramercy Park, famous bar*

Greenwich Village Home [GS,GO]
877/878-2263 *B&B in private guest cottage*

Holiday Inn [GF,F] 138 Lafayette St (btwn Canal & Howard, in Chinatown) **212/966-8898**

Hotel Washington Square [GF,F]
103 Waverly Pl (at MacDougal St)
212/777-9515, 800/222-0418 *renovated 100-yr-old hotel, also North Square restaurant*

➤ **Incentra Village House** [MW,NS,GO]
32 8th Ave (at W 12th St)
212/206-0007

Soho Grand Hotel [GF,WC] 310 W Broadway (at Canal St) **212/965-3000, 800/965-3000** *big, glossy, over-the-top hotel*

Southern Comforts [GF,WC,GO]
310/305-2984, 800/889-7359 *condo in heart of Village*

Tribeca Grand [GS] 2 Avenue of the Americas **212/519-6500, 800/965-3000**

■ BARS

The Bar [M,NH] 68 2nd Ave (at 4th St) **212/254-5766** *4pm-4am*

Bar d'O [GF,S] 29 Bedford St (at Downing St) **212/627-1580** *6pm-3am, theme nights*

Barracuda [★M,S] 275 W 22nd St (at 8th Ave) **212/645-8613** *4pm-4am, live DJs*

The Boiler Room [★M,NH] 86 E 4th St (at 2nd Ave) **212/254-7536** *4pm-4am, Pure Pop Mon w/ DJ & videos*

Boots & Saddle [M,NH] 76 Christopher St (at 7th Ave S) **212/929-9684** *noon-4am, from 8am Sat*

Colonial House Inn

"A gem of a guesthouse" - The Guide Magazine

- Bed and Breakfast
- All rooms equipped with Phones, Cable-TV & A/C
- Private/Shared Baths
- Art Gallery Lounge
- Roof Sundeck
- Some rooms with Refrigerators and Fireplace
- Internet Access
- Rooms from $80.00
- VISA / MC
- Conveniently located
- Reservations suggested

Winner **Out & About**
Editor's Choice Award
1994 - 2003

THE "INN" PLACE TO STAY

www.colonialhouseinn.com

318 West 22nd Street • New York City, New York 10011
Phone: 212-243-9669 • Fax: 212-633-1612 • Toll Free: 1-800-689-3779
email: houseinn@aol.com

NEW YORK

A charming 1841 Guest House located in New York's Greenwich Village Historic District.

All rooms with private baths, most with fireplaces and kitchenettes, all airconditioned.

$119 single/$169 double
Suites $149/$199

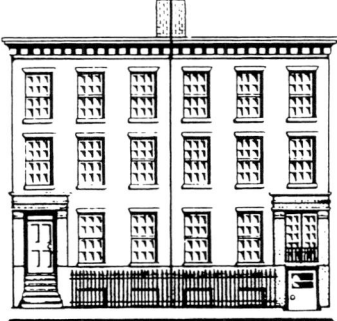

INCENTRA VILLAGE HOUSE

32 Eighth Avenue, NYC 10014
(between West 12th and Jane St.)
Tel 212/206-0007
Fax 212/604-0625

see us at: iloveinns.com

Prices may increase during Holiday and
Special Event periods and are subject to change.

New York • USA

Chi Chiz [M,NH,MR-AF,F,K,S]
135 Christopher St (at Hudson)
212/462-0027 *4pm-4am*

The Cock [M,K,S] 188 Ave 'A' (at 12th St) **212/946-1871** *10pm-4am, a 'sleazy rock 'n roll bar', live DJs*

Dick's Bar [M] 192 2nd Ave (at 12th St) **212/475-2071** *2pm-4am, porno nights Tue & Th, digital jukebox*

The Dugout [M,NH,B,WC]
185 Christopher St (at Weehawken St) **212/242-9113** *4pm-2am, from 1pm Sun, bear/ sports bar*

Duplex [GF,C,P,$] 61 Christopher St (at 7th Ave) **212/255-5438** *4pm-4am, piano bar from 9pm, from 4pm wknds*

G Lounge [★M] 225 W 19th St (at 7th Ave) **212/929-1085** *4pm-4am, lounge, live DJs, juice bar*

The Hangar [M,NH] 115 Christopher St (at Bleecker) **212/627-2044** *3pm-4am, live DJs*

Hell [MW] 59 Gansevoort St (at Washington) **212/727-1666** *7pm-4am, from 5pm Fri, swanky lounge, DJ Tue-Th & Sun*

The Hole [MW,D] 29 2nd Ave (at 2nd St) **212/473-9406** *10pm-4am Th-Sat*

Julius [M,NH,F,OC] 159 W 10th St (at Waverly) **212/929-9672** *8am-4am*

Marie's Crisis [MW,P] 59 Grove St (at 7th Ave) **212/243-9323** *4pm-4am, piano bar from 9:30pm, from 5pm Fri-Sun*

▶ **The Monster** [★M,D,C,P,WC] 80 Grove St (at W 4th St, Sheridan Square) **212/924-3558** *4pm-4am, from 2pm wknds, piano bar, T-dance Sun*

Phoenix [MW,NH] 447 E 13th (at Ave 'A') **212/477-9979** *4pm-4am, patio*

Pieces [M,NH,K,C] 8 Christopher St (btwn 6th-7th) **212/929-9291** *2pm-4am, karaoke Tue, cabaret Wed, DJ Th-Sat*

Rose's Turn [M,C,P] 55 Grove St (btwn 7th & Bleecker) **212/366-5438** *4pm-4am*

THE MONSTER®
80 Grove St. • NY NY • (212) 924-3558

GONZO

Offering a warm, unique dining experience with impeccable food, service and atmosphere. This is assured by the presence of Gonzo's renowned chef/owner, Vincent Scotto.

Gonzo was named one of New York Magazine's top 10 Italian restaurants for 2003.

Traditional Tuscan cuisine, prepared from a seasonal point of view, utilizing the freshest of local ingredients.

Come with friends, and enjoy the 'cicchetti', or Italian tapas. Thin-crust pizzas, fresh fish, pasta, and eye-popping steaks will satisfy any appetite.

Over 60 wines by the glass, a full bar, and great atmosphere.

Gonzo is open nightly from 5:30-midnight, and Sunday from 4-10:30.

'Gonzo' — Italian for cool!

140 West 13th Street, New York, NY 10011
212-645-4606

New York • USA

SBNY—Splash Bar New York [★MO,D,S,V,YC] 50 W 17th St (at 6th Ave) **212/691-0073** *5pm-5am*

Spyder & the Fly [GS,D] 225 Ave 'B', 2nd flr (at Uncle Mings) **212/979-8506** *6pm-close Wed only*

Starlight Bar & Lounge [MW,E] 167 Ave 'A' (at 11th St) **212/475-2172** *7pm-3am, till 4am Fri-Sun, live DJs*

Stonewall Inn [M,D,F,P] 53 Christopher St (at 7th Ave) **212/463-0950** *2:30pm-4am, 4 bars, piano bar, martini bar*

Ty's [M,NH,L,GO] 114 Christopher St (btwn Bleecker & Hudson) **212/741-9641** *2pm-4am, from 1pm wknds*

Urge [M,NH,S] 33 2nd Ave (at 2nd St) **212/533-5757** *5pm-4am, also cafe from 7am, cruisy lounge*

View Bar [★M,V] 232 8th Ave (at 22nd St) **212/929-2243** *3pm-4am, from 1pm wknds, theme nights*

Wonder Bar [★MW,WC] 505 E 6th St (at Ave 'A') **212/777-9105** *6pm-4am, trendy*

XL [★M,D,S] 357 W 16th St (btwn 8th & 9th) **212/995-1400** *4pm-4am, great lights, fab restrooms w/ fish tanks*

■ NIGHTCLUBS

13 Bar & Lounge [GF,D] 35 E 13th St (at University Pl) **212/979-6677** *4pm-4am, from 5pm wknds, more gay Th*

Big Apple Ranch [MW,D,CW,BW,$] 39 W 19th St, 5th flr (btwn 5th & 6th, at Dance Manhattan) **212/358-5752** *8pm-1am Sat only, two-step lessons*

Centro Fly [GS,D,F] 45 W 21st St (btwn 5th & 6th) **212/627-7770** *10pm-5:30am*

Heaven [W,D,MR,S,GO] 579 6th Ave (btwn 16th St & 17th St) **212/539-3982, 212/243-6100** *5pm-4am Wed & Fri, 5pm-midnight Sun, Latin night Wed, Fri Kaleidoscope [25+], Fantasy T-dance Sun*

New York City's Gay Books, Movies, and Gifts Store

Creative Visions Books

Photo: Bruce of LA

548 Hudson Street
2 Blocks North of Christopher St.
New York, NY 10014
www.creativevisionsbooks.com

WITH MORE THAN 40 YEARS AS THE CROSSROADS OF THE INTERNATIONAL GAY COMMUNITY, THERE'S NOTHING LIKE

CHRISTOPHER STREET SHOP

DVDs, VIDEOS, INTIMATE ACCESSORIES, NOVELTIES AND SO MUCH MORE

Udo Light ©David Hubert/ChampionStudios.net Grayscale Graphics

THE GAY LANDMARK
500 HUDSON ST
(AT CHRISTOPHER) NYC
212-463-0657 **NO MAIL ORDER**

THE OLDEST GAY ALL-MALE MEETING PLACE WITH SOMETHING FOR EVERYONE

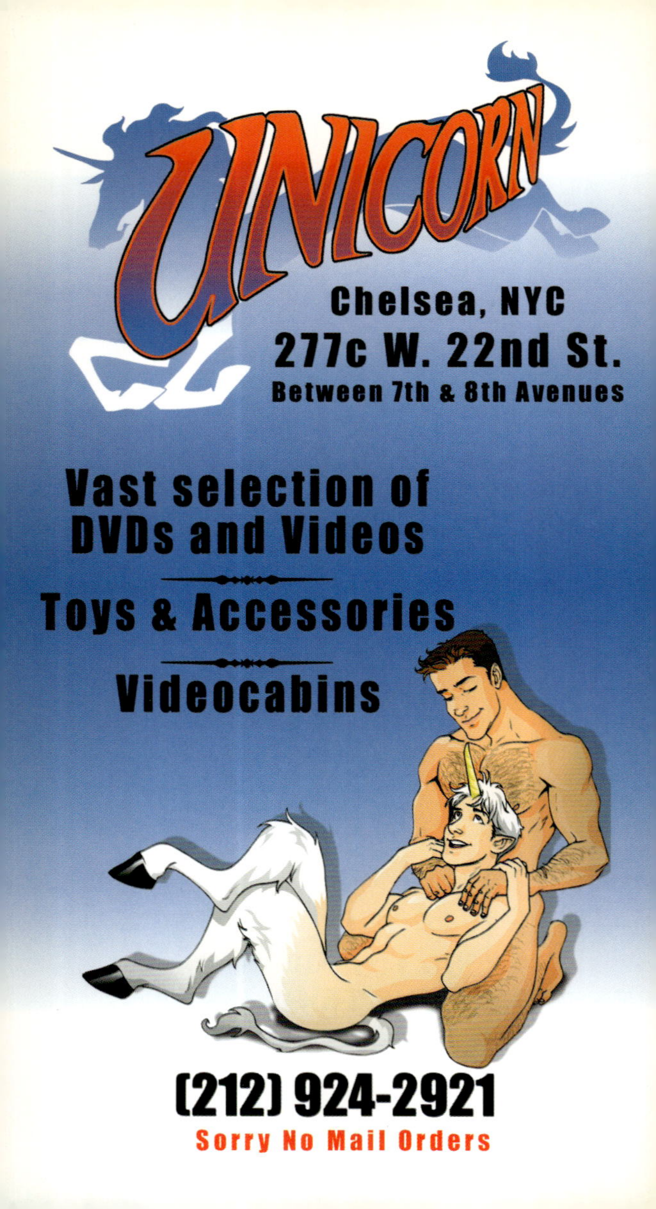

ENTERTAINMENT CENTER

YOUR STOP IN THE FINANCIAL DISTRICT FOR QUALITY INTIMATE ENTERTAINMENT PRODUCTS

21 ANN STREET
BET. B'WAY & NASSAU
212-267-9760
MON-FRI 7 AM-11PM
SAT 10 AM-11 PM
SUN 10 AM- 7 PM

Image: Danny Foxen © David Hubert / ChampionStudios.net Grayscale Graphics

LES HOMMES

**LARGE VARIETY!
DVDs,
Videos, Toys
Novelties, etc.**

**Adult / Non-Adult
Video Rentals**

**Special Selection
of Non-Adult
Gay Themed Titles**

217-B West 80th Street, 2nd Floor NYC
Between Broadway and Amsterdam Avenue
212-580-2445   No Mail Order

"THE" One-Stop Uptown All-Male Shop

Kurt Angle © David Hubert / ChampionStudios.net Design: GRAYSCALE Graphics

NYC—Soho, Greenwich & Chelsea • New York

Nowbar [M,TG,DS,$] 22 7th Ave S (at Leroy St) 212/802-9502 *10pm-4am Th-Sat, drag shows*

Plaid [M,D,E,DS,$] 76 E 13th St (at Broadway) 212/388-1060

Pyramid [GF] 101 Ave 'A' (at 7th Ave) 212/462-9077 *10pm-4am, more gay Fri & 1984, New Wave party*

Roxy [★GS,D,A,S,$] 515 W 18th St (at 10th Ave) 212/645-5156 *11pm-4am Fri-Sat, rollerdisco from 7pm Wed, gay Sat*

Saint-At-Large [★M,D] 212/674-8541 *2 huge annual parties: White Party in Feb & Black Party in March*

Sea Tea [M,D,MR,F,P,S,GO,$] leaves from Pier 40 (at Christopher St) 212/675-4357 *6pm-10pm Sun (June-Oct)*

The Slide [MW,S] 356 Bowery (at 4th Ave) 212/420-8885 *5pm-4am, lounge, go-go dancers*

■ CAFES

Big Cup [★M] 228 8th Ave (at 22nd St) 212/206-0059 *7am-2am, boy central*

Caffe Raffaella 134 7th Ave S (at Charles St) 212/929-7247 *11am-2am, armchair cafe*

■ RESTAURANTS

7A [★] 109 Ave 'A' (at 7th St) 212/673-6583 *24hrs*

Angelica Kitchen 300 E 12th St (at 1st Ave) 212/228-2909 *lunch & dinner, vegetarian/ vegan*

Around the Clock 8 3rd Ave (at 9th St) 212/598-0402 *24hrs*

Benny's Burritos 93 Ave 'A' (at 6th Ave) 212/254-2054 *11:30am-midnight, bar till 2am, cheap & huge; also 113 Greenwich (at Jane), 212/727-0584*

Blue Ribbon [WC] 97 Sullivan St (at Spring St) 212/274-0404 *4pm-4am, cont'l/ American, chef hangout*

Brunetta's [★MW] 190 1st Ave (btwn 11th & 12th Sts) 212/228-4030 *affordable Italian, patio*

Chelsea Bistro & Bar 358 W 23rd St (at 9th Ave) 212/727-2026 *lunch & dinner, trendy French, full bar*

The Cloister Cafe 238 E 9th St (at 2nd Ave) 212/777-9128 *10am-midnight, garden dining*

Cola's [★] 148 8th Ave (at 17th St) 212/633-8020 *4:30pm-11pm, Italian*

Cowgirl Hall of Fame 519 Hudson St (at W 10th) 212/633-1133 *lunch, dinner, wknd brunch*

East of Eighth 254 W 23rd St (at 8th) 212/352-0075 *lunch, dinner till midnight, till 2am wknds*

Eighteenth & Eighth 159 8th Ave 212/242-5000 *boys, boys, boys*

Empire Diner 210 10th Ave (at 22nd St) 212/243-2736 *24hrs*

First 87 1st Ave (at 6th St) 212/674-3823 *6pm-2am, till 3am Fri-Sat, Sun brunch, cont'l, hip crowd*

Flamingo East [D] 219 2nd Ave (at 13th St) 212/533-2860 *2:30pm-close, also bar w/ dancing & 'offbeat rec room'*

Florent [★] 69 Gansevoort St (at Washington) 212/989-5779 *9am-5am, 24hrs Fri-Sat, French diner*

Food Bar 149 8th Ave (at 17th St) 212/243-2020 *11am-midnight, Mediterranean*

Garage [E] 99 7th Ave S (at Grove St) 212/645-0600 *lunch Mon-Fri, dinner Th-Sun, brunch wknds, contemporary American, live jazz*

Global 33 99 2nd Ave (at 5th St) 212/477-8427 *5pm-midnight, int'l tapas*

➤ **Gonzo** [★] 140 W 13th St (btwn 6th & 7th Aves) 212/645-4606 *noon-1am, till 11pm Sun, clsd Mon, great Tuscan menu, over 60 wines by the glass, full bar*

LaVagna 545 E 5th St (btwn 'A' & 'B') 212/979-1005 *affordable Italian*

Life Cafe 343 E 10th St (at Ave 'B') 212/477-8791 *10am-1am, till 3am Fri-Sat, full bar, vegetarian, artist hangout*

Lips [DS] 2 Bank St (at Greenwich) 212/675-7710 *dinner nightly, Disco Fever Brunch Sun, full bar, 'the ultimate in drag dining'*

New York • USA

Lucky Cheng's [★K,DS] 24 1st Ave (at 2nd St) 212/473-0516 *5:30pm-midnight, Asian/fusion, full bar, drag shows*

Marion's Continental 354 Bowery St (btwn E 3rd & E 4th Sts) 212/475-7621 *6pm-11pm, bar till 2am, monthly Fashion Brunch*

Miracle Grill 112 1st Ave (at 6th St) 212/254-2353 *dinner, brunch, Southwestern, full bar, garden dining*

The Pink Tea Cup 42 Grove St (btwn Bleecker & Bedford) 212/807-6755 *8am-midnight, till 1am Fri-Sun, Southern homestyle*

Restivo [GO] 209 7th Ave (at 22nd St) 212/366-4133 *noon-midnight, Italian, intimate*

Sacred Chow [WC] 522 Hudson St (at W 10th St) 212/337-0863 *7:30am-11pm, gourmet vegan*

Sazerac House Bar & Grill 533 Hudson (at Charles) 212/989-0313 *lunch & dinner, Cajun, full bar*

Stingy Lulu's 129 St Marks Pl (at Ave 'A') 212/674-3545 *11am-4am, funky American diner, popular brunch, drag queen servers*

Stonewall Bistro [MW,D,P] 113 7th Ave S 917/661-1335 *5pm-11pm, Sun brunch from 11am, full bar*

Trattoria Pesce Pasta 262 Bleecker St (at 6th Ave) 212/645-2993 *noon-midnight*

Tribeca Grill [★R] 375 Greenwich St (btwn N Moore & Franklin) 212/941-3900 *chic neighborhood restaurant co-owned by Robert DeNiro, full bar, extensive wine list*

The Viceroy [★] 160 8th Ave (at 18th St) 212/633-8484 *noon-midnight, fusion, full bar*

Waikiki Wally's [E] 101 E 2nd St (at 1st Ave) 212/673-8908 *6pm-10pm, till 11pm Fri-Sat, tiki bar open later, new Polynesian, fun island atmosphere*

Welcome to Manhattan's WEST SIDE OASIS!

- Absolutely Free Indoor Parking
- Fitness Center
- Minutes to Theatres, shopping & Sightseeing
- Gay Friendly
- Great Value!

IGTA

515 W42nd St., NYC 10036
(212) 695-7171 (800)869-4630
Fax: (212) 967-5025

TRAVEL INN

Visit our website at www.newyorkhotel.com

NYC—Midtown • New York

■Entertainment & Recreation

Leslie-Lohman Gay Art Foundation & Gallery 127-B Prince St, lower level 212/673-7007 *1pm-6pm, clsd Sun-Mon*

PS 122 150 1st Ave (at E 9th St) 212/477-5829, 212/477-5288 *it's rough, it's raw, it's real New York performance art*

■Bookstores

➤ **Creative Visions Books** 548 Hudson St (btwn Perry & Charles) 212/645-7573, 800/434-7126 *noon-10pm, till 11pm Fri-Sat, lgbt*

Oscar Wilde Bookshop 15 Christopher St (at 7th Ave) 212/255-8097 *11am-8pm, noon-7pm Sun, lgbt*

■Retail Shops

Crush 860 Lexington Ave, 2nd flr (btwn 64th & 65th) 212/535-8142 *11:30am-7pm, till 6pm wknds, clsd Tue, retro-kitsch*

DeMask 135 W 22nd St (btwn 6th & 7th Aves) 212/352-2850 *11am-7pm, European fetish fashion*

Flight 001 96 Greenwich (btwn Jane & 12th) 212/691-1001 *11am-8:30pm, noon-6pm Sun, travel gear*

Rainbows & Triangles 192 8th Ave (at 19th St) 212/627-2166 *11am-10pm, noon-9pm Sun*

Universal Gear 140 8th Ave 212/206-9119 *casual, club, athletic & designer clothing*

Whittall & Shon 113 Christopher St 212/691-6964 *funky clothes & clubwear for boys*

■Gyms & Health Clubs

19th St Health & Fitness [MW] 22 W 19th St (btwn 5th & 6th) 212/414-5800 *also day passes*

David Barton Gym [MW] 552 6th Ave (btwn 15th & 16th) 212/727-0004 *also day passes*

New York Sports Club [M] 128 8th Ave (btwn 16th & 17th) 212/627-0065 *day passes available*

■Men's Clubs

➤ **West Side Club** [★M,PC] 27 W 20th St, 2nd flr (at 6th Ave) 212/691-2700 *24hrs*

■Erotica

➤ **Ann St Entertainment Center** 21 Ann St (at Broadway) 212/267-9760

➤ **Christopher Street Shop** 500 Hudson St (at Christopher) 212/463-0657

Leather Man 111 Christopher St (at Bleecker) 212/243-5339

The Noose 261 W 19th St (at 8th Ave) 212/807-1789

Pleasure Chest 156 7th Ave S (at Charles) 212/242-2158

➤ **Unicorn** 277-C W 22nd St (at 8th Ave) 212/924-2921

NYC—Downtown

■Accommodations

➤ **Holiday Inn Wall Street District** [GS,WC] 15 Gold St 212/232-7700, 800/465-4329 *all suites & rooms have 'virtual offices,' also Platinum Cafe*

■Bars

Pussycat Lounge [M] 96 Greenwich St (at Rector) 212/349-4800 *gay Th for Ultra*

■Men's Clubs

Wall Street Sauna [★] 1 Maiden Ln, 11th flr (at Broadway) 212/233-8900 *clsd Sun*

NYC—Midtown

■Accommodations

Belvedere Hotel [GF] 319 W 48th St (at 8th Ave) 212/245-7000, 888/468-3558

Buckingham Hotel [GF] 101 W 57th St (at 6th Ave) 212/246-1500, 888/511-1900 *studios & 1-bdrm suites, concierge, fitness center*

Gershwin Hotel [GF] 7 E 27th St (at 5th Ave) 212/545-8000

Habitat Hotel [GF] 130 E 57th St (at Lexington) 212/753-8841, 800/497-6028 *upscale budget hotel*

"Still One of the Most Reliable Good Time Sex Palaces in the United States."

Kyle Madison

STEAM

TEMPORARY MEMBERSHIPS AVAILABLE to out-of-town men with proper I.D.

east side club
227 E. 56 St. New York 212•PL3•2222

west side club
27 West 20th Street 2nd floor
Chelsea, New York City

A Hard Man is Good to Find

24 Hours

Private Membership

Photo: Jake Sorentino

New York • USA

Holiday Inn Martinique on Broadway [GS] 49 W 32nd St (btwn Broadway & 5th) 212/736-3800, 888/694-6543 *also restaurant, cafe & cocktail lounge*

The Hotel Metro [GF] 45 W 35th St (at 5th Ave) 212/947-2500, 800/356-3870 *slick art deco hotel*

Lambda Mews [MW,GO] 24 W 30th St (at 5th Ave & Broadway) 212/229-9339, 212/213-8798 *B&B in private home, views of Empire State Bldg*

Park Central Hotel [GF,WC] 870 7th Ave (at 56th St) 212/247-8000, 800/346-1359 *also restaurant*

➤ **Travel Inn** [GF,SW] 515 W 42nd St (at 10th Ave) 212/695-7171, 800/869-4630 *fitness center*

■ BARS

Bar Nine [GF,F,E] 807 9th Ave (at W 53rd St) 212/399-9336 *5pm-4am, also restaurant*

Barrage [M] 401 W 47th St (at 9th Ave) 212/586-9390 *4pm-close*

Cleo's Saloon [M,NH] 656 9th Ave (at 46th St) 212/307-1503 *11am-4am, from noon Sun*

Cosmo [M,WC] 359 W 54th St (btwn 8th & 9th) 212/582-2200 *6pm-4am, also downstairs lounge*

Danny's Skylight Room [GF,C,P,S] 346 W 46th St (at 9th Ave) 212/265-8133 *4pm-midnight, brunch Wed & wknds, piano bar from 6pm, cover + 2 drink minimum*

Don't Tell Mama [★GF,C,P,YC,$] 343 W 46th St (at 9th Ave) 212/757-0788 *4pm-4am, cover + 2 drink minimum*

Dusk [GS] 147 W 24th St (btwn 6th & 7th) 212/924-4490 *6pm-close, clsd Sun*

The Eagle [M,L] 554 W 28th St (btwn 10th & 11th) 646/473-1866 *10pm-4am*

Foot Friends/ Boot Bros [M,$] 133 W 33rd St (at Red Zone) 212/760-5952 *8pm-2am Sun*

Hannah's Lava Lounge [MW] 923 8th Ave (at 55th St) 212/974-9087 *noon-4am, theme nights, art exhibits*

OW Bar [M,V,GO] 221 E 58th St (at 2nd Ave) 212/355-3395 *4pm-4am, digital jukebox*

Pegasus [M,E,K,C,P] 119 E 60th St (at Lexington) 212/888-4702 *4pm-4am, open mic Fri-Sun, piano bar*

Posh [M,NH] 405 W 51st St (at 9th Ave) 212/957-2222 *4pm-4am, popular happy hour, theme nights, DJ Fri-Sun*

Red [M,S] 305 E 53rd St, 2nd flr (btwn 2nd & 3rd Ave) 212/688-1294 *6pm-4am, from 8pm wknds*

Regents [M,C,P] 317 E 53rd St (at 2nd Ave) 212/593-3091 *4pm-4am, noon-midnight Sun, also restaurant*

Stella's [M,S] 266 W 47th St (at 8th Ave) 212/575-1680 *noon-4am, go-go boys, hustlers*

Townhouse Bar [M,E,C,P] 236 E 58th St (btwn 2nd & 3rd Ave) 212/754-4649 *4pm-3am, till 4am Th-Sat, 3 bars, club bar clsd Sun-Mon*

The Web [M,D,MR-A,K,S] 40 E 58th St (at Madison) 212/308-1546 *4pm-3am, till 4am Fri-Sun, theme nights, go-go boys*

Xth Ave Lounge [M,F] 642 10th Ave (at 45th St) 212/245-9088 *6pm-4am, DJ Th-Sat, lounge*

■ NIGHTCLUBS

Escuelita [M,D,MR-L,TG,DS,S,$] 301 W 39th St (at 8th Ave) 212/631-0588 *10pm-5am, 7pm-4am Sun, T-dance from 5pm Sun, clsd Mon-Th*

■ RESTAURANTS

44 & X Hell's Kitchen [WC,GO] 626 10th Ave (at 44th St) 212/977-1170 *5:30pm-midnight, brunch wknds, American comfort food*

Cafe Un Deux Trois [★] 123 W 44th St (at Broadway) 212/354-4148 *noon-midnight, brunch wknds, bistro*

Mangia e Bevi 800 9th Ave (at W 53rd St) 212/956-3976 *noon-midnight, Italian*

Revolution [E] 611 9th Ave (at 43rd St) 212/489-8451 *5pm-midnight, bar till 3am, new American, DJ/ live entertainment nightly*

NYC—Brooklyn • New York

Rice 'N' Beans [NS,BW] 744 9th Ave (at 50th St) **212/265-4444** *11am-10pm, Latin/ Brazilian, plenty veggie*

Townhouse Restaurant [★MW] 206 E 58th St (at 3rd Ave) **212/826-6241** *lunch & dinner, Sun brunch, open late wknds*

■ Entertainment & Recreation

Sex and the City Tour 5th Ave, in front of Pulitzer Fountain (at 58th St) **212/209-3370** *Sat & Mon, 3 hours, reservations a must!*

■ Men's Clubs

➤ **East Side Club** [★PC] 227 E 56th St, 6th flr (btwn End & 3rd) **212/753-2222, 212/888-1884** *24hrs, day passes available*

■ Erotica

Gaiety Burlesk 201 W 46th St (at Broadway) **212/221-8868** *famed strip shows—you never know which celebrity you'll see on stage or in the crowd*

NYC—Uptown

■ Accommodations

Country Inn the City [GF] W 77th St (at Broadway) **212/580-4183** *studio apts in restored 1891 town house*

The Harlem Flophouse [NS] 242 W 123rd St **212/662-0678** *guest house, near Apollo Theatre*

Home of the Healing Fire [NS] 208 W 137th St **212/926-1049** *(ask for Ms Faison)*

Hotel Newton [GF] 2528 Broadway **212/678-6500, 800/643-5553**

On The Ave Hotel [GF] 2178 Broadway (at 77th St) **212/362-1100, 800/497-6028**

The Urban Jem Guest House [GF] 2005 Fifth Ave (at 125th in Harlem) **212/831-6029, 888/264-8811** *B&B, renovated brownstone in heart of Harlem's renaissance, some shared baths*

■ Bars

Brandy's Piano Bar [M,P] 235 E 84th St (at 2nd Ave) **212/650-1944** *4pm-4am*

Candle Bar [★M,NH] 309 Amsterdam (at 74th St) **212/874-9155** *2pm-4am, cruisy*

Eight of Clubs [M,NH,V] 230 W 75th St (at Broadway) **212/580-7389** *noon-4am, from 4pm Mon-Tue, patio*

Saints [M,NH] 992 Amsterdam (at 109th St) **212/961-0599** *4pm-4am*

Tool Box [M,NH,V] 1742 2nd Ave (at 91st St) **212/348-1288** *8pm-4am, cruisy*

The Works [★M,V] 428 Columbus Ave (at 81st St) **212/799-7365** *2pm-4am, theme parties*

■ Restaurants

Orbit East Harlem [E,MR,C,P,R] 2257 1st Ave E (at E 116th St) **212/348-7818** *11am-2am, till 4am Fri-Sat, creative cuisine, some veggie, also full bar, open-mic piano cabaret Th, jazz*

■ Men's Clubs

Mt Morris Baths [MO,MR-AF] 1944 Madison Ave (nr 124th) **212/534-9004** *also lecture series*

■ Erotica

➤ **Les Hommes** 217-B W 80th St, 2nd flr (at Broadway) **212/580-2445**

■ Cruisy Areas

The Ramble [AYOR] in Central Park

NYC—Brooklyn

■ Info Lines & Services

Audre Lorde Project 85 S Oxford St **718/596-0342** *10am-6pm, till 9pm Tue-Th, 1:30pm-9pm Sat, clsd Sun, lgbt center for people of color*

■ Bars

The Abbey [GS,NH,D] 536 Driggs Ave (btwn N 7th & 8th), Williamsburg **718/599-4400** *from 3pm, more gay Sun night*

Bar 4 [GS,NH,E] 444 7th Ave (at 15th St, in Park Slope) **718/832-9800** *6pm-4am, DJ Fri-Sat*

New York • USA

Excelsior [MW] 390 5th Ave (btwn 6th & 7th), Brooklyn **718/832-1599** *6pm-4am, from 2pm wknds, patio*

Ginger's Bar [MW,NH,E] 363 5th Ave (btwn 5th & 6th Sts, in Park Slope) **718/788-0924** *5pm-4am, from 2pm wknds*

Metropolitan [MW,NH,D] 559 Lorimer St, Williamsburg **718/599-4444** *3pm-4am, comfy bar w/ fireplaces, DJ Wed*

Rising Cafe [GS,F,E] 186 5th Ave (at Sackett) **718/789-6340** *5pm-1am, from 10am wknds, also Sweet Mama's Griddle*

That Bar [MW,D,F] 116 Smith (btwn Dean & Pacific) **718/260-8900** *5pm-2am, from noon wknds, Sun brunch, more men Fri for TBIF & Sat for Flirt, garden*

■ NIGHTCLUBS

Berliniamsburg at Club Luxx [GS,D] 256 Grand St (btwn Driggs & Roebling), Williamsburg **718/599-1000** *8pm-close Sat*

Spectrum [MW,D,K,DS,S] 802 64th St (at 8th Ave) **718/238-8213** *9:30pm-4am Th-Sat*

■ CAFES

Halcyon [BW] 227 Smith (at Butler), Carroll Gardens **718/260-9299** *11am-1am, till 2am Fri-Sat, also antiques & record store*

■ RESTAURANTS

200 Fifth [E] 200 5th Ave (btwn Union & Sackett) **718/638-0023, 718/638-2925** *4pm-close, eclectic, full bar*

Aunt Suzie [E] 247 5th Ave (at Garfield Pl) **718/788-2868** *dinner only, Italian*

ChipShop/ The Curry Shop [★] 383 5th Ave (at 6th St), Brooklyn **718/244-7746** *noon-10pm, till 11pm Th-Sat, from 11am wknds, English/ Indian, home of the famous fried Twinkie!*

Johnny Mack's [E] 1114 8th Ave (btwn 11th & 12th) **718/832-7961** *4pm-11pm, till 1am Fri-Sat, Sun brunch*

Santa Fe Grill 62 7th Ave (at Lincoln) **718/636-0279** *5pm-close, from 3pm wknds, also bar*

Superfine [E,GO] 126 Front St **718/243-9005** *lunch Wed-Fri, dinner Tue-Sat, noon-5pm Sun, clsd Mon, relaxed atmosphere*

■ GYMS & HEALTH CLUBS

The Training Academy 525 Waverly Ave (btwn Fulton Ave & Atlantic Ave), Brooklyn **718/638-3888**

NYC—Queens

■ INFO LINES & SERVICES

Queens LGBT Pride Community Center 102-09 Northern Blvd, 2nd flr, Corona **718/429-2300** *by appointment only*

■ BARS

Albatross [GS,NH,GO] 36-19 24th Ave (at 37th), Astoria **718/204-9045** *6pm-4am, more gay wknds*

Chueca [W,MR-L,K,S,GO] 69-04 Woodside Ave (at 69th St), Woodside **718/424-1171** *4pm-4am, also restaurant till 10pm, karaoke Wed, more men Th*

Friend's Tavern [M,NH,MR-L] 78-11 Roosevelt Ave, Jackson Hts **718/397-7256** *4pm-4am, DJ Wed-Sun*

Music Box [M,MR-L,DS] 40-08 74th St (at Roosevelt Ave), Jackson Hts **718/429-9356** *4pm-4am, drag Sun*

Zodiacs Tavern [M,DS,S] 69-19 Roosevelt Ave (at 69th St), Jackson Hts **718/899-4724** *9pm-4am, clsd Mon & Wed, DJ Fri-Sat, drag shows, go-go boys*

■ NIGHTCLUBS

Atlantis 2010 [MW,D,MR-L,DS] 76-19 Roosevelt Ave (at 77th St), Jackson Hts **718/457-3939** *10pm-4am Fri-Sun only*

Krash [MW,D,MR,TG,DS,S] 34-48 Steinway St (at 35th Ave), Astoria **718/937-2400** *open Mon & Th-Sat*

Lucho's Club [M,NH,D,TG,C,DS,18+,YC] 38-19 69th St, Woodside **718/424-9181** *10pm-4am*

■ MEN'S CLUBS

Northern Men's Sauna [PC] 3365 Farrington St, Flushing **718/445-9775**

Rochester • New York

NYC—Bronx

■NIGHTCLUBS

G-Vibe [MW,D] 1854 Westchester Ave **914/422-0024** 9pm-4am Mon & Wed only

The Warehouse [M,D,F,MR,$] 141 E 140th St (btwn Grand Concourse & Walton) **718/992-5974** 11pm Fri-Sat, [W] Fri, [M] Sat, patio

NYC—Staten Island

■NIGHTCLUBS

Mardi Gras Lounge [MW,D] 523 Bay St, Staten Island **718/442-9196** 8pm-4am

Niagara Falls

see also Buffalo, New York & Niagara Falls, Ontario, Canada

■EROTICA

Horizon Books 8601 Niagara Falls Blvd (at Military Rd) **716/297-2077** 24hrs

Nineteen St Books & News 641 19th St (at Pine Ave) **716/284-2214** 24hrs

Nyack

■NIGHTCLUBS

Barz [MW,D,E,WC] 327 Rte 9 W **845/353-4444** 8pm-4am, from 3pm Sun, live music Tue

Orange County

■NIGHTCLUBS

Zippers [MW,D,WC,18+] 658 Rte 211 E (exit 120, off Rte 17), Middletown **845/692-9093** 9pm-4am Fri-Sat only

■RESTAURANTS

Gigi's Folderol [P,WC] 795 Rte 284, Westtown **845/726-3822** 5pm-close, clsd Tue-Wed, Sun brunch, piano Fri-Sat

■EROTICA

Exotic Gifts & Videos 658 Rte 211 E (exit 120, off Rte 17), Middletown **845/692-6664**

Exotic Gifts & Videos Old Rte 52 (at Rte 52), Liberty **845/292-1140**

Plattsburgh

■BARS

Backstreet [MW,D,TG,S,18+,WC,GO] 30 Marion St (btwn Clinton & Court) **518/563-8211** 5pm-2am, also Luminary Lounge downstairs 11pm-close Fri-Sat

Port Chester

see also Greenwich & Stamford, Connecticut

■BARS

Sandy's Old Homestead [GF,F,WC] 325 N Main St (at Wilkins) **914/939-0758** noon-4am

Poughkeepsie

■INFO LINES & SERVICES

Poughkeepsie GALA (Gay/ Lesbian Association) 20 Carrol St (at Christ Episcopal Church) **845/431-6756** 7:30pm Tue, call for events

■BARS

Congress [MW,NH,WC] 411 Main St (off Academy) **845/486-9068** 3pm-4am, from 7:30pm Sun

Ripley

■EROTICA

➤ **The Lion's Den Adult Bookstore** 6306 Shortman Rd (Exit 61, off I-90, 1st exit in NY) **716/736-6400** 24hrs

Rochester

■INFO LINES & SERVICES

AA Gay/ Lesbian 244 Alexander St (at Genesee Hospital) **585/232-6720** (AA#)

Gay Alliance of the Genesee Valley (GAGV) 179 Atlantic Ave (at Elton) **585/244-8640** 10am-9pm, till 6pm Fri, clsd wknds, community center, also info line

■BARS

Anthony's 522 [MW,NH,K] 522 E Main St (at Scio) **585/325-2060** noon-2am

Avenue Pub [★M,NH,D] 522 Monroe Ave (at Goodman) **585/244-4960** 4pm-2am, patio

New York • USA

The Bachelor Forum [M,B,L]
670 University Ave (at Atlantic)
585/271-6930 *2pm-2am*

Motor [MW,NH,V] 113 State St (at Andrews) 585/262-2650 *4pm-2am, from 2pm wknds*

Muther's [★MW,D,DS,GO] 40 S Union St (at Gardiner Park) 585/325-6216 *4pm-2am, till 3am Fri-Sun, patio*

RJ's Pub [M,NH,D,GO] 140 Alexander St 585/256-1000 *4pm-2am, noon-9pm Sun, also restaurant*

Tara Lounge [★MW,NH,E,P,OC] 153 Liberty Pole Wy (at Andrews) 585/232-4719 *noon-2am*

■ CAFES

Little Theatre Cafe [★E,BW,WC] 240 East Ave 585/258-0412 *5:30pm-10pm, noon-midnight Fri-Sat, live jazz*

■ RESTAURANTS

Edibles 704 University Ave (at Oxford) 585/271-4910 *lunch & dinner, bar*

Triphammer Grill 60 Browns Race (btwn Platt & Commercial) 585/262-2700 *clsd Sun, full bar, patio*

■ RETAIL SHOPS

Outlandish [GO] 274 N Goodman St (in the Village Gate) 585/760-8383 *11am-11pm, noon-5pm Sun, videos, pride items, books, toys*

The Pride Connection 728 South Ave (1 blk from Gregory) 585/242-7840 *noon-9pm, from 10am Sat, till 6pm Sun, lgbt gifts & books*

■ PUBLICATIONS

Empty Closet 585/244-9030 *lgbt newspaper, resource listings*

■ MEN'S CLUBS

Rochester Spa & Body Club [PC] 109 Liberty Pole Wy 585/852-2153 *24hrs*

■ MEN'S SERVICES

▶ **Megaphone Rochester** 800/289-1489 *Call for the local # nearest you! Meet Hot Men in your area! FREE to Browse & Respond to voice ads. Use code 3087. Also try MEGAMATES.COM*

■ EROTICA

Monroe Show World 585 Monroe Ave 585/473-0160

Saratoga Springs

■ ACCOMMODATIONS

The Mansion [GS,NS,WC,GO] Rte 29, Rock City Falls 518/885-1607, 888/996-9977 *1860 Victorian mansion, full brkfst*

Saratoga B&B/ Saratoga Motel [GF,NS,GO] 434 Church St 518/584-0920, 800/584-0920 *1850 farmhouse, full brkfst*

Shenteng B&B [GS,GO] 128 Southline Rd (at Antioch Rd), Middle Grove 518/882-1853, 888/769-0112 *hot tub, workshops & classes*

The Westchester House 102 Lincoln Ave 518/587-7613, 888/302-1717

■ BOOKSTORES

Nahani [WC] 482 Broadway 518/587-4322 *10am-7pm, noon-5pm Sun*

■ CRUISY AREAS

Congress Park [AYOR] *summers after dusk*

Schenectady

see Capital District

Seneca Falls

■ ACCOMMODATIONS

Guion House [GF,NS] 32 Cayuga St 315/568-8129, 800/631-8919 *full brkfst*

Sharon Springs

■ ACCOMMODATIONS

American Hotel [GS,F,WC,GO] Main St/ Rte 10 518/284-2105

Edgefield [GS,NS,GO] 518/284-3339 *well-appointed English Country house, near opera*

New Yorker Guest House & Spa [GF,NS] Center St 518/284-2126 *seasonal, full brkfst*

The TurnAround Spa [MW,F,NS,GO] 201 Washington St 518/284-9708, 212/628-9008 *small hotel & health spa, full brkfst, hot tub*

Woodstock • New York

■RESTAURANTS

The Roseboro [NS] Main St/ Rte 10 (at Washington St) **518/284-2020** *lunch & dinner, wknd brunch, full bar, veranda*

■RETAIL SHOPS

The Finishing Touch 165 Main St (Rte 10) **518/284-2884** *11am-5pm, clsd Mon, gallery & gift shop*

Syracuse

■INFO LINES & SERVICES

AA Gay/ Lesbian 315/463-5011 (AA#)

Pride Community Center 745 N Salina St **315/426-1650** *6pm-9pm Tue-Fri, noon-6pm Sat, hours vary*

■BARS

Charades [MW,TG,DS,S,18+,GO] 116 St Marks Ave (at W Fayette St) **315/468-8661** *8pm-2am, clsd Mon, lunch & dinner, DJ wknds, 18+ Th-Sat*

Rain Lounge [M,NH,MR,TG,E,K,P,V,GO] 218 N Franklin St (at Herald Pl) **315/474-3487** *4pm-2am*

Spirits [MW,D,NH,E] 205 N West St (at W Genessee) **315/471-9279** *3pm-2am, from noon wknds*

■NIGHTCLUBS

Trexx [M,D,DS,V,18+,WC] 319 N Clinton St (exit 18, off Rte 81) **315/474-6408** *8pm-2am, till 4am Fri-Sat, T-dance from 4pm Sun, clsd Mon-Tue, go-go dancers, drag shows Sun, patio*

■CAFES

Happy Endings [E,WC] 317 S Clinton St (at W Fayette) **315/475-1853** *noon-midnight, from 1pm wknds*

■BOOKSTORES

My Sisters' Words 304 N McBride St (near James) **315/428-0227** *10am-6pm, till 8pm Fri, open Sun (in winter)*

■PUBLICATIONS

OutWords 709 E Genessee St #209 **315/476-6582** *monthly lgbt paper*

■MEN'S SERVICES

▶ **Megaphone Syracuse** **800/289-1489** *Call for the local # nearest you! Meet Hot Men in your area! FREE to Browse & Respond to voice ads. Use code 3087. Also try MEGAMATES.COM*

■EROTICA

Boulevard Books 2576 Erie Blvd E (at Seeley) **315/446-1595** *24hrs*

South City Book & Video 2807 Brewerton Rd **315/454-0629** *24hrs*

■CRUISY AREAS

Thornden Park [AYOR] *pink triangle rock*

Troy

see Capital District

■BARS

Ferry Street Pub [M,NH,D,F,GO] 95 Ferry St (at Fourth St) **518/272-8250** *4pm-2am, till 4am wknds, friendly, no attitude*

Utica

■NIGHTCLUBS

That Place [M,D,L,YC,WC] 216 Bleecker St (at Genessee) **315/724-1446** *8pm-2am, from 4pm Fri*

Watertown

■BARS

Clueless [M,NH,D,V] 545 Arsenal St **315/782-9006** *8pm-2am, clsd Sun-Tue*

Webster

■RESTAURANTS

The Grill at Union Hill Country Store 1891 Ridge Rd **585/265-4443** *6am-10pm, 7am-9pm Sun*

White Plains

■INFO LINES & SERVICES

The Loft 180 E Post Rd (lower level) **914/948-4922** *lgbt community center, also newsletter*

Woodstock

see Catskill Mtns

North Carolina • USA

NORTH CAROLINA

Statewide

PUBLICATIONS

➤ **The Front Page** 919/829-0181
lgbt newspaper for the Carolinas

➤ **TLW Magazine** 727/522-8888
Southeast's largest entertainment magazine for gay men

Arden

EROTICA

Southeastern Fantasy & Video 2317 Henderson Rd **828/684-2821** *toys*

Asheville

includes Black Mountain

INFO LINES & SERVICES

Lambda AA All Souls Church, Biltmore Village **828/254-8539 (AA#)** *8pm Fri*

ACCOMMODATIONS

➤ **1889 WhiteGate Inn & Cottage** [★GS,GO] 173 E Chestnut St **828/253-2553, 800/485-3045** *full-service B&B, 3-course brkfst*

The 1900 Inn on Montford [★GF] 296 Montford Ave **828/254-9569, 800/254-9569** *English cottage, full brkfst*

Abbington Green [GF] 46 Cumberland Circle (at Cumberland Ave) **828/251-2454, 800/251-2454** *B&B in Montford historic district*

Acorn Cottage B&B [GS,NS] 25 St Dunstans Cir **828/253-0609, 800/699-0609** *1925 granite home, full brkfst*

Biltmore Village Inn [GF,NS,GO] 119 Dodge St (at Irwin) **828/274-8707, 866/274-8779** *historic inn near Biltmore Estate*

Bodhi Tree House [W,TG,NS,GO] 395 Lakey Gap Acres, Black Mountain **828/669-3889** *private, near Asheville*

Gay Owned and Operated
Bed and Breakfast
on the National Register
173 East Chestnut St.

Innkeepers:
Ralph Coffey & Frank Salvo

website: http://www.whitegate.net
email: innkeeper@whitegate.net

Rates: $165-$275
Phone: 1-800-485-3045

1889
WhiteGate Inn
& Cottage

AAA Approved

➤ *Award Winning Fully Restored 1889 shingle-style home.*
➤ *5 luxurious guest rooms with Private baths.*
➤ *3 course Gourmet breakfast.*
➤ *Evening social hour.*
➤ *Separate cottage for complete Privacy.*
➤ *Greenhouse/ Conservatory Filled with Orchids and Tropicals.*
➤ *Exotic landscaping with Waterfalls and Koi Pond.*
➤ *Closest inn to downtown Asheville and it's 150 plus Art galleries, antique stores, restaurants, bookstores, sidewalk cafés and Gay bars.*
➤ *3 miles to the Biltmore Estate*
➤ *5 miles to the Blue Ridge Parkway*

Asheville • North Carolina

Cottage at Woodhaven [GS,NS,GO]
828/299-8757, 828/215-3532 (cell)
cottage rental

The Hawk & Ivy B&B [GS,SW,NS,WC]
133 N Fork Rd, Barnardsville
828/626-3486, 888/395-7254
full brkfst

Monthaven Guest Suite Apartments
[M,NS,GO] 21 Arborvale Rd #4 (at Montford Ave) 828/236-9089
located in historic neighborhood

Mountain Laurel B&B [MW,NS,GO] 139 Lee Dotson Rd, Fairview
828/628-9903, 828/712-6289
25 miles from Asheville, full brkfst

The Old Mill [GF,GO] 100 Lake Lure Hwy (at 64 Junction), Bat Cave
828/625-4256

Owl's Nest Inn & Engadine Cabins
[★GS,GO] 2630 Smokey Park Hwy (off I-40, at exit 37), Candler 828/665-8325, 800/665-8868 *full brkfst, fireplace*

Rock Bottom B&B [MW,GO] 712 Main St (at Hwy 64 & Hwy 72-A), Chimney Rock 828/625-0958 *B&B, full brkfst*

Wolf Pines Mountain Lodging [GF,GO]
2153 Memorial Hwy, Lake Lure
828/625-0090, 888/309-0547
studio

■ BARS

O'Henry's [MW,NH,D,DS,PC] 237 Haywood St 828/254-1891 *2pm-2am*

Tressa's [GS,E] 28 Broadway
828/254-7072 *4pm-2am, from 7pm Sat, clsd Sun, jazz/ cigar bar*

■ NIGHTCLUBS

Club Hairspray [MW,D,E,K,C,DS] 38 N French Broad Ave (at Patton Ave)
828/258-2027 *8pm-3am, fetish night last Fri*

Scandals [MW,D,DS,V,18+,PC,WC] 11 Grove St (at Patton) 828/252-2838
9pm-3am, from 10pm Fri-Sat, clsd Mon-Tue, 3 bars

■ CAFES

Beanstreets Coffee 3 Broadway (at College) 828/255-8180 *7:30am-6pm, till 10pm Wed, till 12:30am Th-Sat, 9am-4am Sun*

Laurey's [★WC,GO] 67 Biltmore Ave
828/252-1500 *10am-6pm, till 4pm Sat, clsd Sun, delicious salads & cookies, dinners-to-go*

■ RESTAURANTS

John Henry's 57 Hayward St
828/255-0010 *open April-Dec, brunch from 11:30am Wed-Sun, dinner Tue-Sat, also Scully's Bar, outside deck, patio*

Laughing Seed Cafe [BW,WC] 40 Wall St (at Haywood) 828/252-3445
11:30am-9pm, till 10pm Fri-Sat, Sun brunch, clsd Tue, vegetarian/ vegan, patio

Picnics Restaurant & Bake Shop
[GF,BW,WC,GO] 371 Merrimon Ave
828/258-2858 *11:30am-7pm, clsd Sun-Mon, catering services available*

Tupelo Honey Cafe 12 College St
828/255-4863 *9am-3pm, open till 3am Fri-Sat, clsd Mon, 'southern home cookin' with an uptown twist'*

■ ENTERTAINMENT & RECREATION

Fine Arts Theatre 36 Biltmore Ave
828/232-1536 *first-run art & independent films*

■ BOOKSTORES

Downtown Books & News 67 N Lexington Ave (btwn Walnut & Hiawassee) 828/253-8654 *8am-6pm, used books & new magazines, lgbt section*

Malaprop's Bookstore & Cafe [E]
55 Haywood St (at Walnut)
828/254-6734, 800/441-9829 *9am-9pm, till 11pm Fri-Sat, till 6pm Sun, readings & performances*

Reader's Corner 31 Montford Ave
828/285-8805 *11am-7pm, 10am-6pm Sat, from 1pm Sun, used books*

■ RETAIL SHOPS

Rainbow's End Gallery & Gifts [GO]
10 N Spruce St 828/285-0005 *11am-5pm, till 6pm Fri-Sat, clsd Sun, lgbt, also gifts & video rentals, gallery exhibiting local lgbt artwork*

■ PUBLICATIONS

Community Connections
828/251-2449 *monthly lgbt magazine*

North Carolina • USA

■Gyms & Health Clubs
Sensibilities Natural Body Care & Day Spa [GF,GO] 59 Haywood (at 240) **828/253-3222, 800/635-0948**

■Erotica
Bedtyme Stories 2334 Hendersonville Rd, Arden **828/684-8250**

■Cruisy Areas
The Blue Ridge Parkway [AYOR] Sleepy Gap & Chestnut Cove overlooks (at mile marker 397 & 398)

The Cage [AYOR] the blk around federal bldg

Atlantic Beach

■Accommodations
Royal Pavilion Resort [GS,F,SW,WC] 125 Salter Path Rd **252/726-5188, 800/533-3700** *oceanfront hotel, hot tub, gym*

Blowing Rock

■Accommodations
Blowing Rock Cabins [GF,GO] 229 Price St (Hwy 221 S) **828/295-4272**

Blowing Rock Victorian Inn [GF,GO] 242 Ransom St (at US 321) **828/295-0034** *B&B, full brkfst, jacuzzi*

Stone Pillar B&B [GS,WC,GO] 144 Pine St **828/295-4141, 800/962-9955** *historic 1920s house, full brkfst*

Burnside

■Accommodations
Riverside Treehouse [GF] 8035 State Hwy 80 S (above Sally's Kitchen) **828/675-1881** *2-bdrm apt overlooking river*

■Restaurants
Sally's Kitchen 8035 State Hwy 80 S **828/675-1881** 8am-8pm, 9am-7pm wknds, 'If it's not good, we don't serve it'

Chapel Hill
see Raleigh/Durham/Chapel Hill

Charlotte

■Info Lines & Services
AA Gay/ Lesbian 3200 Park Rd (at St Luke's Lutheran Church) **704/332-4387** (AA#) 8pm Fri

Gay/ Lesbian Switchboard **704/535-6277** 6:30pm-10pm Sun-Th

The Lesbian/ Gay Community Center 1401-B Central Ave (at Clement Ave) **704/333-0144** 4pm-9pm, 10am-6pm Sat, 1pm-7pm Sun

■Accommodations
The Morehead Inn [GF,WC,GO] 1122 E Morehead St **704/376-3357, 888/667-3432** *antique-filled suites*

Morgan Suites Hotel [GS] 315 E Woodlawn Rd **704/522-0852**

Vanlandingham Estate [GF,NS,WC,GO] 2010 The Plaza **704/334-8909, 888/524-2020** *Bungalow-style estate*

■Bars
Central Station [MW,NH,MR,PC] 2131 Central Ave (at The Plaza) **704/377-0906** 5pm-2am

▶ **Charlotte Eagle** [★M,D,CW,B,L,F,V,GO] 4544-H South Blvd (at Woodlawn) **704/679-9901** 8pm-2am, from 6pm Fri-Sun, theme nights

DAKS Tavern [MW,NH,E] 1704 Shamrock Dr **704/347-6826** 6:30pm-2:30am, clsd Mon, patio

Hartigan's Irish Pub [★GS,NH,F,GO] 601 S Cedar St **704/347-1841**

Liaisons [★MW,NH,F,V,PC] 316 Rensselaer Ave (at South Blvd) **704/376-1617** 5pm-1am, restaurant Wed-Sun

The Woodshed [M,NH,B,L,F,PC,WC] 4000 S I-85 Service Rd (at Little Rock) **704/394-1712** 5pm-2:30am, from 3pm Sun, also patio bar

■Nightclubs
Chaser's [M,D,S,V,PC,WC] 3217 The Plaza (at 36th) **704/339-0500** 5pm-2am, till 10pm Sun

Club Myxx [MW,D,MR-AF,S,PC] 3110 S Tryon St **704/525-5001** 10pm-4am Sat & 9pm-close Sun

Charlotte • North Carolina

Mecca [GS,D] 300 E Morehead St (btwn South Blvd & S Tryon) **704/334-2655** *10pm-close Wed, Fri-Sun*

Mythos [GF,D,A,S,18+,PC,WC] 300 N College St (at 6th) **704/375-8765** *10pm-3am, till 4am wknds, 11pm-4am Sun, clsd Mon, more gay Sat*

Scorpios [MW,D,MR,DS,V,18+,PC,WC] 2301 Freedom Dr **704/373-9124** *9pm-3:30am, clsd Mon-Tue, also Diva's*

Velocity [★M,D,PC,WC] 935 S Summit Ave (at Morehead St) **704/333-0060** *from 10pm Fri-Sat only*

■CAFES

Caribou Coffee 1531 East Blvd (near Scott) **704/334-3570** *6am-11pm, till midnight Fri-Sat*

Tic Toc Coffeeshop 512 N Tryon St (btwn 8th & 9th) **704/375-5750** *7am-3pm, clsd wknds*

■RESTAURANTS

300 East 300 East Blvd (at Cleveland) **704/332-6507** *11:30am-10pm, till 11pm Tue-Th, till midnight Fri-Sat, bar*

Alexander Michael's 401 W 9th St (at Pine) **704/332-6789** *lunch & dinner, clsd Sun, pub fare, full bar*

Cosmos Cafe 300 N College (at 6th) **704/372-3553** *11am-2am, from 5pm wknds, also martini lounge*

Fat City 3127 N Davidson St (at 35th) **704/343-0240** *noon-2am, from 2pm Sun*

Lupie's Cafe 2718 Monroe Rd (near 5th St) **704/374-1232** *11am-11pm, from noon Sat, clsd Sun, homestyle*

■BOOKSTORES

Paper Skyscraper [WC] 330 East Blvd (at Euclid Ave) **704/333-7130** *10am-7pm, till 6pm Sat, noon-5pm Sun, books & funky gifts*

White Rabbit Books & Things 1401 Central Ave **704/377-4067** *10am-9pm, noon-8pm Sun, lgbt, gifts*

■RETAIL SHOPS

Urban Evolution 1500 Central Ave (at Pecan) **704/332-8644** *10am-9pm, 1pm-6pm Sun, clothing & more*

North Carolina • USA

PUBLICATIONS

➤ **The Front Page** 919/829-0181 *lgbt newspaper for the Carolinas*

Q Notes 704/531-9988 *bi-weekly lgbt newspaper for the Carolinas*

MEN'S SERVICES

➤ **Megaphone Charlotte** 800/289-1489 *Call for the local # nearest you! Meet Hot Men in your area! FREE to Browse & Respond to voice ads. Use code 3087. Also try MEGAMATES.COM*

EROTICA

Carolina Video Source 8829 E Harris Blvd 704/566-9993

Hwy 74 Video & News 3514 Barry Dr 704/399-7907

Independence News 3205 The Plaza (at 36th) 704/332-8430

Queen City Video & News 2320 Wilkinson Blvd 704/344-9435 *24hrs*

CRUISY AREAS

Freedom Park [AYOR]

Park on Eastway & Shamrock Dr [AYOR]

Plaza Road [AYOR]

Columbia

ACCOMMODATIONS

The River House B&B [GS] 202 Bridge St (at Hwy 64) 252/796-1855 *full brkfst, shared baths*

Duck

ACCOMMODATIONS

Advice 5¢, a B&B [GF] 111 Scarborough Ln 252/255-1050, 800/238-4235 *seaside cottage on North Carolina's outer banks*

Durham

see Raleigh/Durham/Chapel Hill

Fayetteville

ACCOMMODATIONS

Sterling's B&B [M,SW,N,GO] 5616 Sheraton Dr 910/864-2321

NIGHTCLUBS

Alias [MW,D,MR,TG,E,S,V,18+,GO] 984 Old McPherson Church Rd (at Raeford Rd) 910/484-7994 *10pm-3am Fri-Sat, also Th in summers*

Club Spektrum [MW,D,MR,DS] 107 Swain St (at Bragg Blvd) 910/868-4279 *8pm-3am, clsd Mon*

EROTICA

Fort Video & News 4431 Bragg Blvd (near 401 overpass) 910/868-9905

Priscilla's 3800 Sycamore Dairy Rd (at Bragg Blvd) 910/860-1776

CRUISY AREAS

Fort Bragg Army Reservation [AYOR] 910/860-1776

Franklin

ACCOMMODATIONS

For Your Pleasure Rentals (Mountain Magic) [GS,WC] 850/231-0254, 866/836-2040

Phoenix Nest [MW,NS,WC,GO] 850/421-1984 *seasonal mtn cabin, sleeps 4*

Gastonia

EROTICA

321 News & Video 1410 N Chester St 704/866-0075

Gastonia Video & News [★] 414 W Main 704/867-9262 *24hrs*

CRUISY AREAS

W Main St [AYOR] from Chester St to Trenton St

Greensboro

INFO LINES & SERVICES

Gay/ Lesbian Hotline 336/855-8558 *7pm-10pm Sun-Th*

Live & Let Live AA 617 N Elm St (at First Presbyterian Church) 336/854-4278 (AA#) *8pm Tue*

ACCOMMODATIONS

Biltmore Greensboro Hotel [GS,GO] 111 W Washington (at Elm St) 336/272-3474, 800/332-0303 *fully restored historic hotel*

Raleigh/Durham/Chapel Hill • North Carolina

■NIGHTCLUBS

The Palms [M,D,S,PC] 413 N Eugene St (at Smith) **336/272-6307** 9pm-2:30am

Warehouse 29 [M,D,DS,S,V,PC] 1011 Arnold St **336/333-9333** 9:30pm-3:30am Fri-Sat only (also open 3pm-3am Sun summers), T-dance Sun (summer), also patio bar

■EROTICA

Gents Video & News [★] 3722 High Point Rd **336/855-9855** 24hrs

New Visions Video 507 Mobile St (off Randleman Rd) **336/274-6443**

Xanadu 1205 E Bessemer **336/373-9849**

■CRUISY AREAS

High Point Rd [AYOR] late

Oka Hester Park [AYOR] Groometown Rd (at I-85)

Greenville

■NIGHTCLUBS

Paddock Club [M,D,A,DS,S,18+,PC,WC] 1008-B Dickinson Ave **252/758-0990** 9pm-2:30am, clsd Mon-Tue, strippers

■CRUISY AREAS

Green Springs Park [AYOR] 5th St (behind Pizza Hut)

Hickory

■NIGHTCLUBS

Club Cabaret [MW,D,S,PC,WC] 101 N Center St (at 1st Ave) **828/322-8103** 10pm-2am, clsd Sun-Tue

Hot Springs

■ACCOMMODATIONS

The Duckett House Inn [GS,NS,GO] **828/622-7621** Victorian farmhouse, full brkfst, creek swimming, also a vegetarian restaurant

Jacksonville

■CAFES

Corner Cafe Coffeehouse [GS] 715 Gum Branch Rd (at Hwy 17) **910/938-2535** 7pm-close, till 3am Fri-Sat, internet access, full bar, patio

■EROTICA

Priscilla's 113-A Western Blvd **910/355-0765**

■CRUISY AREAS

Camp Lejeune [AYOR] Main Field House days

Morehead City

■CRUISY AREAS

Fort Macon St Park Beach [AYOR] Morehead summers

Morehead City Park [AYOR] Morehead

New Bern

■ACCOMMODATIONS

Harmony House Inn [GF,NS] 215 Pollock St **252/636-3810, 800/636-3113** 1850 Greek Revival, full brkfst

Raleigh/Durham/Chapel Hill

■INFO LINES & SERVICES

Gay/ Lesbian Helpline of Wake County 919/821-0055 6:30pm-9:30pm Sun-Th

Steps, Traditions & Promises AA 80 Watts St (at Watts Baptist Church), Durham **919/286-9499** 8pm Fri

■ACCOMMODATIONS

Fickle Creek Farm [GS,GO] **919/304-6287** passive solar B&B, full brkfst, some shared baths, jacuzzi

Joan's Place [GS,NS,GO] **919/942-5621** 2 guest rooms w/ shared bath

Morehead Manor B&B [GS,NS] 914 Vickers Ave (at Morehead), Durham **919/687-4366, 888/437-6333** splendid Colonial home, full brkfst

The Oakwood Inn B&B [GF] 411 N Bloodworth St (at Oakwood), Raleigh **919/832-9712, 800/267-9712** Victorian in the heart of Raleigh, full brkfst

The FRONT PAGE

Serving the Carolina's Gay & Lesbian Communities for Over **20 Years.**

Local, National and World News • Opinion
AIDS/HIV Coverage • Features • Cartoons
Film, Music & Book Reviews • Calendar
Community Resources via our Website
Horoscope • Ms. Behavior • Classifieds

To send news, letters, or Calendar Items
and for advertising information:
P.O. Box 27928 • Raleigh, NC 27611
(919) 829-0181 • Fax (919) 829-0830
E-mail: frntpage@aol.com

Check out our website:
FrontPageNews.com

Available Free across the Carolinas
and by Subscription.

Biweekly - 26 issues per year
$30 – Bulk Rate • $52 – First Class Rate
$2 – Sample copy

LEGENDS

330 W. Hargett St • Raleigh, NC
919.831.8888

www.legends-club.com

Great People
Music &
Shows!

Open 7 days a week, 9pm until...

FLEX

MEN'S BAR OF THE CAROLINAS

2 S. West St • Raleigh, NC
919.832.8855
www.flex-club.com

North Carolina • USA

BARS

➤ **Flex** [★M,B,L,E,S,PC] 2 S West St (at Hillsborough), Raleigh **919/832-8855** *5pm-close, from 2pm Sun, 18+ Mon & Th*

Retail Bar [MW,D,PC] 14 W Martin St (btwn Salisbury & Wilmington), Raleigh **919/828-7622** *8pm-close, also martini lounge*

NIGHTCLUBS

The Capital Corral (CC) [M,D,MR,P,18+,PC,WC] 313 W Hargett St (at Harrington), Raleigh **919/755-9599** *8pm-close, from 6pm Sun, piano bar, more diverse Th*

➤ **Legends** [MW,D,S,YC,PC,WC] 330 W Hargett St (at Harrington), Raleigh **919/831-8888** *9pm-close, theme nights, deck*

The Oasis [M,D,CW,E,GO] 3201 New Bern Ave (at Milburnie), Raleigh **919/255-1314** *9pm-3am, 8pm-midnight Sun, clsd Mon-Wed, patio*

RESTAURANTS

Crooks Corner [WC] 610 Franklin St (at Merritt Mill Rd), Chapel Hill **919/929-7643** *dinner nightly, Southern cooking, full bar, patio*

Elmo's Diner 776 9th St (in the Carr Mill Mall), Chapel Hill **919/929-2909** *6:30am-10pm, till 11pm wknds*

Irregardless Cafe 901 W Morgan St (at Hillsborough), Raleigh **919/833-8898**

Magnolia Grill [WC] 1002 9th St (at Knox), Durham **919/286-3609** *6pm-9:30pm, clsd Sun-Mon, upscale Southern, full bar*

Vertigo Diner 426 S McDowell St (at Cabarrus), Raleigh **919/832-4477** *lunch Tue-Fri, dinner Wed-Sat, bar till 2am, retro*

Weathervane Cafe [WC] Eastgate Shopping Center, Chapel Hill **919/929-9466** *10am-9pm, till 10pm Fri-Sat, till 6pm Sun, full bar, great brunch*

BOOKSTORES

Internationalist Books & Community Center 405 W Franklin St (at Columbia), Chapel Hill **919/942-1740** *11am-8pm, noon-6pm Sun, from 2pm Mon, progressive/ alternative, readings & events*

Quail Ridge Books 3522 Wade Ave (at Ridgewood Center), Raleigh **919/828-1588, 800/672-6789** *9am-9pm, lgbt section*

Reader's Corner 3201 Hillsborough St (at Rosemary), Raleigh **919/828-7024** *10am-8pm, noon-6pm wknds, used books*

Regulator Bookshop 720 9th St (btwn Hillsborough & Perry), Durham **919/286-2700** *9am-9pm, till 6pm Sun, also cafe*

White Rabbit Raleigh [WC] 309 W Martin St (btwn Dawson & Harrington), Raleigh **919/856-1429** *11am-9pm, 1pm-8pm Sun, lgbt, music, movies, cards & gifts*

PUBLICATIONS

➤ **The Front Page 919/829-0181** *lgbt newspaper for the Carolinas*

MEN'S SERVICES

➤ **Megaphone Raleigh 800/289-1489** *Call for the local # nearest you! Meet Hot Men in your area! FREE to Browse & Respond to voice ads. Use code 3087. Also try MEGAMATES.COM*

EROTICA

Atlantis Video & News 522 E Main St (near Dillard), Durham **919/682-7469**

Capitol Blvd News 2236 Capitol Blvd, Raleigh **919/831-1400**

Castle Video & News 1210 Capitol Blvd, Raleigh **919/836-9189** *24hrs*

Movie Town 3615 Chapel Hll Blvd (at University), Durham **919/489-9945**

Our Place 327 W Hargett (at Harrington), Raleigh **919/833-8968** *24hrs*

Videos for the Mature 9016 Glenwood Ave, Raleigh **919/787-0016** *24hrs*

Rocky Mount

NIGHTCLUBS

Liquid Nightclub [M,D] 313 Falls Rd **252/266-6464** *9pm-close, till 2:30 am Fri, till 4am Sat, clsd Mon-Wed*

Fargo • North Dakota

Sanford

■ EROTICA

Sanford Video & News 667 S Horner Blvd **919/774-9124** *24hrs*

Spruce Pine

■ ACCOMMODATIONS

The Lemon Tree Inn [GS,GO] 872 Greenwood Rd **828/765-6161**

Statesville

■ ACCOMMODATIONS

Madelyn's in the Grove [GS,NS] 1836 W Memorial Hwy, Union Grove **704/539-4151, 800/948-4473** *B&B, full brkfst, 'murder mystery' wknds*

Wilmington

■ ACCOMMODATIONS

Coastline Inn [GS,WC,GO] 503 Nutt St **910/763-2800, 800/617-7732**

Fifteenth St B&B [GF,NS] 111 N 15th St **910/763-2136, 877/506-3974** *1921 Colonial, full brkfst*

Hidden Treasure Beach [GS,SW,NS] 113 S 4th Ave (at 'K' Ave), Kure Beach **910/458-3216** *3 private units w/ kitchens*

The Taylor House Inn [GS,NS] 14 N 7th St **910/763-7581, 800/382-9982** *romantic 1905 house, full brkfst*

■ BARS

Club Mixers [M,MR,TG,K,DS,S,V,18+,GO] 2325 Burnett Blvd (at Shipyard Blvd) **910/362-0200** *5pm-2am, clsd Sun, karaoke Mon, strippers Wed & Fri-Sat*

Costello's [M,NH,E,P,V,PC,WC,GO] 211 Princess St (btwn 2nd & 3rd) **910/362-9666** *7pm-close*

■ NIGHTCLUBS

Ibiza [M,D,K,DS,YC,WC,GO] 118 Market St (rear) **910/251-1301** *5pm-3am, clsd Mon, karaoke Wed*

■ RESTAURANTS

Caffé Phoenix [GO] 9 S Front St **910/343-1395**

The Forks [BW,GO] 3151 S 17th St (at Louise Wells Cameron Museum) **910/395-5999** *11:30am-3pm, also open for dinner Fri 5pm-10pm, jazz brunch Sun, clsd Mon, upscale Southern*

■ BOOKSTORES

Bristol Books 1908 Eastwood Rd, Ste 116 (in Lumina Station) **910/256-4490** *9am-8pm, from 8am Sun, also cafe*

Winston-Salem

■ INFO LINES & SERVICES

Gay/ Lesbian Hotline **336/855-8558** *7pm-10pm Sun-Th*

■ BARS

Satellite [MW,D,E,K,S] 701 N Trade St (at 7th) **336/722-8877** *5pm-2:30am, karaoke Tue*

■ NIGHTCLUBS

Club Odyssey [★MW,D,S,18+] 4019-A Country Club Rd **336/774-1077** *9pm-3am, clsd Mon*

■ EROTICA

New Visions Videos 1045 N Cherry St **336/725-8034** *also 3061 Kennersville Rd, 336/788-0020*

Parkview Video & News 3051 Waughtown St **336/788-9100**

NORTH DAKOTA

Statewide

■ PUBLICATIONS

Lavender Magazine **612/871-2237** (MN#), **877/515-9969** *lgbt newsmagazine for MN, WI, IA, ND, SD*

Fargo

■ INFO LINES & SERVICES

Pride Collective & Community Center 116 12th St S (at Main Ave), Moorhead, MN **218/287-8034** *3pm-5pm Tue & Sat, referrals, support/ social groups*

■ NIGHTCLUBS

I-Beam [MW,D,K] 1021 Center Ave (at 11th), Moorhead, MN **218/233-7700** *8pm-1am, clsd Sun*

North Dakota • USA

■RESTAURANTS
Fargo's Fryn' Pan [★WC] 301 E Main St (at 4th) **701/293-9952** *24hrs*

■RETAIL SHOPS
One World Imports [GO] 618 Main Ave (at Broadway) **701/297-8882** *10:30am-6pm, clsd Sun*

Zandbroz Variety 420 Broadway **701/239-4729** *9am-9pm, noon-5pm Sun, books & gifts*

■MEN'S SERVICES
➤ **Megaphone Fargo 800/289-1489** *Call for the local # nearest you! Meet Hot Men in your area! FREE to Browse & Respond to voice ads. Use code 3087. Also try MEGAMATES.COM*

■EROTICA
Romantix ABC Fargo 417 N Pacific Ave **701/232-9768** *24hrs*

■CRUISY AREAS
Broadway [AYOR] *nights*

Island Park [AYOR] *near pool*

Grand Forks

■EROTICA
Romantix Plain Brown Wrapper 102 S 3rd St (at Kittson) **701/772-9021** *24hrs*

■CRUISY AREAS
South Washington [AYOR]

Mandan

■EROTICA
Bookstore of Mandan 116 E Main St (near Collins) **701/663-9013**

Minot

■EROTICA
Risque's 1514 S Broadway **701/838-2837**

■CRUISY AREAS
Rest Area [AYOR] Hwy 2 (10 miles E of town)

OHIO

Statewide

■PUBLICATIONS
Exposé Magazine 330/459-0296 *covers Cleveland, Akron, Canton, Pittsburgh (PA), Warren & Youngstown*

Gay People's Chronicle 216/631-8646, 800/426-5947 *Ohio's largest weekly lgbt newspaper w/ extensive listings*

Outlines Magazine 4472 W 160th St (at Puritas Ave), Cleveland **216/433-1280** *free bi-weekly club magazine covering Akron, Cleveland, Columbus, Sandusky, Toledo & more*

Akron

■INFO LINES & SERVICES
AA Intergroup 330/253-8181 (AA#)

Akron Pride Center 71 N Adams St (off E Market St) **330/253-2220** *10am-5:30pm, 11am-9pm Th, call for wknd hours*

■BARS
Adams Street Bar [★M,D,DS,P,S] 77 N Adams St **330/434-9794** *4:30pm-2:30am, from 9pm Sun, piano bar Wed*

Club Amsterdam [MW,NH] 358 S Main St **330/535-6776** *4pm-2:30am, from 6pm Sat, from 11am Sun*

Cocktails [M,D,DS,V] 1009 S Main St **330/376-2625** *2pm-2:30am, clsd Sun, The Zone [D] upstairs*

Lydia's [MW,NH,E] 1348 S Arlington St (in Arlington Plaza) **330/773-3001** *5pm-2:30am, from 6pm Mon, from 8pm Tue-Th, live blues Th*

Tear-Ez [MW,NH,DS,S,WC] 360 S Main St (near Exchange St) **330/376-0011** *11am-2:30am, from noon Sun, male strippers Mon & Wed*

■NIGHTCLUBS
Babylon [M,D,E,DS,S,V,WC,GO] 820 W Market St (btwn Portage Pass & Rhodes Ave) **330/252-9000** *4pm-2:30am*

Interbelt [MW,D,S,V,18+] 70 N Howard St (near Perkins & Main) **330/253-5700** *9:30pm-2:30am, from 3pm Sun, clsd Tue, patio*

Cincinnati • Ohio

■CAFES

Angel Falls Coffee Company [WC,GO]
792 W Market St (btwn S Highland & Grand) 330/376-5282 *patio*

■RESTAURANTS

Aladdin's Eatery 782 W Market St
330/535-0110 *11am-10:30pm, till 11:30pm Fri-Sat, till 9pm Sun, Middle Eastern*

Bruegger's Bagels 1821 Merriman Rd
330/867-8394 *6am-7pm, 7am-4pm Sun*

Two Amigos Mexican Grill 804 W Market St 330/762-8226 *11:30am-9pm, till 10pm Fri-Sat, till 7:30pm Sun, clsd Mon*

■MEN'S CLUBS

Akron Steam & Sauna [PC] 41 S Case (near River) 330/784-0777 *noon-midnight, till 6am Fri-Sat*

■MEN'S SERVICES

➤ **Megaphone Akron** 800/289-1489
Call for the local # nearest you! Meet Hot Men in your area! FREE to Browse & Respond to voice ads. Use code 3087. Also try MEGAMATES.COM

■EROTICA

XTC Video & Theatre [MW]
1167 Britain Rd, NE 330/633-7311
24hrs, also magazines & toys

Athens

■ACCOMMODATIONS

Rose Cottage Inn B&B [GS]
10764 Hooper Ridge Rd, Glouster
740/448-7673, 866/225-9624
historic 1880s country inn

Brunswick

see also Akron & Cleveland

■RESTAURANTS

Pizza Marcello 67-A Pearl Rd (near Boston Rd) 330/225-1211 *4pm-10pm, till midnight Fri-Sat, from 1pm wknds, Italian*

Canton

■ACCOMMODATIONS

Tudor Rose Estate [MO,GO]
2210 Market Ave N 330/455-0104
guest house, jacuzzi

■NIGHTCLUBS

540 Eagle [M,NH,B,L] 540 Walnut Ave NE (at 6th) 330/456-8622 *9pm-2:30am, 10pm-close Sun, home bar of the The Iron Eagles* [L]

Boardwalk [M,D,18+,WC] 1227 W Tuscarawas 330/453-8000 *5pm-2:30am, DJ Th-Sat, 18+ wknds*

Studio 704 [MW,D,DS,S] 704 4th St SW 330/453-1220 *9pm-2:30am, clsd Sun-Tue, male strippers Th-Sat*

■EROTICA

Market Street News 440 Market St (at 5th) 330/453-1275

Tower Bookstore 219 12th St NE (near Walnut) 330/455-1254

XTC 3255 Cleveland Ave NW
330/493-6404

Chillicothe

■EROTICA

➤ **The Lion's Den Adult Bookstore**
3216 S Bridge St (US 23 & Three Locks Rd) 740/663-5060 *24hrs*

Cincinnati

■INFO LINES & SERVICES

AA Gay/ Lesbian 320 Resor Ave (in St John's Unitarian Church), Clifton
513/351-0422 (AA#) *8pm Mon, Wed & Fri, call for locations of wknd mtgs*

Gay/ Lesbian Community Center of Greater Cincinnati 4119 Hamilton Ave (near Blue Rock) 513/591-0200 *6pm-9pm, noon-4pm Sat, clsd Sun*

■ACCOMMODATIONS

Cincinnatian Hotel [GF] 601 Vine St (at 6th St) 513/381-3000,
800/942-9000 *restaurant & lounge*

The Vernon Manor Hotel [GF]
400 Oak St 513/281-3300,
800/543-3999 *restaurant, pub, gym*

Ohio • USA

■ BARS

Golden Lion [M,NH,D,K,S] 340 Ludlow (at Telford), Clifton **513/281-4179** *11am-2:30am*

Hamburger Mary's [MW,F] 909 Vine St (at Court St) **513/381-6279** *11am-2am*

Junkers Tavern [GF,NH] 4156 Langland (at Pullan) **513/541-5470** *7:30am-1am*

Milton's [GF,NH] 301 Milton St (at Sycamore) **513/784-9938** *4pm-2:30am*

Plum St Pipeline [★M,NH,D,S,V] 241 W Court (at Plum) **513/241-5678** *4pm-2:30am, till 4am Fri, till 5am Sat, DJ wknds*

The Serpent [M,L] 4042 Hamilton Ave (at Blue Rock) **513/681-6969** *7pm-2:30am, clsd Mon, dress code Fri-Sat*

Shooters [M,D,CW,K,S] 927 Race St (at Court) **513/381-9900** *4pm-2:30am, karaoke Wed, dance lessons 7pm Th*

Simon Says [★M,NH,P,WC] 428 Walnut (at 5th) **513/381-7577** *11am-2:30am, from 1pm Sun*

Spurs [★M,L,F,WC] 1121 Race St (N of Central Pkwy) **513/621-2668** *4pm-2:30am, cruisy, patio*

The Subway [M,NH,D,F,S] 609 Walnut St (at 6th) **513/421-1294** *6am-2:30am, from noon Sun*

■ NIGHTCLUBS

The Dock [★MW,D,K,S,19+,WC] 603 W Pete Rose Wy (near Central) **513/241-5623** *4pm-2:30am, till 4am wknds, (from 8pm winter)*

Jacobs on the Avenue [M,D,E,K,S,V,WC,GO] 4029 Hamilton Ave (at Blue Rock) **513/591-2100** *6pm-2:30am, till 1am Mon*

Warehouse [GF,D,A,F,V,18+] 1313 Vine St (2 blks N of Central Pkwy) **513/684-9313** *10pm-2:30am Wed, till 4am Fri-Sat, patio*

■ CAFES

Kaldi's Cafe & Books [E,WC] 1204 Main St (at 12th) **513/241-3070** *9am-1am, 10am-2am Fri-Sat, till midnight Sun, full bar*

■ RESTAURANTS

Boca 4034 Hamilton Ave (btwn Knowlton St & Broadway) **513/542-2022** *lunch & dinner, clsd Mon, nouvelle int'l, patio, full bar*

Carol's on Main [★WC,GO] 825 Main St (btwn 8th & 9th) **513/651-2667** *11am-1am, till 2:30am Th-Sat, from 5pm wknds, bistro*

Mullane's Parkside Café [BW,WC] 723 Race St (btwn 7th & Garfield) **513/381-1331** *11:30am-11pm, till midnight Fri-Sat, from 5pm Sat, clsd Sun*

■ ENTERTAINMENT & RECREATION

Alternating Currents WAIF 88.3 FM **513/333-9243, 513/749-1444** *3pm Sat, lgbt public affairs radio program*

■ RETAIL SHOPS

Pyramids 907 Race St (btwn 9th & Court) **513/621-7465** *noon-9pm, till 11pm Fri-Sat, 1pm-8pm Sun, pride items, also leather*

■ MEN'S SERVICES

▶ **Megaphone Cincinnati** **800/289-1489** *Call for the local # nearest you! Meet Hot Men in your area! FREE to Browse & Respond to voice ads. Use code 3087. Also try MEGAMATES.COM*

Cleveland

■ INFO LINES & SERVICES

AA Gay/ Lesbian 7801 Detroit Ave (at St Augustine Manor) **216/241-7387** *8:30pm Fri*

Cleveland Lesbian/ Gay Community Center [WC] 6600 Detroit Ave **216/651-5428** *noon-10pm, 6pm-9pm Sun*

■ ACCOMMODATIONS

▶ **Bourbon House** [M,NS,GO] 6116 Franklin Blvd (at W 65th) **216/939-0535** *1901 Victorian, full brkfst*

Clifford House [GS,NS,GO] 1810 W 28th St (at Jay) **216/589-4432, 216/589-0121** *near downtown*

Edgewater Estates [GS] 9803 Lake Ave **216/961-1764** *English Tudor on Lake Erie, full brkfst*

Cleveland • Ohio

Grandmother's Heaven [GF,NS] 3560 W 45th St (at I-71 & Fulton) **216/631-1231**

Greystone B&B [GS,GO] 10405 Lake Ave (at W 104th St) **216/939-0405** *full brkfst, weekly rates available*

Radisson Hotel Cleveland–Gateway [GF,WC] 1651 Huron Rd **216/377-9000, 800/333-3333**

Stone Gables B&B [GS,WC,GO] 3806 Franklin Blvd (at W 38th) **216/961-4654, 877/215-4326** *sauna*

■ BARS

A Man's World [MW,D] 2909 Detroit Ave (at 29th St) **216/574-2203** *7am-2:30am, from noon Sun-Tue, DJ wknds, patio*

Deco [MW,NH,D,DS,S] 11213 Detroit Ave **216/221-8576** *9am-2:30am*

The Hawk [MW,NH,WC] 11217 Detroit Ave (at 112th St) **216/521-5443** *10am-2:30am, from 1pm Sun*

➤ **Leather Stallion Saloon** [★M,NH,B,L,F,S] 2205 St Clair Ave (near E 21st St) **216/589-8588** *3pm-2:30am, DJ wknds, patio*

Longevity [M,NH,S,WC] 2032 W 25th St (at Lorain & 24th) **216/781-9191** *11am-2:30am, from noon Sun, strippers*

MJ's Place [★M,NH,E,S] 11633 Lorain Ave (at W 117th St) **216/476-1970** *4pm-2:30am, clsd Sun, theme nights Mon, 'Cleveland's gay Cheers'*

Muggs [GF,NH] 3194 W 25th St (near Clark) **216/398-7012** *11am-2:30am, from 9am wknds*

Paradise Inn [W,NH] 4488 State Rd (Rte 94, at Rte 480) **216/741-9819** *11am-close*

➤ **Rockies Bar** [★M,D,F,K,S,V] 9208 Detroit Ave (at W 93rd St) **216/961-3115** *4pm-2:30am, patio, 'Cleveland's only Sun T-dance'*

Twist [★MW,D,P] 11633 Clifton (at 117th St) **216/221-2333** *9am-2:30am, from noon Sun*

Bourbon House

This elegant, antique-filled home is located in a historic district only a few minutes from downtown, restaurants, antiques district, beach, sporting arenas, museums, and gay nightlife.

- King, queen or double beds
- Free local calls
- Snacks & soft drinks provided
- Rooms or Suites
- Control your own a/c
- Full breakfast included
- Non-smoking (indoors)
- Cable & premium movie channels
- Credit cards accepted
- Weekly, monthly & other discounts available

6116 Franklin Boulevard
Cleveland, OH 44102
(216) 939-0535
E-mail: Robert_Bourbon_House@msn.com

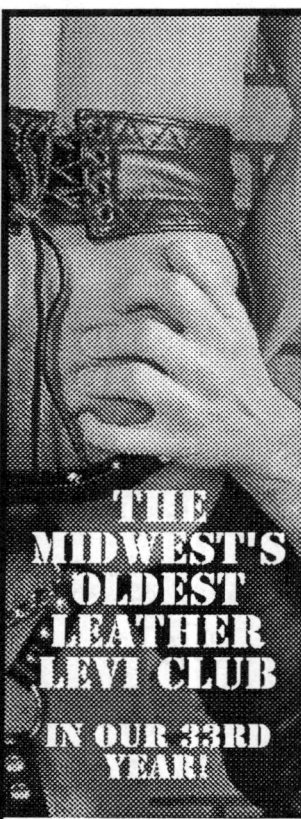

CLEVELAND

World-Famous Patio Bar

Within Walking Distance To
- Cleveland's Scenic Lakefront
- The Rock 'N Roll Hall Of Fame
- Gund Arena
- Jacob's Field
- Downtown

THE MIDWEST'S OLDEST LEATHER LEVI CLUB IN OUR 33RD YEAR!

Home Of
UNICORN M.C. • EXCALIBUR RANGERS, INC. TRIDENT-CLEVELAND
Leather Clubs

OPEN DAILY 3 P.M. - 2:30 AM
Enjoy Our Festive Happy Hour Daily
Everyone Welcome!
2205 St. Clair Ave • Cleveland, OH 44114
(216) 589-8588
Visit Us At... http://leatherstallion.com

Cleveland's Party Place!

Join Us for Cleveland's
Fabulous Happy Hour
Daily 4 to 8 p.m.

Karaoke Wednesdays
Thunderous Thursdays
Super Sunday Tea Dance
Expanded Game Room

2 Pool Tables

Garden Patio

D.J. & Music Videos every
Thursday, Friday, Saturday,
& Sunday with Dance Floor

Open everyday   Never A Cover
4:00p.m. to 2:30a.m.   Charge

(Corner of West 93rd & Detroit Ave)
9208 Detroit Ave. Cleveland OH 44102
(216) 961-3115
Visit us at : WWW.ROCKIES-CLEV.COM

Setting A New Standard

Always Open
Guest Memberships
Steam Room
Sauna
Whirlpool
Private Dressing Rooms
Indoor Pool
Sun Deck
Gym
18+ only

THE CLUB CLEVELAND

A PRIVATE MEN'S CLUB
3219 Detroit Ave. • Cleveland, Ohio • (216)961-2727
www.the-clubs.com

Cleveland • Ohio

Union Station Video Café [★MW,F,V] 2814 Detroit Ave (at W 28th) 216/357-2997 *5pm-3am, also Sun brunch; also Bounce [D,DS] Th-Sun & Pump [DS] clsd Th*

■ NIGHTCLUBS

Fuse [GS,NH,D] 6757 W 130th St, Parma Hts 440/842-4669 *5pm-2:30am*

The Grid [★M,D,S,V] 1437 St Clair Ave 216/623-0113 *5pm-close, also Orbit [D,18+]*

Tool Shed [M,NH,D,CW,L,WC] 2901-2909 Detroit Ave (enter on W 29th St) 216/771-7812, 216/574-2203 *7pm-2:30am, cruise bar, CW Sun, also Crossover [MO,L] from 10pm Fri-Sat, dress code*

■ CAFES

Johnny Mango [WC] 3120 Bridge Ave (btwn Fulton & W 32nd) 216/575-1919 *11am-10pm, till 11pm Fri-Sat, from 9am wknds, healthy world food & juice bar, also full bar*

■ RESTAURANTS

Cafe Tandoor 2096 S Taylor Rd (at Cedar), Cleveland Hts 216/371-8500, 216/371-8569 *lunch & dinner, Indian*

Harmony Bar & Grille [E] 3359 Fulton 216/398-5052 *lunch & dinner, clsd Sun-Mon, eclectic*

Hecks [★WC] 2927 Bridge Ave (at W 30th) 216/861-5464 *lunch & dinner, gourmet burgers*

The Inn on Coventry [WC] 2785 Euclid Heights Blvd (at Coventry), Cleveland Hts 216/371-1811 *7am-9pm, from 8:30am Sat, 9am-3pm Sun, 8am-3pm Mon, Sun brunch, homestyle, popular Bloody Marys*

My Friend's Deli & Restaurant 11616 Detroit Ave 216/221-2575 *24hrs*

Vina Noté [E] 2025 University Hospital Rd (at Euclid Ave) 216/229-1177 *lunch Mon-Fri & dinner nightly, clsd Sun, Italian, live jazz wknds*

■ ENTERTAINMENT & RECREATION

Rock & Roll Hall of Fame 1 Key Plaza 216/781-ROCK *even if you don't like rock, be sure to stop by & check out IM Pei's architectural gift to Cleveland*

■ BOOKSTORES

Bookstore on W 25th St 1921 W 25th St (at Lorain) 216/566-8897 *10am-6pm, noon-5pm Sun, lgbt section*

Borders Bookshop & Espresso Bar 2101 Richmond Rd (at Cedar, in LaPlace Mall), Beachwood 216/292-2660 *9am-11pm, till 9pm Sun*

■ RETAIL SHOPS

Bank News 4025 Clark Ave (at W 41st St) 216/281-8777 *10:30am-8:30pm, clsd Sun*

Big Fun 1827 Coventry Rd 216/371-4386 *variety store*

Body Language 11424 Lorain Ave (at W 115th St) 216/251-3330, 888/420-7733 *11am-10pm, till 6pm Sun, 'an educational store for adults in alternative lifestyles'*

Body Work Productions 2710 Detroit Ave (at W 28th) 216/623-0744 *1pm-8pm, noon-9pm wknds, piercing*

City Dweller [GO] 12005 Detroit Ave, Lakewood 216/226-7106 *10am-9pm, 11am-6pm Sun, cards, gifts & home decorations*

The Clifton Web 11512 Clifton Blvd (at W 115th) 216/961-1120 *11am-8pm, from 10am Sat, till 5pm Sun, cards & gifts*

Diverse Universe [WC,GO] 12011 Detroit Ave (at Hopkins), Lakewood 216/221-4297 *10am-9pm, 11am-6pm Sun, lgbt books, videos, music & gifts*

■ PUBLICATIONS

Erie Gay News 814/456-9833 *covers news & events in the Erie, Cleveland, Pittsburgh, Buffalo & Chautauqua County, NY region*

Exposé Magazine 330/459-0296 *covers Cleveland, Akron, Canton, Pittsburgh (PA), Warren & Youngstown*

Gay People's Chronicle 216/631-8646, 800/426-5947 *Ohio's largest weekly lgbt newspaper w/ extensive listings*

Outlines Magazine 4472 W 160th St (at Puritas Ave) 216/433-1280 *free bi-weekly club magazine covering Akron, Cleveland, Columbus, Sandusky, Toledo & more*

Ohio • USA

■ MEN'S CLUBS
► **The Club Cleveland** [★PC]
1448 W 32nd St (off Detroit Ave)
216/961-2727 *24hrs*

► **Flex** [MR,V,PC] 1293 W 9th St (btwn Lakeside & St Clair) **216/696-0595** *24hrs, lounge*

■ MEN'S SERVICES
► **Megaphone Cleveland**
800/289-1489 *Call for the local # nearest you! Meet Hot Men in your area! FREE to Browse & Respond to voice ads. Use code 3087. Also try MEGAMATES.COM*

■ EROTICA
Brookpark News & Video [AYOR] 16700 Brookpark Rd (at W 150th) **216/267-9019**

Laws Leather Shop 11112 Clifton Blvd **216/961-0544** *1pm-9pm, clsd Sun-Tue*

Rocky's Entertainment & Emporium [AYOR] 13330 Brookpark Rd (at W 130th) **216/267-4936**

Columbus

■ INFO LINES & SERVICES
AA Gay/ Lesbian 614/253-8501

Stonewall Columbus Community Center/ Hotline [WC] 1160 N High St (at E 4th Ave) **614/299-7764** *10am-7pm, till 5pm Fri, clsd wknds*

■ ACCOMMODATIONS
The Brewmaster's House [MO,GO] **614/449-8298** *full brkfst, historic house*

Columbus B&B [GF,GO] 763 S 3rd St **614/444-8888** *in historic district*

Courtyard by Marriott [GF,WC] 35 W Spring St (at Front St) **614/228-3200, 800/321-2211**

The Gardener's House [M,NS,GO] 556 Frebis Ave (at Ann St) **614/444-5445, 800/547-6737** *hot tub*

Columbus • Ohio

BARS

AWOL [M,NH,WC] 49 Parsons Ave (at Oak) **614/621-8779** *1pm-2:30am*

Blazer's Pub [MW,NH,K] 1205 N High St (at 5th) **614/299-1800** *4pm-2:30am, 3pm-9pm Sun*

Club 20 [M,NH,K] 20 E Duncan (at High) **614/261-9111** *noon-2:30am, from 1pm Sun, patio*

Club Diversity [MW,E,P] 863 S High St **614/224-4050** *5pm-midnight, 6pm-2am Fri-Sat, clsd Sun-Mon, piano bar*

➤ **Columbus Eagle Bar** [★M,D,DS,S,18+,WC] 232 N 3rd St (at Hickory) **614/228-2804** *8pm-2:30am*

Downtown Connection [M,NH] 1126 N High St (at 4th Ave) **614/299-4880** *5pm-2am, from 3pm wknds, sports bar*

Eagle in Exile (Patrick's) [M,NH,WC] 893 N 4th St (at 2nd Ave) **614/294-0069** *9pm-2:30am, clsd Mon-Tue*

The Far Side [W,NH,F,E,K,GO] 1662 W Mound St (at Reed) **614/276-5817** *5pm-1am, till 2:30am Fri-Sat, from 6pm Sat, live bands wknds*

Havana Video Lounge [★MW,NH,S,V] 862 N High (at 1st Ave) **614/421-9697** *5pm-2:30am, martini & cigar lounge, male strippers Sun*

The Pyramid Night Club [M,NH,DS,S] 196-1/2 E Gay St (at 5th St, enter rear) **614/228-6151** *4pm-2:30am, from 1pm wknds, strippers Tue & Sun*

Remo's [MW,NH,K,DS,S] 1409 S High St (at Jenkins) **614/443-4224** *7am-2:30am, clsd Sun*

Slammers Pizza Pub [MW,F,E,WC] 202 E Long St (at 5th St) **614/469-7526** *11am-2:30am, from 2:30pm wknds, open mic Tue, patio*

The South Bend Tavern [M,NH,WC] 126 E Moler St (at 4th St) **614/444-3386** *noon-2:30am*

Tremont II [M,NH,OC] 708 S High St (at Frankfort) **614/445-9365** *noon-2:30pm, 1pm-midnight Sun*

Setting A New Standard

Always Open
Guest Memberships
Steam Room
Sauna
Whirlpool
Private Dressing Rooms
Outdoor Pool & Patio
Gym
18+ only

THE CLUB COLUMBUS

A PRIVATE MEN'S CLUB
795 West 5th Avenue • Columbus, Ohio • (614)291-0049
www.the-clubs.com

Columbus • Ohio

Union Station Video Cafe
[★MW,F,V,WC] 630 N High St (at Goodale) **614/228-3740** *11am-2am, video bar, internet access*

The Vine Cocktails & Café
[MW,F,K,DS,WC] 73 E Gay St (at 3rd St) **614/221-8463** *5pm-1am, Sun brunch, martinis, boy's night Wed*

■NIGHTCLUBS

Axis [★M,D,18+,WC,GO] 775 N High St (at Hubbard) **614/291-4008** *10pm-2:30am, Varsity Night Th w/ dancers*

Odyssey [M,D] 747 Chambers Rd (off King Ave) **614/291-7867** *after-hours Fri-Sat only (2:30am-5am)*

Tradewinds II [M,D,B,L,V,WC] 117 E Chestnut (at 3rd St) **614/461-4110** *4pm-2:30am, clsd Mon, 3 bars & restaurant*

Wall Street [★MW,D,CW,DS,P,YC,WC] 144 N Wall St (at Long) **614/464-2800** *8pm-2:30am, from 9pm Wed & Sun, clsd Mon-Tue, more men Wed*

■CAFES

The Coffee Table [MW] 731 N High St (at Buttles) **614/297-1177** *7:30am-midnight, till 1am Fri-Sat, 8am-10pm Sun*

Cup-O-Joe Cafe 627 3rd St (at Sycamore) **614/221-1563** *6:30am-11pm, till midnight Fri-Sat, from 7:30am Sun*

■RESTAURANTS

Chinese Village 2124 Lane St (at High) **614/297-7979** *11am-10pm*

Fresno's [★] 782 N High St (at Buttles Ave) **614/298-0031** *11am-11pm, from 4pm Sat, clsd Sun*

L'Antibes [WC,GO] 772 N High St #106 (at Warren) **614/291-1666** *dinner from 5pm, clsd Sun-Mon, French*

Lemon Grass [★R] 641 N High (N of Goodale St) **614/224-1414** *lunch & dinner, from 3pm Sat, dinner only Sun, Asian cuisine*

ADULT SUPERSTORES

Columbus, OH
3015 Morse Rd.
(614) 475-1943

Columbus, OH
4315 Kimberly Parkway
(614) 861-6770

Columbus, OH
973 Harrisburg Pike
(614) 272-1373

Columbus, OH
Roberts Rd. & I-270
(614) 475-1943

Findlay, OH
Exit 164 off I-75
(419) 299-8080

Washington C.H., OH
Exit 65 off I-71
(740) 948-2446

Marengo, OH
Exit 140 off I-71
(419) 253-5200

Quaker City, OH
Exit 193 off I-70
(740) 758-5210

Heath, OH
Exit 129b off I-70
(740) 928-4404

Chillicothe, OH
US23 & 3 Locks Rd.
(740) 663-5060

Shippensburg, PA
Penn Exit 24 off I-81
(717) 530-8032

Nelson, MO
Exit 84 off I-70
(660) 859-2741

Waynesville, MO
Exit 153 off I-44
(573) 774-9957

Bowman, SC
Exit 159 off I-26
(803) 829-1781

Coldwater, MI
Exit 16 off I-69
(517) 278-9577

Sawyer, MI
Exit 12 off I-94
(269) 426-6099

Atkinson, IL
Exit 27 off I-80
(309) 936-7066

Buckley, IL
Exit 272 off I-57
(217) 394-2601

Marion, IL
Exit 45 off I-57
(618) 995-1586

Montrose, IL
Exit 105 off I-70
(217) 924-4524

Newton, IA
Exit 159 off I-80
(641) 792-9301

Milton, WV
Exit 28 off I-64
(304) 743-0190

Mineral Wells, WV
Exit 170 off I-77
(304) 489-9690

Louisville, KY
2517 7th Street Rd.
(502) 636-9002

Louisville, KY
626 W. Broadway
(502) 681-5111

Upton, KY
Exit 76 off I-65
(270) 369-8171

Ripley, NY
Exit 61 off I-90
(716) 736-6400

OPEN 24HRS.
MUST BE
18 TO ENTER.

WWW.LIONSDENADULT.COM

Dayton • Ohio

■ Entertainment & Recreation

The Reality Theatre 775 N High St (at Axis) **614/265-7337** *lgbt plays & new releases*

■ Bookstores

An Open Book [WC] 685 N High St (at Lincoln) **614/221-6339** *11am-9pm, till midnight Fri-Sat, noon-5pm Sun, lgbt, also pride items, music & gifts, coffee bar*

The Book Loft of German Village 631 S 3rd St (at Sycamore) **614/464-1774** *10am-11pm, till midnight Fri-Sat, lgbt section*

■ Retail Shops

ACME Art Company 1129 N High St (at 4th Ave) **614/299-4003** *noon-5pm, clsd Mon-Wed, alternative art space*

Creative-A-Tee 874 N High St **614/297-8844** *noon-7pm, till 5pm Sat, clsd Sun-Mon, gay pride T-shirts, silkscreening*

Hausfrau Haven 769 S 3rd St (at Columbus) **614/443-3680** *10am-6:30pm, till 5pm Sun, cards, wine & gifts*

Metro Video 848 N High St (at Hubbard) **614/291-7962** *noon-midnight, large selection of lgbt videos*

Pierceology 872 N High St (S of 1st, 2nd flr) **614/297-4743** *noon-8pm, till 9pm Fri-Sat, 1pm-7pm Sun, body-piercing studio*

Torso 772 N High St (at Warren) **614/421-7663** *11am-9pm, till 10pm Fri-Sat, from noon Sat, 1pm-5pm Sun, clothing*

■ Publications

Outlines Magazine 4472 W 160th St (at Puritas Ave), Cleveland **216/433-1280** *free bi-weekly club magazine covering Akron, Cleveland, Columbus, Sandusky, Toledo & more*

Outlook News **614/268-8525, 866/452-6397** *statewide lgbt newspaper*

Spotlight Magazine **614/805-5664** *bi-weekly lgbt paper for Central Ohio*

The Stonewall Journal **614/299-7764**

■ Men's Clubs

► **The Club Columbus** [SW] 795 W 5th Ave (at Olentangy Rd) **614/291-0049** *gym, steam, sauna*

► **Flex** [V,PC] 1567 E Livingston **614/252-0730** *24hrs, lounge*

■ Men's Services

► **Megaphone Columbus** **800/289-1489** *Call for the local # nearest you! Meet Hot Men in your area! FREE to Browse & Respond to voice ads. Use code 3087. Also try MEGAMATES.COM*

■ Erotica

Garden 1186 N High St (at 5th Ave) **614/294-2869** *adult toys*

IMRU 235 N Lazelle (at Hickory, above the Eagle) **614/228-9660** *clsd Sun-Wed, leather, pride & fetish store*

► **The Lion's Den Adult Bookstore** 3015 Morse Rd **614/475-1943** *24hrs*

► **The Lion's Den Adult Bookstore** 4315 Kimberly Pkwy (off Hamilton Rd) **614/861-6770** *24hrs*

► **The Lion's Den Adult Bookstore** 973 Harrisburg Pike (just S of Five Points shopping center) **614/272-1373** *24hrs*

► **The Lion's Den Adult Bookstore** 4375 Roberts Rd (Exit 10, off I-270) **614/529-8501** *24hrs*

North Campus Video 2465 N High St (at Hudson) **614/268-4021** *24hrs*

Zodiac 1565 Alum Creek Dr (at Livingston) **614/252-0281** *24hrs*

Dayton

■ Info Lines & Services

AA Gay/ Lesbian 20 W 1st St (off Main, at Christ Episcopal Church) **937/222-2211** *8pm Sat*

Dayton Lesbian/ Gay Hotline **937/274-1776** *24hr hotline, 7pm-11pm (volunteer staff)*

■ Bars

City Cafe [M,K,WC] 121 N Ludlow St (in Talbot Tower Bldg) **937/223-1417** *5pm-2:30am, DJ Fri-Sat, cruisy*

Ohio • USA

Club Diva [W,GO] 6303 Rip Rap Rd (off I-75, Little York exit) **937/235-9511** *7pm-close, from 4pm Fri-Sat, clsd Sun-Mon*

DJ's Saloon [M,CW,B,S] 237 N Main St **937/223-7340** *3pm-2:30am, deck*

Right Corner [M,NH,WC] 105 E 3rd St (at Jefferson) **937/228-1285** *noon-2:30am*

Stage Door [M,L,WC] 44 N Jefferson (at 2nd) **937/223-7418** *noon-2:30am, from 2pm Wed & Sat-Sun*

■ NIGHTCLUBS

1470 West [★MW,D,DS,V,WC] 34 N Jefferson St (btwn 2nd & 3rd) **937/461-1470** *9pm-2:30am, till 4am Th & Sat, clsd Mon-Wed*

Jessie's Celebrity Showbar [★M,D,K,DS,S,18+,WC] 850 N Main St (off I-75) **937/461-2582** *9pm-2:30am, till 4am Fri-Sat, clsd Sun-Tue*

■ CAFES

Gloria Jean's Coffee Bean [GO] 2727 Fairfield Commons (in mall), Beavercreek **937/426-1672** *9:30am-9pm, noon-6pm Sun*

■ RESTAURANTS

Cold Beer & Cheeseburgers [WC] 33 S Jefferson St (at 4th St) **937/222-2337** *11am-11pm, noon-8pm Sun, grill, full bar*

The Spaghetti Warehouse 36 W 5th St (at Ludlow) **937/461-3913** *11:30am-10pm, till 11pm Fri-Sat, more gay Tue w/ 'Friends of the Italian Opera'*

■ BOOKSTORES

Books & Co 350 E Stroop Rd (at Farhills) **937/298-6540** *9am-11pm, till 8pm Sun*

■ RETAIL SHOPS

Q Gift Shop 1904 N Main St (at Ridge Ave) **937/274-4400** *noon-7pm, till 5pm Sun, lgbt gifts*

■ MEN'S SERVICES

➤ **Megaphone Dayton** **800/289-1489** *Call for the local # nearest you! Meet Hot Men in your area! FREE to Browse & Respond to voice ads. Use code 3087. Also try MEGAMATES.COM*

Findlay

■ ACCOMMODATIONS

Zelkova Country Manor [★GS,NS] 2348 S CR 19 (off 224), Tiffin **419/447-4043** *full brkfst*

■ EROTICA

Findlay Adult Books & Video 623 Trenton Ave (at I-75, exit 159) **419/422-1301** *24hrs*

➤ **The Lion's Den Adult Bookstore** 11681 SR 613 (Exit 164, off I-75) **419/299-8080** *24hrs*

■ CRUISY AREAS

Riverside Park [AYOR]

Heath

■ EROTICA

➤ **The Lion's Den Adult Bookstore** 6762 Hebron Rd/ SR 79 (exit 129b, off I-70) **740/928-4404** *24hrs*

Kent

■ BARS

The Zephyr Cafe [GF,E,WC] 106 W Main St **330/678-4848**

Lima

■ NIGHTCLUBS

Somewhere in Time [MW,D,DS,S] 804 W North St **419/227-7288** *6pm-2:30am, from 8pm wknds*

Logan

■ ACCOMMODATIONS

Glenlaurel—A Scottish Country Inn & Cottages [GS,NS,WC,GO] 14940 Mt Olive Rd (off State Rte I-80), Rockbridge **740/385-4070, 800/809-7378** *full brkfst, hot tub*

Lorain

■ BARS

Tim's Place [MW,NH,D,DS,WC] 2223 Broadway (btwn 22nd & 23rd) **440/246-9002** *8pm-2:30am, clsd Mon, patio*

Toledo • Ohio

Marengo

■EROTICA
➤ **The Lion's Den Adult Bookstore**
511 State Rte 61 (exit 140, off I-71)
419/253-5200 *24hrs*

Monroe

■BARS
Old Street Saloon [MW,NH,D,DS]
13 Old St **513/539-9183** *8pm-2am Wed-Sat*

Niles

■EROTICA
Niles Books 5970 Youngstown Warren Rd (off Rte 46) **330/544-3755**

Oberlin

■RETAIL SHOPS
Stitch by Stitch 31 S Main St
440/774-4544 *noon-9pm, till 4pm Sun, many lgbt items*

Oxford

■CRUISY AREAS
Hueston Woods State Park [AYOR]
mornings & at dusk

Pickerington

■CAFES
Planet Coffee & Tea Coffee Company 1252 Hill Rd N
614/861-2040 *5:30am-9pm*

Quaker City

■EROTICA
➤ **The Lion's Den Adult Bookstore**
65799 Batesville Rd (exit 193, off I-70)
740/758-5210 *24hrs*

Sandusky

■ACCOMMODATIONS
2-Twelve Guesthouse [MW,GO]
212 Decatur St **419/627-0636** *1890s house, near pier*

■NIGHTCLUBS
Xcentricities [MW,D,K,DS,S]
306 W Water St **419/624-8118** *8pm-2:30am, patio*

■CRUISY AREAS
Boeckling Boat Dock [AYOR]

Springfield

■NIGHTCLUBS
Chances [GF,D,E,K] 1912-14 Edwards Ave (at N Belmont Ave)
937/324-0383 *8:30pm-2:30am, clsd Tue, patio*

■CRUISY AREAS
Clarence J Brown Reservoir Beach
[AYOR]

Steubenville

■NIGHTCLUBS
Club 2000 [MW,D,K,S,V] 122 N 6th St (at Market) **740/284-1291** *8pm-close, till 4am Fri-Sat, clsd Sun-Tue*

Toledo

■INFO LINES & SERVICES
AA Gay/ Lesbian 2272 Collingwood Blvd (at St Mark's Episcopal Church)
419/380-9862 *8pm Wed & Sun*

Pro Toledo Info Line 419/344-6415
lgbt info line

■BARS
Blu Jean Cafe [★MW,TG,K,WC,GO]
3606 Sylvania Ave (near Monroe)
419/474-0690 *4pm-2:30am, clsd Sun-Mon, also seasonal restaurant 5pm-11pm*

Hooterville Station [M,D,B,K]
119 N Erie St (btwn Jeff & Monroe)
419/241-9050 *5:30am-2:30am, patio*

'R' House [M,D,P] 5534 Secor Rd (btwn Laskey & Alexis) **419/474-2929** *4pm-2:30am, patio, also piano bar*

Rip Cord [M,NH,K,DS,S] 115 N Erie (btwn Jefferson & Monroe)
419/243-3412 *1pm-2:30am, free Sun brunch*

Ohio • USA

■NIGHTCLUBS
Bretz [MW,D,K,DS,S,V,18+,WC]
2012 Adams St **419/243-1900**
4pm-2:30am, till 4:30am Fri-Sat, clsd Mon-Tue, patio

Caesar's Show Bar [MW,D,S,WC]
725 Jefferson **419/241-5140** *8pm-2:30am, clsd Mon-Th*

■BOOKSTORES
Thackeray's [WC] 3301 W Central Ave (at Secor, in Westgate Shopping Center) **419/537-9259** *9am-9pm, 10am-6pm Sun*

■MEN'S CLUBS
Diplomat Health Club [PC]
1313 N Summit (along Maumee River) **419/255-3700** *24hrs*

■MEN'S SERVICES
➤ **Megaphone Toledo**
800/289-1489 *Call for the local # nearest you! Meet Hot Men in your area! FREE to Browse & Respond to voice ads. Use code 3087. Also try MEGAMATES.COM*

Warren

■BARS
The Queen of Hearts [MW,NH,D,K,S]
132-136 Pine St (btwn Market & Franklin) **330/395-1100** *3pm-2:30am, also Queen's Dungeon, Levi/ leather bar Fri-Sat downstairs, patio*

■NIGHTCLUBS
The Alley [MW,D,S,WC] 441 E Market St (enter rear) **330/394-9483** *4pm-2:30am, from 2pm Fri-Sun*

Washington Court House

■EROTICA
➤ **The Lion's Den Adult Bookstore**
9021 W Lancaster Rd NW (exit 65, off I-71) **740/948-2446** *24hrs*

Yellow Springs

■RESTAURANTS
Winds Cafe & Bakery [WC] 215 Xenia Ave **937/767-1144** *lunch & dinner, Sun brunch, clsd Mon, full bar*

Youngstown

■INFO LINES & SERVICES
The Pride Center of Greater Youngstown 1105 Elm St (basement of First Unitarian Church) **330/747-7433**

■BARS
Club Blue Note [MW,D,F,WC]
2810 Market (at Hilda) **330/782-3694** *4pm-2:30am, patio*

The Mixx [MW,NH,D,K,DS,WC] 21 W Hylda Ave (off Market) **330/782-6991** *4pm-2:30am, 2 bars*

■EROTICA
Uptown Book Store 2597 Market St (at Princeton) **330/783-2533** *24hrs*

OKLAHOMA

Statewide

■PUBLICATIONS
Gayly Oklahoman **405/528-0800** *lgbt newspaper*

Bartlesville

■CRUISY AREAS
Jo Allyn Lowe Park [AYOR]

Johnstone Park [AYOR]

El Reno

■ACCOMMODATIONS
The Good Life RV Resort [GF,SW,GO]
Exit 108 I-40 (1/4 mile S)
405/884-2994, 405/893-2345
campsites & RV hookups

Enid

■EROTICA
Priscilla's 4810-A W Garriott (at Garland) **580/233-5511** *toys & more*

■CRUISY AREAS
Meadowlake Park [AYOR] N side

Lawton

■BARS
Triangles [★MW,NH,D,K,DS] 8-1/2 NW 2nd St (enter rear) **580/351-0620** *9pm-2am, from 3pm Sun, clsd Mon-Tue*

Oklahoma City • Oklahoma

BOOKSTORES
Ingrid's Books 1124 NW Cache Rd 580/353-1488 *10am-10pm, clsd Sun, also adult novelties, magazines*

CRUISY AREAS
The Strip [AYOR] Fort Sill Blvd, near Cache Rd *by car*

Lexington

ACCOMMODATIONS
Blue Sky Ranch [W,SW,WC,GO] 14001 Banner 405/872-2583 *cabin, camping & 2 RV hookups*

Norman

see also Oklahoma City

INFO LINES & SERVICES
OU GLBT & Friends 405/325-4452

BOOKSTORES
Borders Books 300 Norman Center 405/573-4907 *lgbt section*

CRUISY AREAS
Lions & Reavers Parks [AYOR]
White St [AYOR] *near OU*

Oklahoma City

INFO LINES & SERVICES
AA Live & Let Live 3405 N Villa 405/947-3834 (club#), 405/525-2437

The Center [WC] 2135 NW 39th St 405/524-6000 *11am-7pm, till midnight Fri, clsd wknds*

ACCOMMODATIONS
America's Crossroads B&B [M,GO] 405/495-1111 *reservation service for private homes*

➤ **Habana Inn** [★MW,SW,WC] 2200 NW 39th Expwy (at Youngs) 405/528-2221, 800/988-2221 (reservations only) *gay resort, also 3 clubs, piano bar, restaurant, gift shop*

BARS
➤ **The Finishline** [MW,D,CW,WC] at Habana Inn 405/525-2900 *noon-2am, CW lessons 7pm Tue & Th, poolside bar*

Hi-Lo Club [MW,NH,D,E,DS] 1221 NW 50th St (btwn Western & Classen) 405/843-1722 *noon-2am, live bands weekly*

➤ **The Ledo** [MW,F,E,K,C,DS,P,WC] at Habana Inn 405/525-0730 *4pm-close, cabaret & lounge*

Levi's [M,NH,L,WC] 2807 NW 36th St (at May Ave) 405/947-1155 *noon-2am, cruise bar, patio*

Rocky's [MW,NH,BW,GO] 3201 N May Ave (at 30th) 405/947-9361 *noon-2am, till midnight Mon-Tue, patio*

Tramps [★M,D,S,WC] 2201 NW 39th St (at Barnes) 405/521-9888 *noon-2am, from 10am wknds*

NIGHTCLUBS
Angles [★MW,D,S,WC] 2117 NW 39th St (at Pennsylvania) 405/524-3431 *9pm-2am, clsd Mon-Wed*

➤ **The Copa** [MW,D,DS,S,WC,$] at Habana Inn 405/525-0730 *9pm-2am, clsd Mon, cover charge Sun*

The Park [M,D,S,V,WC] 2125 NW 39th St (at Barnes/ Pennsylvania) 405/528-4690 *5pm-2am, from 3pm Sun, patio, cruisy*

Wreck Room [★MW,D,S,YC] 2127 NW 39th St (at Pennsylvania) 405/525-7610 *10pm-close Th-Sat, 18+ after 1am*

CAFES
Grateful Bean Cafe & Soda Fountain [E] 1039 Walker (at 10th) 405/236-3503 *11am-5pm, clsd wknds, 'Seattle-style' espresso*

RESTAURANTS
Bricktown Brewery Restaurant [E] 1 N Oklahoma (at Sheridan) 405/232-2739 *11am-10pm, till 2am wknds, clsd Sun, live bands wknds*

Gusher's Bar & Grill [WC] at Habana Inn 405/528-2221 x411 *11am-10:30pm, from 9am wknds, till 3:30am Fri-Sat (after-hours brkfst)*

Terra Luna Grille 7408 N Western (at 73rd) 405/879-0009 *lunch & dinner, clsd Sun-Mon*

OKLAHOMA CITY'S HABANA INN

The Southwest's Largest All Gay Resort

175 Guest Rooms ★ Two Swimming Pools
Poolside Rooms ★ Suites ★ Cable TV

Park Once And Party All Night!
Located In The Habana Inn Complex

THE COPA

OKC's Hottest Dance Club
Newly Redecorated

- Tuesday Amatuer Strip-Off
- Wednesday Kitty's Comedy Capers
- Thursday Open Talent Dong Show
- Friday HOT - HOT Male Dancers
- Saturday HOT - HOT Male Dancers
- Sunday The COPA Show

Open 9pm 2am   Closed Mondays

Finishline

OKC's Only Country Dance Floor
OPEN 7 days a week

COUNTRY MUSIC & DANCING
POOL BAR during season

Darts **Noon - 2am** Pool

GUSHER'S Bar & Grill

Finest Prime Rib in OKC

OPEN
Mon - Fri 11am
Sat & Sun 9am

SERVING UNTIL
Sun - Thurs 10:30pm
Fri & Sat 3:30am

The Ledo Cabaret & Lounge

Open 4pm Daily

- Karaoke Every Thursday & Friday from 9pm — Join the Fun Sing Along!
- OKC'S Only Piano Bar — Best Martini's in Town
- ShowBiz Saturday's 10:00pm — OKC's Top Female Impersonators with host Ginger Lamar

2200 NW 39th Expressway, Oklahoma City, OK 73112
Call for rates and information
(405) 528-2221   Reservations only: 1-800-988-2221
Website: www.habanainn.com

Tulsa • Oklahoma

■ RETAIL SHOPS

23rd St Body Piercing 411 NW 23rd St (at N Hudson) **405/524-6824**

Ziggyz 4005 N Pennsylvania (at I-240) **405/521-9999** *novelty gifts & smokeshop; also 924 SW 59th, 405/632-0810*

■ PUBLICATIONS

Gayly Oklahoman 405/528-0800 *lgbt newspaper*

■ MEN'S SERVICES

➤ **Megaphone Oklahoma City 800/289-1489** *Call for the local # nearest you! Meet Hot Men in your area! FREE to Browse & Respond to voice ads. Use code 3087. Also try MEGAMATES.COM*

■ EROTICA

Christie's Toy Box 3126 N May Ave (at 30th) **405/946-4438** *also 1039 S Meridian, 405/948-3333*

Jungle Red [WC] at Habana Inn **405/524-5733** *novelties, leather, gifts*

Naughty & Nice 3121 SW 29th St (at I-44) **405/686-1110** *24hrs*

Priscilla's 615 E Memorial **405/755-8600**

■ CRUISY AREAS

Penn Square [AYOR]

Trosper Park [AYOR]

Shawnee

■ CRUISY AREAS

Shawnee Reservoir [AYOR]

Tulsa

■ INFO LINES & SERVICES

Gay/ Lesbian AA 2545 S Yale Ave (at Community of Hope) **918/747-6300**

The Tulsa LGBT Community Center [WC] 2114 S Memorial **918/743-4297** *touchtone info, center open 6pm-9pm, 3pm-9pm Sat, many activites*

Voted TULSA'S BEST CLUB

New Age Renegade

Renegade Room...Rainbow Room...Patio Lounge
Video Dance Music

17th & Main...DownTown

Tulsa, OK

Shows, Karaoke, Pool, Video Games, Cabaret & Dancers

Open Daily 2p-2a - **918-585-3405** - Tulsa, Oklahoma

Oklahoma • USA

ACCOMMODATIONS
Holiday Inn Select [GF,SW,WC]
5000 East Skelly Dr (at I-44 & Yale Ave)
918/622-7000, 800/836-9635
full brkfst

BARS
Bamboo Lounge [M,NH,D,S,WC]
7204 E Pine **918/836-8700** *noon-2am, dancers*

Heads or Tails [MW,NH] 7944 E 21st St (at Memorial) **918/660-7878**

► **New Age Renegade/ The Rainbow Room** [★MW,NH,K,C,S] 1649 S Main St (at 17th) **918/585-3405** *2pm-2am, patio*

Play-Mor Lounge [M,NH]
424 S Memorial (at 4th) **918/838-9792** *2pm-2am, cruisy*

The Tool Box [★M,NH,D,S,WC] 1338 E 3rd (at Peoria) **918/584-1308** *noon-2am, cruisy*

The Yellow Brick Road
[MW,NH,D,K,S,WC] 2630 E 15th (at Harvard) **918/293-0304** *2pm-2am, strippers Fri*

NIGHTCLUBS
Silver Star Saloon [M,D,S,WC] 1565 S Sheridan **918/834-4234** *9pm-2am, clsd Sun*

RESTAURANTS
St Michael's Alley 3324 E 31st (in Ranch Acres) **918/745-9998** *lunch & dinner, clsd Sun*

Wild Fork [WC] 1820 Utica Square **918/742-0712** *7am-10pm, clsd Sun*

ENTERTAINMENT & RECREATION
Gilcrease Museum 1400 Gilcrease Museum Rd **918/596-2787** *one of the best collections of Native American & cowboy art in the US*

Philbrook Museum of Art 2727 S Rockford Rd (1 blk E of Peoria, at end of 27th St) **918/749-7941** *clsd Mon, Italian villa built in the '20s oil boom complete w/ kitschy lighted dance flr, now a museum—the gardens are a must in spring & summer*

RETAIL SHOPS
Body Piercing by Nicole 2727 E 15th St (btwn Harvard & Lewis)
918/712-1122 *11am-9pm, noon-6pm Sun*

The Pride Store [WC] 2114 S Memorial (in LGBT Community Center)
918/743-4297 *6pm-9pm, clsd Sun, lgbt cards, gifts, shirts & some books*

PUBLICATIONS
Tulsa Family News **918/583-1248**
monthly lgbt newspaper

MEN'S SERVICES
► **Megaphone Tulsa 800/289-1489**
Call for the local # nearest you! Meet Hot Men in your area! FREE to Browse & Respond to voice ads. Use code 3087. Also try MEGAMATES.COM

EROTICA
Dreamland Video 8807 E Admiral (btwn Memorial & traffic circle)
918/834-1051 *24hrs*

Elite Bookstore 812 S Sheridan Rd (at 11th) **918/838-8503** *24hrs*

Midtown Theatre 319 E 3rd St (at Elgin) **918/584-3112** *24hrs*

Whittier News Stand 1 N Lewis St (at Admiral) **918/592-0767** *24hrs*

Watonga

CRUISY AREAS
Trails [AYOR] W of truck stop

Bend • Oregon

OREGON

Statewide

■PUBLICATIONS
Just Out 503/236-1252 *lgbt newspaper w/ resource directory*

Albany

■CRUISY AREAS
Hyak Park [AYOR] Hwy 20

Ashland

■INFO LINES & SERVICES
The Abdill-Ellis Lambda Community Center 717 Siskiyou Blvd (at Congregational Church) **541/488-6990** *3pm-7pm, noon-4pm Sat, clsd Sun, mtgs, events, library*

Gay/ Lesbian AA 175 N Main St upstairs (at Methodist Church) **541/482-3647** *7pm Mon*

■ACCOMMODATIONS
The Arden Forest Inn [GS,NS,SW,WC,GO] 261 W Hersey St **541/488-1496, 800/460-3912** *full brkfst*

Blue Moon B&B [GF,NS,GO] 312 Helman St (at Hersey) **541/482-9228, 800/460-5453** *full brkfst*

Country Willows Inn [GF,SW,NS,WC,GO] 1313 Clay St **541/488-1590, 800/945-5697** *full brkfst, jacuzzi*

Lithia Springs Inn [GS,NS] 2165 W Jackson Rd **541/482-7128, 800/482-7128** *full brkfst, natural hot-springs-fed whirlpools*

Neil Creek House B&B [GF,SW,NS] 341 Mowetza Dr **541/482-6443, 800/460-7860** *full brkfst*

Romeo Inn B&B [GF,SW,NS] 295 Idaho St **541/488-0884, 800/915-8899** *full brkfst, jacuzzi*

■CAFES
Ashland Bakery/ Cafe [WC] 38 E Main **541/482-2117** *7:30am-8pm*

■RESTAURANTS
The Black Sheep 51 N Main St (on the Plaza) **541/482-6414** *lunch & dinner, full bar till 1am, eclectic pub fare*

Geppetto's [WC] 345 E Main **541/482-1138** *8am-midnight, Italian, full bar*

Greenleaf Restaurant [BW] 49 N Main St (on The Plaza) **541/482-2808** *8am-9pm, Mediterranean/ Italian, creekside dining*

■BOOKSTORES
Bloomsbury Books 290 E Main St (btwn 1st & 2nd) **541/488-0029** *8am-10pm, 9am-9pm Sat, 10am-9pm Sun*

■RETAIL SHOPS
Travel Essentials 264-A E Main St **541/482-7383** *10am-5:30pm, 11am-4pm Sun, luggage, books, accessories*

■CRUISY AREAS
Lithia Park [AYOR]

Astoria

■INFO LINES & SERVICES
North Coast Pride Network Gay/ Lesbian Resource Center 10 6th St #209 **503/338-0161**

■ACCOMMODATIONS
Rosebriar Hotel [GF,WC] 636 14th St **503/325-7427, 800/487-0224** *upscale classic hotel in former convent, full brkfst*

Beaverton

■RESTAURANTS
Swagat Indian Cuisine [BW] 4325 SW 109th Ave **503/626-3000** *lunch & dinner*

Bend

■INFO LINES & SERVICES
Out & About **541/388-2395** *lgbt info*

■CAFES
Royal Blend 1075 NW Newport **541/383-0873** *6:30am-6pm*

■CRUISY AREAS
Drake Park [AYOR] Riverside Dr *clsd winter*

Sawyer Park [AYOR] *evenings*

Damron Men's Travel Guide 2004   **489**

Oregon • USA

Corvallis

■BOOKSTORES
Book Bin 228 SW 3rd (btwn Madison & Jefferson) **541/752-0040** *9am-9pm, till midnight Fri-Sat, noon-5pm Sun*

Grass Roots Bookstore [WC] 227 SW 2nd St (btwn Jefferson & Madison) **541/754-7668** *9am-7pm, till 9pm Fri, till 5:30pm Sat, 11am-5pm Sun, music section, espresso bar*

■CRUISY AREAS
Willamette River [N,AYOR] N of Willamette Park

Eugene

■INFO LINES & SERVICES
Gay/ Lesbian AA 1414 Kincaid (at Koinonia Center) **541/342-4113** *7pm Wed*

LGBTQ Alliance [WC] **541/346-3360** *9am-5pm, various drop-in groups*

■RESTAURANTS
Glenwood Restaurant 1340 Alder St (at 13th St) **541/687-0355** *7am-10pm*

Keystone Cafe 395 W 5th (at Lawrence) **541/342-2075** *7am-3pm, popular brkfst*

■BOOKSTORES
Mother Kali's Books [WC] 720 E 13th Ave (at Hilyard) **541/343-4864** *10am-6pm, clsd Sun, lgbt*

■RETAIL SHOPS
High Priestess Piercing 675 Lincoln St (at 7th St) **541/342-6585** *noon-8pm, 11am-10pm Fri-Sat, piercing studio*

■EROTICA
Exclusively Adult 1166 S 'A' St (at 10th St), Springfield **541/726-6969** *24hrs*

■CRUISY AREAS
Skinner Butte Park [AYOR]

Willamette River Beach [AYOR] *on the coast fork* take 30th Ave, exit E off I-5, turn left at stop sign, right at Texaco station & park past the recycling center, then follow paths to paved road to beach

Grants Pass

■CAFES
Sunshine Natural Foods Cafe 128 SW 'H' (btwn 5th St & 6th St) **541/474-5044** *9am-6pm, till 4pm Sat, 11am-4pm Sun*

■CRUISY AREAS
Riverside Park [AYOR] *near art museum*

Klamath Falls

■CRUISY AREAS
Haglestein Park [AYOR] Hwy 97 (about 10 miles N of town, past Klamath Lake)

Moore Park [AYOR] *summers*

Lincoln City

■RESTAURANTS
Dory Cove Restaurant [BW] 75819 Logan Rd (at 59th St) **541/994-5180** *11:30am-8pm, till 9pm Fri-Sat, noon-8pm Sun, steak & seafood*

Key West 2945 NW Jetty Ave **541/994-3877** *8am-10pm, lounge open later wknds*

McMinnville

■ACCOMMODATIONS
Brightridge Farm B&B [GS] 18575 SW Brightridge Rd, Sheridan **503/843-5230** *full brkfst, in the rural heart of Oregon wine country*

Middle Creek Run [GS,SW,GO] 25400 Harmony Rd, Sheridan **503/843-7606** *full brkfst*

Medford

■ACCOMMODATIONS
The Bybee House B&B [GF,NS] 4491 Jackson Hwy, Central Point **541/773-3026**

Kalles Family Ranch [MW,GO] 233 Jackson Creek Rd, Tiller **541/825-3271** *campsites & RV hookups, btwn Medford & Roseburg*

Portland • Oregon

■NIGHTCLUBS

Ground Zero [GF,D,E] 123 S Front St **541/779-4827** *8pm-2am, from 9pm Sat, clsd Sun-Tue, more gay Th at Alternative Night, comedy Fri*

■RESTAURANTS

Cadillac Cafe 207 W 8th St (at Holly) **541/857-9411** *7am-2pm Mon-Fri*

Mac's Rock & Rod Diner 2382 Jacksonville Hwy **541/608-7625** *6am-10pm, till 11pm wknds*

■EROTICA

Castle Megastore 1113 Progress Dr (at Bittle) **541/608-9540**

■CRUISY AREAS

Jackson County Sports Park [AYOR]

Touvelle Park [AYOR] *along Rogue River*

Newport

■ACCOMMODATIONS

The Beach House B&B [MW,NS,WC,GO] 107 SW Coast St **541/265-9141, 866/215-6486** *full brkfst, jacuzzi*

Cliff House B&B [GF,NS] **541/563-2506** *oceanfront, full brkfst, hot tub*

■RESTAURANTS

Mo's Annex 657 SW Bay Blvd **541/265-7512** *great chowder*

■CRUISY AREAS

Yaquina Bay State Park [AYOR] *off Hwy 101 (at N end of Yaquina Bay Bridge)*

Ontario

■CRUISY AREAS

Ontario State Park [AYOR] *on the Snake River*

Port Orford

■CRUISY AREAS

Battle Rock Wayside Park [AYOR] *S edge of town*

Portland

see also Vancouver, Washington

■INFO LINES & SERVICES

Live & Let Live Club 2940-A SE Belmont St **503/238-6091** *12-step mtgs*

Sexual Minority Youth Recreation Center (SMYRC) 2100 SE Belmont **503/872-9664** *4pm-8pm Mon, 4pm-9pm Wed, 4pm-midnight Fri-Sat, drop-in center for lgbtq youth*

■ACCOMMODATIONS

The Clyde Hotel [GS,NS] 1022 SW Stark St (at 10th) **503/224-8000** *some shared baths*

Fifth Avenue Suites Hotel [GF] 506 SW Washington (at 5th Ave) **503/222-0001, 866/861-9514** *also restaurant, gym*

The Grand Ronde Place [GS,GO] 250 NE Tomahawk Island Dr Slip A-15 (I-5, at N Jantzen Beach exit) **503/901-9802** *B&B on 34-ft yacht, also private charter cruises*

Hotel Vintage Plaza [★GF,WC] 422 SW Broadway **503/228-1212, 800/263-2305** *upscale, also restaurant*

MacMaster House [GF,NS] 1041 SW Vista Ave (at Park Pl) **503/223-7362, 800/774-9523** *historic mansion*

The Mark Spencer Hotel [GF] 409 SW Eleventh Ave (near Stark) **503/224-3293, 800/548-3934**

Sullivan's Gulch B&B [MW,GO] 1744 NE Clackamas St (at 17th) **503/331-1104** *1907 Portland home, decks*

■BARS

Boxxes [★M,D,K,V,WC] 1035 SW Stark (at SW 11th Ave) **503/226-4171** *noon-2:30am, also Brig [MW,D], also Red Cap Garage*

Brazen Bean [GS,F] 2075 NW Glisan St (at 21st Ave) **503/294-0636** *5pm-midnight, till 1am Fri-Sat, swank cigar & martini bar*

Damron Men's Travel Guide 2004

Oregon • USA

Candlelight Bar & Cafe [GF,F,E] 2032 SW 5th (at Lincoln) 503/222-3378 *10am-2:30am, from 11am wknds, live blues, hamburgers*

CC Slaughter's [★M,D,CW,F,K,V] 219 NW Davis (at 3rd) 503/248-9135 *4pm-2:30am, after-hours brkfst Sat, [CW] Wed, Latino night Sun, also martini lounge & restaurant*

Darcelle XV [GS,F,DS,WC] 208 NW 3rd Ave (at NW Davis St) 503/222-5338 *5pm-11pm, 6pm-2am Sat, clsd Sun-Tue*

Eagle PDX [M,L,V] 1300 W Burnside (at 13th Ave) 503/241-0105 *4pm-2:30am*

Fox & Hound [★M,WC] 217 NW 2nd Ave (btwn Everett & Davis) 503/243-5530 *9:30am-2am, from 8:30am wknds, also restaurant, brunch Sun*

Gail's Dirty Duck Tavern [M,NH,B,L,OC,BW,WC] 439 NW 3rd (at Glisan) 503/224-8446 *3pm-midnight, till 1:30am Fri-Sat, from noon wknds, 'home of the bears,' hanky night & leather social 1st & 3rd Fri*

Hobo's [GS,P,WC] 120 NW 3rd Ave (btwn Davis & Couch) 503/224-3285 *4pm-2:30am, piano bar, also restaurant*

JOQ's Tavern [M,NH,F,WC] 2512 NE Broadway (at NE 24th Ave) 503/287-4210 *11am-2:30am*

Scandals Tavern [M,NH,F,WC,GO] 1038 SW Stark St (at SW 11th Ave) 503/227-5887 *noon-2:30am, friendly bar, also Other Side Cafe Bar*

Silverado [★M,D,F,K,S,WC] 1217 SW Stark St (btwn SW 11th & 12th Aves) 503/224-4493 *9am-2:30am, strippers*

Starky's [★MW,NH,F,WC] 2913 SE Stark St (at SE 29th Ave) 503/230-7980 *11am-2am, also restaurant, Sun brunch, patio*

Three Sisters Tavern [M,NH,D,S] 1125 SW Stark St (at 12th) 503/228-0486 *1pm-2:30am, DJ & strippers Tue-Sat*

Tiger Bar [★GF,WC] 317 NW Broadway (btwn Everett & Flanders) 503/222-7297 *5pm-2:30am*

■ NIGHTCLUBS

Embers Avenue [★M,D,F,DS,WC] 110 NW Broadway (at NW Couch St) 503/222-3082 *11:30am-2:30am, also restaurant*

Klub Z [MW,D,F,E,DS,V,YC,WC,$] 333 SW Park (btwn SW Oak & SW Stark) 503/241-1153 *Th-Sun, drag shows Fri-Sat, smoke & alcohol-free*

Panorama [★GF,D,WC] 341 SW 10th Ave (at Stark) 503/221-7262 *9pm-4am Fri-Sat, call for events*

■ CAFES

Bread & Ink Cafe [★BW,WC] 3610 SE Hawthorne Blvd (at 36th) 503/239-4756 *hours vary*

Cup & Saucer Cafe [★NS] 3566 SE Hawthorne Blvd (btwn 34th & 36th) 503/236-6001 *7am-9pm*

Haven Coffee [W,E,WC,GO] 3551 SE Division St 503/236-6890 *7:30am-10pm, till 11pm Sat*

Marco's Cafe & Espresso Bar 7910 SW 35th (at Multnomah Blvd), Multnomah 503/245-0199 *7am-9:30pm, from 8am wknds, till 2pm Sun*

The Pied Cow 3244 SE Belmont (at 33rd Ave) 503/230-4866 *4pm-midnight, till 1am Fri, from noon Sun, funky Victorian, great desserts, patio*

Saucebox [MW,WC] 214 SW Broadway (at Stark) 503/241-3393 *5pm-10pm, clsd Sun-Mon, pan-Asian, full bar, DJ nightly*

Three Friends Coffeehouse 201 SE 12th Ave 503/236-6411 *7am-10pm, till midnight Fri-Sat, from 9am wknds*

Touchstone Coffee House [E,GO] 7631 NE Glisan St 503/262-7613 *6:30am-9pm, till 10pm Th-Fri, 7am-10pm Sat, 8am-6pm Sun, live music Th-Sat*

■ RESTAURANTS

The Adobe Rose [BW] 1634 SE Bybee Blvd (at Milwaukee) 503/235-9114 *11:30am-2pm, also 5pm-9pm Fri-Sat, clsd Sun-Mon, New Mexican cuisine*

Assaggio [BW] 7742 SE 13th (at Lambert) 503/232-6151 *5pm-9:30pm, clsd Sun-Mon, Italian*

Portland • Oregon

Bastas Trattoria 410 NW 21st (at Flanders) 503/274-1572 *lunch Th-Fri & dinner nightly, northern Italian, full bar till 1am*

Bijou Cafe [★] 132 SW 3rd Ave (at Pine St) 503/222-3187 *7am-2pm, from 8am wknds, also 6pm-10pm Tue-Sat*

Blue Hour 250 NW 13th Ave (at NW Everett St) 503/226-3394 *5pm-10pm, till 10:30pm Fri-Sat, bar open till midnight, extensive wine list*

Brasserie Montmartre 626 SW Park (at Alder) 503/224-5552 *lunch & dinner, brunch wknds, bistro menu, live jazz, full bar*

Daydream Cafe [★GO] 1740 SE Hawthorne (at 17th) 503/233-4244 *7am-5pm, clsd Tue*

Delta [WC] 4607 SE Woodstock 503/771-3101 *5pm-10pm, from noon wknds, Southern*

Dingo's Mexican Grill 4612 SE Hawthorne Blvd (at SE 39th) 503/233-3996 *11:30am-10pm, till midnight Th-Sat*

Dot's Cafe [★] 2521 SE Clinton (at 26th) 503/235-0203 *lunch & dinner till 2am, full bar*

Esparza's Tex-Mex Cafe [★] 2725 SE Ankeny St (at 28th) 503/234-7909 *11:30am-10pm, clsd Sun-Mon*

Fish Grotto [★] 1035 SW Stark (at SW 11th Ave, at Boxxes) 503/226-4171 *5pm-close, clsd Mon, full bar*

Hobo's [★GS,E,WC] 120 NW 3rd Ave (btwn Davis & Couch) 503/224-3285 *4pm-2:30am*

Mayas Taqueria 1000 SW Morrison 503/226-1946 *11am-9:30pm*

Montage [★WC] 301 SE Morrison 503/234-1324 *lunch & dinner till 2am, till 4am Fri-Sat, Louisiana-style cookin'*

Nicholas' 318 SE Grand 503/235-5123 *11am-9pm, noon-8pm Sun, Middle Eastern*

Old Wives Tales [BW,WC] 1300 E Burnside St (at 13th) 503/238-0470 *8am-9pm, till 10pm Fri-Sat, multi-ethnic vegetarian*

The Original Pancake House 8600 SW Barbur Blvd 503/246-9007 *7am-3pm, clsd Mon-Tue, great brkfst*

Paradox Palace Cafe [★] 3439 SE Belmont 503/232-7508 *8am-9pm, till 10pm Fri-Sat, vegetarian diner, killer Reuben*

Pizzacato [★BW] 505 NW 23rd (at Glisan) 503/242-0023 *11:30am-10pm, till 11pm Fri-Sat, many locations*

The Roxy [★MW,WC] 1121 SW Stark St 503/223-9160 *24hrs, clsd Mon, American*

Starky's [MW] 2913 SE Stark St 503/230-7980 *11am-2pm & 5:30pm-9:30pm, from 9:30am Sun, full bar till 2:30am*

Vista Spring Cafe [BW] 2440 SW Vista (at Spring) 503/222-2811 *11am-10pm, from noon wknds, till 9pm Sun*

Wildwood [★R] 1221 NW 21st Ave (at Overton) 503/248-9663 *lunch & dinner, full bar*

■ ENTERTAINMENT & RECREATION

Sauvie's Island Beach 25 miles NW (off US 30) *follow Reeder Rd to the Collins beach area, park at the farthest end of the road, then follow path to beach*

■ BOOKSTORES

Countermedia 927 SW Oak (btwn 9th & 10th) 503/226-8141 *11am-7pm, noon-6pm Sun, alternative comics, vintage gay books/ periodicals*

Gai-Pied 2544 NE Broadway (at 26th) 503/331-1125 *11am-8pm, till 9pm Fri-Sat, till 7pm Sun, gay bookstore*

Laughing Horse Bookstore [WC] 3652 SE Division (at 37th) 503/236-2893 *11am-7pm, clsd Sun, alternative/ progressive*

Looking Glass Bookstore 318 SW Taylor (btwn 3rd & 4th) 503/227-4760 *9am-6pm, from 10am Sat, clsd Sun, general, some lgbt titles*

Powell's Books [★WC] 1005 W Burnside St (at 10th) 503/228-4651, 800/878-7323 *9am-11pm, huge new & used bookstore, cafe*

Oregon • USA

Reading Frenzy [WC] 921 SW Oak St (at 9th) 503/274-1449 *11am-7pm, noon-6pm wknds, zines, comics*

Twenty-Third Ave Books [WC] 1015 NW 23rd Ave (at Lovejoy) 503/224-5097 *9:30am-9pm, from 10am Sat, 11am-7pm Sun, lgbt section*

■ RETAIL SHOPS

The Jellybean [WC] 721 SW 10th Ave (at Morrison) 503/222-5888 *10am-6pm, noon-5pm Sun, T-shirts & gifts*

Presents of Mind [WC] 3633 SE Hawthorne (at 37th Ave) 503/230-7740 *10am-7pm, jewelry & unique gifts*

■ PUBLICATIONS

Just Out 503/236-1252 *lgbt newspaper w/ resource directory*

■ GYMS & HEALTH CLUBS

Inner City Hot Tubs [GF,R] 2927 NE Everett St (btwn 29th & 30th) 503/238-1065 *wellness center*

Nelson Nautilus Plus [GF] 614 SW 11th Ave (at Alder) 503/222-2639 *$10 day pass*

■ MEN'S CLUBS

Club Portland [★18+,PC] 303 SW 12th Ave 503/227-9992 *24hrs*

Xes [MO,18+,PC] 415 SW 13th St (behind the Eagle PDX) 503/226-6969 *5pm-4am Tue-Sun*

■ MEN'S SERVICES

➤ **Megaphone Portland** 800/289-1489 *Call for the local # nearest you! Meet Hot Men in your area! FREE to Browse & Respond to voice ads. Use code 3087. Also try MEGAMATES.COM*

■ EROTICA

Fantasy for Adults 3137 NE Sandy Blvd (near NE 39th) 503/239-6969

Hard Times Video 311 NW Broadway (at Everett) 503/223-2398

Spartacus Leathers 302 SW 12th Ave (at Burnside) 503/224-2604

Tim's Hideaway 4229 SE 82nd Ave, #3 (at Holgate) 503/771-9774

Tim's Hideaway Downtown 330 SW 3rd Ave (btwn Stark & Oak) 503/224-2338

■ CRUISY AREAS

Kelly Point [AYOR] on Marine Dr *follow trail to left of parking lot*

West Delta Park [AYOR] W Delta Park Rd (btwn Portland Int'l Raceway & Expo Center)

Roseburg

■ INFO LINES & SERVICES

Gay/ Lesbian Switchboard 541/672-4126 *24hrs, also newsletter*

■ CRUISY AREAS

Stewart Park [AYOR] *river trails & under bridge*

Salem

■ NIGHTCLUBS

300 Club [GS,D,F,E,C,DS,YC,WC] 300 Liberty St SE (at Trade St) 503/365-9721 *5pm-2am, men's night Wed, also Right Side Showbar, [C] Fri*

■ RESTAURANTS

Off Center Cafe [★WC] 1741 Center St NE (at 17th) 503/363-9245 *brkfst & lunch daily, dinner Th-Sat*

■ BOOKSTORES

Rosebud & Fish 524 State St (at High) 503/399-9960 *10am-7pm, noon-5pm Sun, alternative bookstore*

■ EROTICA

Bob's Adult Bookstore 3815 State St (at Lancaster) 503/363-3846

■ CRUISY AREAS

Bush Park [AYOR] 12th & State Sts *days only*

Seaside

■ CRUISY AREAS

Cannon Beach [AYOR] 10 miles S *summers only*

Seaside Beach [AYOR] *area under turn-around summers*

Sunriver

■ ACCOMMODATIONS

DiamondStone Guest Lodge & Gallery [GF,NS] 16693 Sprague Loop, La Pine 541/536-6263, 800/600-6263 *Western hotel-style B&B, full brkfst*

Bethlehem • Pennsylvania

Warrenton

■CRUISY AREAS
Carruthers Park [AYOR] Warrenton Dr

Yachats

■ACCOMMODATIONS
Ocean Odyssey [GF,NS]
541/547-3637, 800/800-1915 *vacation rental homes in Yachats & Waldport, on the coast*

The Oregon House [GF,NS,WC] 94288 Hwy 101 **541/547-3329** *ocean views*

See Vue Motel [GS,NS,WC,GO] 95590 Hwy 101 **541/547-3227** *oceanview*

Shamrock Lodgettes [GF,WC,GO] 105 Hwy 101 S (at Yachats Ocean Rd) **541/547-3312, 800/845-5028** *5-acre resort, hot tub*

PENNSYLVANIA

Adamstown

■ACCOMMODATIONS
The Barnyard Inn [GS,NS]
2145 Old Lancaster Pike, Reinholds **717/484-1111, 888/738-6624** *150-yr-old restored German school house, full brkfst, petting zoo*

Allentown

see also Bethlehem

■BARS
Candida's [MW,NH,F,K] 247 N 12th St (at Chew) **610/434-3071** *2pm-2am*

Moose Lounge/ Stonewall [★MW,D,F,E,K,S,V] 28-30 N 10th St (at Hamilton) **610/432-0706** *7pm-2am, clsd Mon*

■EROTICA
Adult World 80 S West End Blvd/ Rte 309, Quakerstown **215/538-1522** *24hrs*

Leather Masters 1023 Hamilton St **610/434-3626** *clsd Mon*

■CRUISY AREAS
The Block [AYOR] 13th & 14th Aves

Lehigh Park [AYOR] near Keck's Bridge

Upper Macungie Park [AYOR] Rte 100 (1 mile N of the I-78 exit)

Upper Terrace Park [AYOR] Union & St Elmo's Sts

Altoona

■NIGHTCLUBS
Escapade [MW,D,GO] 2523 Union Ave, Rte 36 **814/946-8195** *8pm-2am, clsd Sun*

Rumors [MW,D,F,GO] 1413 11th Ave (enter rear) **814/941-0803** *9pm-2am, clsd Sun-Tue, patio*

■RESTAURANTS
Michael's Cafe [GO] 1413 11th Ave **814/941-0803** *11am-9pm, from 2pm Mon, clsd Sun, upscale, full bar*

■EROTICA
Adult World Old Rte 220 (Bellwood exit, off I-99) **814/742-7781**

Beaver Falls

■EROTICA
Video Hobby Land 7211 Big Beaver Blvd (on Rte 18) **724/847-3777**

Berwick

■CRUISY AREAS
Wetlands Pennsylvania Power & Light Park [AYOR] Rte 11

Bethlehem

■NIGHTCLUBS
Diamonz [W,D,F,E,WC] 1913 W Broad St (at Pennsylvania Ave) **610/865-1028** *4pm-2am, from 3pm wknds, also restaurant (clsd Tue)*

■EROTICA
Cupid's Treasure's 1162 Pembroke Rd **610/865-5855**

Cupids 1861 Stefko Blvd (btwn Irene St & Gresham St) **610/868-6616**

Pennsylvania • *USA*

Bridgeport

■NIGHTCLUBS

The Lark [MW,D,K,DS] 302 Dekalb St/ Rte 202 N **610/275-8136** *8pm-2am*

Bristol

■EROTICA

Bristol News World 576 Bristol Pike/ Rte 13 N **215/785-4770**

■CRUISY AREAS

Silver Lake Park [AYOR]

Butler

■CRUISY AREAS

Moraine State Park [AYOR] Bear Run area (south shore)

Cornwells Heights

■CRUISY AREAS

Neshaminy Park [AYOR]

East Stroudsburg

■ACCOMMODATIONS

Curt & Wally's Guest House [M,SW,N,GO] Primrose Dr, Marshalls Creek **570/223-1395**

Rainbow Mountain Resort [★MW,D,TG,E,K,SW,GO] **570/223-8484** *atop Pocono mtn on 26 acres, also restaurant & bar, DJ Fri-Sat*

■BARS

Secrets [M,D,F,SW,GO] Business Rte 209 **570/420-8716** *8pm-2am, from 9pm wknds, clsd Mon-Tue, game room, theme nights, also motel*

Edgemont

■CRUISY AREAS

Ridley Creek State Park [AYOR] Rte 3, W Chester Pike

Edinboro

■CRUISY AREAS

Lakeside Commons [AYOR] Rte 6 N (behind the mall overlooking the lake), Waterford *days*

Erie

■ACCOMMODATIONS

The Boothby Inn [GF] 311 W 6th St **814/456-1888, 866/266-8429**

The Castle Guest House [MW,NS,GO] 231 W 21st St **814/461-8770**

■NIGHTCLUBS

The Village Supper Club [MW,D,DS,S,WC] 133 W 18th St (at Peach) **814/452-0125** *9pm-2am*

The Zone [MW,D,F] 1711 State St (at 17th) **814/459-1711** *4pm-2am, from 8pm Sat, clsd Sun*

■CAFES

Aroma's Coffeehouse 2164 W 8th St **814/456-5282** *7am-11pm, 9am-1am Sat, till 4pm Sun, light fare*

■RESTAURANTS

Matthew's Trattoria 153 E 13th St (at Lovell Place) **814/459-6458** *dinner, clsd Sun-Mon, martini lounge, live music*

Papermoon [E,P,R] 1325 State St (at 14th) **814/455-7766** *4:30pm-9pm, till 10pm Th-Sat, brunch Sun, seafood/ int'l, live jazz*

Pie in the Sky Cafe [BYOB,R,WC] 463 W 8th St (at Walnut) **814/459-8638** *7:30am-2pm, dinner from 5:30pm Fri-Sat, clsd Sun*

■PUBLICATIONS

Erie Gay News 814/456-9833 *covers news & events in the Erie, Cleveland, Pittsburgh, Buffalo & Chautauqua County (NY) region*

Gay People's Chronicle 216/631-8646, 800/426-5947 *Ohio's largest weekly lgbt newspaper w/ extensive listings*

■EROTICA

Eastern Adult Books 1313 State St (btwn 13th & 14th) **814/459-7014** *24hrs*

Modern News 1113 State St (at 12th) **814/453-6932**

■CRUISY AREAS

Erie Zoo [AYOR] *park on the hill (overlooking the zoo)*

Presque Isle Park Beach [AYOR] *non-guarded area (E of Beach 2)*

Lancaster • Pennsylvania

Gettysburg

■ ACCOMMODATIONS

Battlefield B&B Inn [GF,GO]
2264 Emmitsburg Rd (at Ridge Rd)
717/334-8804, 888/766-3897
Civil War home, full brkfst

Maplecrest Farm [GS,SW,GO] 749 Dicks Dam Rd, New Oxford **717/624-3339**

Sheppard Mansion B&B [GS,NS]
117 Frederick St (at High St), Hanover
717/633-8075, 877/762-6746
B&B, full brkfst

Greensburg

■ NIGHTCLUBS

RK's Lounge [★M,D,DS,S,WC]
108 W Pittsburgh St (at Pennsylvania Ave) **724/837-6614** *9pm-2am, clsd Sun, strippers, patio*

■ CRUISY AREAS

Harrison Ave [AYOR] off Otterman St

Harrisburg

■ INFO LINES & SERVICES

Gay/ Lesbian Switchboard
717/234-0328 *6:30pm-9pm Mon-Fri (volunteers permitting)*

■ BARS

704 Strawberry [★M,V,OC,WC] 704 N 3rd St **717/234-4228** *2pm-2am*

The Brownstone Lounge [MW,F,WC]
412 Forster St (btwn 3rd & 6th)
717/234-7009 *11am-2am, 1pm-2am wknds*

Neptune's Lounge [★MW,NH,D,YC] 268 North St (at 3rd) **717/233-0581** *4pm-2am*

The Pink Lizard [MW,D,TG,F,E,DS,V]
891 Eisenhower Blvd (near exit 19)
717/939-1123 *7pm-2am, clsd Sun-Tue*

■ NIGHTCLUBS

Stallions [★M,D,E,K,YC,WC] 706 N 3rd St (enter rear) **717/232-3060** *7pm-2am, clsd Sun, also Shimmer 10pm-2am Fri-Sat [M,D,V,18+,YC]*

■ EROTICA

Rural Book & News 315 Market St (at 3rd) **717/255-9121**

■ CRUISY AREAS

Riverfront Park [AYOR] Front & State Sts

Johnstown

■ NIGHTCLUBS

Lucille's [MW,D,DS,S] 520 Washington St (near Central Park) **814/539-4448**
6pm-2am, clsd Sun, strippers

■ CRUISY AREAS

Babcock Park [AYOR]

Kutztown

■ ACCOMMODATIONS

Grim's Manor B&B [MW,NS,GO]
10 Kern Rd **610/683-7089** *stone farmhouse on 5 acres, full brkfst*

Lancaster

■ ACCOMMODATIONS

Cameron Estate Inn [GS,NS,WC,GO]
1855 Mansion Ln (at Donegal Springs Rd), Mount Joy **717/492-0111** *B&B inn, full brkfst, located on 15 acres of lawn & woods, jacuzzi, restaurant*

Candlelight Inn B&B [GF]
2574 Lincoln Hwy E (at Rte 896/ Hartman Bridge Rd) **717/299-6005, 800/772-2635** *full brkfst, jacuzzi*

Casual Corners B&B [GF] 301 N Broad St (at Market St), Lititz **717/626-5299, 800/464-6764**

The Noble House B&B [GS,NS] 113 W Market St, Marietta **717/426-4389, 888/271-6426** *full brkfst*

■ BARS

Tally Ho [★MW,D,YC] 201 W Orange (at Water) **717/299-0661** *8pm-2am*

■ RESTAURANTS

The Loft above Tally Ho bar
717/299-0661 *lunch & dinner, clsd Sun, contemporary American / French*

■ BOOKSTORES

Borders Bookshop 940 Plaza Blvd (at Harrisburg Pike) **717/293-8022** *9am-11pm, till 9pm Sun, lgbt section*

Pennsylvania • USA

■ RETAIL SHOPS
The Green Room 246 W King St
717/394-8311, 866/394-7336 *3pm-8pm, till 9pm Fri, 9am-6pm Sat, clsd Sun-Mon, pride items, books, DVDs*

■ CRUISY AREAS
Lancaster County Park [AYOR]
Long's Park [AYOR] Rte 30 at Harrisburg Pike

Lebanon

■ EROTICA
Hobeze Lebanon Adult Gifts 1604 E Cumberland St (at 15th Ave)
717/273-6398

■ CRUISY AREAS
Coleman's Park [AYOR]
Union Canal Tunnel Park [AYOR]

Meadville

■ EROTICA
Central News 1206 Park Ave
814/724-4690 *large selection of lgbt & adult publications*

Monroeville

■ EROTICA
Monroeville News 2735 Stroschein Rd (off Rte 22) **412/372-5477** *24hrs*

Montgomeryville

■ EROTICA
Adult World Book Store Rtes 202 & 309 **215/362-9560** *24hrs*

Mt Pleasant

■ BARS
Yuppie's [MW,NH,F] 241 E Main St
724/547-0430 *9pm-2am, from 8pm Fri-Sat, till 1am Sun*

New Castle

■ CRUISY AREAS
McConnell's Mill State Park [AYOR]
summers

New Hope

see also Lambertville & Sergeantsville, New Jersey

■ ACCOMMODATIONS
Ash Mill Farm B&B [GF] 5358 York Rd (at Rte 202), Holicong **215/794-5373**

Best Western New Hope Inn
[GF,SW,WC] 6426 Lower York Rd/ Rte 202
215/862-5221, 800/467-3202 *also restaurant & lounge*

Cordials B&B of New Hope
[MW,WC,GO] 143 Old York Rd (at Sugan Rd) **215/862-3919, 877/219-1009**
hot tub

Fox & Hound B&B [GF,NS]
246 West Bridge St **215/862-5082, 800/862-5082** *1850s stone manor, full brkfst wknds*

The Lexington House [GS,SW,NS,GO]
6171 Upper York Rd **215/794-0811**
1749 country home, full brkfst

The Mansion Inn [MW,SW,NS,GO]
9 S Main (at Bridge St) **215/862-1231**
B&B inn, full brkfst, jacuzzi

The New Hope Motel [GS,SW] 400 W Bridge St/ Rte 179 **215/862-2800**
lounge

Silver Maple Organic Farm & B&B
[GS,SW,NS,WC,GO] 483 Sergeantsville Rd (Rte 523), Sergeantsville, NJ
908/237-2192 *200-yr-old farmhouse, full brkfst, hot tub*

The Victorian Peacock B&B
[GS,SW,NS,GO] 309 E Dark Hollow Rd, Pipersville **215/766-1356** *spa*

The Wishing Well Guesthouse
[GS,NS,WC,GO] 144 Old York Rd
215/862-8819 *B&B in restored farmhouse*

York Street House B&B [GF]
42 York St, Lambertville, NJ
609/397-3007, 888/398-3199
1909 Manor house

■ BARS
➤ **The Raven Bar & Restaurant**
[M,GO] 385 West Bridge St
215/862-2081 *11am-2am, also motel* [SW]

New Hope • Pennsylvania

■ NIGHTCLUBS

The Cartwheel [★MW,D,F,DS,P,S,WC]
437 Old York Rd/ US 202
215/862-0880 *5pm-2am, also piano bar, full restaurant*

■ RESTAURANTS

Havana [E,K] 105 S Main St
215/862-9897 *noon-midnight, from 11am wknds, bar till 2am, karaoke Mon*

Karla's 5 W Mechanic St (at Main)
215/862-2612 *lunch, dinner & late-night brkfst Fri-Sat, Mediterranean, full bar*

Mother's 34 N Main St 215/862-5270
11am-9pm, clsd Mon

Nouveau Country Diner [WC]
463 Old York Rd/ Rte 202
215/862-5575 *7am-10pm*

Odette's [C,P,WC] South River Rd
215/862-3000 *11am-10pm, Sun brunch, cont'l, piano bar till 1am*

➤ **The Raven** [★GS,SW,GO] 385 West Bridge St 215/862-2081 *noon-3pm & 6pm-10pm, cont'l*

Wildflowers 8 W Mechanic St
215/862-2241 *seasonal, noon-9:30pm, full bar*

■ RETAIL SHOPS

Bucks County Video & CD Exchange
[GO] 415-C York Rd 215/862-0919
10am-10pm

■ PUBLICATIONS

➤ **EXP Gayzette** 302/227-5787, 877/397-6244 *bi-weekly gay magazine for Mid-Atlantic*

Visions Today 302/656-5876, 800/241-5803 *quarterly, covers Rehoboth, Philadelphia, New Hope, Wilmington & surrounding area*

■ EROTICA

Grownups [GO] 4 E Mechanic St (at Main) 215/862-9304

Le Chateau Exotique 27 W Mechanic St 215/862-3810 *fetishwear*

Raven Hall
385 West Bridge St., New Hope, PA 18938

Lodging • Restaurant • Pub
215 862-2081

Pennsylvania • USA

New Kensington

■ BARS

Zebra Lounge [MW,D] 910 Constitution Blvd (at 9th) **724/339-0298** *4pm-2am, clsd Sun*

New Milford

■ ACCOMMODATIONS

Oneida Camp & Lodge [M,SW,N,GO] **570/465-7011** *April-Oct, oldest gay-owned campground dedicated to our community, also 1 guest cottage*

Philadelphia

■ INFO LINES & SERVICES

AA Gay/ Lesbian 215/923-7900

William Way LGBT Community Center 1315 Spruce St (at Juniper) **215/732-2220** *noon-10pm, till 7pm Sat, till 8pm Sun*

■ ACCOMMODATIONS

➤ **Alexander Inn** [GS,GO] Spruce (at 12th) **215/923-3535, 877/253-9466**

Antique Row B&B [GF] 341 S 12th St (at Pine) **215/592-7802** *1820s town house, full brkfst*

Doubletree Hotel [GF] 237 S Broad St (at Locust) **215/893-1600, 800/222-8733**

Embassy Suites Center City [GF] 1776 Ben Franklin Pkwy (at 18th) **215/561-1776, 800/362-2779**

Gaskill House B&B [GS,NS,GO] 312 Gaskill St (btwn Lombard & South St) **215/413-0669** *full brkfst, on Society Hill*

Danny's
CELEBRATING 24 YEARS

Philly's #1
Adult Leather & DVD Shop

- *DVD*
- *Video*
- *Leather*
- *Novelties*
- *Mags (Sold, Traded)*
- *Private Viewing Booths*

MC • VISA • DISCOVER • AMX
-MAC-

Open 365 Days

133 South 13th Street
(Between Walnut & Sansom)

215-925-5041
Philadelphia, PA 19107

Philadelphia • Pennsylvania

Glen Isle Farm [GS,F,NS,GO]
30 miles out of town, in Downingtown
610/269-9100, 800/269-1730
full brkfst

Latham Hotel [GF] 135 S 17th St (at Walnut) **215/563-7474, 800/528-4261**

Philadelphia Marriott [GF,SW,WC] 1201 Market St (btwn 12th & 13th) **215/625-2900, 800/228-9290** *near the gay area in Philly*

Rittenhouse Hotel [GF,F] 210 W Rittenhouse Square (at 19th) **215/546-9000, 800/635-1042**

Rodeway Inn [MW] 1208 Walnut St (btwn 12th & 13th) **215/546-7000, 800/887-1776**

Uncles Upstairs Inn [M,GO] 1220 Locust St (at 12th) **215/546-6660** *downtown town house*

■ BARS

12th Air Command Headquarters for Men [M,D,A,F,K] 254 S 12th St (btwn Locust & Spruce) **215/545-8088** *4pm-2am, from 2pm Sun*

Bump [MW,F,DS] 1234 Locust St (at 13th) **215/732-1800** *5pm-2am, clsd Mon, also restaurant, Sun brunch*

Key West [MW,NH,D,F,P,WC] 207-209 S Juniper (btwn Walnut & Locust) **215/545-1578** *noon-2am, from 2pm Sun, 4 bars, lunch served, also sports bar*

The Khyber [GF,E] 56 S 2nd St (btwn Market & Chestnut) **215/238-5888** *noon-2am, live bands*

The Post [M,NH,F,S,WC] 1705 Chancellor St (at 17th) **215/985-9720** *noon-2am, lunch daily, dancers Th-Sat*

Tavern on Camac [MW,D,C,P] 243 S Camac St (at Spruce) **215/545-0900** *noon-2am, DJ wknds, also restaurant*

Tyz [M,D] 1418 Rodman St (near 15th & Richmond) **215/546-4195** *11pm-3am*

Uncle's [M,NH] 1220 Locust St (at 12th) **215/546-6660** *11am-2am*

Venture Inn [MW,NH,F] 255 S Camac (at Spruce) **215/545-8731** *11am-2am*

The Westbury [M,NH,F,WC] 261 S 13th (at Spruce) **215/546-5170** *10am-2am, dinner till 10pm, till 11pm wknds*

➤ **Woody's** [★M,D,CW,F,K,S,V,YC,WC] 202·S 13th St (at Walnut) **215/545-1893** *11am-2am, 18+ Wed, Latin Th*

■ NIGHTCLUBS

2-4 Club [M,D,PC,$] 1221 St James St (off 13th & Locust) **215/735-5772** *1am-3am Mon-Wed, from midnight Th & Sun, from 10pm Fri-Sat*

Bike Stop [★M,D,L] 204-206 S Quince St (btwn 11th & 12th, Walnut & Locust) **215/627-1662** *4pm-2am, from 2pm wknds, cruisy, 4 flrs, also The Gear Box custom leather shop*

Fluid [GF,D,S,$] 613 S 4th St (at South) **215/629-3686** *10pm-2am, more gay wknds, theme nights*

G-Room [MW,D,MR,TG,E,C,YC,GO] **215/977-9009** *10pm-2am 2nd Sat, local artists, performers & talent, call for location*

Lounge 125 [GS,D,S] 125 S 2nd St (at Chestnut) **215/351-9026** *8pm-close Fri-Sat*

Palmer Social Club [GF,D,PC] 601 Spring Garden St (at 6th) **215/925-5000** *11pm-3am Fri-Sun only, 3 flrs*

Shampoo [GF,D,A] 417 N 8th St (at Willow) **215/922-7500** *9pm-2am, clsd Mon-Tue & Th, more gay Fri*

Sisters [W,D,E,K,WC] 1320 Chancellor St (at Juniper) **215/735-0735** *5pm-2am, also restaurant, dinner Wed-Sat, Sun brunch*

■ CAFES

10th Street Pour House 262 S 10th St (at Spruce) **215/922-5626** *7:30am-3pm, from 8:30am wknds*

The Arts Café [GS] 1431 Spruce St (across from The Kimmel Center) **215/732-5585** *8am-8pm, till 9pm Mon, till midnight Fri-Sat, 10am-6pm Sun, upscale*

Millennium Coffee 212 S 12th St (btwn Locust & Walnut) **215/731-9798** *open till midnight*

Stellar Coffee 1101 Spruce St (at 11th) **215/625-7923** *6:30am-9pm*

Pennsylvania • USA

■RESTAURANTS

The Adobe Cafe [E] 4550 Mitchell St (at Greenleaf), Roxborough **215/483-3947** *lunch & dinner, till 11pm Fri-Sat, plenty veggie*

Astral Plane 1708 Lombard St (btwn 17th & 18th) **215/546-6230** *lunch & dinner, full bar*

Circa [E,WC] 1518 Walnut St (btwn 15th & 16th) **215/545-6800** *lunch Tue-Fri, dinner nightly*

The Continental 138 Market St (at 2nd) **215/923-6069** *lunch & dinner, wknd brunch, also bar*

Cresheim Cottage Cafe [TG,NS,WC] 7402 Germantown Ave (at Gowen Ave) **215/248-4365** *lunch & dinner, Sun brunch, eclectic menu, full bar*

The Happy Rooster [GF,K] 118 S 16th St (at Sansom St) **215/963-9311** *lunch & dinner, clsd Sun, cont'l, upscale, karaoke Th, full bar*

Harmony Vegetarian 135 N 9th St (at Cherry) **215/627-4520** *11am-10pm, till midnight Fri-Sat*

The Inn Philadelphia 251 S Camac St (btwn Locust & Spruce) **215/732-2339** *5pm-10pm, Sun brunch, clsd Mon, cont'l, full bar*

Judy's Cafe 627 S 3rd St (at Bainbridge) **215/928-1968** *5:30pm-11pm, Sun brunch from 10:30am, full bar*

L2 [E] 2201 South St (at 22nd) **215/732-7878** *dinner nightly, also bar*

Lansdowne Station Café [GO] 36 E Baltimore Pike, Lansdowne **610/259-8240** *8am-7pm Tue-Fri, till 2pm wknds, clsd Mon, homestyle*

Latimer's Deli 255 S 15th St (at Latimer) **215/545-9244** *9am-9pm, till 11pm Fri, Jewish deli*

Liberties [E] 705 N 2nd St (at Fairmount) **215/238-0660** *lunch & dinner, full bar*

My Thai 2200 South St (at 22nd) **215/985-1878** *5pm-10pm, till 11pm Fri-Sat, full bar*

Palladium/ Gold Standard [WC] 3601 Locust Walk (at 36th) **215/387-3463** *lunch & dinner, bar till 12:30am*

PREMIER ESCORTS

SERVING PA, NJ, DE & MD
SINCE 1987

www.PremierEscorts.com

888.765.6665

Philadelphia • Pennsylvania

Roosevelt's Pub 2222 Walnut (at 23rd) **215/636-9722** *lunch & dinner, full bar*

Sisters [W] 1320 Chancellor St (at Juniper) **215/735-0735** *dinner 5pm-10pm Wed-Sat, Sun brunch*

Striped Bass 1500 Walnut St (at 15th) **215/732-4444** *lunch, dinner & Sun brunch, upscale*

Swanky Bubbles 10 S Front St (at Market) **215/928-1200** *dinner nightly, also bar*

Trust [C,DS] 121-127 S 13th St (at Sansom) **215/629-1300** *lunch & dinner, Sun brunch, more gay Tue for cabaret*

Valanni 1229 Spruce St **215/790-9494** *dinner nightly, Sun brunch, Mediterranean/ Latin, full bar*

White Dog Cafe 3420 Sansom St (at Walnut) **215/386-9224** *lunch & dinner, brunch wknds, full bar, eleectic American*

■ ENTERTAINMENT & RECREATION

Q Zine WXPN-FM 88.5 **215/898-6677** *10pm Sun, lgbt radio*

The Walt Whitman House 328 Mickle Blvd (btwn S 3rd & S 4th Sts), Camden, NJ **856/964-5383** *the last home of America's great & controversial poet, just across the Delaware River*

■ BOOKSTORES

Afterwords 218 S 12th St (btwn Locust & Walnut) **215/735-2393** *11am-10pm*

Giovanni's Room [★] 345 S 12th St (at Pine) **215/923-2960** *open daily, legendary lgbt bookstore*

■ RETAIL SHOPS

Infinite Body Piercing 626 S 4th St (at South) **215/923-7335**

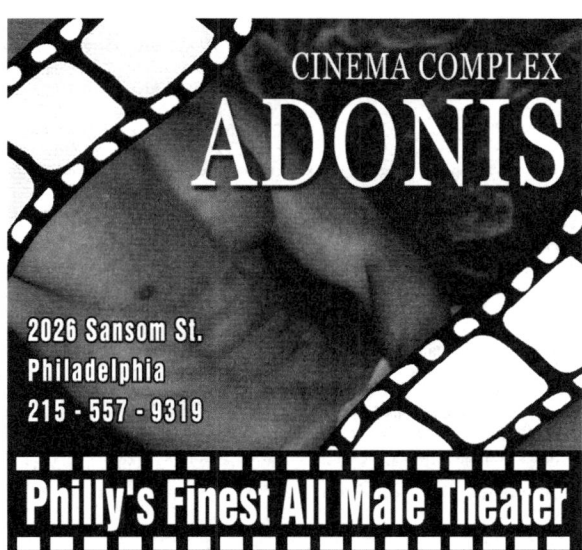

Pennsylvania • USA

PUBLICATIONS

➤ **EXP Gayzette** 302/227-5787, 877/397-6244 *bi-weekly gay magazine for Mid-Atlantic*

PGN (Philadelphia Gay News) 215/625-8501 *lgbt newspaper w/ extensive listings*

Visions Today 302/656-1809, 800/944-0100 *quarterly, covers Rehoboth, Philadelphia, New Hope, Wilmington & surrounding area*

GYMS & HEALTH CLUBS

12th St Gym [GF] 204 S 12th St (btwn Locust & Walnut) 215/985-4092 *5:30am-11pm, day passes*

MEN'S CLUBS

Club Body Center [PC] 1220 Chancellor St (at 12th) 215/735-7671 *24hrs*

LR Fitness 105 S 18th St (at Sansom) 215/564-0225 *24hrs*

Philly Jacks [MO,18+,PC] 1318 Walnut St (near 13th) 215/618-1519 *3 sex parties per month*

MEN'S SERVICES

➤ **Megaphone Philadelphia** 800/289-1489 *Call for the local # nearest you! Meet Hot Men in your area! FREE to Browse & Respond to voice ads. Use code 3087. Also try MEGAMATES.COM*

➤ **Premier Escort Service** 215/733-9779, 888/765-6665

EROTICA

➤ **Adonis Cinema Complex** 2026 Sansom St (at 20th) 215/557-9319 *24hrs*

Condom Kingdom 437 South St (at 5th) 215/829-1668 *safer sex materials & toys*

➤ **Danny's New Adam & Eve Books** 133 S 13th St (at Walnut) 215/925-5041 *24hrs*

Fantasy Island Adult Books 7363 State Rd 215/332-5454

Fetishes Boutique 704 S 5th St (at Bainbridge) 215/829-4986, 877/2-CORSET

The Pleasure Chest 2039 Walnut (btwn 20th & 21st) 215/561-7480 *clsd Sun-Mon*

Spruce Street Video [M,GO] 1201 Spruce St 215/985-2955

Phoenixville

NIGHTCLUBS

Frank Jeffrey's [MW,F] 233 Bridge St (at Hotel Washington) 610/935-8000 *7pm-2am, from 5pm Sun, clsd Mon-Th*

Pine Grove

CRUISY AREAS

Public Park [AYOR] hiking area off I-81 E (exit 34)

Swatara Falls [AYOR]

Pittsburgh

INFO LINES & SERVICES

AA Gay/ Lesbian 412/471-7472

Gay/ Lesbian Community Center 5808 Forward Ave (at Murray, 2nd flr) 412/422-0114 *6:30pm-9:30pm, 3pm-6pm Sat, clsd Sun*

ACCOMMODATIONS

Arbors B&B [MO,NS,GO] 745 Maginn St 412/231-4643 *in restored farmhouse, hot tub*

Camp Davis [MW] 311 Red Brush Rd, Boyers 724/637-2402 *1 hour from Pittsburgh, cabin & campsites, variety of events*

The Inn on the Mexican War Streets [MW,F,GO] 604 W North Ave 412/231-6544 *on gay-friendly North Side, also restaurant*

The Priory [GF] 614 Pressley (near Cedar Ave) 412/231-3338 *Victorian, fitness center*

BARS

Brewery Tavern [GF] 3315 Liberty Ave (at Herron Ave) 412/681-7991 *10am-2am, from noon Sun*

Holiday Bar [★M,NH,S] 4620 Forbes Ave (at Craig) 412/682-8598 *4pm-2am, from 2pm wknds, patio*

Pittsburgh • Pennsylvania

Images [M,K,S,V] 965 Liberty Ave (at 10th St) **412/391-9990** *2pm-2am, from 5pm Sat, from 6pm Sun, karaoke Mon & Th, go-go boys*

Leather Central [★M,L,F,V] 1226 Herron Ave (at Liberty, in Donny's basement) **412/682-9869** *9pm-2am Fri-Sat, 5pm-midnight Sun*

Liberty Avenue Saloon [MW,NH,S] 941 Liberty Ave (at Smithfield) **412/338-1533** *11am-2am, from 5pm Sat, from 1pm Sun, also restaurant*

New York, New York [★MW,P] 5801 Ellsworth Ave (at Maryland) **412/661-5600** *4pm-2am, from 2pm Sun, also restaurant, piano sing-along Sat*

Pittsburgh Eagle [★M,D,L,WC] 1740 Eckert St (near Beaver) **412/766-7222** *9pm-2am, clsd Sun-Tue*

Real Luck Cafe [MW,NH,F,WC] 1519 Penn Ave (at 16th) **412/566-8988** *4pm-2am*

Sidekicks [MW,F,P] 931 Liberty Ave (at Smithfield) **412/642-4435** *5pm-midnight, clsd Sun, also restaurant*

■ NIGHTCLUBS

CJ Deighan's [W,D,F,E,S,WC] 2506 W Liberty Ave, Brookline **412/561-4044** *8pm-2am, clsd Sun-Mon, men welcome*

Donny's Place [★MW,D,L,F,E] 1226 Herron Ave (at Liberty) **412/682-9869** *4pm-2am, from 3pm Sun, leather bar downstairs*

House of Tilden [MW,D,PC] 941 Liberty Ave, 2nd flr (at Smithfield) **412/391-0804** *10pm-3am*

Pegasus Night Club [★M,D,DS,YC] 818 Liberty Ave (at 9th) **412/281-2131** *9pm-2am, clsd Sun-Mon, 18+ Tue & Th*

Studio 54 [MW,D] 2604 Josephine St (at 26th St) **412/488-2700** *8pm-2am Fri-Sat*

■ CAFES

Tuscany Cafe 1501 E Carson St (at 15th) **412/488-4475** *7am-2am, from 8am wknds, full bar*

Welcome to Pittsburgh!

Get

Since 1973, *the* gay news and information source

- **Local news**
- **Entertainment**
- **Classified ads**
- **"Nightlife" guide**
- **"What's Happening" calendar of events**

Visit our Web site at www.outpub.com

Out, 1000 Ross Ave., Pittsburgh, PA 15221
Phone: (412) 243-3350; fax: (412) 243-7989
E-mail: out@outpub.com

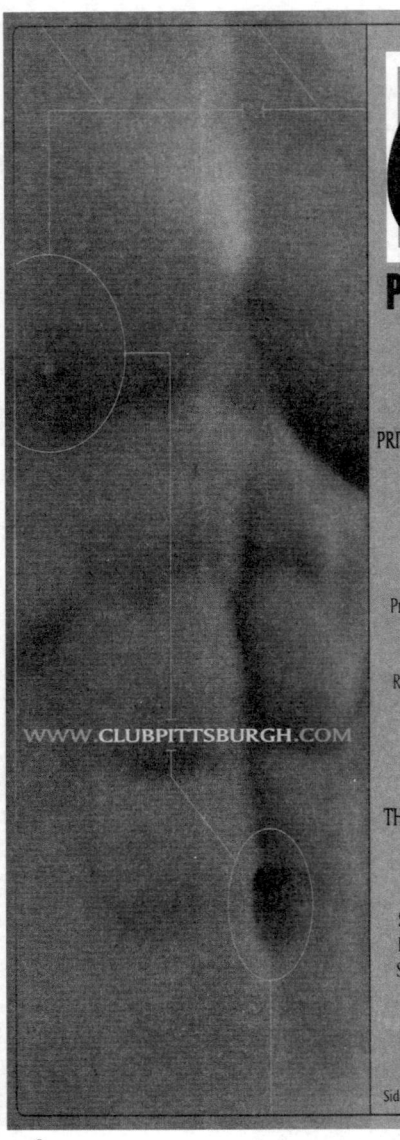

Club Pittsburgh

1139 Penn Ave
Pittsburgh, PA
412-471-6790

PRIVATE GAY MEN'S CLUB
Open 24 Hours

Four Social Areas
Video Lounge
Private Changing Rooms
Steam Room
Whirlpool and Sauna
Roof Top Tanning Deck
Fully Equipped Gym

WWW.CLUBPITTSBURGH.COM

THEME NIGHT SPECIALS
Lockers only $8
6pm - Midnight

Sunday: Leather Night
Monday: Locker Night
Student Special **DAILY!**

Located near Greyhound
bus station and Amtrak
Side entrance of Penn Ave & 12th

Schaefferstown • Pennsylvania

■ RESTAURANTS

Rosebud [E,WC] 1600 Smallman St **412/261-2221** *dinner nightly, clsd Mon*

■ ENTERTAINMENT & RECREATION

Andy Warhol Museum
117 Sandusky St (at General Robinson) **412/237-8300** *clsd Mon, is it soup or is it art?—see for yourself*

■ BOOKSTORES

The Bookstall 3604 5th Ave (at Meyran) **412/683-2644** *9:30am-5:45pm, till 4:30pm Sat, clsd Sun, general*

■ RETAIL SHOPS

A Pleasant Present [WC] 2301 Murray Ave (at Nicholson) **412/421-7104** *10am-8pm, till 6pm Fri-Sat*

Ellenbee's Rainbow Gifts & Books [GO] 5831 Forward Ave **724/224-4569** *11am-8pm, till 9pm Fri-Sat, 1pm-6pm Sun, pride items, books*

Slacker [WC] 1321 E Carson St (btwn 13th & 14th) **412/381-3911** *11am-9pm, till 11pm Fri-Sat, noon-6pm Sun, magazines, leather, piercing*

■ PUBLICATIONS

Erie Gay News **814/456-9833** *covers news & events in the Erie, Cleveland, Pittsburgh, Buffalo & Chautauqua County, NY region*

▶ **EXP Gayzette** **302/227-5787, 877/397-6244** *bi-weekly gay magazine for Mid-Atlantic*

▶ **Out** **412/243-3350** *lgbt newspaper*

■ MEN'S CLUBS

▶ **Club Pittsburgh** [PC] 1139 Penn Ave (enter side) **412/471-6790** *24hrs, 3 flrs, gym, rooftop tanning deck*

■ MEN'S SERVICES

▶ **Megaphone Pittsburgh** **800/289-1489** *Call for the local # nearest you! Meet Hot Men in your area! FREE to Browse & Respond to voice ads. Use code 3087. Also try MEGAMATES.COM*

■ EROTICA

Boulevard Videos & Magazines
346 Blvd of the Allies (at Smithfield) **412/261-9119** *24hrs, leather & toys*

Golden Triangle News 816 Liberty Ave (at 9th) **412/765-3790** *24hrs*

■ CRUISY AREAS

Schenley Park [AYOR]

Poconos

■ ACCOMMODATIONS

The Arrowheart Inn [GS,NS,GO]
3021 Valley View Dr (at Fox Gap Rd), Bangor **610/588-0241** *B&B near skiing, hiking, biking, river, 1 1/2 hours from NYC*

Frog Hollow [MW,GO] **570/595-2814** *secluded 1920s cottage*

Milanville House B&B [GS,GO]
River Rd, Milanville **717/729-8236, 800/820-5111** *restored 19th-c inn, 5 minutes from Delaware River, full brkfst*

Rainbow Mountain Resort [★MW,D,TG,E,K,SW,GO] **570/223-8484** *atop Pocono mtn on 26 acres, also restaurant & bar, DJ Fri-Sat*

Stoney Ridge [MW,GO] **570/629-5036** *secluded log home*

Quakertown

■ RESTAURANTS

The Brick Tavern Inn 2460 Old Bethlehem Pike (at Brick Tavern Rd) **215/538-0865** *11am-9pm, full bar open later*

Reading

■ NIGHTCLUBS

Scarab [★MW,D,DS,YC] 724 Franklin (at Lemon) **610/375-7878** *9pm-2am, clsd Sun-Tue*

Rochester

■ CRUISY AREAS
Brady's Run Park [AYOR]

Schaefferstown

■ CRUISY AREAS
Middle Creek Wildlife Preserve [AYOR]

Pennsylvania • *USA*

Scranton

■ ACCOMMODATIONS
Hillside Campgrounds
[★MO,D,SW,N,GO] 570/756-2007
campground, cabins, disco Fri-Sat

■ BARS
Silhouette Lounge [M,NH,L]
523 Linden St (at N Washington Ave)
570/344-4259 *3pm-2am, from 10am Sat, clsd Sun*

■ CRUISY AREAS
Court House Square [AYOR]

Shippensburg

■ EROTICA
➤ **The Lion's Den Adult Bookstore**
8071 Olde Scotland Rd, exit 24 (Penn exit 24, off I-81) 717/530-8032

State College

■ BARS
Chumley's [★M,NH,WC] 108 W College
814/238-4446 *5pm-2am, from 6pm Sun*

■ NIGHTCLUBS
Players [GS,D,V,YC] 112 W College Ave
814/234-1031 *9pm-2am, clsd Mon & Wed, more gay Sun*

■ CRUISY AREAS
The Wall [AYOR] 100 blk of College Ave

Sunbury

■ CRUISY AREAS
Market St & Park [AYOR] *downtown*
Shikellamy State Park [AYOR]

Valley Forge

■ CRUISY AREAS
Betzwood Park [AYOR]

West Chester

■ CRUISY AREAS
Court House Wall [AYOR] *late nights*

Wilkes-Barre

■ INFO LINES & SERVICES
Coming Home (AA) 97 S Franklin Blvd
(at Presbyterian Church) *noon Th*

■ NIGHTCLUBS
Twist [★M,D,F,WC] Fox Ridge Plaza
570/825-7300 *8pm-2am, from 6pm Sun, patio, also restaurant*

■ RETAIL SHOPS
The Coming Out [MW,GO] 493 Johnson St (at Rte 309) 570/970-2663 *11am-7pm, till 5pm Sat, clsd Sun, pride items, adult novelties, clothing, books, videos*

■ EROTICA
Cinema 309 [AYOR] Rte 309 (W-B/Mountaintop exit, off I-81) *behind Kmart, unconfirmed*

■ CRUISY AREAS
Francis Slocum State Park [AYOR]
Carverton Rd, Kingston Township

Nesbitt Park [AYOR] Susquehanna River (N of Pierce St bridge), Kingston

Williamsport

■ BARS
Peachie's [MW,D,F,WC] 144 E 4th St
570/326-3611 *3pm-2am, from 7pm Sat, clsd Sun, DJ wknds*

■ CRUISY AREAS
Scenic Overlook [AYOR] 3 miles S, on Rte 15 N

York

■ INFO LINES & SERVICES
York Area Gay Info 717/846-2560

■ NIGHTCLUBS
Altland's Ranch [MW,D] 8505 Orchard Rd, Spring Grove 717/225-4479 *8pm-2am Fri-Sat only*

The Velvet Rope [MW,D,TG,F,K,DS]
36-38 W 11th St 717/812-1474 *6pm-2am Tue-Sun, retro night 1st & 3rd Fri, karaoke 3rd Th*

■ EROTICA
Cupid's Connection Adult Boutique
244 N George St (at North)
717/846-5029

Providence • Rhode Island

RHODE ISLAND

Statewide

■ PUBLICATIONS
▶ **In Newsweekly** 617/426-8246 *New England's largest lgbt newspaper*

Options 401/781-1193 *extensive resource listings*

Bristol

■ RESTAURANTS
Hotpoint Restaurant 31 State St (in Bristol Harbor area) **401/254-7474** *lunch & dinner, clsd Mon, American*

East Greenwich

■ RETAIL SHOPS
Scrumptions Bakery 5600 Post Rd **401/884-0844** *9am-5pm*

Newport

■ INFO LINES & SERVICES
Sobriety First 135 Pelham St (at Channing Memorial Church) **401/438-8860** *8pm Fri*

■ ACCOMMODATIONS
Brinley Victorian Inn [GF,NS] 23 Brinley St **401/849-7645, 800/999-8523**

Captain James Preston House [GF,NS] 378 Spring St (at Pope) **401/847-7077**

Hydrangea House Inn [★GS,GO] 16 Bellevue Ave **401/846-4435, 800/945-4667** *full brkfst, near beach*

The Melville House Inn [★GS,NS,GO] 39 Clarke St **401/847-0640, 800/711-7184** *full brkfst*

The Spring Seasons Inn [GF] 86 Spring St (at Marty St) **401/849-0004** *B&B, full brkfst, jacuzzi*

■ CAFES
Java Bob's Cafe [GF,F] 435 Thames St **401/846-5402** *6am-6pm, internet*

■ RESTAURANTS
Restaurant Bouchard 505 Thames St **401/846-0123** *dinner, clsd Tue*

Whitehorse Tavern 26 Marlborough (at Farewell) **401/849-3600**

■ CRUISY AREAS
Purgatory Chasm [AYOR] E on Purgatory Rd (past St George's school), Middletown *turn right before going downhill to beach*

North Kingstown

■ EROTICA
Amazing 6774 Post Rd/ Rte 1 **401/885-0209**

Pawtucket

■ INFO LINES & SERVICES
Gay & Lesbian AA 71 Park Place (at Congregational church) **401/438-8860**

Providence

■ INFO LINES & SERVICES
Brothers in Sobriety 372 Wayland (at Lloyd, at Central Baptist Church) **401/438-8860** *7:30pm Sat*

GLBT Helpline of Rhode Island **401/751-3322** *7pm-10pm Mon, Wed & Fri*

■ BARS
Deville's [★W,NH,D,WC] 150 Point St **401/751-7166** *7pm-1am, till 2am Fri-Sat, clsd Mon-Tue*

European Tavern [MW,NH] 828 Charles St (at Raphael) **401/831-3327** *4pm-midnight, clsd Sun*

The Providence Eagle [M,L,WC] 200 Union St (at Weybosset) **401/421-1447** *3pm-1am, from noon wknds, till 2am Fri-Sat*

Union Street Station [M,D,S,WC] 69 Union St (at Washington) **401/331-2291** *noon-1am, till 2am Fri-Sat*

University Pub [M,NH] 17 Snow St (at Washington) **401/273-0951** *11:30am-1am, till 2am Fri-Sat, hustlers*

Wheels [MW,D,K,V,WC] 125 Washington (at Mathewson) **401/272-6950** *noon-1am, till 2am Fri-Sat, DJ wknds*

Yukon Trading Co [★M,D,B,L] 124 Snow St (at Weybosset) **401/274-6620** *5pm-1am, till 2am Fri-Sat, from 4pm wknds, uniform & bear bar*

Rhode Island • USA

■NIGHTCLUBS

Bar One [GS,D,18+] 1 Throop Alley (off S Main St) 401/621-7112 *more gay Sun, call for events*

Gerardo's [GS,D,E,WC] 1 Franklin Square (btwn Allens & Eddy) 401/274-5560 *8pm-1am, till 2am Fri-Sat*

Kamp [★MW,D,K] 235 Promenade St 401/621-4141 *9pm-2am, clsd Sun-Tue, karaoke Wed, more men Fri for Boyz, Boyz, Boyz & Asylum Sat, [18+] Wed-Fri*

Mass at Zoom [M,D,18+] 172 Pine St 401/225-5692 *6pm Sun only*

Mirabar [M,D,K,S,WC] 35 Richmond St (at Weybosset) 401/331-6761 *3pm-1am, till 2am Fri-Sat, male dancers*

NV@ The Strand [M,D,S,18+,$] 79 Washington 401/751-2700 *9pm-1am Sun only, go-go boys, huge space*

Pulse [M,D,K,S,18+,$] 86 Crary St (at Plain) 401/272-2133 *9pm-close, from 6pm Sun, clsd Mon-Tue, all-male review Sun & Wed [21+]*

Saints & Sinners [M,S] 257 Allens Ave 401/780-8823 *8pm-close, clsd Mon-Tue, strippers*

Therapy/ INSANE [GS,D] 7 Dike St (at Troy) 401/490-7202 *9pm-2am Tue-Th, till 4am wknds, also gallery & cafe from 10am*

■CAFES

Coffee Cafe [GO] 257 S Main St (at Power) 401/421-0787 *7am-5pm, 8am-4pm Sat, clsd Sun, patio*

Nicks on Broadway 259 Broadway 401/421-0286 *brkfst & lunch Wed-Sat, Sun brunch*

Reflections Cafe [F] 8 Governor St (at Wickenden) 401/273-7278 *7am-11pm, till midnight Fri-Sat, also sidewalk seating*

White Electric 150 Broadway 401/453-3007 *7am-5:30pm, from 8am Sat, clsd Sun*

■RESTAURANTS

Al Forno [★] 577 S Main St 401/273-9760 *dinner only, clsd Sun-Mon, Little Rhody's best dining experience*

Camille's 71 Bradford St (at Atwell's Ave) 401/751-4812 *lunch & dinner, dinner only Sat, full bar*

Downcity Diner [WC] 151 Weybosset St 401/331-9217 *lunch & dinner, popular Sun brunch (very gay), full bar*

Intermezzo [S] 220 Weybosset St (at Matthewson St) 401/331-5100 *11am-10pm, clsd Mon-Tue, popular 'dragtime' Sun 11am-3pm*

Julian's 318 Broadway (at Vinton) 401/861-1770 *9am-1am, gourmet*

Rue de l'Espoir [★] 99 Hope St (at John) 401/751-8890 *lunch & dinner, clsd Mon, full bar*

Viola's 58 DePasquale Plaza (on Federal Hill) 401/861-5766 *lunch Th-Sun, dinner Th-Mon, patio*

■BOOKSTORES

Books on the Square 471 Angell St (at Wayland) 401/331-9097 *9am-9pm, till 10pm Fri-Sat, 10am-6pm Sun, some lgbt*

■RETAIL SHOPS

Esta's on Thayer St 257 Thayer St (across from Avon cinema) 401/831-2651 *videos, pride items & Tarot readings*

■PUBLICATIONS

➤ **In Newsweekly** 617/426-8246 *New England's largest lgbt newspaper*

➤ **Metroline** 860/233-8334 *covers CT, RI & MA*

Options 401/781-1193

■MEN'S CLUBS

Club Body Center [PC] 257 Weybosset (at Richmond) 401/274-0298 *24hrs*

The Gay Mega-Plex [PC,WC,GO] 257 Allens Ave 401/780-8769 *24hrs*

■MEN'S SERVICES

➤ **Megaphone Providence** 800/289-1489 *Call for the local # nearest you! Meet Hot Men in your area! FREE to Browse & Respond to voice ads. Use code 3087. Also try MEGAMATES.COM*

■SEX CLUBS

Black Key Club [NS,PC] 401/274-3700 *call for hours, playspace for lesbian, gay, bi, transgendered & straight couples & singles*

■EROTICA

Adult Video & News 255 Allens Ave (at Point) 401/785-1324

Charleston • South Carolina

Amazing 262 Charles St (at Orms) 401/273-0610

Amazing Express 1954 Westminster (at Manton Ave) 401/861-0739

Amazing Super Store 15 Thurbers Ave (at Rte 1A) 401/467-7631

Miko 653 N Main St (at Doyle) 401/421-6646, 800/421-6646 *fetishwear, sex toys, classes*

■ CRUISY AREAS
State House [AYOR] *nights*

Smithfield

■ BARS
The Loft [MW,D,SW,WC] 325 Farnum Pike 401/231-3320 *noon-1am, from 10am wknds & summers*

Warwick

■ BOOKSTORES
Barnes & Noble 1441 Bald Hill Rd/ Rte 2 401/828-7900 *9am-11pm, 11am-7pm Sun, lgbt section*

■ EROTICA
Amazing 2318 Post Rd/ Rte 1 401/739-3080

■ CRUISY AREAS
Salter Grove Park [AYOR] Narragansett Pkwy (off Post Rd)

Westerly

■ ACCOMMODATIONS
The Villa [GF,SW,NS] 190 Shore Rd 401/596-1054, 800/722-9240 *near beach, hot tub*

■ RESTAURANTS
Mary's Rte 1 & Post Rd (off 1-A) 401/322-0444 *5pm-close, from 3pm Sun, Italian*

■ CRUISY AREAS
Misquamicut State Beach [AYOR] *go left before the bridge (at Fenway Beach)*

Woonsocket

■ BARS
Kings & Queens [MW,NH,D,K] 285 Front St (at Vernon) 401/762-9538 *7pm-1am, till 2am Fri-Sat, DJ wknds*

SOUTH CAROLINA

Statewide

■ PUBLICATIONS
▶ **The Front Page** 919/829-0181 *lgbt newspaper for the Carolinas*

▶ **TLW Magazine** 727/522-8888 *Southeast's largest entertainment magazine for gay men*

Aiken

see also Augusta, Georgia

■ NIGHTCLUBS
Marlboro Station [MW,D,S,18+] 141 Marlboro St 803/644-6485 *8pm-5am, till 3am Sat, clsd Mon-Tue*

Anderson

■ NIGHTCLUBS
The Cove II Lounge & Club [MW,D,S,PC,WC] 818 Hwy 28 Bypass S (1/2 mile N of Wal-Mart) 864/224-9050 *8pm-2am Th-Sat only, patio*

Augusta

■ BARS
The Shack [M,NH,D,PC] 425 Carolina Springs Rd (at Aiken-Augusta Hwy), North Augusta 803/441-0053 *8pm-close, after-hours*

Bowman

■ EROTICA
▶ **The Lion's Den Adult Bookstore** 803/829-1781

Charleston

■ INFO LINES & SERVICES
Acceptance Group (Gay AA) St Stephen's Episcopal on Anson St (btwn Society & George) 843/762-2433, 843/723-9633 (AA#) *7pm Mon, 8pm Tue & 6:30pm Sat*

South Carolina • USA

ACCOMMODATIONS

1854 B&B [MW,GO] 34 Montagu St
843/723-4789 *in the historic district*

65 Radcliffe Street [MW,NS,GO]
65 Radcliffe St 843/577-3372 *1880s home*

A B&B @ 4 Unity Alley [GS,NS]
4 Unity Alley 843/577-6660
full brkfst, parking inside

Blue Heron Inn [GF,NS] 122 E Arctic Ave (corner of E Artic Ave, E Ashley Ave & 2nd St), Folly Beach 843/588-3343 *1-bdrm villas w/ ocean view*

The Gateway House Inn [GF,NS]
20 Burns Ln (at King & Calhoun St)
843/722-3969, 800/706-1802
B&B, some shared baths, pets ok

Height of Folly [MO,GO] 1309 E Ashley Ave, Folly Beach 843/588-6200
beachfront apts, hot tub

BARS

Dudley's on Ann [M,NH,18+,GO]
42 Ann St (at King St) 843/577-6779
4pm-late

Patrick's Pub [MW,NH,TG,E,K,S,WC]
1377 Ashley River Rd/ Hwy 61
843/571-3435 *5pm-2am, patio bar*

NIGHTCLUBS

Club Pantheon [M,D,MR,E,DS,18+,GO]
28 Ann St (at King) 843/577-2582
9pm-2am Th-Sun

Deja Vu II [W,D,F,E,K,PC,WC,GO]
4628 Spruill Ave 843/554-5959 *5pm-3am, from 8pm Fri-Sat, clsd Sun-Tue*

CAFES

Bear E Patch [WC] 801 Folly Rd
843/762-6555 *7am-8pm, 9am-3pm Sun, patio*

Tomato Shed Cafe [GO] 842 Main Rd (at Stono Farm Market & Bakery), Johns Island 843/559-9999,
866/877-8666 *9am-6pm (lunch 11:30am-3pm), crabcakes & more, on-site bakery*

RESTAURANTS

Blossom Cafe 171 E Bay St
843/722-9200 *11:30am-11pm, till midnight wknds*

Cafe Suzanne [E] 4 Center St
843/588-2101 *5:30pm-9:30pm, Sun brunch, clsd Mon, live jazz*

Joe Pasta 428 King St (at John)
843/965-5252 *lunch & dinner, also full bar*

St Johns Island Cafe [★BW]
3140 Maybank Hwy, St Johns Island
843/559-9090 *brkfst, lunch & dinner, Sun brunch, Southern*

Sweetwater Cafe [★] 137 Market St (at King St) 843/723-7121 *7am-3pm, till 4pm Fri-Sat*

Vickery's of Beaufain Street [★]
15 Beaufain St (at St Philip)
843/577-5300 *11:30am-2am, Cuban influence, full bar*

ENTERTAINMENT & RECREATION

Historic Charleston Foundation
108 Meeting St 843/723-1623
call for info on city walking tours

Spoleto Festival USA 843/722-2764
2-week avant-garde art festival in late May-early June

PUBLICATIONS

▶ **The Front Page** 919/829-0181
lgbt newspaper for the Carolinas

The Loop 843/571-6942 *Charleston's gay newspaper*

Q Notes 704/531-9988 *bi-weekly lgbt newspaper for the Carolinas*

EROTICA

C&C Adult Video 904 St Andrews Blvd
843/763-0344 *24hrs*

CRUISY AREAS

The Battery [AYOR] White Point Garden

Folly Beach [AYOR] western tip of island (make a right at the island's only traffic light & drive all the way to county park)

Waterfront Park [AYOR] pier & promenade

Myrtle Beach • South Carolina

Columbia

■ INFO LINES & SERVICES

AA Gay/ Lesbian 5220 Clemson (in the house behind St Martin's Church) **803/254-5301**(AA#) *8pm Fri*

South Carolina Pride Center 1108 Woodrow St **803/771-7713** *24hr message, live 2pm-10pm Sat*

■ BARS

Capital Club [M,NH,P,PC,WC] 1002 Gervais St **803/256-6464** *5pm-2am*

■ NIGHTCLUBS

Candy Shop [M,D,MR-AF,PC] 1903 Two Notch Rd *Fri-Sat only, unconfirmed*

Metropolis/ OZ [MW,D,S,PC] 1800 Blanding St (at Barnwell) **803/799-8727** *9pm-4am, 7pm-2am Sun, clsd Mon-Th, also Oz from 9pm*

PTS 1109 [MW,D,MR,TG,S,PC,GO] 1109 Assembly St (at Gervais St) **803/253-8900** *5pm-4am, till 2am Sat-Sun*

The Revolution [MW,D,MR,E,K,DS,S,V, 18+,PC,WC,GO] 920 Lady St (at Park St) **803/254-4645** *10pm-4am Fri-Sat only, 2 levels*

■ RESTAURANTS

Alley Cafe [E] 911 Lady St **803/255-0257** *dinner Wed-Sat, full bar*

■ RETAIL SHOPS

Moxie 631-C Harden St **803/929-0644** *11am-6pm, clsd Sun-Mon*

■ MEN'S SERVICES

➤ **Megaphone Columbia** **800/289-1489** *Call for the local # nearest you! Meet Hot Men in your area! FREE to Browse & Respond to voice ads. Use code 3087. Also try MEGAMATES.COM*

■ EROTICA

Video Magic 5445 Two Notch Rd **803/786-8125**

■ CRUISY AREAS

Lake Murray Dam [AYOR]

Senate Street [AYOR] near the university

Florence

■ NIGHTCLUBS

Warehouse 250 [MW,D,S,PC] 1719 Irby St **843/667-3214** *9pm-2am, till 3am Fri*

■ CRUISY AREAS

Jeffries Creek Park [AYOR]

Timrod Park [AYOR]

Greenville

■ ACCOMMODATIONS

Walnut Lane Inn [GF,GO] 110 Ridge Rd (at Groce Rd), Lyman **864/949-7230** *full brkfst*

■ NIGHTCLUBS

The Castle [★MW,D,DS,S,V,YC,PC] 8-B Legrand Blvd **864/235-9949** *9:30pm-4am, till 3am Sun, clsd Mon-Th*

Club 621 [★M,D,V,SW,PC,WC] 621 Airport Rd **864/234-6767** *7pm-4am, till 5am Fri, 3pm-2am Sun*

New Attitude [★MW,D,MR-AF,PC] 706 W Washington St **864/233-1387** *10pm-4:30am Th-Sun*

■ MEN'S SERVICES

The Confidential Connection®! **864/370-2218** *The hottest local guys! 18+ Record & Listen FREE! Use access code 499*

➤ **Megaphone Greenville** **800/289-1489** *Call for the local # nearest you! Meet Hot Men in your area! FREE to Browse & Respond to voice ads. Use code 3087. Also try MEGAMATES.COM*

Hilton Head

■ CRUISY AREAS

Coligny Circle Beach [AYOR] S of the Holiday Inn (at the end of Pope Ave)

Pinckney Island Park [AYOR] Hwy 278 *days*

Myrtle Beach

■ ACCOMMODATIONS

The Lilly Pad [GS,GO] 407 12th Ave S **843/450-4225** *1 blk to beach, kitchenettes*

South Carolina • USA

Pondview Chalet [GS,SW,N,NS,GO]
1200 Horry Rd (at Rte 501), Conway
877/311-5478, 866/945-7355 *guest house, hot tub*

Teakwood Inn [GS,SW,GO]
7201 N Ocean Blvd (at 72nd Ave)
843/449-6700, 800/868-0046 *hotel*

■ BARS

Club Blue [GS,D,F,K,DS,S,WC,GO]
515 9th Ave N (at N Kings Hwy)
843/448-0077 *5pm-5am, till 2am wknds*

Time Out [★M,NH,D,K,S,PC,WC]
520 8th Ave N (at Oak) **843/448-1180**
5pm-close, till 2am Sat, patio bar

■ NIGHTCLUBS

Rainbow House [MW,D,K,WC]
815 N Kings Hwy **843/626-7298**
3pm-5am, till 2am wknds, patio

■ EROTICA

X-citement Video 2123 Hwy 501
843/448-7756 *also 3106 Hwy 17 S, 843/272-0744, 24hrs*

■ CRUISY AREAS

Beach at 82nd Ave [AYOR]

Huntington Beach State Park
[AYOR] Hwy 17 S *Mon-Fri*

Hurl Rock Park [AYOR] at 21st Ave S (south end)

Rock Hill

■ BARS

Hideaway [MW,NH,PC] 405 Baskins Rd
803/328-6630 *8pm-close Th-Sat*

Spartanburg

■ NIGHTCLUBS

The Cove Lounge & Club
[MW,D,S,PC,WC] 9112 1H Abernathy Rd
864/576-2683 *8pm-2am, patio*

■ CRUISY AREAS

Millikan Park [AYOR] off I-85 *days*

Walhalla

■ ACCOMMODATIONS

Country Place B&B [MO,SW,N,GO] 490 Country Place Dr **864/944-6924** *full brkfst, on 100 acres, primitive camping*

SOUTH DAKOTA

Statewide

■ PUBLICATIONS

Lavender Magazine 612/871-2237 (MN#), 877/515-9969 *lgbt newsmagazine for MN, WI, IA, ND, SD*

Aberdeen

■ BARS

Baby Boomers [GF] 208 S Main St
605/226-2140 *2pm-2am, clsd Sun, more gay late*

Batesland

■ ACCOMMODATIONS

Wakpamni B&B [GF,NS] (on the Pine Ridge Indian Reservation)
605/288-1800 *rooms & tipis, full brkfst, dinner available*

Belle Fourche

■ ACCOMMODATIONS

Back to Nature Ranch & Campground [MO,NS,WC,GO] Water Tank Rd 57717-0039 **605/723-2867**
B&B, full hookup campsite

Hot Springs

■ ENTERTAINMENT & RECREATION

Springs Bath House [GF]
146 N Garden St **605/745-4424, 888/817-1972** *10am-9pm (seasonal), 1880s bathhouse w/ hot mineral-water soaking pools (indoor & outdoor), massage center, day-spa services*

Pierre

■ CRUISY AREAS

LaFramboise Island [AYOR] *off the causeway*

Rapid City

■ INFO LINES & SERVICES

Gay/ Lesbian Talk Line
605/721-6743 *6pm-10pm*

Unified Live & Let Live AA
605/381-1325 *8pm Fri, call for info*

Gatlinburg • Tennessee

■ACCOMMODATIONS
Camp Michael B&B [MW,GO] 13051 Bogus Jim Rd **605/342-5590** *peaceful getaway, full brkfst, shared baths*

■NIGHTCLUBS
TW's [MW,D,CW,B,L,K,S,GO] 702 Box Elder Rd W (I-90 E, exit 63), Box Elder **605/923-2153** *8pm-2am, clsd Sun-Mon, also camping & RV*

■EROTICA
Heritage Bookstore 912 Main St **605/394-9877**

■CRUISY AREAS
Main & St Joe Sts [AYOR] btwn 6th & 8th

Salem

■ACCOMMODATIONS
Camp America [GF,GO] 25495 US 81 **605/425-9085** *35 miles W of Sioux Falls, camping, RV hookups*

Sioux Falls

■INFO LINES & SERVICES
The Center 309 W 43rd St #107 **605/331-1153** *support groups, counseling, library & more*

Rainbow Wildbunch AA 400 N Western **605/332-4017** *7pm Wed & Sat*

■NIGHTCLUBS
Touchez [★MW,D,F,K] 323 S Phillips Ave (enter rear) **605/335-9874** *8pm-2am, from 5pm Fri, clsd Sun, also Downstairs Bar from 10pm Sat*

■EROTICA
Studio One Book Store 311 N Dakota Ave (btwn 6th & 7th) **605/332-9316** *24hrs*

■CRUISY AREAS
Faywick Park [AYOR] 2nd Ave & 11th St
Sherman Park [AYOR] Kiwanis (btwn 12th & 26th Sts)

Spearfish

■CAFES
The Bay Leaf Cafe 126 1/2 W Hudson St **605/642-5462** *lunch & dinner, plenty veggie, espresso bar*

TENNESSEE

Statewide

■PUBLICATIONS
➤ **Southern Voice** **404/876-1819** *weekly lgbt newspaper for AL, FL (panhandle), GA, LA, MS, TN w/ resource listings*

➤ **TLW Magazine** **727/522-8888** *Southeast's largest entertainment magazine for gay men*

Chattanooga

■BARS
Chuck's II [MW,NH,D,K,OC] 27-1/2 W Main (at Market) **423/265-5405** *6pm-1am, till 3am Fri-Sat, leather night Sat, patio*

■NIGHTCLUBS
Alan Gold's [★MW,D,F,DS,YC,WC] 1100 McCallie Ave (at Central) **423/629-8080** *4:30pm-3am, drag shows Tue-Sun*

Images [MW,D,F,DS,WC] 6005 Lee Hwy **423/855-8210** *5pm-3am, also restaurant*

■EROTICA
Rossville News 2437 Rossville Blvd **423/266-7639** *24hrs*

Clarksville

■CRUISY AREAS
Fairground Park & MacGregor Park [AYOR]

Gatlinburg

■ACCOMMODATIONS
Big Creek Stables & Big Creek Outpost [GS,WC,GO] 5019 Rag Mtn Rd, Hartford **423/487-5742, 423/487-3490** *cabins, camping, horseback-riding*

Stonecreek Cabins [MW,NS,GO] **865/429-0400** *23-acre paradise*

Tennessee • *USA*

Greeneville

ACCOMMODATIONS

Timberfell Lodge [★MO,F,SW,N,NS,GO] 2240 Van Hill Rd (exit 36, off I-81) **800/437-0118** *also camping & RV hookups, full brkfst, hot tub*

Jackson

BARS

The Other Side [MW,K,DS,18+] 3883 Hwy 45 N (at Ashport) **731/668-3749** *5pm-midnight, till 3am Fri-Sat, from 7pm Fri-Sun, clsd Mon-Tue*

EROTICA

I-40 Bookstore [18+] Exit 68, W of Jackson **731/424-7226**

CRUISY AREAS

Muse Park [AYOR]

Johnson City

ACCOMMODATIONS

Safehaven Farm [GF] 336 Stanley Hollow Rd, Roan Mountain **423/725-4262** *cabins, creekside privacy, fireplace, wraparound porch*

NIGHTCLUBS

New Beginnings [★M,D,F,DS,WC] 2910 N Bristol Hwy **423/282-4446** *9pm-3am, from 8pm Fri-Sat, clsd Mon*

Pharaohs [M,F,DS,P,V,WC] 215 E Main St (at Roan St) **423/926-2541** *3pm-3am, noon-midnight Sun, clsd Mon*

RETAIL SHOPS

Spikes Gift Shop 2910 N Bristol Hwy (inside New Beginnings) **423/282-4446** *10pm-3am Fri-Sat only, pride gifts*

CRUISY AREAS

Buffalo Mountain Park [AYOR] end of Buffalo Mountain Park Rd

Jonesborough

RESTAURANTS

Dogwood Lane Cafe 109 Courthouse Square **423/913-1629** *brkfst & lunch Tue-Sun, dinner served Fri-Sat, clsd Mon, Southern*

Kingsport

CRUISY AREAS

Broad St [AYOR] near library

Knoxville

INFO LINES & SERVICES

AA Gay/ Lesbian 865/522-9667 *7:30pm Wed, call for location*

Gay/ Lesbian Helpline 865/531-2539 (MCC#) *7pm-11pm*

BARS

Kurt's Bar [M,NH,D,F,E,K,WC,GO] 4928 Homberg Dr (at Kingston Pike) **865/558-5720** *6pm-3am, from 9pm Mon-Tue, restaurant, patio*

NIGHTCLUBS

Carousel II [★MW,D,DS] 1501 White Ave (on U Tenn campus, behind the law library) **865/522-6966** *9pm-3am, also restaurant till 4am*

Electric Ballroom [M,D,F,K,DS,WC,18+] 1213 Western Ave **865/525-6724** *9pm-3am, from 6pm Fri-Sat, clsd Mon & Wed*

The New Rainbow Club West [MW,D,F,K,DS,WC] 7211 Kingston Pike **865/588-8030** *5pm-3am*

RESTAURANTS

Adrian's Cafe 10133 Kingston Pike #104 (at Center Park Dr) **865/693-6888** *11am-6pm, clsd Sun, eclectic*

EROTICA

Town & Country News 7011 Clinton Hwy **865/947-9153** *24hrs*

West Knoxville News 5005 Kingston Pike **865/588-1972** *24hrs*

CRUISY AREAS

Downtown [AYOR] btwn post office & library

Fort Dickerson [AYOR] off Chapman Hwy, S Knoxville

Gay St [AYOR] lower end, close to bridge

I C King Park [AYOR] off Alcoa Hwy

Sharps Ridge [AYOR] off N Broadway

The Square [AYOR] intersection of Church, Market, Walnut & Union Sts

Memphis • Tennessee

Memphis

■ INFO LINES & SERVICES

AA Intergroup 5119 Summer Ave #315 **901/454-1414**

Memphis Gay/ Lesbian Community Center 892 S Cooper **901/278-4297** *groups, 24hr recorded info*

■ ACCOMMODATIONS

French Quarter Suites [GF] 2144 Madison **901/728-4000, 800/843-0353** *also Bourbon St Cafe*

Madison Hotel [GF,SW] 79 Madison Ave **901/333-1200, 866/446-3674**

Talbot Heirs Guesthouse [GF,NS] 99 S Second St (btwn Union & Peabody Pl) **901/527-9772, 800/955-3956** *suites w/ kitchens, funky decor*

■ BARS

Crossroads [MW,NH,K,DS] 1278 Jefferson (at Claybrook) **901/276-1882** *noon-3am, beer & set-ups only, karaoke Th, also Crossroads II at 111 N Claybrook*

J Wags Bar [M,D,F,DS] 1268 Madison (btwn Claybrook & Montgomery) **901/725-1909** *24hrs, beer & set-ups only, patio*

The Jungle [M,NH,D,L,F] 1474 Madison (at McNeil) **901/278-4313** *4pm-3am, from 3pm wknds, dancing/DJ wknds, beer & set-ups only*

Lorenz [MW,D,CW,E] 1528 Madison Ave (at Avalon) **901/274-8272** *24hrs, patio*

Madison Flame [MW,NH,D] 1588 Madison (at Avalon) **901/278-9839** *7pm-3am Wed-Sun*

The Metro [MW,D,F,K,WC] 1349 Autumn St (at Cleveland) **901/274-8010** *6pm-3am, karaoke Mon-Tue*

One More [GF,NH,MR,F] 2117 Peabody Ave (at Cooper) **901/278-6673** *11am-3am, from noon Sun, patio*

The Paragon [M,D,F,E,K] 2865 Walnut Grove Rd (at Tillman) **901/320-0026** *8pm-close, dancing Fri, karaoke Th*

Pumping Station [M,D,WC] 1382 Poplar (at Cleveland) **901/272-7600** *4pm-3am, from 3pm wknds, courtyard*

■ NIGHTCLUBS

Allusions [MW,D,DS,18+,BYOB] 3204 N Thomas (in Northgate Shopping Center) **901/357-8383** *from 10pm Fri-Sat only*

Backstreet [MW,D,WC] 2018 Court Ave (at Morrison) **901/276-5522** *8pm-3am, till 6am wknds, clsd Tue-Th, beer & set-ups only*

■ CAFES

Buns on the Run 2150 Elzey Ave (at Cooper) **901/278-2867** *7am-2pm, till 1:30pm Sat, clsd Sun*

Java Cabana [E] 2170 Young Ave (at Cooper) **901/272-7210** *11am-10pm, till midnight wknds, from noon Sun, also art gallery*

Otherlands Coffee Bar [★F,E] 641 S Cooper (at Central) **901/278-4994** *7am-8pm*

P&H Cafe [F,E,BW,WC] 1532 Madison (at Adeline) **901/726-0906** *11am-3am, from 5pm Sat, clsd Sun*

■ RESTAURANTS

Automatic Slim's Tonga Club [WC] 83 S 2nd St (at Union) **901/525-7948** *lunch & dinner Mon-Fri, dinner till 11pm Fri-Sat, clsd Sun, Caribbean & Southwestern, full bar*

Cafe Society [WC] 212 N Evergreen Ave (btwn McLean & Belvedere) **901/722-2177** *lunch & dinner, till 10pm Fri-Sat, full bar*

Leonard's Pit Barbeque 5465 Fox Plaza Dr **901/360-1963** *11am-9pm, Elvis ordered the pork sandwich at the original Leonard's (now closed), but the food is just as good here!*

Melange 948 S Cooper (at Young) **901/276-0002** *dinner till 10:30pm, bar till 3am*

Saigon Le 51 N Cleveland **901/276-5326** *11am-9pm, clsd Sun, pan-Asian*

■ ENTERTAINMENT & RECREATION

Center for Southern Folklore [F] 119 S Main St (at Peabody Pl) **901/525-3655** *11am-7pm, till 11pm Th-Sat, live music, gallery, also cyber-cafe*

Tennessee • *USA*

Graceland PO Box 16508 38186
901/332-3322, 800/238-2000
no visit to Memphis would be complete w/out a trip to see The King

■BOOKSTORES

Davis-Kidd Booksellers 397 Perkins Rd Ext (at Poplar & Walnut Grove) **901/683-9801** *9am-10pm, 10am-8pm Sun, some lgbt titles, also cafe*

■RETAIL SHOPS

Inz & Outz [WC] 553 S Cooper **901/728-6535** *10am-6pm, from 1pm Sun, pride items, books*

■PUBLICATIONS

Family & Friends 901/682-2669 *lgbt newsmagazine*

Triangle Journal News 901/454-1411 *lgbt newspaper, extensive resource listings*

■MEN'S SERVICES

The Confidential Connection®! 901/578-8900 *The hottest local guys! 18+ Record & Listen FREE! Use access code 499*

➤ **Megaphone Memphis 800/289-1489** *Call for the local # nearest you! Meet Hot Men in your area! FREE to Browse & Respond to voice ads. Use code 3087. Also try MEGAMATES.COM*

■EROTICA

Airport Book Mart 2214 Brooks Rd E (at Airways) **901/345-0657**

Cherokee Books 2947 Lamar **901/744-7494**

Getwell Books 1275 Getwell (at Park) **901/454-7765**

Paris Theater 2432 Summer Ave (at Hollywood) **901/323-2665**

Tammy's 2 2220 E Brooks Rd **901/396-9050**

Tammy's 3 1617 Getwell Rd **901/744-4513**

Tammy's 4 5939 Summer Ave **901/373-5760**

Nashville

■INFO LINES & SERVICES

AA Gay/ Lesbian 1808 Woodmont (at Unitarian church) **615/831-1050** *7:30pm Th & 8pm Mon*

Rainbow Community Center 961 Woodland St **615/297-0008** *daily mtgs & events, phone staffed 6pm-9pm Wed & Fri*

■ACCOMMODATIONS

Brentwood Suites [GF] 622 E Church St, Brentwood **615/277-4000**

Savage House [GS,GO] 167 8th Ave N (btwn Church & Commerce) **615/244-2229** *full brkfst, also Gas Lite Lounge*

■BARS

The Cabaret: Episode 2 [MW,D,K,DS] 833 Murfreesboro Rd **615/367-1995** *8pm-3am, clsd Mon-Tue*

The Gas Lite Lounge [M,F] 167-1/2 8th Ave N (btwn Church & Commerce) **615/254-1278** *4:30pm-3am*

Jaded Mary's [MW,D,F,E,K] 1713 Church St (at 17th & 18th) **615/320-3808** *5pm-1am, 7pm-3am Sat, 1pm-6pm Sun, clsd Mon-Tue, Sun brunch, popular Wed trivia night, karaoke Th, patio*

Jungle Lounge & Restaurant [M,D,F,DS] 306 4th Ave S (at Molloy) **615/256-9411** *11am-3am, from noon Sun*

The Nut House [M,DS] 339 Wilhagen Rd (at Murfeesboro) **615/361-3616** *4pm-3am, cruise bar*

TC's Triangle [MW,NH,F,WC] 1401 4th Ave S (btwn Lafayette & Chestnut) **615/242-8131** *1pm-3am, from noon wknds*

Tribe [MW,F,E,V,WC,GO] 1517 Church St (at 15th Ave S) **615/329-2912** *4pm-midnight, till 2am wknds, upscale, full restaurant*

Sewanee • Tennessee

NIGHTCLUBS

The Chute Complex
[★M,D,CW,L,K,DS,P,WC] 2535 Franklin Rd (at Wedgewood) **615/297-4571** *5pm-3am, 6 bars, patio, also restaurant w/ piano bar*

Connection Complex
[★MW,D,CW,DS,V,WC] 901 Cowan St (at Jefferson) **615/742-1166** *8pm-3am, clsd Mon-Tue, 3 clubs, also restaurant & gift shop*

Excess/ Orbit [MW,D,18+] 909 Church St (at 9th) **615/255-4331** *2am-6am Fri, 2am-8am Sat, alcohol-free, juice bar*

Nashville Nightlife [MW,F,DS,GO] 2620 Music Valley Dr **615/885-5201** *gay Tue only from 9pm*

CAFES

Bongo Java [E] 2007 Belmont Blvd **615/385-5282** *coffeehouse, deck, also serves brkfst, lunch & dinner*

RESTAURANTS

Calypso Cafe 2305 Elliston Pl **615/321-3878** *11am-9pm, Caribbean*

International Market 2010 Belmont Blvd (at International) **615/297-4453** *lunch & dinner, Thai/Chinese, plenty veggie*

The Mad Platter [R,WC] 1239 6th Ave N (at Monroe) **615/242-2563** *lunch Tue-Sat, dinner, clsd Mon*

Mirror 2317 12th Ave S (at Linden) **615/383-8330** *dinner only, clsd Sun*

Towne House Tea Room 165 8th Ave N (btwn Church & Commerce) **615/254-1277** *brkfst & lunch Mon-Fri, clsd wknds, buffet*

BOOKSTORES

Davis-Kidd Booksellers 4007 Hillsboro Rd (at Abbot-Martin) **615/385-2645** *9am-10pm, till 11pm Fri-Sat, 10am-7pm Sun, lgbt section*

Outloud Books & Gifts 1709 Church St (btwn 17th & 18th Ave) **615/340-0034** *11am-9pm, till 10pm Fri-Sat, noon-6pm Sun, lgbt*

PUBLICATIONS

Out & About Nashville **615/596-6210** *lgbt newspaper for Nashville region, monthly*

Query **615/298-4532** *lgbt newspaper*

Xenogeny/ Southern X-posure **615/831-1806** *lgbt newspaper & bar guide*

MEN'S SERVICES

➤ **Megaphone Nashville** **800/289-1489** *Call for the local # nearest you! Meet Hot Men in your area! FREE to Browse & Respond to voice ads. Use code 3087. Also try MEGAMATES.COM*

EROTICA

Purple Onion 2807 Nolansville Rd (at SE Jeep Eagle) **615/259-9229** *24hrs; also 2702 Dickerson Rd location,* **615/227-8832**

Southern Vibe 700 Division (at 8th Ave S) **615/256-5775**

CRUISY AREAS

Cedar Hill Park [AYOR]

Percy Priest Dam [AYOR]

Newport

ACCOMMODATIONS

Christopher Place, An Intimate Resort [GS,SW,NS,WC,GO] 1500 Pinnacles Wy **423/623-6555, 800/595-9441** *full brkfst*

Pigeon Forge

ENTERTAINMENT & RECREATION

Dollywood 1020 Dollywood Ln **865/428-9488** *Dolly Parton's 'wholesome Smoky Mtn theme park,' 35 miles SE of Knoxville*

Sewanee

ACCOMMODATIONS

Boxwood Cottage B&B [MO,NS,GO] 293 Anderson Cemetery Rd **931/598-5012** *clsd Dec-Feb, full brkfst*

Texas • USA

TEXAS

Statewide

PUBLICATIONS

Qtexas 214/855-4990 *hip glossy entertainment magazine, weekly*

Texas Triangle 214/946-0401, 877/903-8407 *lgbt weekly newspaper w/ arts calendar & resource list*

Abilene

EROTICA

Romantix Adult Etc IV 3305 Hwy 80 E 915/672-5380 *24hrs*

CRUISY AREAS

Kirby Park [AYOR]

Amarillo

BARS

212 Club [MW,NH,D,DS,WC] 212 W 6th St (at Taylor) 806/372-7997 *2pm-2am*

Sassy's [MW,D,K,DS] 309 W 6th St 806/374-3029 *3pm-2am*

T Time [MW,NH,K,GO] 521 E 10th St 806/371-3535 *2pm-2am, karaoke Th*

Whiskers [MW,NH] 1219 W 10th Ave 806/371-8482 *4pm-2am*

NIGHTCLUBS

Open Mind [GS,D,WC] 519 E 10th St (at Buchanan) 806/374-2435 *call for hours*

RESTAURANTS

Italian Delight [BW,WC] 2710 W 10th Ave (at Georgia) 806/372-5444 *lunch & dinner, clsd Sun*

EROTICA

Boulevard Book Store & Video 601 N Eastern (at Eastern) 806/379-9002 *24hrs*

Romantix Adult Etc II I-40, exit 80 806/335-3155 *24hrs*

Studio One 9000 Triangle Dr 806/372-0648 *24hrs*

Arlington

see also Fort Worth

INFO LINES & SERVICES

Tarrant County Lesbian/ Gay Alliance 817/877-5544 *info line*

ACCOMMODATIONS

Country Inn & Suites—Arlington [GS,SW,WC] 1075 Wet N' Wild Wy (Hwy 30 & Collins 157 N) 817/307-4606 *all-studio hotel*

NIGHTCLUBS

The 1851 Club [M,D,K,DS,V,WC] 1851 W Division (at Fielder) 817/801-9303 *3pm-2am, karaoke Th*

Austin

INFO LINES & SERVICES

Lambda AA (Live & Let Live) 2700 W Anderson Ln #412 (in the Village Shopping Center) 512/444-0071 *8pm nightly & 1pm Sun*

ACCOMMODATIONS

1888 Miller Crockett House [GF,WC,GO] 112 Academy Dr (at Congress Ave) 512/441-1600, 888/441-1641 *full brkfst*

A Summit House B&B [MW,R,NS,GO] 1204 Summit St (at Lupine) 512/445-5304 *reservations req'd, full brkfst, bear-friendly*

Austin Folk House [GS,NS,WC] 506 W 22nd St 512/472-6700, 866/472-6700 *B&B in restored 1880 house*

Austin's Wildflower Inn [GS,GO] 1200 W 22 1/2 St (at Longview) 512/477-9639, 800/995-6171 *B&B, full brkfst*

Carrington's Bluff [GF,WC] 1900 David St (at W 22nd St) 512/479-0638, 888/290-6090 *full brkfst*

Days Inn North [GF,SW,WC] 820 E Anderson Ln (Hwy 183) 512/835-4311, 866/835-4311 *200-car (free) parking lot, good for truckers & tour buses*

Austin • Texas

Driskill Hotel [GF,F,WC] 604 Brazos St (at 6th) **512/474-5911, 800/252-9367** *even if you don't stay in this landmark hotel, be sure to check out the lobby*

Governor's Inn [GF] 611 W 22nd St (at Rio Grande) **512/477-0711, 800/871-8908** *neo-classical Victorian, full brkfst*

Hotel San Jose [GS,SW,WC] 1316 S Congress Ave **512/444-7322, 800/574-8897** *small boutique hotel*

Lazy Oak Inn [GF] 211 W Live Oak (btwn S 1st & Congress) **512/447-8873, 877/947-8873** *1911 plantation-style farmhouse, full brkfst*

Omni Hotel [GF,F,SW,WC] 700 San Jacinto (at 7th) **512/476-3700, 800/843-6664** *rooftop pool*

Park Lane Guest House [GS,SW,WC,GO] 221 Park Ln (at Drake) **512/447-7460, 800/492-8827** *full brkfst, also cottage, lesbian-owned/ run*

■ **BARS**

'Bout Time [★MW,NH,TG,DS,WC] 9601 N IH-35 (at Rundberg) **512/832-5339** *2pm-2am, drag shows, volleyball court*

Boyz Cellar [M,D,S,18+] 213 W 4th St (btwn Colorado & Lavaca) **512/479-8482** *all-male strip contest Th*

Casino El Camino [GF,NH,F] 516 E 6th St (at Red River) **512/469-9330** *4pm-2am, psychedelic punk jazz lounge*

Chain Drive [M,L,WC] 504 Willow St (at Red River) **512/480-9017** *4pm-2am daily, grill 5pm-8pm Sun, Bear Bust 2nd Sun*

Charlie's [★M,D,DS,S,YC,WC] 1301 Lavaca (at 13th) **512/474-6481** *2pm-2am, patio*

The Forum [★M,D,DS,S] 408 Congress Ave (at 4th) **512/476-2900** *4pm-2am, after-hours Fri-Sat, patio*

Rainbow Cattle Company [MW,D,CW] 305 W 5th St (btwn Guadalupe & Lavaca) **512/472-5288** *2pm-2am, classes Tue & Th*

■ **NIGHTCLUBS**

1920's Club [MW,P] 918 Congress Ave (btwn 9th & 10th) **512/479-7979** *5pm-midnight, till 2am wknds, from 6pm Sun, jazz club, piano Th*

Dick's Dejà Disco [M,D] 113 San Jacinto Blvd (btwn 1st & 2nd) **512/457-8010** *noon-2am, patio*

Oil Can Harry's [★M,D,A,YC,WC] 211 W 4th St (btwn Lavaca & Colorado) **512/320-8823** *2pm-2am, till 4am Fri-Sat, patio*

■ **CAFES**

Joe's Bakery & Coffeeshop 2305 E 7th St **512/472-0017** *7am-3pm, clsd Mon, Tex-Mex*

Little City Espresso Bar & Cafe 916 Congress Ave (at E 11th St) **512/476-2489** *popular gay hangout*

■ **RESTAURANTS**

Castle Hill Cafe 1101 W 5th St (at Baylor) **512/476-0728** *lunch & dinner, clsd Sun*

Eastside Cafe [BW,WC] 2113 Manor Rd (at Coleto, by bright yellow gas station) **512/476-5858** *lunch & dinner*

El Sol y La Luna [E,WC,GO] 1224 S Congress Ave (at Academy) **512/444-7770** *7am-3pm, till 10pm Wed-Sat, great brkfst*

Fonda San Miguel [GO] 2330 W North Loop (at Hancock Rd) **512/459-4121** *dinner only, popular Sun brunch, Mexican, full bar*

Jo's Coffee Shop [GO] 1300 S Congress Ave **512/444-3800** *7am-9pm*

Katz's [WC] 618 W 6th St (at Rio Grande) **512/472-2037** *24hrs, NY-style deli, full bar*

Mother's Cafe & Garden [★] 4215 Duval St (at 43rd) **512/451-3994** *lunch & dinner, vegetarian*

Romeo's [BW,WC] 1500 Barton Springs Rd (near Lamar) **512/476-1090** *lunch & dinner, Italian*

Starlite [GO] 624 W 34th St (at Guadalupe) **512/374-9012** *6pm-11pm, Sun brunch till 3pm, located in a hip, refurbished vintage 1930s home*

Texas • USA

Threadgill's 6416 N Lamar (at Koenig) **512/451-5440** *11am-10pm, till 9pm Sun, great chicken-fried steak*

West Lynn Cafe [BW] 1110 W Lynn (at W 12th St) **512/482-0950** *lunch & dinner, wknd brunch, vegetarian*

ENTERTAINMENT & RECREATION

Barton Springs [N] Barton Springs Rd *natural swimming hole*

Bat Colony Congress Ave Bridge (at Barton Springs Dr) *everything's bigger in Texas—including the colony of bats that flies out from under this bridge every evening March-Oct*

Historic Austin Tours 201 E 2nd St (in the Visitor Information Center) **512/478-0098, 800/926-2282 x4577** *free guided & self-guided tours of the Capitol, Congress Ave & 6th St, Texas State Cemetery, Hyde Park*

Zachary Scott Theatre Center 1510 Toomey Rd **512/476-0541** *diverse theater*

BOOKSTORES

Lobo [WC] 3204-A Guadalupe (btwn 32nd & 33rd) **512/454-5406** *10am-10pm, till 11pm Fri-Sat, from noon Sun, lgbt*

RETAIL SHOPS

Tapelenders [GO] 1114 W 5th St, #201 **512/472-0844** *10am-10pm, till midnight Th-Sat, lgbt videos, novelties*

PUBLICATIONS

Texas Triangle 611 W 6th St **512/476-0576, 877/903-8407** *lgbt weekly newspaper w/ arts calendar & statewide resource list*

GYMS & HEALTH CLUBS

Hyde Park Gym [GF] 4125 Guadalupe (at 42nd St) **512/459-9174** *day passes $7.50*

MEN'S CLUBS

➤ **Midtowne Spa—Austin** [PC] 5815 Airport Blvd (at Koenig) **512/302-9696** *24hrs*

OPEN 24 HOURS
VIDEO ROOMS
TEMPORARY MEMBERSHIPS
EXECUTIVE SUITE
W/PRIVATE BATHS

MIDTOWNE SPA AUSTIN
5815 AIRPORT BLVD. • AUSTIN, TX 78752
(512) 302-9696
AMEX/VISA/MC ACCEPTED   www.midtowne-spa.com
Locations: AUSTIN, DALLAS, DENVER, HOUSTON, LOS ANGELES & MILWAUKEE

Dallas • Texas

MEN'S SERVICES
➤ **Megaphone Austin**
800/289-1489 *Call for the local # nearest you! Meet Hot Men in your area! FREE to Browse & Respond to voice ads. Use code 3087. Also try MEGAMATES.COM*

EROTICA
Forbidden Fruit 512 Neches (btwn 5th & 6th) **512/478-8358**

CRUISY AREAS
Hippy Hollow-Lake Travis [AYOR]

Beaumont

INFO LINES & SERVICES
Lambda AA 1385 Calder Ave **409/866-6165** *8pm Wed & Sat*

NIGHTCLUBS
Copa [★MW,D,E,DS,WC] 304 Orleans St (at Liberty) **409/832-4206** *5pm-2am, till 3am Fri-Sat, talent night Wed*

RESTAURANTS
Carlo's [E] 2570 Calder (btwn 9th & 10th) **409/833-0108** *11am-10pm, clsd Sun, Italian/ Greek, full bar*

Buffalo

ACCOMMODATIONS
Buffalo RV Park & Campground [GF,SW,WC] 9928 US Hwy 79E, Oakwood **903/322-3854** *hot tub*

Corpus Christi

INFO LINES & SERVICES
Clean & Serene AA 1315 Craig (at MCC Corpus Christi) **361/882-8255** *8pm Fri*

ACCOMMODATIONS
Anthony's By The Sea [GS,SW,WC,GO] 732 S Pearl St, Rockport **361/729-6100, 800/460-2557** *full brkfst, hot tub*

Christy Estates Suites [GF,SW,WC] 3942 Holly St (at Weber) **361/854-1091, 800/678-4836** *hot tubs & spas, non-smoking rooms available*

BARS
The Hidden Door [M,NH,WC] 802 S Staples St (at Coleman) **361/882-5002** *3pm-2am*

The Rose [MW,NH] 213 S Staples **361/881-8181** *6pm-2am, from 3pm Sun*

MEN'S SERVICES
➤ **Megaphone Corpus Christi**
800/289-1489 *Call for the local # nearest you! Meet Hot Men in your area! FREE to Browse & Respond to voice ads. Use code 3087. Also try MEGAMATES.COM*

CRUISY AREAS
Seawall [AYOR]

Dallas

see also Fort Worth

INFO LINES & SERVICES
John Thomas Gay/ Lesbian Community Center [WC] 2701 Reagan St (at Brown) **214/528-9254** *9am-9pm, till 5pm wknds, from noon Sun*

Lambda AA 2438 Butler #106 **214/267-0222**

ACCOMMODATIONS
The Courtyard on the Trail [GS,SW,NS,GO] 8045 Forest Trail (at White Rock Trail) **214/553-9700** *full brkfst*

Holiday Inn Select Dallas Central [GS] 10650 N Central Expwy (at Meadow) **214/373-6000, 888/477-STAY**

Melrose Hotel [GF,P,SW,WC] 3015 Oak Lawn Ave (at Cedar Springs) **214/521-5151, 800/635-7673** *full brkfst, smokefree rooms available, also piano bar & lounge*

BARS
After Dark [MW,P,WC] 4026 Cedar Springs (at Throckmorton) **214/219-1099** *10am-2am, from noon wknds, piano & jazz bar*

Crews Inn [★M,D,S,WC] 3215 N Fitzhugh (at Travis) **214/526-9510** *noon-2am, popular Tue nights, patio*

Setting A New Standard

Always Open
Guest Memberships
Steam Room
Sauna
Whirlpool
Private Dressing Rooms
Outdoor Pool & Patio
Gym
18+ only

THE CLUB DALLAS

A PRIVATE MEN'S CLUB
2616 Swiss Ave. • Dallas, Texas • (214)821-1990
www.the-clubs.com

Dallas • Texas

Dallas Eagle [M,L] 2515 Inwood #107 (at Maple, enter rear) **214/357-4375** *4pm-2am, after-hours Fri-Sat*

Dewayne's Oasis Bar & Grill [M,NH,D,F,K,DS,S] 5334 Lemmon Ave (at Hudnall) **214/528-6234** *11am-2am, male dancers*

Hideaway Club [MW,P,OC] 4144 Buena Vista (at Fitzhugh) **214/559-2966** *8am-2am, from noon Sun, upscale piano bar*

JR's Bar & Grill [★M,F,E,DS,WC] 3923 Cedar Springs Rd (at Throckmorton) **214/528-1004** *11am-2am, grill till 4pm*

Moby Dick [MW,K,DS,V,WC] 4011 Cedar Springs Rd (btwn Douglas & Throckmorton) **214/520-6629** *noon-2am, karaoke Sun*

Pub Pegasus [M,NH,WC] 3326 N Fitzhugh (at Travis) **214/559-4663** *9am-2am, from noon Sun*

Side 2 Bar [GS,NH,K,WC] 2615 Oak Lawn Ave, Ste 101 (btwn Fairmount & Brown) **214/528-2026** *9am-2am, from 8am Fri-Sat, from noon Sun, karaoke Sat*

Sue Ellen's [★W,D,E,WC] 3903 Cedar Springs Rd (at Reagan) **214/559-0707** *5pm-2am, from noon wknds, patio*

Throckmorton Mining Co [★M,L] 3014 Throckmorton (at Cedar Springs) **214/521-4205** *5pm-2am, from 3pm Sun*

Trestle [M,NH,L] 412 S Haskell **214/826-9988** *11pm-4am, from 9pm Sun, after-hours Fri-Sat*

Zippers [M,NH,S] 3333 N Fitzhugh (at Travis) **214/526-9519** *noon-2am, dancers*

■ NIGHTCLUBS

The Brick [M,D,WC,$] 4117 Maple Ave (at Throckmorton) **214/521-2024** *9pm-4am, patio*

Male Boxx [M,S] 5006 Lemmon Ave (at Inwood) **214/219-8269** *3pm-2am*

OPEN 24 HOURS

VIDEO ROOMS
TEMPORARY MEMBERSHIPS
EXECUTIVE SUITE
W/PRIVATE BATHS

MIDTOWNE SPA DALLAS
2509 PACIFIC • DALLAS, TX 75226
(214) 821-8989
AMEX/VISA/MC ACCEPTED   www.midtowne-spa.com
Locations: AUSTIN, DALLAS, DENVER, HOUSTON, LOS ANGELES & MILWAUKEE

Texas • USA

One [GS,D,A,18+,$] 3025 Main (in Deep Ellum) **214/741-1111** *10pm-4am Fri-Sat only, more gay Fri*

Round-Up Saloon [★M,D,CW,K,WC] 3912 Cedar Springs Rd (at Throckmorton) **214/522-9611** *3pm-2am, from noon wknds*

Village Station [★MW,D,C,DS,S,V,18+] 3911 Cedar Springs Rd **214/526-7171** *9pm-3am Wed-Sun, also Rose Room cabaret, patio*

■ CAFES

Dream Cafe [WC] 2800 Routh St (in the Quadrangle) **214/954-0486** *7am-10pm, brkfst served till 5pm*

■ RESTAURANTS

Ali Baba Cafe 1905 Greenville Ave (near Ross) **214/823-8235** *lunch & dinner, clsd Sun-Mon, Middle Eastern*

Black-Eyed Pea [WC] 3857 Cedar Springs Rd (at Reagan) **214/521-4580** *11am-10pm, Southern homecookin'*

Blue Mesa Grill 5100 Beltline Rd (at Tollway), Addison **972/934-0165** *11am-10:30pm, 10am-9:30pm Sun, great fajitas, full bar*

Bread Winners [GS,WC] 3301 McKinney **214/754-4940** *7am-4pm, till 11pm Wed-Sun, Sun brunch, int'l, full bar*

The Bronx Restaurant & Bar [WC,GO] 3835 Cedar Springs Rd (at Oak Lawn) **214/521-5821** *lunch & dinner, Sun brunch, clsd Mon*

Cremona Bistro & Cafe 3136 Routh St (at Cedar Springs) **214/871-1115** *11am-10pm, till midnight Fri-Sat, from 4pm Sun, Italian, full bar*

Fresh Start Market & Deli [WC,GO] 4108 Oak Lawn (near Avondale) **214/528-5535** *7:30am-7:30pm, 9am-6pm Sat, noon-6pm Sun, organic, plenty veggie*

Hunky's [★BW,WC,GO] 4000 Cedar Springs Rd (at Throckmorton) **214/522-1212** *11am-10pm, till 11pm Fri-Sat, from noon Sun, patio*

Monica Aca y Alla [★TG,E,WC] 2914 Main St (at Malcolm X) **214/748-7140** *clsd Mon, trendy, contemporary Mex, full bar, live music Th-Sun, Latin jazz/salsa*

Sushi on McKinney [WC] 4500 McKinney Ave (at Armstrong) **214/521-0969** *lunch & dinner, Fri-Sat till 11pm, full bar*

Thai Soon 101 S Coit, Ste 401 (at Beltline) **972/234-6111** *lunch & dinner*

Vitto's [BW,WC,GO] 316 W 7th St (at Bishop) **214/946-1212** *lunch & dinner, Italian*

Ziziki's [WC] 4514 Travis St, #122 (in Travis Walk) **214/521-2233** *11am-11pm, till 9pm Sun, Sun brunch, Greek, full bar*

■ ENTERTAINMENT & RECREATION

Conspiracy Museum 110 S Market (in the Katy Bldg) **214/741-3040** *dedicated to infamous US assassinations since 1835 & their cover-ups*

Lambda Weekly KNON 89.3 FM *1pm Sun, lgbt radio show for northern TX*

Turtle Creek Chorale (TCC) 3630 Harry Hines Blvd (at Sammons Center for the Arts) **214/526-3214** *world-famous male choir w/ several subscription concerts yearly & many CDs*

■ BOOKSTORES

Crossroads Market Bookstore/ Cafe [WC] 3930 Cedar Springs Rd (at Throckmorton) **214/521-8919** *9am-9:30pm, till 11pm Fri-Sat, lgbt*

■ RETAIL SHOPS

An Occasional Piece 3922 Cedar Springs Rd (at Throckmorton) **214/520-0868** *gifts, cards, collectibles*

Off the Street 4001-B Cedar Springs (at Throckmorton) **214/521-9051** *10am-9pm, noon-6pm Sun, lgbt gifts*

Tapelenders [GO] 3926 Cedar Springs Rd (at Throckmorton) **214/528-6344** *9am-midnight, lgbt T-shirts, books, video rentals*

■ PUBLICATIONS

Dallas Voice **214/754-8710** *lgbt newspaper w/ extensive resource listings*

Texas Triangle 1012 N Bishop Ave **214/946-0401, 877/903-8407** *lgbt weekly newspaper w/ arts calendar & statewide resource list*

El Paso • Texas

GYMS & HEALTH CLUBS
Centrum Sports Club [GF,SW]
3102 Oak Lawn (at Cedar Springs)
214/522-4100

MEN'S CLUBS
➤ **Club Dallas** [★SW,PC] 2616 Swiss Ave (at Good Latimer) **214/821-1990** *24hrs*

➤ **Midtowne Spa—Dallas** [★PC] 2509 Pacific (at Hawkins) **214/821-8989** *24hrs*

MEN'S SERVICES
➤ **Megaphone Dallas**
800/289-1489 *Call for the local # nearest you! Meet Hot Men in your area! FREE to Browse & Respond to voice ads. Use code 3087. Also try MEGAMATES.COM*

EROTICA
Alternatives 1720 W Mockingbird Ln (at Hawes) **214/630-7071** *24hrs*

Leather by Boots—Dallas
2525 Wycliff #124 (at Maple)
214/528-3865

Shades of Grey Leather [WC] 3930-A Cedar Springs Rd (at Throckmorton) **214/521-4739**

CRUISY AREAS
Lee Park [AYOR] Turtle Creek (at Hall) *foot trails off Hall, across from main park*

Denison

BARS
Good Time Lounge [MW,K,DS]
2520 Hwy 91 N **903/463-9944** *7pm-2am, clsd Mon*

Denton

BARS
Geronimo's [★MW,NH,YC,PC]
1803 N Elm St **940/566-5969**, **940/390-5057** *5pm-2am, from noon wknds, 18+ from 9pm Th only*

NIGHTCLUBS
Mable Peabody's Beauty Parlor & Chainsaw Repair [MW,D,E,WC,GO] 1215 E University Dr **940/566-9910** *8pm-2am, clsd Sun-Mon*

CAFES
Cupboard Natural Foods 200 W Congress St (at Elm) **940/387-5386** *9am-9pm, 11am-6pm Sun, health food store & cafe*

CRUISY AREAS
Lake Lewisville-Queens Pt [AYOR] *clsd in winter*

El Paso
see also Ciudad Juárez, Mexico

INFO LINES & SERVICES
GLBT Community Center [F] 216 S Ochoa **915/562-4297** *24hr hotline, events, pride store, cafe (10am-6pm, till 3am Fri-Sat)*

Lambda Line **915/562-4297** *24hrs*

BARS
Briar Patch [MW,NH] 508 N Stanton (at Missouri) **915/577-9555** *noon-2am, patio*

Chiquita's Bar [MW,NH,MR-L,WC]
602 Magoffin (at Ochoa)
915/351-0095 *2pm-2am*

The Whatever Lounge [M,D,K,MR-L,WC] 701 E Paisano St (at Ochoa) **915/533-0215** *2pm-2am*

NIGHTCLUBS
The New Old Plantation
[★MW,D,DS,V,WC] 301 S Ochoa St (at Paisano) **915/533-6055** *9pm-2am, till 4am Fri-Sat, clsd Mon-Wed, drag shows Sun, also Generation Q II pride store upstairs*

San Antonio Mining Co
[★MW,D,DS,V,WC] 800 E San Antonio Ave (at Ochoa) **915/533-9516** *3pm-2am*

CAFES
Ol' Gay Cafe 216 S Ochoa (at GLBT Community Center) **915/562-4297** *10am-6pm, till 3am Fri-Sat*

RESTAURANTS
The Little Diner 7209 7th St, Canutillo **915/877-2176** *11am-8pm, clsd Wed, true Texas fare*

Texas • USA

MEN'S SERVICES
➤ **Megaphone El Paso**
800/289-1489 *Call for the local # nearest you! Meet Hot Men in your area! FREE to Browse & Respond to voice ads. Use code 3087. Also try MEGAMATES.COM*

EROTICA
Eros Adult Book Store 4812 Montana (at Reynolds) **915/565-2929**

Trixx Adult Cinema 2230 Texas Ave (at Palm) **915/532-6171**

Venus Adult Theatre & Books 4812 Montana (near Reynolds) **915/566-8061**

Fort Worth

see also Dallas

INFO LINES & SERVICES
Tarrant County Lesbian/ Gay Alliance 817/877-5544 *info line & newsletter*

BARS
The Corral Club & Patio Bar [M,CW,B,L,K,E,DS,V,WC] 621 Hemphill St (at Pennsylvania) **817/335-0196** *11am-2am, from noon Sun, shows wknds, patio*

Crossroads [M,NH] 515 S Jennings Ave **817/332-0071** *11am-2am, from noon Sun*

NIGHTCLUBS
651 Club Fort Worth [M,D,CW,WC] 651 S Jennings Ave (at Pennsylvania) **817/332-0745** *4pm-2am*

Magnolia Station [M,S] 600 W Magnolia **817/332-0415** *9pm-2am, clsd Mon-Tue*

CAFES
Paris Coffee Shop 704 W Magnolia (at Hemphill) **817/335-2041** *6am-2:30pm, till 11am Sat, clsd Sun*

MEN'S SERVICES
➤ **Megaphone Fort Worth**
800/289-1489 *Call for the local # nearest you! Meet Hot Men in your area! FREE to Browse & Respond to voice ads. Use code 3087. Also try MEGAMATES.COM*

EROTICA
The Bright Lights II 10355 N Freeway (I-35W) **817/232-5584** *24hrs*

The New Video [MR] 6704 Lindale Rd (I-20 E, take exit 442-A) **817/483-8206** *24hrs*

Fredericksburg

ACCOMMODATIONS
Town Creek B&B [GS] 304 N Edison (at W Travis) **830/997-6848** *full brkfst*

Galveston

ACCOMMODATIONS
Cottage by the Beach [GF,WC,GO] 810 Ave 'L' (at Seawall & 8th) **409/770-9332** *6 private rental homes*

Hollywood at Galveston [GF,SW,GO] 3028 Seawall Blvd **409/750-8900, 888/899-0899**

Oasis Beach Cottage [GF,NS,GO] 1322 Ave N 1/2 (at Seawall Blvd) **713/256-3000** *on the Gulf of Mexico*

Oh! Susana's [GF,SW,WC] 2315 Ave 'P' **409/763-3406, 866/787-2627** *hot tub*

Paradise Guesthouse & Resort [MW,SW,NS,WC,GO] 2317 Ave 'P' **409/762-6677, 877/919-6677** *1 blk from beach*

BARS
Boulevard Saloon [MW,S,GO] 3102 Seawall Blvd (at 31st) **409/750-8571** *4pm-2am, from 2pm Fri-Sun, on the beach, male dancers Fri-Sun*

Robert's Lafitte [M,DS,WC] 2501 'Q' Ave (at 25th St) **409/765-9092** *8am-2am, from noon Sun, drag shows wknds*

NIGHTCLUBS
Garza's Kon Tiki [MW,NH,D,MR,TG,E,K,DS,S] 315 23rd St (at Market) **409/765-5805** *noon-2am, drag shows Fri-Sun, male dancers wknds*

RESTAURANTS
Mosquito Cafe 628 14th St (at Winnie) **409/763-1010** *7am-2pm, till 10pm Th-Sat, 8am-3pm Sun*

CRUISY AREAS
The Dunes [AYOR]

Houston • Texas

Granbury

■ACCOMMODATIONS

A Bit of Rest Guesthouse [GF]
817 Switzer St **817/579-7465**
full brkfst, hot tub

Groesbeck

■ACCOMMODATIONS

Rainbow Ranch Campground
[MW,GO] 1662 LCR 800
254/729-5847, 888/875-7596
campsites & RV hookups, on Lake Limestone

Gun Barrel City

■ACCOMMODATIONS

Triple 'B' Cottages [GS]
903/451-5105 *78 miles from Dallas on Cedar Creek Lake, motor homes & travel trailers welcome*

■BARS

Friends [MW,NH,F,K,WC] 410 S Gun Barrel/ Hwy 198 **903/887-2061** *4pm-midnight, till 1am Sat, from 3pm wknds, karaoke Wed, patio*

Houston

■INFO LINES & SERVICES

Gay/ Lesbian Switchboard
713/529-3211 *24hrs*

Houston LGBT Center 3400 Montrose, Ste 207 **713/521-1000** *2pm-9pm, noon-5pm Sat, 10am-6pm Sun*

Lambda AA Center [WC] 1201 W Clay (btwn Montrose & Waugh)
713/521-1243

■ACCOMMODATIONS

Crocker Street Inn [M,SW,V,GO] 2609 Crocker St (at Pacific) **713/529-3277, 877/642-9466** *B&B, near popular gay bars & restaurants*

The Lovett Inn

Houston's Only Gay-Owned Inn Hosting Gay & Lesbian Travelers

Jacuzzi Suites ▼ Pool and Hot Tub ▼ Continental Breakfast
Walking Distance to Bars and Restaurants
Close to Museums, Downtown, and Medical Center

You'll Love It!

501 Lovett Blvd. • Houston, Texas • 77006 • 713.522.5224
800.779.5224 • lovettinn@aol.com • www.lovettinn.com

Texas • USA

Gar-Den Suites [MO,SW,NS,GO]
2702 Crocker St #1 (at Westheimer)
713/528-2302, 800/484-1036
x2669 *nudity ok at hot tub & pool*

▶ **The Lovett Inn** [★GS,SW,NS,GO]
501 Lovett Blvd, Montrose (at Whitney)
713/522-5224, 800/779-5224
sundeck, hot tub

Montrose Inn [M,GO] 408 Avondale (at Taft) 713/520-0206, 800/357-1228 *full brkfst, 'our motto: basic & butch'*

Patrician B&B Inn [GF]
1200 Montrose Blvd (at San Jacinto)
713/523-1114, 800/553-5797
1919 three-story mansion, full brkfst

■ BARS

The 611 Club [★M,NH] 611 Hyde Park (at Stanford) 713/526-7070 *7am-2am, from noon-2am Sun*

Brazos River Bottom (BRB)
[★M,D,CW] 2400 Brazos (btwn Hadley & McIlhenny) 713/528-9192 *noon-2am*

Briar Patch [M,NH,P] 2312 Crocker St (at Fairview) 713/665-9678 *4pm-2am*

The Bricks II [M,NH,CW] 617 Fairview (at Stanford) 713/528-8102 *7am-2am, from noon Sun, patio*

Chances [MW,D,E,WC] 1100 Westheimer (at Waugh) 713/523-7217 *2pm-2am, from noon wknds*

Cousins [MW,NH,DS] 817 Fairview (at Converse) 713/528-9204 *11am-2am, from noon Sun*

Decades [MW,NH] 1205 Richmond (btwn Mandel & Montrose)
713/521-2224 *11am-2am, from noon Sun*

EJ's [M,D,E] 2517 Ralph (at Westheimer) 713/527-9071 *7am-2am, from 10am Sun*

Guava Lamp [MW,K,C,DS,WC]
2159 Portsmouth (btwn Shepherd & Greenbriar, in Shepherd Plaza)
713/524-3359 *4pm-2am, swanky lounge, karaoke Wed & Sun*

JR's [★M,K,DS,S,V,WC] 808 Pacific (at Grant) 713/522-2519 *noon-2am, karaoke Th-Sun, patio*

Keys West [MW,NH,P] 817 W Dallas (btwn Arthur & Crosby) 713/571-7870 *3pm-2am, large 2-level deck*

Mary's [★MW,NH,L,S,WC]
1022 Westheimer (at Waugh)
713/527-9669 *7am-2am, from 10am Sun, also patio bar*

Meteor [M,V,GO] 2306 Genesee (at Fairview) 713/521-0123 *4pm-2am, from 6pm Sat, 3pm-midnight Sun*

Michael's Outpost [M,NH,CW,DS] 1419 Richmond (at Mandell) 713/520-8446 *11am-2am, from noon Sun*

Montrose Mining Co [★M,L]
805 Pacific (at Grant) 713/529-7488 *4pm-2am, from 1pm wknds, patio*

Ripcord [M,L,WC] 715 Fairview (at Crocker) 713/521-2792 *1pm-2am, till 4am Fri-Sat*

■ NIGHTCLUBS

Inergy [★MW,D,MR-L,K,DS,V]
5750 Chimney Rock (at Glenmont)
713/666-7310 *8pm-2am, clsd Mon-Tue*

Numbers [GF,D,E,YC] 300 Westheimer (at Taft) 713/526-6551 *live music*

O [M,D,MR,TG,DS,S,V,WC] 710 Pacific St (at Crocker) 713/523-0213 *3pm-2am, from 1pm Sun, garden patio, after-hours wknds, 18+ Th & Sat*

Ranch Hill Saloon
[MW,NH,D,CW,E,K,W,SO,GO] 2111 Airport Rd (at N Loop 336), Conroe
936/441-6426 *4pm-2am, from 6pm Sat, from 2pm Sun, karaoke Th*

Rich's [★M,D,A,E,DS,S,V,18+] 2401 San Jacinto (at McIlhenny) 713/759-9606 *9pm-4am, clsd Sun-Wed, 18+ Th-Fri*

South Beach Nightclub [M,D,S]
810 Pacific 713/529-7236 *9pm-5am, clsd Mon-Tue*

Toyz [M,D,MR-LS] 5322 Glenmont (at Chimney Rock) 713/668-4892 *Th-Sun*

Viviana's Night Club [M,D,MR-L] 5219 Washington 713/862-0203 *5pm-2am*

■ CAFES

Diedrich Coffee 4005 Montrose (btwn Richmond & W Alabama)
713/526-1319 *5:30am-11pm, till midnight Fri-Sat, 7am-10pm Sun*

■ RESTAURANTS

Baba Yega's [★WC] 2607 Grant (at Pacific) 713/522-0042 *11am-10pm, till 11pm Fri-Sat, full bar, patio*

Houston • Texas

Barnaby's Cafe [★BW,WC]
604 Fairview (btwn Stanford & Hopkins St) **713/522-0106** *11am-10pm, till 11pm Fri-Sat; also 1701 S Shepard, 713/520-5131*

Black-Eyed Pea [★WC] 2048 W Gray (at Shepherd) **713/523-0200** *11am-10pm, Southern*

Brasil [BW] 2604 Dunlavy (at Westheimer) **713/528-1993** *9am-2am, bistro, plenty veggie*

Cafe Annie 1728 Post Oak Blvd (at San Felipe) **713/840-1111** *lunch Mon-Fri, dinner Mon-Sat, clsd Sun*

Captain Benny's Half Shell [BW] 8506 S Main **713/666-5469** *lunch & dinner, clsd Sun*

Chapultepec [BW] 813 Richmond (btwn Montrose & Main) **713/522-2365** *24hrs, Mexican*

House of Pies [★] 3112 Kirby (at Richmond/ Alabama) **713/528-3816** *24hrs*

Java Java Cafe [★] 911 W 11th (at Shepherd) **713/880-5282** *brkfst & lunch*

Magnolia Bar & Grill [WC] 6000 Richmond Ave (at Fountain View Dr) **713/781-6207** *Cajun, full bar*

Ming's Cafe 2703 Montrose (at Westheimer) **713/529-7888** *11am-10pm, Chinese*

Mo Mong 1201 Westheimer #B (at Montrose) **713/524-5664** *11am-11pm, till midnight Fri-Sat, Vietnamese, full bar*

Ninfa's [★] 2704 Navigation **713/228-1175** *11am-10pm, Mexican, full bar*

Ninos 2817 W Dallas (btwn Montrose & Waugh Dr) **713/522-5120** *lunch Mon-Fri, dinner Mon-Sat, clsd Sun, Italian, full bar*

Spanish Flower [BW] 4701 N Main (at Airline) **713/869-1706** *24hrs, till 10pm Tue, Mexican*

Longview • Texas

■ ENTERTAINMENT & RECREATION

After Hours KPFT 90.1 FM **713/526-4000** *midnight-3am Sat, lgbt radio, also Queer Voices 8pm Mon*

■ BOOKSTORES

Lobo—Houston [WC] 3939 Montrose Blvd (at Alabama) **713/522-5156** *9am-midnight, lgbt books & videos, also cafe*

■ RETAIL SHOPS

Lucia's Garden 2216 Portsmouth (at Greenbriar) **713/523-6494** *clsd Sun, spiritual herb center*

■ PUBLICATIONS

Houston Voice **713/529-8490** *lgbt newspaper*

OutSmart **713/520-7237** *free monthly lgbt newsmagazine*

Texas Triangle 315 W Alabama, Ste 101 **713/521-5822, 877/903-8407** *lgbt weekly newspaper w/ arts calendar & statewide resource list*

■ GYMS & HEALTH CLUBS

Fitness Exchange [GF] 4040 Milam **713/524-9932**

Houston Gym [GF,GO] 1501 Durham Rd (at Washington & Shepherd) **713/880-9191** *6am-10pm, 8am-6pm wknds*

YMCA Downtown [GF,SW] 1600 Louisiana St (btwn Pease & Bell) **713/659-8501**

■ MEN'S CLUBS

➤ **The Club Houston** [★SW,PC] 2205 Fannin (at W Gray) **713/659-4998** *24hrs*

The Meat Rack [B,L,MR,18+,PC,GO] 2915 San Jacinto (at Elgin) **713/528-2028** *24hrs wknds*

➤ **Midtowne Spa—Houston** [★SW,PC] 3100 Fannin (at Elgin) **713/522-2379** *24hrs*

■ MEN'S SERVICES

➤ **Megaphone Houston** **800/289-1489** *Call for the local # nearest you! Meet Hot Men in your area! FREE to Browse & Respond to voice ads. Use code 3087. Also try MEGAMATES.COM*

■ EROTICA

BJ's 24 Hour News 6314 Gulf Fwy **713/649-9241** *24hrs*

Diners News 240 Westheimer (at Mason) **713/522-9679** *24hrs*

Eros 1207 [GO] 1207 Spencer Hwy (at Allen Genoa) **713/944-6010**

Leather Forever 604 Westheimer **713/526-6940**

Kilgore

■ EROTICA

Texas Adult Video [GS,GO] 1907 Industrial Blvd **903/986-2090** *10am-1am, large selection of gay erotica*

Lampasas

■ CRUISY AREAS

William Brook Park at Sulphur Creek [AYOR]

Laredo

■ CRUISY AREAS

Lake Casa Blanca [AYOR]

Lexington

■ ACCOMMODATIONS

Hoot-N-Holler Ranch [M,GO] 2143 County Rd 413 (at County Rd 412) **512/446-4614** *camping, guest rooms & bunkhouse, full brkfst, hot tub*

Longview

■ BARS

Decisions [MW,D,CW,DS,WC] 2103 E Marshall (2 blks E of Eastman Rd) **903/757-4884** *5pm-2am, DJ Fri-Sun, 3 bars, drag shows Fri & Sun*

Down South [M,NH,BW,BYOB,GO] 1204 S Hwy 31 **903/553-1546** *4pm-midnight, till 2am Fri-Sat, clsd Sun-Mon*

■ CRUISY AREAS

Hensley Park [AYOR]

Teague Park [AYOR]

Texas • USA

Lubbock

INFO LINES & SERVICES
AA Lambda 4501 University Ave (at MCC) **806/792-5562** *8pm Fri*

NIGHTCLUBS
Club Luxor [GS,D,DS] 2211 4th St (at V) **806/744-3744** *9pm-close Th-Sun*

CRUISY AREAS
McKenzie Park [AYOR]

Merkel

EROTICA
Adult Etc I 9210 I-20/ Rte 1 Box 5-E (exit 270) **915/928-3894** *24hrs*

Mt Vernon

ACCOMMODATIONS
The Veranda [MW,F,SW,NS] Hwy 21 (at Country Rd 4115) **903/588-2402** *B&B on 68 private acres, lake, jacuzzi, gourmet restaurant Fri-Sat*

Odessa/Midland

EROTICA
B&L Adult Bookstore 5890 W University Blvd (at Mercury) **915/381-6855**

County Line 6947 Commerce **915/552-0055** *24hrs*

Plano

RESTAURANTS
Roy's Hawaiian Seafood [WC] 2840 Dallas Pkwy (btwn Park & Parker) **972/473-6263** *5:30pm-9pm, till 10pm Wed-Th, till 11pm Fri-Sat, Hawaiian fusion*

Port Aransas

ACCOMMODATIONS
The Belles by the Sea [GS,SW,NS] **361/749-6138** *Euro-style inn on dunes of Mustang Island & Port Aransas, hot tub*

Rio Grande Valley

ACCOMMODATIONS
La Mirada Country Estates [GF,SW,NS,GO] 8901 W Business Hwy 83 (at Tamm Ln), Harlingen **956/343-5059** *hot tub, clubhouse, also camping & RV hookups*

BARS
PBD's [M,D,DS,S,WC] 2908 Ware Rd (at Daffodil), McAllen **956/682-8019** *8pm-2am, strippers Fri-Sat*

San Angelo

CRUISY AREAS
Downtown River [AYOR]

San Antonio

INFO LINES & SERVICES
Gay/ Lesbian Community Center of San Antonio (GLCCSA) [WC] 611 E Myrtle **210/223-6106** *11am-8pm, noon-6pm Sun*

Lambda Club AA 210/223-6106 (Ctr #)

ACCOMMODATIONS
Adams House B&B [GS] 231 Adams St (at S Alamo) **210/224-4791, 800/666-4810** *full brkfst, also carriage house*

Alamo Condo [MW,SW,GO] 102 Vassar Ln #1 **210/826-2066, 800/708-4681 x81** *fully furnished private 1-bdrm luxury condo*

Arbor House Suites B&B [GS,WC,GO] 109 Arciniega (btwn S Alamo & S St Mary's) **210/472-2005, 888/272-6700** *hot tub*

The Garden Cottage [GF,SW,NS] **210/828-7815** *private cottage*

➤ **The Painted Lady Inn on Broadway** [★MW,GO] 620 Broadway (at 6th) **210/220-1092** *full brkfst, private art deco suites, rooftop deck & spa*

Shady Lady Lakeshore Lodge [MW,GO] 118 Lakeshore Dr (at Whartons Dock Rd), Bandera **830/796-7001** *guest house, located on Lake Medina*

San Antonio • Texas

■BARS

2015 Place [M,NH] 2015 San Pedro (at Woodlawn) **210/733-3365** *4pm-2am, patio*

The Annex [M,NH,WC] 330 San Pedro Ave (at Euclid) **210/223-6957** *2pm-2am, cruise bar, patio*

Cobalt Club [MW,NH,S,WC] 2022 McCullough **210/734-2244** *10am-2am, from noon Sun*

Fusion [MW,D,CW,WC] 1818 N Main (at Dewey) **210/732-0333** *8pm-2am Wed-Sun, also martini bar*

Gotham [GS,NH,WC] 223 3rd St (at N Alamo) **210/527-1707** *11am-2am, from noon Sun*

The Hideout [MW,NH,D,WC] 5307 McCullough (near Basse) **210/828-4222** *4pm-2am, patio*

One-Oh-Six Off Broadway [M,NH,F,OC] 106 Pershing St (at Broadway) **210/820-0906** *noon-2am, steak night Th*

Pegasus [M,S] 1402 N Main (btwn Laurel & Evergreen) **210/299-4222** *2pm-2am, strippers*

Silver Dollar Saloon [M,D,CW,K,S,WC] 1418 N Main Ave (at Laurel) **210/227-2623** *2pm-2am, 2-story patio bar*

■NIGHTCLUBS

The Bonham Exchange [★MW,D,V,18+,GO] 411 Bonham St (at 3rd/ Houston) **210/271-3811** *4pm-2am, from 8pm wknds, till 4am Fri-Sat, in 111-yr-old mansion*

Heat [M,D,S] 1500 N Main Ave (at Evergreen) **210/227-2600** *2pm-2am, Sun T-dance from 7pm*

The Saint [MW,D,A,S,18+] 1430 N Main (at Evergreen) **210/225-7330** *9pm-2am, till 4am Sat*

■CAFES

Candlelight Coffeehouse 3011 N St Mary's (at Rte 281) **210/738-0099** *4pm-midnight, till 1am wknds, clsd Mon*

VOTED MOST ROMANTIC AND BEST B&B IN SAN ANTONIO*

The Painted Lady Inn

Luxurious suites and guestrooms, some with jacuzzi tubs and fireplaces. Six blocks to the River Walk. Near major convention hotels, convention center, bars, clubs. Rates $109-$219, includes breakfast delivered to your room.

210-220-1092
WWW.THEPAINTEDLADYINN.COM

*BY "TEXAS TRIANGLE" AND "SA CURRENT"

Texas • USA

■ RESTAURANTS

Giovanni's Pizza & Italian Restaurant 913 S Brazos (at Guadalupe) **210/212-6626** *10am-8pm, clsd wknds*

Lulu's Jailhouse Cafe [WC] 918 N Main (at W Elmira) **210/224-5001** *7am-5pm, till 10pm Fri-Sun, Tex-Mex*

Madhatter's Tea [BYOB,WC] 320 Beauregard **210/212-4832** *7am-9pm, 9am-10pm wknds, Sun brunch, patio*

El Mirador [BW,WC] 722 S St Mary's St (at Durango St) **210/225-9444** *6:30am-9pm, till 3pm Mon, till 10pm Fri-Sat, 9am-2pm Sun, Tex-Mex, plenty veggie, patio*

■ RETAIL SHOPS

Backbone Body Mods 4741 Fredericksburg Rd (off Loop 10) **210/349-6637** *2pm-9pm, till 11pm Fri-Sat, clsd Sun, piercing*

Dark Fire Gallery 7126 Eckhert Rd #8 **210/682-3500** *2pm-7pm Wed or by appt, pride, BDSM & fetish items*

On Main 2514 N Main (btwn Woodlawn & Mistletoe) **210/737-2323** *10am-6pm, till 5pm Sat, clsd Sun, gifts, cards & T-shirts*

ZEBRAZ.com 1608 N Main **210/472-2800, 800/788-4729** *10am-10pm, lgbt dept store, also online version*

■ MEN'S CLUBS

Alternative Clubs [SW,PC] 827 E Elmira St (at St Mary's) **210/223-2177** *24hrs wknds*

Executive Health Club [PC] 1121 Basse Rd (at San Pedro) **210/732-4433** *24hrs*

■ MEN'S SERVICES

➤ **Megaphone San Antonio** **800/289-1489** *Call for the local # nearest you! Meet Hot Men in your area! FREE to Browse & Respond to voice ads. Use code 3087. Also try MEGAMATES.COM*

■ EROTICA

Apollo News 2376 Austin Hwy (at Walzem) **210/653-3538** *24hrs*

Broadway News 2202 Broadway (at Appler St) **210/223-2034**

Encore Video 1031 NE Loop 410 **210/821-5345**

■ CRUISY AREAS

Please Note: All cruisy areas for San Antonio have been removed because the San Antonio Park Rangers aggressively police these areas.

Shelbyville

■ ACCOMMODATIONS

English Bay Marina [GS,F,WC,GO] 186 D English Ln **936/368-2554** *motel, cabins & RV hookups, also cafe*

South Padre Island

■ ACCOMMODATIONS

New Upper Deck Hotel & Bar [M,SW,N,WC,GO] 120 E Atol (at Padre Blvd) **956/761-5953** *bar open from 2pm (5pm off-season)*

■ CRUISY AREAS

Andy Bowie Beach [AYOR]

Atol Beach [AYOR]

The Jetties [AYOR] County Park, at S end

Terrel

■ EROTICA

Romantix Adult Etc V 6086 W Hwy 80 **972/524-1449**

Tyler

■ NIGHTCLUBS

Outlaws [GF,D,18+] Hwy 110 (4 miles S of Loop 323) **903/509-2248** *more gay Wed*

■ CRUISY AREAS

Bergfield Park [AYOR]

Fun Forest Park [AYOR]

Waco

■ INFO LINES & SERVICES

Gay/ Lesbian Alliance of Central Texas **254/715-6501** *info, newsletter*

■ CRUISY AREAS

Cameron Park [AYOR]

Midway Park [AYOR]

Park City • Utah

Wichita Falls

BARS
Odds [MW,D,K,DS,BW] 1205 Lamar (at 12th) **940/322-2996** *3pm-2am*

NIGHTCLUBS
Club Cloud 9 [M,D,K,DS,V,18+,BW,BYOB,GO] 311 E Scott (at Jacksboro Hwy) **940/723-2264** *3pm-2am, till 3am Fri-Sat*

CRUISY AREAS
Lucy Park [AYOR]

Wimberley

ACCOMMODATIONS
Bella Vista [MW,SW,NS,WC,GO] 2121 Hilltop **512/847-6425**

UTAH

Boulder

ACCOMMODATIONS
Eagle Star Ranch [GF,GO] 330 E Boulder Pines Rd **435/335-7438** *working 350-acre ranch*

Capitol Reef

ACCOMMODATIONS
Capitol Reef Inn & Cafe [GF] 360 W Main St, Torrey **435/425-3271** *seasonal, hot tub, also restaurant* [BW]

Escalante

ACCOMMODATIONS
Rainbow Country B&B [GF,NS] **435/826-4567, 800/252-8824** *full brkfst, hot tub*

Logan

CRUISY AREAS
Logan Canyon [AYOR] *Zanavoo loop*

Moab

ACCOMMODATIONS
Los Vados Canyon House [GS,SW,NS,GO] **801/971-3325** *retreat house in a red rock canyon*

Mayor's House B&B [GF,SW,NS,GO] 505 East Rosetree Ln (at 400 E) **435/259-3019, 888/791-2345** *hot tub, full brkfst*

Mt Peale Resort Inn & Spa [★GS,NS,GO] 1415 East Hwy 64, mile post 14.1 (at mile mark 14.1), Old La Sal **435/686-2284, 888/687-3253** *B&B, full brkfst, hot tub*

Red Cliffs Lodge [GF,SW,WC] Hwy 128, mile post 14 **435/259-2002, 866/812-2002** *resort, on Colorado River, hot tub*

Monument Valley

ACCOMMODATIONS
Pioneer House Inn [GF] **435/672-2446, 888/637-2582** *full brkfst, also guided tours*

Ogden

ACCOMMODATIONS
North Fork B&B [M,NS,GO] **801/745-8350** *in 4,000-sq-ft home, 1 hour from Salt Lake, jacuzzi, weight room*

BARS
Brass Rail [★MW,D,F,DS,PC] 103 27th St (at Wall) **801/399-1543** *5:30pm-1am, 3pm-2am Fri-Sat, 2pm-midnight Sun, DJ Th-Sat, women's night Fri*

CRUISY AREAS
Mount Ogden Park [AYOR]

Pine View Reservoir [AYOR] *Cemetery Point*

Park City

ACCOMMODATIONS
1904 Imperial Hotel [GF] 221 Main St **435/649-1904, 800/669-8824** *B&B, full brkfst, hot tub*

The Old Miners Lodge—A B&B Inn [GF,NS] **435/645-8068, 800/648-8068** *full brkfst, hot tub*

Resort Property Management **800/243-2932**

Utah • USA

Salt Lake City

■ INFO LINES & SERVICES

Gay & Lesbian Community Center of Utah 355 N 300 W, 1st flr 801/539-8800, 888/874-2743 *info, resource center, mtgs, coffee shop, programs & much more*

■ ACCOMMODATIONS

Anton Boxrud B&B [GF] 57 S 600 E (at S Temple) 801/363-8035, 800/524-5511 *full brkfst, hot tub*

Hotel Monaco Salt Lake City [GF,WC] 15 W 200 S 801/595-0000, 877/294-9710 *restaurant & bar, gym*

Maple Grove B&B [GF,NS,GO] 539 E 3rd Ave 801/322-5372 *hot tub, shared baths*

Parrish Place [GS,NS,GO] 720 E Ashton Ave 801/832-0970, 888/832-0869 *Victorian mansion, hot tub*

Peery Hotel [★GF,WC] 110 W 300 S 801/521-4300, 800/331-0073 *full brkfst, also 2 restaurants, full bar*

Ric's Place [MO,NS,GO] 1272 E 1300 S (at 13th E) 801/466-6747 *private home*

Saltair B&B/ Alpine Cottages [★GF,NS] 164 S 900 E 801/533-8184, 800/733-8184 *full brkfst, hot tub*

Under the Lindens [M,NS,GO] 128 S 1000 E 801/355-9808 *studios, hot tub*

■ BARS

Bourbon St Bar & Grille [GS,NH,F,V] 372 S State St 801/521-8358 *11am-2am*

Club Try-Angles [M,NH,D,F,PC,GO] 251 W 900 S 801/364-3203 *2pm-2am*

The Galley [MW,F,BW] 64 W 400 S 801/961-9900 *24hrs, also diner & cafe*

Radio City [M,WC] 147 S State St (btwn 1st & 2nd) 801/532-9327 *10am-1am, beer only*

Todd's Bar & Grill [GF,NH,D,F,E,K,V,PC,GO] 1051 S 300 W (at 900 S) 801/328-8650 *10am-2am, more gay Wed*

The Trapp Door [MW,D,CW,PC,WC] 615 W 1st S 801/531-8727, 801/531-8728 *11am-1am, patio, food Sun*

■ NIGHTCLUBS

Bricks Tavern [★GS,D,E,K,V,18+,PC] 579 W 200 S (at 600 W) 801/328-0255 *9:30pm-2am, patio, live bands*

Club Axis [★GS,D,S,V,18+,PC] 100 S 500 W (at 100 S) 801/519-2947 *9:30pm-close, gay night Fri*

Club Manhattan [GF,D,F] 5 E 400 S 801/364-7651 *lunch & dinner, live music*

Club Naked [GS,D,PC] 326 S West Temple 801/521-9292 *9:30pm-2am, clsd Mon*

Club Splash [M,D,DS] 404 S West Temple 801/363-2623 *gay Tue only*

Zipperz [M,D,K,S,V,PC,GO] 155 W 200 S (at 200 W) 801/521-8300 *4pm-2am, strippers Sat*

■ CAFES

Angles 511 W 200 S 801/961-8218 *also deli & gallery*

Coffee Garden [WC] 898 E 900 S 801/355-3425 *6:30am-11pm, till midnight wknds*

Cup of Joe 353 W 200 S (btwn 300 & 400 W) 801/363-8322 *7am-midnight, internet access*

■ RESTAURANTS

Baci Trattoria [WC] 134 W Pierport Ave 801/328-1333 *lunch & dinner, dinner only Sat, clsd Sun, full bar*

Lambs Restaurant [WC] 169 S Main St 801/364-7166 *7am-9pm, till 8pm Sat, clsd Sun*

Market St Grill [WC] 48 W Market St 801/322-4668 *brkfst, lunch & dinner, Sun brunch, seafood/ steak, full bar*

Rio Grande Cafe [★] 270 S Rio Grande 801/364-3302 *lunch & dinner, Mexican, full bar*

■ ENTERTAINMENT & RECREATION

Concerning Gays & Lesbians KRCL 90.9 FM 801/363-1818 *12:30pm Wed*

Salt Lake City • Utah

Lambda Hiking Club 700 E 200 S (S of Chevron station) **801/532-8447** *9am 1st & 3rd Sat (May-Nov), 10am (Dec-April)*

■ BOOKSTORES

Golden Braid Books 151 S 500 E **801/322-1162, 801/322-0404 (cafe)** *10am-9pm, also Oasis Cafe, 7am-9pm, from 8am wknds*

■ RETAIL SHOPS

Cahoots [WC,GO] 878 E 900 S (at 900 E) **801/538-0606** *10am-9pm, unique gift shop*

Cockers 602 E 500 S (on upper level of Trolley Square) **801/359-0406** *10am-9pm, noon-5pm Sun, men's athletic wear, club clothing, underwear, etc*

Gypsy Moon Emporium 1011 E 900 S **801/521-9100** *hours vary, New Age*

■ PUBLICATIONS

The Pillar of the Gay/Lesbian Community 801/265-0066 *lgbt*

■ MEN'S SERVICES

➤ **Dennis Massage** [MO] **801/598-8344** *full-body massage for men*

➤ **Megaphone Salt Lake City 800/289-1489** *Call for the local # nearest you! Meet Hot Men in your area! FREE to Browse & Respond to voice ads. Use code 3087. Also try MEGAMATES.COM*

■ EROTICA

All For Love [TG,WC] 3072 S Main St (at 33rd St S) **801/487-8358** *clsd Sun, lingerie & S/M boutique*

Blue Boutique 2106 S 1100 E (at 2100 S) **801/485-2072** *also piercing*

Hayat's Magazines & Gifts 1350 S State St (at 13th St S) **801/486-9925**

Mischievous 559 S 300 W (at 6th S St) **801/530-3100** *clsd Sun*

Video One 484 S 900 W **801/524-9883** *also cult & art films*

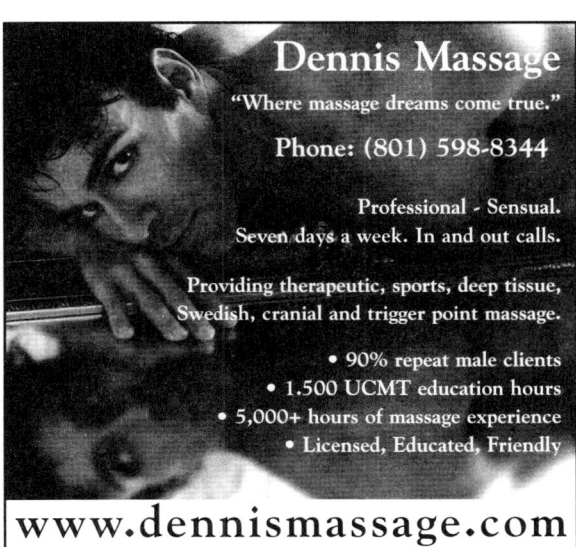

Dennis Massage
"Where massage dreams come true."

Phone: (801) 598-8344

Professional - Sensual.
Seven days a week. In and out calls.

Providing therapeutic, sports, deep tissue, Swedish, cranial and trigger point massage.

- 90% repeat male clients
- 1.500 UCMT education hours
- 5,000+ hours of massage experience
- Licensed, Educated, Friendly

www.dennismassage.com

Utah • USA

■ CRUISY AREAS

Memory Grove [AYOR] Canyon Rd (below the Capitol, on the E side)

Sugarhouse Park [AYOR] 21st S *also btwn 13th & 17th E*

Torrey

■ ACCOMMODATIONS

SkyRidge Inn B&B [GF,NS] 435/425-3222 *full brkfst, hot tubs, near Capitol Reef Nat'l Park*

Zion Nat'l Park

■ ACCOMMODATIONS

Red Rock Inn [GS,NS,WC,GO] 998 Zion Park Blvd, Springdale 435/772-3139 *cottages w/ canyon views, full brkfst, hot tub*

VERMONT

Statewide

■ ENTERTAINMENT & RECREATION

The Vermont Rainbow Connection 802/849-2739 x3 *TV show by & for VT's lgbt community, call for channels & show times*

■ PUBLICATIONS

► In Newsweekly 617/426-8246 *New England's largest lgbt newspaper*

Out in the Mountains (OITM) PO Box 1078, Richmond 05477-1078 *monthly newspaper covering Vermont & beyond*

Andover

■ ACCOMMODATIONS

The Inn At HighView [GS,F,SW,NS,GO] 753 E Hill Rd 802/875-2724 *full brkfst*

Arlington

■ RESTAURANTS

Arlington Inn Rte 7-A 802/375-6532, 800/443-9442 *dinner from 5:30pm, clsd Sun-Mon*

■ CRUISY AREAS

Battenkill River Beach [N,AYOR] *trails too*

Brattleboro

■ ACCOMMODATIONS

The Maples of Poocham [GS,GO] Poocham Rd (at Paine Rd), Westmoreland, NH 603/399-8457, 800/659-6810 *B&B, near hiking & ski trails*

■ BARS

Rainbow Cattle Company [MW,D,K,DS,WC] Rte 5 (btwn exits 3 & 4, off I-91), Dummerston 802/254-9830 *8pm-2am, clsd Mon-Wed*

■ RESTAURANTS

Common Ground [BW] 25 Elliott St (at Main) 802/257-0855 *lunch & dinner, Sun brunch, vegetarian/ vegan*

Peter Haven's [GO] 32 Elliott St (at Main) 802/257-3333 *6pm-10pm, clsd Sun-Mon, cont'l*

■ BOOKSTORES

Everyone's Books [WC] 25 Elliott St 802/254-8160 *9:30am-6pm, till 8pm Fri, from 10am Sat, 11am-5pm Sun*

Bridgewater Corners

■ RESTAURANTS

Blanche & Bill's Pancake House US Rte 4 802/422-3816 *7am-2pm Wed-Sun, great flapjacks & maple syrup*

Burlington

■ INFO LINES & SERVICES

R.U.1.2? Community Center 802/860-RU12 (7812) *social/ support groups, events*

■ ACCOMMODATIONS

The Black Bear Inn [GS,SW,NS,WC,GO] 4010 Bolton Access Rd, Bolton Valley 802/434-2126, 800/395-6335 *full brkfst, hot tub*

■ BARS

135 Pearl [GS,D,K,C] 135 Pearl St 802/863-2343 *7:30pm-2am, from 5pm Fri-Sat, smokefree dance flr Fri-Sat*

Manchester • Vermont

■ RESTAURANTS

Daily Planet 15 Center St (at College) 802/862-9647 *11:30am-10:30pm, dinner only summers, bar till 1am*

Loretta's [GO] 44 Park St (near 5 Corners), Essex Junction 802/879-7777 *lunch Tue-Fri, dinner Tue-Sat, Italian*

Parima Thai 185 Pearl St 802/864-7917 *5pm-9pm, till 10pm Fri-Sat, courtyard garden*

Silver Palace 1216 Williston Rd 802/864-0125 *lunch & dinner, Chinese, full bar*

■ RETAIL SHOPS

Peace & Justice Store 21 Church St (at Pearl) 802/863-8326 *10am-6pm, till 8pm Fri-Sat, noon-5pm Sun, pride store, books*

■ CRUISY AREAS

Battery Park [AYOR] N Public Beach

The Fruit Loop [AYOR] downtown Bank, College & St Pauls Sts

Chester

■ ACCOMMODATIONS

Chester House Inn [GS,NS,WC,GO] 266 Main St 802/875-2205, 888/875-2205 *inn circa 1780, also restaurant* [BW]

The Stone Hearth Inn [GS,GO] 698 Rte 11 W 802/875-2525, 888/617-3656 *full brkfst, hot tub*

Dorset

■ CRUISY AREAS

Dorset Quarry [AYOR] on Rte 30 & Kelly Rd

Jay Peak

■ ACCOMMODATIONS

Grey Gables Mansion [GF] 122 River St, Richford 802/848-3625 *ca-1888 B&B inn, full brkfst, available for civil unions & receptions*

Killington

■ ACCOMMODATIONS

Cortina Inn & Resort [GF,F,WC] Rte 4 802/773-3333, 800/451-6108 *hot tub, also tavern*

The Salt Ash Inn [GS,F,SW,GO] 4758 Rte 100A (at Rte 100) 802/672-3748, 800/725-8274 *1830s country inn, full brkfst, hot tub, pub, near skiing*

Ludlow

■ ACCOMMODATIONS

Happy Trails Motel [GF] 321 Rte 103 S 802/228-8888 *seasonal hot tub, near skiing*

■ CRUISY AREAS

Buttermilk Falls [AYOR] off Rte 103, toward Rutland

Lyndonville

■ RESTAURANTS

Miss Lyndonville Diner Rte 5 802/626-9890 *6am-8pm*

Manchester

■ CAFES

Little Rooster Cafe Rte 7-A, Manchester Center 802/362-3496 *7am-2:30pm, clsd Wed (winters)*

■ RESTAURANTS

Bistro Henry [R] Manchester Village 802/362-4982 *dinner only, clsd Mon, Mediterranean, also bar*

The Black Swan [WC] Rte 7-A S 802/362-3807 *dinner from 5:30pm, clsd Wed, cont'l/ game*

Chanticleer Rte 7-A N, Manchester Center 802/362-1616 *clsd Mon-Tue (winter), clsd Tue (summer)*

■ BOOKSTORES

Northshire Bookstore 4869 Main St, Manchester Center 802/362-2200 *10am-9pm, till 7pm Sun-Th (seasonal)*

Vermont • USA

Marlboro

ACCOMMODATIONS

Colonel Williams Inn [GS,F,NS,WC] Rte 9 (at Staver Rd) **802/257-1093, 877/765-6639** *1769 farmhouse, full brkfst, hot tub, also restaurant*

RESTAURANTS

Skyline Restaurant [WC] Rte 9, Hogback Mountain **802/464-5535** *8am-3pm, till 8pm Fri-Sat, 7:30am-5pm Sun, clsd Tue-Wed (winters)*

Montgomery Center

ACCOMMODATIONS

Phineas Swann B&B [GS,NS,GO] **802/326-4306** *full brkfst*

Montpelier

RESTAURANTS

Julio's 54 State **802/229-9348** *lunch & dinner till midnight, from 4pm Sun, Mexican*

Sarducci's [WC] 3 Main St **802/223-0229** *11:30am-9:30pm, till 10pm wknds, from 4:30pm Sun, Italian, full bar*

Wayside Restaurant [WC] Rte 302 **802/223-6611** *6:30am-9:30pm*

RETAIL SHOPS

Phoenix Rising [GO] 34 State St **802/229-0522** *10am-5:30pm, till 6pm Fri, 11am-5pm Sat, 11am-3pm Sun, metaphysical, jewelry, gifts, pride items*

Newfane

CRUISY AREAS

Rock River [AYOR] Williamsville Rd *nude sunbathing & cruisy woods, park before bridge, cross Rte 30 & walk up Williamsville Rd, take 1st road toward river, follow path about a mile, 3rd & 4th swimming holes are gay*

Richmond

ACCOMMODATIONS

The Spa [GS,SW,NS,GO] 961 Hinesburg-Richmond Rd (at Huntington Rd) **802/434-3846** *mostly women, overnight health spa, exercise room*

Rutland

ACCOMMODATIONS

The Inn of the Six Mountains [GF,SW,WC] 2617 Killington Rd, Killington **802/422-4302, 800/228-4676** *hotel, full brkfst, jacuzzi*

Lilac Inn 53 Park St, Brandon **802/247-5463, 800/221-0720** *full brkfst*

Maplewood Inn [GF,NS] Rte 22-A S, Fair Haven **802/265-8039, 800/253-7729** *1843 Greek Revival B&B w/ beautiful antiques, full brkfst*

EROTICA

AA Video & Books 156 West St **802/773-8990** *clsd Sun*

CRUISY AREAS

Gorge Rd [AYOR] off Rte 7 by airport (1 mile to the Flats) *nude sunbathing by Mill River*

St Albans

RESTAURANTS

Jeff's Maine Seafood 65 N Main St **802/524-6135** *lunch Mon-Sat, dinner Tue-Sat, clsd Sun*

Stowe

ACCOMMODATIONS

Arbor Inn [GS,SW,NS] 3214 Mountain Rd **802/253-4772, 800/543-1293** *full brkfst, hot tub*

Fitch Hill Inn [GS] **802/888-3834, 800/639-2903** *full brkfst, hot tub*

Gardner's Eden [GF,NS] 150 Upper Sky Acres Dr **802/253-8464** *luxury apt rental, hot tub*

The Green Mountain Inn [GF,F,SW] 18 Main St **802/253-7301, 800/253-7302**

Honeywood Inn [GS,SW,NS] 4583 Mountain Rd **802/253-4846, 800/821-7891** *full brkfst, jacuzzi*

Northern Lights Lodge [GF,SW,GO] 4441 Mountain Rd **802/253-8541, 800/448-4554** *full brkfst, hot tub, sauna*

Windham • Vermont

The Old Stagecoach Inn [GF].
18 N Main St (at Stowe St), Waterbury
802/244-5056, 800/262-2206
historic village inn, full brkfst, also full bar

➤ **Timberholm Inn** [GS,GO]
452 Cottage Club Rd **802/253-7603, 800/753-7603** *full brkfst, hot tub*

Winding Brook, A Classic Mountain Lodge [GS,NS,GO] 199 Edson Hill Rd **802/253-7354, 800/426-6697** *rustic mtn retreat*

Stratton Mountain

■ACCOMMODATIONS

Stratton Mountain Inn [GF,SW]
61 Middle Ridge Rd **802/297-2500, 877/887-3767** *resort*

Townshend

■ACCOMMODATIONS

Townshend State Park [GF] 2755 State Forest Rd **802/365-7500** *mid-May to mid-Oct, campground, hiking*

Waterbury

■ACCOMMODATIONS

Grünberg Haus B&B & Cabins [GS,NS] 94 Pine St, Rte 100 S
802/244-7726, 800/800-7760
full brkfst, hot tub

Moose Meadow Lodge [GS,GO]
607 Crossett Hill **802/244-5378** *log home on 86-acre wooded estate, hot tub*

Wilmington

■ACCOMMODATIONS

Averill Stand B&B [MW,GO] 236 Rte 9 East (at Rte 100) **802/464-9951** *1787 farmhouse, near Mt Snow, full brkfst, some shared baths*

Windham

■ACCOMMODATIONS

A Stone Wall Inn [GS,NS,GO] RFD 133
802/875-4238 *B&B inn, hot tub*

Tucked into a quiet, wooded hillside... the perfect place to enjoy a civil union or a romantic Stowe getaway in the beautiful Green Mountains.

800-753-7603
452 Cottage Club Road
Stowe, VT 05672
www.timberholm.com

Gay-Owned and Operated

Vermont • USA

Woodstock

■ACCOMMODATIONS

The Ardmore Inn [GF,NS] 23 Pleasant St **802/457-3887, 800/497-9652** *1880s Greek Revival, full brkfst, jacuzzi*

Cabin in the Woods [GF,SW] 1944 Chateauguay Rd, Bridgewater **802/672-5141** (no calls after 9pm) *secluded rustic cabin, hot tub, swimming hole, fireplace, seasonal May-Oct*

Rosewood Inn [GF,NS] **802/457-4485** *full brkfst*

VIRGINIA

Statewide

■PUBLICATIONS

Shout! 540/529-6363 *entertainment & personals for the Virginias & Carolinas*

➤ **TLW Magazine** 727/522-8888 *Southeast's largest entertainment magazine for gay men*

The Virginia GayZette **804/355-7939** (Richmond #), **757/622-3701** (Norfolk #) *statewide*

Abingdon

■ACCOMMODATIONS

Hunters Island Campground [GF,GO] Hwy 65 (at Coeburn Rd), Dungannon **276/452-2344** *1-bunk cabin & his/her toilets/showers (exclusively for 1 group at a time)*

Alexandria

see also Washington DC

Arlington

see also Washington, District of Columbia

■INFO LINES & SERVICES

Arlington Gay/ Lesbian Alliance **703/522-7660** *monthly mtgs*

■ACCOMMODATIONS

Best Western Arlington Hotel [GF,SW,WC] 2480 S Glebe Rd (at 24th St) **703/979-4400, 800/486-6228** *restaurant & lounge*

■BARS

Freddie's Beach Bar & Restaurant [MW,K,DS,WC] 555 S 23rd St **703/685-0555** *11am-2am, from 4pm Mon, patio*

■CAFES

Java Shack [MW] 2507 N Franklin Rd (at Wilson Blvd & N Barton) **703/527-9556** *7am-10pm, from 8am wknds*

■CRUISY AREAS

Columbia Island Marina [AYOR]

Iwo Jima Memorial [AYOR] *woods*

Ashland

■CAFES

Coffee Talk Cafe 10396 Leadbetter Rd **804/550-0887** *7am-5pm, 7:30am-2pm Sat, clsd Sun, pasta, plenty veggie*

Cape Charles

see also Norfolk & Virginia Beach

■ACCOMMODATIONS

Cape Charles House B&B [GF,NS] 645 Tazewell Ave (at Fig) **757/331-4920** *1912 Colonial Revival home w/ antiques*

Sea Gate B&B [GF,GO] 9 Tazewell Ave **757/331-2206** *full brkfst*

Sterling House B&B [GS,GO] 9 Randolph Ave (at Bay Ave) **757/331-2483** *1913 beach bungalow, full brkfst, hot tub*

Wilson-Lee House B&B [GS,NS,GO] 403 Tazewell Ave **757/331-1954** *full brkfst*

Charlottesville

■INFO LINES & SERVICES

Gay AA 434/293-8227

LGBT Helpline 434/982-2773 *active during school yr*

■ACCOMMODATIONS

Fiddlestick Lane [GS,GO] 1889 Fiddlestick Ln (at 5th St) **434/296-6545** *B&tB, full brkfst*

The Inn at Court Square [GF] 410 E Jefferson St **434/295-2800, 866/466-2877** *period antiques, jacuzzi*

Norfolk • Virginia

Mark Addy Inn [GS,SW,NS,WC,GO]
56 Rodes Farm Dr, Nellysford
434/361-1101, 800/278-2154
full brkfst, tennis, hot tub

The Summer Kitchen B&B [GS,NS,GO]
6482 Dick Woods Rd **540/456-7009**
full brkfst, hot tub, sauna

■ NIGHTCLUBS

Club 216 [★MW,D,S,PC,WC]
218 W Water St (enter on South St)
434/296-8783 *10pm-5am Fri-Sat, some Sun events*

■ RESTAURANTS

Bistro 151 [E] Valley Green Center, Nellysford **434/361-1463** *lunch & dinner, clsd Mon, full bar*

Eastern Standard/ Escafe [E,GO] in West End mall (next to the Omni Hotel) **434/295-8668** *5:30pm-10pm Wed-Sat, Asian/American, also Escafe*

■ CRUISY AREAS
Lee Park [AYOR]

Christiansburg

■ ACCOMMODATIONS

River's Edge [GF,NS] 6208 Little Camp Rd, Riner **540/381-4147, 888/786-9254** *full brkfst*

Danville

■ CRUISY AREAS
Ballou Park [AYOR]

Fairfax

■ CRUISY AREAS
Turkey Run Park [AYOR] off GW Pkwy

Fredericksburg

■ RESTAURANTS

Merrimans [★MW,D,WC] 715 Caroline St (btwn Charlotte & Hanover) **540/371-7723** *lunch & dinner, full bar*

Hampton

see also Newport News

■ CRUISY AREAS
Grandview Shores Beach Park [AYOR]
nude beach past rock mounds

Harrisonburg

■ CAFES

Artful Dodger Coffeehouse [WC]
47 W Court Square **540/432-1179**
8am-11pm, from noon Sun

Lynchburg

■ INFO LINES & SERVICES

Gay/ Lesbian Helpline
434/847-5242 *live 7pm-10pm Mon, Wed & Fri, info for central & SW VA*

■ CRUISY AREAS
Blackwater Creek area [AYOR]
Court Street area [AYOR]

Newport News

see also Norfolk & Virginia Beach

■ BARS

Corner Pocket [MW,NH,F,WC]
3516 Washington Ave (at 36th)
757/247-6366 *4pm-2am, full menu till midnight*

■ EROTICA

Mr D's Leather & Novelties
9902-A Warwick Blvd (at Randolph Rd)
757/599-4070

Norfolk

see also Virginia Beach

■ INFO LINES & SERVICES

Saturday Night Live Gay/ Lesbian AA 1301 Colley Ave (at First Lutheran Church) **757/625-1953 (church #)**
8pm Sat

■ ACCOMMODATIONS

Tazewell Hotel & Suites [GF,WC]
245 Granby St (at Tazewell St)
757/623-6200 *full brkfst*

■ BARS

The Garage [M,NH,F,WC] 731 Granby St (at Brambleton) **757/623-0303** *8am-2am, from noon wknds*

Hershee Bar [W,D,F,E,K,WC]
6117 Sewells Pt Rd (at Norview)
757/853-9842 *4pm-2am*

Nutty Buddy's [M,D,MR,F,DS,WC]
143 E Little Creek Rd **757/588-6474**
4pm-2am Wed-Sun, also restaurant

Virginia • USA

The Wave [M,D,F,S,WC] 4107 Colley Ave (at 41st St) **757/440-5911** *4pm-2am, from 5pm Sat, clsd Sun, male dancers Wed, also restaurant*

CAFES

Oasis Cafe [GO] 142 W York St #101A (in York Center bldg) **757/627-6161** *7:30am-4pm Mon-Fri*

RESTAURANTS

Charlie's Cafe [BW] 1800 Granby St (at 18th) **757/625-0824** *7am-2pm, till 3pm wknds*

Uncle Louie's [E,K,WC] 132 E Little Creek Rd (at Granby) **757/480-1225** *8am-11pm, till midnight Fri-Sat, till 10pm Sun, Jewish fine dining, also bar & deli*

BOOKSTORES

Lambda Rising [WC] 322 W 21st St (at Llewellyn) **757/626-0969** *10am-10pm, lgbt*

Phoenix Rising East 619B Colonial Ave (at Olney) **757/622-3701** *noon-8pm, till 7pm Sun, clsd Mon, lgbt*

MEN'S SERVICES

➤ **Megaphone Norfolk**
800/289-1489 *Call for the local # nearest you! Meet Hot Men in your area! FREE to Browse & Respond to voice ads. Use code 3087. Also try MEGAMATES.COM*

EROTICA

Leather & Lace 149 E Little Creek Rd (at Granby) **757/583-4334** *clsd Sun*

Petersburg

ACCOMMODATIONS

The High Street Inn [GF] 405 High St (at Cross St) **804/733-0505**, **888/733-0505** *Victorian mansion, full brkfst*

➤ **Walker House B&B** [GF,NS,GO] 3280 S Crater Rd (at Wagner) **804/861-5822** *antebellum farmhouse*

Walker House
BED & BREAKFAST
Circa 1815

- 4 lg suites w/new private baths
- Window unit AC, telephones
- Cable TV, VCRs, mini stereos
- Full breakfasts everyday
- Community kitchenette
- Major credit cards accepted

1 mile off I-95 at Exit 48B in Petersburg, Virginia
804-861-5822 • **www.walker-house.com**

Shenandoah Valley • Virginia

■ EROTICA

Thriller Books 1919 E Washington (on Rte 36) **804/733-0064**

Richmond

■ INFO LINES & SERVICES

AA Gay/ Lesbian 804/355-1212

■ ACCOMMODATIONS

Bellmont Manor B&B Inn [GS,SW,NS,WC,GO] 6600 Belmont Rd, Chesterfield **804/745-0106, 800/809-9041 x69** *full brkfst*

■ BARS

Babe's of Carytown [W,D,F,E,WC] 3166 W Cary St (at Auburn) **804/355-9330** *11am-midnight, till 2am Th-Sat, 9am-3pm Sun*

Barcode [M,NH,K,V] 6 E Grace St (btwn 1st & Foushee Sts) **804/648-2040** *11am-2am, from 3pm wknds*

Broadway Cafe & Bar [M,NH,F,BW,WC] 414 E Main St (btwn 4th & 5th) **804/643-9667** *5pm-2am*

Cosmopolitan [MW,NH,TG,F,DS,GO] 3156 West Cary St (at Alburn) **804/355-5527** *11am-2am*

Godfrey's [MW,D,CW,F,K,DS] 308 E Grace St (btwn 3rd & 4th) **804/648-3957** *5pm-2am, lunch daily, drag brunch Sun, clsd Mon-Tue, also restaurant*

■ NIGHTCLUBS

Club Colours [MW,D,MR-AF,F,S,WC] 536 N Harrison St (at Broad) **804/353-9776** *11:30pm-3am Sat*

Fielden's [★M,D,S,BYOB,PC,WC] 2033 W Broad St **804/359-1963** *midnight-close, clsd Mon-Wed, 3 levels*

■ RESTAURANTS

The Village 410 N Harrison **804/353-8204** *8:30am-11:30pm, bar till 2am, American*

■ BOOKSTORES

Carytown Books [WC] 2930 W Cary St (at Sheppard) **804/359-4831** *10am-7pm, till 5pm Sun, lgbt section*

Phoenix Rising [WC] 19 N Belmont Ave **804/355-7939, 800/719-1690** *11am-7pm, lgbt*

■ PUBLICATIONS

Shout! 540/529-6363 *entertainment & personals for the Virginias & Carolinas*

The Virginia GayZette 804/355-7939 (Richmond #), 757/622-3701 (Norfolk#) *statewide lgbt newspaper*

■ MEN'S SERVICES

➤ **Megaphone Richmond** 800/289-1489 *Call for the local # nearest you! Meet Hot Men in your area! FREE to Browse & Respond to voice ads. Use code 3087. Also try MEGAMATES.COM*

■ CRUISY AREAS

Forest Hill Park [AYOR]

Roanoke

■ BARS

Backstreet Cafe [MW,NH,F] 356 Salem Ave (off Jefferson) **540/345-1542** *7pm-2am, till midnight Sun*

Cuba Pete's [GF,NH,F,K,WC] 120 Church Ave SW (at First St SW inside Macado's) **540/342-7231** *11am-2am, more gay wknds, also Macado's restaurant, karaoke Sun*

■ NIGHTCLUBS

The Park [★MW,D,DS,V,YC,WC] 615 Salem Ave **540/342-0946** *9pm-close Fri-Sun*

■ BOOKSTORES

Out Word Connections 129 Salem Ave SW **540/985-6886** *noon-8pm, lgbt*

■ PUBLICATIONS

Blue Ridge Lambda Press 540/344-4444 *covers western VA*

Shout! 540/529-6363 *entertainment & personals for the Virginias & Carolinas*

Shenandoah Valley

■ INFO LINES & SERVICES

SVGLA (Shenandoah Valley Gay/ Lesbian Assoc) 540/574-4636 *24hr touchtone info & weekly mtgs, also dances & potlucks*

Virginia • USA

■ ACCOMMODATIONS

Frog Hollow B&B [GS,GO] 492 Greenhouse Rd (at Rte 11), Lexington **540/463-5444** *full brkfst*

The Olde Staunton Inn [GS] 260 N Lewis St, Staunton **540/886-0193, 866/653-3786** *B&B, hot tub*

Piney Hill B&B [GS,GO] 1048 Piney Hill Rd (at Mill Creek Crossroads), Luray **540/778-5261** *1750s farmhouse in Shenandoah Valley, hot tub*

Twelfth Night Inn [GF] 402 E Beverley St (at Coalter), Staunton **540/885-1733** *full brkfst*

White Fence B&B [GF,NS] 275 Chapel Rd, Stanley **540/778-4680, 800/211-9885** *full brkfst, jacuzzi*

Virginia Beach

see also Norfolk

■ BARS

In Between [MW,F,DS,GO] 5266 Princess Anne Rd (btwn Witchduck & Newton Rds) **757/490-9498** *4pm-2am, from 10am Sun, also restaurant*

Klub Ambush [M,NH,D,F,K,DS,GO] 475 S Lynnhaven Rd (at Lynnhaven Pkwy) **757/498-4301** *5pm-2am*

Rainbow Cactus [M,D,CW,F,K,WC] 3472 Holland Rd (at Diana Lee) **757/368-0441** *7pm-2am, clsd Mon-Tue*

■ PUBLICATIONS

Lambda Directory **757/486-3546**

■ EROTICA

Oceana Video & News 1301 Oceana Blvd **757/428-1498**

Windsor

■ ACCOMMODATIONS

Blackwater Campground [GF,SW] 7651 Whispering Pines Trail **757/357-7211** *RV hook-ups & primitive camping*

WASHINGTON

Auburn

■ CRUISY AREAS

Isaac Evans Park [AYOR] Green River Rd (off 104th Ave SE)

Bellevue

see also Seattle

Bellingham

■ BARS

Rumours [MW,D,F,WC] 1119 Railroad Ave (at Chestnut) **360/671-1849** *4pm-2am*

■ CAFES

Tony's Coffee [WC] 1101 Harris Ave (at 11th), Fairhaven **360/738-4710** *7am-8pm, till 10pm wknds*

■ RESTAURANTS

Skylark's Hidden Cafe [BW] 1308-B 11th St (at McKenzie) **360/715-3642** *7am-9pm, till 10pm Fri-Sat, outdoor seating*

■ BOOKSTORES

Village Books 1210 11th St (at Harris) **360/671-2626** *9am-10pm, 10am-8pm Sun, new & used*

■ RETAIL SHOPS

Kalamalka Studio 2518 Meridian **360/733-3832** *11am-7pm, clsd Sun-Mon, tattoos & piercing*

■ EROTICA

Great Northern Bookstore 1308 Railroad Ave (at Holly) **360/733-1650**

■ CRUISY AREAS

Cornwall Park [AYOR]

Teddy Bear Cove [AYOR]

Whatcom Falls Park [AYOR]

Blaine

■ CRUISY AREAS

Lincoln Park [AYOR] across from the mall (on 'H' St)

Rest Stop [AYOR] off I-5 (northbound)

La Conner • Washington

Bremerton

■ INFO LINES & SERVICES
AA Gay/ Lesbian 700 Callahan Dr (at St Paul's Episcopal) **360/475-0775** *7:30pm Tue*

OutKitsap 360/373-6150 *weekly social events*

■ BARS
Brewski's [GF,NH,F,WC] 2810 Kitsap Wy (enter off Wycuff St) **360/479-9100** *11am-2am*

■ CRUISY AREAS
Waterfront Boardwalk/ Pier [AYOR] across from ferry terminal

Centralia

■ CRUISY AREAS
Fort Borst Park [AYOR] Harrison Ave

Edmonds

■ CRUISY AREAS
Edmonds Beach Park [AYOR] by ferry dock

Everett

■ INFO LINES & SERVICES
AA Gay/ Lesbian 2624 Rockefeller **425/252-2525** *7pm Sun*

■ NIGHTCLUBS
Everett Underground [MW,D,MR,F,K,DS,WC] 1212 California St (at Grand Ave) **425/339-0807** *4pm-2am*

■ EROTICA
Airport Video 11732 Airport Rd (1 blk W of Hwy 99, at 128th St) **425/290-7555** *24hrs*

■ CRUISY AREAS
Forest Park [AYOR] off 41st St

Glacier

■ ACCOMMODATIONS
Mt Baker B&B [GS] 9447 Mt Baker Hwy **360/599-2299** *modern chalet, full brkfst, hot tub*

Hoquiam

■ ACCOMMODATIONS
Rivendell Ranch [GS,GO] 100 Hensel Rd (at Hwy 101) **360/987-0088** *campground & working ranch on Olympic Peninsula*

Issaquah

■ CRUISY AREAS
Lake Sammamish State Park [AYOR] I-90 & SR 900

Kennewick

■ CRUISY AREAS
Columbia Park [AYOR] *days only, cops & bashers after dark*

Kent

■ BARS
The Trax Terminal [MW,D,K,DS] 226 1st Ave S (btwn Titus & Gowe) **253/854-8729** *3pm-2am, karaoke Wed, DJ wknds, also Cha Cha Palace [D,DS] 9pm-close Fri-Sat & Iron Horse Saloon [NH,CW] 9pm-close Fri-Sat*

■ EROTICA
The Voyeur 604 Central Ave S **253/850-8428** *videos, toys, clothing*

■ CRUISY AREAS
Grandview Park [AYOR] 228th & Military Rd *along trail off path to soccer field*

La Conner

■ ACCOMMODATIONS
The White Swan Guesthouse [GF,NS] 15872 Moore Rd, Mt Vernon **360/445-6805** *farmhouse B&B, also cottage*

The Wild Iris [GF,NS,WC] 121 Maple Ave **360/466-1400** *inn, also restaurant w/ dinner wknds only*

Damron Men's Travel Guide 2004

Washington • USA

Long Beach Peninsula

■ACCOMMODATIONS

Anthony's Home Court [GS,GO] 1310 Pacific Hwy N, Long Beach **360/642-2802, 888/787-2754** *cabins & RV hookups*

The Historic Sou'wester Lodge, Cabins & RV Park [GF,NS] Beach Access Rd/ 38th Pl (PO Box 102), Seaview **360/642-2542** *inexpensive suites, cabins w/ kitchens & vintage trailers*

Shakti Cove Cottages [MW,GO] **360/665-4000** *cabins on the peninsula*

Lynnwood

■RETAIL SHOPS

Lynnwood Tattoo 15315 Hwy 99, #7 (at 153rd) **425/742-8467**

■CRUISY AREAS

Flag Pavilion Park [AYOR]

Mt Vernon

■RESTAURANTS

Deli Next Door [WC] 210 S 1st St (at Memorial Hwy) **360/336-3886** *8am-9pm, 9pm-8pm Sun*

■BOOKSTORES

Scott's Bookstore 121 Freeway Dr **360/336-6181** *9am-8pm, till 5pm Sun, till 6pm Mon*

■CRUISY AREAS

Lions Park [AYOR] Freeway Dr (along the river)

Oak Harbor

■CRUISY AREAS

Joseph Whidbey Park [AYOR] Swantown & Crosby

Olympia

■INFO LINES & SERVICES

Free at Last AA 11th & Washington (at United Church) **360/352-7344** *7pm Mon*

Gay Men's Social Network **360/923-1267** *events, newsletter*

■BARS

Hannah's [GS,NH,F] 123 5th Ave W (at Columbia) **360/357-9890** *11am-2am, from 10am Fri-Sat, till midnight Sun-Mon*

■CAFES

Darby's Cafe [GS,GO] 211 SE 5th Ave (at Washington) **360/357-6229** *7am-3pm, 8am-2pm wknds, clsd Mon-Tue*

Otto's 111 Washington St NE **360/352-8640** *7am-6pm, espresso & freshly baked bagels*

■RESTAURANTS

Saigon Rendez-Vous 117 5th Ave SW (btwn Columbia & Capitol Wy) **360/352-1989** *Vietnamese, plenty veggie*

Urban Onion [WC] 116 Legion Wy SE (at Capitol) **360/943-9242** *6am-10pm, till 11pm wknds, plenty veggie*

■RETAIL SHOPS

Dumpster Values 117 Washington St NE **360/705-3772** *11am-7pm, noon-5pm Sun, clothing, zines, records, toys*

■EROTICA

Desire Video 3200 Pacific Ave SE (off I-5, at exit 107) **360/352-0820** *24hrs, videos, toys, 100-channel video arcade, extensive lgbt section*

■CRUISY AREAS

Capitol Lake Marathon Park *take 5th Ave E to the parkway, follow signs to park*

Pasco

■NIGHTCLUBS

Out & About Restaurant & Lounge [MW,D,F,K,C,DS,WC] 327 W Lewis **509/543-3796, 877/388-3796** *6pm-2am, DJ wknds, karaoke Tue & Th, Latin night Mon, all ages welcome Fri & Sun, also restaurant*

Port Townsend

■ACCOMMODATIONS

Bearheart Inn B&B [GS] 1290 Gardiner Beach Rd (at Hwy 101 & Diamond Pt Rd), Sequim **360/797-7500, 888/206-0899** *full brkfst*

Seattle • Washington

The James House [GF,NS]
1238 Washington St **800/385-1238, 360/385-1238** *Victorian B&B, full brkfst, gardens*

Ravenscroft Inn [GF,NS] 533 Quincy St (at Clay St) **360/385-2784, 800/782-2691** *seaport inn w/ views of Puget Sound, gourmet brkfst, hot tub*

Redmond

■ CRUISY AREAS

Marymoore Park [AYOR] *days (cops evenings)*

San Juan Islands

■ ACCOMMODATIONS

Blue Rose B&B [GF] 1811 9th St, Anacortes **360/293-5175, 877/293-3285** *full brkfst*

Lopez Farm Cottages & Tent Camping [GS,NS] 555 Fisherman Bay Rd, Lopez Island **360/468-3555, 800/440-3556** *hot tub, also camping*

Spring Bay Inn on Orcas Island [GS] **360/376-5531** *full brkfst, hot tub, kayak tour included in price*

The Whidbey Inn [GS,NS] 106 1st St, Langley **360/221-7115, 888/313-2070** *full brkfst*

Seattle

■ INFO LINES & SERVICES

Capitol Hill Alano 1222 E Pine St, 2nd flr (at 13th) **206/587-2838 (AA#), 206/860-9560 (club)** *12-step mtgs daily*

Seattle LGBT Community Center [WC] 1115 E Pike St (btwn 11th & 12th Aves) **206/323-5428**

■ ACCOMMODATIONS

Ace Hotel [GS,GO] 2423 1st Ave (at Wall St) **206/448-4721** *modern & stylish, some shared baths*

Alexis Hotel [GF,WC] 1007 1st Ave (at Madison) **206/624-4844, 800/426-7033** *luxury hotel w/ Aveda spa*

Amaranth Inn [GS,NS] 1451 S Main St (at 16th) **206/720-7161, 800/720-7161**

Artist's Studio Loft B&B [GF,NS] 16529 91st Ave SW, Vashon Island **206/463-2583** *not tub*

Bacon Mansion [GS,WC] 959 Broadway E (at E Prospect) **206/329-1864, 800/240-1864** *Edwardian-style Tudor*

Bed & Breakfast on Broadway [GF,NS] 722 Broadway Ave E (at Aloha) **206/329-8933** *full brkfst*

Chambered Nautilus B&B Inn [GF] 5005 22nd Ave NE (at N 50th St) **206/522-2536, 800/545-8459** *full brkfst, sundecks*

Gaslight Inn [★GS,SW,NS,GO] 1727 15th Ave (at E Howell St) **206/325-3654** *also Howell St Suites next door*

Gypsy Arms B&B [GS,L,NS,GO] 3628 Palatine Ave N **206/547-8194** *Victorian inn w/ full dungeon, hot tub*

Hill House B&B [GF,NS] 1113 E John St (at 12th Ave) **206/720-7161, 800/720-7161** *full brkfst*

Hotel Monaco [GF,WC] 1101 4th Ave (at Spring St) **206/621-1770, 800/945-2240** *gym*

Hotel Vintage Park [GS,WC] 1100 5th Ave (at Spring) **206/624-8000, 800/454-8401** *ultra-luxe sleep in Seattle*

Inn at Queen Anne [GS] 505 1st Ave N (at Republican) **206/282-7357, 800/952-5043** *kitchenettes*

Landes House B&B [MW,GO] 712 11th Ave E (at Aloha) **206/329-8781, 888/329-8781** *two 1906 houses joined by deck, hot tub*

Madrigal Inn B&B [GS] 14421 SE 232nd St, Kent **253/638-6566** *full brkfst*

Pioneer Square Hotel [GF,WC] 77 Yesler Wy (btwn 1st Ave & Alaskan Wy) **206/340-1234, 800/800-5514** *gym, restaurants & saloon*

Seattle Suites [GS,NS] 1400 Hubbell Pl **206/232-2799** *studio, 1 & 2-bdrm condos*

The Shafer-Baillie Mansion [GF,NS] 907 14th Ave E (at Aloha) **206/322-4654, 800/922-4654**

Washington • *USA*

Sweet Suite Seattle [GS,GO]
1400 Hubbell Pl, Ste 812 (at Pike)
206/909-9047 *condo, close to convention center*

The Warwick Hotel [GS,SW,WC]
401 Lenora St (at 4th) **206/443-4300** *full brkfst, jacuzzi*

Wild Lily Ranch B&B
[★MW,SW,NS,GO] **360/793-2103** *cabins & authentic Sioux tipis (w/ electricity) on Skykomish River, 1 hour from Seattle, riverside jacuzzi*

■ BARS

The Bad Juju Lounge [GS,D,F]
1518 11th Ave (at Pike) **206/709-9951** *4pm-2am*

The Baltic Room [GS,E] 1207 Pine St (at Melrose) **206/625-4444** *5pm-2am, clsd Mon*

Beacon Pub [MW,WC] 3057 Beacon Ave S **206/726-0238**

CC Attle's [★M,NH,V,WC] 1501 E Madison (at 15th Ave) **206/726-0565** *8am-2am, patio, also Veranda Room & Men's Room*

Changes [M,NH,F,K,V,WC] 2103 N 45th St (at Meridian) **206/545-8363** *noon-2am*

The Crescent Tavern [M,NH,WC]
1413 E Olive Wy (at Bellevue)
206/720-8188 *noon-2am, from 8am wknds*

➤ **The Cuff** [★M,D,WC] 1533 13th Ave (at Pine) **206/323-1525** *2pm-2am, after-hours wknds, Levi crowd, 5 bar areas, also patio*

Double Header [M,NH] 407 2nd Ave S Extension (at Washington)
206/464-9918 *10am-midnight, till 2am wknds, 'one of the oldest gay bars in the US'*

Elite Tavern [MW,NH,BW,WC] 622 Broadway East (at Roy) **206/324-4470** *noon-2am, from 10am wknds*

Guppy's [MW,NH,F,K,DS] 4752 California Ave SW (at Edmonds Ave)
206/932-6996 *2pm-2am, from noon Sat, Sun brunch, theme nights*

Hana's Restaurant & Lounge
[M,D,F,WC] 1914 8th Ave (at Stewart)
206/340-1591 *noon-2am, Korean food 11am-6pm*

Jade Pagoda [M,NH,F,WC] 606 Broadway (at Mercer) **206/322-5900** *5pm-2am, from noon Th-Fri, Chinese/American*

Madison Pub [★M,NH,OC,WC] 1315 E Madison St (at 13th) **206/325-6537** *noon-2am*

Manray [M,F,V] 514 E Pine (at Belmont) **206/568-0750** *4pm-2am*

R Place [M,NH,D,F,K,V,WC] 619 E Pine St (at Boylston) **206/322-8828** *2pm-2am, 3 flrs, video sports bar, Sun brunch*

Rendezvous [GF,NH,F,E] 2320 2nd Ave (at Battery) **206/441-5823** *6am-2am, live bands Th-Sat, also restaurant*

The Seattle Eagle [M,L,WC] 314 E Pike St (at Bellevue) **206/621-7591** *2pm-2am, patio, rock 'n' roll*

The Seawolf Saloon & Gallery
[M,NH,F,WC] 1413 14th Ave (at Madison) **206/323-2158** *11am-2am*

Sonya's Bar & Grill [M,NH] 1919 1st Ave (btwn Virginia & Stewart)
206/441-7996 *11am-2am*

Thumpers [★M,V,WC,GO] 1500 E Madison St (at 15th) **206/328-3800** *11am-2am, also restaurant*

Timberline Spirits [MW,D,C] 1828 Yale Ave (at Howell) **206/883-0242** *6pm-close, from 4pm Sun, CW Fri, disco T-dance Sun*

Watertown [GF,D] 106 1st Ave N (at Denny) **206/284-5003** *5pm-2am, 8pm-3am wknds*

■ NIGHTCLUBS

BLU Video Bar [M,D,E,P,V] 722 E Pike St (at Harvard) **206/568-4258** *4pm-2am*

Catwalk Club [GS,F,$] 172 S Washington St (at 2nd) **206/622-1863** *Fri-Sun, call for events*

Chop Suey [GF,D,E,YC,$] 1325 E Madison (btwn 13th Ave & 14th Ave)
206/324-8000 *8pm-2am, clsd Mon*

Jazz Alley [GF,F,E,$] 2033 6th Ave (at Lenora) **206/441-9729** *call for events & reservations*

Neighbours Dance Club
[★MW,D,YC,WC] 1509 Broadway (at Pike & Pine) **206/324-5358** *9pm-2am, till 4am Fri-Sat, 2 flrs*

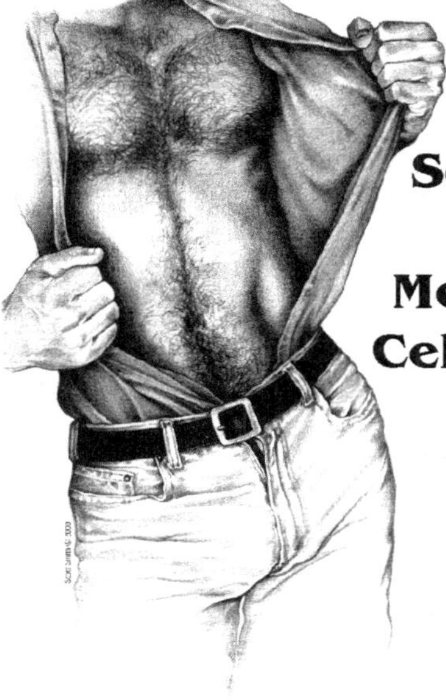

Washington • USA

Re-bar [★GS,D,E,K,C] 1114 Howell (at Boren Ave) 206/233-9873 *6pm-2am, DJ Th-Sun*

Showbox [GF,E,$] 1426 1st Ave (at Pike) 206/628-3151 *live music venue*

The Vogue [GF,D,A,E] 1516 11th Ave (at Pine) 206/324-5778 *6pm-2am, theme nights*

■ CAFES

Espresso Vivace 901 E Denny Wy #100 206/860-5869 *6:30am-11pm*

■ RESTAURANTS

1200 Bistro & Lounge [★MW,GO] 1200 E Pike St (at 12th Ave) 206/320-1200 *dinner only, also lounge*

Addis Cafe [★] 61224 E Jefferson (at 12th) 206/325-7805 *lunch & dinner, Ethiopian*

Al Boccalino 1 Yesler Wy (at Alaskan) 206/622-7688 *lunch Tue-Fri, dinner nightly, classy southern Italian*

Broadway New American Grill [★] 314 Broadway E (at E Harrison) 206/328-7000 *9am-3am, from 8am wknds, full bar*

Cafe Septieme [★MW] 214 Broadway Ave E (at Thomas & John) 206/860-8858 *9am-midnight, till 2am wknds, also bar*

Campagne [R] 86 Pine St (at 1st) 206/728-2800 *5:30pm-10pm, French, also Cafe Campagne, lunch & dinner, wknd brunch*

Dahlia Lounge 1904 4th Ave (at Virginia) 206/682-4142 *lunch Mon-Fri, dinner nightly, full bar*

Gravity Bar [WC] 415 Broadway E (at Harrison) 206/325-7186 *10am-10pm, vegetarian, juice bar*

Kokeb [BW] 9261 12th Ave 206/322-0485 *lunch & dinner, clsd Sun, Ethiopian*

Mae's Phinney Ridge Cafe [★WC] 6410 Phinney Ridge N (at 65th) 206/782-1222 *7am-3pm, brkfst menu*

Mama's Mexican Kitchen 2234 2nd Ave (in Belltown) 206/728-6262 *lunch & dinner, cheap & funky*

Queen City Grill [★WC] 2201 1st Ave (at Blanchard) 206/443-0975 *dinner only, fresh seafood*

Rosebud Restaurant & Bar 719 E Pike St (at Harvard Ave) 206/323-6636 *lunch Mon-Fri, dinner nightly, wknd brunch*

Sunlight Cafe [BW,WC] 6403 Roosevelt Wy NE (at 64th) 206/522-9060 *7am-9:30pm, vegetarian*

Szmania's 3321 W McGraw St (in Magnolia Bluff) 206/284-7305 *dinner nightly, clsd Mon*

Wild Ginger Asian Restaurant & Satay Bar [★] 1400 Western Ave (at Union) 206/623-4450 *lunch Mon-Sat, dinner nightly, bar till 1am*

■ ENTERTAINMENT & RECREATION

Gay Bingo 15th & E Union (at Temple De Hirsch Sinai) 206/323-0069, 206/328-8979 *monthly, run by the Chicken Soup Brigade*

Harvard Exit 807 E Roy St 206/323-8986 *rep film theater*

Northwest Lesbian & Gay History Museum Project 206/903-9517 *exhibits & free newsletter*

Seattle Men's Chorus PO Box 20146 98102 206/323-0750 *world's largest & most successful gay men's chorus*

Tacky Tourist Clubs 800/807-5214 *fabulous social events*

■ BOOKSTORES

Bailey/ Coy Books [WC] 414 Broadway Ave E (at Harrison) 206/323-8842 *10am-10pm, till 11pm Fri-Sat*

Beyond the Closet Bookstore 518 E Pike St (at Belmont) 206/322-4609, 800/238-8518 *10am-10pm, lgbt*

Edge of the Circle 701 E Pike (at Boylston) 206/726-1999 *noon-9pm, alternative spirituality store*

Fremont Place Book Company 621 N 35th (at Fremont Ave N) 206/547-5970 *10am-8pm, till 9pm Wed-Sat, till 6:30pm Sun*

Left Bank Books 92 Pike St (at 1st Ave) 206/622-0195 *10am-7pm, noon-6pm Sun, worker-owned collective, lgbt section*

Spokane • Washington

■RETAIL SHOPS

Archie McPhee 2428 NW Market (in Ballard) **206/297-0240** *9am-7pm, 10am-6pm Sun, weird & wonderful toys & trinkets*

Broadway Market [★] 401 E Broadway (at Harrison & Republican) *funky, queer & hip stores*

Metropolis 7220 Greenwood Ave N (at 73rd) **206/782-7002** *10am-8pm, cards & gifts*

The Pink Zone 909 E Denny Wy (at Nagle Pl) **206/325-0050** *11am-9pm, pride items, underwear, cards, gifts, adult items*

Sunshine Thrift Shops [WC] 1718 12th Ave (at Pike/ Broadway) **206/324-9774** *10am-6pm, nonprofit for AIDS groups*

■PUBLICATIONS

Pride Magazine 773/769-6328 *also publish Seattle Pink Pages*

SGN (Seattle Gay News) 206/324-4297 *weekly lgbt newspaper*

The Stranger 206/323-7101 *queer-positive alternative weekly*

■GYMS & HEALTH CLUBS

Every Body Heath & Fitness Inc [WC,GO] 2609 S Jackson St (btwn 23rd Ave & Martin Luther King) **206/324-6062**

Gold's Gym [GF] 825 Pike St (at 8th Ave) **206/583-0640**

■MEN'S CLUBS

Basic Plumbing 1505 10th Ave (btwn Pike & Pine) **206/323-2799** *6pm-3am, from 1pm wknds*

Club Seattle [★PC] 1520 Summit Ave (btwn Pine & Pike) **206/329-2334** *24hrs*

Club Z [PC] 1117 Pike St (at Boren) **206/622-9958** *4pm-9am, 24hrs wknds, discounts for out-of-towners*

■EROTICA

Castle Superstore 613 Fairview Ave N **206/621-7236** *24hrs*

The Crypt 1113 10th Ave E (at Denny) **206/325-3882**

Deja Vu Love Boutique 1510 1st Ave (at Pike) **206/624-1784** *24hrs*

Fantasy Unlimited 2027 Westlake Ave (at 7th) **206/682-0167** *24hrs*

■CRUISY AREAS

Arboretum [AYOR] *days*

Boy Beach [N,AYOR] 110th St, off 3rd Ave NW (1 mile N of Carkeek Park) *along RR tracks*

Edmonds Ferry Pier [AYOR] bluffs (above parking lot & beach)

Green Lake Park [AYOR] 5500 blk of W Green Lake Wy (btwn putting course & aqua theater) *evenings*

Madison Beach [AYOR] 43rd & Madison

Volunteer Park [AYOR] top of Capitol Hill (btwn Prospect & Boston, 15th & Federal) *days only*

Seaview

■ACCOMMODATIONS

Senator TC Bloomer's Mansion [GF,GO] 1004 41st Pl (at Oceanfront) **360/642-3471** *rental home*

Spokane

■INFO LINES & SERVICES

AA Gay/ Lesbian 411 S Washington (at church) **509/624-1442** *7pm Mon*

Rainbow Regional Community Center 508 W 2nd Ave **509/489-1914** *10am-6pm, from 2pm Sat, clsd Sun, support groups, events, also art gallery*

■ACCOMMODATIONS

Sun Flower Cottage [MW,NS,GO] 4114 N Wall St **509/326-7707** *full brkfst*

■NIGHTCLUBS

Dempsey's Brass Rail [★MW,D,F,S,WC] 909 W 1st St (btwn Lincoln & Monroe) **509/747-5362** *3pm-2am, till 4am Fri-Sat, DJ Th-Sat, also restaurant*

■CAFES

Tryst Coffee House & Juice Bar [GF,E,BW,GO] 122 S Monroe (at 1st Ave) **509/455-5699** *9am-11pm, till midnight Fri-Sat, 11am-9pm Sun*

Damron Men's Travel Guide 2004

Washington • USA

■RESTAURANTS
Mizuna 214 N Howard **509/747-2004** *lunch Mon-Fri, dinner Tue-Sat, full bar*

The Top Notch Cafe 825 N Monroe **509/327-7988** *8am-2pm, home-cookin'*

■BOOKSTORES
Auntie's Bookstore & Cafe [WC] 402 W Main St (at Washington) **509/838-0206** *9am-9pm, till 10pm Fri, 11am-6pm Sun*

■PUBLICATIONS
Stonewall News Northwest **509/456-8011** *monthly lgbt newspaper for Spokane & NW*

■MEN'S SERVICES
The Confidential Connection®! **509/325-6900** *The hottest local guys! 18+ Record & Listen FREE! Use access code 499*

■EROTICA
Best Buy Adult Entertainment 2425 Springfield Ave **509/624-7522**

Castle Superstore 11324 E Sprague (btwn Gillis & Bowdish) **509/893-1180**

■CRUISY AREAS
High Bridge [AYOR] People's Park

Manito Park [AYOR]

Mission Park [AYOR]

Suquamish

■INFO LINES & SERVICES
Kitsap Lesbian/ Gay AA 18732 Division Ave NE (at Geneva St) **360/475-0775** *7:30pm Sun*

Tacoma

■INFO LINES & SERVICES
AA Gay/ Lesbian 209 S 'J' St (at the church, enter on alley) **253/474-8897** *7:30pm Fri*

Rainbow Center 308 Tacoma Ave S **253/383-2318** *drop-in hours 9am-noon, till 6pm Tue & Th, clsd wknds, community center, call for meetings & events*

■ACCOMMODATIONS
Chinaberry Hill [GF,NS] 302 Tacoma Ave N **253/272-1282** *full brkfst, jacuzzis in rooms, romantic*

Sheraton Tacoma Hotel [GF,WC] 1320 Broadway Plaza (at S 15th) **253/572-3200, 800/325-3535** *restaurants & bars*

■BARS
Airport Tavern [MW,NH] 5406 S Tacoma Wy (at 54th) **253/475-9730** *2pm-2am*

■NIGHTCLUBS
Club Silverstone [MW,D,F,K,DS] 739 1/2 St Helens Ave **253/404-0273** *11am-2am, also restaurant, karaoke Mon & Wed-Th*

Destiny's [MW,D,F,DS] 754 Pacific Ave (at 9th) **253/627-0987** *5pm-2am, till 4am Fri-Sat, also restaurant*

■EROTICA
Castle Superstore 6015 Tacoma Mall Blvd **253/471-0391**

Jerry's Mecca Theater 755 Broadway **253/272-4700**

■CRUISY AREAS
Wright Park [AYOR] 6th & 'G' Sts

Tukwila

■EROTICA
The Voyeur 10315 E Marginal Wy S **206/768-1360**

Vancouver

see also Portland, Oregon

■BARS
North Bank [MW,D,F,K,DS,WC] 106 W 6th St **360/695-3862** *4pm-2am, from noon wknds, CW Th, karaoke Mon & Fri*

Walla Walla

■CRUISY AREAS
Fort Walla Walla Park [AYOR]

Pioneer Park [AYOR]

Wildwood Park [AYOR]

Charleston • West Virginia

Wenatchee

CAFES
The Cellar Café [BW,GO] 249 N Mission St (at 5th) **509/662-1722** *9am-5pm, 10am-4pm Sat, clsd Sun, patio*

CRUISY AREAS
River Walk [AYOR] at 19th St

Washington & Miller Sts [AYOR]

Whidbey Island

ACCOMMODATIONS
Whidwood Inn [GS,NS,GO] **360/679-7472** *near historic Coupeville*

Winthrop

ACCOMMODATIONS
Chewuch Inn [GF,NS] 223 White Ave **509/996-3107, 800/747-3107** *E of N Cascades Mtns*

Yakima

EROTICA
Yakima Magazine Center 18 S 1st St **509/248-8598**

WEST VIRGINIA

Beckley

NIGHTCLUBS
Hideaway [MW,D,TG,E,K,DS,18] 2011 Harper Rd (at West Virginia Tpke) **304/256-9707** *7pm-3am, karaoke Wed*

EROTICA
Blue Moon Video 3427 Robert C Byrd Dr (at New River Dr) **304/255-1200**

Bluefield

CRUISY AREAS
Kee Dam (Cattail Hollow) [AYOR] State Rte 123, 3 miles E of airport

Raleigh St [AYOR] near Norfolk & Sou RR

Charleston

INFO LINES & SERVICES
COGLES (Community Oriented Gay/ Lesbian Events/ Services) **304/345-0491** *local info & resources*

West Virginia Lesbian/ Gay Coalition **304/343-7305** *recording of bars & resources*

BARS
The Tap Room/ Quarrier Diner [M,NH,B,L] 1022 Quarrier St **304/342-7453** *6pm-close, from 7pm Sun, bears 1st Sat, leather 3rd Sat*

NIGHTCLUBS
Broadway [M,D,S] 210 Leon Sullivan Way (at Lee) **304/343-2162** *3:30pm-3am, from 1pm wknds*

Grand Palace [MW,D,V,S] 617 Brook St (near Lee; take Broad St exit, off I-64) **304/342-9532** *noon-3am, till 2:30am Sun*

Trax [MW,DS,S] 504 W Washington (at Maryland) **304/345-8931** *4pm-3am, till 2:30am Sat*

ENTERTAINMENT & RECREATION
Living AIDS Memorial Garden corner of Washington St E (at Sidney Ave) **304/346-0246, 877/543-5264**

PUBLICATIONS
About PO Box 2624 25329

Graffiti 1427 Lee St **304/342-4412** *alternative entertainment guide, mostly non-gay*

Shout! **540/529-6363** *entertainment & personals for the Virginias & Carolinas*

MEN'S SERVICES
➤ **Megaphone Charleston** **800/289-1489** *Call for the local # nearest you! Meet Hot Men in your area! FREE to Browse & Respond to voice ads. Use code 3087. Also try MEGAMATES.COM*

CRUISY AREAS
The Block [AYOR] Summers, Donnally, Capitol & Christopher Sts

Daniel Boone Park [AYOR] Rte 60 E *evenings*

West Virginia • USA

Fairmont

ACCOMMODATIONS
Travelodge Inn & Suites [GS,SW,WC]
1117 Fairmont Ave **304/363-0100**
hot tub

Huntington

BARS
The Driftwood-Beehive Lounge
[MW,D,K,DS,V,YC,WC] 1121 7th Ave (at 11th St) **304/696-9858** *5pm-3am*

Polo Club [M,D,DS,PC,WC] 733 7th Ave (enter rear) **304/522-3146** *5pm-1am*

The Stonewall [★MW,D,K,DS,WC] 820 7th Ave (enter rear) **304/523-1069** *8pm-3am*

RESTAURANTS
Calamity Cafe [E,WC] 1555 3rd Ave **304/525-4171** *11am-10pm, till 3am wknds*

EROTICA
House of Video 1109 4th Ave (at 11th) **304/525-2194**

CRUISY AREAS
Rotary Park [AYOR] off Rte 60 E

Lewisburg

ACCOMMODATIONS
Lee Street Inn B&B [GF,GO] 200 N Lee St **304/647-5599, 888/228-7000** *grand 1876 house, jacuzzi, garden*

Lost River

ACCOMMODATIONS
The Guesthouse [MW,SW,NS] Settlers Valley Wy **304/897-5707** *full brkfst, hot tub*

Martinsburg

EROTICA
Variety Books & Video 255 N Queen St (at Race) **304/263-4334** *24hrs*

Milton

EROTICA
➤ **The Lion's Den Adult Bookstore** 325 Summers Addition (exit 28, off I-64) **304/743-0190** *24hrs*

Mineral Wells

EROTICA
➤ **The Lion's Den Adult Bookstore** State Rte 14 & I-77 (exit 170, off I-77) **304/489-9690** *24hrs*

Morgantown

BARS
Weezie's Pub & Club [W,NH,F,K]
3117 University Ave, downstairs **304/598-0919** *6pm-3am, food served till 10pm*

NIGHTCLUBS
Vice Versa [MW,D,K,DS,PC,18+,WC]
335 High St (enter rear)
304/292-2010 *8pm-3am Th-Sun*

Parkersburg

BARS
Genders Video Bar [MW,D,K,DS]
316 5th St (at Market) **304/485-2929** *9pm-close, clsd Tue*

EROTICA
Pioneer Adult Books & Videos
6603 Emerson Ave **304/428-8604**

CRUISY AREAS
The Boat Ramp [AYOR]

Princeton

EROTICA
Exotic Illusions Adult Bookstore 853 Frontage Rd/ Rte 460 (btwn Bluefield & Princeton) **304/487-2170** *24hrs*

Proctor

ACCOMMODATIONS
Roseland Guesthouse & Campground [MO,F,SW,N,GO]
304/455-3838 *222 secluded acres w/ scenic mtn-top views, unlimited campsites, theme wknds, hot tub*

Shepherdstown

ACCOMMODATIONS
Thomas Shepherd Inn [GF]
300 W German St (at Duke St)
304/876-3715, 888/889-8952
B&B, full brkfst

Geneva Lakes • Wisconsin

■ BOOKSTORES
On the Wings of Dreams
129 W German St **304/876-0244**
metaphysical

Vienna

■ BARS
True Colors [MW,D,DS,18+,PC] 102 12th St (at Grand Central) **304/295-8783** *8:30pm-3am, clsd Mon-Tue*

Wheeling

■ EROTICA
Fritz The Cat [GO] Coventry Rd (at I-70), Dallas Pike **304/547-0250**

Market St News 1437 Market St (at 14th St) **304/232-2414**

WISCONSIN

Statewide

■ PUBLICATIONS
IN Step 414/278-7840
lgbt newspaper

Lavender Magazine 612/871-2237 (MN#), 877/515-9969 *lgbt newsmagazine for MN, WI, IA, ND, SD*

Appleton

■ BARS
Rascals Bar & Grill [MW,F] 702 E Wisconsin Ave (at Meade) **920/954-9262** *5pm-2am, from noon Sun, patio*

■ EROTICA
Eldorado's 2545 S Memorial Dr (at Hwys 47 & 441) **920/830-0042**

■ CRUISY AREAS
Lutz Park [AYOR]

Ashland

■ CRUISY AREAS
Prentice Park [AYOR]

Baileys Harbor

■ ACCOMMODATIONS
Blacksmith Inn B&B [GF,NS,WC] 8152 Hwy 57 **920/839-9222, 800/769-8619**

Clinton

■ ACCOMMODATIONS
Carvers Rock B&B [MW,NS,WC,GO] 11044 E Creek Rd **877/296-9048** *full brkfst, sundeck*

Eagle River

■ ACCOMMODATIONS
The Edgewater Hotel & Resort [GS,GO] 5054 Hwy 70 W **715/479-4011, 888/334-3987** *also waterfront cottages*

Eau Claire

■ INFO LINES & SERVICES
LGBT Community Center of the Chippewa Valley 510 S Farwell St **715/552-5428** *drop-in 7pm-10pm Fri, call for other hours, library, events*

■ BARS
Wolfe's Den [M,NH,B,K,DS,S] 302 E Madison **715/832-9237** *6pm-2:30am, home bar of the Chippewa Bears*

■ NIGHTCLUBS
Scooters [MW,D,C,DS,WC] 411 Galloway (at Farwell) **715/835-9959** *3pm-2am*

■ EROTICA
Adult Video Unlimited 1518 Bellinger St **715/834-3393**

Geneva Lakes

■ ACCOMMODATIONS
Allyn Mansion Inn [GS,NS,GO] 511 E Walworth Ave (btwn 5th & 6th), Delavan **262/728-9090** *full brkfst*

Eleven Gables Inn on the Lake [GF,NS,WC] 493 Wrigley Dr, Lake Geneva **262/248-8393** *lakeside inn, full brkfst wknds*

■ CRUISY AREAS
Riviera Beach [AYOR]

Waterfront & Flat Iron Park [AYOR]

Wisconsin • USA

Green Bay

INFO LINES & SERVICES
Gay AA 920/494-9904

BARS
Brandy's II [MW,NH,WC] 1126 Main St (near Webster Ave) **920/437-3917** *4pm-2am, from 11am wknds*

The Historic West Theater [GS,D,F,V] 405 W Walnut St **920/435-1057** *films, full bar, dancing wknds*

Napalese Lounge [M,NH,F,DS,WC] 1351 Cedar St **920/432-9646** *11am-2am, till 2:30am Fri-Sat, DJ Fri-Sat*

Sass [MW,D] 840 S Broadway **920/457-7277** *6pm-2am, from 5pm Sun (winters)*

NIGHTCLUBS
XS [M,D,TG,DS,S,V,YC,WC,GO] 1106 Main St (at Clay St) **920/884-2949** *7pm-close, 2 flrs*

PUBLICATIONS
Quest **920/433-0611, 800/578-3785**

MEN'S SERVICES
The Confidential Connection®! **920/431-9000** *The hottest local guys! 18+ Record & Listen FREE! Use access code 499*

EROTICA
Adult Movieland/Books 'N' Things 836 S Broadway (at 5th) **920/433-9640**

Main Attraction Book & Video/ Nite Owl Motel 1614 E Main (at Elizabeth) **920/465-6969**

Hayward

ACCOMMODATIONS
The Lake House [MW,SW,NS,WC,GO] 5793 Division, Stone Lake **715/865-6803** *full brkfst*

Hazelhurst

BARS
Willow Haven Resort/ Supper Club [GF,F] 4877 Haven Dr (at Willow Dam Rd) **715/453-3807** *11:30am-close, lunch & dinner*

Hurley

ACCOMMODATIONS
Anton-Walsh House [GF] 202 Copper St (at US Hwy 51) **715/561-2065, 715/561-9977** *historic B&B, full brkfst*

Kenosha

see also Racine

BARS
94 North [MW,D,DS,S] 6305 120th Ave (on E frontage road of 94) **262/857-3240** *7pm-2am, till 2:30am Fri-Sat, 3pm-2am Sun, clsd Mon*

CAFES
Becca's Cafe [GO] 4015 80th St **262/694-7160** *7am-6pm, till 1pm Sat, till 11am Sun*

La Crosse

ACCOMMODATIONS
Rainbow Ridge Farms B&B [GF,NS] N 5732 Hauser Rd (at County S), Onalaska **608/783-8181** *restored farmhouse, full brkfst, hot tub*

Trillium B&B [GF] **608/625-4492** *cottage, full brkfst, 35 miles from La Crosse*

BARS
My Place [MW,NH,K,GO] 3201 South Ave (at East Ave) **608/788-9073** *3pm-close, friendly bar*

Players [★MW,D,MR,TG,E,DS,WC,GO] 214 Main **608/784-2353** *5pm-2am, from 3pm Fri-Sun, till 2:30am Fri-Sat*

Rainbow's End [MW,NH] 417 Jay St (at 4th) **608/782-5105** *2pm-2am, from noon wknds*

BOOKSTORES
Pearl Street Books 323 Pearl St **608/782-3424** *9:30am-8pm, till 9pm Fri, from noon Sun, mostly used, lgbt section*

EROTICA
Best Buy Books 314 Jay St (at 3rd) **608/784-6350**

CRUISY AREAS
Pettibone Park [AYOR] on the Mississippi River (off of North Beach, across from the Holiday Inn) *days only*

Madison • Wisconsin

Madison

■ INFO LINES & SERVICES

LesBiGay Campus Center 800 Langdon, 2nd flr Memorial Union, UW **608/265-3344** *drop-in 9am-5pm, clsd wknds*

OutReach 600 Williamson St #P-1 **608/255-8582** *9am-9pm, noon-3pm Sat, clsd Sun, drop-in center, library, newsletter, referrals, call for AA mtgs*

■ ACCOMMODATIONS

Hawks Nest Log Home Rentals [GS,NS,GO] 2455 & 2459 Fairview (at Door Creek Rd), Stoughton **608/445-7468, 608/877-0925** *log homes on Lake Kegonsa*

➤ **Prairie Garden B&B** [MW,NS,GO] W 13172 Hwy 188, Lodi **608/592-5187, 800/380-8427** *full brkfst, hot tub, 30 minutes N of Madison*

■ BARS

➤ **Club 5** [MW,D,K,DS,V] 5 Applegate Ct (btwn Fish Hatchery Rd & W Beltline Hwy) **608/277-9700, 877/648-9700** *4pm-2am, dance club & restaurant, also Barracks leather bar & Planet Q video bar, Tue 18+*

Green Bush [GF,F] 914 Regent St (at Park) **608/257-2874** *4pm-midnight, clsd Sun*

Rainbow Room [MW,D,WC] 121 W Main (at Fairchild) **608/251-5838** *10am-2am*

Ray's Bar [MW,NH] 2526 E Washington **608/241-9335** *3pm-2am, from noon wknds*

Shamrock [MW,F] 117 W Main St (at Fairchild) **608/255-5029** *2pm-2am, Sun brunch from 10am*

Experience the Quiet Beauty Close to Nude Beach

Prairie Garden Bed & Breakfast
Outdoor Spa, Fantastic Breakfasts, Farm Animals
1/2 Hour North of Madison

Rooms starting at $70
www.prairiegarden.com

Your innkeeper: Todd   **1-800-380-8427**   W13172 Hwy. 188, Lodi, WI 53555

Wisconsin • USA

■ NIGHTCLUBS

Cardinal [GF,D] 418 E Wilson St (at S Franklin) **608/251-0080** *8pm-2am, clsd Mon, more gay 2nd Tue & early Fri, call for events*

Club Majestic [MW,D,S] 115 King St **608/251-2582** *9pm-2am, from 4pm Fri-Sun, clsd Mon-Tue*

■ RESTAURANTS

Fyfe's [★] 1344 E Washington (at Dickinson) **608/251-8700** *lunch Mon-Fri, dinner nightly, full bar*

La Hacienda [★] 515 S Park St **608/255-8227** *8am-3am, Mexican, popular & cruisy post-Club 5 spot*

Monty's Blue Plate Diner [BW,WC] 2089 Atwood Ave (at Winnebago) **608/244-8505** *7am-10pm, till 9pm Sun-Tue, from 7:30am wknds*

■ ENTERTAINMENT & RECREATION

High Tea & Talk 2089 Atwood Ave (at Monty's Blue Plate Diner) *3:30pm Fri, social group for older gay men*

■ BOOKSTORES

Mimosa 210 N Henry **608/256-5432** *11am-6pm, from 10am Sun, spiritual*

■ RETAIL SHOPS

Piercing Lounge 461 W Gilman (at University) **608/284-0870** *11am-11pm, till midnight Fri, noon-7pm Sun*

■ EROTICA

Red Letter News 2528 E Washington (at North) **608/241-9958** *24hrs*

State Street Arcade [AYOR] 113 State (btwn Mifflin & Broom) **608/251-4540** *24hrs, active back alley*

■ CRUISY AREAS

Burrows Park [AYOR]

Nude beach (Mazomanie) [AYOR] *30 miles NW on Hwy 4, then 4 miles N to Laws Rd, turn left & go 1/2 mile to gravel rd*

Olin Park [AYOR] W shore of Lake Monona (parking lot near Sheraton) *afternoons*

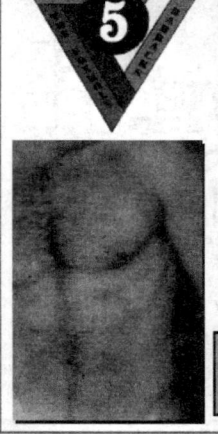

CLUB 5

MADISON'S PREMIER GAY ENTERTAINMENT PLACE

FEATURING

BARRACKS MEN'S BAR
FEATURING MALE PORNO
FOXHOLE WOMYN'S BAR
PLANET Q DANCE & VIDEO BAR
WITH STATE OF THE ART SOUND
MADISON'S EDIBLE COMPLEX
DINNER RESTAURANT
OUTDOOR PATIO - LIVE SHOWS
EXOTIC DANCERS
FEMALE IMPERSONATORS

5 APPLEGATE COURT
MADISON, WISCONSIN 53713
club5q@aol.com
ph 608.277.9700 / 877.648.9700
fax 608.277.8704
http://www.club-5.com

Milwaukee • Wisconsin

Manitowoc

■ BARS

RiverBank Lounge [GF,NH,F,GO]
902 Jay St (at 9th St) **920/482-0032**
5:30pm-2am Th-Sat, homemade hors d'oeuvres & desserts, in converted 1901 Victorian bank

Milwaukee

■ INFO LINES & SERVICES

AA Galano Club 315 W Court #201 (in LGBT Community Center)
414/276-6936 *call after 5pm for mtg schedule*

Gay People's Union Hotline
414/645-0585

Milwaukee LGBT Community Center
315 W Court #101 (btwn W Sherry & Galena) **414/271-2656** *10am-10pm, till 6pm Sat*

■ ACCOMMODATIONS

Layton Guest House [M,GO] 2146 S Layton Blvd (at Grant) **414/389-0900** *full brkfst*

The Milwaukee Hilton [GF,F,SW]
509 W Wisconsin Ave (at 5th St)
414/271-7250, 800/445-8667

Park East Hotel [GF,NS,WC] 916 E State St (at Marshall) **414/276-8800, 800/328-7275** *also restaurant*

■ BARS

Ballgame [M,NH] 196 S 2nd St (at Pittsburgh) **414/273-7474** *2pm-2am, from 11am wknds*

Barossa [★GS,D,A,WC] 235 S 2nd St (at Oregon) **414/272-8466** *11:30am-2am, winebar & restaurant, dancing/DJ upstairs*

Boot Camp Saloon [M,NH,L] 209 E National Ave (at Barclay)
414/643-6900 *4pm-2am, from 9pm Sat*

C'est La Vie [M,DS] 231 S 2nd St (at Pittsburgh) **414/291-9600** *5pm-2:30am, 1pm-2am Sun*

Club Boom [MW,NH,F,V] 625 S 2nd St (at W Bruce) **414/277-5040** *5pm-2am, from 11am Sun, patio*

Harbor Room [M,L] 117 E Greenfield Ave **414/672-7988** *7am-2am*

Henry's Pub & Grill [GS,F,WC]
2523 E Belleview Pl (at Downer)
414/332-9690 *3pm-2am, full menu*

M&M Club [M,F,WC] 124 N Water St (at Erie) **414/347-1962** *11am-2am, from 10:30am Sun, full restaurant, Sun brunch, patio*

The Nomad [GF,E] 1401 E Brady St (at Warren) **414/224-8111** *3pm-2am, from noon wknds*

Pulse [MW,D,F,DS,S] 200 E Washington St **414/649-9547** *3pm-4am, till 6am Th-Sun, 2 bars, male dancers Sun, patio*

Redroom Cocktail Lounge [GF,WC]
1875 N Humboldt (at Kane)
414/224-7666 *5pm-2:30am, also coffee bar, patio*

South Water Street Dock [M,NH,WC]
354 E National (at Water St)
414/225-9676 *3pm-2am, till 2:30am wknds*

Switch [MW,NH,K] 124 W National Ave (at 1st) **414/220-4340** *5pm-2am, from 2pm wknds, patio*

Taylor's Bar [GS,NH,WC,GO] 795 N Jefferson St (at Wells) **414/271-2855** *4pm-2am, from 5pm wknds, patio*

This Is It [★M] 418 E Wells St (at Jefferson) **414/278-9192** *3pm-2am*

Triangle Bar [M,NH,WC] 135 E National Ave (at Barclay) **414/383-9412** *noon-2am, from 6am wknds*

Walker's Pint [MW,E,K,GO] 818 S 2nd St **414/643-7468** *4:30pm-2am, till 2:30am Fri-Sat, till midnight Sun, clsd Mon*

Woody's [MW,NH] 1579 S 2nd St (at Lapham St) **414/672-0806** *4pm-2am, from 2pm wknds, sports bar*

■ NIGHTCLUBS

Club 219 [MW,D,MR,DS,S]
219 S 2nd St (btwn Florida & Pittsburgh) **414/276-2711** *7pm-2am, 4pm-2:30am wknds*

La Cage (Dance, Dance, Dance)
[★M,D,S,V,YC,WC] 801 S 2nd St (at National) **414/383-8330** *5pm-2am, from 8pm wknds, 2-bar complex*

Orbit [MW,D,GO] 739 S 2nd St (at National) **414/202-7600** *6pm-close*

Wisconsin • *USA*

■CAFES

Alterra Coffee Roasters 2211 N Prospect Ave (at North) **414/273-3753** *7am-10pm, 8am-11pm Fri-Sat, till 9pm Sun*

Fuel Cafe 818 E Center St **414/374-3835** *7am-11pm, from 9am wknds, infamous for their strong coffee*

■RESTAURANTS

Cafe Vecchio Mondo 1137 N Old World Third St (at Juneau) **414/273-5700** *lunch & dinner, full bar*

Coquette Cafe 316 N Milwaukee St (btwn Buffalo & St Paul) **414/291-2655** *lunch Mon-Fri, dinner nightly, clsd Sun*

The Knick [★WC] 1030 E Juneau Ave (at Waverly) **414/272-0011** *11am-midnight, from 9am wknds, full bar*

La Perla 734 S 5th St (at National) **414/645-9888** *11am-10:30pm, till 11:30pm Fri-Sat, 10am-10pm Sun, Mexican*

Sanford Restaurant 1547 N Jackson St **414/276-9608** *dinner only, clsd Sun, elegant Milwaukee Euro-style*

■ENTERTAINMENT & RECREATION

Boerner Botanical Gardens 5879 S 92nd St (in Whitnall Park), Hales Corners **414/525-5601** *8am-dusk, 40-acre garden & arboretum, garden clsd in winter*

Mitchell Park Domes 524 S Layton Blvd (27th St) (at Pierce) **414/649-9830** *9am-5pm, botanical gardens*

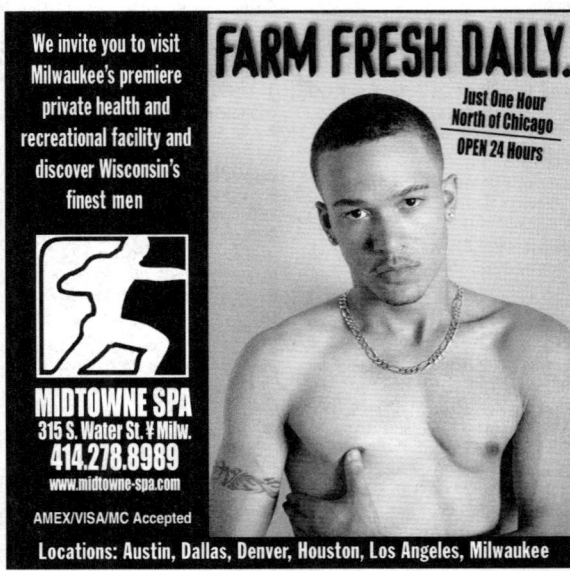

Sheboygan • Wisconsin

BOOKSTORES

OutWords Books, Gifts & Coffee [WC] 2710 N Murray (at Park) **414/963-9089** *11am-10pm, till 6pm Sun, lgbt, pride items*

Peoples' Books 2122 E Locust St (at Maryland) **414/962-0575** *11am-7pm, till 6pm Sat, clsd Sun*

Schwartz Bookstore 2559 N Downer Ave **414/332-1181** *9am-10pm, till 11pm Fri-Sat, till 9pm Sun*

RETAIL SHOPS

Adambomb Gallery 524 S 2nd St (at Bruce) **414/276-2662** *11am-9pm, clsd Mon, tattoo studio*

Miss Groove [GO] 1225 E Brady (btwn Arlington & Franklin) **414/298-9185** *11am-7pm, 10am-6pm Sat, 11am-4pm Sun, clsd Mon, accessories & gifts*

Out of Solitude [GO] 918 E Brady (at Astor) **414/223-3101** *11am-6pm, till 4pm Sat, clsd Sun, jewelry & gifts*

Yellow Jacket 2225 N Humboldt Ave (at North Ave) **414/372-4744** *noon-7pm, till 5pm Sun, vintage clothes*

PUBLICATIONS

IN Step **414/278-7840** *lgbt newspaper*

Quest **800/578-3785, 920/433-0611** *good bar list*

MEN'S CLUBS

➤ **Midtowne Spa–Milwaukee** [PC,WC] 315 S Water **414/278-8989** *24hrs*

MEN'S SERVICES

➤ **Megaphone Milwaukee** **800/289-1489** *Call for the local # nearest you! Meet Hot Men in your area! FREE to Browse & Respond to voice ads. Use code 3087. Also try MEGAMATES.COM*

EROTICA

Booked Solid 7035 Greenfield Ave (at 70th), West Allis **414/774-7210**

Water St Video 225 N Water St (at Buffalo) **414/278-0636** *toys & videos*

CRUISY AREAS

Juneau Park [AYOR] *beware after 10pm*

Underwood Parkway [AYOR]

Warnimont Park [N,AYOR] *beach*

Oshkosh

see also Appleton

EROTICA

Pure Pleasure 1212 Oshkosh Ave (off Hwy 21) **920/235-9727**

CRUISY AREAS

Menomonee Park [AYOR]

Racine

ACCOMMODATIONS

Lochnaiar Inn [GF,WC] 1121 Lake Ave (at 11th St) **262/633-3300** *English Tudor on Lake Michigan, full brkfst*

BARS

What About Me? [MW,NH] 600 6th St (at Villa) **262/632-0171** *3pm-2am, from 7pm Wed-Th, clsd Mon*

NIGHTCLUBS

JoDee's International [MW,D,E,K,DS,S] 2139 Racine St/ S Hwy 32 (at 22nd) **262/634-9804** *7pm-close, park in rear*

EROTICA

Racine News & Video 316 Main St (at State) **262/634-9827**

Rhinelander

ACCOMMODATIONS

Woodwind Health Spa & Resort [GS,NS,WC,GO] 3033 Woodwind Wy (at S River Rd & Hwy 8) **715/362-8902** *resort, full gourmet brkfst*

Sheboygan

BARS

The Blue Lite [MW,NH,D] 1029 N 8th St (off Rte 143) **920/457-1636** *7pm-2am, from 3pm Sun*

CRUISY AREAS

Fountain Park [AYOR]

North Beach [AYOR] *summers*

Wisconsin • USA

Stevens Point

■EROTICA

Eldorado's 3219 Church St (at Business 51 S) **715/343-9877**

Sturgeon Bay

■ACCOMMODATIONS

The Chadwick Inn [GF,NS,GO] 25 N 8th Ave **920/743-2771** *1890 Queen Anne*

The Chanticleer Guest House [★GF,SW,NS,WC,GO] 4072 Cherry Rd **920/746-0334, 866/682-0384** *hot tub, on 70 acres*

Superior

■BARS

JT's Bar & Grill [★MW,D] 1506 N 3rd St (at Blaknik Bridge) **715/394-2580** *3pm-2am, till 2:30am Fri-Sat, patio*

The Main Club [★M,D,CW,L,WC] 1217 Tower Ave (at 12th) **715/392-1756** *3pm-2am, till 2:30am Fri-Sat, internet access*

Molly & Oscar's [GF,NH] 405 Tower Ave **715/394-7423** *5pm-2am, till 2:30am Fri-Sat*

Wausau

■NIGHTCLUBS

Oz [M,D,V] 320 Washington **715/842-3225** *7pm-2am, from 5pm Sun*

Wisconsin Dells

■ACCOMMODATIONS

Captain Dix Resort [MW] 4125 River Rd **608/253-1818, 866/553-1818** *cottages, restaurant & nightclub (Th-Sat)*

WYOMING

Cheyenne

■INFO LINES & SERVICES

United Gays & Lesbians of Wyoming **307/778-7645** *9am-6pm Mon-Sat, info, referrals & newsletter, support groups, quarterly social activities*

■CRUISY AREAS

Holiday Park [AYOR] *near bandstand*

Lions Park [AYOR] *near skating pond*

Etna

■RETAIL SHOPS

Blue Fox Studio & Gallery 107452 Hwy 89 **307/883-3310** *open 7 days, hours vary, pottery & jewelry studio, local travel info*

Freedom

■ENTERTAINMENT & RECREATION

Fool's Gold Excursions [GS,GO] **307/883-3783** *day hiking & outdoor retreats*

Jackson

■ACCOMMODATIONS

Bar H Ranch [W] **208/354-2906, 888/216-6025** *seasonal, authentic working cattle ranch*

Spring Creek Ranch [★GF,F,SW,WC] 1800 Spirit Dance Rd **307/733-8833, 800/443-6139** *non-smoking rooms available*

Riverton

■RESTAURANTS

Country Cove [WC] 301 E Main (at First) **307/856-9813** *7am-3pm, clsd Sun*

INTERNATIONAL
SECTION

Canada
Caribbean
Mexico
Central America
Europe

Alberta • CANADA

Canada

ALBERTA

Provincewide

■ INFO LINES & SERVICES
Xtensions Calgary **877/882-2011 (in Canada only)** *provincewide lgbt info line*

■ PUBLICATIONS
Outlooks 403/228-1157, 888/228-1157 *lgbt magazine available in Alberta & in Vancouver, BC*

Banff

■ ACCOMMODATIONS
The Pigeon Hole [GS,NS,GO] **403/246-4036** *condo, some shared baths*

Calgary

■ INFO LINES & SERVICES
Front Runners AA 1227 Kensington Close NW (at Hillhurst United Church) **403/777-1212** *8:30pm Tue, Th & Sat*

Gay/ Lesbian Centre & Info Line 223 12th Ave SW #206 **403/234-8973** *9am-9pm, till 5pm Fri, clsd wknds, many groups*

Xtensions 403/777-9499, 877/882-2011 (in Canada only) *provincewide lgbt info line*

■ ACCOMMODATIONS
11th Street Lodging [GS,NS,GO] **403/209-0111** *'no shoe' policy inside*

Calgary Westways Guest House [GS,NS,GO] 216 25th Ave SW **403/229-1758, 866/846-7038** *full brkfst, hot tub*

The Foxwood B&B [MW,NS,GO] 1725 12th St SW (17th Ave SW) **403/244-6693** *B&B, spa, some shared baths*

Westpoint Executive B&B [GF,NS,GO] 101 Westpoint Gardens SW (at Old Banff Coach Rd SW) **403/248-5668, 866/592-3974** *some shared baths*

■ BARS
The Backlot [M,WC] 209 10th Ave SW (at 1st St SW) **403/265-5211** *2pm-2am, from 4pm winters, martini lounge, patio*

Calgary Eagle [M,B,L,F,OC,GO] 424 'A' 8th Ave SE **403/263-5847** *4pm-midnight, till 2am wknds, clsd Mon, dress code Fri-Sat from 10pm, dark night Fri, cruisy*

Detour/ Loading Dock [M,NH,D,DS] 318 17th Ave SW **403/244-8537** *3pm-3am, drag show Sun*

Ming [GF] 520 17th Ave SW **403/229-1986** *4pm-2am, martini lounge*

Money Pennies [MW,NH,F,WC] 1742 10th Ave SW (near 14th St) **403/263-7411** *11am-2am, till midnight Sun-Wed, rooftop patio*

The Rekroom [M,PC] 213-A 10th Ave SW (at 1st St) **403/265-4749** *4pm-3am*

Texas Lounge [MO] 308 17th Ave SW (enter rear) **403/229-0911** *11am-2am*

The Verge [MW,NH,F,GO] 2500 4 St SW, 4-A **403/245-3344** *4pm-midnight, clsd Mon, martini bar*

■ NIGHTCLUBS
Boyztown: Metro [M,D,S,PC] 213 10th Ave SW **403/265-2028** *9pm-4am*

The Warehouse [GF,D,YC,PC] 731 10th Ave SW (alley entrance) **403/264-0535** *9pm-3am, after-hours Fri-Sat, clsd Sun-Tue*

■ CAFES
Arena Coffee Bar 310 17th Ave SW **403/228-5730** *4pm-11pm, noon-10pm wknds*

Cafe Beano [WC] 1613 9th St SW (at 17th Ave) **403/229-1232** *6am-midnight, from 7am wknds*

Timothy's World Coffee [MW,WC] 1610 10th St SW (btwn 16th & 17th Ave) **403/244-7750** *7am-11pm, from 8am Sun, patio, more gay in evenings*

■ RESTAURANTS
Melrose Cafe 730 17th Ave SW (at 7th St) **403/228-3566** *11am-midnight, from 10am wknds, full bar till 2am, patio*

Edmonton • Alberta

Thai Sa-On 351 10th Ave SW (at 4th) **403/264-3526** *lunch & dinner, Thai*

Victoria's [WC] 306 17th Ave SW **403/244-9991** *lunch, dinner, wknd brunch, homecooking, full bar*

Wicked Wedge Pizza 618 17th Ave SW (at 6th St) **403/228-1024** *open late*

■ BOOKSTORES

A Woman's Place [WC] 1404 Centre S (at 14th Ave) **403/263-5256** *10am-5:30pm, clsd Sun, many gay titles*

Daily Globe News Shop 1004 17th Ave SW **403/244-2060** *9am-11pm, periodicals*

With the Times 2203 4th St SW (at 22nd Ave) **403/244-8020** *9am-11pm; also at 118 10 St NW, 403/ 282-9257*

■ RETAIL SHOPS

Priape 1322 17th Ave SW (enter on 16th) **403/215-1800, 800/461-6969** *noon-9pm, from 10am Sat, till 6pm Sun, clubwear, leather, books, toys & more*

Rainbow Pride Resource Centre [GO] 1229 16th Ave SW, 2nd flr **403/266-5685** *11am-10pm, noon-6pm Sun, pride items & info*

■ PUBLICATIONS

Perceptions 306/244-1930 *covers the Canadian prairies*

■ MEN'S CLUBS

Goliath's Saunatel [F,PC,AYOR] 308 17th Ave SW (enter rear) **403/229-0911** *24hrs, cocktails*

■ EROTICA

Adult Depot 3505 32 St NE **403/264-7399** *clsd Sun; also 626 58th Ave SE, 403/258-2777*

B&D Emporium 426 8th Ave SE **403/265-7789** *clsd Mon, drag/ fetish*

■ CRUISY AREAS

North Glenmore Park [AYOR] S end of Crowchild *down the ravine*

Prince's Island [AYOR] at 4th St

Edmonton

■ INFO LINES & SERVICES

AA Gay/ Lesbian 12530 110th Ave (at Unitarian church, Green Room) **780/424-5900** *8pm Fri*

Gay & Lesbian Community Centre of Edmonton 9912 106th St, #45 **780/488-3234** *1:30pm-5:30pm & 7pm-10pm, clsd wknds, also youth group 7pm Sat*

Xtensions 877/882-2011 (in Canada only) *provincewide lgbt info*

■ ACCOMMODATIONS

Labyrinth Lake Lodge [GS] **780/878-3301** *lodge on private lake, hot tubs*

Northern Lights B&B [MW,SW,GO] 8216 151st St **780/483-1572** *full brkfst*

■ BARS

Boots/ Garage Burger Bar [M,D,F,DS,S,PC,WC] 10242 106th St (at 103rd Ave) **780/423-5014** *3pm-2am, cafe 11am-8pm, till 10pm Fri, male strippers*

The Roost [MW,D,DS,S,PC] 10345 104th St **780/426-3150** *8pm-3am, clsd Mon, patio, strippers Wed*

Woody's Pub & Cafe [MW,NH,F,K] 11723 A Jasper (above Buddy's) **780/488-6557** *noon-midnight, till 3am Fri-Sat, karaoke Sun-Wed*

■ NIGHTCLUBS

Buddy's Nite Club [MW,D] 11725 B Jasper **780/488-6636** *8pm-3am*

■ CAFES

Urban Grind 10124 124th St **780/451-1039** *10am-midnight, 11am-10pm Sun*

■ RESTAURANTS

Cafe de Ville [NS,R] 10137 124th St (side entrance) **780/488-9188** *11:30am-10pm, till 11pm Th, till midnight Fri-Sat, Sun brunch*

■ ENTERTAINMENT & RECREATION

Gaywire CJSR FM 88.5 **780/492-5244** *6pm-7pm Th, lgbt radio*

Alberta • CANADA

BOOKSTORES

Audrey's Books [WC] 10702 Jasper Ave (at 107th) **780/423-3487** *9am-9pm, 9:30am-5:30pm Sat, noon-5pm Sun, large lgbt section*

The Front Page 10356 Jasper Ave (at 104th St) **780/426-1206** *9am-8pm, clsd Sun*

Greenwood's Bookshoppe 7925 104th St (at 80th) **780/439-2005** *9am-9pm, till 5:30pm Sat, noon-5pm Sun*

RETAIL SHOPS

Divine Decadence 10441 82nd Ave (at 105th) **780/439-2977** *hip fashions, accessories*

PUBLICATIONS

Times .10 10121 124th St, Ste 402 **780/415-5616**

MEN'S CLUBS

Down Under [MO] 12224 Jasper Ave **780/482-7960** *24hrs*

Steamers [MO] 9668 Jasper Ave (at 97th St) **780/422-2581** *24hrs*

EROTICA

Pride Video 10121 124th St, 2nd flr **780/452-7743**

CRUISY AREAS

River Road [AYOR] near Victoria Golf Course

Lethbridge

INFO LINES & SERVICES

GALA/LA (Gay/ Lesbian Alliance of Lethbridge & Area) **403/308-2893** *peer support line 7pm-10pm Mon & Wed, coffee night Wed, dance last Sat, youth group, also newsletter*

Medicine Hat

INFO LINES & SERVICES

LGBT Society of Medicine Hat [18+] 550 C Allowance Ave **403/581-5428** *coffee nights 2nd Tue, activities, resources*

Rocky Mtn House

ACCOMMODATIONS

Country Cabin B&B [GF,SW] **403/845-4834** *full brkfst, hot tub*

BRITISH COLUMBIA

Birken

ACCOMMODATIONS

Birkenhead Resort [GF,SW,GO] Portage Rd **604/452-3255** *cabins & campsites, hot tub, also restaurant*

Campbell River

CRUISY AREAS

Quadra Ferry Landing [AYOR] *wknds & evenings*

Fairmont Hot Springs

ACCOMMODATIONS

Chalet in the Rockies [GF,NS] 5021 Fairmont Close **250/345-9553, 800/856-9551** *some shared baths*

Gibsons

ACCOMMODATIONS

Gower Point Seaside Cottage [GS,NS,GO] **604/687-7798, 866/587-7798** *3 self-contained suites in cottage or whole cottage, 20 miles from Vancouver*

Gulf Islands

INFO LINES & SERVICES

Gays & Lesbians of Salt Spring Island (GLOSSI) **250/537-7773**

ACCOMMODATIONS

Anne's Oceanfront Hideaway B&B [GF,WC] 168 Simson Rd, Salt Spring Island **250/537-0851, 888/474-2663** *full bkfst, hot tub*

The Blue Ewe Private Cabin [MW,NS,GO] 1207 Beddis Rd, Salt Spring Island **250/537-9344** *hot tub*

Clare's Cottage [GS,NS,GO] 425 Fulford Ganges Rd, Salt Spring Island **250/537-5912, 877/537-5912** *B&B*

Clare's Cottage B&B [MW,NS,GO] 425 Fulford Ganges Rd, Salt Spring Island **250/537-5912, 877/537-5912** *rental house & cottage*

Hawthorne House [GS,NS,WC,GO] 6436 Porlier Pass Rd, Galiano Island **250/539-5815** *rental home, sleeps 10*

Prince George • British Columbia

Tutu's B&B [GS,SW] 3198 Jemima Rd, Denman Island **250/335-0546, 877/560-8888** *lakefront*

The Wheatley's Cottage [MW,NS,GO] 2154 Sturdies Bay Rd, Galiano Island **250/537-5912, 877/537-5912** *rental house & cottage*

The Wheatley's Country Home [MW,NS,GO] 2154 Sturdies Bay Rd, Galiano Island **888/539-5980, 866/539-5988** *rental house & cottage*

■ BARS

Moby's Pub [GF,NH,F] 124 Upper Ganges, Salt Spring Island **250/537-5559** *10am-midnight, 11am-1am Fri-Sun*

Kelowna

■ INFO LINES & SERVICES

Okanagan Rainbow Coalition 991 Richter St **250/860-8555** *24hr recorded info, support groups, social events & dances*

■ ACCOMMODATIONS

The Flags B&B [MO,SW,N,GO] 2295 McKinley Rd (at Glenmore Rd) **250/762-8184, 866/762-8184** *full brkfst, hot tub, patio*

The Quails' Nest B&B [M,SW,GO] 2535 Winnipeg Rd **250/769-9171**

■ CAFES

Bean Scene [WC] 274 Bernard Ave **250/763-1814** *7am-10pm, till 11pm Fri-Sat*

■ RESTAURANTS

Greek House 3159 Woodsdale Rd **250/766-0090** *11am-10pm, from 4pm wknds, cont'l*

Maple Ridge

■ EROTICA

XXXtreme Adult 11955 207 St **604/465-5811**

Mission

■ EROTICA

XXXtreme Adult 115 'B' 32423 Lougheed Hwy **604/814-0488**

Nanaimo

■ ACCOMMODATIONS

Dorchester Hotel [GF] 70 Church St **250/754-6835, 800/661-2449**

■ BARS

Blackbeards [MW,NH,D,E,K,V] 70 Church St (under hotel) **250/716-0505** *7pm-close, karaoke Wed*

■ CRUISY AREAS

Bowen Park [AYOR]

Maffeo Sutton Park [AYOR]

Penticton

■ ACCOMMODATIONS

Bear's Den B&B [GS,NS,WC,GO] **250/497-6721, 866/232-7722** *full brkfst, hot tub, great views*

Port Alberni

■ CRUISY AREAS

Harbor Quay Promenade [AYOR]

Powell River

■ ACCOMMODATIONS

Beacon B&B [GF,NS,WC] 3750 Marine Ave **604/485-5563, 877/485-5563** *full brkfst, hot tub*

Wilde Road Farm & Guesthouse [GS] 7420 Wilde Rd **604/483-4923** *farmhouse & cabin, full brkst*

Prince George

■ INFO LINES & SERVICES

GALA North 250/562-6253 *24hr recorded info, call for drop-in hours & location*

■ BOOKSTORES

Mosquito Books 131-1600 15th Ave (Parkwood Place Mall) **250/563-6495, 800/451-6495** *9am-6pm, some gay titles*

■ EROTICA

XXXtreme Adult 1412 Patricia Blvd **250/614-1411** *24hrs*

British Columbia • CANADA

Prince Rupert

■ INFO LINES & SERVICES
Prince Rupert Gay Info Line
250/627-8900

Qualicum Beach

■ ACCOMMODATIONS
Bahari B&B [GF,NS] 5101 Island Hwy W
877/752-9278 *full brkfst, hot tub, apt rental*

Richmond

■ CRUISY AREAS
Richmond Nature Park [AYOR]

Tofino

■ ACCOMMODATIONS
Alder View Suite/ B&B [GF,GO] 1108 Abraham Dr **250/725-4427** *hot tub*

Beachwood [GF,GO] 1368 Chesterman Beach Rd **250/725-4250** *private house, steps to the beach*

BriMar B&B [GS] 1375 Thornberg Crescent **250/725-3410, 800/714-9373** *on the beach, full brkfst*

Lone Cone Guest Suites [GS,NS] 170 2nd St **250/725-3394**

West Wind [M,N,NS,GO] 1321 Pacific Rim **250/725-2224** *hot tub, gym, 5 minutes from beach*

■ RESTAURANTS
Blue Heron [WC] 634 Campbell St **250/725-4266** *5am-2pm & 5pm-9pm, full bar*

Vancouver

■ INFO LINES & SERVICES
AA Gay/ Lesbian 604/434-3933

The Greater Vancouver Pride Line
604/684-6869, 800/566-1170
7pm-10pm, info & support

Vancouver Gay/ Lesbian Centre 1170 Bute St (btwn Davie & Pendrell Sts) **604/684-5307, 800/566-1170** *9am-10pm, also Out on the Shelves lgbt lending library*

■ ACCOMMODATIONS
A Place at Penny's [GF,NS,WC] 810 Commercial Dr (at Venables) **604/254-2229**

Aberdeen Mansion [GF] 1110 Victoria Dr **604/254-2229** *B&B*

The Albion Guest House [GF,NS] 592 W 19th Ave (at Ash) **604/873-2287, 877/717-2287** *hot tub*

Anthem House/ 'O Canada' House [GS,GO] 1114 Barclay St (at Thurlow) **604/688-0555, 877/688-1114** *restored Victorian, full brkfst*

Barclay House B&B [GS,NS,GO] 1351 Barclay St (at Jervis) **604/605-1351, 800/971-1351** *restored Victorian, full brkfst*

Barefoot Moon Guesthouse [GS,NS] 1620 Adanac St (at Commercial Dr) **604/251-9774**

The Buchan Hotel [GF,NS] 1906 Haro St (btwn Denman & Gilford) **604/685-5354, 800/668-6654**

Columbia Cottage B&B [GF,NS] 205 W 14th Ave (at Manitoba) **604/874-5327** *1920s Tudor, full brkfst*

Comfort Inn Downtown [GS,F] 654 Nelson St (at Granville St) **604/605-4333, 888/605-5333** *hip boutique-style hotel in the heart of entertainment district, also Doolin's Irish Pub & Restaurant, ask for IGLTA Pride rate*

Downtown Accommodations/ Furnished Suites [GF,SW] 515 Pender, Ste 247 **604/694-8806, 877/454-8179** *condos*

Dufferin Hotel [GS] 900 Seymour St (at Smithe) **604/683-4251, 877/683-5522** *also 3 bars [M,S]*

The Langtry [GS,NS,GO] 968 Nicola St **604/687-7892** *B&B apts in West End, full brkfst*

Listel Vancouver [GS,F,SW] 1300 Robson St (at Jervis) **604/684-8461, 800/663-5491** *boutique hotel, gym*

Nelson House B&B [MW,GO] 977 Broughton St (btwn Nelson & Barclay) **604/684-9793, 866/684-9793** *Edwardian mansion, full brkfst*

Vancouver • British Columbia

Opus Hotel [GF,WC] 322 Davie St (Yaletown) **604/642-6787, 866/642-6787** *hip luxury boutique hotel, also bar & Elixer French brasserie*

The Park Ridge At Queen Elizabeth Park [MO,GO] 4438 Yukon St **604/420-6367** *upscale B&B, clothing-optional hot tub*

Penny Farthing Inn [GS,NS] 2855 W 6th Ave (at MacDonald) **604/739-9002, 866/739-9002** *1912 heritage house in Kitsilano, full brkfst*

River Run Cottages [GF,WC] 4551 River Rd W, Ladner **604/946-7778** *on the Fraser River, full brkfst*

Rural Roots B&B [MW,NS,N,WC,GO] 4939 Ross Rd, Mt Lehman **604/856-2380** *full brkfst, hot tub, 1 hour from Vancouver*

The West End Guest House [GS,NS,GO] 1362 Haro St (at Broughton) **604/681-2889, 888/546-3327** *full brkfst*

■ BARS

Dufferin Hotel [MW,E,K,DS,S] 900 Seymour St (at Dufferin Hotel) **604/683-4251** *from noon, 3 bars (tavern, pub & lounge)*

The Fountainhead Pub [MW,NH,TG] 1025 Davie St **604/687-2222** *11am-midnight, till 1am Fri-Sat, patio*

The Oasis [M,F,E] 1240 Thurlow **604/685-1724** *3:30pm-midnight, till 1am Fri-Sat, martini bar, tapas menu*

The PumpJack Pub [M,NH,L,19+,WC] 1167 Davie St (off Bute) **604/685-3417** *1pm-midnight, till 1am Fri-Sat*

■ NIGHTCLUBS

23 West [MW,D] 23 W Cordova (at Carrall) **604/662-3277** *9pm-2am, 7pm-midnight Sun, clsd Mon-Wed, call for events, P-CAN naked parties [M,D], patio*

816 Granville [M,D] 816 Granville *2am-6am Sat*

Ms T's Cabaret [GS,D,TG,E] 339 W Pender St **604/682-8096** *8pm-2am, punk bands, theater*

Numbers [★M,D,S,V] 1042 Davie (btwn Thurlow & Burrard) **604/685-4077** *9pm-2am, from 8pm Fri-Sat, till midnight Sun*

The Odyssey [★M,D,DS,S,YC] 1251 Howe St (at Davie) **604/689-5256** *9pm-2am, patio*

Skybar 670 Smithe St (Yaletown) **604/697-0990** *3 flrs, rooftop patio*

■ CAFES

Delany's 1105 Denman St **604/662-3344** *8am-11pm, from 6:30am wknds, coffee shop*

Melriches Coffeehouse 1244 Davie St **604/689-5282** *7am-11pm*

■ RESTAURANTS

Accents Restaurant [E, GO] 1967 W Broadway (at Arbutus) **604/734-6660** *lunch noon-3pm Wed-Fri, dinner 5:30pm-close Tue-Sun, European/ int'l*

Big C Grill [GO] 3941/43 Main St (at 23rd) **604/871-9096** *8am-10pm, diner, patio*

Cafe Luxy [WC] 1235 Davie St (btwn Bute & Jervis) **604/669-5899** *11am-10pm, till 11pm wknds, brunch 9am-3pm wknds, full bar*

Chianti's 1850 W 4th Ave (at Burrard) **604/738-8411** *lunch & dinner*

Cincin 1154 Robson St (off Bute) **604/688-7338** *11am-11pm, Italian/ Mediterranean, full bar*

Delilah's [WC] 1789 Comox St (at Denman) **604/687-3424** *5:30pm-11pm, full bar, extensive martini menu*

The Dish [GO] 1068 Davie St **604/689-0208** *7am-9pm, from 9am Sun, veggie fast food*

Elbow Room Café 560 Davie St (at Seymour) **604/685-3628** *8am-4pm, till 5pm wknds, great brkfst*

Glowbal Grill & Satay Bar 1079 Mainland St (Yaletown) **604/602-0835** *lunch, dinner, brunch wknds, eclectic menu, martinis, extensive wine list; also check out Afterglow next door, nightly 5pm-late*

Hamburger Mary's 1202 Davie St (at Bute) **604/687-1293** *7am-3am, till 4am Fri-Sat, till 2pm Sun, full bar*

British Columbia • CANADA

Havana [★] 1212 Commercial Dr 604/253-9119 *11am-midnight, from noon wknds, Cuban fusion, full bar, patio*

India Gate 616 Robson St (at Granville) 604/684-4617 *lunch & dinner*

Lickerish 903 Davie 604/696-0725 *5pm-midnight, till 1am Th-Sun, global cuisine, cocktail lounge*

Mario's 33555 S Fraser Wy (at Kent Ave) 604/852-6919 *lunch & dinner, Italian*

Martini's 151 W Broadway (btwn Cambie & Main) 604/873-0021 *11am-2am, from 2pm Sat, till 1am Sun, great pizza & full bar*

Naam [WC] 2724 W 4th St (at MacDonald) 604/738-7151 *24hrs, vegetarian*

Octane [★MW,D,E,DS,GO] 1188 Davie St 604/688-0677 *5:30pm-1am, later wknds, brunch wknds, full bar, very popular for Stare [M,D]*

Shiraz [GS,E] 911 Denman St (at Barclay, upstairs) 604/697-0501 *noon-midnight, live jazz, full bar*

■ ENTERTAINMENT & RECREATION

Cruisey T [MW,D,F,E,$] *leaves from N foot of Denman St (at Harbor Cruises)* 604/551-2628 *Sun (seasonal), 4-hour party cruise around Vancouver Harbour tickets at Little Sister's, 1238 Davie St*

Lotus Land Tours 1251 Cardero St #2005 604/684-4922, 800/528-3531 *day paddle trips, whale-watching trips, no experience necessary (price includes pick-up & gourmet meal)*

Queer FM CITR 101.9 FM 604/822-1242 *6pm-8pm Sun, political & social issues in queer community*

Rockwood Adventures 839 W 1st St #C, North Vancouver 604/980-7749, 888/236-6606 *rain forest walks for all levels w/ free hotel pick-up*

Sunset Beach *right in the West End*

■ BOOKSTORES

Little Sister's [★WC] 1238 Davie St (btwn Bute & Jervis) 604/669-1753, 800/567-1662 (in Canada only) *10am-11pm, lgbt*

Spartacus Books 311 W Hastings (at Hamilton) 604/688-6138 *10am-8:30pm, 11am-7pm Sat, noon-7pm Sun, lgbt section*

■ RETAIL SHOPS

Gay-Mart 1148 Davie St (btwn Bute & Thurlow) 604/681-3262, 877/429-6278 *11am-9pm, clothing, books, jewelry, etc*

Mack's Leathers 1043 Granville (at Nelson) 604/688-6225 *11am-7pm, noon-8pm Th-Fri, also body piercing*

Next Body Piercing 1068 Granville St (at Nelson) 604/684-6398 *noon-6pm, 11am-7pm Fri-Sat, also tattooing*

State of Mind 1100 Davie St (at Thurlow) 604/682-7116 *9am-6pm, designer queer clothes*

TopDrawers [WC] 1030 Denman St #115 604/684-4861 *10am-7pm, till 9pm Th-Sat, men's clothing & underwear*

■ PUBLICATIONS

Rainbow Choices Directory 416/762-9994 *lgbt entertainment & business directory for Canada*

➤ **Xtra! West** 604/684-9696 *lgbt newspaper*

■ GYMS & HEALTH CLUBS

Fitness World [GF] 1214 Howe St (at Davie) 604/681-3232 *day passes $15*

■ MEN'S CLUBS

Club Vancouver [★] 339 W Pender St (at Homer) 604/681-5719 *24hrs*

Fahrenheit 212° [PC] 1048 Davie (at Burrard) 604/689-9719 *24hrs; also 430 Columbia St, 604/540-2117*

M2M [LPC] 1210 Granville, downstairs 604/684-6011 *24hrs*

■ EROTICA

Love's Touch 1069 Davie St 604/681-7024

Source Video 2838 E Hastings St 604/251-9191 *24hrs; also 7994 Granville St, 604/ 264-4446*

Womyn's Ware [GO] 896 Commercial Dr (at Denables, in East End) 604/254-2543, 888/WYM-WARE (orders only) *11am-6pm, till 7pm Th-Fri, till 6pm Sat, till 5pm Sun, toys for men too*

Victoria • British Columbia

■Cruisy Areas
Central Park [AYOR] S side of the Boundary & Kingsway intersection *on the Vancouver/ Burnaby border*

English Bay [AYOR]

Stanley Park [AYOR] Lee's Trail

Wreck Beach [AYOR] below UBC

Vernon

■Accommodations
Rainbow's End [MW,WC,GO] 8282 Jackpine Rd 250/542-4842 *full brkfst, hot tub*

■Cruisy Areas
White Rock Beach [AYOR] on Kalamalka Lake

Victoria

■Info Lines & Services
Front Runners AA 1112 Caledonia Ave (at St Nicholas Church) 250/383-7744 (AA#) *8pm Tue*

■Accommodations
Arts & Antiques B&B [GF,NS,GO] 58 Government St (at Battery) 250/385-0410, 877/438-7795

Begbie Cottage [GS] 250/519-0309, 866/519-0309

The Consulate, A Historic B&B [GF] 528 Goldstream (at Hwy 14) 250/474-9796 *full brkfst, pagoda-shaped home*

Eden Guest House [MW,GO] 325 Moss St 877/382-6077 *full brkfst*

The Fairmont Empress [GF,SW,WC] 721 Government St 250/384-8111, 800/441-1414 *Victoria landmark, famous afternoon tea*

Howard Johnson Hotel & Suites Victoria [GF,SW,WC] 4670 Elk Lake Dr 250/704-4656, 866/300-4656 *hot tub, restaurant & lounge*

Ifanwen B&B [MW,GO] 44 Simcoe St 250/384-3717 *full brkfst, gardens*

Oak Bay Guest House [GF,NS] 1052 Newport Ave 250/598-3812, 800/575-3812 *1912 Tudor-style house, full brkfst, near beaches*

■Bars
Prism Lounge [MW,D,K,DS,V,WC] 642 Johnson (enter on Broad St) 250/388-0505 *noon-2am, till midnight Sun, karaoke Mon, drag bingo Wed*

■Nightclubs
Electric Avenue [MW,NH,D,18+,YC] 1601 Store St (at Pandora) 250/920-0018 *7pm-2am, 8pm-midnight Sun*

Hush [GS,D,DS] 1325 Government St (in basement) 250/385-0566 *9pm-2am, till midnight Sun, clsd Mon-Tue, more gay Sun*

■Restaurants
Green Cuisine 560 Johnson St #5 (in Market Square) 250/385-1809 *10am-8pm, vegan, also juice bar, bakery*

Rosie's Diner [WC,GO] 235 Cook St 250/384-6090 *8am-9pm, '50s & '60s music & videos*

Santiago's Cafe [GO] 660 Oswego St 250/388-7376 *8am-10pm, from 7am summers, tapas bar, patio*

■Bookstores
Bleeding Rose Books & Multimedia [GO] 102/102-764 Yates St (on alley btwn Yates & Johnson) 250/385-3099 *10am-10pm, new & used books, video rentals, also coffee shop*

Bolen Books 1644 Hillside Ave #111 (in shopping center) 250/595-4232 *8:30am-10pm, lgbt section*

■Publications
Outviews 250/385-3099 *Victoria's lgbt magazine*

Victoria Rainbow News PO Box 5339, Station B V8R 6S4 250/598-6490 *lgbt monthly*

■Men's Clubs
Steamworks [MO,V] 582 Johnson St (at Gov't St, look for red alley) 250/383-6623

British Columbia • CANADA

■EROTICA

Bleeding Rose Afterdark [MW,GO] 764 A Yates 250/385-3099 *10am-10pm, adult toys, clothing, leather, fetish*

Kiss & Tell 531 Herald St 250/380-6995

Rubber Rainbow Condom Co 560 Johnson St #100 (in Market Square) 250/388-3532

■CRUISY AREAS

Beacon Hill [AYOR]

Gay Beach Dallas Rd, W of stairway at Cook

Thetis Lake Park [AYOR] Highland Rd exit, towards Duncan (off Hwy 1) *look for parked cars & pathway to 'Blowjob Hill'*

Whistler

■ACCOMMODATIONS

Coast Whistler Hotel [GF,SW,WC] 4005 Whistler Wy 604/932-2522, 800/663-5644 *full-service resort hotel, full bar & restaurant*

■RESTAURANTS

Boston Pizza 2011 Innsbruck Dr 604/932-7070 *11am-11pm, till midnight wknds, full bar*

La Rua 4557 Blackcomb Blvd 604/932-5011 *6pm-close, clsd Mon-Tue, Italian/cont'l*

Monks Grill base of Blackcomb 604/932-9677 *11:30am-10pm, grill menu, full bar*

White Rock

■CRUISY AREAS

Marine Dr [AYOR] at Balsam & Kent

MANITOBA

St Pierre-Jolys

■RESTAURANTS

La Table Des Bonnes Soeurs [WC,GO] 432 Joubert St (at Hwy 59, in St Pierre Museum) 204/433-3878, 888/528-2253 *lunch & dinner, clsd Mon-Tue, eclectic*

Winnipeg

■INFO LINES & SERVICES

Rainbow Resource Centre 1-222 Osborne St S 204/284-5208, 888/399-0005 *7:30pm-10pm, clsd Sun, also info line, many social/support groups*

■ACCOMMODATIONS

Winged Ox Guest House [MW,NS,GO] 82 Spence St 204/783-7408 *full brkfst, shared baths*

■BARS

Club 200 [MW,D,F,K,DS,S,WC] 190 Garry St (at St Mary Ave) 204/943-6045 *4pm-2am, from 11am Th-Fri, till midnight Sun, karaoke Wed, go-go dancers Tue*

■NIGHTCLUBS

Gio's Club & Bar [MW,D,E,DS,PC] 155 Smith St 204/786-1236 *4pm-3am, from 2pm wknds, till midnight Sun, clsd Mon, screened patio*

Happenings [MW,D,K,DS,S,PC] 274 Sherbrook St (upstairs) 204/774-3576 *9pm-2am, till 4am Sat, clsd Sun, 2 levels, karaoke Mon, male dancers Fri*

■CAFES

Theatro Café [WC] 126 Sherbrook St 204/775-3375 *11am-11pm, till midnight Fri-Sat, 2-story cafe w/ balcony, salads & sandwiches*

■RESTAURANTS

Step'N Out [WC] 283 Bannatyne Ave (at King St) 204/956-7837 *lunch & dinner, clsd Sun*

■BOOKSTORES

Dominion News 262 Portage Ave 204/942-6563 *8am-9pm, from 9am Sat, from noon Sun*

McNally Robinson [WC] 1120 Grant Ave #4000 (in the mall) 204/453-2644 *9am-10pm, till 11pm Fri-Sat, noon-6pm Sun*

■PUBLICATIONS

Perceptions 306/244-1930 *covers the Canadian prairies*

Swerve 204/942-4599 *lgbt newspaper*

St John • New Brunswick

■ MEN'S CLUBS

Adonis Spa [MO] 1060 Main St (at Burrows), **204/589-6133** *24hrs*

Aquarius Bath [MO] 457 Notre Dame Ave **204/947-1763** *24hrs*

■ EROTICA

Discreet Boutique 340 Donald (at Ellice) **204/947-1307, 800/247-0454** *also Discreet Video next door*

Love Nest 172 St Anne's Rd **204/254-0422** *also 1341 Main St, 204/589-4141, Portage & Westwood, 204/837-6475*

■ CRUISY AREAS

Assiniboine Ave [AYOR] parking lot (btwn Main & Fort Sts) *nights by car*

Assiniboine Park [AYOR] parking lot of central picnic area (1/4 km W of pavilion) *weekday afternoons*

Bonnycastle Park [AYOR]

Osborne St Village [AYOR]

Parliament Grounds—The Hill [AYOR]

NEW BRUNSWICK

Fredericton

■ ACCOMMODATIONS

Hatfield Heritage Inn [GS,GO] 370 Main St (at Queen), Hartland **506/375-8000, 877/637-8200** *1870s antique-filled home*

■ BOOKSTORES

Beegie's Books 370 Prospect St (in Fredericton Mall) **506/459-3636** *9:30am-9pm, clsd Sun (summers), some lgbt titles*

■ EROTICA

X-Citement 558 Queen St **506/458-2048** *videos, magazines, adult novelties*

■ CRUISY AREAS

The Green [AYOR]

Lower Sackville

■ EROTICA

X-Citement 295 Sackville Dr **902/864-4159** *videos, magazines, adult novelties*

Moncton

■ NIGHTCLUBS

Triangles [MW,D,K] 234 St George St (at Archibald) **506/857-8779** *7pm-2am, from 8pm wknds, clsd Mon, more men Wed*

■ RETAIL SHOPS

Rainbow Gift Shop 245 Lutz St **506/863-1888, 866/756-7277** *pride items, also Cafe du Village*

■ EROTICA

X-Citement 203 St George St **506/855-2333** *videos, magazines, adult novelties*

X-Citement 651 Mountain Rd **506/388-2226**

■ CRUISY AREAS

The Block [AYOR] Main St (btwn Highland & Fleet Sts)

Champlain Place [AYOR]

Petit-Rocher

■ NIGHTCLUBS

Club GNG [MW,D,19+] 702 rue Principle, Bloc C **506/783-7440** *Sat 9pm-2am, internet access*

St Andrews

■ ACCOMMODATIONS

Windsor House of St Andrews [GS,GO] 132 Water St (at Edward) **506/529-3330, 888/890-9463** *comfortable inn, full brkfst, massage*

St John

■ ACCOMMODATIONS

Mahogany Manor [GS,NS,WC,GO] 220 Germain St **506/636-8000, 800/796-7755** *full brkfst*

■ NIGHTCLUBS

Club Montreal [M,D,S] 9 Sydney St (off King Square, upstairs) **506/696-1900** *8pm-2am, clsd Mon-Tue*

■ CRUISY AREAS

Carleton St [AYOR] btwn YMCA & Old Stone Church

City Market [AYOR]

Rockwood Park [AYOR] at beach & on trails

Newfoundland • CANADA

NEWFOUNDLAND

St John's

■ACCOMMODATIONS

A Gower House B&B [GS,NS] 180 Gower St (at Prescott St) **709/754-0058, 800/563-3959** *in downtown, full brkfst, some shared baths*

Abba Inn St John's [GS,NS] 36 Queen's Rd (at Prescott St) **709/754-0058, 800/563-3959** *B&B, full brkfst, fireplaces*

Banberry House [GS,GO] 116 Military Rd (at Rawlins Cross) **709/579-8006, 877/579-8226** *full brkfst*

Bluestone Inn [GF,GO] 34 Queen's Rd (at Water St) **709/754-7544, 877/754-9876**

NaGeira House [GF,NS] 7 Musgrave St (at Water St), Carbonear **709/596-1888, 800/600-7757** *B&B, full brkfst, jacuzzi*

■BARS

Schroders Piano Bar [GF,E] 10 Bates Hill (off Queens Rd) **709/753-0807** *4:30pm-1am, till 2am Fri-Sat, till midnight Sun, also Zapata's Mexican restaurant*

■NIGHTCLUBS

Zone 216 [MW,D] 216 Water St **709/754-2492** *9pm-3am, till 4:30am Fri-Sat, clsd Sun-Wed*

■BOOKSTORES

Bennington Gate Bookstore 8-10 Rowan St, Churchill Square (lower level, Terrace on the Square) **709/576-6600** *10am-6pm, till 9pm Th-Fri, 12:30pm-5pm Sun, lgbt section*

NOVA SCOTIA

Annapolis Royal

■ACCOMMODATIONS

King George Inn [MW,NS] **902/532-5286, 888/799-5464** *seasonal, full brkfst, jacuzzi*

Baddeck

■ACCOMMODATIONS

The Dunlop Inn [GF] 552 Chebucto St **902/295-1100, 888/263-9840** *waterfront B&B inn*

Bear River

■ACCOMMODATIONS

Lovett Lodge Inn [GF,SW,NS,GO] 1820 Main St **902/467-3917, 866/467-3917** *seasonal, full brkfst*

Chéticamp

■ACCOMMODATIONS

Seashell Housekeeping Units [GS,NS,GO] 125 Chéticamp Island Rd **902/224-3569 (summer)** *seasonal*

Dartmouth

■RETAIL SHOPS

Wolfgang Leathers 148 Windmill Rd **902/463-0942** *noon-5pm Mon-Fri & by apt*

■EROTICA

X-Citement 155 Main St **902/435-5312** *videos, magazines, adult novelties*

Digby

■ACCOMMODATIONS

Harbourview Inn [GF,SW,WC] 25 Harbourview Rd (at Hwy 1), Smith's Cove **902/245-5686, 877/449-0705** *century-old country inn*

Guysborough

■ACCOMMODATIONS

Barrens at Bay Coastal Cottages [GS,WC,GO] 6870 Hwy 16 (at Halfway Cove) **902/358-2157** *jacuzzi*

Halifax

■ACCOMMODATIONS

Centretown Guest House [M,NS,GO] 2016 Oxford St (at Quinpool Rd) **902/422-2380** *hot tub, French spoken*

Yellowknife • NW Territories

The Old Fisher House B&B [GS] 204 Paddys Head Rd, RR 1, Indian Harbour **902/823-2228** *125-yr-old fisherman's home*

BARS

Reflections Cabaret & Cigar Bar [MW,D,E,C,DS,WC] 5184 Sackville St (at Barrington) **902/422-2957** *1pm-4am, from 4pm Sun*

The Toolbox East [M,D,L] 2104 Gottingen St, upstairs **902/423-1083** *noon-2am*

NIGHTCLUBS

Club NRG [MW,D,TG,F,K,DS,GO] 2099 Gottingen St **902/422-4368** *4pm-2am, karaoke Tue & Th, drag shows Sun*

CAFES

The Daily Grind 5686 Spring Garden Rd (near South Park) **902/429-6397** *7am-10pm, from 8am wknds, also newsstand*

The Second Cup 5425 Spring Garden Rd **902/429-0883** *7am-midnight, internet access*

RESTAURANTS

Le Bistro [WC] 1333 South Park (near Spring Garden Rd) **902/423-8428** *11am-10pm, till 11pm Fri-Sat, till 9pm Sun-Mon, some veggie, full bar*

Satisfaction Feast 1581 Grafton St (off Blower St) **902/422-3540** *11:30am-9pm, till 4pm Wed, till 10pm Fri, from 4pm Sun, vegetarian, patio*

Soho [E] 1582 Granville St (at Sackville) **902/423-3049** *11:30am-10pm, clsd Sun, cont'l*

Sweet Basil 1866 Upper Water St (near Duke) **902/425-2133** *11:30am-10pm, full bar*

BOOKSTORES

Atlantic News 5560 Morris St (at Queen) **902/429-5468** *8am-10pm daily, periodicals*

Frog Hollow Books 5657 Spring Garden Rd (at Dresden Row) **902/429-3318** *9:30am-6pm Mon-Wed, till 9:30pm Th-Fri, noon-5pm Sun*

Smithbooks 5201 Duke St (in Scotia Square) **902/423-6438** *9am-6pm, till 9pm Fri-Sat*

Trident Booksellers & Cafe 1256 Hollis St (at Morris St) **902/423-7100** *8:30am-5pm, from noon Sun*

MEN'S CLUBS

Apollo Sauna Bath 1547 Barrington (at Blowers) **902/423-6549** *clsd Sun*

SeaDog's Sauna & Spa [MO,18+,V,PC,GO] 2199 Gottingen St (at Cunard St) **902/444-3647, 888/837-1388** *24hr wknds, steam, darkroom, internet access*

EROTICA

Night Magic Fashions 5268 Sackville St **902/420-9309** *clsd Sun, lingerie, toys, videos*

X-Citement 6260 Quinpool Rd **902/492-0026** *videos, magazines, adult novelties*

CRUISY AREAS

Citadel Hill [AYOR] *evenings*

Crystal Crescent Beach [N,AYOR] *20 min from Halifax*

Public Gardens [AYOR] *summers*

Lunenburg

ACCOMMODATIONS

Brook House [GF,GO] 3 Old Blue Rocks Rd **902/634-3826** *seasonal*

Yarmouth

ACCOMMODATIONS

Charles C Richards House Historic B&B [GS,GO] 17 Collins St **902/742-0042** *brick mansion, full brkfst, some shared baths*

Murray Manor B&B [GF] 225 Main St (at Forest St) **902/742-9625, 877/742-9629** *heritage home w/ lovely gardens & greenhouse, full brkfst, shared baths*

NW TERRITORIES

Yellowknife

ACCOMMODATIONS

Ptartan Ptarmigan [GS,NS,GO] 5120 51st St (at 52nd Ave) **867/669-7222** *B&B, shared baths*

Ontario • CANADA

ONTARIO

Provincewide

■ PUBLICATIONS

fab 416/925-5221 *Ontario's glossy gay scene magazine*

The Voice *monthly lgbt paper serving South Central/ Western Ontario*

Belleville

■ CRUISY AREAS

Zwick's Park [AYOR]

Brighton

■ ACCOMMODATIONS

Apple Manor [GF,SW,NS] 96 Main St, Box 11 613/475-0351 *150-yr-old Victorian, full brkfst, shared baths*

Butler Creek Country Inn [GF,NS,GO] 613/475-1248, 877/477-5827 *full brkfst*

■ BOOKSTORES

Lighthouse Books 65 Main St 613/475-1269 *9:30am-5:30pm, clsd Sun-Mon*

Brockville

■ ACCOMMODATIONS

The Calico Cat B&B [GF,NS] 193 Brockmere Cliff (at Hwy 401) 613/342-0363 *located in the beautiful 1000 Islands*

Cambridge

■ ACCOMMODATIONS

Blairview B&B [GF] 519/621-9335 *antique-filled home, full brkfst*

Dutton

■ ACCOMMODATIONS

Victorian Court B&B [MW,NS] 235 Main St 519/762-2244 *restored Victorian*

Gananoque

■ ACCOMMODATIONS

Boathouse Country Inn & Heritage Boat Tours [GS,NS,WC] 17-19 Front St, 1000 Islands, Rockport 613/659-2348, 800/584-2592 *full brkfst, also tavern*

Trinity House Inn [GF,NS,GO] 90 Stone St S, 1000 Islands 613/382-8383, 800/265-4871 (ON only) *historic country inn & sailing charters*

Grand Valley

■ ACCOMMODATIONS

Rainbow Ridge Resort [MW,F,SW,GO] Country Rd 109 (at Hwy 25 S) 519/928-3262 *trailers & tents, located on 72 acres on Grand River, restaurant, dance hall, day visitors welcome, seasonal*

Guelph

■ INFO LINES & SERVICES

Out Line 519/836-4550 *volunteer hours vary*

■ ACCOMMODATIONS

Dr WF Savage House B&B [MW,NS,GO] 45 Colborne St, Elora 519/846-5325 *full brkfst*

■ BOOKSTORES

Bookshelf Cafe 41 Quebec St 519/821-3311 *9am-10pm, 10:30am-9pm Sun, cinema, also restaurant & bar*

Hamilton

■ ACCOMMODATIONS

The Cedars Tent & Trailer Park [MW,D,SW] 1039 5th Concession W Rd, Waterdown 905/659-3655 *private campground, also bar, restaurant wknds*

The Twisted Magnolia B&B [GS,SW] 971 Lowers Lions Club Rd (at Wilson & Main W) 905/304-6130 *Victorian farmhouse, full brkfst, fireplaces*

■ BARS

The Embassy Club [MW,D,TG,K,DS,V] 54 King St E (at Houston) 905/522-1100 *8pm-2am, patio bar 9pm-2am Fri-Sat*

Mississauga • Ontario

M [M,NH,E,GO] 164 James St S
905/570-0404 *1pm-2am, lounge, live jazz Th*

The Werx [MW,NH,D,K,GO] 121 Hughson St N (at Canon)
905/972-9379, 866/796-0701 *2pm-2am, pub, dance bar & dungeon [M,B,L]*

The Windsor [MW,NH,K,DS] 31 John St N (at King William) **905/308-9939** *11am-2am, karaoke Tue & Th*

■ BOOKSTORES

Gomorrah's 233 Locke St S (near Charlton) **905/526-1074, 888/338-8278** *11am-6pm, till 8pm Fri, noon-5pm Sun, books, magazines, videos, pride gifts & jewelry, toys*

■ MEN'S CLUBS

Warehouse Spa [GO] 401 Main W
905/523-7636 *24hrs Th-Sat*

■ CRUISY AREAS

Dundern Park [AYOR] near bridge

Jackson St [AYOR] from Catherine to City Hall

Kingston

■ CRUISY AREAS

City Park [AYOR] near Bagot St

MacDonald Park [AYOR]

Kitchener

■ NIGHTCLUBS

Club Renaissance [MW,D,F,DS] 24 Charles St W **519/570-2406, 877/635-2352** *9pm-3am, clsd Mon-Tue, also billiards lounge*

London

■ INFO LINES & SERVICES

Halo Gay/ Lesbian Community Centre 388 Dundas St #206
519/433-3551 *9am-4pm, clsd wknds, also bi-monthly newsletter*

■ BARS

The Junction [MO,F,WC] 722 York St (at Complex 722) **519/438-2625** *24hrs*

■ NIGHTCLUBS

Club 181 [M,D] 181 King St
519/672-5182 *2pm-2am*

■ RESTAURANTS

Blackfriars Cafe [★] 46 Blackfriars (2 blks S of Oxford) **519/667-4930** *lunch & dinner, Sun brunch, full bar*

The Green Tomato 172 King St (at Richmond) **519/660-1170** *11am-11pm, 5pm-10pm Sun, plenty veggie, full bar*

Marla Jane's [GO] 460 King St (at Maitland) **519/858-8669** *lunch Wed-Fri, dinner Wed-Sun, clsd Mon-Tue, French/ Cajun cuisine*

Murano [GO] 394 Waterloo St (at Dundas) **519/434-7565** *dinner only, clsd Sun, northern Italian cuisine, terrace*

Veranda [GO] 546 Dundas St (at William St) **519/434-6790** *lunch & dinner, dinner only Sat, clsd Sun-Mon*

■ BOOKSTORES

Mystic Book Shop 612 Dundas St (at Adelaide) **519/673-5440** *11am-6pm, clsd Sun, spiritual*

■ MEN'S CLUBS

Club London [F] 722 York St (rear) (at Complex 722) **519/438-2625** *24hrs, also bar w/ light meals*

■ EROTICA

Adonis 722 York St (at Complex 722)
519/438-2625 *24hrs, video sales/ rentals*

■ CRUISY AREAS

Reservoir Park [AYOR] SW London

Maynooth

■ ACCOMMODATIONS

Wildewood Guesthouse [W,NS,WC,GO] 613/338-3134 *brkfst & dinner included, hot tub*

Mississauga

■ EROTICA

Lovecraft 2200 Dundas St E (west of Hwy 427) **905/276-5772** *toys, lingerie, videos*

Stag Shop 6020 Hurontario Rd
905/501-9855

Ontario • CANADA

Morrisburg

■ACCOMMODATIONS

The Village Antiques & Tea Room B&B [GF,F,GO] 4326 County Rd 31, Williamsburg 613/535-2463, 877/264-3281 *B&B inn, full brkfst, dining room w/ excellent wine list, also antique shop & tea room*

Niagara Falls

see also Niagara Falls & Buffalo, New York, USA

■ACCOMMODATIONS

Amelia's [GS,SW,GO] 15526 Niagara River Pkwy, Niagara-on-the-Lake 905/468-5550 *full brkfst*

Angels Hideaway [GS,NS] 4360 Simcoe St (at River Rd) 905/354-1119 *B&B, full brkfst, jacuzzi*

Avec Chateau Pebbles [GS] 1059 Hwy 8, Stoney Creek 905/643-6627 *B&B*

Bampfield Hall B&B [GS,GO] 4761 Zimmerman Ave 905/352-8522, 877/353-8522 *historic Gothic home near Niagara Falls, full brkfst, jacuzzi*

Britaly B&B [GF,GO] 57 The Promenade (at Charlotte & John), Niagara-on-the-Lake 905/468-8778 *B&B, full bkfst*

Fairbanks House/ Ellis House [GS,NS,GO] 4965 River Rd 905/371-3716, 866/246-6616 *1877 restored Victorian*

Gretna Green B&B [GS,NS] 5077 River Rd 905/357-2081 *full brkfst*

Niagara Inn B&B [GF,GO] 4300 Simcoe St (at River Rd) 905/353-8522, 877/353-8522 *restored Victorian near Niagara Falls, full brkfst*

Oasis Niagara B&B [M,NS,GO] 4266 Elgin St (at River Rd) 905/353-0223 *close to falls, hot tub*

■CRUISY AREAS

Clifton Hill [AYOR]

Dufferin Islands [AYOR]

Queen Victoria Park [AYOR]

Niagara-on-the-Lake

■ACCOMMODATIONS

302 Nassau St B&B [GS,NS,GO] 302 Nassau St (at Johnson) 905/468-5080, 800/505-9274 *full brkfst*

The Pride of Niagara B&B [GS,SW,NS,GO] 279 Nassau St, Box 485 (at Johnson) 905/468-8181, 877/586-1212 *full brkfst*

■CRUISY AREAS

Simcoe Park [AYOR]

Oshawa

■NIGHTCLUBS

Club 717 [MW,D,K,DS] 717 Wilson Rd S #7 905/434-4297 *9pm-2am Th, till 3am wknds, till midnight Sun*

■MEN'S CLUBS

Continental Spa/ Sauna 16-A Ontario St 905/728-0545 *clsd Sun*

■EROTICA

Forbidden Pleasures 1268 Simcoe St N 905/728-0834

Ottawa

see also Hull, Province of Québec

■INFO LINES & SERVICES

237-XTRA 613/237-9872

Gayline/ Télégai 613/238-1717 *7pm-10pm Mon-Th, bilingual helpline*

Pink Triangle Services 177 Nepean St #508 (at Bank St) 613/563-4818 *many groups & services, library*

■ACCOMMODATIONS

Ambiance B&B [GS,NS,GO] 330 Nepean St 613/563-0421, 888/366-8772 *some shared baths*

Home Sweetland Home B&B [GS,GO] 62 Sweetland Ave (at Laurier Ave) 613/234-1871 *full brkfst*

Inn on Somerset [GS,NS] 282 Somerset St W (at Elgin) 613/236-9309, 800/658-3564 *3-story Victorian, full brkfst, some shared baths*

Rideau Inn [GS,NS,GO] 177 Frank St 613/688-2753, 877/580-5015 *Victorian town house, some shared baths*

Peterborough • Ontario

■ Bars

Centretown Pub [MW,D,V]
340 Somerset St W (at Bank)
613/594-0233 *2pm-2am, also Cell Block [L] & Silhouette Lounge [P] Th-Sat*

The Lookout [MW,F,WC,GO] 41 York, 2nd flr **613/789-1624** *noon-2am, balcony*

Swizzles [MW,D,K,DS,S] 246 Queen St **613/232-4200** *11am-2am, karaoke Tue, male dancers Mon & Wed*

VIP [MW,NH] 313-315 Bank St **613/594-8287** *11am-2am*

■ Nightclubs

Circus [M,D,F,DS,S] 21 Jacques-Cartier **613/224-4056** *Mon only, go-go boys, patio, call for info*

Club AWOL [MW,D,C] 212 Sparks St (at Bank) **613/266-2965** *9pm-2am, cabaret Sun, rooftop terrace*

Icon [★MW,D,S,V] 366 Lisgar St (at Bank) **613/235-4005** *8pm-3am, clsd Mon, martini lounge, DJ Wed-Fri*

Zaphod Beeblebrox [GS,NH,D,S] 27 York **613/562-1010** *4pm-2am, live music*

■ Cafes

AE Micro Internet Cafe 288 Bank St (at Somerset) **613/230-9000** *24hrs, clsd Mon-Tue*

Bridgehead Coffee [GO] 365 Bank St (at Gilmour) **613/569-5600** *7am-9pm*

■ Restaurants

Alfonsetti's 5830 Hazeldean Rd, Stittsville **613/831-3008** *lunch & dinner, clsd Sun, plenty veggie*

Fairouz 343 Somerset St W (btwn Bank & O'Connor) **613/233-1536** *lunch & dinner, dinner only wknds, Lebanese*

Manfred's 2280 Carling Ave **613/829-5715** *lunch & dinner, dinner only wknds, cont'l, full bar*

■ Bookstores

After Stonewall 370 Bank St (near Gilmour) **613/567-2221** *10am-6pm, till 8pm Fri, noon-5pm Sun, lgbt*

Mags & Fags 254 Elgin St (btwn Somerset & Cooper) **613/233-9651** *gay magazines*

Octopus Books 116 3rd Ave (at Bank) **613/233-2589** *10am-6pm*

■ Retail Shops

Classic Body Piercing 369 Bank St (next door to Wildes) **613/594-3555** *11am-5pm*

One in Ten [V] 216 Bank St (at Nepean) **613/563-0110** *1pm-8pm, pride gifts, T-shirts, videos, toys, also all-male XXX theater*

Wilde's [WC] 367 Bank St **613/234-5512** *11am-9pm, noon-6pm Sun, pride items, magazines, leather*

■ Publications

▶ **Capital Xtra!** **613/237-7133** *lgbt newspaper*

Rainbow Choices Directory **416/762-9994** *lgbt entertainment & business directory for Canada*

■ Men's Clubs

Club Ottawa Health Club [★PC] 1069 Wellington St **613/722-8978** *24hrs*

Steamworks 487 Lewis (at Bank St) **613/230-8431** *24hrs*

Steamworks 487 Lewis (at Bank St) **613/230-8431** *24hrs*

■ Cruisy Areas

Elgin St [AYOR]

Perth

■ Accommodations

Perth Manor Heritage Inn- Accommodation & Reception Facility [GS,GO] 23 Drummond St W (at D'Arcy & Boulton) **613/264-0050** *B&B inn, English gardens*

Stonegarden Retreat [GS,NS,GO] 2236 Old Brooke Rd, Maberly **613/268-2828** *peaceful country location, jacuzzi*

Peterborough

■ Info Lines & Services

Rainbow **705/876-1845, 877/554-4210 (Canada only)** *phoneline from 9pm, many social events*

■ Erotica

Forbidden Pleasures 91 George St N **705/742-3800**

Ontario • CANADA

Picton

■ACCOMMODATIONS

Henderson House B&B [GF,GO] 116 Main St (at Hwy 33), Consecon **613/394-5093** *full brkfst, along Consecon River,*

Puslinch

■ACCOMMODATIONS

Cedarbrook Farm B&B [GS,NS,GO] 812 8th Conc Rd W, RR 3 **905/659-1566** *full brkfst, lesbian-owned/ run*

Sault Ste-Marie

■ACCOMMODATIONS

St. Christopher's Inn B&B [GS,GO] 923 Queen St E (at Church St) **705/759-0870** *gay/ lesbian marriages can be performed on-site*

Stratford

■ACCOMMODATIONS

A Hundred Church Street [GS,NS,GO] 100 Church St **519/272-8845** *full brkfst, hot tub*

■RESTAURANTS

Down the Street 30 Ontario St **519/273-5886** *11am-midnight, dinner only Mon, bar till 2am, int'l*

■CRUISY AREAS

Shakespeare Memorial Gardens [AYOR]

Tom Patterson Island [AYOR]

Sudbury

■ACCOMMODATIONS

Rainbow Guest House [M,GO] 43 Lorne St **705/673-8681, 705/688-0561** *some shared baths*

■NIGHTCLUBS

Zig's [MW,NH,D,B,L,TG,K,DS] 54 Elgin St (at Elm St) **705/673-3873** *8pm-close*

Thunder Bay

■EROTICA

Rainbow DVD & Video 264 Bay St (at Court St) **807/345-6272** *11am-10pm, noon-6pm Sun, some books*

Toronto

■INFO LINES & SERVICES

519 Church St Community Centre [WC] 519 Church St (on Cawthra Park) **416/392-6874** *9am-10pm, till 5pm wknds, also cafe*

925-XTRA 416/925-9872 *touch-tone lgbt visitors info*

AA Gay/ Lesbian 416/487-5591

Canadian Lesbian/ Gay Archives 56 Temperance St, # 201 **416/777-2755** *7:30pm-10pm Tue-Th & by appt*

Toronto Area Gay/ Lesbian Phone Line 416/964-6600 *7pm-10pm Mon-Fri*

■ACCOMMODATIONS

104 Earl Place Toronto B&B [GS,GO] 104 Earl Place (at Jarvis St & Wellesley St) **416/323-8898, 877/500-0466** *jacuzzi, 1 block to gay village*

213 Carlton Street—Toronto Townhouse [GS,NS,WC,GO] **416/323-8898, 877/500-0466** *upscale town house, full brkfst, some shared baths*

A Seaton Dream [GS,NS,GO] 243 Seaton St (at Sherbourne & Gerrard) **416/929-3363, 866/878-8898** *B&B, full brkfst, garden patio*

Aberdeen Guest House B&B [GS,NS] 52 Aberdeen Ave **416/922-8697** *in historic Cabbagetown, shared baths, secret garden*

Allan Gardens B&B [GF] 106A Pembroke St (at Jarvis & Gerrard) **416/964-1470** *B&B in private home, close to gay village, full brkfst*

Amazing Space B&B [MW,NS] 246 Sherbourne St (at Dundas) **416/925-3799, 800/205-3694**

Annex Townhouse B&B [GS,GO] 384 Clinton St (at Bloor) **416/323-8898, 877/500-0466** *jacuzzi*

Au Beauregard B&B [GF,MR,TG,NS,GO] 12 Prospect St (at Parliament) **416/960-5682**

Banting House Inn [MW,GO] 73 Homewood Ave (at Wellesley) **416/924-1458** *restored Edwardian home, private entrances*

Toronto • Ontario

Bent Inn [M,L,GO] 552 Church St, #90 (at Wellesley St) **416/925-4499, 866/743-5357** *B&B*

Bonnevue Manor B&B [GS] 33 Beaty Ave (at Queen St & Roncesvalles) **416/536-1455, 800/603-3837** *B&B, full brkfst*

Burwood Inn B&B [GS,GO] 10 Monteith St (near Church & Wellesley) **416/351-1503, 877/580-5015** *Victorian town house, some shared baths, garden, deck*

➤ **Cawthra Square Bed & Breakfast Inns** [MW,NS,GO] **416/966-3074, 800/259-5474** *includes Ten Cawthra & 512 Jarvis, some shared baths*

➤ **Dundonald House** [M,NS,GO] 35 Dundonald St (at Church) **416/961-9888, 800/260-7227** *full brkfst, hot tub, sauna, gym, shared baths*

Executive Apartments [GS,WC] **416/918-8467** *full kitchens*

House on McGill [GS,NS,GO] 110 McGill St (at Church & Carlton) **416/351-1503, 877/580-5015** *Victorian town house, shared baths, garden w/ deck*

Howard Johnson Selby [GF,SW] 592 Sherbourne St (at Selby) **416/921-3142, 800/387-4788**

Immaculate Reception B&B [MW,NS,GO] 34 Monteith St (at Church) **416/925-4202, 800/335-9190** *full brkfst*

The Mansion [GS] 46 Dundonald St (at Church) **416/963-8385** *B&B, elegant Victorian, also 2 apts*

Mike's on Mutual [MW,NS,GO] 333 Mutual St (at Maitland) **416/944-2611** *B&B-private home*

Muther's [MO,N,NS,GO] 508 Eastern Ave (btwn Carlaw & Logan) **416/466-8616** *above Tool Box bar*

Ontario • CANADA

Pimblett's Rest B&B [GS,NS,GO] 242 Gerrard St E **416/929-9525, 416/921-6896** *Victorian, full brkfst, hot tub, theme rooms*

Toronto Downtown Bed & Breakfast® [GS,NS,GO] 57 Chicora Ave **416/921-3533, 877/950-6200** *luxurious, full brkfst*

Two Aberdeen B&B [MW,NS] 2 Aberdeen Ave **416/944-1426** *Victorian in historic Cabbagetown, full brkfst*

Victoria's Mansion Guest House [GF] 68 Gloucester St **416/921-4625** *converted mansion*

■BARS

Babylon [GS,F] 553 Church St **416/923-2626** *3pm-2am, martini bar, also restaurant*

Bar 501 [MW,NH,DS] 501 Church (at Wellesley) **416/944-3272** *11am-2am, infamous Window Show Sun*

The Black Eagle [M,B,L,F] 457 Church St (btwn Maitland & Alexander) **416/413-1219** *2pm-2am, 3 bars, theme nights, dress code after 8pm, heated rooftop patio*

Carrington's [M,NH] 618 Yonge, upstairs (at St Joseph) **416/944-0559** *11am-2am, sports bar*

The Cellblock/ Yard [M,D,DS,P] 72 Carlton St (behind Zipperz) **416/921-0066** *noon-2am, drag shows Mon & Wed, DJ Th-Sun, also lounge*

Ciao Edie [GS,F] 489 College St (at Markham) **416/927-7774** *cocktail lounge w/ DJ*

Crews/ Tango [M,NH,D,K,DS] 508 Church **416/972-1662** *noon-2am, deck overlooks Church St, Tango [W] from 8pm Tue-Sat, popular Sat*

The Hair of the Dog [MW,NH,F] 425 Church St **416/964-2708** *11:30am-2am, pub & restaurant, patio*

Voted Best Bed & Breakfast

DUNDONALD HOUSE
BED & BREAKFAST

- Full Breakfast
- Parking Available
- Touring Bikes
- Hot tub
- Sauna
- Work Out Room
- Right In the gay village

Your Hosts: **David & Warren**

35 DUNDONALD ST. TORONTO, ON M4Y 1K3

email: dh@dundonaldhouse.com http://www.dundonaldhouse.com

(416) 961-9888 OR 1-800-260-7227

Toronto • Ontario

The House On Parliament Pub [GS,NH,F] 456 Parliament St **416/925-4074** *patio*

Inspire [GS] 491 Church **416/963-0044** *5pm-1am, ultra-hip, cocktails, also restaurant, pan-Asian*

The Looking Glass [★GS,D,E,C,DS] 582 Church St **416/929-4779** *4pm-2am, from 11am wknds, also restaurant, brunch wknds, cabaret Th, fireplaces, patios*

Midtown [GF,NH,F] 552 College St (W of Euclid) **416/920-4533** *5pm-2am, from 3pm Fri-Sun, pool bar, tapas served*

Pegasus on Church [MW,NH] 489-B Church St (at Wellesley, upstairs) **416/927-8832** *noon-2am*

Queen's Head Pub (aka Pimblett's Restaurant & Pimblett's Rest Guest House) [GS,NH,F,GO] 263 Gerrard St E (btwn Seaton & Parliament) **416/929-9525** *4pm-2am, friendly pub, patio, also restaurant & B&B*

Red Spot Lounge & Bar [MW,NH,D,MR,TG,F,E,DS] 459 Church St (at Alexander) **416/967-7768** *4pm-2am, Latin music Fri-Sat, Shemale 2nd Th [TG]*

Remington's Men of Steel [MO,S,WC,GO] 379 Yonge St (at Gerrard) **416/977-2160** *3pm-2am, strip bar*

Slack Alice [★MW,D,F,E,V] 562 Church St (at Wellesley) **416/969-8742** *4pm-2am, from 11am wknds, also restaurant, int'l fusion, brunch wknds, comedy Th*

Sneakers [M,NH,TG] 502-A Yonge St (at Alexander) **416/961-5808** *11am-2am, cruisy*

Statlers [M,E,P,OC] 471 Church St (at Maitland) **416/925-0341** *2pm-2am*

Toolbox [★M,B,L,F,NS] 508 Eastern Ave **416/466-8616** *5pm-2am, from 2pm Fri, from noon wknds, Sun brunch, theme nights, cruisy patio*

Trade [GS,F] 76 Wellesley St E (above Cellar) **416/968-6665** *4pm-2am, also cafe*

Trax V [★M,DS,P,OC,WC] 529 Yonge St (at Maitland) **416/963-5196** *11am-2am, drag shows nightly, bingo, 2 piano bars*

Woody's/ Sailor [★M,NH,E,DS,V, 18+,WC] 465-467 Church (at Maitland) **416/972-0887** *1pm-2am, Bad Boy's Night Out Tue, Best Chest Contest Th, cruisy*

Zipperz [M,D,DS,P] 72 Carlton St (at Church) **416/921-0066** *noon-2am, patio*

■ NIGHTCLUBS

5ive [★M,D,$] 5 St Josephs St (at Yonge) **416/964-8685** *10pm-3:30am, clsd Mon-Tue*

AsianXpress [M,D,MR-A,S] *last Fri, check listings for location, 'for Gay Asians & their friends'*

The Barn/ Stables [★M,D,L,V] 418 Church (at Granby) **416/977-4684, 416/977-4702** *9pm-3am, till 4am Fri-Sat, from 4pm Sun, 3 flrs*

El Convento Rico [★GS,D,MR,TG,DS] 750 College St (at Crawford) **416/588-7800** *9pm-3:30am, clsd Sun-Wed, drag shows at 1am Fri, 12:30am Sat*

Fly [★M,D,$] 8 Gloucester St (at Yonge) **416/410-5426** *10pm-3am, till 7am Sat, clsd Mon-Wed, circuit crowd*

It Nightclub [M,D,S] 167 Church St **416/410-1902** *10pm-close Fri only for It's a Boy's Life, 3 flrs, check web for other events: www.itsaboyslife.com*

Tallulah's Cabaret [M,D,C] 12 Alexander St (at Buddies in Bad Times Theatre) **416/975-8555** *10:30pm Fri-Sat only, eclectic performances*

■ CAFES

Cafe Diplomatico [★] 594 College (at Clinton, in Little Italy) **416/534-4637** *8am-3am, patio*

The Second Cup [★] 548 Church St (at Wellesley) **416/964-2457** *open late, 24hrs Th-Sat*

Sweet City Bakery 24 Wellesley St W (at Yonge) **416/962-0358** *6:30am-5:30pm, 8am-4pm Sat, clsd Sun*

Timothy's [★] 500 Church St (at Alexander) **416/925-8550**

Ontario • CANADA

■ RESTAURANTS

Allen's Restaurant [E] 143 Danforth Ave (at Broadview) **416/463-3086** *lunch & dinner, great scotch selection, patio*

Avalon [NS] 270 Adelaide St W (at John) **416/979-9918** *dinner nightly, lunch Th only, clsd Sun, contemporary cont'l, intimate dining*

Bistro 422 422 College St **416/963-9416** *4pm-2am, full bar*

Byzantium [M,GO] 499 Church St (S of Wellesley) **416/922-3859** *5:30pm-11pm, chic, cont'l/ global, also martini bar till 2am, patio*

Fire on the East Side [MW] 6 Gloucester St (at Yonge) **416/960-3473** *11am-11pm, till 4pm wknds, brunch wknds, Southern comfort food, trendy, patio*

Flo's Diner [GO] 70 Yorkville Ave (near Bay St) **416/961-4333** *7:30am-10pm, till 7pm Mon, from 8am Sat, from 9am Sun*

Golden Thai 105 Church St (at Richmond) **416/868-6668** *11:30am-10:30pm, from 5pm wknds*

The Gypsy Co-Op [GS] 817 Queen St W (W of Bathurst) **416/703-5069** *noon-3am, 6pm-2am Mon, clsd Sun, also bar, eclectic & kitschy*

Hughie's Burgers, Fries & Pies 777 Bay St (at College) **416/977-2242** *11:30am-11pm, clsd Sun, full bar, patio*

Il Fornello 1560 Yonge St (1 blk N of St Clair) **416/920-7347** *11:30am-10pm, no lunch Sat, Italian, plenty veggie; also 214 King W (at Simcoe), 416/977-2855 & 576 Danforth Ave (at Carlaw), 416/466-2931*

Joy Bistro [NS] 884 Queen St E **416/465-8855** *8am-11pm, brunch wknds, patio*

La Hacienda 640 Queen St W (near Bathurst) **416/703-3377** *lunch & dinner, sleazy, loud & fun Mexican restaurant*

The Living Well Restaurant & Bar [MW] 692 Yonge St (at Isabella) **416/922-6770** *11:30am-1am, also bar, open 6pm-2am, live DJ, 2 patios*

Mitzi's Sister [★GO] 1554 Queen St W **416/532-2570** *10am-2am, till midnight Sun, popular wknd brunch, upscale pub eats, full bar*

Oasis [E] 294 College St (at Spadina) **416/975-0845** *5pm-2am, eclectic tapas, also bar*

PJ Mellon's [WC] 489 Church St (at Wellesley) **416/966-3241** *11:30am-11pm, from 11am Sun, full bar*

Solo on Yonge [R] 605 Yonge St **416/920-0607** *creative seafood & pasta dishes, int'l wine list*

Splendido [WC] 88 Harbord St (at Spadina) **416/929-7788** *5pm-11pm, clsd Mon, great decor & gnocchi, full bar*

The Superior Restaurant [WC] 253 Yonge St (across from Eaton Center) **416/214-0416** *11:30am-midnight, oysters, full bar*

Tantra 634 Church St (at Isabella) **416/926-0313** *lunch & dinner, also bar & lounge, patio*

Trattoria Al Forno 459 Church St (at Carlton) **416/944-8852** *lunch Mon-Fri & dinner nightly, full bar*

The Village Rainbow 477 Church St (at Maitland) **416/961-0616** *7am-midnight, till 1am Th-Sat, from 8am Sun, full bar, big patio*

Wilde Oscars [GS] 518 Church St (at Maitland) **416/921-8142** *11am-2am, casual dining, huge patio, also lounge upstairs*

Zelda's [★MW] 542 Church St **416/922-2526** *11am-2am, from 10am wknds, all-you-can-eat Sun brunch, full drag service Tue, full bar, big patio*

ZiZi Trattoria 456 Bloor St W (E of Bathurst) **416/533-5117** *5pm-close, from noon Fri-Sat, clsd Sun*

■ ENTERTAINMENT & RECREATION

AIDS Memorial in Cawthra Park

Buddies in Bad Times Theatre 12 Alexander St **416/975-8555** *lgbt theater, also bar*

Gay/ Lesbian History Walking Tour **416/651-2223** *2-hour tour, meets at 519 Church St Community Centre*

Toronto • Ontario

Hanlan's Pt Beach Toronto Islands *nude beach 10 minutes from downtown*

■ BOOKSTORES

Glad Day Bookshop [★] 598-A Yonge St (at Wellesley) **416/961-4161, 877/783-3725** *10am-7pm, till 9pm Th-Fri, from noon Sun, lgbt*

The Omega Centre 29 Yorkville Ave (btwn Yonge & Bay) **416/975-9086, 888/663-6377 (in Canada)** *10am-9pm, till 6pm Sat, 11am-5pm Sun, metaphysical*

This Ain't The Rosedale Library [★] 483 Church St (at Wellesley) **416/929-9912** *10am-10pm, till 11pm Fri-Sat, 1pm-9pm Sun, lgbt*

■ RETAIL SHOPS

Out on the Street 551 Church St **416/967-2759, 800/263-5747** *10am-8pm, from 11am Sun, lgbt accessories*

Passage Body Piercing 473 Church St, 2nd flr **416/929-7330** *noon-7pm, clsd Mon, also tattoos & scarification*

Planet Earth 473 Church St (S of Maitland St) **416/929-2007, 877/503-7374 (mail-order)** *11am-6pm, till 5pm Sun, clsd Mon, all-natural body care products*

Take A Walk On the Wild Side [TG] 161 Gerrard St E (at Jarvis) **416/921-6112** *'hotel, boutique & club for crossdressers, transvestites, transexuals & other persons of gender'*

Vixon 620 Yonge St (at St Joseph) **416/960-6464** *11am-8pm, clubwear*

■ PUBLICATIONS

The Pink Pages **416/972-7418** *annual lgbt directory*

Rainbow Choices Directory **416/762-9994** *lgbt entertainment & business directory for Canada*

➤ **Xtra!** **416/925-6665** *lgbt newspaper*

■ GYMS & HEALTH CLUBS

Epic Fitness [GF] 9 St Josephs (at Yonge) **416/960-1705**

Canada's **gay & lesbian** media group

1-800-268-XTRA

XTRA! · XTRA! west · capital XTRA! · xtra.ca

Windsor • Ontario

■ MEN'S CLUBS

The Barracks [L] 56 Widmer St (at Richmond) **416/593-0499** *24hrs, spa, theme nights*

The Bijou [AYOR] 370 Church St (btwn Granby & Gerrard) **416/971-9985** *9pm-4am, bathhouse*

Cellar 78 Wellesley St E **416/975-1799** *24hrs, no sign, enter through black door*

Central Spa 1610 Dundas St W **416/588-6191** *noon-3am*

Club Toronto Baths & Health Club [SW,PC] 231 Mutual St (at Carlton) **416/977-4629** *24hrs, gym equipment*

Spa Excess [★] 105 Carlton St **416/260-2363, 877/867-3301** *24hrs, 4 flrs*

St Marc Sauna [★WC] 543 Yonge St, 4th flr (at Wellesley) **416/927-0210** *24hrs*

➤ **Steamworks** 540 Church/ 66 Maitland (level 2) **416/925-1571** *24hrs*

■ EROTICA

Aslan Leather 135 Tecumseth St, Unit 6 (rear) **416/306-0462** *leather, rubber & vinyl dildo harnesses, fine bondage gear*

Barbwire XXX Cinema 543 Yonge St, 1st flr (below St Marc Spa) **416/934-1359** *also private booths & cruise area*

Come As You Are 701 Queen St W (at Bathurst) **416/504-7934** *co-op-owned sex store*

Lovecraft 27 Yorkville Ave (btwn Bay & Yonge) **416/923-7331** *toys, lingerie, videos*

New Release-Wega 489 Church St **800/730-5528**

North Bound Leather [WC] 586 Yonge (W of Wellesley St) **416/972-1037** *toys & clothing*

Priape [★] 465 Church St (at Wellesley, above Woody's) **416/586-9914, 800/461-6969** *clubwear, leather, books, toys & more*

Seduction 577 Yonge St **416/966-6969**

Stag Shop 239 Yonge St **416/368-3507**

■ CRUISY AREAS

Balfour Park [AYOR]

Cawthra Park [AYOR] Church St *summer sunbathing*

Gibraltar Point [AYOR] Toronto Islands *nude gay beach*

Hanlan's Pt Beach [AYOR] Toronto Islands *summers*

High Park [AYOR]

Yonge Street Walkway [AYOR] E of Yonge (from Charles to Alexander)

Turkey Point

■ ACCOMMODATIONS

The Point Tent & Trailer Resort [M,L,SW,N,GO] 918 Charlotteville Rd #2, RR 1, Vittoria **519/426-7275** *on 50 acres*

Waterloo

■ RESTAURANTS

Ethel's Lounge 114 King St N (at Spring) **519/725-2361** *11:30am-2am, full bar, patio*

Windsor

see also Detroit, Michigan

■ BARS

The Honest Lawyer [GF,F] 300 Ouellette Ave **519/977-0599** *11am-2am, from 4pm Sun*

■ NIGHTCLUBS

The Complex [★MW,D,F,K,DS,V,GO] 634 Chilver Rd (at Wyandotte East) **519/252-1774** *2pm-2am, DJ from 10pm Tue & Fri-Sat, karaoke Th & Sun*

The Loop [GF,D,A,E,YC] 156 Chatham St W (at Ferry St) **519/256-9844** *9pm-2am, theme nights*

■ ENTERTAINMENT & RECREATION

Queer Radio CJAM 91.5 FM **519/253-4232** *9pm Mon*

■ MEN'S CLUBS

Vesuvio Steam Bath [PC] 563 Brant St **519/977-8578** *24hrs*

Ontario • CANADA

■CRUISY AREAS

Jackson Park [AYOR] area at Ouelette Overpass

River Front Park [AYOR] at foot of Ouelette St *evenings*

Woodstock

■ACCOMMODATIONS

Nunn's Hollow Guest Suites [M,GO] 21 Delatre St (Dundas St) **519/539-9780** *full brkfst, jacuzzi*

PRINCE EDWARD ISLAND

Albany

■ACCOMMODATIONS

Evening Primrose [GF,NS,GO] 114 Lord's Pond Rd **902/437-3134** *40 minutes from Charlottetown, B&B, cottage & studio, full brkfst*

Blooming Point

■ENTERTAINMENT & RECREATION

Blooming Point *nude beach*

Charlottetown

■INFO LINES & SERVICES

Abegweit Rainbow Collective 902/894-5776, 877/380-5776 *24hr info line, staffed 7pm-10pm Tue & Th, monthly dances & other social activities*

■ACCOMMODATIONS

Blooming Breezes Executive Cottage [GS,GO] 108 Lowe Ln, Blooming Point **902/626-4475** *cottage, close to beach*

Charlottetown Hotel [GF,SW,WC] 75 Kent St (at Pownall) **902/894-7371, 800/565-7633** *also restaurant & lounge (clsd Sun)*

Rainbow Lodge [MW,NS,GO] **902/651-2202, 800/268-7005** *full brkfst, 15 minutes outside of town*

■BARS

Baba's Lounge [GF,F] 81 University Ave **902/892-7377** *noon-2am, 5pm-midnight Sun, live bands, also Cedars Canadian/ Lebanese restaurant*

■BOOKSTORES

Book Mark 172 Queen St (in mall) **902/566-4888** *9am-9pm, 9am-5:30pm Sat, noon-5pm Sun*

■EROTICA

Afternoon Delight 218 University Ave, Charlotte **902/892-3469, 877/424-5469** *woman-owned/ run*

Cornwall

■ACCOMMODATIONS

The Rainbow Inn PEI [GO] 4992 Rte 19 Nine Mile Creek **902/675-2393** *renovated farm house*

Souris

■ACCOMMODATIONS

Johnson Shore Inn [GS,WC,GO] RR #3 Rte16 **902/687-1340, 877/510-9669** *full brkfst, ocean views*

PROVINCE OF QUÉBEC

Provincewide

■INFO LINES & SERVICES

Gay Line/ Gai Ecoute 888/505-1010 *7pm-11pm*

Alma

■CRUISY AREAS

Carcajou Bridge [AYOR]

Parc de la Falaise [AYOR] beach of Dam-en-terre

Baie-des-Sables

■ACCOMMODATIONS

Gîte aux Trois Pains [GS,GO] 3 rue des Pins CP 127 **418/772-6047, 877/210-2910** *1880 renovated home, full brkfst, shared baths*

Chicoutimi

see also Jonquière

■NIGHTCLUBS

L'Arlequin [MW,D] 574 boul du Saguenay O **418/696-2072** *4pm-3am, from 9pm wknds, clsd Mon-Tue*

Magog • Province of Québec

Drummondville

ACCOMMODATIONS
Motel Alouette [GS,GO] 1975 boul Mercure **819/478-4166**

BARS
Bar 'G' Pob [MW,NH,D,DS,18+,YC,WC] 901 Mercure Blvd **819/471-4252** *8pm-3am, clsd Mon-Tue, terrace*

CRUISY AREAS
Woodyat Park [AYOR]

Granby

ACCOMMODATIONS
Le Campagnard B&B [GF] 146 Denison Ouest J2G 4C8 **450/770-1424** *in a quiet village, bikes available, also camping*

Hull
see also Ottawa, Ontario

BARS
Le Pub de Promenade [MW,NH,D,K] 175 Promenade de Portage **819/771-8810** *noon-2am, karaoke Th-Fri*

CRUISY AREAS
Meach Lake Beach [AYOR]
Place du Centre [AYOR]

Joliette

ACCOMMODATIONS
L'Oasis des Pins [MW,SW] 381 boul Brassard, St-Paul-de-Joliette **450/754-3819** *camping May-Sept, restaurant open yr-round*

Jonquière
see also Chicoutimi

CRUISY AREAS
Rue St-Aime & rue St-Dominique [AYOR]

Laurentides (Laurentian Mtns)

ACCOMMODATIONS
Auberge de la Gare [MW,SW] 1694 chemin Pierre-Peladeau, Ste-Adèle **450/228-3140, 888/825-4273 (in Québec only)** *B&B, superb ancestral home, near slopes*

B&B du Mont Sauvage [GF,SW] 2340 chemin du Mont Sauvage, Ste-Adèle **450/229-7821**

Le Grand Boisé [MO,SW,N] 246 rang 4 ouest, Chertsey **514/823-1190** *seasonal, lakeside w/ beach, camping sites*

Le Septentrion B&B [MW,SW,NS,GO] 901 chemin St-Adolphe, Morin-Heights/ St-Sauveur **450/226-2665** *Victorian, full brkfst*

St Adolphe Inn [GS,GO] 1777 Chemin du Village (at Tour du Lac), St-Adolphe d'Howard **819/327-2816, 866/327-2816** *country inn across street from Lac St-Joseph, full brkfst*

NIGHTCLUBS
Différent [MW,D] 257 St-Georges (Autoroute 15, take exit 'sortie 43'), St-Jérôme **450/569-8769** *9pm-3am, from 5pm Fri-Sun, clsd Mon-Tue*

RESTAURANTS
Restaurant Zeste [GO] 1777 Chemin du Village (at St Adolphe Inn), St-Adolphe-D'Howard **819/327-2816, 866/327-2816** *6pm-10pm Th-Sun, Sun brunch in summer, overlooking Lac St-Joseph, fireplace, terrace*

Magog
see also Sherbrooke

ACCOMMODATIONS
Au Gîte du Cerf Argenté [GS,GO] 2984 chemin Georgeville Rd (off Rte 10) **819/847-4264, 514/521-2712** *B&B in century-old farmhouse*

The Mascul'inn/ Auberge au Masculin [MO,GO] 202 Bolton Pass (near Lac Brome, on Rt 243), Bolton Ouest **450/243-5904** *luxurious retreat, full brkfst, 1 hour from Montréal*

Province of Québec • CANADA

Montréal

■ INFO LINES & SERVICES

AA Gay/ Lesbian 514/376-9230 *call for mtg times & locations (in French or English)*

Gay/ Lesbian Community Centre of Montréal 2075 rue Plessis, local 110 (at Ontario) 514/528-8424 *10am-noon & 1pm-5pm, clsd wknds, library*

Gay Line/ Gai Ecoute 514/866-5090 (English), 888/505-1010 (in Canada only) *7pm-11pm*

■ ACCOMMODATIONS

Accommodations International B&B [MO,GO] 2002 Champlain #1 (at Ontario, above Citibar) 514/596-2317, 888/334-0348 *outside terrace*

Angelica Blue B&B [GS,NS] 1213 Ste-Elisabeth (at Ste-Catherine) 514/844-5048, 800/878-5048 *theme rooms, full brkfst, some shared baths*

Au Stade B&B [M] 514/899-4636

Auberge Belles Vues B&B 1407 Panet #2 514/521-9998 *in the gay Village*

Auberge Cosy [★MO,GO] 1274 Ste-Catherine Est (at de la Visitation) 514/525-2151 *hot tub*

Auberge de la Fontaine [GS,WC] 1301 rue Rachel Est (at Chambord) 514/597-0166, 800/597-0597

➤ **Auberge du Centre-Ville** [★MO,GO] 1070 rue Mackay (at René Lévesque) 514/938-9393, 800/668-6253 *high sexual atmosphere, also bar & sauna*

Auberge La Raveaudiere B&B [GS,GO] 11 Hatley Center, North Hatley 819/842-2554 *19th-c country inn, full brkfst, 1.5 hours from Montréal*

Aubergell.com [MO,F,GO] 1641 Amherst (at de Maisonneuve) 514/597-0878, 514/525-7744 *also full bar & restaurant, rooftop terrace*

la Conciergerie GUEST HOUSE

Your resort in the city!

1019 rue Saint-Hubert, Montréal (Qc)
Tel.: (514) 289-9297 Fax: (514) 289-0845
www.laconciergerie.ca

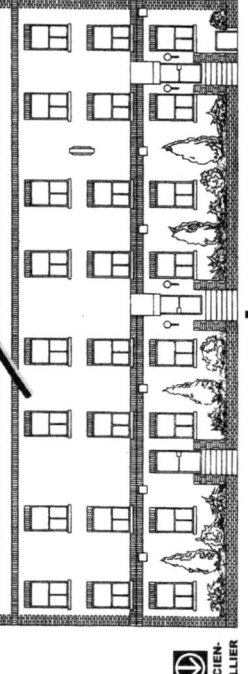

Province of Québec • CANADA

B&B Le Cartier [GS,GO]
1219 rue Cartier (at Ste-Catherine Est) **514/917-1829, 877/524-0495**
newly renovated 100-yr old stone building in gay village

BBV (B&B du Village) [M]
1279 rue Montcalm (at Ste-Catherine) **514/522-4771, 888/228-8455**
jacuzzi

Le Chasseur B&B [M,GO]
1567 rue St-André (at Maisonneuve) **514/521-2238, 800/451-2238**
Victorian row house, summer terrace

Chateau Cherrier [MW,GO] 550 rue Cherrier (at St-Hubert) **514/844-0055, 800/816-0055** *seasonal, full brkfst*

Chez Roger Bontemps [GS]
1441 Wolfe (at Ste-Catherine) **514/598-9587, 888/634-9090**
B&B & furnished apts

➤ **La Conciergerie Guest House** [★MO,N,NS,GO] 1019 rue St-Hubert (at Viger) **514/289-9297** *hot tub, gym & sundeck*

Crowne Plaza Metro Centre [GF,SW,WC] 505 rue Sherbrooke Est (at Berri) **514/842-8581, 800/561-4644** *full brkfst, breathtaking views of Montréal*

Delta Montréal [GF,SW,WC] 475 President Kennedy (at City Councilor) **514/286-1986, 877/814-7706** *hot tub, restaurant, bar, garden terrace*

Gingerbread House B&B [MW,NS,GO]
1628 St-Christophe (at Maisonneuve) **514/597-2804** *full brkfst, shared bath*

Hébergement Touristique du Plateau Mont-Royal [GF]
1131 rue Rachel Est **514/527-2394, 800/597-0597** *reservation service*

Hotel Bourbon [★M] 1574 rue Ste-Catherine Est (at Champlain) **514/523-4679, 800/268-4679** *also Bar Cajun & popular La Track disco, also Club Sandwich 24hrs, also sauna, cybercafe, theater & more*

Hotel du Fort [GS,WC] 1390 rue du Fort (at Ste-Catherine) **514/938-8333, 800/565-6333**

Hotel Kent [GF] 1216 rue St-Hubert (at Ste-Catherine) **514/845-9835**

Hotel Lord Berri [GF] 1199 rue Berri (at Ste-Catherine) **514/845-9236, 888/363-0363** *also European-style resto-bar*

Hotel Manoir des Alpes [GF]
1245 rue St-André (at Ste-Catherine) **514/845-9803, 800/465-2929**

Hotel Pierre [GF] 169 Sherbrooke Est (btwn St-Denis & St-Laurent) **514/288-8519, 877/288-8577**

Hotel Visitel Network
1617 rue St-Hubert (at Maisonneuve) **514/529-0990** *hotel & reservation service*

The House of Angels B&B [M,GO]
1640 rue Alexandre de Sève (at Maisonneuve) **514/527-9890**
rooms in cozy apt, shared baths

Le Houseboy B&B [M,NS,GO]
1281 rue Beaudry (at Ste-Catherine Est) **514/525-1459, 866/525-1459**
full brkfst, shared baths

Loews Hotel Vogue [GF] 1425 rue de la Montagne (near Ste-Catherine) **514/285-5555, 800/465-6654**
full-service 5-star hotel

Maison Chablis [MO,F,GO]
1641 rue St-Hubert (at Maisonneuve) **514/527-8346** *some shared baths*

Renaissance Montréal Hotel [GF,SW]
3625 av du Parc (at Prince Arthur) **514/288-6666, 800/363-0735**

Ruta Bagage [GS] 1345 rue Ste-Rose (at Panët) **514/598-1586** *Victorian B&B, full brkfst, shared baths*

Le St-Christophe [MO,N,NS,GO]
1597 St-Christophe (at Maisonneuve) **514/527-7836, 888/521-7836**
full brkfst, hot tub, sundeck

Le Traversin [GS,NS,GO] 4124 rue St-Hubert (at Duluth) **514/597-1546**
B&B & urban spa, full brkfst, some shared baths, hot tub

Turquoise B&B [M,GO] 1576 rue Alexandre de Sève (at Maisonneuve) **514/523-9943, 877/707-1576**
Victorian B&B, shared baths

Montréal • Province of Québec

■ BARS

L' Adonis [MO,S] 1681 rue Ste-Catherine Est (at Papineau) **514/521-1355** *3pm-3am, nude dancers, couples shows Th-Sun*

Agora [M,NH,K] 1160 rue Mackay (at Réné Lévesque) **514/934-1428** *4pm-3am, karaoke Sat*

Bar Cajun [MW] 1574 rue Ste-Catherine Est (at Hotel Bourbon) **514/523-4679** *3pm-3am*

Black Eagle Bar (Aigle Noir) [M,L,PC] 1315 Ste-Catherine Est (at Visitation) **514/529-0040** *8am-3am, theme nights*

Cabaret Mado [★MW,D,K,DS,WC] 1115 Ste-Catherine Est (below Le Campus, at Amherst) **514/525-7566** *1pm-3am, theme nights, owned by the fabulous Mado!*

Le Campus [M,S] 1111 rue Ste-Catherine Est, 2nd flr (at Amherst) **514/526-3616** *3pm-3am, nude dancers, couples shows Th-Sun*

Citibar [GS,NH] 1603 Ontario Est (at Champlain) **514/525-4251** *11am-3am*

Club Bolo [MW,D,CW,PC,$] 960 rue Amherst (at Viger) **514/849-4777** *7:30pm-1am Fri, 9pm-3am Sat, T-dance from 4pm-9pm Sun*

Club Date [MW,NH,K,S] 1218 rue Ste-Catherine Est (at Beaudry) **514/521-1242** *8am-2am*

Le Drugstore [★MW,F] 1366 rue Ste-Catherine Est (at Panêt) **514/524-1960** *9am-3am, 8 bars on 3 flrs*

Foufounes Electriques [GF,D,E] 87 Ste-Catherine Est (at St-Laurent) **514/844-5539** *4pm-3am, patio*

Fun Spot [MW,NH,D,TG,K,DS] 1151 rue Ontario Est (at Wolfe) **514/522-0416** *11am-3am, poker machines*

Météor [MW,D,F,K,DS,OC] 1661 rue Ste-Catherine Est (at Champlain) **514/523-1481** *11am-3am, '60s themed bar, ballroom dancing, square dancing*

Le Mystique [GS,NH] 1424 rue Stanley (at Maisonneuve) **514/844-5711** *4pm-3am, English underground pub, poker machines*

La Relaxe [M,NH] 1309 Ste-Catherine Est, 2nd flr **514/523-0578** *noon-3am, open to the street—as the name implies, a good place to relax & people-watch*

Stock Bar [MO,S] 1171 Ste-Catherine **514/842-1336** *3pm-3am, nude dancers*

Le Stud [MO,B,L,K] 1812 rue Ste-Catherine Est (at Papineau) **514/598-8243** *10am-3am, karaoke Mon, leather party Fri-Sat, underwear party Sun from 5pm*

Taboo [MO,S] 1950 boul de Maisonneuve Est (at Dorion) **514/597-0010** *8pm-3am, nude dancers*

Taverne Rocky [M,V,OC] 1673 rue Ste-Catherine Est (at Papineau) **514/521-7865** *3pm-3am*

Vox Pub [M,NH,V] 1295 Amherst (at Ste-Catherine) **514/522-2766** *11am-midnight, terrace, one of Montréal's oldest taverns, popular happy hour*

West Side [M,S] 1071 Beaver Hall (at Belmont) **514/866-4963** *4pm-3am, from 7pm wknds, nude dancers, ladies night Wed*

■ NIGHTCLUBS

Bar Exceso Latino [★MW,D,MR-L,E] 1333 rue Ste-Catherine Est, 2nd flr (at Panêt) **514/529-4460** *shows Fri*

Chez Cleopatra [M,D,TG,DS] 1230 boul St-Laurent (at Ste-Catherine) **514/871-8066** *8pm-3am*

Club BackTrack [★MW,D] 1592 Ste-Catherine E **514/523-4679** *3pm-3am, '70s, '80s & '90s club disco, 3 flrs w/ large back patio*

Club Parking [★M,D,L] 1296 rue Amherst **514/282-1199** *3pm-3am, 2 flrs*

Red-Lite (After Hours) [★GF,D,$] 1755 rue de Lierre, Laval **450/967-3057** *Fri-Sun only, after-hours club*

Sky Complex [★MW,D,A,L,F,C,DS,S] 1474 rue Ste-Catherine Est **514/529-6969** *11am-3am, 3 levels, also Resto Bisous bistro, cabaret Th-Sun, nude dancers 6pm-3am Wed-Sun in Nirvana, dance club Fri-Sun*

Province of Québec • CANADA

Sona [GS,$] 1439 rue Bleury (at Place des Arts, across from the Imperial Cinema) 514/282-1000 *Fri-Sat only, after-hours club*

Stéréo [MW,$] 858 rue Ste-Catherine Est 514/282-3300 *after-hours, inquire locally*

Unity II [★MW,D,S,YC] 1171 Ste-Catherine Est 514/523-2777 *10pm-close Th-Sat, from 4pm Sun, clsd Mon-Wed, 4 flrs & great rooftoop terrace*

■CAFES

Café Titanic [★] 445 St-Pierre (in Old Montréal) 514/849-0894 *7am-5pm, clsd wknds, salads & soups*

The Second Cup [NS] 1351 Ste-Catherine Est 514/598-7727 *très gay coffee shop*

■RESTAURANTS

L' Anecdote [MW] 801 rue Rachel Est (at St-Hubert) 514/526-7967 *8am-10pm, burgers*

Après le Jour [MW,BYOB] 901 rue Rachel Est (at St-Andre) 514/527-4141 *5pm-10pm, till 11pm Th-Sun, Italian/ French, seafood*

Area [R] 1429 rue Amherst 514/890-6691 *lunch Mon-Fri, dinner nightly, French/ Italian/ Asian fusion*

L' Armoricain [BW,WC] 1550 Fullum (at Maisonneuve) 514/523-2551 *lunch & dinner, clsd Sun, gourmet French*

Bato Thai [★MW,BW] 1310 rue Ste-Catherine Est 514/524-6705 *lunch & dinner*

Bazou [BYOB] 1310 de Maisonneuve Est 514/526-4940 *5pm-10pm, clsd Mon, California fusion, terrace*

Chablis 1639 rue St-Hubert (at Maisonneuve) 514/523-0053 *11am-11pm, from 5pm wknds, Spanish/ French, full bar, terrace*

Chuchai 4088 rue St-Denis (at Rachel) 514/843-4194 *lunch & dinner, vegetarian Thai, full bar*

Commensal 1720 St-Denis (at Ontario) 514/845-2627 *11am-11pm, vegetarian*

L' Exception 1200 rue St-Hubert (at Réné-Lévesque) 514/282-1282 *burgers & sandwiches, plenty veggie, terrace*

L' Express [★R] 3927 rue St-Denis (at Duluth) 514/845-5333 *8am-2am, 1pm-10pm Sun, French bistro & bar, great pâté*

La Paryse [MW] 302 rue Ontario Est (near Sanguinet) 514/842-2040 *11am-11pm, from noon wknds, (from 2pm in July), '50s-style diner*

Piccolo Diavolo [★] 1336 rue Ste-Catherine Est (at Panêt) 514/526-1336 *5pm-2am, lunch Tue & Fri, Italian, charming waiters*

Le Planète [YC,BW] 1451 rue Ste-Catherine Est (at Plessis) 514/528-6953 *lunch & dinner, brunch only Sun, global cuisine*

Le Queen [DS] 1329 rue Ste-Catherine Est (at Panêt) 514/526-6011 *noon-midnight, fusion, drag shows Sat*

Le Saloon [★] 1333 rue Ste-Catherine Est (at Panêt) 514/522-1333 *11am-midnight, till 2am Fri-Sat, int'l cuisine, big dishes & even bigger drinks*

Thai Grill 5101 boul St-Laurent (at Laurier) 514/270-5566

■ENTERTAINMENT & RECREATION

Ça Roule 27 rue de la Commune Est 514/866-0633 *join the beautiful people skating up & down Ste-Catherine*

Cinéma du Parc 3575 Parc (btwn Milton & Prince Arthur) 514/281-1900 *repertory film theater*

Prince Arthur Est at boul St-Laurent, not far from Sherbrooke Métro station *closed-off street w/ tons of outdoor restaurants & cafés–it's touristy but oh-so-European*

■RETAIL SHOPS

Cuir Mont-Royal 826-A Mont Royal Est (at St Hubert) 514/527-0238, 888/338-8283 *leather, fetish*

Priape [★] 1311 Ste-Catherine Est (at Visitation) 514 /521-8451 *clubwear, leather, books, toys & more*

Screaming Eagle 1424 boul St-Laurent 514/849-2843 *leather shop; also 3915 Blvd Samson, Laval, 450/ 978-9237*

U-Bahn 1285 rue Amherst (at Ste-Catherine) 514/529-0808 *leather & rubber clothing, accessories & toys*

Québec • Province of Québec

■ PUBLICATIONS

Fugues 514/848-1854, 888/848-1854 *glossy lgbt bar/ entertainment guide*

The Mirror 514/393-1010 *free queer-positive weekly, reviews, event listings & more in English*

Rainbow Choices Directory 416/762-9994 *lgbt entertainment & business directory for Canada*

RG 514/523-9463 *monthly newsmagazine*

■ GYMS & HEALTH CLUBS

Physotech Plus [MW] 1657 rue Amherst (near Maisonneuve) 514/527-7587

■ MEN'S CLUBS

5018 Sauna [V] 5018 boul St-Laurent (at St-Joseph) 514/277-3555 *24hrs, hot tub*

Aux Berges 1070 rue Mackay (at Auberge du Centre-Ville) 514/938-9393 *also hotel*

Colonial Bath 3963 av Colonial (at Napoléon) 514/285-0132 *1pm-6am, 24hrs wknds*

Le Millénium Econo-Spa [★MO] 1166 Ste-Catherine Est 514/528-3326

L' Oasis [★V,PC] 1390 Ste-Catherine Est 514/521-0785 *24hrs, jacuzzi*

Sauna 1286 [V] 1286 chemin Chambly (at Breggs), Longueuil 450/677-1286 *24hrs, 3 flrs, hot tub*

Sauna 226 [V] 226 boul des Laurentides, Laval 514/975-4556 *24hrs Th-Sat*

Sauna 456 [★SW,PC] 456 rue de la Gauchetière Ouest (at Metro Square) 514/871-8341 *24hrs, 3 flrs, hot tub, also gym*

Sauna Centre-Ville 1465 rue Ste-Catherine Est (at Plessis) 514/524-3486 *24hrs*

Sauna du Plateau 961 rue Rachel Est (at Boyer) 514/528-1679 *24hrs*

Sauna Le Bronx [★L,E,V,PC] 1166 Ste-Catherine Est 514/528-3326 *24hrs, hot tub, specials for leather crowd, also Millénium*

Sauna Pont-Viau [V] 15-A boul des Laurentides, Laval 450/663-3386 *24hrs*

Sauna St-Hubert [V] 6527 rue St-Hubert (at Beaubien) 514/277-0176 *24hrs Th-Sun*

■ EROTICA

La Capoterie 2061 St-Denis 514/845-0027 *adult novelties, condoms*

Il Bolero 6842-46 St-Hubert (btwn St-Zotique & Bélanger) 514/270-6065 *fetish & clubwear emporium, ask about monthly fetish party*

■ CRUISY AREAS

Angrignon Park [AYOR]

De Maisonneuve Park [AYOR]

Mont Royal [AYOR] Park Ave *summer nights*

Phillips Square [AYOR]

Place Dupuis [AYOR]

North Hatley

see Sherbrooke

Québec

■ ACCOMMODATIONS

Le 727 Guest House (Chambres et Pension) [M,GO] 727 rue d'Aiguillon (btwn St-Augustin & Côte Ste-Geneviève) 418/523-7705, 866/523-7705 *B&B in private home, full brkfst, terrace*

L' Auberge du Quartier [GF,NS] 170 Grande Allée Ouest (at av Cartier) 418/525-9726, 800/782-9441 (in Québec only) *buffet brkfst*

Le Coureur des Bois Guest House [MW,GO] 15 rue Ste-Ursule (at St-Jean, in Old Québec) 418/692-1117, 800/269-6414 *also apts, shared baths*

Domaine Vagabond [MO,SW] 1878 rang 5 Ouest (exit 266, off Rte 20), Joly 418/728-5522 *camping, full brkfst, also bar & restaurant*

Hoel-Motel Le Voyageur [GS,SW] 2250 boul Sainte-Anne (at Estimauville) 418/661-701, 800/463-5568 *sauna, restaurant, 2 bars*

Province of Québec • CANADA

Hôtel Dominion 1912 [GF,WC]
126 rue St-Pierre 418/692-2224, 888/833-5253 *boutique hotel in city's 1st skyscraper*

Hôtel Germain Des Prés [GF,WC]
1200 Ave Germain des Prés (at Laurier Blvd), Sainte-Foy 418/658-1224, 800/463-5253 *modern & elegant hotel, restaurant*

Loews Le Concorde [GF,SW,WC]
1225 cours du Général De Montcalm 418/647-2222, 800/463-5256 *4-stars, located on Grand Allée, w/ revolving restaurant*

La Lucarne Enchantée [GS,SW] 225 chemin Royal, St-Jean-De-L'Ile d'Orléans 418/829-3792 *full brkfst, near beach, shared baths*

Le Moulin de St-Laurent Chalets [GF,SW] 754 Chemin Royal, St Laurent, Ile d' Orleans 418/829-3888, 888/629-3888 *cottages, also restaurant*

■BARS

L' Amour Sorcier [★MW,NH,F,V]
789 côte Ste-Geneviève (at St-Jean) 418/523-3395 *2pm-3am, cafe-bar, terrace*

Bar 321 [M,NH,TG,S] 321 de la Couronne (at La Salle) 418/525-5107 *noon-3am*

Bar 889 [MW,NH,E] 889 côte Ste-Geneviève 418/524-5000 *8am-3am, patio, live music Mon-Tue*

Bar de la Couronne [★M,S] 310 rue de la Couronne (btwn rues de la Reine & de la Salle) 418/525-6593 *8pm-3am, nude dancers, men only Th-Sat*

Bar L' Eveil [W,NH] 670 rue Bouvier #118 418/628-0610 *4pm-close, from 5pm wknds, clsd Mon-Wed, patio*

Bar Le Drague [★M,NH,D,F,DS,WC]
815 rue St-Augustin (at St-Joachim) 418/649-7212 *10am-3am, 3 bars, DJ Fri-Sun, terrace*

■NIGHTCLUBS

Zazou Cabaret Club [★MW,D,F,E]
811 rue St-Jean (at St-Augustin) 418/524-4982 *4pm-3am, terrace*

■RESTAURANTS

Cafe Zorba [BYOB,WC] 854 rue St-Jean (near Dufferin) 418/525-5509 *24hrs, Canadian, Greek & Italian*

Le Commensal 860 rue St-Jean 418/647-3733 *11am-10pm, vegetarian/ vegan*

Le Hobbit 700 rue St-Jean (at Ste-Geneviève) 418/647-2677 *8am-close*

La Playa [GO] 780 rue St-Jean (at St-Augustin) 418/522-3989 *lunch Th-Fri, dinner nightly, 'West Coast cuisine,' martini bar, heated terrace*

Poisson d'Avril 115 rue St-André (at St-Paul) 418/692-1010 *lunch & diner, French for 'April Fools'*

Restaurant Diana [★] 849 rue St-Jean (at St-Augustine) 418/524-5794 *8am-1am, till 2am Fri-Sat, Italian & Greek*

■ENTERTAINMENT & RECREATION

Le Château Frontenac [GF,SW] 1 rue des Carrières 418/692-3861, 800/441-1414 *this hotel disguised as a castle remains the symbol of Québec—even if you can't afford the princess' ransom to stay the night, you can come & enjoy the view from outside*

Ice Hotel [GF] Sainte-Catherine-de-la-Jacques-Cartier 418/875-4522, 877/505-0423 *sometimes getting put on ice isn't a bad thing—check it out before it melts away, 9 km E of Québec City in Montmorency Falls Park (Jan-March only)*

■RETAIL SHOPS

FinFinaud 847 rue St-Jean 418/649-9526 *club & fetish clothes*

■MEN'S CLUBS

Bloc 225 [PC] 225 St-Jean (at Turnbull) 418/523-2562, 877/523-2562 *24hrs, also Capital Gym*

Sauna Backboys [V] 264 rue de la Couronne (at Prince Edward) 418/521-6686, 877/523-6686 *24hrs during week*

Sauna/ Hotel Hippocampe [★V]
31 rue McMahon 418/692-1521, 888/388-1521 *24hrs, bar, also small hotel*

Ste-Marthe • Province of Québec

■EROTICA

Empire Lyon 873 rue St-Jean (at St-Augustin) **418/648-2301** *videos, toys, books, clothing & more*

Importation André Dubois [TG,WC] 46 côte de la Montagne (at Frontenac Castle) **418/692-0264**

Importation Delta 762 rue St-Jean **418/647-6808, 877/647-6808** *videos, magazines, books, underwear*

■CRUISY AREAS

Boardwalk [AYOR] by Château Frontenac

Rue Grande Allée [AYOR] btwn rue Montcalm & Place George V *summers only, at the outdoor cafes*

Rue St-Denis [AYOR]

Rouyn-Noranda

■BARS

Station D [MW,D,K,DS] 82 Perreault Ouest **819/797-8696** *4pm-close, clsd Mon-Tue, drag shows, terrace*

Sherbrooke

■BARS

L' Otre Zone [MW,D,F] 252 rue Dufferin **819/565-5333** *3pm-1am, till 3am Th-Sat, clsd Mon-Tue, more men Sat*

■NIGHTCLUBS

Complex 17-13 [MW,D,S] 13-15-17 Bowen Sud (at rue King) **819/569-5580** *11am-3am, pub & dance club, strippers Fri-Sun, also sauna*

■RESTAURANTS

Café Bla-Bla 2 rue Wellington S (at Ramada) **819/565-1366** *11am-12:30am, till 2am wknds, full bar*

■CRUISY AREAS

Wellington St [AYOR] *downtown*

St-Alphonse-de-Granby

■ACCOMMODATIONS

Bain Gai de Nature [MO,SW,N,GO] 127 rue Lussier **450/375-4765** *seasonal, all meals included, hot tub*

St-Donat

■ACCOMMODATIONS

Havre du Parc Auberge [GS,F,GO] 2788 Rte 125 N **819/424-7686** *quiet lakeside inn for nature lovers, full brkfst*

St-François-du-Lac

■ACCOMMODATIONS

Domaine Gay Luron [MO,F,SW,N,GO] **450/568-3634** *seasonal, cabins, camping, RV spots & rental condos, also restaurant & bar*

St-Hubert

■MEN'S CLUBS

3481 Sauna [MO] 3481 St-Hubert **450/462-3481** *24hrs*

St-Hyacinthe

■BARS

La Main Gauche [MW,D,S] 470 rue Mondor **450/774-5556** *3pm-3am*

Ste-Catherine-de-Hatley

■ACCOMMODATIONS

L' Auberge Ste-Catherine-de-Hatley [GF] 2 rue Grand **819/868-1212** *also bar & restaurant, terrace*

Ste-Julienne

■ACCOMMODATIONS

Camping de la Fierté [MO,SW,N,18+] 2905 Montée Hamilton **450/834-2888** *theme wknds summers, tent & RV spots, cabin, also bar/ restaurant/ rec hall*

Ste-Marthe

■ACCOMMODATIONS

Camping Plein Bois [MO,D,SW,N,GO] 550 chemin St-Henri **450/459-4646, 888/459-4646** *seasonal, DJ Fri-Sat, also restaurant, 350 campsites & 200 trailer sites*

Province of Québec • CANADA

Trois Rivières

■ INFO LINES & SERVICES

Gay Ami 819/373-0771 *lgbt social contacts*

■ ACCOMMODATIONS

Le Gîte du Huard [GF] 42 rue St-Louis 819/375-8771 *B&B*

■ BARS

La Station [M,D,F,K] 1198 rue Champflour 819/376-0481 *3pm-3am*

SASKATCHEWAN

Ravenscrag

■ ACCOMMODATIONS

Spring Valley Guest Ranch [★GF,F,GO] 306/295-4124 *1913 character home, also cabin, full brkfst*

Regina

■ INFO LINES & SERVICES

The Gay & Lesbian Community of Regina 2070 Broad St (at Victoria) 306/569-1995, 306/522-7343 *4pm-2am, from 2pm Th-Sat, also lounge & Homo-Depot gay store, deck*

Pink Triangle Community Services 2070 Broad St 306/525-6046 *7pm-10pm, clsd wknds, also store, library*

■ NIGHTCLUBS

The Outside [MW,D] 2070 Broad St (at Victoria) 306/569-1995, 306/522-7343 *10:30pm-3am Fri-Sat only, Homo-Depot gay store inside 7pm-10pm, also lounge*

■ BOOKSTORES

Buzzword Books 2926 13th Ave 306/522-6562 *11am-6pm, clsd Sun*

■ CRUISY AREAS

Victoria Park [AYOR]

Wascana Park [AYOR]

Saskatoon

■ INFO LINES & SERVICES

Circle of Choice Gay/ Lesbian AA 10th St & Broadway (at Grace Westminster United Church) 306/665-5626 *8pm Wed*

Gay/ Lesbian Line & Drop-In 203-220 3rd Ave S (at Gay/ Lesbian Health Services) 306/665-1224, 800/358-1833 *noon-10pm, till 6pm Sat, clsd Sun, library, social/ support*

■ ACCOMMODATIONS

Brighton House [GF,NS,GO] 1308 5th Ave N 306/664-3278 *hot tub*

■ NIGHTCLUBS

Diva's [MW,D,DS,PC] 220 3rd Ave S #110 (alley entrance) 306/665-0100 *8pm-2am, clsd Tue*

■ ENTERTAINMENT & RECREATION

Rainbow Radio 90.5 FM CFCR 306/664-6678 (station #) *8:30pm Sun*

■ RETAIL SHOPS

Out of the Closet 203-220 3rd Ave S, 3rd flr 306/665-1224 *boutique run by the Gay/ Lesbian Line, lgbt gifts, magazines, art, etc*

The Trading Post 226 2nd Ave S 306/653-1769 *10am-5:30pm, clsd Sun, clothing*

■ PUBLICATIONS

Perceptions 306/244-1930 *covers the Canadian prairies*

■ MEN'S CLUBS

Steam Works [MO] 122B 20th St W (behind the Antique Emporium) 306/955-0090, 866/955-0090 *24hrs*

■ CRUISY AREAS

Kiwanis Park [AYOR] *along river bank*

YUKON

Whitehorse

■ INFO LINES & SERVICES

Gay/ Lesbian Alliance of the Yukon Territory PO Box 31678 Y1A 6L3 867/667-7857 *events, newsletter, check web for current event listings: www.gaycanada.com/galayukon*

■ ACCOMMODATIONS

Inn on the Lake [GF,NS] Lot 76 McClintock Pl, Marsh Lake 867/660-5253 *luxury log inn*

Caribbean

BAHAMAS

Eleuthera

■ACCOMMODATIONS

Cigatoo Resort [GF,SW]
Governor's Harbour 242/332-3060, 800/688-4752 *high atop hill overlooking the Atlantic Ocean*

Nassau

■BARS

Club Waterloo [GF,D,F,E,SW] E Bay St (1/2 mile E of Paradise Island Bridge) 242/393-7324 *11:30am-4am, indoor/outdoor complex w/ 5 bars, 2 dance flrs, live music & restaurant*

The Drop-Off Pub [GF,D,F] Bay St (at East St, downstairs, across from Planet Hollywood) 242/322-3444 *11am-6am, dancing from 10pm, also restaurant, lunch & dinner, English/Bahamian*

■NIGHTCLUBS

Endangered Species [MW,D,DS,18+,GO] West Bay St (in Cable Beach Shopping Center, no sign) 242/327-0127 *11pm-close Fri-Sat*

BARBADOS

Bridgetown

■RESTAURANTS

The Waterfront Cafe [E] The Careenage 246/427-0093 *clsd Sun, trendy, also bar, live music, outdoor seating (not surprisingly, on the waterfront)*

St James

■ACCOMMODATIONS

Hogarth House [GF] Holders Hill, West Coast Barbados 246/432-6402 *sauna*

Fort Recovery Villas
Tortola, British Virgin Islands

Luxury 3-4 bedroom house on beach from $560–$797 per night.
Featured on *Discovery's Travel Channel* 1 and 2 bedroom beachfront villas from $160–$522 per night

Inquire Super Deluxe Package for Two:
$1,995 (4/15–12/17) – per couple – $2,810 (12/18–4/14) includes:
Villa, Tax, Jeep, B'fast, 3 Dinners, Boat Trip, Massage, Yoga, Pedicure, Pool, AC, TV, Kitchen, Maid.

(284) 495-4354 Fx (284) 495-4036
(800) 367-8455 (wait for ring) **www.fortrecovery.com**

British Virgin Islands • CARIBBEAN

BRITISH VIRGIN ISLANDS
see also US Virgin Islands

Tortola

■ACCOMMODATIONS

➤ **Fort Recovery Villa Estate** [GF,SW,WC] 284/495-4354, 800/367-8455 (wait for ring) *grand home on beach & private beachfront villas*

■ENTERTAINMENT & RECREATION

Yacht Ferdinand [GF] PO Box 3069 Road Town, Tortola 284/499-4941

DOMINICAN REPUBLIC

Puerto Plata

■ACCOMMODATIONS

Club Escape Caribe [MW,SW] Playa Las Canas (at Cabarete Rd) 809/739-0129 *hotel, located on coconut plantation, hot tub, private beach*

Tropix Hotel [GF,SW,GO] Camino Libre #7 (at Pedro Clisante), Sosua, Puerto Plata 809/571-2291 *garden setting near center of town & beach, full brkfst*

Santo Domingo

■ACCOMMODATIONS

El Duque de Wellington Hotel [GF] Av Independencia #304 809/682-4525 *in the Colonial City*

Hotel Aida [GF] Calle El Conde 464 809/685-7692 *quite a dump but cheap & near gay bars*

Renaissance Jaragua Hotel & Casino [GF] 367 George Washington Ave 809/221-2222, 800/468-3571 *14-acre resort w/ tropical gardens, lagoon & waterfalls*

Residencial El Candil [GS,SW,GO] Calle el Candil #2 (at 20 de Deciembre), Boca Chica 809/523-4252, 808/523-4253 *apts, 5 minutes from beach*

■BARS

Llego [M,NH,S,V] Jose Reyes 10, Zona Colonial 809/689-8250

The Phoenix [M,NH] Calle Polvorin 10, Zona Colonial 809/689-7572 *7pm-1am, friendly bar*

■NIGHTCLUBS

Aire Club [M,D,MR,YC,GO] Mercedes 313 (N of El Conde) 809/689-4163 *9pm-3am*

■RESTAURANTS

Café Coco [E] 53 Padre Billini (in Colonial Zone) 809/687-9624 *noon-10pm, English, full bar*

■CRUISY AREAS

Calle el Conde *evenings*

DUTCH WEST INDIES

Aruba

■BARS

The Hide Out [MW,D] Fergusonstraat (in Dakota Shopping Paradise), Oranjestad

Jimmy's Place [★GF,NH,D,F] Kruisweg 15, Oranjestad 297/82-25-50 *4pm-2am, more gay late*

The Paddock [GS,NH,F] LG Smith Blvd #13, Oranjestad 297/83-23-34 *10am-2am*

■NIGHTCLUBS

Club E [GS,D] Westraat 7A 297/93-67-84 *9:30pm-late*

■ENTERTAINMENT & RECREATION

Shhh Don't Tell Mama [GF,DS,$] La Cabana Resort & Casino (in the Tropicana showroom), Oranjestad 297/87-90-00, 800/835-7193 *shows 9:30pm, from 11pm Wed, clsd Sun*

■CRUISY AREAS

California Dunes [N,AYOR] behind lighthouse (at the rocks), Oranjestad

Caya GF Croes [AYOR] Main St, Oranjestad *after-hours*

Eagle Beach [AYOR] btwn La Quinta Resort & Dutch Village Hotel, Oranjestad *afternoons*

Manchebo Beach Oranjestad

St Martin • French West Indies

Bonaire

■ACCOMMODATIONS

Ocean View Villas [GS,R,GO] Kaya Statius van Eps 6 599/717-6105 *luxury apts*

Saba

■RESTAURANTS

YIIK Bakery & Grill [GO] The Road 599/416-2539 *clsd Sun*

St Maarten

■ACCOMMODATIONS

Delfina Hotel [M,SW,GO] Tigris Rd 14-16, Lowlands/ Cupecoy, Philipsburg 599/545-3300

Holland House [GF] 43 Front St, Philipsburg 599/542-2572 *on the beach, restaurant, bar*

■RESTAURANTS

Cheri's Cafe [★D,E,WC] Maho Reef 599/54-53-361 *11am-1:30am, clsd Tue, full bar, live music*

Wajang Doll [GO] 167 Front St, Philipsburg 599/54-22-687 *lunch & dinner, dinner only Mon/Sat, Indonesian*

FRENCH WEST INDIES

Guadeloupe

■ACCOMMODATIONS

Eurolangue Caraibe [GS] 27 bis Rue de la République, Pointe à Pitre 590-590/68-19-55 *apt, hot tub, kitchen, also French lessons*

St Barthelemy

■ACCOMMODATIONS

Hotel Normandie [GF] 590-590/27-61-66

Hotel St-Barth Isle De France [GF,F] Plage des Flamands 508/528-7727, 800/421-3396 *ultra-luxe hotel*

St Barth's Beach Hotel [GF,SW] Grand Cul de Sac 508/528-7727, 800/421-3396

Village St-Jean [GF,SW] 590-590/27-61-39 *hotel & cottages*

■NIGHTCLUBS

Le Sélect [GF] Gustavia 590-590/27-86-87 *more gay after 11pm*

■ENTERTAINMENT & RECREATION

Anse Gouverneur St-Jean Beach [N]

Anse Grande Saline Beach [N] *gay section on the right side of Saline*

L'Orient Beach *gay beach*

St Martin

■ACCOMMODATIONS

Meridien L'Habitation [GF,SW] Anse Marcel 590-590/87-67-67, 800/543-4300 *beachfront resort*

Orient Beach [GF] Mont Vernon 1 590-590/87-31-10, 800/818-5992 *1 & 2-bdrm villas*

■NIGHTCLUBS

In's Club [M,D,GO] Auberge de mer-Marigot, upstairs 590-590/87-08-39, 590-590/55-27-03 *Th-Sat, 2 bars*

L' Alibi [GS,D,GO] Auberge de mer-Marigot, upstairs 590-590/87-08-39, 590-590/55-27-03 *11pm-late, clsd Sun*

■RESTAURANTS

L'Escapade [R] 94 Blvd de Grand Case 590-590/87-75-04 *French*

Le Pressoir 30 Blvd de Grand Case 590-590/87-76-62 *French*

Rainbow 176 Blvd de Grand Case (at W end of beach) 590-590/87-55-80 *lunch & dinner, French/ int'l*

■ENTERTAINMENT & RECREATION

Cupecoy Beach *gay beach*

Damron Men's Travel Guide 2004

Jamaica • CARIBBEAN

JAMAICA

Montego Bay

ACCOMMODATIONS

Half Moon Golf, Tennis & Beach Club [GF] 876/953-2211, 866/648-6951 *upscale resort*

Moun Tambrin Retreat [GS,F,SW] set in the mtns 28 miles from Montego Bay 876/918-4486 *art deco estate formerly owned by Alex Haley*

Negril

ACCOMMODATIONS

Seagrape Villas [GF] West End Rd 831/625-1255 (US#) *3 seafront villas*

Tingalaya's B&B [GF,SW,N] West End Rd, Negril, Westmoreland 414/924-4269 *rustic thatched cottages*

Ocho Rios

ACCOMMODATIONS

Golden Clouds Villa [GF,SW,WC,GO] North Coast Rd, Oracabessa 941/922-9191, 888/625-6007 *private estate, full brkfst*

Port Antonio

ACCOMMODATIONS

Hotel Mocking Bird Hill [GF,F,SW,WC] 876/993-7267 *eco-friendly inn*

PUERTO RICO

Note: For those w/ rusty or no Spanish, 'carretera' means 'highway.' 'Calle' means 'street.'

PUBLICATIONS

➤ **Puerto Rico Breeze** 787/722-5759 *islandwide lgbt paper*

Aguadilla

EROTICA

Condom World Crta 2, km 124.7 787/819-1418 *condoms, toys, videos & more—18 locations in Puerto Rico*

CRUISY AREAS

Beach Park [AYOR]

Bayamón

BARS

Gilligan's Pub [MW,D,E,S] Av Betances D-18, Hnas Davila (near Pepin Ct) 787/786-5065 *8pm-close Wed-Sat, strippers*

EROTICA

Condom World Santa Rosa Mall 787/787-2224 *condoms, toys, videos & more—18 locations in Puerto Rico*

Boqueron

ACCOMMODATIONS

A Boqueron Bay Guest House [MW,SW,GO] 10 Quintas del Mar (at SR 307, Km 7.6, Interior) 787/255-0224 *jacuzzi*

Coamo

ACCOMMODATIONS

Baños de Coamo [GF,F,WC] end of Rte 546 787/825-2186 & 825-2239, 877/797-3434 *resort w/ mineral baths, public baths*

Hormigueros

BARS

Station Bar [D,E,DS,S] Casablanca Shopping Center, Rd #2 *from 7pm Wed-Sun*

Puerto Rico • CARIBBEAN

■NIGHTCLUBS
Faces [★M,D,DS,S] Hwy 2 (at km 164) 787/849-2005 *9pm-late Th-Sun, patio*

Luquillo

■ACCOMMODATIONS
Villas Margarita [GS,SW,NS] 787/889-2098 *tree house villa*

■CRUISY AREAS
Luquillo Beach [AYOR] *walk toward town*

Manati

■CRUISY AREAS
Playa de los Tubos [AYOR]

Mayaguez

■EROTICA
Condom World Marginal 2 (at Plaza Masso) 787/265-5325 *condoms, toys, videos—18 locations in Puerto Rico*

■CRUISY AREAS
Plaza Colon [AYOR] *by City Hall*

Moca

■NIGHTCLUBS
Style [MW,D,DS] Carr 111, Km 72 *10pm-close Fri-Sat only*

Patillas

■ACCOMMODATIONS
Caribe Playa Beach Resort [GF,SW] Road #3, Km 112.1 Guardarraya 787/839-6339 *hotel, full brkst, jacuzzi*

Ponce

■NIGHTCLUBS
Backstage [M,D,DS,S] Ave Ponce de Leon, Las Delicias 787/647-6576 *Th-Sun*

■CRUISY AREAS
Off Main Plaza [AYOR] *near Cathedral*

San German

■BARS
Norman's Bar [MW,NH,D] Ctra 318, Barrio Maresúa *6pm-1am, salsa & merengue*

San Juan

■ACCOMMODATIONS
At Home Vacation [GS,MR,TG,GO] 1131 Ashford Ave, Apt 505 (at Calle Vendig) 787/633-8906, 787/635-1462 (cell) *furnished apts*

At Wind Chimes Inn [GF,SW,WC] 1750 McLeary Ave, Condado 787/727-4153, 800/946-3244 *restored Spanish Villa, 1 blk from Condado beach*

Atlantic Beach Hotel & Bar [MW] Calle Vendig 1, Condado (off Av Ashford) 787/721-6900, 888/611-6900

Caribe Mountain Villas [GF,SW,GO] Carr 857, km 6.0, Carolina 787/769-0860 *resort in Carolina rain forest (25 miles from San Juan)*

Casa del Caribe Guest House [GF] Calle Caribe 57, Condado 787/722-7139, 877/722-7139

Condado Inn [MW,GO] Av Condado 6 (at Av Ashford) 787/724-7145 *also bar*

E & G's Place [GS] Condo Condado Ave #54, apt 8-C (at Ashford Ave) 718/984-3497 *studio, 1 blk to beach*

El San Juan Hotel & Casino [GF,F,SW,WC] 6063 Isla Verde Ave (at Baldorioty de Castro), Carolina 787/791-1000, 800/468-2818 (reservations only) *resort on ocean, Asian restaurant & cigar bar*

Hotel El Convento [★GF,SW] Calle Cristo 100, Old San Juan (btwn Caleta de las Monjas & Calle Sol) 787/723-9020, 800/468-2779 *17th-c former Carmelite convent*

Hotel Iberia [GS,NS,WC,GO] Av Wilson 1464, Condado (btwn Avs de Diego & Washington) 787/723-5380, 787/723-0200 *also restaurant & bar*

Jose's Apartment [GF,SW,GO] 1302 Ashford Ave, Condado (at Calle Caribe) 787/722-1352

L' Habitation Beach Guesthouse [MW,GO] Calle Italia 1957, Ocean Park (near Santa Ana) 787/727-2499 *also restaurant & bar*

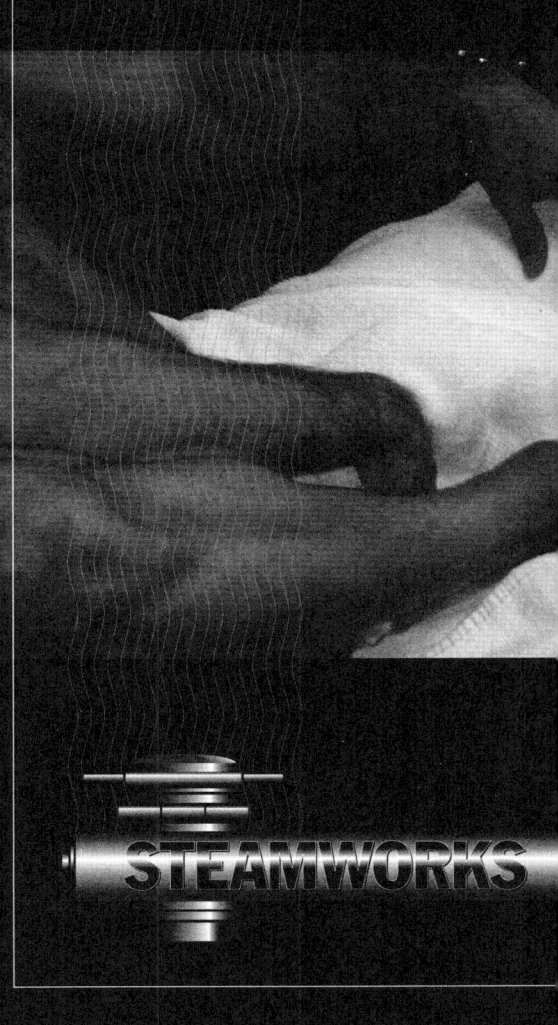

24/7 MEN'S GYM/SAUNA   205 CALLE LUNA   OLD SAN JUAN
787.725.4993   WWW.STEAMWORKSONLINE.COM

Puerto Rico • CARIBBEAN

Numero Uno on the Beach [GS,SW,WC] Calle Santa Ana 1, Ocean Park (near Calle Italia) 787/726-5010, 866/726-5010 *also Pamela's restaurant & bar*

■BARS

Bebo's Playa [MW,NH,D,DS,S,V] Piñones, Isla Verde *Th, Sat-Sun only, beachfront, fun crowd*

Café Bohemio [GF,E] Calle Cristo 100, Old San Juan (in Gran Hotel El Convento) 787/723-9200 *11am-2am, popular Tue, also restaurant, food till 11pm, professional crowd, live music Th-Sat*

Downstairs Lounge [M] Av Condado 6 (at Condado Inn) 787/724-7145 *noon-4am, near beach, hustlers*

Junior's [MW,NH,DS,S] Calle Condado 602, Santurce (btwn Calle Benito Alonso & Av Ponce de León) 787/723-9477 *5:30pm-6:30am, local crowd*

Maroma [GS] 1060 Av Ponce de Leon (go left into alley after Marshalls) 787/721-7115 *Th-Sat, upcale & trendy*

Nuestro Ambiente [W,D,E] Av Ponce de León 1412, Santurce (across from Central High School) 787/724-9093

Tia Maria's [★MW,NH] Av Jose de Diego 326, Stop 22, Santurce (at Ponce de León) 787/724-4011 *noon-2am, professional crowd, also liquor shop*

■NIGHTCLUBS

Byach Nights at Machu Picchu Cafe [M,DS] Puntas las Marias, Isla Verde 787/728-1041 *Mon only*

Club Lazer [GF,D] Calle Cruz 251, Old San Juan 787/725-7581 *8pm-close, popular w/ gay cruises*

Concepts (The Downtown Club) [MW,D,E] Av Chardón 9, Hato Rey (in Le Chateau), Hato Rey 787/763-7432 *Sun only, popular drag shows*

Eros [★MW,D,DS,S,V,GO] Av Ponce de León 1257, Santurce (btwn Calles Villamil & Labra) 787/722-1131 *10pm-5am, clsd Sun-Tue, theme nights*

Kouros [D] 1515 Ponce de Leon Ave, Santurce *10pm-close Wed-Sun*

Pink Flamingo [★M,D,S] Calle Barranquitas 53, Condado (btwn Calle Mayagüez & Av Ashford) *4pm-close, Sun T-dance*

El Teatro [GS,D,DS] Av Ponce de León 1420, Santurce 787/722-1130 *9pm-late, clsd Mon-Wed*

■CAFES

Café Berlin [★] Calle San Francisco 407, Plaza Colón, Old San Juan (btwn Calles Norzagary & O'Donnel) 787/722-5205 *9am-11pm*

■RESTAURANTS

Al Dente Calle Recinto S, Old San Juan 787/723-7303 *lunch & dinner, Italian*

La Bombonera [★] Calle San Francisco 259, Old San Juan 787/722-0658 *7:30am-8pm, come for the strong coffee & pastries, since 1903!*

Café Amadeus [★GO] Calle San Sebastián 104, Old San Juan (btwn Calles San José & del Cristo) 787/723-8635 *lunch & dinner, bar noon-midnight Tue-Sat*

Dragonfly 364 S Fortaleza St (across from Parrot Club) 787/977-3886 *lunch & dinner, Latin/ Asian fusion*

Mona's 510 Ponce de Leon, Hato Rey 787/282-0207 *Mexican*

The Parrot Club [E] Calle Fortaleza 363, Old San Juan (btwn Plaza Colón & Callejón de la Capilla) 787/725-7370 *chic Nuevo Latino bistro & bar, live music*

Sam's Patio Calle San Sebastián 102, Old San Juan 787/723-1149 *Mexican*

Transylvania Restaurant [E] Recinto Sur 317, Old San Juan 787/977-2328 *lunch Tue-Sat & dinner nightly, Romanian, also bar & gallery, live music*

Yukiyu 311 Recinto Sur, Old San Juan 787/722-1423 *Japanese, also locations in Guaynabo & Hato Rey*

■BOOKSTORES

Bookworm Av Ashford 1129, Condado (at Calle Vendig) 787/711-3344 *11am-7pm*

Trinidad • Trinidad & Tobago

■ RETAIL SHOPS

Eros Clothing Ashford Ave (at Vendig St), Condado 787/722-0662 *clothes, clubwear*

The Rainbow Shop Av Ponce de León 1412, Santurce (inside Nuestro Ambiente) 787/721-0401, 787/721-2982

■ PUBLICATIONS

➤ **Puerto Rico Breeze** 787/725-5759 *lgbt newspaper*

■ GYMS & HEALTH CLUBS

Fitness City [GF] 1959 Calle Loiza, 4th flr, Ocean Park (above Post Office) 787/268-7773 *day passes*

International Fitness [GS] Av Ashford 1302, Condado (btwn Avs Cervantes & Caribe) 787/721-0717 *6am-10pm*

■ MEN'S CLUBS

➤ **Steamworks** [V,PC] Calle Luna 205, 2nd flr, Old San Juan (btwn Calle San Justo & Calle de la Cruz, ring to enter) 787/725-4993 *24hrs, sauna & spa*

■ EROTICA

Condom World 311 Roosevelt Ave, Hato Rey 787/751-0997 *condoms, toys, videos & more— 18 locations in Puerto Rico*

Pleasure Paradise Av Roosevelt 1367 (in Plazoleta Julio Garriga) 787/706-0855

■ CRUISY AREAS

Condado Beach [AYOR]

Ocean Park Beach [AYOR]

La Playita [AYOR] in front of capitol bldg in Old San Juan

Toa Baja

■ NIGHTCLUBS

Obsessions The Club [MW] Ave Rios Roman #12, Sabana Seca 787/261-6319 *from 8pm Th only*

Vieques Island

■ ACCOMMODATIONS

Crow's Nest Inn [GF,SW,NS] PO Box 1521, 00765 787/741-0033, 877/276-9763 *restaurant*

Inn on the Blue Horizon [GF,SW,F] 787/741-3318

Rainbow Realty [GS,GO] HC-01 Box 6307 787/741-4312 *20 fully equipped properties available, most w/ views, some on the water*

Villas of Vieques Island [GS] 787/741-0023

■ RESTAURANTS

Chef Michael's 787/741-3318 *most elegant restaurant on island*

TRINIDAD & TOBAGO

Tobago

■ ACCOMMODATIONS

Grafton Beach Resort [GF,F,SW] 868/639-0191

Kariwak Village Hotel & Holistic Haven [GF,F,SW] Store Bay Local Rd, Crown Point 868/639-8442, 868/639-8545 *1-room cabañas, outdoor jacuzzi w/ waterfall*

■ RESTAURANTS

Rouselles Bacolet St, Scarborough 868/639-2839 *West Indian/ int'l*

Trinidad

■ BARS

Pelican Pub [GF] 2-4 Coblentz Ave (next to the Hilton), Port of Spain 868/624-7486

Pier One [★GF] on ocean, Chaguanas 868/634-4426 *also party cruises*

St Thomas • US Virgin Islands

US VIRGIN ISLANDS
see also British Virgin Islands

St Croix

■ ACCOMMODATIONS

Cormorant Beach Club & Hotel [★MW,F,SW,GO] 4126 La Grande Princesse, Christiansted 340/778-8920, 800/548-4460 *beachfront resort*

King Christian Hotel [GF,F,SW] 59 Kings Wharf, Christiansted 340/773-6330, 800/524-2012 *also restaurant*

Pink Fancy Hotel [GF,SW] 27 Prince St, Christiansted 340/773-8460, 800/524-2045

➤ **Sand Castle On The Beach** [GF,SW,GO] 127 Smithfield, Frederiksted 340/772-1205, 800/524-2018 *hotel*

■ RESTAURANTS

Le St-Tropez 227 King St (at Pier 69), Frederiksted 340/772-3000, 340/772-3335 *French cuisine, full bar*

■ CRUISY AREAS

Old Fortress [AYOR] Christiansted

Park along waterfront [AYOR] Frederiksted *nights*

St John

■ ACCOMMODATIONS

Gallows Point Suite Resort [GF,F,SW,WC] Cruz Bay 340/776-6434, 800/323-7229 *beachfront resort*

Island's End [GS,NS,GO] Hansen's Bay 888/205-2729 *vacation villa w/ panoramic views, lesbian-owned/ run*

Maho Bay Camps & Harmony Studios [GF] VI National Park 340/776-6226, 800/392-9004 *environmentally aware resort*

Sago Palms [GF] Estate 2B, Denis Bay 340/776-6384, 340/776-6876 *private homes*

St John Inn [GF,SW,NS] 800/666-7688

■ RESTAURANTS

Asolare Rte 20, Cruz Bay 340/779-4747 *Asian/ French fusion*

Château Bordeaux Centerline Rd, Jct 10 340/776-6611 *5:30pm-8:30pm, great view*

■ ENTERTAINMENT & RECREATION

Solomon Bay *nude beach, 20-minute hike on Solomon Beach Trail*

St Thomas

■ ACCOMMODATIONS

Danish Chalet Guest House [GS] 340/774-5764, 800/635-1531 *overlooking harbor*

Hotel 1829 [GF,F,SW] Government Hill 340/776-1829, 800/524-2002

The Inn at Blackbeard's Castle [GS,F] 340/776-1234, 800/344-5771

Pavilions & Pools Hotel [GF,SW] 6400 Estate Smith Bay 340/775-6110, 800/524-2001 *1-bdrm villas each w/ own private swimming pool*

■ BARS

Cabana Lounge [★MW,F] at Blackbeard's Castle Hotel *Mon-Sat*

■ NIGHTCLUBS

R&R [MW,F] Back St (at Baker Square) *10pm-close Fri-Sat only, also Lemon Grass Cafe*

■ ENTERTAINMENT & RECREATION

Little Magens Beach *gay nude beach, near main beach at Magens Bay*

Morning Star Beach *popular gay beach*

Acapulco • MEXICO

Mexico

MEXICO

Please Note: Mexican cities are often divided into districts or 'Colonias,' which we abbreviate as Col. Please use these when giving addresses for directions.

Acapulco

■ACCOMMODATIONS

Acapulco Casa del Mar [MO,N,GO] Calle La Bocana 12-18, Fracc Las Playas (at Av Gran Via Tropical) 52-744/482.16.36 *on Acapulco Bay*

Acapulco Las Palmas Resort Hotel [MO,F,SW,N,GO] Av Las Conchas 155, Fracto Farrallón (next to Restaurant El Chivo) 52-744/487-0843 *private villas, near gay beach, also bar*

Acapulco-Villa Roqueta [MO,GO] 305/226-6006 (US#), 52-744/483-8503 *former estate of disco queen Gloria Gaynor, jacuzzi*

Casa Condesa [M] Bella Vista 125 52-744/484-1616 *full brkfst*

Fiesta Americana Condesa [★GF,F,SW] Av Costera Miguel Alemán 1200 52-744/484.28.28, 800/343-7821 *deluxe hotel above the gay beach, 4-star dining, no guests allowed in room*

Hotel Acapulco Tortuga [GF,F,SW] Av Costera Miguel Alemán 132 52-744/484.88.89, 800/832-7491 *across from the gay beach*

Las Brisas [GF,SW,WC] 52-744/469.69.00, 888/559-4329 (US#) *luxury resort, private pools*

Quinta Encanto [GF,SW] Privada Roca Sola 108, Col Club Deportivo (off Costera Blvd) 52-744/484.65.08, 310/657-1945 (US#) *small house rental*

Sunscape Acapulco [GF,F,SW] Calle Caracol 70, Fracc Amiento Farallón 52-744/484.37.07

■BARS

El Bar/ Sunset Bar [MO,F,SW,N,GO] at Acapulco Las Palmas 52-744/487.08.43 *24hrs*

Picante [★GS,D,S,AYOR] Privada Piedra Picuda 16 (behind Demas) *9pm-5am, hustlers*

■NIGHTCLUBS

Demas [★MO,D,S,$] Privada Piedra Picuda#17 (behind Carlos & Charlie's) 52-744/484.13.70 *10pm-3am*

Relax [★MW,D,DS,S,V,YC] Calle Lomas de Mar 4 (Zona Dorada) 52-744/484.04.21 *10pm-late, clsd Mon-Wed, drag & strip shows wknds*

■RESTAURANTS

Beto's Beach Restaurant [MW] Av Costera Miguel Alemán 33 (at Condesa Beach) 52-744/484.04.73 *11am-midnight, full bar, palapas*

El Cabrito Restaurante Avenida Costera M Aleman 1480 (near Convention Center) 52-744/484.77.11

Carlos & Charlie's [E] Costera Miguel Aleman #112 52-744/84.00.39 *lunch & dinner, int'l*

Coyuca 22 Avenida Coyuca 22 52-744/482.34.68, 52-7/483.50.30 *open Nov-April, dress code, great views*

Le Jardin des Artistes Yanez Pinzon 11 52-744/484.83.44 *French*

Kookaburra [★] Carretera Escénica (at Marina Las Brisas) 52-744/46.60.20 *int'l, expensive*

Le Bistroquet [MW,GO] Calle Andrea Doria 5, Fracc Costa Azul 52-744/484.68.60 *French*

Su Casa/ La Margarita Av Anahuac 110 52-744/484.12.61 *great views*

Suntory de Acapulco Costera Miguel Aleman 52-744/484.80.88 *Japanese, gardens*

■CRUISY AREAS

Playa Condesa & Beto's Beach *cruisy by the rocks, at sundown*

Plaza Alvarez/ Zócalo [AYOR] *hustlers (chichifos)*

Cancún • Mexico

Aguascalientes

■NIGHTCLUBS

Mandiles [MW,D] Av Lopez Mateos 730 W (btwn Agucate & Chabacano) 52-449/15.32.81

■CRUISY AREAS

Jardin de San Marcos [AYOR] Calle Carraza & Calle Arturo J Pani

Plaza Principal [AYOR]

Cabo San Lucas

■ACCOMMODATIONS

Chile Pepper Inn [GS,NS,WC] 16 de Septiembre y Abasolo 52-624/143-8611, 143-8612 or 143-8613, 888/708-1918

Hotel Hacienda Beach Resort [GF] Playa el Medano 52-624/143-0663, 800/733-2226 (US#) *upscale*

■BARS

The Rainbow Bar & Grill [★MW,D] Blvd de la Marina #39-E (Marina Cabo Plaza) 52-624/3.14.55 *8pm-3am, patio*

■RESTAURANTS

Mi Casa Av Cabo San Lucas 52-624/3.19.33 *great chicken mole*

■CRUISY AREAS

Playa Medano [AYOR] btwn Las Palmas restaurant & the Hacienda Hotel

Campeche

■CRUISY AREAS

Plaza Principal/ Plaza de Independencia [AYOR]

Cancún

see also Cozumel & Playa del Carmen

■ACCOMMODATIONS

Camino Real [GF,SW] Paseo Kukulcán 52-998/48.70.00, 877/722-6466 (US#) *2 beaches, 3 restaurants*

Cancun Luxury Villas [GF,SW] Palenque #17 #1-B, SM 29 52-998/892.41.02

Casa Cancún [GS,NS] 212/598-0469 (US#) *rental home on the beach, 20 minutes S of Cancún*

Takul Villas [GF] Blvd Kukulcan km 5.5 (in Zona Hotelera) 52-998/883.00.00, 800/842-0193 *gardens, restaurant*

Zona Hotelera (The Hotel Zone) Blvd Kukulcán *Cancún's answer to the Las Vegas Strip: resorts ranging from the Sheraton Cancún's Mayan pyramids to small boutique hotels*

■BARS

Picante Bar [★M,D,YC] Av Tulum 20, Centro (E of Av Uxmal, next to Plaza Galeriás) 52-998/45.55.87 *9am-5am, clsd Mon, hustlers*

■NIGHTCLUBS

Karamba [★MW,D,DS,S] Av Tulum 9 altos, 2nd flr (near Azucentas St) 52-998/84.00.32 *10pm-7am, clsd Mon, go-go boys wknds, drag shows Wed & Sun*

Sebastian's [D,DS,S] in Zona Hotelera

■RESTAURANTS

Avenida Tulum *take a stroll & take your pick*

Modern Art Cafe Kukulcan Blvd km 12.5 (at La Isla Shopping Center) 52-998/83.45.12 *full bar, gallery*

■ENTERTAINMENT & RECREATION

Chichén Itza *the must-see Mayan ruin 125 miles from Cancún*

Playa Delfines in the Hotel Zone (next to Hilton's beach) *gay beach*

■CRUISY AREAS

Avenida Tulum [AYOR] Centro *late*

Gay Dunes [AYOR] beach near Holiday Inn

El Mirador [AYOR] behind the Hotel Camino Real on Blvd Kukulcán, Punta Cancún (near the lighthouse)

Parque de las Palapas [AYOR] *1 blk W of Ave Tulum, in center of SM22, downtown*

Playa Chac-Mool [AYOR] *afternoons*

Celaya • MEXICO

Celaya

■BARS
Los Caballos [M,D,S,$] Hidalgo 220 (Centro) 52-461/331.08 *Fri-Sat only*

Chihuahua

■CRUISY AREAS
Plaza de la Constitución [AYOR] Plaza Hidalgo

Ciudad del Carmen

■CRUISY AREAS
Bajamita Beach [AYOR]

Ciudad Juárez
see also El Paso, Texas, USA

■BARS
Club La Escondida [GS,NH] Calle Ignacio de la Peña 366 W

Club Olímpico [★M,NH,P] Av Lerdo 210 S 52-656/12.57.42 *noon-2am*

■NIGHTCLUBS
G&G Disco [★M,D,S,V,$] Av Lincoln 1252, Córdoba-Américas *9pm-3am, strippers wknds*

■MEN'S CLUBS
Baños Roma [GS] Calle Ignacio Mejía 881 E (at Calle Constitución) 52-16/12.77.32

■CRUISY AREAS
Gay Zone [AYOR] area around intersection of Calle Ignacio de la Peña & Av Lerdo *late nights*

Monument to Benito Juárez [AYOR] Avs Lerdo & Vicente Guerrero

Parque de la Mision [AYOR] in front of the Mision de Nuestra Señora de Guadalupe (btwn Av 16 de Septiembre & Av Vicente Guerrero)

Colima

■CRUISY AREAS
Jardins Publico [AYOR]

Cordoba

■BARS
Salon Bar El Metro [MW,D] Av 7 #117-C,1 & 3

■CRUISY AREAS
Mercado Juárez [AYOR] btwn Calles 7 & 9

Sidewalk Cafés [AYOR] El Portal Zevallos

Cozumel
see also Cancún & Playa del Carmen

■ACCOMMODATIONS
El Cid La Ceiba Cozumel [GF,SW] km 4.5 Caraterra a Chankanaab 52-987/87 20844, 800/435-3240 *5-star beachfront resort*

Villa Las Anclas [GF] S 5th Ave #325 (btwn 3rd & 5th Sts) 52-987/872-5476, 52-987/872-6130 *B&B, 1 blk from main plaza*

■CRUISY AREAS
Zócalo [AYOR]

Cuernavaca

■ACCOMMODATIONS
Las Mañanitas [GF,SW] Ricardo Linares 107 52-777/12.46.46, 52-73/14.14.66 *gardens, restaurant, peacocks!*

Nido de Amor [GF] 52-777/18.06.31 *suites in private home*

La Nuestra [GS,SW,GO] Calle Mesalina 18 (at Calle Neptuno) 52-777/315.22.72, 404/806-9694 *B&B, full brkfst*

Quinta Las Flores [GF,SW] Tlaquepec 1 52-777/314.12.44, 52-777/312.57.69 *gardens, near downtown*

Las Quintas [GF,SW,F] 9 Diaz Ordaz Blvd 52-777/18.39.49, 800/990-1888 *hotel & spa, restaurant, botanical gardens*

Guadalajara • Mexico

■BARS
La Casa del Dictador [D] Jacarandas 4 (at Av Emiliano Zapata) 52-777/17.23.77 wknds only

■NIGHTCLUBS
Oxygen Dance Hall & Lounge [M,D,F,E,DS,S,V,18+,YC] 1303 Ave Vincente Guerrero (near Sam's Club) 52-777/374-0649, 773/528-0001 (US#) 10pm-close, Fri-Sat only

■RESTAURANTS
La India Bonita Calle Dwight Morrow 52-777/18.69.67 clsd Mon, in historic home of former US ambassador & father-in-law of Charles Lindbergh

■ENTERTAINMENT & RECREATION
Diego Rivera Murals Plaza de Museo (in Cuauhnáhuac Regional Museum)

■CRUISY AREAS
Jardin Juárez [AYOR]

Mercado [AYOR]

Plaza Morelos [AYOR]

Zócalo [AYOR] also adjacent bar, Fri-Sat only

Durango

■BARS
Arthur's [GF,D,DS,$] Blvd Domingo Arrieta 809 (upstairs, in front of the Soria Madero) drag shows, cover Fri-Sat

Ensenada

■BARS
La Ola Verde [MW,F,E] Calle 2a #459 (btwn Av Castelo & Calle Miramar, Zona Roja) 9pm-2am Fri-Sun only, popular late, live music, small dance flr, hustlers

■NIGHTCLUBS
Club Ibis [M,D,S,$] at Blvd Costero & Av Sangines 9pm-2am Th-Sun

■RESTAURANTS
Casamar [★] Blvd Lázaro Cárdenas 987, Centro (at Blvd Costero) 52-646/74.04.17

■CRUISY AREAS
Gay Beach [AYOR] past the Corona Beer Distrib, turn right on dirt road (Farmacia San Jorge) before pedestrian bridge–do not swim in the water!

Parque Revolución [AYOR] Calle 7 & Av Obregón evenings

Guadalajara

■ACCOMMODATIONS
Hacienda Aldama [GS,NS,WC,GO] Aldama 22 (off Main Crta), Ajijic 52-376/766-0944 3 rooms in private home, full brkfst

Hotel Calinda Roma [GF] Av Juárez 170 (Sector Juárez) 52-33/614.86.50 also rooftop restaurant

■BARS
Amelia's [M,AYOR] Madero 25 (Calzada Independencia) 52-33/613.67.64 after-hours till 6am

Arizona Saloon [M,B,DS,$] Av de la Paz 1985 (at Chapultepec, Zona Rosa) 52-33/3826.37.44 10pm-3am, clsd Mon

El Botanero [M,D,DS,YC,$] Calle Javier Mina 1348 (at Calle 54, Sector Libertad) 52-33/643.95.46 7pm-11pm, clsd Mon, drag shows, T-dance Sun

Caudillos Bar [★M,D,F,YC] Calle Prisciliano Sánchez 407, Centro (at Ocampo) 52-33/613.54.45 2pm-3am, friendly bar, also restaurant

Chivas [★M,NH,F] Calle Degallado 150 (at López Cotiolla) 52-33/614.19.65 8am-2am, till 3am Fri-Sun, cruisy & friendly

El Ciervo [M,D] 20 de Noviembre 797 (at Los Angeles, Sector Reforma) 52-33/619.67.65

Flama Latina [D] Degollado 187 (btwn Madero & Lopez Cotillo) Fri (Centro)

Kike's [★M,TG,S] Calle Galeana 159 (upstairs) 8pm-2am, clsd Mon, drag shows Th-Sun, also men's bathhouse

Los Panchos Jr [M,D,F,S] Calle Galeana 180-A, 2nd flr (Centro) 52-33/613.53.25 9pm-2am, hustlers

Mascara's [MW,NH,F,E] Calle Maestranza 238 (at Prisciliano Sánchez) 52-33/614.81.03 8am-2am, colorful atmosphere, live music

Guadalajara • MEXICO

■NIGHTCLUBS

Angel's [★M,D,F,S,V,$] Lopez Cotillo 1459-B, Col Americana 52-33/615.25.25, 52-3/630.78.79 *9pm-4am, clsd Sun-Mon, strippers wknds, restaurant open from 1pm*

Candilejas [GS,D,S,$] Calle Prisciliano Sánchez 407, Centro 52-33/614.55.12 *8pm-4am, clsd Mon, lavish drag shows*

The Louvre [M,D,S,$] Madero 676 (at Federalismo) 52-33/826-8530 *clsd Mon-Tue*

La Malinche [M,D,DS] Av Álvaro Obregón 1230 (btwn Calles 48 & 50, Sector Libertad; look for the large black canopy) 52-33/643.65.62 *9pm-3am, clsd Mon-Wed, drag shows wknds, hustlers*

Monica's Disco Bar [★M,D,DS,S,YC,$] Av Álvaro Obregón 1713 (btwn Calles 68 & 70, Sector Libertad; no sign, look for canopy under a big palm tree) 52-33/643.95.44 *10pm-5am, clsd Mon-Tue, packed after midnight, drag/ strip shows wknds, take a taxi to & from*

SOS Club [★MW,D,DS,$] Av La Paz 1413 (Sector Hidalgo) 52-33/826.41.79 *9pm-3am, clsd Mon-Wed, drag shows wknds, patio*

El Taller [MO,D,S,V] Calle 66 #30 (btwn Calles Gigantes Eje & 12 de Octubre, Sector Reforma) 52-33/655.95.49 *10pm-5am, cruisy, makeout booths*

■RESTAURANTS

Mondo Caffe [GF,MR,BW] Av Chapultepec 48 (at Pedro Moreno) 52-333/630.22.32 *8am-11pm, brkfst, lunch & dinner, coffee, smoothies, free internet access*

El Paraíso at Angel's club 52-33/615.25.25 *7pm-2am, clsd Sun-Mon*

Sanborn's Av Juárez 305 (at Av 16 de Septiembre)

Sanborn's Café Av Vallarta 2037

■GYMS & HEALTH CLUBS

La Academia [PC] Priscilo Sanchez 484 (btwn Donato Guerra & Enrique Gonzalez M) *gym, steam, massage, darkroom, private rooms*

■MEN'S CLUBS

Baños Galeana [★GS,YC,GO] Calle Galeana 159 (in Kike's Bar) 52-33/613.62.86

Banos La Fuente Calle Manuel Acuna #1107 (btwn Nicolas Romero & Gregoria Davila) 52-33/826.36.18 *clsd Sun*

■EROTICA

Mundo Cool Ocampo 245 (at Prisciliano Sánchez) 52-33/614.74.81

Super Tienda De Videos Av La Paz 1527 52-33/825.99.80 *also at 1485 Mexicaltzingo (at Diaz de Leon), 52-33/825.59.28*

■CRUISY AREAS

Parque Revolución [AYOR] Av Juárez at Av Federalismo

Plaza Tapatía [AYOR] near Degollado Theater *days*

Guanajuato

■BARS

La Lola [GS,F,GO] Ancha de San Antonio #31, San Miguel de Allende 52-473/2.40.50 *1pm-2am, clsd Mon*

■NIGHTCLUBS

La Cueva [GF,D,MR,F,18+,YC,GO] Calle Alonso 48 (at Barranca) 52-473/32.76.47 *6pm-4am*

El Paraiso [M] Tepetapa (past Tepetapa's Bridge, before Ferrocarril Station)

■RESTAURANTS

La Mancha Galarza 7 (at Pocitos & San Roque Square) 52-473/32.46.33 *8am-midnight, also bar*

Irapuato

■BARS

Blanco y Negro [GF,D] Av Ejército National 890 52-462/4.23.81 *Th-Sun only*

Mazatlán • Mexico

Isla Mujeres

ACCOMMODATIONS
Villas Allure [GF,SW,GO] Fracz Paraiso lte 55 & 56 **52-998/877.0615** *intimate & luxurious hotel on its own private Caribbean island (20-minute boat ride from Cancun)*

Jalapa

NIGHTCLUBS
D K Ché [★MW,D,S,$] at Calles Zaragoza & Prolongación (take road to Banderilla, 2 blks S of the hwy, at the town border, on a rough dirt road) *10pm-close Fri-Sat*

La Mansión [MW,D,S,$] take a cab toward Banderilla (20 minutes NW of town, turn right at sign for El Paraíso Campestre & go past RR tracks) *9pm-4am Fri-Sat only*

CRUISY AREAS
Parque Juárez/ Zócalo [AYOR] at Enriquez & Zaragoza

La Paz

ACCOMMODATIONS
La Casa Mexicana Inn [GS,NS,WC] Calle Bravo 106 (btwn Madero & Mutualismo) **52-612/125-2748** *open Nov-June*

Hotel Mediterrane [GS,F,GO] Allende 36 (at Malecón) **52-612/125-1195** *sundeck*

BARS
Bar Neon [MW,NH,YC,GO] Allende 36 (at Hotel Mediterrane) **52-612/125-1195** *7pm-1am*

¡No Que No! [MW,D] Marcelo Rubio (btwn Cuauhtemoc & Sonora)

NIGHTCLUBS
Las Varitas [GS,D,E] Calle Independencia 111 (at Malecón) **52-612/125-2025** *9pm-3am, clsd Mon*

RESTAURANTS
La Pazta Allende 36 (at Hotel Mediterrane) **52-612/5.11.95** *7am-11pm, Italian & Swiss*

CRUISY AREAS
Malecón (Seawall) [AYOR] *afternoon & early evening*

León

BARS
La Movida [M] Belisario Domínguez 417, 2nd flr **52-477/14.21.41** *10am-midnight*

NIGHTCLUBS
Bagoas [M,D,PC,$] Mar Baltico 1332, Col Rinconada del Sur (at Alfredo Valadez) **52-477/71.01.53** *Fri-Sat only*

La Bizantina [M,D,S] 20 de Eñero 204, Centro (off Calle Pedro Moreno) **52-477/13.44.85** *Fri-Sun only*

Manzanillo

ACCOMMODATIONS
Las Hadas [GF] Santiago Peninsula **52-314/31.01.01, 888/559-4329** *great resort & location*

Mexico's Villa Montaña Adventure Outpost [GF] 46 Los Angeles Locos, La Manzanilla **206/932-7012** *2-bdrm hilltop villa, ocean views*

BARS
OK [M,D,DS,$] Independencia 42 (Centro) *Th-Sun only, drag shows*

San Luis Av de la Republica (near Zaragoza & Lopez Mateos)

CRUISY AREAS
Santiago Beach [AYOR]

Matamoros

CRUISY AREAS
Mercado & Zócalo [AYOR]

Mazatlán

ACCOMMODATIONS
El Cid Resort [GF] **800/525-1925** *4 hotels*

Hotel Los Sábalos [★GF,SW] Rodolfo T Loaiza #190 (Zona Dorada) **52-669/983.53.33, 800/528-8760 (US#)** *upscale resort w/ 2 pools, beach, health club, also popular Joe's Oyster Bar*

Mazatlán • *MEXICO*

The Pueblo Bonito Emerald Bay [GF,SW] Ernesto Coppel Compaña **52-669/989.05.25, 800/990-8250** *resort on 20 acres, jacuzzi, gym, also piano bar*

■BARS

La Alemana [GS] Calle Zaragoza 16 (at Benito Juarez & Serdan) *sports bar*

Pepe Toro [★M,D,DS,S] Av de las Garzas 18, Zona Dorada (1 blk W of Av Camarón Sábalo) **52-669/914.41.76** *9pm-4am, clsd Mon-Wed*

Vitrolas Bar [MW,F,DS,S] Heribertos Frias 1608 (in El Centro) **52-669/85.22.21** *lunch menu, drag shows & strippers Sun*

■RESTAURANTS

Panama Restaurant Pasteleria [GS] at Avs de las Garzas & Camarón Sábalo **52-669/13.69.77**

Roca Mar [★] Av del Mar (at Calle Isla de Lobos, Zona Costera) **52-669/81.60.08** *till 2am, seafood, full bar*

Señor Frogs [D] Av del Mar, Zona Costera **52-669/82.19.25, 52-69/82.11.10** *noon-midnight, expensive menu, seafood, full bar*

■MEN'S CLUBS

Baños Juan Carlos [AYOR] Calle Genaro Estrada #702 *sleazy*

■CRUISY AREAS

Avenida Del Mar [AYOR] along malecón (sea wall)

Mérida

■ACCOMMODATIONS

Casa Ramos 59 [M,GO] Calle 59 #541 (btwn Calle 66 & Calle 68) **52-999/928-3626** *guest house*

Casa San Juan B&B [GS,NS,WC,GO] 545A Calle 62 (at Calle 69 & Calle 71) **52-999/23.68.23**

Gran Hotel [GF,F] Calle 60 #496 **52-999/24.77.30** *historic turn-of-the-century hotel, courtyard w/ balconies, also restaurant*

■BARS

Kumbala Calle 16 # 519 (btwn 64 and 66)

■NIGHTCLUBS

Status/ Prince [M,D,S] Avenida Colon (behind cinema)

■RESTAURANTS

La Bella Época Calle 60 #447 (upstairs in the Hotel del Parque) **52-999/28.19.28** *4pm-1am, Yucatécan, try for a balcony table*

■MEN'S CLUBS

El Baño Azul 514 Calle 70 (3 blks from Parque Santiago) **52-999/23.39.57**

Hotel Colón Calle 62 #483 (btwn 57 & 59 Centro) **52-999/23.43.55** *3pm-9pm, also hotel*

■CRUISY AREAS

Hidalgo Park [AYOR]

Santa Lucia Park [AYOR]

Zócalo [AYOR] near corner of Calle 60 & 61

Mexicali

■BARS

Cantine Tare [M,NH,S] at Calle Uxmal & Av Jalisco, Pueblo Nuevo (across the Rio Nuevo from downtown) *6pm-3am, clsd Mon, cruisy, drag shows*

Galerie 232 [D,V,BW] Av Zuazua 232 (in zona Centro) **52-686/543.01.61** *1pm-midnight*

La Linterna [M,NH,OC,AYOR] Blvd Juárez (btwn Calles Azueta & Altamirano) *1pm-2am, hustlers*

El Rey de Copas [MW,NH] Av Baja California (at Av Tuxtla Gutierrez, Pueblo Nuevo) *open till 3am*

El Taurino [★M,D] Av Juan de Zuazua 480 (near Morelos) *1pm-2am, cruisy*

■NIGHTCLUBS

Mirage Disco [★D] Av Lerdo #430 (in zona Centro) *6pm-2am Wed-Sun*

■MEN'S CLUBS

Baños San Jose [GS] Av Juan de Zuazua 475 (enter rear) *7am-8pm*

Mexico City • Mexico

■ CRUISY AREAS

Chapultepec Park [AYOR] *afternoons*

Parque Madero [AYOR] *Sun afternoons*

Mexico City

Note: Mexico City is divided into 'Zonas' (ie, Zona Rosa) & 'Colonias' (abbreviated here as Col). Remember to use these when giving addresses to taxi drivers.

■ INFO LINES & SERVICES

Centro Cultural de la Diversidad Sexual Colima 267, Col Roma 52-55/514.25.65

Gay/ Lesbian AA Av Universidad 1900, Federal Dist 52-55/658.86.85 *times vary, call for info, meeting for persons living w/ AIDS/ HIV*

■ ACCOMMODATIONS

Hotel Casa Blanca [GF,F,SW] Lafragua 7 52-55/705.13.00, 800/972-2162 (US#)

Hotel Krystal Rosa [GF,F,SW] Liverpool 155 52-55/228.99.28, 800/231-9860 (US#) *upscale, 2 restaurants & nightclub*

Hotel Majestic [GF] Madero 73, Col Centro 52-55/521.86.00, 800/528-1234

Marco Polo [GF] Amberes 27, Col Juarez (Zona Rosa) 52-55/511.18.39, 800/223-0888 (US#) *upscale hotel*

Suites Michelangelo [GF] Calle Rio Amazonas 78 (Zona Rosa) 52-55/566.98.77 *kitchen*

■ BARS

La Cantina del Vaquero [M,D,L] Calle Algéciras 26, Col Insurgentes Mixcoac (in Centro Armand) 52-55/598.21.95

La Cantina del Vaquero [★MO,L,S,V] Calle Algéciras 26, Col Insurgentes Mixcoac (in Centro Armand) 52-55/598.21.95 *5pm-close, strict leather/ Levi dress code (cowboy heaven)*

El Celo [M,NH,D,F,S,$] Calle Londres 104 (Zona Rosa) 52-55/514.47.66 *5pm-close, clsd Mon*

Enigma [MW,D,S,$] Calle Morelia 111, Col Roma (4 blks from Metro Niño Héroes, Zona Rosa) 52-55/207.73.67 *9pm-3:30am, 6pm-2am Sun, clsd Mon*

Living [★MW,D,DS] Orizaba 146, Col Roma 52-55/584.74.03, 52-55/584.74.68 *Fri-Sat only*

Los Rosales [MW,D,TG,S,AYOR] Calle Pensador Mexicano 11 (Centro Historico, next to Teatro Blanquito) *9pm-close, clsd Mon, drag shows, dicey area*

Pigalles [M,D] Insurgentes Sur 1281 (at Felix Cuevas) 52-5/563.25.63

Tom's Leather Bar [M,L,S,V,$] Av Insurgentes 357, Col la Condesa

Viena Bar [★M] República de Cuba 3 (Centro Historico) *11am-11pm, beer bar, packed nightly*

■ NIGHTCLUBS

Anyway/ Exacto/ The Doors [★MW,D,F,DS,S,$] Calle Monterrey 47, Col Roma (Zona Rosa) 52-55/533.16.91 *9pm-4am, 3 flrs: The Doors, 1st flr, is mostly women; Exacto, 2nd flr, is mixed; Anyway, 3rd flr, is men's bar w/ drag & strip shows*

Box [MW,D] Moliere 425 (Col Polanco) 52-55/203.33.56, 52-55/203.33.65 *huge club, call for info*

Cabaré-Tito [MW,D,S] Calle Londres 161 & 117, Plaza del Angel (Zona Rosa) 52-55/514.94.55, 52-55/207.25.54 *Th-Sat only, go-go dancers*

El Punto [MW,F,S,YC,BW] Insurgentes Sur 226, Col. Roma (at Colima) 52-55/525.18.36 *Mon-Sun, live shows, young crowd, beer only, also La Rockola cafe & soda fountain*

■ RESTAURANTS

Fonda San Ángel Plaza San Jacinto 3, Col San Ángel (across from Bazar San Ángel) 52-55/550.19.42 *popular after 7pm Fri-Sat, classic Mexican dishes*

La Opera [P] Calle 5 de Mayo 10 (Centro Historico) 52-55/512.89.59 *noon-midnight, clsd Sun*

PK II Mayran 224 (Mariano Escobedo) 52-55/1055.83.52 *also bar*

Mexico City • *MEXICO*

Sanborn's Madera 4 (in Casade los Azulejos) 52-55/**512.22.33** *often cruisy, especially in magazine/newsstand section*

■ENTERTAINMENT & RECREATION

The Great Temple Museum Calle Seminario 8 (Zocalo) 52-55/**542.47.84** *9am-5pm, clsd Mon, artifacts from the central Aztec temple at Tenochtitlán*

El Hábito [S] Madrid 13 (Coyoácan District) 52-55/**659.11.39** *avantegarde theater & bar*

Museo de Arte Carrillo Gil Av Revolución 1608 (San Angel) 52-55/**550.62.60**, 52-55/**550.39.83** *10am-6pm, clsd Mon, contemporary art*

Museo de Arte Moderno Paseo de la Reforma (at Gandhi, Chapultepec Forest) 52-55/**553.62.33**, 52-55/**211.87.29** *10am-6pm, clsd Mon*

National Museum of Anthropology Paseo de la Reforma (at Gandhi) 52-55/**553.62.66**, 52-55/**553.62.43** *9am-7pm, clsd Mon*

■PUBLICATIONS

Ser Gay 52-55/**534.38.04** *covers all Mexico nightlife, limited resources*

■GYMS & HEALTH CLUBS

Club San Francisco [M] Calle Rio Panuco 207, Col Cuauhtémoc 52-55/**519.86.82**

■MEN'S CLUBS

Baños Finisterre [AYOR] Calle A Contreras 11, Col San Rafael (4 blks W of Metro San Cosme) 52-55/**535.87.59**

Baños San Juan [F,AYOR] Calle López 120 (N of Metro Salto de Agua, in Centro Historico) 52-55/**521.33.76** *also salon*

Baños Señorial [AYOR] Calle Isabel La Católica 52 (Centro Historico) 52-55/**709.07.32**, 52-55/**709.31.20** *erotic massages available*

La Casita [V,YC,PC,AYOR] Viaducto Miguel Alemán 72, Col Algarín (near Bolivar—no sign/ number on door) 52-55/**519.86.82** *24hrs, gym equipment, porn shop, ages 18-35 only*

La Escuelita [V,PC] Rio Tiber 98, Col Cuauhtémoc *24hrs*

Fuck [S] Paseo de la Reforma 169, Col Insurgentes 52-55/**566.73.42**, 52-55/**559.77.18** *name says it all*

La Nueva Casita II [V,YC,PC,AYOR] Insurgentes S 228, Col Roma 52-55/**514.46.39**, 52-55/**514.45.91** *24hrs, gym equipment, bar, porn shop, ages 18-35 only*

La Toalla [V,PC,AYOR] Calle Rio Panuco 207, Col Cuauhtémoc (at Club San Francisco) 52-55/**525.18.94** *wknds only, cruisy bath house*

■EROTICA

Sexy Video [AYOR] Calle Génova 20-3 (Zona Rosa) 52-55/**514.80.40**, 52-55/**525.47.32 (orders)** *private booths*

■CRUISY AREAS

Alameda Central [AYOR] W side of park (Centro Historico) *afternoons & early evenings, dangerous later*

Bosque de Chapultepec [AYOR] either side of gate to monument (Zona Rosa) *afternoons*

Metro Hidalgo [AYOR] (Centro Historico) *hustlers afternoons & early evenings, dangerous later*

Metro Insurgentes [AYOR] (Zona Rosa)

Zona Rosa [AYOR] *nights, anywhere & everywhere, but especially Calle Florencia btwn Reforma & Liverpool, also Calles Génova, Hamburgo & Londres*

Mineral de Pozos

■ACCOMMODATIONS

Casa Montana [GF] Plaza Principal, Jardin Juarez #4A (at Ocampo) 52-442/**293.0032**, 52-442/**293.0033** *boutique hotel, garden restaurant & bar*

Nogales • Mexico

Monterrey

ACCOMMODATIONS

Hotel Rio [GF,SW] Calle Padre Mier 194 N (at Garibaldi, Centro) **800/432-2520 (US#)** *also restaurant, near Zona Rosa*

BARS

Charao's [MW,D,S] at Calles Isaac Garza E & Zaragoza W (Centro) *10pm-6am, clsd Sun, popular after-hours*

La Florida [M,NH] Calle Juan Méndez 1131 N (btwn Av Colón & Clzda Madero) *24hrs, popular after-hours Fri-Sat*

El Kloster [M,NH,YC] Av Benito Juárez 916 (btwn Calle Arteaga & Madero) *straight by day & gay by night (after 10pm)*

Napoleón [M,V] Calle Garibaldi 727 S (btwn Matamoros & Padre Mier) **52-81/342.68.36** *10am-late, cruisy*

La Ópera [M,NH] at Calles Colegio Civil W & Áramberri W **52-81/340.85.30** *10pm-4am, clsd Sun*

Pato Lucas [M,S,AYOR,$] Calle Zaragoza (at Tapia, Centro) *open late*

El Taurus [M,NH,YC] Calle Arteaga 117 N (btwn Colegio Civil & Juárez) *11am-1am, packed wknds*

NIGHTCLUBS

Arcanos [MW,D,S,V,$] Calle Ruperto Martínez 845 (at Calle Cuauhtémoc) *open Wed-Sat, drag shows Sat, video bar downstairs*

Extremo [MO,D,S,$] Av Fidel Velazquez 318 (200 meters N of Pulga Mitras) *7pm-2am, clsd Wed-Th, strippers Sat*

Milenium [D,S] Ruiz Cortines 3135 **52-81/354.16.61** *shows on Sat, dancing/DJ Sun*

Vongolé [M,D,S,AYOR,$] Av Constitución (at Santa Bárbara) **52-81/336.03.35** *Wed-Sat, live shows Sat*

EROTICA

Cine Chaplin [AYOR] Calle Héroes de 47 815 N (N of Zona Rosa, btwn Calles Arteaga E & Carlos Salazar E) **52-81/375.62.57** *rundown but cruisy*

Cinema Cometa [GS] Felix U Gomez (at Magnolia) *gay/ straight, cruisy in balcony*

CRUISY AREAS

Avenida Juárez [AYOR] btwn Calle Matamoros & Calle Padre Mier (Centro) *part of 'El Circuito,' hustlers*

Parque Alameda [AYOR] Av Pino Suárez S (at Calle Aramberri N) *late afternoons & evenings*

Plaza Hidalgo [AYOR] Zona Rosa *late afternoons & early evenings*

Morelia

NIGHTCLUBS

Con la Rojas [M,D,$] Aldama 343 (Centro) **52-443/12.15.78** *11pm-2am, clsd Sun-Wed, upscale*

RESTAURANTS

La Capilla Ignacio Zaragoza 90 (at Posada de la Soledad Hotel) **52-443/12.18.18** *in charming old hotel in converted convent*

Fonda de las Mercedes [★] Calle Leon Guzmán 47 **52-443/12.61.13, 52-443/13.32.22** *inside beautiful colonial home*

Sanborn's Plaza de las Américas shopping center *popular w/ gay men evenings*

MEN'S CLUBS

Baños Mintzicuri Calle Vasco de Quiroga 227 (enter through the Hotel Mintzicuri) **52-443/12.06.64** *gay area through door marked 'Ruso General'*

CRUISY AREAS

Central Camionera [AYOR] *the central bus station, late nights wknds*

Plaza de Armas [AYOR] *late afternoons & early evenings, hustlers*

Nogales

ACCOMMODATIONS

Motel Miami [AYOR] Av Ingenieros & Campillo **52-631/312-5450**

Nogales • *MEXICO*

■MEN'S CLUBS
Baños Ana [GS] Av Lopez Mateos (at Av Abregon) *7am-9pm, small but clean*

Nuevo Laredo

■CRUISY AREAS
Plaza de Armas [AYOR] *late afternoons & early evenings, hustlers*

Oaxaca

■ACCOMMODATIONS
El Camino Real Oaxaca [★GF,F,SW] Calle 5 de Mayo 300 52-951/**6.06.11**, 800/**722-6466** (US reservations) *5-star hotel in restored 16th-century convent, frescoes & courtyards abound*

Mision de los Angeles Hotel [GF,F,SW] Calzada Porfirio Díaz 102 52-951/**5.15.00** or **5.10.00**, 800/**221-6509** (US#) *resort w/ bungalows, restaurant & dance club, tennis courts*

■BARS
Bar Jardin [GS,F] Portal de Flores 10 (on the zócalo) 52-951/**6.20.92** *7:30am-1am, sidewalk cafe, more gay as day goes by, also restaurant*

■NIGHTCLUBS
Disco Snob [M,D] Calzada Niños Héroes de Chupultepec (1 blk W of bus station) *gay from 10pm Wed only*

El Numerito (aka Disco 502) [MO,D,PC,$] Calle Porfirio Díaz 502 (Centro, ring to enter) *10pm-close, tourists welcome w/ proper ID*

■CRUISY AREAS
Bustamante [AYOR] Zaragoza to Periférico *late evenings*

Parque Alemeda & Zócalo [AYOR] *early evenings*

Orizaba

■NIGHTCLUBS
Sky Drink [M,D,DS,S,$] Madero N 1280 *clsd Sun-Tue, drag/ strip shows Sat*

■CRUISY AREAS
Parque del Castillo [AYOR]

Pachuca

■BARS
Chez-Lui [GF,D] Calle Suárez Molina 105-B 52-771/**1.08.80** *Fri-Sat only*

■CRUISY AREAS
Zócalo [AYOR]

Pátzcuaro

■CRUISY AREAS
Mercado [AYOR]

Plaza Principal/ Plaza Grande [AYOR]

Playa del Carmen
see also Cancún & Cozumel

■ACCOMMODATIONS
Aventura Mexicana Resort [GF,SW,N,WC] Av 10 (at Calle 22) 52-984/**873-1876** *jacuzzi, 15 minutes to gay nude beach, also restaurant & bar*

Pension San Juan [GF,NS] 5a Av 165 (btwn Calles 6 & 8 N) 52-984/**3.06.47**

■NIGHTCLUBS
Playa 69 [M,D,GO] Fifth Ave (btwn 4th & 6th Sts, ground flr) 52-984/**876-9466** *9pm-4am, cruisy, int'l crowd*

■RESTAURANTS
100% Natural 5th Ave (btwn 10 & 12) *vegetarian*

Poza Rica

■NIGHTCLUBS
El 42 [GF,D,S,$] Plaza 18 de Marzo (Centro) *Fri-Sat only*

Paladium [GF,D,S,$] 16 de Septiembre 119, upstairs, Col El Tajín 52-782/**4.11.76** *Th-Sat only*

Puebla

■BARS
La Cigarra [★M,S] Calle 5 W 538 (at Calle 7, Centro) *5pm-3am, clsd Sun, beer bar*

Franco's Bar [E,DS,S] Sur 15 Oriente 52-222/**40.56.67** *8pm-close*

Puerto Vallarta • Mexico

■ NIGHTCLUBS

Cherri's [GF,D,DS,$] Prolongacion 11, Col Mayorazgo (at Zapotecas) 52-222/**28.89.37** *Fri-Sat only*

Garrotos [GF,D,$] 22 Orient E 602 (close to Blvd 5 de Mayo, Xenenetla) 52-222/**42.42.32** *Fri-Sat only*

Jaleo's [M,D,DS,S,$] Av Reforma 3121 S, Col La Paz *10pm-3am Fri-Sat*

■ MEN'S CLUBS

Baños Las Termas [MO,V,PC] Av 5 de Mayo 2810, Centro 52-222/**32.95.62** *clsd Mon, gym, sauna, '100% gay'*

■ CRUISY AREAS

Mercado Garibaldi [AYOR] Calle 14 E

Zócalo/ Main Park [AYOR] at cathedral *late evenings*

Puerto Vallarta

■ ACCOMMODATIONS

ARCO IRIS Accommodations [MW,F,SW,N,GO] Paseo de los Delfines #115, Colonia Conchas Chinas 52-322/**221-5579** *rooms, apts & houses, tropical brkfst*

Blue Chairs Beach Resort [M,SW,WC] Malecon & Almendro #4 (on Playa Los Muertos) 229/**336-9979** (US#), 866/**514-7969** *beachfront resort in Puerto Vallarta, hot tub*

Bugambilia Blanca Condo Apartments [GS,GO] Carretera Barra de Navidad #602, Col Emiliano Zapata (Off Hwy 200) 52-322/**222-1152** *4 levels, suites, 2 & 3-bdrm apts, full brkfst, 6-minute walk to gay beach*

Casa Boana Torre Malibu [★GS,F,SW] Calle Amapas 325 52-322/**222-0099**, 52-322/**222-6695** *condo-hotel w/ bay views, poolside bar, near gay beach*

Casa Cupula [M,SW,NS,GO] 129 Callejon de la Igualdad, Colonia Amapas 52-322/**294-0942** *luxury guest house*

Casa de los Arcos [GS,SW] 52-322/**222-5990** *private villa, sleeps 8, terrace w/ amazing view of Bandera Bay*

Casa dos Comales [GF,SW,GO] Calle Aldama 274 52-322/**223-2042**, 888/**881-1822** (US#) *guest house & apts, near Old Town*

Casa Fantasía [GS,SW,NS,WC,GO] 203 Pino Suarez, Col Emiliano Zapata (near Rio Cuale) 52-322/**223-2444** *B&B made up of 3 haciendas, terrace*

Casa Palapa, A B&B [MO,SW,NS,GO] Paseo de Las Conchas Chinas #107, Colonia Conchas Chinas 909/**921-5033** (in US), 52-322/**221-5561** *B&B, full brkfst, ocean views*

Casa Tres Vidas [GS,SW] 888/**640-8100** (US#), 801/**536-5850** *3 luxury beachfront villas, hot tub*

Casa Ventana [GF,SW,GO] 135 Calle Hortencias, Penthouse 649/**376-6230** *luxury condo, sleeps 6*

Condominios Plazamar [GF,SW,GO] Lázaro Cárdenas #155 702/**496-4432** (NV#) *1 & 2-bdrm beachfront condos*

David's Beach Condo in PV [GF,SW] 156 Amapas St #402 415/**487-0800** *on gay beach*

Discovery Vallarta 52-322/**222-6918** *gay accommodations reservation service*

Doin' It Right Travel 941/**918-2166** (US#), 800/**936-3646** (US#) *Puerto Vallarta gay travel specialist, villas & condos, also great website at www.doinitright.com*

Hotelito Desconocido [GS,SW] Carretera a Mismaloya 479-102, 48380 Cruz de Loreto 52-322/**222-2526**, 800/**851-1143** *eco-resort on the beach, sauna*

Paco Paco Descanso del Sol Hotel [★MW,SW,GO] Pino Suárez #583, Zona Romantica 52-322/**223-0277**, 52-322/**222-5229** *apts, casitas & tents, rooftop bar*

Paco's Hidden Paradise [MW,F,GO] 30 minutes S of Puerto Vallarta 52-322/**223-0277** & **222-1899** *secluded beach resort accessible only by boat, also bar & restaurant*

Damron Men's Travel Guide 2004

Puerto Vallarta • *Mexico*

Quinta Maria Cortez [GS,SW] 132 Calle Sagitario, Playa Conchas Chinas 801/536-5850 (US#), 888/640-8100 (US#) *'Mexaterranian Villa' w/ sunny terraces & spectacular ocean views*

Vallarta Cora [MO,SW,N,GO] Calle Pilitas 174, Col Emiliano Zapata 52-322/223-2815, 52-322/222-6234 *basic apts, often sexually charged atmosphere*

Villa del Cielo [GS,SW,GO] Paseo de los Delfines 121 (at Residencial Conchas Chinas) 206/285-3503 (US#) *private villa*

Villa Felíz [MW,SW] Privada del Bosque #149 (Colonia Altavista) 52-322/222-0798, 916/684-0312 (US#) *full brkfst, great views, in Old Town*

Villas David B&B [M,SW,GO] Calle Galeana 348 (at Calle Miramar) 724/573-4693 (US#), 52-322/223-0315 *rooftop jacuzzi & pool, nude sunbathing*

■ BARS

Los Amigos Bar [MW,NH] Calle Carranza 237 (upstairs, next to Paco's Ranch) 52-322/222-7802 *5pm-2am, Mexican cantina, patio*

Apaches [GS,F,GO] Olas Altas 439 (at Rodriguez) 52-322/222-5235 *5pm-2am, till 1am Sun-Mon, classy cocktail bar, martinis & margaritas, tapas*

Blue Sunset Rooftop Bar [M,F,K,DS] S Los Muertos Beach, at Blue Chairs Resort *2pm-10pm, T-dance wknds*

La Bola [★M,F] Calle Pilitas 174 (at Vallarta Cora hotel) 52-322/223-2815 *4pm-11pm, poolside big spot, popular mtg spot after Amadeus day cruises, rumored to get quite wild some nights*

Cafe Bohemio [MW,18+,GO] Rodolfo Gomez 127 (at Olas Altas) 52-322/223-4676 *5pm-2am, clsd Mon, grilled food, patio*

Frida [GS,F,GO] Lazaro Cardenas 361 (at Insurgentes) *noon-2am, from 7pm Mon-Tue, more gay later in evening*

Garbo [GS,E,P] Pulpito 142 52-322/222-6142 *6:30pm-2am, upscale, live jazz Fri-Sat*

Kit Kat Bar [★MW,F,DS,GO] Pulpito 120 (next door to Chiles restaurant) 52-322/223-0093 *5pm-1:30am, swanky New York-style cocktail lounge, drag shows some nights, also restaurant, pricey but fun*

Paco's Sunset Bar [★MW,F,SW,GO] Calle Pino Suárez 583 (on rooftop of Paco Paco Descanso del Sol) 52-322/223-0277 *noon-10pm, the spot to watch the sun set*

The Palm [MW,D,F,E,DS,V,GO] Olas Altas 508 (at Rodolfo Gomez) 52-322/223-4818 *7pm-2am*

Santa Barbara Bar & Restaurant [GS,F,P,GO] 351 Olas Altas (S side) 52-322/222-4477, 52-322/222-2048 *8am-2am, Mexican/ American food, piano bar 10:30pm-1:30am Tue-Sat*

■ NIGHTCLUBS

Anthropology [MW,DS,S,YC] Calle Morelos 101, Plaza Río (at Rodriguez) 52-322/222-6392 *noon-4am, 3 levels: intimate rooftop bar, game bar, basement disco*

Los Balcones [★M,D,S] Calle Juárez 182, 2nd flr (at Calle Libertad) 52-322/222-4671 *9pm-3am, till 4am wknds, T-dance 6pm-11pm Sun, popular strippers late night*

Club Paco Paco [★M,D,P,GO,$] Calle Ignacio Vallarta 278 (at Carranza) 52-322/222-1899 *1pm-6am, cantina on 2nd flr, disco downstairs from 10pm, also rooftop terrace w/ live piano*

The Ranch [★M,D,S,V,GO,$] Calle Carranza 239 (walk thru Club Paco Paco to back of dance flr) 52-322/223-0537 *9pm-6am, packed for nightly strip shows, also upstairs bar*

■ CAFES

A Page in the Sun [★] Olas Altas 299 52-322/222-3608 *8am-10pm, coffee shop & English bookstore, also location at 950 Morelos w/ internet access*

Este Cafe [★GO] Libertad 336, Centro (around corner from flea market) 52-322/222-4261 *8am-10pm, clsd Sun, espresso & juice bar, desserts, ice cream*

Puerto Vallarta • Mexico

The Net House [★GO,F] Calle Ignacio Vallarta 232   52-322/222-6953   *7am-2am, cybercafe, organic coffee & baked goods, also Buona Pizza*

■ RESTAURANTS

Adobe Café [★GO] Calle Basilio Badillo 252 (at Ignacio Vallarta)   52-322/222-6720   *6pm-11pm, clsd Tue (also clsd Aug-Sept), full bar*

Bombo's [R,GO] Corona 327, Centro (at Matamoros)   52-322/222-5164   *4pm-midnight, upscale French, great views of Bandera Bay*

Cafe de Olla [★] Calle Basilio Badillo 168   52-322/223-1626   *10am-11pm, clsd Tue, Mexican, wait list an hour*

Café des Artistes [R] Calle Guadalupe Sánchez 740 (at Leona Vicario)   52-322/222-3228   *upscale French w/ a Mexican twist*

Chez Elena [GO] Matamoros 520, Centro (at Los Quatros Vientos)   52-322/222-0161   *6pm-11pm, seasonal, garden restaurant, Mexican/ int'l, also rooftop bar*

¡Chiles! [★GO] Pulpito 122 (at Olas Altas)   52-322/223-0373   *11am-6pm, clsd Sun, seasonal (clsd July-Sept), roasted chicken, sandwiches, hamburgers, large patio*

Daiquiri Dick's [★] Olas Altas 314 (on Playa Los Muertos)   52-322/222-0566   *9am-10:30pm, clsd Wed, Cal-Mex*

Le Bistro Jazz Café [★GO] Isla Rio Cuale 16-A (on the island, at the East Bridge)   52-322/222-0283   *9am-midnight, clsd Sun, PV's classiest*

Memo's Casa de los Hotcakes [★] Calle Basilio Badillo 289   52-322/222-6272   *8am-2pm, long lines for cheap & good brkfst, indoor patio, cooking classes*

Planeta Vegetariano Iturbide 270   52-322/222-3073   *buffet-style*

Red Cabbage [GO] Calle Rio Ribera 206-A (at Basilio Badillo)   52-322/223-0411   *Mexican, on Rio Cuale w/ great kitschy decor*

Santa Barbara Bar & Restaurant [GS,P,GO] 351 Olas Altas (S side)   52-322/222-4477, 52-322/222-2048   *8am-2am, Mexican/ American, full bar, piano bar 10:30pm-1:30am Tue-Sat*

Trio Guerrero 264   52-322/222-2196   *6pm-midnight, clsd Sun, Mediterranean/ Mexican, patio, live music*

■ ENTERTAINMENT & RECREATION

Boana Tours Calle Amapas 325 (at Casa Boana Torre Malibu)   52-322/222-0099   *horseback tours daily, hotspring tour (Tue)*

Diana's Cruise the Bay Tour [MW] meet at Los Muertos pier   52-322/222-1510   *10:30am-6pm Th, cruise on 33-ft trimaran, limited to 20 people, food served, open bar*

Paco Paco's Gay Hot Springs Tour [N] Calle Ignacio Vallarta 278 (at Club Paco Paco)   52-322/222-1899   *7pm-midnight Tue, trip to hot spring N of Puerto Vallarta, includes dinner & open bar*

Playa Los Muertos/ Playa del Sol [★] S of Rio Cuale   *the gay beach, now spans 'Blue Chairs' & 'Green Chairs'*

■ RETAIL SHOPS

La Rosa de Cristal [GO] Insurgentes 272 (at Cardenas)   52-322/222-5698   *10am-8pm, local handicrafts & beautiful blown-glass items*

Safari Accents [GO] Olas Altas 224   52-322/223-2660   *10am-11pm, pricey but beautiful home furnishings*

■ CRUISY AREAS

Malecón (Seawall) [AYOR] facing Calle Morelos (esp near benches across from Presidencia Municipal at Iturbide)   *evenings*

Playa Los Muertos [AYOR] near green chairs at The Beach Café & further S by the rocks   *afternoons*

Plaza Caracol Mall [AYOR]

Querétaro • MEXICO

Querétaro

■BARS
Villa Jardín/ Bar Oz [M,D,$] Blvd Bernardo Quintana 556, Col Arboledas (across from Cinemark) 52-442/24.13.96 *Sat only*

■NIGHTCLUBS
La Creación [GF,D,$] Monte Sinai 113, Col Vista Hermosa (before Disco Qu) 52-442/13.51.90 *Fri-Sat only*

La Iguana [GF,D,S] Av Universidad 308 (at Hotel Maria Teresa) *9pm-2am Fri-Sat*

■CRUISY AREAS
Alameda Parque [AYOR]

El Jardín Guerrero [AYOR] 3 blks from Centro Historico

Plaza de Armas [AYOR]

Zócalo/ Obregón Plaza [AYOR]

Reynosa

■BARS
Eurobar [M,D]

Ocean [M,D] Ocampo St

■MEN'S CLUBS
Baños Colon [F] Colon St (across from bus station) *small but clean*

■CRUISY AREAS
Plaza [AYOR] Main Square (opposite American Hotel aka 'The Circuit')

Rosarito Beach

■ACCOMMODATIONS
Rosarito Beach Hotel [GF] 31 Benito Juarez Blvd 52-661/612-0144, 800/343-8582

■BARS
Ricardo's Siete Mares [M,NH,D,MR,TG,F,DS,18+,GO] 46-5 Benito Juarez Blvd (across from Rosarito Beach Hotel) 52-661/612-0774 *mostly straight until 10pm, drag shows Th, cruisy late*

San Luis Potosí

■BARS
Boy's House [M] Zacatecas 347

Sheik [M,D,DS,$] Prolongación Zacatecas 347 52-444/2.74.57, 52-444/4.49.85 *10pm-3am Fri-Sat, drag shows Fri, strippers Sat*

■CRUISY AREAS
El Jardín San Francisco [AYOR]

San Miguel de Allende

■ACCOMMODATIONS
Casa de Sierra Nevada [GF,SW] Calle Hospicio 35 52-415/2.04.15, 800/223-6510 (US#) *suites w/ fireplaces, horseback riding, also spa*

Casa Schuck Luxury B&B Inn [GF,SW] Bajada Garita 3 52-415/2.06.57 *B&B*

Casita La Madeja [GS,GO] Carlos del Castillo 1 (at Col Guadalupe) 52-415/154-4536 *apt, near center of town*

Las Terrazas San Miguel [GS,NS,GO] Santo Domingo #3 52-415/152-5028 *4 rental homes*

■BARS
La Lola [GS,F,YC] Calle Ancha de San Antonio 31 (across from the Instituto Allende) 52-415/2.40.50 *1pm-2am, clsd Mon, also restaurant*

■NIGHTCLUBS
Cien (100) Ángeles [M,D,S,$] Tinajitas 24, Col San Antonio (across from Hotel Real de Minas) *9pm-3am Fri-Sat*

Tampico

■CRUISY AREAS
Zócalo/ Plaza de Armas [AYOR]

Tapachula

■CRUISY AREAS
Zócalo [AYOR]

Veracruz • Mexico

Tenancingo

■ACCOMMODATIONS

Casa Mora B&B Malinalco [GF,SW]
18 Calle de la Cruz , Malinalco
52-714/147-0002 *full brkfst*

Tepic

■BARS

Club Tepic [MO] Calle Veracruz N 131 *more gay after 11pm*

La Posta Emiliano Zapata 193 Poniente

Tijuana

■INFO LINES & SERVICES

Gay/ Lesbian Social Resource Center Calle 1 #7648 (Zona Centro) 52-664/80.99.63

■BARS

DF [M,NH,OC] Plaza Santa Cecilia 781 (near Calle 3) *open late*

Emilio's Cafeteria Musical [MW,F,E,BW] Calle 3/ Puerto Ste 1810 #11 (in entry to Parking América complex) 52-664/88.02.67 *8pm-4am, live music, also cafe, open 8am-6pm, many local lgbt groups meet here*

Noa Noa [★MW,D,DS,YC] Av 'D'/ Miguel F Martínez 678 (at Calle 1) 52-664/81.79.01 *5pm-3am, till 4am Fri, till 5am Sat, drag shows*

El Ranchero Bar [★M,NH,D,F,AYOR] Plaza Santa Cecilia 769 (btwn Calles 1 & 2 and Revolución & Constitución) *10am-late, cruisy cantina, hustlers, use caution in bathrooms*

El Taurino Bar [M,NH,S] at Calles 1 & Constitución 52-664/85.24.78 *3pm-2am, till 5am Fri-Sat, cruisy, hustlers*

Villa Garcia [M,D] Plaza Santa Cecilia 751 (next to El Ranchero) *10am-late, small dance flr, cruisy*

■NIGHTCLUBS

Los Equipales [★MW,D,DS,YC] Calle 7/ Galeana #8236 (at Av Revolución, opposite Jai Alai Palace) 52-664/88.30.06 *9pm-3am, clsd Mon-Tue*

Extasis [★M,D,S,$] Larroque 213 (in Plaza Viva Tijuana, next to the border) 52-664/82.83.39 *8pm-late, from 6pm Sun, clsd Mon-Wed, go-go boys, more women Th*

Mike's Disco [★MW,D,DS,V] Av Revolución 1220 (at Calle 6A) 52-664/85.35.34 *8pm-5am, till 3am Th, clsd Wed*

Terraza 9 [MW,D,DS,S,$] Calle 6/ Flores Magón #8150 (at Av Revolución) 52-664/85.35.34 *5pm-2am, till 5am Fri-Sat, clsd Mon*

■MEN'S CLUBS

Baños Enva Av Revolucion *mostly straight*

Toluca

■BARS

Open House [D] Pino Suarez S 2014, Col Juarez

■CRUISY AREAS

Mercado [AYOR]

Zócalo/ Plaza de Los Martires [AYOR]

Tuxtla Gutierrez

■BARS

Sandy's Bar [GF,TG] Calle 9 S & 8 N (inside Via Fontana)

■CRUISY AREAS

Cristobal Colón [AYOR]

Plaza Bellsario Dominguez [AYOR]

Veracruz

■ACCOMMODATIONS

Hotel Imperial [GF,F] Portales de Miguel Lerdo de Tejada 153 (N side of the Plaza de Armas) 52-229/32.12.04 *expensive*

Hotel Villa del Mar [GF,SW] Blvd Miguel Ávila Camacho 2707, Col Zaragoza (across street from Playa del Mar beach) 52-229/32.71.35

■NIGHTCLUBS

Deeper [★M,D,S,$] Calle Icazo 1005 (btwn Avs Victoria & Revillagigedo N) 52-229/35.02.65 *9pm-4am Th-Sun, strippers Fri-Sat*

Veracruz • MEXICO

Shooters [★MW,D,DS,S] Calle 3 #1221 (btwn Enriquez & Alcocer) *warehouse club in a residential neighborhood, 10-minute cab ride from downtown*

■ ENTERTAINMENT & RECREATION

San Juan de Ulua Fortress 9am-4:30pm, clsd Mon, *impressive early colonial-era fortress*

Veracruz Aquarium Blvd Avila (at Xicolencat) 52-229/**32.79.84** *10am-7pm, one of the largest & best in the world; don't miss it!*

■ MEN'S CLUBS

Baños El Edén [AYOR] Av Hidalgo•1113, Centro (btwn Calles Juan Soto & Hernán Cortés) 52-229/**32.44.00** *buy tickets at rear counter of music store*

■ CRUISY AREAS

Plaza de Armas/ Zócalo [AYOR]

Waterfront & Av República [AYOR]

Zacatecas

■ NIGHTCLUBS

Escándalo [MW,D,S] Feria Zacatecan, Terraza 4 52-492/**4.14.76** *9pm-3am Fri-Sat*

■ CAFES

Café Acropolis Av Hidalgo

■ CRUISY AREAS

Av Juárez [AYOR] E from Av Hidalgo for 2 blks

Zihuatanejo

■ ACCOMMODATIONS

Hotel Las Palmas [GF,SW] Calle de Aeropuerto (at lot 5) 52-755/**557-0443** *B&B inn, full brkst*

■ NIGHTCLUBS

Tequila Town [GF,K,V] Cuauhtehoc 3 (off Malecon) *more gay after 11pm*

■ RESTAURANTS

Paul's [P] Benito Juarez #23 52-755/**554-6528** *also El Mascarero Piano Bar from 9pm*

Central America

COSTA RICA

Alajuela

see also San José

■ BARS

Marguiss [★MW,NH] (250 meters S of Almacénes Llobet, on 2nd flr) 506/**443-5310** *6pm-close, clsd Mon*

Arenal

■ ACCOMMODATIONS

Arenal Lodge [GF] 506/**253-5080** *volcano views*

■ ENTERTAINMENT & RECREATION

The Arenal Volcano *hourly eruptions*

Tabacon Hot Springs La Fortuna (at Tabacon Resort) 506/**256-1500** *10am-10pm*

Guanacaste

■ ACCOMMODATIONS

Villa Decary [GF,GO] Nuevo Arenal, 5717 Tilaran 506/**383-3012** *former coffee farm on 7 acres overlooking Lake Arenal*

Manuel Antonio, Quepos

■ ACCOMMODATIONS

➤ **Big Ruby's La Plantacion** [M,SW,F,GO] Pacific Coast 506/**777-1332** or 506/ **777-1115**, 800/**477-7829** (US#) *full brkfst*

Casa Bumerango [GS,WC,GO] 213/**330-0231**

Casa Lydia Luxury Oceanview Villa [GS,SW,NS] 407/**897-3638** *luxury 3-story villa*

Casa Romano [GS,SW,WC,GO] 510/**665-6162** *near gay beach*

Condominium Villas Mymosa Apdo 271-6350 506/**777-1254**

Géminis del Pacifico [GF,SW,NS,GO] 773/**472-7127** *luxurious vacation home, near beaches & bars*

Costa Rica • CENTRAL AMERICA

➤ **Hotel Casa Blanca** [MW,SW,GO] 506/777-0253, 506/777-1790 *helpful local info at* www.hotelcasablanca.com/Hotel/

Hotel Del Mar [GS] 200 Meters Playa Espadilla, apdo 6350-31 506/777-0543 *near beach & Manuel Antonio Nat'l Park*

Hotel Parador [GF,SW] 506/777-1414 *large luxury resort w/ mini golf course, health club, private helicopter pad (!), also restaurant*

Hotel Villa Roca [M,SW,GO] 506/777-1349, 506/777-2335 *great ocean views*

Makanda by the Sea [GF,SW] 506/777-0442 *private oasis*

The New Kekoldi Beach Hotel (El Dorado Mojado) [GF,SW] 506/248-0804 *rooms & villas in forest*

El Parque [GF,F,SW] 506/777-0096 *hillside condos w/ ocean views, waterfall pool, restaurant*

Si Como No [★GF,SW] 506/777-0777

Villa Titi [GS,SW,GO] Manuel Antonio Rd 206/938-8603 *located above Manuel Antonio's gay beach*

Villas las Estrellas [GS] 506/777-1286 *2-bdrm villas*

Villas Nicolas [GF] 506/777-0481

■ BARS

Cockatoo Bar [MW,D] across from Escuela d'Amore Spanish-language school (near Manuel Antonio Park) *4pm-close*

Hotel Vela Bar [GF,F] 1st Beach (at Vela Bar Hotel) 506/777-0413 *7am-10:30pm, also restaurant*

Los Jocotes [M,B] 506/296-8258, 506/356-9360 *6pm-close Th-Sat*

Mar y Sombra [GF,D,F] on Playa Espadilla *7pm-close, local flavor, [D] Nov-April, also full restaurant*

■ RESTAURANTS

El Barba Roja [★] 506/777-0331 *great sunset location*

El Gran Escape & Fish Head Bar 506/777-0395 *clsd Tue, full bar*

Hotel Casa Blanca

Gay owned & managed Hotel
at the Central Pacific Coast of Costa Rica
For our gay/lesbian guests, their families and friends.
Panoramic ocean views to the National Park & Beaches
Walking distance to the Gay Beach

For more information contact us:
Hotel Casa Blanca de Manuel Antonio S.A.
Apdo. 194 - Entrada la Mariposa
6350 Quepos - Ml. Ant., Costa Rica, Central America
Phone/Fax: (+506) 777-1316, 777-1790, 777-0253
Internet: cblanca@sol.racsa.co.cr
www.hotelcasablanca.com

San José • Costa Rica

Karola's [GO] top of hill right in front of Cafe Milagro 506/777-1557 *11am-11pm, clsd Wed, lunch & dinner w/ a view, full bar*

Madres at La Plantacion Big Ruby's 506/777-1332 *8am-9pm, bar till 10pm, int'l*

The Plinio at the Hotel Plinio 506/777-0055 *int'l, full bar*

Rico Tico paved road to national park (in Hotel Sí Como No) *6:30am-9:30pm, Tex/Mex, includes use of pool bar*

■ ENTERTAINMENT & RECREATION

La Playita [N] N end of Playa Espadilla (w/ a steep hike over rocks) *the gay beach (impassable 2 hours before & after high tide)*

Playa Jaco

■ ACCOMMODATIONS

Hotel Poseidon [GF,SW] Calle del Bohio (30 meters W of Jaco Centro) 506/643-1642, 888/643-1642 *also bar & restaurant, 50 meters to beach*

Puntarenas

■ CRUISY AREAS

Beach [AYOR] from the port to the jetties (malecones)

Calle el Paseo de los Turistas [AYOR]

San José

■ INFO LINES & SERVICES

Uno @ Diez Calle 3 (at Aveda 7) 506/258-4561 *Mon-Sat 9:30am-9pm, lgbt tourist info center w/ internet access, cafeteria*

■ ACCOMMODATIONS

➤ **Colours Oasis Resort** [★M,SW,F,E,GO] El Triangulo Noroeste, Blvd Rohrmoser (200 meters before end of blvd) 506/232-3504 & 506/296-1880, 877/932-6652 & 305/532-9341 (US#) *full brkfst*

Don Carlos B&B [★GF] 506/221-6707

Hotel Amon Plaza [GF,F] Ave 11 & Calle 3 bis 800/575-1253 *modern hotel, quiet location*

Costa Rica • CENTRAL AMERICA

Hotel Kekoldi [GF] Avda 9 (Calle 3 Bis, Barrio Amón) 506/248-0804

Joluva Guesthouse [MW,GO] Barrio Amón 506/223-7961

Melia Cariari [GF,SW] 506/290-0798 *luxury resort, great golfing*

■BARS

La Casita [M,S] 11th St (at Ave 6 & 8) 506/223-1537 *8pm-close, darkroom*

Coconut Grove [MW,F,S] 100 meters E & 50 meters S of Acueductos & Alcantarillados 506/221-0437 *4pm-2:30am, clsd Sun-Mon, strippers Sat*

■NIGHTCLUBS

La Avispa [MW,D] 834 Calle 1 (pink house btwn Avdas 8 & 10) 506/223-5343 *7pm-2:30am, clsd Mon & Th, popular T-dance Sun*

El Bochinche [MW,D,V] Calle 11 (btwn Avdas 10 & 12, Paseo de los Etudiantes), San Pedro 506/221-0500 *7pm-2am, clsd Sun-Mon, also full restaurant, Mexican, dancing/DJ after 10pm*

Dejá Vú [★MW,D,S] Calle 2 (btwn Avdas 14 & 16) 506/223-3758 *8pm-close Fri-Sun, 2 dance flrs, men-only Wed 9pm-midnight, strippers Fri, take taxi to avoid bad area*

Los Cucha [MW,D,TG,F,DS] Avda 6 (btwn Calles Central & 1, 75 meters E of Farmacia Jara—no sign; look for big, black wooden doors & enter) 506/233-4310 *7pm-2am, clsd Mon-Tue*

Puchos [MW,F,DS,S] Calle 11 (btwn Avdas 8 & 10, knock to enter) 506/256-1147 *6pm-2:30am, clsd Sun, also restaurant*

■CAFES

Café Ruisenor in Teatro Nacional 506/223-4488 *lunch*

■RESTAURANTS

Anochecer 2 km from Centro Aserri on Carretera A Tarbaca (near Colours) 506/230-5232

El Bochinche [MW,D,V] Calle 11 (btwn Avdas 10 & 12, Paseo de los Etudiantes), San Pedro 506/221-0500 *7pm-2am, clsd Sun-Mon, Mexican, dancing/DJ after 10pm, also 3 bars*

Café Mundo [GO] Avda 9 & Calle 15 (200 meters E of parking lot for INS, Barrio Amón) 506/222-6190 *Italian, garden seating, also cafe/ bar*

La Cocina de Leña [★] in El Pueblo complex 506/255-1360 *5 minutes from downtown, Costa Rican*

Olio [GF] Escalante 506/281-0541 *also full bar*

Vishnu Vegetarian Restaurant [★] Avda 1 (btwn Calles 3 & 1) 506/221-7605

■PUBLICATIONS

Gente 10 Apdo Postal 1910-2100, Sector Guadalupe 506/280-8886 *bi-monthly lgbt magazine, also map w/ listings*

■MEN'S CLUBS

Paris Sauna corner of 7th St & 7th Ave (1 blk from Morazan Park) 506/257-5272

Sauna Hispalis [★V] 1762 Avda 2 (E of the Plaza de la Democracia, btwn Calles 17 & 19) 506/256-9540 *noon-2am, till 4am Fri-Sat*

■EROTICA

Tabú 50 meters N of Farmacia Fischel (in XXX World) 506/221-7165

■CRUISY AREAS

Parque La Sabana [AYOR] next to Municipal Stadium (btwn airport & San José) *evenings & wknds*

Parque Nacional [AYOR] N of Avda 1 (btwn Calles 15 & 19)

Plaza de la Cultura [★AYOR] in front of the Nat'l Theater (btwn Calles 3 & 5) *late afternoons & early evenings*

Uvita • Costa Rica

Tamarindo

ACCOMMODATIONS

Cala Luna Hotel & Villas [GF,SW] Playa Langosta (at Playa Tamarindo) 506/653-0214 *hotel*

Hotel Sueño del Mar [GF,SW] Playa Langosta 506/653-0284 *private hacienda on the beach, full brkfst*

Laz Divaz Casitas [GO] Apdo 05-5235, Playa Sámara, Guanacaste 506/656-0295 *B&B, full brkfst*

Uvita

ACCOMMODATIONS

Tucan Hotel [GF] Frente Ebais De Uvita (across from church) 506/743-8140

Austria • EUROPE

Europe

AUSTRIA

Vienna

■ INFO LINES & SERVICES

Gay & Lesbian AA 43-1/799.55.99

Hosi Zentrum Novarragasse 40
43-1/216.66.04 *many groups & events, also publishes quarterly news magazine*

Rosa-Lila-Villa Linke Wienzeile 102 (near Hofmühlgasse, U4-Pilgramgasse)
43-1/586.81.50 (women),
43-1/585.43.43 (men) *lgbt center, staffed 5pm-8pm Mon-Fri, info, gay city maps, also mtg place for various groups, also cafe-bar*

■ ACCOMMODATIONS

Hotel Urania [GF,F,WC] Obere Weißgerberstr 7 (U-Schwedenplatz)
43-1/713.17.11 *centrally located & inexpensive, rooms also rented by hour, bar & restaurant (pizza) on premises*

Pension Wild [M,F,GO] Lange Gasse 10 (off Lerchenfelder Str)
43-1/406.51.74 *small, friendly pension in the heart of Vienna, clean rooms at a reasonable price, also sauna*

Das Tyrol [GF] Mariahilfer Str 15
43-1/587.54.15 *small luxury hotel*

■ BARS

Alte Lampe [★M,P,OC] Heumühlgasse 13 (at Rechte Weinzeile, U4-Kettenbrückengasse) 43-1/587.34.54 *6pm-1am, 8pm-3am Fri-Sat, clsd Mon-Tue, piano bar wknds, Vienna's oldest gay bar*

Bip [GS,F] Opernring 6
43-1/512.84.60 *9am-3am, from 2pm Sun*

Boy Zone [M,YC] Schikanedergasse 12
43-1/585.75.67 *9pm-6am, darkroom, hustlers*

Brot & Rosen [MW,F] Ratschkygasse 48/ 2-4
43-1/966.28.24 *6pm-midnight, cafe-bar*

Café Berg [★MW,F,YC] Berggasse 8 (at Wasagasse, U2-Schottentor)
43-1/319.57.20 *10am-1am, cafe-bar*

Café Reiner [M,NH,F] Kettenbrückengasse 4 (at Grüngasse, U4-Kettenbrückengasse)
43-1/586.23.62 *9pm-4am, hustlers, darkroom*

Café Savoy [★MW,F] Linke Wienzeile 36 (at Köstlergasse) 43-1/586.73.48 *5pm-2am, from 9am Sat, clsd Sun, upscale cafe-bar*

Café Stein [GF,F] Währinger Str 6-8 (near U-Schottentor) 43-1/319.72.41 *7am-1am, from 9am Sun, internet access, terrace*

Café X Bar [M] Mariahilfer Str 45 (enter on Stiegengasse, U3-Neubaugasse) 43-1/585.24.37 *4pm-2am*

Chamaleon [M,YC] Stiegengasse 8 (near Naschmarkt) 43-1/585.11.80 *5pm-2am, till 4am Fri-Sat, American bar, theme nights*

Eagle Bar [★M,L,V] Blümelgasse 1 (at Gumpendorfer Str, U3-Neubaugasse)
43-1/587.26.61 *9pm-4am, darkroom, also sex shop*

Goldener Spiegel [★M,F,YC] Linke Wienzeile 46 (enter on Stiegengasse, U4-Kettenbrückengasse)
43-1/586.66.08 *7pm-2am, hustlers*

Hyde Park [M] Sonnenfelsgasse 17 (near Stephansplatz) 43-1/512.95.17 *8pm-4am*

Lo:sch [MO,L] Fünfhuasgasse 1 (at Sechshauserstr) 43-1/895.99.79 *Fri-Sat, also Sun in winter, call for events, leather/ uniform/ fetish club, strict dress code*

Mango Bar [★M,YC,GO] Laimgrubengasse 3 (U4-Kettenbrückengasse) 43-1/587.44.48 *9pm-4am*

Nanu Bar [M,NH,F] Schleifmühlgasse 11
43-1/587.29.87 *4pm-2am, cybercafe*

Nightshift [★MO,L,V] Corneliusgasse 8 (at Kopernikusgasse, look for unmarked black door at bottom of stairs)
43-1/586.23.37 *11pm-4am, till 5am Fri-Sat, darkroom*

Vienna • Austria

Operncafé Hartauer [GS,F] Riemergasse 9 (at Singer) 43-1/512.89.81 *8am-5pm, till 2am Fri, 7pm-2am Sat, clsd Sun, terrace*

Stiefelknecht [MO,L,V] Wimmergasse 20 (enter on Stolberggasse) 43-1/545.23.01 *10pm-2am, till 4am Fri-Sat, darkroom*

Le Swing [M,TG,V,$] Hannovergasse 5 (at Wallensteinstr) 43-1/332.16.70 *gay Tue only 9pm-2am, sauna*

Das Versteck [GS,YC] Grünangergasse 10, downstairs (at Nikolaigasse, U1-Stephansplatz) 43-1/513.40.53 *6pm-midnight, till 4am Fri-Sat, clsd Sun*

Wiener Freiheit [M,D,F,V] Schönbrunner Str 25 (U4-Kettenbrückengasse) 43-1/931.91.11 *8pm-midnight, clsd Sun-Mon, 3 flrs, disco open 10pm-4am Fri-Sat*

■ NIGHTCLUBS

Heaven Gay Night at U4 [★M,D,TG,S,V,YC,WC] Schönbrunner Str 222 (at Meidlinger, U4-Meidlinger Haupstr) 43-1/815.83.07 *11pm-5am Th only, 3 bars, 2 dance flrs, darkroom*

Why Not? [M,D,S,V] Tiefer Graben 22 (at Wipplinger, U-Schottentor) 43-1/925.30.24 *10pm-close Fri & Sat before public holidays, darkroom*

■ CAFES

Smart Cafe [GS] Kostlergasse 9 43-1/585.71.65 *4pm-2am, Fri-Sat till midnight, clsd Sun, fetish cafe*

■ RESTAURANTS

Café-Restaurant Willendorf [MW] Linke Wienzeile 102 (near Hofmuhlgasse, U4-Pilgramgasse) 43-1/587.17.89 *6pm-2am, from 10am wknds, food served till midnight, plenty veggie, full bar, terrace*

The Living Room [M] Franzensgasse 18 (at Grüngasse, U4-Kettenbrückengasse) 43-1/585.37.07 *6pm-3:30am, bar open till 2am*

Motto [★GS,R] Schönbrunner Str 30 43-1/587.06.72 *6pm-4am, trendy, also bar, terrace*

Orlando [★MW,GO] Mollardgasse 3 (U-Pilgramgasse) 43-1/941.99.88 *6pm-2am (food served till midnight), bar, terrace*

■ ENTERTAINMENT & RECREATION

House of Music Seilerstätte 30 43-1/516.48.10 *10am-10pm, interactive museum*

Kunsthistorisches Museum Maria-Theresien-Platz 43-1/525.24.403 *10am-6pm, till 11pm Th, not to be missed*

■ BOOKSTORES

American Discount Rechte Wienzeile 5 (at Paniglgasse) 43-1/587.57.72 *9:30am-6:30pm, 9am-5pm Sat, clsd Sun, int'l magazines & books; also Neubaugasse 39 , 43-1/523.37.07; also Donaustadt Str 1, 43-1/203.95.18*

Löwenherz Berggasse 8 (next to Cafe Berg, enter on Wasagasse, U2-Schottentor) 43-1/317.29.82 *10am-7pm, till 5pm Sat, clsd Sun, lgbt, large selection of English titles*

■ PUBLICATIONS

Vienna Gay Guide 43-1/789.97.37 *city-map & guide*

■ MEN'S CLUBS

Apollo City Sauna [SW,V] Wimbergergasse 34 43-1/523.08.14 *bar, darkroom, gym equipment*

Kaiserbründl [F,V,SW] Weihburggasse 18-20 (at Grünangergasse, U1-Stephansplatz) 43-1/513.32.93 *2pm-midnight, till 2am Fri, 24hrs Sat, 3 flrs, 2 bars, darkroom maze, gym equipment*

Kino Labyrinth [M,TG,V] Favoritenstr 164 43-1/920.40.88 *[MO] Wed, gay & [TG] Fri, darkrooms, huge cruising area*

Sport Sauna [F,V,YC] Lange Gasse 10 (at Pension Wild, U2-Lerchenfelderstr) 43-1/406.71.56 *bar, gym equipment*

■ EROTICA

Art-X Percostr 3 43-1/258.04.44, 43-2622/88.555 *erotic supermarket, clsd Sun*

Condomi Otto-Bauer-Gasse 24 (near Mariahilfer Str, U3-Zieglergasse) 43-1/581.20.60 *clsd Sun*

Austria • *Europe*

Gay Markt [V] Mariahilfer Str 72 (btwn Neubaugasse & Andreasgasse, U-Neubaugasse) 43-1/**523.75.00** *clsd wknds, cabins, hustlers, also mail order*

Man for Man [V] Hamburgerstr 8 (at Rechte Wienzeile, U-Kettenbrückengasse) 43-1/**585.20.64** *clsd Sun, books, toys, videos, DVDs, private rooms*

Sexworld International [GS,V] Mariahilfer Str 49 43-1/**587.66.56** *clsd Sun, cabins, darkroom, cruisy, special gay section*

Spartacus XXL Store Mariahilfer Str 49 (enter through Sexworld) 43-1/**587.66.56** *clsd Sun, toys, leather, books, videos, DVDs*

Tiberius Leather, Latex & Tools [WC] Lindengasse 2 (at Stiftgasse, U3-Neubaugasse) 43-1/**522.04.74** *clsd Sun*

■ Cruisy Areas

Albertina Passage [AYOR] next to the Opera

Donauinsel [AYOR] Lobau (accessible by U1 metro line) *nude beach*

Rathauspark [AYOR] *evenings only*

Schweizer Garten [AYOR] next to Südbanhof

Venediger Au [AYOR] at Praterstern (next to the Big Wheel)

Czech Republic

Prague (Praha)

Prague is divided into 10 city districts: Praha—1, Praha—2, etc.

Praha—Overview

■ Accommodations
Toucan Apartments [M,GO] 36-309/**32.33.34** *self-catering apts*

■ Publications
Amigo 420/**284.82.83.61** *bi-monthly magazine w/ guide to gay scene in Czech Republic & Slovakia, personals*

Maxx 420/**284.82.83.61** *monthly erotica magazine, classified ads (in Czech)*

Praha—1

■ Accommodations
Old Town Prague [M] Dusni 1 (at Old Town Square) 420/**224.81.49.12** *apts*

Prague Center Guest Residence [MW,GO] Stepanska Street (at Zitna) 36-309/**32.33.34** *apt, near Wencelas Square*

■ Bars
Friends Bar [MW] Naprstkova 1 (at Karoliny Svetle, downstairs) 420/**221.63.54.08** *4pm-3am, DJ Wed-Sat, internet access*

U Rudolfo [M,BW,OC] Mezibránské 3 420/**605.87.24.92** *4pm-2am*

■ Nightclubs
Escape Club [MO,D,F,S,$] V Jame 8 (off Vaclavske namesti) 420/**602.40.37.44** *8pm-5am, disco from 10pm, go-go boys, also restaurant, hustlers*

■ Cafes
Café 'Erra [GS,F] Konviktská 11 420/**222.22.05.68** *10am-midnight, from 11am wknds, salads, sandwiches & entrées*

Downtown Cafe [GO] Juncmannova Namesti 21 420/**724.111.276** *10am-11pm, till midnight Fri-Sat, terrace*

Kafirna U Ceského Pána [★M] Kozí 13, Stare Mesto 420/**222.32.82.83** *noon-11pm, from 3pm wknds, small bar popular w/ locals*

■ Restaurants
Petrinské Terasy [GO] Seminariská Zahrada 13, Petrin 420/**290.00.04.57**, 420/**290.05.99.96** *11am-1pm, in a former monastery, great view*

La Provence [GO] Stupartska 9 (near Old Town Square) 420/**257.53.50.50** *11am-midnight, bar open till 1am, French, also Banana Cafe & Tapas Bar upstairs*

■ Men's Clubs
Sauna Babylonia [★V] Martinská 6 420/**224.23.23.04** *popular w/ tourists, gym equipment, bar*

Praha–3 • Czech Republic

■ EROTICA
Amigo Shop Princná 7
420/222.23.32.50 *clsd Sun-Mon, videos, DVDs, magazines*

Lambda City Man Rimská 16
420/737.45.71.45, 420/224.21.68.09
clsd Sun, sex shop, videos

■ CRUISY AREAS
Hlavni Nadrazi [AYOR] Main Railway Station *gallery above ticket counters*

Petrin Hill, Petrin Park [AYOR] *paved walkways & bathroom*

Praha–2

■ ACCOMMODATIONS
Prague Gay, Lesbian & Transvestite Apartments [M,GO] 44–7802/225917 **(UK#)** *20 centrally located apartments*

■ BARS
Bar 21 [MW] Rimska 21
420/724.25.40.48 *6pm-4am, cellar bar, mostly Czechs*

Fajn Bar [M,F,DS,S] Dittrichova 5 (near river) 420/224.91.74.09, 420/603.52.21.17 *1pm-1am, from 4pm wknds, cafe-bar, occasional drag or strip shows*

Stella Club [MW,F] Luzická 10 (in Vinohrady) 420/224.25.78.69
8pm-5am, cozy bar/ cafe, terrace

■ NIGHTCLUBS
Gejzee..r [★MW,D,S,V,$] Vinohradska 40 (in Vinohrady) 420/222.51.60.36
8pm-late, from 9pm Fri-Sat, clsd Sun-Wed, darkroom

■ RESTAURANTS
Celebrity Cafe [GS] Vinohradska 40 (in Vinohrady) 420/222.51.13.43 *8am-2am, noon-3am Sat, till midnight Sun, also bar, right next door to Gejzee..r nightclub*

Radost FX [GS] Belehradska 120, Vinohrady 420/224.25.47.76, 420/603.18.15.00 *straight nightclub, but fabulous wknd brunch!*

Reviera [MW] Balbínova 26
420/222.25.44.18, 420/606.81.77.53
5pm-4am, also music club

■ MEN'S CLUBS
Cannes Club Salmovská 6
420/224.92.01.27 *6pm-4am*

Marco [★V] Lublanská 17, Vinorady
420/224.26.28.33 *2pm-3am, also bar, booths, small but popular*

■ EROTICA
Heaven [★] Gorazdova 11
420/224.92.12.82 *cinema, toys, books, videos, many US titles, darkroom*

Praha–3

■ ACCOMMODATIONS
Studio Henri [M,GO] Jeseniova 52
420/271.77.38.37 *apt, jacuzzi, great view of Old Town Prague*

■ BARS
Piano Bar [★M,F] Milesovská 10
420/222.72.74.96 *5pm-close, mostly Czech*

Pinocchio [★M,D,DS,S,V,AYOR] Seifertova 3   420/602.96.93.74 *3pm-6am, hustlers, also sex shop, rent boys*

■ CAFES
Duhova Cajovna [MW] Chlumova 13
420/222.78.30.25 *4pm-10pm, clsd Mon, teahouse*

Galerie Cafe [GS] Jagellonska 20, Vinohrady 420/222.73.00.56, 420/605.10.82.96 *8:30am-10pm, from 5pm Sun, clsd Sat, works by gay artists*

■ GYMS & HEALTH CLUBS
Bravo Fitness [MW,GO] Srobarova 9, Zizkov (at Piseckà) 420/271.73.14.12
9am-10pm, 2pm-9pm wknds

■ MEN'S CLUBS
Alcatraz [MO,L,V,S] Borivojova 58 (off Seifertova, in Zizhkov)
420/222.71.14.58 *9:30pm-4am, S/M club, theme nights*

■ EROTICA
City Fox Pribenicka 12, Zizkov
420/222.54.03.58 *clsd Sun-Mon, small video store, Czech & US titles, cabins*

Czech Republic • EUROPE

Praha—4

MEN'S CLUBS
Plavecky Stadion Podoli [GS,F]
Podolská 74 420/261.21.43.43
public baths, men's sauna 9am-6:30pm

Praha—5

BARS
Angel Club [M,D,K,V,AYOR] Kmochova 8
(at Holeckova, in Smichov)
420/257.31.61.27 *7pm-2am, open later Fri-Sat, karaoke Th, gypsies*

SEX CLUBS
Drake's [MO,F,S,V,$] Zborovska 50
(at Petrinska) 420/257.32.68.28
24hrs, darkroom, maze, sex shop, free Sun buffet from 8pm

Praha—6

CRUISY AREAS
Sarka Lake [AYOR] by Metro to Dejvicka & tram 26 to endstation *nude bathing*

Praha—7

NIGHTCLUBS
Calimero Night [MW,D,V] Bubenska 21
420/737.73.83.40 *7pm-4am*

CRUISY AREAS
Park Letna [AYOR] Park Letna *near Metronom & next to Belvedere Palace*

Praha—8

ACCOMMODATIONS
Hotel Villa Mansland Prague [M,GO]
Stepnicná 9, Liben 420/286.88.44.05
sauna, also restaurant

NIGHTCLUBS
Mansland [MO,D,F,S] Stepnicná 11, Liben 420/02.50.48.93 *6pm-3am, clsd Sun-Wed, strippers, hustlers*

MEN'S CLUBS
Sauna David [V] Sokolovská 44, Kárlin
420/222.31.78.69 *noon-midnight, oldest sauna in Prague, gym*

Praha—10

ACCOMMODATIONS
Arco Guest House [M,GO] Voronézská 24 (in Vinohrady) 36.309/32.33.34
(English & German) *internet access, dance club*

Ron's Rainbow Guest House [GS,GO]
Bulharska 4 (at Finská)
420/271.72.56.64 *jacuzzi*

Praha—11

CRUISY AREAS
Seberak Lake [AYOR] *from endstation in Seberak, go to opposite side of lake to nude beach*

ENGLAND

LONDON

London is divided into 6 regions:
London—Overview
London—Central
London—West
London—North
London—East
London—South

London—Overview

INFO LINES & SERVICES
Black Lesbian/ Gay Centre 5/5A
Westminster Bridge Rd, Rm 113
44-020/7620-3885 *helpline staffed 2pm-5:30pm Sat*

London Lesbian/ Gay Switchboard
44-020/7837-7324 *24hrs*

ACCOMMODATIONS
London First Choice Apartments [GF]
44-020/8990-9033 *short-term apt rentals, also hotel reservations*

PUBLICATIONS
Boyz 44-020/7845-4300 *fab gay boy newspaper w/ extensive club & event listings*

Gay Times 44-020/7424-7400, 44-020/8340-8644 *gloricus gay glossy*

The Pink Paper 44-020/7845-4300
free lgbt newspaper

London—Central • England

QX International
44-020/7379-7887

Time Out 44-020/7813-3000
weekly city scene guide w/ gay section

London—Central

London—Central includes Soho, Covent Garden, Bloomsbury, Mayfair, Westminster, Pimlico & Belgravia

■ ACCOMMODATIONS

Central London Guestrooms & Apts [MW,NS,GO] Tottenham Court Rd (at Charing Cross Rd)
44-020/7497-7000 *also apt*

Clone Zone Luxury Apts [MW] 64 Old Compton St (at Whitcomb)
44-020/7287-3530 *fully equipped apts above Clone Zone retail store*

London Gay Accommodation [MW,GO] 44-020/7486-0855 *room in private apt, shared bath, hot tub*

Manors & Co [GF,WC] 1 Baker St
44-020/7486-5982, 800/454-4385
luxury apts

Rainbowstay Guest House [MW,GO] 14 Thornhill Bridge Wharf (Islington)
44-020/7713-5287

Waverley House Hotel [GF,F] 130-134 Southampton Row (Bloomsbury) 44-020/7833-3691, 44-020/7833-2579

■ BARS

Note: 'Pub hours' usually means 11am-11pm Mon-Sat and noon-3pm & 7pm-10:30pm Sun

79 CXR [★M,D,WC] 79 Charing Cross Rd (Soho) 44-020/7734-0769
1pm-2am, till 10:30pm Sun, 2 flrs, cruisy

The Admiral Duncan [★MW,NH,TG] 54 Old Compton St (Soho)
44-020/7437-5300 *pub hours*

Bar Aquda [★MW] 13-14 Maiden Ln (btwn Bedford & Southampton, Covent Garden) 44-020/7577-9891 *cafe-bar*

Bar Code [MW,F,E,K,V] 3-4 Archer St (btwn Windmill & Rupert, off Shaftesbury, Soho)
44-020/7734-3342 *open till 1am, karaoke Wed, Comedy Camp Tue*

The Box [★MW,D,F,V,WC] 32-34 Monmouth St, Seven Dials (near Shaftesbury Ave, Covent Garden)
44-020/7240-5828 *6pm-3am, 3pm-midnight Sun, cafe-bar*

Compton's of Soho [★M,L,F,WC] 53 Old Compton St 44-020/7479-7961
noon-11pm, 7pm-10:30pm Sun, cruisy

The Edge [MW,D,WC] 11 Soho Square 44-020/7439-1313 *noon-1am, till 10:30pm Sun, open later Th-Sat, 4 flrs, cafe-bar, live music, outdoor seating*

The Escape [★M,D,V] 8-10 Brewer St (near Regent St) 44-020/7734-2626
3pm-3am, clsd Sun

The G.A.Y Bar [MW,F,V] 30 Old Compton St 44-020/7494-2791
3 flrs, soap operas & videos shown

Halfway 2 Heaven [★M,NH,K,OC,GO] 7 Duncannon St (at Charing Cross, West End) 44-020/7321-2791 *pub hours*

King's Arms [M,NH,B,F,K,V] 23 Poland St (Soho) 44-020/7734-5907 *pub hours, bears Wed & Fri*

Ku Bar [MW,YC] 75 Charing Cross Rd (at Shaftesbury, Soho)
44-020/7437-4303 *pub hours, trendy cafe-bar*

Kudos [★MW,F,V,WC,GO] 10 Adelaide St (off the Strand) 44-020/7379-4573
pub hours, trendy cafe-bar, basement video bar open from 4pm

The Quebec [M,NH,OC] 12 Old Quebec St (at Marble Arch)
44-020/7629-6159 *pub hours, live DJs Th-Sun*

The Retro Bar [★MW,NH,D,A,K] 2 George Ct (off the Strand)
44-020/7321-2811 *pub hours*

Rupert Street [MW,F,WC] 50 Rupert St (off Brewer) 44-020/7734-5614 *pub hours, 'fashiony-types'*

Sanctuary [★MW,D,P] 3-5 Greek St (Soho) 44-020/7434-3323 *noon-3am, till midnight Sun, 3 flrs, lounge area*

England • *Europe*

The Stag [M] 15 Bressenden Pl (near Victoria Stn) 44-020/7828-7287 *noon-midnight, till 2am Fri, from 5pm Sat, till 10pm Sun, terrace*

Star at Night [MW,F,E] 22 Great Chapel St 44-020/7434-3749 *Italian restaurant during day, 6pm-midnight, clsd Sun-Mon, women-only Fri-Sat, relaxed cafe/ bar*

The Village Soho [★M,F,YC,WC] 81 Wardour St (at Old Compton) 44-020/7434-2124 *pub hours, cafe menu till 5pm*

West Central [MW,D,TG,DS] 29-30 Lisle St (behind Leicester Square cinemas) 44-020/7479-7981 *pub hours, Underground Club open 10:30pm-3am*

The Yard [★MW,F,E,YC,WC] 57 Rupert St (off Brewer) 44-020/7437-2652 *pub hours, 2 levels*

■ NIGHTCLUBS

G.A.Y. [★M,D,E,YC,$] 157 Charing Cross Rd (at Old St, in London Astoria theatre complex) 44-020/7734-6963 *10:30pm-4am Mon & Th-Sat, this is a HUGE club*

The Ghetto [MW,D,A] 5-6 Falconberg Court (off Charing Cross, behind G.A.Y) 44-020/7272-0093 *10:30pm-3:30am, till 5am Fri-Sat, theme nights*

Heaven [★M,D] The Arches (off Villiers St) 44-020/7930-2020 *the mother of all London gay clubs, call for hours/ events*

Off the Hook [★M,D,$] 143 Charing Cross Rd (at Velvet Underground) 44-020/7973-628585 *10pm-3am Mon, diverse crowd & funky music*

Sound on Sunday [★MW,D,YC] At The Sound, Swiss Centre (Leicester Square) 44-020/7287-1010 *7pm-2am Sun only, T-dance*

■ CAFES

First Out [MW,F] 52 St Giles High St (btwn Charing Cross & Shaftesbury) 44-020/7240-8042 *10am-11pm, noon-10:30pm Sun, cont'l cafe, full bar*

Freedom Cafe-Bar [S,YC] 60-66 Wardour St (off Old Compton St) 44-020/7734-0071 *9am-11pm, till 10:30pm Sun, trendy scene cafe, also downstairs bar open till 3am Mon-Sat*

Old Compton Cafe [★MW] 34 Old Compton St 44-020/7439-3309 *24hrs, terrace*

■ RESTAURANTS

Balans [★TG,S,WC] 60 Old Compton St 44-020/7439-2183 *8am-5am, till 6am Fri-Sat, till 2am Sun, cafe-bar*

Food for Thought 31 Nea St, downstairs (Covent Garden) 44-020/7836-9072 *noon-8pm, vegetarian*

The Gay Hussar [WC] 2 Greek St (on Soho Square) 44-020/7437-0973 *lunch & dinner, clsd Sun, Hungarian*

Mildred's [★] 45 Lexington 44-020/7494-1634 *noon-11pm, clsd Sun*

Nusa Dua 11-12 Dean St (Oxford Circus) 44-020/7437-3559 *pan-Asian*

Steph's 39 Dean St 44-020/7734-5976 *lunch Mon-Fri & dinner Mon-Sat, clsd Sun, English*

Wagamama Noodle Bar [NS] 10a Lexington St 44-020/7292-0990, 44-020/7631-3140 *noon-11pm, till midnight Fri-Sat, 12:30pm-10pm Sun, Japanese; also locations in Bloomsbury, Covent Garden*

■ ENTERTAINMENT & RECREATION

Prince Charles Cinema [GF] 7 Leicester Pl (off Leicester Square) 44-020/7494-3654 *sing-alongs, often show lgbt & alternative films*

■ BOOKSTORES

Gay's the Word 66 Marchmont St (near Russell Square) 44-020/7278-7654 *10am-6:30pm, 2pm-6pm Sun, lgbt*

■ RETAIL SHOPS

American Retro 35 Old Compton St 44-020/7734-3477 *10am-7:30pm, clsd Sun, clothing & gifts*

London—West • England

Metal Morphosis 10-11 Moor St (at Old Compton St) 44-020/7434-4554 *tattooing, piercing studio, body jewelry, toys*

Prowler Soho [★] 3-7 Brewer St (behind Village Soho bar) 44-020/7734-4031 *large gay dept store*

■ GYMS & HEALTH CLUBS

London Central YMCA [GF,SW] 112 Great Russell St 44-020/7343-1700

Soho Athletic Club [★M] 10-14 Macklin St (at Drury Ln, Covent Garden) 44-020/7242-1290

■ MEN'S CLUBS

Pleasuredrome [NS] 125 Alaska St (Waterloo) 44-020/7633-9194 *24hrs, also gym, $7 day pass*

The Sauna Bar 29 Endell St 44-020/7836-2236 *sauna, steam, solarium, jacuzzi, holistic services, also bar*

■ EROTICA

RoB London [WC] 24-25 Wells St (near Berwick St) 44-020/7735-7893 *leather/fetish shop*

Soho Cinemas [V] 7-12 Walkers Court (off Brewer St, Soho) 44-020/7439-0835

London—West

London—West includes Earl's Court, Kensington, Chelsea & Bayswater

■ ACCOMMODATIONS

Lincoln House Hotel [GS,WC] 33 Gloucester Pl, Marble Arch (at Baker St) 44-20/7486-7630 *B&B, full brkfst*

The Philbeach Hotel [M] 30-31 Philbeach Gardens (Earl's Court) 44-20/7373-1244, 44-020/7244-6884 *Thai restaurant & bar on premises*

■ BARS

Bromptons [★M,D,F,S] 294 Old Brompton Rd (at Warwick Rd) 44-020/7370-1344 *8pm-2am, till midnight Sun*

Champion [M,NH,S] 1 Wellington Ter (at Bayswater Rd) 44-020/7229-5056, 44-020/7243-9531 *pub hours, cruisy*

The Coleherne [★M,NH,L,WC] 261 Old Brompton Rd (at Coleherne Rd) 44-020/7244-5951 *pub hours, cruisy*

The George Music Bar [M,TG,C] 114 Twickenham Rd 44-020/8560-1456 *5pm-11pm, from noon Sat, noon-10:30pm Sun, George Cabaret every Fri-Sat & every other Sun*

Queen's Head [M,NH,OC] 27 Tryon St (btwn King's Rd & Sloane Ave, Chelsea) 44-020/7589-0262 *pub hours, professional crowd*

Richmond Arms [MW,D,K,C,DS] 20 The Square (at Princess) 44-020/8940-2118 *pub hours, professional crowd*

West Five (W5) [MW,F,C,P] 5 Popes Ln (Ealing) 44-020/8579-3266 *pub hours, till 1am Fri-Sat, lunch served Sun, lounge & cabaret, garden*

■ RESTAURANTS

Balans West [MW] 239 Old Brompton Rd 44-020/7244-8838 *8am-1am, till 2am Th-Sat, English*

Phoenicia 11-13 Abingdon Rd 44-020/7937-0120 *Lebanese/Mediterranean*

Thai Princess [MW,WC] 30-31 Philbeach Gardens (at the Philbeach Hotel) 44-020/7835-1858, 44-020/7373-1244

■ ENTERTAINMENT & RECREATION

Walking Tour of Gay SOHO 56 Old Compton St 44-020/7437-6063 *2pm Sun, £5*

■ RETAIL SHOPS

Adonis Art Gallery 1b Coleherne Rd 44-020/7460 3888 *gay art*

Clone Zone 266 Old Brompton Rd (Earl's Court) 44-020/7373-0598 *10am-8pm, noon-6pm Sun, magazines, videos, toys, solarium, tattooing; also Soho location (64 Old Compton St, 44-020/7287-3530)*

■ GYMS & HEALTH CLUBS

Soho Athletic Club [GF] 254 Earls Ct Rd 44-020/7370-1402 *also at 193 Camden High St, 44-020/7482-4524*

England • EUROPE

London—North

London—North includes Paddington, Regents Park, Camden, St Pancras & Islington

■ACCOMMODATIONS

The Town House [M,GO] Caledonian Rd (Islington) 44-020/7609-9082

■BARS

Bar Fusion/ Diffusion [MW,NH,D,F] 45 Essex Rd (at Queen's Head St, Islington) 44-020/7688-2882 *1pm-midnight, trendy cafe-bar*

The Black Cap [★MW,D,TG,F,C,DS] 171 Camden High St (Camden Town) 44-020/7428-2721 *noon-2am, till 3am Fri-Sat, till midnight Sun, London's leading cabaret*

Blush [MW,NH,F,K] 8 Cazenove Rd (Stoke Newington) 44-020/7923-9202 *5pm-midnight, brunch from noon wknds, clsd Mon, friendly cafe-bar, karaoke Fri*

Duke of Wellington [MW,NH] 119 Balls Pond Rd (Islington) 44-020/7254-4338 *noon-midnight, till 11:30pm Sun*

The Flag [MW,NH] 29 Crouch Hill 44-020/7272-4748 *friendly pub*

King Edward VI/ Sunroom [★M,NH,F,WC] 25 Bromfield St (at Parkfield St, Islington) 44-020/7704-0745 *noon-midnight, Sun lunch from 2pm-5pm, cafe-bar, terrace*

The Oak Bar [MW,D,F,K,S,V] 79 Green Lanes 44-020/7354-2791 *5pm-midnight, till 2am Fri-Sat, from 1pm Sun*

The Ram Club Bar [GS,WC] 39 Queen's Head St 44-020/7354-0576 *pub hours, terrace*

Y-Bar [★MW,D] 142 Essex Rd (Islington) 44-020/7359-2661 *4pm-midnight, till 1am Fri-Sat*

■NIGHTCLUBS

Central Station [★MW,D,TG,F,C,DS,S,V] 37 Wharfedale Rd (King's Cross) 44-020/7278-3294, 44-020/7833-8925 *5pm-2am, till 3am Th, till 4am Fri-Sat, 1am-midnight Sun, complex includes Sports Bar, Cabaret & The Underground [M], theme nights including Strictly Handbag Fri*

Club Kali [★MW,D,TG,$] 1 Dartmouth Park Hill (at The Dome) 44-020/7272-8153 (Dome #) *10pm-3am 1st & 3rd Fri, South Asian music*

The Egg [GS,D] 13 Vale Royal (off York Way) 44-020/7428-7574 *3 flrs, more gay Sat for Spin & Sun for Picochet*

Fiction at The Cross [★MW,D,$] Bagleys Yard (Kings Cross) 44-020/7837-0828 *11pm-late Fri, see-and-be-seen*

Popstarz [★MW,D,$] 275 Pentonville Rd (at Scala, Kings Cross) 44-020/7956-549246 *10pm-5am Fri, 4 rooms*

■MEN'S CLUBS

Pacific 33 [V] 33 Hornsey Rd (Holloway) 44-020/7609-8011 *24hrs wknds, bar*

■EROTICA

Prowler Camden 283 Camden High St (Camden Town) 44-020/7284-0537, 44-020/7267-0021 (mail order) *clsd Sun, fetishwear, books, videos, sex toys & more, also mail order*

Regulation 17a St Albans Pl (Islington Green) 44-020/7226-0655 *fetish gear & toys 'made to measure'*

■CRUISY AREAS

Hampstead Heath [AYOR]

London—East

London—East includes City, Tower, Clerkenwell & Shoreditch

■ACCOMMODATIONS

The Penthouse: Private B&B [MO] 44-020/7251-3535 *centrally located, single, dbl & triple rooms available*

London—South • England

■ BARS

Backstreet [MO,PC] Wentworth Mews, Burdett Rd (at Mile End Rd, Bow) 44-020/8980-8557, 44-020/8980-7880 *10pm-3am, till 1am Sun, clsd Mon-Wed, strict leather/ rubber dress code*

The Black Horse [M,NH,D,TG,K,C,DS,S,V,WC] 168 Mile End Rd (across from the Globe Centre, Stepney Green) 44-020/7790-1684 *8pm-1am, till 3am Fri-Sat, 4pm-midnight Sun*

Royal Oak [★MW,NH,TG,F] 73 Columbia Rd (Bethnal Green, in the flower market) 44-020/7739-8204 *11am-late, from 8am Sun*

The Ship [MW,NH,C,DS,WC] 17 Barnes St (in Stepney) 44-020/7790-4082 *6pm-11pm, from 7:30pm Sat, 1:30pm-10:30pm Sun*

The Spiral [★MW,NH,D,K,DS,S,V] 138 Shoreditch High St (across from Shoreditch Church) 44-020/7613-1351 *10pm-2am, till 4am Fri-Sat, till 3:30am Sun, clsd Mon*

The White Swan [M,D,TG,F,C,DS,S,V,WC] 556 Commercial Rd (near Bromley St) 44-020/7780-9870 *9pm-2am, till 1am Mon-Tue, till 3am Fri-Sat*

■ NIGHTCLUBS

Benjy's 2000 [★MW,D,YC] 562a Mile End Rd 44-020/8980-6427 *9pm-1am Sun only*

DTPM [★MW,D,YC,$] 77a Charterhouse St, Smithfield Mkt (at Fabric) 44-020/7439-9009 (info line) *8pm-late Sun, huge, stylish techno club*

Way Out Club [MW,D,TG,S,PC,$] 9 Crosswall (at Charlie's) 44-020/8363-0948 *9pm-4am Sat only, TV/TS & their friends*

■ RESTAURANTS

Café Spice Namaste 16 Prescott St 44-020/7488-9242 *Indian*

Cantaloupe [★] 35-42 Charlotte Rd 44-020/7729-5566 *noon-midnight, till 10:30pm Sun, also bar*

SoSho [★] 2 Tabernacle St 44-020/7920-0701 *11am-midnight Wed, till 2am Th-Fri, 7pm-2am Sat, clsd Sun-Tue, also bar*

■ MEN'S CLUBS

Chariots I [★SW,F] Chariots House, Fairchild St 44-020/7247-5333 *sauna, steam, jacuzzi, gym equipment, also Chariots Café-Bar*

Chariots III [F,V] 57 Cowcross St (across from Farringdon tube) 44-020/251-5333

The Health Club 6 Leytonstone Rd 44-020/8555-5455 *jacuzzi, steam-room, garden, also bar*

Sailors Sauna 572-574 Commercial Rd (near Limehouse tube) 44-020/7791-2808 *24hrs wknds, sauna, tanning & jacuzzi, sundeck*

■ EROTICA

Centaurus 100 Old St (Clerkenwell) 44-020/7251-3535 *clsd Sun, videos, books, photos, gallery, video cabins*

Expectations 75 Great Eastern St (Shoreditch) 44-020/7739-0292 *London's premier leather/ rubber store & mail order company*

London—South

London—South includes Southwark, Lambeth, Kennington, Vauxhall, Battersea, Lewisham & Greenwich

■ BARS

Bar 68 [MW,NH,D,K] 68 Brigstock Rd (Thornton Heath) 44-020/8665-0683 *karaoke Sun*

Battersea Barge [GF,F,E,C,GO] Nine Elms Ln 44-020/7498-0004 *11:30am-late, clsd Mon, cabaret, comedy on the Thames River!*

Buzz Bar [MW,F,K,C] 136 Battersea High St 44-020/7207-3895 *bar & restaurant, karaoke Fri-Sat, food served noon-8pm*

Dukes [M,NH,B,L,S] 349 Kennington Ln (Vauxhall) 44-020/7793-0903 *8am-1am, 9am-2am Wed-Sat, 2pm-10:30pm Sun*

England • EUROPE

The Fort [M,L] 131 Grange Rd (off Tower Bridge Rd, Bermondsey) 44-020/7237-7742 *pub hours, darkroom, theme nights, strict dress code, cruisy*

Fridge Bar [★GS,D] 22 Town Hall Parade (Brixton Hill) 44-020/7326-5100 *10am-11pm, till 2am Th, till 4am Fri-Sat, clsd Sun; also The Fridge Club next door, which hosts Love Muscle Sat [M,D]*

The Gloucester [M,NH,F,E,WC] 1 King William Walk (btwn Greenwich Pk & Footway Tunnel, Greenwich) 44-020/8858-2666, 44-020/8293-6131 *pub hours*

Kazbar [MW,TG,V] 50 Clapham High St (Clapham) 44-020/7622-0070 *4pm-midnight, from noon Sat, till 11:30pm Sun, cafe-bar*

The Little Apple [MW,D,TG,F,WC] 98 Kennington Ln 44-020/7735-2039 *noon-midnight, till 10:30pm Sun, terrace*

Man Bar [★MO,B,L,F,$] 82 Great Suffolk St 44-020/7928-3223 *8pm-1am, from 2pm wknds, clsd Mon, weekly underwear nights, theme nights, cruisy, food served Sun*

The Two Brewers [MW,D,K,C] 114 Clapham High St (Clapham) 44-020/7498-4971 *6pm-1am, noon-3am Fri-Sat, lunch open-6pm Sun*

■ NIGHTCLUBS

Crash [★MW,D,V,$] Arch 66, Goding St 44-020/7820-1500 *10:30pm-late Fri-Sat*

Duckie [★MW,D,C] 372 Kennington Ln (at Vauxhall Tavern) 44-020/7737-4043 *9pm-2am every Sat, retro indie*

Ego [MW,D] 82 Norwood High St 44-020/8761-5200 *open late, women-only Fri*

The Hoist [M,L] Railway Arch 47c, S Lambeth Rd (Vauxhall) 44-020/7735-9972 *10pm-4am Fri-Sat & 9pm-2am Sun, S/M club w/ strict dress code*

Royal Vauxhall Tavern [M,NH,D,TG,DS,WC] 372 Kenrington Ln (Vauxhall) 44-020/7582-0833 *8pm-1am, till 2am Sat, noon-midnight Sun, popular Sat evenings & Sun afternoons*

The Substation South [★M,D,L,PC] 9 Brighton Terr (Brixton) 44-020/7737-2095 *10:30pm-late, Blackout Th, Queer Nation [MR] Sat, strict fetish dress code some nights, cruisy*

■ CAFES

Surf.Net Cafe [BW] 13 Deptford Church St 44-020/8488-1200 *11am-9pm, till 7pm Sat, clsd Sun, cybercafe/ wine bar*

■ ENTERTAINMENT & RECREATION

Oval Theatre Cafe Bar 52-54 Kennington Oval 44-020/7582-7680 *6pm-8pm, till 11pm Th-Sun, clsd Wed*

■ RETAIL SHOPS

London Piercing Clinic 13 Portland Rd (S Norwood) 44-020/8656-7180 *11am-7pm, 2pm-6pm Sun, also branches in Croydon & Camden*

■ GYMS & HEALTH CLUBS

Paris Gymnasium [MO] Arch 73, Goding St (behind Vauxhall Tavern, Vauxhall) 44-020/7735-8989 *£7 day pass*

■ MEN'S CLUBS

A-Maze! Bathhouse [V] 57 Camberwell Rd 44-020/7703-1100 *jacuzzi, gym, bar*

Chariots II 292 Streatham High Rd (at Babington Rd, enter rear) 44-020/8696-0929 *24hrs wknds*

The Locker Room [V] 8 Cleaver St (Kennington) 44-020/7582-6288

Star Steam [V] 38 Lavender Hill (Battersea) 44-020/7924-2269 *seasonal terrace*

Paris—Overview • France

FRANCE

PARIS

Note: M°=Métro station

Paris is divided by arrondissements (city districts); 01=1st arrondissement, 02=2nd arrondissement, etc

Paris—Overview

Note: When phoning Paris from the US, dial the country code + the city code + the local phone number

■ INFO LINES & SERVICES

Centre gai et lesbien 3 rue Keller (M°Bastille) 33-1/**43.57.21.47** *drop-in 4pm-8pm, clsd Sun, many groups/ events, also wine bar*

Ecoute Gaie 33-1/**44.93.01.02** *helpline staffed 6pm-10pm Mon-Fri*

Gay AA 7 rue August Vacquerie (at St George's Anglican) 33-1/**46.34.59.65** *7:30pm Tue*

■ ACCOMMODATIONS

A Parisian Home 12 rue Mandar 33-1/**45.08.03.37** *furnished apts in Paris, short-term rentals*

Gay Accommodation Paris [GO] 271, rue du Faubourg Saint Antoine, 33-1/**43.48.13.82** *studios for rent in central Paris*

➤ **Mas du Petit Grava** [GS,SW,GO] Route de Saint Hippolyte, Moules 33-4/**90.98.35.66** *300-year-old country house on 7 acres in Provence, full brkfst, kids ok, open March-Oct*

Paris Marais Studios [MW,GO] Marais District *apt rentals, romantic flats in historic homes*

Paris Séjour Réservation [GF] 312/**587-7707 (US#)**, 800/**582-7274 (fax #)** *short-term apt rentals*

■ PUBLICATIONS

Têtu 33-1/**56.80.20.80** *stylish & intelligent lgbt monthly (en français)*

Mas du Petit Grava
Your Favorite Guest House in Provence, France
www.masdupetitgrava.net Tel.: 33(0)490-983566

France • EUROPE

Paris—01

ACCOMMODATIONS

Hôtel Louvre Richelieu [GS]
51 rue de Richelieu (M°Palais-Royal)
33-1/**42.97.46.20**

Hotel Louvre Saint-Honoré [GS,WC]
141 rue Saint-Honoré (at rue du Louvre)
33-1/**42.96.23.23**

BARS

Le Banana Café [★MW,D,E,P,S,YC,WC]
13-15 rue de la Ferronnerie (near rue St-Denis, M°Châtelet)
33-1/**42.33.35.31** *6pm-dawn, go-go boys Th-Sat, theme nights, terrace*

Café Cargo [MW,D,F,K]
37 rue des Lombards (M°Châtelet)
33-1/**40.28.02.52** *noon-2am, cafe-bar w/ naval decor, karaoke Th & Sun, T-dance Sun*

Le Tropic Café [MW,D,TG,F,YC,WC]
66 rue des Lombards (M°Châtelet)
33-1/**40.13.92.62** *noon-5am, tapas, terrace*

Le Vagabond [M,F,OC] 14 rue Thérèse (at av de l'Opera, M°Pyramides)
33-1/**42.96.27.23** *6pm-close, clsd Mon, oldest gay bar & restaurant in Paris*

NIGHTCLUBS

Le Club 18 [★M,D,YC,PC,$] 18 rue du Beaujolais (at rue Vivienne, M°Palais-Royal) 33-1/**42.97.52.13** *midnight-dawn Th-Sun*

L' Insolite [★M,D] 33 rue des Petits-Champs (at du Beaujolais, enter through back courtyard, M°Pyramides)
33-1/**40.20.98.59** *11pm-5am, till 6am Fri-Sat, clsd Mon-Wed, cover charge Fri-Sat*

Le Club [MW,D,MR,F,S,YC,PC,$]
14 rue St-Denis (at rue des Lombards, M°Châtelet) 33-1/**45.08.96.25**
midnight-close, till 7am Sat, theme nights, Butch [M,L] Fri

Le London [M,D,F,$] 33 rue des Lombards, in basement (look for red door) 33-1/**42.33.41.45** *11pm-5am, till 7am Fri-Sat, clsd Mon, theme nights, Asian night Tue, also restaurant/ bar upstairs (open from 8:30pm), darkroom, hustlers*

RESTAURANTS

L' Amazonial [MW,C,DS,WC] 3 rue Ste-Opportune (at rue Ferronnerie, M°Châtelet) 33-1/**42.33.53.13** *lunch Mon-Fri & dinner nightly, brunch wknds, Brazilian/ int'l, bingo Mon-Tue, cabaret Th, drag shows Sat, heated terrace*

Au Diable des Lombards 64 rue des Lombards (at rue St-Denis, M°Châtelet)
33-1/**42.33.81.84** *11am-2am, French/ Tex-Mex, brunch till 6pm daily, full bar, terrace*

Au Rendez-Vous des Camionneurs [M] 72 quai des Orfèvres (M°Pont Neuf)
33-1/**43.54.88.74** *lunch & dinner, traditional bistro*

Caribbean Coffee [MW] 15 rue du Roule 33-1/**42.33.21.30** *clsd Mon, Creole bistro, also bar*

La Mondetour [★MW] 14 rue Mondetour 33-1/**42.36.01.63** *lunch & dinner, also bar*

La Poule au Pot 9 rue Vauvilliers (M°Les Halles) 33-1/**42.36.32.96**
7pm-5am, clsd Mon & Aug, bistro, French

ENTERTAINMENT & RECREATION

Les Halles *underground sports/ entertainment complex w/ museums, theater, shops, clubs, cafes & more*

GYMS & HEALTH CLUBS

Club Med Gym [GS]
147b rue St-Honoré (M°Louvre)
33-1/**40.20.03.03** *day passes available, many locations throughout city*

MEN'S CLUBS

Le Tilt [V] 41 rue Ste-Anne (near av de l'Opera, M°Pyramides)
33-1/**42.96.07.43** *6pm-7am, bar*

L' Univers Gym & Sauna [★S,V,YC]
20-22 rue des Bons Enfants (M°Palais Royal) 33-1/**42.61.24.83** *gym equipment, bar, theme parties, strippers Sat*

Paris—03 • France

EROTICA

Boxx Man 2 rue de la Cossonnerie (M°Châtelet) 33-1/**42.21.47.02** *videos, toys & fetish gear, also sex club, internet access*

IEM Les Halles 43 rue de l'Arbre Sec (near rue de Rivoli, M°Louvre) 33-1/**42.96.05.74**

Yanko 54 rue de l'Arbre Sec (near rue de Rivoli, M°Louvre) 33-1/**42.60.55.28** *toys & videos*

CRUISY AREAS

Jardin des Tuileries [AYOR] on promenade de l'Orangerie (M°Tuileries)

'Tata Beach' [AYOR] on the waterfront by the Louvre & Tuileries (M°Concorde)

Paris—02

ACCOMMODATIONS

Frendy [MW,GO] 7 rue Paul Lelong (at rue Montmartre) 33-1/**45.08.90.77**

BARS

Alexander's Bar [M,NH,OC,GO] 2 rue de Marivaux (at Blvd des Italiens) 33-1/**42.96.40.79** *8pm-2am*

L' Impact [M,O,N,V] 18 rue Grenéta (M°Châtelet) 33-1/**42.21.94.24** *8pm-3am, 3pm-6am Sat, from 5pm Sun, cruise bar, 100% naked, backroom, theme nights, free brkfst wknds*

NIGHTCLUBS

Le Scorp [M,D,E,DS,YC] 25 bd Poissonnière (M°Grands-Blvds) 33-1/**40.26.01.50** *midnight-7am, shows Sun-Tue, Oh La La on Th w/ old French hits*

RESTAURANTS

Aux Trois Petits Cochons [★MW,R,GO] 31 rue Tiquetonne (at rue St-Denis, M°Etienne-Marcel) 33-1/**42.33.39.69** *8pm-1am, clsd Mon, gourmet French*

Le Dénicheur 4 rue Tiquetonne (M°Etienne-Marcel) 33-1/**42.21.31.01**

L' Homosapiens 29 rue Tiquetonne (M°Etienne-Marcel) 33-1/**40.26.94.85** *lunch Mon-Fri & dinner Mon-Sat, clsd Sun (also clsd all Aug), French*

Le Loup Blanc [★MW] 42 rue Tiquetonne (M°Etienne-Marcel) 33-1/**40.13.08.35** *7:30pm-midnight, till 1am Sat, also brunch 11am-4:30pm Sun, French/ int'l*

Mi Cayito 10 rue Marie-Stuart 33-1/**42.21.98.86** *7pm-midnight, Cuban*

Le Monde à l'envers [M] 35 rue Tiquetonne (M°Etienne-Marcel) 33-1/**40.26.13.91** *lunch & dinner, dinner only Sat, clsd Mon, traditional French*

RETAIL SHOPS

Galerie au Bonheur du Jour 11 rue Chabanais 33-1/**94296 5864** *gay art*

MEN'S CLUBS

Euro Men's Club [V,SW,OC] 8-10 rue St-Marc (M°Bourse) 33-1/**42.33.92.63** *run-down*

Paris—03

ACCOMMODATIONS

Absolu Living [MW,GO] 3 passage de l'ancre 33-1/**44.54.97.00** *fully furnished apts in central Paris, short & long-term stays*

Adorable Apartment in Paris [★GF,NS,GO] 415/**397-6454 (US#)** *2-bdrm flat in heart of Marais (sleeps 4-6)*

BARS

Le Dépot [M,D,S,$] 10 rue aux Ours (btwn bd de Sébastopol & rue St-Martin, M°Rambuteau) 33-1/**44.54.96.96** *2pm-8am, huge cruise bar on 3 flrs, backroom, T-dance 5pm Sun, go-go boys*

Le Duplex [MW,NH,S] 25 rue Michel-le-Comte (at rue Beaubourg, M°Rambuteau) 33-1/**42.72.80.86** *8pm-2am, friendly, cruisy, internet access*

One Way [M,NH,B,L,F,V,OC] 28 rue Charlot (at rue des 4 Fils, M°République) 33-1/**48.87.46.10** *5pm-2am, cruisy, darkroom, tapas*

La Petite Vertu [MW,D,F] 15 rue des Vertus (M°Arts-et-Métiers) 33-1/**48.04.77.09** *5pm-2am, from noon wknds, clsd Mon*

France • EUROPE

Villa Keops [MW,D,F] 58 bd de Sébastopol 33-1/**40.27.99.92** *noon-2am, till 5am Fri-Sat, 4pm-3am Sun (clsd Aug), also restaurant*

■ NIGHTCLUBS

Les Bains [★GF,D,F,$] 7 rue du Bourg-l'Abbé (at bd de Sébastopol, M°Étienne-Marcel) 33-1/**48.87.01.80** *midnight-close, gay Sun-Mon*

■ RESTAURANTS

Les Epicuriens du Marais 19 rue Commines (M°Filles-du-Calvaire) 33-1/**40.27.00.83** *lunch & dinner, traditional French*

La Fontaine Gourmande 11 rue Charlot 33-1/**42.78.42.40** *lunch Tue-Fri & dinner Tue-Sun, French*

■ ENTERTAINMENT & RECREATION

Musée Picasso [WC] 5 rue de Thorigny (in the Hôtel Salé, M°St-Paul) 33-1/**42.71.25.21** *clsd Tue*

■ MEN'S CLUBS

The Glove [L] 34 rue Charlot (M°St-Sebastien-Froissard) 33-1/**48.87.31.36** *open late, clsd Mon-Wed, strict dress code, leather/ rubber/ uniform, theme nights, also bar, brkfst wknds*

■ EROTICA

Rexx 42 rue de Poitou (at rue Charlot, M°St-Sébastien-Froissard) 33-1/**42.77.58.57** *clsd Sun, new, custom & secondhand leather & S/M accessories*

Paris—04

■ ACCOMMODATIONS

Historic Rentals [GF] 100 W Kennedy Blvd #260, Tampa, FL 33602 800/**537-5408 (US#)** *1-bdrm apt, in the heart of the Marais*

Hôtel Beaubourg [GS] 11 rue Simon le Franc (btwn rue Beaubourg & rue du Temple, M°Hôtel-de-Ville) 33-1/**42.74.34.24**

Hôtel Central Marais [M,GO] 33 rue Vieille du Temple, upstairs (at 2 rue Ste Croix de la Bretonnevie M°Hotel-de-Ville) 33-1/**48.87.56.08** *central location, some shared baths, also gay bar*

■ BARS

AccesSoir Café [MW,F,DS,S] 41 rue des Blancs-Manteaux (M°Rambuteau) 33-1/**42.72.12.89** *6pm-2am, theme nights*

L' Amnésia Café [★MW,D,F] 42 rue Vieille du Temple (at rue des Blancs-Manteaux, M°Hôtel-de-Ville] 33-1/**42.72.16.94** *10:30am-2am, brunch daily*

Le Bar du Palmier [MW,F] 16 rue des Lombards (at bd de Sébastopol, M°Châtelet) 33-1/**42.78.53.53** *5pm-5am*

Le Bazooka Café [MW,F] 15 rue des Lombards (near rue St-Martin, M°Châtelet) 33-1/**42.74.45.82** *11am-2am, terrace*

Bears' Den [MO,D,B,V] 6 rue des Lombards (at rue St-Martin, M°Hôtel-de-Ville) 33-1/**42.71.08.20** *4pm-2am, theme nights, T-dance Sun, darkroom, terrace*

Bliss Kfe [MW,D] 30 rue du Roi de Sicile (M°Hôtel-de-Ville) 33-1/**42.78.49.36** *5:30pm-2am, stylish new bar*

Le Carré [MW,F] 18 rue du Temple (M°Hôtel-de-Ville) 33-1/**44.59.38.57** *10am-2am, Sun brunch from 11am, lounge & restaurant, terrace*

Le Central [★M] 33 rue Vieille du Temple (below Hôtel Central Marais) 33-1/**48.87.99.33** *4pm-2am, from 2pm Fri-Sun, int'l crowd, a Marais landmark*

Cox Café Bar [★M] 15 rue des Archives (at rue Ste-Croix-de-la-Bretonnerie, M°Hôtel-de-Ville) 33-1/**42.72.08.00** *1pm-2am, cruisy, terrace*

Le Feeling [MW,NH] 43 rue Ste-Croix-de-la-Bretonnerie (M°Hôtel-de-Ville) 33-1/**48.04.70.03** *3pm-2am*

Paris—04 • France

Full Metal [M,L] 40 rue des Blancs-Manteaux (M°Rambuteau) *5pm-4am, till 6am Fri-Sat, from 3pm Sun, well-stocked 'hard backroom bar', theme parties, dress code*

Le Mic-Man [M,NH,W] 24 rue Geoffroy-l'Angevin (at rue du Renard, M°Rambuteau) 33-1/**42.74.39.80** *noon-2am, open later wknds, friendly bar w/ cruisy cave downstairs*

Le Mixer Bar [★MW,D,YC] 23 rue Ste-Croix-de-la-Bretonnerie (at rue des Archives, M°Hôtel-de-Ville) 33-1/**48.87.55.44** *4pm-2am, 3-flr techno/ house bar, theme nights*

Morri's bar [MW,NH,F] 27 rue Quincampoix 33-1/**42.72.80.50** *11am-2am, from 5pm Mon-Tue*

Okawa [★GS,F,C,P,YC] 40 rue Vieille du Temple (at rue Ste-Croix-de-la-Bretonnerie, M°Hôtel-de-Ville) 33-1/**48.04.30.69** *9am-2am, trendy cafe-bar in 12th/ 13th-century caves, theme nights, cabaret, piano bar Tue-Wed, also restaurant*

L' Open Café [★MW,F] 17 rue des Archives (at rue Ste-Croix-de-la-Bretonnerie, M°Hôtel-de-Ville) 33-1/**42.72.26.18** *11am-2am, Sun brunch, sidewalk cafe-bar; also L'Open Coffee Shop, 23 rue du Temple (33-1/48.87.80.25), salads & sandwiches*

Le Piano Zinc [MW,P,NS] 49 rue des Blancs-Manteaux (at rue du Temple, M°Hôtel-de-Ville) 33-1/**40.27.97.42** *noon-2am, T-dance Sun*

Le Polystar [D,K,S] 94 rue St-Martin (M°Hôtel-de-Ville) 33-1/**44.54.99.30** *8:30pm-2am, strippers*

Le QG [MO,L,V] 12 rue Simon le Franc (at rue du Renard, M°Rambuteau) 33-1/**48.87.74.18** *4pm-8am, theme parties Fri, dress code, sex bar*

Quetzal [★M,NH,S] 10 rue de la Verrerie (at rue des Archives, M°Hôtel-de-Ville) 33-1/**48.87.99.07** *5pm-5am, cruise bar, internet access, Latino night Mon, go-go boys/ shows Tue & Th, darkroom, terrace*

Rainbow Cafe [M,NH,TG,F] 16 rue de la Verrerie (M°Hôtel-de-Ville) 33-1/**40.29.05.55** *5pm-2am, clsd Mon, dancing/DJ downstairs wknds, theme nights*

La Station Q [★MO,S,V,PC] 80 quai de l'Hôtel de Ville (at rue Vieille du Temple, M°Hôtel-de-Ville) 33-1/**42.78.88.49** *2pm-7am, 3 levels, strippers, cruisy*

Le Thermik Bar [M] 7 rue de la Verrerie (at rue des Archives, M°Hôtel-de-Ville) 33-1/**44.78.08.18** *4pm-2am, theme nights, club downstairs [D]*

La Traverse [GF] 62 rue Quincampoix 33-1/**42.71.76.00** *5pm-2am, clsd Mon, also restaurant & nightclub*

■ NIGHTCLUBS

Le Déclic [M,D] 12 rue Quincampoix (M°Rambuteau) 33-1/**40.27.82.67** *midnight-close, clsd Mon-Tue, theme nights*

■ CAFES

Coffee-Shop [MW,V] 3 rue Ste-Croix-de-la-Bretonnerie (at rue Vieille du Temple, M°Hôtel-de-Ville) 33-1/**42.74.24.21** *10am-2am, full bar*

■ RESTAURANTS

Au Tibourg 29 rue du Bourg-Tibourg (M°Hôtel-de-Ville) 33-1/**42.74.45.25** *dinner nightly, lunch wknds from 11am, French, quiet & romantic setting*

Le Chant des Voyelles [GF] 4 rue des Lombards (M°Châtelet) 33-1/**42.77.77.07** *lunch & dinner, traditional French, terrace*

Le Crocman [M] 6 rue Geoffroy l'Angevin (M°Rambuteau) 33-1/**42.77.60.02** *7pm-close, clsd Tue-Wed*

Le Dos de la Baleine 40 rue des Blancs-Manteaux (M°Rambuteau) 33-1/**42.72.38.98** *lunch Tue-Fri, dinner Tue-Sun, clsd Mon (also clsd Aug), gourmet seafood*

Equinox [DS,P] 33-35 rue des Rosiers (M°St-Paul) 33-1/**42.71.92.41** *7pm-midnight, Québecois/ French, full bar, piano bar, shows Th-Fri*

Le Gai Moulin [MW] 4 rue St-Merri (at rue du Temple, M°Hôtel-de-Ville) 33-1/**48.87.47.59** *dinner, French/ int'l*

Damron Men's Travel Guide 2004

France • EUROPE

Le Parisiennes [MW] 10 rue Brise-Mich (M°Rambuteau) 33-1/**42.78.44.11** *full bar, terrace*

Le Petit Picard [MW] 42 rue Ste-Croix-de-la-Bretonnerie (M°Hôtel-de-Ville) 33-1/**42.78.54.03** *lunch Tue-Fri & dinner Tue-Sun, clsd Mon*

Les Piétons [GS] 8 rue des Lombards (M°Châtelet) 33-1/**48.87.82.87** *11am-2am, brunch noon-6pm Sun, Spanish/ tapas, also bar, [D] Wed*

■ ENTERTAINMENT & RECREATION

Gay Beach E end of Ile St-Louis *sunbathing*

■ BOOKSTORES

Les Mots à la Bouche 6 rue Ste-Croix-de-la-Bretonnerie (near rue du Vieille du Temple, M°Hôtel-de-Ville) 33-1/**42.78.88.30** *11am-11pm, 2pm-8pm Sun, lgbt, English titles*

■ RETAIL SHOPS

Boy'z Bazaar 5 rue Ste-Croix-de-la-Bretonnerie (at rue Vieille du Temple, M°Hôtel-de-Ville) 33-1/**42.71.34.00** *noon-midnight, 2pm-9pm Sun, clubwear to drag to leather; also Boy'z Bazaar Videostore, 38 rue Ste-Croix-de-la-Bretonnerie, 33-1/42.71.80.23*

Factory's 3 rue Ste-Croix-de-la-Bretonnerie (M°Hôtel-de-Ville) 33-1/**48.87.29.10** *10am-8pm, till 10pm Fri-Sat, from 2pm Sun, clothing & accessories*

■ MEN'S CLUBS

Athletic World [V] 20 rue du Bourg-Tibourg (M°Hôtel-de-Ville) 33-1/**42.77.19.78** *noon-2am, from 4am wknds, gym equipment*

■ EROTICA

IEM Marais 16 rue Ste-Croix-de-la-Bretonnerie (M°Hôtel-de-Ville) 33-1/**42.74.01.61** *leather, latex, uniforms & fetish gear, also bar, sauna wknds*

Projection Video 21 rue des Lombards 33-1/**40.27.98.09** *videos, DVDs, toys*

■ CRUISY AREAS

Square du Pont de Sully [AYOR] at the end of Ile St-Louis (M°Sully-Morland) *along the side paths at night*

Paris—05

■ ACCOMMODATIONS

Historic Rentals [GF] 100 W Kennedy Blvd #260, Tampa, FL 33602 800/**537-5408 (US#)** *1-bdrm apts, steps to Notre Dame & Luxembourg Gardens*

■ CAFES

Clickside 14 rue Domat (off rue Dante, M°Maubert-Mutualite) 33-1/**56.81.03.00** *noon-10pm, 2pm-8pm wknds, cyber-cafe, printing services, English keyboards available*

■ RESTAURANTS

Restaurant le Petit Prince de Paris [★] 12 rue de Lanneau (M°Maubert-Mutualité) 33-1/**43.54.77.26** *7:30pm-midnight, French*

■ ENTERTAINMENT & RECREATION

Open-Air Sculpture Museum 33-1/**42.71.25.21** *along the Seine btwn the Jardin des Plantes & the Institut du Monde Arabe*

Paris—06

■ BARS

Le Trap [M,S,V,YC,PC] 10 rue Jacob (at rue des Saints-Pères, M°St-Germain-des-Près) 33-1/**43.54.53.53** *10pm-close, cruise bar, large backroom, go-go boys Mon & Wed, strippers Mon, cover Fri-Sat*

■ BOOKSTORES

The Village Voice 6 rue Princesse (M°Mabillon) 33-1/**46.33.36.47** *10am-8pm, from 2pm Sun-Mon, till 7pm Sun, English-language bookshop*

Paris—07

■ CRUISY AREAS

Champs de Mars [AYOR] (M°Pont-de-l'Alma)

Paris—08

■NIGHTCLUBS

Le Queen [★M,D,TG,DS,YC,$] 102 av des Champs-Élysées (btwn rue Washington & rue de Berri, M°Georges-V) 33-1/82.70.73.30 *11:30pm-dawn, very trendy, selective door, theme nights, drag shows, go-go boys*

■MEN'S CLUBS

La Banque Club [V] 23 rue de Penthièvre (off Champs d'Elysées, M°Miromesnil) 33-1/42.56.49.26 *4pm-2am, from 2pm Sun, 3 levels, maze, theme nights, also bar*

■EROTICA

French Art [V] 64 rue de Rome (M°Europe) 33-1/45.22.57.35 *clsd Sun*

IEM Liège 33 rue de Liège (M°Liège) 33-1/45.22.69.01 *clsd Sun*

Vidéovision 62 rue de Rome (M°Europe) 33-1/42.93.66.04 *clsd Sun*

Paris—09

■BARS

Mec Zone [M,L,V] 27 rue Turgot (M°Anvers) 33-1/40.82.94.18 *9pm-6am, from 6pm Sun, cruisy, theme nights, darkroom*

■NIGHTCLUBS

Folies Pigalle [GS,D,MR,$] 11 place Pigalle (M°Pigalle) 33-1/48.78.55.25, 33-1/42.80.12.03 **(BBB info line)** *midnight-dawn Tue-Sat, more gay at popular Black, Blanc, Beur T-dance 6pm-midnight Sun & Escualita [MR-L,TG] from midnight Sun*

■MEN'S CLUBS

IDM [★V] 4 rue du Faubourg-Montmartre (at bd St-Martin, M°Grand-Blvds) 33-1/45.23.10.03 *3 levels, full gym, jacuzzi, bar*

Le Mandala [V,SW] 2 rue Drouot (at rue Montmartre, M°Richelieu-Drouot) 33-1/42.46.60.14 *gym equipment, bar*

■EROTICA

Yanko 10 pl de Clichy 33-1/45.26.71.19 *videos & cinema*

Paris—10

■ACCOMMODATIONS

Hotel Louxor [GF] 4 rue Taylor (at bd St-Martin, M°République) 33-1/42.08.23.91 *near Marais, free internet access*

Hôtel Moderne du Temple [GS,GO] 3 rue d'Aix 33-1/42.08.09.04 *economy-class hotel*

■BARS

Café Moustache [M,NH,B,V] 138 rue du Faubourg St-Martin (at bd de Magenta, M°Gare-de-l'Est) 33-1/46.07.72.70 *4pm-2am, darkroom, patio*

Les Rangers [MO,L,DS,S,V,OC,$] 6 bd St-Denis (M°Strasbourg) 33-1/42.39.83.30 *1pm-midnight, till 2am Fri, from 2pm wknds, cruise bar & sex club*

■RESTAURANTS

Le Châlet Maya [MW] 5 rue des Petits Hôtels (M°Gare de l'Est) 33-1/47.70.52.78 *lunch Mon-Fri, dinner Mon-Sat, clsd Sun, French*

■MEN'S CLUBS

Key West Sauna [★V,SW] 141 rue Lafayette (M°Gare-du-Nord) 33-1/45.26.31.74 *gym equipment, jacuzzi, 3 levels*

■EROTICA

IEM St-Maur 208 rue St-Maur (M°Goncourt) 33-1/40.18.51.51 *clsd Sun, huge sex shop, whole flr of leather/latex items*

■CRUISY AREAS

Canal St-Martin Jean-Jaurès [AYOR] (M°Jaurès) *on the quais btwn the Jean-Jaurès & Louis-Blanc bridges*

Paris—11

■ACCOMMODATIONS

Hôtel Beaumarchais [GS] 3 rue Oberkampf (btwn bd Beaumarchais & bd Voltaire, M°Filles-du-Calvaire) 33-1/53.36.86.86

Hôtel Mondia [GF] 22 rue du Grand-Prieuré (M°République) 33-1/47.00.93.44

France • *EUROPE*

Studio in Paris [GS,GO] 41 rue Saint Bernard 33-1/**43.79.67.44** *studio in Bastille area*

■BARS

Interface [M,S] 34 rue Keller (M°Bastille) 33-1/**47.00.67.15** *3pm-2am*

Keller's [MO,L,$] 14 rue Keller (M°Bastille) 33-1/**47.00.05.39** *10:30pm-2am, till 4am Th-Sat, raunchy cruise bar, theme parties, strict dress code, darkroom*

■NIGHTCLUBS

Le Gibus Club [GF,D,E,P,$] 18 rue du Faubourg-du-Temple (M°République) 33-1/**47.00.78.88** *midnight-close, clsd Mon-Tue, gay Th & Sat, also piano bar, live music Sat*

■RESTAURANTS

L' ArtiShow [C] 3 cite Souzy 33-1/**43.48.56.04** *lunch & dinner, French/ Thai, cabaret theater*

Le Temps Au Temps [MW,E,R] 13 rue Paul Bert (M°Faidherbe-Chaligny) 33-1/**43.79.63.40** *8pm-11pm, clsd Sun, French bistro*

Le Sofa 21 rue St-Sabin (M°Bastille) 33-1/**43.14.07.46** *6pm-midnight, till 2am Th-Sat, also bar*

■MEN'S CLUBS

Bastille Sauna [MR,V] 4 passage St-Antoine (near rue Keller, M°Ledru-Rollin) 33-1/**43.38.07.02** *gym equipment, bar*

Les Docks [V] 150 rue St-Maur (M°Goncourt) 33-1/**43.57.33.82** *4pm-2am, till 4am Fri, till 5am Sat, backroom, theme nights*

■EROTICA

Kingdom [V] 19 rue Keller (M°Bastille) 33-1/**48.07.07.08** *clsd Sun, leather, latex, military gear*

Paris—12

■MEN'S CLUBS

Alantide [GS,V] 13 rue Parrot 33-1/**43.42.22.43** *cabins, tanning, women welcome*

■CRUISY AREAS

Bois de Vincennes [AYOR]

Place de la Nation [AYOR] (M°Nation)

Paris—13

■RESTAURANTS

Au Pet de Lapin 2 rue Dunois (M°Massena) 33-1/**45.86.58.21** *lunch & dinner, clsd Sun-Mon (also clsd Aug), foies gras & seafood*

■CRUISY AREAS

Quai d'Austerlitz [AYOR] Quai d'Austerlitz

Les Sablières [AYOR] *along the quai d'Austerlitz, from library to blvds Perijheriques, at night only*

Paris—14

■ENTERTAINMENT & RECREATION

Catacombes 1 place Denfert Rochereau 33-1/**43.22.47.63** *a ghoulish yet intriguing tourist destination, these burial tunnels were the headquarters of the Résistance during World War II*

Paris—15

■ACCOMMODATIONS

ParisCondo.com [GS,SW,WC,GO] rue Gaston de Caillavet (at Quai de Grenelle) 212/**594-6369 (US#)** *fully furnished high-rise apt w/ view of Seine*

■MEN'S CLUBS

Le Steamer [MO] 5 rue du Dr Jacquemarie Clemenceau 33-1/**42.50.36.49** *clsd Sun, also bar*

Paris—16

■CRUISY AREAS

Bois de Boulogne [AYOR]

Jardins du Trocadéro [AYOR] (M°Trocadéro) *on rue le-Nôtre & av des Etats-Unis*

Berlin—Overview • Germany

Paris—17

MEN'S CLUBS
King Sauna [V] 21 rue Bridaine (near place de Clichy, M°Rome)
33-1/**42.94.19.10** *1pm-7am, bar*

CRUISY AREAS
Place des Batignolles [AYOR]
(M°Brochant)

Paris—19

ACCOMMODATIONS
A Week or More in Paris [GS,GO]
33-1/**43.42.21.56**, 33-6/**13.62.90.98**
studio

CRUISY AREAS
Parc des Buttes-Chaumont [AYOR]
(M°Buttes-Chaumont)

Paris—20

ACCOMMODATIONS
A Pink Froggy B&B [MW,GO]
Gambetta Place (at rue des Pyrénées)
33-1/**43.58.34.56**

ENTERTAINMENT & RECREATION
Père Lachaise Cemetery bd de Ménilmontant (M°Père-Lachaise)
perhaps the world's most famous resting place, where lie such notables as Chopin, Oscar Wilde, Sarah Bernhardt, Isadora Duncan, Gertrude Stein & Jim Morrison

MEN'S CLUBS
Le Riad [SW,V] 184 rue des Pyrénées (M°Gambetta) 33-1/**47.97.25.52**

GERMANY

BERLIN

Berlin is divided into 5 regions:
Berlin—Overview
Berlin—Kreuzberg
Berlin—Prenzlauer Berg-Mitte
Berlin—Schöneberg-Tiergarten
Berlin—Outer

Berlin—Overview

INFO LINES & SERVICES
Gay AA for English Speakers at M-O-M 49-30/**216.80.08** *5pm Tue, also Gay AA 8pm Th*

Mann-O-Meter Bülowstr 106 (at Nollendorfplatz) 49-30/**216.80.08**
open 5pm-10pm, from 4pm wknds, gay switchboard & center, also cafe, also B&B referral service

Sonntags Club Greifenhagener Str 28 (S/U-Schönhauser Allee)
49-30/**449.75.90**, 49-30/**442.37.02** **(transgender line)** *info line 10am-6pm daily, lgbt info & counseling, mtgs, also cafe-bar [MW,TG,S,V] open 5pm-midnight Mon-Sun, regular parties*

ACCOMMODATIONS
Enjoy B&B [MW] Bülowstr 106 (at M-O-M center) 49-30/**23.62.36.10**
accommodations referral service, 'on-the-cheap'

ENTERTAINMENT & RECREATION
The Jewish Museum Berlin Lindenstr 9-14 49-30/**30.87.85.681**
10am-8pm, till 10pm Mon

Schwules (Gay) Museum U6/U7 Mehringdamm 49-30/**69.59.90.50**
2pm-6pm, till 7pm Sat, clsd Tue, guided tours 5pm Sat (in German)

PUBLICATIONS
Sergej 49-30/**44.31.98.0**
free monthly gay magazine

➤ **Siegessäule** 49-30/**23.55.39-0**, 49-30/**23.55.39-32** *free monthly lgbt city magazine (in German), awesome maps*

Germany • *Europe*

Berlin—Kreuzberg

■ACCOMMODATIONS

Hotel Transit [GF] Hagelberger Str 53-54 (U-Mehringdamm) 49-30/789.04.70 *loft-style hotel, also bar*

■BARS

Barbie Bar [MW] Mehringdamm 77 49-30/69.56.86.10 *4pm-close, lounge, terrace*

Bargelb [MW] Mehringdamm 62 (U-Mehringdamm) 49-30/788.99.299 *8pm-close*

Bierhimmel [GS,YC] Oranienstr 183 (U-Kottbusser Tor) 49-30/615.31.22 *1pm-3am*

Club Trommel [M,D,TG] Thomasstr 53 49-30/686.73.45 *7pm-close*

Ficken 3000 [M,D,L,V,YC] Urbanstr 70 (at Hermannplatz) 49-30/69.50.73.35 *10pm-close, cruisy, large darkroom*

Kumpelnest 3000 [GF,D,TG,YC] Lützowstr 23 (at Potsdamer Str, U-Kurfürstenstr) 49-30/261.69.18 *5pm-5am, till 8am Fri-Sat, cocktail bar*

Mobel Olfe [★MW] Kottbusser Tor/ Dresden Str (U-Kottbusser Tor) *6pm-close Wed-Sun*

Mondschein [M,NH,F] Urbanstr 101 (at Hermannplatz) 49-30/693.23.55 *8pm-3am, till 5am Fri-Sat, darkroom, Safer Sex Party 2nd & 4th Sat*

Roses [★MW,TG,YC] Oranienstr 187 (Kottbusser Tor) 49-30/615.65.70 *10pm-close*

Triebwerk [M,L,V,WC] Urbanstr 64 (at Leinestr, U-Hermannplatz) 49-30/69.50.52.03 *10pm-close, cruise bar w/ darkroom*

■NIGHTCLUBS

Böse Buben [MO] Lichtenrader Str 32 (at Kienitzer Str) 49-30/62.70.56.10 *darkroom*

Club Culture Houze [MW] Görlitzer Str 71 (off Skalitzer Str) 49-30/61.70.96.69 *also darkroom*

Erotic Sunday at Adagio Scandal [M,D,S] Reichpietschufer 22 (off Linkstrasse, Potsdamer Platz) *7pm-close Sun only, go-go boys*

SchwuZ (SchwulenZentrum) [★M,D,S,YC,$] Mehringdamm 61 (enter through Café Sundstroem) 49-30/69.50.78.92 *11pm Fri-Sat, 2 dance flrs, cocktail lounge, theme nights include Bump (retro) 1st Sat, PopStaRrZ (pop, indie, electronic) 1st Fri*

SO 36 [★GS,D,TG,S,V,YC,WC] Oranienstr 190 (at Kottbusser Tor) 49-30/61.40.13.06, 49-30/61.40.13.07 *theme nights, also live music venue*

■CAFES

Melitta Sundström [MW,WC] Mehringdamm 61 (at Gneisenaustr, U-Mehringdamm) 49-30/692.44.14 *10am-8pm, till 4pm Sat, clsd Sun, terrace, also gay bookstore*

Muvuca [F] Gneisenaustr 2a (at Mehringdamm) 49-30/63.90.17.56 *4pm-close, radical/ political int'l cafe*

■RESTAURANTS

Abendmahl [WC] Muskauer Str 9 (U-Görlitzer Bahnhof) 49-30/612.51.70 *6pm-11:30pm, vegetarian & seafood, also bar (open till 1am), terrace*

Kaiserstein Mehringdamm 80 49-30/78.89.58.87 *int'l*

Locus [★MW] Marheinekeplatz 4 49-30/691.56.37 *10am-2am, Mexican, full bar*

Berlin—Prenzlauer Berg-Mitte

■ACCOMMODATIONS

Le Moustache [M] Gartenstr 4 (at Rosenthaler Platz, U-Oranienburger Tor) 49-30/281.72.77 *also Moustache Bar [M,L,F], open 8pm-close, clsd Mon-Tue*

Schall & Rauch Pension [MW] Gleimstr 23 (at Schönhauser Allee) 49-30/443.39.70, 49-30/448.07.70 *also bar & restaurant*

Transit Loft [GF] Greifswalder Str 219 (enter on Immanuelkirchstrasse) 49-30/4849.37.73 *hotel in restored 19th-c factory*

Berlin—Prenzlauer Berg-Mitte • Germany

■ BARS

Bärenhöhle [M,B,BW] Schönhauser Allee 90 49-30/44.73.65.53 *5pm-2am, beer bar*

Besenkammer Bar [MW] Rathausstr 1 (at Alexanderplatz, under the S-Bahn bridge) 49-30/242.40.83 *24hrs, tiny 'beer bar'*

Cafe Amsterdam [GS,TG,F,YC,WC] Gleimstr 24 (at Schönhauser Allee) 49-30/44.00.94.54, 49-30/231.67.96 *9am-3am, till 5am Fri-Sat, cafe-bar, terrace, also pension*

DarkRoom [MO,L] Rodenbergstr 23 (at Schönhauser Allee) 49-30/444.93.21 *10pm-6am, uniform bar, darkroom, theme parties wknds*

Flax [MW,F] Chodowieckistr 41 (off Greifswalder Str) 49-30/44.04.69.88, 49-30/441.98.56 *3pm-3am, till 4am Sat, brunch 10am-5pm Sun*

Gay-Point [MO] Dolziger Str 24 (at Voight Str, in Friedrichshain) 49-30/48.62.24.88 *sex parties, darkroom*

Goldrausch [MW] Rosenthaler Str 72a (U-Rosenthaler Platz) *cocktail lounge*

Greifbar [MO,L,V] Wichertstr 10 (at Greifenhagener Str, S/U-Schönhauser Allee) 49-30/444.08.28 *10pm-6am, darkroom*

Guppi [M,D,F] Gleimstr 31 (at Schönhauser Allee) 49-30/43.73.96.11 *1pm-close, from 11am wknds, terrace*

The Midnight Sun [MO,D,V,PC] Paul Robeson Str 50 (at Schönhauser Allee) 49-30/44.71.63.95 *10pm-close, 24hrs wknds, darkroom, cruisy*

Offenbar [MW] Schreinerstr 5 (U-Samariterstr) 49-30/426.09.30 *10am-4am, brunch buffet wknds*

SIEGESSÄULE
Europe's Biggest Queer City Mag
Presents OUT IN BERLIN
Queer Guide Berlin
www.out-in-berlin.com

Germany • EUROPE

Pick ab! [★M,V] Greifenhagener Str 16 (S/U-Schönhauser Allee)
49-30/445.85.23 *10pm-close, cruise bar w/ darkroom*

Reingold [GS,GO] Novalisstr 11 (U-Oranienburger Str)
49-30/28.38.76.76

Romeo [M,F] Greifenhagener Str 16 (S/U-Schönhauser Allee)
49-30/447.67.89 *11pm-8am*

Schoppenstube [M,D] Schönhauser Allee 44 (at Eberswalder Str)
49-30/442.82.04 *8pm-close, from 10pm Fri-Sun, theme nights, terrace, cruisy*

Sonderbar [MW,F,YC] Käthe-Niederkirchner-Str 34 (near Märchenbrunnen) 49-30/42.80.64.25 *8pm-8am, terrace*

Stahlrohr [MO] Greifenhagener Str 54 (off Wicherts Str, U-Schonhauser Allee)
49-30/44.73.27.47 *10pm-close, sex parties*

Stiller Don [★MW,NH,L,F] Erich-Weinert-Str 67 (at Schönhauser Allee)
49-30/445.59.57 *7pm-close, terrace*

■ NIGHTCLUBS

Ackerkeller [★MW,D,YC] Ackerstr 12 (Hinterhaus, enter at Ackerstr 12, U-Rosenthaler Platz) 49-30/280.72.16 *10pm-2am Tue & 10pm-4am Fri*

Cafe Moskau (GMF) [M,D] Karl-Marx-Allee 34 (U-Schillingstr) *Sun T-dance*

E5 Club at BKA Theater [MW,D] Schlossplatz (at U-Alexanderplatz or U-Friedrichst) 49-30/20.22.00.44 *1st & 3rd Fri only*

Sage Club [GS,D,TG] Köpenicker Str 76 (at Brückenstr) 49-30/278.98.30 *11pm-7am Th-Sun, more gay wknds*

■ CAFES

Kapelle [GS,YC] Zionskirchplatz 22-24 (U-Rosenthaler Platz)
49-30/44.34.13.00 *10am-3am, food served till midnight, also cocktail bar from 8pm*

November [MW] Husemannstr 15 (at Sredzkistr) 49-30/442.84.25 *10am-2am, cafe-bar, terrace, brkfst buffet wknds*

■ RESTAURANTS

Drei Lychener Str 30 (U-Eberswalder Str) 49-30/44.73.84.71 *pan-Asian*

Rice Queen Danziger Str 13 (U-Eberswalder Str) 49-30/44.04.58.00 *Asian*

Schall & Rauch Wirtshaus [MW,BW] Gleimstr 23 (at Schönhauser Allee)
49-30/443.39.70, 49-30/448.07.70 *10am-close*

Thüringer Stuben Stargarder Str 28 (at Dunckerstr, S/U-Schönhauser Allee)
49-30/44.63.33.91 *4pm-1am, from noon wknds, full bar*

■ BOOKSTORES

Adam-Buchladen Gleimstr 27 (S/U-Schönhauser Allee) 49-30/448.07.67 *10am-8pm, till 4pm Sat, clsd Sun, lgbt*

■ MEN'S CLUBS

Gate Sauna [F,V] Wilhelmstr 81 (near Brandenburger Tor, U-Mohrenstr)
49-30/229.94.30 *24hrs wknds, also bar, theme nights*

Treibhaus Sauna [F,V,YC] Schönhauser Allee 132 (U-Eberswalder Str) 49-30/448.45.03 *24hrs wknds, also bar, student discount*

■ EROTICA

Bad Boy'z [V] Schliemannstr 38 (U-Eberswalder Str) 49-30/440.81.65 *toys, videos, cruising, safer sex party 3rd Sat (dress code)*

Black Style Seelower Str 5 (S/U-Schönhauser Allee)
49-30/44.68.85.95 *clsd Sun, latex & rubber wear, also mail order*

Duplexx Schönhauser Allee 131 (U-Eberswalder Str) 49-30/48.49.42.00 *videos, cruisy*

Lustwandel [GO] Raumerstr 20 (off Prenzlauer Allee & Danziger Str)
49-30/44.04.08.60

■ CRUISY AREAS

Volkspark Friedrichshain [AYOR] (at Märchenbrunnen, in Friedrichshain)

Berlin–Schöneberg-Tiergarten • **Germany**

Berlin–Schöneberg-Tiergarten

■ ACCOMMODATIONS

Arco Hotel [GS,WC,GO] Geisbergstr 30 (at Ansbacherstr, U-Wittenbergplatz) 49-30/235.14.80 *centrally located*

Art-Hotel Connection [M,L,WC,GO] Fuggerstr 33 (near Welser Str, U-Wittenbergplatz) 49-30/210.21.88.00, 49-30/217.70.29 *also special 'fantasy' apt for kink & S/M types, some shared baths*

Gaybed.de [GS,GO] Perleberger Str (at Stephan Str) 49-30/81.85.19.88 *B&B, hot tub, shared bath*

Hotel Hansablick [GF] Flotowstr 6 (at Bachstr, off Str des 17 Juni) 49-30/390.48.00 *full brkfst*

Hotel Sachsenhof [GS] Motzstr 7 (at Nollendorfplatz) 49-30/216.20.74

Pension Niebuhr [GS,GO] Niebuhrstr 74 (at Savignyplatz) 49-30/324.95.95, 49-30/324.95.96

Tom's House Berlin [MO,L,GO] Eisenacher Str 10 (at Winterfeldstr, above Tom's Bar, U-Nollendorfplatz) 49-30/218.55.44 *spacious rooms on the 3rd flr of a turn-of-the-century bldg (no elevator)*

■ BARS

Ajpnia eV [MO] Eisenacher Str 23 (U-Eisenacher Str) 49-30/425.52.41 *sex parties*

Andreas Kneipe [★M,NH,L] Ansbacher Str 29 (at Wittenbergplatz) 49-30/218.32.57 *11am-3am, till 4am Fri-Sat*

Bear [MO,B,L] Fuggerstr 34 (at Welserstr, U-Wittenbergplatz) 49-30/21.96.87.53 *8pm-2am*

Blue Boy Bar [M,V] Eisenacher Str 3a (at Fuggerstr, U-Nollendorfplatz) 49-30/218.74.98 *24hrs, ring bell, hustlers; also Fugger-Eck* [GS,NH], *1pm-6am, clsd Sun, terrace*

CC 96 [MO,TG,DS,S,V,PC,WC] Lietzenburger Str 96 (at Sächsische Str, U-Uhlandstr) 49-30/883.26.50 *noon-3am, clsd Wed, strip shows & drag shows from 8pm*

Chez Nous [GS,DS,$] Marburger Str 14 (at Tauentzienstr, U-Wittenbergplatz) 49-30/213.18.10 *famous drag revue, shows 8:30pm & 11pm nightly, pricey 1-drink minimum*

Dreizehn [M] Welserstr 27 (at Fuggerstr, U-Wittenbergplatz) 49-30/218.23.63 *5pm-5am, terrace*

E116 [M,L,F] Eisenacher Str 116 (at Motzstr, U-Nollendorfplatz) 49-30/217.05.18 *8pm-3am, from 3pm wknds, cafe-bar, terrace, hustlers*

Eldorado [M,F,E] Motzstr 20 (U-Nollendorfplatz) 49-30/213.25.18 *24hrs, terrace*

Flipflop [M,F] Kulmer Str 20a (at Yorckstr) 49-30/216.28.25 *7pm-close, from 11am Sun*

Hafen [★M,TG,S,YC] Motzstr 19 (at Eisenacher Str, U-Nollendorfplatz) 49-30/211.41.18 *8pm-close*

Harlekin [M,NH,F] Schaperstr 12-13 (at Lietzenburger Str, U9-Spichernstr, in Wilmersdorf) 49-30/218.25.79 *4pm-close, from 2pm Sun, terrace*

Heile Welt [MW,F] Motzstr 5 49-30/21.91.75.07 *6pm-close*

Lenz...die Bar [★M,WC] Eisenacher Str 3 (at Nollendorfplatz) 49-30/217.78.20 *8pm-close, cocktail bar*

Memory's [M,F] Fuggerstr 37 (U-Wittenbergplatz) 49-30/213.52.71 *4pm-close, cafe-bar, terrace, bears 4th Sun*

Mutsch Mann's [MO,L] Martin-Luther-Str 19 (at Motzstr, U-Nollendorfplatz) 49-30/21.91.96.40 *11pm-close, also bar, darkroom*

New Action [★MO,L,V] Kleiststr 35 (at Eisenacher Str, U-Nollendorfplatz) 49-30/211.82.56 *8pm-close, from 1pm Sun, uniform bar, darkroom, very cruisy*

Prinzknecht [★M] Fuggerstr 33 (U-Nollendorfplatz) 49-30/236.27.44 *6pm-close, theme nights*

Germany • *EUROPE*

Pussy-Cat [MW,D,TG,F,E] Kalkreuthstr 7 (at Nollendorfplatz) 49-30/213.35.86 *6pm-6am, clsd Tue, terrace*

Scheune [★MO,L,V] Motzstr 25 (at Nollendorfplatz) 49-30/213.85.80 *9pm-7am, till 9am Fri-Sat, uniform bar, darkroom, Naked Sex Party from 5:30pm Sun, rubber party last Fri*

Spot [M,NH,F] Eisenacher Str 2 (at Nollendorfplatz) 49-30/213.22.67 *4pm-4am, open later wknds, from 6pm in winter, terrace*

Tabasco [M,F,AYOR] Fuggerstr 3 (at Schönhauser Allee, U-Nollendorfplatz) 49-30/214.26.36 *6pm-6am, 24hrs wknds, hustlers*

Together [MW] Hohenstauffenstr 53 (off Luther Str, U-Viktoria Luise Platz) 49-30/21.91.63.00

Tom's Bar [★MO,L,V] Motzstr 19 (at Eisenacherstr, U-Nollendorfplatz) 49-30/213.45.70 *10pm-6am, open later Fri-Sat, very cruisy, downstairs maze*

■NIGHTCLUBS

Connection [★MO,D,L,V,$] Fuggerstr 33 (at Art-Hotel Connection) 49-30/218.14.32 *11pm-close Fri-Sat only, cruisy, darkroom; also sex shop & cinema*

■CAFES

Café Berio [★WC] Maaßenstr 7 (at Winterfeldtstr, U-Nollendorfplatz) 49-30/216.86.54 *8am-1am, int'l, brkfst all day, seasonal terrace, also bar*

Café PositHiv Alvenslebenstr 26 (at Potsdamer Str, U-Bülowstr) 49-30/216.86.54 *3pm-close, from 1pm Th, from 6pm Sat, clsd Mon, for HIV+ & friends*

Café Savigny Grolmanstr 53-54 (at Savignyplatz) 49-30/312.81.95 *9am-1am, full bar, terrace*

Windows [MW] Martin-Luther-Str 22 (at Motzstr, U-Wittenbergplatz) 49-30/214.23.94 *2pm-4am, from 11am Sun, full bar, terrace*

■RESTAURANTS

Art [MW,WC] Fasanenstr 81-A (at Kantstr, in S-Bahn arches, Charlottenburg, S/U-Zoologischer Garten) 49-30/313.26.25 *8am-2am, from 10am wknds, also bar, internet access, terrace*

LukiLuki [MW,TG,S] Motzstr 28 (U-Nollendorfplatz) 49-30/23.62.20.79 *6pm-2am, full bar, topless hardbody & drag-queen servers, brunch buffet Sun, internet access*

■ENTERTAINMENT & RECREATION

Xenon Kino Kolonnenstr 5-6 49-30/792.88.50 *gay & lesbian cinema*

■BOOKSTORES

Bruno's Bülowstr 106 (U-Nollendorfplatz) 49-30/21.47.32.93 *10am-10pm, clsd Sun, many beautiful books w/ beautiful pictures of beautiful boys, also video/ DVD rentals*

Prinz Eisenherz Buchladen [WC] Bleibtreustr 52 (in Charlottenburg, S-Savignyplatz) 49-30/313.99.36 *10am-7pm, till 4pm Sat, clsd Sun, lgbt books & magazines 'in all languages'*

■RETAIL SHOPS

Galerie Janssen Pariser Str 45 (at Nollendorfplatz, U1/9-Spichernstr) 49-30/881.15.90 *clsd Sun, books & artwork for men*

■MEN'S CLUBS

Apollo City Sauna [F,V] Kurfürstenstr 101 (in Charlottenburg, U-Wittenbergplatz) 49-30/213.24.24 *gym equipment, tanning booths, also bar*

Steam Sauna Club [L,F,V] Kurfürstenstr 113 (U-Wittenbergplatz) 49-30/218.40.60 *24hrs wknds, jacuzzi, also bar*

■EROTICA

Beate Uhse International Joachimstaler Str 4 (at Kantstr, at Erotic Museum) *cinema, video cabins & bar*

City Men Fuggerstr 26 49-30/218.29.59 *videos, magazines, toys*

Rome • Italy

Man's Pleasurechest [V]
Kalckreuthstr 15 (U-Nollendorfplatz)
49-30/211.20.25

Mazeworld Kurfürstenstr 79 (at Keithstr)

Mister B Nollendorfstrasse 23
49-30/21.99.77.04 *clsd Sun, leather, rubber, toys*

New Man [V] Joachimstaler Str 1-3 (in Charlottenburg, U-Zoologischer Garten)
49-30/480.08.54 *darkroom*

Pool Berlin [V] Schaperstr 11
(at Joachimsthaler Str, in Wilmersdorf, U-Kurfürstendamm) 49-30/214.19.89
clsd Sun, gay emporium

■ CRUISY AREAS

Tiergarten [AYOR] along Str de 17 Juni (near the Siegessäule monument)

Berlin—Outer

■ BARS

Himmelreich [MW] Simon Dach Str 36 (off Warschauer Str, in Friedrichshain, U-Frankfurter Tor) 49-30/29.00.08.72 *from 6pm Mon-Fri, 2pm-close wknds*

HT [MW,F] Kopernikusstr 23 (in Friedrichshain) 49-30/29.00.49.65
5pm-2am, terrace

Stonewall [MW,GO] Ott Suhr Allee 125 (in Charlottenburg)
49-30/34.70.55.30

■ NIGHTCLUBS

Die Busche [★MW,D,S,$]
Mühlenstr 11-12 (at Kurfürstenstr, in Friedrichshain, S/U-Warschauer Str)
49-30/296.08.00 *9:30pm-5am Wed & Sun, 10pm-6am Fri-Sat, terrace; also Kleine (Little) Busch at Warschauer Platz 18*

■ CAFES

Schrader's [GO] Malplaquetstr 16b (at Utrechter Str, Wedding)
49-30/45.08.26.63

■ RESTAURANTS

Cafe Rix Karl-Marx-Str 141 (in Neükolln) 49-30/686.90.20 *10am-5pm, Mediterranean, plenty veggie, also bar, open till 1am*

■ CRUISY AREAS

Volkspark Wilmersdorf [AYOR]

ITALY

Rome

■ INFO LINES & SERVICES

Circola Arcigay Ora Via Goito 35b
39-06/340.347.57.10 *sells the arcigay membership required for entry to some bars & clubs*

Circolo di Cultura Omosessual Mario Mieli Via Efeso 2a (Metro San Paolo) 39-06/541.39.85 *10am-5:30pm Mon-Fri, switchboard, mtgs & discussion groups*

■ ACCOMMODATIONS

Albergo Del Sole al Pantheon [GF]
Piazza della Rotonda 63
39-06/678.04.41

Bologna B&B [GS] 6 Piazza Bologna (at Via Sambucuccio D'Alando)
39-06/442-40244

Domus International [GS]
39-06/6889.2918 *short-term apt rentals in the heart of Rome*

Gayopen B&B [GS,GO] Via dello Statuto 44, Apt 18 (at Via Merulana, Piazza Vittorio) 39-06/482.00.13
full brkfst

Hotel Altavilla [GF] Via Principe Amedeo 9 39-06/474.11.86

Hotel Derby [GF,WC] Via Vigna Pozzi 7 (Largo delle Sette Chiese)
39-06/513.49.55 *small hotel in heart of Rome*

Hotel Eden [GF,WC] Via Ludovisi 49
39-06/478.121, 800/543-4300(US#)
restaurant & rooftop bar

Hotel Edera [GF] Via A Poliziano 75
39-06/7045.3888, 800/448-8355

Hotel Scott House [GF] Via Gioberti 30
39-06/446.53.92

Loft Colosseum [GF] Rione Monti-Colosseum neighborhood (Piazza degli Zingari)

Rainbow B&B [GF,GO] Via Accademia Ambrosiana 41 (at Via Leonori)
39-06/540.54.84

Italy • *Europe*

Scalinata di Spagna [GF] Piazza Trinità dei Monti 17 (Metro Piazza di Spagna) 39-06/6994.0896, 39-06/679.30.06 (booking #) *roof garden*

Valadier [GF] Via della Fontanella 15 39-06/361.19.98, 800/448-8355 *4-star hotel, 2 restaurants & piano bar*

Villa Appennini [GS] 32 Via Appennini 39-06/855-1262

■ BARS

Apeiron [M,TG,F,DS,S,V,PC] Via dei Quattro Cantoni 5 (Metro Cavour) 39-06/482.88.20 *10:30pm-3am, clsd Sun, darkroom*

Coming Out [MW,TG,F,E,K,V,GO] Via San Giovanni in Laterano 8 (near Colosseum) 39-06/700.98.71

Garbo [MW,F,GO] Vicolo di Santa Margherita 1a (in Trastevere, Tram 8) 39-06/5832.0782, 39-06/581.67.00 *10pm-3am, clsd Mon, cocktail bar*

Hangar [★M,L,V,YC] Via In Selci 69 (Metro Cavour) 39-06/48.81.397 *10:30pm-2am, clsd Tue, int'l crowd, cruisy, live DJs*

Matisse [MW,D,F,V] Via Montebello 68 39-06/347.94.92.601 *8pm-3am, clsd Mon, karaoke Th*

Shelter [MW,TG,F,S,PC] Via dei Vascellari 35 (in Trastevere, Tram 8) *9pm-4am, from 5pm wknds, internet access*

Side Meeting Point [★MW,D,F,YC] Via Pietro Verri 1 (near Coliseum) 39-06/348.692.94.72 *8pm-3am, clsd Mon, internet access*

Skyline [M,L,S,V,PC] Via degli Aurunci 26-28 (in San Lorenzo district, Metro Policlinico) 39-06/444.08.17 *10:30pm-2am, till 3am Fri-Sat, clsd Sun, 2-flr American bar, backroom, monthly sex parties*

■ NIGHTCLUBS

L' Alibi [★MW,D,S,YC] Via di Monte Testaccio 40-44 (Metro Piramide) 39-06/574.34.48 *11pm-4am, clsd Mon-Tue, rooftop garden in summer*

Max's Bar [MO,D,L,V,$] Via Achille Grandi 7a (near Porta Maggiore, below Center Hotel 3, Metro Manzoni) 39-06/7030.1599 *10:30pm-close, clsd Wed*

Muccassassina [★MW,D,K,S,YC,$] Via del Comercio 32 39-06/541.39.85 *10:30pm-5am Fri only (Sept-June), location changes so call ahead, darkroom*

■ CAFES

Oppio Café [★MW,E] Via delle Terme di Titi 72 39-06/474.52.62 *brkfst, lunch & dinner, open 24hrs in Aug, full bar, terrace w/ great view*

TreviNet Pl@ce Internet Point [GO,WC] Via in Arcione 103 (btwn Trevi Fountain & Via del Traforo) 39-06/699.22320 *10:30am-10:30pm, from 4pm Sun, internet cafe*

■ RESTAURANTS

Asinocotto Ristorante [R,GO] Via dei Vascellari 48 (in Travestere, Tram 8) 39-06/589.89.85, 212/858-5771 (US reservations fax line) *dinner, lunch Sun, clsd Mon, creative gourmet Mediterranean*

La Cicala e la Formica Via Leonina 17 39-06/481.74.90 *7pm-midnight, clsd Sun*

Ditirambo Piazza della Cancelleria 74-75 (near Campo dei Fiori) 39-06/687.16.26

Edoardo II [MW,WC] Vicolo Margana 14 39-06/6994.2419 *7pm-12:30am, clsd Tue, full bar*

Gelateria San Crispino Via della Panetteria 42 (near Trevi Fountain) *gelato!*

Jeliel [WC] Vicolo Montevecchio 8 (Plaza Navona) 39-06/68.80.70.25 *noon-1am, Italian, large pizza selection*

Taverna del Campo Campo dei Fiori 16 39-06/687.44.02 *lunch & dinner, Italian*

■ ENTERTAINMENT & RECREATION

Settimo Cielo Castel Porziano (btwn Ostia Lido & Torvaianica) *gay beach*

■ BOOKSTORES

La Libreria Babele Via dei Banchi Vecchi 116 39-06/687.66.28 *10am-7:30pm, clsd Sun, lgbt, some English titles*

Amsterdam—Overview • Netherlands

Queer Via del Boschetto 25 (at Via Nazionale) 39-06/474.06.91 *9:30am-7:30pm, from 2:30pm Mon, clsd Sun, lgbt, also videos, pride items, T-shirts, cards & gadgets*

Rinascita Via delle Botteghe Oscure 1 39-06/679.74.60 *large lgbt section*

■ PUBLICATIONS

Aut 39-06/541.39.85 *monthly magazine w/ news & event listings, free around Rome*

■ GYMS & HEALTH CLUBS

Roman Sport Center [GS] Via del Galoppatoio 33 39-06/320.16.67

■ MEN'S CLUBS

Apollion Bath [V] Via Mecenate 59a (at Via Carlo Botta, Metro Piazza Vittorio) 39-06/482.53.89 *gym equipment, bar*

Balnea Club [M,PC] Via dei Pescatori 495a 39-06/335.80.09.714 *gay Sun*

EMC-Europa Multiclub [V,SW,YC,PC] Via Aureliana 40 (Metro Repubblica) 39-06/482.36.50 *1pm-1am, till 6am Fri-Sat, 3 flrs, fountain whirlpool, gym, bar, massage, solarium, private rooms*

Excess [F] Via Ombrone 1 (Metro Policlinico) 39-06/885.83.98 *3pm-10pm Fri-Sat only, also bar, internet access*

K Sex Club [L,V,PC] Via Amato Amati 6-8 (at Via Dulceri), Casilina 39-06/278.002.92 *10pm-4am, S/M club & bar, maze, darkroom*

Mediterraneo Sauna [F,V,PC] Via Pasquale Villari 3 (btwn Via Merulana & Via Labicana, Metro Manzoni) 39-06/772.059.34 *3 flrs, full bar, jacuzzi, maze*

Terme di Roma Internazionale [V] Via Persio 4 (Metro Arco di Travertino) 39-06/718.43.78, 39-06/339.886.97.51 *jacuzzi, gym equipment, bar, labyrinth, popular Sun*

■ SEX CLUBS

Gender [GS,TG,S,PC] Via Faleria 9 39-06/7049.7638, 39-06/702.58.29 *Th-Sat only, S/M club & bar, performances, darkroom*

■ EROTICA

La Bancarella di Andy Capp Piazza Alessandria 2 (near Porta Pia, Metro Repubblica) 39-06/853.03.71 *erotic comics & lgbt magazines*

Cobra Via Barletta 23 (Metro Ottaviano) 39-06/3751.7350 *clsd Sun, underwear, magazines, videos; also Via Aurelio Cotta 22-24 location (39-6/764.357); also Via G Giolitti 307-313 location (39-6/4470.0636)*

Pussycat Via Cairoli 96/98 (Metro Vittorio) 39-06/446.49.61 *cinema*

Studio Know How Via di San Gallicano 13 39-06/58.33.56.92

■ CRUISY AREAS

Colosseo Quadrato [AYOR] (near Palazzo della Civiltà del Lavoro park)

Monte Caprino Park [AYOR] Capidoglio Hill

Parco di Villa Borghese [AYOR] (in front of the Architecture Academy)

NETHERLANDS

AMSTERDAM

Amsterdam is divided into 5 regions:
Amsterdam—Overview
Amsterdam—Centre
Amsterdam—Jordaan
Amsterdam—Rembrandtplein
Amsterdam—Outer

Amsterdam—Overview

■ INFO LINES & SERVICES

COC Amsterdam Rozenstr 14 (in the Jordaan) 31-20/626.30.87 *info line 10am-5pm, also cafe 8pm-11:30pm Wed-Fri*

Gay/ Lesbian Switchboard 31-20/623.65.65, 31-20/422.65.65 (TTY) *2pm-10pm, English spoken*

Pink Point Westermarkt (in the Jordaan by Homomonument) *noon-6pm (April 1-Sept 30), gay info kiosk & souvenirs*

Netherlands • EUROPE

ENTERTAINMENT & RECREATION

The Anne Frank House Prinsengracht 263 (in the Jordaan) 31-20/556.71.00, 31-20/626.45.33 *the final hiding place of Amsterdam's most famous resident*

Homomonument Westermarkt (in the Jordaan) *moving sculptural tribute to lesbians & gays killed by Nazis*

The van Gogh Museum Paulus Potterstr 7 (on the Museumplein) 31-20/570.52.52 *a must-see museum dedicated to this Dutch master painter*

PUBLICATIONS

Gay News 31-20/679.15.56 *bilingual paper, extensive listings*

Gay & Night 31-20/622.53.64 *free monthly bilingual entertainment paper w/ club listings*

Shark 31-20/420.6775 *monthly queer-oriented alternative culture guide & calendar (in English)*

Amsterdam—Centre

ACCOMMODATIONS

Amsterdam Canal Apartments [M,GO] Kloveniersburgwal 55 31-20/471.02.72 *close to museums & nightlife*

Amsterdam Escape [GS] Geldersekade 106 (at Centrum) 31-20/320.64.02 *luxury apts & canal houses*

Amsterdam Lodge [GF] Eerste Boomdwarsstraat 10-I (at Westerstraat) 31-20/620.64.41 *B&B*

Anco Hotel-Bar [MO,L,N,GO] OZ Voorburgwal 55 (across from the Oude Kerk) 31-20/624.11.26 *1640 canal house, some shared baths, also bar*

The Black Tulip Guesthouse [★MO,L,GO] Geldersekade 16 31-20/427.0933 *Europe's classiest hotel for leather guys, all rooms w/ sling & bondage hooks, fantasy suite available*

Centre Apartments Amsterdam [GS,GO] Heintje Hoekssteeg 31-20/627.25.03

Clemens Hotel [GF] 39 Raadhuisstraat (at Herengracht) 31-20/624.60.89 *small hotel in Amsterdam's center, some shared baths*

The Collector B&B [GF,GC] De Lairessestr 46 (in museum area) 31-6/110.10.105 *full brkfst*

Crowne Plaza Amsterdam City Centre [GF,SW,WC] NZ Voorburgwal 5 31-20/620.05.00, 800/227-6936 (US#)

▶ **Drake's Guesthouse** [M,GO] Damrak 61 (above cinema) 31-20/638.23.67 *rates include videos & free tickets to cruisy cinema downstairs*

▶ **Drake's Guesthouse** [M,GO] Nieuwendijk 20 31-20/638.23.67 *rates include videos & free tickets to cruisy cinema*

E&D City Apartments [MO,L] Singel 34 31-20/624.73.35 *'for the 'eatherboy & his friend'*

Maes B&B [GS,NS,GO] Herenstr 26 31-20/427.51.65

Stablemaster Hotel [MO,L] Warmoesstr 23 31-20/625.01.48 *shared baths, also bar*

Sunhead of 1617 [GS,GO] Herengracht 152 (at Leliegracht & Raadshuisstraat) 31-20/626.18.09 *B&B, full brkfst*

Victoria Hotel Amsterdam [GF,SW,WC] Damrak 1-5 (opposite Central Station) 31-20/623.42.55, 800/814.70000 *gym, restaurants, bar*

BARS

Argos [★MO,L] Warmoesstr 95 31-20/622.65.95 *10pm-3am, till 4am Fri-Sat, the oldest leather bar in Europe, popular darkroom*

Bar Why Not/ Blue Boy Club [M,S,V,GO] NZ Voorburgwal 28 (near Centraal Station) 31-20/627.43.74 *noon-1am, till 2am wknds, casual bar, strip shows, cinema & escort services*

De Barderij [M,NH] Zeedijk 14 31-20/420.51.32 *4pm-1am, till 3am Fri-Sat, large brown café*

Casa Maria [M,L] Warmoesstr 60 31-20/627.68.48 *noon-1am, till 3am Fri-Sat, from 2pm Sun*

Amsterdam—Centre • Netherlands

The Cuckoo's Nest [MO,L,V] NZ Kolk 6
31-20/**627.17.52** *1pm-1am, till 2am Fri-Sat, cruisy, large play cellar*

Dirty Dick's [MO,L] Warmoesstr 86
31-20/**627.86.34** *midnight-4am Fri-Sat, 10pm-3am Sun, very cruisy, darkroom*

The Eagle Amsterdam [MO,L]
Warmoesstr 90   31-20/**627.86.34**
10pm-4am, till 5am Fri-Sat, darkroom

Getto [★MW,F,K] Warmoesstr 51
31-20/**421.51.51** *4pm-1am, from 7pm Tue, 1pm-midnight Sun, also restaurant, some veggie, live DJs, Tarot readings Sun, Sun brunch*

Queen's Head [M,S] Zeedijk 20 (off Nieuwmarkt)   31-20/**420.24.75** *5pm-1am, till 3am Fri-Sat, from 4pm wknds, bingo Tue*

Stablemaster Bar [MO,L]
Warmoesstr 23   31-20/**625.01.48**
8pm-1am, 2pm-2am Fri-Sat, clsd Tue-Wed, very cruisy, nightly jack-off parties

Vrankrijk [GS,A] Spuistr 216 *rowdy, friendly squat bar, more gay Mon*

The Web [MO,B,L,V] St Jacobsstr 4-6 (btwn Nieuwendijk & NZ Voorburgwal)
31-20/**623.67.58** *2pm-1am, till 3am Fri-Sat, darkroom, bears Sat*

■ NIGHTCLUBS

Club Trash [★MO,D,L,$] *monthly sex parties, strict dress code, get info at Mr B, RoB, Black Body, Drake's, Stringslip or in the Gay News*

Cockring [★MO,D,S,V] Warmoesstr 96
31-20/**623.96.04** *11pm-4am, till 5am Fri-Sat, cruisy darkroom, strippers/ sex shows Th & Sun*

■ RESTAURANTS

Camp Cafe [★MW,GO] Kerkstr 45 (at Leidsestr)   31-20/**622.15.06** *8am-1am, till 3am Fri-Sat, also bar, terrace*

Cock & Feathers Geldersekade 23
31-20/**624.31.41** *5pm-1am, till 3am Fri-Sat, Dutch cuisine, also bar*

Netherlands • *Europe*

Hemelse Modder [WC] Oude Waal 9 31-20/624.32.03 *6pm-10pm, French/ int'l*

La Strada [★] NZ Voorburgwal 93 31-20/625.02.76 *4pm-1am, till 2am wknds, Mediterranean, full bar, terrace*

't Sluisje [★MW,TG,DS] Torensteeg 1 31-20/624.08.13 *6pm-close, clsd Mon-Tue, steak house, full bar, drag shows nightly*

Song Kwae Kloveniersburgwal 14a (near Nieuwmarkt & Chinatown) 31-20/624.25.68 *1pm-10:30pm, Thai, full bar, terrace*

■ BOOKSTORES

The American Book Center [WC] Kalverstr 185 (at Heiligeweg) 31-20/625.55.37 *10am-8pm, till 9pm Th, 11am-6:30pm Sun, books & magazines in English imported from US & UK, large lgbt section*

Boekhandel Vrolijk Gay & Lesbian Bookshop Paleisstr 135 (near Dam Square) 31-20/623.51.42 *10am-6pm, from 11am Mon, till 9pm Th, till 5pm Sat, clsd Sun, lgbt books, videos & gadgets, also mail order*

Intermale Gay Bookstore Spuistr 251-253 31-20/625.00.09 *10am-6pm, till 9pm Th, wide selection of gay men's titles in English & Dutch*

■ RETAIL SHOPS

Conscious Dreams Kokopelli Warmoesstr 12 31-20/421.70.00 *11am-10pm, 'smart warehouse'*

Magic Mushroom Spuistr 249 31-20/427.57.65 *11am-7pm, till 8pm Fri-Sat, 'smartshop': magic mushrooms & more*

■ MEN'S CLUBS

Blowbuddies [MO,L] Warmoesstr 121 *10pm-4am 1st & 3rd Sat only, also bar*

■ EROTICA

4men Spuistr 21 31-20/625.87.97 *cinema, darkroom, all-day ticket, private cabin, large sexshop*

Adonis [V] Warmoesstr 92 31-20/627.29.59 *cinema, darkroom, large sexshop*

Condomerie Het Gulden Vlies Warmoesstr 141 31-20/627.41.74 *'world-wide condom specialists'*

DeMask Zeedijk 64 31-20/620.56.03 *clsd Sun, fetish fashion*

Drake's [★] Damrak 61 31-20/627.95.44 *videos & magazines, video cabins, cinema*

Mister B [WC] Warmoesstr 89 31-20/422.00.03 *leather & rubber, also tattoo & piercing*

RoB Accessories Warmoesstr 32 31-20/420.85.48 *leather, rubber, toys*

Robin & Rik Runstr 30 31-20/627.89.24 *by appointment only, custom leatherwear*

Le Salon Nieuwendijk 20-22 (near the Spui) 31-20/622.65.65 *sex supermarket, cinema*

Amsterdam—Jordaan

■ ACCOMMODATIONS

Amsterdam Barangay B&B [GS,NS,GO] 31-0-62/504.5432 *1777 town house near tourist attractions*

Canal Apartments [GF] Lijnbaansgracht 55 31-20/626.45.32 *studio, 1-bdrm & 2-bdrm apts*

Flatmates Amsterdam [MO,SW,NS,WC,GO] Java Island 31-20/620.15.45 *full brkfst*

Hotel Pulitzer [GF] Prinsengracht 315-331 31-20/523.52.35, 800/325-3535 (US#) *occupies 24 17th-c bldgs facing the Prinsengracht & Keizersgracht—2 of Amsterdam's most picturesque canals*

Rainbow Palace Hotel [GF] Raadhuisstr 33 31-20/625.43.17 *centrally located near the Homomonument, some shared baths*

Rembrandt Residence Hotel [GS] Herengracht 255 31-20/622.17.27 *near Dam Square*

The Townhouse B&B [GF] Akoleienstraat 2 31-20/612.93.20

■ BARS

Bar/ Restaurant 5 [MW] Prinsengracht 10 31-20/428.24.55 *noon-1am, clsd Tue*

Amsterdam—Rembrandtplein • Netherlands

■NIGHTCLUBS

COC [MW,D,$] Rozenstr 14
31-20/623.40.79, 31-20/626.30.87
10pm-5am Fri, [WO] 10pm-4am Sun, multicultural disco 8pm-2am Sun, HIV+ 8pm-12:30am Th, call for many other parties/events

Mazzo [GF,D,YC,$] Rozengracht 114
(near Westermarkt) 31-20/626.75.00
11pm-4am, till 5am Fri-Sat, clsd Mon-Tue

de Trut [MW,D,A,YC] Rozengracht 114
31-20/612.35.24
11pm-4am Sun only, hip underground party, call for location

■CAFES

Café 't Smalle Egelantiersgracht 12
31-20/623.96.17 *10am-1pm, brown cafe, full bar, outdoor seating*

Reibach [GO] Brouwersgracht 139
31-20/626.77.08 *10am-6pm, from 11am Sun, lunchroom*

Tops Prinsengracht 480
31-20/627.3436 *smoking internet cafe*

■RESTAURANTS

De Bolhoed Prinsengracht 60 (at Tuinstr) 31-20/626.18.03 *vegetarian/vegan*

Burger's Patio 2e Tuindwarsstr 12
31-20/623.68.54 *Italian, plenty veggie*

Granada [E] Leidsekruisstr 13
31-20/625.10.73 *5pm-close, clsd Tue, Spanish, tapas, also bar*

De Vliegende Schotel Nieuwe Leliestr 162 31-20/625.20.41 *5pm-11pm, vegetarian*

■ENTERTAINMENT & RECREATION

De Looier Art & Antiques Centre Elandsgracht 109 31-20/624.90.38
11am-5pm, clsd Fri

■MEN'S CLUBS

Boomerang Heintje Hoeksteeg 8
31-20/622.61.62 *gay sauna & suntanning studio*

Modern [OC] Jacop van Lennepstr 311
31-20/612.17.12 *clsd Sun, sauna*

■EROTICA

Black Body [WC] Lijnbaansgracht 292
(across from Rijksmuseum)
31-20/626.25.53 *clsd Sun, rubber clothing specialists*

Amsterdam—Rembrandtplein

■ACCOMMODATIONS

Aero Hotel [M] Kerkstr 49
(off Leidsestr) 31-20/662.77.28 *some shared baths, opposite Thermos Night Sauna*

➤ **Drake's Guesthouse** [M,GO]
Keizersgracht 669 31-20/638.23.67
rates include videos & free tickets to cruisy cinema

The Golden Bear [M,GO] Kerkstr 37 (at Leidsestr) 31-20/624.47.85 *formerly the Hotel Unique, the oldest gay hotel in Amsterdam, some shared baths*

Greenwich Village [M] Kerkstr 25
31-20/626.97.46

Hotel Amistad [M,WC,GO] Kerkstraat 42 (at Leidsestraat) 31-20/624.80.74
friendly staff, some shared baths

Hotel Monopole [GF] Amstel 60
31-20/624.62.71 *also Cafe Rouge [M], 31-20/624.64.51, open 4pm-1am, till 3am Fri-Sat*

Hotel Orfeo [M] Leidsekruisstr 14 (at Prinsengracht) 31-20/623.13.47
some shared baths, also bar & 24hr sauna

Hotel Orlando [GF,GO]
Prinsengracht 1099 (at Amstel River)
31-20/638.69.15

ITC Hotel [MW,GO] Prinsengracht 1051 (at Utrechtsestr) 31-20/623.02.30
18th-c canal house, great location, also bar & lounge

■BARS

Amstel Taveerne [M,NH] Amstel 54 (at Rembrandtplein) 31-20/623.42.54
4pm-1am, till 3am Fri-Sat

April [★M,V] Reguliersdwarsstr 37 (at Rembrandtplein) 31-20/625.95.72
2pm-1am, till 3am Fri-Sat, 3 bars, cruisy back bar

Netherlands • *Europe*

ARC [★GS,D,F] Reguliersdwarsstr 44
31-20/**689.70.70** *10am-1am, till 3am Fri-Sat, brkfst, lunch & dinner served*

The Back Door Cafe [GS,NH,GO] Amstelstr 28-30 (beneath Back Door nightclub) 31-20/**620-2333** *6pm-1am, till 3am Fri-Sat, clsd Mon-Tue, great cocktails*

Entre-Nous [MW,NH] Halvemaansteeg 14 (at Rembrandtplein) 31-20/**623.17.00** *8pm-3am, till 4am Fri-Sat*

Exit Cafe [M] Reguliersdwarsstr 42 31-20/**625.87.88** *11am-4am, till 5am Fri-Sat, upscale*

Gaiety [★M,YC] Amstel 14 31-20/**624.42.71** *4pm-1am, till 3am Fri-Sat, cafe-bar, terrace*

Habibi Ana [MW,E,MR] Lange Leidsedwarsstraat 4-6 31-06/**620.17.88** *5pm-1am, till 3am Fri-Sat, Arabian clientele, Arabian & int'l music, bellydancing shows wknds*

Hot Spot Café [M,NH] Amstel 102 31-20/**622.83.35** *8pm-3am, till 4am Fri-Sat*

de Krokodil [M,NH,OC] Amstelstr 34 31-20/**626.22.43** *4pm-1am, till 2am Fri-Sat*

Lellebel [M,NH,TG,F,K,DS] Utrechtsestr 4 31-20/**427.51.39** *9pm-4am, from 10pm Fri-Sun, till 4am Fri-Sat, drag bar*

Mix Cafe [★MW] Amstel 50 31-20/**420.33.88** *8pm-3am, till 4am Fri-Sat*

Le Montmartre [★M,NH,YC] Halvemaansteeg 17 31-20/**620.76.22**, 31-20/**624.92.16** *5pm-1am, till 3am wknds, very Dutch*

Music Box [M,AYOR] Paardenstr 9 (near Rembrandtplein) 31-20/**620.41.10** *8pm-2am, till 3am Fri-Sat, hustlers*

Night Life [GS,AYOR] Paardenstr 7 31-20/**622.17.89** *9pm-2am, till 3am Fri-Sat, hustlers*

Reality [M,NH,MR-AF] Reguliersdwarsstr 129 31-20/**639.30.12** *8pm-3am, till 4am Fri-Sat*

Shako [M,NH,B] Gravelandseveer 2 31-20/**624.02.09** *10pm-3am, till 4am Fri-Sat, terrace*

Soho [★MW,YC] Reguliersdwarsstr 36 31-20/**616.12.13** *10pm-3am, 2 flrs*

Spijker [★MO,NH,L,V] Kerkstr 4 31-20/**620.59.19** *1pm-1am, till 3am Fri-Sat, darkroom, TVs showing hardcore porno & cartoons*

■ NIGHTCLUBS

The Back Door [M,D,F,GO,$] Amstelstr 32 (near Rembrandtplein) 31-20/**620-2333** *clsd Mon-Tue & Th, T-dance 10pm-4am Sun*

Club LA [M,D,F,E,DS,YC] Kerkstr 50-52 *6pm-1am, till 3am Fri-Sat, from 5pm Sun, dinner served Mon*

Exit [★MO,D,$] Reguliersdwarsstr 42 31-20/**625.87.88** *11pm-4am, till 5am Fri-Sat, 4 bars, 4 kinds of music, darkroom*

IT [★GS,D,PC,$] Amstelstr 24 31-20/**618.60.40** *11pm-6am Fri-Sat, more gay Sat*

You II [MW,D] Amstel 178 (at Wagenstraat) 31-20/**421.09.00** *10pm-4am, till 5am Fri-Sat, 4pm-1am Sun, clsd Mon-Wed*

■ CAFES

Downtown [★M] Reguliersdwarsstr 31 31-20/**622.99.58** *10am-8pm, till 10pm Fri-Sat, terrace open in summer*

Global Chillage Kerkstr 51 31-20/**777.97.77** *smoking coffee shop*

The Other Side [M,GO] Reguliersdwarsstr 6 31-20/**421.10.14** *10am-1am, gay smoking coffee shop*

■ RESTAURANTS

Garlic Queen Reguliersdwarsstr 27 31-20/**422.64.26** *5pm-close, clsd Mon-Tue, even the desserts are made w/ garlic!*

Golden Temple [NS] Utrechtsestr 126 31-20/**626.85.60** *5pm-10pm, noon-3pm Tue & Sat, Indian-influenced vegetarian & vegan*

De Jaren [GS,YC] Nieuwe Doelenstr 20-22 31-20/**625.57.71** *10am-1am, French, full bar, terrace, also cafe*

Rose's Cantina [★] Reguliersdwarsstr 38-40 (near Rembrandtplein) 31-20/**625.97.97** *5pm-11pm, Mexican, full bar*

Saturnino [MW] Reguliersdwarsstr 5 31-20/639.01.02 *noon-midnight, Italian, full bar*

■ Entertainment & Recreation

Bridge-Sociëteit de Looier Lijnbaansgracht 187 31-20/420.69.88 *gay prize bridge 7:30pm Wed*

■ Retail Shops

Conscious Dreams Dreamlounge Kerkstr 93 31-20/626.69.07 *11am-7pm, till 8pm Th-Sat, noon-5pm Sun, 'psychedelicatessen,' internet access*

■ Men's Clubs

Thermos Day [SW,F] Raamstr 33 31-20/623.91.58 *noon-11pm, till 10pm wknds, cruisy sauna on 5 flrs, also bar & cafe, bears 3rd Sat*

Thermos Night Kerkstr 58-60 (near Leidseplein) 31-20/623.49.36 *11pm-8am, till 10am Sun, sauna on 3 flrs, also bar*

■ Erotica

The Bronx Kerkstr 53-55 (near Leidseplein) 31-20/623.15.48 *huge gay shop for sex supplies, videos, magazines & toys, also cinema*

Der Stringslip Reguliersdwarsstr 59 31-20/638.11.43 *underwear, clothing, leather, rubber, accessories*

Amsterdam—Outer

■ Accommodations

Amsterdam Room Service [GS,GO] 2e van der Helststraat 26 III 31-20/679.49.41 *apt & B&B rooms in Amsterdam*

Johanna's B&B [GS,NS] Van Hogendorpplein 62 31-20/684.85.96, 31-0/624.13.30.56

Prinsen Hotel [GF] Vondelstr 36-38 (near Leidseplein) 31-20/616.23.23

Toro Hotel [GF] Koningslaan 64 (next to Vondelpark) 31-20/673.72.23

■ Bars

Mankind [M,F] Weteringstr 60 31-20/638.47.55 *noon-midnight, clsd Sun, cafe-bar, canal-side terrace*

■ Restaurants

De Vrolijke Abrikoos Weteringschans 76 31-20/624.46.72 *5pm-11:30pm, eclectic organic cuisine, plenty veggie, patio*

■ Entertainment & Recreation

Gallery Faubourg Overtoom 426 31-20/676.19.18 *gay art gallery*

■ Erotica

RoB Weteringschans 253 (at Reguliersgracht) 31-20/625.46.86 *clsd Sun, Amsterdam's first leathershop*

■ Cruisy Areas

Oosterpark [AYOR] at Linnaeusstr *(behind the Tropenmuseum)*

Sarphatipark [AYOR] *near baseball field*

Vondelpark [AYOR] at Vondelstr *in the rose garden*

Westerpark [AYOR] *at night, N of lake*

Spain

Barcelona

■ Info Lines & Services

Casal Lambda Verdaguer y Calle 10 (Metro Drassanes) 34/933.195.550 *5pm-9pm, till 11pm Sat, clsd Sun, community center & cafe, archives & library, also publish magazine*

Colectivo Gay de Barcelona (CGB) 34/93.453.41.25 *staffed 7pm-9pm Mon-Sat, also publish Info Gai*

Coordinadora Gai Lesbiana Finlandia 45, E-08014 34/93.298.00.29, 34/902.120.140 *nat'l gay group*

Telefono Rosa 34-900/601.601 (in Spain), 34/932.981.088 *6pm-10pm Mon-Fri*

Spain • EUROPE

ACCOMMODATIONS

Aparts B&B Barcelona [GF]
Gran Via de las Corts Catalanes
34/677.286.263 *hostel in city center*

▶ **Beauty & the Beach B&B**
[M,NS,WC,GO] 34/93.266.05.62 *B&B, full brkfst, right across from gay nude beach*

California Hotel [GS]
Rauric 14 (at Fernando, Metro Liceu)
34/93.317.77.66

Cama Catalana [GF,NS]
34/93.318.79.03 *bdrm in private home in heart of Barcelona*

Casa.nova [M] Carrer de Diputació (at Casanova) 34/650.165.078,
34/93.451.57.17

Catalonia Albinoni [GF] Avenida Portal de L'Angel 17 34/93.318.41.41 *3-star hotel*

Central Town Rooms & Apartments
[M,WC,GO] Ronda San Pau 51
34/93.442.70.57, 24/677.80.20.40
guest house

Centre Apartments Barcelona
[GS,GO] 31–20/627.25.03
(Amsterdam #)

Éos [M,GO] Gran Via de los Corts Catalanes 575 (at Unversitat Place)
34/93.451.87.72 *B&B in gay district*

Hostal Absolut Centro [M,GO]
Calle Balmes y Calle Casanova
34/649.55.02.38 *hostel, some shared baths*

Hostal Que Tal [M] Mallorca 290 (at Bruch) 34/93.459.23.66

Hotel Axel [MW,SW,WC] Aribau 33 (at Consell de Cent) 34/93.323.93.93 *full brkfst, jacuzzi*

Regencia Colon Hotel [GF,SW]
Sagristans 13–17 (in the Barri Gotic, Metro Jaume I) 34/93.318.98.58,
800/223–1356 *some shared baths*

The Seven Balconies (Natalia's) [MW]
Cervantes 7 34/93.654.23.81.61
B&B, full brkfst, some shared baths

**Beauty and the Beach
Bed & Breakfast
Barcelona, Spain
(34) 93 266 05 62**

**Exclusively gay B&B
Across from gay nude beach Mar Bella
Lavishly appointed penthouse apartment
Air-conditioned rooms with queen beds
Beautiful terrace and internet access
Easy walk to Cultural Forum 2004**

**Visit us at www.beautyandthebeach.net
reservations@beautyandthebeach.net**

Barcelona • Spain

Tony's & Alex Place [MO,GO]
Provença (at Enrique Granados)
34/**661.69.28.36** *guest houses in center of Barcelona*

■ BARS

Aire/ Sala Diana [W,F,S,YC]
Enrique Granados 48/ Valencia 236
34/**93.451.84.62**

Átame [M,V] Consell de Cent 257
34/**93.454.92.73** *6pm-2:30am, till 3am wknds*

Café de la Calle [MW,F,YC] Vic 11
(Metro Gracia) 34/**93.218.38.63**
6pm-3am

Dietrich [★MW,D,F,DS] Consell de Cent 255 (btwn Muntaner & Aribau, Metro Universitat) 34/**93.451.77.07** *6pm-3am, upscale, theater-cafe*

Eagle [M,L,S,V] Passeig Sant Joan 152 (Metro Verdaguer) 34/**93.207.58.56**
8pm-2:30am, till 3am Fri-Sat, darkroom

Espai Magic [M,D,L,DS,S,V,YC] San Marcos 18-20 (Metro Fontana)
34/**93.415.36.10** *9pm-3am, darkroom*

Fenix [M,F] Casanova 64 *6pm-3am, underwear party Th from midnight*

La Luna [M,D,S,V] Av Diagonal 323 (Metro Verdaguer) *9pm-3am, till 4am wknds, darkroom*

Machín [MW,D,F] Casanova 48
34/**93.530.46.56** *6pm-3am, clsd Mon, many events*

Mandarina [MW,F] Diputación 157
34/**93.323.33.93** *9pm-3am, terrace*

New Chaps [M,L,S,V] Av Diagonal 365 (Metro Diagonal) 34/**93.215.53.65**
9pm-3am, till 3:30am Fri-Sat, from 7pm Sun, darkroom

NQN (Nois Quina Nit) [M,D,S,V] Riera de Sant Miquel 59 (Metro Fontana)
34/**93.207.01.20** *10pm-3am, clsd Mon*

Oui Café [M,F] Consell de Cent 247
34/**93.451.45.70** *6pm-3am, terrace*

Padam Padam [MW] Rauric 9
34/**93.302.50.62** *7pm-3am, clsd Sun, also cafe*

Punto BCN [★M,WC] Muntaner 63-65 (enter on Consejo de Ciento Yragón, Metro Universitat) 34/**93.453.61.23**
6pm-2:30am, till 3am wknds, upscale cafe-bar

Sweet Café [MW,D,F] Casanova 75 (Metro Gran Vía) *6pm-midnight, till 3am Th-Sat, clsd Mon*

Topxi [M,D,DS,V] València 358
34/**93.207.01.20** *10pm-5am, dance bar, drag shows nightly*

■ NIGHTCLUBS

Arena [★M,D,F,S,V,YC,$] Balmes 32 (at Diputació, Metro Universitat)
34/**93.487.83.42** *12:30am-5am, clsd Mon (except in Aug), darkroom*

Arena Classic [★M,D,S,V,YC,$]
Diputación 233 (at Balmes, Metro Universitat) 34/**93.487.83.42**
12:30am-6am Th-Sat only, theme nights

Arena Dandy [MO,D] Gran Vía 593
34/**93.487.83.42** *1am-6:30am Fri-Sat*

Arena VIP [★M,D,S,V,YC,$] Gran Vía 593 (Metro Universitat) 34/**93.487.83.42**
1am-6am Fri-Sat only

Martin's [M,D,L,S,V] Passeig de Gràcia 130, lower level (Metro Diagonal)
34/**93.218.71.67** *midnight-5am, 3 flrs, huge darkroom*

Metro [★M,D,L,F,DS,V,YC,$]
Sepúlveda 185 (Metro Universitat)
34/**93.323.52.27** *midnight-5am, T-dance 7pm-10:30pm Sun, drag shows*

Salvation [M,D,F,DS,S,V,YC,$] Ronda San Pere 19-21 (at Plaza Urquinaona)
34/**93.318.06.86** *midnight-close Fri-Sat only*

Tatu [M,D,TG,DS,V,$] Cai Celi 7 (Metro Plaza d'Espanya) 34/**93.425.33.50**
10pm-4am, from 7pm Sun, patio, drag shows, darkroom

Z:eltas [M,D] Casanova 75 (Metro Gran Vía/ Urgell) 34/**93.454.19.02**
10:30pm-3am, clsd Mon-Tue

■ CAFES

De Blanco [M,YC] Villarroel 71
34/**93.451.59.86** *6pm-3am, full bar*

■ RESTAURANTS

7 Portes Passeig d'Isabel II, 14
34/**93.319.30.33** *1pm-1am, Catalan*

Botafumeiro [R] Mayor de Gràcia 81
34/**93.218.42.30** *1pm-1am, Galician seafood specialities, full bar*

Spain • *EUROPE*

Café Miranda [★MW,DS] Casanova 30 (btwn Gran Vía & Sepúlveda, Metro Gran Vía) 34/93.453.52.49 *9pm-1am, int'l/ Mediterranean, full bar, campy decor*

Castro [M,L,S] Casanova 85 (Metro Urgell) 34/93.323.67.84 *1pm-4pm & 9pm-11:30pm, clsd Sun, Mediterranean, full bar*

Comme-Bio Gran Via Corts Catalanes 603 34/93.301.03.76 *vegetarian; also location at Via Laietana 28, 34/93.319.89.68*

dDivine [MW,DS,R] Balmes 24 34/93.317.22.48 *9pm-midnight, clsd Mon-Tue, dinner show hosted by 'Divine'*

La Diva [★MW,TG,C,DS,R] Diputació 172 (Metro Universitat) 34/93.454.63.98 *lunch & dinner, clsd Mon, creative Mediterranean, fabulous drag cabaret*

Little Italy Rec 30 (near Plaza del Born) 34/93.319.79.73 *lunch & dinner*

La Veronica Avinyo 30 34/93.412.11.22 *lunch & dinner, clsd Mon-Tue, terrace*

■ BOOKSTORES

Antinous [WC] Josep Anselm Clavé 6 (btwn Las Ramblas & Ample, Metro Drassanes) 34/93.301.90.70 *lgbt, books & gifts, also cafe*

Cómplices Cervantes 2 (at Avinyó, Metro Liceu) 34/93.412.72.83 *10:30am-8:30pm, from noon Sat, clsd Sun, lgbt, Spanish & English titles*

Nosotr@s Casanova 56 34/93.451.51.34 *lgbt books, magazines, gifts, videos, DVDs*

■ RETAIL SHOPS

Ovlas [★] Laietana 33 34/93.268.76.91 *clothing, also cafe, Italian (DJ & shows Sat)*

■ PUBLICATIONS

Info Gai 34/96.681.23.03 *free monthly newspaper in Catalan*

MENsual 34/93.412.53.80 *slick monthly w/ complete listings for Spain (in Spanish)*

Nois 34/93.454.38.05 *free gay monthly*

■ MEN'S CLUBS

Casanova [F,V] Casanova 57 (at Diputació, Metro Universitat) 34/93.323.78.60 *24hrs, gym equipment, also bar*

Condal [F,V,SW] Espolsasacs 3 (at Carrer Condal, Metro Catalunya) 34/93.301.96.80 *24hrs wknds, 3 flrs, gym equipment, also bar*

Corinto [F,V] Pelaya 62 (at Rambla, Metro Catalunya) 34/93.318.64.22 *24hrs wknds, jacuzzi, maze, bar*

Galilea Sauna [F,V] Calabria 59 (Metro Rocafort) 34/93.426.79.05 *24hrs wknds, bar, internet access*

Lesseps [V,SW] Mauricio Serrahima 9 (Metro Lesseps) 34/93.218.05.92 *also bar*

Thermas [F,V,SW] Diputación 46 (at Entenza, Metro Rocafort) 34/93.325.93.46 *24hrs wknds, jacuzzi, gym equipment, also bar, restaurant, hustlers*

■ EROTICA

Blue Star Av Roma 2-4 (Edificio Torre Catalunya) 34/93.292.60.90

Erotic Museum of Barcelona Ramblas 96 34/93.318.98.65 *10am-midnight*

Kitsch Muntaner 17-19 (at Gran Vía) 34/93.451.20.48

Nostromo Diputació 208 (downstairs, Metro Universitat) 34/93.323.31.94 *video cabins*

Sestienda Rauric 11 (at Farran, Metro Liceu) 34/93.318.86.76 *clsd Sun, ask for gay map*

Skorpius Gran Vía 384-390 34/93.423.40.40 *video cabins*

Zeus Gay Shop Riera Alta 20 (Metro Sant Antoni) 34/93.442.97.95 *clsd Sun, ask for 'MENsual' gay map, also info center*

■ CRUISY AREAS

Parc de Montjuïc [AYOR] btwn Avs del Estadio & Rius y Taulet *behind the archaeology museum*

Parc Sagrada Familia [AYOR]

Plaça de les Glòries [AYOR]

Las Ramblas [AYOR]

Madrid • Spain

Madrid

■ INFO LINES & SERVICES

COGAM (Colectivo de Lesbianas y Gays de Madrid) Fuencarral 37 (Metro Tribunal) 34/91.522.45.17 *lgbt center, groups, library, also cafe-bar*

Gai Inform 34/91.523.00.70 *5pm-9pm, helpline*

■ ACCOMMODATIONS

Gay Hostal Puerta del Sol [M,WC,GO] Plaza Puerta del Sol 14, 4° (at Calle de Alcalá, Metro Sol) 34/91.522.51.26 *centrally located*

Hostal Hispano [GF] Hortaleza 38, 2° izq (at Perez Galdos, Metro Chueca) 34/91.531.48.71

Hostal La Fontana [MW] Valverde 6, 1° (Metro Gran Via) 34/91.521.84.49, 34/91.523.15.61

Hostal la Zona [M,GO] Calle Valverdi 7, 1 & 2 (at Gran Via) 34/91.521.99.04 *full bkfst*

Hostal Odesa [★M] Hortaleza 38, 3° izq (at Perez Galdos) 34/91.521.03.38, 34/91.532.08.28

Hostal Oporto [GF] Calle Zorilla 9, 1st flr (Metro Sol) 34/91.429.78.56 *10-minute walk to gay scene, some shared baths*

Hostal Sonsoles [M] Fuencarral 18, 2° dcha (Metro Chueca) 34/91.532.75.23

Hotel A Gaudí Gran Via 9 (at Alcalá) 34/91.531.22.22 *4-star hotel in the heart of the city*

Hotel Villa Real [M] Plaza de Las Cortes, 10 34/91.420.37.67 *located in the cultural, political & financial center of Madrid, full bkfst*

Pensión HispaDomus [M,GO] San Bartolomé 4, 2° izda 34/91.523.81.27

■ BARS

Bajo Cuerda [★M,NH,S,V,OC] Pérez Galdós 8 (Metro Chueca) 34/91.523.19.01 *9pm-3am, darkroom*

Black & White (Blanco y Negro) [★M,D,DS,S,YC] Libertad 34 (at Gravina, Metro Chueca) 34/91.531.11.41 *8pm-5am, till 6am Fri-Sat, disco downstairs*

Copper [MO,D,L] San Vincente Ferrer 34 (Metro Tribunal) *8pm-3am, till 3:30am Fri-Sat, theme nights, dress code*

Cruising [★M,D,L,V] Pérez Galdós 5 (Metro Chueca) 34/91.521.51.43 *7pm-3am, till 3:30am Fri-Sat, cruise bar, darkroom*

Dumbarton [M,NH,P] Zorrilla 7 (behind Congress bldg, Metro Sevilla, ring to enter) 34/91.429.81.91 *7pm-2am*

Eagle Madrid [M,L,F,V,PC] Pelayo 30 (Metro Chueca) 34/91.531.62.96 *2pm-2am, till 3am Fri-Sat, from 5pm wknds, [MO] after 10pm, theme nights, darkroom*

Hot [M,B,L,V] Infantas 9 (Metro Chueca, ring to enter) *8pm-3am, till 4am Fri-Sat, cruise bar, bears 1st Sat*

Leather Club [MO,D,L,S,V] Pelayo 42 (at Gravina, Metro Chueca) 34/91.308.14.62 *8pm-3am, till 3:30am wknds, strippers Th-Sat, darkroom*

Liquid [M,D,F,V,YC] Barquillo 8 (Metro Banco) 34/91.532.74.28 *9pm-4am, friendly bar*

Lucas [MW,D,S,YC] San Lucas 11 (Metro Chueca) *8:30pm-3:30am*

El Mojito [MW,NH] Olmo 6 (Metro Antón Martin) 34/91.539.46.17 *9pm-2:30am, till 3:30am Fri-Sat, cocktail bar*

Museo Chicote [GS,F] Gran Via 12 *10pm-3am, hip, historic cocktail bar, also restaurant*

PK2 [M,D,V] Libertad 28 (at Augusto Figueroa, next to Truck, Metro Chueca) 34/91.531.86.77 *11pm-5am, darkroom*

Priscilla [GS,D] San Bartolomé 12 (Metro Gran Via) *10pm-6am, till 8am Fri-Sat, trendy dance bar*

Rimmel [M,NH,V] Luis de Góngora 2 (Metro Chueca) *7pm-3am, darkroom, hustlers*

El Sueño Eterno [M,NH,F,S] Pelayo 37 (Metro Chueca) *8pm-3am, also cafe*

Sunrise [MW,D,S] Barbieri 7 (btwn San Marcos & Infantas, Metro Chueca) 34/91.523.28.08 *midnight-close, clsd Mon-Tue*

Damron Men's Travel Guide 2004 675

Spain • *EUROPE*

Troyans/ Bear's Bar [MO,B,L,V] Pelayo 4 (Metro Chueca, ring to enter) **34/91.521.73.58** *9:30pm-3am, 8pm-4am Fri-Sat, clsd Mon, 3 bars, darkroom, cruisy*

Truck [M,D,TG,DS,S,V,$] Libertad 28 (Metro Chueca) **34/91.531.18.70** *10pm-5:30am, clsd Mon, dance bar, drag shows, go-go boys, darkroom*

Why Not? [★GF,$] San Bartolomé 6 (Metro Gran Vía) **34/91.523.05.81** *10pm-6am, till 8am Fri-Sat, fun dance bar*

XXX Café [M,F,C] Clavel 4 (Metro Gran Vía) **34/91.532.84.15** *9:30am-2am, from 4pm Sun, cabaret wknds*

■ NIGHTCLUBS

Cream [MW,D,$] Plaza del Callao 4 (at Sala Bash, Metro Callao) **34/91.531.48.27** *1am-6am Th only*

Escape [MW,D,DS] Gravina 13 (at Plaza de Chueca) *11pm-4:30am Th & 1am-7am Fri-Sat, drag shows*

Mito [MW,NH,D,DS] Augusto Figueroa 3 **34/91.532.88.51** *8pm-close*

Ohm [★M,D] Plaza del Callao 4 (at Sala Bash, Metro Callao) *midnight-close Fri-Sat*

Pasapoga [M,D,YC] Gran Vía 37 (Metro Callao) **34/91.547.57.11** *12:30am-6am Fri-Sat only*

Rick's [★M,D,YC] Clavel 8 (at Infantas, Metro Gran Vía, ring to enter) **34/91.531.91.86** *11pm-5am, 'see-and-be-scene'*

Sachas [M,D,DS] Plaza de Chueca 1 (Metro Chueca) *8pm-5am Th-Sun, bar open 8pm-5am nightly, terrace*

Shangay Tea Dance [★M,D,S,YC,$] Isabel la Catolica 6 **34/91.445.17.41** *9pm-3am Sun*

Strong Center [M,D,L,S,V,$] Trujillos 7 (Metro Santo Domingo) **34/91.541.54.15** *12:30am-7am, till 9am Fri-Sat, the main attraction is its enormous darkroom*

Tábata [M,D,YC,$] Vergara 12 (next to Teatro Real, Metro Opera) **34/91.542.78.32** *10:30pm-late Wed-Sat*

Week-end [★MW,D,A,$] Plaza del Callao 4 (at Sala Bash, Metro Callao) *midnight-6am wknds*

■ CAFES

Baires Café [MW] Gravina 4 (Metro Chueca) **34/91.532.98.79** *also bar*

Bonamara [MW] Hortaleza 51 (Metro Gran Vía, Chueca) **34/91.521.25.64** *2:30pm-2:30am, also bar*

Cafe Acuarela [MW] Gravina 8-10 (Metro Chueca) **34/91.532.87.35, 34/91.570.69.07** *3pm-3am, till 4am Fri-Sat, bohemian cafe-bar*

Cafe Figueroa [★MW] Augusto Figueroa 17 (at Hortaleza, Metro Chueca) **34/91.521.16.73** *noon-1:30am, till 2:30am Fri-Sat, also bar*

Café la Troje [★MW] Pelayo 26 (at Figueroa, Metro Chueca) *4pm-2am, till 3am Wed, full bar*

Color [M] Augusto Figueroa 11 (Metro Chueca) **34/91.522.48.20** *cafe-bar, tapas & desserts*

El Jardin [MW] Infantas 9 **34/91.521.90.45**

Mama Inés [GS] Hortaleza 22 (Metro Chueca) **34/91.523.23.33** *9am-2am, 10am-3am Fri-Sat, sandwiches, pies*

La Sastrería [★MW] Hortaleza 74 (at Gravina, Metro Chueca) **34/91.532.07.71** *10am-2am, till 3am Fri-Sat, from 11am wknds, trendy, internet access*

Star's [MW,D] Marqués de Valdeiglesias 5 (at Infantas, Metro Banco) **34/91.522.27.12** *9am-2am, till 4am Th-Fri, 8pm-4am Sat, clsd Sun, cafe-bar, DJ Th-Sat*

Urania's Cafe [MW] Fuencarral 37 (at COGAM center, Metro Tribunal) **34/91.522.45.17** *5pm-midnight, till 1am Fri-Sat, cafe-bar*

■ RESTAURANTS

A Brasileira Pelayo 49 (Metro Chueca) **34/91.308.36.25** *lunch & dinner, Brazilian*

Abaco Jovellanos 6 **34/91.420.11.64** *dinner Mon-Sat, clsd Sun, int'l cuisine, elegant*

Madrid • Spain

Al Natural Zorrilla 11 (Metro Sevilla) 34/91.369.47.09 *lunch & dinner, vegetarian*

El Armario [MW,S] San Bartolomé 7 (btwn Figueroa & San Marcos, Metro Chueca) 34/**91.532.83.77**

Artemisa [MW] Ventura de la Vega 4 (at Zorrilla) 34/**91.429.50.92** *vegetarian*

Café Miranda [MW,DS] Barquillo 29 (downstairs) 34/**91.521.29.46** *9pm-close, drag shows, kitschy decor*

El Castro de San Francisco [MW] Hernán Cortés 19 (Metro Chueca) 34/**91.531.27.40**, 34/**63.628.52.32** *11am-1:30am, clsd Sun, upscale cafebar & restaurant*

Chez Pomme Pelayo 4 (Metro Chueca) 34/**91.532.16.46** *lunch & dinner, int'l/vegetarian*

La Coqueta [MW] Libertad 6 34/**91.523.06.47** *lunch & dinner, Mediterranean*

La Dame Noire Pérez Galdós 3 (Metro Gran Vía) 34/**91.531.04.76** *9pm-2am, clsd Mon, creative French*

Divina La Cocina [MW] Colmenares 13 (at San Marcos, Metro Chueca) 34/**91.531.37.65** *elegant & trendy*

La Dolce Vita Cardenal Cisneros 58 (Metro Quevedo) 34/**91.445.04.36** *lunch & dinner, Italian, full bar*

Ecocentro Esquilache 4 (at Pablo Iglesias, Metro Rios Rosas) 34/**91.553.55.02** *open till midnight, natural foods, also shop, herbalist school*

Los Girasoles Hortaleza 106 34/**91.308.44.94** *clsd Sun, creative Spanish, tapas*

Gula Gula [★MW,DS] Infante 5 34/**91.420.29.19** *lunch & dinner, clsd Mon, buffet/salad bar, full bar; also Gran Vía 1 location (34/**91.522.87.64**)*

Hudson [M,S] Hortaleza 37 (Metro Gran Vía) 34/**91.532.33.46** *11:30am-3am, clsd Mon, American food, pizza, also bar*

Lombok Augusto Figueroa 32 34/**91.531.35.66** *lunch & dinner, int'l*

Momo [NS,GO] Augusto Figueroa 41 (Metro Chueca) 34/**91.532.71.62** *lunch & dinner*

El Rincón de Pelayo [MW] Pelayo 19 (Metro Chueca) 34/**91.521.84.07** *lunch & dinner*

■ BOOKSTORES

A Different Life Pelayo 30 (Metro Chueca) 34/**91.532.96.52** *11am-2pm & 5pm-10pm, till midnight Sat, clsd Sun, lgbt, books, magazines, music, videos, sex shop downstairs*

Berkana Bookstore [WC] Hortaleza 64 34/**91.522.55.99** *10:30am-9pm, from 11:30am Sat, from noon Sun, lgbt, Spanish & English titles, ask for free gay map of Madrid*

■ RETAIL SHOPS

Ovlas Augusto Figueroa 1 (Metro Chueca) 34/**92.268.76.91** *9:30am-8:30pm, men's clothing, clubwear*

■ PUBLICATIONS

MENsual 34/**93.412.53.80** *slick monthly w/ complete listings for Spain, in Spanish*

Shangay Express 34/**91.445.17.41** *free biweekly gay paper, also publishes Shanguide*

Zero 34–91/**701.00.89** *stylish & intelligent lgbt monthly (en español)*

■ GYMS & HEALTH CLUBS

Energy Gym Hortaleza 19 (Metro Gran Vía, Chueca) 34/**91.532.38.23**

Holiday Gym [GF] Princesa 40 34/**91.547.40.33** *also locations at Plaza de Carlos Trias Bertran 4 & Plaza Republica Dominicana 8*

■ MEN'S CLUBS

Adán [V,SW] San Bernardo 38 (Metro Noviciado) 34/**91.532.91.38** *24hrs wknds, 3 flrs, also bar, hustlers*

Alameda Alameda 20 34/**91.429.87.45** *darkroom, also bar*

Caldea [F,V] Valverde 32 (at Gran Vía, Metro Chueca) 34/**91.522.99.56** *24hrs, gym equipment, bar*

Comendadoras [V] Plaza Comendadoras 15 (Metro Noviciado) 34/**91.532.88.92** *24hrs, also bar*

Cristal [V] Augusto Figueroa 17 (Metro Chueca) 34/**91.531.44.89** *24hrs, also bar*

Spain • *Europe*

Hell Buenavista 14 (Metro Antón Martín) *10:30pm-2:30am, till 3:30am Fri-Sat, rubber/ leather/ uniforms welcome, selective entry policy*

Into the Tank [MO,D,L] 29 Calatrava St (Toledo) *11pm-6am Th, 2am-8am Fri-Sat, 6pm-6am Sun, clsd Mon-Wed, theme nights, basement, dress code*

Men [V] Pelayo 25 (Metro Chueca) **34/91.531.25.83** *bar*

Querella [M,V] Lavapiés 12 (Metro Tirso de Molina) **34/91.528.38.60** *sex parties Wed, darkroom*

Sauna Paraíso [★V] Norte 15 (at San Vicente F, Metro Noviciado) **34/91.522.42.32** *gym equipment, also bar*

Sauna Plaza [V] Gran Vía 88 (in Edificio España, Metro Sevilla) **34/91.548.37.41** *gym equipment, bar*

Sauna Príncipe [F,V] Travesia de las Beatas 3 **34/91.547.91.85** *also bar*

EROTICA

Barco-43 Sex Shop Gay Barco 43 (Metro Gran Via) **34/91.531.49.88** *books, videos, etc*

California [V] Valverde 20 (at Gran Via)

Happy Sex [V] Fuencarral 101, downstairs (Metro Tribunal) **34/91.448.69.02**

SR [GO] Pelayo 7 **34/91.531.59.26** *fetish, military, leather*

CRUISY AREAS

Casa de Campo [AYOR]

Jardín de Atenas [AYOR] *near the Campo del Moro*

Parque del Buen Retiro [AYOR] (Metro Atocha) *days*

Plaza de la Lealtad [AYOR] *near the obelisk, nights*

Plaza de Toros [AYOR] *car cruising*

Sitges

ACCOMMODATIONS

Antonio's Guesthouse [MW,GO] Passeig Vilanova 58 **34/93.894.92.07** *full brkfst*

Casa Sitges [M,GO] Carrer de Francesc Guma 20 (by Sitges Train Station) **34/65.161.04.56** *B&B*

Los Globos [MW,GO] **34/93.894.93.74** *also bar, terrace*

Hotel Liberty [★MW,WC,GO] Isla de Cuba 45 (at A Carbonell) **34/93.811.08.72** *seasonal*

Hotel Romàntic [★GS] Sart Isidre 33 **34/93.894.83.75** *full brkfst, some shared baths, seasonal, also full bar*

Masia Casanova [M,SW,N,GO] Pasaje Casanova 8, Canyelles **34/93.818.80.58** *guest house,10 minutes from town, full brkfst, jacuzzi, ('hetero-friendly' Oct 1−June 1)*

Sitges Holiday Apts [GF] Francisco Gum 25, 08870 **34-93/894-1333** *centrally located 1-brdm apts, near beach*

Sitges, Spain Condo [MW,GO] 32 Pasco de la Ribera **954/563-1576 (US#)** *beach condo*

BARS

Azul [★M,NH,V] Sant Bonaventura 10 **34/93.894.76.34** *9pm-3am, till 3:30pm Fri-Sat*

B-Side [M,F,V] San Gaudencio 7 **34/61.799.09.26** *6pm-3am, clsd Mon, cafe-bar, darkroom*

Bear's Bar [M,B] Bonaire 17 **34/93.894.62.96** *10pm-3am, topless night Th, dark night Sun*

Bourbon's [★M,D,V,YC] Sant Bonaventura 13 **34/93.894.33.47** *10:30pm-3:30am (Sat & Wed only off-season), darkroom*

Casablanca [GS,NH,F] Pau Barrabeitg 5 **34/93.894.70.82** *8:30pm-3am (clsd Tue-Wed off-season), cafe-bar*

Comodín [M,D,DS] Tacó 4 **34/93.894.16.98** *10pm-3:30am, drag shows Sat, darkroom*

Sitges • Spain

El Horno [★M,B,L,F,V] Joan Tarrida Ferratges 6   34/93.894.09.09   *5:30pm-3am, underwear parties Tue & Th, darkroom*

Le Male à Bar [M,D,F,V] Centro Comercial Oasis 28   *7pm-3am (only wknds in winter), terrace, salad bar, dancing till 10am, darkroom*

Mediterraneo [★M,D,YC] Sant Bonaventura 6   34/93.894.33.47   *10pm-3:30am, patio*

Parrot's Pub [★MW,L,S] Plaza Industria 2 (at Primero de Mayo)   34/93.894.78.81   *seasonal, 5pm-3am, from 3pm wknds, patio*

Perfil [M,NH,D,L,DS,V,YC] Espalter 7   34/656.376.791   *10:30pm-3am, drag shows Fri, darkroom*

Phillip's [GS,F] Port Alegre 10 (at San Sebastian Beach)   34/93.894.97.43   *10:30am-3am, terrace, seasonal*

Reflejos [★M,D,YC] Sant Bonaventura 19   *10:30pm-3am, clsd Nov*

Seven [M,D,S,V] Nueva 7   *10pm-3am, till 3:30am Fri-Sat (Wed & Sat only off-season), clsd Nov, terrace, darkroom*

XXL [★M,D,L,V] Joan Tarrida Ferratges 7   *11:30pm-3:30am (clsd Mon-Wed in off-season), industrial-style bar, darkroom, popular underwear parties Tue*

■ NIGHTCLUBS

Organic [M,D,TG,S] Bonaire 15   34/93.894.22.30   *2am-6am (Wed & Sat only off-season), singles party Th*

Trailer [★M,D,YC] Angel Vidal 36   *midnight-6am, seasonal, foam parties in summer*

■ RESTAURANTS

La Borda San Buenaventura 5   34/93.811.20.02   *lunch & dinner*

Can Pagès [MW] Sant Pere 24-26   34/93.894.11.95   *1pm-4pm & 8pm-midnight, clsd Mon*

Casa Hidalgo [WC] San Pablo 12   34/93.894.38.95   *Galician, seafood*

Chez Jeanette Sant Pau 23   34/93.894.00.48   *lunch & dinner, clsd Nov-Dec*

Flamboyant [M] Pau Barrabeitg 16   34/93.894.58.11   *8pm-11:30pm, int'l, full bar, terrace dining, seasonal*

Ma Maison [★MW] Bonaire 28   34/93.894.60.54   *1:30pm-3:30pm & 8:30pm-12:30am, French, full bar, terrace, clsd Nov*

Sucré-Salé [MW] Sant Pau 39   34/93.894.23.02   *lunch & dinner, clsd Tue, crepes & salads*

El Trull [★MW] Mossèn Felix Clará 3 (off Major)   34/93.894.47.05   *dinner only, French*

■ RETAIL SHOPS

Boyzone Sant Bonaventura 18   34/93.894.64.66   *clubwear, swimwear*

Jazz Boutique Bonaire 20   34/93.894.99.63   *men's clothing*

Oscar Marqués de Montroig 2 (at Plaza Industria)   34/93.894.19.76   *designer clothing*

■ GYMS & HEALTH CLUBS

Gym Squash Sitges Barrachina 10   34/93.894.50.05   *gym, also sauna & bar*

■ MEN'S CLUBS

Sauna Sitges [V] Espalter 11   34/93.894.28.63   *bar, darkroom, theme parties*

■ CRUISY AREAS

Calles Primero de Mayo & Marqués de Montroig [AYOR]   *beware of cops!*

Gay Beach [AYOR]   *in front of Calipolis Hotel & Picnic cafe—beware of cops!*

Playa del Muerto [AYOR]   *inquire locally—beware of cops!*

2004 Tours & Tour Operators

Custom Tours 681
Cruises 682
Luxury Tours 683
Great Outdoors Adventures 683
Spiritual/Health Vacations 685
Thematic Tours 685
Various Tours 687

2004 Calendar

Events 688
Film Festivals 697
Leather, Fetish & Bears 701
Conferences & Retreats 705
Spiritual Gatherings 706
The Circuit 707

Custom Tours

Mostly Men

Northmen VIP Travel ☎877/VIP-MEN1 trip planning • concierge services • companion guides in major cities, including New York, Chicago, Seattle & more

Fantasy City Vacations Lijnbaansgracht 64B, 1015 Amsterdam, Netherlands ☎31-20/672 3993, *fax:* 31-20/672 3992 customized hotel & tour packages in Amsterdam

Gay/Lesbian

Qvacations 325 W 16th St #4-W, New York City, NY 10011 ☎212/645-4909, 866/690-6999, *fax:* 212/691-0733 top quality, exciting, affordable tours for the discriminating gay traveler

Straight/Gay

Costa Rica Experts 3166 N Lincoln Ave #424, Chicago, IL 60657 ☎773/935-1009, 800/827-9046, *fax:* 773/935-9252

Embassy Travel 927 N Kings Rd #310, West Hollywood, CA 90069 ☎323/656-0743, 800/227-6668, *fax:* 323/654-4091 personalized tours to Southern Africa & other worldwide destinations

Tour Operators • Cruises

CRUISES

Men Only

Naked Magazine Cruises Nazca Plains Corp, 4640 Paradise Rd #141, Las Vegas, NV 89109 ☎800/863-7080, *fax:* 210/342-4931 naked gay cruises

Mostly Men

Atlantis Events 8490 Sunset Blvd, Ste 610, West Hollywood, CA 90069 ☎310/659-4400, 800/628-5268, *fax:* 310/659-4888 all-gay cruises, resorts & tours • see ad in front color section

Pied Piper Tours 330 W 42nd St, Ste 1804, New York, NY 10036 ☎212/239-2412, 800/874-7312, *fax:* 212/239-2275 gay group cruises

Windjammer Barefoot Cruises 1759 Bay Rd, Miami Beach, FL 33139 ☎305/672-6453, 800/327-2601, *fax:* 305/674-1219

Gay/Lesbian

Bounty International PO Box 21516, Fort Lauderdale, FL 33335 ☎954/763-8663, 888/725-7777, *fax:* 954/763-8693 gay & lesbian yacht charter company • worldwide

Gayribbean Cruises PO Box 192506, Dallas, TX 75219 ☎214/824-8765, 888/813-9947 gay & lesbian group cruises to great destinations around the world

Journeys By Sea PO Box 7500, Fort Lauderdale, FL 33338 ☎954/522-5865, 800/825-3632, *fax:* 954/522-5836 sailing in the Caribbean with gay captain & crew

Ocean Voyager 1275 Bloomfield Ave #26-A, Fairfield, NJ 07004 ☎973/882-5959, 800/435-2531, *fax:* 973/439-2770 hosted gay groups on mainstream upscale cruise ships

Port Yacht Charters 9 Belleview Ave, Port Washington, NY 11050 ☎516/883-0998, 877/DO-A-BOAT, *fax:* 516/883-0998 custom charters worldwide, specializing in the Caribbean • commitment ceremonies • gourmet cuisine

Rainbow Charters 939 Kawaiki Pl, Honolulu, HI 96825 ☎808/396-5995, *fax:* 808/396-5995 gay & lesbian weddings • custom sailing cruises • whale-watching • snorkeling

RSVP 2800 University Ave SE, Minneapolis, MN 55414 ☎612/729-1113, 800/328-7787, *fax:* 612/729-2809 cruises & all-gay/ lesbian resorts in the Caribbean, Mexico & Alaska • see ad in front color section

Sailing Affairs ☎917/453-6425 sailboat charters, day trips, sunset sails & sailing vacations

Straight/Gay

Amazon Tours & Cruises 275 Fontainebleau Blvd #173, Miami, FL 33172 ☎305/227-2266, 800/423-2791, *fax:* 305/227-1880 weekly cruises in the upper Amazon

Whitney Yacht Charters 3214 Casey Key Rd, Nokomis, FL 34275 ☎941/966-9767, 800/223-1426 yacht charters in the Caribbean, Mediterranean & New England states

Great Outdoors Adventures • TOUR OPERATORS

LUXURY TOURS

Men Only

Hanns Ebensten Travel, Inc 513 Fleming St #2, Key West, FL 33040 ☎305/294-8174, 866/294-8174, *fax:* 305/292-9665 worldwide adventures for the uncommon traveler • Peru, Tahiti, Southeast Asia, Greece, Egypt & more

Mostly Men

World Guest 8 75th St, N Bergen, NJ 07047 ☎201/861-5059, 800/873-9691, *fax:* 201/861-4983 indulgent vacations for men • exclusive departures to Cuba

Gay/Lesbian

DavidTours 310 Dahlia Pl, Ste A, Corona del Mar, CA 92625-2821 ☎949/723-0699, 888/723-0699, *fax:* 949/723-0666 luxury small group tours to Europe, Africa, South America, Canada, Asia & the South Pacific

GREAT OUTDOORS ADVENTURES

Men Only

Adventure Bound Expeditions 711 Walnut St, Boulder, CO 80302 ☎303/449-0990, 877/440-0990, *fax:* 303/449-9038 mountain tours & hiking excursions

Mostly Men

Exilio Tours ☎866/265-1915 exclusive gay multisport spa retreats
Touring Cairns Kewarra Beach, QLD, Australia ☎61-7/4055 6462, *fax:* 61-7/4055 6472 rain forest tours in the Cairns hinterland

Mostly Women

Mountain Trek Fitness Retreat & Health Spa Box 1352, Ainsworth Hot Springs, BC V0G 1A0, Canada ☎250/229-5636, 800/661-5161, *fax:* 250/229-5246 a vacation for the mind & body • comprehensive health programs

Gay/Lesbian

Alaska Fantastic Fishing Charters PO Box 2807, Homer, AK 99603 ☎800/478-7777 deluxe cabin cruiser for big-game fishing (halibut)
Alyson Adventures PO Box 1638, Key West, FL 33041-1638 ☎305/296-9935, 800/825-9766, *fax:* 305/292-9665 active adventure vacations
Big Daddy Scuba Tours 1778 Ala Moana Blvd, Lower Lobby, Honolulu 96815 ☎808/922-2600, 888/922-3483, *fax:* 808/949-3483 diving trips in Hawaii
OutWest Global Adventures PO Box 2050, Red Lodge, MT 59068 ☎406/446-1533, 800/743-0458, *fax:* 406/446-1338 specializing in active outdoor vacations worldwide
Rainbow Adventures, Inc PO Box 983, Pahoa, HI 96778 ☎808/965-9011, *fax:* 808/965-9013 intimate hikes for 1 or more women • Volcano Nat'l Park • coastline lava tubes • ancient sacred sites • snorkeling • swimming with dolphins • also B&B
Undersea Expeditions PO Box 9455, Pacific Beach, CA 92169 ☎858/270-2900, 800/669-0310, *fax:* 858/490-1002 warm-water diving & scuba trips worldwide

Tour Operators • Great Outdoors Adventures

Straight/Gay

10,000 Waves PO Box 7924, Missoula, MT 59807 ☎406/549-6670, 800/537-8315 white water & scenic rafting • kayaking • on Montana's premier rivers

Adventure Photo Tours 3111 S Valley View Blvd #X-106, Las Vegas, NV 89102 ☎702/889-8687, 888/363-8687, *fax:* 702/889-6900 off-road sightseeing tours

Ahwahnee Whitewater PO Box 1161, Columbia, CA 95310 ☎209/533-1401, 800/359-9790, *fax:* 209/533-1409 women-only, co-ed & charter rafting

Alpenglow Adventure Tours PO Box 6961, Stateline, NV 89449 ☎530/582-5670, *fax:* 530/582-5670 outdoor adventure at Lake Tahoe & the Sierras • small groups

Amphibious Horizons 600 Quiet Waters Park Rd, Annapolis, MD 21403 ☎410/267-8742, 888/458-8786, *fax:* 410/222-1545 lesbian-owned sea kayaking & adventure travel in the Chesapeake Bay Region • all levels • groups of any type welcome • 30 gorgeous paddle locations

Backroads 801 Cedar St, Berkeley, CA 94710 ☎510/527-1555, 800/462-2848, *fax:* 510/527-1444

Blue Moon Explorations 4658 Blank Rd, Sedro-Woolley, WA 98284 ☎360/856-5622 sea kayaking & x-country ski trips in Pacific Northwest & Hawaii • women-only & co-ed trips • also accommodations

Bluff Expeditions PO Box 219, Bluff, UT 84512 ☎435/672-2446, 888/637-2582 guided back-country archaeological tours by foot, bike, skis, or van

GoNorth Alaska Adventure Travel Center 3500 Davis Rd, Fairbanks, AK 99709 ☎907/479-7272, 866/236-7272, *fax:* 970/474-1041 guided tours throughout Alaska & the Arctic • air taxis & transportation • camper, canoe & bike rentals • hostel accommodations

Great Canadian Ecoventures PO Box 2481, Yellowknife, NT X1A 2P8, Canada ☎867/920-7110, 800/667-9453, *fax:* 867/920-7180 wildlife photography tours

Greentracks 10 Town Plaza, Ste 231, Durango, CO 81301 ☎970/884-6107, 800/9-MONKEY Amazon expeditions

Natural Habitat Adventures 2945 Center Green Ct, Ste H, Boulder, CO 80301 ☎303/449-3711, 800/543-9917, *fax:* 303/449-3712 up-close encounters worldwide with wildlife in their natural habitats

Open Eye Tours PO Box 324, Makawao, HI 96768 ☎808/572-3483 customized private land tours of Maui • visit places seldom seen • refreshing, unique & fun, sharing Maui's best-kept secrets since 1983

Outland Adventures PO Box 16343, Seattle, WA 98116 ☎206/932-7012 ecologically sensitive cultural tours with snorkeling & biking in Central America, Canada, Alaska & Washington State

Paddling South & Saddling South PO Box 827, Calistoga, CA 94515 ☎707/942-4550, 800/398-6200, *fax:* 707/942-8017 horseback, mountain biking & sea kayak trips in Baja • call for complete calendar

Passage to Utah 1338 S Fooothill Dr, Salt Lake City, UT 84108 ☎801/519-2400, 800/677-0553, *fax:* 801/519-2500 custom trips in the West including hiking, horseback riding & river riding

Planet Explorer PO Box 8659, Victoria, BC V8W 3S2, Canada ☎250/656-5181, 877/732-5238, *fax:* 250/656-5182 worldwide adventure travel

Puffin Family Charters PO Box 232813, Anchorage, AK 99523 ☎907/278-3346, 800/978-3346

Rockwood Adventures 839 W 1st St #C, North Vancouver, BC V7P 1A4, Canada ☎604/980-7749, 888/236-6606, *fax:* 604/980-7721 rain forest walks for all levels with free hotel pick-up

Thematic Tours • TOUR OPERATORS

Snow Lion Expeditions Oquirrh Pl, 350 South 400 East #G-2, Salt Lake City, UT 84111 ☎801/355-6555, 800/525-8735, *fax:* 801/355-6566 tours, treks & active vacations in the Himalayas, Tibet, SE Asia, China & more • gay and mixed tours available

Voyager North Outfitters 1829 E Sheridan, Ely, MN 55731 ☎218/365-3251, 800/848-5530 canoe outfitting & trips

Wildlife Safari 346 Rheem Blvd, Moraga, CA 94556 ☎925/376-5595, 800/221-8118, *fax:* 925/376-5059 photographic safaris • Eastern & Southern Africa, Egypt, Mauritius & Seychelles Islands

SPIRITUAL/HEALTH VACATIONS

Gay/Lesbian

Spirit Journeys PO Box 3046, Asheville, NC 28802 ☎828/258-8880, 800/490-3684, *fax:* 828/281-0334 spiritual retreats, workshops & adventure trips

Tellardians GB 197, RR 4, Huntsville, ON P1H 2J6, Canada ☎705/789-8596 guided spiritual retreats with rustic camping • into Algonquin Park & beyond • also motorhome retreats

THEMATIC TOURS

Men Only

Absolute Sultans 465 Hidivyal Palace, 80020 Beyoglu, Istanbul, Turkey ☎90-212/292-9860, *fax:* 90-212/292-9861 luxury tours to Turkey

Pete's Tours PO Box 14373, San Francisco, CA 94114 ☎415/621-2915 full-service travel agency specializing in vacation packages

Toto Tours 1326 W Albion Ave #3W, Chicago, IL 60626 ☎773/274-8686, 800/565-1241, *fax:* 773/274-8695 unique worldwide adventures for gay men

Travel Keys Tours PO Box 162266, Sacramento, CA 95816-2266 ☎916/452-5200 tours of dungeons & castles in Europe • also antique tours (gay/straight)

Mostly Men

Coda International Tours, Inc 255 W 23rd St #3-GW, New York City, NY 10011 ☎212/741-5040, 888/677-2632, *fax:* 212/929-0960 intellectually focused travel programs

Connections Tours 14362 SW 96 Terrace #1, Miami, FL 33186 ☎305/385-3844, 800/688-8463 (OUT-TIME), *fax:* 305/382-1149 discount hotel reservations in Miami, Orlando & more

Tours to Paradise PO Box 3656, Los Angeles, CA 90078 ☎323/962-9169, *fax:* 323/962-3236 tours to Thailand & SE Asia • call for complete itinerary

Ursa Travel 285 Governor St, Providence, RI 02906 ☎401/274-1646 x124, 800/333-5929 x124, *fax:* 401/331-2838 tour & cruise packages & events for the bear & gay communities • individual & group planning

X'otic Destinations 32 Bridgewood Ln, Watervliet, NY 12189 ☎518/782-4975, *fax:* 603/698-8160 specializing in Egypt, Morocco & Middle East • gay-owned

Gay/Lesbian

Adventure Tours, Inc PO Box 6538, Scarborough, ME 04070-6538 ☎207/885-9889, 888/206-6523, *fax:* 207/885-5062 custom individual & group packages to Costa Rica

Tour Operators • Thematic Tours

African Outing 5 Alcyone Rd, Claremont, Capetown 7700, South Africa ☎27-21/671-4028, fax: 27-21/683-7377 gay/lesbian safaris & more • tours customized to your needs

Aloha Lambda Weddings PO Box 159005, Honolulu, HI 96830 ☎808/922-5176, 800/982-5176 all-inclusive wedding ceremonies in Hawaii

Arco Iris Gay Mexico Travel Experts 1286 University Ave, #154, San Diego, CA 92103 ☎619/297-0897, 800/765-4370, fax: 619/297-6419 the original gay Mexico experts • group tours & individual trips to all of Mexico

Brazil Fiesta Tours 323 Geary St #711, San Francisco, CA 94102 ☎415/986-1134, 800/200-0582, fax: 415/986-3029 tours to Brazil & Central & South America

Cruisin' the Castro 375 Lexington St, San Francisco, CA 94110 ☎415/550-8110 award-winning, guided walking tour of the Castro • includes lunch

DaSi Tours PO Box 2307, Seal Beach, CA 90740-1307 ☎877/276-6636, fax: 562/430-0031 independent & group tours in Spain & Portugal

Doin' It Right – In Puerto Vallarta 1010 University Ave #C113-741, San Diego, CA 92103 ☎941/918-2166 (US#), 800/936-3646 1st ('95) Gay, condo villa Puerto Vallarta Specialist • clients receive our
150+ page Vallarta Guide • $100 free coupons • honest descriptions & a live person on the phone! We've slept there!!

GayTravelOne 880 E Sunny Dunes Rd, Palm Springs, CA 92264 ☎760/320-4158, fax: 760/320-5161 all-gay cruises & tours • individual packages to anywhere • Palm Springs getaways • deluxe China with Yangtze River cruise • European river cruises

Going Your Way Tours 109 Dayton Rd #A, Waterford, CT 06385 ☎860/447-1845, fax: 860/447-1845 upscale customized group & individual itineraries worldwide

MexGay Vacations 611 S Catalina St #222, Los Angeles, CA 90005 ☎213/383-9491, 866/639-4299, fax: 213/383-9406 specializing in gay travel to Mexico

National Gay Pilots Association 13140 Coit Rd #320, LB 120, Dallas, TX 75240 ☎972/233-9107 x203, fax: 972/490-4219 several annual gatherings • call for more info

Pacific Ocean Holidays Honolulu, HI ☎808/923-2400, 800/735-6600, fax: 808/923-2499 Hawaii vacation packages

Pro Musica Tours 48 Eighth Ave #127, New York, NY 10014 ☎800/916-0312 gay-only or mixed • performing arts/cultural tours • gay-owned/run

Touristic Service Center Centro Comercial Churriana, Oficina 2, Crta C-344, 29140 Malaga, Spain ☎34 952/43 70 67, fax: 34 952/62 31 05 gay/ lesbian dream vacations in Spain

Venture Out 575 Pierce St #604, San Francisco, CA 94117 ☎415/626-5678, 888/431-6789, fax: 415/626-5679 cultural & easy-adventure tours in Europe

Victorian Home Walks 335 Powell, at Westin St Francis Hotel, San Francisco, CA ☎415/252-9485 historical walking tour of San Francisco's Victorian homes

Way To Go Costa Rica 2801 Blue Ridge Rd, Raleigh, NC 27607 ☎919/782-1900, 800/835-1223, fax: 919/787-1952 personalized itineraries

Winelovertours.com 109 Dayton Rd #A, Waterford, CT 06385 ☎860/447-1845, fax: 860/444-0538 upscale group tours & individual itineraries for foodies & winelovers

Straight/Gay

Alaska Railroad Scenic Tours PO Box 107500, Anchorage, AK 99510-7500 ☎907/265-2494, 800/544-0552, fax: 907/265-2323

Earth Walks PO Box 8534, Santa Fe, NM 87504 ☎505/988-4157 custom, guided tours of American Southwest & Mexico

Various Tours • Tour Operators

Ecotour Expeditions, Inc PO Box 128, Jamestown, RI 02835-1822 ☎401/423-3377, 800/688-1822, *fax:* 401/423-9630 small group boat tours of the Amazon & more • call for color catalog

Heritage Tours 121 W 27th St #1201, New York, NY 10001 ☎212/206-8400, 800/378-4555, *fax:* 212/206-9101 custom trips to Turkey, Spain, South Africa & Morocco

Holbrook Travel 3540 NW 13th St, Gainesville, FL 32609 ☎352/377-7111, 800/451-7111, *fax:* 352/371-3710 natural history tours in Central America, South America & Africa • small groups

Kenny Tours, Ltd 5530 Abbey Ln, Salisbury, MD 21801-2323 ☎410/548-2200, 800/648-1492, *fax:* 410/548-2209 trips to Ireland

Lima Tours Belen 1040, Lima 1, Peru ☎51-1/424-5110, *fax:* 51-1/330-4488 customized, gay-friendly tours to Peru

New England Vacation Tours PO Box 560, West Dover, VT 05356 ☎802/464-2076, 800/742-7669, *fax:* 802/464-2629 gay/lesbian tours (including fall foliage) conducted by a mainstream tour operator

Pacha Tours 1560 Broadway #316, New York, NY 10036 ☎800/722-4288, *fax:* 212/764-5642 trips to Turkey

Quality Tours 5003 Palmetto Ave #83, Pacifica, CA 94044 ☎650/994-5054, *fax:* 650/992-8033 tours of Northern California

Skunk Train- California Western Railroad 299 E Commercial St, Willits, CA ☎707/777-5865 (Willits), 707/964-6371 (Fort Bragg) scenic train trips in Northern California

Stockler Expeditions 10266 NW 4th Ct, Plantation, FL 33324 ☎954/472-7163, 800/591-2955, *fax:* 954/472-7579 trips to Brazil, Argentina & Chile

SunTrips 2350 Paragon Dr, San Jose, CA 95131 ☎408/432-1101, 800/SUN-TRIP, *fax:* 408/436-7825 specializing in Hawaii & Mexico

Turisaven Lerida 381, Quito, Ecuador, *fax:* 593-2/2502 234 tours to Galapagos Islands, rain forest, Peru, Bolivia & more

VIP Tours of New York 205 W 57th St, New York, NY 10019 ☎212/247-0366, 800/300-6203, *fax:* 212/397-0851 private, custom-designed tours of New York • specializing in theater, architecture, gay life & more • groups from one to 100+

VARIOUS TOURS

Gay/Lesbian

Above & Beyond Tours 230 N Via Las Palmas, Palm Springs, CA 92262 ☎760/325-0702, 800/397-2681, *fax:* 760/325-1702 several departures/year to South Pacific, Latin America, South Africa & Europe • cruises • also independent vacations year-round

Footprints 23 College St, Toronto, ON M5G 2B3, Canada ☎416/962-8111, 888/962-6211, *fax:* 416/585-9809 group & independent adventures throughout Asia, Latin America, Africa & more

Friends of Dorothy Travel® 1177 California St #B, San Francisco, CA 94108 ☎415/864-1600, *fax:* 415/864-1601 unique gay & lesbian adventures • individual & group arrangements

Out & About Travel 161 Federal Street, Providence, RI 02903 ☎800/842-4753, *fax:* 401/751-5624 full service gay owned & operated travel agency specializing in gay & lesbian tours, cruises, adventure travel, ski trips & more!

Postcard Destinations 188 Crystal St, Johnstown, PA 15906 ☎814/539-4999, 800/484-3250 x2621, *fax:* 814/532-8882

EVENTS — 2004 Calendar

EVENTS

January 2004

7-11: Utah Gay/ Lesbian Ski Week — *Park City, UT*
☎877/**429-6368**
Email: wehojohn@aol.com **Web:** www.gayskiing.org

25-Feb 1: Aspen Gay Ski Week — *Aspen, CO*
lgbt • 2000+ attendees ☎970/**925-9249**, 800/**367-8290**
✉ c/o *Aspen Gay/Lesbian Community Fund*, PO Box 3143, Aspen, CO 81612
Email: aspengay@rof.net **Web:** www.gayskiweek.com

25-331: GLBT Together Cruise — *Miami, Grand Cayman, and Cozumel, Mexico*
7 days on the Norwegian Dawn for LGBT sports enthusiasts age 35+ • produced by the NCLR, Homophobia in Sports Project & ECWC (a division of Pride Sports)
☎203/**378-6218**, 800/**277-5218** x39
Email: bren927@aol.com **Web:** www.bookavacation.com

February 2004

1: Sydney Gay Mardi Gras — *Sydney, Australia*
extravagant season of festivities, arts & culture, culminating in the parade & world-famous Mardi Gras party • 25th anniversary! ☎011-61-2/**9549-2110**
✉ PO Box 557, Newtown, NSW, Australia 2042
Email: newmardigras@mardigras.org.au **Web:** www.mardigras.org.au

1-9: Whistler Gay Ski Week: Altitude 2004 — *Whistler, BC, Canada*
annual gay/lesbian ski week • parties for boys & girls! • top-notch DJs & venues • popular destination 75 miles N of Vancouver • lgbt • 3000+ attendees
☎604/**899-6209**, 888/**258-4883** ✉ c/o *Out On The Slopes Productions*, 101-1184 Denman St #190, Vancouver, BC, Canada V6G 2M9
Email: altitude@outontheslopes.com **Web:** www.outontheslopes.com

24: Mardi Gras — *New Orleans, LA*
North America's rowdiest block party • mixed gay/straight ☎504/**566-5011**, 800/**672-6124** ✉ c/o *New Orleans Convention & Visitors Bureau*, 1520 Sugarbowl Dr, New Orleans, LA 70112 **Web:** www.neworleanscvb.com

March 2004

7-14: Winterfest — *Lake Tahoe, NV*
nightly entertainment • comedy show • Tahoe Cruise party boat • & of course skiing, at 6 world-class ski resorts • lgbt • 1000 attendees ☎877/**777-4950**
✉ c/o *Nevada Gay/ Lesbian Visitor & Convention Bureau*, PO Box 2215, Carson City, NV 89702
Email: nglvcb@aol.com **Web:** www.LakeTahoeWinterfest.com

14-23: European Gay Ski Week — *the Alps, Italy*
6 days of skiing in the Alps • full board included • ski lessons & stretching classes • health center • disco & evening entertainment • mostly men
☎44-208/**795-6567** ✉ c/o *Alternative Holidays Ltd*, PO Box 16393, London, United Kingdom SE1 4NU
Email: info@alternative-holidays.com **Web:** www.alternative-holidays.com

2004 Calendar EVENTS

26-28: Rainbow Ski Weekend — *Mammoth Mountain, CA*
3 days of fun on the slopes in Northern California • complete packages available • book early • lgbt • $399 ☎619/**435-0996** ✉ c/o *Rainbow Ski Weekend*, PO Box 182170, Coronado, CA 92178-2170
Email: Leftie69@aol.com **Web:** www.rainbowski.com

31-April 4: OutBoard — *TBA, CO*
annual lesbian/ gay snowboarding festival • 300+ attendees
Email: webmaster@outboard.org **Web:** www.outboard.org

TBA: Desert AIDS Walk — *Palm Springs, CA*
benefits Desert AIDS Project • lgbt ☎760/**325-4402** ✉ c/o *Desert AIDS Project*, PO Box 2890, Palm Springs, CA 92263
Email: information@desertaidsproject.org **Web:** www.desertaidsproject.org

April 2004

17: AIDS Walk St Louis — *St Louis, MO*
☎314/**367-7273** ✉ c/o *AIDS Foundation of St Louis*, 5615 Pershing Ave #11, St Louis, MO 63112 **Email:** aidstl@earthlink.net **Web:** www.aidstl.org

26-May 2: Equality Forum — *Philadelphia, PA*
annual forum on lgbt culture • film, performances, literature, sports, seminars, parties & more ☎215/**732-3378**, 800/**990-3378** ✉ c/o *PrideFest America*, 200 S Broad St #600, Philadelphia, PA 19102
Email: info@equalityforum.com **Web:** www.equalityforum.com

30: Queensday — *Amsterdam, Netherlands*
huge street festival to celebrate what was originally the birthday of the Queen Mother • lgbt

TBA: AIDS Walk Miami — *Miami, FL*
lgbt ☎305/**667-9296** ✉ c/o *CARE Resource*, 225 NE 34 St #201, Miami, FL 33137
Email: info@careresource.org **Web:** www.careresource.org

TBA: Philadelphia Black Gay Pride — *Philadelphia, PA*
a weekend of social & cultural activities • films, BBQ, spoken word, parties & more • lgbt ☎215/**496-0330** ✉ c/o *Philadelphia Black Pride, Inc*, 1201 Chestnut St, 5th Fl, Philadelphia, PA 19107
Email: pride@coloursinc.org **Web:** www.phillyblackpride.org

May 2004

1: Bad Boys Pool Party — *Palm Springs, CA*
gay porn stars mingle w/ fans to raise money for a great cause • mostly men
Email: willclark3@aol.com **Web:** www.badboyspoolparty.com

1: Boybutante Ball — *Athens, GA*
lgbt • 1000+ attendees ☎706/**227-3530** ✉ c/o *Boybutante AIDS Foundation, Inc*, PO Box 6013, Athens, GA 30604-6013
Email: missthing@boybutante.org **Web:** www.boybutante.org

2: Splash Days — *Austin, TX*
weekend of parties in clothing-optional Hippie Hollow, highlighted by the beer barge on Sunday ☎512/**474-6481** ✉ c/o *Tavern Guild*, PO Box 13004, Austin, TX 78711
Email: splash2000@aol.com

EVENTS — 2004 Calendar

6-10: Cancun Int'l Gay Festival — *Cancun, Mexico*
lgbt ☎619/297-0897, 800/765-4370
Email: Info@ArcoIrisTours.com **Web:** www.ArcoIrisTours.com

25-31: Annual Gay Bowling Tournament — *Phoenix, AZ*
☎703/820-8313 ✉ c/o *IGBO*, PO Box 312, Westerville, OH 43086
Email: president@igbo.org **Web:** www.igbo.org

27-31: Pensacola Memorial Day Weekend — *Pensacola, FL*
many parties on beaches & in bars • lgbt • 35,000+ attendees ☎850/438-0333

28-31: Armory Sports Classic — *Atlanta, GA*
softball & many other sports competitions • mostly men ☎404/881-9280
✉ c/o *Armory Bar*, 836 Juniper St NE, Atlanta, GA 30308

28: Gay/ Lesbian Night at Great America — *Santa Clara, CA*
join 10,000 men & women for a special night at Northern California's favorite amusement park • live performances • dancing till 3am • lgbt

TBA: AIDS Walk — *Long Island, NY*
lgbt ☎631/385-2451 ✉ c/o *LIAAC*, PO Box 2859, Huntington Stn, NY 11746
Email: info@aidswalkli.org **Web:** www.AIDSwalkLongIsland.org

TBA: AIDS Walk New York — *New York City, NY*
AIDS benefit • mixed gay/straight ☎212/807-9255 ✉ c/o *Gay Men's Health Crisis*, PO Box 10, Old Chelsea Stn, New York, NY 10113-0010
Email: info@gmhc.org **Web:** www.gmhc.org

TBA: Art for AIDS/ Art for Change — *Pittsburgh, PA*
huge party benefitting AIDS charities • lgbt ☎412/441-9786 ✉ c/o *Persad Center*, 5150 Penn Ave, Pittsburgh, PA 15224

TBA: Minnesota AIDS Walk — *Minneapolis, MN*
enjoy a walk through Minnehaha Park & raise money for local AIDS organizations • mixed gay/straight • 12,000 attendees ☎612/373-2411 ✉ c/o *Minnesota AIDS Project*, 1400 Park Ave, Minneapolis, MN 55404
Email: info@mnaidsproject.org **Web:** www.mnaidsproject.org

TBA: Splash: Houston Black Gay Pride — *Houston, TX*
lgbt ☎713/237-9431, 832/443-1016 ✉ c/o *Houston Splash*, PO Box 35431, Houston, TX
Email: info@houstonsplash.com **Web:** www.houstonsplash.com

TBA: Spoleto Festival USA — *Charleston, SC*
one of the continent's premier avant-garde cultural arts festivals • mixed gay/straight ☎843/579-3100 ✉ c/o *Spoleto Festival USA*, PO Box 157, Charleston, SC 29402-0157
Email: receptionist@spoletousa.org **Web:** www.spoletousa.org

June 2004

on-going: LGBT Pride — *Everywhere, USA*
celebrate yourself & attend one – or many – of the hundreds of Gay Pride parades & festivities happening in cities around the continent
Email: info@interpride.org **Web:** www.interpride.org

2004 Calendar — EVENTS

on-going: Music in the Mountains — *Nevada City, CA*
summer music festival • mixed gay/straight ☎530/**265-6124**, 800/**218-2188** ✉ c/o *Music in the Mountains*, PO Box 1451, Nevada City, CA 95959
Email: mim@musicinthemountains.org **Web:** www.musicinthemountains.org

1-7: Gay Days Orlando — *Orlando, FL*
including Gay Day at Disney & Islands of Adventure • 4 days of parties & fun for boys & girls alike! • lgbt ☎407/**896-8431** ✉ c/o *GayDays, Inc*, 1011 Virginia Dr #101, Orlando, FL 32803
Email: info@gaydays.com **Web:** gaydays.com

1-July: National Queer Arts Festival — *San Francisco, CA*
performances & exhibitions in the San Francisco Bay Area highlighting artists from around the country • lgbt ☎415/**552-7709**, 415/**552-7200** ✉ c/o *Queer Cultural Center & Harvey Milk Inst*, 1800 Market St, San Francisco, CA 94102
Email: nqaf@aol.com **Web:** www.QueerCulturalCenter.org

3-27: SNAP! Fest — *Omaha, NE*
local theater festival • mixed gay/straight ☎402/**341-2757** ✉ c/o *SNAP! Productions*, 3225 California St, Omaha, NE 68105
Email: info@snapproductions.com **Web:** www.snapproductions.com

4-20: Juneteenth Jamboree of New Plays — *Louisville, KY*
annual theater festival • new works about the African-American experience • many with gay themes • mixed gay/straight ☎502/**636-4200** ✉ c/o *Juneteenth Legacy Theatre*, PO Box 3463, Louisville, KY 40201
Email: juneteenthlegacy@aol.com **Web:** www.juneteenthlegacytheatre.com

6-12: AIDS LifeCycle — *San Francisco to Los Angeles, CA*
bike from San Francisco to Los Angeles to raise money for HIV/AIDS services ☎866/**BIKE-4AIDS** ✉ c/o *San Francisco AIDS Foundation*, PO Box 7151, San Francisco, CA 94120
Email: info@aidslifecycle.org **Web:** www.aidslifecycle.org

6: AIDS Walk & 5K Run Boston — *Boston, MA*
mixed gay/straight • 12,000 attendees ☎617/**424-WALK** ✉ c/o *AIDS Action Committee*, 294 Washington Street, 5th floor, Boston, MA 02108
Email: walkinfo@aac.org **Web:** www.aidswalkboston.org

12: Razzle Dazzle Dallas — *Dallas, TX*
dance party & carnival benefits PWAs • 10,000+ attendees • $8-12 ☎214/**520-7336** ✉ c/o *Razzle Dazzle Dallas*, 2429 Reagan St #211, Dallas, TX 75219
Email: rddpresident@yahoo.com **Web:** www.razzledazzledallas.com

20-27: Black Pride NYC — *New York City, NY*
multicultural LGBT festival with a wide array of entertainment, forums, workshops & events • lgbt ☎212/**613-0097** ✉ c/o c/o *GMHC*, 119 W 24th St, New York City, NY 10011
Email: blackpridenyc@aol.com **Web:** www.blackpridenyc.com

20: Unofficial Gay Day at Cedar Point — *Sandusky, OH*
wear red to show your support on the unofficial Gay Day at this popular amusement park • mixed gay/straight
Email: info@lgcsc.org

EVENTS   2004 Calendar

23: Pearl Day at Six Flags *Atlanta, GA*
unofficial gay celebration at Six Flags amusement park • show your support with a string of Commemorative Pearls • proceeds go to local charities • lgbt
☎404/**885-6800** ext 232, 404/**872-3975**
Email: claudia.zevallos@aidatlanta.org **Web:** www.pearlday.com

24-28: Mexico City Gay Pride Week *Mexico City, Mexico*
5 days of parties & more • lgbt ☎619/**297-0897**, 800/**765-4370**
Email: arcoiris7@aol.com **Web:** www.mexcity.8m.com

26-27: Black Lesbian/ Gay Pride *San Francisco, CA*
celebrate with a weekend of conferences, awards ceremonies & parties • lgbt
☎510/**268-0646** ✉ c/o *californiablackprides.org*, 484 Lakepark Ave #1, Oakland, CA 94610
Email: bglt@pacbell.net **Web:** www.californiablackprides.org

26-27: San Francisco LGBT Pride Parade/ Celebration *San Francisco, CA*
lgbt ☎415/**864-3733** ✉ c/o *SFLGBTPCC*, 1390 Market St #903, San Francisco, CA 94102
Email: sfpride@aol.com **Web:** www.sfpride.org

TBA: Black Gay Pride *Memphis, TN*
lgbt ☎901/**521-6922** **Web:** www.chocolatecityusa.com

TBA: Gay Day at Six Flags *Jackson, NJ*
unofficial Gay Day at this popular amusement park • wear red to show your support • lgbt

TBA: Midwest Male Nudist Gathering *Camp Gaea, KS*
men only • 175+ attendees • $145 ☎763/**263-2282** ✉ c/o *MMNG*, PO Box 52, Big Lake, MN 55309
Email: to_attend@nakedmn.org **Web:** www.nakedmn.org

TBA: PrideFest *Milwaukee, WI*
celebrate lgbt pride at Henry W Maier Festival Park • lgbt ☎414/**645-FEST**
✉ c/o *PrideFest*, PO Box 511763, Milwaukee, WI 53203-0301
Email: info@pridefest.com **Web:** www.pridefest.com

TBA: Tampa Jamz *Tampa, FL*
celebrate African-American gay pride in sunny Tampa • lgbt **Web:** www.clikque.com

July 2004

1-4: At the Beach Weekend *Los Angeles, CA*
celebrate a weekend of Black gay pride in Malibu • lgbt ☎323/**293-4282**
✉ c/o *ATB*, 4745 W Slauson Ave, Los Angeles, CA 90056
Email: atbla@aol.com **Web:** www.atbla.com

1-4: Int'l Association of Country Western Dance Clubs Annual Convention *Columbus, OH*
check website for other events during the year • lgbt • 400-600 attendees
☎972/**395-7045**, 416/**923-8247** (in Canada) ✉ c/o *IAGLCWDC*, 5534 Edmondson Pike, PMB 107, Nashville, TN 37211
Email: info@iaglcwdc.org **Web:** www.outcountrydance.com

2004 Calendar   EVENTS

17-24: Black & White Men Together Convention *Atlanta, GA*
mostly men • 200+ attendees ☎800/**624-2968**, 412/**421-1000** ✉ c/o *National Association of Black & White Men Together*, PO Box 81236, Pittsburgh, PA 15217
Email: nabwmt@mindspring.com **Web:** www.nabwmt.com

28-Aug 3: Adventure Summer Camp Week *Whistler, BC, Canada*
5-day outdoor adventure in Whistler, followed by 2 days of partying in Vancouver for Pride Weekend • top-notch DJs & venues • 75 miles N of Vancouver • mostly men ☎604/**899-6209**, 888/**258-4883**
Email: info@outontheslopes.com **Web:** www.outontheslopes.com

TBA: AIDS Walk San Francisco *San Francisco, CA*
mixed gay/straight • 27,000+ attendees ☎415/**392-9255** ✉ c/o *Miller Zeichik & Assoc*, PO Box 193920, San Francisco, CA 94119-3920
Email: aidswalksf@yahoo.com **Web:** www.aidswalk.net

TBA:Crape Myrtle Festival *Raleigh-Durham, Chapel Hill, NC*
weeklong festival to raise money for AIDS & lgbt concerns • gala Saturday • also supporting events throughout the year • mixed gay/straight • 1500+ attendees ☎919/**832-2103** ✉ c/o *Crape Myrtle Festival, Inc*, PO Box 10043, Raleigh, NC 27605
Email: info@crapemyrtlefest.org **Web:** www.crapemyrtlefest.org

TBA: EuroPride 2004 *Cologne, Germany*
parties, politics, performance & more • there is something for everyone at this massive celebration of gay pride ☎49-177/**317 0943** ✉ c/o *European Pride Organisers Assoc*, Buelowstrasse 106, Berlin, Germany D-10783
Email: presse@europride.de **Web:** www.europride.de

TBA: Hotter Than July Weekend *Detroit, MI*
celebrate African-American gay pride in the Motor City • lgbt ✉ c/o *Hotter Than July*, PO Box 3025, Detroit, MI 48231 **Web:** www.hotterthanjuly.com

TBA: Independence 2004:
Celebrate the African-American LGBT Community *Chicago, IL*
a weekend of parties, seminars & more • lgbt ☎773/**731-8665** ✉ c/o *Chicago Black Pride, Inc*, 7836 S Kingston Ave, Chicago, IL 60649
Email: chicagobp@aol.com **Web:** www.windycitypride.org

TBA: Paradise Ride Hawaii *4 islands, HI*
7-day cycling event to raise funds for HIV/AIDS service • 390 miles on the islands of Oahu, Kauai, Maui & Molokai ☎888/**285-9866** ✉ c/o *Life Foundation*, 233 Keawe St #226, Honolulu, HI 96813
Email: info@paradiseridehawaii.org **Web:** www.paradiseridehawaii.org

August 2004

6-8: Minnesota AIDS Trek *St Paul, MN*
annual 175-mile bike ride to fight AIDS • mixed gay/straight ☎651/**917-3504** ✉ 499 Lynhurst Ave W, St Paul, MN 55104
Email: info@aids-trek.org **Web:** www.aids-trek.org

13-15: Black Pride *Jacksonville, FL*
celebrate African-American gay/lesbian culture • 2nd wknd in August • lgbt ☎904/**318-0045**
Email: ycluby@aol.com **Web:** www.jaxxblackpride.com

EVENTS — 2004 Calendar

13-22: GNI (Gay Naturist Int'l) Gathering — *TBA, USA*
weeklong gathering of gay nudists • price includes food, lodging & entertainment • workshops • men only • 800 attendees ☎ 954/567-2700 ✉ c/o *GNI*, PMB #F-5, 1007 N Federal Hwy, Ft Lauderdale, FL 33304-1422
Email: gni@gaynaturists.org **Web:** www.gaynaturists.org

16-22: 'Camp' Camp — *Kezar Falls, ME*
summer camp for lgbt adults • sports, pottery, theater, yoga & more • gbt • $924 ☎ 888/924-8380 ✉ c/o *Camp Camp*, 8 Perkins Ave, Hyde Park, MA 02136
Email: info@campcamp.com **Web:** www.campcamp.com

16-22: Provincetown Carnival — *Provincetown, MA*
☎ 800/637-8696, 508/487-2313 ✉ c/o *Provincetown Business Guild*, PO Box 421, Provincetown, MA 02657
Email: pbguild@capecod.net **Web:** www.ptown.org

19-22: Black Gay Pride — *Minneapolis/St Paul, MN*
lgbt ☎ 612/827-1666 ✉ 3515 Chicago Ave S, Minneapolis, MN 55407
Email: mwhswm@hotmail.com **Web:** www.blackpridemn.com

22-23: Sunset Junction Fair — *Los Angeles, CA*
carnival, arts & information fair on Sunset Blvd in Silverlake benefits Sunset Junction Youth Center • 75,000 attendees ☎ 323/661-7771 ✉ c/o *Sunset Junction*, PO Box 26565, Los Angeles, CA 90026
Email: sunsetjunction@sunsetjunction.org **Web:** www.sunsetjunction.org

27-30: Atlanta Black Pride Weekend — *Atlanta, GA*
celebrate Black Pride over Labor Day weekend in Atlanta • lgbt ☎ 404/872-6410 ✉ c/o *In The Life Atlanta*, PO BOX 7206, Atlanta, GA 30357
Email: info@inthelifeatl.com **Web:** www.inthelifeatl.com

TBA: AIDS Walk Colorado — *Denver, CO*
☎ 303/837-0166 ✉ c/o *Colorado AIDS Project*, PO Box 18529, Denver, CO 80218-0529
Email: info@aidswalkcolorado.org **Web:** www.aidswalkcolorado.org

TBA: Black Unity Pride Celebration — *Cleveland, OH*
Ohio's oldest & largest event celebrating African-American gay/lesbian culture • lgbt ☎ 216/462-0257, 888/825-5226 ✉ c/o *Black Out*, PO Box 14553, Cleveland, OH 44114
Email: shakaspr94@aol.com **Web:** www.chocolatecityusa.com

TBA: National Gay Softball World Series — *TBA, USA*
lgbt ☎ 412/362-1247 ✉ c/o *NAGAAA*, 1014 King Ave, Pittsburgh, PA 15206
Email: board@nagaaa.org **Web:** www.nagaaa.org

TBA: Northalsted Market Days — *Chicago, IL*
a good ol' summer block party on Main St of Boys' Town, USA • lgbt ☎ 773/883-0500 ✉ c/o *Chicago Area Gay & Lesbian Chamber of Commerce*, 3713 North Halsted, Chicago, IL 61613

TBA: Rendezvous 2004 — *Medicine Bow Nat'l Forest, WY*
5-day camping festival to celebrate lgbt pride • 400+ attendees ☎ 307/778-7645 ✉ c/o *United Gays & Lesbians of Wyoming*, PO Box 6837, Cheyenne, WY 82003
Email: info@uglw.org **Web:** www.uglw.org

2004 Calendar — EVENTS

September 2004

1-6: Southern Decadence — *New Orleans, LA*
gay end of summer blow out • Southern Decadence parade • mostly men
☎504/**522-8049** ✉ c/o *Official Southern Decadence*, 828-A Bourbon St, New Orleans, LA 70116
Email: info@southerndecadence.com **Web:** www.southerndecadence.com

3-6: Great Alberta Campout — *Red Deer, AB, Canada*
3 days of friendly camping fun • meet & greet Friday • special meals all wknd • games, dances, more • presented by Gay & Lesbian Assoc of Central Alberta • always Labor Day wknd • lgbt ✉ c/o *GALACA*, Box 1078, Red Deer, AB, Canada T4N 6S5
Email: gacampout@hotmail.com **Web:** members.shaw.ca/GACampout/

3-6: Labor Day LA — *Los Angeles, CA*
weekend-long AIDS fundraising celebration with many events • lgbt
☎800/**522-7329** ✉ c/o *Foundation for Educational Research*, PO Box 69504, Los Angeles, CA 90069-9504

5: Last Splash — *Austin, TX*
weekend of parties in clothing-optional Hippie Hollow, highlighted by the beer barge on Sunday ☎512/**474-6481** ✉ c/o *Tavern Guild*, PO Box 13004, Austin, TX 78711
Email: webmaster@charliesaustin.com **Web:** www.charliesaustin.com

19: AIDS Walk Toronto — *Toronto, ON, Canada*
walk in Toronto & cities across Canada to raise money to fight AIDS • lgbt
☎416/**340-8484 x263** ✉ c/o *AIDS Committee of Toronto*, 399 Church St, Toronto, ON, Canada M5B 2J6
Email: ebruce@actoronto.org **Web:** www.aidswalktoronto.org

19: Out in the Park — *Springfield, MA*
unofficial gay day at Six Flags New England • wear red to show your support • lgbt • 1000+ attendees
Email: beproud@masspride.net **Web:** www.masspride.net/outinthepark

24: Gay Night at Six Flags Magic Mountain — *Valencia, CA*
lgbt ☎661/**222-7788** ✉ c/o *Odyssey Adventures*, PO Box 221477, Newhall, CA 91322
Email: odsyadv@pacbell.net **Web:** www.odysseyadventures.com

TBA: AIDS Walk Seattle — *Seattle, WA*
mixed gay/straight • 7000+ attendees ☎206/**329-6923** ✉ c/o *Lifelong AIDS Alliance*, 1002 E Seneca, Seattle, WA 98122
Email: aidswalk@lifelongaidsalliance.org **Web:** www.aidswalk2002.org

TBA: Camp WillowSwish — *Lake Murray, OK*
3-day camping extravaganza • anything goes! • mostly men
Email: info@willowswish.com **Web:** www.willowswish.com

TBA: Gay Day at Paramount Kings Island — *Cincinnati, OH*
lgbt ☎513/**591-0200** ✉ c/o *Gay & Lesbian Community Center*, 4119 Hamilton Ave, Cincinnati, OH 45223
Email: mail@glbtcentercincinnati.com **Web:** www.glbtcentercincinnati.com

EVENTS — 2004 Calendar

TBA: Gay Ski Week Queenstown — *Queenstown, New Zealand*
☎ 64-4/**917-9176**
Email: info@gayskiweeknewzealand.com **Web:** www.gayskiweeknewzealand.com

TBA: New York to the Hamptons Challenge — *Long Island, NY*
100-mile bike ride to benefit victims of hate crimes & HIV/AIDS • ☎877/**612-BIKE** ✉ c/o *LINCS*, PO Box 4169, Huntington Stn, NY 11743
Email: info@bikechallenge.com **Web:** www.BikeChallenge.com

October 2004

3: Castro Street Fair — *San Francisco, CA*
arts & community groups street fair • co-founded by Harvey Milk
☎415/**467-3354**

8-11: Baltimore Black Gay Pride — *Baltimore, MD*
lgbt ☎443/**524-1555** ✉ c/o *BBGP Inc*, 714 Park Ave Lower Level, Baltimore, MD 21201
Email: bmoreblackgaypride@aol.com **Web:** bmoreblackgaypride.org

9-11: Black Lesbian/ Gay Pride — *Oakland, CA*
celebrate with a weekend of conferences, awards ceremonies & parties • lgbt
☎510/**268-0646** ✉ c/o *californiablackprides.org*, 484 Lakepark Ave #1, Oakland, CA 94610
Email: bglt@pacbell.net **Web:** www.californiablackprides.org

11: National Coming Out Day — *Everytown, USA*
check local listings for events in your area or visit www.hrc.com/ncop
☎202/**628-4160**, 800/**866-6263** ✉ c/o *Human Rights Campaign*, 1640 Rhode Island Ave, Washington, DC 20036
Email: ncop@hrc.org **Web:** www.hrc.org

17: AIDS Walk Atlanta — *Atlanta, GA*
mixed gay/straight • 10,000+ attendees ☎404/**870-7700** ✉ c/o *MZA Events, Inc*, 1438 W Peachtree St NW #100, Atlanta, GA 30309
Email: aidswalkat@mzainc.com **Web:** www.aidswalk.net

17: AIDS Walk Philly — *Philadelphia, PA*
lgbt ☎215/**731-9255** ✉ c/o *AIDSFUND*, 1227 Locust St, Philadelphia, PA
Email: aidsfund@aidsfundphilly.org **Web:** www.aidsfundphilly.org

22-31: Fantasy Fest — *Key West, FL*
10 days of parties, costume contests, street fairs, masquerade balls & parades • 70,000 attendees ☎305/**296-1817** ✉ c/o *Fantasy Fest*, PO Box 230, Key West, FL 33040
Email: kwfanfest@aol.com **Web:** www.fantasyfest.net

30-Nov 7: Annual Black Lesbian/ Gay Cruise — *Caribbean*
lgbt ☎415/**922-2916**, 888/**922-2916**
Email: bgc@songmaster1.com **Web:** www.bgl.com

TBA: AIDS Walk LA — *Los Angeles, CA*
annual AIDS fundraiser at Paramount Pictures • mixed gay/straight
☎213/**201-9255** ✉ c/o *AIDS Walk LA*, 3550 Wilshire Blvd #890, Los Angeles, CA 90010
Email: lainfo@aidswalk.net **Web:** www.aidswalk.net

2004 Calendar — FILM FESTIVALS

TBA: Black Gay Pride — *Dallas, TX*
lgbt ☎214/742-2101 ✉ c/o *Underground Station*, PO Box 224571, Dallas, TX 75222 **Web:** www.chocolatecityusa.com

TBA: Fantasia Fair — *Provincetown, MA*
annual 10-day fair for trannies & those who love them • costume ball, workshops, talent show, wine tasting • all genders welcome ☎207/621-0858 ✉ c/o *Outreach Institute of Gender Studies*, 126 Western Ave #246, Augusta, ME 04330 **Web:** www.ptown.org

TBA: International Gay Rodeo Finals — *TBA, USA*
check with local chapters for events throughout the year in your area ☎303/832-4472 ✉ c/o *International Gay Rodeo*, 900 E Colfax, Denver, CO 80218
Email: spokesman@igra.com **Web:** www.igra.com

November 2004

1-14: Glasgay — *Glasgow, Scotland*
UK's largest lesbian & gay multi-arts festival
Email: info@glasgay.org.uk **Web:** www.glasgay.co.uk

6-7: Greater Palm Springs Pride — *Palm Springs, CA*
come out for a weekend of gay films, dance parties, and a parade on Sunday ☎760/416-8711 ✉ 1 Pavillion Way, Palm Springs, CA 92264
Email: PSPride@dc.rr.com **Web:** www.PSPride.org

TBA: Divas in the Desert: Black Gay Pride Weekend — *Phoenix, AZ*
mostly men ✉ c/o *FinWill Productions*, 5713 W Zoe Ella Wy, Glendale, AZ 85306

December 2004

3-5: Holly Folly — *Provincetown, MA*
gay & lesbian holiday celebration • fabulous parties • holiday concert • open houses ☎888/887-8696
Email: info@davidflower.com **Web:** www.davidflower.com

31: Mummer's Strut — *Philadelphia, PA*
big New Year's Eve party • followed by New Year's Day Parade • mixed gay/straight • $40-50 ☎215/732-3378
Email: parade@mummers.com **Web:** mummers.com

TBA: IAGLBC Annual Bridge Tournament — *Palm Springs, CA*
Int'l Association of Gay & Lesbian Bridge Clubs ☎877/429-6368
Email: wehojohn@aol.com **Web:** www.GayBridge.org

FILM FESTIVALS

February 2004

13-15: Out Far! — *Phoenix, AZ*
Phoenix Int'l lesbian & gay film festival ☎602/410-1074 ✉ c/o *Vision Events, Inc*, 619 E Vista Ave, Phoenix, AZ 85020
Email: OutFarFilmFest@aol.com **Web:** www.outfar.org

Film Festivals — 2004 Calendar

27-29: Reel Identities — *New Orleans, LA*
gay/lesbian ☎504/**945-1103** ✉ 2114 Decatur St, New Orleans, LA
Email: info@lgccno.net **Web:** www.lgccno.net

March 2004

5-7: Wingspan/ Tucson LGBT Film Festival — *Tucson, AZ*
showcasing the best in new queer cinema ☎520/**624-1779** ✉ c/o *Wingspan LGBT Center*, 300 E 6th St, Tucson, AZ 85705
Email: filmfest@wingspan.org **Web:** www.wingspan.org

TBA: Out in Africa — *Cape Town, South Africa*
the only film festival of its kind on the African continent • also in Johannesburg & Durban ☎/27 21 465 9289 ✉ 924-926 Groote Kerke Gebou, 39 Adderley St, 8000 Cape Town, South Africa
Email: info@oia.co.za **Web:** www.oia.co.za

April 2004

23-May 2: Miami Gay & Lesbian Film Festival — *Miami, FL*
☎305/**534-9924** ✉ 1521 Alton Rd #147, Miami Beach, FL 33139
Email: info@miamigaylesbianfilm.com **Web:** www.MGLFF.com

May 2004

20-30: Inside Out — *Toronto, ON, Canada*
annual lesbian & gay fim fest ☎416/**977-6847**, 416/**925-XTRA ext 2229** ✉ c/o *Inside Out*, 401 Richmond St W #219, Toronto, ON, Canada M5V 3A8
Email: inside@insideout.on.ca **Web:** www.insideout.on.ca

TBA: Honolulu Gay/ Lesbian Film Festival — *Honolulu, HI*
☎808/**941-0424 ext 18** ✉ c/o *Honolulu Gay & Lesbian Cultural Foundation*, 1877 Kalakaua Ave, Honolulu, HI 96815
Email: info@hglcf.org **Web:** www.hglcf.org

June 2004

3-13: New York Lesbian & Gay Film Festival — *New York City, NY*
10-day fest in early June ☎212/**571-2170** ✉ c/o *The New Festival*, 139 Fulton St #PH-3, New York, NY 10038
Email: info@newfestival.org **Web:** www.newfestival.org

4-12: Connecticut Gay/ Lesbian Film Festival — *Hartford, CT*
lgbt ☎860/**586-1136**, 860/**232-3402** ✉ c/o *Alternatives, Inc*, PO Box 231192, Hartford, CT 06123
Email: glff@yahoo.com **Web:** www.CTGLFF.org

17-20: Q Cinema — *Fort Worth, TX*
annual celebration of lgbt-themed movies ☎817/**462-3368** ✉ c/o *Q Cinema Inc*, 9 Chase Ct, Fort Worth, TX 76110
Email: tcamp@star-telegram.com **Web:** www.qcinema.org

2004 Calendar — FILM FESTIVALS

17-27: **San Francisco Int'l Lesbian/ Gay Film Festival** *San Francisco, CA*
get your tickets early for a slew of films about us • lgbt • 85,000+ attendees
☎ 415/**703-8650** ✉ c/o *Frameline*, 145 9th St, San Francisco, CA 94103
Email: info@frameline.org **Web:** www.frameline.org

July 2004

8-19: **Outfest** *Los Angeles, CA*
Los Angeles' lesbian/gay film & video festival in mid-July ☎ 213/**480-7088**
✉ c/o *Outfest*, 3470 Wilshire Blvd #1022, Los Angeles, CA 90010
Email: outfest@outfest.org **Web:** www.outfest.org

15-26: **Philadelphia Gay/ Lesbian Film Festival** *Philadelphia, PA*
☎ 215/**733-0608**, 800/**333-8521** ext 237 ✉ c/o *Philadelphia Film Society*,
234 Market St, Philadelphia, PA 19106
Email: ray@phillyfests.com **Web:** www.phillyfests.com/piglff

August 2004

10-15: **Rhode Island International Film Festival** *Providence, RI*
don't miss the Gay & Lesbian Film Fest sidebar • mixed gay/straight
☎ 401/**861-4445** ✉ c/o *RIIFF*, PO Box 162, Newport, RI 02840
Email: info@film-festival.org **Web:** www.film-festival.org

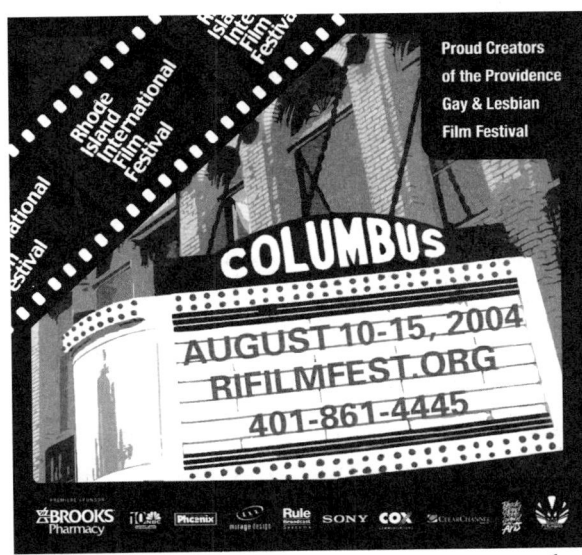

Film Festivals — 2004 Calendar

- **12-15: North Carolina Gay/ Lesbian Film Festival** — *Durham, NC*
  ☎919/560-3040 ext 226 ✉ c/o *Carolina Theatre*, 309 W Morgan St, Durham, NC 27701
  Email: steve@carolinatheatre.org **Web:** www.carolinatheatre.org

- **26-Sept 6: Austin Gay/ Lesbian International Film Festival** — *Austin, TX*
  ☎512/302-9889 ✉ c/o *AGLIFF*, 1216 E 51st St, Austin, TX 78723
  Email: kino@agliff.org **Web:** www.agliff.org

- **TBA: Vancouver Queer Film & Video Festival** — *Vancouver, BC, Canada*
  lgbt ☎604/844-1615 ✉ c/o *Out on Screen*, 405-207 West Hastings St, Vancouver, BC, Canada V6B 1H7
  Email: general@outonscreen.com **Web:** www.outonscreen.com

September 2004

- **9-12: Bent Lens: The Boulder Gay & Lesbian Film Festival** — *Boulder, CO*
  ☎303/494-1518 ✉ 2118 14th St, Boulder, CO 80302
  Email: info@boulderfilms.org **Web:** www.boulderfilms.org

- **15-19: Fresno Reel Pride** — *Fresno, CA*
  annual lesbian & gay film festival in central California ☎559/488-6562
  ✉ PO Box 4647, Fresno, CA 93744
  Email: info@reelpride.com **Web:** www.reelpride.com

- **16-19 & 23-26: Making Scenes** — *Ottawa, ON, Canada*
  Ottawa's queer film & video festival ☎613/566-2113
  ✉ c/o *Making Scenes* c/o Arts Court, 2 Daly Ave, Ottawa, ON, Canada K1N 6E2
  Email: scenes@magma.ca **Web:** www.makingscenes.ca

- **24-Oct 4: International Film & Video Festival** — *Montréal, QC, Canada*
  lgbt ☎514/285-9466 ✉ c/o *Image + Nation*, 4067 boul St Laurent #404, Montréal, QC H2W 1Y7
  Email: info@image-nation.org **Web:** www.image-nation.org

- **TBA: St Louis Int'l Lesbian/ Gay Film Festival** — *St Louis, MO*
  ☎314/997-9846 ✉ c/o *SLILAG*, PMB 388, 6614 Clayton Rd, St Louis, MO 63117
  Email: slilagff@aol.com **Web:** www.slilagfilmfestival.org

October 2004

- **3-13: Tampa Int'l Gay/ Lesbian Film Festival** — *Tampa Bay, FL*
  ☎813/879-4220 ✉ c/o *Friends of the Festival*, PO Box 18445, Tampa, FL 33679
  Email: joe@tiglff.com **Web:** www.tiglff.com

- **7-17: Portland Lesbian & Gay Film Festival** — *Portland, OR*
  ☎503/345-9393 ✉ c/o *Sensory Perceptions*, 818 SW 3rd Ave #1224, Portland, OR 97204
  Email: info@sensoryperceptions.org **Web:** www.sensoryperceptions.org

- **14-24: Reel Affirmations Film Festival DC** — *Washington, DC*
  lesbian/gay films ☎202/986-1119 ✉ c/o *One In Ten*, PO Box 73587, Washington, DC 20056
  Email: info@reelaffirmations.org **Web:** www.reelaffirmations.org

- **TBA: Barcelona Gay & Lesbian Film Festival** — *Barcelona, Spain*
  ☎877/276-6636
  Email: info@da-sitours.com **Web:** www.da-sitours.com

2004 Calendar — LEATHER, FETISH & BEARS

TBA: Out on Film — *Atlanta, GA*
lgbt ☎404/352-4225 ✉ c/o *IMAGE Film & Video Center*, 75 Bennett St NW, Ste N-1, Atlanta, GA 30309
Email: aff@imagefv.org **Web:** www.outonfilm.com

TBA: Pittsburgh International Lesbian & Gay Film Festival *Pittsburgh, PA*
lgbt ☎412/232-3277 ✉ c/o *PILGFF*, PO Box 81237, Pittsburgh, PA 15217
Email: pilgff@aol.com **Web:** www.pilgff.org

TBA: Seattle Lesbian/ Gay Film Festival — *Seattle, WA*
lgbt ☎206/323-4274 ✉ c/o *Three Dollar Bill Cinema*, 1122 E Pike St #1313, Seattle, WA 98122
Email: filmfest@seattlequeerfilm.com **Web:** www.seattlequeerfilm.com

November 2004

TBA: Mix: New York Lesbian/ Gay Experimental Film/ Video Fest — *New York City, NY*
film, videos, installations & media performances • write for info ☎212/571-4242
✉ 29 John St PMB 132, New York, NY 10038
Email: info@mixnyc.org **Web:** www.mixnyc.org

TBA: Reeling 2004: Chicago Lesbian and Gay Int'l Film Fest *Chicago, IL*
☎773/293-1447 ✉ c/o *Chicago Filmmakers*, 5243 N Clark St, 2nd flr, Chicago, IL 60640
Email: reeling@chicagofilmmakers.org **Web:** www.chicagofilmmakers.org/reeling

TBA: Seeing Queerly — *Denver, CO*
Mountain State's annual lesbian/gay film festival ☎303/733-7743 ext 15
✉ c/o *The Center*, PO Box 9798, Denver, CO 80209
Email: kevin @coloradoglbt.org

December 2004

1: Blowing Bubbles — *Italy*
international film & video contest promoting AIDS prevention & education • lgbt
☎0039-051/649-4416 ✉ c/o *Il Cassero- Gay & Lesbian Centre*, via Don Minzoni 18, 40121 Bologna, Italy
Email: blowingbubbles@cassero.it **Web:** www.blowingbubbles.it

LEATHER, FETISH & BEARS

January 2004

16-19: La Fiesta de Los Osos — *Tucson, AZ*
winter bear gathering in the warmth of the desert sun • men only
☎520/327-1620 ✉ c/o *Bears of the Old Pueblo*, PO Box 43910, Tucson, AZ 85733-3910
Email: fiesta@botop.com **Web:** www.botop.com

16-19: Mid-Atlantic Leather Weekend — *Washington, DC*
lgbt ☎202/388-1010 ✉ c/o *Centaur MC*, PO Box 34193, Washington, DC 20043
Email: registration@leatherweekend.com **Web:** www.leatherweekend.com

Leather, Fetish & Bears — 2004 Calendar

24-31: Beef Dip: Int'l Leather & Bear Week — *Puerto Vallarta, Mexico*
beach parties, BBQs & hot DJs • local tours • cruises • bring sunscreen! • mostly men ☎416/**925-0229** ✉ c/o *LeatherAndBearTours.com*, 511 Church Street # 202, Toronto, ON, Canada M4Y 2C9
Email: info@leatherandbeartours.com **Web:** www.leatherandbeartours.com

February 2004

13-16: Int'l Bear Rendezvous 2004 — *San Francisco, CA*
☎415/**541-5000** ✉ c/o *Bears of San Francisco*, 2215-R Market St PMB 266, San Francisco, CA 94114
Email: ibr@bosf.org **Web:** www.bosf.org

13-15: Pantheon of Leather — *Chicago, IL*
annual SM community service awards • mixed gay/straight ✉ 5306 Romaine, Hollywood, CA 90029
Email: tljandcuir@aol.com **Web:** www.TheLeatherJournal.com/pantheon.htm

13-15: Portland Uniform Weekend — *Portland, OR*
lgbt ☎503/**228-6935** ✉ c/o *In Uniform Magazine*, PO Box 3226, Portland, OR 97208
Email: uniformmag@aol.com **Web:** www.inuniform.net

March 2004

TBA: Washington State Leather Pride Week — *Seattle, WA*

April 2004

2-4: Leather Leadership Conference — *Boston, MA*
join us to develop & strengthen problem-solving & camaraderie in the leather community • lgbt ✉ c/o *LLC c/o John Weis*, 265 W 19 St, New York, NY 10011
Email: lolitassc@aol.com **Web:** www.leatherleadership.org

8-12: Easter 2004 Berlin — *Berlin, Germany*
annual leather & fetish weekend • German Mr Leather contest ☎49 30/**215 0099** ✉ c/o *Berlin Leder und Fetisch*, Nollendorfstrasse 28, Berlin, Germany 10777
Email: info@blf.de **Web:** www.blf.de

TBA: Rubbout 13 — *Vancouver, BC, Canada*
don't miss this annual pansexual rubber weekend • mostly men • 60-100 attendees ☎604/**683-8000** ✉ PO Box 2253, Vancouver, BC, Canada V6B 3W2
Email: mkenyon@miabc.org **Web:** www.rubbout.ca

May 2004

27-31: International Mr Leather — *Chicago, IL*
weekend of leather events, capped by contest Sunday, Black & Blue Ball on Monday ☎800/**545-6753** ✉ c/o *International Mr Leather*, 5015 N Clark St, Chicago, IL 60640 **Email:** info@imrl.com **Web:** www.imrl.com

28-31: Bear Pride — *Chicago, IL*
1000+ attendees ☎773/**509-5135** ✉ c/o *Great Lakes Bears*, PO Box 578840, Chicago, IL 60657 **Email:** BP@GLBears.com **Web:** www.GLBears.com

2004 Calendar — LEATHER, FETISH & BEARS

28-31: International Mr Bootblack Contest
Chicago, IL
contest takes place during International Mr Leather weekend ☎800/**545-6753** ✉ c/o *International Mr Leather*, 5015 N Clark St, Chicago, IL 60640
Email: info@imrl.com **Web:** www.imrl.com

June 2004

22: Folsom Street East
New York City, NY
New York City's answer to the famous San Francisco fetish street fair • lgbt
☎212/**727-9878** ✉ c/o *GMSMA*, 332 Bleecker St #D-23, New York City, NY 10014
Email: info@gmsma.org **Web:** www.folsomstreeteast.org

TBA: Southeast Leatherfest
Atlanta, GA
lgbt ☎800/**279-1106 x01** ✉ c/o *Southeast Leatherfest*, PO Box 78974, Atlanta, GA 30357
Email: bruiser01@aol.com **Web:** www.seleatherfest.com

July 2004

2-6: Bear All
Atlanta, GA
men only ☎770/**908-3381** ✉ c/o *Southern Bears*, PO Box 13964, Atlanta, GA 30324-0964 **Email:** alphabear@attbi.com
Web: www.southernbears.org/southernbears/index.htm

3-5: Bear Games
Bucks County, PA
men only ☎202/**337-8046** ✉ c/o *Chesapeake Bay Bears*, PO Box 34725, Washington, DC 20043
Email: webmaster@chesapeakebaybears.com **Web:** www.chesapeakebaybears.com

16-18: Thunder in the Mountains
Denver, CO
weekend of pansexual leather events & seminars • kinky comedy revue • Mr & Ms Rocky Mountain Leather contest • lgbt • 800+ attendees ☎303/**698-1207** ✉ c/o *Thunder in the Mountains, LLC*, 258 Acoma St, Denver 80223-1339
Email: MrLthrCO@aol.com **Web:** www.thunderinthemountains.com

25: Up Your Alley Fair
San Francisco, CA
local SM/leather street fair held in Dore Alley, South-of-Market • thousands of local kinky men & women attendees ☎415/**861-3247** ✉ c/o *Folsom Street Events*, 584 Castro, PMB 553, San Francisco, CA 94114
Email: smmile@folsomstreetfair.com **Web:** www.folsomstreetfair.com

TBA: Lazy Bear Weekend 2004
Russian River, CA
'no contests, no pageants, no frills—just fur!' • benefits AIDS charities in Northern California • check web for details • mostly men ✉ c/o *Castrobear Presents*, 584 Castro St PMB 374, San Francisco, CA 94114
Email: lazybearweekend@aol.com **Web:** www.lazybearweekend.com

TBA: Living in Leather
TBA, USA
national conference for the leather, SM & fetish communities • lgbt • 600 attendees • $150-300 ✉ c/o *National Leather Association: International*, 4038 Cedars Springs #961, Dallas, TX 75219
Email: info@livinginleather.org **Web:** www.livinginleather.org

LEATHER, FETISH & BEARS — 2004 Calendar

August 2004

16: Leather Ball *Toronto, ON, Canada*
hot parties all weekend, featuring Leather Ball on Sat • mostly men
☎416/**890-2326** ✉ c/o *MLTC, Inc*, 552 Church St, PO Box 500-35, Toronto, ON, Canada M4Y 2H0
Email: info@leatherball.com **Web:** www.leatherball.com

26-30: Big Apple Bearfest *New York City, NY*
the fur flies during this packed weekend in New York City • live music, museums, city tours, bar crawls & more
Email: info@bigapplebearfest.com **Web:** www.bigapplebearfest.com

September 2004

10-12: Bears on the Beach *Rehoboth Beach, DE*
men only ☎202/**337-8046** ✉ c/o *Chesapeake Bay Bears*, PO Box 34725, Washington, DC 20043
Email: webmaster@chesapeakebaybears.com **Web:** www.chesapeakebaybears.com

26: Folsom Street Fair *San Francisco, CA*
huge SM/leather street fair, topping a week of kinky events • lgbt • thousands of local & visiting kinky men & women attendees ☎415/**861-3247** ✉ c/o *Folsom Street Events*, 584 Castro, PMB 553, San Francisco, CA 94114
Email: smmile@folsomstreetfair.com **Web:** www.folsomstreetfair.com

27-Oct 3: Leather Week *Russian River, CA*
weekend of demonstrations, play parties, & the North Coast Leather Title contest • lgbt • 300+ attendees ☎707/**869-3400** ✉ c/o *Russian River Productions*, PO Box 858, Guerneville, CA 95446
Email: info@russianrivereagle.com **Web:** www.russianrivereagle.com

October 2004

1-3: OctobearFest *Denver, CO*
men only ☎303/**331-2705** ✉ c/o *Front Range Bears*, PO Box 100551, Denver, CO 80250-0551
Email: obfcom@frontrangebears.org **Web:** www.frontrangebears.org

7-10: International Leather Sir & Leather Boy *St Petersburg, FL*
international leather title contest & vendors ☎412/**889-9605** ✉ c/o *DCI Productions*, PO Box 99307, Pittsburgh, PA 15233
Email: mike@leathersir.com **Web:** www.leathersir.com

November 2004

5-7: Leather Pride Amsterdam *Amsterdam, Netherlands*
2 days of hot leather events • men only ☎31-020/**422-3737** ✉ c/o *Leather Pride Nederland*, PO Box 2674, 1000 CR Amsterdam, Netherlands
Email: info@leatherpride.nl **Web:** www.leatherpride.nl

2004 Calendar — CONFERENCES & RETREATS

25-28: Mr Leatherman Toronto Competition — Toronto, ON, Canada
hot parties all weekend, including the competition & Victory Ball on Saturday • mostly men ☎416/890-2326 ✉ c/o *MLTC, Inc*, 552 Church St, PO Box 500-35, Toronto, ON, Canada M4Y 2H0
Email: info@leatherball.com **Web:** www.leatherball.com

TBA: Hibearnation — St Louis, MO
weekend of bear events • 400+ attendees ✉ c/o *Show-Me Bears*, 3858-A Market St, St Louis, MO 63110
Email: smb@gaystlouis.com **Web:** www.showmebears.com

TBA: Rubber Blowout — Chicago, IL
largest rubber event in US • market, parties • Mr Int'l Rubber contest • men only ☎773 ✉ c/o *Mr Int'l Rubber, Inc*, 3023 N Clark, #201, Chicago, IL 60657
Email: cellblock@cellblock-chicago.com
Web: www.cellblock-chicago.com/html/rubber.html

TBA: Santa Clara County Leather Weekend — San Jose, CA
3 days of leather celebration in the South Bay • lgbt ✉ c/o *Santa Clara Leather Assoc*, 938 The Alameda, San Jose, CA 95126
Email: info@sccleather.org **Web:** www.SCCLeather.org

CONFERENCES & RETREATS

April 2004

2-4: National Lesbian & Gay MBA Conference — Los Angeles, CA
discussions of sexual orientation in the workplace by MBA students & representatives from big-name companies • lgbt • 300+ attendees
☎212/765-8880
Email: info@reachingoutmba.org **Web:** www.gaybiz.org

May 2004

TBA: Lambda Literary Awards — Chicago, IL
the 'Lammies' are the Oscars of lgbt writing & publishing • lgbt ☎202/682-0952 ✉ c/o *Lambda Literary Foundation*, PO Box 73910, Washington, DC 20056
Email: LLF@lambdalit.org **Web:** www.lambdalit.org

June 2004

24-27: National Lesbian & Gay Journalists Association Convention
New York City, NY
workshops • keynote speakers • entertainment • lgbt ☎202/588-9888 ✉ c/o *NLGJA*, 1420 'K' St NW #910, Washington, DC 20005
Email: info@nlgja.org **Web:** www.nlgja.org

October 2004

TBA: Lambda Literary Festival — TBA, USA
lgbt ☎202/682-0952 ✉ c/o *Lambda Literary Foundation*, PO Box 73910, Washington, DC 20056
Email: llf@lambdalit.org **Web:** www.lambdalit.org

SPIRITUAL — 2004 Calendar

TBA: National Latino/a Lesbian/Gay Conference *TBA, FL*
come together to strengthen, empower & mobilize the Latina/o LGBT community • lgbt ☎202/**408-5380** ✉ c/o *LLEGO*, 1420 'K' St NW #400, Washington, DC 20005
Email: encuentro@llego.org **Web:** www.llego.org

November 2004

TBA: Creating Change Conference *TBA, USA*
for lesbians, gays, bisexuals, transgendered people & queers into social activism • lgbt • 2500+ attendees ☎202/**332-6483 x3301** ✉ c/o *National Gay/Lesbian Task Force*, 1700 Kalorama Rd NW, Washington, DC 20009
Email: creatingchange@ngltf.org **Web:** www.creatingchange.org

July 2005

TBA: RAD Conference: Rainbow Alliance of the Deaf *Washington, DC*
workshops • conferences • keynote speakers • social events • come celebrate deaf culture & identity
Email: secretary@rad.org **Web:** www.rad.org

SPIRITUAL

February 2004

13-16: PantheaCon *San Jose, CA*
pagan convention • mixed gay/straight ☎510/**653-3244** ✉ c/o *Ancient Ways*, 4075 Telegraph Ave, Oakland, CA 94609
Email: store@ancientways.com **Web:** www.ancientways.com

June 2004

3-7: Ancient Ways Festival *Harbin Hot Springs, CA*
annual 4-day mixed gender/orientation spring festival • pan-pagan rituals, workshops & music w/ lesbian/gay campsite • mixed gay/straight ☎510/**653-3244** ✉ c/o *Ancient Ways*, 4075 Telegraph Ave, Oakland, CA 94609
Email: store@ancientways.com **Web:** www.ancientways.com

20-27: Pagan Spirit Gathering *near Athens, OH*
summer solstice celebration in Ohio • primitive camping • workshops • rituals • advance registration required • mixed gay/straight ☎608/**924-2216** ✉ c/o *Circle Sanctuary*, PO Box 219, Mt Horeb, WI 53572
Email: psg@circlesanctuary.org **Web:** www.circlesanctuary.org/psg

July 2004

TBA: BC Witchcamp *near Vancouver, BC, Canada*
weeklong Wiccan intensive • mixed gay/straight ☎604/**253-7189**, 604/**253-7195** ✉ c/o *BCWC*, PO Box 21510, 1850 Commercial Dr, Vancouver, BC, Canada V5N 4A0
Email: bcwcinfo@yahoo.ca **Web:** www.bcwithcamp.org

2004 Calendar — THE CIRCUIT

October 2004

29-31: Real Witches Ball — *Columbus, OH*
weekend pagan celebration of Samhain • mixed gay/straight ☎614/**421-7557**
✉ c/o *Salem West*, 1209 N High St, Columbus, OH 43201
Email: ajdrew@neopagan.com **Web:** www.neopagan.com

THE CIRCUIT

January 2004

23-25: Blue Ball — *Philadelphia, PA*
AIDS benefit weekend highlighted by Saturday night dance • mostly men
☎215/**985-4448** ✉ c/o *Philadelphia Fight*, 1233 Locust St, 5th Fl, Philadelphia, PA 19107
Email: jeremy@blueballphilly.com **Web:** www.blueballphilly.com

February 2004

1-9: Whistler Gay Ski Week: Altitude 2004 — *Whistler, BC, Canada*
annual gay/lesbian ski week • top-notch DJs & venues • popular destination 75 miles N of Vancouver • lgbt • 3000+ attendees ☎604/**899-6209**, 888/**258-4883** ✉ c/o *Out On The Slopes Productions*, 101-1184 Denman St #190, Vancouver, BC, Canada V6G 2M9
Email: altitude@outontheslopes.com **Web:** www.outontheslopes.com

12-15: Red Party Weekend — *Montreal, QC, Canada*
AIDS benefit dance • mostly men • 2500+ attendees • $50+ ☎514/**875-7026**
✉ c/o *Bad Boy Club Montreal*, PO Box 1253, Stn B, Montreal, QC, Canada H3B 3K9
Email: information@bbcm.org **Web:** www.bbcm.org

14: Saint-at-Large White Party — *New York City, NY*
mostly men • $30-50 ☎212/**674-8541** ✉ c/o *Saint-at-Large*, 8 St Mark's Pl, Ste 1A, New York, NY 10003
Email: nyctstal@aol.com **Web:** www.saintatlarge.com

TBA: Fireball (previously Hearts Party) — *Chicago, IL*
a weekend of dance parties to raise money for local AIDS organizations • mostly men ☎773/**244-6000**
Email: info@heartsfoundation.com **Web:** www.thefireball.com

March 2004

5-7: Volcano Party — *Island of Oahu, HI*
also March 13, 2004 on the Island of Maui • mostly men ☎877/**242-4900 ext 102** ✉ c/o *Maui AIDS Foundation*, 1935 Main St #101, Wailuku, HI 96793
Email: info@mauiaids.org **Web:** www.volcanoparty.com

10-15: Winter Party Week South Beach — *Miami Beach, FL*
AIDS benefit dance on the beach • 18,000 attendees • $75-275 ☎305/**572-1841**
✉ c/o *Dade Human Rights Foundation*, 4500 Biscayne Blvd #300, Miami, FL 33157
Email: manager@dhrf.com **Web:** www.winterparty.com

THE CIRCUIT   2004 Calendar

TBA: Saint-at-Large Black Party   *New York City, NY*
lgbt • $80-100 ☎212/**674-8541** ✉ c/o *Saint-at-Large*, 8 St Mark's Pl, Ste 1A, New York, NY 10003
Email: nyctstal@aol.com **Web:** www.saintatlarge.com

April 2004

8-12: White Party   *Palm Springs, CA*
weekend of buffed, tan & beautiful party circuit queens, benefits Desert AIDS Project & Aides for AIDS etc • mostly men ☎323/**653-0800** ✉ c/o *JeffreySanker Enterprises*, 8344 Melrose Ave #20, West Hollywood, CA 90069
Email: feedback@jeffreysanker.com **Web:** www.jeffreysanker.com

23-25: Cherry Weekend   *Washington, DC*
mostly men
Email: info@cherryfund.com **Web:** www.cherryfund.com

May 2004

13-17: Hot & Dry   *Montreal, QC, Canada*
AIDS benefit dance • mostly men • 5000+ attendees • $50+ ☎514/**875-7026** ✉ c/o *Bad Boy Club Montreal*, PO Box 1253, Stn B, Montreal, QC, Canada H3B 3K9
Email: information@bbcm.org **Web:** www.bbcm.org

28-30: Colossus Memorial Day Weekend   *San Francisco, CA*
San Francisco's original circuit party weekend returns w/ 3 days & nights in incredible venues all over town • mostly men ✉ c/o *Gus Presents*, 1459 18th St PMB#141, San Francisco, CA 94107
Email: gus@guspresents.com **Web:** www.guspresents.com

28-30: Meltdown 2004   *Austin, TX*
lgbt ☎512/**478-1791**, 888/**558-1791** ✉ c/o *Ben Parsley & Splash Productions*, 1212 Guadalupe St #1003, Austin, TX 78701
Email: ben@partyaustin.com **Web:** www.partyaustin.com

TBA: Motorball   *Detroit, MI*
annual AIDS fundraising parties in the Motor City • 1000+ attendees
☎248/**358-9849** ✉ c/o *Geared 4 Life*, PO Box 21938, Detroit, MI 48221-0938
Email: contactus@geared4life.org **Web:** www.geared4life.org

TBA: Purple Party   *Dallas, TX*
a weekend of parties benefits the Resource Center of Dallas ☎877/**U-GO-GIRL**
Email: purplepartydallas@yahoo.com **Web:** www.dallaspurpleparty.com

June 2004

5: One Mighty Party   *Orlando, FL*
celebrate Gay Day at Disney • mostly men ☎323/**653-0800** ✉ c/o *JeffreySanker Enterprises*, 8344 Melrose Ave #20, West Hollywood, CA 90069
Email: feedback@jeffreysanker.com **Web:** www.jeffreysanker.com

2004 Calendar   THE CIRCUIT

THE CIRCUIT — 2004 Calendar

24-27: Gus Presents Gay Pride Events *San Francisco, CA*
Temple, Mass & Sanctuary parties are bigger than ever this weekend • fabulous locations • mostly men ✉ c/o *Gus Presents*, 1459 18th St PMB#141, San Francisco, CA 94107
Email: gus@guspresents.com **Web:** www.guspresents.com

26: Pride SPLASH! *San Francisco, CA*
a daytime 'sip & twirl' at the Phoenix Hotel • mostly men ☎415/**674-1214 Web:** www.barstoclubs.com/SPLASHsf

26: ReUNION *San Francisco, CA*
celebrate gay pride in San Francisco's beautiful City Hall • mostly men • 2000 attendees ☎415/**674-1214 Web:** www.noblebeast.org

July 2004

1-4: Freedom Party *Charleston, SC*
4-day festival of circuit DJs, movies, special performances & parties • benefiting local lgbt service organizations • mostly men • 1000+ attendees ☎843/**425-6920**
Email: info@freedomfundsc.com **Web:** www.freedomfundsc.com

2-4: Laguna Beach Independance *Laguna Beach, CA*
celebrate the 4th of July with 3 days of parties • mostly men ☎323/**866-7018** ✉ c/o *Will Gorges & Canboy Productions*, PO Box 5943, Beverly Hills, CA 90209
Email: wgorges@earthlink.net **Web:** www.willgorges.com

3-9: Summer Camp *Provincetown, MA*
celebrate the week of the 4th with cute boys & big name DJs ☎508/**487-9601**
Email: info@davidflower.com **Web:** www.davidflower.com

23: Pride Ball *San Diego, CA*
party at the San Diego Cruise Ship Terminal • mostly men • 4000 attendees • $25-35 ☎619/**220-2137** ✉ c/o *Powerhouse Productions*, 7140 Engineer Rd, San Diego, CA 92111 **Email:** info@powerhouse-productions.com
Web: www.powerhouse-productions.com

24: Circuit Daze *San Diego, CA*
party at the San Diego Sports Arena • mostly men • 7000 attendees • $40-75 ☎619/**220-2137**, 858/**623-9547** ✉ c/o *Powerhouse Productions*, 7140 Engineer Rd, San Diego, CA 92111 **Email:** info@powerhouse-productions.com
Web: www.powerhouse-productions.com

25: Fete Accompli, Official After Zoo Party *San Diego, CA*
On Broadway Event Center • mostly men • 1500 attendees • $30-50 ☎619/**220-2137**, 858/**623-9547** ✉ c/o *Powerhouse Productions*, 7140 Engineer Rd, San Diego, CA 92111 **Email:** info@powerhouse-productions.com
Web: www.powerhouse-productions.com

gus presents

SUNDANCE

the seventh annual russian river **MORNING PARTY**

AUGUST 6-8 2004 * GUERNEVILLE CALIFORNIA

WWW.GUSPRESENTS.COM

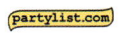

THE CIRCUIT — 2004 Calendar

25: Zoo Party — *San Diego, CA*
party at the world-famous San Diego Zoo • mostly men • 4000 attendees • $75-100 ☎619/**220-2137**, 858/**623-9547** ✉ c/o *Powerhouse Productions*, 7140 Engineer Rd, San Diego, CA 92111 **Email:** info@powerhouse-productions.com **Web:** www.powerhouse-productions.com

29-Aug 1: Twist Party Weekend — *Montreal, QC, Canada*
celebrate gay pride in Montreal • several dance events, including Mega T-Dance Saturday afternoon • mostly men • $40+ ☎514/**875-7026** ✉ c/o *Bad Boy Club Montreal*, PO Box 1253, Station B, Montreal, QC, Canada H3B 3K9 **Email:** information@bbcm.org **Web:** www.bbcm.org

TBA: Moonshot — *Huntsville, AL*
annual dance event to benefit local HIV/AIDS organizations • mostly men • 400 attendees ☎256/**536-0060** ✉ c/o *Moonshot, Inc*, PO Box 757, Huntsville, AL 35804 **Email:** info@moonshot.org **Web:** www.moonshot.org

August 2004

6-8: Sundance — *Russian River, CA*
a weekend of indoor & outdoor dance events in the heart of the Russian River • party with 4,000+ gay boys in Guerneville ✉ c/o *Gus Presents*, 1459 18th St PMB#141, San Francisco, CA 94107 **Email:** gus@guspresents.com **Web:** www.guspresents.com

15: Morning Party at Laguna Beach — *Laguna Beach, CA*
mostly men ☎323/**866-7018** ✉ c/o *Will Gorges & Canboy Productions*, PO Box 5943, Beverly Hills, CA 90209 **Email:** wgorges@earthlink.net **Web:** www.willgorges.com

TBA: Hotlanta River Expo — *Atlanta, GA*
mostly gay men • AIDS benefit • parties, events & river-rafting parade • mostly men • $150-175 ☎404/**872-1792** ✉ c/o *Hotlanta River Expo*, PO Box 8375, Atlanta, GA 31106 **Email:** inquiry@hotlanta.org **Web:** www.hotlanta.org

September 2004

3-6: Perfect Day 2004 — *Austin, TX*
during 'Last Splash' weekend • lgbt ☎512/**478-1791**, 888/**558-1791** ✉ c/o *Ben Parsley & Splash Productions*, 1212 Guadalupe St #1003, Austin, TX 78701 **Email:** ben@partyaustin.com **Web:** www.partyaustin.com

25 Magnitude — *San Francisco, CA*
sexy men in leather dance the night away at this Folsom Street Fair weekend party c/o *Folsom Street Events*, 584 Castro, PMB 553, San Francisco, CA 94114 **Email:** smmile@folsomstreetfair.com **Web:** www.folsomstreetfair.com

26 Real Bad Party — *San Francisco, CA*
lots of real bad boys in leather at this popular fundraising event following the Folsom Street Fair • mostly men • c/o *Grass Roots Gay Rights West*, 584 Castro, PMB 495, San Francisco, CA 94114 **Web:** www.realbad.org

October 2004

6-12 : Black & Blue Party — *Montreal, QC, Canada*
North America's biggest & most innovative dance event & cultural festival • mostly men • 25,000+ attendees • $60-100+ ☎514/**875-7026** ✉ c/o *Bad Boy Club Montreal*, PO Box 1253, Stn B, Montreal, QC, Canada H3B 3K9 **Email:** information@bbcm.org **Web:** www.bbcm.org

GRGRWest Presents

REAL BAD XVI

SUNDAY SEPTEMBER 26, 2004
IMMEDIATELY FOLLOWING
FOLSOM STREET FAIR

FRIENDS JOINING FRIENDS IN CELEBRATION TO BENEFIT COMMUNITY

JOIN THE REAL BAD CIRCLE OF FRIENDS AT:
WWW.REALBAD.ORG

GRASS ROOTS GAY RIGHTS WEST
GRGR*West* is an all-volunteer organization dedicated to broadening the base of fundraising benefiting the gay and lesbian community.

GOLD FRIENDS

FALCON
www.falconstudios.com

www.MANHUNT.net

JockStudBoys.com

PYRAMID Printing & Graphics
www.pyramidgraphics.net

vitaminwater
www.glaceau.com

MARKETING FRIENDS

Graphic Design: Chris Tyler - www.threedkid.com
Photos: Rick Rediske - JockStudBoys.com

THE CIRCUIT — 2004 Calendar

25: Hell Ball — *San Francisco, CA*
a gathering of the tribes • all-night costume party • mostly men
Email: hellball@hotmail.com **Web:** www.hellball.org

28-31: Halloween in New Orleans — *New Orleans, LA*
weekend of parties • Sat costume extravaganza • Sun Gospel brunch • 3- & 4-day passes available • mostly men • 5000+ attendees ☎504/**949-3609** ✉ c/o *Halloween in New Orleans*, PO Box 52171, New Orleans, LA 70152-2171
Email: halloween@halloweenneworleans.com
Web: www.halloweenneworleans.com-

31: Mass-ive Halloween — *San Francisco, CA*
official Hell Ball weekend closing party • costume optional, flesh mandatory • mostly men ✉ c/o *Gus Presents*, 1459 18th St PMB#141, San Francisco, CA 94107
Email: gus@guspresents.com **Web:** www.guspresents.com

TBA: Better Than Wet Party — *Tampa Bay, FL*
mostly men ✉ c/o *Pride Tampa Bay*, PO Box 172553, Tampa, FL 33672
Web: www.betterthanwet.com

TBA: Viva Las Vegas — *Las Vegas, NV*
3-day party in America's biggest adult playground • lgbt ☎310/**659-4400**, 800/**628-5268** ✉ c/o *Atlantis Events, Inc*, 8490 Sunset Blvd, Ste 610, West Hollywood, CA 90069
Email: info@atlantisevents.com **Web:** www.atlantisevents.com

November 2004

24-29: White Party Week — *Miami Beach, FL*
6 days of festivities capped by the annual 'White Party at Vizcaya' • benefitting Care Resource • lgbt ☎305/**667-9296** ✉ c/o *CARE Resource*, 225 NE 34 St #201, Miami, FL 33137
Email: info@careresource.org **Web:** www.whiteparty.net

26: White Dreams — *Miami Beach, FL*
Thanksgiving wknd • benefits local charities • mostly men • 6000 attendees
☎323/**653-0800**, 323/**653-0800** ✉ c/o *JeffreySanker Enterprises*, 3344 Melrose Ave #20, West Hollywood, CA 90069
Email: feedback@jeffreysanker.com **Web:** www.jeffreysanker.com

December 2004

26-Jan 1: Bal Des Boys Weekend — *Montreal, QC, Canada*
AIDS benefit dance • mostly men • 5000+ attendees • $40+ ☎514/**875-7026**
✉ c/o *Bad Boy Club Montreal*, PO Box 1253, Stn B, Montreal, QC, Canada H3B 3K9
Email: information@bbcm.org **Web:** www.bbcm.org

31: Metropolis New Year's Eve 2005 — *San Francisco, CA*
12-hour dance marathon • largest gay New Year's party in San Francisco • mostly men ✉ c/o *Gus Presents*, 1459 18th St PMB#141, San Francisco, CA 94107
Email: gus@guspresents.com **Web:** www.guspresents.com

31: Miami New Years — *Miami Beach, FL*
celebrate New Year's Eve • mostly men ☎323/**653-0800** ✉ c/o *JeffreySanker Enterprises*, 8344 Melrose Ave #20, West Hollywood, CA 90069
Email: feedback@jeffreysanker.com **Web:** www.jeffreysanker.com

JEFFREY SANKER
PRESENTS

NEW YEAR'S EVE...
LOS ANGELES, CA

NEW YEAR'S EVE...
MIAMI, FL

WHITE PARTY XV...
APRIL 8-12, 2004 · PALM SPRINGS, CA

ONE MIGHTY PARTY...
DISNEY'S MGM STUDIOS, ORLANDO, FL

WHITE DREAMS...
WHITE PARTY WEEK, MIAMI, FL

WILTERN THEATER...
LOS ANGELES, CA

WWW.JEFFREYSANKER.COM
888.777.8886

Damron City Guide

Our new City Guide is the perfect companion to the **Men's Travel Guide** and the **Women's Traveller**! This attractive full-color guide features **more than 140 maps** with color-coded dots that pinpoint lesbian & gay bars, accommodations, and bookstores in **over 75 cities** and resorts worldwide. Also included are restaurants, cafés, gyms, travel agencies, publications and more. "Info boxes" detail major annual gay events, local tourist attractions and food, transit, weather, best views of the city, and directions from the airport. It is also the only Damron guide that contains websites within its listings. 1st Edition: only **$21.95**.

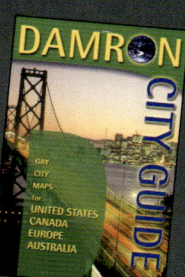

Damron Accommodations

Now you'll always have a home away from home! The first and only **full-color guide** to gay-friendly B&Bs, inns, hotels, and other accommodations in North America, Europe, Central America, South Africa, and Australia. Most listings include **color photographs** (not even straight B&B guides do this!) and a comprehensive description. Sophisticated travellers will appreciate the handy multiple cross-referenced index. Over 500 pages. **$22.95**.

To order, call **(800) 462-6654**
Ask for your **FREE** Damron catalog of international lesbian & gay travel guides!